Sociological Perspectives on Sport

Sociological Perspectives on Sport: The Games Outside the Games seeks not only to inform students about the sports world but also to offer them analytical skills and the application of theoretical perspectives that deepen their awareness and understanding of social processes linking sports to the larger social world. With six original framing essays linking sport to a variety of topics, including race, class, gender, media, politics, deviance, and globalization, and 37 reprinted articles, this text/reader sets a new standard for excellence in teaching sports and society.

David Karen is Professor of Sociology at Bryn Mawr College. In addition to his interest in sports, he also studies social inequality, the sociology of education, and social movements. He has been elected to four consecutive terms as a School Director in Upper Merion Area School District.

Robert E. Washington is Professor of Sociology and Africana Studies at Bryn Mawr College. His areas of scholarly interest are sociology of sports, race relations, social deviance, and the sociology of culture. With David Karen, he co-edited *The Sport and Society Reader* (Routledge) and *Sport, Power, and Society* (Westview).

Contemporary Sociological Perspectives

*Edited by **Douglas Hartmann**, University of Minnesota and **Jodi O'Brien**, Seattle University*

This innovative series is for all readers interested in books that provide frameworks for making sense of the complexities of contemporary social life. Each of the books in this series uses a sociological lens to provide current critical and analytical perspectives on significant social issues, patterns, and trends. The series consists of books that integrate the best ideas in sociological thought with an aim toward public education and engagement. These books are designed for use in the classroom as well as for scholars and socially curious general readers.

Published:

Political Justice and Religious Values by Charles F. Andrain

GIS and Spatial Analysis for the Social Sciences by Robert Nash Parker and Emily K. Asencio

Hoop Dreams on Wheels: Disability and the Competitive Wheelchair Athlete by Ronald J. Berger

The Internet and Social Inequalities by James C. Witte and Susan E. Mannon

Media and Middle Class Mom: Images and Realities of Work and Family by Lara Descartes and Conrad Kottak

Watching T.V. Is Not Required: Thinking about Media and Thinking about Thinking by Bernard McGrane and John Gunderson

Violence Against Women: Vulnerable Populations by Douglas Brownridge

State of Sex: Tourism, Sex and Sin in the New American Heartland by Barbara G. Brents, Crystal A. Jackson and Kate Hausbeck

Sociologists Backstage: Answers to 10 Questions about What They Do by Sarah Fenstermaker and Nikki Jones

Surviving the Holocaust: A Life Course Perspective by Ronald Berger

Stargazing: Celebrity, Fame, and Social Interaction by Kerry Ferris and Scott Harris

The Senses in Self, Society, and Culture by Phillip Vannini, Dennis Waskul and Simon Gottschalk

Surviving Dictatorship by Jacqueline Adams

The Womanist Idea by Layli Maparyan

Social Theory Re-Wired: New Connections to Classical and Contemporary Perspectives by Wesley Longhofer and Daniel Winchester

Religion in Today's World: Global Issues, Sociological Perspectives by Melissa Wilcox

Understanding Deviance: Connecting Classical and Contemporary Perspectives edited by Tammy L. Anderson

Social Statistics: Managing Data, Conducting Analyses, Presenting Results, Second Edition by Thomas J. Linneman

Transforming Scholarship: Why Women's and Gender Studies Students Are Changing Themselves and the World, Second Edition by Michele Tracy Berger and Cheryl Radeloff

Who Lives, Who Dies, Who Decides? Abortion, Neonatal Care, Assisted Dying, and Capital Punishment, Second Edition by Sheldon Ekland-Olson

Life and Death Decisions: The Quest for Morality and Justice in Human Societies, Second Edition by Sheldon Ekland-Olson

Gender Circuits: Bodies and Identities in a Technological Age, Second Edition by Eve Shapiro

Migration, Incorporation, and Change in an Interconnected World by Syed Ali and Douglas Hartmann

Sociological Perspectives on Sport: The Games Outside the Games by David Karen and Robert E. Washington

Forthcoming:

Social Worlds of Imagination by Chandra Mukerji

All Media are Social by Andrew Lindner

Sociological Perspectives on Sport

The Games Outside the Games

David Karen and Robert E. Washington

LONDON AND NEW YORK

First published 2015
by Routledge
711 Third Avenue, New York, NY 10017

and by Routledge
2 Park Square, Milton Park, Abingdon, Oxon, OX14 4RN

Routledge is an imprint of the Taylor & Francis Group, an informa business

Library of Congress Cataloging in Publication Data
A catalog record for this book has been requested

ISBN: 978-0-415-71839-4 (hbk)
ISBN: 978-0-415-71841-7 (pbk)
ISBN: 978-1-315-87085-4 (ebk)

Typeset in Utopia and Trade Gothic
by Florence Production Ltd, Stoodleigh, Devon, UK

Printed and bound in the United States of America
by Edwards Brothers Malloy

CONTENTS

LIST OF FIGURES

LIST OF TABLES

SERIES FOREWORD

This innovative series is for all readers interested in books that provide frameworks for making sense of the complexities of contemporary social life. Each of the books in the series uses a sociological lens to provide current critical and analytical perspectives on the best ideas in sociological thought with an aim toward public education and engagement. These books are designed for use in the classroom as well as for scholars and socially curious general readers.

David Karen and Bob Washington's book on sport, *Sociological Perspectives on Sport: The Games Outside the Games,* is an exciting addition to our series. Though much maligned and sometimes ignored in the academy, sport is clearly one of the most prominent, complex, and revealing institutions of the modern world. A quick look at any newspaper, cable television package, or list of global brands or internationally known celebrities will tell you that. Fortunately in recent years, a vast and sophisticated new body of research and writing has emerged to help us unpack and understand sport's complex social structure as well as its broader role and significance in contemporary social life.

In this volume Karen and Washington provide a rich, wide-ranging sampling of the most important and exciting work in this field. They have chosen these pieces carefully, and edited them closely so as to provide a comprehensive and yet accessible representation of this scholarship. Moreover, their innovative six section organizational scheme and penetrating framing essays provide an indispensible roadmap to this work and its various component parts.

In a landmark lecture delivered in the early 1980s, Pierre Bourdieu described the sociology of sport as trapped in a "golden ghetto." According to the great French sociologist, those folks who love sport are typically unwilling or unable to be critical of it, while those who have the tools to be more analytical—that is, most of us social scientists—generally refuse to take sport seriously as a social form and force. Karen and Washington's wonderful, wide-ranging collection helps us realize that Bourdieu's depiction has now been rendered a half-truth at best. Our hope and expectation is that this volume will not only provide inspiration and guidance for the next generation of sport scholars, it will help all social scientists—as well as those outside of the academy—better appreciate the social structure, cultural significance, and public impact of sport in our constantly changing world.

Douglas Hartmann
Jodi O'Brien
Series Editors

PREFACE

This is a comprehensive text/reader that provides an integrated approach to understanding the linkages between sport and society. It goes beyond standard anthologies by providing not only a unique conception of the field but a concise and compelling introduction of sociology's basic concepts—for example, social class, race/ethnicity, gender, deviance, and community—applied to the world of sport. And, it goes beyond standard textbooks by including a range of well-written, insightful articles on a variety of topics on sports/society. Laying out a broad view of the "games outside the games," the book is organized into six Sections—each reviewing the relevant literature and presenting multiple perspectives in response to key analytical questions.

The book opens with an introductory essay that provides both a brief overview of the sociological study of sports and a discussion of the analytical perspective that informs our approach to the field. In contrast to earlier sociologists who regarded sport as an insignificant social activity, we view it as a unique and significant social institution. It is unique because, at the level of the individual contest, it is transparent (its performances are open to public observation and assessment) and it embodies meritocratic principles (selecting the most talented players in order to achieve optimal outcomes). Based on these two attributes of competitive sports, which are linked directly to their sociological significance, we argue that these sports not only exemplify the highest normative development of meritocratic practices of fair competition in contemporary societies, but that they also influence the subsequent normative development of those practices in other institutions. Further, because they operate in this way, they play the role of legitimating a *limited* conception of fairness that is entirely consistent with ideologies of justice in contemporary capitalist democracies.

Seen from this perspective, we believe it is hardly coincidental that the familiar sports expression—"level playing field"—is invoked often in informal discourse as an overarching metaphor for fairness. Sports tend to become our normative frame of reference for assessing all competition. Hence, we argue that competitive sports matter sociologically—not simply because they are entertaining and popular, but because they exemplify norms of fair competition and social justice that influence our perceptions of other institutions (e.g., political, economic, educational, etc.). In the United States, for example, this was perhaps most dramatically demonstrated by the racial integration of major league baseball and other major sports a decade before the civil rights movement and subsequent legislation outlawing racial segregation. So, sport played the role of a leading institution in the struggle against racial exclusion even as it reinforced a narrow conception of distributive justice.

Building from insights about the meritocratic attributes of sports, we explore how professional competitive sports—governed by equitably enforced rules—is shaped by gatekeeping controls at three levels: standardizing access to teams and leagues; regulating team resources that determine player movement; and broadening opportunities for talent development. Overall, based on this broader perspective on fairness, the *ideal* competitive sport consists of the best players, selected and coached by teams that have relatively equal resources, drawn from a population in which all individuals have every opportunity to develop their potential. This conception of sports, as we will show, opens for inquiry the influences on sports of the "games outside the games"—especially, the societal opportunity structure and the power relations that sustain it—which is a major theoretical focus of this text/reader.

In the five additional Sections, we focus on the ways that sport and society intertwine. Beginning with "Biases and Barriers" in the second Section, we explore the various ways that racial/ethnic, social class, gender, and disability have affected who plays which sport—and at what level. Highlighting the socially determined marginalization and exclusion that shape sports participation, we demonstrate the ways these barriers in sports have been supported and reinforced by key societal institutions.

We turn next, in the third Section, to address the generative issues of fandom and community galvanized by sports. Here, we explore the ways that sports, through allegiances to teams, often bond diverse individuals into groups with shared feelings of support and collective identity—which, in some contexts, may be expressed as fanaticism, bigotry, and antagonism that glorify wider social divisions. Expanding on this theme of sports teams as symbolic representations of social communities, we also focus in this Section on the role of the media as technological instruments that have not only increased dramatically direct fan access to sports contests, but also transformed the boundaries of sports communities in the modern world, with the result that it is hardly unusual to discover that professional teams, like Manchester United (soccer) and the Los Angeles Lakers (basketball), have fans in Africa, North America, and Asia. Closely related to this global development of sports communities, we also address the increasing linkages of sports media conglomerates to neo-liberal corporate capitalism, and its consequences for global sports broadcasts.

In the fourth Section, we focus on two of the most neglected topics in the popular sports media discourse—the political economy and the politics of sports. Here we expand on the above discussion of the corporate–media–sports complex that has emerged in sports in response to the enormous potential wealth generated by sports contests. Also, closely related to the growth of corporate sports media, we examine an array of sports–economic developments ranging from sports leagues' economics and player labor union struggles to the expanding international sports labor market and player mobility. On a different note, we explore the often underreported and politically controversial issues surrounding the construction of professional sports teams stadiums at taxpayers' expense, arrangements that reflect the enormous leverage professional teams often have over the cities where they play. Viewing this political theme from a somewhat different angle, we address the link between sports and politics, with particular emphasis on governmental interventions in sports and the often controversial political roles of athletes.

In the fifth Section, we examine perhaps the hottest and most complex phenomenon confronting the contemporary sports world, namely the problem of rule-breaking or deviance. Here, we explore not only varied types of deviance, extending from gambling and fixing contests to illegal player recruitment and the use of prohibited performance-enhancing drugs; but, also, and perhaps most sociologically important, we examine the danger to sports posed by unchecked deviance. Viewing this deviance from the standpoint of meritocratic norms, we discuss the implications of sports deviance for undermining the core meaning of the sports contest as competition conducted on a level playing field. This Section considers both the operation of meritocratic norms as well as mechanisms of social control—negative sanctions—that deter deviance in competitive sports as key factors for assessing the level of a sport's institutional development. Drawing from the insights of the meritocratic theoretical perspective noted above, we argue that those societies whose dominant competitive sports have attained high levels of institutional development are most likely to evidence high levels of meritocratic norms in their other major institutions. Our discussion of deviance in this Section includes issues of gambling, drugs, and violence.

Finally, we address sports globalization as a dynamic and complex process of expanding transnational organization. In this Section, we explore the early historical background of international diffusion of sports through colonialism, the growth of international sports competition through the Olympics and the more recent international expansion of professional sports leagues such as FIFA, and the unprecedented increase of player migration. We also examine the growing divide between the wealthy "haves" (sports enterprises in the global North) and poor "have-nots" (sports enterprises in the global South) and explore the consequences of this development for future directions of sports globalization. Throughout this Section, we address the many ways that competitive sporting events that occurred formerly within national settings are occurring now in multiple national settings. They are sponsored by transnational leagues and conferences, reflecting the diffusion of sports and the changing configurations of sports fandoms, resulting in the global diffusion of normative standards and cultural values.

PEDAGOGICAL GOALS

This text/reader aims to introduce students to a fascinating multidisciplinary field. By presenting coherent analytical essays and reading selections that illuminate the complex interconnections between sports and society, it addresses such phenomena as: the relationship between social movements and changes in sports; the social processes that sustain the institutional stability and integrity of sports; the role of sports in creating group identity and bonds of social community; the enormous growth of sports in modern society as sources of entertainment and wealth; and, perhaps most far reaching, the influence of sports on the development of meritocratic normative practices in other social institutions.

In short, this text/reader constitutes a unique undertaking. Combining the best features of textbooks and edited readers, it has the advantage of flexibility, which makes it suitable for a variety of course objectives and audiences. The framing essays will introduce analytical concepts and theoretical perspectives that the student will encounter in the reading selections. They will also demonstrate how to employ those concepts and theories. The reading selections have been chosen for their topicality, clarity, and excellent integration of theoretical and empirical material. Seeking not only to inform students about the sports world but also to teach them analytical skills and the application of theoretical perspectives that deepen their awareness and understanding of social processes linking sports to the larger social world, this text/reader aims to appeal to both undergraduates and graduate students.

Our approach aims to combine in one place all an instructor would need to provide a comprehensive representation of the major topics and issues characterizing the field of sport and society. By combining our original framing essays with the previously published articles, it introduces students to intellectual frameworks that transcend the commonsense interpretations of sports-relevant events, both on and off the field. Indeed, we hope that the format provides the flexibility that instructors need to present a deep understanding of the relationship between sport and society and a critical approach to the "games outside the games."

Instructors: We have organized this book in a way that provides the opportunity to map its contents onto your current syllabi. Depending on the level of your class, you may choose to assign small sections of the framing essays for given class meetings along with an article from the associated readings in that Section. You may elect to assign for a given week an entire Section essay and then spend the next few weeks reading through the additional articles. Though the articles are organized in given Sections, many of them are quite relevant for other topical areas. For example, the article about the Green Bay Packers' unique fan base and ownership structure (Chapter 14) is relevant to our fandom Section and our political economy/politics Section. In short, we hope that this book's design appeals to a wide range of course needs and objectives.

ACKNOWLEDGMENTS

Over the many years of thinking about how to develop a book that would meet the needs of our course on Sports and Society, we have relied heavily on our students' feedback about the materials that have been most helpful and unhelpful in deepening their understanding of sport as a social institution. Our first debt is to them. Second, we wish to thank our research assistants—Hannah Smith and Sonia Giebel—for the breadth of their searching for *just* the right articles for this volume. A number of colleagues helped us arrange free or reduced costs for the publication of their contributions: Michael Messner, Ben Carrington, Doug Hartmann, Sherri Grasmuck, Loic Wacquant, Andy Markovits, and Malcolm Gladwell deserve mention in this regard. For reading, providing comments, and preventing some errors or, as one of them called it, some "real clunkers," we thank Andy Markovits, David Swartz, Doug Hartmann, and Katherine McClelland. Barbara Burns and, especially, Karen Sulpizio (who also helped in the article searches) were very helpful during the last stage of manuscript preparation. Steve Rutter's insight, encouragement, and vision for the project were key elements to the project's initiation and ultimate success. His prodding (!) was, in the end, much appreciated. We thank Margaret Moore and Fred Courtright for their assistance with a range of organizational challenges. Elsa Peterson's editing was a boon to the finished product. Also, a thank you to the reviewers:

Reuben A. Buford May	Texas A&M
Jeff Montez de Oca	University of Colorado, Colorado Springs
Nicole M. LaVoi	University of Minnesota
Barbara Thomas Coventry	University of Toledo

Finally, on a personal level, Karen would like to thank his family for supporting him in every way possible: thanks to Katherine, Rachel, and Josh for being Katherine, Rachel, and Josh. Washington thanks Rose for enduring a summer without Key West and other adventurous journeys.

SECTION 1

Sport and Sociology: Meanings and Dimensions

You are probably taking this course and reading this book because you're involved in playing or following sports. If that is the case, you are certainly not alone for many millions of Americans are similarly involved in sports to some degree. The range of activities that could plausibly fall under the category "sports" is wide and its economic impact is enormous.

By any economic accounting, sport is a huge industry in the United States. According to the US Census Bureau, the "spectator sports" industry had receipts/revenues of almost $32 billion in 2009 (US Census Bureau, 2012). If we compare that to the Census category that is focused on "performing arts companies," (which includes theater, musical groups, etc.) their receipts/revenues are less than half ($14.1 billion). Plunkett Research, Ltd. suggests that "[a] reasonable estimate of the total U.S. sports market would be $485 billion yearly (and $1.5 trillion for the entire world)" (Plunkett Research, 2014). This estimate comes from revenues from the four big professional sports leagues (Major League Baseball, National Hockey League, National Football League, and National Basketball Association) including sales of sports-related equipment, licensed jerseys and uniforms, video games, advertising, endorsement income, stadium income, NCAA-related income, health club revenue, other spectator sports, and other sports-related items.

While the precise numbers are not important here, the vastness of the industry and the number of people who are employed by or consume the products of this industry (including consuming the newspaper and web reports of the games that the consumers/fans have attended) is considerable. The attention paid to sport, the emotional energy invested, and the money spent translate to sport being a ubiquitous—and emotionally charged—feature of contemporary society.

WHAT IS THE SOCIOLOGY OF SPORT?

In this section, we introduce alternative definitions of sport and discuss what it means to examine *sociological* dimensions of sport. We present different theoretical perspectives on sport so that you have a variety of tools available as you analyze the social context within which a sporting event occurs. We challenge you to think not only about the games that your favorite team plays but also about the opportunities (or lack thereof) your team has to improve by acquiring new players, using new training techniques, or adopting new rationalistic approaches to analyzing the game (e.g., the approach known as "moneyball"). We ask that you think critically about three things: your team's revenues and its sources, how player mobility is accomplished, and how the available pool of talent developed. We provide you with concepts that will help you analyze a range of questions about sports and that you will want to use in comparative perspective (across amateur and professional levels, different sports, and different countries). At the end of the section, we offer a new way of thinking critically about different dimensions of the fairness that we expect to see on sport's "level playing field."

WHAT IS SPORT?

Before setting out on a discussion of the **sociology of sport**, it is important to decide what is a **sport**. As you will see throughout this book, sociologists pay close attention to definitions of concepts because they are not just neutral descriptions of words, as we tend to think about dictionary definitions. Concepts may be more or less historically, culturally, and socially based and their definition connects them to other concepts in complex ways. Let's think about different definitions.

As indicated in the opening paragraph of this section, the US Census and the Plunkett research firm have different definitions of sport. If we want to have a conversation about sports, how do we decide what is a sport? Just imagine this hypothetical conversation: You tell me that the greatest athlete ever was Willie Shoemaker . . . and I say WHO? You explain that Shoemaker was one of the greatest jockeys ever, that he won 11 Triple Crown races and held the record for most victories ever by a jockey. And I say . . . isn't the real athlete the horse? What did Shoemaker do?[1] If Willie Shoemaker is the best athlete ever, I might even go so far as to suggest that Stuey Ungar (poker) or Willie Mosconi (billiards) were the best.

ESPN, the Entertainment and Sports Programming Network, covers all the major world sports: soccer/football, American football, baseball, basketball, and hockey. It also broadcasts skiing, tennis, lacrosse, cheerleading, bowling, golf, and rugby. Even though the human involved (just) sits, ESPN also shows auto racing and horse racing. Finally, you can turn on ESPN to see poker and the US national spelling bee, competitions that don't involve any obvious athleticism. We don't want to decide on our definition of sports based on what ESPN broadcasts, do we? After all, the ESPN lineup has changed over the years, based on its perception of what would be most profitable to put on the air. We wouldn't want to eliminate a particular sport as a *sport*, simply because of ESPN's profit-maximizing behavior or its contractual arrangements with an organization's governing body.

Or, consider the Olympics, a much more international and seemingly "official" credentializer of "what is a sport." Here, we see a plethora of sports that enter our consciousness once every four years only to disappear again. Many of the shooting sports, synchronized swimming, and rhythmic gymnastics come to mind. Some sports gain apparent legitimacy with their inclusion and then disappear . . . and sometimes appear again. Tennis, for example, was an Olympic sport from 1896 till 1924 and resumed official status (beyond being a "demonstration sport") in 1988. Softball was an Olympic sport only from 1996 until 2008. The world's most popular sport, soccer, is in the Olympics but the important championship is the other quadrennial event: the World Cup.

Definitions for bolded terms can be found in the glossary/index at the back of the book.

So, how would we go about deciding what criteria to use in deciding whether a given activity is or isn't a sport? Many definitions of sport have been proposed. We offer five here:

1. Coakley (2009: 6) suggests a general definition that many scholars have relied on: Sports are "well-established, officially governed competitive physical activities in which participants are motivated by internal and external rewards."
2. Coakley (2009: 10) also offers a "contested" version of a definition of sport, wherein "sports are contested activities" and there are disagreements over the "meaning, purpose, and organization of sports." These disagreements play out as well with respect to who should be allowed to play, the conditions under which they can play, and who provides the resources for playing.
3. Curry and Jiobu (1984: 8) suggest that "[s]port is a physical activity that is fair, competitive, nondeviant, and that is guided by rules, organization, and/or tradition."
4. Guttmann (2004: 2) argues that "sports can be defined as autotelic [it has its own purpose] physical contests." He admits that this is an ahistorical definition and adds that a comparative historical framework is necessary to understand the many variations that have occurred across time and space.
5. According to Giulianotti (2005: xii–xiii), sport is:
    1. structured by rules and codes of conduct, spatial and temporal frameworks (playing fields and time limits on games), and institutions of government;
    2. goal-oriented: aimed at particular objectives (e.g., scoring goals, winning contests, increasing averages), thus winners and losers are identifiable;
    3. competitive: rivals are defeated, records are broken;
    4. ludic, enabling playful experiences, generating excitement;
    5. culturally situated, in that factors 1–4 correspond closely to the value systems and power relations within the relevant sport's host society.

If we think through these different definitions, we can see that they all imply—sometimes by avoiding the issue—that sports are socially and historically situated. The first definition simply sidesteps the social and historical question by saying that sports are "well-established" and "officially governed." We are encouraged to accept that the establishment and governance exist without questioning how that sport became well established and how it became governed in that particular, official manner. Curry and Jiobu's definition similarly avoids a host of sociological questions: what is fair; what is nondeviant; and how do rules, organization, and tradition get instituted? Guttmann's definition, by including the idea of contests, suggests that sports are also play, also rule-bound, but definitely competitive. The other definitions explicitly include a social and historical contextual element. All the definitions agree that sports are rule-bound, competitive activities but differ about whether or not they are physical. Giulianotti explicitly includes games like darts and snooker in his definition since they do have a physical component and accord with the other criteria.[2] His last criterion, that sport is "culturally situated," is his most important one. We don't call a sport a sport unless criteria 1–4 "fit" within the value systems and power relations in the given society. Coakley's "contested" definition is another way of thinking about this "fit."

It is worthwhile to acknowledge that there are many activities that are physical and athletic but are not sports and many competitions that are playful, goal-oriented, and have rules and leagues but are not sports. Dance is probably the clearest example of an athletic activity that lacks a competitive aspect. Scrabble and chess are highly organized, goal-oriented, exciting competitions that lack intense physical engagement and hence would not be sports, according to most definitions.

It is also important to consider that the very definition of sport is socially and historically variable. "What is a sport" has changed over time and is different in different societies. Activities vie to become sports. Yes, there is a competition among activities to become sports (even beyond getting on to ESPN or being slated for the Olympics). And this has everything to do with how those activities "fit" into their host societies. To give a simple example, we would not expect Buzkashi, the national sport of Afghanistan, which involves horse riders moving a goat carcass to a scoring area, to be prevalent in contemporary, dense, US metropolitan areas.

WHAT IS SOCIOLOGY?

The definitions of sport that we've offered reference the larger social context in which the sports are played. ***Sociology*** focuses on the many ways that individuals' motivations and actions are shaped by the society in which they live as well as the ways that individuals contribute to the way society is organized. A simple way of seeing this is to notice how "normal" it is for children in Brooklyn, New York to learn basketball and how "normal" it is for children of the same age in Rio de Janeiro, Brazil to grow up playing soccer/football. Different societies have different histories and the people in those societies who have made those histories have produced different societies. There's certainly nothing except the larger social context that can explain why the bat that the Pakistani athlete picks up is probably so that he can play cricket and the one that the Japanese athlete picks up is most likely used to play baseball. Sociology is focused on providing us with the conceptual tools to dissect exactly how we can understand that larger social context.

One idea that is central to sociology is the concept of **social institution**. Social institutions such as language, the family, education, government, religion, and sport are enduring relationships, stories, meanings, and social forms that people create together but that exist independent of them.[3] In fact, we can think about sociology as the study of the relationship between individuals and social institutions (Scott, 2008). The problem, though, is that social institutions exist at many levels of abstraction and they manifest themselves in many ways. So, for example, we can talk about language as a social institution insofar as it is rooted in and created by social relationships, is enduring, carries meanings, and takes various social forms (think of the differences between family talk and talk with a government official). As that parenthetical phrase suggests, however, we cannot look at social institutions in isolation, as they are each related to and set contexts for one another.

If we only focus on the three institutions just mentioned—language, family, government—we can think about an immigrant family's communication processes: US-born children speaking flawless English to parents and grandparents, whose English skills are at various stages of development and whose residency/citizenship is legally/governmentally fraught. Certainly, we can focus on family *or* language *or* government to understand the immigrants' situations—but if we do, we certainly have to account for the other institutions if we are to attain a complete understanding. Sociology gives us the means to foreground any given social phenomenon and see it in its embedded complexity. This initial chapter will help you do that with sports.

WHAT IS THE SOCIOLOGY OF SPORT?

The **sociology of sport** is focused on the study of sport as a social institution. Yes, we want to understand the game; but we also want to focus on the "games outside the games," which means that we must understand sport as it relates to other institutions. These set the context for the game itself and we can't understand the game without understanding that larger social context.

Sociologists differ in their theoretical understandings of the nature and dynamics of society. In this brief introductory chapter, we will lay out the general ideas from ***functionalist*, *conflict*,** and ***symbolic interactionist*** theoretical perspectives. We will also introduce some variations within each of those theories. Theories tell us what in particular we should look for as we explore the relationships between sports and society.

Functionalist perspective. In the functionalist framework, sociologists focus their attention on what holds society together; they are interested in the problem of social order. Since individuals have all sorts of interests, proclivities, and inclinations—many of which conflict with one another, how do we ever get to a point that there is enough cooperation to make society even viable, let alone a flourishing phenomenon?

Emile Durkheim (1858–1917). Emile Durkheim, considered one of the founders of sociology, suggested that society is like a human organism, insofar as its parts must work in harmony for the greater good of the organism. His idea of "organic solidarity" is based on the idea that the society, deriving especially from the industrial division of labor, binds each person to play particular roles in the society. So, just as each individual performs a critical function on the assembly line so, also, does each person play a critical role in, say, the family, school, and church. Ultimately, Durkheim believed that societies are held together because there are some basic, underlying values that everyone believes in and these values are reinforced through rituals that people practice in their everyday lives.

In his book *Elementary Forms of Religious Life*, Durkheim (1965/1915) describes how Australian aboriginal tribes engaged in collective rituals. They would choose an object—a totem—designate it as *sacred* (separate and apart from profane daily life), and organize collective rituals around the totem that bound the society together and reinforced the sacredness of that object.

This kind of ritualism may seem far removed from twenty-first century society, but we can easily apply it to two examples of sports-related social solidarity. First, we can think about the kind of cooperation necessary for a football team to play a game—11 players, with different roles, functioning as a unit. If we broaden this a bit to think about all the players that aren't on the field at the same time, we can think about the various activities that players engage in as a team—their practice and pre-game rituals—that reinforce their collective solidarity. Second, we can think about the fans that gather to watch their favorite sports team. On the way into the stadium, we pass statues and iconic plaques that memorialize great moments and players—*sacred* moments and players. We sit or stand, body to body, with people we don't know (and who, if we knew them, we might not even like!) and experience elation and despair together as we practice our sports-related rituals in support of our sacred team.

Conflict perspective. The conflict perspective focuses on the social divisions that exist in society and is concerned with the sources and dynamics of social change. Three theorists are particularly important in the context of conflict perspective: Marx, Weber, and Bourdieu. We will consider each in turn.

Karl Marx (1818–1883). Karl Marx considered conflict among **social classes** to be the engine of history. He analyzed societies by looking at the key cleavages that existed in their primary economic systems. These cleavages—usually, between owners and non-owners—demarcated the main social classes in those societies. In contemporary society, dominated by capitalism, he saw the main conflict as occurring between two classes: capitalists (owners of **capital**) and workers (who own nothing but their labor power). In this system, he saw competition among capitalists as driving them continually to expand to new markets and to exploit the workers in ever newer ways in a search for greater profits. Capitalists who "won" would have greater resources to win more in the future and those who lost would be eliminated (and, perhaps, be forced to join the working class). Workers, on the other hand, would be "free" to sell their labor power in the marketplace for the best price possible. Ultimately, they would be driven to join unions and political parties to resist the speed-up, de-skilling, and dehumanization of their jobs imposed on them by the capitalists. Since, over time, there would be fewer and fewer capitalists and more and more workers organizing against the capitalists and the system that exploited them, Marx believed that this conflict would lead to the victory of the workers over the capitalists and would establish a new, socialist society. This society would not have the kinds of radical inequalities and power differentials of capitalist society. Marx's relative inattention to other kinds of conflicts (e.g. **race**, ethnic, and **gender** inequalities) is a major limitation of his approach.

Marx's theory suggested that, in contemporary society, the power of the capitalist class and the dynamics of the capitalist economic system would shape all of the other social institutions of the society. He expected that, for instance, the educational system, culture, and the state (the government and its agencies) would all work in ways that ultimately reinforced the capitalist system. So, from a Marxist perspective, the educational system would produce workers that could be easily slotted into the capitalist workplace. The kinds of culture that are produced (books, theater, music, and ideas, more generally—sports would be included here) would tend to reinforce the idea that the individual has the capacity to sink or swim in a society that ostensibly provides equal opportunity for all (we are all equal as individuals in the marketplace). Marxist theorists would refer to this notion as an ideology that helps the capitalists maintain their power by providing justification for their actions.

To the extent that the population has bought into this ideology, we can say that the capitalists maintain their power through consent rather than force. Marxists call this ***hegemony***. Indeed, when institutions simply operate according to "natural" stories and narratives, we can think about them as being embedded in a hegemonic system. Finally, the state would produce and enforce public policies that would protect the property of the capitalists by, for example, limiting corporate taxes and constraining the political organization of the workers.

From a Marxist perspective, the contemporary sociological analysis of sports would focus primarily on two key aspects: the conditions of athletic production and the nature and effects of sports consumption. The former would highlight the ways that athletes have been pushed toward greater specialization and decreased autonomy in pursuing their craft. This has led in the major professional sports to major owner-worker conflict and the eventual establishment of players' unions. Sports consumption, from a Marxist perspective, contributes to societal stability in two ways. First, the collective passion toward sports distracts people from the vagaries and exploitation of everyday life: when the workday is over, I can root for my beloved Rangers/Giants/Titans and not think about my nasty boss. Second, even as the fans are all equal and equally committed to their team, the organization of the fans in the stadium reinforces and normalizes class divisions by having the many cheap bleacher seats and the few, expensive/luxury boxes.

Max Weber (1864–1920). Max Weber also focused on conflict as the most important aspect of society, but he broadened Marx's focus on economic class to include race/ethnic/national conflicts as well. While Weber saw economically based cleavages as critically important, he also saw ideas and values as main drivers of social change and individual motivation. His idea of **social closure** suggests that groups can seize on any characteristic to engage in exclusionary behavior (see Parkin, 1979). So, one's class or race or **ethnicity** or gender (or language or neighborhood) might be seized on by a dominant group in order to exclude any other group(s) from scarce, valued resources.[4] And the excluded, **subordinate groups** will also mobilize to attempt to usurp the resources from which they have been excluded. These struggles can lead to significant social change, as when **dominant groups** lose some of their power to monopolize those scarce resources.

The conflicts often involve the use of symbols and ideologies—for example, equal treatment based on ability—seen to reflect the interests of given groups. An excellent example from baseball is the struggle to racially integrate the "national pastime." A Weberian analysis would focus on the patterns and processes of **exclusion** and **usurpation** that had been in place prior to Jackie Robinson's becoming a Brooklyn Dodger. Weber's attention to the varied social bases of group formation gives his framework the flexibility to be applied to many situations but at the expense of not knowing specifically where to look to find the most salient conflicts in any given society.

Weber foresaw that modern society would witness a vast expansion of bureaucracy in all areas of social life. Bureaucratic organizations are characterized by highly developed divisions of labor, clear lines of hierarchy, and rule by experts. These organizations develop as part of the increasing rationalization of everyday life, wherein more and more decisions are subjected to a formal, means-end, **instrumental rationality** that is oriented toward specific ends. So, the small neighborhood hardware store would be overtaken by the super-efficient, larger national chain. Weber was concerned that bureaucratic rationality in the context of rule by experts would lead to a decline in democratic participation. With greater development of scientific rationality, Weber also expected a decline in the importance of religion, a process he thought of as part of a progressive "disenchantment of the world."

A Weberian perspective on sport would surely focus our attention on all the ways that "scientific rationality" has been leveraged in the pursuit of success on the field, court, and pitch. Although consistent with a Marxian approach as well, a "moneyball" (see Lewis, 2003) orientation toward winning, whereby "old," untested knowledge is replaced by empirically verifiable results, is at one with a Weberian perspective that expects rationalization processes to dominate all aspects of social life. In terms of fandom and community, a Weberian sociologist of sports would not be surprised at all by the fervor with which fans of different teams confront each other. The symbols and ideologies associated with different teams would be important foci for the relevant communities.[5] At the same time, while fans want their teams to use every possible means to make the best decisions so as to maximize likelihood of victory (using the most rational means available), they are also often imprisoned by superstitious behavior that they believe is necessary for victory (suggesting that Weber was wrong in predicting the decline of religion!).

Pierre Bourdieu (1930–2002). As opposed to Marx and Weber, who ignored sports, Pierre Bourdieu directly discussed the role of sports in social life. In line with Marx and Weber, his theoretical approach is focused on inequality and power.[6] Bourdieu sees one's position in the class structure determined by where one is located in the distribution of economic (income and wealth), cultural (education, tastes, and habits), and social (resources in one's networks) capital. So, to the extent that we have a group of people located at the very top of the three distributions (high in economic *and* cultural *and* **social capital**), that group would be the dominant class. The subordinate class would be composed of those who are low across all three of these distributions, while intermediate classes would be located between these two extremes.

In more recent decades, **cultural capital** has become a more important determinant of one's position in the overall class structure and, indeed, the classes with high cultural capital have become more powerful in the society. Since many occupational positions have specific educational requirements and employers use personal interviews to assess the style and habits of potential hires, one's cultural capital plays a key role in determining one's overall social standing. Bourdieu makes clear that, though no particular cultural style is inherently more valuable than any other, the dominant groups in a society have the power to certify particular cultural practices and knowledge as highly valued, which, of course, gives them a major advantage in reproducing their high status—yes, they tend to be good at the things that are deemed valuable (having been able to deem those things valuable).

Bourdieu's attention to the different capitals (and forms of capital) that people use in their attempts to maintain or advance their class position manifests itself in sports as we look at which sports people play and how they play those sports. Bourdieu roots people's sports choices in their experiences growing up in particular social spaces—in the US, playing golf versus playing basketball is connected strongly to one's social class and the social space it occupies—and he further highlights the differences between playing tennis, say, at an exclusive club (wearing "whites") versus playing in tattered shorts and everyday sneakers at a public court (Bourdieu, 1988).

Struggles of individuals and classes to enhance or reproduce their status or, as Bourdieu might put it, to gain "**distinction**," are only one aspect of Bourdieu's analysis of power. These struggles take place within ***fields***, which are structured social spaces in which people strategize and attempt to use the resources at their disposal to gain advantage. People's perceptions of their resources and how relevant they are to their struggles are based on their ***habitus***, a socially structured set of dispositions toward the world that facilitates and constrains one's actions. One's habitus is a somewhat conscious and somewhat unconscious perception of one's opportunity structure and how one might best navigate one's relevant fields. So, an upper middle class, white, urban male, following his habitus, may take up squash as his sport, since that seems to be what the "cool" kids are doing in his elite private school (the micro-field in which he is operating). A black working-class urban male may take up basketball, since that is dominant in his neighborhood (the micro-field in which he is operating).

Every society is constituted by a series of fields—for example, the political field, the artistic field, the religious field, and others—in which actors and organizations vie for dominance by attempting to monopolize the resources at hand. The resources are the capitals relevant to that field. We can imagine sport competing for resources with health and education in the political field, as relevant contestants vie for money and other perquisites from the government or other political agencies. In the sport field in the United States, we can think of the various professional leagues as competing to be dominant in this social space. In 2014, the National Football League would be seen as dominant, capturing the most revenue and media attention, easily outpacing the other three major sports leagues (see Gaines, 2014). Soccer, boxing, Mixed Martial Arts, and X Games would be much smaller blips in that field. If we were to compare this field to what it was in, say, 1960, we'd see enormous differences. Major League Baseball would be dominant, with the NFL barely visible. Even less visible at that time was the American Football League, which began operation in that year with such teams as the New York Titans (later called the Jets), the Los Angeles Chargers (who moved to San Diego), and the Dallas Texans (soon relocated to Kansas City as the Chiefs). The NHL (with six teams—four in the US and two in Canada) and the NBA (with eight teams and only one west of the Mississippi) were also struggling entities compared to MLB. Boxing would have been a much more powerful presence in 1960 than it is now, and MMA and the X Games did not even exist.

Bourdieu helps us understand these historical changes by referring to a "field of power." The "field of power" structures the ways that power and resources operate within other fields in the society. The rise of media/communication corporations in the economic field has led to the dominance of their form of capital in the field of power and, therefore, in the society as a whole. So, in the sports field, the increased importance of the media forms the backdrop for how the NFL began its rise to prominence and how the X Games is even visible.

Bourdieu's perspective helps us address, for example, the question of why the US, a sports-crazed nation, is not crazy about the sport soccer—that most of the rest of the world is totally crazy about (Markovits and Hellerman, 2001), and how and why that might be changing. Understanding this notion of fields also helps us think about how new sports compete for legitimacy and popularity with more central, powerful sports. Or, we can think about whether and how Major League Soccer in the US might, over time, be able to become more central and more powerful in the sports field.

Neo-institutional theory. Building on Bourdieu's concept of "field" as well as the concept of institution, neo-institutional theory is a theoretical perspective related to the conflict perspective. In neo-institutional theory, a key empirical focus is the **organizational field** (DiMaggio and Powell, 1983), defined as

> those organizations that, in the aggregate, constitute a recognized area of institutional life: key suppliers, resource and product consumers, regulatory agencies, and other organizations that produce similar products or services.
>
> (1983:143)

Bringing together our definition of institutions with this notion of organizational field, we can see that we are talking about organizations that are necessarily relating to one another, sharing stories and meanings, and being subject to similar sets of constraints—both coercive (for example, economic constraints) and normative (say, the rules of the game in certain industries). So, within a given field, the organizational actors share a common set of assumptions—an **institutional logic**—about how they can and should relate to one another and they have similar conceptions about how the world works.[7] These **institutional logics** (Friedland and Alford, 1991: 248–9), which are the underlying, taken-for-granted principles and practices of a given institutional environment, are very strong orienting mechanisms for these organizations. It is also important to recognize, however, that, at any given time, an organization—since it is not located in just one organizational field—may be subject to competing logics, even contradictory, logics.

In the context of sports, let's take the example of a team in a professional sports league. As the definition above suggests, its organizational field would include the other teams in the league, potential team members (athletes from around the world), fans, the league office as well as any government agencies that regulate the team's activities (local, state, national), and, more broadly, other organizations that vie for the entertainment dollar of the public. The primary institutional logic of a sports team is, as Al Davis, the long-time owner (until he died) of the Oakland Raiders football team put it, "just win, baby." The institutional logic could more formally be presented as maximizing instrumental rationality (efficiently using the resources at hand to achieve a given goal) toward the goal of winning games and, ultimately, championships. It would seem obvious that this institutional logic is a given for sports teams. But sports teams are also business enterprises and such organizations generally have profit maximization as the dominant institutional logic. A neo-institutional perspective would allow the analyst to tease out how the various pressures from these competing logics play themselves out in given situations.[8]

Symbolic interactionist perspective. The last of the three sociological perspectives explored here, the symbolic interactionist perspective, focuses much more on the "micro level"—the direct relationship among individuals and between the individual and society. It considers the subjective understandings that develop among individuals to be the primary means by which society is "socially constructed"; indeed, it is the basis of social order. The world exists as it does by virtue of the understandings that are implicitly agreed and acted on by the individuals in given societies. Symbolic interaction theorists focus on inter-personal relationships, with particular emphasis on the development of conceptions of self through interactions with significant others. This is especially evident in athletic peer groups, as Michael Messner discusses in Chapter 28. There, he provides examples of misogynistic behavior by male athletes, focusing on how the various individuals interact with one another and how they mutually encourage and permit behavior that is normally not acceptable.

A key insight from this perspective is W. I. Thomas's dictum: "if [humans] define situations as real, they are real in their consequences." This is the idea that people's "definition of the situation" is critical to understanding how and why they act as they do. Symbolic interaction theorists attempt to understand how individuals co-construct their shared meanings and they see this process as part and parcel of the construction of society and of social change.

From a symbolic interactionist perspective, we might compare how Division I college athletes think about their Sports in Society class compared to their athletically inclined, intramural-playing classmates. Although both types probably find the content of the course interesting, the D-I athletes are probably much more focused on studying enough to get a grade that enables them to maintain their athletic eligibility while the other students, perhaps, are focused entirely on truly understanding the content and concepts offered by the professor (they also may pay just a bit of attention to their grades!). The students' different definitions of the situation—derived especially from their peers—play a determining role in their behaviors.

SPORT AS A SOCIAL INSTITUTION

Returning to the general idea of how sports fit into the larger society, we wish to highlight the importance of *sport as a social institution.* This means that we wish to understand its enduring qualities as a phenomenon that is composed of individuals in society and that has clear effects on individuals in determining behaviors, motivations, meanings, and relationships. When we understand sport as a social institution, we are highlighting both its effects on the people involved in sporting endeavors and on its relationship to other sectors of society. Most important, it is not simply the sum of the behaviors of the individuals involved; it exists apart from and, in a real sense, above those individuals.

Essentially, we are suggesting that one has to consider the social space within which individual sports are located, in which they compete with one another for power and advantage, and then view sports' collective social space as located within a larger societal field that includes other institutions such as other parts of the entertainment industry, the educational system, and, say, religion. Sport is one of many institutions in society and is affected not only by the ones with which it has direct contact but also, as noted earlier, by the larger, societal field of power. Sport may get marginalized during certain periods not because some other institution directly "nudged it aside" but because other institutions became more central to some larger social issues (as an obvious example, sports tend to get marginalized during wars).

SPORT AND POWER IN SOCIETY

A major focus in this book is how sport affects, is affected by, and is imbued with relations of power in the larger society. Underlying our analysis of sport, then, is a recognition that the society's "field of power" is central to a sociology of sport (Bourdieu, 1988). This means that, in order to understand sport in a given society, we have to take into account the patterns and dynamics of power and stratification—who controls power and resources, how the powerful exercise their dominance, and how "the excluded" struggle for access—in that society.

Sports that are dominant in a given society are not only those that most people play and attend to but also those that are important to the elite. If given sports are important to the elite and to affluent consumers, they will get much more commercial attention from corporate sponsors and therefore television time from media corporations. Thus, in the US, golf gets much more prominent exposure than, say, bowling. A proper analysis would take into account not only the resources of the main organizations of each sport but how they are connected to global media. Sometimes, this connection takes the form of a contractual relationship to broadcast given events and sometimes the connection manifests itself in the form of ownership (for example, James L. Dolan is the Chief Executive Officer of Cablevision and the Executive Chairman of Madison Square Garden Company, which owns the New York Knicks [National Basketball Association] and the New York Rangers [National Hockey League]).

We also wish to draw attention to the many different spheres in which power dynamics are important. In subsequent sections of this book we will address, for example, conflicts between team owners and players; these days, sports fans hear all the time about CBAs (collective bargaining agreements). We examine differences between sports in societies that strongly control them compared to societies where sports markets are less regulated (see, especially, Chapter 19 by Baird). Or, one could examine the power relations involved in the power of the media over sports (see Chapter 16 by Rowe), as when, for example, games are rescheduled based on media profit expectations or significantly extended in order to accommodate more commercial interruptions.

SPORT AS AN OSTENSIBLE MERITOCRACY

While sport constitutes one of many social institutions, we wish to draw attention to one of its most unique aspects: that it is an *ostensible* meritocracy whose contests are public and transparent.[9] The goal of sports competitions is to win—a clear, agreed-upon, measurable outcome—and the public viewing the contests, having played and watched those sports, can assess whether the team or a given player is performing according to the norms of instrumental rationality. The audience assesses whether the players' or team's efforts and skills are up to the tasks at hand. Contrast this to another, ostensibly meritocratic institution: education. If a teacher asks a student to read a paragraph, there are a multitude of ways for the teacher to evaluate the student: accuracy, pronunciation, and tone, for example. On the other hand, if a coach asks a player to shoot foul shots, the success rate will be the issue—if the form is off, no matter. Further, there is no audience that is viewing and evaluating the student's reading of the paragraph but, even in Little League, there is an audience at the game.[10] So, here we wish to emphasize that the sports contest is the one place where there is real *transparency* about meritocratic processes.

Let's clarify what we mean by "**meritocracy**." Its most common meaning is a form of social organization in which people get ahead by virtue of their talents, abilities, and efforts, rather than through bribes or special favors. The assumption is that, if people are evaluated and succeed based on their own efforts, then the competition among individuals is a fair one.[11] In capitalist democracies, there is strong emphasis on this idea of fair competition, or, as it has become known, a "level playing field." Yes, the most common way of expressing that the competition is fair is to use a sports metaphor. Our current understanding of fair competition for societal resources is rooted in a set of generally agreed-upon, or *normative*, practices that rewards productivity and merit and avoids the effects of inheritance, nepotism, or any other ascriptive ties. Indeed, in a "pure meritocracy," the focus on success and on winning should produce a carefully designed and executed plan to use the best—meaning most efficient and effective—strategies (and, in a collective context, the best employees or players) within the constraints of the rules of the game. And such rules should be enforced fairly and universally both within the organization and across the society (or, in sports, within the game and across the league).

It is our claim that the sports contest—the level playing field on which teams compete in public—exemplifies a particular notion of fair competition. We further claim that this sports-contest-derived idea of fairness represents a normative ideal in modern capitalist democracies, playing a key ideological role in "naturalizing" individuals' conceptions of what a fair and just society looks like. So, we argue that the institution of sport's underlying institutional logic is a meritocratic one, wherein competition takes place on the "level playing field" and "winning is everything." We are not suggesting that "meritocratic fairness" is the only or best notion of fairness; we do argue that it is hegemonic in modern capitalist democracies and that the institution of sport helps reinforce and legitimate that particular, and we believe quite flawed, conception of fairness.

Daniel Bell (1973: 409) claims that "the post-industrial society is, in its initial logic, a meritocracy." On what basis does he make this claim? Essentially, the argument is that no one is given high income and/or high status in our society unless they have *earned* it. Bell claimed that the university has "become the arbiter of class position" (1973: 410) and, since the university selects students on the basis of their previous academic achievements, the entire system is fair, meritocratic, and has none of the taint of nepotistic or other kinds of personal favoritism. In sports, as we can see when we watch the contests, we *know* that the owner of the team did not simply put his kid on the team and demand that the manager/coach put him in the lineup. When an owner turns the ownership of the team to his kids, however, no one raises an eyebrow—in fact, this is expected.[12] So, we're suggesting that there is a specific kind of fairness that people come to expect in our kind of society and that we expect it in certain places (and not in others).

During the course of this book, we will be exploring the institutional nature of sport—how its norms, practices, narratives, and beliefs shape how sport is produced but also how it relates to the rest of society. In effect, our focus in this exploration is on the "games outside the games" and *power* will be a central concern.

Before moving on, let's think more analytically about the idea of meritocratic fairness in relation to sports.[13] We need to make a number of points:

1. We do not regard meritocracy as a utopian—or even, as a desirable—social order because it has major flaws and blind spots.
2. We do believe that a meritocratic approach in sport has much to recommend it compared to practices that rely on ascriptive criteria (familial, tribal, or ethno-racial) for selecting personnel and managing competition.
3. We believe meritocratic fairness to be an ideological cover for true egalitarian competition: not only does meritocracy hide various types of inequalities but it ends up legitimating them by claiming that equality and ultimate fairness have been achieved.

To make these points more concrete, let's distinguish four dimensions of fair competition and equality in sport: 1. Contest fairness; 2. Access fairness; 3. Resource fairness; 4. Pipeline fairness.

Contest fairness. The first dimension focuses on equality and fair competition in actual sports contests. This dimension poses questions about the integrity of the contest, how the games are played. Cheating, either by or on behalf of certain contest participants or corruption among officials, is the major problem threatening fairness at this level. If cheating is simply taken for granted and rationalized by a widespread belief that "everyone does it," the sport operates at a predatory level, which is sometimes associated with bribery and gambling. Professional boxing, for example, had a long history of such predatory practices. When all players are equally subject to the same strictly enforced rules and regulations, the sport contests exhibit fair competition. This is routinely expected and evidenced in major sports in modern democratic capitalist societies.[14] Suspicions of cheating tend to be investigated; guilty athletes and sports organizations are subject to sanctions. Within this level of fairness, sport showcases the rule of law and legal equality of participants, which models the democratic capitalist legal order.

Access fairness. The second dimension points to a different pattern of equality and fair competition, focusing on the issue of whether there is open access to participate for all who demonstrate the requisite ability in the sport. The major problem threatening equality and fair competition at this level is discrimination. Much of the twentieth-century history of race relations in American sport highlights this level, as talented African-American athletes struggled for access to both college and professional sports. Jackie Robinson's entry into Major League Baseball marked a watershed in that struggle, breaking the racial barrier to the nation's most popular sport, which was followed by gradual opening of access for talented racial and ethnic minorities to all major sports.

The meritocratic model in sport was based on the institutionalization of these two levels of sport equality and fair competition. All participants in sport contests were subject to the same rules and regulations and access to participation was based on the individual's demonstrated talent rather than his class, ethnicity, or race. It seems reasonable to suggest that these meritocratic developments in sports influenced other major institutions in American society as they were followed by the Supreme Court's unanimous decision in *Brown v. Board of Education* and civil rights legislation, which institutionalized formal legal protections against non-meritocratic practices in education and employment.

But these two levels, important as they are, hardly constitute a full development of equality and fair competition in sport. That is because they fail to include two crucially important dimensions of fairness and equality. To move beyond these two aspects of meritocratic fairness to a more universalistic model of sport, we must consider the third and fourth dimensions of sport's potential development that have been much less visible on the radar screen of sports discourse in American society.

Resource fairness. The third level refers to the distribution of resources among sports competitors. Under the conditions of the meritocratic model, particularly when sports are subjected to the institutional logic of neo-liberal capitalism (all individuals and organizations are equal and they can "vote" with however many dollars they have[15]), sports oligopolies will tend to form, giving wealthier teams distinct advantages over poorer teams in acquiring talented players and winning games. This is a problem because it threatens the fundamental essence of sports: the principle of uncertainty of outcomes on a level playing field. We see this illustrated in Major League Baseball, where the unequal distribution of wealth among teams (in 2014, the Yankees and Dodgers far outspent the other teams) has created a relatively permanent structure of unfair competition. It is hardly coincidental that this resembles the meritocratic free market system of democratic capitalist economies. If the institutional development of sport is to advance to a more universalistic standard of fair competition, it must create conditions for an equitable distribution of resources among teams. Some sports organizations have moved further in this direction than others (the National Football League and the National Basketball Association, for example, have much "harder" salary caps, which attempt to preserve competitiveness, compared to MLB).

Pipeline fairness. The fourth dimension focuses on the development of talent and the expansion of the pipeline for sport participation. A universalistic standard of equality and fair competition should mean not merely that every person in the society should have an equal opportunity to *participate* in established sports but also, most importantly, to *develop one's talents* to play sports. The meritocratic model of sports in democratic capitalist societies—like the meritocratic model of education—falls short of that standard because it is based only on the (formal) equal opportunity to participate rather than on the (substantive) equal opportunity to develop one's talents in diverse ways, and thereby, increase one's possibilities for "success" in given endeavors.[16]

This model of fair competition in sport raises many questions about the conditions under which pressures for a more universalistic standard of equality and fair competition in sport is likely to emerge. How would this expanded standard of equality and fairness in sport affect the neo-liberal institutional logic, which is now a dominant force in major college and professional sports? Which sports and which societies have made progress in moving beyond the meritocratic model of fair competition in sports? Not until sports focus on developing practices that incorporate the third and fourth dimensions can we say that sports represent a truly level playing field. We will explore these issues, among others, throughout this book.

THE PLAN OF THE BOOK

In the sections that follow, we will review the literature and introduce theoretical perspectives that relate to different aspects of understanding sport as a social institution. Our goal is to consider the "games outside the games" in relation to the perspectives that we have already developed.

In Section 2, "Biases and Barriers in Sport: Class, Race, Gender, and Disability," we will discuss the ways that these divisions in society articulate with the development of sport. In particular, we will examine the ways that patterns of inclusion and exclusion have manifested themselves and what narratives have been used to explain those patterns. We will pay particular attention to instances when the institution of sport plays a central role in opening new spaces for previously excluded peoples. This section will also touch on the **socialization** of youth into the institution of sport. The readings in this section provide concrete, substantive examples of the various ways that class, race, gender, and (dis)ability affect and are incorporated into the institution of sport. From the ways that people use sport to cement or advance their social status to the ways that sport serves as a canvass upon which gender expectations are reproduced, the essays introduce the reader to the ways that sociologists analyze biases and barriers in the context of sports.

In Section 3, we will focus on "The Social Bonds Generated by Sports: Fandom, Community, and Media." These bonds range from the relatively ephemeral ties among strangers at a ballgame who connect in the context of the tension of a given contest to the international ties created in far-flung communities via media conglomerates as they shape the experience of sports audiences. And, of course, as groups gather in support of given teams, other groups gather in support of the opponents. We will explore the nature and dynamics of community-building (and separation) in this media-inflected sports world. The readings in this section attempt to capture the dynamics of how sports and communities intersect. Obviously, as media relationships have changed, so, too, have the connections between people and teams.

Section 4, "**Political Economy** and the Politics of Sports: Dynamics and Diffusion," focuses on the counter-intuitive relationship between the ways that politics are central to sport as a social institution and the ways that the political context of sport and the politics of the participants are marginalized. Even as sports team owners rely so fundamentally on political connections to produce and popularize its product—for everything from parking arrangements with municipalities to funding stadiums with state monies—owners attempt to keep sports pure and especially do not appreciate their players speaking out on political issues. We will examine how these conflicting institutional logics play out.

In this chapter, we focus on a range of connections between the economic and political spheres: union struggles; cross-national player mobility; public funding of sports; and international sports–media–corporate relations. The readings in this section underscore the centrality of politics to sports and attempt to convey the many situations in which people contest power relations in sports-related contexts.

In Section 5, "Breaking the Normative Rules: The Problems of **Deviance** in Sports," we explore a broad range of behaviors that conflicts with the generally accepted "rules of the game"—including those that are part and parcel of a meritocratic institutional logic. A basic, but extreme, form of deviance occurs when a game official is being paid off or gambles on a game he is officiating. Thinking about the range of deviant behaviors, some involve transgressions within the contest, which are generally sanctioned by the officials who are regulating the game, while others involve trying to gain an advantage through, say, pharmacological means. We will also explore behaviors of athletes off the field. This section's readings provide excellent examples of how different forms of deviance—from violence to drugs to sexualities—articulate with sport as a social institution. They convey the way that sociologists study and contextualize these behaviors that occur in the realm of sports.

Section 6, "Globalization and Sports," focuses on the myriad ways that sports have become a global institution. We will examine the connections that have developed across nations within sports (FIFA) and across sports (Olympics). We are especially interested in the effects on community-building and on changes in cultural values and normative standards as a result of the spread of sports. Finally, we consider whether and how sports can be a greater force for democratic empowerment within and across societies. The readings in this section are especially focused on situations in which sports are imported to "new" places and fans are exposed to "new" sports.

NOTES

1 In *Seabiscuit*, Laura Hillenbrand (2001) provides an excellent description of the athletic challenges that jockeys face as they attempt to guide an "athlete" that weighs, perhaps, 12 times as much as they do to a victory over the course of a mile-long racecourse.

2 It is unclear whether Giulianotti would include games like chess and Scrabble in his definition of sport. He wants an inclusive definition but he also mentions "intensive physical engagement and proficiency in hand-eye coordination" (2005: xiii) in his justification for including games like darts, bowling, and pool. It is not in his five criteria, however.

3 Conley (2013), Friedland and Alford (1991), and Scott (2008) were all helpful in defining "institution."

4 The history of African Americans' exclusion from construction trades—for example, plumbing, plastering, and tile layers—would be a good example of social closure. Many unions had kin- and ethnic-based hiring practices. See Sugrue, 2004.

5 While Marx and Weber would both see ideologies as relevant in interpreting fan behavior, Weber would be much more likely than Marx to expect conflicts among fans of different teams since they are often rooted in neighborhood or geographical associations. Marx would see conflicts among fans as part of the *disorganizing* effects of ideology on working class unity as well as a means of smoothing conflicts between capitalists and workers.

6 Our discussion of Bourdieu owes much to Swartz (1997; 2013). Also, see Chapter 1 by Bourdieu.

7 Part of this may be related to the **hegemonic ideology** of the society.

8 In Section 4, we present the organizational field of a fictitious football program at Football State University. There, all the various pressures and constraints on the team are indicated and it becomes clear that the organization is subject to multiple institutional logics. See p. 289.

9 In this section, we draw on Washington and Karen (2012).

10 In Section 2, we will provide concrete empirical examples of the implications of this aspect of competitive sports. See p. 31.

11 Kristen Purcell (1996) argues that a number of mental leveling processes are involved in making these kinds of comparisons and measurements.

12 However, in the event the team does poorly, we might expect fans to complain about how the kid isn't doing as well as the father and that this is what happens when inheritance and nepotism are at work.

13 The next few paragraphs rely directly on Washington and Karen (2012).

14 The recent allegations about football/soccer are particularly troubling in this regard. See Hill and Longman (2014).

15 This institutional logic is summarized best by the following famous quote from Anatole France: "The law, in its majestic equality, forbids the rich as well as the poor to sleep under bridges, to beg in the streets, and to steal bread."

16 This fourth dimension implies a very different standard of success than one implied in a meritocratic model. Indeed, incorporating this fourth dimension essentially means valorizing and respecting all individuals for their unique personhood.

REFERENCES

Bell, Daniel. 1973. *The Coming of Post-Industrial Society.* New York, NY: Basic.

Bourdieu, Pierre. 1988. "Program for a Sociology of Sport." *Sociology of Sport Journal* 5(2): 153–161.

Coakley, Jay. 2009. *Sports in Society: Issues and Controversies.* 10th edition. New York, NY: McGraw Hill.

Conley, Dalton. 2013. *You May Ask Yourself: An Introduction to Thinking Like a Sociologist.* New York, NY: W. W. Norton.

Curry, Timothy J. and Robert M. Jiobu. 1984. *Sports: A Social Perspective.* Englewood Cliffs, NJ: Prentice-Hall, Inc.

DiMaggio, Paul J. and Walter W. Powell. 1983. "The Iron Cage Revisited: Institutional Isomorphism and Collective Rationality in Organizational Fields." *American Sociological Review* 48(2) (April): 147–160.

Durkheim, Emile. 1965. *The Elementary Forms of Religious Life.* New York, NY: Free Press. (Originally published by George Allen and Unwin, 1915.)

Friedland, Roger, and Robert R. Alford. 1991. "Bringing Society Back in: Symbols, Practices, and Institutional Contradictions." Pp. 232–266 in *The New Institutionalism in Organizational Analysis,* edited by Walter W. Powell and Paul J. DiMaggio. Chicago, IL: University of Chicago Press.

Gaines, Cork. 2014. "CHART: English Soccer Lags Way Behind Top American Sports in Revenue." March 18. *Business Insider.* www.businessinsider.com/premier-league-sports-mlb-nfl-nba-nhl-revenue-2014-3

Giulianotti, Richard. 2005. *Sport: A Critical Sociology,* Cambridge, UK: Polity Press.

Guttmann, Allen. 2004. *Sports: The First Five Millennia.* Massachusetts, MA: University of Massachusetts Press.

Hill, Declan and Jeré Longman. 2014. "Fixed Soccer Matches Cast Shadow Over World Cup." 2 parts. May 31, June 1. *New York Times.* www.nytimes.com/2014/06/01/sports/soccer/fixed-matches-cast-shadow-over-world-cup.html

Hillenbrand, Lauren. 2001. *Seabiscuit: An American Legend.* New York, NY: Random House.

Lewis, Michael. 2003. *Moneyball: The Art of Winning an Unfair Game.* New York, NY: W. W. Norton.

Markovits, Andrei S. and Steven Hellerman. 2010. *Offside: Soccer and American Exceptionalism.* Princeton, NJ: Princeton University Press.

Messner, Michael. 2002. *Taking the Field: Women, Men, and Sports.* Minneapolis, MN: U. of Minnesota Press.

Parkin, Frank. 1979. *Marxism and Class Theory: A Bourgeois Critique.* New York, NY: Columbia University Press.

Plunkett Research. 2014. http://www.plunkettresearch.com/sports-recreation-leisure-market-research/industry-and-business-data

Purcell, Kristen. 1996. "In a League of Their Own: Mental Leveling and the Creation of Social Comparability in Sport." *Sociological Forum* 11(3): 435-–456.

Scott, W. Richard. 2008. *Institutions and Organizations.* Thousand Oaks, CA: Sage. 2nd edition.

Sugrue, Thomas J. 2004. "Affirmative Action from Below: Civil Rights, the Building Trades, and the Politics of Racial Equality in the Urban North, 1945–1969." *J. of American History* 91(1): 145–173.

Swartz, David. 1997. *Culture and Power: The Sociology of Pierre Bourdieu.* Chicago, IL: University of Chicago Press.

—— 2013. *Symbolic Power, Politics and Intellectuals: The Political Sociology of Pierre Bourdieu.* Chicago, IL and London: University of Chicago Press.

U.S. Census Bureau, Statistical Abstract of the United States. 2012. Table 1228. Arts, Entertainment, and Recreation Services—Estimated Revenue: 2004 to 2009. P. 758. Washington, D.C.

Washington, Robert and David Karen. 2012. "Sport as a Model of Meritocracy: Theoretical Implications and a Research Agenda." Pp. 133–162 in *A Mirror of Our Culture: Sport and Society in America*, edited by Kevin Quinn and Michael Marsden. DiPere, WI: St. Norbert College Press.

SECTION 2

Biases and Barriers in Sport: Class, Race, Gender, and Disability

In today's world, it is quite obvious that society's scarce and valued resources are unequally distributed. Many sociologists would argue that this inequality reflects the power relations of the society: those with power have benefited from the way society is organized and can advance their interests even further thanks to their advantaged situation. Those without power are disadvantaged not only in their access to valued resources but also in being able to affect the societal arrangements that confer privilege.

In this section, we introduce you to the biases and barriers that affect sport participation. We do this, first, by reviewing how sociologists have conceived of class, race/ethnicity, gender, and disability. We explain different theories that use these concepts so that they can be applied as we discuss their value later in the section. We will also assess the relative importance of sport participation's biases and barriers and examine how they have changed over time.

SOCIAL INEQUALITY IN THE UNITED STATES

Whether we assess inequality in terms of wealth, income, or other measures, the distribution of resources in many societies—among economically advantaged societies, perhaps especially the United States—is highly unequal.[1] In the US, the top 1 percent of wealth[2] holders in 2010 controlled 35.4 percent of all wealth, while the bottom 90 percent held 23.3 percent of all wealth. Income is also unequally distributed. In 2010, the households in the top 1 percent of income[3] received 17.2 percent of all income, while the bottom 90 percent received only 55.5 percent of all income.

Economic resources are also unequally distributed by race/ethnicity. Since the distributions of income and wealth in most societies are highly "skewed" (that is, there are a very few individuals or families with a very large share of the wealth and income), social scientists often use the *median* to compare economic resources across groups. The median is the exact middle of the distribution; thus, it is not as sensitive to outliers (or distributions with long tails) as is the mean. In 2010, median white family wealth was $97,000, compared with $4,900 for blacks and $1,300 for Latinos. In addition, approximately one-third of black and Latino families had zero wealth or were in debt compared with less than one-fifth of white families. In 2010, the black median family income was 61 percent of whites' and the Latino median family income was 63 percent of whites'.

Finally, despite major advances in women's labor force participation and compensation since the 1960s, there remain some major differences between men's and women's experience in the labor force. In 2011, women's hourly wage rate was 84 percent of men's, and female college graduates in that year earned about 24 percent less than male college graduates. Over 55 percent of those who worked at minimum-wage jobs in 2011 were women, even though women made up less than 47 percent of the labor force.

The question for us here is: how does social inequality—in particular, inequality related to social class, race/ethnicity, gender, and disability—affect the institution of sport? We also examine the flip side of this question: how does sport as a social institution affect social relations—especially with respect to these power-related divisions—in the larger society? In essence, then, this section focuses on the relationship between sport and social power, focusing especially on these various biases and barriers.

We begin by examining how social class, race/ethnicity, and gender affect the extent and nature of participation in sport, at both the amateur and professional levels. Does bias affect the distribution of people into (different) sports and, if so, how? Are there differences in how different groups orient toward sports with more/less bodily contact, more/less teamwork, or, say, more/less cost? In team sports, do athletes from different backgrounds play different positions? What are the differences between *how* various groups play given sports: tennis in a public park versus tennis at a country club, for example. Is sport a social escalator that enables those from disadvantaged backgrounds to be upwardly mobile? To the extent that barriers have been overcome, how has that happened? What barriers remain? What biases and barriers are associated with ability/disability, age, sexual orientation, or with any other "differences"? How do these patterns change over time and why?

We will also ask questions about spillover effects from sports to the larger society. Do changes in biases and barriers within sport come from changes in the larger society, or can the reverse take place? What kinds of social divisions are overcome or reinforced through different patterns of sport participation?

These questions relate directly to the issues we raised in Section 1 about sports, inclusion, and the four dimensions of fairness (see p. 13 ff.). How do factors such as class, race/ethnicity, gender, and disability affect the likelihood that one would have exposure and access to the full range of sporting activities in given societies? A society that realized the most inclusive dimension—the "pipeline" dimension—of fairness would organize sports in ways that would provide opportunities for all to be trained in the sports they favor. Thus, it makes sense to begin our discussion with a look at how sociologists have conceptualized the biases and barriers that prevent these dimensions of fairness from being realized.

SOCIAL CLASS

Some sociologists who are interested in the sources and nature of the unequal distribution of resources focus on ***social stratification***. This term implies that there is a smooth distribution of individuals along an advantage–disadvantage continuum. In the functionalist framework (introduced in Section 1, p. 5), there is an assumption of equal opportunity for all; thus, each generation starts anew in the race for social advantage. Individuals are arrayed along a prestige continuum with greater rewards allocated to those with jobs with higher prestige. Often there is an assumption that one's place in this stratification system is temporary, with an expectation of mobility, if not within one's lifetime, then certainly for the next generation.

Other sociologists—from the conflict perspective—argue that opportunities are not equally distributed, and that groups such as social classes fight over the distribution of resources, with the winners passing on their advantages from generation to generation. As explained in Section 1, Marx's distinction between capitalists (business owners . . . the bourgeoisie) and workers (working class . . . the proletariat) within capitalism is the most famous two-class schema. Insofar as his perspective highlights the power of the largest corporate interests, it is most useful in helping us think about the larger field of power within contemporary societies. Capitalists operate in a social context that is organized for their success, in part because, through their political power, they can shape the rules governing property rights.[4] Their power is also embedded institutionally in a range of ways, one of the most important being our conceptualizations of what is normal and "natural" as far as social arrangements are concerned.

Through what Italian Marxist Antonio Gramsci called ***ideological hegemony***, the major belief systems of the society are sufficiently accepted by the populace that the ruling class can be said to have "the consent of the governed."[5] Marxian theorists have focused on the power that corporations and owners of sports teams exercise with respect to tax breaks, special antitrust deals, stadium construction projects, and favorable infrastructure arrangements (e.g., parking and roads around stadiums). That "regular people" are excluded from conversations on these topics would be expected from this perspective.

Max Weber suggested that people organize themselves in the struggle for power in classes, **status groups**, and/or political parties. We will leave Weber's focus on parties aside and examine briefly his perspective on **social classes** and status groups. For Weber, social classes are defined in terms of "common mobility chances"—groups of people who have similar resources (and these could be of various sorts—for example, property, income, or educational credentials) that advantage or disadvantage the next generation's likelihood of achieving the same class standing. Weber's notion of status groups enables us to think more broadly about how groups form in the pursuit of power. According to Weber, virtually any characteristic can be the basis of group formation—including, but not limited to, race/ethnicity and gender—but his primary focus is on groups that form on the basis of common lifestyles. So, groups that have similar patterns of consumption—they value and invest in the same *things*—form status groups. As we discuss class, race, and gender, it is important to remember that, for Weber, classes and status groups are *competing* modes of group formation in the pursuit of power (Giddens, 1973: 44). So, for example, an African-American female doctor may decide, for particular political goals at a particular time, that it would be best for her to mobilize as a woman. At another point, for a different goal, she may decide that she should ally with other professionals. It is also important to remember that groups that are powerful (**dominant groups**) are mobilizing to exclude those without power (**subordinate groups**) and that subordinate groups are attempting to usurp the privileges of the dominant groups; this is a process that Weber called *social closure* (see Parkin, 1979).

Following Weber's insights, Bourdieu developed a conception of class that is particularly useful for our purposes. As discussed briefly in Section 1, Bourdieu defines class in terms of three components: **economic capital** (money and wealth), cultural capital (education and cultural participation), and social capital (the resources of the people with whom one interacts). Social classes, for Bourdieu, are best characterized as social divisions that reflect the population's most common locations in the distribution of economic, social, and cultural capital. So, the people who are located at the very highest points across the three distributions would be the most powerful, dominant group. The people at the lowest point would be the least advantaged, subordinate group.

The advantage of this schema over other conceptualizations of social class is that we can think about how people with different sets of resources strategically confront the world in their quest for "distinction."[6] These strategic moves, rooted in a group's habitus, manifest themselves as differences over art, music, dress, language, and leisure activities, including sports. On the one hand, our choices of favored sports reflect our backgrounds, both in terms of our tastes for particular sports and our access to them. On the other hand, our choices tend to reinforce stratification patterns: they announce to the world who we are, who plays these sports, and who does *not* play these sports.

These patterns, therefore, help not only to reproduce our sporting choices for given classes but also to bind those classes together. For example, Bourdieu contrasts the sport choices of two advantaged groups—professionals (e.g., doctors) and employers—that are probably similar in economic capital but differ in that the professionals are likely to be higher in cultural capital and the employers are higher in social capital. He suggests that professionals, who can certainly afford to engage in expensive activities, tend toward health-enhancing activities like yachting, open-sea swimming, and cross-country skiing, while their economic equals—employers—tend toward golf, where social capital accumulation is reinforced (Bourdieu, 1984: 219).[7]

RACE/ETHNICITY

Race/ethnicity also affects the nature of one's relationship to sport. In part through its relationship to social class but also due to its relationship to other ways that powerful groups monopolize resources, race/ethnicity is associated with many aspects of sport and its historical development. As Weber suggests, race/ethnicity is one of those characteristics around which groups organize for social closure in the pursuit of power. Though hardly universally accepted, there is a tendency in the US to talk about "whites" as a dominant group that engages in *exclusion* and "people of color" (e.g., African-Americans; Latinos; Asian-Americans; Native Americans) as subordinate groups that organize for *usurpation.*

Let's begin by clarifying what we mean when we talk about race/ethnicity. Though they overlap in various ways, race and ethnicity are *different.* From a Weberian perspective, they would both be considered status groups, but power issues differentiate them in important ways. For sociologists, the most important point to make about race *and* ethnicity is that they are *socially constructed.* There is nothing inherent in a given person's genes or background that determines race or ethnic group membership; her identity (both how others see her and how she sees herself) is determined by the historical and social context in which she lives. This can be clearly seen in the changes over time of the official categories used by the US Census. In 1890, there was a category for "Whites" and four categories for African-Americans ("Black"; "Mulatto"; "Quadroon"; "Octoroon"). Native Americans were labeled "Indian"; and Asian-Americans were either "Chinese" or "Japanese" (Lee, 1993). In 2010, the US Census (US Census Bureau, 2010) asked two questions about race/ethnic background: one focusing on "Hispanic origin" and one about "race." The instructions indicated that people of Hispanic or Latino origin may be of any race. A person who is "Hispanic or Latino" could indicate his origin as "Mexican, Mexican Am., or Chicano"; "Puerto Rican"; "Cuban"; and "Another Hispanic, Latino, or Spanish origin." For race, the following categories were included: "White," "Black or African American," "American Indian or Alaska Native," "Asian," and "Native Hawaiian or Other Pacific Islander." "Some other race" was also an option. The 2010 US Census allowed respondents to indicate more than one race (this was done for the first time in 2000) and reported that over nine million people indicated two or more races as their race background.

For our purposes, it is sufficient to recognize that races and ethnic groups are created historically through "us versus them" processes, respectively, of **racialization** and **ethnicization** (Cornell and Hartmann, 2007: 34–5). Both race and ethnicity tend to be used to describe groups characterized by common descent and/or common physical characteristics; thus, they may tend to appear as "natural" phenomena. But, as we have seen, historical variations within nations and social variations across nations quickly undermine that conception. At various points, Jews and Irish were considered different races in the US, while now they are both considered white. The four official races in South Africa established during the apartheid era ("Whites," "Blacks," "Coloured," and "Indian") and the occasional use of "honorary whites" for certain favored non-whites underlines this notion of social construction and its link to power relations.

The key difference between races and ethnic groups lies in who is doing the "defining"—that is, in the origin of the categorization. Processes of racialization (the creation of racial groups) take place when a group defines another group as inferior (*assigns* it inferior status); by contrast, ethnicization (the creation of ethnic groups) is accomplished by the group members themselves—an affirmative assertion that *we* are different and equal. The dynamics and results of these processes of identity assignment and assertion are historically variable (see Cornell and Hartmann, 2007).

This distinction between assignment and assertion relates to Appiah's (1992) distinction between what he calls "**extrinsic racism**" and "**intrinsic racism**." Both of these derive from what he calls "racialism," the belief that there are different races and that each has certain essences. Extrinsic racism involves the claim that a particular *other* group's essence is associated with negative characteristics and is thus the source of one's "racism" toward them. So, if a group is deemed greedy or lazy, it's not that the group is hated *per se*, it's that one hates that characteristic and therefore hates the group. One's *own* group would display positive characteristics and would therefore be "better" than the other groups. Intrinsic racism, on the other hand, involves a belief that one's race is tied to a particular moral status. So, just by virtue of being of a given race may mean that one has a preference to hang with one's own group (and its essence) and for others to hang with theirs (and its essence). We might think of this as a kind of "tribalism." The question is whether and under what conditions this kind of tribalism leads to biases and barriers.

So, depending on the power and competition among the groups involved, patterns of racialism (or racialization or ethnicization) have implications for sports. It would be difficult to explain, for example, historical patterns of participation of different race and ethnic groups in different sports or the current centrality of basketball in African-American neighborhoods without at least passing reference to these factors. Further, as we will see later, the intersection of race/ethnicity with social class[8] produces particular patterns of sport participation as well, for example, with swimming, polo, and water polo.

GENDER

Another very consequential social division is gender. From the time a baby is born and we ask "is it a boy or a girl?" to the time one enters sex-segregated lavatories in public places to the differential experiences in the labor market and in marriage, one's gender is a key aspect of one's identity and a major determinant of one's behavior. Let's immediately clarify that "sex" is generally taken to mean one's biological sex and "gender" is taken to mean the socially constructed experience of being a boy/girl, man/woman. Sociologists generally focus on gender—rather than sex—insofar as that is of most relevance for one's behavior and experience in the world. Although sociologists accept that biology has effects (hormonal and gene differences between men and women interact with social influences to produce differences between women and men), they are much more focused on exactly how social context affects identity, behavior, and outcomes. And, even as gender has become the socially relevant factor, its status as a binary variable has come into question.

Most discussions of how gender comes to be so important involve different kinds of learning theories that are linked to socialization. Socialization suggests that, as we grow up, we learn "gender roles." Some theorists argue that we mimic the behaviors of the same-sex parent so that girls learn how to become feminine and boys masculine. Others suggest that, because we live in a gender-segregated society, girls and boys are exposed to different situations and therefore learn different, gendered ways of adapting to society. Some versions of this theory build in a developmental component so that we can see girls and boys developing "appropriate" gender identities over time.

Michael Kimmel (2009) suggests that the focus on gender *roles* is misguided for many reasons. First, the notion of normative definitions of masculinity and femininity is too restrictive; there are many versions of masculinity and femininity and they vary over time, cross-culturally, and in intersection with race, ethnicity, and social class. Second, gender has much deeper meaning than to talk about it simply in terms of roles—we all play different roles: father, sister, student, worker. Gender is much more consequential than these "hats" that we put on and take off, even during the course of a day. Third, gender roles imply separate spheres, yet femininity is often expressed in the context of the masculinity with which it interacts—so it is relational and situational. Finally, the notion of gender roles doesn't deal with the significant differences in power between men and women and how these may change over time. It implies that the roles are simply different, not unequal nor differentially connected to valued resources. It omits the idea that social movements—for example, feminism—may have very consequential effects on what men and women do.

So, if a focus on gender roles does not help us understand the ways that gender is socially constructed, how should we think about gender and, more specifically, about gender and sport? There are two important perspectives that will help us understand how gender and sport articulate with one another. First, there is Connell's work on *Gender and Power* (1987) and *Gender* (2009). Connell suggests that our biological selves interact with society at many levels: for example, family, education, and employment. Due to the ways that people interact in these contexts, men and women develop different personality characteristics, different psychological orientations, and different perceptions of the opportunity structure—using Bourdieu's term, a different habitus. Connell makes the point that there are many masculinities and femininities but that ***hegemonic***

masculinity—a version of masculinity that highlights power, marriage, and heterosexuality—occupies the central space in a gender order (the particular way that gender power is exercised in a given field in a given society). One key manifestation of hegemonic masculinity is fluency in sports; indeed, this is so central that a lack of fluency is often considered non-masculine, feminine, or homosexual (a subordinated masculinity).[9]

The most common mode of expressing femininity—**emphasized femininity**—involves compliance, empathy, and nurturance. Because men dominate gender regimes, Connell doesn't want to attach "hegemonic" to *any* form of femininity, not least to one—even the most common one—that focuses on sociability and ego-stroking of men. So, for Connell, there are many ways that gender gets expressed, but the power associated with it is held in place largely by hegemonic masculinity. It is, so to speak, the 800-pound gorilla in the room that all other masculinities and femininities must deal with. Barbara Risman (1998) also sees gender as fundamental and considers it to be "a structural property of society" that has effects at the level of individuals, interactions, and institutions. No matter our individual intentions or motivations, we must deal with gender's embeddedness at all levels of society.[10]

Similarly, Michael Messner (2000; 2002) argues that gender is constituted at three levels of society: the interactional level, the cultural level, and the structural level. His argument is that all three contribute to the ways that gender is expressed and affects social life. The cultural meanings and symbols that develop historically work with (and within) gendered institutions that are sex-segregated and have different rules, jobs, and rewards for men and women. So, we develop ideas about women's work and men's work, women's sports and men's sports. With cultural and structural levels setting the context, interaction among individuals actually "allows gender to happen." People "do gender" (West and Zimmerman, 1987) in interaction and this is necessary for its social accomplishment as well as being a requirement of all actors. We do gender in gendered institutions. And sport, of course, is one of those gendered institutions. As we will discuss later, historical changes in gender participation in sport as well as women's inclusion in softball and exclusion from baseball speak to gender's articulation with the sports field.

DISABILITY

Disability, involving a relatively permanent impairment of a person's capacities to engage in given activities, has been an important factor in affecting people's access to the rewards and opportunities of the society. According to 2010 US Census data, more than one in five persons 15 years and older have some kind of communicative, physical, or mental disability (Brault, 2012). In regulated sports, disabilities matter if the person cannot participate in the ways that the governing bodies of the sport allow. Notice we are not saying that the people cannot *play* the sport; disability has been defined by the powers that be in given sports. If the rules or field or court is not designed to accommodate people with given limitations, then they would be labeled "disabled" and therefore ineligible. Perhaps the most famous example of a "disabled" player being *able* to play a sport but not *allowed* to play was the golfer Casey Martin. He had to sue the Professional Golfers Association to be allowed to use a golf cart to play in order to accommodate his congenital circulatory disorder. Under the Americans with Disabilities Act, the Supreme Court ruled that the PGA must accommodate Martin's disability and upheld his right to play with a cart. So, Martin went from being *ineligible* due to his disability to *eligible*.

Though most Americans no longer even notice the "curb cuts" in sidewalks at intersections, these were virtually unknown in the United States before the disability rights movement mobilized in the 1970s. The recognition, integration, accommodation, and mainstreaming of people with disabilities have been important outcomes of this ongoing social movement. In sports, the range of organizational contexts in which athletes with disabilities have taken part has continued to expand since the 1960s.

Howard Nixon (2007) has elaborated a series of models of potential sport opportunities for people with disabilities. These range from Special Olympics, which accommodates in North America over a half-million people with intellectual disabilities in 30 sports (Special Olympics), to integrating elite athletes into mainstream sports competitions—like Casey Martin or Major League Baseball's ten-year veteran pitcher Jim Abbott, who was born without a right hand and who had two seasons when he didn't make an error in the field!

As we will see, struggles over access and opportunity across these socially constructed categories has been a major feature of the history of sports. Fay and Wolff (2009) discuss how the "sport opportunity spectrum" for persons with disabilities has changed over time and how continuing struggles by athletes, advocates, and allies will affect a more inclusive and equitable spectrum. The selection by Le Clair (Chapter 11) highlights important aspects of this process.

OTHER BIASES AND BARRIERS

Social class, race/ethnicity, gender, and disability do not exhaust the barriers that athletes must overcome in order to participate in specific sports. Age is another. As people age, their access to sports declines and this happens more or less depending on their other social characteristics. Similarly, as children play in different levels of given sports, they are encouraged or discouraged from continuing.[11] Obviously, different sports require different levels of concrete economic investment (and families' capacities to meet these requirements differ radically) but, in general, as children mature and transition to high school, to higher education, and/or to the labor market, studies from a number of different countries report a decline in sports participation (Telama and Yang, 2000; Sport England; Physical Activity Council, 2012).

Another barrier to sports participation is sexual orientation. With the dominance of hegemonic masculinity in the gender order, gay and lesbian athletes are marginalized in various ways (Curry, 1991; Pronger, 1990). Since sports are considered to be the ultimate masculine domain, those who don't conform to the fundamental "requirements" of hegemonic masculinity (which of course, includes all women as well as non-heterosexual males) are marginalized in and by sport.[12] Women who play sports may be assumed to be lesbian and men who don't are assumed to be gay. For non-heterosexual athletes, the challenges are daunting: whether through coaches' biases[13] or locker room harassment,[14] they are "informed" that they are not welcome to play. Nevertheless, athletes like Martina Navratilova, Sheryl Swoopes, and Britney Griner have come out during their active careers and, in 2013, Jason Collins became the first active US professional athlete to acknowledge publicly that he is gay. While it has been easier for lesbians to come out during their active careers than for gay male athletes, concerns about how they will be treated by coaches, fellow players, the media, and potential corporate sponsors have discouraged athletes to acknowledge their sexual orientation. Mobilization by gay athletes has been critical to a broadening of sports' inclusiveness.

INTERSECTIONALITIES

Until this point, we have considered how each of these biases and barriers should be defined and how we might apply them to the sports field. Patricia Hill Collins (1990) argues that these biases and barriers should not be considered in isolation from one another. Suggesting that there is a matrix of domination that manifests itself differently for different populations, Collins' perspective implies that we must think through how, for example, class, race, gender, disability, and sexual orientation may *simultaneously* operate in the lives of individuals. She argues against an *additive* notion of inequality and oppression; considering the ways that black women, for example, experience oppression is NOT the simple addition of race oppression plus gender oppression. We will examine each of the biases and barriers that we introduced and, when data are available, we will also examine intersectional variations.[15]

SOCIAL CLASS AND SPORT PARTICIPATION

Data on social class participation in sport and physical activity are difficult to come by. Perhaps the most comprehensive compilation is the 2005 publication *Sports Participation in the European Union* (Bottenburg et al., 2005). Not only does it report data for each member state for each sport, but data by age, gender, and (less often) socioeconomic characteristics are reported as well. A number of findings stand out. First, across countries, the higher one's socioeconomic standing, the more likely one is to be playing sports. Second, the richer the country, the higher the overall participation rate, and the less apparent the socioeconomic differences in participation. Finland, for example, shows *no* class differences in participation.

Another rich source of data on sports participation and social class comes from England. A collaboration between Street Games (private) and Sport England (public), the Active People Survey (APS) has been administered six times since 2005 and has focused on bringing sport to poorer communities. The general findings, similar to those of the aforementioned European Union publication, are that the higher the class background of the individual,[16] the more they participate in physical activities. This is a very robust finding, true for rates of participation across ages and genders (see the streetgames.org website). However, there are also variations in terms of who plays which sports, based on the monetary and social barriers to participation. Two sports show a predominance of participation from those from lower social backgrounds: football/soccer and boxing. Rugby shows a class-differentiated pattern of participation in its two major organizations; the traditionally working class rugby (League) has higher participation rates among the lower classes while the traditionally more middle class rugby (Union) shows a predominance of higher class participation. Sports like golf and tennis show participation among the higher groups at more than double the rate of participation of the lower groups.

The influence of social class on sports *preferences* has been observed in many societies. In Belgium, Scheerder et al. (2002; 2005) found that significant social class differences exist in sports participation, with upper classes being more likely to be involved in sports with "status sticks" (golf, fencing, squash, tennis, skiing) and lower classes more likely to be involved in cycling, angling, boxing, and karate (see Figure 2.1). In a study of sports preferences in the US, Stempel (2005) found that those in the category of highest economic and cultural capital were most different from those lowest in cultural and economic capital in their preference for tennis and golf. In general, though, Stempel found that the upper classes are quite omnivorous in their sports tastes but do distinguish themselves in their orientation toward working on their bodies (with a goal of health) in ways that those from lower classes do not (who are more inclined toward strength displays).

Figure 2.1 Social status pyramid of sport among male adults in 1999 (Scheerder et al., 2002: 237)

The US Census Bureau's (2011) *Statistical Abstract of the United States* presented 2009 data from a survey by the National Sporting Goods Association about the relationship between type of sports participation and income and between type of sport and gender.[17] The NSGA included household members who were 7 years old and older and used a very weak measure of participation: the respondent only had to indicate participating in a given activity more than once per year. As we reported with the European Union and UK data, the NSGA found an association between participation and economic status: the higher one's income, the more likely one participates in a sport. Second, those with incomes below $25,000 were overrepresented among football players by almost 34 percent. This same group was underrepresented (by over ten percentage points) in sports such as snowboarding, golf, tennis, cross-country skiing, hockey, and "working out at a club." Respondents at the other end of the income distribution—$100,000 and over—were, by contrast, overrepresented in golf, soccer, tennis, and alpine skiing. Though this income category is very active across most sports, they are underrepresented in football and softball participation.

Table 2.1 Sports Activity by Income Category

	<$25,000	*$25,000–$49,999*	*$50,000–$74,999*	*$75,000–$99,999*	*$100,000 & Over*	*Total*
Aerobic Exercise	11.6	18.7	22.4	19.0	28.3	100.0
Baseball	8.9	24.7	21.5	20.6	24.3	100.0
Basketball	11.8	22.7	20.8	19.4	25.2	100.0
Bicycle Riding	11.3	20.4	21.8	18.0	28.4	100.0
Billiards	15.6	23.8	21.2	17.3	22.2	100.0
Bowling	12.8	22.5	23.2	18.7	22.8	100.0
Exercise Walking	14.9	22.2	21.4	18.0	23.5	100.0
Exercising W/Equipment	10.1	21.9	21.3	18.7	28.0	100.0
Football	24.9	24.9	18.4	14.4	17.5	100.1
Golf	5.7	18.5	20.7	20.6	34.5	100.0
Hiking	12.2	18.7	22.3	19.8	27.0	100.0
Hockey	5.3	11.1	39.8	14.8	28.9	100.0
Running/Jogging	9.2	19.8	18.0	24.7	28.3	100.0
Skateboarding	12.4	24.5	21.5	14.4	27.2	100.0
Skiing—Alpine	9.0	13.8	15.6	15.5	46.2	100.0
Skiing—Cross Country	7.2	10.9	36.6	20.8	24.5	100.0
Snowboarding	3.9	22.8	21.9	22.9	28.6	100.0
Soccer	11.0	17.5	18.6	19.2	33.8	100.0
Softball	13.4	25.7	22.5	19.9	18.5	100.0
Swimming	11.6	16.0	23.4	18.9	30.1	100.0
Table Tennis/Ping Pong	10.0	15.5	32.3	18.0	24.3	100.0
Tennis	7.8	16.7	19.9	18.1	37.5	100.0
Volleyball	12.6	22.0	18.8	18.3	28.2	100.0
Weightlifting	12.0	21.9	20.2	20.8	25.0	100.0
Work Out At Club	7.6	18.8	25.4	17.8	30.4	100.0
Yoga	12.9	19.9	22.4	16.4	28.4	100.0
Total	18.6	24.8	20.2	15.4	21.1	100.1

Source: US Census Bureau (2011), Statistical Abstract of the United States.

SPORT, EDUCATION, AND SOCIAL MOBILITY

One of the many misperceptions about professional sports in the US today involves its role in producing upward mobility. We look at our sports celebrities and we notice that many of them have come from lower social classes. While there probably is an overrepresentation of athletes from the lower parts of the social structure who make it to the professional level, the odds of making it to the professional level remain exceedingly long. According to the latest NCAA data (updated in 2012), the *best* chance to make it into professional sports occurs in baseball, where 1 out of 200 of the high school baseball players *get drafted* by a big league team. The other sports for which they have compiled data—men's and women's basketball, men's ice hockey, men's soccer, and football—all have likelihoods of movement from high school player to being drafted at the pro level of less than 1 in 1000.[18] So, strategically, trying to move from the lower social classes to make it in professional sports is a lottery-like process. Those who win may make it big; but the likelihood of making it *at all* is exceedingly low.

Scholars have also examined the influence of sports on educational attainment. The results are somewhat inconsistent, primarily due to the challenges associated with getting adequate sample sizes, longitudinal data, and proper control variables. Some studies have suggested that, like some other extracurricular activities, participation in sport leads to greater orientation to and engagement with school and so leads to greater likelihood of graduation and educational attainment (Broh, 2002; McNeal, 1999; Mackin and Walther, 2011). Other studies find little effect of sports participation on educational outcomes. When the influence of class, race, and gender have been incorporated into these studies, the most common finding is that white males benefit the most from sports participation.[19]

At the same time, Guest and Schneider (2003) remind us of the importance of social context on these outcomes: they demonstrate that school and community contextual factors may affect a student's self-identity as an extra-curricular sports participant (with different effects for students of different races), which may affect educational attainment. Eitle and Eitle (2002) also show how the race and class backgrounds of students affect the ways that students use sports as an investment and how sports participation affects education. So, the short (and somewhat incomplete) answer about sports and status attainment is that participation likely helps students bond more to school, which might lead to higher educational attainment, which is associated with higher socioeconomic outcomes.

RACE/ETHNICITY AND SPORT

In the United States, because of their prominent, public nature, sports have played an important historic *symbolic* role both in reinforcing and in attacking racial barriers.[20] African-Americans' exclusion from big-time sports (especially Major League Baseball, the pre-eminent sport for the first half of the twentieth century) affirmed and reinforced a racialist and racist society. Along with the legal and organizational imposition of segregation across sectors of society, this symbolic exclusion is a good example of ***institutionalized racism***.[21] Whites imposed segregation in mainstream institutions (*de jure* in the South and *de facto* in the North) and blacks developed parallel institutions—schools, churches, businesses, and sports leagues.

The stirrings of African-Americans' struggle for civil rights were characterized by court challenges to segregation in schools, black union pressures on President Franklin

Roosevelt to create a Fair Employment Practices Commission, and the stirrings of mass mobilization (the Congress of Racial Equality—CORE—was organized in 1942). In this context, Jackie Robinson's entry into Major League Baseball in 1947 (signed in 1945 by Brooklyn Dodgers' general manager Branch Rickey) is an excellent example of the powerful symbolic role of sports. If Robinson could break the color barrier in baseball, what other barriers could be overcome? If sport represents a level playing field and Robinson was considered an important part of the Dodgers' (instrumentally rational) plan to emerge victorious, what might this change mean for race relations in the larger society?[22] The fact that Robinson's entry into the game was followed very shortly by Major League Baseball signing another Negro League player, Larry Doby, symbolized a very public movement toward an acknowledgment of excellence as the sole legitimate basis for professional sports participation and a conferral by the larger society of respect and dignity for African-Americans. The integration of major league baseball by no means resolved the problems of racial inequality; but the Robinson–Rickey revolution was an enormous symbolic event that challenged decades of Jim Crow racism.

Since that time, three of the four major US sports—baseball, basketball, and football—have witnessed a huge increase in African-American participation. Racist ideologies now focus on the various ways that African-Americans have a genetic physical advantage—sometimes associated with claims of mental disadvantage—in certain sports.[23] For example, in 1987 when Al Campanis, a former Dodger roommate and friend of Jackie Robinson, appeared on the late-night national TV show *Nightline* and was asked why there aren't more African-American managers in baseball, he said that "they lacked the necessities to be a field manager."[24] The point here is not to highlight Campanis' racism; it is to highlight how "routine" and "natural" it was for someone to express such sentiments on national television 40 years after Robinson broke down the color barrier in baseball.

When we look at racial and ethnic patterns of sports participation over the course of the twentieth century, we see some interesting changes over time. Boxing is probably the clearest example of a sport in which racial/ethnic succession[25] has occurred. Irish boxing champions were followed by Jewish, Italian, African-American, and Latino champs. Eisen (1994: xiii) suggests that, in addition, the Jews were trained by the Irish and the Italians were trained by the Jews. We see a similar pattern in baseball, with the Bergs and Greenbergs being followed by the DiMaggios and Garagiolas, who, in the context of the Robinson opening, were followed by the Mayses and Aarons, who were followed by the Pujols and Ortizes.[26] As groups gain greater access to stable and rewarding educational and occupational opportunities, the attractiveness of sports declines and the winning-the-lottery orientation of getting a professional contract gives way to aspirations for positions that offer a higher likelihood of positive outcomes.[27]

One of the best data sources for current sports preferences by race/ethnicity is from the National Collegiate Athletic Association (NCAA). The NCAA compiles data for collegiate athletes sport by sport and, together, by race/ethnicity and gender. While this does not necessarily illuminate racial patterns among younger, pre-college players (and thus misses the patterns of local community sports development), we believe that these data reflect reasonably well the current distribution of sports preferences by race/ethnicity. As we report the data, think about the kinds of neighborhoods that support the different sports that these college athletes play.

Table 2.2 reports some of the NCAA findings. Perhaps the most surprising is that white women are the most overrepresented—by 30 percent—among the athletes relative to their

Table 2.2 Race-Ethnic Sport Participation—NCAA—2011 by Race and Gender

Sport	*White*	*White*	*Black*	*Black*	*American Indian/ Alaskan Native*	*American Indian/ Alaskan Native*	*Asian*	*Asian*	*Hispanic/ Latino*
	Men	*Women*	*Men*	*Women*	*Men*	*Women*	*Men*	*Women*	*Men*
Baseball	84.7	0	3.9	0	0.4	0	0.9	0	5.6
Basketball	43.5	55.7	45.5	32.7	0.2	0.4	0.5	0.8	2.8
Bowling	100	54.5	0	35.7	0	0.5	0	0.5	0
Cross Country	77.1	77.5	8.1	8.1	0.4	0.4	1.5	1.5	6
Equestrian	87.5	92	6.3	1	0	0.5	0	0.7	0
Fencing	66.5	60.5	3.5	5.3	0.3	0.2	12.4	15.4	6
Field Hockey	0	87.8	0	1.5	0	0.1	0	1.1	0
Football	55.1	0	35.4	0	0.5	0	0.7	0	3
Golf	83	75.7	1.9	2.4	0.3	0.3	2.5	5.1	2.4
Gymnastics	74.2	74.4	3.8	5.8	0.6	0.6	7	4	5
Ice Hockey	74.8	75	0.5	0.3	0.2	0.4	0.8	0.8	0.7
Lacrosse	88.2	88.2	2.7	2.8	0.3	0.2	0.9	1.2	1.5
Rifle	83.1	76.1	2.1	2.3	0	0	5.1	6.3	3.4
Rowing	78	77.2	1.3	2.4	0.3	0.5	4.1	3.9	3.7
Rugby	72	66.3	6	6	0	1.8	0	1.2	6
Sailing	84.2	0	0.6	0	0	0	1.5	0	3.4
Sand Volleyball	0	70.6	0	2.9	0	1	0	2.5	0
Skiing	83.6	86.3	0.2	0.5	0.2	0	0.9	0.2	0
Soccer	68.5	80.7	7.2	3.7	0.2	0.3	1.6	1.5	9.9
Softball	0	81.1	0	5.8	0	0.7	0	1.2	0
Squash	65	64.8	1.3	2.2	0.4	0	8.2	10	3.6
Swimming	80.8	83.1	1.6	1.2	0.3	0.3	3	3.1	4.1
Synchronized Swimming	0	55.6	0	0	0	0	0	22.2	0
Tennis	61.4	64.4	4.3	6.7	0.1	0.3	5.4	4.6	5.4
Track, Indoor	66.7	67.2	20.8	20	0.3	0.3	1.3	1.1	3.6
Track, Outdoor	64.9	66.2	21.6	20.4	0.4	0.4	1.4	1.3	4.6
Volleyball	69.3	77.7	6.3	9.4	0.4	0.3	4.4	1.4	10
Water Polo	75.9	73.3	1.3	1.1	0.4	0.4	3.5	3.6	6.5
Wrestling	80.1	0	6.4	0	1	0	1.1	0	5.8
Athletes in all divisions (2010–11)	69.9	76.9	15.6	8.9	0.4	0.4	1.7	2.1	4.4
All under-graduates (Fall 2010)	62.1	58.9	12.5	16.5	0.9	1	6.2	5.3	13.8

Percentages add to 100 in each row for each gender separately. Sport-by-sport participation data comes from NCAA Race and Gender Demographic's Search website (http://web1.ncaa.org/rgdSearch/exec/saSearch). Data on overall athletic participation by race is from Lapchick (2011); historically black institutions are excluded. Overall, undergraduate enrolment data are from Snyder and Dillow (2012), Digest of Education Statistics 2011(Table 237).

Sport	*Hispanic/ Latino*	*Native Hawaiian/ Pacific Islander*	*Native Hawaiian/ Pacific Islander*	*Two or More Races*	*Two or More Races*	*Non-resident Alien*	*Non-resident Alien*	*Other*	*Other*
	Women	*Men*	*Women*	*Men*	*Women*	*Men*	*Women*	*Men*	*Women*
Baseball	0	0.3	0	1.2	0	0.7	0	2.3	0
Basketball	3	0.2	0.4	2.2	2.6	3.1	2	2.1	2.5
Bowling	2.1	0	0	0	1.2	0	1.8	0	3.6
Cross Country	5.4	0.1	0.2	1.2	1.4	2.6	2.4	3	3
Equestrian	1.9	0	0	6.3	0.8	0	1.1	0	2
Fencing	6.5	0.2	0.2	1.6	2.9	3.8	3.5	5.8	5.6
Field Hockey	1.6	0	0.1	0	1.1	0	3.1	0	3.7
Football	0	0.8	0	1.8	0	0.4	0	2.4	0
Golf	3.3	0.2	0.2	0.7	0.8	6.8	9.7	2.3	2.5
Gymnastics	3.4	0.3	0.3	2.1	3	2.6	3.3	4.4	5.1
Ice Hockey	0.8	0	0	0.9	1.2	17.1	16.6	5	4.8
Lacrosse	2.1	0.1	0.1	0.6	1.2	1.7	0.6	4	3.6
Rifle	6.8	0	0	0	1.1	3	5.7	3.4	1.7
Rowing	4.3	0.3	0.2	1.2	1.8	3.9	2.6	7.2	7.2
Rugby	3	0	0	2	5.4	2	1.8	12	14.5
Sailing	0	0	0	2.3	0	0.6	0	7.4	0
Sand Volleyball	4.4	0	2.5	0	3.4	0	7.8	0	4.9
Skiing	0.5	0.2	0.2	0.4	0.5	9.4	8.2	5.1	3.7
Soccer	5.6	0.2	0.3	1.5	1.9	7.6	3.1	3.3	2.8
Softball	6	0	0.6	0	1.8	0	0.7	0	2
Squash	4.4	0	0	2.1	2.4	13.9	7.9	5.5	8.3
Swimming	3.5	0.2	0.2	1.6	1.4	4.5	3.6	3.8	3.6
Synchronized Swimming	0	0	11.1	0	0	0	11.1	0	0
Tennis	4.4	0.2	0.3	1.2	1.5	18	14.5	4	3.2
Track, Indoor	3.4	0.1	0.3	1.5	1.8	2.5	2.6	3.1	3.3
Track, Outdoor	4.1	0.1	0.3	1.7	1.9	2.4	2.5	3	3
Volleyball	4.1	1	0.8	1.8	2	2.8	2	4.1	2.3
Water Polo	8.6	0.2	1	2.8	2.9	5.9	4.6	3.5	4.6
Wrestling	0	0.2	0	1.6	0	0.5	0	3.3	0
Athletes in all divisions (2010–11)	4	N/A	N/A	1.6	1.5	2.9	3	3.2	3.1
All under-graduates (Fall 2010)	14.3	0.3	0.3	1.6	1.7	2.6	1.9	N/A	N/A

representation among undergraduates (they make up 58.9 percent of undergraduate students but 76.9 percent of student-athletes). African-American men are also overrepresented, but by only 25 percent (they make up 12.5 percent of the undergraduate population but 15.6 percent of student-athletes).[28] Not surprising to observers of the US sports scene, we see that African-American men and women are overrepresented in basketball and track relative to their overall athletic participation and that African-American men are overrepresented in football. The sports in which white athletes were very overrepresented (by 10 percentage points or more relative to their overall athletic participation[29]) were: baseball (men), wrestling (men), golf (men), skiing (men and women), swimming (men), rifle (men), lacrosse (men and women), field hockey (women), sailing (men), and equestrian (men). Foreign students, identified in this table as "nonresident aliens," seem to be recruited for specific sports: while they make up about 3 percent of all athletes, they are overrepresented in ice hockey, skiing, squash, soccer (men only), and tennis. The only other notable overrepresentations by race are Asians in fencing, tennis, rifle, golf (women only) and squash; and Latinos in water polo.

These patterns are largely consistent with what we would expect based on differences in socioeconomic status and the types of neighborhoods that people from different race/ethnic groups grow up in. In a study of sports participation in high school, Goldsmith (2003) found that "structural inequalities" (rooted in socioeconomic status, neighborhood, and school resource differences) largely explain differences between whites' and blacks' sports participation patterns. In addition, though, he found that there were even larger differences between blacks and whites in boys' basketball and football participation when race relations were more competitive (for example, in schools with a larger percentage of blacks).

Following up on the above discussion of social class, education, and sports, it is worth noting the ways that race affects graduation rates of postsecondary student-athletes. At the college level, there are 76 institutions of higher education in the top six athletic conferences in NCAA Division I (ACC, Big Ten, Big East, Pac 12, SEC, and Big 12). "Between 2007 and 2010, Black men were 2.8% of full-time, degree-seeking undergraduate students, but 57.1% of football teams and 64.3% of basketball teams" (Harper et al., 2013: 1). Almost all of these institutions' black student-athletes graduated at rates lower than other student-athletes (73 of 76 institutions) and of other students overall (74 of 76 institutions). The recruitment of athletes with lower academic credentials than their peers (Gurney, 2011)[30] is a recipe for exploitation, even aside from the fact that NCAA players aren't paid. At the same time, when we look at Division I athletes more broadly, we find that athlete graduation rates have improved over time (even in men's basketball and football) and that athletes generally graduate at rates higher than the general student population (NCAA Research Staff, 2011: 22–23).[31] Race differences in graduation rates are still stark: using the 2004 entering cohort, the six-year white male basketball or football player Federal Graduation Rate is 15–16 percentage points higher than the one for African-Americans. For women basketball players, the rate for whites is four percentage points higher than for African-Americans. The most notable difference here is that African-American female basketball players graduate at a rate 16 percentage points higher than African-American females in the larger student body. Overall, across all African-American students, male athletes have a six-year graduation rate (entering 2004) of 50 percent compared to 38 percent for the overall male graduation rate, and women athletes' rate is 20 percentage points higher than the rate for African-American women in the general student body (66 to 46).

RACE AND GENDER IN SPORTS MANAGEMENT

A somewhat separate issue involving race and gender in sport is the question of who is running the various organizations that, to use corporate-speak, "put the product on the field." So, beyond the socially structured choices that individuals make regarding what sport to play and/or watch and the implications these have for larger questions of power in the society, there are specific issues about who has the power to hire and fire players within given sports and who makes the rules that govern professional sports. Richard Lapchick's *Racial and Gender Report Card* has for the last 30 years focused attention on the gender and racial composition of the management and administration of college and professional sports in the United States. In the 2011 Racial and Gender Report Card,[32] Lapchick (2011) reports that the five professional leagues—Major League Baseball, National Football League, National Basketball Association, Women's NBA, and Major League Soccer—receive a grade of "A" for racial/ethnic diversity of players (meaning that player representation in the league matched the representation of people of color in the US). Over the years, leagues and teams have also made huge improvements in diversifying their office employees, managements, and administrations. The place where very little progress has been made is with respect to top administrators. For example, Lapchick reports that Chief Executive Officers/Presidents are predominantly white. No people of color occupy these positions in MLB and the NFL; 39 of 45 are white in NBA; 23 of 24 are white in the WNBA; and 15 of 18 are white in MLS. Reflecting the wealth inequality in the larger society, it is very rare for people of color to *own* teams in these leagues (across all teams in these leagues, the only persons of color who owned teams were Arturo Moreno in MLB and Michael Jordan in the NBA).[33]

Women's administrative participation in the four men's leagues has increased tremendously over the last few decades. Many league and team offices have women in about one-third of these positions. At the top levels, however, women are quite scarce: the NBA had two women presidents, MLB and the NFL had one, and MLS had none. In the WNBA, of course, women make up 100 percent of the players but only eight of the owners are women. Half or more of the head coaches and general managers are women as well.

GENDER AND SPORT PARTICIPATION

As noted already, men's athletic participation far outpaces women's. According to the Statistical Abstract of the US (US Census Bureau, 2011), men outpace women by over 35 percentage points in the following sports: baseball, basketball, football, golf, weightlifting, hockey, skateboarding, and snowboarding. Women outpace men by this margin only in aerobics and yoga.

The biggest changes in sports participation among women are associated with the enactment in 1972 of **Title IX** of the Educational Amendments:

> No person in the United States shall, on the basis of sex, be excluded from participation in, be denied the benefits of, or be subjected to discrimination under any education program or activity receiving Federal financial assistance . . .
>
> (Title IX)

This landmark legislation mandated that equal monies be expended on men's and women's education by entities receiving federal funding—and this included sports. It gave schools until 1978 to comply with this mandate, with the Office for Civil Rights of the Department of Education responsible for enforcement. Since that time, in the context of confusion and/or of resistance, OCR has clarified the criteria that institutions must follow to be in compliance. The three-prong test, issued in 1979 but still in use, requires that:

> a. male and female participation opportunities in given institutions are in "numbers substantially proportionate to their respective enrollments"; or
> b. when there has been an historic underrepresentation, that the institution "can show a history and continuing practice of program expansion which is demonstrably responsive to the developing interests and abilities" of the underrepresented sex; or
> c. if there is underrepresentation and there is no evidence of prong "b," that the institution can demonstrate that the interests and abilities of the underrepresented "sex have been fully and effectively accommodated by the present program."
>
> (Office for Civil Rights)

The effect of Title IX has been nothing short of revolutionary in its effects on women's participation in athletics. In 1971–72, 3.67 million boys but only 294,015 girls participated in high school sports. By 1977–78, boys' participation reached 4.37M and girls' participation was over two million. The most recent data from the National Federation of State High School Associations reports 4.48M boys and 3.21M girls participating in high school athletics in 2011–12. In only 40 years, then, the overrepresentation of boys relative to girls went from about 1150 percent greater (boys' participation was 12.48 times girls' participation) to about 40 percent greater (boys' participation was just 1.4 times girls' participation). Even more telling is the simple increase in girls' participation: more than *ten times* the number of girls participate nowadays than did so in the early 1970s (National Federation of State High School Associations).

Similar changes occurred at the collegiate level. In 1971, there were about 30,000 women participating in intercollegiate athletics, compared to over 170,000 men (women made up about 15 percent of the total). In 2011–12, there were over 195,000 women and more than 257,000 men competing (NCAA, 2012b). Overall, in 2011–12, the average institution that fielded intercollegiate teams had 238 men and 180 women on its teams, women making up approximately 43 percent of the total. Though there are many differences across NCAA Divisions, the remarkable increase in women's participation has been hailed as compelling proof that, at least in this domain, opportunity begets aspiration and attainment.[34]

At the same time, even beyond the remaining differences in participation rates of athletes, Title IX did not magically end gender inequality in athletics. There remain large differences in expenditures for men's and women' recruiting and scholarships. The 120 institutions in the Football Bowl Subdivision of Division I spent a median of $498,700 on recruiting for men's teams but only $219,100 on women's teams. In terms of scholarships, these same institutions gave out about one-third more scholarships to men than to women and spent about one-third more on their male athletes than on their female athletes (median=$4,006,300 for men and $2,939,400 for women) (NCAA, 2012a).

Additionally, coaching and administrative positions in NCAA institutions are radically unequally distributed between men and women. On this point, some historical perspective is in order. On the one hand, there has been a notable increase in the number of women throughout the athletic administrations of colleges and universities. Acosta and Carpenter (2013) highlight that, in 2012, almost 92 percent of higher education institutions—the highest ever—had a female athletic administrator. One of five in the top job—athletic director—was female, though the female ADs were concentrated in Division III programs. Women were least likely to be ADs in Football Bowl Subdivision schools; here, less than 1 in 20 were women. In 2012, less than a third of schools had a female head athletic trainer and less than 1 in 10 had a female sports information director. Perhaps the most troubling data in terms of gender equity from the Acosta and Carpenter report (2013) is the decline in the percentage of women coaches during the course of Title IX's enforcement. As they point out, "(i)n 1972, the year Title IX was enacted, more than 90% of women's teams were coached by females" (Acosta and Carpenter, 2013: 17). In 2012, over 57 percent of the coaches of women's teams were male. The percentage of women coaching men's teams, however, has not changed much during the course of the 40 years of Title IX, topping out below 4 percent throughout the period. Not surprisingly, the percentage of women coaches coaching women's teams is highest in sports that are exclusively female (e.g., field hockey) or where the rules of the men's and women's games are significantly different (e.g., lacrosse).

POWER AND THE SPORTS FIELD

Needless to say, not all sports are equally valued in a given society We all know that football/soccer is the global game and holds a place of enormous popularity and status in almost every country.[35] In the US, by contrast, basketball, football, and baseball are the staples of community sports programs, and the people who play them professionally are considered celebrities. Those who are champion curlers or runners or swimmers may be honored in Olympic years, but they are recognized in very few nations and revered by only a few. In Bourdieu's terms, when we are examining the sports "field" we see that different sports occupy positions of greater and lesser power. Bourdieu's notion of the **cultural arbitrary**, which he uses to reinforce the idea that the kinds of knowledge, language, and cultural objects that are most valued in a given society at a given time are not *inherently* more valuable than other forms, directs us to examine the styles and preferences of the upper classes as *arbitrary* measures of evaluating "good taste." Educational institutions valorize *that* knowledge, employers select on certain forms of dress, and the whole society comes to "appreciate" *that* knowledge and *that* fashion as the best way to know and to dress.

In the field of sports, one might say that there's an *athletic arbitrary* that operates such that certain sports are more highly valued and become the standard against which other endeavors are measured. In general, the sports that are most visible, most highly remunerated, and considered most valuable within a society are ones that men tend to excel in. They also tend to be associated with more privileged classes, races/ethnicities, and those considered "able-bodied." Men developed sports that were consistent with the skills and bodily practices that they were fluent in.[36] Were women in control of the society, perhaps sports might have been developed more in line with women's bodies in which, as Jane English argues, "small size, flexibility and low center of gravity combine to give women the kind of natural hegemony [in sports activities such as the balance beam] that men enjoy in football" (English, 1978: 275). English also argues that our entire conception of sport—focused on size, speed, strength—might not have developed in this way if women had been dominant in society. "Competitions emphasizing flexibility, balance, strength, timing, and small size might dominate Sunday afternoon television and offer [high] salaries. . . . Men could be clamoring for equal press coverage of their champions" (English, 1978: 276).

SPORTS AS A CONTINUUM

The reigning hegemonic model that assumes that there are simply two kinds of sports—men's sports and women's sports—has come under increased scrutiny. Why is that model so strong and so resistant to change? Willis (1982) argues that, in the context of obvious physical differences reinforced socially in myriad ways, the "objective data" of heights, times, and percentages in different sports don't lie and they tell a story of masculine advantage. He explains that this perspective and this advantage reifies the particular notion of what sport is, which privileges men. Mary Jo Kane (1995), attempting to move beyond Willis, suggests that societies should move to a conception of sports as a *continuum*, not focusing on men's performances versus women's performances. She suggests, for example, observing marathon races in terms of *all* the runners instead of focusing on the winner of the male race and the slower winner of the female race. The latter approach focuses on how many men ran faster than the fastest woman; the continuum approach would acknowledge and even underline that the vast majority of male runners were bested by a woman.[37] The title of Mariah Nelson's (1995) book comes to mind: *The Stronger Women Get, The More Men Love Football.* She argues that women's athletic accomplishments are continually marginalized by male, couch-potato football fans (these are the easiest target) who are "overwhelmed" by the supposed huge increase in women's sports on television and who *know* that women couldn't compete in the NFL.

An approach that looked at sports as a continuum could potentially organize competition in terms of ability levels, undermining the gender binary in almost all contests and creating social space for the transformation of what being female and an athlete means. Perhaps we would be less likely to hear from announcers that a great female athlete "plays just like a man." Perhaps we would move away from sex-testing (if everyone were tested, how would high-scoring men be labeled?) and whispers about lesbianism—what Kane refers to as the "deviant-mutant label."[38]

McDonagh and Pappano (2008) argue forcefully that sports should be integrated, not least because sex segregation of sports reinforces gender inequality—specifically, female inferiority—in the larger society. While Title IX has certainly affected massive changes in women's sports participation, it reinforces sex segregation and hegemonic masculinity in sports. Such segregation, McDonagh and Pappano suggest, encourages men's and women's sports to have different demands (grand slam men's tennis [best of five sets] and women's tennis [best of three sets], rules [compare men's and women's lacrosse], and events [heptathlon versus decathlon or women's versus men's gymnastics]). Though market considerations are certainly at play, McDonagh and Pappano also criticize the implementation of Title IX by allowing different promotion strategies and ticket prices for, say, women's and men's basketball games.

IS CHANGE POSSIBLE?

A key issue here, then, is how the sports field is structured in a given society and how the field of power affects its organization. The broader the conception of what is central to the sports field, the more inclusive sport would be. As we discussed in the context of "disability in sport," much of the power that inheres in a given society's sports space is rooted in sports' classification system: the names and everyday understandings of the sport give it the power of an institution (see Scott, 2008; Bourdieu, 1991). It becomes the "natural" way to think about sports. Power relations in the larger society have determined the distribution of opportunities and outcomes within sports. Bourdieu suggests that those who have the power to name—those who hold a monopoly of legitimate symbolic violence—are in a particularly unique and powerful position in struggles over classification because the challengers must operate according to the rules and naming conventions of the dominant groups. So, subordinate groups are not only marginalized in sports; they are not only operating in alien territory; they are even disadvantaged in their quest to establish new and different sports and new and different conceptions of already existing sports.

Much progress has been made. We have discussed breakthroughs in sports participation among various subordinate groups. Jackie Robinson's integration of Major League Baseball, gay and lesbian players in professional sports leagues, and the Supreme Court ruling on Casey Martin demonstrate that change is possible and that movements toward greater inclusion are possible. The playing field is becoming more level.

To reach a level of fairness across the four dimensions outlined in Section 1, there would need to be a variety of sports available and they would have to allow for a broad range of talents to develop and compete. Different body types and capacities would be emphasized so that given sports could recruit from across the population and athletes would be attracted to a wide variety of sports, being challenged toward—and trained for—excellence, perhaps, in many. This struggle for fairness would have to be focused not only on democratizing training but also on democratizing the classifications (and the social space) themselves. If all four dimensions of fairness were realized, there would be no barriers for training opportunities and a broad conception of the activities that would be available.[39]

NOTES

1 The data in this section come from the Economic Policy Institute's State of Working America website: www.stateofworkingamerica.org/fact-sheets/inequality-facts.
2 Wealth includes the value of all the assets one owns (stocks, bonds, real estate, cars, etc.) minus one's debts (e.g., how much is owed on a mortgage).
3 Income is money received on an annual basis. It includes salary, wages, money from investments, etc.
4 We will explore this idea much more in Section 4 on political economy.
5 By "consent," we do not mean to imply that people eagerly embrace the power arrangements; we are simply acknowledging that "pragmatic acceptance" (Mann, 1970) is sufficient for a degree of legitimacy. There is no implication that conflict is absent from the society.
6 Bourdieu's sociology focuses on the struggle for power by individuals and groups, which primarily takes the form of struggles for social distinction. (See Swartz, 1997: 6.)
7 See Chapter 1 by Bourdieu from *Distinction*.
8 We will introduce this idea of "intersectionality" later.
9 We are referring here to the strong association between sports and the ideology and practice of hegemonic masculinity. When we refer to "fluency" in sport, we mean both talking and playing.

10 Chapter 6 by Messner and Chapter 8 by Hartmann develop this argument about gender's "natural" embeddedness and demonstrate how our "normal" practices reinforce the gender order.

11 Here is a good example of how the structure of sports as it currently exists violates the "pipeline" dimension of fairness. Obviously, there are class, race, ethnicity, gender, and disability aspects to this but age is clearly another one. Clark, in Chapter 9, shows how levels and ability assessments affect girls' sport participation.

12 See, for example, Chapter 10 by Connell, which explores some of the ways that "hegemonic masculinity" articulates with the demands of being an athlete.

13 For example, Rene Portland, Penn State's women's basketball coach for 27 years, had a "no lesbians" rule. Portland resigned after one of her players filed suit against her (Associated Press, 2007).

14 Though not about sexuality, see, for example, the remarkable Ted Wells report (Wells et al., 2014) about the "workplace bullying"of Jonathan Martin in the Miami Dolphins' locker room.

15 Chapter 7 by Bederman examines intersectionality by addressing the ways that black heavyweight champion Jack Johnson challenged white male superiority.

16 In most of the reports, the social class comparison is between categories 1–4 and categories 5–8. Here is the breakdown: 1. Higher managerial and professional occupations; 2. Lower managerial and professional occupations; 3. Intermediate occupations; 4. Small employers and own account workers; 5. Lower supervisory and technical occupations; 6. Semi-routine occupations; 7. Routine occupations; 8. Never worked and long-term unemployed; 9. Full-time students and Occupations not stated or inadequately described.

17 In Table 2.1, we have eliminated less competitive activities, such as camping, fishing, mountain biking, etc.

18 The rates of high school to pro mobility are as follows: men's basketball—3 in 10,000; women's basketball—2 in 10,000; football—8 in 10,000; men's ice hockey—1 in 1000; and men's soccer—3 in 10,000. See NCAA (2012c). Note that these figures are about being *drafted*; they do not take into account whether or not you have any kind of career in the major professional leagues.

19 See, for example, Sabo et al. (1993). They also found positive effects for suburban white females and rural Latino females.

20 You can think about this in relation to "symbolic interaction," which was introduced in Section 1. The symbolic action that we're talking about here occurs because of the meanings that are created in interaction.

21 In introducing the idea of institutionalized racism here, we do not mean to minimize the direct racism expressed and experienced by individuals and groups at this time. Even in the absence of direct discrimination, institutionalized racism is evident when the normal operations of organizations systematically produce racially unequal outcomes.

22 Patrick Miller (2004) makes a similar argument.

23 See Chapter 3 by Gladwell for an interesting challenge to this ideology.

24 Miller, in Chapter 4, mentions the Campanis incident in the context of a larger argument about racialist thinking.

25 Racial/ethnic succession is a term that has been used to describe patterns of residential movement within cities. As new groups arrive, they tend to live in the poorest areas and they move to better areas as their economic situation improves, leaving their original areas for newer groups. See, for example, White (1984).

26 Certainly, one could make a similar case for the early domination of basketball by Jews who gave way to African-Americans.

27 See Gems in Chapter 5 for the Italian-American example, which includes a less straightforward process of "segmented assimilation."

28 Female nonresident aliens are actually the most overrepresented (1.9 percent of the undergrad population and 3 percent of student-athletes) but this is a very small category. In reporting these results, we gloss over the smallest sports but they may be seen in the table.

29 Of course, the bar to reach "overrepresentation" is much higher for women (overall athletic participation was 76.9 percent) than for men (69.9 percent).

30 This pattern is true at Division III institutions as well. In fact, the more selective the institution, the greater the disparity between the academic credentials of the recruited athletes and the non-recruits. See College Sports Project (2010).

31 The NCAA reports two different graduation rates: the Graduation Success Rate (GSR) and the Federal Graduation Rate (FGR). The former takes into account that there are transfers in and out of institutions and that transfers out may be in good academic standing. The latter does not acknowledge these transfers but it does allow for comparisons between the athletes and the general student body. For our purposes, we will focus more on the FGR.

32 The *Racial and Gender Report Card* is often released separately for each sport. We rely here on the last "complete" version.

33 MLS doesn't have a structure of individual team owners so they would be ineligible for this comparison.

34 This idea is central to Bourdieu's concept of habitus.

35 In the US, people *play* soccer but they don't *follow* soccer. See Markovits and Hellerman (2001).

36 For a class-inflected argument about sport and bodily practices, see Chapter 2 by Wacquant.

37 In the 2012 Chicago Marathon, for example, the women's winner came in 35th place, besting 37,420 other participants. The focus of the results, however, was that the men's winning time was a bit more than seventeen seconds (!) faster than the women's winning time. Data come from the Chicago Marathon website: http://www.chicagomarathon.com/. Kane (1995) uses an older example.

38 Travers (2008) also discusses the barriers to (and recommendations for achieving) gender justice in the world of sports and how these articulate with larger issues of inclusion and justice. See Blinde and Taub (Chapter 32).

39 We raise this again in Section 4, especially when we note the "sport for development and peace" movement.

REFERENCES

Acosta, R. Vivian and Linda Jean Carpenter. 2013. "Women in Intercollegiate Sport. A Longitudinal, National Study, Thirty-Six Year Update. 1977–2013." Unpublished manuscript. Available for downloading at www.acostacarpenter.org

Appiah, Kwame Anthony. 1992. *In My Father's House: Africa in the Philosophy of Culture.* New York, NY: Oxford University Press.

Associated Press. 2007. Penn State's Portland Makes Difficult Decision to Quit. March 25. www.sports.espn.go.com/ncw/news/story?id=2808075

Bottenburg, Maarten van, Bas Rijnen, Jacco van Sterkenburg. 2005. *Sports Participation in the European Union: Trends and Differences.* Niewegein, The Netherlands: Michel vanTroost, Arko Sports Media.

Bourdieu, Pierre. 1984. *Distinction: A Social Critique of the Judgment of Taste.* Translated by Richard Nice. Cambridge, MA: Harvard University Press.

Bourdieu. Pierre. 1991. *Language and Symbolic Power.* Cambridge, MA: Harvard University Press.

Brault, Matthew W. 2012. "Americans with Disabilities: 2010." *Current Population Reports,* Pp. 70–131, Washington, D.C.: US Census Bureau.

Brittain, Ian. 2004. "Perceptions of Disability and their Impact upon Involvement in Sport for People with Disabilities at all Levels." *Journal of Sport and Social Issues* 28(4): 429–452.

Broh, Beckett A. 2002. "Linking Extracurricular Programming to Academic Achievement: Who Benefits and Why?" *Sociology of Education* 75(1): 69–95.

College Sports Project. 2010. "College Sports Project updates findings about Athletics and academics in NCAA Division III." www.middlebury.edu/newsroom/archive/2010/node/266828

Collins, Patricia Hill. 1990. *Black Feminist Thought: Knowledge, Consciousness, and the Politics of Empowerment.* New York, NY: Taylor and Francis.

Connell, R. W. 1987. *Gender and Power: Society, the Person, and Sexual Politics.* Stanford, CA: Stanford University Press.

Connell, Raewyn. 2009. *Gender: In World Perspective.* 2nd edition. Cambridge, UK and Malden, MA: Polity Press.

Cornell, Stephen and Douglas Hartmann. 2007. *Ethnicity and Race: Making Identities in a Changing World.* 2nd edition. Thousand Oaks, CA: Pine Forge Press.

Curry, Timothy. 1991. "Fraternal Bonding in the Locker Room: A Profeminist Analysis of Talk about Competition and Women." *Sociology of Sport Journal* 8(2): 119–135.

Economic Policy Institute. State of Working America. www.stateofworkingamerica.org/fact-sheets/inequality-facts

Eisen, George. 1994. "Introduction." Pp. 1–19 in George Eisen and David K. Wiggins, eds., *Ethnicity and Sport in North American History and Culture.* New York, NY: Praeger.

Eitle, Tamela McNulty and David Eitle. 2002. "Race, Cultural Capital, and the Educational Effects of Participation in Sports." *Sociology of Education* 75(2): 123–146.

English, Jane. 1978. "Sex Equality in Sports." *Philosophy & Public Affairs* 7(3) (Spring): 269–277.

Fay, Ted and Eli Wolff. 2009. "Disability in Sport in the Twenty-first Century: Creating a New Sport Opportunity Spectrum." *Boston University International Law Journal* 27(2): 231–248.

Giddens, Anthony. 1973. *The Class Structure of the Advanced Societies.* New York, NY: Harper & Row, Publishers.

Goldsmith, Pat Antonio. 2003. "Race Relations and Racial Patterns in School Sports Participation." *Sociology of Sports Journal* 20(2): 147–171.

Guest, Andrew and Barbara Schneider. 2003. "Adolescents' Extracurricular Participation in Context: The Mediating Effects of Schools, Communities, and Identity." *Sociology of Education* 76(2): 89–109.

Gurney, Gerald S. 2011. "Stop Lowering the Bar for College Athletes." *Chronicle of Higher Education.* April 10. www.chronicle.com/article/Stop–Lowering–the–Bar–for/127058

Harper, S. R., C. D. Williams, and H. W. Blackman. 2013. *Black Male Student-Athletes and Racial Inequities in NCAA Division I College Sports.* Philadelphia, PA: University of Pennsylvania, Center for the Study of Race and Equity in Education.

Kane, M. J. 1995. "Resistance/Transformation of the Oppositional Binary: Exposing Sport As a Continuum." *Journal of Sport and Social Issues* 19(1): 191–218.

Kimmel, Michael. 2009. *The Gendered Society.* 4th edition. New York, NY: Oxford University Press.

Lapchick, Richard E. 2011. *Racial and Gender Report Card.* The Institute for Diversity and Ethics in Sport, DeVos Sport Business Management Program in the College of Business Administration of the University of Central Florida.

Lee, Sharon. 1993. "Racial Classification in the US Census: 1890–1990." *Ethnic and Racial Studies* 16(1): 75–94.

Mackin, Robert Sean and Carol S. Walther. 2011. "Race, Sport and Social Mobility: Horatio Alger in Short Pants?" *International Review for the Sociology of Sport* 47(6): 670–689.

Mann, Michael. 1970. "The Social Cohesion of Liberal Democracy." *American Sociological Review* 35(3) (June): 423–439.

Markovits, Andrei S. and Steven Hellerman. 2001. *Offside: Soccer and American Exceptionalism.* Princeton, NJ: Princeton University Press.

McDonagh, Eileen and Laura Pappano. 2008. *Playing With the Boys: Why Separate is Not Equal.* New York, NY: Oxford University Press.

McNeal, Ralph B. 1999. "Participation in High School Extracurricular Activities: Investigating School Effects." *Social Science Quarterly* 80(2): 291–309.

Messner, Michael. 2002. *Taking the Field: Women, Men, and Sports.* Minneapolis, MN: U. of Minnesota Press.

Messner, Michael A. 2000. "Barbie Girls versus Sea Monsters: Children Constructing Gender." *Gender and Society* 14(6) (Dec.): 765–784.

Miller, Patrick B. 2004. "Muscular Assimilationism: Sport and the Paradoxes of Racial Reform." Pp. 146–182 in Charles K. Ross, ed., *Race and Sport: The Struggle for Equality on and off the Field.* Jackson, MS: University Press of Mississippi.

National Center for Education Statistics. 2011. *Digest of Education Statistics.* Washington, D.C.

National Collegiate Athletics Association Research Staff. 2011. "Trends in Graduation-Success Rates and Federal Graduation Rates at NCAA Division I Institutions." October. Washington, D.C. www.ncaa.org/wps/wcm/connect/e9eb8a0048d2623fb424ffb1fe52de76/GSR+and+Fed+Trends+2011+-+Final+10_20_11.pdf?MOD=AJPERES&CACHEID=e9eb8a0048d2623fb424ffb1fe52de76

National Collegiate Athletic Association. 2012a. "NCAA Gender-Equity Report 2004–2010." Indianapolis, IN: January 2012. www.ncaa.org

—— 2012b. "NCAA Sports Sponsorship and Participation Rates 1981–1982 – 2011–2012." Indianapolis, IN: October 2012. www.ncaa.org.

—— 2012c. "Estimated Probability of Competing in Athletics Beyond the High School Interscholastic Level." www.ncaa.org/wps/wcm/connect/public/NCAA/Resources/Research/Probability+of+Going+Pro

National Federation of State High School Associations. www.nfhs.org/content.aspx?id=3282

Nelson, Mariah Burton. 1995. *The Stronger Women Get, the More Men Love Football: Sexism and the American Culture of Sports.* New York, NY: Avon Books.

Nixon, Howard L. II. 2007. "Constructing Diverse Sport Opportunities for People with Disabilities." *Journal of Sport and Social Issues* 31(4): 417–433.

Office for Civil Rights. http://www2.ed.gov/about/offices/list/ocr/docs/t9interp.html

Parkin, Frank. 1979. *Marxism and Class Theory: A Bourgeois Critique.* New York, NY: Columbia University Press.

Physical Activity Council. 2012. "2012 Participation Report." www.physicalactivitycouncil.com/PDFs/2012 PACReport.pdf

Pronger, Brian. 1990. *The Arena of Masculinity: Sports, Homosexuality and the Meaning of Sex.* New York, NY: St. Martin's Press.

Risman, Barbara. 1998. *Gender Vertigo: American Families in Transition.* New Haven, CT: Yale University Press.

Sabo, Donald F., Merrill J. Melnick, and Beth E. Vanfossen. 1993. "High School Athletic Participation and Post-Secondary Educational and Occupational Mobility: A Focus on Race and Gender." *Sociology of Sport Journal* 10(1): 44–56.

Scheerder, Jeroen, Bart Vanreusel, Marijke Taks, and Roland Renson. 2002. "Social Sports Stratification in Flanders 1969–1999: Intergenerational Reproduction of Social Inequalities?" *International Review for the Sociology of Sport* 37(2): 219–245.

Scheerder, Jeroen, Bart Vanreusel, and Marijke Taks. 2005. "Stratification Patterns of Active Sport Involvement among Adults: Social Change and Persistence." *International Review for the Sociology of Sport* 40(2): 139–162.

Scott, W. Richard. 2008. *Institutions and Organizations.* 3rd edition. Thousand Oaks, CA: Sage.

Snyder, T. D., and S. A. Dillow. 2012. *Digest of Education Statistics 2011* (NCES 2012–001). National Center for Education Statistics, Institute of Education Sciences, U.S. Department of Education. Washington, D.C.

Special Olympics. www.specialolympics.org/Regions/north-america/_Region-Front/North-America.aspx#ProgramList

SportEngland website. www.sportengland.org/research/encouraging-take-up/key-influences/age/sport-and-young-people

Stempel, Carl. 2005. "Adult Participation Sports as Cultural Capital: A Test of Bourdieu's Theory of the Field of Sports." *International Review for the Sociology of Sport* 40(4): 411–432.

Street Games. www.streetgames.org/www/category/sg-categories/academic-research

Swartz. David. 1997. *Culture and Power: The Sociology of Pierre Bourdieu.* Chicago, IL: University of Chicago Press.

Telama, Risto and Xiaolin Yang. 2000. "Decline of Physical Activity from Youth to Young Adulthood in Finland." *Medicine and Science in Sports and Exercise.* http://www.msse.org

Title IX. www.dol.gov/oasam/regs/statutes/titleix.htm

Travers, Ann. 2008. "The Sport Nexus and Gender Injustice." *Studies in Social Justice* 2(1): 79–101.

U.S. Census Bureau, 2010. www.census.gov/prod/cen2010/briefs/c2010br-02.pdf

—— 2011. *Statistical Abstract of the United States: 2012* (131st Edition) Washington, D.C. www.census.gov/compendia/statab

Wells, Theodore V., Jr., Brad S. Karp, Bruce Birenboim, David W. Brown. 2014. *Report to the National Football League Concerning Issues of Workplace Conduct at the Miami Dolphins.* New York, NY: Paul, Weiss, Rifkind, Wharton & Garrison LLP.

West, Candace and Don Zimmerman. 1987. "Doing Gender." *Gender and Society* 1(2): 125–151.

White, Michael J. 1984. "Racial and Ethnic Succession in Four Cities." *Urban Affairs Review* 20(2) (December): 165–183.

Willis, Paul. 1982. "Women in Sport and Ideology." Pp. 117–135 in J. Hargreaves, ed., *Sport, Culture and Ideology.* London: Routledge and Kegan Paul.

CHAPTER 1

Distinction: A Social Critique of the Judgement of Taste

Pierre Bourdieu

Translated by Richard Nice

THE UNIVERSES OF STYLISTIC POSSIBLES

The spaces defined by preferences in food, clothing or cosmetics are organized according to the same fundamental structure, that of the social space determined by volume and composition of capital. Fully to construct the space of life-styles within which cultural practices are defined, one would first have to establish, for each class and class fraction, that is, for each of the configurations of capital, the generative formula of the habitus which retranslates the necessities and facilities characteristic of that class of (relatively) homogeneous conditions of existence into a particular life-style. One would then have to determine how the dispositions of the habitus are specified, for each of the major areas of practice, by implementing one of the stylistic possibles offered by each field (the field of sport, or music, or food, decoration, politics, language, etc.). By superimposing these homologous spaces one would obtain a rigorous representation of the space of life-styles, making it possible to characterize each of the distinctive features (e.g., wearing a cap or playing the piano) in the two respects in which it is objectively defined, that is, on the one hand by reference to the set or features constituting the area in question (e.g., the system of hairstyles), and on the other hand by reference to the set of features constituting a particular life-style (e.g., the working-class life-style), within which its social significance is determined.

For example, the universe of sporting activities and entertainments presents itself to each new entrant as a set of ready-made choices, objectively instituted possibles, traditions, rules, values, equipment, symbols, which receive their social significance from the system they constitute and which derive a proportion of their properties, at each moment, from history.

> A sport such as rugby presents an initial ambiguity. In England, at least, it is still played in the elite 'public schools', whereas in France it has become the characteristic sport of the working and middle classes of the regions south of the Loire (while preserving some 'academic' bastions such as the Racing Club or the Paris Université Club). This ambiguity can only be understood if one bears in mind the history of the process which, as in the 'elite schools' of nineteenth-century England, leads to the transmutation of popular games into elite sports, associated with an aristocratic ethic and world view ('fair play', 'will to win', etc.), entailing a radical change in meaning and function entirely analogous to what

happens to popular dances when they enter the complex forms of 'serious' music; and the less well-known history of the process of popularization, akin to the diffusion of classical or 'folk' music on LPs, which, in a second phase, transforms elite sport into mass sport, a spectacle as much as a practice.

The 'aristocratic' image of sports like tennis, riding or golf can persist beyond a—relative—transformation of the material conditions of access, whereas *pétanque* (a game similar to bocce) doubly stigmatized by its popular and southern origins and connections, has a distributional significance very similar to that of Ricard or other strong drinks and all the cheap, strong foods which are supposed to give strength.

But distributional properties are not the only ones conferred on goods by the agents' perception of them. Because agents apprehend objects through the schemes of perception and appreciation of their habitus, it would be naive to suppose that all practitioners of the same sport (or any other practice) confer the same meaning on their practice or even, strictly speaking, that they are practising the same practice. It can easily be shown that the different classes do not agree on the profits expected from sport, be they specific physical profits, such as effects on the external body, like slimness, elegance or visible muscles, and on the internal body, like health or relaxation; or extrinsic profits, such as the social relationships a sport may facilitate, or possible economic and social advantages. And, though there are cases in which the dominant function of the practice is reasonably clearly designated, one is practically never entitled to assume that the different classes expect the same thing from the same practice. For example, gymnastics may be asked—this is the popular demand, satisfied by body-building—to produce a strong body, bearing the external signs of its strength, or a healthy body—this is the bourgeois demand, satisfied by 'keep-fit' exercises or 'slimnastics'—or, with the 'new gymnastics', a 'liberated' body—this is the demand characteristic of women in the new fractions of the bourgeoisie and petite bourgeoisie. Only a methodical analysis of the variations in the function and meaning conferred on the different sporting activities will enable one to escape from abstract, formal 'typologies' based on universalizing the researcher's personal experience; and to construct the table of the sociologically pertinent features in terms of which the agents (consciously or unconsciously) choose their sports.

The meaning of a sporting practice is linked to so many variables—how long ago, and how, the sport was learnt, how often it is played, the socially qualified conditions (place, time, facilities, equipment), how it is played (position in a team, style, etc.)—that most of the available statistical data are very difficult to interpret. This is especially true of highly dispersed practices, such as pétanque, which may be played every weekend, on a prepared pitch, with regular partners, or improvised on holiday to amuse the children; or gymnastics, which may be simple daily or weekly keep-fit exercises, at home, without special equipment, or performed in a special gymnasium whose 'quality' (and price) vary with its equipment and services (not to mention athletic gymnastics and all the forms of 'new gymnastics'). But can one place in the same class, given identical frequency, those who have skied or played tennis from early childhood and those who learnt as adults, or again those who ski in the school holidays and those who have the means to ski at other times and off the beaten track? In fact, it is rare for the social homogeneity of the practitioners to be so great that the populations defined by the same activity do not function as fields in which the very definition of the legitimate practice is at stake. Conflicts over the legitimate way of doing it, or over the resources for doing it (budget allocations, equipment, grounds, etc.) almost always retranslate social differences into the specific logic of the field. Thus sports which are undergoing 'democratization' may cause to coexist (generally in separate spaces or times) socially different sub-populations which correspond to different ages of the sport. In the case of tennis, the members of private clubs, long-standing practitioners who are more than ever attached to strict standards of dress (a Lacoste shirt, white shorts or skirt, special shoes) and all that this implies, are opposed in every respect to the new practitioners in municipal clubs and holiday clubs who demonstrate that the ritual of clothing is no superficial aspect of the legitimate practice. Tennis played in Bermuda shorts and a tee shirt, in a track suit or even swimming trunks, and Adidas running-shoes, is indeed another tennis, both in the way it is played and in the satisfactions it gives. And so the necessary circle whereby the meaning of a practice casts light on the class distribution of practices and this distribution casts light on the differential meaning of the practice cannot be broken by an appeal to the 'technical' definition. This, far from escaping the logic of the field and its struggles, is most often the work of those who, like physical-education teachers, are required to ensure the imposition and methodical inculcation of the schemes of perception and action which, in practice, organize the practices, and who are inclined to present the explanations they produce as grounded in reason or nature.

In any case, one only needs to be aware that the class variations in sporting activities are due as much to variations in perception and appreciation of the immediate or deferred profits they are supposed to bring, as to variations in the costs, both economic and cultural and, indeed, bodily (degree of risk and physical effort), in order to understand in its broad outlines the distribution of these activities among the classes and class fractions. Everything takes place as if the probability of taking up the different sports depended, within the limits defined by economic (and cultural) capital and spare time, on perception and assessment of the intrinsic and extrinsic profits of each sport in terms of the dispositions of the habitus, and more precisely, in terms of the relation to the body, which is one aspect of this.

The relationship between the different sports and age is more complex since it is only defined—through the intensity of the physical effort called for and the disposition towards this demand, which is a dimension of class ethos—in the relationship between a sport and a class. The most important property of the 'popular' sports is that they are tacitly associated with youth—which is spontaneously and implicitly credited with a sort of temporary licence, expressed, inter alia, in the expending of excess physical (and sexual) energy—and are abandoned very early (generally on entry into adult life, symbolized by marriage). By contrast, the common feature of the 'bourgeois' sports, mainly pursued for their health-maintaining functions and their social profits, is that their 'retirement age' is much later, perhaps the more so the more prestigious they are (e.g., golf).

The instrumental relation to their own bodies which the working classes express in all practices directed towards the body—diet or beauty care, relation to illness or medical care—is also manifested in choosing sports which demand a high investment of energy, effort or even pain (e.g., boxing) and which sometimes endanger the body itself (e.g., motor cycling, parachute jumping, acrobatics, and, to some extent, all the 'contact sports').

Rugby, which combines the popular features of the ball-game and a battle involving the

> body itself and allowing a—partially regulated—expression of physical violence and an immediate use of 'natural' physical qualities (strength, speed, etc.), has affinities with the most typically popular dispositions, the cult of manliness and the taste for a fight, toughness in 'contact' and resistance to tiredness and pain, and sense of solidarity ('the mates') and revelry ('the third half') and so forth. This does not prevent members of the dominant fractions of the dominant class (or some intellectuals, who consciously or unconsciously express their values) from making an aesthetico-ethical investment in the game and even sometimes playing it. The pursuit of toughness and the cult of male values, sometimes mingled with an aestheticism of violence and man-to-man combat, bring the deep dispositions of first-degree practitioners to the level of discourse. The latter, being little inclined to verbalize and theorize, find themselves relegated by the managerial discourse (that of trainers, team managers and some journalists) to the rôle of docile, submissive, brute force ('gentle giant', etc.), working-class strength in its approved form (self-sacrifice, 'team spirit' and so forth). But the aristocratic reinterpretation which traditionally hinged on the 'heroic' virtues associated with the three-quarter game encounters its limits in the reality of modern rugby, which, under the combined effects of modernized tactics and training, a change in the social recruitment of the players and a wider audience, gives priority to the 'forward game', which is increasingly discussed in metaphors of the meanest industrial labour ('attacking the coal-face') or trench warfare (the infantryman who 'dutifully' runs headlong into enemy fire).

Everything seems to indicate that the concern to cultivate the body appears, in its elementary form—that is, as the cult of health—often associated with an ascetic exaltation of sobriety and controlled diet, in the middle classes (junior executives, the medical services and especially schoolteachers, and particularly among women in these strongly feminized categories). These classes, who are especially anxious about appearance and therefore about their body-for-others, go in very intensively for gymnastics, the ascetic sport par excellence, since it amounts to a sort of training (*askesis*) for training's sake. We know from social psychology that self-acceptance (the very definition of ease) rises with unselfconsciousness, the capacity to escape fascination with a self possessed by the gaze of others (one thinks of the look of questioning anxiety, turning the looks of others on itself, so frequent nowadays among bourgeois women who *must not* grow old); and so it is understandable that middle-class women are disposed to sacrifice much time and effort to achieve the sense of meeting the social norms of self-presentation which is the precondition of forgetting oneself and one's body-for-others.

But physical culture and all the strictly health-oriented practices such as walking and jogging are also linked in other ways to the dispositions of the culturally richest fractions of the middle classes and the dominant class. Generally speaking, they are only meaningful in relation to a quite theoretical, abstract knowledge of the effects of an exercise which, in gymnastics, is itself reduced to a series of abstract movements, decomposed and organized by reference to a specific, erudite goal (e.g., 'the abdominals'), entirely opposed to the total, practically oriented movements of everyday life; and they presuppose a rational faith in the deferred, often intangible profits they offer (such as protection against ageing or the accidents linked to age, an abstract, negative gain). It is therefore understandable that they should find the conditions for their performance in the ascetic dispositions of upwardly mobile individuals who are prepared to find satisfaction in effort itself and to take the deferred gratifications of their present sacrifice at face value. But also, because they can be performed in solitude, at times and in places beyond the reach of the many, off the beaten track, and so exclude all competition (this is one of the differences between running and jogging), they have a natural place among the ethical and aesthetic choices which define the aristocratic asceticism of the dominated fractions of the dominant class.

Team sports, which only require competences ('physical' or acquired) that are fairly equally distributed among the classes and are therefore equally accessible within the limits of the time and energy available, might be expected to rise in frequency, like individual sports, as one moves through the social hierarchy. However, in accordance with a logic observed in other areas—photography, for example—their very accessibility and all that this entails, such as undesirable contacts, tend to discredit them in the eyes of the dominant class. And indeed, the most typically popular sports, football and rugby, or wrestling and boxing, which, in France, in their early days were the delight of aristocrats, but which, in becoming popular, have ceased to be what they were, combine all the features which repel the dominant class: not only the social composition of their public, which redoubles their commonness, but also the values and virtues demanded, strength, endurance, violence, 'sacrifice', docility and submission to collective discipline—so contrary to bourgeois 'rôle distance'—and the exaltation of competition.

Regular sporting activity varies strongly by social class, ranging from 1.7 percent for farm workers, 10.1 percent for manual workers and 10.6 percent for clerical workers to 24 percent for junior executives and 32.3 percent for members of the professions. Similar variations are found in relation to educational level, whereas the difference between the sexes increases, as elsewhere, as one moves down the social hierarchy. The variations are even more marked in the case of an individual sport like tennis, whereas in the case of soccer the hierarchy is inverted: it is most played among manual workers, followed by the craftsmen and shopkeepers. These differences are partly explained by the encouragement of sport in schools, but they also result from the fact that the decline in sporting activity with age, which occurs very abruptly and relatively early in the working classes, where it coincides with school-leaving or marriage (three-quarters of the peasants and manual workers have abandoned sport by age 25), is much slower in the dominant class, whose sport is explicitly invested with health-giving functions (as is shown, for example, by the interest in children's physical development). (This explains why, in the synoptic table—Table 1—the proportion who regularly perform any sporting activity at a given moment rises strongly with position in the social hierarchy, whereas the proportion who no longer do so but used to at one time is fairly constant, and is even highest among craftsmen and shopkeepers.)

Attendance at sporting events (especially the most popular of them) is most common among craftsmen and shopkeepers, manual workers, junior executives and clerical workers (who often also read the sports paper *L'Equipe*); the same is true of interest in televised sport (soccer, rugby, cycling, horse-racing). By contrast, the dominant class watches much less sport, either live or on TV, except for tennis, rugby and skiing.

Just as, in an age when sporting activities were reserved for a few, the cult of 'fair play', the code of play of those who have the self-control not to get so carried away by the game that they forget that it is 'only a game', was a logical development of the distinctive function of sport, so too, in an age when participation is not always a sufficient guarantee of the rarity of the participants, those who seek to prove their excellence must affirm their disinterestedness by remaining aloof from practices devalued by the appearances of sheep-like conformism which they acquired by becoming more common. To distance themselves from common amusements, the privileged once again need only let themselves be guided by the horror of vulgar crowds which always leads them elsewhere, higher, further, to new experiences and virgin spaces, exclusively or firstly theirs, and also by the sense of the legitimacy of practices, which is a function of their distributional value, of course, but also of the degree to which they lend themselves to aestheticization, in practice or discourse.

All the features which appeal to the dominant taste are combined in sports such as golf, tennis, sailing, riding (or show-jumping), skiing (especially its most distinctive forms, such as cross-country) or fencing. Practised in exclusive places (private clubs), at the time one chooses, alone or with chosen partners (features which contrast with the collective discipline, obligatory rhythms and imposed efforts of team sports), demanding a relatively low physical exertion that is in any case freely determined, but a relatively

Table 1.1 Class Variations in Sports Activities and Opinions on Sport, 1975.

	Positive responses (%) by class fraction						
Sports characteristics of respondents	*Farm workers*	*Manual workers*	*Craftsmen, small shopkeepers*	*Clerical, junior execs.*	*Senior execs., professions*	*Positive responses (%) by sex*	
						Men	*Women*
Attend sports events fairly or very often	20	22	24	18	16	26	10
Watch or listen to sports events (on TV or radio) often or fairly often	50	62	60	60	50	71	47
Would like their child to become sports champion	50	61	55	44	33	52	47
Think that physical education ought to have a bigger place in the school curriculum	23	48	41	60	71	47	39
Regularly practise one or more sports (other than swimming if only on holiday)	17	18	24	29	45	25	15
Practise no sport now but used to	26	34	41	34	33	42	21
Have never regularly practised any sport	57	48	35	37	22	33	64
Regularly practise:							
tennis	0	1.5	2.5	2.5	15.5	2	2.5
riding	1.5	0.5	1	1.5	3.5	1	1
skiing	3.5	1.5	6.5	4.5	8	3	3
swimming	2.0	2 5	3.5	6.5	10	4	3
gymnastics	0.5	3	0.5	5	7	1.5	4
athletics	0	1.5	0.5	2.5	4	2	0.5
football	2.5	6	4.5	4	4	7	0.5

Source: CS. XXXVIII (1975).

high investment—and the earlier it is put in, the more profitable it is—of time and learning (so that they are relatively independent of variations in bodily capital and its decline through age), they only give rise to highly ritualized competitions, governed, beyond the rules, by the unwritten laws of fair play. The sporting exchange takes on the air of a highly controlled social exchange, excluding all physical or verbal violence, all anomic use of the body (shouting, wild gestures, etc.) and all forms of direct contact between the opponents (who are often separated by the spatial organization and various opening and closing rites). Or, like sailing, skiing and all the Californian sports, they substitute man's solitary struggle with nature for the man-to-man battles of popular sports (not to mention competitions, which are incompatible with a lofty idea of the person).

The statistics available only indicate the most general tendencies, which are confirmed in all cases, despite variations due to vague definition of the practice, frequency, occasions, etc. (It may also be assumed that the rates are over-estimated, to an unequal extent in the different classes, since all the surveys are based on the respondents' statements and are no substitute for surveys of the actual practitioners or spectators.) For this reason a synoptic table is used to show the proportion of each class or sex of agents who present a given characteristic according to the most recent survey on sporting activities and opinions on spoil (C.S. XXXVIII). Italic figures indicate the strongest tendency in each row.

Thus it can be seen that economic barriers—however great they may be in the case of golf, skiing, sailing or even riding and tennis—are not sufficient to explain the class distribution of these activities. There are more hidden entry requirements, such as family tradition and early training, or the obligatory manner (of dress and behaviour), and socializing techniques, which keep these sports closed to the working class and to upwardly mobile individuals from the middle or upper classes and which maintain them (along with smart parlour games like chess and especially bridge) among the surest indicators of bourgeois pedigree.

> In contrast to belote (and, even more so, manille), bridge is a game played more at higher levels of the social hierarchy, most frequently among members of the professions (IFOP, 1948). Similarly, among students of the grandes écoles, bridge, and especially intensive playing, with tournaments, varies very strongly by social origin. Chess (or the claim to play it) seems less linked than bridge to social traditions and to the pursuit of the accumulation of social capital. This would explain why it increases as one moves up the social hierarchy, but chiefly towards the area of social space defined by strong cultural capital (C.S. VII).

The simple fact that, at different times, albeit with a change in meaning and function, the same practices have been able to attract aristocratic or popular devotees, or, at the same time, to assume different meanings and forms for the different groups, should warn us against the temptation of trying to explain the class distribution of sports purely in terms of the 'nature' of the various activities. Even if the logic of distinction is sufficient to account for the basic opposition between popular and bourgeois sports, the fact remains that the relationships between the different groups and the different practices cannot be fully understood unless one takes account of the objective potentialities of the different institutionalized practices, that is, the social uses which these practices encourage, discourage or exclude both by their intrinsic logic and by their positional and distributional value. We can hypothesize as a general law that a sport is more likely to be adopted by a social class if it does not contradict that class's relation to the body at its deepest and most unconscious level, i.e., the body schema, which is the depository of a whole world view and a whole philosophy of the person and the body.

Thus a sport is in a sense predisposed for bourgeois use when the use of the body it requires in no way offends the sense of the high dignity of the person, which rules out, for example, flinging the body into the rough and tumble of 'forward-game' rugby or the demeaning competitions of athletics. Ever concerned to impose the indisputable image of his own authority, his dignity or his distinction, the bourgeois treats his body as an end, makes his body a sign of its own ease. Style is thus foregrounded, and the most typically bourgeois deportment can be recognized by a certain breadth of gesture, posture and gait, which manifests by the amount of physical space that is occupied; the place occupied in social space; and above all by a restrained, measured, self-assured tempo. This slow pace, contrasting with working-class haste or petit-bourgeois eagerness, also characterizes bourgeois speech, where it similarly asserts awareness of the right to take one's time—and other people's.

And just as a history of the sporting practices of the dominant class would no doubt shed light on the evolution of its ethical dispositions, the bourgeois conception of the human ideal and in particular the form of reconciliation between the bodily virtues and the supposedly more feminine intellectual virtues, so too an analysis of the distribution at a given moment of sporting activities among the fractions of the dominant class would bring to light some of the most hidden principles of the opposition between these fractions, such as the deep-rooted, unconscious conception of the relationship between the sexual division of labour and the division of the work of domination. This is perhaps truer than ever now that the gentle, invisible education by exercise and diet which is appropriate to the new morality of health is tending to take the place of the explicitly ethical pedagogy of the past in shaping bodies and minds. Because the different principles of division which structure the dominant class are never entirely independent—such as the oppositions between the economically richest and the culturally richer, between inheritors and parvenus, old and young (or seniors and juniors)—the practices of the different fractions tend to be distributed, from the dominant fractions to the dominated fractions, in accordance with a series of oppositions which are themselves partially reducible to each other: the opposition between the most expensive and smartest sports (golf, sailing, riding, tennis) or the most expensive and smartest ways of doing them (private clubs) and the cheapest sports (rambling, hiking, jogging, cycling, mountaineering) or the cheapest ways of doing the smart sports (e.g., tennis on municipal courts or in holiday camps); the opposition between the 'manly' sports, which may demand a high energy input (hunting, fishing, the 'contact' sports, clay-pigeon shooting), and the 'introverted' sports, emphasizing self-exploration and self-expression (yoga, dancing, 'physical expression') or the 'cybernetic' sports (flying, sailing), requiring a high cultural input and a relatively low energy input.

Thus, the differences which separate the teachers, the professionals and the employers are, as it were, summed up in the three activities which, though relatively rare—even in the fractions they distinguish, appear as the distinctive feature of each of them, because they are much more frequent there, at equivalent ages, than in the others. The aristocratic asceticism of the teachers finds an exemplary expression in mountaineering, which even more than rambling, with its reserved paths (one thinks of Heidegger) or cycle-touring, with its Romanesque churches, offers for minimum economic costs the maximum distinction, distance, height, spiritual elevation, through the sense of simultaneously mastering one's own body and a nature inaccessible to the many. The health-oriented hedonism of doctors and modern executives who have the material and cultural means of access to the most prestigious activities, far from vulgar crowds, is expressed in yachting, open-sea swimming, cross-country skiing or underwater fishing; whereas the employers expect the same gains in distinction from golf, with its aristocratic etiquette, its English vocabulary and its great exclusive spaces, together with extrinsic profits, such as the accumulation of social capital.

Since age is obviously a very important variable here, it is not surprising that differences in social age, not only between the biologically younger and older in identical social positions, but also, at identical biological ages, between the dominant and the dominated fractions, or the new and the established fractions, are retranslated into the opposition between the traditional sports and all the new forms of the classic sports (pony trekking, cross-country skiing, and so on), or all the new sports, often imported from America by members of the new bourgeoisie and petite bourgeoisie, in particular by all the people working in fashion—designers, photographers, models, advertising agents, journalists—who invent and market a new form of poor-man's elitism, close to the teachers' version but more ostentatiously unconventional.

The true nature of this counter-culture, which in fact reactivates all the traditions of the typically cultivated cults of the natural, the pure and the authentic, is more clearly revealed in the equipment which one of the new property-rooms of the advanced life-style—the FNAC ('executive retail' shops), Beaubourg, *Le Nouvel Observateur*, holiday clubs, etc.—offers the serious trekker: parkas, plus-fours, *authentic* Jacquard sweaters in *real* Shetland wool, *genuine* pullovers in *pure natural* wool, Canadian trappers' jackets, English fishermen's pullovers, U.S. Army raincoats, Swedish lumberjack shirts, fatigue pants, U.S. work shoes, rangers, Indian moccasins in supple leather, Irish work caps, Norwegian woollen caps, bush hats—not forgetting the whistles, altimeters, pedometers, trail guides, Nikons and other essential gadgets without which there can be no natural return to nature. And how could one fail to recognize the dynamics of the dream of social weightlessness as the basis of all the new sporting activities—foot-trekking, pony-trekking, cycle-trekking, motorbike-trekking, boat-trekking, canoeing, archery, windsurfing, cross-country skiing, sailing, hang-gliding, microlights, etc.—whose common feature is that they all demand a high investment of cultural capital in the activity itself, in preparing, maintaining and using the equipment, and especially, perhaps, in verbalizing the experiences, and which bear something of the same relation to the luxury sports of the professionals and executives as symbolic possession to material possession of the work of art?

In the opposition between the classical sports and the Californian sports, two contrasting relations to the social world are expressed, as clearly as they are in literary or theatrical tastes. On the one hand, there is respect for forms and for forms of respect, manifested in concern for propriety and ritual and in unashamed flaunting of wealth and luxury, and on the other, symbolic subversion of the rituals of bourgeois order by ostentatious poverty, which makes a virtue of necessity, casualness towards forms and impatience with constraints, which is first marked in clothing or cosmetics since casual clothes and long hair —like the minibus or camping-car, or folk and rock, in other fields—are challenges to the standard attributes of bourgeois rituals, classically styled clothes, luxury cars, boulevard theatre and opera. And this opposition between two relations to the social world is perfectly reflected in the two relations to the natural world, on the one hand the taste for natural, wild nature, on the other, organized, signposted, cultivated nature.

Thus, the system of the sporting activities and entertainments that offer themselves at a given moment for the potential 'consumers' to choose from is predisposed to express all the differences sociologically pertinent at that moment: oppositions between the sexes, between the classes and between class fractions. The agents only have to follow the leanings of their habitus in order to take over, unwittingly, the intention immanent in the corresponding practices, to find an activity which is entirely 'them' and, with it, kindred spirits. The same is true in all areas of practice: each consumer is confronted by a particular stare of the supply side, that is, with objectified possibilities (goods, services, patterns of action, etc.) the appropriation of which is one of the stakes in the struggles between the classes, and which, because of their probable association with certain classes or class fractions, are automatically classified and classifying, rank-ordered and rank-ordering. The observed state of the distribution of goods and practices is thus defined in the meeting between the possibilities offered at a given moment by the different fields of production (past and present) and the socially differentiated dispositions which—associated with the capital (of determinate volume and composition) of which, depending on the trajectory, they are more or less completely the product and in which they find their means of realization—define the interest in these possibilities, that is, the propensity to acquire them and (through acquisition) to convert them into distinctive signs.

CHAPTER 2

The Boys Who Beat the Street

Loïc Wacquant

It is well known that the overwhelming majority of boxers come from popular milieus, and especially from those sectors of the working class recently fed by immigration. Thus, in Chicago, the predominance first of the Irish, then of central European Jews, Italians, and African Americans, and lately of Latinos closely mirrors the succession of these groups at the bottom of the class ladder.[1] The upsurge of Chicano fighters (and the strong presence of Puerto Ricans) over the past decade, which even a casual survey of the program of the great annual tournament of the Chicago Golden Gloves immediately reveals, is the direct translation of the massive influx of Mexican immigrants into the lowest regions of the social space of the Midwest. Thus, during the finals of the 1989 edition of that joust, clearly dominated by boxers of Mexican and Puerto Rican extraction, DeeDee [The manager of the gym, Eds.] points out to me that "if you want to know who's at d'bottom of society, all you gotta to do is look at who's boxin'. Yep, Mexicans, these days, they have it rougher than blacks." A similar process of "ethnic succession" can be observed in the other major boxing markets of the country, the New York–New Jersey area, Michigan, Florida, and southern California. By way of local confirmation, when they first sign up at the gym, each member of the Woodlawn Boys Club must fill out an information sheet that includes his marital status, his level of education, his occupation and those of his parents, and mention whether he was raised in a family without a mother or father as well as the economic standing of his family: of the five precoded income categories on the questionnaire, the highest begins at $ 12,500 a year, which is *half* the average household income for the city of Chicago.

It is necessary to stress, however, that, contrary to a widespread image, backed by the native myth of the "hungry fighter" and periodically validated anew by selective media attention to the more exotic figures of the occupation, such as former heavyweight champion Mike Tyson,[2] boxers are generally not recruited from among the most disenfranchised fractions of the ghetto subproletariat but rather issue from those *segments of its working class that are struggling at the threshold of stable socioeconomic integration.* This (self-)selection, which tends de facto to exclude the most excluded, operates not via the constraint of a penury of monetary means but through the *mediation of the moral and corporeal dispositions* that are within reach of these two fractions of the African-American population. In point of fact, there is no direct economic barrier to participation to speak of: yearly dues to enroll at the Woodlawn Boys Club amount to 10 dollars; the mandatory license from the Illinois Amateur Boxing Federation costs an additional 12 dollars per annum, and all the equipment necessary for training is graciously lent by the club—only the hand-wraps and the mouthpiece have to be purchased in one of the few sporting-goods stores that carry them, for a total outlay of less than ten dollars.[3] Youngsters issued from the most disadvantaged families are eliminated because they lack the habits and inclinations demanded by pugilistic practice: to become a boxer requires a regularity of life, a sense of discipline, a physical and mental asceticism that cannot take root in social and economic conditions marked by chronic instability and temporal disorganization. Below a certain threshold of objective personal and family constancy, one is highly unlikely to acquire the corporeal and moral dispositions that are indispensable if one is to successfully endure the learning of this sport.[4]

Preliminary analysis of the profile of the 27 professional boxers (all but two of them African-American, ages ranging from 20 to 37) active in the summer and fall of 1991 in Chicago's three main gyms confirms that prizefighters do, on the whole, stand above the lower tier of the male ghetto population. One-third of them grew up in a family receiving public aid and 22 percent were currently jobless, the remainder being either employed or drawing a "weekly salary" from their manager. Thirteen of them (or 48 percent) had attended a community college (if only for a brief period and with little if any educational and economic gain to show for it); one had earned an associate degree and another a bachelor of science.[5] Only three (or 11 percent) had failed to graduate from high school or obtain a GED, and about half held a current checking account. For comparison, of men ages 18 to 45 living in Chicago's South Side and West Side ghettos, 36 percent have grown up in a household receiving welfare, 44 percent do not hold a job, half have not completed their high school education, and only 18 percent have a current checking account.[6] The educational, employment, and economic status of professional boxers is thus quite a bit higher than that of the average ghetto resident. Most distinctive about their background is that none of their fathers received a high school degree and nearly all held typical blue-collar working-class jobs (with the exception of the son of a wealthy white entrepreneur from the suburbs). And sketchy evidence culled from biographies and native accounts suggests that the social recruitment of fighters tends to rise slightly, rather than descend, as one climbs up the pugilistic ladder. "Most of my boys," says veteran trainer and founder of the world-renowned Kronk gym in Detroit, Emanuel Steward, "contrary to what people think, are not that poor. They come from good areas around the country."[7]

By and large, then, professional boxers do not belong to that disorganized and desocialized "dangerous class" the fear of which fed the recent pseudoscientific discourse on the consolidation of a black "underclass" supposedly cut off from "mainstream society."[8] Everything tends to indicate instead that most of them differ from other ghetto youths by virtue of their stronger social integration relative to their low cultural and economic status, and that they come from traditional working-class backgrounds and are attempting to maintain or recapture this precarious status by entering a profession that they perceive as a skilled manual trade, highly regarded by their immediate entourage, which furthermore offers the prospect—however illusory–of big financial earnings. The great majority of adults at the Woodlawn Boys Club are employed (if only part-time) as a security guard, gas station attendant, bricklayer, janitor, stockman, fireman, messenger, sports instructor for the city's Park District, copy shop clerk, bagger at Jewel's food store, counselor at a youth detention center, and steel mill worker.

To be sure, these proletarian attachments are in most cases tenuous, for these jobs are as a rule insecure and low paying, and they do not obviate the chronic need for "hustling" in the street economy to make ends meet at the end of the month.[9] And a contingent of professional fighters does come from the lower fractions of the working class, namely, large female-headed families raised on public aid in stigmatized public housing projects for most of their youth and plagued with endemic and quasi-permanent joblessness. But they are not the majority; nor are they the more successful competitors in the pugilistic field in the medium run.

Furthermore, if their mediocre income and early educational disaffection do not differentiate them clearly from the mass of ghetto residents of their age category, prizefighters come more often from intact families and are much more likely to be married fathers living with their children. And they have the privilege of belonging to a formal organization—the boxing gym—whereas the overwhelming majority of the black residents of the city's poorest neighborhoods belong to none, with the partial exception of their few remaining middle-class members.[10] However, conjugal and familial integration wields its influence in a subtly contradictory manner: a necessary condition for practicing the sport regularly, it must be sufficiently strong to enable the acquisition of the dispositions and motivations necessary for prizefighting but at the same time not so strong as to allow work and household life to compete too intensely with investment in boxing.

> "No, Ashante, he don't come ev'ry day, you know that, Louie,"* explains DeeDee. "It's only them young guys in high school who come regularly ev'ry afternoon. Tha's what's wrong with them grownups: they're married, they got a family, kids, they can't be in d'gym ev'ry day. Rents are high, same with food, an' you gotta go out make some money for all that. They gotta have some job on the side, they gotta find themselves a job that give 'em the money they need for their wife and kids. An' when you got a chance to bring some money home, you gotta go, you ain't gonna come to work out. Tha's Ashante's problem right there. Ashante, he got two kids. He gets jive jobs here an' there. He missed the last event, where he was on the card, cause he had an opportunity to work three-four days in a row and make himself a lil' money. It's a warehouse, when they lookin' for overtime, they call him up [to work as a stockman on a day-to-day basis]. He ain't no regular employee, but they call him often, yep, soon as they need somebody. He can make more workin' that jive job than he can gettin' in d'ring. [A preliminary fight guarantees a purse of about $150 to $300 to each of the contestants.] And he don't have to get beat up. So he gotta take it."
>
> [Field notes, 13 January 1989]

The conversation turns to Mark—a new guy who has been working as an attendant in a photocopy shop since he left high school without finishing three years ago. He arrived really late but DeeDee let him start his workout anyway. He boxes with fervor, leaning over the sandbag, machine-gunning it with short hooks, which earns him praise from DeeDee. "This dude's good. He move well. *He's a natural.* Look at his moves. He's strong. Good hands. Tha's cause he used to fight in d'streets. He's comin' along quick. But he got stiff legs, he don't know how to bend his legs. An' then he got a job, which mean he can only come in late like this. He's gotta train more than that but he don' have the time. It's a real pity, a real pity, yep, 'cause he could make a good boxer. If only I had had 'im earlier, when he was younger . . ." "How old is he?" "He's twenty-two. He was tellin' me hisself how he wish he coulda gone to d'gym when he was fifteen-sixteen years old. But there was no gym where he lived, so he didn' do nuthin'. He hung 'round an' spent his time fightin' in his neighborhood. He weighs 127 pounds, he's not big

> but he's stocky, tha's why. He played football on his high-school team. He can lose some more weight, but it's a shame that he don't have d'time to train more . . . Unfortunately, with guys like him, tha's often the case."
>
> [Field notes, 22 March 1989]

DeeDee articulates here in passing one of the factors that differentiate "street fighters" who eventually fall into petty or serious delinquency from those who exercise their skill in the ring and participate, however irregularly, in the wage-labor economy: the same dispositions can lead to one or the other career depending on the space of activities on offer, here deeply rooted gangs that rule a housing project, there a gym that "stays busy" in a comparatively quiet neighborhood.

The enrollment of the Woodlawn Boys Club fluctuates markedly and irregularly from one month to the next. Anywhere from 100 to 150 boys and men sign up over the course of a year, but most of them stay for no more than a few weeks as they soon find out that the workout is too demanding for their taste—an attrition rate in excess of 90 percent is commonplace for a boxing gym.[11] Attendance is at its highest in winter, just before the Golden Gloves (whose preliminaries take place in early February every year), and in the late spring. A nucleus composed of a score of "regulars," including an inner circle of eight older members who recently turned professional after rising through the amateur ranks together, forms the backbone of this shifting membership. The motivations of participants vary according to their status. Most of the regulars compete officially in the amateur and professional divisions; for them the gym is the locus of an intensive preparation for competition. The others come to the club to get or to keep in shape, sometimes with the explicit design of seducing members of the opposite sex (as does Steve, a massive, twenty-nine-year-old black Puerto Rican who is there "to lose weight, for the chicks. I wanna lose this belly, you know, for the women: that's what they want, man, they're the ones who decide"), to stay in touch with boxing friends (this is the case of several retired "pros" who spend more time talking in the back room than working out on the bags), or to learn techniques of self-defense.[12] In addition to the fighters and trainers, many former pugilists in their old age drop by the gym to chat with DeeDee, spending countless hours in the windowless office reminiscing about the olden days, "when fighters were fighters." For the veteran Woodlawn coach, only competitive boxing really counts. And although he attentively monitors the progress of those who come to the gym only for the sake of exercise, he does not hide his preference for the real pugilists. When the occasion arises, DeeDee does not hesitate to try and entice the "fitness boxers" to the pleasures of the virile embrace of the ring. The following conversation offers a good characterization of this attitude.

> 6 December 1988. As I'm returning to the back room, a tall black man in his forties, very elegantly dressed in a light brown suit and a matching dark brown tie, graying, hairline receding at the temples, with a curly, well-trimmed beard, a little on the plump side, looking very much like an upper-level manager in the public transportation sector, cranes his neck across the door to ask to see "Mister Armour." DeeDee replies that he's he and invites him to seat himself on the little red stool in front of his desk. I pretend to read that day's *Chicago Sun-Times* in order to discreetly listen in on their conversation.
>
> "I'd like some information about boxing lessons for adults. Do you give them yourself?"
>
> "Yep, it depends on what you wanna do: you jus' wanna keep in shape or you wanna fight? How old 're you?"
>
> "I'm forty-one. No, it wouldn't be to fight, not at forty-one years old. . . . It's more for

stayin' in shape and also for self-defense on the street."

"Okay, but later you might get interested in fightin', you know. It's quite a few guys who're pretty old, forty-nine, fifty, even fifty-three—we got T-Jay at fifty-three—who come in to keep their selves in shape an' then after three-four months, they wanna do d'Golden Gloves. Of course [in a matter-of-fact tone], they're gonna find themselves squarin' off with these young guys who're gonna cut'em to pieces and bust'em up, but then they lovin' it: they don' care, all they want to do (hissed with an undertow of admiration) is *fight*."

"At forty-nine years old? Isn't that a little old to fight?"

"Yeah, but it depen's, we got young kids as well as adults . . ."

The mustachioed executive retorts: "No thanks. What I'm interested in is self-defense, that's all, to fight in the street if I get attacked." He will never be seen in the gym again.

Within the Woodlawn Boys Club, indigenous perception establishes a distinction first, among "serious" boxers, between youth who are still in high school and adults who are free of academic obligations but subject to the more constraining obligation of work and family. The youngest is 13 years old, the oldest 57, with the median age hovering around 22.[13] All members are men, as the gym is a *quintessentially masculine space* into which the trespassing of the female sex is tolerated only so long as it remains incidental. "Boxing is for men, and is about men, and *is* men. . . . Men who are fighting men to determine their worth, that is, masculinity, exclude women."[14] While there exists no formal obstacle to their participation—some trainers will even verbally deny having any reticence toward female boxing—women are not welcome in the gym because their presence disrupts if not the smooth material operation of the pugilistic universe then its symbolic organization.

Only under special circumstances, such as the imminence of a big-time fight or the morrow of a decisive victory between the ropes, will the girlfriends and wives of boxers have license to attend their man's training session. When they do so, they are expected to remain quietly seated, motionless, on the chairs that line the flanks of the ring; and they typically move carefully along the walls so as to avoid penetrating the actual training "floor," even when the latter is vacant. It goes without saying that they are not to interfere in any manner with the training, except to help extend its effects into the home by taking full charge of household maintenance and the children, cooking the required foods, and providing unfailing emotional and even financial support. If a woman is present at the Woodlawn Boys Club, boxers are not allowed to walk out of the dressing room bare-chested to come weigh themselves on the scale in the back room—as if men's half-naked bodies could be seen "at work" on the public scene of the ring but not "at rest" in the backstage of the workshop. In another professional gym located near Chicago's Little Italy, the head coach resorts to this heavy-handed method to keep women at a distance: he firmly warns his boxers to not bring their "squeeze" to the gym; if they disobey him, he sends them into the ring to spar with a much stronger partner so that they receive a beating in front of their girlfriend and lose face. At the Windy City Gym, on the edge of the West Side ghetto, a separate area, enclosed by a waist-high wall, is officially reserved for "visitors" to sit in; in practice, it serves only to park the female companions of boxers in training. The famed Top Rank Gym in Las Vegas formally bars entrance to women.

Among regular practitioners, the main division separates amateurs from professionals. These two types of boxing form neighboring universes that, though they are tightly interdependent, are very distant from each other at the level of experience.

A pugilist may spend years fighting in the amateur ranks yet know next to nothing about the mores and factors that mold the careers of their "pro" colleagues (especially when it comes to their financial aspects, which all conspire to keep in the dark).[15] Moreover, the rules that govern competition in these two divisions are so different that it would scarcely be an exaggeration to consider them two different sports. To put it simply, in amateur boxing the goal is to accumulate points by hitting one's opponent as many times as possible in rapid flurries, and the referee enjoys ample latitude to stop the contest as soon as one of the protagonists appears to be in physical difficulty; among professionals, who do not wear protective headgear and whose gloves are notably smaller and lighter, the main objective is to "hurt" one's opponent by landing heavy blows, and the battle continues until one of the fighters is no longer able to carry on. As the head trainer from Sheridan Park puts it, "professional boxers don't screw around, they'll knock you *outa your mind*, you know. It's a rough game, you turn professional, it's a rough game: (abruptly catching himself) it's *not* a game. Amateur, you have your fun. Professional (whispering by way of warning) they're tryin' to kill you." The vast majority of amateur boxers never "turn pro," so that those who do constitute a highly (self-) selected group. Here again, the transition from one category to the other has a better chance of being successful if the fighter can rely on a family environment and social background endowed with a minimum of stability.

Within each of these categories, the other distinctions current in the gym refer to style and tactics in the ring: "boxer" (or "scientific boxer") against "brawler" or "slugger," "counterpuncher," "banger," "animal," and so on. Beyond those differentiations, the gym culture is ostensibly egalitarian in the sense that all participants are treated alike: whatever their status and their ambitions, they all enjoy the same rights and must acquit themselves of the same duties, particularly that of "working" hard at their craft and displaying a modicum of bravery between the ropes when the time comes. To be sure, those who benefit from the services of a personal trainer are in a position to command added attention, and the professionals go through a more demanding and more structured workout. But DeeDee is as keen to teach a 16-year-old novice who might never set foot in the gym again after a week of trial how to throw a left jab as he is on polishing the defensive moves of a ring veteran preparing for a televised bout. Whatever their level of pugilistic competency, all those who "pay their dues" are wholeheartedly accepted as full-fledged members of the club.

As he progresses, each apprentice boxer finds his comfort zone: some are content to stick to the role of "gym fighter," one who trains and "gloves up" more or less frequently to spar and enter an occasional tournament; others decide to venture further in competition and launch themselves onto the amateur circuit; still others crown their amateur careers by "turning pro." The differentiation between the mere dabbler boxer and the full-fledged pugilist is made visible by the expenses each consents to acquire his gear and by the use of a permanent locker. Only competitive fighters train with their own gloves (of which they generally own several worn pairs accumulated over the years), their personal head guard and jumprope, which they keep preciously under lock and key in their individual lockers. The purchase of boxing boots (which cost 35 to 60 dollars) and, even more so, sparring headgear (60 dollars minimum) suffices to signal a long-term commitment to fighting for both the boxer and his entourage. Training outfits also provide a good clue as to the degree of involvement in the sport, although this is easier to manipulate and therefore less reliable. The firm

Ringside, which supplies boxing equipment by mail order, sells a wide range of custom-made gear (trunks, tank tops, jerseys, and robes), and anyone can order a sweatsuit cut to a unique pattern or emblazoned with the likeness of a great champion. Moreover, professional boxers never wear their fighting apparel during workouts. It nonetheless remains that the amount of money spent on training gear is usually a faithful measure of a boxer's material and moral investment in the pugilistic field.

We have seen how the ecology of the ghetto environment and its street culture predispose the youths of Woodlawn to conceive of boxing as a meaningful activity that offers them a stage on which to enact the core values of its masculine ethos. Viewed from that angle, the ghetto and the gym stand in a relation of contiguity and continuity. However, once *inside* the gym, this relation is ruptured and reversed by the Spartan discipline that boxers must obey, which harnesses street qualities to the pursuit of different, more astringently structured and distant goals. Thus the first thing that trainers always stress is what one is *not* supposed to do in the gym. Eddie, the coach-in-second at Woodlawn, offers the following enumeration of the prohibitions of the gym: "Cursin'. Smokin'. Loud talkin'. Disrespect for the women, disrespect for the coaches, disrespect for each other. No animosity, no braggin'." To which one could add a host of lesser and often implicit rules that converge to *pacify* the conduct of the gym's members.

Without having to display his severity, DeeDee sees to it that an iron discipline reigns in the Woodlawn gym as regards both behavior and training routines: it is forbidden to bring food or beverages into the club, to drink or talk during workouts, to rest sitting on the edge of a table, to alter the sequence of drills (for instance, to start a session by skipping rope instead of loosening up and shadowboxing) or modify a standard technical figure. There is no using of the equipment in an unconventional fashion, firing punches at objects, or sparring if one is not in full gear for it or, worse yet, faking a fight or tussling outside the ring. (Indeed, such "floor incidents" are so rare that they remain inscribed in the collective memory of the gym, unlike the routine violence of the street.) It is mandatory to wear a jockstrap under one's towel when coming out of the shower room and a dry change of clothes when leaving the gym. Finally, the children from the day-care center or the neighborhood who come in to admire the efforts of their elders must not under any pretext get near the bags. One must even watch closely one's language: DeeDee will not allow the expression "to fight" to be used in lieu of "to box" (or "to spar" for sparring sessions); and neither he nor the club regulars use vulgar language or curse words in their conversations in the gym.

Most clauses of these implicit "internal regulations" of the club are visible only in the deportment and demeanor of the regulars who have gradually internalized them, and they are brought to explicit attention only when violated.[16] Those who do not manage to assimilate this unwritten code of conduct are promptly dismissed by DeeDee or strongly advised to transfer to another gym. The gym functions in the manner of a *quasi-total institution* that purports to regiment the whole existence of the fighter—his use of time and space, the management of his body, his state of mind, and his most intimate desires. So much so that pugilists often compare working out in the gym to entering the military.

> Butch: In the gym, you learn discipline, self-control. You learn tha' you s'pose to go to bed early, git up early, do your road work, take care of yerself, eat the right foods. Uh, yer body is a *machine*, it's s'pose to be well-tuned. You learn to have some control

so far as rippin' an' runnin' the streets, social life. It jus' gives you kin' of like an *army, soldier mentality,* an' [chuckling] tha's real good for folks.

Curtis: The average guy tha' trains in this gym, kid or man, he matures, see, 85 perzent, 85 perzent more than if he was out on d'street. 'Cause it discipline him to try to be a young man, to try to have sportsmanship, ring generalship, you know, uh, I don' know . . . [stumbles] It's more like, I coul' sit up here an' give you a line of thin's, you know, but [you can] break it down to: it works *like bein' in the military,* it show you how to be *a gentleman* and all, and learn *respect.*

The *boxing gym thus defines itself in and through a relation of symbiotic opposition to the ghetto* that surrounds and enfolds it: at the same time that it recruits from among its youth and draws on its masculine culture of physical toughness, individual honor, and bodily performance, it stands opposed to the street as order is to disorder, as the individual and collective regulation of passions is to their private and public anarchy, as the constructive—at least from the standpoint of the social life and sense of self of the fighter—and controlled violence of a strictly policed and clearly circumscribed agonistic exchange is to the violence, seemingly devoid of rhyme or reason, of the unpredictable and unbounded confrontations symbolized by the rampant crime and drug trafficking that infest the neighborhood.

NOTES

* "Louie" is Loïc Wacquant's nickname in the gym, Eds.

1. S. K. Weinberg and Henri Arond, "The Occupational Culture of the Boxer," *American Journal of Sociology* 57, 5 (March 1952): 460–469 (for statistics on the period 1900 to 1950); T. J. Jenkins, "Changes in Ethnic and Racial Representation among Professional Boxers: A Study in Ethnic Succession," M.A. thesis, University of Chicago, 1955; Nathan Hare, "A Study of the Black Fighter," *Black Scholar* 3 (1971): 2–9; John Sugden, "The Exploitation of Disadvantage: The Occupational Subculture of the Boxer," in Sport, *Leisure, and Social Relations,* eds. John Horne, David Jay, and Andrew Tomlinson (London: Routledge and Kegan Paul, 1987), 187–209; and Jeffrey T. Sammons, *Beyond the Ring: The Role of Boxing in American Society* (Urbana-Champaign, IL: University of Illinois Press, 1990), chapters 2–6. On the trajectory of American Jews in boxing in the first half of the twentieth century, see Stephen A. Reiss, "A Fighting Chance: The Jewish American Boxing Experience, 1890–1940." *American Jewish History* 74 (1985): 233–254, and, for the broader context, Benjamin G. Rader, *American Sports: From the Age of Folk Games to the Age of Spectators* (Englewood Cliffs, N.J.: Prentice-Hall, 1983).
2. It would be difficult to overstate the influence of the Tyson phenomenon on boxing in the black ghetto in the late 1980s. The veritable media tidal wave that accompanied his rise (out of the ghetto of Brooklyn and out of prison where, as a teenager, he was initiated into boxing), his conjugal and financial troubles with the African-American actress Robin Givens (featured in several prime-time television specials), his economic ties to the white New York real estate billionaire Donald Trump, his acquaintances in the artistic milieu (via the agency of Spike Lee), and his personal and legal conflicts with his former entourage made him a legendary character who not only fed a continual flood of rumors, stories, and discussions but who was furthermore capable, by the sole virtue of his symbolic value, of stimulating vocations en masse (as did Joe Louis and Muhammad Ali, who were, in their days, the inspirations of thousands of apprentice boxers). The phenomenon has since gone through a spectacular reversal following Tyson's stunning defeat at the hands of James "Buster" Douglas in February 1990, then his sentencing to six years of prison for rape, and the series of bizarre incidents that followed. See Peter Niels Heller, *Bad Intentions: The Mike Tyson Story* (New York: Da Capo Press, 1995), and, on the multiple meanings of Tyson's trajectory as a living emblem of rough masculinity, the stim-

ulating article by Tony Jefferson, "Muscle, 'Hard Men' and 'Iron' Mike Tyson: Reflections on Desire, Anxiety and the Embodiment of Masculinity," *Body and Society* 4, 1 (March 1998): 77–98.

3. The boxing gyms of the city's Park District are even less costly since they levy no dues; one other professional gym in Chicago requires monthly payments of $5 for amateurs and $20 for professionals but allows many waivers. In other cities, some gyms post notably higher dues: for example, $55 per quarter at the Somerville Boxing Club in a working-class suburb of Boston, where I boxed from 1991 to 1993, and $50 a month at a gym in the Tenderloin, a disreputable area in downtown San Francisco.
4. Or else lack of internal government must be compensated by truly exceptional aggressivity, physical prowess, and ring "toughness." Such fighters, however, tend to "burn out" prematurely and rarely fulfill their potential, pugilistic as well as economic. The ring prodigy and three-time world champion Wilfredo Benitez, the son of a Puerto Rican sugar cane cutter, is an exemplary case in point: though he turned "pro" at age fourteen and was world champion by his seventeenth birthday, his irregularity in training and notorious lack of eating discipline quickly cut his career short.
5. Though they are purported to offer a bridge to four-year campuses, community colleges (or junior colleges) function as remedial courses for high school education and deliver degrees that are largely devoid of value on the labor market. Stephen Brint and Jerry Karabel, "Les 'community colleges' américains et la politique de l'inégalité," *Actes de la recherche en sciences sociales* 86–87 (September 1987): 69–84.
6. Loïc J. D. Wacquant and William Julius Wilson, "The Cost of Racial and Class Exclusion in the Inner Annals of the American City," *Academy of Political and Social Science* 501, *The Ghetto Underclass: Social Science Perspectives* (Jan., 1989), pp. 8–25, here 17, 19, 22.
7. Cited in David Halpern, "Distance and Embrace," in *Reading the Fights,* eds. Joyce Carol Oates and David Halpern (New York: Prentice-Hall, 1988), 279.
8. For a methodical critique of this bogus concept and its social usages, see Loïc Wacquant, "L''*underclass*' urbaine dans l'imaginaire social et scientifique americain," in *L'Exclusion: l'état des savoirs* (Paris: La Découverte, 1996), 248–262.
9. Betty Lou Valentine, *Hustling and Other Hard Work: Life Styles in the Ghetto* (New York: Free Press, 1978).
10. Wacquant and Wilson, "The Cost of Racial and Class Exclusion in the Inner City," 24.
11. The rate for the Woodlawn Boys Club is comparable to that of the East Harlem gym described by Plummer, *Buttercups and Strong Boys,* 57, in which the annual turnover hovers around 80 percent.
12. I explain to the director of the day-care center adjoining the gym, who is inquiring as to why I got into this "sport for brutes," that I come here mostly to get back in shape. She immediately adds, as if it went without saying: "Oh, yes, and then it can't hurt to know a little bit of self-defense in *this* neighborhood. You also got to keep that in mind" (field notes, 8 October 1988). While I am jumping rope to wind down after a sparring session, Oscar, Little Keith's manager, asks me if I want to turn pro (I reassure him, I'm only a dilettante boxer but I would like to go as far as to have a few amateur fights): "'Cuz you box pretty good, you doin' a good job, ya know . . . And then it give ya confidence in the street 'cuz you can defend yo'self better" (field notes, 17 June 1989).
13. One can obtain an amateur license at age thirteen, and some tournaments allow the participation of children as young as ten, who are called "sub-novices." According to Henri Allouch, "Participation in Boxing among Children and Young Adults," *Pediatrics* 72 (1984): 311–312, nearly 30,000 children under fifteen are licensed and tally more than twenty fights a year in North America.
14. Joyce Carol Oates, *On Boxing* (Garden City, N.Y.: Doubleday, 1987), 72. Boxing pundits and commentators sometimes complain about the increasingly constraining regulation of pugilistic violence, which they depict and denounce as a "feminization" of prizefighting apt to pervert it: the reduction from fifteen to twelve rounds for championship bouts, the increased role of physicians, the mandatory forty-five-day waiting period after suffering a defeat by knockout, and especially the growing latitude given to the referee to stop a fight as soon as one of the protagonists appears unable to defend himself or is at risk of serious injury.
15. Professional boxers never reveal the amount of their purses, even to their regular sparring partners; all monetary negotiations and transactions among fighters, trainers, managers, and promoters take place *sub rosa.* See Loïc Wacquant, "A Flesh Peddler at Work: Power, Pain and Profit in the Prizefighting Economy," *Theory and Society* 27, 1 (February 1998): 1–42.
16. Most of the other gyms I have observed in Chicago and visited in other cities broadcast their rules in the form of a standardized list posted on the entrance door or on a wall, or yet hung from the ceiling for all to see. It appears that the more unstable and socially disparate the membership of a boxing club, the more explicit and conspicuous its regulations.

CHAPTER 3

The Sports Taboo: Why Blacks Are Like Boys and Whites Are Like Girls

Malcolm Gladwell

The education of any athlete begins, in part, with an education in the racial taxonomy of his chosen sport—in the subtle, unwritten rules about what whites are supposed to be good at and what blacks are supposed to be good at. In football, whites play quarterback and blacks play running back; in baseball whites pitch and blacks play the outfield. I grew up in Canada, where my brother Geoffrey and I ran high-school track, and in Canada the rule of running was that anything under the quarter-mile belonged to the West Indians. This didn't mean that white people didn't run the sprints. But the expectation was that they would never win, and, sure enough, they rarely did. There was just a handful of West Indian immigrants in Ontario at that point—clustered in and around Toronto—but they *owned* Canadian sprinting, setting up under the stands at every major championship, cranking up the reggae on their boom boxes, and then humiliating everyone else on the track. My brother and I weren't from Toronto, so we weren't part of that scene. But our West Indian heritage meant that we got to share in the swagger. Geoffrey was a magnificent runner, with powerful legs and a barrel chest, and when he was warming up he used to do that exaggerated, slow-motion jog that the white guys would try to do and never quite pull off. I was a miler, which was a little outside the West Indian range. But, the way I figured it, the rules meant that no one should ever out-kick me over the final two hundred metres of any race. And in the golden summer of my fourteenth year, when my running career prematurely peaked, no one ever did.

When I started running, there was a quarter-miler just a few years older than I was by the name of Arnold Stotz. He was a bulldog of a runner, hugely talented, and each year that he moved through the sprinting ranks he invariably broke the existing four-hundred-metre record in his age class. Stotz was white, though, and every time I saw the results of a big track meet I'd keep an eye out for his name, because I was convinced that he could not keep winning. It was as if I saw his whiteness as a degenerative disease, which would eventually claim and cripple him. I never asked him whether he felt the same anxiety, but I can't imagine that he didn't. There was only so long that anyone could defy the rules. One day, at the provincial championships, I looked up at the results board and Stotz was gone.

Talking openly about the racial dimension of sports in this way, of course, is considered unseemly. It's all right to say that blacks dominate sports because they lack opportunities elsewhere. That's the "Hoop Dreams" line, which says whites are allowed to acknowledge black athletic success as long as they feel guilty about it. What you're not supposed to say is what we were saying in my track days—that we were better *because* we were black, because of something intrinsic to being black. Nobody said anything like that publicly last month when Tiger Woods won the Masters or when, a week later, African men claimed thirteen out of the top twenty places in the Boston Marathon. Nor is it likely to come up this month, when African-Americans will make up 80 per cent of the players on the floor for the N.B.A. playoffs. When the popular television sports commentator Jimmy (the Greek) Snyder did break this taboo, in 1988—infamously ruminating on the size and significance of black thighs—one prominent N.A.A.C.P. official said that his remarks "could set race relations back a hundred years." The assumption is that the whole project of trying to get us to treat each other the same will be undermined if we don't all agree that under the skin we actually are the same.

The point of this, presumably, is to put our discussion of sports on a par with legal notions of racial equality, which would be a fine idea except that civil-rights law governs matters like housing and employment and the sports taboo covers matters like what can be said about someone's jump shot. In his much heralded new book "Darwin's Athletes," the University of Texas scholar John Hoberman tries to argue that these two things are the same, that it's impossible to speak of black physical superiority without implying intellectual inferiority. But it isn't long before the argument starts to get ridiculous. "The spectacle of black athleticism," he writes, inevitably turns into "a highly public image of black retardation." Oh, really? What, exactly, about Tiger Woods's victory in the Masters resembled " a highly public image of black retardation"? Today's black athletes are multimillion-dollar corporate pitchmen, with talk shows and sneaker deals and publicity machines and almost daily media opportunities to share their thoughts with the world, and it's very hard to see how all this contrives to make them look stupid. Hoberman spends a lot of time trying to inflate the significance of sports, arguing that how we talk about events on the baseball diamond or the track has grave consequences for how we talk about race in general. Here he is, for example, on Jackie Robinson:

> The sheer volume of sentimental and intellectual energy that has been invested in the mythic saga of Jackie Robinson has discouraged further thinking about what his career did and did not accomplish. . . . Black America has paid a high and largely unacknowledged price for the extraordinary prominence given the black athlete rather than other black men of action (such as military pilots and astronauts), who represent modern aptitudes in ways that athletes cannot.

Please. Black America has paid a high and largely unacknowledged price for a long list of things, and having great athletes is far from the top of the list. Sometimes a baseball player is just a baseball player, and sometimes an observation about racial difference is just an observation about racial difference. Few object when medical scientists talk about the significant epidemiological differences between blacks and whites—the fact that blacks have a higher incidence of hypertension than whites and twice as many black males die of diabetes and prostate cancer as white males, that breast tumors appear to grow faster in black women than in white women, that black girls show signs of puberty sooner than white girls. So why aren't we allowed to say that there might be athletically significant differences between blacks and whites?

According to the medical evidence, African-Americans seem to have, on the average, greater bone mass than do white

Americans—a difference that suggests greater muscle mass. Black men have slightly higher circulating levels of testosterone and human-growth hormone than their white counterparts, and blacks overall tend to have proportionally slimmer hips, wider shoulders, and longer legs. In one study, the Swedish physiologist Bengt Saltin compared a group of Kenyan distance runners with a group of Swedish distance runners and found interesting differences in muscle composition: Saltin reported that the Africans appeared to have more blood-carrying capillaries and more mitochondria (the body's cellular power plant) in the fibres of their quadriceps. Another study found that, while black South African distance runners ran at the same speed as white South African runners, they were able to use more oxygen —89 per cent versus 81 per cent—over extended periods: somehow, they were able to exert themselves more. Such evidence suggested that there were physical differences in black athletes which have a bearing on activities like running and jumping, which should hardly come as a surprise to anyone who follows competitive sports. To use track as an example—since track is probably the purest measure of athletic ability—Africans recorded fifteen out of the twenty fastest times last year in the men's ten-thousand-metre event. In the five thousand metres, eighteen out of the twenty fastest times were recorded by Africans. In the fifteen hundred metres, thirteen out of the twenty fastest times were African, and in the sprints, in the men's hundred metres, you have to go all the way down to the twenty-third place in the world rankings—to Geir Moen, of Norway—before you find a white face. There is a point at which it becomes foolish to deny the fact of black athletic prowess, and even more foolish to banish speculation on the topic. Clearly, something is going on. The question is what.

If we are to decide what to make of the differences between blacks and whites, we first have to decide what to make of the word "difference," which can mean any number of things. A useful case study is to compare the ability of men and women in math. If you give a large, representative sample of male and female students a standardized math test, their mean scores will come out pretty much the same. But if you look at the margins, at the very best and the very worst students, sharp differences emerge. In the math portion of an achievement test conducted by Project Talent—a nationwide survey of fifteen-year-olds—there were 1.3 boys for every girl in the top 10 per cent, 1.5 boys for every girl in the top 5 per cent, and seven boys for every girl in the top 1 per cent. In the fifty-six-year history of the Putnam Mathematical Competition, which has been described as the Olympics of college math, all but one of the winners have been male. Conversely, if you look at people with the very lowest math ability, you'll find more boys than girls there, too. In other words, although the average math ability of boys and girls is the same, the distribution isn't: there are more males than females at the bottom of the pile, more males than females at the top of the pile, and fewer males than females in the middle. Statisticians refer to this as a difference in variability.

This pattern, as it turns out, is repeated in almost every conceivable area of gender difference. Boys are more variable than girls on the College Board entrance exam and in routine elementary-school spelling tests. Male mortality patterns are more variable than female patterns; that is, many more men die in early and middle age than women, who tend to die in more of a concentrated clump toward the end of life. The problem is that variability differences are regularly confused with average differences. If men had higher average math scores than women, you could say they were better at the subject. But because they are only more variable the word "better" seems inappropriate.

The same holds true for differences between the races. A racist stereotype is the assertion of average difference—it's the claim that the typical white is superior to the typical black. It allows a white man to assume that the black man he passes on the street is stupider than he is. By contrast, if what racists believed was that black intelligence was simply more variable than white intelligence, then it would be impossible for them to construct a stereotype about black intelligence at all. They wouldn't be able to generalize. If they wanted to believe that there were a lot of blacks dumber than whites, they would also have to believe that there were a lot of blacks smarter than they were. This distinction is critical to understanding the relation between race and athletic performance. What are we seeing when we remark black domination of elite sporting events—an average difference between the races or merely a difference in variability?

This question has been explored by geneticists and physical anthropologists, and some of the most notable work has been conducted over the past few years by Kenneth Kidd at Yale. Kidd and his colleagues have been taking DNA samples from two African Pygmy tribes in Zaire and the Central African Republic and comparing them with DNA samples taken from populations all over the world. What they have been looking for is variants—subtle differences between the DNA of one person and another—and what they have found is fascinating. "I would say, without a doubt, that in almost any single African population—a tribe or however you want to define it—there is more genetic variation than in all the rest of the world put together," Kidd told me. In a sample of fifty Pygmies, for example, you might find nine variants in one stretch of DNA. In a sample of hundreds of people from around the rest of the world, you might find only a total of six variants in that same stretch of DNA—and probably every one of those six variants would also be found in the Pygmies. If everyone in the world was wiped out except Africans, in other words, almost all the human genetic diversity would be preserved.

The likelihood is that these results reflect Africa's status as the homeland of *Homo sapiens*: since every human population outside Africa is essentially a subset of the original African population, it makes sense that everyone in such a population would be a genetic subset of Africans, too. So you can expect groups of Africans to be more variable in respect to almost anything that has a genetic component. If, for example, your genes control how you react to aspirin, you'd expect to see more Africans than whites for whom one aspirin stops a bad headache, more for whom no amount of aspirin works, more who are allergic to aspirin, and more who need to take, say, four aspirin at a time to get any benefit—but far fewer Africans for whom the standard two-aspirin dose would work well. And to the extent that running is influenced by genetic factors you would expect to see more really fast blacks—and more really slow blacks—than whites but far fewer Africans of merely average speed. Blacks are like boys. Whites are like girls.

There is nothing particularly scary about this fact, and certainly nothing to warrant the kind of gag order on talk of racial differences which is now in place. What it means is that comparing élite athletes of different races tells you very little about the races themselves. A few years ago, for example, a prominent scientist argued for black athletic supremacy by pointing out that there had never been a white Michael Jordan. True. But, as the Yale anthropologist Jonathan Marks has noted, until recently there was no black Michael Jordan, either. Michael Jordan, like Tiger Woods or Wayne Gretzky or Cal Ripken, is one of the best players in his sport not because he's like the other members of his own ethnic group but precisely because he's not like them—or like anyone else, for that matter. Élite athletes are élite athletes because, in some sense, they are on the fringes of genetic variability. As it happens, African populations seem to create more of these genetic outliers than white populations do, and this is what underpins the claim that blacks are better athletes than whites. But that's all the claim amounts to. It doesn't say anything at all about the rest of us, of all races, muddling around in the genetic middle.

There is a second consideration to keep in mind when we compare blacks and whites. Take the men's hundred-metre final at the Atlanta Olympics. Every runner in that race was of either Western African or Southern African descent, as you would expect if Africans had some genetic affinity for sprinting. But suppose we forget about skin color and look just at country of origin. The eight-man final was made up of two African-Americans, two Africans (one from Namibia and one from Nigeria), a Trinidadian, a Canadian of Jamaican descent, an Englishman of Jamaican descent, and a Jamaican. The race was won by the Jamaican-Canadian, in world-record time, with the Namibian coming in second and the Trinidadian third. The sprint relay—the 4 x 100—was won by a team from Canada, consisting of the Jamaican-Canadian from the final, a Haitian-Canadian, a Trinidadian-Canadian, and another Jamaican-Canadian. Now it appears that African heritage is important as an initial determinant of sprinting ability, but also that the most important advantage of all is some kind of cultural or environmental factor associated with the Caribbean.

Or consider, in a completely different realm, the problem of hypertension. Black Americans have a higher incidence of hypertension than white Americans, even after you control for every conceivable variable, including income, diet, and weight, so it's tempting to conclude that there is something about being of African descent that makes blacks prone to hypertension. But it turns out that although some Caribbean countries have a problem with hypertension, others—Jamaica, St. Kitts, and the Bahamas—don't. It also turns out that people in Liberia and Nigeria—two countries where many New World slaves came from—have similar and perhaps even lower blood-pressure rates than white North Americans, while studies of Zulus, Indians, and whites in Durban, South Africa, showed that urban white males had the highest hypertension rates and urban white females had the lowest. So it's likely that the disease has nothing at all to do with Africanness.

The same is true for the distinctive muscle characteristic observed when Kenyans were compared with Swedes. Saltin, the Swedish physiologist, subsequently found many of the same characteristics in Nordic skiers who train at high altitudes and Nordic runners who train in very hilly regions—conditions, in other words, that resemble the mountainous regions of Kenya's Rift Valley, where so many of the country's distance runners come from. The key factor seems to be Kenya, not genes.

Lots of things that seem to be genetic in origin, then, actually aren't. Similarly, lots of things that we wouldn't normally think might affect athletic ability actually do. Once again, the social-science literature on male and female math achievement is instructive. Psychologists argue that when it comes to subjects like math, boys tend to engage in what's known as ability attribution. A boy who is doing well will attribute his success to the fact that he's good at math, and if he's doing badly he'll blame his teacher or his own lack of motivation—anything but his ability. That makes it easy for him to bounce back from failure or disappointment, and gives him a lot of confidence in the face of a tough new challenge. After all, if you think you do well in math because you're good at math, what's stopping you from being good at, say, algebra, or advanced calculus? On the other hand, if you ask a girl why she is doing well in math she will say, more often than not, that she succeeds because she works hard. If she's doing poorly, she'll say she isn't smart enough. This, as should be obvious, is a self-defeating attitude. Psychologists call it "learned helplessness"—the state in which failure is perceived as insurmountable. Girls who engage in effort attribution learn helplessness because in the face of a more difficult task like algebra or advanced calculus they can conceive of no solution. They're convinced that they can't work harder, because they think they're working as hard as they can, and that they can't rely on their intelligence, because they never thought they were that smart to begin with. In fact, one of the fascinating findings of attribution research is that the smarter girls are, the more likely they are to fall into this trap. High achievers are sometimes the most helpless. Here, surely, is part of the explanation for greater math variability among males. The female math whizzes, the ones who should be competing in the top 1 and 2 per cent with their male counterparts, are the ones most often paralyzed by a lack of confidence in their own aptitude. They think they belong only in the intellectual middle.

The striking thing about these descriptions of male and female stereotyping in math, though, is how similar they are to black and white stereotyping in athletics—to the unwritten rules holding that blacks achieve through natural ability and whites through effort. Here's how *Sports Illustrated* described, in a recent article, the white basketball player Steve Kerr, who plays alongside Michael Jordan for the Chicago Bulls. According to the magazine, Kerr is a "hard-working over-achiever," distinguished by his "work ethic and heady play" and by a shooting style "born of a million practice shots." Bear in mind that Kerr is one of the best shooters in basketball today, and a key player on what is arguably one of the finest basketball teams in history. Bear in mind, too, that there is no evidence that Kerr works any harder than his teammates, least of all Jordan himself, whose work habits are legendary. But you'd never guess that from the article. It concludes, "All over America, whenever quicker, stronger gym rats see Kerr in action, they must wonder, How can that guy be out there instead of me?"

There are real consequences to this stereotyping. As the psychologists Carol Dweck and Barbara Licht write of high-achieving schoolgirls, "[They] may view themselves as so motivated and well disciplined that they cannot entertain the possibility that they did poorly on an academic task because of insufficient effort. Since blaming the teacher would also be out of character, blaming their abilities when they confront difficulty may seem like the most reasonable option." If you substitute the words "white athletes" for "girls" and "coach" for "teacher," I think you have part of the reason that so many white athletes are underrepresented at the highest levels of professional sports. Whites have been saddled with the athletic equivalent of learned helplessness—the idea that it is all but fruitless to try and compete at the highest levels, because they have only effort on their side. The causes of athletic and gender discrimination may be diverse, but its effects are not. Once again, blacks are like boys, and whites are like girls.

When I was in college, I once met an old acquaintance from my high-school running days. Both of us had long since quit track, and we talked about a recurrent fantasy we found we'd both had for getting back into shape. It was that we would go away somewhere remote for a year and do nothing but train, so that when the year was up we might finally know how good we were. Neither of us had any intention of doing this, though, which is why it was a fantasy. In adolescence, athletic excess has a certain appeal—

during high school, I happily spent Sunday afternoons running up and down snow-covered sandhills—but with most of us that obsessiveness soon begins to fade. Athletic success depends on having the right genes and on a self-reinforcing belief in one's own ability. But it also depends on a rare form of tunnel vision. To be a great athlete, you have to *care*, and what was obvious to us both was that neither of us cared anymore. This is the last piece of the puzzle about what we mean when we say one group is better at something than another: sometimes different groups care about different things. Of the seven hundred men who play major-league baseball, for example, eighty-six come from either the Dominican Republic or Puerto Rico, even though those two islands have a combined population of only eleven million. But then baseball is something that Dominicans and Puerto Ricans care about—and you can say the same thing about African-Americans and basketball, West Indians and sprinting, Canadians and hockey, and Russians and chess. Desire is the great intangible in performance, and unlike genes or psychological affect we can't measure it and trace its implications. This is the problem, in the end, with the question of whether blacks are better at sports than whites. It's not that it's offensive, or that it leads to discrimination. It's that, in some sense, it's not a terribly interesting question; "better" promises a tidier explanation than can ever be provided.

I quit competitive running when I was sixteen—just after the summer I had qualified for the Ontario track team in my age class. Late that August, we had travelled to St. John's, Newfoundland, for the Canadian championships. In those days, I was whippet-thin, as milers often are, five feet six and not much more than a hundred pounds, and I could skim along the ground so lightly that I barely needed to catch my breath. I had two white friends on that team, both distance runners, too, and both, improbably, even smaller and lighter than I was. Every morning, the three of us would run through the streets of St. John's, charging up the hills and flying down the other side. One of these friends went on to have a distinguished college running career, the other became a world-class miler; that summer, I myself was the Canadian record holder in the fifteen hundred metres for my age class. We were almost terrifyingly competitive, without a shred of doubt in our ability, and as we raced along we never stopped talking and joking, just to prove how absurdly easy we found running to be. I thought of us all as equals. Then, on the last day of our stay in St. John's, we ran to the bottom of Signal Hill, which is the town's principal geographical landmark—an abrupt outcrop as steep as anything in San Francisco. We stopped at the base, and the two of them turned to me and announced that we were all going to run straight up Signal Hill *backward*. I don't know whether I had more running ability than those two or whether my Africanness gave me any genetic advantage over their whiteness. What I do know is that such questions were irrelevant, because, as I realized, they were willing to go to far greater lengths to develop their talent. They ran up the hill backward. I ran home.

Excerpted from Malcolm Gladwell, "The Sports Taboo: Why Blacks are like Boys and Whites are like Girls" in *The New Yorker* (May 19, 1997). Reprinted with the permission of the author.

CHAPTER 4

The Anatomy of Scientific Racism: Racialist Responses to Black Athletic Achievement

Patrick B. Miller

[. . .]

When African-American artists and athletes pursued excellence within the boundaries of Western aesthetic and agonistic traditions, they encountered more than customary biases and myriad discriminatory acts. They confronted a discourse of difference, which, inscribed as a set of "racial constants," effectively discounted the efforts of black Americans or denied the cultural significance of their achievements.

Ultimately, this particular dimension of the politics of culture has engaged a vast scholarship that ranges far beyond the history of racial relations in the United States. Within one frame of analysis, the origins and development of the discourse of difference have been examined specifically with regard to the Nazi eugenic theories that finally marked Jews and gypsies, as well as homosexuals, for extermination. Such cultural boundary marking has also been assessed with consideration of the linkages between gender and race in the construction of hierarchies of privilege and subordination over time. As scholars of postcolonial ideology and experience have demonstrated, furthermore, the ranking of racial traits—especially as it has elaborated the dichotomy between mind and body—continues to serve as a means of suppressing the claims of people of color around the world. What remains is the relationship between the pseudo-science of racial difference and the pernicious social policies it both inspires and informs.[1]

It is significant, then, that even those who endeavor to expose and thus dispose of the cultural hierarchies predicated on the tired old versions of ethnicity and race have lately become involved in earnest and extensive debates over Charles Murray and Richard Herrnstein's *The Bell Curve,* an elaborate ranking of so-called racial and ethnic groups in terms of IQ—with African Americans at the bottom of the list. Scholars have also felt compelled to address the claims made by Dinesh D'Souza, who in *The End of Racism,* has gone so far as to describe the civilizing and Christianizing effects of slavery on the majority of blacks in the United States.[2] In such instances, progressive writers and educators must still regularly engage the persistent stereotypes concerning the "natural" physical abilities of blacks, which are said to explain the "dominance" of African Americans in sports such as basketball and football.

To account for achievement in biologically essentialist terms effectively discounts the traits identified with "character": discipline, courage, sacrifice. And therein lies the significance of inquiries into racial science when they have been applied to athletics.[3]

Ultimately, the questions of who can run faster or jump higher are simplistic, but they are pernicious as well as foolish if conceived as measures of innate racial difference.

[. . .]

Since "race matters," as the title of one of Cornel West's recent books avows, we need to discuss not only why it should but when it should not—in judgments of individual abilities and accomplishments. With regard to the historical construction of racial categories, we ought to consider that the *body* continues to loom large in many people's thinking about difference. TV sports reports often provide the most obvious marker of distinctions associated with race and ethnicity. In basketball, the trope of the white point guard—court savvy, disciplined, and controlled—has stood in striking contrast to prevailing images of black male athletes, able and all too willing to shatter backboards with their slam dunks. And if that juxtaposition appears too stark and simple—in light of the widespread recognition of what was Michael Jordan's mastery, not just of the mechanics of his game, but also of modern media techniques—we can turn to the lecture hall. "I don't know whether or not most white men can jump," the historian of science Stephen Jay Gould wrote during *The Bell Curve* controversy:

> And I don't much care, although I suppose that the subject bears some interest and marginal legitimacy in an alternate framing that avoids such biologically meaningless categories as white and black. Yet I can never give a speech on the subject of human diversity without attracting some variant of this inquiry in the subsequent question period. I hear the "sports version," I suppose, as an acceptable surrogate for what really troubles people of good will (and bad, although for other reasons).[4]

The "sports version" of human diversity, still placing population groups up and down a vertical axis of accomplishment, suggests another significant topic. Without discussing the economic and educational practices that mark "racial" distinctions in the United States, without examining the concepts of whiteness and blackness in cultural terms, and without recognizing the facts of mixed heritage, most racialist formulations have had as their objective the demonstration of African-American inferiority, for example, on intelligence tests. But judgments about culture or ideologies of success also come in response to *black achievement*. Frequently, in reaction to triumphs by African Americans, we hear explanations that qualify excellence fashioned out of the notion of "natural ability."

When African Americans began to register an increasing number of victories on the playing fields during the first decades of the twentieth century, mainstream commentators abandoned the athletic creed that linked physical prowess, manly character, and the best features of American civilization. Although many African Americans had subscribed to the ideal that achievement in sport constituted a proof of equality, a mechanism of assimilation, and a platform for social mobility, the recognition successful black athletes actually received from many educators and journalists explained away their prowess by stressing black anatomical and physiological advantages or legacies from a primitive African past.[5]

Many academicians, beginning in the mid-nineteenth century, thus turned away from the discourse of culture when interpreting the physical talents of blacks—and other Others. As they became engrossed in the "scientific" analysis of racial difference, various anthropologists and anthropometrists reached for their calipers and tape measures in search of a gastrocnemius muscle with a certain diameter or of an elongated heel bone in order to explain the success of certain sprinters or jumpers. In the dominant discourse, an individual's performance was bound to attributes ascribed to the group of his or her origin. Such a racialized view of excellence defined the physical accomplishments of Europeans in terms of diligence and forethought, the application of the mind to the movements of the body, while it framed the achievements of people of color with words such as "natural" and "innate." Ultimately, then, racialized responses to the athletic as well as the artistic accomplishments of blacks have served both to shape and reinforce prevailing stereotypes. In so doing, they have also served to rationalize exclusionary social practices and discriminatory public policies.

THE HISTORY OF RACIAL RANKING

The construction of racial typologies can be traced in general terms to Aristotle's attempt to justify slavery. Pictorial representations of Africans dating back to Greek antiquity, as well as the patterns of thought that shaped the characterization of Caliban and Othello, for instance, undergird modern European racism. Such images speak to a lengthy history of racial boundary marking and the color coding of culture. Yet it is in the mid nineteenth-century writings of Joseph Arthur, Comte de Gobineau, that many scholars perceive the racist ideologies that first alluded to measurable distinctions and pretended to scientific objectivity. In *The Inequality of Human Races* (1853–1855), Gobineau asked: "Is there an inequality in physical strength?" His answer, according to the intellectual historian Elazar Barkan, "mixed aristocratic pessimism, romanticism, theology together with biology, all of which became part of a shared European value system based on racial differentiation."[6] "The American savages, like the Hindus, are certainly our inferiors in this respect, as are also the Australians. The Negroes, too, have less muscle power; and all these people are infinitely less able to bear fatigue."[7]

[. . .]

At the turn of the century, standard reference books continued to include broad generalizations about racial difference based on observations and measurements. Under the subject heading "Negro," the canonical *Encyclopaedia Britannica* of 1895 distinguished between cranial capacities (an average European, 45 ounces; Negro, 35; highest gorilla, 20) and underscored a differential development of the cranial sutures wherein the "premature ossification of the skull" was said to account for the intellectual limitations of blacks. Significantly, such prematurity was said to result in "the inherent mental inferiority of the blacks, an inferiority which is even more marked than their physical differences."[8] Later versions of these notations would accentuate the so-called primitive features of the Negro physiognomy in order to explain the relative failure of African Americans—in the aggregate —on intelligence tests. Such references would also inform the doctrine of racial eugenics as it was elaborated on both sides of the Atlantic.[9]

By 1900, however, another dimension of scientific racism could be discerned. Rather than simply reinforce prevailing notions of Negro inferiority, experts felt compelled to account for the extraordinary achievements of some black athletes. In the face of an increasing number of victories posted by African Americans, the mainstream culture began to *qualify* the meanings of excellence in sport. The *Encyclopaedia Britannica* had described "the abnormal length of the arm, which in the erect position sometimes reaches the kneepan, and which on an average exceeds that of the Caucasian by about two inches," and "the low instep, divergent and somewhat prehensile great toe, and heel projection backwards ('lark heel')." Increasingly, these specifications would be advanced as reasons for black success in sports. Thus, in 1901 the champion sprint cyclist Marshall "Major" Taylor was X-rayed, as well as measured up and down by a number of French medical anthropologists, in an effort to reveal the source of his triumphs in the velodrome. In similar terms, comment on the speed of the black Olympian John Taylor, and on the prepossessing strength of the heavyweight champion boxer Jack Johnson a few years later, included "scientific" speculation.

Throughout the twentieth century, it would often be the accomplishments of people of color in the realm of sport that particularly vexed and intimidated those who endeavored to defend a long-standing racial hierarchy. The response would not be subtle. Indeed, the Western discourse of racial difference carefully juxtaposed black athletic achievement—assessed in terms of compensation—to the supposed intellectual disabilities or cultural shortcomings of African Americans.

Critically, the initial forays into the anthropometry of athletic difference were expounded against the backdrop of increasing segregation in the United States, which involved—beyond the enforcement of Jim Crow in housing, transportation, and education—the exclusion of the vast majority of African-American ballplayers, jockeys, and boxers from mainstream sporting competitions. The cyclist Major Taylor, for instance, competed when he could in Europe and Australia because of the hostility he encountered at home. Hypocrisy was piled upon paradox when those who spoke for the dominant culture began to contrast the alarming vitality of African Americans (as well as immigrant newcomers to the United States) to the alleged degeneration of Anglo-America. Such works as Madison Grant's *The Passing of the Great Race* and Lothrop Stoddard's *The Rising Tide of Color against White World Supremacy* reflected nearly hysterical feelings about the links between demography and democracy. Vaguely informed by statistical data, such discussions of the relative birthrates among the Mayflower descendants, the sons and daughters of the shtetl, and those who were moving from southern farms to northern cities revealed a deep fear about the claims black Americans and "hyphenated" Americans might well make against hallowed ideals such as equality and opportunity.[10]

Black leaders like W. E. B. Du Bois—alongside the guiding lights of the new immigrant groups—did indeed seek full participation in the social, economic, and political mainstream, though they demanded fairness not merely as a measure of their numbers but on the basis of their contributions to American culture. And according to the "muscular assimilationists" among them, there was no better argument for inclusion than success in the "national" pastimes. Major Taylor and Jack Johnson were not the first African Americans to make their mark in sports, and it was clear to racial reformers that they would not be the last to tread "the hard road to glory." Well before the appearance of Joe Louis and Jesse Owens in the 1930s, and a decade later, of Jackie Robinson, black leaders saw in athletics a platform for social change.[11]

Resistance to such assertions was formidable, however. Those who would maintain Jim Crow guarded the portals of the stadium just as they stood at the schoolhouse door. Others reinforced racial hierarchy by constructing elaborate frameworks to distinguish between the laurels won by whites and blacks in sport. During the interwar period, anatomy and physiology were frequently invoked to explain the athletic success of African Americans, circumscribing declarations that prowess in contests of speed, strength, and stamina bespoke fitness for other realms of endeavor. In the idiom of sports, to deny the correspondence between athletics and other accomplishments (more profound and long-standing), numerous mainstream commentators "moved the goal posts."

By the 1930s, generalizations from individual performances to group characteristics dominated many descriptions of black prizefighters, such as the heavyweight champion Joe Louis. Likewise, to account for the medals won by the sprinters Eddie Tolan and Ralph Metcalfe during the 1932 Olympics and by Jesse Owens, Metcalfe, and many other African-American champions at the Berlin Games of 1936, white commentators insisted that black success derived from innate biological advantages. Early in the decade, E. Albert Kinley—whose claim to expertise was that he was an X-ray specialist—repeated the canard about the elongated heel bone, then predicted more world records for African Americans in events that depended on a certain kind of anatomical leverage. Working from a similar premise, Eleanor Metheny, a well-known physical educator, conducted a number of studies on body proportions. Though somewhat guarded in her conclusions, she asserted that kinesiological differences—in the movements generated by individuals with longer legs and narrower hips, for instance—could account for black dominance in sport. Significantly, and ultimately ironically, Metheny would declare that a different, somehow deficient chest construction, as well as lower breathing capacity among blacks, handicapped them in endurance events such as distance running. In David Wiggins's apt phrase, "great speed but little stamina" became the watchword for many white commentators on black athletics. In formulations repeated both in scholarly journals and the popular press, the science of sport further insinuated itself into the broader history of racism in the United States.[12]

If experiments like those conducted by Metheny were as flawed in their conception as in their conclusions, other writers appeared just as intent on defending myths of Anglo-Saxon or Aryan superiority. "It was not long ago," wrote the track-and-field coach Dean Cromwell in 1941, "that his [the black athlete's] ability to sprint and jump was a life-and-death matter to him in the jungle. His muscles are pliable, and his easygoing disposition is a valuable aid to the mental and physical relaxation that a runner and jumper must have." The attempt thus to "historicize" racial difference in sport revealed a significant strand of popular thought. To invoke an African past, the primitive Other, a state-of-being predicated solely on physical prowess, was literally to denigrate what flowed from it. By extension, it was also to exalt its presumed obverse—civilization and the attributes of the dominant order.[13]

Cromwell's interpretation was a curious notion of nature and culture at odds. It imagined that when blacks in Africa had been off running and hunting, the ancestors of white athletes were composing symphonies and building cathedrals, which placed their descendants at a substantial disadvantage at the modern-day Olympics. If the black athlete's "easy-going disposition" lay at or near the center of his success, then again by contrast, white competitors may have been thwarted from starting blocks to finish line by their particular worries about the fate of Western civilization.

Such luridly imagined observations as Cromwell's never stood alone or without amplification. In the ensuing years, black athleticism fell prey to the Harvard anthropologist Carleton S. Coon, who began his commentary on the inherited advantages of African Americans in sport with a depiction of their slender calves and loose jointedness. But what started with anatomy ended with a striking analogy, as was so often the case with racial scientists. The biological features that suited African Americans for certain sports, Coon declared, were characteristic of "living things (cheetahs, for instance) known for their speed and leaping ability." Two later chroniclers of the history of college football continued to rely on gross stereotype, though they had relocated their analogies from the African jungle to the

American palladium. "Because of their tap-dancer sense of rhythm and distinctive leg conformation, blacks excel as sprinters," John McCallum and Charles Pearson averred. "It follows naturally that on the football field they stand out as broken field runners."[14]

After mid-century, racial science often focused on the triumph of black athletes in the track-and-field events of the Olympic Games. The stopwatch and the tape measure seemed to offer a certain validation to the claims of the hereditarians that significant and fixed anatomical and physiological differences accounted for the medals won by black Americans in the sprints and jumps. But then, rather suddenly, racial commentators were confronted by the stellar efforts and world records of African distance runners. On the heels of successive gold medal performances in the marathon, steeplechase, and 10,000-meter race by competitors from Ethiopia and Kenya during the 1960s, the notion of fast-twitch and slow-twitch muscle fibers—which had for a time been used to distinguish between the speed of blacks and stamina of whites—was displaced as a frame of analysis. Substituted for it were assertions that strove to mark differences between East-African and West-African physiques, long and lithe versus compact and muscular. From the vantage not so much of a later era but of a different ideological stance, this swift shift in explanations suggests that the persistence of scientific racism lay not so much in the consistency of the science but in the constancy of its racism.

At odds with such racially essentialist notions, an increasing emphasis on cultural interpretations of African-American success in sports characterized the social science of sport as well as mainstream journalism. A five-part series by Charles Maher in the *Los Angeles Times*, March 24–29, 1968, that surveyed current biological studies of black athletic performance concluded that hard training and motivational factors accounted for the increasing success of African-American athletes. Mainstream sociological opinion had begun to yield the same conclusions.[15] These were noteworthy developments whose stress on black struggle and triumph within the boundaries marked by the athletic establishment reflected the growing influence of the civil rights movement and its integrationist appeal.

[. . .]

RESPONSES TO THE RACIAL "SCIENTISTS"

References to innate athletic differences between population groups persisted well beyond the era of desegregation in sport. But such ways of thinking have also provoked a variety of reactions, often passionate and profound, from black Americans. From Du Bois at the turn of the century to educators and athletes such as Harry Edwards and Arthur Ashe in our own time, most African-American commentators have objected to the use of stereotype and the misuse of science to distinguish the accomplishments of black and white athletes. Urgently and insistently, many intellectuals and activists in the civil rights movement have asserted that the claims made by excellent black athletes against the mainstream rhetoric of equality and opportunity have stood for the larger aspirations of Afro-America. They have also drawn upon the findings of numerous physical scientists and social scientists, who have disproved the allegations of biodeterminism and dismissed the idea of legacies from a primitive past.

During the early years of the century Du Bois enlisted a new generation of anthropologists led by Franz Boas to refute the tenets of scientific racism. In 1906, at the invitation of Du Bois, Boas delivered a paper titled "The Health and Physique of the Negro American" at the eleventh annual Atlanta University Conference. Emphasizing the significance of culture in perceived racial differences, he was instrumental in prompting young African-American scholars, such as Zora Neale Hurston, to undertake research in black folklore and culture. Through the first half of the century, Boasians were popular speakers on the campuses of historically black colleges. The environmentalism embraced by an increasing number of social scientists in the ensuing years seemed to remove black athletic accomplishment from the shaky anthropometrical foundations first advanced by ideologues like Gobineau and to place excellence in sport, for instance, within the sturdier frames of analysis that address social circumstance and cultural innovation.[16]

At the same time, biological scientists also challenged the generalizations based on anthropometry. Few if any offered findings more emphatic or timely than the African-American scholar W. Montague Cobb. Drawing on his experiments in physiology and anatomy, particularly his biopsies of the muscle tissue of Jesse Owens during the late 1930s, Cobb assailed the proposition that specific biological determinants could account for black athletic success. With reference to the prevailing classification systems, the Howard University professor declared without equivocation that the "Negroid type of calf, foot, and heel bone" could not be found in the Olympic champion; if anything, Cobb asserted, the diameter of Owens's gastrocnemius conformed to "the caucasoid type rather than the negroid."[17]

In professional as well as popular journals, Cobb extended his analysis in important ways. He was neither the first scientist, nor the last, to underscore the salience of physical variations *within* population groups as well as between them. Nevertheless, he discussed that notion within the context of sporting accomplishment and thus engaged, at an early date, the athletic typologies then in place. What is more, Cobb indicated his clear sense that racial mixing subverted any assertion about fixed and isolated genetic determinants of muscular or mental prowess. Howard Drew had been a co-record holder in the 100-yard-dash and the first black sprinter to be acclaimed "the world's fastest human," Cobb noted in 1936. But Drew was also light-skinned and "usually taken for a white man by those not in the know." Edward Gourdin, the Harvard sprinter and former world-record holder in the broad jump, was similarly light skinned. "There is not one single physical feature, including skin color, which all our Negro champions have in common which would identify them as Negroes," Cobb asserted. A mixed heritage, he concluded, obviously removed such stellar athletes from consideration when rigid racial dichotomies were being cast, thus exposing as arbitrary and contrived the very principles of racial taxonomy.[18]

[. . .]

The massive resistance to the efforts of the integrationists might begin to explain why other African-American commentators have come to subscribe to essentialist considerations of physical hardihood and athletic prowess. The attempt to strategically appropriate the notion of racial difference —to turn it on its head, as it were—may have been born of frustration. It was clearly sustained by considerations of cultural nationalism and Black Power during the late 1960s and 1970s. But today such racialism is not only manifest in African-centered assertions regarding distinctive patterns of cultural development; it also makes its appeal through the notions of melanin theory, no less weird or pernicious than the pronouncements of coach Cromwell or the journalist Kane. Although the various tenets of Afrocentrism certainly speak to racial pride, it is important not to confuse such a sociological phenomenon with a solidly grounded school of critical analysis; while Afrocentrism may be good therapy, as one prominent scholar has noted, it is not good history.[19]

[. . .]

RECENT DEVELOPMENTS

[. . .] Al Campanis stated that blacks performed well on the field but lacked "the necessities" to occupy managerial positions or places of responsibility and authority in the front offices of sports organizations. Jimmy "the Greek" Snyder, a bookmaker turned loose on television, linked the heritage of slavery to the modern playing field. "The slave owner would breed his big black with his big woman so that he could have a big black kid," Snyder maintained. The consternation evinced by their respective interviewers and the summary firing of both men indicated a shift of values and standards toward such public declarations and their racist underpinnings. Yet many Americans continue to mark racial differences in the athletic arena in terms both calculated and crude. Toward the end of the 1996–1997 basketball season, a sportscaster was fined by the NBA for his retrograde appraisal of black athletic ability. Commenting on a stellar play by one athlete, David Halberstam, who announced the games for the Miami Heat, remarked that "Thomas Jefferson would have been proud of that pass. When Thomas Jefferson was around basketball was not invented yet, but those slaves working at Thomas Jefferson's farm, I'm sure they would have made good basketball players."[20]

Clearly, such instances draw attention to the prevalence of racialist thinking about athletic accomplishment. Other commentary has been less forthright in addressing the meaning of the success of blacks in sport. In the aftermath of the firing of Jimmy the Greek, the syndicated columnist Richard Cohen vaguely suggested that civil rights activists would want to steer clear of any assessment of the racial dimension of physical attributes for fear of having to engage intellectual and psychological distinctions. Raising the issue of "political correctness," Cohen then shied away from further speculation about racial difference in sport or other endeavors.[21]

Cohen's comments nevertheless made their way into the much more purposive arguments of Dinesh D'Souza in *The End of Racism*, a book that deals with scientific racism principally by repeating its most atrocious pronouncements and ignoring its critics. Thus in a short section concerning athletics, intended to set up his selective digest of IQ statistics, D'Souza not only recapitulated the "categorical imperative" that has long prevailed among racial scientists, he also reiterated the notion of compensation. "It stands to reason that groups that are unlike each other in some respects may also differ in other respects," D'Souza contends offhandedly. "Why should groups with different skin color, head shape, and other visible characteristics prove identical in reasoning ability or the ability to construct an advanced civilization? If blacks have certain inherited abilities, such as improvisational decision making, that could explain why they predominate in certain fields such as jazz, rap, and basketball, and not in other fields, such as classical music, chess, and astronomy." The end of racism indeed.[22]

The racial essentialism that continues to shadow much of the commentary on sport is confined neither to American culture nor to considerations of the achievements of African Americans. A 1993 article from a popular New Zealand magazine, for example, titled "White Men Can't Jump"—how ironically it is hard to tell—documented the increasing prominence of native peoples in rugby, a sport long identified with British colonialism as a means of toughening those who administered the Empire. Amid a wide-ranging discussion of changing demographics in New Zealand as well as an analysis otherwise sensitive to Maori and

Samoan cultural patterns, several white sports figures speculate, first, on the innate abilities vis-a-vis the acquired skills of Polynesian squads. "Polynesian players were naturally superior to us in talent," one former player declared, "but a lot of them aren't there now because they didn't have the discipline for physical conditioning. They lacked the right kind of mental attitude. They'd just turn up and play." Said another, it was once the case that "your typical Polynesian rugby team would have just lost their head in a pressure situation. It was almost as if it was the Polynesian way to do something really stupid that gave the game away." Another passage indicates the malleability of such typologies, however. Polynesians have come to excel at the sport because they are bigger now and play a "more physical and confrontational" brand of the game. Inevitably size will win out in such appraisals: "The Polynesian is basically mesomorphic, tending to be big-boned, muscular, of average height, wide shoulders, thin waist," one trainer asserts. "They have a higher proportion of fast twitch muscle fibre which is the source of their explosive style and the reason they are fast over short distances." Contrasting feats of character to mere physicality, the article offers yet another instance where innatist constructs can be placed in comparative perspective, encouraging us to generalize somewhat about the phenomenon of racial essentialism. In New Zealand as in the United States, athletic competition has offered a way for people of color to fashion significant emblems of identity and pride as well as to challenge the discriminatory practices of old. It is a critical commentary on both social systems that those initiatives are still contested, that racialist thinking continues to qualify such hallowed notions as sportsmanship and fair play, equality, and opportunity.[23]

Significantly, taxonomic conventions in the representation of population groups have long stood as the predicate of social authority. That the dominant culture can employ them—and modify them when necessary—to maintain hierarchies of privilege and subordination means that minority cultures cannot use such typologies in the same way. If the strategy of "muscular assimilationism"—a prominent element of the civil rights campaigns of the twentieth century—has not been entirely successful in creating a level playing field, it is more certain still that the separatism manifest in Afrocentrism and melanin theory is patently self-defeating in the long run. Moreover, to the extent that many African-American youth exalt athletic heroes over other role models—spending their formative years in "hoop dreams"—the emphasis on athletic striving has been overplayed. What remains is yet another troubling fact. Even as sociological surveys and a new generation of biographies and memoirs tell us about the increasingly *multiracial* character of U.S. society, the discourse of innate and immutable racial difference still looms large in the popular consciousness. A recent addition to the long shelf of pseudoscientific racism, Jon Entine's *Taboo: Why Black Athletes Dominate Sports and Why We're Afraid to Talk About It* promises that future genetic research will provide the evidence he begs for—mainly concerning the success of Kenyan runners in the marathon and steeplechase. Though historians, anthropologists, and sociologists shredded the book, it received a mild reception by most sports columnists, which may reveal the deep-rootedness of racial lore in America.[24]

Ultimately, for intellectual historians, cultural theorists, social scientists, as well as journalists who hope to engage entrenched modes of racialist thought and to create a more expansive conception of culture, it may be well as a first step to adopt a new perspective regarding the texts devoted to innatist thinking. Central to this undertaking would be the compilation of a roster of phrases and pronouncements that clearly links academic racism, past and present. To be sure, as we strive to move beyond category, the idea of an index of racialist literature involves a troubling dimension. Yet it is nevertheless crucial that progressive, or expansive, thinkers on the subject—rather than institute- and foundation-based conservative ideologues—become the cartographers of the contemporary discussion of race. Better still, though from a different interpretive position, we might start erasing racial boundaries altogether.

[. . .]

Excerpted from Patrick B. Miller, "The Anatomy of Scientific Racism: Racialist Responses to Black Athletic Achievement" in the *Journal of Sport History* 25.1 (Spring 1998): 119–151.

NOTES

1. See, for example, Stephen Jay Gould, *The Mismeasure of Man* (New York: Norton, 1981); Nancy Stepan, *The Idea of Race in Science: Great Britain, 1800–1860* (London: MacMillan, 1982); Nancy Leys Stepan and Sander Gilman, "Appropriating the Idioms of Science: The Rejection of Scientific Racism," in Dominick LaCapra, ed., *The Bounds of Race: Perspectives on Hegemony and Resistance* (Ithaca: Cornell University Press, 1991), 72–103; Gilman, *Difference and Pathology: Stereotypes of Sexuality, Race, and Madness* (Ithaca: Cornell University Press, 1985); *idem., The Jew's Body* (New York: Routledge, 1991); *idem., Picturing Health and Illness: Images of Identity and Difference* (Baltimore: Johns Hopkins University Press, 1995); *idem., Smart Jews: The Construction of the Image of Jewish Superior Intelligence* (Lincoln: University of Nebraska Press, 1996); William H. Tucker, *The Science and Politics of Racial Research* (Urbana: University of Illinois Press, 1994). See also George Mosse, *Toward the Final Solution: A History of European Racism* (New York: Harper, 1980) and Michael Adas, *Machines as the Measure of Men: Science, Technology, and Ideologies of Western Dominance* (Ithaca: Cornell University Press, 1989); Laura Nader, ed., *Naked Science: Anthropological Inquiries into Boundaries, Power, and Knowledge* (New York: Routledge, 1996); Ivan Hannaford, *Race: The History of an Idea in the West* (Baltimore: Johns Hopkins University Press, 1996). See also William R. Stanton, *The Leopard's Spots: Scientific Attitudes Toward Race in America, 1815–1859* (Chicago: University of Chicago Press, I960); Thomas Gossett, *Race: The History of an Idea in America* (New York: Schocken, 1965); John S. Haller, *Outcasts from Evolution: Scientific Attitudes of Racial Inferiority, 1859–1900* (Urbana: University of Illinois Press, 1971); and George Fredrickson, *The Black Image in the White Mind: The Debate on Afro-American Character and Destiny, 1817–1914* (New York: Harper & Row, 1971).
2. See Charles Murray and Richard J. Herrnstein, *The Bell Curve: Intelligence and Class Structure in American Life* (New York: Free Press, 1994); *idem.*, "Race and I.Q.," *The New Republic* (October 31, 1994): 10–37; Russell Jacoby and Naomi Glaubermarn, eds., *The Bell Curve Debate: History, Documents, Opinions* (New York: Times Books, 1995); Steven Fraser, *The Bell Curve Wars: Race, Intelligence, and the Future of America* (New York: Basic Books, 1995); Ashley Montagu, *Race and IQ* (New York: Oxford University Press, 1995); Robert Newby, ed., *The Bell Curve: Laying Bare the Resurgence of Scientific Racism,* special issue of *American Behavioral Scientist* 39 (October 1995); John L. Rury, "IQ Redux," *History of Education Quarterly* 35 (Winter 1995): 423–38; Leon J. Kamen, "Behind the Curve," *Scientific American* 272 (February 1, 1995); 99–103; Claude S. Fischer, Michael Hour, Martin S. Anchez Jankowski, Samuel R. Lucas, Ann Swidler, and Kirm Voss, *Inequality by Design: Cracking the Bell Curve Myth* (Princeton, NJ: Princeton University Press, 1996). See also Marek Kohn, *The Race Gallery: The Return of Racial Science* (London: Jonathan Cope, 1995) and Dinesh D'Souza, *The End of Racism: Principles for a Multiracial Society* (New York: Free Press, 1995).
3. See, for example, "The Black Athlete Revisited," *Sports Illustrated* August 5, 12–19, 1991, pp. 38–77, 26–73, 40–51. The prevailing representation of black and white athletes had not changed significantly, the authors discovered, since 1968, when the magazine published its first expose of racism in the realm of U.S. sport.
4. Gould, "Ghosts of Bell Curves Past," *Natural History* (February 1995): 12.
5. See, for example, Patrick B. Miller, "'To Bring the Race along Rapidly': Sport, Student Culture, and Educational Mission at Historically Black Colleges during the Interwar Years," *History of Education Quarterly* 35 (Summer 1995): 111–33.

6. Elazar Barkan, *The Retreat of Scientific Racism: Changing Concepts of Race in Britain and* the *United States between the World Wars* (Cambridge, UK; Cambridge University Press, 1992), 16. See Michael D. Biddiss, *Father of Racist Ideology: The Social and Political Thought of Count Gobineau* (London: Weidenfeld and Nicolson, 1970).
7. Gobineau, *The Inequality of Human Races* (London: William Heinemann, 1915), 151–3. I am indebted to Scott Haine for bringing this passage to my attention.
8. *Encyclopaedia Britannica*, American edition, vol. 17 (New York, 1895): 316–20.
9. See, for instance, Thurman B. Rice, *Racial Hygiene: A Practical Discussion of Eugenics and Race Culture* (New York: MacMillan, 1929). For historical assessments of eugenics, see Mark H. Haller, *Eugenics: Hereditarian Attitudes in American Thought* (New Brunswick, NJ: Rutgers University Press, 1963); Gould, *The Mismeasure of Man*; Daniel J. Kevles, *In the Name of Eugenics: Genetics and the Uses of Human Heredity* (New York: Alfred A. Knopf, 1985); Troy Duster, *Backdoor to Eugenics* (New York: Routledge, 1990); Tucker, *The Science and Politics of Racial Research*, 54–137; Joseph Graves, Jr., *The Emperor's New Clothes: Biological Theories of Race at the Millennium* (New Brunswick, NJ: Rutgers University Press, 2001).
10. Madison Grant, *The Passing of the Great Race; or The Racial Basis of European History* (New York: Scribner, 1916); Lothrop Stoddard, *The Rising Tide of Color against White World Supremacy* (New York: Scribner 1920).
11. The "contributionist" writings of George Washington Williams and Carter G. Woodson, for example, closely parallel those of immigrant American authors. With respect to sport, see Edwin Bancroft Henderson, the foremost chronicler of black achievements: *The Negro in Sports* (Washington: Associated Publishers, 1939) and *The Black Athlete: Emergence and Arrival* (New York: Publishers Co., 1968).
12. On Kinley, see the *New York World*, March 14, 1931. Eleanor Metheny, "Some Differences in Bodily Proportions between American Negro and White male college students as Related to Athletic Performance," *Research Quarterly* 10 (December 1939): 41–53; David K. Wiggins, "'Great Speed but Little Stamina': The Historical Debate over Black Athletic Superiority," *Journal of Sport History* 16 (Summer 1989): 162–4.
13. Dean Cromwell and Al Wesson, *Championship Technique in Track and Field* (New York, London: McGraw-Hill, 1941), 6; Wiggins, "Great Speed But Little Stamina," 161.
14. Coon quoted in Marshall Smith, "Giving the Olympics an Anthropological Once-Over," *Life*, October 23, 1964, p. 83; John McCallum and Charles H. Pearson, *College Football, USA, 1869–1973* (New York: Hall of Fame Publishers, 1973), 231.
15. See D. Stanley Eitzen and George Sage, *Sociology of American Sport* (Dubuque, IA: W. C. Brown, 1978), 300; Jay Coakley, *Sport in Society: Issues and Controversies* (St. Louis: Times Mirror/Mosby College, 1986), 146–50.
16. See David Levering Lewis, *W. E. B. Du Bois: Biography of a Race, 1868–1919* (New York: Holt, 1993), 351–52. See Boas, *The Real Race Problem from the Point of View of Anthropology* (New York: National Association for the Advancement of Colored People, 1912) and *Race and Nationality* (New York: American Association for International Conciliation, 1915).
17. W. Montague Cobb, "Race and Runners," *Journal of Health and Physical Education* 7 (January 1936): 3–7, 52–56.
18. *Ibid.* See also W. Montague Cobb, "The Physical Constitution of the American Negro," *Journal of Negro Education* 3 (1934): 340–88, and "Does Science Favor Negro Athletes?" *Negro Digest* 5 (May 1947): 74–7.
19. On African-centered social commentary, see Molefi Kete Asante, *Afrocentricity: The Theory of Social Change* (Buffalo, NY: Amulefi, 1980) and *The Afrocentric Idea* (Philadelphia: Temple University Press, 1987; rev. ed., 1997). See also Cheikh Anta Diop, *Civilization or Barbarism: An Authentic Anthropology* (Brooklyn, NY: Lawrence Hill Books, 1991); Bernal, *Black Athena.* An impressive introduction to the mode of thought can be found in Carl Pedersen, "Between Racial Fundamentalism and Ultimate Reality: The Debate over Afrocentrism," *Odense American Studies International Series*, Working, Paper no. 4 (1993). And, concerning its appeal, see Gerald Early, "Understanding Afrocentrism: Why Blacks Dream of a World Without Whites," *Civilization* (July/August 1995): 31–39. See also Clarence E. Walker, "You Can't Go Home Again: The Problem with Afrocentrism," *Prospects* 18 (1993), 535–43; on "therapy" and "history," see Leon Litwack, "The Two-Edged Suspicion," *American Historical Association Perspectives* 31 (September 1993), 13–14. For a somewhat different view of this strand of black nationalism, see bell hooks, *Black Looks: Race and Representation* (Boston: South End Press, 1992), 30.
20. On these episodes, see Wiggins, "Great Speed but Little Stamina," 179–81; Phillip M. Hoose, *Necessities: Racial Barriers in American Sports* (New York: Random House, 1989); *New York Times*, March 27, 1997.
21. See Richard Cohen, "The Greek's Defense," *Washington Post*, January 19, 1988.

22. D'Souza, *The End of Racism*, 440–1.
23. Tom Hyde, "White Men Can't Jump," *Metro: Essentially Auckland*, September 1993, 63–9. I am indebted to Charles Martin for pointing this work out to me. More recently still, the New Zealand anthropologist Phillip Houghton has spoken of the ways Polynesians, such as the great rugby player Jonah Lomu, have finally reached their "genetic potential." Houghton, *People of the Ocean: Aspects of Human Biology of the Early Pacific* (Cambridge, UK: Cambridge University Press, 1996). See also Julia Leilua, "Lomu and the Polynesian Power packs," *New Zealand Fitness* (February/March 1996), 24–7, I am grateful to Douglas Booth for sharing this article with me. In broader terms, Marek Kohn discusses the "race science system" directed at the control of the Romani (gypsy) population that has in recent years been established in parts of Southern and Eastern Europe; see Kohn, *The Race Gallery*, 178–252. On issues of classification and discrimination, see also Saul Dubow, *Scientific Racism in Modern South Africa* (Cambridge, UK: Cambridge University Press, 1995).
24. Entine, *Taboo* (New York: Public Affairs, 2000); Paul Spickard (review), *Journal of Sport History* 27 (Summer 2000), 338–400; Mark Dyreson, "American Ideas About Race and Olympic Races from the 1890s to the 1950s: Shattering Myths or Reinforcing Scientific Racism?" *Journal of Sport History* 28 (Summer 2001), 173–215. The historians of science who have made the most telling rebuttals to the new scientific racists include Jonathan Marks, *Human Biodiversity: Genes, Race, and History* (New York: Aldine De Gruyter, 1995); *idem.*, *What It Means To be 98% Chimpanzee: Apes, People, and Their Genes* (Berkeley: University of California Press, 2002), esp. ch. 6. See also Graves, *The Emperor's New Clothes.*

CHAPTER 5

Sport and the Italian American Quest for Whiteness[1]

Gerald R. Gems

INTRODUCTION

In 1861 military forces led by Giuseppe Garibaldi liberated Italy from centuries of foreign rule; but Italians still lacked any sense of a national identity and had no allegiance to the new government. Faced with more taxes, grinding poverty and epidemics, oppressed peasants sought a better life. Between 1880 and 1924 more than 4,000,000 migrated to the United States. Uneducated and largely illiterate, they had only their bodies, in the form of physical labour, to offer in return. They arrived unwashed and unwanted by the white Anglo-Saxon Protestants who enjoyed hegemony over American society. This study analyses the role of sport as a means to gain greater group recognition and eventual acceptance of Italians within the polity. That process differed markedly from the Jewish pursuit of education or the Irish involvement in politics as other ethnics' means of gaining social capital. The study utilises English- and Italian-language sources, such as newspapers that provided middle-class perceptions, values and goals; oral histories that gave voice to working-class families, their values and generational conflicts in identity and purpose; and archival materials to trace the journey from a lack of a national identity to the development of an Italian identity, a liminal identity as Italian Americans, and the question of full inclusion in the Americanisation process, which necessitated a transition from racial to ethnic classification and evolution from non-white to white status.

Whiteness studies have been prominent within the scholarly literature for two decades, and Italians have drawn their share of attention without consensus. Jennifer Guglielmo and Salvatore Salerno asked 'Are Italians White?', while Thomas Guglielmo concluded that Italians were 'White on Arrival' in the United States.[2] This study disagrees with the latter contention. Whiteness extends beyond one's skin colour; to include the norms, values, standards and practices of a dominant social group, what Pierre Bourdieu refers to as habitus, a lifestyle and taste that is deeply embedded in one's social class, though not entirely fixed. The standards of whiteness in American society derived from the beliefs, principles, values and decorum of white, Anglo, middle-class Protestant (WASP) culture largely established before the arrival of Italian immigrants. Cheryl Harris has stated that 'the law's construction of whiteness defined and affirmed critical aspects of identity (who is white); of privilege (what benefits accrue to that status); and of property (what legal entitlements arise from that status)'.[3] While Italians may have been designated as white on immigration records, they did not arrive with the privileges of whiteness and were not accepted as such.

Southern and eastern European peasants faced an uphill battle in pursuit of social acceptance. Many migrants were distinguished by their poverty, lack of education, Catholic or Jewish religion, and communal lifestyle that deemed them to be unacceptable 'others'. Scholars continue to disagree as to when Italians gained whiteness. It is clear, however, that the racialisation of Italians appeared by the mid-nineteenth century with the rise of anthropology that focused on differences rather than similarities among humans and the consequent categorisation of the species. Southern Italians and Sicilians were especially labelled with derogatory stereotypes even before they embarked for America and such denigration continued upon and after their arrival.[4] As early as 1830 a New Yorker remarked that 'A dirty Irishman is bad enough, but he's nothing comparable to a nasty . . . Italian loafer'. By mid-century another common comparison viewed the Italians unfavourably: 'The lowest Irish are far above the level of these creatures [Italians].' By 1876 even the *New York Times* promoted the image of Italian criminality by stating that 'The knife with which he cuts his bread he also uses to lop off another dago's finger or ear. . . . He is quite as familiar with the sight of human blood as with the sight of the food he eats.'[5] In the media and popular culture Italians were characterised as less than white in slang and jokes, and, especially in the South, treated similarly to blacks. The term 'guinea', previously used for African slaves, ascribed an equally low status to Italians by the 1890s. Many Sicilians took work on the sugar cane plantations of Louisiana. Their willingness to assume dirty, physical labour equated them with blacks and bosses referred to them as 'niggers'. Hard, physical labour became 'nigger work' and 'dago work'. They worked every day of the week for 12–16 hours (18 during harvest season) to earn just 75 cents to one dollar per day. At the 1898 Louisiana state constitutional convention, representatives admitted a measure of whiteness in the skin colour of Italians; but 'according to the spirit of our meaning when we speak of white man's government [the Italians] are as black as the blackest negro [*sic*] in existence'; and they consequently denied suffrage to Italians by instituting poll taxes, literacy tests and residency requirements. Neither blacks nor Italians were allowed to serve on the New Orleans police force.[6] In 1922 an Alabama judge acquitted Jim Rollins, a black man, of miscegenation charges when he determined that the Sicilian women with whom he cohabited was as dark as Rollins, and therefore inconclusively white.[7]

Bias was not limited to the South. An 1895 public notice for labourers to build a reservoir in New York City advertised daily wages of $1.30–1.50 for whites, $1.25–1.40 for 'coloreds' and $1.15–1.25 for Italians. In 1902 a Minneapolis fraternal lodge excluded both blacks and Italians. In 1907 residents of Sumrall, Mississippi protested against Italian children in the public schools, and Frank Scaglioni, a crippled shoemaker and leader of the Italian community, was beaten and dragged for a mile with a rope. The California lumber industry also considered Italians to be non-white as well; and both Italians and Greeks were ascribed non-white status in the Minnesota mining towns until the First World War era. In the Arizona mines Italians got the lowest wages; and in the Alabama steel mills an immigration commission report of 1911 claimed that it was 'practically universal opinion among employers that South Italians are . . . the most inefficient of all races, whether immigrant or native'. Such treatment forced Italians to confront their ascribed difference from other groups, a step in reaching a collective identity.[8]

POPULAR CULTURE AS AN ASSIMILATIVE PROCESS

Initially the immigrant Italians had little concept of an Italian nation. They maintained an allegiance to family and friends, and perhaps their fellow villagers or *paesani* with whom they shared a lifestyle and a linguistic dialect at odds with the Tuscan language adopted by the national government. Residents of the Mezzogiorno, the region south of Rome, considered the northern-based government to be as exploitative as the previous foreign occupiers. Early migrants, therefore, did not consider themselves to be beholden to any 'Italian' state. Editors of Italian American newspapers, mostly northern Italians, attempted to develop an Italian identity in America by proposing the celebration of Columbus Day without great success.

Popular culture, however, had always allowed the lower classes to entertain their social superiors via music, theatre and sport, and the advent of the vaudeville stage provided an early opportunity for Italians to garner notice. Anglos feared an increasing feminisation of culture in the late nineteenth century which they perceived to be an emasculating influence. Consequently, the well-developed masculine physique drew the scrutiny of large audiences. Romolo or Romulus (Cosimo Molino), known as the Sicilian Hercules, and his partner Remus (Giacomo Zaffarana), were both born in Catania, but embarked on an international tour, thrilling onlookers with their feats of strength. The diminutive Romulus stood only five feet tall and weighed 167 lb, but lifted 119-lb dumbbells with each arm, and pressed a 168-lb weight 20 times in succession. In the United States he even took to wrestling bulls, feats that drew admiration but also reinforced the physical nature of the Italian body, and the perception that Italian labourers were fit enough to construct the roadways, railways and subways of America.[9] Italians also began to assume an increasing role in American popular culture by the latter nineteenth century, and Lawrence Brignoli(a), the son of an immigrant peddler, gained notice as the winner of the Boston Marathon in 1899. Brignolia spent much of the next century engaged in sporting enterprises. After his marathon victory he continued to compete as an oarsmen and a baseball player before taking up harness racing. He owned his own stable of trotting horses and also promoted boxing matches.[10] Larry Brignolia, Jr. attempted to emulate his father as a distance runner before baseball attracted his attention. He proved good enough to earn a try-out with the Chicago Cubs professional team; but when that quest failed, he turned to professional boxing, where rewards were more immediate. Despite his father's attainment of social and economic capital, physical prowess apparently remained central to the identity of the son. Such early Italian athletic stars continued to provide role models for the aspiring youth of the second and third generations, but the emphasis on physicality marked the self-perceptions of most immigrants and their children.[11]

The appearance of athletes from Italy also stirred a greater recognition among the immigrants of their Italian heritage. Italian cyclists and the famed runner Dorando Pietri drew crowds of Italian supporters in their competitions versus other ethnics in the United States. The social Darwinian beliefs of the era, grounded in the ideology of the 'survival of the fittest', rationalised the superiority of one group over another and engaged sport as a means to determine the physical qualities of different races. Scientists of the era divided the multitude of peoples into various races, as the concept of ethnicity had not yet gained currency.[12]

Marathon racing provided one of the greatest tests of human endurance and a means to test racial comparisons. Pietri had first gained international fame as the near winner of the 1908 Olympic marathon in London and he soon embarked on a tour of the United States to compete against a variety of other ethnic runners in commercialised spectacles. Italians of various regions and occupations turned out to support, cheer and fete him in dinners as one of their own, promoting a pan-Italian identity. Perhaps in emulation of Pietri, Gaston Strobino, another immigrant, took up distance running and performed well enough to win a bronze medal for the US Olympic team in 1912, an event that signalled a symbolic transition in identity. Upon his return Strobino was feted as an 'American' hero. Second-generation Italian youths also began to appear on Major League baseball diamonds by the twentieth century, further galvanising an Italian American identity and a presence in the national game. The gradual inclusion of Italians in the sport distanced them from African American players who had been banned since the late nineteenth century, and gave the Italians an increasing claim to the status of whiteness.[13]

Boxing offered yet another means to establish a greater sense of unity among the multitude of immigrants. The ethnic rivalries of the city streets transferred readily to the boxing ring and promoters capitalised on such animosities that focused attention on one's national identity. Sicilians, Neapolitans, Apulians and Tuscans might all be drawn to an event that featured an 'Italian' athlete. Casper Leon (Gaspare Leoni), born in Palermo in 1872, boxed throughout the United States from 1891 to 1909 as 'the Sicilian Swordfish'. Fighting in Italian areas throughout the Northeast and the Midwest, he provided the residents with a greater sense of identity. Others initially assumed Irish aliases due to the domination of that group in boxing circles; but by the 1920s Italian fighters would assume their own names, generating a great sense of pride in the Little Italies of America as many rose to championship status.

Fearing the loss of power and culture as millions of European immigrants seemingly overwhelmed America, the US Congress imposed an immigration quota in 1924. The law effectively impaired the flow of immigrants that had sustained the European ethnic cultures in the United States. Ethnic communities gradually eroded as second-generation youth, educated in American schools, turned to the English language outside the home and adopted new lifestyles and interests, particularly the popular culture of music, movies and sport. Such transitions were already evident in the Italian American youth who adopted sport in the nineteenth century.

SPORT AS AN ASSIMILATIVE FACTOR

Some ethnic groups, such as the Germans, brought a well-developed sporting culture, such as the *turner* movement, when they migrated to America. Like the German *turners*, the Czech *sokols* and Polish falcons practised a nationalistic form of gymnastics that reinforced their European languages, literature and identities. The educated Germans, many of whom were skilled craftsmen, had preceded the Italians by several decades, and their middle-class value systems fit more readily into the American mainstream. Germans introduced their gymnastics system into the American public schools and introduced the concept of early childhood kindergartens. Italians, however, brought little in the way of established sporting practices and generally eschewed education in favour of child labour that contributed more immediately to the family coffers.[14] Sport came more easily than some other aspects of WASP culture to Italian youth familiar with physical labour and the use of their bodies. Progressive era (1880–1920) social reformers embarked upon a mission to assimilate ethnic youth via the legislative process, which initially removed children from the industrial workforce through child labour laws, required them to attend school and instituted physical education in the curriculum. The latter included sports and games that inculcated competition, the basis for the capitalist economy; deference to authority in the person of a coach, referee or umpire; and teamwork that encouraged elements of self-sacrifice, leadership and democracy. Baseball, the American national game, proved particularly effective in rationalising the confusing American culture for the familial Italians as a team had to cooperate communally while on defence; but on offence each player performed individually and was rewarded according to his production, similar to one's role in the commercialised economy. Increasingly exposed to American sports in the public schools, parks and playgrounds, boys and girls readily adopted activities that allowed for greater integration without violating the norms of their residual Italian culture. By the 1920s the Italo-American Union sponsored baseball, basketball and football teams, and Catholic parishes fielded a variety of athletic teams that brought greater inclusion in the mainstream society. Competition in athletic leagues might maintain ethnic rivalries, but did so within an American framework, and as winning assumed greater importance even ethnic teams integrated to attract the best players.[15]

Visible Americanisation efforts proved essential as Italians confronted charges of anarchism and criminality in the aftermath of the controversial Sacco and Vanzetti trial of 1921, which sent two Italian labourers to their death despite specious charges of theft and murder.[16] A gradual transition to an American identity became noticeable with the representation of Frankie Genaro (Di Gennaro) and Fidel La Barba on the US Olympic boxing team in 1920 and 1924 respectively. Ray Barbuti was the lone star on a disappointing 1928 Olympic track team. The assimilation process accelerated with the establishment of the Catholic Youth Organization (CYO) in Chicago in 1930, which soon reached national and international proportions in its athletic endeavours. Three of the eight members of the 1936 Olympic boxing team, including Andy Scrivani, had been CYO boxers; and Louis Laurie (Lauria) brought home a bronze medal. Tony Terlazzo won a gold medal as a weightlifter in 1936. Such public displays of whiteness countered the perceptions of Italians as gangsters and greatly aided their gradual inclusion, acceptance and identity as Americans.[17]

Within the field of sport Italians competed not only with native-born Americans but with other ethnics in pursuit of recognition, status and a measure of power. Pierre Bourdieu's concept of a field envisioned a social arena in which groups or individuals competed for resources. It had both vertical and horizontal dimensions. On the vertical plane Italians contended with the Anglos and upper classes who set policies and controlled most resources. On the horizontal plane they vied with multiple other ethnic and working-class groups for income, space and social acceptance. Unlike the Jews, who placed an emphasis on education, and the Irish, who spoke English and gained access to political power, sport and popular culture afforded a means other than crime to achieve recognition. Without the benefit of education, southern Italians and Sicilian peasants developed a particular habitus over the centuries that revolved around their physicality, which regulated social practices. Humour, for example, might revolve around bodily functions or slapstick forms of comedy. Physical labour earned their sustenance; while physical power might generate a level of respect, honour and self-esteem, i.e. a means to gaining social capital without upsetting the familial hierarchy that acceded to paternal authority in contrast to educational attainments that surpassed parental achievements.[18]

Parents initially opposed children's participation in games and sports, deemed frivolous when children might be earning a paycheck to help support the family. That changed when athletes on semi-pro teams or boxers began to provide more money than parents earned at hard labour. Willie Pep (Papaleo) started boxing at the age of 15 in 1937. He anglicised his name as a marketing device, which garnered a protest from his immigrant father. As an employee of the Works Progress Administration (WPA), a Depression-era government programme that put the unemployed to work, the elder Papaleo earned $15 per week. The son earned $50 by fighting two bouts in one night and presented his father with $40 from his winnings. The father responded with his approval by stating: 'If you fought tonight and you got 40 dollars see if you can fight twice a week from now on.'[19] Other pro fighters used their earnings to buy new homes for their ageing parents and remove them from the Little Italies of the inner city, another step towards the achievement of whiteness.

The Italians' embattled quest for whiteness might be contrasted to that of African Americans to whom they were so often compared. The black banishment from Major League Baseball (MLB) forced them to initiate their own Negro National League in 1920; but Italians found increasing, if grudging acceptance for their physical skills within the mainstream. The early professional players who encroached upon the enclaves of power in the sports world had to endure the animosity of more established groups or their own families. Ping Bodie (Francesco Pizzola), the first of the Italians to achieve a level of baseball stardom in the First World War era, suffered the ostracism of his own family when his father disowned him for anglicising his name.[20] Babe Pinelli (Rinaldo Paolinelli) broke into the National League with Cincinnati in 1922 and later became a major league umpire; but bemoaned 'a lot of strife in both the minor and major leagues'.[21] Pinelli stated that 'From 1922 to 1925 I was the only Italian in the National League. I'd taken a riding from the bench jockeys and I'd had to keep my fist cocked.'[22] Such taunting led to a fight with Bob Smith of the Boston Braves. Pinelli insisted 'that the riding he had to take because of it (being Italian) equals or surpasses anything dished out to the first Negro players'. Such reactions illustrate the Italian reliance on physicality; but Pinelli learned to be more judicious as an umpire. In both roles as a player and an umpire he confronted the established Irish and Germans who had long dominated the playing fields. Nativist fans and players presented a more troublesome obstacle for Italians. In that era some opposing players held membership in the Ku Klux Klan.[23] Years later, when Don Mossi, an Italian American, took the field for the minor league team in Tulsa, Oklahoma a fan turned to his wife and exclaimed 'Good God, Maude, they got three niggers now'.[24] The growing number of Italians in professional baseball provided greater visibility of the assimilation process, greater social mobility for gifted athletes and a greater, but gradual, measure of acceptance. Tony Lazzeri became a star second baseman with the New York Yankees in the 1920s, the golden age of American sport. The New York media provided ready recognition to such symbols of ethnic pride during the era. References to Italian stars, although sometimes derogatorily reinforcing stereotypes, fostered a greater awareness of Italian presence and success in the American national game. Oscar Melillo, second baseman for the St Louis Browns, set a new record for fielding average in 1933, and Gus Mancuso, New York Giants catcher, along with Frank Crosetti, the Yankees shortstop, and the inimitable Joe DiMaggio further established Italian credibility among baseball fans. By the 1930s so many Italians appeared in MLB that Italian newspapers started naming all-Italian all-star teams. A sports reporter for the *Corriere D'America* proudly informed his readers that 'all in all the Italian boys have certainly made the grade in baseball and their prowess on the diamond is known to all sports lovers'.[25] Meanwhile, the typical Italian construction labourer earned $294 in 1935 working for a private contractor, and $768 working for the federal government. Joe DiMaggio the year before made $6,500 playing baseball, and Italian boys increasingly aspired to such wealth and recognition.[26] Even for the multitudes that did not earn a paycheck as professional baseball players, the game represented a badge of Americanism. Oral histories attest to the love of the game. An Italian mother of a 14-year-old lamented: 'Nick no wanta work. He big man, fourteen and wanta play ball all the day. Father say, "You go today and work in restaurant with your uncle". . . . He make faces, cusses, laughs, and runs out to play ball. . . . He very bad boy. . . . He no wants work. . . . He like nothing but ball.'[27] In New York Angelo Rucci endured the insults and fights at school because of his ethnicity, yet he endured to play baseball and football, and run track on the school teams to become 'American'. Angelo Vacca learned to play baseball when his father bought equipment for that purpose, as baseball presented a clear sign of integration into mainstream culture. In Chicago Anthony Sorrentino faced similar issues with antagonistic Anglos at school. Baseball provided some respite; but he lamented that the injurious treatment affected both him and his sister long afterward.[28] The adoption of American sport forms brought a greater measure of integration and inclusion; but did not guarantee acceptance for the working classes, who still had to contend with ethnic rivalries.

Like baseball, Italian boys were introduced to American football early in the assimilation process. Throughout the late nineteenth and early twentieth centuries, football had a particular social cache, as it was associated with colleges and high schools, symbols of the educated upper classes. A sport club in the Italian colony in New York City offered American football as early as 1906, and Italian high school stars appeared on the New Orleans gridirons that same year. Paul Gallico, the son of immigrants and educated at Columbia University, became one of the famed sportswriters who spawned the 'Golden Age'. He played football as a youth; and extolled the values of sport for much of his career. Good athletes soon learned that they could make more money on a multitude of professional and semi-pro teams than in industrial labour, long before the advent of the American Professional Football Association (NFL) in 1920. Carl 'Squash' Cardarelli, a centre for the Akron, Ohio high-school football team, soon joined the local pro contingent. Murray Battaglia and Art Pascolini were among other pioneers of the early pro circuit with the Evanston North Ends, a Chicago suburban team in the First World War era. Performance on the football field sometimes garnered notice and advantage elsewhere. Historian Keith McClellan claimed that 'Battaglia went from being a peddler's son to foreman for the Bowman Milk Company, at least in part because of the leadership skills he developed on the football field'.[29] Another early pro player, Lou Little (Luigi Piccolo), a First World War veteran, assumed the head coaching duties at Georgetown University in 1924 before moving to Columbia University in 1930, where he produced the 1934 Rose Bowl winner (mythical national champion) en route to a hall of fame career. The association of Italian players and coaches with institutions of higher education further distinguished them from their parents' generation, marking them as Americans and affording them the privileges of whiteness.[30]

While the semi-pro players enjoyed local celebrity, the Italian college stars became nationally recognised courtesy of the English- and Italian-language newspapers, as well as the burgeoning radio networks that broadcast the games. In 1922 Elmer Mitchell, a University of Michigan professor, wrote an article entitled 'Racial Traits in Athletics', in which he claimed that

> the Italian was better fitted for games of quickness, dexterity, and skill, rather than of rugged strength. He lacked self-discipline and was too fiery and impulsive of feeling for contact sports. . . . Italians' tendency to the extreme of elation, or to the opposite extreme of despondency, made them fearless, daring, and reckless but also more easily stampeded into a rout if beaten.[31]

By the end of the decade Italian players had largely dispelled such notions. In 1930, John Billi, a reporter for *Il Progresso Italo-American,* stated that 'Experts claim that Notre Dame University has the greatest backfield of the American gridiron. . . . Two Italians are the pivots of that backfield, the formidable fullback (Joe Savoldi), and Frank Carideo, the famous quarterback.' Carideo won All-American honours in 1929 and 1930, leading Notre Dame to two undefeated seasons and two national championships. Billi went on to list a host of Italians starring on other college teams throughout the country. By 1932 he counted 56 Italian players and named an Italian all-star team. Within a few years Billi could pick his all stars from at least 115 Italian players on college teams.[32]

In contrast to the elitism of early college teams, by the 1920s football coaches recruited talent rather than ethnicity or social class in their quest to win. In the northern schools, even African American stars were awarded athletic scholarships. Many of the Italians played for Catholic colleges, and contests with secular rivals gradually dismantled religious barriers, as Catholic teams, most conspicuously Notre Dame, scheduled secular institutions in the quest for national glory. Sport, in that sense, proved more inclusive in its incorporation of Italians and Catholics than other spheres of American life; and sport provided one means for Italian athletes to gain a college education.[33]

Hank Luisetti, the son of Italian immigrants, won an athletic scholarship to the elite Stanford University, after his high-school basketball team won the San Francisco city championship. There Luisetti won All-American and player of the year honours during the 1930s as he became the first collegian to ever score 50 points in a single game. In an era when the two-handed set shot was the norm, Luisetti revolutionised the game with his leaping, one-handed attempts. Youthful emulators soon adopted his style, modernising and changing the nature of the game.[34]

In the inner cities, impoverished youth who had little hope and perhaps little interest in attending college formed neighbourhood teams, often sponsored by local businessmen or politicians, who sought their support. In Chicago, one study found that 22 chartered athletic clubs were all involved in politics. The clubs numbered from 15 to 300 members and 'work for the politician who promises the most'.[35] Such involvement further incorporated the second generation within mainstream political culture.

Italian teams often battled ethnic rivals, transferring school and workplace rivalries to the athletic fields in some cases. Such altercations transferred animosities to regulated contests within the sphere of organised sporting practices rather than the gang fights of the streets. In such contexts athletic stars might replace gangsters as community heroes. In the Bloomfield area of Pittsburgh Martin 'Hooks' Donatucci's athletic fame spanned generations: 'In a neighborhood that reveres athletes, Hooks is known as one of the greatest athletes that Bloomfield ever produced.' The son of immigrants from Abruzzi brought pride to the community with his athletic prowess; and historians concluded that 'Bloomfield's proud athletic past looms large in the community's consciousness, making the athletic field nearly as much of a unifying symbol as Immaculate Conception Church'.[36]

Sports teams even united disparate ethnic and religious groups previously at odds. In Chicago the Wizard Arrows club emanated from a multicultural neighbourhood that brought Italians together with a variety of other ethnics as the former residents of Little Sicily spilled into a previously German area. Its teams resembled the American melting pot envisioned by earlier sociologists, and included Germans, Italians, Poles, Irish, Jews and Greeks. Like many of the more than 1,000 Chicago gangs studied by University of Chicago sociologist Frederic Thrasher, it was sponsored by a local politician, and merchants who equipped the men's baseball and football teams, and women's softball team, in uniforms in return for expected patronage. The club joined a disparate group of second-generation ethnics in a common pursuit that elicited local community pride. Two of its members became city billiards champions; while the football team had been unscored upon in 34 straight games as of 1936. Some members earned cash as boxers in club fights during the Depression; while several community residents won national boxing honours in the CYO and Golden Gloves competition.[37]

Similar clubs in Italian neighbourhoods implemented sport as a means to endure the Depression, earning money through dances as fund raisers, softball leagues sponsored by local bookmakers or tavern owners, and gambling operations. Typical stakes on athletic contests amounted to $25; but larger bets reached $3,000 on occasion. Mario Bruno claimed that he once won $1,600 on one game when the local bank would not give him a $100 mortgage on a paid-up home. Bruno parlayed his athletic skills and organisational abilities into political office in a Chicago suburb.[38]

Such community athletic clubs distanced their members from their parents' generation psychologically and ideologically: 'When Chicago's working class youth were not socializing in movie houses, they could be found at their neighborhood clubs . . . young people built their social lives around clubs . . . away from parental eyes and ears, club members played cards, held "socials", and planned sports contests and annual dances.' Extensive betting on ball games and horse races provided expendable income for winners. One Chicago club reported winning more than $100 on a football game; while another in an Italian neighbourhood claimed that 'We played ball for money only against black teams and other area gangs'.[39]

Unlike their parents, second-generation Italians, bereft of European memories, adopted new means of coping with their liminal identities. For many unemployed people sport, more so than work, allowed for greater, if temporary, socio-economic gain and greater self-esteem. Aspirations to bourgeois status seemed irrelevant and out of reach during the Depression. Life proved hard and too often short, and many sought immediate gratification, a lifestyle popularised by the hedonism of the 1920s and the gangsters of the inter-war era. The emphasis on the body as a source of pleasure and the means to social as well as economic capital continued to reinforce the class differences with the middle-class Anglo culture for most Italians.[40] Sport, however, provided a mutual interest and an entrée into the American mainstream.

Within the contested field of sports young Italian women even challenged their prescribed gender roles. In a clear departure from Italian lifestyles Maud Nelson (Clementine Brida) also learned and loved to play baseball. By 1897, at the age of 16, she began pitching for the Boston Bloomer Girls. She pitched and played third base for a number of barnstorming teams for 25 years, playing with and against male teams from coast to coast. In 1911 she became manager and co-owner of her own Chicago-based team. Upon her death her second husband returned to Italy; but the attraction of American sports had turned a young Italian girl into an athletic entrepreneur, which would have been an impossibility in Italy.[41]

Nelson's entrepreneurial ventures proved to be more than the efforts of an isolated iconoclast, for she spawned social change over the next generation of young women. In 1929 sports promoter Dick Jess formed a semi-pro baseball team centred around Josephine Parodi, who assumed the moniker of Josie Caruso, possibly to capitalise on the fame of Enrico Caruso, the popular opera star. The team drew large crowds to its games and Parodi enjoyed some celebrity in newsreels until her marriage in 1931, when she returned to a more traditional domestic life. Other women stretched the gender boundaries thereafter. Margaret Gisolo starred at second base for an Indiana town team in the 1928 American Legion baseball tournament. Her winning hit in a championship game prompted a protest by males; but a tribunal that included Kenesaw Mountain Landis, the commissioner of baseball, supported Gisolo's team. The case drew national attention and spurred a multitude of other girls to take up the game. When the American Legion banned girls from its competitions the next year, Maud Nelson hired Gisolo for her barnstorming teams during the 1930s. Gisolo used her ball-playing salary to gain a college education; she then became a lieutenant commander in the Navy WAVES (female auxiliary corps) during the Second World War. Gisolo later became a college coach, inspiring women's teams through the Title IX era. Such Italian women had been among the pioneers of women's sport in America, challenging the hegemonic perceptions of gender roles and female physical abilities; while the *Federazione Medici Sportivi* (official sport medicine federation) in Italy warned in 1930 that 'Italian women were first and foremost Italians and should, therefore, avoid any "Americanization"' regarding their sport participation.[42] Despite the admonitions of the Italian government Italian American women such as Eleanor Garatti-Saville represented the United States on the Olympic swimming teams in 1928 and 1932; while three Italian American women competed for the US gymnastics team in 1936.[43] Such second-generation Italian American girls and women had clearly transcended the traditional domestic roles to which they would have been assigned in Italy. The third generation would reap even greater benefits, as evidenced by the career of Donna Lopiano, multi-sport star, collegiate coach, Ph.D., president of the Association for Intercollegiate Athletics for Women, chief executive officer of the Women's Sports Foundation, entrepreneur and selectee to several halls of fame. Lopiano has been deemed one of the ten most powerful women in sports.[44]

Just as young women crossed previously imposed boundaries, a few Italian men managed to bridge the gulf between the proletarian and the elite sports, particularly in the sport of golf, a conspicuous symbol of whiteness in that era. Fred Ebetino grew up in Connecticut across from a golf course, where he became a caddy and a professional by the age of 19. Anthony Corica reached the professional ranks in a similar fashion. Johnny Revolta won the 1935 Professional Golfers' Association (PGA) championship as well as the Western Open, and Tony Manero won the PGA tournament in 1936. Both represented the United States on the Ryder Cup team in 1937. Vic Ghezzi played on the 1939 and 1941 Ryder Cup teams; but the most successful was Gene Sarazen (Eugenio Saraceni), a dominant figure in the game for half a century as a player and promoter. Sarazen, too, learned the game as a working-class caddy; but proved good enough despite his diminutive size (5 ft 5 in,

145 lb) to win both the US Open and the PGA tournament in 1922 at the age of 20. His fame reached such proportions that he was invited to play golf with President Warren Harding. Sarazen competed on six Ryder Cup teams, and was the first player to achieve the modern Grand Slam (winner of all four major tournaments). As a member of the US national team in the international Ryder Cup Sarazen earned Italians even greater recognition and symbolic capital as Americans.[45]

Despite such excursions into the upper class, Italians won their greatest recognition in the sport of boxing. A parade of Italians followed the Irish and then the Jews as boxing champions after the turn of the twentieth century. John Sugden explained the symbiotic relationship between boxing and poverty, in which the latter feeds the former. Only the poor are willing to put their bodies on the line for the meagre rewards of such punishment. Other ethnic groups (with perhaps the exception of the Irish) eschewed boxing as they gained greater socio-economic status, but Italians persisted throughout the remainder of the century, contesting with blacks and Hispanics for the spoils of the ring. Despite a litany of Italian fighters (many fighting under Irish aliases) throughout the 1920s, the first Italian of international magnitude hailed from South America. Luis Angel Firpo, the son of Italian immigrants to Argentina, burst upon the American boxing scene in spectacular fashion. His heavyweight world championship bout with Jack Dempsey in 1923 is still considered among the most thrilling boxing matches of all time and featured a dozen knockdowns in only two rounds. In an era of open nativism, sportswriters characterised Firpo in racialist terms. A supposed psychological study claimed

> the man is a combination of a Patagonian giant and a Genoese wild man. Like his progenitors, who were some of the most famous of Italian vendettists, he has the ability to curb his strength and his passions and disguise his feelings until the proper moment for action is arrived. . . . He is absolutely cold blooded.[46]

When Firpo fell in defeat a journalist stated:

> If Luis Angel Firpo had the brain power in proportion to his tremendous strength, there is no denying that he and not Jack Dempsey would be world's heavyweight champion this morning. Endowed with the mentality which would enable him to think and think quickly in emergencies, Firpo could afford to be slow moving and cumbersome. But Firpo with all his great strength to give and take punishment, lacked that one essential—a fighting brain.[47]

Firpo gradually faded from the public eye and although a host of Italian champions thereafter had greater success, Italians remained grounded in the pursuit of physical excellence. That perception was reinforced with the rise of Primo Carnera, a 6 ft 7 in, 270 lb mesomorphic Italian strongman turned boxer, who made two tours to the United States starting in 1930 and fought before packed houses. In the second tour in 1932 Carnera killed Ernie Schaaf in a Madison Square Garden bout, and when he beat Jack Sharkey for the championship in 1933 he assumed the symbolic stature of Mussolini's fascist superman: 'He returned to Rome to a hero's welcome and, on the eve of Italy's invasion of Abyssinia, was feted by the Italian dictator as an icon of Italian prowess.'[48] To Paul Gallico, 'His skin was brown and glistening and he invariably smelled of garlic'. For Gallico, perhaps reinforcing his own sense of acquired whiteness, Carnera represented a 'big, stupid Wop', whose victories were too often arranged by gangsters.[49]

THE PHENOMENON OF JOE DIMAGGIO

The increasing number of Italian baseball players served to counter such depictions;

but even Tony Lazzeri, a star for the New York Yankees in the 1920s, was coined 'the walloping Wop'.[50] The most valuable player in a symbolic sense proved to be Joe DiMaggio, one of three sons of a Sicilian fisherman, who made it to the major leagues. DiMaggio joined the New York Yankees in 1936 as a reticent and humble high school dropout. Mired in the Great Depression, America needed a hero. DiMaggio made an immediate impact upon Italians, who bought seats in the nearby bleachers, waved Italian flags and sent loads of fan mail. One such letter stated: 'Dear Joe, I want to stop here and congratulate you for the great name you have made for yourself. You hold a very important place in the heart of every true Italian.' The Yankees won four World Series titles in a row, while DiMaggio got the Most Valuable Player award in 1939.[51]

Despite his immense success, a 1939 article by Noel Busch in the popular *Life* magazine continued to stereotype his abilities as due to natural talent and genetic advantages rather than assiduous devotion to his craft. The author not only referred to him as a freak, but stated that 'Joe was lazy, rebellious and endowed with a weak stomach. . . . Joe refused to go fishing because it made him seasick . . . refused to clean the boat, saying that it smelled bad.'[52] Busch claimed that 'Joe DiMaggio's rise in baseball is a testimonial to the value of general shiftlessness . . . the very indolence which later helped him to succeed almost ruined his career', and that 'like heavyweight champion Joe Louis, DiMaggio is lazy, shy, and inarticulate'.[53] The writer further denigrated his limited education by stating that 'It cannot be said, however, that he has ever worried his employers by an unbecoming interest in literature or the arts, nor does he wear himself down by unreasonable asceticism. In laziness, DiMaggio is still a paragon.' Busch described DiMaggio's apparent Americanisation by asserting that 'Instead of olive oil or smelly bear grease he keeps his hair slick with water. He never reeks of garlic and prefers chicken chow mein to spaghetti.'[54] The article could hardly have been less flattering by minimising DiMaggio's greatness and reinforcing negative and stereotypical perceptions of Italians.

DiMaggio's stellar play and all-round ability, and the grace with which he played the game, matched with his proud yet dignified and humble demeanour, eventually won over the American media and a multitude of baseball fans as he confronted the Italian stereotype. In the 13 years that he played for the Yankees they won ten American League pennants and nine World Series. DiMaggio was awarded the Most Valuable Player trophy three times, and he set perhaps the most enduring record in all of sports with his 56-game hitting streak in 1941. That achievement has never been equalled and might represent the tipping point for Italians' achievement of whiteness. He became the new role model for countless American boys, Italians and otherwise. Schoolchildren in Cincinnati even voted him 'the greatest American of all time' after the eventful season. Whereas Italians had only aspired to a good job, a good marriage, their own home and a wealth of children, DiMaggio gave hope for equal acceptance in the American polity.[55] Teammate Lefty Gomez stated that 'All the Italians in America adopted him. Just about every day at home and on the road there would be an invitation from some Italian-American club.' Actor Ben Gazzara claimed that 'He was our god, the god of all Italian Americans.'[56] George Pataki, later to become governor of New York, remembered that 'he was every American boy's hero, including mine'.[57] Mussolini allied with Hitler as the Second World War erupted in Europe, forcing Italians in America to make difficult choices as to their loyalty. With the US entry into the war non-citizens such as DiMaggio's parents were restricted as 'enemy aliens', removed from their coastal homes in California and placed under curfew and travel restraints.[58] Joe DiMaggio joined the US military during the Second World War, along with hundreds of thousands of other Italian American men and women who asserted their allegiance to their land of birth rather than their land of ancestry. DiMaggio's career exemplified the Italian quest and the attainment of whiteness in American society, notably marked by his brief marriage to the Hollywood sex symbol Marilyn Monroe in 1954.

The 1950s represented the golden age for Italian Americans. Their allegiance was no longer questioned. The ascendance of singer/actor Frank Sinatra in the post-war years as a matinee idol, the proliferation of Italian Americans on the professional baseball and football fields, combined with Rocky Marciano's rule of the heavyweight boxing ranks in the 1950s, further solidified Italians' claim to whiteness. Marciano's accepted whiteness contrasted with the abundance of black aspirants to the title, as an Italian American represented the fabled white hope as blacks had held the symbolic championship for two decades.

In the aftermath of the Second World War rock 'n' roll music emerged as a new genre in American popular culture, with musical groups often headed by Italian youth, and Italians proliferated on the new medium of television as singers, actors and comedians. Ex-boxing champions Rocky Graziano and Jake LaMotta and former basketball star and boxer Lou Costello each conveyed their troubled past through comedy. Both sport and entertainment provided forms of expression that allowed Italians to demonstrate their physicality, still an essential element of the Italian habitus.

EPILOGUE AND CONCLUSION

By the 1970s changing residential patterns, intermarriage rates and general acceptance of Italians indicated that they had secured the status of whiteness; but a whiteness that retained the elements of *Itatianità* in ethnic expressions of style, food and lifestyle that persist to this day. The third and fourth generations of Italian Americans affected a resurgence of ethnicity that sociologists have termed a segmented assimilation. Traditional religious festivals continue in Italian Catholic parishes and celebrations of Italian identity maintain an ancestral allegiance in numerous metropolitan areas of the United States. The Italian sport of bocce ball continues to grow rather than dissipate, and Italian American athletes have chosen to represent Italy rather than the United States in Olympic and international competition, most notably soccer star Giuseppe Rossi. The most popular television shows in the past decade have been those that continued to portray Italians as gangsters and the negative stereotype of the youthful *guido* subculture, suggesting that the processes of whiteness and full assimilation may be incomplete.[59] Italians had helped to build much of the American transport network through their physicality, but got little recognition for their efforts. That physical prowess, however, transferred more easily to sport, where their efforts earned a greater measure of recognition and acceptance, and even fame, celebrity and fortune for some. While their immigrant parents laboured in anonymity for meagre wages, their US-born offspring found their physicality rewarded on the athletic fields. Unlike their Italian parents, both young men and women pursued sport as a means to achieve whiteness. The Italians differed from other ethnic groups in their adherence to physicality as a means towards social and, for some, economic capital. Jews pursued education as a vehicle for social mobility, while the Irish engaged in politics. African Americans, to whom the Italians were often compared, also lacked education and often pursued sport as a means to recognition, celebrity and greater acceptance. Such a strategy emanated from one's habitus and social class, a quest for acceptance based on working-class perceptions of worth and value in a democracy that might allow for pluralism rather than the WASP hegemony that Anglos had attempted to impose.

NOTES

1. Parts of this article are excerpted from Gerald R. Gems, *Sport and the Shaping of Italian American Identity* (Syracuse, NY: Syracuse University Press, forthcoming).
2. Jennifer Guglielmo and Salvatore Salerno, eds. *Are Italians White? How Race Is Made in America* (New York: Routledge, 2003); Thomas A. Guglielmo, *White on Arrival: Italians, Race, Color, and Power in Chicago, 1890–1945* (New York: Oxford University Press, 2003). Other scholars had posed similar questions concerning other ethnic groups in the preceding decade. See Noel Ignatiev, *How the Irish Became White* (New York: Routledge, 1995); and Karen Brodkin, *How Jews Became White Folks and What That Says About Race in America* (New Brunswick, NJ: Rutgers University Press, 1998).
3. Whiteness studies and their debates can be followed in Reginald Horsman, *Race and Manifest Destiny: The Origins of American Racial Anglo-Saxonism* (Cambridge, MA: Harvard University Press, 1981); David R. Roediger, *The Wages of Whiteness: Race and the Making of the American Working Class* (London: Verso, 1999 [1991]); Theodore W. Allen, *The Invention of the White Race: Racial Oppression and Social Control* (London: Verso, 1998); Lee D. Baker, *From Savage to Negro: Anthropology and the Construction of Race, 1896–1954* (Berkeley, CA: University of California Press, 1998); Matthew Frye Jacobson, *Whiteness of a Different Color: European Immigrants and the Alchemy of Race* (Cambridge, MA: Harvard University Press, 1998); Matthew Frye Jacobson, *Barbarian Virtues: The United States Encounters Foreign Peoples at Home and Abroad, 1876–1917* (New York: Hill and Wang, 2000); David R. Roediger, *Working Toward Whiteness: How America's Immigrants Became White, The Strange Journey from Ellis Island to the Suburbs* (New York: Basic Books, 2005); Eric Arnesen, 'Whiteness and the Historians' Imagination', *International Labor and Working Class History* 60 (Fall 2001), 3–32; Peter Kolchin, 'Whiteness Studies: The New History of Race in America', *Journal of American History* 89, no. 1 (June 1990): 154–173; C. Richard King, 'Cautionary Notes on Whiteness and Sport Studies, *Sociology of Sport Journal,* 22 no. 3 (September 2005), 397–408; Ian Haney Lopez, *White By Law: The Legal Construction of Race* (New York: New York University Press, 2006), 4–5 (quote).
4. As the title suggests, Guglielmo, *White on Arrival,* argues for instant recognition; while David A.J. Richards, *Italian America: The Racializing of an Ethnic Identity* (New York: New York University Press, 1999) disagrees; and Jacobson, *Whiteness of a Different Color,* opts for the achievement of whiteness in the inter-war period, 1918–1945.
5. Quotes are from Salvatore J. La Gumina, *Wop! A Documentary History of Anti-Italian Discrimination* (Toronto: Guernica, 1999 [1973]), 24, as is the *New York Times* citation, April 16, 1876, 31. While the Irish were similarly denigrated as non-whites upon their arrival, they had the benefit of speaking English which accorded them quicker access to the American mainstream and entry into vehicles of power, such as the Democratic political party and the labour union movement.
6. Baker, *From Savage to Negro,* 73–80, 88; Richard Gambino, *Vendetta: The True Story of the Largest Lynching in US History* (Toronto: Guernica, 1998 [1977]), 64, 133; James R. Barrett and David Roediger, 'Inbetween Peoples: Race, Nationality, and the "New Immigrant" Working Class', *Journal of American Ethnic History* 16, no. 3 (Spring 1997), 3–44 (quote, from Academic Search Premier #9706064070); Roediger, *Working Toward Whiteness,* 37–9.
7. Jacobson, *Whiteness of a Different Color,* 4.
8. Richard Gambino, *Blood of My Blood: The Dilemma of the Italian-Americans* (Garden City, NY: Anchor Books, 1975 [1974]), 77; Donna R. Gabaccia, 'Race, Nation, Hyphen: Italian-Americans and American Multiculturalism in Comparative Perspective', in *Are Italians White? How Race Is Made in America,* eds Jennifer Guglielmo and Salvatore Salerno (New York: Routledge, 2003), 44–59; Alexander De Conde, *Half Bitter, Half Sweet: An Excursion into Italian-American History* (New York: Charles Scribner's Sons, 1971), 91; clipping, *Outlook,* November 16, 1907, 556, in Schiavo Papers, Box: Italian American Renaissance Foundation Archives, New Orleans, Immigration Studies Articles, Report of Commissioner-General of Immigration, 1903 folder; Patrick J. Gallo, *Old Bread, New Wine: A Portrait of the Italia-Americans* (Chicago: Nelson-Hall, 1981), 118;

Jerre Mangione and Ben Morreale, *La Storia: Five Centuries of the Italian American Experience* (New York: Harper Collins, 1992), 212; Roediger, *Working Toward Whiteness*, 47, 74, 76 (quote), 77. Roediger indicates that 11% of Hispanic miners and 43% of Anglo miners in Arizona got $3 or more per day; while only 6% of Italians did so. Among the New York subway workers Italians were also paid less than black and Irish labourers in 1896.

9. See *L'Italia*, March 2–3, and March 9–11, 1895; March 16–17, 1895 (all in Foreign Language Press Survey, Chicago Public Library) on Romulus's appearance in Chicago. Other data on Romulus come from Edmond Desbonnet, *Les rois de la force* (1912), graciously supplied and translated by David Chapman. See David L. Chapman, *Sandow the Magnificent: Eugen Sandow and the Beginnings of Body Building* (Urbana, IL: University of Illinois Press, 1994); and Robert Ernst, *Weakness Is a Crime: The Life of Bernarr Macfadden* (Syracuse, NY: Syracuse University Press, 1991), on the early physical culture movement.
10. *Boston Daily Globe*, July 31, 1916, 7; 'Brignolia Recalls His Many Sports Feats', *Portland Press Herald*, July 20, 1950, 17. The surname is spelled variously across publications.
11. 'Fans Await Resumption of Boxing Bouts Here Tonight', *Lowell Sun*, December 1, 1927, 40; *Oakland Tribune*, January 25, 1933, 9; February 27, 1933, 10. See Monika Stodolska and Alexandris Konstsntinos, 'The Role of Recreational Sport in the Adaptation of First Generation Immigrants in the United States', *Journal of Leisure Research* 36, no.3 (2004), 403, on the continued adherence to athletic role models in contemporary immigrant populations.
12. Matthew P. Llewellyn, 'Viva Italia! Viva Italia! Dorando Pietri and the North American Professional Marathon Craze, 1908–10', *International Journal of the History of Sport* 25, no. 6 (2008), 710–36. Pietri had gained international attention as the apparent winner of the 1908 Olympic marathon when British officials assisted him across the finish line after he collapsed. American Johnny Hayes was declared the winner upon appeal. The federal Dillingham Commission issued its report after a four-year study in 1911 and proclaimed 45 separate races among the immigrants to the United States.
13. *New York Times*, Jan. 12, 1909, 7; *Chicago Tribune*, Feb. 26, 1909, 10. The occupations of Italians in Chicago was ascertained by comparing names and addresses of those mentioned in the *Chicago Tribune* account to the *Chicago City Directory* (Chicago: Chicago Directory Co., 1909), which elicited matches for Oscar Durante, editor of the *L'Italia* newspaper, as well as saloon owners, a tailor, a printer, a bartender and a liquor salesman. See David E. Martin and Roger W.H. Gynn, *The Olympic Marathon* (Champaign, IL: Human Kinetics, 2000), 94; *Waterloo Times-Tribune* (IA), July 30, 1912, 2; and *Janesville Daily Gazette* (WI), August 8, 1912, 3, on Strobino. Physical separation no less than symbolic distance from blacks, with whom Italians had shared urban ghettoes, proved essential in the transition to whiteness.
14. See Annette Hofmann, *The American Turner Movement: A History from its Beginnings to 2000* (Indianapolis, IN: Printing Edge, 2010) for a comprehensive treatment of the turners; and Gerald R. Gems, *Windy City Wars: Labor, Leisure, and Sport in the Making of Chicago* (Lanham, MD: Scarecrow Press, 1997), for German activities in that city.
15. See Gems, *Windy City Wars* for a case study of Americanisation of ethnic groups via sport.
16. Paul Avrich, *Sacco and Vanzetti: The Anarchist Background* (Princeton, NJ: Princeton University Press, 1991). The Italian anarchists were convicted of armed robbery and murder in a 1921 trial presided over by a decidedly anti-Italian judge. Despite further appeals and international protests the labourers were executed in 1927.
17. *Bulletin Italo-American National Union* (January 1928), FLPS; Don W. Riggs, *History of St. Donatus Parish* (n.p., 1981), indicates that the Chicago area Italian parish produced at least 11 professional athletes after the First World War. Gerald R. Gems, 'Sport, Religion, and Americanization: Bishop Sheil and the Catholic Youth Organization', *International Journal of the History of Sport* 10, no. 2 (August, 1993), 233–41; www.en.wikipedia.org/wiki/Louis_Laurie, June 9, 2009). See Peter T. Alter, 'Serbs, Sports, and Whiteness', in *Sports in Chicago*, ed. Elliott J. Gorn (Urbana, IL: University of Illinois Press, 2008), 113–27, on public displays of whiteness.
18. Pierre Bourdieu, *Outline of a Theory of Practice* (Cambridge: Cambridge University Press, 1977).
19. Willie Pep with Robert Sacchi, *Willie Pep remembers. . . Friday's Heroes* (New York: Friday's Heroes, Inc., 1973), 4–8, 5 (quote).
20. Ping Bodie file, Baseball Hall of Fame, Cooperstown, NY; Ira Berkow, 'The Extraordinary Life and Times of Ping Bodie', in *Reaching for the Stars: A Celebration of Italian Americans in Major League Baseball*, ed. Larry Freundlich, ed. (New York: Ballantine Books, 2003), 49–64; Sam Weller, 'Ping Bodie Hero of Sox Victory', *Chicago Tribune*, May 15, 1911, 12; *Chicago Tribune*, February 8, 1912, C2.
21. John J. Pinelli, 'From San Francisco Sandlots to the Big Leagues: Babe Pinelli', in *Baseball and*

the American Dream: Race, Class, Gender and the National Pastime, ed. Robert Elias (Armonk, NY: M.E. Sharpe, 2001), 135–40 (quote, 138).

22. Lawrence Baldassaro and Richard A. Johnson, eds., *The American Game: Baseball and Ethnicity* (Carbondale, IL: University of Southern Illinois Press, 2002), 101.
23. Sidney Fields, 'Hat's Off', *New York Daily Mirror*, clipping in Pinelli file, Baseball Hall of Fame.
24. Samuel O. Regalado, *Viva Baseball: Latin Major Leaguers and Their Special Hunger* (Urbana, IL: University of Illinois Press, 1998), 72.
25. *Corriere D'America*, December 21, 1933, 7; *Corriere D'America*, October 4, 1936, 11 (quote). Freundlich, *Reaching* for *the Stars*, 204–300, lists at least 47 Italians on major league teams during the decade.
26. Joseph A. Burger, 'Baseball and Social Mobility for Italian Americans in the 1930s', unpublished manuscript in the Center for Migration Studies, Staten Island, New York, 10–11.
27. Leonard Covello, *The Social Background of the Italo-American School Child* (Totowa, NJ: Rowman & Littlefield, 1971), 300 cites the stereotypical quote from the Report of the Causes of Crime, National Commission on Law Observance and Enforcement (Washington, DC, 1931), vol. II, 3, 4–5.
28. Rucci interview AKRF-83; Vacca interview EI-200, both in Ellis Island Oral History Collection; Anthony Sorrentino Papers, 8–9, Chicago History Museum.
29. Italian American Directory Company, *Gli Italiani Negli Stati Uniti D'America* (New York: Andrew Kellogg Co., 1906), 164; Ron Brocato, *The Golden Game: When Prep Football Was King in New Orleans*, 48, photocopy in Italian American Renaissance Foundation Library, New Orleans, miscellaneous folder; Paul Gallico, *Farewell to Sport* (New York: Alfred A. Knopf, 1950), 290; Keith Mc Clellan, 'Thomas J. Holleran, The Akron Pros' Signal Caller', *Coffin Corner* 30, no. 6 (2008), 14; Mc Clellan, *The Sunday Game: At the Dawn of Professional Football* (Akron, OH: University of Akron Press, 1998), 366 (quote).
30. www.hickoksports.com/biograph/littlelou.shtml, accessed April 19, 2009.
31. Mitchell cited in Michael Oriard, *King Football: Sport and Spectacle in the Golden Age of Radio and Newsreels, Magazines, the Weekly and the Daily Press* (Chapel Hill, NC: University of North Carolina Press, 2001), 256.
32. John Billi, 'US Sports Firmament is Dotted with Many First Magnitude Stars of Italian Origin', *Il Progresso Italo-Americano*, November 9, 1930, n.p. (quote); G. Billi, 'Per l'All-Italian 1937', *Il Progresso Italo-Americano*, November 26, 1937, n.p.; *Corriere D'America*, November 1, 1932, 7; November 3, 1932, 7; November 4, 1932, 7; November 5, 1932, 7; November 8, 1932, 7; November 10, 1932, 7; November 11, 1932, 7; November 13, 1932, 13; November 17, 1932, 17; November 22, 1932, 7; November 26, 1932, 7; November 27, 1932, 9; November 29, 1932, 7. Billi did not include any southern schools in his survey: http://www.und.com/sports/m-footbl/mtt/carideo_frank00.html, accessed April 21, 2009. Savoldi was expelled from Notre Dame for marrying before graduation and soon capitalised on his fame as a professional wrestler.
33. An athletic scholarship provided free tuition, books, room and board to athletes in exchange for their participation on the university's athletic teams. Both blacks and Italians generally relied on their physicality in the form of sport or expressive musical talents to achieve a measure of inclusion in the larger society.
34. www.stanfordalumni.org/news/magazine/2003/marapr/departments/examinedlife.html, accessed June 2, 2009.
35. Sayler, 'A Study of Behavioral Problems of Boys in Lower North Community', Burgess Papers, Box 135, University of Chicago Library, Special Collections, folder 4, 24–26.
36. William Simons, Samuel Patti and George Hermann, 'Bloomfield: an Italian Working Class Neighborhood', *Italian American*, VII. no. 1 (Fall/Winter, 1981), 102–116 (quotes, 104, 112 respectively).
37. Frederic M. Thrasher, *The Gang* (Chicago: University of Chicago Press, 1963 [1927]), considered neighbourhood social-athletic clubs to be gangs due to their engagement in petty crimes; although some were involved in felonious activities. Gerald R. Gems, 'The Neighborhood Athletic Club: An Ethnographic Study of a Working-Class Athletic Fraternity in Chicago, 1917–1984', *Colby Quarterly* 32, no. 1 (March 1996), 36–44; *Chicago American*, November 14, 1936, 16; personal papers of Frank Di Benedetto, club officer.
38. Frank Di Liberto interview, Chicago Oral History Project, University of Illinois; Nick Zaranti interviews, Box 2, 13; Mario Bruno interview, Box 3, 47–59.
39. Andrew J. Diamond, *Mean Streets: Chicago Youths and the Everyday Struggle for Empowerment in the Multiracial City, 1908–1969* (Berkeley, CA: University of California Press, 2009), 46, 316, en. 12; Lizabeth Cohen, *Making a New Deal Industrial Workers in Chicago*, 1919–1939 (New York: Cambridge University Press, 1990), 145 (quote). Wizard Arrows' football game programmes indicated that they played throughout the Chicago metropolitan area against rival clubs and black teams, including a contest with the Indiana state prison team.

40. Hedonism is apparent in Elliott Gorn, *Dillinger's Wild Ride* (New York: Oxford University Press, 2009); and Joshua Zeitz, *Flapper: The Madcap Story of Sex, Style, Celebrity, and the Women Who Made America Modern* (New York: Crown Publishers, 2006); and sport stars. On the latter, see Leigh Montville, *The Big Bam: The Life and Times of Babe Ruth* (New York: Doubleday, 2006), and Robert W. Creamer, *Babe: The Legend Comes to Life* (New York: Simon & Schuster, 1974).
41. www.exploratorium.edu/baseball/nelson.html; www.barbaragregorich.com/clem.htm, accessed June 6, 2009. Sarah Bair, 'American Sports, 1910–1919', in *Encyclopedia of Sports in America: A History from Foot Races to Extreme Sports*, ed. Murry Nelson (Westport, CT: Greenwood Press, 2009), 160–1.
42. Gail Ingham Berlage, 'From Bloomer Girls' Baseball to Women's Softball: A Cultural Journey resulting in Women's Exclusion from Baseball', in *The Cooperstown Symposium on Baseball and American Culture*, 1999, ed. Peter M. Rutk (Jefferson, NC: Mc Farland & Co., 2000), 245–60; 'Margaret Gisolo', photocopy adopted from Barbara Gregorich, *Women at Play*, 30–31, in Italian American Renaissance Foundation Library, miscellaneous folder; www.niashf.org/index2.cfm?ContentID=58&InducteeID=100, accessed June 6, 2009; Angela Teja and Marco Impiglia, 'Italy', 139–59 (quote, 145–6) in *European Cultures in Sport: Examining the Nations and Regions*, eds James Riordan and Arnd Kruger (Bristol: Intellect Books, 2003). Title IX was a federal law enacted in 1972 that assured equal opportunity in all federal programmes, including education, with great ramifications for females' sports participation.
43. www.ishof.org/honorees/92/92egsaville.html, accessed August 6, 2009; www.hickoksports.com/history/usgymchamps.shtml, accessed August 2, 2010; www.sports-reference.com/olympics/athletes/ca/connie-carucciolenz-1.html, accessed August 2, 2010. Thanks to Gertrud Pfister for alerting me to the gymnasts.
44. www.sportmanagementresources.com, accessed September 11, 2012.
45. *Corriere D'America*, November 8, 1932, 7; December 8, 1933, 6; December 12, 1933, 7; December 25, 1933, 7; October 11, 1933, 11s; November 22, 1936, 11s; Fred Ebetino interview EI 481, Ellis Island Oral History Collection; La Gumina, *Wop!*, 122; Joe McGuigan, 'Vic Ghezzi Is Golf's Victor Mature', in Box Sol-Sz, Giovanni Schiavo Papers; John Sayle Watterson, *The Games Presidents Play: Sports and the Presidency* (Baltimore, MD: Johns Hopkins University Press, 2006), 110; George Kirsch, *Golf in America* (Urbana, IL: University of Illinois Press, 2009), 88, 119–20; www.wgv.com/hof/member.php?member=1102, accessed April 20, 2009.
46. John Sugden, *Boxing and Society: An International Analysis* (Manchester: Manchester University Press, 1996), 5, 7, 54–88, 182–185, 194–196; Dr Juan Reilly quoted in 'Frank Klaus Sees Firpo in Action', *New York Times*, September 2, 1923, 18.
47. 'Firpo Had The Title Within His Grasp', *New York Times*, September 15, 1923, 1; also see Sid Sutherland, 'Latin Lacks Ring Wit to Cope with Yank, the Experienced', *Chicago Tribune*, September 15, 1923, 11.
48. Joseph S. Page, *Primo Carnera: The Life and Career of the Heavyweight Boxing Champ* (Jefferson, NC: Mc Farland & Co., 2011); Arne K. Lang, *Prizefighting: An American History* (Jefferson, NC: McFarland & Co., 2008), 90–5; Sugden, *Boxing and Society: An International Analysis*, 36 (quote).
49. Gallico, *Farewell to Sport*, 58, 66 respectively. See Jeffrey T. Sammons, *Beyond the Ring: The Role of Boxing in American Society* (Urbana, IL: University of Illinois Press, 1988), 86–91, for a critical assessment of Carnera's boxing career.
50. Stephen Fox, *Big Leagues: Professional Baseball, Football, and Basketball in National Memory* (New York: William Morrow & Co., 1994), 106–7; Lawrence Baldassaro, 'Go East Paesani: Early Italian Major Leaguers from the West Coast', in *The Impact of Locale on Ethnicity* ed. Janet E. Worrall, Carol Bonomo Albright and Elvira G. Di Fabio (Cambridge, MA: Italian American Historical Association, 2003), 100–108 (quote, 106).
51. David Jones, *Joe DiMaggio A Biography* (Westport, CT: Greenwoood Press, 2004), 26.
52. Noel F. Busch, 'Joe DiMaggio: Baseball's Most Sensational Big League Star Starts What Should Be His Best Year So Far', *Life*, May 1, 1939, 62–69 (quote, 64).
53. Ibid., 66–7.
54. Ibid., 68. Numerous other players reported being subjected to ethnic slurs and bigotry during the era, see Lawrence Baldassaro, *Beyond DiMaggio, Beyond DiMaggio: Italian Americans in Baseball* (Lincoln, NE: University of Nebraska Press, 2011), 38, 111–12, 125–7, 134, 136, 183, 267.
55. Jones, *Joe DiMaggio*, 68. DiMaggio's adulation crossed ethnic and class boundaries; and Italian Americans' military service against their ancestral homeland in the Second World War solidified their claims to whiteness and citizenship.
56. Baldassaro, *Beyond DiMaggio*, 226, 228 respectively on the quotes.
57. Simons, 'Joe DiMaggio and the Ideal of American Masculinity', in *The Cooperstown Symposium on*

Baseball and American Culture, 1999, ed. Peter M. Rutkoff (Jefferson, NC; McFarland & Co., 2000), 227–44 (quote).

58. The government classified Italians as enemy aliens similar to the non-white Japanese, who were actually interred in concentration camps for much of the war. The sheer number of Italians and Germans in the United States precluded the government from incarcerating them as well.
59. The popular television shows are a reference to *The Sopranos*, about a family of gangsters, and the hedonistic youth culture depicted in *Jersey Shore*.

CHAPTER 6

Barbie Girls versus Sea Monsters: Children Constructing Gender

Michael A. Messner

[. . .] The purpose of this article is to use an observation of a highly salient gendered moment of group life among four- and five-year-old children as a point of departure for exploring the conditions under which gender boundaries become activated and enforced. I was privy to this moment as I observed my five-year-old son's first season (including weekly games and practices) in organized soccer. Unlike the longterm, systematic ethnographic studies of children conducted by Thorne (1993) or Adler and Adler (1998), this article takes one moment as its point of departure. I do not present this moment as somehow "representative" of what happened throughout the season; instead, I examine this as an example of what Hochschild (1994, 4) calls "magnified moments," which are "episodes of heightened importance, either epiphanies, moments of intense glee or unusual insight, or moments in which things go intensely but meaningfully wrong. In either case, the moment stands out; it is metaphorically rich, unusually elaborate and often echoes [later]." A magnified moment in daily life offers a window into the social construction of reality. It presents researchers with an opportunity to excavate gendered meanings and processes through an analysis of institutional and cultural contexts. The single empirical observation that serves as the point of departure for this article was made during a morning. Immediately after the event, I recorded my observations with detailed notes. I later slightly revised the notes after developing the photographs that I took at the event.

I will first describe the observation—an incident that occurred as a boys' four- and five-year-old soccer team waited next to a girls' four- and five-year-old soccer team for the beginning of the community's American Youth Soccer League (AYSO) season's opening ceremony. I will then examine this moment using three levels of analysis.

- *The interactional level:* How do children "do gender," and what are the contributions and limits of theories of performativity in understanding these interactions?
- *The level of structural context:* How does the gender regime, particularly the larger organizational level of formal sex segregation of AYSO, and the concrete, momentary situation of the opening ceremony provide a context that variously constrains and enables the children's interactions?
- *The level of cultural symbol:* How does the children's shared immersion in popular culture (and their differently gendered locations in this immersion) provide sym-

bolic resources for the creation, in this situation, of apparently categorical differences between the boys and the girls?

Although I will discuss these three levels of analysis separately, I hope to demonstrate that interaction, structural context, and culture are simultaneous and mutually intertwined processes, none of which supersedes the others.

BARBIE GIRLS VERSUS SEA MONSTERS

It is a warm, sunny Saturday morning. Summer is coming to a close, and schools will soon reopen. As in many communities, this time of year in this small, middle- and professional-class suburb of Los Angeles is marked by the beginning of another soccer season. This morning, 156 teams, with approximately 1,850 players ranging from 4 to 17 years old, along with another 2,000 to 3,000 parents, siblings, friends, and community dignitaries have gathered at the local high school football and track facility for the annual AYSO opening ceremonies. Parents and children wander around the perimeter of the track to find the assigned station for their respective teams. The coaches muster their teams and chat with parents. Eventually, each team will march around the track, behind their new team banner, as they are announced over the loudspeaker system and are applauded by the crowd. For now though, and for the next 45 minutes to an hour, the kids, coaches, and parents must stand, mill around, talk, and kill time as they await the beginning of the ceremony.

The Sea Monsters is a team of four- and five-year-old boys. Later this day, they will play their first-ever soccer game. A few of the boys already know each other from preschool, but most are still getting acquainted. They are wearing their new uniforms for the first time. Like other teams, they were assigned team colors—in this case, green and blue—and asked to choose their team name at their first team meeting, which occurred a week ago. Although they preferred "Blue Sharks," they found that the name was already taken by another team and settled on "Sea Monsters." A grandmother of one of the boys created the spiffy team banner, which was awarded a prize this morning. As they wait for the ceremony to begin, the boys inspect and then proudly pose for pictures in front of their new award-winning team banner. The parents stand a few feet away—some taking pictures, some just watching. The parents are also getting to know each other, and the common currency of topics is just how darned cute our kids look, and will they start these ceremonies soon before another boy has to be escorted to the bathroom?

Queued up one group away from the Sea Monsters is a team of four- and five-year-old girls in green and white uniforms. They too will play their first game later today, but for now, they are awaiting the beginning of the opening ceremony. They have chosen the name "Barbie Girls," and they also have a spiffy new team banner. But the girls are pretty much ignoring their banner, for they have created another, more powerful symbol around which to rally. In fact, they are the only team among the 156 marching today with a team float—a red Radio Flyer wagon base, on which sits a Sony boom box playing music, and a 3-foot-plus-tall Barbie doll on a rotating pedestal. Barbie is dressed in the team colors—indeed, she sports a custom-made green-and-white cheerleader-style outfit, with the Barbie Girls' names written on the skirt. Her normally all-blonde hair has been streaked with Barbie Girl green and features a green bow, with white polka dots. Several of the girls on the team also have supplemented their uniforms with green bows in their hair.

The volume on the boom box nudges up and four or five girls begin to sing a Barbie song. Barbie is now slowly rotating on her pedestal, and as the girls sing more gleefully and more loudly, some of them begin to hold hands and walk around the float, in sync with Barbie's rotation. Other same-aged girls from other teams are drawn to the celebration and, eventually, perhaps a dozen girls are singing the Barbie song. The girls are intensely focused on Barbie, on the music, and on their mutual pleasure.

As the Sea Monsters mill around their banner, some of them begin to notice, and then begin to watch and listen as the Barbie Girls rally around their float. At first, the boys are watching as individuals, seemingly unaware of each other's shared interest. Some of them stand with arms at their sides, slack-jawed, as though passively watching a television show. I notice slight smiles on a couple of their faces, as though they are drawn to the Barbie Girls' celebratory fun. Then, with side-glances, some of the boys begin to notice each other's attention on the Barbie Girls. Their faces begin to show signs of distaste. One of them yells out, "NO BARBIE!" Suddenly, they all begin to move —jumping up and down, nudging and bumping one other—and join into a group chant: "NO BARBIE! NO BARBIE! NO BARBIE!" They now appear to be every bit as gleeful as the girls, as they laugh, yell, and chant against the Barbie Girls.

The parents watch the whole scene with rapt attention. Smiles light up the faces of the adults, as our glances sweep back and forth, from the sweetly celebrating Barbie Girls to the aggressively protesting Sea Monsters. "They are SO different!" exclaims one smiling mother approvingly. A male coach offers a more in-depth analysis: "When I was in college," he says, "I took these classes from professors who showed us research that showed that boys and girls are the same. I believed it, until I had my own kids and saw how different they are." "Yeah," another dad responds, "Just look at them! They are so different!"

The girls, meanwhile, show no evidence that they hear, see, or are even aware of the presence of the boys who are now so loudly proclaiming their opposition to the Barbie Girls' songs and totem. They continue to sing, dance, laugh, and rally around the Barbie for a few more minutes, before they are called to reassemble in their groups for the beginning of the parade.

After the parade, the teams reassemble on the infield of the track but now in a less organized manner. The Sea Monsters once again find themselves in the general vicinity of the Barbie Girls and take up the "NO BARBIE!" chant again. Perhaps put out by the lack of response to their chant, they begin to dash, in twos and threes, invading the girls' space, and yelling menacingly. With this, the Barbie Girls have little choice but to recognize the presence of the boys—some look puzzled and shrink back, some engage the boys and chase them off. The chasing seems only to incite more excitement among the boys. Finally, parents intervene and defuse the situation, leading their children off to their cars, homes, and eventually to their soccer games.

THE PERFORMANCE OF GENDER

It has become increasingly fashionable among academic feminists to think of gender not as some "thing" that one "has" (or not) but rather as situationally constructed through the performances of active agents. The idea of gender as performance analytically foregrounds the agency of individuals in the construction of gender, thus highlighting the situational fluidity of gender: here, conservative and reproductive, there, transgressive and disruptive. Surely, the Barbie Girls versus Sea Monsters scene described above can be fruitfully analyzed as a moment of crosscutting and mutually constitutive gender performances: The girls—at least at first glance—appear to be performing (for each other?) a conventional four- to five-year-old version of emphasized femininity. At least on the surface, there appears to be nothing terribly transgressive here. They are just "being girls," together. The boys initially are unwittingly constituted as an audience for the girls' performance but quickly begin to perform (for each other?—for the girls, too?) a masculinity that constructs itself in opposition to Barbie, and to the girls, as not feminine. They aggressively confront—first through loud verbal chanting, eventually through bodily invasions—the girls' ritual space of emphasized femininity, apparently with the intention of disrupting its upsetting influence. The adults are simultaneously constituted as an adoring audience for their children's performances and as parents who perform for each other by sharing and mutually affirming their experience-based narratives concerning the natural differences between boys and girls.

In this scene, we see children performing gender in ways that constitute themselves as two separate, opposed groups (boys vs. girls) and parents performing gender in ways that give the stamp of adult approval to the children's performances of difference, while constructing their own ideological narrative that naturalizes this categorical difference. In other words, the parents do not seem to read the children's performances of gender as social constructions of gender. Instead, they interpret them as the inevitable unfolding of natural, internal differences between the sexes. That this moment occurred when it did and where it did is explicable, but not entirely with a theory of performativity. As Walters (1999, 250) argues:

> The performance of gender is never a simple voluntary act. . . . Theories of gender as play and performance need to be intimately and systematically connected with the power of gender (really, the power of male power) to constrain, control, violate, and configure. Too often, mere lip service is given to the specific historical, social, and political configurations that make certain conditions possible and others constrained.

Indeed, feminist sociologists operating from the traditions of symbolic interactionism and/or Goffmanian dramaturgical analysis have anticipated the recent interest in looking at gender as a dynamic performance. As early as 1978, Kessler and McKenna developed a sophisticated analysis of gender as an everyday, practical accomplishment of people's interactions. Nearly a decade later, West and Zimmerman (1987) argued that in people's everyday interactions, they were "doing gender" and, in so doing, they were constructing masculine dominance and feminine deference. As these ideas have been taken up in sociology, their tendencies toward a celebration of the "freedom" of agents to transgress and reshape the fluid boundaries of gender have been put into play with theories of social structure (e.g., Lorber 1994; Risman 1998). In these accounts, gender is viewed as enacted or created through everyday interactions, but crucially, as Walters suggested above, within "specific historical, social, and political configurations" that constrain or enable certain interactions.

The parents' response to the Barbie Girls versus Sea Monsters performance suggests one of the main limits and dangers of theories of performativity. Lacking an analysis of structural and cultural context, performances of gender can all too easily be interpreted as free agents acting out the inevitable surface manifestations of a natural inner essence of sex difference. An examination of structural and cultural contexts, though, reveals that there was nothing inevitable about the girls' choice of Barbie as their totem, nor in the boys' response to it.

THE STRUCTURE OF GENDER

In the entire subsequent season of weekly games and practices, I never once saw adults point to a moment in which boy and girl soccer players were doing the *same* thing and exclaim to each other, "Look at them! They are *so similar!*" The actual similarity of the boys and the girls, evidenced by nearly all of the kids' routine actions throughout a soccer season—playing the game, crying over a skinned knee, scrambling enthusiastically for their snacks after the games, spacing out on a bird or a flower instead of listening to the coach at practice—is a key to understanding the salience of the Barbie Girls versus Sea Monsters moment for gender relations. In the face of a multitude of moments that speak to similarity, it was this anomalous Barbie Girls versus Sea Monsters moment—where the boundaries of gender were so clearly enacted—that the adults seized to affirm their commitment to difference. It is the kind of moment—to use Lorber's (1994, 37) phrase—where "believing is seeing," where we selectively "see" aspects of social reality that tell us a truth that we prefer to believe, such as the belief in categorical sex difference. No matter that our eyes do not see evidence of this truth most of the rest of the time.

In fact, it was not so easy for adults to actually "see" the empirical reality of sex similarity in everyday observations of soccer throughout the season. That is due to one overdetermining factor: an institutional context that is characterized by informally structured sex segregation among the parent coaches and team managers, and by formally structured sex segregation among the children. The structural analysis developed here is indebted to Acker's (1990) observation that organizations, even while appearing "gender neutral," tend to reflect, recreate, and naturalize a hierarchical ordering of gender. Following Connell's (1987, 98–99) method of structural analysis, I will examine the "gender regime"—that is, the current "state of play of sexual politics"—within the local AYSO organization by conducting a "structural inventory" of the formal and informal sexual divisions of labor and power.[1]

ADULT DIVISIONS OF LABOR AND POWER

There was a clear—although not absolute—sexual division of labor and power among the adult volunteers in the AYSO organization. The Board of Directors consisted of 21 men and 9 women, with the top two positions—commissioner and assistant commissioner—held by men. Among the league's head coaches, 133 were men and 23 women. The division among the league's assistant coaches was similarly skewed. Each team also had a team manager who was responsible for organizing snacks, making reminder calls about games and practices, organizing team parties and the end-of-the-year present for the coach. The vast majority of team managers were women. A common slippage in the language of coaches and parents revealed the ideological assumptions underlying this position: I often noticed people describe a team manager as the "team mom." In short, as Table 6.1 shows, the vast majority of the time, the formal authority of the head coach and assistant coach was in the hands of a man, while the backup, support role of team manager was in the hands of a woman.

These data illustrate Connell's (1987, 97) assertion that sexual divisions of labor are interwoven with, and mutually supportive of, divisions of power and authority among women and men. They also suggest how people's choices to volunteer for certain positions are shaped and constrained by previous institutional practices. There is no formal AYSO rule that men must be the leaders, women the supportive followers. And there are, after all, *some* women coaches and *some* men team managers.[2] So, it may appear that the division of labor among adult volunteers simply manifests an accumulation of individual choices and

Table 6.1 Adult Volunteers as Coaches and Team Managers, by Gender (in Percentages) (*N* = 156 teams)

	Head coaches	*Assistant coaches*	*Team managers*
Women	15	21	86
Men	85	79	14

preferences. When analyzed structurally, though, individual men's apparently free choices to volunteer disproportionately for coaching jobs, alongside individual women's apparently free choices to volunteer disproportionately for team manager jobs, can be seen as a logical collective result of the ways that the institutional structure of sport has differentially constrained and enabled women's and men's previous options and experiences (Messner 1992). Since boys and men have had far more opportunities to play organized sports and thus to gain skills and knowledge, it subsequently appears rational for adult men to serve in positions of knowledgeable authority, with women serving in a support capacity (Boyle and McKay 1995). Structure—in this case, the historically constituted division of labor and power in sport—constrains current practice. In turn, structure becomes an object of practice, as the choices and actions of today's parents recreate divisions of labor and power similar to those that they experienced in their youth.

THE CHILDREN: FORMAL SEX SEGREGATION

As adult authority patterns are informally structured along gendered lines, the children's leagues are formally segregated by AYSO along lines of age and sex. In each age-group, there are separate boys' and girls' leagues. The AYSO in this community included 87 boys' teams and 69 girls' teams. Although the four- to five-year-old boys often played their games on a field that was contiguous with games being played by four- to five-year-old girls, there was never a formal opportunity for cross-sex play. Thus, both the girls' and the boys' teams could conceivably proceed through an entire season of games and practices in entirely homosocial contexts.[3] In the all-male contexts that I observed throughout the season, gender never appeared to be overtly salient among the children, coaches, or parents. It is against this backdrop that I might suggest a working hypothesis about structure and the variable salience of gender: The formal sex segregation of children does not, in and of itself, make gender overtly salient. In fact, when children are absolutely segregated, with no opportunity for cross-sex interactions, gender may appear to disappear as an overtly salient organizing principle. However, when formally sex-segregated children are placed into immediately contiguous locations, such as during the opening ceremony, highly charged gendered interactions between the groups (including invasions and other kinds of border work) become more possible.

Although it might appear to some that formal sex segregation in children's sports is a natural fact, it has not always been so for the youngest age-groups in AYSO. As recently as 1995, when my older son signed up to play as a five-year-old, I had been told that he would play in a coed league. But when he arrived to his first practice and I saw that he was on an all-boys team, I was told by the coach that AYSO had decided this year to begin sex segregating all age-groups, because "during half-times and practices, the boys and girls tend to separate into separate groups. So the league thought it would be better for team unity if we split the boys and girls into separate leagues." I suggested to some coaches that a similar dynamic among racial ethnic groups (say, Latino kids and white kids clustering as separate groups during halftimes) would not similarly result in a decision to create racially segregated leagues. That this comment appeared to fall on deaf ears illustrates the extent to which many adults' belief in the need for sex segregation—at least in the context of sport—is grounded in a mutually agreed-upon notion of boys' and girls' "separate worlds," perhaps based in ideologies of natural sex difference.

The gender regime of AYSO, then, is structured by formal and informal sexual divisions of labor and power. This social structure sets ranges, limits, and possibilities for the children's and parents' interactions and performances of gender, but it does not determine them. Put another way, the formal and informal gender regime of AYSO made the Barbie Girls versus Sea Monsters moment possible, but it did not make it inevitable. It was the agency of the children and the parents within that structure that made the moment happen. But why did this moment take on the symbolic forms that it did? How and why do the girls, boys, and parents construct and derive meanings from this moment, and how can we interpret these meanings? These questions are best grappled within in the realm of cultural analysis.

THE CULTURE OF GENDER

The difference between what is "structural" and what is "cultural" is not clear-cut. For instance, the AYSO assignment of team colors and choice of team names (cultural symbols) seem to follow logically from, and in turn reinforce, the sex segregation of the leagues (social structure). These cultural symbols such as team colors, uniforms, songs, team names, and banners often carried encoded gendered meanings that were then available to be taken up by the children in ways that constructed (or potentially contested) gender divisions and boundaries.

TEAM NAMES

Each team was issued two team colors. It is notable that across the various age-groups, several girls' teams were issued pink uniforms—a color commonly recognized as encoding feminine meanings—while no boys' teams were issued pink uniforms. Children, in consultation with their coaches, were asked to choose their own team names and were encouraged to use their assigned team colors as cues to the theme of the team name (e.g., among the boys, the "Red Flashes," the "Green Pythons," and the blue-and-green "Sea Monsters"). When I analyzed the team names of the 156 teams by age-group and by sex, three categories emerged:

1 Sweet names: These are cutesy team names that communicate small stature, cuteness, and/or vulnerability. These kinds of names would most likely be widely read as encoded with feminine meanings (e.g., "Blue Butterflies," "Beanie Babes," "Sunflowers," "Pink Flamingos," and "Barbie Girls").
2 Neutral or paradoxical names: Neutral names are team names that carry no obvious gendered meaning (e.g., "Blue and Green Lizards," "Team Flubber," "Galaxy," "Blue Ice"). Paradoxical names are girls' team names that carry mixed (simultaneously vulnerable *and* powerful) messages (e.g., "Pink Panthers," "Flower Power," "Little Tigers").
3 Power names: These are team names that invoke images of unambiguous strength, aggression, and raw power (e.g., "Shooting Stars," "Killer Whales," "Shark Attack," "Raptor Attack," and "Sea Monsters").

As Table 6.2 illustrates, across all age-groups of boys, there was only one team name coded as a sweet name—"The Smurfs," in the 10- to 11-year-old league. Across all age categories, the boys were far more likely to choose a power name than anything else, and this was nowhere more true than in the youngest age-groups, where 35 of 40 (87 percent) of boys' teams in the four-to-five and six-to-seven age-groups took on power names. A different pattern appears in the girls' team name choices, especially among the youngest girls. Only 2 of the 12 four-to five-year-old girls' teams chose power names, while 5 chose sweet names and 5 chose neutral/paradoxical names. At age six to seven, the numbers begin to tip toward the boys' numbers but still remain different, with half of the girls' teams now choosing power names. In the middle and older girls' groups, the sweet names all but disappear, with power names dominating, but still a higher proportion of neutral/paradoxical names than among boys in those age-groups.

BARBIE NARRATIVE VERSUS WARRIOR NARRATIVE

How do we make sense of the obviously powerful spark that Barbie provided in the opening ceremony scene described above? Barbie is likely one of the most immediately identifiable symbols of femininity in the world. More conservatively oriented parents tend to happily buy Barbie dolls for their daughters, while perhaps deflecting their sons' interest in Barbie toward more sex-appropriate "action toys." Feminist parents, on the other hand, have often expressed open contempt—or at least uncomfortable ambivalence—toward Barbie. This is because both conservative and feminist parents see dominant cultural meanings of emphasized femininity as condensed in Barbie and assume that these meanings will be imitated by their daughters. Recent developments in cultural studies, though, should warn us against simplistic readings of Barbie as simply conveying hegemonic messages about gender to unwitting children (Attfield 1996; Seiter 1995). In addition to critically analyzing the cultural values (or "preferred meanings") that may be encoded in Barbie or other children's toys, feminist scholars of cultural studies point to the necessity of examining "reception, pleasure, and agency," and especially "the fullness of reception contexts" (Walters 1999, 246). The Barbie Girls versus Sea Monsters moment can be analyzed as a "reception context," in which differently situated boys, girls, and parents variously used Barbie to construct

Table 6.2 Teams Names, by Age-Groups and Gender

	4–5		*6–7*		*8–13*		*14–17*		*Total*	
	n	*%*	*n*	*%*	*n*	*%*	*n*	*%*	*n*	*%*
Girls										
Sweet names	5	42	3	17	2	7	0	0	10	15
Neutral/ paradoxical	5	42	6	33	7	25	5	45	23	32
Power names	2	17	9	50	19	68	6	55	36	52
Boys										
Sweet names	0	0	0	0	1	4	0	0	1	1
Neutral/ paradoxical	1	7	4	15	4	12	4	31	13	15
Power names	13	93	22	85	29	85	9	69	73	82

pleasurable intergroup bonds, as well as boundaries between groups.

[. . .]

Recent Third Wave feminist theory sheds light on the different sensibilities of younger generations of girls and women concerning their willingness to display and play with this apparently paradoxical relationship between bodily experience (including "feminine" displays) and public empowerment. In Third Wave feminist texts, displays of feminine physical attractiveness and empowerment are not viewed as mutually exclusive or necessarily opposed realities, but as lived (if often paradoxical) aspects of the same reality (Heywood and Drake 1997). This embracing of the paradoxes of post–Second Wave femininity is manifested in many punk, or Riot Grrrl, subcultures (Klein 1997) and in popular culture in the resounding late 1990s' success of the Spice Girls' mantra of "Girl Power." This generational expression of "girl power" may today be part of "the pleasures of girl culture that Barbie stands for" (Spigel forthcoming). Indeed, as the Barbie Girls rallied around Barbie, their obvious pleasure did not appear to be based on a celebration of quiet passivity (as feminist parents might fear). Rather, it was a statement that they—the Barbie Girls—were here in this public space. They were not silenced by the boys' oppositional chanting. To the contrary, they ignored the boys, who seemed irrelevant to their celebration. And, when the boys later physically invaded their space, some of the girls responded by chasing the boys off. In short, when I pay attention to what the girls *did* (rather than imposing on the situation what I *think* Barbie "should" mean to the girls), I see a public moment of celebratory "girl power."

And this may give us better basis from which to analyze the boys' oppositional response. First, the boys may have been responding to the threat of displacement they may have felt while viewing the girls' moment of celebratory girl power. Second, the boys may simultaneously have been responding to the fears of feminine pollution that Barbie had come to symbolize to them. But why might Barbie symbolize feminine pollution to little boys? A brief example from my older son is instructive. When he was about three, following a fun day of play with the five-year-old girl next door, he enthusiastically asked me to buy him a Barbie like hers. He was gleeful when I took him to the store and bought him one. When we arrived home, his feet had barely hit the pavement getting out of the car before an eight-year-old neighbor boy laughed at and ridiculed him: "A *Barbie?* Don't you know that Barbie is a *girl's toy?*" No amount of parental intervention could counter this devastating peer-induced injunction against boys playing with Barbie. My son's pleasurable desire for Barbie appeared almost overnight to transform itself into shame and rejection. The doll ended up at the bottom of a heap of toys in the closet, and my son soon became infatuated, along with other boys in his preschool, with Ninja Turtles and Power Rangers.

Research indicates that there is widespread agreement as to which toys are appropriate for one sex and polluting, dangerous, or inappropriate for the other sex. When Campenni (1999) asked adults to rate the gender appropriateness of children's toys, the toys considered most appropriate to girls were those pertaining to domestic tasks, beauty enhancement, or child rearing. Of the 206 toys rated, Barbie was rated second only to Makeup Kit as a female-only toy. Toys considered most appropriate to boys were those pertaining to sports gear (football gear was the most masculine-rated toy, while boxing gloves were third), vehicles, action figures (G. I. Joe was rated second only to football gear), and other war-related toys. This research on parents' gender stereotyping of toys reflects similar findings in research on children's toy preferences (Bradbard 1985; Robinson and Morris 1986).

Children tend to avoid cross-sex toys, with boys' avoidance of feminine-coded toys appearing to be stronger than girls' avoidance of masculine-coded toys (Etaugh and Liss 1992). Moreover, preschool-age boys who perceive their fathers to be opposed to cross-gendertyped play are more likely than girls or other boys to think that it is "bad" for boys to play with toys that are labeled as "for girls" (Raag and Rackliff 1998).

By kindergarten, most boys appear to have learned—either through experiences similar to my son's, where other male persons police the boundaries of gender-appropriate play and fantasy and/or by watching the clearly gendered messages of television advertising—that Barbie dolls are not appropriate toys for boys (Rogers 1999, 30). To avoid ridicule, they learn to hide their desire for Barbie, either through denial and oppositional/pollution discourse and/or through sublimation of their desire for Barbie into play with male-appropriate "action figures" (Pope *et al.* 1999). In their study of a kindergarten classroom, Jordan and Cowan (1995, 728) identified "warrior narratives . . . that assume that violence is legitimate and justified when it occurs within a struggle between good and evil" to be the most commonly agreed-upon currency for boys' fantasy play. They observe that the boys seem commonly to adapt story lines that they have seen on television. Popular culture—film, video, computer games, television, and comic books—provides boys with a seemingly endless stream of Good Guys versus Bad Guys characters and stories—from cowboy movies, Superman and Spiderman to Ninja Turtles, Star Wars, and Pokémon—that are available for the boys to appropriate as the raw materials for the construction of their own warrior play.

In the kindergarten that Jordan and Cowan studied, the boys initially attempted to import their warrior narratives into the domestic setting of the "Doll Corner." Teachers eventually drove the boys' warrior play outdoors, while the Doll Corner was used by the girls for the "appropriate" domestic play for which it was originally intended. Jordan and Cowan argue that kindergarten teachers' outlawing of boys' warrior narratives inside the classroom contributed to boys' defining schools as a feminine environment, to which they responded with a resistant, underground continuation of masculine warrior play. Eventually though, boys who acquiesce and successfully sublimate warrior play into fantasy or sport are more successful in constructing what Connell (1989, 291) calls "a masculinity organized around themes of rationality and responsibility [that is] closely connected with the 'certification' function of the upper levels of the education system and to a key form of masculinity among professionals."

In contrast to the "rational/professional" masculinity constructed in schools, the institution of sport historically constructs hegemonic masculinity as *bodily superiority* over femininity and nonathletic masculinities (Messner 1992). Here, warrior narratives are allowed to publicly thrive—indeed, are openly celebrated (witness, for instance, the commentary of a televised NFL [National Football League] football game or especially the spectacle of televised professional wrestling). Preschool boys and kindergartners seem already to know this, easily adopting aggressively competitive team names and an us-versus-them attitude. By contrast, many of the youngest girls appear to take two or three years in organized soccer before they adopt, or partially accommodate themselves to, aggressively competitive discourse, indicated by the 10-year-old girls' shifting away from the use of sweet names toward more power names. In short, where the gender regime of preschool and grade school may be experienced as an environment in which mostly women leaders enforce rules that are hostile to masculine fantasy play and physicality, the gender regime of sport is experienced as a place where masculine styles and values of physicality, aggression, and competition are enforced and celebrated by mostly male coaches.

A cultural analysis suggests that the boys' and the girls' previous immersion in differently gendered cultural experiences shaped the likelihood that they would derive and construct different meanings from Barbie—the girls through pleasurable and symbolically empowering identification with "girl power" narratives; the boys through oppositional fears of feminine pollution (and fears of displacement by girl power?) and with aggressively verbal, and eventually physical, invasions of the girls' ritual space. The boys' collective response thus constituted them differently, *as boys*, in opposition to the girls' constitution of themselves *as girls*. An individual girl or boy, in this moment, who may have felt an inclination to dissent from the dominant feelings of the group (say, the Latina Barbie Girl who, her mother later told me, did not want the group to be identified with Barbie, or a boy whose immediate inner response to the Barbie Girls' joyful celebration might be to join in) is most likely silenced into complicity in this powerful moment of border work.

What meanings did this highly gendered moment carry for the boys' and girls' teams in the ensuing soccer season? Although I did not observe the Barbie Girls after the opening ceremony, I did continue to observe the Sea Monsters' weekly practices and games. During the boys' ensuing season, gender never reached this "magnified" level of salience again—indeed, gender was rarely raised verbally or performed overtly by the boys. On two occasions, though, I observed the coach jokingly chiding the boys during practice that "if you don't watch out, I'm going to get the Barbie Girls here to play against you!" This warning was followed by gleeful screams of agony and fear, and nervous hopping around and hugging by some of the boys. Normally, though, in this sex-segregated, all-male context, if boundaries were invoked, they were not boundaries between boys and girls but boundaries between the Sea Monsters and other boys' teams, or sometimes age boundaries between the Sea Monsters and a small group of dads and older brothers who would engage them in a mock scrimmage during practice. But it was also evident that when the coach was having trouble getting the boys to act together, as a group, his strategic and humorous invocation of the dreaded Barbie Girls once again served symbolically to affirm their group status. They were a team. They were the boys.

CONCLUSION

The overarching goal of this article has been to take one empirical observation from everyday life and demonstrate how a multilevel (interactionist, structural, cultural) analysis might reveal various layers of meaning that give insight into the everyday social construction of gender. This article builds on observations made by Thorne (1993) concerning ways to approach sociological analyses of children's worlds. The most fruitful approach is not to ask why boys and girls are so different but rather to ask how and under what conditions boys and girls constitute themselves as separate, oppositional groups. Sociologists need not debate whether gender is "there"—clearly, gender is always already there, built as it is into the structures, situations, culture, and consciousness of children and adults. The key issue is under what conditions gender is activated as a salient organizing principle in social life and under what conditions it may be less salient. These are important questions, especially since the social organization of categorical gender difference has always been so clearly tied to gender hierarchy (Acker 1990; Lorber 1994). In the Barbie Girls versus Sea Monsters moment, the performance of gendered boundaries and the construction of boys' and girls' groups as categorically different occurred in the context of a situation systematically structured by sex segregation, sparked by the imposing presence of a shared cultural symbol that is saturated with gendered meanings, and actively supported and applauded by adults who basked in the pleasure of difference, reaffirmed.[4]

I have suggested that a useful approach to the study of such "how" and "under what conditions" questions is to employ multiple levels of analysis. At the most general level, this project supports the following working propositions.

Interactionist theoretical frameworks that emphasize the ways that social agents "perform" or "do" gender are most useful in describing how groups of people actively create (or at times disrupt) the boundaries that delineate seemingly categorical differences between male persons and female persons. In this case, we saw how the children and the parents interactively performed gender in a way that constructed an apparently natural boundary between the two separate worlds of the girls and the boys.

Structural theoretical frameworks that emphasize the ways that gender is built into institutions through hierarchical sexual divisions of labor are most useful in explaining under what conditions social agents mobilize variously to disrupt or to affirm gender differences and inequalities. In this case, we saw how the sexual division of labor among parent volunteers (grounded in their own histories in the gender regime of sport), the formal sex segregation of the children's leagues, and the structured context of the opening ceremony created conditions for possible interactions between girls' teams and boys' teams.

Cultural theoretical perspectives that examine how popular symbols that are injected into circulation by the culture industry are variously taken up by differently situated people are most useful in analyzing how the meanings of cultural symbols, in a given institutional context, might trigger or be taken up by social agents and used as resources to reproduce, disrupt, or contest binary conceptions of sex difference and gendered relations of power. In this case, we saw how a girls' team appropriated a large Barbie around which to construct a pleasurable and empowering sense of group identity and how the boys' team responded with aggressive denunciations of Barbie and invasions.

Utilizing any one of the above theoretical perspectives by itself will lead to a limited, even distorted, analysis of the social construction of gender. Together, they can illuminate the complex, multileveled architecture of the social construction of gender in everyday life. For heuristic reasons, I have falsely separated structure, interaction, and culture. In fact, we need to explore their constant interrelationships, continuities, and contradictions. For instance, we cannot understand the boys' aggressive denunciations and invasions of the girls' space and the eventual clarification of categorical boundaries between the girls and the boys without first understanding how these boys and girls have already internalized four or five years of "gendering" experiences that have shaped their interactional tendencies and how they are already immersed in a culture of gendered symbols, including Barbie and sports media imagery. Although "only" preschoolers, they are already skilled in collectively taking up symbols from popular culture as resources to be used in their own group dynamics—building individual and group identities, sharing the pleasures of play, clarifying boundaries between in-group and out-group members, and constructing hierarchies in their worlds.

Furthermore, we cannot understand the reason that the girls first chose "Barbie Girls" as their team name without first understanding the fact that a particular institutional structure of AYSO soccer preexisted the girls' entrée into the league. The informal sexual division of labor among adults, and the formal sex segregation of children's teams, is a preexisting gender regime that constrains and enables the ways that the children enact gender relations and construct identities. One concrete manifestation of this constraining nature of sex segregated teams is the choice of team names. It is reasonable to speculate that if the four- and five-year-old children were still sex integrated, as in the pre-1995 era, no team would have chosen "Barbie Girls" as its team name, with Barbie as its symbol. In other words, the formal sex segregation created the conditions under which the girls were enabled—perhaps encouraged—to choose a "sweet" team name that is widely read as encoding feminine meanings. The eventual interactions between the boys and the girls were made possible—although by no means fully determined—by the structure of the gender regime and by the cultural resources that the children variously drew on.

On the other hand, the gendered division of labor in youth soccer is not seamless, static, or immune to resistance. One of the few woman head coaches, a very active athlete in her own right, told me that she is "challenging the sexism" in AYSO by becoming the head of her son's league. As post-Title IX women increasingly become mothers and as media images of competent, heroic female athletes become more a part of the cultural landscape for children, the gender regimes of children's sports may be increasingly challenged (Dworkin and Messner 1999). Put another way, the dramatically shifting opportunity structure and cultural imagery of post-Title IX sports have created opportunities for new kinds of interactions, which will inevitably challenge and further shift institutional structures. Social structures simultaneously constrain and enable, while agency is simultaneously reproductive and resistant.

NOTES

1. Most of the structural inventory presented here is from a content analysis of the 1998–99 regional American Youth Soccer League (AYSO) yearbook, which features photos and names of all of the teams, coaches, and managers. I counted the number of adult men and women occupying various positions. In the three cases where the sex category of a name was not immediately obvious (e.g., Rene or Terry), or in the five cases where simply a last name was listed, I did not count it. I also used the AYSO yearbook for my analysis of the children's team names. To check for reliability, another sociologist independently read and coded the list of team names. There was disagreement on how to categorize only 2 of the 156 team names.
2. The existence of some women coaches and some men team managers in this AYSO organization manifests a less extreme sexual division of labor than that of the same community's Little League baseball organization, in which there are proportionally far fewer women coaches. Similarly, Saltzman Chafetz and Kotarba's (1999, 52) study of parental labor in support of Little League baseball in a middle-class Houston community revealed an apparently absolute sexual division of labor, where nearly all of the supportive "activities off the field were conducted by the women in the total absence of men, while activities on the field were conducted by men and boys in the absence of women." Perhaps youth soccer, because of its more recent (mostly post-Title IX) history in the United States, is a more contested gender regime than the more patriarchally entrenched youth sports like Little League baseball or youth football.
3. The four- and five-year-old kids' games and practices were absolutely homosocial in terms of the kids, due to the formal structural sex segregation. However, 8 of the 12 girls' teams at this age level had male coaches, and 2 of the 14 boys' teams had female coaches.
4. My trilevel analysis of structure, interaction, and culture may not be fully adequate to plumb the emotional depths of the magnified Barbie Girls

versus Sea Monsters moment. Although it is beyond the purview of this article, an adequate rendering of the depths of pleasure and revulsion, attachment and separation, and commitment to ideologies of categorical sex difference may involve the integration of a fourth level of analysis: gender at the level of personality (Chodorow 1999). Object relations theory has fallen out of vogue in feminist sociology in recent years, but as Williams (1993) has argued, it might be most useful in revealing the mostly hidden social power of gender to shape people's unconscious predispositions to various structural contexts, cultural symbols, and interactional moments.

REFERENCES

Acker, Joan. 1990. Hierarchies, jobs, bodies: A theory of gendered organizations. *Gender & Society* 4: 139–58.

Adler, Patricia A., and Peter Adler. 1998. *Peer power: Preadolescent culture and identity.* New Brunswick, NJ: Rutgers University Press.

Attfield, Judy. 1996. Barbie and Action Man: Adult toys for girls and boys, 1959–93. In *The gendered object,* edited by Pat Kirkham, 80–89. Manchester, UK, and New York: Manchester University Press.

Boyle, Maree, and Jim McKay. 1995. "You leave your troubles at the gate": A case study of the exploitation of older women's labor and "leisure" in sport. *Gender & Society* 9:556–76.

Bradbard, M. 1985. Sex differences in adults' gifts and children's toy requests. *Journal of Genetic Psychology* 145:283–84.

Campenni, C. Estelle. 1999. Gender stereotyping of children's toys: A comparison of parents and nonparents. *Sex Roles* 40:121–38.

Chodorow, Nancy J. 1999. *The power of feelings: Personal meanings in psychoanalysis, gender, and culture.* New Haven, CT, and London: Yale University Press.

Connell, R.W. 1987. *Gender and power.* Stanford, CA: Stanford University Press.

——. 1989. Cool guys, swots and wimps: The interplay of masculinity and education. *Oxford Review of Education* 15:291–303.

DuCille, Anne. 1994. Dyes and dolls: Multicultural Barbie and the merchandising of difference. *Differences: A Journal of Cultural Studies* 6:46–68.

Dworkin, Shari L., and Michael A. Messner. 1999. Just do . . . what?: Sport, bodies, gender. In *Revisioning gender,* edited by Myra Marx Ferree, Judith Lorber, and Beth B. Hess, 341–61. Thousand Oaks, CA: Sage.

Etaugh, C., and M. B. Liss. 1992. Home, school, and playroom: Training grounds for adult gender roles. *Sex Roles* 26:129–47.

Heywood, Leslie, and Jennifer Drake, Eds. 1997. *Third wave agenda: Being feminist, doing feminism.* Minneapolis: University of Minnesota Press.

Hochschild, Arlie Russell. 1994. The commercial spirit of intimate life and the abduction of feminism: Signs from women's advice books. *Theory, Culture & Society* 11:1–24.

Jordan, Ellen, and Angela Cowan. 1995. Warrior narratives in the kindergarten classroom: Renogotiating the social contract? *Gender & Society* 9:727–43.

Kessler, Suzanne J., and Wendy McKenna. 1978. *Gender: An ethnomethodological approach.* New York: John Wiley.

Klein, Melissa. 1997. Duality and redefinition: Young feminism and the alternative music community. In *Third wave agenda: Being feminist, doing feminism,* edited by Leslie Heywood and Jennifer Drake, 207–25. Minneapolis: University of Minnesota Press.

Lorber, Judith. 1994. *Paradoxes of gender.* New Haven, CT, and London: Yale University Press.

Messner, Michael A. 1992. *Power at play: Sports and the problem of masculinity.* Boston: Beacon.

Pope, Harrison G., Jr., Roberto Olivarda, Amanda Gruber, and John Borowiecki. 1999. Evolving ideals of male body image as seen through action toys. *International Journal of Eating Disorders* 26:65–72.

Raag, Tarja, and Christine L. Rackliff. 1998. Preschoolers' awareness of social expectations of gender: Relationships to toy choices. *Sex Roles* 38:685–700.

Risman, Barbara. 1998. *Gender vertigo: American families in transition.* New Haven and London: Yale University Press.

Robinson, C. C., and J. T. Morris. 1986. The gender-stereotyped nature of Christmas toys received by 36-, 48-, and 60-month-old children: A comparison between nonrequested vs. requested toys. *Sex Roles* 15:21–32.

Rogers, Mary F. 1999. *Barbie culture.* Thousand Oaks, CA: Sage.

Saltzman Chafetz, Janet, and Joseph A. Kotarba. 1999. Little League mothers and the reproduction of gender. In *Inside sports,* edited by Jay Coakley and Peter Donnelly, 46–54. London and New York: Routledge.

Seiter, Ellen. 1995. *Sold separately: Parents and children in consumer culture.* New Brunswick, NJ: Rutgers University Press.

Spigel, Lynn. Forthcoming. Barbies without Ken: Femininity, feminism, and the art-culture system. In *Sitting room only: Television, consumer culture and the suburban home*, edited by Lynn Spigel. Durham, NC: Duke University Press.

Thorne, Barrie. 1993. *Gender play: Girls and boys in school.* New Brunswick, NJ: Rutgers University Press.

Walters, Suzanna Danuta. 1999. Sex, text, and context: (In) between feminism and cultural studies. In *Revisioning gender*, edited by Myra Marx Ferree, Judith Lorber, and Beth B. Hess, 222–57. Thousand Oaks, CA: Sage.

West, Candace, and Don Zimmerman. 1987. Doing gender. *Gender & Society* 1:125–51.

Williams, Christine. 1993. Psychoanalytic theory and the sociology of gender. In *Theory on gender, gender on theory*, edited by Paula England, 131–49. New York: Aldine.

CHAPTER 7

Remaking Manhood through Race and "Civilization"

Gail Bederman

At 2:30 p.m. on July 4, 1910, in Reno, Nevada, as the band played "All Coons Look Alike to Me," Jack Johnson climbed into the ring to defend his title against Jim Jeffries. Johnson was the first African American world heavyweight boxing champion. Jeffries was a popular white former heavyweight champion who had retired undefeated six years before. Although it promised to be a fine match, more than mere pugilism was at stake. Indeed, the Johnson-Jeffries match was the event of the year. Twenty thousand men from across the nation had traveled to Reno to sit in the broiling desert sun and watch the prizefight. Five hundred journalists had been dispatched to Reno to cover it. Every day during the week before the fight, they had wired between 100,000 and 150,000 words of reportage about it to their home offices. Most had assured their white readership that Jeffries would win. On the day of the fight, American men deserted their families' holiday picnics. All across America, they gathered in ballparks, theaters, and auditoriums to hear the wire services' round-by-round reports of the contest. Over thirty thousand men stood outside the *New York Times* offices straining to hear the results; ten thousand men gathered outside the *Atlanta Constitution*. It was, quite simply, a national sensation.[1]

Ever since 1899, when Jeffries first won the heavyweight championship, he had refused to fight any Negro challengers. Jack Johnson first challenged him as early as 1903. Jeffries replied, "When there are no white men left to fight, I will quit the business. . . . I am determined not to take a chance of losing the championship to a negro."[2] Jeffries' adherence to the color line was not unique. Ever since 1882, when John L. Sullivan had won the title, no white heavyweight champion had fought a black challenger, even though black and white heavyweights had previously competed freely.[3] Sullivan had announced he would fight all contenders—except black ones. "I will not fight a negro. I never have and never shall."[4] It was in this context that Jack Johnson began his career, and eventually defeated every fighter, black or white, who faced him.

For two years Jeffries refused to fight Johnson, but when Jeffries retired in 1905, the remaining field of white contenders was so poor that the public temporarily lost interest in prizefighting. Finally in 1908, the reigning white champion, Tommy Burns, agreed to fight Johnson. By accepting Johnson's challenge, Burns hoped to raise both interest and prize money. Johnson promptly and decisively thrashed Burns, however, and won the title. Faced with the unthinkable—

a black man had been crowned the most powerful man in the world—interest in pugilism rebounded. The white press clamored for Jeffries to return to the ring. "Jeff must emerge from his alfalfa farm and remove that smile from Johnson's face. Jeff, it's up to you," implored Jack London in the *New York Herald*.[5] In April 1909, the *Chicago Tribune* printed a drawing of a little blond girl begging the former champion: "Please, Mr. Jeffries, are you going to fight Mr. Johnson?"[6] Across America, white newspapers pleaded with Jeffries to vindicate Anglo-Saxon manhood and save civilization by vanquishing the upstart "Negro."

Eventually the aging, reluctant Jeffries agreed to fight, reportedly explaining. "I am going into this fight for the sole purpose of proving that a white man is better than a negro."[7] From its inception, then, the Johnson-Jeffries fight was framed as a contest to see which race had produced the most powerful, virile man. Jeffries was known as the "Hope of the White Race," while Johnson was dubbed the "Negroes' Deliverer."[8] With few exceptions, predictions of the fight's outcome focused on the relative manliness of the white and the black races. For example, *Current Literature* predicted Jeffries would win because "the black man . . . fights emotionally, whereas the white man can use his brain after twenty rounds."[9] White men were confident that Jeffries's intrinsic Anglo-Saxon manhood would allow him to prevail over the (allegedly) flightier, more emotional Negro.

Thus, when Johnson trounced Jeffries—and it was a bloody rout—the defenders of white male supremacy were very publicly hoist by their own petards. They had insisted upon framing the fight as a contest to demonstrate which race could produce the superior specimen of virile manhood. Johnson's victory was so lopsided that the answer was unwelcome but unmistakable. After the fight, the black *Chicago Defender* exulted that Johnson was "the first negro to be admitted the best man in the world."[10]

The ensuing violence showed what a bitter pill that was for many white American men to swallow. Race riots broke out in every Southern state, as well as in Illinois, Missouri, New York, Ohio, Pennsylvania, Colorado, and the District of Columbia. Occasionally, black men attacked white men who were belittling Johnson. In most of the incidents, however, rampaging white men attacked black men who were celebrating Johnson's victory.[11] In Manhattan, the *New York Herald* reported: "One negro was rescued by the police from white men who had a rope around his neck. . . . In Eighth Avenue, between Thirty-Seventh and Thirty-Ninth Streets, more than three thousand whites gathered, and all the negroes that appeared were kicked and beaten, some of them into insensibility. . . . Three thousand white men took possession of Eighth Avenue and held against police as they attacked every negro that came into sight."[12] Contemporary reports put the overall national toll at eighteen people dead, hundreds more injured.[13]

Even the United States Congress reacted to the implicit aspersions Johnson's victory cast on white manhood. Before the Johnson-Jeffries fight, Congress had refused even to consider a bill suppressing motion picture films of prizefights. The prospect of the filmic reenactment of the "Negroes' Deliverer" thrashing the "White Hope" in hundreds of movie theaters across the nation was too much for them, however. Within three weeks, a bill suppressing fight films had passed both houses and was soon signed into law.[14]

Soon after Johnson won the championship, an even more scandalous public controversy arose: the "Negroes' Deliverer" was making no secret of his taste for the company of white women. White men worried: Did Johnson's success with white women prove him a superior specimen of manhood? The spectacle of dozens of white women in pursuit of Johnson's favor pleased Johnson and infuriated many whites. These women were mostly prostitutes, but racial etiquette held all white women were too "pure" for liaisons with black men.[15] It seemed bad enough that Johnson's first wife was white, although antimiscegenist doomsayers felt smugly vindicated when she committed suicide in 1912.[16] But when authorities discovered Johnson was having an affair with an eighteen-year-old blond from Minnesota, Lucille Cameron, they charged him with violating the Mann Act—that is, with engaging in white slavery. The white American public, north and south, was outraged. In Johnson's hometown, Chicago, a man threw an ink-well at him when he made an appearance at his bank. Effigies of Johnson were hung from trolley and electric poles around the city. Wherever Johnson went he was greeted with cries of "Lynch him! Lynch the nigger!"[17] It didn't matter that Lucille Cameron insisted she was in love with Johnson and soon married him. It made no difference that she turned out to have been an established prostitute, not a seduced virgin. It didn't even matter that no violations of the Mann Act had occurred, and the original charges had to be dropped. By winning the heavyweight championship and by flaunting his success with white women, Johnson had crossed the line, and the white public demanded punishment.[18]

The national Bureau of Investigation was ordered to conduct a massive search to find *something* to pin on Johnson. After an expensive and exhaustive inquiry, it dredged up some old incidents in which Johnson had crossed state lines with a long-time white mistress. Although the government usually invoked the Mann Act only to combat white slavery and commercial prostitution, officials made an exception for Johnson. He was convicted of crossing state lines with his mistress and of giving her money and presents. For most American men, these were perfectly legal activities. Johnson, however, was sentenced to a year in prison and a thousand-dollar fine. Hoping to get rid of him, government employees tacitly encouraged him to jump bail and leave the country, which he did. For the next seven years, all Johnson's efforts to make a bargain and turn himself in were rebuffed. Only in 1920 was Johnson allowed to return to the United States to serve his sentence, an impoverished and greatly humbled former champion.[19] The photograph of him losing his last championship bout to white fighter Jess Willard in Havana in 1915 was a standard feature in white bars and speakeasies for many years thereafter.[20]

By any standard, white Americans' response to Jack Johnson was excessive. Why should a mere prizefight result in riots and death? What was it about Jack Johnson that inspired the federal government to use the Bureau of Investigation to conduct a vendetta against him? That moved Congress to pass federal legislation to mitigate his impact? That impelled prominent leaders like former President Theodore Roosevelt to condemn him in print?[21] That caused so many respected Americans to describe Johnson's activities as "a blot on our 20th century American Civilization?"[22] That caused American men to celebrate his ultimate defeat in their saloons for decades?

The furor over Jack Johnson was excessive, yet it was not unique. During the decades around the turn of the century, Americans were obsessed with the connection between manhood and racial dominance. This obsession was expressed in a profusion of issues, from debates over lynching, to concern about the white man's imperialistic burden overseas, to discussions of child-rearing. The Jack Johnson controversy, then, was only one of a multitude of ways middle-class Americans found to explain male supremacy in terms of white racial dominance and, conversely, to explain white supremacy in terms of male power.

This book will investigate this turn-of-the-century connection between manhood and race. It will argue that, between 1890 and 1917, as white middle-class men actively worked to reinforce male power, their race became a factor which was crucial to their gender. In ways which have not been well understood, whiteness was both a palpable fact and a manly ideal for these men. During these years, a variety of social and cultural factors encouraged white middle-class men to develop new explanations of why they, as men, ought to wield power and authority. In this context, we can see that Johnson's championship, as well as his self-consciously flamboyant, sexual public persona, was an intolerable—and intentional—challenge to white Americans' widespread beliefs that male power stemmed from white supremacy. Jack Johnson's racial and sexual challenge so upset the ideology of middle-class manhood that both the white press and the United States government were willing to take extraordinary measures in order to completely and utterly annihilate him.

The Jack Johnson controversy, then, simply exemplifies one of many ways Progressive Era men used ideas about white supremacy to produce a racially based ideology of male power. Hazel Carby has called for "more feminist work that interrogates sexual ideologies for their racial specificity and acknowledges whiteness, not just blackness, as a racial categorization."[23] This study attempts precisely that task.

In order to understand why turn-of-the-century middle-class Americans were so interested in using race to remake manhood, we need to outline a larger historical and analytical context. Thus, we will consider a question which is not as self-evident as it appears: precisely what do we mean by "manhood," and how do we study its history?

"MANHOOD": WHAT IS IT, AND HOW DOES IT WORK?

What do we mean by manhood? This question is not as simpleminded as it appears. Although most people can easily identify certain human beings as men, manhood has been defined quite differently in different times, places, and contexts.[24] Moreover, historians of American manhood have based their analyses on very disparate assumptions about the meaning of manhood, which has led to confusion and misunderstanding. (I am purposely using the term "manhood" instead of "masculinity" here because, as we will see, the noun "masculinity" was only beginning to be widely adopted by 1890 and had very specific connotations which have been largely forgotten today.)

Many historians have simply assumed that manhood is an unproblematic identity—an unchanging essence—inherent in all male-bodied humans. These historians see manhood as a normal aspect of human nature, transparent and self-evident, which simply needs to be expressed without inhibiting factors like "anxiety." Although they recognize that manhood might be expressed differently at different times, they nonetheless assume that its underlying meaning remains basically the same. Historians using this sort of theoretical approach have tended to write about what men have done, historically, to express their manhood. For example, they have written fine accounts of men's activities in fraternal organizations and in the Boy Scouts. Moreover, these historians, by raising such questions as whether the Progressives experienced a "masculinity crisis," were among the first to identify male gender issues as proper subjects of historical analysis—in itself, a major contribution. However, their approach has the drawback of *assuming* what it ought to *investigate.* What did "masculinity" mean to men in organizations like the Boy Scouts? Why was it so important to them? Why would its presumed loss be painful enough to cause a "crisis"? Does power or authority have anything to do with manhood? By ignoring these historically important questions, this approach leaves the impression that manhood is a transhistorical essence, substantially unchanging over time, rooted in biology, and therefore not amenable to historical analysis—or to human efforts to change gender relations.[25]

Other historians have seen manhood as a culturally defined collection of traits, attributes, or sex roles. For example, one historian renders the Victorian definition of manhood as a list of adjectives: "a man was self-reliant, strong, resolute, courageous, honest."[26] These historians often analyze how the traits or occupations which are seen as masculine change from period to period or class to class. For example, colonial American men were socialized to be strong patriarchal fathers, while nineteenth-century middle-class men were shunted off to a "separate sphere" to be competitive businessmen. By investigating how manhood changes over time, historians using this approach encourage readers to see gender relations as mutable and improvable. Yet this approach, too, has its limitations. Attempting to define manhood as a coherent set of prescriptive ideals, traits, or sex roles obscures the complexities and contradictions of any historical moment. For example, some historian argue that middle-class Progressive manhood was most characterized by chest-thumping virility, vigorous outdoor athleticism, and fears of feminization. Others disagree, and stress Progressive men's growing interest in erstwhile "feminine" occupations like parenthood and domesticity. Envisioning manhood as a unified set of traits gives us no way to consider the relations between these two coexisting but contradictory aspects of Progressive manhood, nor does it give us a way to understand how men themselves negotiated the contradictions.[27]

This study is based on the premise that gender—whether manhood or womanhood—is a *historical, ideological process*.[28] Through that process, individuals are positioned and position themselves as men or as women. Thus, I don't see manhood as either an intrinsic essence or a collection of traits, attributes, or sex roles. Manhood—or "masculinity," as it is commonly termed today—is a continual, dynamic process. Through that process, men claim certain kinds of authority, based upon their particular type of bodies. At any time in history, many contradictory ideas about manhood are available to explain what men are, how they ought to behave and what sorts of powers and authorities they may claim, as men. Part of the way gender functions is to hide these contradictions and to camouflage the fact that gender is dynamic and always changing. Instead, gender is constructed as a fact of nature, and manhood is assumed to be an unchanging, transhistorical essence, consisting of fixed, naturally occurring traits. To study the history of manhood, I would argue, is to unmask this process and study the historical ways different ideologies about manhood develop, change, are combined, amended, contested—and gain the status of "truth."[29]

To define manhood as an ideological process is not to say that it deals only with intellectuals or ideas. It is, rather, to say that manhood or masculinity is the cultural process whereby concrete individuals are constituted as members of a preexisting social category—as men. The ideological process of gender—whether manhood or womanhood—works through a complex political technology, composed of a variety of institutions, ideas, and daily practices. Combined, these processes produce a set of truths about who an individual is and what he or she can do, based upon his or her body. Individuals are positioned through that process of gender, whether they choose to be or not. Although some individuals may reject certain aspects of their positioning, rare indeed is the person who considers "itself" neither a man nor a woman. And with that positioning as "man" or "woman" inevitably comes a host of other social meanings, expectations, and identities. Individuals have no choice but to act upon these meanings—to accept or reject them, adopt or adapt them—in order to be able to live their lives in human society.

Another way to say this is to define manhood as the process which creates "men" by linking male genital anatomy to a male identity, and linking both anatomy and identity to particular arrangements of authority and power. Logically, this is an entirely arbitrary process. Anatomy, identity, and authority have no intrinsic relationship. Only the process of manhood—of the gender system—allows each to stand for the others.

We can see more concretely how this cultural process works by returning to our discussion of Jack Johnson and considering how Johnson's championship was construed by his culture's historically specific way of linking male anatomy, identity, and authority. Late Victorian culture had identified the powerful, large male body of the heavyweight prizefighter (and not the smaller bodies of the middleweight or welterweight) as the epitome of manhood. The heavyweight's male body was so equated with male identity and power that American whites rigidly prevented all men they deemed unable to wield political and social power from asserting any claim to the heavyweight championship. Logically, there was no reason to see a heavyweight fighter's claim to bodily strength as a claim to public power. Yet the metonymic process of turn-of-the-century manhood constructed bodily strength and social authority as identical. Thus, for twenty-seven years African American men, whom whites saw as less manly than themselves, were forbidden to assert any claim to this pugilistic manhood. When Johnson actually won the heavyweight title, white men clamored for Jeffries to ameliorate the situation and restore manhood to what they believed was its proper functioning.

Yet Johnson was not only positioned by these cultural constructs—he also actively used them to position himself. Embittered by years of vainly seeking a title bout, Johnson consciously played upon white Americans' fears of threatened manhood by laying public claim to all three of the metonymic facets of manhood—body, identity, and authority. During his public sparring matches, Johnson actually wrapped his penis in gauze to enhance its size. Clad only in his boxing shorts, he would stroll the ring, flaunting his genital endowments for all to admire, displaying his superior body to demonstrate his superior manhood.[30] In his private life, Johnson also took great pleasure in assuming a more conventional middle-class manly identity, sometimes taking on the persona of a successful self-made man. In 1912, he publicly claimed the right to move into an exclusive white suburb until the horrified residents took steps to prevent him.[31] He also dressed both his beautiful blond wives in jewels and furs and paraded them in front of the press. Johnson, who grew up in Texas, was well aware that throughout the South black men were regularly tortured and lynched for consorting with white women, and that even Northern whites feared that black men lusted irrepressibly after pure white womanhood. Therefore, he made certain the public could not view his wives as pathetic victims of Negro lust. Instead, he presented his wives as wealthy, respectable women whose husband was successful and manly enough to support them in comfort and luxury.

Johnson was equally insistent upon his masculine right to wield a man's power and authority. He treated minor brushes with the law—his many speeding tickets and automobile violations—contemptuously, as mere inconveniences which he was man enough to ignore.[32] In his autobiography, he claims (falsely, according to his biographer) to have "mingled . . . with kings and queens; monarchs and rulers of nations have been my associates."[33] On a more sinister note, he physically beat and emotionally maltreated his wives and mistresses, implicitly claiming a man's right to dominate women.[34] In short he recognized that dominant white usage prevented him from being treated as the epitome of manhood, as a white heavyweight champion would be treated. Nevertheless he scornfully refused to accept this racial slight. Defiantly, Johnson positioned himself as a real man by laying ostentatious claim to a male body, male identity, and male power.

NOTES

1. Al-Tony Gilmore, *Bad Nigger! The National Impact of Jack Johnson* (Port Washington, N.Y.: Kennikat Press, 1975), 41; Randy Roberts, *Papa Jack: Jack Johnson and the Era of White Hopes* (New York: Free Press, 1983), 99. Both books provide excellent broader discussions of Johnson's life and cultural importance.
2. Roberts, *Papa Jack,* 31.
3. Gilmore, *Bad Nigger!* 25–6; Elliot J. Gorn, *The Manly Art: Bare-Knuckle Prizefighting in America* (Ithaca, N.Y: Cornell University Press, 1986), 218, 238–9.
4. Gilmore, *Bad Nigger!* 26
5. Jack London, *Jack London Reports: War Correspondence, Sports Articles, and Miscellaneous Writings,* ed. King Hendricks and Irving Shepard (Garden City: Doubleday, 1970), 264.
6. Roberts, *Papa Jack,* 85–6.
7. "Is Prize-Fighting Knocked Out?" *Literary Digest* 41 (16 July 1910): 85.
8. "A Review of the World," *Current Literature* 48 (June 1910): 606.
9. "The Psychology of the Prize Fight," *Current Literature* 49 (July 1910): 57.
10. Roberts, *Papa Jack,* 114.
11. On the riots, see Gilmore, *Bad Nigger!* 59–73; "Is Prize-Fighting Knocked Out?" 85; Roberts, *Papa Jack,* 108–9.
12. *New York Herald,* 5 July 1910, quoted in Gilmore, *Bad Nigger!* 65–6.
13. "Is Prize-Fighting Knocked Out?" 85.
14. Gilmore, *Bad Nigger!* 75–93.
15. Gilmore, *Bad Nigger!* 14; Roberts, *Papa Jack,* 74–5.
16. See, e.g., "Reflections on Suicide," *New York Times,* 14 September 1912, 12.
17. Roberts, Papa Jack, 146; "Mob Threatens Johnson," *New York Times,* 20 October 1912, 12.
18. Roberts, *Papa Jack,* 138–54; Gilmore, *Bad Nigger!* 95–116.
19. Roberts, *Papa Jack,* 158–219; Gilmore, *Bad Nigger!* 117–33.
20. Gilmore, *Bad Nigger!* 148
21. Theodore Roosevelt, "The Recent Prizefight," *Outlook* 95 (16 July 1910) 550–1.
22. Gilmore, *Bad Nigger!* 81, 108
23. Havel V. Carby, *Reconstructing Womanhood: The Emergence of the Afro-American Woman Novelist* (New York: Oxford University Press, 1987), 18. A number of important recent theoretical articles have thoughtfully considered the relation between race and gender in history. They include Evelyn Brooks Higginbotham, "African-American Women's History and the Metalanguage of Race," *Signs* 17 (December 1992): 251–74; Iris Berger, Elsa Barkely Brown, and Nancy A. Heweitt, "Symposium – Intersections and Collision Courses: Women, Blacks, and Workers Confront Gender, Race, and Class," *Feminist Studies* 18 (Summer 1992): 283–326; and Gerda Lemer, "Reconceptualizing Differences Among Women," *Journal of Women's History* 1 (Winter 1990): 106–22. Two fine articles utilizing these sorts of approaches are Laura F. Edwards, "Sexual Violence, Gender, Reconstruction, and the Extension of Patriarchy in Granville County, North Carolina," *North Carolina Historical Review* 68 (July 1991): 237–60; and Ruth Feldstein, "'I wanted the Whole World to See': Race, Gender, and Constructions of Motherhood in the Death of Emmett Till," in *Not June Cleaver; Women and Gender in Postwar America, 1945–1960,* ed. Joanne Meyerowitz, (Philadelphia: Temple University Press, 1994).
24. For a cross-cultural anthropological discussion, see David D. Gilmore, *Manhood in the Making: Cultural Concepts of Masculinity* (New Haven, Conn.:Yale University Press, 1990).
25. For two otherwise useful examples, see Mark C, Carnes, *Secret Ritual and Manhood in Victorian America* (New Haven, Conn.: Yale University Press,

1989), and Jeffrey P. Hantover, "The Boy Scouts and the Validation of Masculinity," in *The American Man*, ed. Elizabeth H. Pleck and Joseph H. Pleck (Englewood Cliffs, N.J.: Prentice-Hall, 1980), 285–302.

26. Peter G. Filene, *Him/Her/Self: Sex Roles in Modern America* (Baltimore: Johns Hopkins University Press, 1986), 70.
27. Two examples of this approach are Michael C. Adams, *The Great Adventure: Male Desire and the Coming of World War I* (Bloomington: University of Indiana Press, 1990); and Filene, *Him/Her/Self.* For debates over whether or not there was a "masculinity crisis," see, for example, Filene, *Him/Her/Self*, 69–93; Michael S. Kimmel, "The Contemporary 'Crisis' of Masculinity in Historical Perspective," in *The Making of Masculinities*, ed. Harry Brod (Boston: Allen and Unwin, 1987), 121–54; Margaret Marsh, "Suburban Men and Masculine Domesticity," *American Quarterly* 40 (June 1988): 165–86, and Clyde Griffen, "Reconstructing Masculinity from the Evangelical Revival to the Waning of Progressivism: A Speculative Synthesis," in *Meanings for Manhood: Constructions of Masculinity in Victorian America*, ed. Mark C. Canres and Clyde Griffen (Chicago: University of Chicago Press, 1990), 183–204.
28. Two fine examples of this approach are Donna Haraway, *Primate Visions: Gender, Race, and Nature in the World of Modern Science* (New York: Routledge, 1989), and Mary Poovey, *Uneven Developments: The Ideological Work of Gender in Mid-Victorian England* (Chicago: University of Chicago Press, 1988).
29. For a more complete discussion of this approach to gender, see Teresa de Lauretis, *Technologies of Gender: Essays on Theory, Film, and Fiction* (Bloomington: University of Indiana Press, 1987), 1–30. See also Judith Butler, *Gender Trouble: Feminism and the Subversion of Identity* (New York: Routledge, 1990); Michel Foucault, *The History of Sexuality, vol. 1: An Introduction* (New York: Vintage, 1978); Denise Riley, *Am I That Name? Feminism and the Category of "Women in History"* (New York: Macmillan, 1988); Joan Wallach Scott, *Gender and the Politics of History* (New York: Columbia University Press, 1988); and Joan W. Scott, "Experience," in *Feminists Theorize the Political*, ed. Judith Butler and Joan W. Scott (New York: Routledge, 1992), 22–40.
30. Gilmore, *Bad Nigger!* 14; Roberts, *Papa Jack*, 74.
31. Roberts, *Papa Jack*, 66–7, 160–1.
32. Roberts, *Papa Jack*, 124–6.
33. Jack Johnson, *Jack Johnson is a Dandy: An Autobiography* (New York: Chelsea House, 1969), 22: Roberts, *Papa Jack*, 185–214.
34. Roberts, *Papa Jack*, 54–67, 122.

CHAPTER 8

The Sanctity of Sunday Football: Why Men Love Sports

Douglas Hartmann

My father, a no-nonsense grade school principal, had little time for small talk, contemplation, or leisure—with one major exception: sports. He spent Sunday afternoons watching football games on television, passed summer evenings listening to Jack Buck announce St. Louis Cardinals baseball games, and took me to every sporting event in town. He coached all the youth sports his children played, and spent hours calculating team statistics, diagramming new plays, and crafting locker room pep talks. Though never a great athlete, his high school varsity letters were displayed in his basement work area; just about the only surefire way to drag dad out of the house after a long day at work was to play "a little catch." Sports were one of the few topics he ever joked about with other men.

My father's fascination with sports was not unique. Though women are increasingly visible throughout the sporting world, more men than women play sports, watch sports and care about sports. Is it any wonder that corporate advertising campaigns, drinking establishments, and movements such as the Promise Keepers all use sports to appeal to men? Or that sports figures so prominently in many books and movies dealing with men and masculinity in America? Nevertheless, there is surprisingly little serious reflection about why this is the case. When asked why so many men are so obsessed with sports, most people—regardless of their gender or their attitudes about sports—say something to the effect that men are naturally physical and competitive, and that sports simply provide an outlet for these inherently masculine traits.

To sociologists, however, men love playing, watching, and talking sports because modern, Western sports—dominated as they are by men and by values and behaviors that are traditionally regarded as masculine—provide a unique place for men to think about and develop their masculinity, to make themselves men, or at least one specific kind of man.

WHERE BOYS BECOME MEN

Ask sports enthusiasts why they participate in sports and you are likely to get a wide variety of answers. "Because it is fun and exciting," some respond. Others say it is because they need the exercise and want to stay physically fit. Still others talk about sports providing them a way to relax and unwind, or about the thrill of competition—these responses are especially common for that large percentage of sports lovers whose "participation" mainly takes the form of being a fan or watching sports on television. These are important parts of sports' value, but they do not really explain why men are, on average, more likely to be involved in sports than women.

For many men, the love of sports goes back to childhood. Sports provided them, as young boys and teens, with a reason to get together, to engage with other boys (and men), and in doing so to begin defining what separates boys from girls: how to act like men. Barrie Thorne's study of grammar school playgrounds illustrates the phenomenon. Thorne finds that pre-adolescent boys and girls use recreation on the schoolyard to divide themselves along gender lines. How they play—for example, running around or quiet games—Thorne suggests, distinguishes male and female child behavior. As they get older, kids become more aware of these distinctions and increasingly use sex-segregated athletics to discuss and act out gender differences. Gary Alan Fine, in *With the Boys*, describes how much of the learning that happens in Little League baseball involves being tough and aggressive and dealing with injuries and other setbacks; and in off-the-field conversations young ballplayers learn about sex and about what it means to be a man as opposed to a "dork," a "sissy" or a "fag."

When Michael Messner interviewed retired athletes and asked them how they initially got involved with sports, they told him it had little to do with any immediate or natural attraction to athletics and was really based upon connecting to other boys and men. "The most important thing was just being out there with the rest of the guys—being friends," said one. Sports, according to Messner, "was something 'fun' to do with fathers, older brothers, uncles and eventually with same-aged peers."

Girls start playing sports for similar reasons, and children of both genders join in other activities, such as choir or community service, for social purposes, too. (Many boys and girls start to drop out of sports at about ages 9 or 10—when the sports they play become increasingly competitive and require them to think of themselves primarily as athletes.) What is distinctive about the experience of boys and young men in sports, however, is that the sporting world is organized and run primarily by men, and that athletic activities require attitudes and behaviors that are typically understood to be masculine.

Of course, not all boys play sports, and boyhood and adolescent experiences in sports are not uniformly positive. A great deal of the sociological research in this area focuses on the downside of youth sports participation. Donald Sabo, for example, has written extensively about the pain and violence, both physical and psychological, experienced by many boys who compete in athletics. And Harry Edwards has long argued that over-investing in sports can divert poor and minority youth from more promising avenues of upward mobility. But, despite the harsh realities, sports remains one of the few socially approved settings in which boys and men, and fathers and sons, can express themselves and bond with each other.

SPORT AS A MASCULINE ENTERPRISE

Once boys and girls separate in physical play, it does not take long for gendered styles of play to emerge. Study after study confirms what most soccer moms and dads already know: boys' athletics tend to be more physical and aggressive and put more emphasis on winning, being tough in the face of adversity, and dealing with injuries and pain. Even in elementary school, Thorne finds boys take up far more of the physical space of the playground with their activities than girls, who tend to play (and talk about their play) in smaller spaces and clusters.

People debate whether there is a physiological component to these differences, but two points are clear. First, parents, coaches, and peers routinely encourage such intensity among boys in youth sports. More than a few single mothers bring their boys to the teams I coach out of concern that their sons are insufficiently tough or physical because they lack a male influence. Messner writes about how he learned—against his inclinations—to throw a ball overhand with his elbow tucked in because his father did not want him to "throw like a girl." Stories about overly competitive, physically abusive coaches may be overplayed in the American media, but in many ways they are the inevitable consequence of the emphases many parents express.

Second, the behaviors and attitudes valued in men's and boys' athletics are not just about sports, but about masculinity more generally. The inherent connection of sports to the body, physical activity and material results, the emphasis on the merit of competing and winning, the attention to rules, sportsmanship and team play, on the one hand, and gamesmanship, outcomes and risk, on the other, are not just the defining aspects of male youth sport culture, but conform to what many men (and women) believe is the essence and value of masculinity. Female reporters, homosexual athletes, and men who challenge the dominant culture of men's sports—especially in the sacred space of the locker room—quickly learn that sports are not just dominated by men but also dominated by thinking and habits understood to be masculine (in opposition to the more nurturing values of compromise, cooperation, sympathy, understanding, and sharing typically associated with femininity). If the military is the quintessential institution of Western masculinity, then sports is surely a close second.

The notion that sports is a masculine enterprise is closely connected with the development of modern Western sports. As historians have detailed, middle- and upper-class men used sports in the 19th and early-20th centuries to present and protect their particular notions of masculinity in both schools and popular culture (the classic literary expression being *Tom Brown's School Days*, a 19th-century English story of boarding school boys' maturation through hard-nosed sports). The media is a critical part of perpetuating sports' masculine ethos today, because most adults participate in sports as spectators and consumers. Not only are female athletes and women's sports downplayed by most sports coverage, but the media accentuates the masculinity of male athletes. For example, Hall of Fame pitcher Nolan Ryan's media coverage, according to a study by Nick Trujillo, consistently described him in terms of the stereotypical American man: powerful, hard-working, family patriarch, a cowboy and a symbol of heterosexual virility. Such images not only define an athlete's personal qualities but legitimate a particular vision of masculinity.

The authority of the masculine ethos is underlined by the fact that so many female athletes believe they can receive no higher compliment than to be told they "play like a man." Many feminists cringe at the irony of such sentiments. But they also realize that, while the explosion of women in sports has challenged their male dominance (2.5 million girls and young women participated in interscholastic sport in 2003, up from 300,000 in 1972—before Title IX's federal mandate for gender equality), women's sports have essentially been based upon the same single-minded, hyper-competitive masculine model. Not surprisingly, they are witnessing the emergence of the same kinds of problems—cheating, physical and emotional stress, homophobia, eating disorders—that have long plagued men's sports.

SPORTS AND MAINTAINING MASCULINITY

As the men Messner interviewed became more committed to being athletes, they began to construct identities and relationships that conformed to—and thus perpetuated—sport's masculine values. Athletes are so bound up with being men that when, in his initial interviews, Messner inadvertently referred to them as "ex-athletes," his interviewees responded as if he were taking away their identities, their very manhood. A professional baseball player expressed a similar sentiment when I asked how he dealt with his time on the disabled list last summer because of a serious arm injury: "I'd throw wiffle balls left-handed to my eight-year-old son—and I had to get him out! Just so I could feel like a man again."

Of course, few men participate in sports with the intensity of professional athletes. Those who cannot move up the competitive ladder can still participate in other ways—in recreational sports, in coaching, and perhaps, most of all, in attending sporting events, watching sports on television, and buying athletic gear and apparel. Indeed, it is in being a fan (derived from *fanatic*) that the male slant of sports is clearest. While women often follow sports, their interest tends to be driven by social ends, such as being with family or friends. Male spectators are far more likely to watch events by themselves, follow sports closely, and be affected by the outcomes of games and the performance of their favored teams and athletes. The basic explanation is similar to the one developed out of sports activity studies: Just as playing sports provides many boys and young men with a space to become men, watching sports serves many men as a way to reinforce, rework, and maintain their masculinity—in these cases, through vicarious identification with masculine pursuits and idealized men. Writing of his obsession with 1950s football star Frank Gifford in *A Fan's Notes*, novelist Fredrick Exley explained: "Where I could not, with syntax, give shape to my fantasies, Gifford could with his superb timing, his uncanny faking, give shape to his." "I cheered for him with inordinate enthusiasm," Exley wrote, because he helped me find "my place in the competitive world of men . . . each time I heard the roar of the crowd, it roared in my ears as much for me as for him."

It was no accident that Exley chose to write about football. With its explicit appropriation of the rhetoric and tactics of combat, the sport supplanted baseball as the most popular spectator sport in the United States in the 1970s. Football's primary ideological salience, according to Messner, "lies in its ability . . . to symbolically link men of diverse ages and socioeconomic backgrounds. . . . Interacting with other men and interacting with them in this male-dominated space . . . [is] a way to assert and confirm one's own maleness. . . ." Being with other men allows males to affirm their masculine identity. Listen to today's sports talk radio. These programs are not only sophomorically masculine, many of them serve as little men's communities unto themselves: Tiger fan Jack; Mike from Modesto; Jay the Packer's guy—even teams' announcers have unique personalities and identities, fostering the impression that this is an actual club where all the guys know each other.

The salience of sports as a medium to validate masculinity may be best illustrated when it is taken away. Journalist Susan Faludi reported on what happened when the original Cleveland Browns football team left town to become the Baltimore Ravens. The mostly working-class men who occupied the section of seats in Cleveland called the "Dawg Pound" talked about the team's departure with an overwhelming sense of loss and powerlessness. As it often is for former athletes, it was as if they'd had their manhood taken from them. In tearful media interviews, John "Big Dawg" Thompson compared the team's departure to witnessing his best friend die in the hospital.

SPORTS AS "CONTESTED TERRAIN"

Critics of sports' heavy masculinity (most scholars doing work in this area are critics) have focused on its neglect or even exclusion of women. The way that golf outings perpetuate the privileges men enjoy in the corporate world is a frequent example. Others have gone so far as to suggest that the powerful appeal of sports for men arises because sports provide them at least symbolic superiority in a world in which men's real authority is in decline. As columnist and former professional basketball player Mariah Burton Nelson put it in the deliberately provocative title of her popular 1994 book, "The stronger women get, the more men love football."

In recent years, sociologists of sports have also begun to identify tensions within the masculine culture of athletics. Looking at Great Britain's soccer stars, for example, Garry Whannel has studied how the hedonism of the "new lad lifestyle" (as represented by players like David Beckham) rubs up against the disciplined masculinity traditionalists perceive to be necessary for international football success. Messner, for his part, has shown how "high status" men (white and from middle-class backgrounds) and "low status" men differently understood themselves as athletes. The former tended to transfer what they learned in sports about being men to pursuing success in other spheres, such as education and career. Men from lower status backgrounds saw sports as their only hope for success as a man—an accomplishment that the higher status men looked down upon as a narrow, atavistic type of masculinity. Expanding from this, some scholars have demonstrated that in popular culture the masculinity of African-American athletes is often exaggerated and linked to racial stereotypes about violence, risk and threat. Basketball star Dennis Rodman, for example, gained notoriety by playing on his persona as a "bad" ball player. While problematic in many respects, these images of black masculinity can also provide African-American men with unique opportunities for personal advancement and broader political visibility (as I have suggested in my work on the 1968 black Olympics protest movement).

Such research has led many scholars to see sports not only as a place where mainstream masculine culture is perpetuated, but also a place where it is challenged and possibly changed. These issues have played out clearly in the debates over the implementation of Title IX legislation for women's equal access to sports. While still hotly contested (as evidenced by the recent controversy surrounding the all-male Augusta National Golf Club, as well as speculation that the legislation may be challenged in court by the Bush administration), Title IX has transformed men's relationship to sports, to women, and even to masculinity itself. Sports' most vital social function with respect to masculinity is to provide a separate space for men to discuss—often indirectly, through evaluations of favorite players or controversial incidents—what it is to be a real man. And that space is increasingly shared with women.

Some scholars envision new, more humane or even feminine sports—marked less by an emphasis on winning, record-setting and spectatorship, and more by open participation, enjoyment and fitness. Cross-cultural studies of sports show that these are real possibilities, that sports are not "naturally" and inherently masculine as Americans have long assumed. Sexism and homophobia, for example, have never been a real problem in Chinese sports, anthropologist Susan Brownell explains, because sports emerged there as a low-status activity that more powerful men felt no special compulsion to control or participate in. As a consequence, it is widely believed that a skilled female practitioner of kung fu should be able to defeat stronger but less-skilled men. At the same time, Brownell points out, the current proliferation of Western, Olympic-style sports in China seems to be contributing to the redefinition of gender roles there nearer the pattern of Western sports and masculinity.

PLAYING DEEPLY

In a famous paper on cockfighting in Bali, American anthropologist Clifford Geertz used the term "deep play" to capture the way fans make sense of such competitions as the cockfight, cricket or American football. As passionate and articulate as they may be, these enthusiasts generally do not attempt to justify their pursuits. Instead, they downplay the significance of sports as separate from the serious concerns of real life. We can learn a great deal from such play, Geertz said, if we think about it as an "art form" which helps us figure out who people really are and what they really care about. Similarly, American men who love sports may not be able to fully articulate and understand how it is part of their being men, but their passion for sports can certainly help us understand them and their masculinity.

This peculiar, "deep play" understanding of sports makes it difficult for most men to recognize or confront the costs and consequences that may come with their sports obsessions. But in many ways isn't this true of masculine culture in general? It makes male advantages and masculine values appear so normal and "natural" that they can hardly be questioned. Therein may lie the key to the puzzle connecting men and the seemingly innocent world of sports: they fit together so tightly, so seamlessly that they achieve their effects—learning to be a man, male bonding, male authority and the like—without seeming to be doing anything more than tossing a ball or watching a Sunday afternoon game.

RECOMMENDED RESOURCES

Birrell, Susan and Cheryl L. Cole, eds. *Women, Sport and Culture*. Champaign, IL: Human Kinetics, 1994. A collection of feminist critiques of sport that includes several influential contributions on men and masculinity.

Brownell, Susan. *Training the Body for China: Sports in the Moral Order of the People's Republic*. Chicago: University of Chicago Press, 1995. The chapters on sex, gender, and the body offer a fascinating cross-cultural contrast, and provide an introduction to sports in the nation that will host the 2008 Olympics.

Burstyn, Varda. *The Rites of Men: Manhood, Politics and the Culture of Sport*. Toronto: University of Toronto Press, 1999. The most comprehensive treatment of the social, cultural, and historical forces that account for the relationship between men and sports in modern society.

Fine, Gary Alan. *With the Boys: Little League Baseball and Preadolescent Culture*. Chicago: University of Chicago Press, 1987. A pioneering field study from a noted sociologist of culture.

Kelley, Robin D. G. "Playing for Keeps: Pleasure and Profit on the Postindustrial Playground," pp. 195–231 in Wahneema Lubiano, ed., *The House that Race Built: Black Americans, U.S. Terrain*. New York: Pantheon, 1997. An ethnographically informed treatment of the opportunities basketball presents to inner-city African-American men produced by the country's preeminent historian of black popular culture.

Klein, Alan M. *Little Big Men: Bodybuilding Subculture and Gender Construction*. Albany, NY: State

University of New York Press, 1993. A vivid ethnography of competitive body builders on the West Coast that draws upon Robert Connell's seminal critique of the intersection of men's bodies, identities and sexualities in masculine culture.

Messner, Michael. *Taking the Field: Women, Men, and Sports.* Minneapolis, MN: University of Minnesota Press, 2002. The latest book from the leading scholar in the field. It exposes the ways in which men and women together use sports to define gender differences.

Pronger, Brian. *The Arena of Masculinity: Sports, Homosexuality and the Meaning of Sex.* London: St. Martin's Press, 1990. Pronger explores the problematic connections between gender and sexuality in sport, highlighting its libidinal dimensions.

CHAPTER 9

Being 'Good at Sport': Talent, Ability and Young Women's Sporting Participation

Sheryl Clark

INTRODUCTION

The participation of young women, a social group identified as 'under-represented' in sport in general, has often been deemed problematic and thus targeted for intervention (Bennett, 2000; Kirk, 2000). Yet, recent feminist research has also demonstrated growth in the levels of intense commitment and skill demonstrated by female athletes participating at high levels of competition (Adams et al., 2005; Scraton et al., 1999; Theberge, 2003). Widespread achievements in women's sport have been used to argue that sport is now largely commensurate with the construction of active young femininities. Azzarito (2010) defines these new 'alpha femininities' as fit, healthy and achievement-oriented identities that girls are increasingly able to take up. This article suggests that such discourses of female sporting achievement are complicated by social constructs of 'ability' as a highly gendered and thus discriminatory sorting mechanism. The girls' experiences reveal the importance of ability discourses or 'being good at sport' as framing their decisions and investments in sport and physical activity.

This emphasis on sporting achievement can be situated in relation to broader constructs of 'talent' and 'ability' within contemporary youth sporting initiatives. As Green (2010: 3) notes, youth sport has 'always served as a conveyor belt for elite sport, showcasing able and talented youth with potential to succeed'. As young people are often positioned as future Olympic and sporting hopefuls, their participation in sport and the identification of young talent remain pressing goals at both local and national policy levels in the UK (Collins and Buller, 2003; DCSF, 2008; Houlihan and Green, 2006). Such strategies may uncomfortably straddle tensions between aims of increased overall participation and those of elite talent identification (MacPhail et al., 2003). Current government policy, such as the Physical Education and Sport Strategy (DCSF, 2008), demonstrates little concern for equity in sport with proposals to replace the wide network of established School Sport Partnerships in Britain with an 'Olympic-style school sport competition' (Gove, 2010).[1]

Regardless of such discrepancies, the focus on youth talent identification remains a strong incentive at the level of both practice and policy. Talent identification programmes that see talent as an innate and identifiable classification are backed up by sophisticated scientific discourses rooted in biometrics, psychology, and intensive training (Peirce 2009). Such discourses serve to reinforce the focus on elite talent development, which has been described as currently dominant in terms of 'funding, facilities and coaching' in youth sport (MacPhail et al., 2003: 252).

This article is concerned with the specifically gendered consequences of ability designations for a group of young women interested in sport. It contributes to recent work that has sought to question the straightforward use of 'ability' as a sorting mechanism within youth sport (Evans et al., 2007; Hay and Macdonald, 2010; Wellard, 2006, 2007). This body of work reveals the ways in which categories of 'ability' are constructed and perpetuated within youth sport and PE [Physical Education], thus setting up juxtapositions between 'able' and 'non-able' participants as well as individualizing success or failure at sport. Ability designations are here seen as inevitably gendered and otherwise normative, thereby creating inequalities for young people's participation and a sense of 'lack' in relation to sporting achievement (Probyn, 2000: 20). Researchers have noted feelings of shame, humiliation and anxiety as common affective traces of PE and sporting experiences described by adults who did not 'fit' the performative and corporeal requirements of school sport and PE lessons (Ennis, 1996; Evans et al., 2007). Influential policy documents such as *Sport: Raising the Game* (DNH, 1995) have in recent years emphasized the competitive elements of PE, thereby placing an increased emphasis on performance and ability within youth sport (Houlihan and Green, 2006). This emphasis was certainly relevant to the girls in this research as they struggled to make sense of their sporting identities over the transition to secondary school.

ABILITY AND GIRLS' SPORTING IDENTITIES

Distinctions between 'able' and 'non-able' participants can be seen to relate to specific social and political meanings in and around sport, gender and young people's participation, which circulate through a range of discourses. As Evans et al. (2007) argue, such distinctions are important since they relate to the allocation of resources as well as according value to specific bodies. Importantly, they question whether there is 'a dominant "ability" or "image" of value, such that some students are unable to recognize themselves as having a "body" or "self" or "ability" of any value?' (2007: 52). The discourse of 'being good at sport' might therefore be seen as representing particular ideals of sporting participation and as containing particular signifiers about who might embody such an identity and what physical performances this requires.

A range of feminist work has demonstrated the ways in which the equation of sporting ability with dominant discourses of masculinity has served to position women's bodies as inferior sporting participants (Choi, 2000; Hargreaves, 1994; Scraton, 1992). Cockburn and Clarke's (2002) research revealed that girls felt it necessary to disinvest from the masculinized connotations of physical education through overt performances of 'girliness' in order to construct their young femininities. Evans (2006) further suggests that any disjunction girls felt in PE was also experienced as an embodied sense of incapacity – that they were unable to physically perform to the standard of ability felt to be required.

Such insights demonstrate the importance of the body and physical capacity in girls' sports participation. However, there remains work to be carried out on our understanding of how sporting ability is embodied by young women within broader social contexts. The research carried out also demonstrates the operation of such processes over time as the girls made the transition to secondary school. I suggest that girls' embodied experiences within the sexually charged and highly regulated adolescent contexts of school and peer settings are particularly important to their sports participation. The study further demonstrates some of the ways these meanings interacted with the girls' physical sense of capacity as potential sporting participants. As the work of Young (2005) and Shilling (2004) has demonstrated, gendered bodies both shape and are shaped by dominant discourses of gendered practices, thus constructing many women's and girls' lack of a sense of capacity or 'ability' in relation to sport.

The research demonstrates how achievement discourses in women's sport are complicated by ability constructs. I argue that current emphases of youth sport on 'talent' and 'ability' may be particularly exclusionary for young women as they operate within the gendered contexts of school and peer settings. Girls' identities within their peer-regulated school and sporting contexts are seen to interact with their sporting participation in specific ways, often mediating against sporting identities as an undervalued or relegated form of identification. Girls often struggled to see their bodies as having any 'value' within these specific contexts as they negotiated the range of physical and sexual meanings circulating around their bodies. The findings demonstrate how processes of team selection, coaching emphases on performance outputs and ongoing expectations of athletic development were particularly constraining for girls' participation as they operated within the gendered context of school and peer settings. These processes can therefore be seen to operate as discriminatory mechanisms of exclusion from sports participation for girls. I focus here on the experiences of three girls involved in the research who were identified as 'good at sport' in primary school and the specific processes that framed their ongoing (dis)-engagement.

THE RESEARCH

The research for this study entailed a longitudinal, qualitative investigation (McLeod and Thomson, 2009) into girls' participation in sport and physical activity. This involved tracing the sports participation of six particularly physically active girls over a period of four years as they moved from Year 5 (10–11 years) to Year 8 (13–14 years) in schools at divergent locations across London, England. Within the article I focus on three of the girls in particular: Lindsay, Lucy and Spirit.

Lindsay's parents had emigrated from Pakistan to the UK before she was born and their subsequent loss of status and income was compensated by a particular interest in their children's schooling and career aspirations. Lindsay had attended an inner city, ethnically diverse comprehensive primary school where she excelled in both schoolwork and a variety of sports. She then carried on to Adlington Secondary School,[2] a mixed-sex comprehensive school nearby.

Spirit and Lucy both attended the same primary school in a sought-after catchment area on the outskirts of London. Spirit went on to attend Folkestone Secondary, a fee-paying, selective, independent day school nearby. Spirit took up running in Year 4 and was subsequently identified as 'talented' in this particular sport.

Lucy went on to attend Wellington Gardens, a high-achieving comprehensive girls' secondary school. She came from an active, middle-class family whose interests centred on a range of outdoor activities including climbing, canoeing and involvement in Scouts with her three brothers.

Semi-structured interviews were held with each girl twice yearly from Year 5 to 8 of her schooling. During the interviews we talked about girls' sports involvement, friendships, schoolwork and other interests with a view to exploring their ongoing gender constructions. This long-term and intimate involvement in the girls' lives allowed me to gain important insights into the shifting, complex processes framing girls' investments in sporting and gendered identities. When the girls were in Year 8, I also distributed a questionnaire in each girls' PE lesson ($N = 54$).

THE IMPORTANCE AND DIFFICULTY OF 'BEING GOOD AT SPORT'

The girls involved in the research had all enjoyed sport at primary school and had participated enthusiastically in a range of physical activities including playtime chase games, cross-country running, football, netball and numerous outdoor activities. Studies have suggested that adolescence, and particularly the transition to upper secondary school, are key points at which girls are likely to drop out or to disengage in sport and physical education (Flintoff and Scraton, 2001; Green et al., 2007; WSFF, 2007). When I did the last set of interviews with the girls in Year 8, most had given up on sport and were noticeably less invested in PE. Despite enjoying football in primary school, Lindsay, like her peers from primary school, felt unable to continue with this participation. Lucy and Spirit continued with their sports participation, but they each had issues around coaching and club selection that differently affected their involvement and enjoyment. Coakley and White (1992: 21) suggest that young people make choices about their sports participation 'through a series of shifting, back and forth decisions made within the structural, ideological and cultural contexts of their worlds'. Participating in sports is often related to material and structural circumstances, yet girls increasingly related their sporting decisions to identity and the idea of 'being good at sport' and their (dis)identifications with this classification.

At this transition into adolescence, sport became more competitive and some girls felt that they were no longer 'good at sports' even if they had participated in a variety of physical activities during primary school and hoped to continue playing. In the questionnaire for Year 8 girls, I asked whether they had ever thought about trying out for a sports team. The class-wide responses suggested that ability or perceptions of ability played a key role in these decisions.

> Not very welcoming as they make you think that you can only go if you're good at it. (Questionnaire, Wellington Gardens)
>
> Yes, but I'm scared if everyone else is much better than me/more advanced.
>
> (Questionnaire, Adlington School)

Several girls' recurrent fear that they would not be 'good enough' can be related to overall feelings of both shame and pride that frequently characterize sports participation as 'a constant lack, or recurring incompleteness' of the athletic body (Probyn, 2000: 20). Girls' responses suggested an either/or positioning in which they felt compelled to align themselves according to estimations of their 'ability' and where the prospect of identifying with 'being good at sport' was increasingly tenuous.

NOT MAKING THE CUT

As the girls moved into secondary school they were presented with a new set of expectations around academics, extracurricular activities and social norms. The teams and sports clubs they might join at this transition often represented one of the first points at which overt competition could function to exclude them from participation, but they also served as messages about a girl's social identifications. 'Not making the cut' could have important implications both for a girl's physical inclusion and for her identity as an athlete and as a gendered subject in school.

In primary school Lucy was also an enthusiastic participant in the cross-country team, netball and rugby. In the hopes of continuing with her running as she moved into Year 7, she went along to Champions

Athletics Club, where both her twin brother and Spirit trained. Lucy quickly discovered that expectations at the club were very high and that they were unwilling to cater to her abilities. As her mother Mary described, 'although Lucy is quite a nice runner and she has stamina, she's not . . . fast' (Interview, September 2006). When I asked later in Year 8 about running, Lucy had decided that she preferred alternative sports that did not have initial sorting mechanisms.

> Lucy: Like running, you don't have to learn to run, you just sort of do it. But things like sailing or climbing or anything like that you have to learn the technique. So I prefer things like that 'cause you have to learn it and show your ability and things like that.
>
> Sheryl: Mmm.
>
> Lucy: Whereas with running it's just like 'right, you're really good you can go in the competition' or 'you're really rubbish, you can't'.
>
> (Interview, Year 8, November 2007)

Here Lucy is clearly critical of discriminatory sorting mechanisms and the process of exclusion she was subjected to at the running club. Lucy recognizes the club's practice of accepting girls who met a certain standard as a fixed notion of ability in which being a good runner is a matter of innate talent rather than a result of practice or training. Lucy expresses a preference for outdoor sports such as sailing or climbing where she envisions more scope for improvement and where she suggests she would have the opportunity to prove herself through 'learning the technique' and thus 'showing your ability'.

In this excerpt Lucy seems to view ability as a bodily skill that can be learned over time but she is also aware that certain sports cannot or will not cater for this process of development. This affects her view of running as something 'you don't have to learn'. In contrast, Lucy had previously described the physical pleasure of running as an experience of 'getting the energy out of me' (Interview, Year 6, 2005), an embodied joy unrelated to a particular performance goal. Thus, ability designations were embodied for Lucy as they served to displace the previous joy of running through movement and energy sensation towards a performative assessment that measures Lucy's physical capacity or speed as unvalued or lacking in value.

Lucy's enthusiasm for running, her stamina and her commitment were unimportant to the running club, who evaluated talent through a lens of fixed ability, were intent on placing high in league standings and in developing local champions. MacPhail et al. (2003: 265) observe the increasing trend towards young people's participation in adult-organized community-based sport and the subsequent need for research into children's experiences of these settings. Adult investments in notions of 'success' or 'failure' alongside perceived needs to uphold the status of the club or team may create exclusionary experiences for young people while they are constructing self-identities that may or may not include sport in the future.

Lucy's experiences of team sports are clearly mediated by adult gatekeepers who are seen to be inflexible in their estimations of ability and the potential for development. Lucy's claim supports her earlier account of running, where a pre-existing ability is not only valued but is also a prerequisite for participation. School sporting accomplishments seem to have been taken up as forms of distinction within the increasingly competitive league tables and standings schools find themselves subject to as well. Lucy's comprehensive [school] overtly competed with the private all-girls' schools nearby and, in line with its perceptions of acceptable and 'ladylike' behaviour, the school encouraged sporting participation but did not allow girls to run around or shout at playtime.

Meanwhile, the boys' school next to it where Lucy's brothers attended made no such restrictions. Within team selection processes, the emphasis on ability took precedence over a girl's enthusiasm or willingness to take part and impacted not only on Lucy's enjoyment and opportunity to play but also on her identity as a potential sports participant. Ability had become the ultimate arbiter of participation and, concurrently, of self-worth. As Lucy puts it, 'you're rubbish, you can't', thus lowering both her motivation and constructing her identity as a 'non-able' participant.

'I'M NOT A GOOD RUNNER ANY MORE'

Categorizations such as 'good at sport' or 'talented' can be seen to be constructed through their opposition to a binary Other – 'bad at sport', thus setting up juxtapositions between participants and forms of participation. Competence plays a key role in individuals to continue sports participation (Coakley and White, 1992) and young people who felt that they were 'good' at something were more likely to carry on as it took on a central role in their lives, forming part of their self-identifications.

When I met her in Year 5 (age 10), Lindsay explained that she would sometimes play basketball and 'champ' [also known as foursquare] at playtime. She took up football under the guidance of a supportive teacher who set aside a girls' pitch time on the playground that had previously been male dominated. Similar to other girls, Lindsay described primary school and the games she had played there as more 'fun' and she recounted, 'In primary we played football, all the girls played football and we all had our own pitch' (Interview, Year 7, June 2007). Lindsay had also enjoyed a high standing amongst her classmates and had been avidly cheered by both male and female peers during class sporting competitions. During our Year 7 and 8 interviews, Lindsay lamented that male classmates no longer paid attention to her, something she connected with her wearing of a headscarf. She was the only Muslim girl in her secondary school form room and this contributed to her sense of difference, as she alluded to in our interviews. Lindsay, along with other girls in the study, expressed a sense of betrayal from boys who had previously been their friends but were now 'too into football' to play with them and more interested in girls' physical appearance.

> Lindsay: But boys talk about like girls having big tits [laughs, embarrassed].
>
> Sheryl: Do they?
>
> Lindsay: They go and hug those girls and it's like you're left out. And they go and hug them but if they don't come to you and hug you then you feel kind of like 'yeah, those boys don't like me and I shouldn't be with them'. Like I shouldn't be with these persons.
>
> Sheryl: Does it make you worry about the way you look?
>
> Lindsay: Yeah, it feels that um, maybe I've got a scarf on, that's why they don't come hug me or maybe I'm a bit too religious or blah, blah, blah.
>
> (Interview, Year 8, November 2007)

Lindsay's experience of not seeming to embody the valued physical attributes possessed by other girls contrasts with her relationships in primary school where she was often revered by male peers for her running and football abilities. The extract suggests some of the complex gendered contradictions for young women of wanting to feel noticed and valued, though not necessarily through the physical touching or 'hug' that is described. As Lindsay moved into Year 9 she stopped wearing her headscarf to school and began to invest more overtly in physical performances of a 'girly' femininity through specific clothing and use of makeup. Although physical attractiveness and sports participation were clearly commensurate for many girls at the school, a position of 'otherness' seemed to make such performances difficult to balance. Yet Lindsay's decisions around sport were also clearly related to a growing sense of her position in a larger competitive pool of physically active girls.

Before beginning secondary school, Lindsay's family had moved to another home outside the area and much further away. She continued to attend Adlington but this entailed long commutes and meant that she could not go to football training after school because of her parents' fears for her safety in travelling back. She was not selected for her class relay team on sports day and this seemed to reinforce her belief that she was no longer athletic or 'good at sport'.

> Sheryl: So what's changed?
>
> Lindsay: I'm not the most athletic girl.
>
> Sheryl: You're not? So is it difficult to think of yourself as a good runner still?
>
> Lindsay: I'm not a good runner any more.
>
> Sheryl: And has that stopped you from running?
>
> Lindsay: Yeah. 'Cause you know you can't run quick, fast enough, 'cause there's so many other girls in Year 8 that can run so fast and you feel like you can't do it.
>
> (Interview, Year 8, November 2007)

Similar to Lucy, Lindsay's experience of being rejected from the class relay team for sports day quickly translated into a negative self-belief and her identification as 'not a good runner any more'. Girls' self-belief in particular seemed to be subject to these external assessments, positioned as they were as already outside the particular norms of sports participation. Lindsay's experiences also suggest the added difficulties for girls who have been positioned outside the dominant constructions of sporting participation due to their racialized identities. The stereotypical association of Asian femininity and passivity has often problematized Asian girls' participation in sport, forcing them to challenge both racialized and gendered perceptions of their abilities and interests (Dwyer, 1998).

The coupling of feminized humility and ever-increasing pools of talent seems to work against girls' positive valuations of their sporting abilities. Within a competitive model of sports it was often difficult for girls to believe in their abilities, even if they were competing at high levels, since there would always be another girl who was 'better' or as Lindsay states, 'so many other girls who can run so fast'. Girls sometimes mentioned specific moments where the idea that they were 'bad' or 'rubbish' at sport had been cemented – often by an adult assessment of their ability. Following Shilling's (2004) understanding of embodied physical capital, negative sporting experiences and public humiliations can quickly translate into negative self-belief and decreased bodily capacity. Both for Lindsay and Lucy, external assessments of their abilities and the process of selection leading to rejection served to constitute fixed and embodied 'unable' sporting identities. Both girls struggled to hold on to the identity of 'being good at sport' and therefore saw little reason to continue, thus investing their efforts and identifications elsewhere.

BEING IDENTIFIED AS 'TALENTED'

Commenting on the 'Excellence in Cities' programme aimed at challenging academically 'gifted' young people, Lucey and Reay (2002) note the burden of expectation placed on young people asked to carry the 'beacon of excellence'. Similarly, for young people identified as 'talented' within sports, expectations around their ongoing improvement in fulfilment of 'potential' can serve to create pressurized contexts. Spirit had described to me how she initially took up running in a bid to lose weight, a goal that had turned compulsive at one point as she simultaneously restricted her food intake. The gendered association between weight loss and physical activity for many young women (Evans et al., 2008) demonstrates again some of the complex discourses that often frame girls' participation in sport.

In Year 7 Spirit was selected to join Champions Athletics Club based on her running performances in local races. While at primary school, she had been able to envision future participation and ongoing success in running and she told me that she hoped to become 'an Olympic runner one day' (Interview, Year 5, June 2005). Throughout primary school Spirit was involved in a wide number of extracurricular activities including basketball, karate and cross-country running. In Year 5 she was seen as one of the fastest runners in her class, thus gaining accolades from teachers and coaches, as well as interest from the youth running club.

In Year 7, Spirit's dreams of becoming an Olympic runner had been quickly dissolved by the running coach at her new club who bluntly informed the girls that none of their times would put them in position for future Olympic glory. Accordingly, Spirit noted her change in orientation towards running: 'But now I'm not doing it for fun anymore, now I'm doing it to get faster' (Interview, Year 7, December 2006). Spirit's orientation is reflective of research into young people's socialization into athletics clubs. MacPhail et al. (2003: 261) noted that boys and girls between 13 and 15 'viewed competition as increasingly important to them', representing a shift from an earlier orientation towards enjoyment and self-improvement.

Girls who were able to compete in elite sports teams seemed to have compelling reasons for continuing, often reinforced by adult expectations of ongoing improvement. This expectation could also create pressure to continue to succeed and perform in successive competitions. The celebration of 'PBs' (personal bests) in Spirit's running club meant that girls were under constant pressure to achieve more highly than they had before. Here Spirit describes her coach's reaction to her performance in the school-wide races.

> And he said to me 'Oh Spirit, I think you're over-training a bit now, that's why you lost' and I said '*I'm not allowed to come second for once?!*' It's really annoying. That's why I hate Mr Sebastian.
>
> (Interview, Year 6, December 2006)

The school-wide acknowledgement that Spirit was the 'fastest runner' in her year had worked to build up a series of expectations around her performances whereby her second place finish in the school races becomes noteworthy as insufficient or even 'losing'. Similarly at her running club, the coaches described Spirit's progress to me as 'disappointing' given her earlier performances. Expectations around Spirit's sporting performances were matched in intensity by those around her academic performances, creating a pressurized context for her ongoing achievements. Spirit keenly sensed the need to keep up her high grades alongside growing extracurricular commitments at school and had described to me the juggling act she performed in order to do so. The burdens, pressures and expectations of participating in a sports progamme of 'excellence' is reflected in research by Walkerdine et al. (2001), which has similarly demonstrated the intense pressure on some middle-class girls to perform across their various activities in outstanding achievements that are simultaneously normalized and expected.

DISCUSSION

The girls' experiences highlight some of the specifically gendered, classed and racialized processes that can impact on girls' sports participation. These included the type and ethos of the secondary school they attended, expectations from parents and coaches and access to teams in practical terms such as costs and transportation. Overall, the transition to secondary school marked a significant point where girls who had previously enjoyed sport were moved into more structured and competitive settings that acted as a sifting mechanism for their participation.

The research findings implicate three key processes in relation to ability that impacted on girls' participation at this important transition. The first of these was the process of team selection where ability designations formed a prerequisite for participation, motivation, and continued participation. Girls who decided to not even try out for sports teams on the assumption that they would not be selected were strongly swayed by these ability designations. These expectations created processes of either self-selected or imposed exclusion based on perceptions of ability across sporting contexts. This exclusion from sport was embodied as it presented a lack of opportunity to develop and improve for girls who had been convinced that they were 'rubbish at sports'.

The second key process was the progression into a larger pool of candidates as the girls moved into a larger school and a more widespread competitive base. It was compounded by the pressures of secondary school where wider expectations were made of the girls around academics and performing adolescent femininities in line with peer social groups. This combination of pressures proved too daunting for girls like Lucy and Lindsay, who attempted but were unable to continue with their sports participation. Although ability designations had proved motivating in primary school, they were unsustainable amidst other pressures.

Finally, girls such as Spirit who did continue with sport were faced with developmental models that placed expectations on their performances. Increased expectations may rest alongside academic commitments, thus creating a pressurized context for this participation. Developmental models also translated into persistent training and rising standards of performance making it ever more difficult for girls trying out new sports or to 'join in' at a later age.

Girls often seemed to regret the loss of physical activity in secondary school but felt powerless to change this. The forms of 'fun' experienced in earlier physical activity participation were not readily available at secondary school and girls therefore felt compelled to shift towards performance or fitness-oriented goals. The emphasis on performative targets such as speed, skill and weight/body size as 'measurable' outcomes might be seen to negate the possibility of other learning-oriented goals such as bodily pleasure, social experiences and even personal development.

CONCLUSION

At a point when the girls were constructing important ideas about both their physical abilities and their identities, schools and outside clubs were clearly implicated in routinely distinguishing young people's experiences, often resulting in exclusion. Here, sporting expectations were upheld by facilitating adults invested in particular models of sporting achievement both in and outside of school (Evans and Davies, 2004). The research demonstrates some of the ways in which secondary schools as spaces shut down possibilities for inclusion and enjoying or feeling as if one can be good at sport. Team selection proved particularly damaging to the girls' already fragile sporting identities in the hierarchical and selective ways they were structured. School teams could much more readily embrace democratic and participatory forms of inclusion that focus on all young people's potential and right to take part in physical activity. The girls came to see themselves and to position themselves in school spaces amidst the highly constraining and conflicting discourses of ability, gender and other social constructs that mediated their sporting participation, including body size and physical appearance. Sports participation was often seen to set girls apart from their peers and therefore the need to both prove one's physical abilities and to sustain social friendships and norms could be particularly difficult for girls.

The emphasis on adult models of sporting participation at this level meant that girls, no matter how much they enjoyed the physical activity, felt they had to make immediate decisions about whether they were 'good at sport' or not, thus dictating whether and which physical activities they continued to participate in. For the girls in this research, 'being good at sport' represented a fragile identity that could be easily interrupted or broken, even as this remained a requirement for much participation in sports. Paradoxically, this meant that girls often did not have the opportunity to disprove their believed incapacity as it became embodied in their sense of personal competency (Shilling, 2004). This has implications for the models of sporting participation that are made available to young people and suggests some of the possible gendered consequences of initiatives that attempt to identify and develop young talent.

The research also offers some insights into the ways in which more girls might become and stay physically active and involved in sports. Girls in particular seem to find it difficult to hold onto notions of ability and are therefore subject to exclusion and the constitution of 'unable' identities. This fragility suggests that girls may require ongoing support from adults and peers in sports settings that are both inclusive and encouraging in and outside of school. Lastly, adult sport gatekeepers were sometimes less attentive to the affective and social aspects of girls' participation. Such adults need to remain reflexive about their own investments in sporting success and failure as well as keeping in mind the social and friendship contexts of girls' participation. Encouraging girls to continue to take part in sport will require remaining sensitive to the social aspects of girls' activities while prioritizing young people's physical enjoyment in a spirit of equity and participation.

NOTES

1 At the time of writing, Michael Gove, the Education Minister, had 'backtracked' on the abolishing of School Sport Partnerships and proposed instead to phase out their funding over a longer period of time while remaining tied to the idea of an 'annual schools Olympics' (Gove, 2010).

2 Names of the schools and all participants are pseudonyms. The girls chose their own pseudonyms in Year 5.

REFERENCES

Adams N, Schmitke A and Franklin A (2005) Tomboys, dykes, and girly girls: Interrogating the subjectivities of adolescent female athletes. *Women's Studies Quarterly* 33(1&2): 17–32.

Azzarito L (2010) Future girls, transcendent femininities and new pedagogies: Toward girls' hybrid bodies? *Sport, Education and Society* 15(3): 261–75.

Bennett A (2000) The national action plan for women's and girls' sport and physical activity. *British Journal of Physical Education* 31(3): 6–8.

Choi YL (2000) *Femininity and the Physically Active Woman*. London: Routledge.

Coakley J and White A (1992) Making decisions: Gender and sport participation among British adolescents. *Sociology of Sport Journal* 9: 20–35.

Cockburn C and Clarke G (2002) 'Everybody's looking at you!': Girls negotiating the 'femininity deficit' they incur in physical education. *Women's Studies International Forum* 25(6): 651–65.

Collins M and Buller J (2003) Social exclusion from high-performance sport: Are all talented young sports people being given an equal opportunity of reaching the Olympic podium? *Journal of Sport and Social Issues* 27(4): 420–42.

DCSF (2008) *PE and Sport Strategy for Young People*. London: Department for Children, Schools and Families. Available at: www.teachernet.gov.uk/docbank/index.cfm?id(12416 (accessed 25 October 2008).

DNH (1995) *Sport: Raising the Game*. London: Department of National Heritage.

Dwyer C (1998) Contested identities: Challenging dominant representations of young British Muslim women. In: Skelton T and Valentine G (eds) *Cool Places: Geographies of Youth Culture*. London: Routledge, 50–65.

Ennis CD (1996) Students' experiences in sport-based physical education: [More than] apologies are necessary. *Quest* 48: 453–6.

Evans B (2006) 'I'd feel ashamed': Girls' bodies and sports participation. *Gender, Place and Culture* 13(5): 547–61.

Evans J and Davies B (2004) Introduction: Pedagogy, symbolic control, identity and health. In: Evans J, Davies B and Wright J (eds) *Body Knowledge and Control: Studies in the Sociology of Physical Education and Health*. London: Routledge, 1–12.

Evans J, Rich E, Allwood R and Davies B (2007) Being 'able' in a performative culture: Physical education's contribution to a healthy interest in sport? In: Wellard I (ed.) *Rethinking Gender and Youth Sport*. London: Routledge, 51–67.

Evans J, Rich E, Davies B and Allwood R (2008) *Education, Disordered Eating and Obesity Discourse: Fat Fabrications*. London: Routledge.

Flintoff A and Scraton S (2001) Stepping into active leisure? Young women's perceptions of active lifestyles and their experiences of school physical education. *Sport, Education and Society* 6(1): 5–21.

Gove M (2010) Open Letter to Baroness Sue Campbell, Youth Sport Trust.

Green K (2010) *Key Themes in Youth Sport*. Abingdon: Routledge.

Green K, Smith A, Thurston M and Lamb K (2007) Gender and secondary school national cur- riculum physical education: Change alongside continuity. In: Wellard I (ed.) *Rethinking Gender and Youth Sport*. London: Routledge.

Hargreaves J (1994) *Sporting Females: Critical Issues in the History of Women's Sport*. London: Routledge.

Hay P and Macdonald D (2010) Evidence for the social construction of ability in physical education. *Sport, Education and Society* 15(1): 1–18.

Houlihan B and Green M (2006) The changing status of school sport and physical education: Explaining the policy change. *Sport, Education and Society* 11(1): 73–92.

Kirk D (2000) Promoting girls' participation in physical education and sport: The girls in sport partnership project. *British Journal of Physical Education* 31(1): 27–9.

Lucey H and Reay D (2002) Carrying the beacon of excellence: Social class differentiation and anxiety at a time of transition. *Journal of Education Policy* 17(3): 321–36.

MacPhail A, Gorely T and Kirk D (2003) Young people's socialisation into sport: A case study of an athletics club. *Sport, Education and Society* 8(2): 251–67.

McLeod J and Thomson R (2009) *Researching Social Change: Qualitative Approaches*. London: Sage.

Peirce N (2009) How to build the perfect athlete. *Observer Sport Monthly* (October): 34–43.

Probyn E (2000) Sporting bodies: Dynamics of shame and pride. *Body and Society* 6(13): 13–28.

Scraton S (1992) *Shaping up to Womanhood: Gender and Girls' Physical Education*. Buckingham: Open University Press.

Scraton S, Fasting K, Pfister G and Bunuel Heras A (1999) It's still a man's game? The experi- ences of top-level European women footballers. *International Review for the Sociology of Sport* 34(2): 99–11.

Shilling C (2004) Physical capital and situated action: A new direction for corporeal sociology. *British Journal of Sociology of Education* 25(4): 473–87.

Theberge N (2003) 'No fear comes': Adolescent girls, ice hockey, and the embodiment of gender. *Youth and Society* 34(4): 497–516.

Walkerdine V, Lucey H and Melody J (2001) *Growing up Girl: Psychosocial Explorations of Gender and Class*. Basingstoke: Palgrave.

Wellard I (2006) Able bodies and sport participation: Social constructions of physical ability for gendered and sexually identified bodies. *Sport, Education and Society* 11(2): 105–19.

Wellard I (2007) Introduction. In: Bailey R (ed.) *Rethinking Gender and Youth Sport*. London: Routledge.

WSFF (2007) *It's Time: Future Forecasts for Women's Participation in Sport and Exercise*. London: Women's Sports and Fitness Foundation, 32.

Young, IM (2005) *On Female Body Experience: 'Throwing Like a Girl" and Other Essays*. New York: Oxford University Press.

CHAPTER 10

An Iron Man: The Body and Some Contradictions of Hegemonic Masculinity

Raewyn Connell

It is a basic proposition of the current research and political work that masculine character is socially constructed, not inherited with the Y chromosome. But it is now clear that the old understanding of how this construction occurred, a more or less smooth and consensual socialization into a unitary male role, is not adequate.

There are different kinds of masculine character within society that stand in complex relations of dominance over and subordination to each other. What in earlier views of the problem passed for the 'male sex role' is best seen as hegemonic masculinity, the culturally idealized form of masculine character (in a given historical setting), which may not be the usual form of masculinity at all. It is also clear that masculinities are constructed through processes that are often discontinuous or contradictory (and often experienced as such), for which the model of a 'socializing agency' will not work. This has been most clearly seen in psychoanalytic thinking about the formation of masculinity (Connell 1994).

In this chapter I hope to add to the understanding of hegemonic masculinity and its construction in personal life, by a case study of a champion sportsman. The case raises interesting questions about the interplay between the body and social process, and suggests some lines of thought about sport and its commercialization as a phenomenon of gender and class relations.

I hope also to illustrate the usefulness of the life-history method for studying these social processes. [. . .] Properly handled, the theorized life history can be a powerful tool for the study of social structures and their dynamics as they impinge on personal life and are reconstituted by personal action.

BEING A CHAMPION

Steve Donoghue is an 'iron man'. This deliberately pretentious phrase is a technical term in surf sports. The iron-man race at surf carnivals is an event involving a combination of swimming, running and surf-craft riding. Both short and long forms of the race exist; the long races may take four and a half hours to complete. In surf sports, this event occupies a position analogous to a combination of the marathon and the pentathlon in track and field. A champion of the iron-man event holds a great deal of prestige. Steve is one of a very small group of athletes who trade the Australian national championships among themselves.

Steve, in his twenties at the time he was interviewed, lives in a beachfront flat with his girlfriend. He gets up at 4.30 every morning to start his training, which takes four to five hours a day. When it is done he has the rest of the day to himself because he has no job. More exactly, his job is to be an iron man and to market himself as a sports personality.

The training schedule is rigorous and, at his level of performance, essential—as Steve explains in a fascinating passage of the interview:

> *The main thing . . . is the discipline and motivation side of it. [If] you can't put the five hours in every day, it doesn't matter how old you are—you're not going to win. You've got to have the talent, you've got to have the technique and the ability and everything—and the training is what counts really. Your natural ability only takes you so far, about 60 to 70 per cent of the way, and the rest is where the training comes in, and you've got to be able to. If you are 28 or 30 you have still got to have the time to train. [If you] haven't got business problems, or kids through marriage, or whatever, well, then you'll be right . . . just as long as you keep loving it, you can keep backing up and wanting to train and really feeling keen the whole time, you've got no troubles.*
>
> Where does the love come from?
>
> *I don't know. 1 love the beach. And I love the sun and everything to do with the water. The waves, the water. I love the idea—I've always loved this, even when 1 was at school—of being able to make a living out of sport. I have loved the idea of not having to work, like a strict nine to five set job, you know, like other people, being indoors . . . Five hours a day is still a lot but it is something which I enjoy that people are not telling me what to do. And there's not a set wage, if I go well I can really make a lot of money out of it. I just like that. I like everything to do with it really. I like the people I get involved with.*

This lyrical picture of pleasure and success in the sun and water is characteristic of Steve's self-presentation in the interview. Though there is ideology here, much of the feeling and tone is genuine enough; Steve has realized a schoolboy dream. It comes as something of a shock, then, to find that he also talks of his regime this way:

> *You're up at 4.30 to go training and that goes most of the day. And you are too tired to go out anyway and you've got to get your rest. It is a pretty disciplined sort of life. It's like being in jail.*

This sudden douche of cold water comes in the middle of a discussion about girlfriends. Steve notes that 'a lot of the guys don't have girlfriends'. It is just too hard to combine with training: 'The girl wants to go out with you all the time and, you know, party here and there.' This affects the athlete's performance. So Steve's coach 'doesn't like it, tries to put it down, tries to stop anything serious'. (The coach has a financial interest in his athlete's performance, although Steve does not mention this.)

Steve has a girlfriend, who drifts in and out during the interview. And that seems to be her status in Steve's life, too. She is given a clear message about what really counts for him:

> *Yes, I've got a girlfriend. I think there is no problem as long as you don't have to go out all the time, [as long as] they understand that, and you've got to take training first, and competition first. That's your living, that's your life. That's what I enjoy the most. It is hard, though . . .*
>
> *It's good if you have a girlfriend that is involved with sport, involved with the same sort of interest that you've got. Not iron man or like that! but the same sort of, doing the training here and there so it can work out. Well, when you're doing some training, well, they'll do something else. And if you have someone who is completely different, which I have had girlfriends in the past like that, it doesn't seem to work. You might start off all right, but you*

end up splitting up, because you fight all the time. It gets on their nerves when you are training all the time, you won't go out here and here. It's just rat shit.

What would be the attraction for the 'girls' in Steve's life (the slightly childish language is also characteristic) in having a lifestyle not far removed from that of an armchair? In the first place, this is par for the course in the Australian surfing subculture, which is male supremacist to a marked degree (Pearson 1982). If a 'girl' stands up for her own interests, Steve disposes of her and acquires another. As he notes complacently elsewhere in the interview, he has 'never had trouble' with sexual relationships. And in conventional terms, he is a real catch. He is handsome, healthy, easygoing, sexually experienced, famous, and on the verge of becoming rich.

Steve's 'job' of being an iron man nets him prizes, sponsorships, and endorsements which add up to a phenomenal income for a young man recently out of high school. Asked where he would see himself in five years' time, he replies simply, 'A millionaire'. His aim is to be this by the time he retires, at about 30. At present he is expanding his sponsorship deals with several large companies, is buying into surf businesses, and has just signed up with a multinational marketing company:

I just want to keep winning, keep winning, and keep rolling the money. So when I do get off I've got something to show for what I've done.

Fame is accepted with the same combination of pleasure and complacency as the cash and the sex. He wanted fame, and now he enjoys it. But there is a problem:

Well, you can go out at night and you've got to set an example for yourself. You can't go stupid like other people can. Like Joe Blow can get away with drunk-driving charges and no one will know. If it was me it would be on the front page. Things may be not even that serious. Because if I was just mucking around down the street—it's hard really, people think, 'He's got to do this', and they set you in a certain way . . . behave in your own limits, you can't go wild or anything. If I go out at night I can't get in a fight. That can happen because people think they can . . . say smart comments, and you can hear them, and they try and big-note themselves with friends. And I've had fights before where people have, I have just snapped. But that's only happened once or twice, that's not bad really, considering some of the situations I've had.

This is very much a problem about masculinity. Steve, the exemplar of masculine toughness, finds that his own exemplary status prevents him from doing exactly what his peer group defines as thoroughly masculine behaviour: going wild, showing off, drunk driving, getting into fights, defending his own prestige.

It is also clear in this passage how social the whole business is—the smart-aleck banter among friends, the social pressure that 'sets you in a certain way'. Here we have a vivid glimpse of the production of an exemplary masculinity as a collective practice. It is an accomplishment not of Steve as an individual (throughout this passage he is kicking against the pricks), but of the whole social network in which Steve finds himself enmeshed.

SOFT PATH, HARD GOAL

How did he get to be an exemplar of masculinity? Steve's own account of his childhood and adolescence portrays a simple progression from active child to schoolboy hero to adult champion. He seems to swim endlessly through a warm bath of admiration from family, teachers and friends. His grandfather was a sporting hero and Steve pictures himself as growing up effortlessly in the same mould.

Without denying the reality of this picture, we may question what it means. Steve's childhood was not a conventional idyll. His parents separated when he was young, and he has few memories of the family together. His clearest childhood memory of his father is in a game of hide-and-seek on the day of the weekly visit, when his father vanished and could not be found for 45 minutes. At the least, this is a memory of anxiety. It is hardly over-interpreting to suggest that this remains a haunting memory because the 'lost father' remained a major emotional issue for Steve.

His mother figures as the main adult in Steve's narrative of growing up. She certainly encouraged and organized his swimming, and paid for his travel to championship meetings. He sees her as having the same qualities as him—'intelligent and strong like I am'—and unwilling to be pushed around. There is some identification here, and she remains an emotional presence for him. Asked near the end of the interview his views on violence, he says the only scene he can imagine that would provoke him to murder would be 'if someone killed my mother'.

Yet Steve also records that she moved to another city after her children had left the nest, and the loss does not seem troubling to him. Indeed, he is now pleased to be reestablishing contact with his father, who is taking an interest in his son's career and helping him negotiate sponsorship deals. Steve has not lacked figures to model himself on.

Thus Steve has been inserted into his career by a close network of family, friends and school. He remembers anxiety about moving up to high school—fear of being physically beaten up by the big boys—but soon formed a group of friends and stuck with them right through school. Physically big as a child, he did well in school sporting events and particularly well in swimming. By age 13 he was far enough advanced in formal competition that he gave up football in order to specialize in swimming—a decision that signals the shift from sport as pleasure to sport as a kind of career.

Sport was a career path that elicited a lot of communal support. Steve was the school swimming champion, and his prowess won the district competition for his school. He was 'a bit of a hero' and a leader among his peers, and was treated with indulgence by his teachers. His mother strongly supported his swimming career, which must have shaped household routine from an early stage. Steve's regime as a teenager involved swimming in the morning, school in the day, then more swimming at night. He didn't much want to study, and he completed high school mainly because his friends were still there. When he left school, the study part simply dropped out of his day and the swimming part went on.

At this point Steve was handed over to a new network, and the transition has been complete. Steve hardly sees the once close-knit group of high-school friends any more. Asked what makes someone decide to take up the iron-man event, Steve describes a social practice rather than a choice:

> *There is no decision really. It's just that you've got to be round the beach for starters. And you have got to be involved with the surf club, so that narrows it right down. You've got to have a love of the water. You've got to have a swimming background, pretty well. And you've got to be disciplined and dedicated enough to put the time and work in.*

The surf club is a key part of the new network. Steve joined it as a teenager and was thus absorbed into a slightly older peer group, a group of young adult men absorbed in a cult of physical masculinity.

The surf club in Australia is a high-profile voluntary organization with a public-service rationale—it organizes beach life-saving services—but also with a strong sporting and social flavour. Its networks merge into competitive sport on one side and consumer capitalism (especially advertising and sporting-goods retailing) on the other. In both directions, Steve was brought into contact with 'older guys' and absorbed some of their sexual, commercial, and technical know-how. His first coital experience was organized at the surf club and witnessed by his friends there, when he was about 17:

> *I remember the first time I had sex with a girl; I was at a toga party down at S Surf Club and I was round the rocks and that—pretty funny, yes—all the guys came round and watched . . . I ran back and I was the hero.*

As his career became focussed and he began to earn big money, Steve's peer group once again narrowed and stabilized, 'My friends are the guys I train with.' The replay is almost conscious: 'All the training you do, and all the time you put in, you are around them nearly as much as you are at school.' With his authoritarian trainer in the role of a schoolmaster, the continuity is striking, though the setting is now different. The peer group travels around the country to the big events, and the classroom furnishings are black leather-upholstered couches, expensive video systems, and live-in girlfriends.

THE BODY AND THE SELF

Masculinity is not inherent in the male body; it is a definition given socially, which refers to characteristics of male bodies. If the body is very much at odds with the social definition, there is trouble, as in the situations of transvestites and transsexuals. If the body complies with the social definition it is easier for the meanings to take hold; and sometimes the body cues the social definition. In Steve's case the cue was being tall and strong as a child.

He remembers this with pleasure. The key to the memory is the social meaning of being big. Steve's bodily attributes were appropriated in quite specific social practices. One was the rough-and-tumble atmosphere of an all-boys school, where Steve's group depended on him. The element of nurturance is very interesting: 'We all stuck together; it was really good. I was sort of—I was always bigger than the rest of the guys, I sort of looked after them.'

The other practice was competitive sport organized by adults. Steve's size meant that he won competitive events early on, consistently enough to define him as a champion in the making. His body was certainly given this definition before adolescence, because at 13 he was making the career decision to specialize in swimming.

In Steve's pseudotechnical discussion of the components of success, quoted above, he acknowledges both elements. He calls the bodily cueing 'natural ability', and he theorizes it as inherited from his grandfather. He also acknowledges the highly specific social practice that appropriates the body (training, feeling keen, not having business problems) and turns it into an engine of competitive success.

To call this discussion pseudotechnical is to say that Steve's representation of this process is highly ideological. (I would guess he is quoting his coach, whose relation to sporting ideology is discussed in the next section.) This is not to deny Steve's precise knowledge of his body and its capacities. All top-level sports performers do have this knowledge. Indeed, it is common among adolescent boys engaged in sport, whatever their level of skill. Teenage football players, for instance, develop a detailed knowledge of their own bodies' capacities, and their exact suitability for different positions in the team.

Steve Donoghue is quite eloquent about the particular kind of skill that is involved in top-level performance in his sport. It is far from being pure brawn:

> *I can spread my energy over a four-hour race to not die, to not have to start up slowly. I can start at a pace and finish at a pace every time. When I swam, I used to do 200 metres, which is four 50-metre laps. I can start off, and any 50 is pretty well to the tenth of a second the same time each lap, and I wouldn't even be looking at a watch . . . It's mental. You've got to be fit to do it, but there are so many guys that are fit and not many are able to do that . . . I'm just lucky naturally. But also distance-wise I can measure the distance out without having to think about it and say, 'Right this pace you are going, you will be able to keep going to the end and you will have no energy left at the end—you will have done the best race yon can do over that distance.' And I've just done that all the time.*

What Steve calls 'being lucky naturally' is in fact a skill developed by ten years of hard practising.

There is more to this than a technical knowledge of skills and capacities. Steve's whole person has become caught up in practices that centre on his body and its performances. Asked 'Where would you like to be as Steve? Nothing to do with business or money, just you?', he fumbles and then starts to grapple with this nexus:

> *I haven't even thought about it. I might be just the way I am, but I don't, I never look to the future. Everything is—not day to day—but season to season. I am more interested in winning and racing than anything, and that takes up my whole time, all the preparation and the time I put in. Last winter I was up at T [surf resort]; we were training five hours a day, and the only thing I was thinking about was getting through that day and getting to the next day. Having to make my body, too much energy and not enough rest, to be functional at as good a rate for the next day's training session. That is all I would be thinking about.*

In effect, the body becomes the focus of the self in quite a radical way. Social life is drastically curtailed to suit the logic of peak bodily performance. As Steve remarked, 'It's like being in jail.' Even more strikingly for a fit young heterosexual, sexual life is monitored and constricted because of its effect on performance. The kind of regime Steve sustained at school, and sustains now, leaves little room or energy for interests outside his sport. Even his casual peer group life is centred on others in the sport. Despite coming from a bourgeois background, he had little interest in schoolwork, seems to have no cultural interests beyond popular music, and cannot sustain a relationship with a woman who has interests outside of sport.

The picture, then, is of a psychological focus on the body together with a severely constricted social world and an impoverished cultural world. This is confirmed by a series of questions, asked at the end of the interview, about Steve's views on current issues:

> Feminists?
>
> *I don't like the ones that dress up in men's clothes and that sort of stuff, but I just think I don't mind women doing that sort of stuff. I'm the sort of guy that opens the car door for a girl all the time.*
>
> Gay men?
>
> *I've got no gay friends—I don't think I have. I'm not into television and hairdressing and anything like that . . . As long as they keep to themselves and away from me I'm happy. I'm against them really. I can't see the reason why they are—I can't understand it—but a lot of*

people say they are born that way so I don't know. I'm [with a laugh] not into bashing them or anything like that.

Politics?

Nothing to do with it whatsoever. The last vote they had here I didn't even know it was on that day. I was down the beach in the surf.

In this bleached, featureless world centred on the care and maintenance of his body, punctuated by races, it is not surprising that Steve's only tangible goal is to collect dollars: 'Keep winning, keep winning, and keep rolling the money.' He has in view no use for the money except being able to live in comfort, so his only way of defining a purpose is to pick an arbitrary figure. Becoming a millionaire is 'just a goal, just something that I might aim for'; he is almost apologetic about its arbitrariness. The business of winning has consumed his life. With everything subordinated to bodily performance as the means of success, there is nothing very tangible that the success is for. So a goal has to be invented within the mechanism of races and dollars to give Steve the impression that his effort is leading to something worthwhile.

This cycle could, of course, be disrupted. The most likely disruptions are an injury (Steve has had some); a pregnancy (Steve could easily afford an abortion but the girlfriend of the day might insist on marriage and in that case would have a lot of social pressure behind her); or the emergence of a new champion who overshadows Steve and thus undermines his worth to sponsors. The last will certainly happen in time, but Steve has specialized in an event in which champions are good for a relatively long period. He has researched this point and has concluded that an iron man does not peak until 'around 30 or close to . . . so in that way I've got at least five years left'.

[. . .]

REFLECTIONS

Steve lives an exemplary version of hegemonic masculinity. To live it does not mean to understand it. Steve has great trouble giving an account of masculinity when directly asked to explain a remark that 'men should be men':

I don't know, I really don't know. I just meant that as—I think just being strong and not—I was talking about gays, I think, don't know. I don't even know why I said it really, just came out.

What do you think it means to be a man, for you?

Not be a gay; I don't know. I've done interviews on that sort of stuff before, people said, 'You're scared of spiders and all that sort of stuff?' Yes I am; I have got fears like any other people. I am scared of heights. So I don't think any of that has got anything to do with being a man.

The best definition he can think of is 'be strong' and 'not be a gay'. Other respondents in our study, less exemplary than Steve, have much more complex and fluent answers to this question.

The exclusion of homosexual desire from the definition of masculinity is, of course, a key feature of modern hegemonic masculinity. It makes sense for Steve to grasp at this straw, especially because his life has long been substantially homo-social (i.e. an all-boys' school, a masculinized surf club and peer group, and a masculinized sport). His consciousness of this pattern is tellingly shown by his specific (and quite unnecessary) exclusion of iron-man events as possible sports for his girlfriends. It is a familiar point that there is a lot of homosexual affect floating around in such milieux. Steve simply blanks this out as we saw in his response to the subject of gay men.

To say that a particular form of masculinity is hegemonic means that it is culturally exalted and that its exaltation stabilizes the gender order as a whole. To be culturally exalted, the pattern of masculinity must have exemplars who are celebrated as heroes. Steve certainly enacts in his own life some of the main patterns of contemporary hegemonic masculinity: the subordination of women, the marginalizationof gay men, and the connecting of masculinity to toughness and competitiveness. He has also been celebrated as a hero for much of his life, in school and in adult sport. He is being deliberately constructed now as a media exemplar of masculinity by the advertisers who are sponsoring him.

It is here that the contradictions poke out. Being an exemplar of masculinity actually forbids Steve to do many things that his peer group and culture define as masculine: 'it's like being in jail'. Steve experiences this prohibition as a very tangible pressure. Similarly, sustaining the training regime that yields the bodily supremacy, giving him his status as a champion, is incompatible with the kind of sexual and social life that is expected by affluent young men: 'you end up splitting up'. [. . .]

At a deeper level, Steve's performance is contradictory. Consider the focussing of both his social and his psychological life on the body, and the inward-turned competitiveness that seems related to his particular sport. There is a definite narcissism here, something often observed about athletes. This is a problem given the dominant cultural construction of masculinity as outward turned and denying the subjective.

Even more of a problem, the narcissism is necessarily unstable, unable to rest in self-admiration or indulgence (which would destroy the performance). In Steve's construction of competition (for instance his remarks about controlling pain), the decisive triumph is over oneself and specifically over one's body.

The magnificent machine of Steve's physique has meaning only when subordinated to the will to win. And the will to win is a curiously hollow construction in Steve's psychological makeup. The will to win does not arise from personal 'drive' (a familiar word in sport talk that Steve, tellingly, does not use at all). It is given to him by the social structure of sporting competition. It is his meaning, as a champion.

So we are returned to the social structures in which masculinities are produced. Indeed, we are led to see masculinity as an aspect of social structure, not just a form of personal character. As a configuration of gender relations, here meshed with consumer capitalism, hegemonic masculinity appropriates Steve's body and gives it a social definition. But it does this in ways that are full of contradiction, visible even behind the euphoria of Steve's tale of pleasure and success.

The long-term effect is hard to judge, but the short-term effect is clear. Steve gets his pleasure and success at the cost of his adulthood. [. . .] He is, of course, young. But most other men his age are facing the problems of earning a livelihood, constructing long-term relationships, building households, making hard choices, and facing social issues.

Steve has been taken in hand by the institutions of competitive sport and commerce and protected from common issues and problems. Though Steve cannot see it, for he has little experience of the world, his employers genuinely do not want an individual. They want someone to occupy a spot constructed by gender symbolism and the needs of commerce: a handsome, happy, nicely spoken, beach-sport hero who will make no difficulties about advertising their products. (Steve is, for example, sponsored by a beer company, which not everyone would see as a responsible move by a sporting champion.) At the moment he neatly fits the spot, and as long as he keeps up his winning status and his image, the money will keep rolling in and Steve will be preserved in his extended adolescence.

Excerpted from Raewyn Connell, "An Iron Man: The Body and Some Contradictions of Hegemonic Masculinity" in M. Messner and D. Sabo, eds, *Sport, Men and the Gender Order* (Champaign, Human Kinetics Books, 1990): 83–95. Reprinted with the permission of the author.

REFERENCES

Connell, Raewyn. 1994. "Psychoanalysis on Masculinity." H. Broad and M. Kaufman, eds., *Theorizing Masculinities*, Thousand Oaks: Sage.

Pearson, Kent. 1982. "Conflict, Stereotypes and Masculinity in Australian and New Zealand Surfing." *Journal of Sociology* 18.2: 117–135.

CHAPTER 11

Transformed Identity: From Disabled Person to Global Paralympian

Jill M. Le Clair

I think the word handicapped is probably a bad word. It's kind of like when you use the 'N' word for a black person. It's outdated. It has no place being in society, there are so many better words.
Veteran Paralympian, 2003

THE GLOBAL DISABILITY SPORT SYSTEM

In 1948, a handful of veterans at Stoke Mandeville Hospital in England competed in the first ever disability sport event held parallel to the Olympic Games. At the time, neurosurgeon Ludwig Guttman was thought to be unrealistic because he envisaged these marginalized men with spinal cord injuries using sport as a route to social inclusion.[1] The naysayers were wrong and Guttman was right. It turns out that the impact of international disability sport movements has been very important because these organizations have helped reframe the meaning of disability, and provided new sport opportunities for elite competition and social inclusion.[2]

This paper presents the personal narratives of Canadian swimmers with a disability (SWAD) team members who were, or became Paralympians.[3] Their careers took place at a time of profound change in the Paralympic Games sport system as it evolved from a relatively little-known disability-based, disability-specific group of organizations to become a genuinely global, sport-based umbrella organization.[4] It is a story of [organizational] transformation and of transformation in the lives of individuals with disabilities. It is also the story of individual hard work with a focus on achieving, and this experience is replicated by athletes in many other countries.

Two main stages or transformations in the careers of Canadian Paralympic swimmers are discussed. The first is the recognition of their socially defined disability identity, and the rejection of the limitations of this label. The second is the transformation to athlete and competitive swimmer, as each individual negotiated the differences between the perceived body and the lived body in relation to the presentation of the self as a person with a disabled body.[5] There is also a brief discussion of the classification process required to obtain the status of a Paralympic swimmer and of the macro-organizational change in International Paralympic Committee (IPC) swimming which switched from disability-based classification to sport-based classification and competition.

BACKGROUND: HISTORICAL MOMENTS

This research resulted from the author attending an Atlanta Sports Council meeting in 1995 that was held at Georgia Tech University, in order to showcase the new Olympic aquatics facility and to see the first international event being held in the pool, the Paralympic Games Swim Trials. This event was quite different from a conventional non-disabled swimming event in which the competitor bodies are very similar – tall, wide shoulders and long, muscular arms. There were athletes of varied sizes and shapes in swimsuits of different designs and colours. When competition began some swimmers stood with arms raised in the conventional start position, others were positioned for the same event in the water. The starts were varied – some held onto a rope in the water, some were steadied by an assistant while standing, and others sat on the starting block, but in the water, all swam unaided, with no fins or prostheses. It was obvious that these athletes had different disabilities, but they were competing in the same pool. The daily newssheet, the *ISPT News,* explained that the swimmers were competing in different classes, so we saw the 'same' event take place more than once as those with different degrees of disability were grouped together.[6] I had stumbled on part of the profound shift in disability swimming.

Once competition started, the swimmers raced through the water and the athletes in the lower classes, with more severe disabilities, we had seen moving carefully or with assistance on land moved surprisingly (to the author) speedily through the water. Perhaps part of the author's reaction was emotional as the author was jealous of their athletic vigour as she sat on a bench hardly able to sit and watch, or move up and down the stands because of a spinal cord injury from a car crash. Early in 1996 an introduction to the coach and team followed, and out of that serendipitous event in Atlanta came a decade of following the team and this research.

The author has lived in two worlds, as a non-disabled person who loved movement and physical activity. Her life was then suddenly transformed into the world of disability where every movement was restricted, painful and challenging. This research is part of a reflexive analysis of the world of international swimming while on her own odyssey she was also experiencing a range of issues including stigma and disability identity,[7] the knowledge/power axis, medical 'disciplining',[8] globalization,[9] odysseys[10] and disability rights[11] symbolized locally in the passage of the Accessibility for Ontarians with Disabilities Act (2005),[12] nationally with the Americans with Disabilities Act (ADA)[13] and globally in the UN Declaration of the Rights of Persons with Disabilities (2006).[14] The lived reality of disability allowed for research insights that were informed by experience.

THE FIELDWORK CONTEXT

The analysis in this article is drawn from participant observation and interviews conducted between 1996 and 2008, the bulk of the interviews being conducted between 2000 and 2003. To understand the lives of these athletes it was necessary to follow them as they travelled from one end of the country to the other, and around the world, as best I could, to attend provincial, national and international competitions, training camps and classification sessions and seminars. Similarly to other researchers in our globalized world, Frohlick describes this as researchers 'chasing' people around the world for interviews, and fieldwork as 'fleeting and transient'[15] because of the required mobility of globalization. Between 2002 and

2004, the swimmers on the team literally travelled around the world. They travelled across Canada, to South America and Europe to train and compete: in Canada the pools ranged from Victoria, British Columbia, Winnipeg, Manitoba, Edmonton, Alberta to Toronto, Ontario; overseas the World Championships took place in Mar del Plata, Argentina, and the Paralympic Games in Athens, Greece, in the autumn of 2004. The interviews were primarily conducted at training camps and also on the telephone, and consisted of open-ended questions that related to the five stages of their swimming careers, including retirement.[16]

STAGE ONE: TRANSFORMATION TO DISABILITY IDENTITY

Link and Phelan argue that the development of disability identity takes place in the context of three mechanisms of discrimination – individual, structural, and discrimination that operates through the stigmatized person's beliefs and behaviours.[17] The series of steps or changes in this process of transformation includes, first their awareness of their own self-conception of disability status and its emotional component; and second, what Goffman describes as the rejection of 'virtual' identity replaced with 'authentic social identity'[18] and true identity through friendship and acceptance. All of this takes place in the context of the dominating 'normate' and the social construction of the 'normal'.[19] The limiting disability or handicap label is rejected through sport, and there is a determination to overcome physical barriers using whatever strategies are necessary. In addition, there are changes specific to the acceptance of body shape and 'difference', especially related to the rejection of the concept of the 'missing' or different limb, or limbs, and there is change through the rejection of stereotypes about the 'feminine' body. The final part in transformation is that each and every one of these individuals has to be publicly recognized as a person with a disability and classified for swimming competition in the Paralympic Games. Sometimes impacting directly in one second, and at other times over a period, these myriad ways culminate in the individual reframing what disability means as a stigmatized public status under the hegemonic 'gaze' of the wider society.[20] Through a multiplicity of paths, there are different ways in which persons with a disability reject marginalization and seek empowerment through the physical activity of swimming, often very early in their lives.

CHILDHOOD TEASING, RIDICULE AND SPORT

The elements in this transition included sometimes being subjected to bullying at school and an increasing awareness of disability. Non-disabled individuals often assume that those with a disability must automatically have a sense of self as a person with a disability from earliest childhood, but this is not necessarily the case. Sometimes the individual did not become aware of their disability until their teens or even early adulthood.[21] The child knows that they may be unable to do some of same physical activities as their schoolmates or their family, but they are 'normal' or 'average' in their own minds. This is at the same time that they are experiencing the reality of their physical challenges. One swimmer[22] describes the growing awareness of a different physical ability.

> I was in my teens. I never really thought about it . . . In grade seven is really when it started to come to my attention. Sort of in grades five, six and seven, but painfully so in grades seven and eight. But I always liked doing things. I loved my swimming lessons; we'd walk everywhere.

> My dad would say, run over to the tree, run back. He'd tell me to ride a bike – I know I fell a lot [laughter]. I had lots of skinned knees and skinned elbows, but I did all that stuff.

Some athletes described being at school as being a form of torture; they only began to make sense of it all as an adult.[23] They were made fun of at school, were the target of jokes, name calling or slurs, and their different motor movements were sometimes mimicked. Some, it must be said, had good friends and felt their disability had no impact. These seem to be those individuals who participated in physical activities and were integrated through team sport. Regardless, for some there was a sense of profound rejection. Some athletes had a miserable time at school because of the other children, teachers or sometimes both.

> My gait has definitely improved, but when I was growing up, they imitated the way I walked all the time in the hallways. They called me retard because the only thing that I knew and understood about my disability, I didn't know that I had cerebral palsy until I was just about twenty-one . . .In grade six we had to write a story of our life. I wrote it, I wrote what it was like to have a disability – I didn't know I had CP – to be teased and to be made fun of, to be called names, and to be ridiculed and judged.

AWARENESS AND SELF-NAMING

Each individual goes through the process of naming and self-naming,[24] and this is unique and occurs at different ages for each person. Each athlete was asked, 'When did you become aware of yourself with a disability?', and a number explained that they had been treated in the same way as other family members, with expectations to work hard and contribute like anyone else, so they had not really become aware of the differences until well into adolescence. Goffman might interpret the family focus on sport and opportunities as a form of 'deviance disavowal' – the ignoring of a dominant and determining factor,[25] but the athletes and their families said their focus was on doing whatever seemed possible and 'normalizing' the child's experience.

However, even though some athletes claimed that they had never experienced discrimination, the term disability or disabled nearly always engendered an emotional response. Goffman[26] states that the public recognition of a status, as for alcoholics at an Alcoholics Anonymous meeting, is an important part of identity making.[27] When each athlete was asked if they saw a parallel, this perspective was firmly rejected. The athletes did not see a parallel at all.

> I don't think it's important like that, because AA is, you know, a sociological problem you have. You have to admit it so you can get help. I don't need help. I'm a disabled person, I have a disability, and I'm swimming with a disability. I need help? No. It doesn't work like that.

The athletes felt there was a clear differentiation between a status that they saw as a choice, such as drinking alcohol or being overweight. These were regarded as lifestyle choices which individuals could change. The disabilities the swimmers had were unchangeable by lifestyle; a missing hand or limb, motor neurological limitations or visual limitations cannot be addressed by making different choices. Some seemed to imply that the use of the word disability indiscriminately diminished the reality of a 'genuine', severe and unchangeable disability. This attitude was also present in the magazines based on disability issues. There were debates at this time about the challenge to the gains made through the Americans with Disabilities Act by actions seen to weaken or demean serious concerns related to disability by conflating them with 'math challenges' or non-medical obesity issues in Americans with a Disability law suits.[28]

STAGE TWO: THE IMPACT OF SPORT ON DISABILITY IDENTITY

REJECTING DISABILITY AND EMBRACING ABILITY

The swimmers with a disability rejected the concept of disability outright. In response to the question 'What do you think of the term disability?' these responses were typical.

> No, I never have and I never will (use the term) and if people use that kind of term, I don't know, it's like they're putting themselves down. It's just that word disgusts me so much that every time people use it, it makes me feel so irritated and so out of control because it just drives me crazy. It's like that word for me signifies low self-esteem. I don't like it. You were born that way? Well, go on with your life and do whatever it is that you have to do . . . and go on.

For those born with a disability it has been part of life from the first day, but what it signifies, represents and symbolizes changes with life experience and struggles. The individual becomes socially aware of their limitations or impairments in physical movement and bodily activity, and these necessitate a presentation of self as a person with a disability. But being physically active in the water and becoming involved in organized swimming challenges the 'victim' or limiting label of disability identity. There is a contradiction between the disability label and the abilities the athletes have in the water. The limitations implicit in the term disability are rejected absolutely, as the athletes see themselves as being able to do what they want and achieve the goals they want. The focus across the board was on what the athletes want to do and feel that they can do. The negative elements that disability identity represents are rejected outright.

> No. I don't see myself as disabled so I don't think there's any difference. I don't like that word. It's a very disgusting word. I will use it as somebody who is unable to jump, or go and run, and do something that you could do, I don't know, it's just I believe that word puts people down, makes their self-esteem low. I don't like using that word, find something else. It's a word in the dictionary, but, I don't like classifying people for who they are, what they do, what they are missing. They are who they are, no matter what. Everybody has a story to tell, everybody has something to learn from everybody, so just, respect everybody for the way they are, and live your life the fullest.

The discussion of the meaning of the term disability by athletes was nuanced. The athletes rejected the more common American term of the 1980s and 1990s 'physically challenged'. It was argued that there is physical challenge in many activities, and often there are physical challenges for those with disabilities, but it is not an accurate term because non-disabled individuals can take on physical challenges, but a person with a disability has no choice. However, it was recognized that each person had different strengths and weaknesses and the label disability was dependent on the context and the expected skills.

> Let's just use that stupid word, disability, everybody has one. (Not everyone) can sing; if you put me to sing people will start crying, I can't sing. I could dance, I'm a good dancer, but I can't sing. So that's it, I'm unable to sing, even if I try my best, I can't, so everybody has that in their life, not everybody knows how to do everything. Does that make them disabled? No. They might have the ability to do something, but they don't have the ability to do something else, so what?

Other athletes accepted their body shape from the start and said they never faced discrimination. They were certain that they had not faced discrimination or barriers.

Perhaps it needs to be remembered that most of the athletes were still relatively young, and most students, but they were clear in their answers, explaining: 'Well, I don't know, not really, nothing.' Another said:

> I've never seen (discrimination), I just view it as just being there (my disability), and I'm different than everybody else, it's just fun. I just always have been very aware of it and I don't really deny it, it's just it's there, right there, and face it and go with it. Go on with it, there's not much you could do.

It could be argued that athletes must adopt a specific frame of mind in order to compete; the athlete must think that it is possible to achieve the goals that they have in mind. So the individuals who participated in these interviews would not have chosen this path if they had not had a positive 'can-do' attitude. They must reject the negativity that discrimination presents in order to continue against the odds of achieving various goals.

Disabilities can be visible or invisible and create social margins. If visible, the athlete is forced to negotiate in each and every social situation. Expecting or feeling anxious about potential rejection can lead to social isolation. This expectation of stereotyping has been called 'stigma consciousnesses'.[29] Some persons with a disability become annoyed or irritated at having to constantly negotiate their disability identity, and others put down the endless questioning to 'lack of information' or 'lack of education'. Sometimes being at the receiving end of people staring was irritating, and some athletes, although comfortable and almost naked on the pool deck, felt different outside the pool. One man in his late twenties still felt uncomfortable about his different body and put it this way: 'I've got better, I mean before I wouldn't wear shorts that were short. I would cover up. I got a lot better'.

Older people will often use the term handicapped, meaning disability, and in training a coach referred to a male swimmer as handicapped. The swimmer found this usage inappropriate and explained why.

> 'I'm not handicapped', I said. I hate that word. I'm not handicapped. Sure I've got a disability (one leg) but am I any more handicapped than somebody who sits on the sofa, who eats a bag of chips and weighs 300 pounds? No. Am I any more handicapped than somebody who's on unemployment and won't go to find work because they feel sorry for themselves, no. And you know I train my ass off every day in the water and I swim 180,000 meters a week, a month, does that make me handicapped? No. So I think the word handicapped is probably a bad word. It's kind of like when you call the 'N' word for a black person. It's outdated you. It has no place being in society – there are so many better words.

ACCEPTANCE OF 'TRUE' IDENTITY THROUGH TRUST AND ACCEPTANCE

The process of swimming and sport activity often facilitated acceptance of disability status. At the swimming pool, it meant that there was an acceptance of difference, and of the person and the body, because of swimming.

> I don't think you can accept yourself right away. I'm still working on it. I think it's just a day-by-day thing. I think throughout your life you kind of deal with everything, one thing at a time. Something new will come up. They (others) might think that it's all going to be bad, but it's not, you know. For me I really met some true friends and the same thing will happen for them.

TRANSFORMATION OF IPC SWIMMING IN THE PARALYMPIC GAMES

FROM DISABILITY-BASED TO SPORT-BASED

Athletes train and compete within organizational structures that support or undermine opportunities and the framing of sport experiences. The first Stoke Mandeville Games focused on paralysed athletes with spinal cord injuries, but year by year sports were added (including volleyball, cycling, wheelchair marathon, tennis, wheelchair rugby and sailing). In addition, athletes with different disabilities began competing (cerebral palsy, amputee, *les autres*, visually impaired). Until the 1980s, international sport organizations had been disability based. Classification was based on a medical model and medical classification. The main sport organizations consisted of:

- Cerebral Palsy International Sport and Recreation (CP-ISRA);
- International Blind Sports Association (IBSA);
- International Association of Sport for Persons with a Mental Handicap (INASFMH; joined in 1992 and later became INAS-FID [suspended in 2000]);
- International Stoke Mandeville Games Federation (ISMGF; later the ISMWSF);
- International Sports Organization for the Disabled (ISOD); and
- Comité International des Sports des Sourds (CISS; World Games for the Deaf) which withdrew without participating in the Paralympic Games and became the separate Deaflympics.[30]

In 1988, these previously independent disability sport organizations, under the leadership of Dr Robert Steadward, reorganized as one umbrella organization the International Paralympic Committee (IPC) that would oversee the Paralympic Games. Later the IPC reorganized to follow the global regions of the Olympic Games.[31] The IPC was to become structured in a way similar to the Olympic Games organized by the International Olympic Committee (IOC) and became structurally and financially formally linked in the Olympic bid process and in the Olympic Games themselves. In 2010, the two events of the Olympic and Paralympic Games were planned together and the official title used was 'The Vancouver Organizing Committee for the 2010 Olympic and Paralympic Games' and in the media this was the official title of the Games, spoken of together.[32]

GLOBALIZATION AND UNIFIED NATIONAL TEAM

It is important to recognize that these changes took place in the context of an increasingly globalized world in which we see disability in what Appadurai calls 'postnational geography' and Gupta calls 'transnational identies'[33] where shared values and identities are not based on territoriality, but on shared values about human rights which play an increasingly important role in disability discourses.[34] The passage of the 2006 UN Convention on the Rights of Persons with Disabilities included a section directly addressing sport and physical activity which also strengthened a rights-based approach for inclusion.[35] As supporters in different countries lobbied (assisted by an exponential growth in communications' technology of the Internet, mobile phones and social networks like Facebook) as part of public discourse for national approval and passage by their own legislative assemblies, awareness of disability issues in sport increases.

Older swimmers had competed in a system in which the teams were disability-based and they had felt frustrated because they had wanted better competition and a greater sport focus. Swimming was divided by disability. In Canada, there had been four swim teams with different coaches, different training and different uniforms. Sports aim to create fair competition, and part of ensuring fairness is that athletes are placed in similar groupings as boxers classified by weight. IPC Swimming explains classification in this way:[36]

> Traditionally there are athletes who belong to six different disability groups in the Paralympic Movement: amputee, cerebral palsy, visual impairment, spinal cord injuries, intellectual disability and a group which includes athletes who do not fit into the aforementioned groups (*les autres*).
>
> Classes are determined by a variety of the 1989 international that may include a physical and technical assessment throughout the athlete's career. Sports certify individuals to conduct the process of classification and they are known as classifiers. Since the 1960s, the development of sport for athletes with a disability has produced and developed; and this continues to evolve to the present day.

By 1992, IPC Swimming had reorganized its classification system for competition to become sport-based. How fast did the athletes swim in the water? How effective was their propulsive force through the water? All athletes were grouped together *regardless of their disability* and were classified together. The focus became sport, not disability:

> Swimming is governed by the IPC and coordinated by the IPC Swimming Technical Committee, which incorporates the rules of the International Swimming Federation (FINA). The FINA rules are followed with a few modifications, such as optional platform or in-water starts for some races and the use of signals or 'tappers' for swimmers with blindness/visual impairment; however, no prostheses or assistive devices are permitted.[37]

With a focus on sport in Canada, this meant that there was only one Canadian swim team and this was the sport system athletes were part of in 1996. The team consisted of swimmers with a variety of disabilities who competed as one team. The 1989 international transformation laid the groundwork for Canadian technical classifier and coach James Hood to propose a Memorandum of Understanding for Swimming Canada to integrate the national Olympic swim team and the SWAD team. Therefore for the first time ever the non-disabled Junior National Team Trials and the SWAD Paralympic Trials were held together in Nepean near Ottawa, in 1996. By 2000, the Olympic and Paralympic Trials were held at the same Olympic pool and at the same time in Montreal. In 2004, at the Etobicoke Olympium, the Olympic and Paralympic Trials events alternated. There had been a sea change in attitude from 1996 as the media alternated in interviewing the athletes who were on the way to compete as either Olympians or Paralympians.[38] This was the kind of inclusion that Guttman had imagined over 60 years earlier.

'COMING OUT' – TRANSFORMATION FROM A PERSON WITH A DISABILITY TO CLASSIFIED SWIMMER

PUBLIC DISABILITY IDENTITY

These international and national organizational changes meant that the pool also provided an interesting contradiction in that everyone is present because of an official disability identity, but each person has a different disability. There is a shared normalcy and ease of social understanding with neither staring nor the need to explain. At the same time, there is a classification which creates a disability ranking. Each athlete is classified by their functioning in the water into a class for the stroke used in the specific event. It can be seen to be somewhat like the grouping in boxing to ensure fairness. The groupings are by number; an S1, SB1 is the most severely disabled and S10 or SB9 the least disabled, and athletes with visual impairments or blind S11 to S13; and the classification includes an on-land component and an in the water assessment. No swimmer can compete in the IPC system without being classified and hence a public statement 'coming out' as an athlete with a disability. There is no hiding of disability in this environment.

Many swimmers explained that although their identity is clearly labelled as a disability identity, they did not like the term as it categorized them and was seen to be restrictive. They saw themselves as capable and independent, not as disabled or limited. They rejected Goffman's premise about the need for a public statement as 'swimmers with a disability' and rejected the disability label as negative.

One of the interesting differences between the literature in the past and the experience of those with disabilities in the last 20 years is that those very signs of disability (Goffman's stigma) have been transformed into symbols of excellence. In sport, the visible artificial Flex-foot is not hidden away because of stigma and shame; it is merely part of a post-modern cyborg elite body.[39] 'Passing' or 'covering' is the opposite to 'coming out'. Some theorists have argued that bodies today are by definition cyborg bodies, what Butryn calls 'post-humans'[40] because the 'so-called "natural" body has been impacted by technology whether minimally through a childhood inoculation or maximally through life support systems, heart transplants or prostheses'.[41]

CLASSIFICATION

In the case of competitive athletes 'coming out' is an institutionalized process, with assessments included in the process of classification. It is conceptualized collectively by society,[42] and specifically in this case by the swimming community. The individual recognizes either from birth or through trauma 'I am a person with a disability' (even if this identity is rejected), and in order to compete in disabled swimming, disability identity must be formally and publicly recognized. Those who participate in any sport must first state that they have a disability identity by presenting themselves as a swimmer with a disability who must be placed in the appropriate competition/skill group by being classified. Linton argues that a great deal of energy is put into 'passing' and that hiding is a response to prejudicial attitudes and it is important for individuals to claim and recognize their disability.[43] One female swimmer wrestled with the meaning of identifying with a disability identity.

> Prior to that time, I had never defined myself as having a disability, so it was an element that I struggled with because in order to participate in Paralympic sport you have to first say I have a disability. It's part of the whole eligibility process and then it's moving from that point. It has certainly coloured the kinds of choices that I've made in my own professional career of moving into a situation of saying you know what? I'm an athlete first and I happen to have a disability, and that's one of the really powerful things about the Paralympic sport movement in our society. It gives you the opportunity to take that societal notion of disability and turn it into something else that is constructive. It allows you to not only get on with your life but also to explore those ideas and those goals of excellence.

ATHLETE IDENTITY AND TEAM MEMBERSHIP

Another athlete described the stressful experience of formally joining a team. The swimmer was nervous and the other non-disabled team members were anxious at having their first swimmer with a disability on the university team.

> For fear of being ignorant, or offending me, and I think too, part of it is me, because when I first started swimming with able-bodied clubs, I was scared out of my wits. I was terrified, terrified, and now, and part of it is that I've established myself, so I feel much more comfortable, I can go into the coach and say, Hi, I'm –––, this is what I've done. I hold these Canadian records, I've swum at these international meets; I have a right to be here, whereas, before, it was very scary. And you're much more worried about what people will think about you, and I think where I did my undergrad, from the perspective of swimming with their able-bodied team and so on, and that was a real boost for me, but also being in an environment where we were encouraged not to judge people on the way that they looked but more on their abilities . . .

It could be argued that we all present and think of ourselves by shaping and stressing those things that are most important, but others could define us as being in denial or unrealistic. For swimmers, regardless of disability, the water is always a source of a framing disability identity differently. The athlete feels and moves in different ways in the water, often 'in a liberating sense', often leading to a different framing of the meaning of disability. 'My disability is different. It still does affect me in the water; it's simply that there are more things that I can do.'

Social marginalization can be a consequence of disability. Historically, the disabled were marginalized in all aspects of society – hidden from view, thought to be unmarriageable and usually unemployed.[44] Because of the global initiatives on the rights of athletes, the 2006 UN Convention on the Rights of Persons with Disabilities and the Sport for Development and Peace initiatives,[45] we have seen a shift in attitudes and opportunities towards sport. So, for those who decide to compete and train in high-performance sport we have an interesting dichotomy. Training to perform well means reaching for an above-average sport performance while being marginalized as a person with a disability. Yet performances of higher classed swimmers are beyond the ability of all except for a small percentage of able-bodied swimmers.

Titchkosky uses the term 'betweenness'[46] to describe the marginality of a person with a disability. My findings are that the overriding aspect for swimmers is their love for the water and the freedom of movement in swimming. Most became exposed to swimming from their earliest memories and enjoyed the water from the start. Water was a medium that had a positive impact on their marginalization in various ways. In addition, because of their success with the physical achievements in sport, the marginality that Titchkosky describes as central is minimized. The swimmers see themselves as independent and empowered. One athlete felt the language of disability was inaccurate for athletes:

> I don't perceive myself as disabled. I feel like I'm able-bodied you know, but I just happen to have one leg, so maybe an able-bodied swimmer with one leg; able-bodied swimmer with one arm, but that's not (a) universal (term).

AGENCY: HIGH-PERFORMANCE ATHLETE IDENTITY

Physicality is personal and experienced uniquely by each individual, although clearly there are shared experiences and values. 'The term rather than concept of physicality'[47] has been taken into use in describing people's experiences during physical activity. The body is a means through which each person experiences and learns about the world. It is also a means through which change can take place. Agency, in the context of learned bodily experiences at the personal level, has 'a transformative capacity that is socially and historically contextualized'.[48] In the recognition that there is human agency in movement (in all ways of moving), individuals present, interpret, choreograph and challenge bodily presentation in a constantly changing fashion; this includes 'the moving body',[49] a 'dynamic perspective on the body',[50] and what Harre calls 'causal powers theory'.[51] Here, the context is the competitive pool.

> Stigma is entirely dependent on social, economic, and political power – it takes power to stigmatize. In some instances the role of power is obvious. However, the role of power in stigma is frequently overlooked because in many instances power differences are so taken for granted as to seem unproblematic. When people think of mental illness, obesity, deafness, and having one leg instead of two, there is a tendency to focus on the attributes associated with these conditions rather than on power differences between people who have them and people who do not. But power, even in these circumstances, is essential to the social production of stigma.[52]

Link and Phelan argue that stigma is totally dependent on power differentials and we have seen that change in swimming as swimmers moved from competing in a disability-based system to one that increasingly viewed swimmers as world champions competing in the same venues in conjunction with the Olympic Games.

According to Hevey,[53] empowerment is part of the transforming aspect of the rejection of the aspects of stigmatization and the celebration of 'enfreakment' and the concept of 'Super Crips'. This transformation of the diminishing terms cripple/crips into something that transcends its demeaning framework has power. It means the symbol of inequity is turned on its head. It is also part of the *transformative process* of self-identifying and the structural redefinition from being a person with a disability to that of a high-performance swimmer with a disability.

There are three other main aspects to the transformation into national team member that are briefly outlined here that are inherent and required to be part of high-performance swimming regardless of the athlete being disabled or not, and these automatically become part of the new elite swimmer identity. First, the individual swimmer's body is 'disciplined' in the ways of swimming. Here the terms of Mauss (the *technique du corp*) and Bourdieu (*habitus*)[54] are used to describe the results from the rigours of daily training at the pool, with the essential self-discipline necessary to master the technical aspects of the various strokes and the skills required for competition. This process is accompanied by a new high-performance team identity guided, or some might say dominated, by coaches. The individual team body is also part of the marketing of the team image while it changes shape and may be inscribed to reflect a changed identity.

The second aspect is the experience of the team, which includes the marketing and commodification of team bodies in the team uniform under the authority of the coach and with the support of the 'service specialists'. The team disciplining of the body is epitomized by the athlete's contract, legally specifying the financial, social and political demands of team membership.

Third is the experience of the events in the environment of the competition sites themselves, the competitive settings. This is the globalized part of the athletes' world as competition is international in nature and the Canadians once they are classified become part of this global system. They have potential competitors from 80 countries and changing sites for the swim meets, World Championships and the Olympic Games.

The speed at which the transformation takes place, the swim club membership, and the attitude of the coaches varies, but there are some shared elements for all athletes regardless of disability and gender. The swimmers and their bodies are now subject to the discipline of the team, and these embodied activities are socially constructed.[55] This discipline is more intense and different from what Mauss calls 'the circumstances of life in common'.[56] There is an increased intensity and seriousness:

> But whatever the level of participation, the formal disciplining of bodies that occurs within sport and dance involves not only the transmission of knowledge about, and the shaping of competence with, given techniques of the body, but also the proselytizing of particular schemes of preference, valuation, and meaning.[57]

CONCLUSION

Assumptions about disability identity are changing. The lives of persons with disabilities changed profoundly because of swimming as the sport reframed their childhood experiences of disability. Although each athlete had unique experiences and different disabilities, the term disability held negative connotations for these athletes, who although officially classified as disabled athletes, rejected the disability label as negative and restricting. Their transforming lives took place as the international disability sport system, the international Paralympic Games also shifted its focus from disability-based to sport-based competition.

ACKNOWLEDGEMENTS

The author would like to acknowledge the support of the Social Science and Humanities Research Council (SSHRC) of Canada for their two-year graduate fellowship and the University of Toronto for their one-year graduate fellowship that supported this research. I'd also like to thank Swimming Canada for its ongoing support and co-operation. The following provided personal assistance and without whose help the field-work research could not have been undertaken: Lilian Le Clair, 1996 Youth Nationals and Paralympic Trials, Ottawa, Canada; Tommy Lord, 1996 Paralympic Games, Atlanta, USA; Daniele Laumann Hart, 2002 Swimming World Championships, Mar del Plata, Argentina; Lindy Allery, 2004 Paralympic Games, Athens, Greece and Li Jing (Patricia) of Renmin University of China, 2008 Paralympic Games, Beijing, China. Most importantly I am very appreciative of the time that the athletes, coaches, officials, sport administrators, classifiers and others so generously spent with me, on what I am sure seemed to be a laboriously slow process, as I tried to document their experiences in their own words.

NOTES

1 Guttman, 'Sport for the Disabled'.

2 This article only addresses issues related to athletes with physical disabilities as the International Sports Federation for Persons with Intellectual Disabilities (INAS-FID) that provides opportunities for persons with intellectual disabilities to compete in sport was suspended from the Paralympic Games in 2000 and its activities are under review.

3 The term 'Swimmers with a Disability' was initiated by the team itself, although there is some discussion about who first came up with the term. This article will use the term swimmers throughout to refer to the team. Conventional usage now is to use the term Paralympians in referring to swimmers with disabilities who compete in the Paralympic Games.

4 Steadward and Peterson, *Paralympics;* Duncan, 'The Sociology of Ability and Disability'.
5 Goffman, *Presentation of Self.*
6 ISPT News, 2.
7 Goffman, *Presentation of Self; Stigma.*
8 Foucault, *Discipline and Punish; The Birth of the Clinic.*
9 Brysk, *Globalization and Human Rights.*
10 Homer, *The Odyssey.*
11 Raphael, Bryant and Rioux, *Staying Alive.*
12 Accessibility for Ontarians with Disabilities Act (AODA), www.aoda.ca
13 Although the Americans with Disability Act (ADA) was only national legislation, it had a worldwide impact as other countries invoked its premise, See Americans with a Disability Act. The US Equal Opportunity Commission. www.ada.gov
14 UN Convention of the Rights of Persons with Disabilities, www.un.org/disabilities
15 Frohlick, 'Negotiating the "Global"', 529.
16 Many of the interviews were conducted at different times for two reasons: (1) the limited time swimmers had available. In training camp, swimmers and coaches have virtually no 'free' time as almost every minute is scheduled. (2) The physical challenges of the author who had limitations due to her own disability.
17 Link and Phelan, 'Conceptualizing Stigma', 379.
18 Goffman, *Stigma,* 2.
19 Garland-Thompson, *Extraordinary Bodies.*
20 'In the twentieth and twenty-first centuries, we are so used to hierarchical rankings based on race and colour it is sometimes forgotten that these rankings are grounded in differences in power. It becomes almost surprising to see that English colonists in the eighteenth century and old-order Americans in the nineteenth century were able to stigmatize the Dutch and the Irish because of their positions of power vis-à-vis these groups'. Link and Phelan, 'Conceptualizing Stigma', 375.
21 This is perhaps not dissimilar to the studies of children of colour who did not become aware of their own colour until their teens. They assumed they were like the white characters they saw on television.
22 The confidentiality and anonymity of the swimmers was part of the research guidelines, as many were actively competing. This was to allow those interviewed to speak more freely and not feel that any criticisms they made might have a negative impact on their swimming careers or funding.
23 Nussbaum, 'Feminotopias', 166. There is a long historical tradition of curiosity about differentness and the displaying of deviant or 'freak' bodies. 'Dwarfs, giants, Siamese twins, hermaphrodites and unusual beings with various physical deformities were regularly exhibited for profit in London in the early decades of the (eighteenth) century' and this continued in Canada until the 1950s. Today television and the Internet have replaced travelling fairs.
24 Singer, 'Why Can't You Be Normal'.
25 Goffman, *Stigma.*
26 Goffman, *Presentation of Self.*
27 In the *New York Times* in 2000 Jennifer Egan writes about the then 'new' phenomenon of multiple identities on the Internet. 'While the Internet provides a safe haven for countless gay teenagers who wouldn't dare confide their sexual orientation to the people around them, it is also a very easy place to get burned'. December 10, 2000, 110–117, 128–133. Many people use aliases or fake identities, and there is a real concern that the Internet is dangerous, no one knows for sure who is responding, and there is the possibility that procurers and 'gay bashers' are using the Internet for these purposes. The SWAD team members told the author that they used the Internet as a source of information on swim events and used email as a means of keeping in touch with their friends and family, but they do not use the disability websites or chat rooms. Probably this experience is different today in that disability agencies now deliberately target youngsters with a disability and put advertisements in public places to reach their audience.
28 At the same time the Disability Rights Education & Defence Fund (DREDF) (www.dredf.org) challenges legal definitions of disability e.g. a lower leg amputee defined by the courts as 'not disabled'.
29 Pinel, 'Social Consciousness'. However, this was not the experience of these informants in Canada in the 1970s to the 1990s.
30 Depauw and Gavron, *Disability and Sport.*
31 The last Far East and South Pacific Games for the Disabled (FESPIC) were held in 2006, after which the regions matched those of the Olympic Games.
32 The official site of the Vancouver Olympic Games, www.vancouver2010.com
33 Appadurai, 'Sovereignty Without Territoriality', 381; Gupta, 'The Song', 322.
34 Brysk, *Globalization and Human Rights.*
35 Wolff, Hums, and Roy, *Sport in the UN Convention.*
36 The IPC provided its rules and regulations online, www.swimmingcoach.org/pdf/ipcrulebook.pdf
37 Paralympic swimming is framed by the rules of the international non-disabled swimming organization FINA with few accommodations, www.ipc-swimming.org/About_the_Sport. Rules also include regulations about approved competition suits over which there has been much controversy.

38 Le Clair, 'High Performance Swimming'. It was clear this integration was not based on some form of political correctness, but competition for the best high performance swimmers in the country.
39 Haraway, 'A Cyborg Manifesto'.
40 Butryn, 'Posthuman Podiums'
41 Figueroa-Sarriera, 'Children of the Mind'.
42 Goffman, *Stigma*, 124.
43 Linton, *Claiming Disability*. Linton's choice of title for her book reflects her insistence that individuals claim or own disability and her emphasis on the power of language.
44 O'Sullivan, 'Messy Business'. Disabling illness became front page news and the target of 24-hour media coverage in March 2005 when an American woman, Terri Schiavo, in a 'persistent vegetative state', became subject to adversarial legal suits within her family about whether to invoke state intervention to terminate artificial feeding that would lead to death. Heated moral and religious debate took place about 'quality' of life versus humane release, which were reminiscent to the practices of Grafeneck (Castle) Hospital in Germany during the 1940s when the families of mentally disabled individuals received form letters after their relatives had been euthanized; 'In view of the nature of his serious, incurable aliment, his death, which saved him from a lifelong institutional sojourn is to be regarded merely as a release'.
45 Sport rights; Peter Donnelly, 'Child Labour, Sport Labour'; Jack Donnelley, *Universal Human Rights;* Kidd, 'A New Social Movement'.
46 Titchkosky, *Disability, Self and Society*, 217.
47 McDermott, 'Toward a Feminist Understanding of Physicality', 12.
48 Ibid., 20
49 Langlan, 'Mobility, Disability'.
50 Aronson, Harre, and Cornell Way, *Realism Rescued.*
51 Harre in Farnell, 'Moving Bodies, Acting Selves', 342.
52 Link and Phelan, 'Conceptualizing Stigma'.
53 Language can also be challenged by inverting the meaning of demeaning words. One of the earliest websites that was a source of information for persons with a disability on the Internet was *Cripworld*, which saw itself as a resource site for information and advocacy, and a site of empowerment through the use of this term.
54 Mauss, Techniques du Corps'; Bourdieu, *Distinction.*
55 Dyck and Archetti, *Sport*, 11.
56 Ibid., 9.
57 Ibid.

REFERENCES

Appadurai, Arjun. 'Sovereignty Without Territoriality: Notes for a Postnational Geography'. In *The Anthropology of Space and Place: Locating Culture*, edited by Setha M. Low and Denise Lawrence-Zuniga, 337–50. Malden, MA: Blackwell, 2003.

Aronson, Jerrold, Rom Harre, and Eileen Cornell Way. *Realism Rescued: How Scientific Progress is Possible.* Chicago and LaSalle, Illinois: Open Court, 1995.

Bourdieu, Pierre. *Distinction: A Social Critique of the Judgement of Taste.* Cambridge, MA: Harvard University Press, 1990.

Brysk, Alison, ed. *Globalization and Human Rights.* Los Angeles: University of California Press, 2002.

Butryn, Ted. 'Posthuman Podiums: Cyborg Narratives of Elite Track and Field Athletes'. *Sociology of Sport Journal* 20, no. 1 (2003): 17–39.

Depauw, Karen, and Susan J. Gavron, eds. *Disability and Sport.* Champaign, IL: Human Kinetics, 2005.

Doll-Tepper, Gudrun, Michael Kroner, and Wenner Sonnenschein, ed. *New Horizons in Sport for Athletes with a Disability. Proceedings of the International VISTA '99 Conference, Cologne, Germany.* Vols 1 and 2. Oxford: Meyer and Meyer Sport, 2001.

Donnelly, Jack. *Universal Human Rights in Theory and Practice.* 2nd edn. Ithaca, NY: Cornell University Press, 2003.

Donnelly, Peter. 'Child Labour, Sport Labour: Applying Child Labour Laws to Sport'. *International Review for the Sociology of Sport* 32, no. 4 (1997): 389–406.

Duncan, Margaret Carlisle. 'The Sociology of Ability and Disability in Physical Activity'. *Sociology of Sport Journal* 18, no. 1 (2001): 51–68.

Dyck, Noel, and Eduardo P. Archetti. *Sport, Dance and Embodied Identities.* New York: Berg, 2003.

Dyck, Noel, and Eduardo P. Archetti. 'Getting into the Game: Anthropological Perspectives on Sport – Introduction'. *Anthropologica* 46, no. 1 (2004): 3–8.

Farnell, Brenda. 'Moving Bodies, Acting Selves'. *Annual Review of Anthropology* 28 (1999): 341–73.

Figueroa-Sarriera, Heidi J. 'Children of the Mind with Disposable Bodies'. In *The Cyborg Handbook*, edited by Chris Hables Gray. New York: Routledge, 1995.

Foucault, Michel. *The Birth of the Clinic: An Archaeology of Medical Perception.* New York: Vintage, 1994.

Foucault, Michel. *Discipline and Punish: The Birth of the Prison.* New York: Vintage, 1995.

Frohlick, Susan E. 'Negotiating the "Global" Within the Global Playscapes of Mount Everest'. *The Canadian Review of Sociology and Anthropology* 40, no. 5 (2003): 525–42.

Garland-Thomson, Rosemarie. *Extraordinary Bodies: Figuring Physical Disability in American Culture and Literature.* New York: Columbia University Press, 1997.

Goffman, Erving. *Stigma: Notes on the Management of Spoiled Identity.* New York: Touchstone Press, 1986.

Goffman, Erving. *The Presentation of Self in Everyday Life.* New York: Anchor Books, 1963.

Gupta, Akhil. 'The Song of the Non-Aligned World: Transnational Identities and the Reinscription of Space in Late Capitalism'. In *The Anthropology of Space and Place: Locating Culture,* edited by Setha M. Low and Denise Lawrence-Zuniga, 321–36. Malden, MA: Blackwell, 2003.

Guttman, Ludwig. 'Sport for the Disabled as a World Problem'. *Rehabilitation* 68 (1969): 29–43.

Haraway, Donna. 'Cyborg Manifesto'. In *The Cultural Studies Reader,* edited by Simon During, 271–91, 2nd edn New York: Routledge, 2000.

Homer. *The Odyssey.* London: Penguin Books, 2003.

ISPT News. *IPST Facts and Figures.* International Paralympic Swim Trials. Thursday, August 17, 1995. Evening session. No 2: 1–2.

Kidd, Bruce. 'A New Social Movement: Sport for Development and Peace'. *Sport in Society* 11, no. 4 (2008): 370–80.

Langlan, Celeste. 'Mobility, Disability'. *Public Culture* 13, no. 3 (2001): 459–484.

Linton, Simi. *Claiming Disability: Knowledge and Identity.* New York: New York University Press, 1998.

Le Clair, Jill. 'High Performance Swimming or Political Correctness'. In *New Horizons in Sport for Athletes with a Disability. Proceedings of the International VISTA '99 Conference, Cologne, Germany,* Vol. 2. edited by Gudrun Doll-Tepper, Michael Kroner, and Wenner Sonnenschein, 465–92. Oxford: Meyer and Meyer Sport, 2001.

Link, Bruce G., and Jo C. Phelan. 'Conceptualizing Stigma'. *Annual Review of Sociology* 27 (2001): 363–85.

Low, Setha M., and Denise Lawrence-Zuniga. *The Anthropology of Space and Place: Locating Culture,* 321–36. Malden, MA: Blackwell, 2003.

Mauss, Marcel. 'Techniques du Corps'. *Economy and Society* 2, no. 1 (1974): 70–88.

McDermott, Lisa. 'Toward a Feminist Understanding of Physicality Within the Context of Women's Physically Active and Sporting Lives'. *Sociology of Sport Journal* 1 (1996): 12–31.

Nussbaum, Felicity. 'Feminotopias: The Pleasures of Deformity in Mid-Eighteenth Century England'. In *The Body and Physical Difference: Discourses of Disability,* edited by David T. Mitchell and Sharon L. Snyder, 161–73. Ann Arbor: University of Michigan Press, 1997.

O'Sullivan, John. 'Messy Business'. *National Post,* March 23, 2005, A22.

Pinel, Elizabeth C. 'Stigma Consciousness: The Psychological Legacy of Social Stereotypes'. *Journal of Personality and Social Psychology* 76 (1999): 114–28.

Raphael, Dennis, Toba Bryant, and Marcia Rioux, eds. *Staying Alive: Critical Perspectives on Health, Illness, and Health Care.* Toronto: Canadian Scholars' Press, 2006.

Singer, Judy. '"Why Can't You Be Normal for Once Once in Your Life": From a Problem With No Name to the Emergence of a New Category with a Difference'. In *Disability Discourse,* edited by Mariaan Corker and Sally French, 59–67. Philadelphia: Open University Press, 1999.

Steadward, Robert, and Cynthia Peterson. *Paralympics: Where Heroes Come.* Edmonton, AB: One Shot Publishing, 1997.

Titchkosky, Tanya. *Disability, Self and Society.* Toronto: University of Toronto Press, 2003.

Wolff, Eli, Mary Hums, Elise Roy. *Sport in the UN Convention on the Rights of Persons with Disabilities.* New York: United Nations Office of Sport for Development & Peace, 2007.

SECTION 3

Social Bonds Generated by Sports: Fandom, Community, and Media

For millions of Americans sport is the subject about which they are the most knowledgeable and enthusiastic. For better or worse, probably for worse, many Americans care about sport more deeply than they care about any other aspect of public life.

(Nathan, "Rooting for the Home Team," p. 1)

Every NFL Sunday, Matt Mikolas prepares for action. If he's attending the Seahawks' game, which he often does, that entails putting on a full Hawks uniform, spray-painting his hair blue and green, and inscribing the number "12" on his face. Other fans aren't as extreme in their adornment. . . . But they're often just as deeply invested in the outcome of every game. The Seahawks have become a regional obsession, with the collective mood largely dependent on their success or failure. In case you hadn't noticed, the "12's" are everywhere these days, loud and proud.

(Stone, Seattle Times, p. 1)

Though sport fans like Matt Mikolas and his fellow "12s" are typically viewed by non-fans as an array of hyper-energized eccentrics, they constitute a special type of social phenomenon in modern urban society which transcends the divisions of class, race, ethnicity, and religion. That is because sports—in their most dynamic and compelling forms—have the ability to galvanize people from diverse backgrounds and lifestyles into extraordinary civic fraternities. Whether the fans are congregating on the smaller scale of Little League baseball and high school basketball or on the larger scale of professional soccer and football, it is through sports that they are able to leave behind the tensions and stresses of modern life.

FANDOM AS A BASIS OF SOCIAL COMMUNITY IN MODERN SOCIETY

Fandom has come to form one of the principal media of collective identification in modern society and one of the principal sources of meaning in life for many people.

(Dunning et al., 1986: 222)

The great French sociologist Emile Durkheim argued in his first major theoretical work *The Division of Labor in Society*, that the development of modern urban society would bring about increasing organizational differentiation, social diversity, and individualism. In Durkheim's view, these developments would not only weaken **social community** by increasing social fragmentation and anomie; they would also result in social problems manifested in higher rates of suicide, family instability, and crime. Though Durkheim speculated that these problems might be mitigated to some extent by new bases of social community organized around occupations, he anticipated a difficult and problematic future for the stability of social communities in modern societies. Durkheim's predictions of increases in such social problems as crime and suicide turned out to be correct: the development of modern urban life is linked to increased individualism and weaker social bonds as well as a greater prevalence of social problems, including some—like drug addiction, homeless street children, and mass homicides—that he did not foresee.

Yet despite his brilliant insights into the effects of modernization on the social fabric, Durkheim failed to foresee the new forms of community such as sport fandom that would emerge and help to counteract the fragmentation of urban industrial society. Major spectator sports and many other modern forms of voluntary associations did not exist during Durkheim's lifetime. Nevertheless, in his later writings on religion (*The Elementary Forms of Religious Life*, 2001), where he focused on the role of sacred symbols and rituals in group life, Durkheim developed important insights into the social process of community formation that have strongly influenced contemporary sociological studies of both religious and non-religious communities, including sport fan communities.

IS SOCIAL CAPITAL IN DECLINE?

Sport fan communities, like other forms of community, constitute what social scientists term **social capital**. According to the definition presented by Robert Putnam, one of the major theorists on community, the term social capital denotes "trust, norms and networks . . ." which "tend to be self-reinforcing and cumulative. Successful collaboration in one endeavor builds connections and trust—social assets that facilitate future collaboration" (Putnam, 2000). In short, social capital constitutes a vital social resource in modern urban society. By bringing people together in collective endeavors, it fosters and sustains civic consciousness and civic identity.

Putnam, however, failed to link spectator sports to social capital in contemporary American society. He argued that social capital was strong in American society up to the mid-twentieth century but declined significantly in the contemporary era, which is characterized by weak and fragmented social communities, along with an increased prevalence of autonomous individuals.

It is noteworthy that Putnam used a recreational sport—league bowling—as the metaphorical symbol of declining social capital in American society. He noted that an unprecedented number of Americans were bowling up to the 1970s but that organized bowling leagues plummeted between 1980 and 1993. The number of bowlers in the United States increased by 10 percent, while bowling leagues declined by 40 percent. This decline of bowling leagues, he argued, reflected a general decline in civic engagement and the increased individualizing and privatizing lifestyles in American society.

OR IS SOCIAL CAPITAL EVOLVING?

Putnam's argument encountered critics who pointed out some of its flaws. We will consider the views of two of those critics who focused on the issue of sport social communities in contemporary American life. Writing in response to Putnam, sport social psychologist David Wann (Wann et al., 2001: 187) argued that American society "was witnessing not so much a decline in social capital but a new stage in its development." Wann agreed that modern society has eroded traditional forms of solidarity; but he argued that people satisfy those needs for interaction and civic engagement differently, in less intimate and personal ways. Wann pointed to what he termed "a modern conception of social community," which consists of "[t]ertiary social networks provided by activities like sports fandom [and which] satisfies an important social imperative . . . [b]y serving as places where strangers assemble both to be entertained and to engage in mutual dialogue.

Perhaps most important, Wann noted that Putnam failed to realize that sports are venues with commercial possibilities. This is especially relevant to sports in the contemporary era. Sport gatherings constitute what has been termed "**third places**," destinations apart from the home and the work place, where people interact and easily engage one another in conversations, breaking through the interpersonal anonymity of urban life. These sport venues are located in not only third place commercial establishments that facilitate social connections but also private homes, in house parties and other social gatherings focused on sports events. And in recent years, there has been a dramatic increase in 24 hour sports talk radio programs, another major commercial venue nurturing urban sports communities. We will address this phenomenon later in the discussion of sports media.

A second and equally incisive critique of Putnam's argument came from Jason Kaufman, who expressed skepticism about Putnam's alleged "golden age" of American social community (Kaufman, 2003: Ch. 9). Kaufman suggested that this was an idealized view of social capital in the earlier era of American history, which ignored the racial, ethnic, and religious biases that created exclusive social spaces. Those were not diverse modern urban social communities but rather exclusive small town social communities that reinforced rather than transcended the social divisions in American society (Kaufman, 2003).

Overall, it seems reasonable to conclude that Putnam failed to comprehend the new forms of social capital in sports fan communities. This may have been due to his focus on a recreational sport. But even here his argument seems flawed because he did not take into account the many Little League, high school, and locally based communities formed around sports in organizations for all ages from Little League Baseball and Softball and Pop Warner Football, to high school intramural athletics, to adult local teams organized by municipal recreation departments, local employers, religious congregations, and the like. In her pioneering study of a fan community generated by a boy's baseball little league in Philadelphia, Sherri Grasmuck echoed Kaufman's criticism of Putnam's argument. She noted that the fan community she studied did not reflect "Putnam's dismal argument" (Grasmuck, 2005: 203).

Perhaps most important, as suggested above, Putnam ignored the enormous growth of big-time spectator sports like professional baseball, football, basketball, hockey, and auto racing, as well as the big-time American college sports; they all operate as powerful magnets of social community.

MANIFESTATIONS OF SOCIAL CAPITAL

Regardless of which view of social capital's evolution one subscribes to, it is clear that the social capital generated by sports can be manifested in different forms and social contexts. The influence of sports as a basis of social community pervades modern societies. Consider the following characteristic examples:

- West Germany's World Cup soccer victory in 1954 helped to solidify a new German collective identity nine years after the defeat of the Nazi regime and thereby exerted major influence in legitimating the new democratic German Federal Republic (Heinrich, 2003).
- The Iraqi soccer team's success in the Asia Cup in July 2007 brought a rare moment of unity among Iraqis despite the sectarian violence that divided the nation at the time (Reuters, 2007).

In the case of West Germany, that social capital had long-term effects in helping to stabilize the fragile democratic political system of a war-ravaged nation. Germany's soccer team became a symbol around which the nation could rally without arousing fears or memories of the dreaded Nazi ideology. In Iraq, the soccer team's achievements generated social capital which in turn provided a period when strong feelings of national identity and solidarity surfaced. Those feelings were short-lived as Iraq again descended into sectarian violence, but the event does suggest that sports could play an important future role in helping to foster national integration in Iraq.

A recent example of the impact of sports on a city was illustrated when NBA superstar LeBron James decided to leave his hometown team, the Cleveland Cavaliers, to play with the Miami Heat. "James' departure from Cleveland in 2010 left deep psychic wounds on the city. On the night of his televised decision, fans burned replicas of his jersey and tossed a memorabilia into the trash bins" (Cacciola, 2014: 1).

As residents of a city that had experienced difficult times due to its economic decline and population loss as well as increased social problems, Cleveland fans felt betrayed by James's departure. But that feeling changed quickly when James, after a four-year hiatus in Miami, decided to return home and play once again for the Cavaliers. In response to the news, noted one news reporter:

> Cleveland tossed aside its hesitant tap dance, one part belligerence and one part please-come-back, and broke into a cathartic jig. This corner of the Rust Belt wears its pride and insecurities like a favorite T-shirt. "Cleveland, you are a winner," proclaimed a caller on talk radio. "No one can call us losers anymore.
>
> (Michael Powell, 2014: 3)

These fan reactions reveal not just their elation on the return of their native son, but also a feeling of status elevation because, as arguably the greatest basketball player in the modern era, LeBron James placed Cleveland in the national spotlight. Now Cleveland would be known for something other than its economic and social problems.

Equally significant are the effects of sports on other urban metropolitan areas like Boston, New York, and New Orleans—where winning sports teams ignite unique feelings of collective identity and unity—despite the class and racial divisions of everyday social life.

On the global scale, we can frequently observe the powerful impact of mega-sports events like the Olympics and World Cup victories in enhancing feelings of national unity and pride in nations like China, Brazil, and Ethiopia which are plagued by social inequality and political tensions. National sports victories create opportunities to bask in reflected glory, which is why many authoritarian governments try to promote national sports to galvanize patriotic feeling of national community.

Sport often eases the strains of social stratification. One study about the powerful effects of sports noted: "The success of an Australian community's rugby team created a positive symbolic image for the city that submerged the perceptions of its divisions and inequalities" (Rowe and McGuirk, 1999: 125). A similar indication of the power of sports was affirmed by the mayor of Youngstown, Ohio, which has suffered decades of economic decline due to deindustrialization: "The (sports) program is vital to our community. Losing the mills took a tremendous psychological toll. We're starting to regain confidence and Youngstown State football has been a big part of this (Wann and Pierce, 2000: 196).

IMPACT ON RACIAL PREJUDICE

Sport also sometimes operates to bridge racial divisions in American cities and towns, in communities with long and bitter histories of racial segregation and racial tensions. We see an example of this power of sports to bring blacks and whites together in racially segregated Indianapolis, Indiana, in 1951. An all-black Indianapolis high school basketball team, the Crispus Attucks Tigers, united the city by winning the state championship. In the words of the Indianapolis Superintendent of Schools, "That basketball team accomplished more for race relations in one season than you could accomplish in ten years of forums and discussions. The white people here have a completely new impression of the colored race. It's marvelous" (Pierce, 2004: 202). The superintendent's amazement at the impact of that black basketball team's victory was echoed by a local news reporter. Writing about that state championship in the *Indianapolis News,* he recalled that the championship was "[t]he thing the 1950–51 Attucks team may eventually be known for—it's a long step toward making Indianapolis one town." Whites in Indianapolis, for the first time, were cheering for a black basketball team because they felt pride in the honor the team brought to the city.

IMPACT ON RACIAL INTEGRATION

Addressing this theme of sports bridging racial divisions from a somewhat different angle, Sherri Grasmuck produced an insightful ethnographic study of a Little League baseball team in a racially segregated neighborhood in Philadelphia (see Chapter 13). She demonstrated how Little League baseball, aided by gentrification, facilitated the development of social capital, in the form of friendships among parents, that led to the racial integration of the neighborhood.

Grasmuck specifically attributed the formation of that racially integrated social community, in large part, to Little League baseball because it possessed certain characteristics that facilitated interactions between parents sitting in the stands. Among those characteristics, baseball lacked a clock. The absence of a clock and the slow pace of the game created waiting time between plays, providing opportunities for parents to socialize and bond. By contrast, observed Grasmuck, if the sport had been basketball or soccer, parents would have had less time to get to know one another, and social community would not have developed. This differed from the racial bridging fostered by basketball in Indianapolis which created feelings of interracial unity, which certainly represented progress. But the racial bridging studied by Grasmuck in Philadelphia went farther by facilitating neighborhood racial integration. Significantly, this more significant change resulted from a recreational sport.

IMPACT ON RACIALLY OPPRESSED MINORITY GROUPS

The final racial–ethnic dimension of sports-generated social capital we will note concerns the impact of sports on racially oppressed minority groups. During the Jim Crow era in the United States, when African Americans had few opportunities for upward social mobility and professional jobs in mainstream American society, great black American athletes led the way in achieving recognition of their talents and were regarded by most black Americans as standard bearers of the community's honor and aspirations. Beginning with Jack Johnson's emergence as the world heavyweight boxing champion in 1910, every major sporting event involving black athletes against white opponents symbolized—in the eyes of most black Americans—the black community's struggle for racial equality. Because these black athletes constituted the few African Americans allowed to compete against whites on a level playing field in the public arena, the athletic contests took on the aura of quasi sacred spectacles.

For example, the 1935 victory of black American boxer Joe Louis over his white German opponent, Max Baer, sparked excited and ecstatic celebrations in black American communities throughout the United States (see Chapter 12). The power of sport to boost the morale and affirm the honor of black social communities was unparalleled during the Jim Crow era of racial segregation in the United States. Great black American athletes who excelled in competition against whites—such as Jesse Owens, Jackie Robinson, Hank Aaron, Althea Gibson, Arthur Ashe, Wilma Rudolph, Wilt Chamberlain, Bill Russell, Willie Mays, Muhammad Ali, and Jim Brown—existed not simply as great athletes but as heroic icons in black American culture. Their athletic achievements no doubt influenced the spirit of resistance that led to the black civil rights movement. Similar examples of athletes operating as heroic icons of ethnic community pride occurred in the Irish American, the Italian American, the Jewish American, the Hispanic American communities—as well as other ethnic communities. Sport emerged as the first mainstream social institution in which marginalized ethnic Americans could achieve elite status.

FANS' EMOTIONAL INVESTMENTS VERSUS OWNERS' BUSINESS INVESTMENTS

> Fans are the only ones who really care. There are no free-agent fans.
>
> (Dick Young, in Billings, 2009: 47)

Dick Young's observation captures a central reality of modern big-time sports in the modern era: fans are the only ones whose involvement is based solely on personal loyalty—an emotional investment that seeks no reward apart from the team's success. Manifestations of fans' emotional investments are sometimes bewildering and profound.

In her study of the emotional attachments of fans to the Pittsburgh Steelers, Marci Cottingham wrote of

> [a woman] who, at the final request of her late husband, brought his ashes to a Steeler's game at Heinz Field. Her husband never attended a Steeler's game in his lifetime and was, therefore, unable to experience peak moments. . . . But he had been a devoted fan even from his home in New England. His sons dressed in Steeler's jerseys for his funeral and his body was covered with a Steeler's blanket.
>
> (Cottingham, 2012:179)

This linkage of sports to rituals is hardly unique. In another example, focused on the death of Pittsburgh's mayor, Cottingham cited a newspaper article which reported:

> the mayor's son will help escort his father's casket during the heavy-hearted procession from mass to graveside. Then, prior to the 8:30 pm kickoff at Heinz Field, he will lead the official waving of Terrible Towels (a Steeler's fan ritual), just as his father led the Steeler's faithful in the incredible playoff run of the last season.
>
> (p. 180)

In light of the fans' intense loyalty, it would be difficult to imagine the city of Pittsburgh without its legendary football team, which forms an integral part of that city's identity.

EMOTIONAL ATTACHMENT TO STADIUMS

Fans' emotional investment in their sports teams often extends to the stadiums where the teams have played. As the sites of some of the fans' most cherished life experiences, these stadiums sometimes acquire the sacred symbolic significance of shrines whose emotional value cannot be determined by economic calculations. This was demonstrated clearly in an ethnographic study of fans' responses to teams' decisions to relocate to new stadiums in the same metropolitan area. Some fans expressed a deep emotional bond with the old stadiums which they could not simply transfer to a new stadium. In response to the Houston Rangers (Major League Baseball) team's decision to shift to a new stadium, a 60-year-old woman lamented, "I've been coming here since the Rangers came back in '72. This place has been a big part of me for 22 years. It's like losing an old friend. It's hard to tell an old friend goodbye" (Triujillo, 2010: 283).

In addition to sadness, fans sometimes also express resentment in response to the decision of team owners to move to a new stadium. This was illustrated by the comments of a Chicago White Sox fan, a young man in his early 20s:

> The ball park means a lot more to me than just baseball. There's a lot of personal things tied up in it, and that's why I feel strongly that it shouldn't have been torn down. Instead of spending 100 million on that monstrosity down the street, they could have sunk it in here and we would have had a ballpark for another hundred years and our ties to the past would have been preserved. I can't just cut the ties with her so early.
>
> (p. 281)

As noted in the discussion of sports social capital, sport venues often exist as important "third place" destinations in the lives of sport fans, places apart from their homes and workplaces, where they form social connections and share precious memories. This sentiment was reflected in the comments of another Chicago White Sox fan on the team's move from Comiskey Park.

> We came here, seven of us, right before I left for 'Nam. I remember I was home on leave and seven of us came down here and we joked that this could be for some of us our last ballgame, so we came to see the Sox. Three of those guys were eventually killed over there, and I guess I'm saying goodbye to them. This park was my bond with them, and now I'm gonna lose that tie. So I know that it's weird that I kiss this wall, but I'm just saying goodbye to some buddies I saw in here for the last time back then.
>
> (p. 287)

Put simply, fans' emotional investment in their teams and the team stadiums, unlike the decisions made by team owners, are not based on economic rationality. However, fans can have worse experiences than the loss of old stadiums. Sometimes fans' emotional investment in their professional sports teams is betrayed for financial reasons. We see examples of this when teams decide to abandon a city and relocate elsewhere. One of the most devastating moves in the history of modern professional sports occurred in 1957 when the legendary Brooklyn Dodgers moved to Los Angeles. Dodger fans were legendary as one of Major League Baseball's most passionate fan communities. "A true Dodger fan," in the words of one observer, "did more than simply root for them. A true Dodger fan was an ardent and enthusiastic devotee of the team; not just of baseball but of the only Major League professional baseball team ever to be named after something other than a city or a state" (Thompson, brooklynboard.com/diary). Brooklyn existed as one of five boroughs in New York City. A large part of Brooklyn's identity and civic consciousness as a community derived from its beloved baseball team. The decision of the Dodgers' owner, Walter O'Malley, to move the team to Los Angeles did more than destroy the Dodgers' sports community; it crushed Brooklyn's civic pride. The gravity of that decision was perhaps best captured by an apocryphal anecdote that was repeated in the 2007 HBO documentary *The Brooklyn Dodgers: The Ghosts of Flatbush*: "If you asked a Brooklyn Dodger fan, if you had a gun with only two bullets in it and were in a room with Hitler, Stalin, and O'Malley, who would you shoot first? The answer: O'Malley twice" (HBO 2007). Though this sentiment was expressed as humor, it resonated the actual emotional outrage of hundreds of thousands of Brooklyn Dodger fans who felt they were victimized by moral injustice.

SIGNIFICANT EXAMPLES OF PROFESSIONAL TEAMS' RELOCATIONS

Because they operate not just as representatives of their cities but also as businesses, professional sport teams sometimes relocate to other cities in search of greener financial pastures. The following denote significant examples of American professional sport teams' relocations over the past 60 years:

A. Major League Baseball

- 1958: Brooklyn Dodgers to Los Angeles
- 1958: New York Giants to San Francisco

- 1961 Washington Senators (original) moved to Twin Cities in Minnesota
- 1966 Milwaukee Braves to Atlanta
- 1968 Kansas City Athletics to Oakland, Calif.
- 1972 Washington Senators (second franchise) to Arlington, Texas
- 2005 Montreal Expos to Washington, D.C., became the Washington Nationals

B. National Basketball Association

- 1957: Rochester Royals to Cincinnati, Ohio
- 1960: Minneapolis Lakers to Los Angeles
- 1962: Philadelphia Warriors to San Francisco
- 1963: Syracuse Nationals to Philadelphia, became the 76ers
- 1968: St. Louis Hawks to Atlanta
- 1972: Cincinnati Royals to Kansas City
- 1973: Baltimore Bullets to Washington, D.C., became Washington Wizards in 1997
- 1979: New Orleans Jazz to Salt Lake City
- 1984, San Diego Clippers to Los Angeles
- 2001: Vancover Grizzlies to Memphis, Tenn.
- 2002: Charlotte Hornets to New Orleans
- 2008: Seattle Supersonics to Oklahoma City, became the Thunder
- 2012: New Jersey Nets to Brooklyn, N.Y., became Brooklyn's first major sports franchise since 1957

C. The National Football League

- 1960: Chicago Cardinals to St. Louis
- 1961: Los Angeles Chargers to San Diego
- 1982: Oakland Raiders to Los Angeles
- 1984: Baltimore Colts to Indianapolis
- 1988: St. Louis Cardinals to Phoenix, Arizona
- 1995: Los Angeles Raiders to Oakland
- 1996: Cleveland Browns to Baltimore, became the Ravens
- 1997: Houston Oilers to Memphis, became the Tennessee Oilers

Several qualifications should be noted to clarify the consequences of these relocations for the fan communities they left behind. Not all of the abandoned fan communities ended up without a team. In some cases (e.g., Washington baseball; Cleveland football; Philadelphia basketball; St. Louis football), a new franchise replaced the one that moved. Though still often traumatic for many fans who had developed strong loyalties to their teams over many years, these changes gave fans opportunities to develop new team loyalties. But this was not the situation of such localities as Brooklyn (baseball), Cincinnati (basketball), and Vancouver (basketball). The abandoned localities were left with diminished social communities.

TWO CONFLICTING CONCEPTIONS OF OWNERSHIP

Decisions to move teams to other cities highlight the two conflicting views of ownership in professional sports. The first and most familiar denotes the conventional economic and legal conception of ownership. The teams are property like other businesses that were purchased by their owners, who acquired legal rights to make all decisions about the location and use of their property. The second conception of ownership, in contrast, denotes a subjective *feeling* of ownership which ignores economic considerations. It consists of an enduring emotional attachment, forming a part of the fan's personal identity, like a family bond or a religious affiliation.

This second notion of subjective emotional ownership is captured in the following discussion of European soccer club fans resistance movements which oppose decisions by legal owners:

> These . . . movements defend the idea, whatever the messy history and actuality of private ownership and commercialization might be, that the club's just that, a club rather than another business, and that its authority as such lies in the fans' history of collective investment of time, emotion, imagination and money.
>
> (Hughson and Free, 2006: 81)

As the anchors who nurture and sustain the team's collective memory and identity amid the turbulent and disruptive market forces of modern sports, fans feel entitled to influence team decision making. In light of their deep emotional investment, some scholars describe fans as stakeholders whose enduring loyalty counteracts the continuous evolution and changes of players, coaches, and owners. Players come and go, coaches come and go, owners come and go. But fans endure.

In a study of a soccer fan community in Florence, Italy, Zagnoli and Radicchi cite the various ways in which the fans constitute "a territorially based tribe," noting that 87 percent of the fans live in the city's metropolitan area (see Chapter 18). Based on their observations of this fan community, the authors identified four types of fans who differed by the levels and patterns of their involvement with the team. Significantly, the intense feelings of some fan stakeholders have led to open conflicts with the owner about the management of the team.

We see another example of this type of fan reaction and conflict in the case of Manchester United, the English Premier League professional soccer team, where some fans strongly objected to a new owner because he had engaged in questionable financial transactions to acquire the team. He purchased the team with leveraged debt, causing some fans to believe that this would result in a sharp increase in ticket prices and severely limit the team's ability to acquire new players and remain competitive. In the words of one fan: "the amount of money to be repaid is huge. . . . It is difficult to see how these sums can be reached without significant increases in ticket prices, which, as we always suspected, means the fans will effectively be paying for someone to borrow money to own their own club" (Tynan, 2014: 1). This is an example of fans mobilizing to represent their interest as stakeholders who have strong emotional investments in the team.

As we have noted, sometimes tensions between fans' emotional investment and the owner's economic investment may persist because professional sport fandom and capitalism exists in an uneasy relationship. An example of this is illustrated in the actions of the Denver Broncos owners:

> Mere months [after the Broncos' Super Bowl win], the newly crowned Super Bowl champions announced they might move the team to another city if Denver fails to come up with $250 million for a new stadium—even though the team itself is valued at only $180 million.

> Denver's predicament is not uncommon. More than 50 million Americans in almost 30 urban areas stand to lose a professional sports team in the near future unless their local governments agree to subsidize new, amenity-laden stadiums. But why should a community pay more than a team is worth simply to keep it local for another 10 to 20 years—especially since tax revenue generated by a stadium is usually less than the cost of the subsidy? How can a team keep its home team without emptying its coffers into the hands of a private owner?
>
> (See Chapter 14; Morris and Krager, 2010: 26–27)

So the predicament of the Brooklyn Dodger fans mentioned earlier is now a potential threat confronting many cities with professional sports teams. Not that most of those threats will ever come to fruition. Nevertheless, the threat of financial blackmail faced by these cities and their fans makes them vulnerable to exploitation by profit-driven owners.

Various critics have raised questions about private capitalist ownership of professional sports teams, as they differ from conventional businesses and economic products. Sports franchises, unlike auto manufacturers or drug companies and other privately owned enterprises, are cultural commodities.

THE GREEN BAY PACKERS MODEL: FAN COMMUNITY OWNERSHIP

The Green Bay Packers deserve attention because they constitute an anomaly in American professional sports: a sport franchise owned by the fan community. As one observer has put it:

> The best town in pro sports is also the smallest: Green Bay, Wisconsin, home of the Packers. The Dallas Cowboys aren't America's team, the Green Bay Packers are. And not just because of their championship history. The Packers are owned by the fans, not a wealthy owner operating with a profit-at-all-costs (PAAC) philosophy. The Green Bay Packers are a publicly owned non-profit with a unique stock ownership structure. Green Bay's by-laws state that the Packers are a "community project, intended to promote community welfare."
>
> (Reed, "League of Fans," p. 1)

That the Green Bay Packers with its radically different ownership structure has attracted little public discussion is curious, particularly in light of the widespread tensions between fans and owners of various sport franchises around the country. Why the relative silence about this alternative which, in the opinion of ESPN's Patrick Hruby, represents "a working model for a better way to organize and admisister pro-sport?" No one can question the success of the Packers franchise.

> The Packers have sold out more than 300 consecutive games and have more than 80,000 names on their season-ticket waiting list. Despite being one of the most successful teams on the field, the Packers ticket prices are among the lowest in the league. Unlike other NFL stadiums that have advertisements everywhere the eyes can see, Lambeau Field is relatively free of corporate sales pitches. The only ads you see are on the scoreboards.
>
> (Reed, "League of Fans," p. 1)

The reason fans in other NFL cities have not adopted the Green Bay model is hardly a mystery. No future Green Bay Packers are possible because its ownership model is now prohibited by the league. In 1960, then-commissioner Pete Rozelle changed the league rules and banned any further attempts of franchises to adopt the Green Bay model. In effect, the new NFL rule prohibits ownership by non-profit charitable organizations. As commissioner, Rozelle was representing the views of the league's team owners, his employers, who felt their financial interests would be threatened if the Green Bay model were allowed to spread. The new rule consolidated the private ownership model. Fans are limited to an emotional investment.

THE PARTNERSHIP-CARTEL MODEL

The major sports teams in the United States operate as enormously profitable economic cartels. Members of the league cartels control the rules of ownership and act in concert to prevent competition. Under NFL bylaws, a team must have at least one general partner who holds a minimum of 30 percent of stake in the team. Partnerships can't number more than 24 persons and corporate ownership is denied.

Why the denial of corporate ownership in the NFL? Some owners fear that this would lead to imbalances in league competition because small market teams would be less likely to attract corporate ownership than large market teams. As a result, large market teams would dominate the league championships ("NFL Owners Debate The Pros and Cons of Corporate Ownership," *Los Angeles Times*).

In recent years, challenges to the sport league monopolies have emerged and sought to mobilize a social movement to promote changes in the private ownership model of professional sports. One of the individuals in the forefront of this challenge is the social critic and consumer advocate Ralph Nader, who argues:

> The fundamental problem in pro sports is that we've given free reign [sic] to owners through a self-regulated monopoly system—including anti-trust exemptions—which allows owners to pursue a profit-at-all-costs agenda at the expense of fans. This system has resulted in owners playing one city off another in the quest for new taxpayer-funded stadiums and other freeloading. A community ownership model, like the Green Bay Packers', works. It's a better way to structure and administer professional sports. It should become an optional mainstay of sports policy in this country.
>
> (Nader, 2011)

Fans Voice, a fans' interest group founded by Ralph Nader, marks an interesting and unprecedented development in American sports. As it points out in its agenda statement, "Sports fans have lost their grip on the games we love. The sports business today is a $200 billion plus business. Isn't it time that the sports fan, the one who pays for all of this, is the only one without a 'seat at the table'" (Nader, 2011).

Fans Voice views the relationship between fans and owners as essentially a power imbalance. In effect, it aims to subject professional sports owners to a more democratic process of accountability, by mobilizing fans to assert their collective interests. We can discern the general perspective of the movement from the eight articles asserted in its Fans' Bill of Rights:

> Sports fans have the right to organize and to formalize their own associations at the local, regional, national, and international levels.

> Sports fans have the right to representation and to have a voice in appropriate forums where sports related issues and matters affecting sports at any level are being debated and decisions are being made. True fan representation should always be invited and included in such forums.
>
> Sports fans have the right to self-expression, to voice their own opinions on any and all aspects of sport in a respectful and deliberate manner.
>
> Sports fans have the right to vote in all national sports ranking systems and honors awarded to franchises, coaches and players.
>
> Sports fans have the right to fast, accurate, and complete public information about players, coaches, owners, league members, games and performance.
>
> Sports fans have the right to demand good sportsmanship and the exhibition of positive moral character from all who engage in or represent organized sports at all levels including athletes and non-athletes.
>
> Sports fans have the right to a wholesome environment for athletic events; free of violence, profane gestures and language or rude and invasive behavior that could in any way interfere with a positive exemplary entertainment experience.
>
> Sports fans have the right to expect a best effort on a consistent basis. This includes every play on the field, every action in the stands, every call in the front office, and every team involvement in the community.
>
> (Fans Voice "Sports Fans Bill of Rights," pp. 1–2)

THE DARK SIDE OF SOCIAL CAPITAL

> Sports plays a role in engendering jingoist and chauvinist attitudes. They're designed to organize a community to be committed to their gladiators.
>
> (Chomsky, 1994: 259)

Though Noam Chomsky's statement was intended as a characterization of sport's role in society, it actually describes a negative aspect of sports community or "the dark side of social capital." This has been defined as "situations in which trust, social ties and shared beliefs and norms that may be beneficial to some persons are detrimental to other(s)" (see Chapter 31). Put simply, sometimes sport social capital is manifested in destructive or harmful social behavior. Here we will examine some of its effects in facilitating and affirming antagonistic fan communities which are oriented to intolerance, bigotry and violence. This seems ironic because sport is predicated on the normative ideals of fairness; yet sport fan communities often fail to adhere to ideals in their own behavior.

FAN RACIAL BIGOTRY

Sports can be potent symbols that mobilize racial tensions, especially when the outcome of the contests challenge the dominant racial group's claim to superiority. This was evidenced historically in American sport contests between white and black athletes. Those contests often embodied powerful racial symbolism because many fans tended to view them as events that determined racial superiority. They generated negative racially based social capital which reinforced racial biases and divisions in the society.

Jack Johnson, the first African American to win the heavyweight boxing championship, was so reviled by white American boxing fans that many rioted and attacked blacks in cities across the country the night Johnson won the title. Shortly afterwards, a movement was launched to find a white boxer—the putative "great white hope"—who could defeat Johnson and regain the title for the white race. Jesse Owens, the African American sprinter, greatly offended pro-Nazi German sport fans during the 1936 Olympic games in Berlin when he won four gold medals, thereby puncturing the Nazi myth of "Aryan racial superiority." German Chancellor Adolf Hitler was so disturbed by Owens's extraordinary performance that he abruptly left the stadium before the awards ceremony. The Nazis had used sports as an instrument for mobilizing social capital to support their racist political movement.

Yet another example of the symbolic potency of sports performances to generate negative social capital occurred when Hank Aaron, the black American Major League Baseball player, received death threats and had to be protected by security guards during the season he broke Babe Ruth's home run record. Because Babe Ruth, who held the record for 60 years existed as the quintessential white male symbol of baseball prowess, was being supplanted by a black man, many white American male fans felt deeply offended. Though Aaron played for a racially integrated team, many baseball fans perceived his achievement within a racial context.

The media frequently report incidents of soccer fan racism in Europe, where it has become a familiar spectacle. In Western Europe, for example, Italy and Spain have acquired infamous reputations for soccer fan racism directed at African players. In 2005 an anti-racist campaign was organized by Belgian and Italian players in response to what was described as "a shameful weekend of racism in Cup soccer," when an African player from Ivory Coast was subjected to racial insults from the fans of his opponent's team. In another incident, "in an Italian stadium, a game turned ugly when a white player called his opponent 'a black monkey'" (Welle, 2005).

According to one news report, "some of the (Italian) fans are notorious. You can hear them boo or grunt when the other team's black players touch the ball." Though less frequent than white–black racial slurs, anti-semitic gestures also constitute part of the fans' arsenal of hateful insults. "At one match, fans waved a banner that said their opponent's Jewish fans belonged in Auschwitz" (ABC News.go.com/wnt/story).

Spain's soccer fans hardly take a back seat to Italian fans in reported incidents of bigoted behavior. Following the experience of fans making monkey chants and throwing bananas in response to his presence, an African player from Senegal commented to reporters that he was not placing the blame on all of the opposition team's fans. But he wanted to explain what happened (CNN, 2014). The article reporting the incident online provoked responses from some Spanish fans. Several defended the behavior.

One of the fans who apparently objected to racial diversity wrote: "I live in a mono-ethnic society and I am happy of this fact." Another who seemed to resent the large salaries received by the African players wrote: "With the money they are being paid, they should be able to take a little verbal abuse without running to the thought-police." In a somewhat odd twist, another fan defended the racial chants as a fan's right of free speech: "So if I go to the movies, according to you I invest in the movies I'm seeing. I should be able to decide what's in the movie, and censor the other viewers' reactions. Talk about thought-police" (CNN, 2014).

While soccer fans' racism in Western Europe may be shocking to some North Americans, the behavior of their counterparts in Eastern Europe has acquired an even worse reputation. It should be noted that these societies have had little contact with people of African ancestry because they lived in isolation from African migrations. Nevertheless, reports of crude xenophobic-racist behavior of Eastern European fans in response to African soccer players appear often in international media. According to one media account, Serbian soccer fans manifest especially toxic racist reactions to African players. A British journalist related that he was told by an acquaintance, before he visited Eastern Europe, about its racist soccer fans. He later wrote:

> As it turned out, he wasn't wrong. Almost every negative aspect humanity can offer was visible that evening. Hatred, intimidation, violence, verbal and physical abuse, arson. It was a melting pot of society's worst traits. . . What struck me in that hate-filled environment was how racism and discrimination go well beyond every other form of taboo.
>
> (CNN, 2013)

Various hypotheses have been advanced to explain European soccer fan racism. One hypothesis places the blame on sports media. "In an international context, the media . . . play a part in encouraging racist xenophobia at football matches and this was recognized in the European Parliament Report. . . The committee noted the media frequently present individual matches as 'war-like confrontations' which thus give rise to jingoism and sometimes violence" (SIRC, www.sirc.org.public/fan/racism.html, p. 2).

A second hypothesis links it to immigration. As one journalist has noted: "there have been incidents across Europe in countries that . . . are unaccustomed to immigration from other parts of the world." Another journalist described "a shocking episode in Poland. . . . Fans pelted a Nigerian player with bananas and then laughed at him." The journalist attributed this behavior to Poles being unaccustomed to immigration. The sight of African players apparently symbolized the intrusion of black people into white Polish society, which provoked their fear and hostility (Richard Gizhart, ABC News.go.com/wnt/story).

Taking a broader political sociological perspective, a third hypothesis attributes European soccer fan racism to right-wing political groups. "It's not just Italy," commented one knowledgeable observer. "In many European countries, soccer stadiums have become theaters of hatred, platforms from which neo-Nazis and racists peddle their ideology." He went on to cite an example of this right-wing ideology in the statement of a French politician: "When the French won the World Cup, one politician branded the team 'unworthy' of France because so many of the players were non-whites" (ABC News.go.com/wnt/story). In effect, this hypothesis of right-wing involvement suggests that sport stadiums are used as settings to propagandize and advance xenophobic racist ideologies. This view is supported by the Social Inquiry Research Committee's Report "Racism and Football Fans":

> The attraction of football matches to right wing groups are obvious. Football games provide a useful platform for the group to make their views heard. From there their views can be directed into millions of homes. It also seems as if football grounds can be a means to recruit young supporters.
>
> (www.sirc.org/fn racism.html, 1996)

While considerable evidence suggests that European soccer stadiums are used by right-wing groups to promote their racist and anti-immigrant ideologies, it would be a mistake to assume European fans' racism derives from fringe elements in otherwise racially tolerant fan communities. It is perhaps more accurate to say that some European soccer fans sympathize with racist gestures toward African players: though only a minority of fans are involved in doing such things as throwing bananas on the field and participating in monkey chants, those behaviors are tolerated by many non-participants where race operates as a strong base of social community. These sympathetic non-participants have been termed "hoolifans" (Rockwood and Pearson, 2012).

Taking a somewhat different perspective, Doug Hartmann argues that sport stadiums are often used to showcase social conflict. Because sport events galvanize the attention of huge numbers of people, they operate as what he terms "contested terrain"—settings where social tensions and conflicts are played out (Hartmann, 2000) Soccer matches apparently have assumed this role in some European countries, revealing the dark side of sports social capital.

Some sport analysts view these hostile acts among European sport fans as anti-cosmopolitan reactions to globalization, which is especially visible in player migration from African and Latin American to national soccer clubs in Europe. We will return to a discussion of anti-cosmopolitanism in Section 6 on globalization.

SPORT FAN VIOLENCE

Racism is not the only dark side of sport social capital. Another dimension of this dark side is manifested in sport fan violence. Though there exist different types of sport fan violence, a significant portion is linked to extreme team loyalty or what sometimes assumes the form of crude "tribal sentiments" aroused by sport. Unlike sport fan racism, which seems most prevalent in Europe, sport fan violence occurs throughout the world—in North America, in Europe, in Latin America, and in Africa.

In Latin America, a region known for having some of the world's most rabid sport fans, deaths among fans at sporting events persist as an unfortunate but familiar reality. In 2013, for example, Argentina suffered 18 soccer-related deaths, Colombia suffered 40, and Brazil suffered 30, the highest in the country's history (Wen, 2014: 2). These deaths represent only a small fraction of the number of sports fans who suffered injuries from violence linked to soccer matches in Latin America. These include fans' attacks on players and referees as well as on other fans. In one horrendous incident in Brazil, several fans decapitated a referee (Associated Press, Huffington Post, July 8, 2013).

But despite the pervasive acts of fan violence in Latin American countries, no country has experienced the number of fatalities that Egyptian fans suffered at a single soccer match, in 2013.

> At least 74 people died and hundreds were injured after Wednesday's game in the seaside city of Port Said, when fans of the home team, Al Masry, rushed the pitch, setting off clashes and a stampede as riot police largely failed to intervene. . . . Witnesses say scores of Egyptian soccer fans were stabbed to death while others suffocated, trapped in a long, narrow corridor trying to flee rival fans armed with knives, clubs, and stones in the country's worst ever soccer violence.
>
> (Associated Press, ESPN Soccer, February 1, 2012)

Like many other incidents of group fan violence, in contrast to individual fan violence, this tragic event in Egypt was linked to tribal/ethnic sentiments associated with the opposing teams. We see another example of sport fan violence between ethnic groups in Malawi, in southern Africa, in 2013 where one fan was killed and 20 were injured at a soccer match (BBC.com, December 2013: 1). Tribal sentiments behind sport fan violence can sometimes reflect nationalistic loyalties. This was what apparently happened in Zimbabwe in 2013 during a soccer match between Zimbabwe and South Africa. According to one media report:

> The incident began when fans hurled bottles and other items onto the field after [the team] scored its second goal in the game . . . [giving them] the lead . . . police fired tear gas at unruly fans during a World Cup qualifying soccer game today between Zimbabwe and South Africa, setting off a stampede that killed 12 people.
>
> (ABC News.go.com)

North American sport fan violence is rarely linked to ethnic bonds or large numbers of deaths as witnessed in Latin America and Africa. Nevertheless, fan violence frequently occurs at American sporting events. Fans at NFL games seem especially prone to violence, as noted in a December 2013 *Bleacher Report*.

> Following the [recent] football game in Denver, *The Denver Post* reported that three people were stabbed outside of Sports Authority Field. . . .
>
> This incident would be merely troubling if it were isolated, but it's yet another in a long line of fan-violence problems that have plagued the NFL not only this season, but for a number of years. . . .
>
> [In December 2013], a fan died at another Broncos game. . . . The very next week, a Detroit Lions fan says he was targeted for wearing a Barry Sanders jersey and eventually knocked unconscious following a Philadelphia Eagles victory at Lincoln Financial Field. At one game this year, a male New York Jets fan punched a female New England Patriots fan.
>
> (*Bleacher Report*, 2013)

One way of approaching an understanding of sport fan violence is to distinguish between "expressive" and "instrumental" violence. Expressive sport fan violence consists of emotional catharses, most often carried out by jubilant fans after a sport victory. These are celebratory acts that may damage cars, shop windows and public transportation, intentionally or accidentally as a result of fans getting emotionally "carried away." If there are injuries, they usually result from the reactions of police who attempt to restrain the individuals and restore public order. These acts do not manifest the dark side of social capital, except when they are extraordinarily destructive and motivated to harm others.

By contrast, instrumental sport fan violence—interpersonal violence that aims to harm others—manifests the dark side of social capital. All of the examples of sport fan violence cited above illustrate instrumental—purposeful—actions which were linked directly to sport events. Eliminating the dark side of social capital stands as a major challenge confronting sport authorities throughout the world.

Probably the most influential hypothesis presented to explain sport fan violence was developed by British sociologist Eric Dunning, who argues in his book, *Sport Matters*, that "athletic events are realms in which other major issues in society, often related to class, religion, ethnicity, politics, regionalism, historic rivalries, etc., can play out among supporters" (Wen, 2014: 1–2). In short, sport fan violence often reflects the major divisions and conflicts in society and needs to be approached in that wider context. From this we may conclude that, in order to understand the deeper sources of much sport fan violence, we must analyze its relationship to major social strains in the wider society.

SPORT AND THE MEDIA

> Media sports has . . . a proven capacity to bring potential consumers to the marketplace in numbers ranging from the respectable to the staggering. It is able at particular moments symbolically to reconstruct disparate human groups to make them feel at one with each other (and perhaps, in the case of the Olympics and the World Cup of association football, in the world).
>
> (Rowe, 2004: 73)

The linkage between sport and the media, which began as a tenuous and uncertain alliance, has evolved with the advent of electronic technology into a permanent and highly lucrative marriage. The historical development of that relationship began with the sport pages of daily newspapers which relayed information about sport events through written descriptions and analyses of sport reporters—who operated as the eyes and ears for fans who were not present in the stadiums. In effect, the sport reporters served as proxies for fans who were unable to experience directly the performances of individual and team sport. This arrangement yielded relatively small fan communities.

The first significant change from this proxy arrangement based on sport reporters occurred with the advent of radio, a major advance in media development. The first sport radio broadcast featured a heavyweight boxing championship in 1921. Radio had the advantage of being able to transmit sport events in real-time accounts of the action—live, play by play. Because radio's direct transmissions enriched fan experiences of sport, radio broadcasts increased both the size and number of fan communities. For the first time, fans experienced live sport events, even if they could not afford to go to the stadiums or lived too far away to travel to a game. This was especially significant for out-of-town sport events such as championships, as well as routine "away" games. In effect, the advent of radio marked the beginning of a serious bond between media and sport; although it remained limited, the relationship was firm. Radio broadcasts became a standard feature of all major sports events. In the process, many sports radio broadcasters such as Major League Baseball's Mel Allen (New York Yankees), Harry Carey (St. Louis Cardinals), and Red Barber (Brooklyn Dodgers) became legendary because of their unique personal styles of sport commentary.

TELEVISION'S EFFECTS ON THE SPORT–MEDIA BOND

Notwithstanding the significance of radio, which certainly enhanced fans' experiences of sport, the sport–media bond did not develop into a true marriage until the 1950s, with the emergence of television. This allowed fans not only to experience sport events in real time, but also to actually see the events with their own eyes. The spectacular touchdown pass, the buzzer-beating jump shot, the towering home run and similar spectacular sport performances—all could be observed by fans sitting in their living rooms.

Interestingly, the owners and executives of sport organizations initially felt wary about television because they feared that it might decrease attendance at sport events. This turned out to be a classical case of organizations underestimating the potential of new technology. Their fears of television vanished once they realized that televised sport would open a veritable gold mine of potential wealth. Not only did it greatly increase the sport fan base; it also opened unanticipated streams of revenue from advertising. Tens of millions of people who seldom went to sport events became sport fans. In fact, televised sport became the primary mechanism behind the development and expansion of sport social capital in modern urban societies.

The sports–media marriage forged by television transformed sport—in ways that no one anticipated—with unsettling consequences in that media–sport now poses the danger of sport's subordination to crass materialism. We will examine five principal ways in which this marriage has played out.

MEDIA AND WEALTH

First, the predominance of television in the sport–media relationship has greatly increased the financial wealth of major sport teams and organizations. For example, the scale of financial payments to the NFL can be discerned from the following data reported in 2011.

Sports Illustrated estimated that the total revenue earned by the NFL in 2011 was $9.3 billion dollars (*Sports Illustrated*, 2011, p. 1). The media corporations are willing to pay such huge sums of money to televise NFL games because those broadcasts yield ample advertising revenues. As we can see in the escalating advertising rates in the case of the Super Bowl—the most watched American media event of the year—the rate for 30-second commercials increased from $42,000 in 1967 to almost $3.5 million in 2012 (*Salt Lake Tribune News*, 2012).

We see a similar escalation of fees for televising the Olympic games as the payment for the summer games went from $394,000 in 1960 to nearly $1 million ($894,000) in 2008. Those advertising rates are based on the size of the television audience. If we look at the number of households viewing Super Bowl games from 1960 to 2000, we see an increase from 43.6 to 75.9 million households. The Super Bowl has become the single most watched American television event each year.

SPORT AND CAPITALIST CONSUMER CULTURE

Driven by advertising and commercialization via the sport–media marriage, sport has become inextricably linked to capitalist consumer culture, with the result that almost every object associated with major sports—from T-shirts, jackets, and replicas of player jerseys to beer mugs and key chains with team colors and logos—is being marketed for profit. By the late twentieth century, sports such as professional football, hockey, and baseball had evolved into major retail enterprises, promoting a vast and ever-expanding pool of consumer merchandise, produced with the objective of exploiting fan loyalties to grow teams' financial wealth. In the words of the sport and media scholar David Rowe, "The key to the commercialization of sports through sponsorship, celebrity endorsements, and merchandising is, of course, the mass media" (Rowe, 2012).

This aggressive commercialization has extended to selling the names of sport stadiums to the highest bidder. The epidemic of stadium naming rights began in the early 2000s, when Cinergy paid $1 million to have the Cincinnati Reds' stadium renamed Cinergy Field, and Compaq paid $900,000 for naming rights to have Houston's Rockets/Comets stadium renamed Compaq Center (ESPN.com, 2014). Perhaps the most controversial naming rights to date is that of the former Shea Stadium in Queens, New York, home of the New York Mets. The stadium opened in 2009 amid criticism for its overly commercial appearance—featuring large logo ads for sponsors including beverages, clothing, cars, and, ironically, a news network—as well as the cost of the naming rights (ESPN.com, 2014).

> Reports have put the value of the deal at $400 million spread out in payments of $20 million per year over the course of the next 20 years. That would make it one of the most lucrative stadium naming arrangements in history. According to the Mets, besides the naming rights for Citi Field, "The fully integrated partnership includes Citi brand and business unit presence throughout the new ballpark."
>
> (CNN, 2009)

SPORT FRANCHISE OWNERSHIP

Perhaps the most far reaching effect of the sports–media marriage is the way in which it is transforming the pattern of sport franchise ownership. Though less discussed publicly than some of the other consequences of the sport–media marriage, this change has enormous implications for the future development of sport. As the wealth generated by media continues to grow and as professional sports become more commercialized, large corporations have begun to purchase sport franchises formerly owned by individuals and families.

Consider the example of Rupert Murdoch's News Corp, which has become one of the major corporate forces in the sport–media marriage.

> News Corp assumed control of the Los Angeles Dodgers in March 1998 and has an interest in the New York Rangers and Knicks under its alliance with Rainbow Media and Madison Square Gardens. News Corp has full ownership of the Los Angeles Dodgers Stadium, and a 40 percent interest in the U.S. $300 million Staples Center, home of the Los Angeles Kings, Lakers and Clippers.
>
> (Law et al., 2002: 114)

These convey only part of News Corp's financial interests in sports; those interests also extend to England, Continental Europe, and Australian sport organizations. Similarly, the Disney Corporation, which began in the business of movie entertainment, has expanded into the sport world.

> We are able to observe an array of sport rights, properties and related distribution channels. . . . Disney's two major North American franchise teams include 100 percent of the Mighty Ducks for 50m from the NHL in 1992 and 25 percent of the Anaheim Angels (then the California Angels) from Gene Autry in 1996. Disney's broadcasting portfolio flows through ESPN and ABC networks. ABC holds rights to over $6 billion of sport coverage in college football, PGA Golf, the NHL, NFL, and major League Soccer over eight years. ESPN extends that with no less than four major broadcasting agreements.
>
> (Law et al., 2002: 115)

Other media conglomerates such as Time Warner, Comcast, Viacom, and Bertelsmann have also acquired major sport properties with the strategic objective of using sport not just to increase their profits but also to expand and boost markets for their other corporate ventures.

Among the possible hazards from the corporate control of media sport, none deserves more concern than the potential loss of critical media voices. In the words of one scholar, this development "may lead to the disappearance of critical accounts of the sports spectacle, thus eliminating what is left from the already limited freedom of the sports press and therefore jeopardizing the rights of the sport consumers to independent sports information" (Law et al, 2002: 127).

STAR PROFESSIONAL ATHLETES

The fourth effect of the media–sport marriage we will examine is the way in which it has greatly increased the wealth and celebrity status of star professional athletes. Proffering multimillion-dollar player contracts, often accompanied by additional millions from advertising endorsements, media sports have made the major sport athlete one of the highest paid professionals in the world. The following list of incomes of some leading NFL players reflects the phenomenal wealth earned by these athletes—and, remember, this list only refers to football.

To say that star athletes earn enormous incomes is hardly intended to suggest that they are overpaid. Quite the contrary. Their incomes are earned because they generate enormous wealth. In the contemporary era of hypercommercialized media sport, they constitute high-priced commodities who command such incomes only if they produce results that attract the interest and admiration of fans. This becomes clearly evident when superstar athletes grow older and become less productive: their value abruptly declines. But when they are playing during their peak years, their value to their team and sport exceeds what they are paid.

The names of such sport superstars as Michael Jordan, David Beckham, Tiger Woods, Serena Williams, and Roger Federer will likely be more familiar to people in New York, Berlin, Tokyo, Paris, and Buenos Aires than the names of most heads of government, cabinet ministers or supreme court justices. Because of their high profiles, star athletes are often media celebrities, attracting media attention beyond their sport performances, extending into their off-field activities because of the seemingly insatiable public appetite for gossip about their personal lives.

This curiosity becomes even more relentless if any trace of unconventional or deviant behavior is linked to a star athlete. Sport talk radio programs, along with other media outlets, immediately gravitate to such stories. As an example, New York Giants receiver Plaxico Burress sparked a media frenzy complete with late-night talk show jokes in November 2008 when he accidentally shot himself in the thigh and tried to cover up the incident (N.Y.Daily News.com). However, it might be argued that media attention can have a positive effect, as in the controversy over Baltimore Ravens running back Ray Rice

NFL Player	*Income*	*From Football*	*Endorsements*
Drew Breese	49.4m	44.4m	5m
Peyton Manning	42.8m	34.4m	10m
Larry Fitzgerald	36.8m	35.3m	1.5m
Tom Brady	27.1m	23.1m	4m
Charles Johnson	34.4m	34.3m	$100,000
Darnelle Revis	28.8m	27m	1.3m

Source: "Highest Paid Players on Forbes List" (www.nfl.com/2012/06/19).

receiving a two-game suspension after his fiancée reported he had assaulted her. "Widely viewed as soft punishment, [this suspension] left many with the impression that the NFL did not understand domestic violence or take it seriously as a crime" (Jane McManus, August 28, 2014, ESPN). As a result, NFL commissioner Roger Goodell announced a domestic violence initiative instituting much stricter penalties.

PROFESSIONALIZATION OF COLLEGE SPORT

Fifth, and finally, the media–sport marriage, and the resulting commercialization of sport, has played a large role in professionalizing college sport. This can be seen perhaps most clearly, on the one hand, in current state of college football and basketball.

To understand the current state of college sport it is necessary to understand the impact of a U.S. Supreme Court Decision in eliminating the NCAA's control over college television contracts. Notes Welch Suggs: "From the earliest days of the medium, the NCAA exercised complete control over which football teams got to play on television" (Suggs, 2010: 131). Some universities became frustrated because the NCAA rules limited each institution to only one or two television appearances a year. This was especially frustrating to some of the strongest college football teams which, because of their potential for drawing large audiences, the networks wanted to televise more frequently. So in 1984, the disagreements led to a legal challenge to the NCAA's control by two state universities (Georgia and Okahoma), who took their cases for undertaking independent television contracts to the U.S. Supreme Court. The Supreme Court sided with the colleges. Though it is doubtful that the Court foresaw its impact, that decision effectively transformed college sport.

> The decision freed colleges to pursue their own broadcast contracts, enabling them to make millions of dollars. In doing so, it brought economic competition to college sports, making money at least as important as games on the field. The "haves" of college sports signed their own television deals, setting one athletic conference against another in the race for network dollars.
>
> (See Chapter 15; Suggs, 2010: 130)

The decision created a split between big-time college sports (e.g., football and basketball) and all the other college sports (which Suggs terms the "have-nots"), as it brought the former under the umbrella of the media–sport marriage. Though college football continued to be defined as an amateur sport, it actually operates as a quasi-professional enterprise. The college conferences compete for lucrative multimillion-dollar media contracts and post-season bowl invitations as they manage, much like their professional counterparts, to generate enormous financial returns. An example of this is reflected in the comments on college football made by a journalist who in 2008 asked, "What's the biggest story in college sports so far this season?" and responded, "I'd nominate the SEC's $2.25 billion deal with ESPN for rights to televise conferences games through 2025. With an additional $55 million annually from CBS, the SEC will get $205 million a year over the life of the television contracts, a little more than $17 million per school" (Oriard in Slate, 2008: 1).

In fact, few people are surprised to learn that some Division I college football and basketball coaches earn more than their professional counterparts and that some star athletes in big-time college sport receive secret payments, gifts, or other perks in violation of NCAA rules. Given the stakes, this simply reflects the value of these star coaches and athletes in commercialized media-driven athletic programs.

Some critics have argued that big-time college sports should stop maintaining the fiction that they are amateur sport. In the view of these critics, the present system is broken because: (1) it encourages hypocrisy and cheating; (2) it betrays the educational mission of the institutions sponsoring big-time college sport; and, perhaps most important, (3) it exploits the players by obliging them to exist on modest stipends while their colleges earn multimillion-dollar incomes which they cannot share.

How should the current college sport system be reformed? Among the many suggestions, we will note several that seem most compelling.

- Pay athletes in big-time college sport in the form of annuities that are invested for them and which they could access when they reach 35 years of age. These annuities would provide especially valuable resources for those athletes who failed to move up to a professional sport career and lack a college degree. The annuity would provide a substantial amount of money the athlete could use for down payment on a home, help finance children's education, or roll over into a retirement fund.
- Classify big-time college sports like football as official minor leagues of the professional sport. Sports such as baseball and hockey have a long history of supporting minor league franchises ("farm teams") which are the source of new players in the major leagues, but college football and basketball currently function as minor leagues for the NFL and NBA. Classifying them as minor leagues would remove the hypocrisy by acknowledging the close linkage between college sports and their professional counterparts.

These are only two among the many possible suggestions for reforming big-time college sport. While it is unlikely that media-driven college sport can be eliminated, the college system can be reformed and moved beyond the hypocrisy and exploitation that remain troubling features of the current system.

POSTMODERN MEDIA SPORTS AND THE CHANGING PATTERNS OF THE FAN COMMUNITY

We have thus far discussed sport fans as though they exist as monolithic groups, drawn together by their shared enthusiasm and commitment to their teams. But in this era of a hyper-commercialized and increasingly global culture of media sport, it seems reasonable to ask: how do fans differ? And most important, how have they changed? In a ground breaking article, Richard Giulianotti presents a typology that marks a significant beginning effort to answer those questions (see Chapter 17; Giulianotti 2010). Although focused on spectators involved with soccer football, the most popular global sport, his typology has relevance to other sports communities. His insightful observations have special pertinence to postmodern media sports.

Rather than explore each of the four types, we will list them briefly and highlight the type of fans he denotes as *flâneurs*; those whose emergence is linked especially to the expansion of sport media and the increasing globalization of sports loyalties.

Giulianotti's first type, which he denotes as *supporters*, are committed deeply to their team as symbolic representatives of the surrounding local community. They display the familiar conventional pattern of team loyalty, a pattern that historically preceded the modern media sport era. The second type, *followers*, tend to be connected to teams through electronic media and are more prone to seeking not just team success but also certain social and cultural values in their loyalty. They are less rooted in local team loyalty than supporters, as some may be committed to a non-local team that exemplifies ideologies that reflect their ideological views (e.g., leftist, neo-Nazi, anarchist, fascist). In contrast, the third type, *fans*, are more consumer- and celebrity-oriented than team-oriented and tend to resemble the fans of musicians, actors, and media personalities. They are heavily committed to purchasing team jerseys, hats, photos, and other consumer products of popular culture.

These three types contrast sharply to *flâneurs*, Giulianotti's fourth and most intriguing type. *Flâneurs* (a French expression for one who strolls or saunters along) are postmodern cosmopolitans who are in pursuit of multiple soccer football experiences. In Giulianotti's words, "they belong to a virtual community of strollers who window shop around clubs" (2002: 307). They are creatures of the postmodern culture, lacking ties to traditional forms of social community.

> Their natural habitat is increasingly the virtual arena, seeking the sensations of football as represented through television. . . . Television presentation of football is tailored toward a *flâneur*-type experience. Television compresses time-space differences, distilling entire matches or tournaments into 100-second transmissions of blinding aestheticized action, to an accompanying backbeat that drifts between techno and opera.
>
> (2002: 307)

Simply put, the *flâneur* represents the blasé sport spectator. An emotionally detached, "cool" consumer, the *flâneur* "seeks relatively thin forms of social solidarity with other fellow fans" (2002: 307). Unlike the passionately committed *supporter* who typically has a deep lifelong win-or-lose commitment to the club, the *flâneur* "evidences the transferable loyalties of the postmodern passenger." The transient fan. Here today, gone tomorrow. Sport matches for the *flâneur* are more aesthetic spectacles like ballet or opera performances than battles for communal honor and affirmation. It would be difficult to imagine *flâneurs* engaged in fan violence.

The *flâneur* type appears to be the outcome of several postmodern social developments: (1) increasing levels of higher education; (2) increasing geographical mobility; (3) weakening ties to local communities; (4) the increasing globalization of media sport; (5) the increasing globalization of sport; (6) the increased geographical migration of athletes, coaches, and owners. They seem to be products of changing forms of social community rather than personality characteristics.

Though most people think of the sport fan as simply a person committed to supporting a particular team, sport fans clearly vary in both the level and type of commitment they display. We will address these issues in more detail in the section on globalization, but at present we should conclude this discussion with several critical questions:

- Are *flâneurs* good or bad for sport, and in what ways?
- Do cosmopolitan *flâneurs* represent a wave of the future or a short-lived phenomenon?
- Which sports seem most likely to attract *flâneurs* (e.g., tennis, golf, soccer football, basketball, baseball, American football)?

- Are *flâneurs* more attracted to globalized sports (e.g., tennis, golf, soccer)?
- Are increasing numbers of *flâneurs*—relative to more traditional fans—a danger to the long-term viability of a sport?
- What portion of modern fandom can be characterized as *flâneurs*?
- What is the gender distribution of *flâneurs*?
- How is sport advertising affected by *flâneurs*?

These are among many questions that require future research because the changing patterns of fandom are likely to have a major impact on the future development of media sport.

SPORT MEDIA RACE AND GENDER BIAS

In concluding this essay, we will consider the problem and implications of gender and racial bias in sport media. Gender and racial biases vary among social institutions as well as societies, but our main concern here is with sport media in American society. To what extent does the powerful modern sport media reflect the gender and racial diversity of both sport fandom and American society? Why does sport media diversity matter?

In reference to race and gender, the answers were addressed—in part—by a study of the gender content and commentary of sport media published in 2000 by Michael A. Messner and colleagues at the University of Southern California (Messner et al. 2000). The study focused specifically on 8- to 17-year-old children as the consumers of media sport programs. Though some girls watch the programs, boys constituted a large majority of the viewers. Among the programs the boys watched were the NFL, NBA, MLB, pro wrestling, men's college basketball, college football, and extreme sports—in that order. The study was interested in answering the question: what messages are being sent by sports media to the young male viewers?

Its findings were disturbing, as they revealed strong racial and gender biases in the programs, biases which projected and reinforced attitudes affirming white male superiority. The analyses of the content of the programs spanned multiple networks. Among the recurrent themes the study discovered were the following:

- white males are the voices of authority
- whites are foregrounded in commercials
- sport is a man's world
- men are foregrounded in commercials
- women are sexy props or prizes for men's successful sport performances
- aggressive guys get the prize; nice guys finish last
- boys will be (violent) boys
- sport is war

(Messner et al., 2000: 380–394).

A different but related study undertaken by The Institute for Diversity and Ethics in Sport provides an important context for understanding the organizational context of racial and gender biases in the sport media. In its 2012 publication, *The Associated Press Sports Editors Racial and Gender Report Card*, the Institute focused on the state of racial and gender diversity in the sport media. Its findings were unsettling as they revealed that sport media

Occupation	*% of White Sport Media Employees*		*% of Male Sport Media Employees*	
	2010	*2012*	*2010*	*2012*
Sports Editor	96.9	90.9	93.9	90.4
Asst. Sports Editor	85.4	86.6	89.6	82.8
Columnist	85.6	83.9	90.0	90.2
Reporter	85.6	86.3	89.4	88.3
Copy Editor/Designer	89.8	86	83.6	80.4

Source: Based on data from *The 2012 Associated Press Sports Editors Racial and Gender Report Card*, accessed at www.tidesport.org.

employment remains heavily dominated by white males. As can be seen in the above table, there has been little progress in diversity. This helps to explain the persisting racial and gender bias in sports media programs.

The assumptions of white male racial and gender superiority evidenced in the content of sports media are unlikely to change significantly until the media organizations become committed to genuine diversity. Not surprisingly, sport media has not featured stories criticizing its own lack of diversity. Thus far fan groups have been largely silent about this problem. Perhaps more than any other stakeholders, fan groups have the potential to exert pressure through organized Internet protests to increase the racial and gender diversity in sport media.

REFERENCES

ABC News. ABCNews.go.com/wnt/story

Associated Press: Huffington Post, "Police Search for Suspects After Referee Was Decapitated in Brazil Soccer Slaying." huffingtonpost.com

Associated Press Sports Edition Racial and Gender Report Card. www.tide.report.org

BBC News. BBC.com, Dec. 13.

Billings, Andrew C. 2009. *Communicating about Sports Media: Culture Collide.* Spain: Editorial Aresta

Bleacher Report. 2013. "NFL Fans, You're Better Than That." December 13. bleacherreport.com

Cacciola, Scott. 2014. "LeBron James to Return to Cavaliers, Leaving Miami Heat." *New York Times*, July 11. www.nytimes.com/2014/07/12/sports/basketball/lebron–james–to–return–to–cleveland–cavaliers–leaving–miami–heat.html

Chomsky, Noam. 1994. Quoted in David Barasamian, *Keeping the Rabble In Line.* Monroe, ME: Common Courage Press.

CNN. 2009. www.cnn.com/2009/us/04/13/metsbaseballpark

—— 2013. "Football Racism in Serbia." edition.cnn.com/2013/06/12/sport/football-racism-serbia—reekie

—— 2014. "Player Called a Black Monkey in Poland." edition.cnn.com/2014/05/05/sport/football

Cottingham. 2012. "Interaction Ritual Theory and Sports Fans: Emotion, Symbols, and Solidarity." *Sociology of Sports* 29(2): 168–185.

Dunning, Eric et al. 1986. "Spectator Violence at Football Matches: Toward a Sociological Explanation" *British Journal of Sociology* 37(2): 221–244.

Durkheim, Emile. 1964. *The Division of Labor in Society.* New York, NY: Free Press of Glencoe.

—— 2001. *The Elementary Forms of Religious Life.* New York, NY: Oxford U. Press

ESPN. 2014. www.espn.go.com/sportsbusiness/s/stadiumnames.html

Fan Voice. "Sports Fans Bill of Rights." FanVoice.com, pp. 1–2.

Giulianotti, Richard. 2002. "Supporters, Followers, Fans, and Flaneurs: A Taxonomy of Spectators in Football." Pp. 297–313 in *Sport, Power, and Society,* edited by Robert Washington and David Karen. Boulder, CO: Westview Press. Originally published in *Journal of Sport and Social Issues* 26(1) (Feb. 2002): 25–46.

Grasmuck, Sherri. 2005. *Protecting Home: Class, Race, and Masculinity in Boy's Baseball.* New Brunswick: NJ: Rutgers University Press.

Hartmann, Douglas. 2000. "Rethinking the Relationship Between Sport and Race in American Culture: Golden Ghettos—Contested Terrain." *Sociology of Sport* 17(3): 229–253.

HBO. 2007. "Brooklyn Dodgers: The Ghosts of Flatbush." imdb.com

Heinrich, A. 2003. "The 1954 Soccer World Cup and the Federal Republic of Germany's Social Democracy." *American Behavior Scientist* 146 (11): 1491–1505

Hughson, John and Marcus Free. 2006. "Paul Willis, Cultural Consumption, and Collective Sports Fandom." *Sociology of Sports* 23(1): 72–85.

Kaufman, Jason. 2003. *For the Common Good: American Civic Life and the Golden Age of Fraternity.* New York, NY: Oxford University Press.

Law, Alan, Jean Harvey, and Stuart Kemp. 2002. "The Global Mass Media Oligopoly." Pp. 109–130 in *Sport, Power, and Society* edited by Robert Washington and David Karen. Boulder, CO: Westview Press. Originally published in *International Review for the Sociology of Sport* 37: 279–302.

L.A. Times. 1998. "NFL Owners Debate the Pros and Cons of Corporate Ownership" L.A.Times.com/1998/08/30

Messner, Michael, Michele Dunbar, and Darnell Hunt. 2000. "The Televised Manhood Forumla." Pp. 229–245 in *Critical Readings: Sport, Culture and the Media* edited by David Rowe. Maidenhead Bershire, England: Open University Press.

Morris, David and Daniel Krager. 2010. "Rooting for the Home Team." Pp. 26–33 in *Sport, Power, and Society* edited by Robert Washington and David Karen. Boulder, CO: Westview. Reprinted from *The American Prospect* 9(40) (September 1, 1998).

Nader, Ralph. 2011. "Nader Announces Push For Community Ownership in Professional Sports," July 13. www.leagueofsportsfans.org/2011/07/13/Ralph–Nader–announces–push–for–legislation–that–will–enable–community–ownershipmodelinprofessionalsports

Nathan, David. "Rooting for the Home Team: American Sport and Civic Identity." http://www.helsinski/home/renvall/biirold/heroes+papers=Nathan.html

"NFL Owners Debate the Pros and Cons of Corporate Ownership." *Los Angeles Times.* L.A. Times.com/1998/08/30

Oriard, Michael. 2008. "Bowling for Dollars—Why College Football is More Cutthroat and Competitive than the NFL." www.slate.com/articles/sports/sport_not/2008/11/bowling-for-dollars.html

Pierce, Richard. 2004. "More than a Game: The Political Meaning of High School Basketball in Indianapolis." Pp. 191–211 in *Sport and the Color Line* edited by Patrick Miller and David K. Wiggins. New York, NY: Routledge.

Powell, Michael. 2014. "Star Reconnects with a Special Place in His Heart." July 11. www.nytimes.com/2014/07/12/sports/basketball/lebron–james–bares–his–soul–in–announcing–return–to–cleveland.html

Putnam, Robert. 2000. *Bowling Alone.* New York, NY: Simon and Schuster.

Reed, Ken. League of Fans "Fans Voice.com." www.fansvoice.com/story.aspx

Reuters. 2007. "Iraqis Ready to Defy Bombs to Back Soccer Team." www.reuters.com/article/latest crisis/usl26780468

Rockwood, Joel and Geoff Pearson. 2012. "The Hoolifan: Positive Fan Attitudes to Football Hooligans." *International Review for the Sociology of Sport* 47(2): 149.

Rowe, David. 2004. *Money, Myth, and the Big Match,* 2nd edition. Berkshire, England: Open University Press.

—— 2012. Britannica.com/ebchecked/topic/61041/sports/mass-media-the-rise-of-professional-sport

Rowe, David and P. McGuirk. 1999. "Drunk for Three Weeks: Sporting Success and City Image." *International Review for the Sociology of Sport* 34(2): 125–141.

Salt Lake Tribune News. 2012.

SIRC. www.sirc.org.public/fn/racism.html, p. 2.

Sports Illustrated. SI.com/nfl/2011/03/11 inside-the-nfl-money-machine

Stone, Larry. *Seattle Times.* seattletimes.com/html/larrystone/202292152—stone16xmhtml

Suggs, Welch. 2010. "Football, Television, and the Supreme Court." Pp. 130–135 in *Sport, Power and Society* edited by Robert Washington and David Karen. Boulder, CO: Westview Press. Originally published in *The Chronicle of Higher Education* (July 9, 2004).

Thompson, Ken. "A Brooklyn Dodger Fan." The Brooklyn Board. brooklynboard.com/diary

Trujillo, Bob Krizek. 2010. "Emotionality in the Stands and in the Field: Expressing Self Through Baseball." Pp. 281–293 in *Sport, Power and Society* edited by Robert Washington and David Karen. Boulder, CO: Westview Press. Originally published in *Journal of Sport and Social Issues* 18(4) (November 1994): 303–325.

Tynan, Gordon. 2014. "Malcolm Glazer Dead: Billionaire Passing Is a Minor Jolt in Manchester United's World." May 28, *The Independent.* www.independent.co.uk/sport/football/news-and commentary/Malcolm-glazer

Wann, Dan and Stephanie Pierce. 2000. "The Relationship Between Sport Fan Identification and Social Well Being: Additional Evidence Supporting the Team Identification—Social Psychological Health Model." *North American Journal of Psychology* 7(1): 117–124.

—— 2001. *Sports Fans: The Psychology and Impact of Spectators.* New York, NY: Routledge.

Welle, Deutsch. 2005. "African Player from the Ivory Coast Subjected to Racist Insults." December 2. www.dw.de/european.soccer.racism-problem

Wen, Tiffany. 2014. "Sociological History of Soccer Violence." *Atlantic Monthly.* www/theatlanticcom/health/2014/07

CHAPTER 12

Joe Louis Uncovers Dynamite

Richard Wright

Wun—tuh—three—fooo—fiiive—seex—seven—eight—nine—thuun!"

"Joe Louis—the winnah!"

On Chicago's South Side five minutes after these words were yelled and Joe Louis's hand was hoisted as victor in his four-round go with Max Baer, Negroes poured out of beer taverns, pool rooms, barber shops, rooming houses and dingy flats and flooded the streets.

"Louis! Louis! Louis!" they yelled and threw their hats away. They snatched newspapers from the stands of astonished Greeks and tore them up, flinging the bits into the air. They wagged their heads. Lawd, they'd never seen or heard the like of it before. They shook the hands of strangers. They clapped one another on the back. It was like a revival. Really, there was a religious feeling in the air. Well, it wasn't exactly a religious feeling, but it was *something*, and you could feel it. It was a feeling of unity, of oneness.

Two hours after the fight the area between South Parkway and Prairie Avenue on 47th Street was jammed with no less than twenty-five thousand Negroes, joy-mad and moving to they didn't know where. Clasping hands, they formed long writhing snake-lines and wove in and out of traffic. They seeped out of doorways, oozed from alleys, trickled out of tenements, and flowed down the street; a fluid mass of joy. White storekeepers hastily closed their doors against the tidal wave and stood peeping through the plate glass with blanched faces.

Something had happened, all right. And it had happened so confoundingly sudden that the whites in the neighborhood were dumb with fear. They felt—you could see it in their faces—that *something* had ripped loose, exploded. Something which they had long feared and thought was dead. Or if not dead, at least so safely buried under the pretence of good-will that they no longer had need to fear it. Where in the world did it come from? And what was worst of all, how far would it go? Say, what's got into these Negroes?

And the whites and the blacks began to feel themselves. The blacks began to remember all the little slights, and discriminations and insults they had suffered; and their hunger too and their misery. And the whites began to search their souls to see if they had been guilty of something, sometime, somewhere, against which this wave of feeling was rising.

As the celebration wore on, the younger Negroes began to grow bold. They jumped on the running boards of automobiles going east or west on 47th Street and demanded of the occupants:

"Who yuh fer—Baer or Louis?"

In the stress of the moment it seemed that the answer to the question marked out friend and foe.

A hesitating reply brought waves of scornful laughter. Baer, huh? That was funny. Now, hadn't Joe Louis just whipped Max Baer? Didn't think we had it in us, did you? Thought Joe Louis was scared, didn't you? Scared because Max talked loud and made boasts. We ain't scared either. We'll fight too when the time comes. We'll win, too.

A taxicab driver had his cab wrecked when he tried to put up a show of bravado.

Then they began stopping streetcars. Like a cyclone sweeping through a forest, they went through them, shouting, stamping. Conductors gave up and backed away like children. Everybody had to join in this celebration. Some of the people ran out of the cars and stood, pale and trembling, in the crowd. They felt it, too,

In the crush a pocketbook snapped open and money spilled on the street for eager black fingers.

"They stole it from us, anyhow," they said as they picked it up.

When an elderly Negro admonished them, a fist was shaken in his face. Uncle Tomming, huh?

"Whut in hell yuh gotta do wid it" they wanted to know.

Something had popped loose, all right. And it had come from deep down. Out of the darkness it had leaped from its coil. And nobody wanted to say. Blacks and whites were afraid. But it was a sweet fear, at least for the blacks. It was a mingling of fear and fulfillment. Something dreaded and yet wanted. A something had popped out of a dark hole, something with a hydra-like head, and it was daring forth its tongue.

You stand on the borderline, wondering what's beyond. Then you take one step and you feel a strange, sweet tingling. You take two steps and the feeling becomes keener. You want to feel some more. You break into a run. You know it's dangerous, but you're impelled in spite of yourself.

Four centuries of oppression, of frustrated hopes, of black bitterness, felt even in the bones of the bewildered young, were rising to the surface. Yes, unconsciously they had imputed to the brawny image of Joe Louis all the balked dreams of revenge, all the secretly visualized moments of retaliation, AND HE HAD WON! Good Gawd Almighty! Yes, by Jesus, it could be done! Didn't Joe do it? You see, Joe was the consciously-felt symbol. Joe was the concentrated essence of black triumph over white. And it comes so seldom, so seldom. And what could be sweeter than long-nourished hate vicariously gratified? From the symbol of Joe's strength they took strength, and in that moment all fear, all obstacles were wiped out, drowned. They stepped out of the mire of hesitation and irresolution and were free! Invincible! A merciless victor over a fallen foe! Yes, they had felt all that—for a moment . . .

And then the cops came.

Not the carefully picked white cops who were used to batter the skulls of white workers and intellectuals who came to the South Side to march with the black workers to show their solidarity in the struggle against Mussolini's impending invasion of Ethiopia; oh, no, black cops, but trusted black cops and plenty tough. Cops who knew their business, how to handle delicate situations. They piled out of patrols, swinging clubs.

"Git back! Gawddammit, git back!"

But they were very careful, very careful. They didn't hit anybody. They, too, sensed *something*. And they didn't want to trifle with it. And there's no doubt but that they had been instructed not to. Better go easy here. No telling what might happen. They swung clubs, but pushed the crowd back with their hands.

Finally, the streetcars moved again. The taxis and automobiles could go through. The whites breathed easier. The blood came back to their cheeks.

The Negroes stood on the sidewalks, talking, wondering, looking, breathing hard. They had felt something, and it had been sweet—that feeling. They wanted some more of it, but they were afraid now. The spell was broken.

And about midnight down the street that feeling ebbed, seeping home—flowing back to the beer tavern, the pool room, the café, the barber shop, the dingy flat. Like a sullen river it ran back to its muddy channel, carrying a confused and sentimental memory on its surface, like water-soaked driftwood.

Say, Comrade, here's the wild river that's got to be harnessed and directed. Here's that *something*, that pent-up folk consciousness. Here's a fleeting glimpse of the heart of the Negro, the heart that beats and suffers and hopes—for freedom. Here's that fluid something that's like iron. Here's the real dynamite that Joe Louis uncovered!

CHAPTER 13

Something About Baseball: Gentrification, "Race Sponsorship," and Competing Class Cultures in Neighborhood Boys' Baseball

Sherri Grasmuck

In the late 1960s White residents of a Philadelphia neighborhood called Fairmount, north of center city, regularly and often with the support of police, ran off Blacks who walked through the neighborhood.[1] A red-faced, Irish-Ukrainian Fairmounter, looking back at his teenage years, described the neighborhood this way:

> They called our neighborhood "White island" because we were surrounded. . . . When I was growing up there would have been fighting no matter what. We fought everyday. We fought our way to school. We fought our way home from school. We fought everyday.

Thirty years later, on a summer evening in 2001, three police cars surrounded and detained a group of four boys in Fairmount, two Black and two White, under suspicion of attempted car theft. As the police aggressively questioned the 14-year-old boys, a group of White Fairmounter adults surrounded the police cars to defend the interracial group of boys against this "police harassment." Among these adults was the same Fairmounter who had, as a teenager in the 1960s, as described above, fought Blacks transgressing the neighborhood. Yet on that summer night in 2001, after this incident, he loudly explained to a group of listeners why the police had really stopped the boys that night: "You want to know what they did wrong? I'll tell you what. They were guilty of 'walking while Black.' Or they were White and hanging with Blacks. That's what they did wrong."

What had happened in this neighborhood and to these adults to produce such surprising changes? One clue comes from the fact that these were not just any boys. They were baseball players, players who had played in the neighborhood baseball league for almost a decade. Another clue is that both of the Black boys were middle-class, and one of them now lived in the neighborhood. Many other clues to understanding this moment are uncovered by a look at the changes that swept Fairmount, along with its adjacent neighborhood, Spring Garden, in the last decades of the 20th century and at how neighborhood baseball changed over the same period.

Scholars who have studied race and sport have often debated whether sports activities promote social integration or merely reflect broader social inequalities within their games, benches, and locker rooms (Coakley, 2001; Gatz, Messner, & Ball-Rokeach, 2002). Depending on the context, sport can facilitate racial harmony or can contribute to racial division. On the negative side, sport events can become venues for racial hostilities, when teams representing different racial groups compete and give fans and players opportunities to vent game frustrations through racial channels. Other sports practices, such as "stacking"—the segregating of Blacks into certain team positions—or the underrepresentation in professional sports of minorities in leadership or "thinking positions," inflame racial resentments (Edwards, 1970, 1973; Eitzen, 1999; Lapchick and Benedict, 1993; Sage, 2001). On the positive side, sport enthusiasts point to the way sports can bring people of different backgrounds together. For example, three fourths of high school athletes told Louis Harris pollsters in 1993 that they had made friends across racial lines through sport (Eitzen, 1999, p. 18). Thus sports become a means of integration, not just for the participants but also for those who identify with the competing teams (Coakley, 2001). Eitzen (1999, p. 18) has identified some contexts in which sports can help build racial understandings, such as when teams permit players of different races to contribute equally to team success, and when the team with mixed races is successful.

Much of what we do know from the field of the sociology of sport, regarding the ameliorative or destructive impact of sport, comes from research on the top-level of sports, the college and professional levels. With this elite focus comes a heavy emphasis on how organized sports, controlled by a dominant class (Goodman, 1979), or corporate sports, controlled by a power elite, directs spectator attention away from social injustices (Hoch, 1972). This emphasis on "sports as opiate" (Coakley, 2001) leaves little maneuverability to human agents who might find pleasure and community amidst the constraints of sports rules and ideologies or even resist the status quo within sport arenas.

Critical sports sociologists, who have weighed extensive evidence on both sides of this debate, point to a more paradoxical verdict: Under certain conditions the consequences of sport can be destructive, by reinforcing dominant power relations and racial and gender inequalities, and under some conditions constructive, by undermining or challenging them (Gatz et al., 2002, p. 5). The answer might well depend on the type of sport and level of sport, whether it is informal, organized, or corporate sports. The challenge is to understand the particular circumstances when sports experiences are positive and healthy and when they are negative and destructive and to explain how and why (Coakley, 2001; Edwards, 2001).

This paper addresses this challenge by exploring two sets of tensions related to a process of racial integration and new class encounters in a neighborhood baseball league in the two gentrifying Philadelphia neighborhoods described above. There are plenty of stories in America of racial conflict and violence after neighborhood change. Here we explore the opposite—the features of neighborhood baseball that might have made a transition toward racial integration a relatively smooth one. Moreover, the encounter of folks of different socioeconomic backgrounds permits not just a look at how sport structured and processed neighborhood tensions but also how the competing class cultures of diverse parents created conflicting expectations about rights in and responsibilities toward public space and voluntary organizations.

METHODS

The findings for this paper are based on a larger study of neighborhood gentrification, baseball, and masculinity in a gentrifying area of Philadelphia.[2] I warmed the bleachers at the baseball field continuously for thirteen years watching the games and practices of my son and daughter between 1987 and 2002. I began an ethnographic study of the ball club in 1997, its changes over time and its relationship to the neighborhood. Working with a graduate student, over the next three years, we observed 121 games of the 7–9 and 10–12 teams and conducted 41 interviews with parents, coaches, and staff of FSA.[3]

I made the decision to present the real names of these two neighborhoods, following norms of journalism rather than sociology, as I believed the actual historical identities of these spaces mattered to the storytelling. One of my broader goals for this project was to prioritize sociological storytelling rather than to use the community to build abstract theory as an equally valid way of telling the truth (Sparkes, 2002; Grasmuck, 2005). However, I did not extend this "real naming" to individuals in the community. Although some neighborhood folks preferred that I use their real names, some did not. For consistency's sake, all of the names of persons presented here are pseudonyms, even in the case of those who played recognized historical roles in establishing FSA as an organization.

NEIGHBORHOOD RACIAL TRANSITION

By the year 2000, most children who played baseball in the Fairmount and Spring Garden neighborhoods of Philadelphia played it on the Von Colin Fields of Fairmount Park, 10 blocks from city hall. Fairmount and Spring Garden physically meet here on their western borders, just opposite the impressive Philadelphia Museum of Art. The ball field is just one block down from the museum at the southwestern corner of the Spring Garden neighborhood. However, before this ball field evolved into a site of social unity for the two neighborhoods, residents of the two neighborhoods lived in different social worlds.

In the early 1950s, both Spring Garden and Fairmount were predominantly White, working-class neighborhoods with a strong representation of Irish, English, Ukrainian, Polish, and Italian ethnic groups. Fairmount remained subdivided into a number of small pockets, where different blocks were often dominated by different first- and second-generation White immigrants (Cybriwsky, 1978, p. 61). As a White enclave bordering poorer Black neighborhoods to the north, Fairmount had a strong race identity. As a 60-year-old barber who had grown up in Fairmount remembered this period:

> You had the Italians living on Aspen Street and 23rd Street. The Irish were throughout the neighborhood. The Ukrainians were down this way and a lot of Greeks were at 27th and 28th. It was pretty mixed with those groups. . . . Blacks would try to come down here, through here and all. This was a tough neighborhood, so it would be like hand-to-hand combat. There *were* some Black families, around 23rd and Oliver, and I went to school with some Blacks and Puerto Ricans, but it was mostly White. This area just seemed to hold on. I called this like "Custer's Last Stand." We got the city here [signaling south], got the park over here [signaling west], Girard College on the north and then the prison [signaling east]. So kind of like boundaries. . . . But things have changed now. The old-timers were more racial than we are.

While Fairmount remained an almost exclusively White area during the 1950s, Spring Garden underwent considerable racial change. First, because of its relative proximity to the first Spanish-speaking church in the city, Spring Garden became the first area of settlement for Puerto Rican migrants arriving from New Jersey agricultural areas in the 1950s (Ericksen et al., 1985), who constituted 31% of the population in Spring Garden by the end of the decade (see Table 13.1). Second, during the same period the proportion of African Americans in the area just to the east of

Table 13.1 Racial Changes in the Neighborhoods of Fairmount, Spring Garden, and Philadelphia, 1950–2000

	FAIRMOUNT				*SPRING GARDEN*				*PHILADELPHIA*[a]		
		%	%	%		%	%	%	%	%	%
Year	*Population*	*White*	*Black*	*Latino*[b]	*Population*	*White*	*Black*	*Latino*[b]	*White*	*Black*	*Latino*[b]
1950	10,764	99.3	0.5	—	16,737	84.5	15.5	—	81.7	18.2	0.1
1960	8,769	97.2	2.5	0.1	9,289	81.8	17.8	30.8	79.0	20.4	0.5
1970	7,620	93.0	6.1	2.1	7,436	82.0	14.9	27.7	68.6	30.1	2.3
1980	6,532	94.1	4.7	1.8	5,694	69.1	10.7	22.4	59.2	35.9	3.7
1990	5,882	91.0	6.7	2.7	5,483	74.2	12.8	14.0	53.5	39.6	5.3
2000	5,962	84.1	8.2	2.9	5,389	73.9	16.0	10.4	45.1	43.1	8.5

Source: Years 1950–1990, compiled from an aggregate file of the U.S. Census created by William Yancey with the assistance of Joshua Freely, Social Science Data Library, Temple University, 2000 data from the U.S. Census 2000 Web site, Summary File 3.

a Philadelphia is defined here as excluding the two census tracts represented by Fairmount (136) and Spring Garden (134).

b Census questions relevant to the categories of race and Latinos changed twice between 1950 and 2000. Throughout the period, "race" and "Hispanic origin" have been operationalized as separate variables in the Census. For the first time in 1960, in addition to the question, respondents were asked, in a separate ethnicity question, if they were "Puerto Rican" as the only possible Hispanic response. Beginning in 1980, respondents were asked, on a 100% basis, if they were "Latino." Before 1980, the Latino origin question was only asked on a sample basis. Therefore, one cannot always find comparable tabulations on Latinos on the census-tract level in the 1960–1970 period and the 1980–2000 period. Starting in 2000, moreover, people could check off more than one race, making new mixed-race categories possible, and lowering the proportions answering "White" or "Black." These changes explain why in this table the categories White, Black, and Latino sometimes surpass 100% in the same year (1960 and 1970) and sometimes drop below 100% (in 2000), when mixed-race categories are added to the census but not reported here.

Spring Garden doubled, growing from 15% to 34% (Whalen, 2001, p. 186).[4] Overall then, while Fairmount remained almost exclusively White in the 1950s, almost half of Spring Garden residents identified as either Latino or Black by the decade's end (Grasmuck, 2005, p. 20).

This racial transition in the Spring Garden area was far from smooth. White residents of Spring Garden, especially the poorer ones, resisted their new neighbors with racial riots and violence. During the summer of 1953, one of the worst riots of the city occurred near the corner of Mt. Vernon and 16th Street, with fighting that involved anywhere from 300 to 1,000 people and lasted more than 2 hours. Shawn, a Spring Garden resident, remembered his youth in the neighborhood this way:

> Twenty years ago this was a bad neighborhood. . . . You wouldn't walk past here. The Puerto Ricans would just jump you. Blacks couldn't walk down through the neighborhood. We had fights at the Art Museum all the time. . . . I had a hard time because I lived above Fairmount (in Spring Garden) and we hung out below Fairmount. But I had to go home at night. Puerto Ricans would actually wait up at night. But we had one Puerto Rican kid who lived on Fairmount Avenue, and he used to walk me home at night. . . . But mostly we used to get in fights just because they were Black and we were White. . . . It was Fairmount. Blacks weren't supposed to walk through Fairmount.

For many Fairmount residents, this racial transition in the area to their south reinforced their long held sense of being a White oasis. The Fairmount area was indeed racially distinct from its surrounding areas. Fairmounters' fears of racial integration were not realized; throughout the period of Spring Garden's racial transformation, Fairmount remained almost 100% White. Cybriwski (1978), who studied Fairmount in the 1970s, identified three factors central to Fairmount's racial stability. First, Fairmounters were much more likely to own their homes, which made the rate of vacancies during this period considerably slower in Fairmount than in Spring Garden.[5] This lower turnover meant fewer opportunities for newcomers in Fairmount than Spring Garden. Second, when vacancies did occur in Fairmount, they were often managed informally through relatives or word of mouth. A village-like cohesiveness made it relatively easy to discriminate against Blacks or Puerto Ricans entering the housing market. Jessie, who lived in the heart of Fairmount all her life, described how it worked:

> Jessie: Thirty years ago this was a very prejudiced neighborhood. I mean everybody in it was prejudiced and that's just . . . the way you were brought up. . . . They kept everything closed mouthed. . . . They called this neighborhood the "Oreo," that's what they used to say, "We're an Oreo cookie." . . . And to hold strong, you stuck together like glue. [You didn't] put a sign on your house if you were selling it. It was word of mouth. . . . I've even been guilty of that. Ten years ago, a woman was renting her house on this block, and I said to her, "Watch what you rent to because while you are out in Bryn Mawr, I'm across the street from the garbage you put in the house."
>
> S.G.: And what you had in mind then was someone Black?
>
> Jessie: Right. And she knew what I was saying, and she said, "I wouldn't do that to you." [laughter] I think she was afraid I'd come for her. [laughter]

Third, beyond the closed housing market, Fairmount's youth had a well-established reputation for violently defending its space against transgressors.[6] Well after Puerto Ricans and Blacks had established a strong presence in surrounding areas, Fairmounter corner youths continued their violent confrontations with Blacks who passed through the neighborhood. And, although lower-class families were often harshly criticized by other Fairmount residents as "white trash," they were also often the ones "taking care of business" by enforcing racial boundaries, just as the poorest Whites in Spring Garden were associated with street fighting with Puerto Ricans in the 1950s (Cybriwsky, 1978; Whalen, 2001). These internal divisions, however, had always paled in comparison with the boundaries drawn between this White enclave and the surrounding areas. Then, as the neighborhood to the south changed again, this time with the arrival of new higher income Whites, a new "other" emerged. This both alleviated the racial fears of Fairmounters and posed a threat of a different nature to the old neighborhood.

GENTRIFICATION

If the high concentration of rental property in Spring Garden helped facilitate the entrance of Puerto Ricans in the 1950s, it also helped push them out. In the 1970s, Spring Garden began to gentrify. With its close proximity to downtown Philadelphia and its large stock of historic townhouses and rental properties, Spring Garden started to attract many young professional newcomers. The rapidly rising rents and housing values of the 1970s hit hard the poorer sectors of Spring Garden, the struggling Puerto Rican community. Despite resistance, the poorer sectors of the Latino population were pushed out and moved toward the growing community of Latinos in northeast Philadelphia. While Latinos constituted 30% of the Spring Garden area in 1970, they represented only 14% by 1990 and 10% by 2000 (Grasmuck, 2005, p. 20).

From a working-class area with significant pockets of poverty, numerous basement bars, corner taverns, small industries, and three neighborhood Catholic schools in the 1960s, grew a visibly more affluent one. As the price of real estate in Spring Garden rose, gentrification also extended into Fairmount. Both neighborhoods were transformed by the arrival of more affluent professional residents but in different degrees. With gentrification proceeding at a more rapid pace in Spring Garden than in Fairmount, the proportion of college-educated residents in Spring Garden was already notably higher by the early 1970s (16.4% compared with 7.4%) and stayed significantly higher throughout the 1980s (Grasmuck, 2005, p. 25). This disparity established new grounds for suspicion between the two areas, disparities now based more on class than on race. But as gentrification continued northward into the Fairmount area throughout the 1980s, these same educational disparities became more salient *within* the two neighborhoods. Just as the arrival of new professionals in the more southern neighborhood, Spring Garden, had pushed out many Puerto Ricans in the 1960s and 1970s, the continued movement of professionals northward into Fairmount in the 1980s also squeezed out many White Fairmounters.

Despite early tensions and suspicions between old-timers and newcomers, the arrival of new White professionals marked a consolidation of Spring Garden as a predominantly White neighborhood again. This gradual transition eased racial fears to the extent that some of the racial riots in the early 1970s in Fairmount against the entrance of new Black families[7] subsided over the next decade. But this was a gradual process, and although more middle-class professionals entered Spring Garden and Fairmount in the 1990s without incident, some of the first Black professionals who had arrived in the 1970s remembered a hostile welcoming. One Black professor, Helena,

Table 13.2 Economic and Housing Changes in Fairmount and Spring Garden Neighborhoods Compared with Citywide Changes, 1960–2000

Year	*FAIRMOUNT*				*SPRING GARDEN*				*PHILADELPHIA*[a]			
	Owner occupied (%)	*Poor (%)*	*Median income ($)*	*Average housing value ($)*	*Owner occupied (%)*	*Poor (%)*	*Median income ($)*	*Average housing value ($)*	*Owner occupied (%)*	*Poor (%)*	*Median income ($)*	*Average housing value ($)*
1960	51.3	16.3	5,015	6,700	14.5	44.1	2,508	7,400	59.9	17.6	6,039	9,842
1970	48.5	9.7	9,009	7,100	10.4	21.1	9,083	9,200	56.2	12.2	9,834	12,683
1980	50.9	10.7	17,249	37,700	16.6	24.0	15,005	73,900	55.4	17.6	17,336	30,760
1990	48.6	9.8	34,503	94,400	31.3	16.8	34,691	168,200	62.0	20.7	24,603	48,400
2000	58.5	11.0	46,250	100,600	40.0	19.9	41,536	191,300	64.4	22.9	30,746	61,000

Note: Poverty was not officially computed in 1960; the 1960 numbers in this table are based on a calculation using the 1970 poverty level, the rate of inflation, and changes in the consumer price index between 1960 and 1970.[a] Philadelphia is defined as excluding the two census tracts represented by Fairmount (136) and Spring Garden (134); "Owner occupied" is based on all housing units; "Median income" is based on the household; "Average housing value" refers only to owner occupied residences. *Source:* Years 1950–1990, compiled from an aggregate file of the U.S. Census created by William Yancey with the assistance of Joshua Freely, Social Science Data Library, Temple University; 2000 data from the U.S. Census 2000 Web site, Summary File 3.

whose family moved into Fairmount in 1973, described how they bypassed the closed real estate market with help from an interracial couple and defended themselves in the early years of their arrival.

> It was rough when we first moved here. We used to live in "Pig Alley," in a house two doors down from here. But we were renting. We entered from the back. The first couple of weeks, the local guys threw something into the window. Earl [her husband] had to go out there and straighten them out . . . the teenagers, the White gang that hung out down at the corner. There was a lot of drugs. . . . He knew who the kid was. Earl went up there and nearly killed him. He ran and got him and really shook him up. . . . And another day, Earl was sitting on the front porch and his wallet was sitting there next to him, and somebody ran by and took the wallet. He chased him down too. He got his wallet back and scared them. After that we haven't had any problems.

As she recounted these events, 30 years later, in the living room of her home that borders the Fairmount-Spring Garden divide, she contrasted these experiences and her early feelings with her current, extremely positive feelings about the neighborhood. She noted the importance of baseball to her integration. Beyond the fact that Helena and her husband were highly educated professionals, another critical piece of information is that her son and daughter were excellent athletes who had played in the neighborhood baseball league. The theme of baseball in this story of a Black professional family's gradual feeling of acceptance in the neighborhood parallels the baseball connection established in the vignette at the beginning of this article about the White Fairmount man who, as a youth, had fought Blacks in the area and yet who, as an adult, defended their right of passage in the 1990s. Both cases of transformation, however understood, are deeply embedded in youth baseball, the centerpiece of recreation in Fairmount.

Over this 30-year period of neighborhood change, the local youth baseball organization changed even more dramatically. Although historically an all-White organization, by the mid-1990s approximately one third of the boys playing in the younger division were children of color. And peace prevailed. Given this neighborhood's past, how did this happen? The answer to this question must begin with a brief history of neighborhood baseball and its evolution from informal play to structured, competitive games.

Table 13.3 Changes in Educational Background of Fairmount and Spring Garden Residents Compared with the City of Philadelphia, 1970–2000

Year	*Fairmount college graduates (%)*	*Spring Garden college graduates (%)*	*Philadelphia[a] college graduates (%)*
1970	7.4	16.4	6.8
1980	19.4	27.8	12.8
1990	45.2	56.7	15.2
2000	54.3	57.4	17.9

a Philadelphia is defined here as excluding the two census tracts represented by Fairmount (136) and Spring Garden (134).

Source: Years 1970–1990, compiled from an aggregate file of the U.S. Census created by William Yancey with the assistance of Joshua Freely, Social Science Data Library, Temple University; 2000 data from the U.S. Census 2000 Web site, Summary File 3.

BASEBALL AS THE SOUL OF THE NEIGHBORHOOD

Neighborhood play in Fairmount in the 1950s centered on baseball. Kids played informal games for years at 24th Street and Fairmount Avenue, a prominent block between the two neighborhoods. Sometime in the early 1960s, a neighborhood man wanted to organize games among the boys. He got together some friends and began a baseball club, originally called simply, the Braves, out of the Catholic War Veterans Post and recruited boys from the families connected to the post. Because there was no longer a field in the neighborhood, the neighborhood guys would have them all meet at a specified corner in Fairmount and drive the boys about 3 miles north to "the Dairy," a section of Fairmount Park off Kelly Drive, in an old station wagon they called the "Fairmount Bomber." They organized teams according to "corners," where different clusters of boys hung out.

Around the same time, when Tom O'Connors,[8] another Fairmounter who had grown up playing ball with these teams, turned 21, he started his own traveling team sponsored by a different veterans' post in the neighborhood, the Parkway VFW, and recruited about 15 of the best players from the original Braves. By the next year, O'Connors had 50 players and had to organize several teams. These traveling teams continued to practice at "the Dairy" and began to play competitive games in South Philadelphia. O'Connors looked to his friends to help him out with the coaching and thereby established a pattern that was to continue for decades in the organization whereby coaches were recruited strictly by word of mouth from neighborhood friendship networks, some of whom were parents and some of whom were not. Both the in-house teams and the traveling teams worked as a loose coalition until 1967, when personality conflicts and internal divisions provoked the men more associated with the travel teams to break away and form a separate organization newly named the Fairmount Sports Association (FSA). Both the Fairmount Braves and FSA coexisted for a brief period, until the original Braves folded, and FSA emerged as the exclusive neighborhood baseball club, still organizationally based at the Catholic War Veterans Post.

The driving of kids back and forth from the neighborhood to the Dairy in Fairmount Park continued until the late 1960s, when the coaches decided they needed to play closer to the neighborhood and selected a nearby city-owned block, formally part of Fairmount Park, the largest urban park in the United States. Their eventual success in securing permission to use this parkland is all the more surprising when one considers that this block is strategically located among major historic landmarks of Philadelphia. It borders a broad, tree-lined boulevard called the Ben Franklin Parkway, which dramatically connects the vast Philadelphia Museum of Art, situated on a granite hill on one end, with the impressive late 19th-century structure, city hall, at the other end. One of the obstacles to the use of this contested space was that, while it was city-owned, it was not controlled by the recreation office of the city but was officially part of Fairmount Park. The Fairmount Park Commission saw it as an open green space visible from the Franklin Parkway (some even described it as the "Champs-Elysées of Philadelphia") and wanted its park image to remain.

Gaining the right to use this public space was a gradual process requiring street smarts, persistence, and a "quiet confrontation" with local police officers. This case stands in sharp contrast to Goodman's (1979) description of the way dominant economic and cultural groups imposed organized sports on working-class youth in the Lower East Side of Manhattan to eliminate immigrant street culture in the early 20th century. Here we have working-class residents fighting dominant cultural groups for rights to public parkland to serve their own definitions of legitimate use of public space, in this case organized baseball. By the early 1970s they had succeeded: FSA received formal permission to use the land and spent two years leveling the field. Neighborhood men built two batting backstops on the property and began devoting themselves to the arduous task of maintaining the rough fields. And they continued to maintain the fields as a condition for the leasing of the grounds for the price of $1 a year from the city for the next 30 years. This block, soon to become known in the neighborhood as "the field," and remain so for the next 40 years, also immediately borders the Rodin Museum, also on the Parkway. Any visitor contemplating the outdoor, gateway statute of Rodin's "Thinker" in the springtime only need glance left to see the ballgames that came to be a regular feature, after the late 1960s, of this vast, open, public space.

The original terms for the use of the public space included a substantial commitment to maintain the physical appearance of the land as parkland. The neighborhood men took up the challenge and transformed the block into a beautiful lush green surface of well-manicured grass and turf. Inevitably, this kind of transformation, built on neighborhood labor, instilled a sense of ownership and territoriality into the space. The claiming of this space for community use left with it collective "memory traces" that established baseball and this voluntary association as central to the "character" of this community (Molotch, Freudenburg, & Paulsen, 2000) and defined baseball as a "beauty asset" that Fairmounters would defend for the next three decades.

LETTING OUTSIDERS IN

In these early years of FSA baseball, all the kids came from the neighborhood and almost exclusively from the three Catholic schools in Fairmount that existed then. Although there was some limited involvement of local Latino families who were part of the same Catholic schools, these children were overwhelmingly White.[9] The organization did not draw upon the large population of Black children from bordering neighborhoods. For one thing, the origins of the organization as an informal operation out of a veterans post meant that it was next to impossible to know when and where to sign up to play in the spring if you were outside of the social networks of these neighborhood men. Up until the mid-1980s, registration for the spring season occurred over two weekends in February at the Catholic War Veterans Post, where all the baseball equipment was stored for the year and where neighborhood men regularly congregated to drink beer together and socialize. The inaccessibility of the registration also fed into a culture of racial exclusion that had dominated in the neighborhood. As one Fairmounter coach described it,

> Listen. We have our own Halloween. We call it "Whiteween." Parents are notified in their mailboxes when our Halloween is, so they don't have to be attacked on regular Halloween, or be run over by wolf packs. We have our own Halloween separate for that reason. . . . Twenty years ago that's how it would be here (with baseball). We would notify who we wanted to about registration. It would be delivery to your house, instead of putting it in the newspaper and publicizing everything. That's how it would have been handled 20 years ago. Registration wouldn't be open. It would be closed.

The tightness of the neighborhood, the reputation for racial exclusion, and the inaccessibility of the sign-ups meant few people needed to be turned away. They simply did not turn up.

Fairmount baseball first started to change in the early 1970s when several things happened that would permanently transform its insular nature. First, the rapid gentrification of the area meant a rather dramatic loss of population, especially in the relative numbers of children in the area. This meant a relative scarcity of children eligible for baseball. Between 1950 and 1990, the population of Fairmount dropped by almost half, from 10,764 to 5,882. Spring Garden's population declined even more sharply over the same period. By 1990 it had dropped to approximately one third of its 1950 size (Table 13.1). As the local population declined, and the social backgrounds of Fairmount and Spring Garden residents changed, the traditional base of the Catholic schools in the area declined dramatically. The lack of children in the area meant the viability of strictly "local" baseball was at risk. This was recognized by the original leadership of FSA in the early 1970s, who made a series of strategic decisions to insure an ample supply of children for the organization and its ability to launch a full spectrum of teams for each division. The organization would have to be "opened" up, first to the children of the new professionals in the area, who were already entering, and second to children from other Center City areas.

Second, beyond the scarcity of children, the friendship networks of local children, newcomers, and Fairmounters expanded to include children from outside the neighborhood. As the neighborhood gentrified, the presence of a growing group of children who attended non-Catholic private schools, Quaker, and secular, public, and nonparish Catholic schools outside the neighborhood also grew. Because a growing proportion of these children attended schools outside the neighborhood, the networks of information about the neighborhood and its recreational opportunities expanded. Many of these children had strong networks to middle-class minority children. These children and their parents played a part in sponsoring middle-class children of color into FSA. Quite a number of Black parents I interviewed mentioned that they learned about FSA's programs through these private school networks. Thus, ironically, although the entry of these largely White professionals into Spring Garden had played a part in pushing out Latino residents from the area, their sponsorship of middle-class children of color into neighborhood baseball also played a part in breaking down the racial isolation of Fairmount. But only a part. In addition, the fact that the one surviving Catholic school in the area, St. Francis, could no longer rely predominantly on neighborhood children to sustain itself, and drew increasingly from neighborhoods of color in the surrounding areas, also played a role. As this school increasingly integrated over time, some White Fairmounter children also sponsored the entrance of their school friends of color into the ranks of FSA. Both of these sources provided a kind of "race sponsorship" into the local space.

Third, several factors combined to give FSA greater visibility and political accountability in the city in the mid-1980s. Before this time, there were no physical markers of the organization at the ball field. Children desperate for restroom facilities were often shepherded to a tolerant neighbor's house a few blocks away. Several years after my family had moved to Spring Garden in 1984, I remember driving by the field and seeing kids playing baseball in uniforms. I tried to find out how to sign up my daughter to play T-ball. No one I asked seemed to know until it occurred to me to ask the mother of two girls on the block who went to the neighborhood Catholic school. She explained that I should go to a smoke-filled backroom, "kind of a bar," up at one of the veterans' posts in Fairmount, on one of two Saturday nights, a few months before the season starts. They would collect the registration fee, and then a coach would call about a month later to tell me what team my daughter was on and where to go to practice. "How would I find all this out if I didn't know you?" I asked. "You wouldn't," she replied.

The ball field remained essentially a large, leveled lot until 1985, when the president of FSA and the local ward leader persuaded John Street, the local city council representative, to secure Mayor Wilson Goode's approval for the construction of a clubhouse with bathroom facilities, a concession area, and a meeting room for the organization. Five years later, in the middle of the season of 1990, the new building with its concession stand and restrooms opened with an agreement from the City that FSA, in exchange for the maintenance of the field, the grounds, and the building by its volunteers, would rent the space and facilities for $1 a year, ratified in five-year contracts.

From that point on, anyone driving by and seeing large groups of children playing organized games could inquire at the concession stand on one side of the new building and receive information about sign-up procedures. It is of no small significance that the city council representative, and the mayor who ultimately supported this neighborhood initiative, were African-American politicians who represented large minority constituencies beyond the neighborhood. The completion of this building, and the involvement of city officials, was a turning point for the organization, as it marked a visible transition of organizational headquarters from an insulated informal club within a Catholic veterans' organization, controlled by a small group of neighborhood men, to a highly visible building constructed with city funds with a new accountability to public officials.

Finally, although White gentrification in Spring Garden had contributed to pushing out many residents of color, largely Puerto Rican, in the 1970s and 1980s, throughout the 1990s growing numbers of Black professional residents began to appear in the area. The entrance of the children of these Black newcomers from Spring Garden into FSA, combined with the other, largely middle-class minority children from outside the area who had already entered FSA, meant that by the mid-1990s, approximately one third of the youngest children playing organized baseball in Fairmount were children of color. Anyone in the 1960s closely monitoring how Blacks were excluded and sometimes violently expelled from this area, would have found such an outcome surprising indeed. One Fairmounter mother who had grown up playing baseball in the neighborhood said the rapid racial change in FSA took her by surprise:

> well I know my reaction to opening day and the day after it was like, "Did they send flyers out all over the city?" I was just like, "Where did they all come from, I mean, where did they all find out about us?" And it's like word of mouth. And I mean there's nothing you can really do. When you have a league and it's opened up for enrollment, that's it.

This racial transformation of neighborhood baseball occurred not only relatively rapidly, compared to the two surrounding neighborhoods, but relatively harmoniously. How was that? Beyond the demographic changes and the new accountability to Black politicians, the answer relates to two factors, "race sponsorship" and the nature of baseball itself.

RACE SPONSORSHIP

The importance of what I call race sponsorship in the smooth integration of FSA cannot be underestimated. Race sponsorship, as I define it, occurs when an individual or family enters a formerly exclusive space aligned with or sponsored by an individual with legitimate membership status. This is similar to the moment Pee Wee Reese of the Brooklyn Dodgers called a timeout to embrace Jackie Robinson in 1947, as a dramatic silent confrontation to screaming bigots in the stands of Cincinnati.[10] In FSA, race sponsors helped create pockets of safe space for new minority members in this early stage of integration. Sometimes this was a "remote sponsorship," where a leader of the organization would extend a welcome to a minority stranger in the face of members who demonstrated a more hostile reception. The motives for this kind of sponsorship are almost irrelevant and might be little more than a strategic move on the part of the sponsor to fill the ranks of the organization. The important function of such a leader or sponsor is to resist the "race bulldogs"—the more overt racists in the organization, those who dedicate themselves to "boundary work," and would exclude Blacks, for example, under almost any circumstance if not kept in check by fellow insiders.

I saw this kind of sponsorship on numerous occasions by strategic leaders of FSA in the 1990s. Several examples can illustrate this. On two weekends in February of every year, organizational leaders of FSA, some insider coaches and their friends from the neighborhood, often congregate in the small, windowless meeting room of the clubhouse to await the arrival of parents signing up their children for the next season of baseball. A good deal of socializing occurs over the course of these two weekends. It is also a good strategic place to be if you're a coach who is looking to pick up new talented kids who might not be known to the other coaches. Once this registration is over, the league selects its coaches, holds a draft, and has no formal obligations to accept any latecomers into the league. Accepting those who come late and charging them a late fee is a discretionary decision. This makes the postregistration period an opportune time for excluding anyone who might be considered undesirable.

During one of these weekends, in the mid-1990s when the number of Black children was just beginning to noticeably increase, I went to this "office" to pay the $80 inscription fee and register my son. There were two chairs seated in front of the sign-up desk for those registering. I was seated at one, filling out forms, while a heavy-set Black mother, filling out a registration form for her son, sat next to me. After she left, a Fairmounter named Carl, who regularly hangs out at the clubhouse and qualifies for what I have called a "race bulldog," softly mumbled to a small group of men standing around something about, "Watch out, that chair is still warm." I glanced up to see the expression of Brian, one of the leaders of the organization seated opposite me. As he looked up he frowned disapprovingly in Carl's direction. The reprimand was subtle and involved no overt loss of face for Carl but served to silence him and the snickers of another listener.

Commentary from two other FSA coaches also confirms the importance of sponsorship by strategic FSA leaders as well as coaches. William, a Black school principal I interviewed whose two sons had played for five years in the league, also stressed the role of certain FSA strategic leaders in welcoming new people of color "without a lot of ruffled feathers,"

> I've heard other people who have complained but when I ask questions about it, I think sometimes they may be overly reacting, you know, overly sensitive to what has been, what someone has said or done to them. . . . If there is a problem, I think that there are ways to deal with that problem. I think Brian is very approachable. I think the commissioners are approachable. But Brian, specifically, is very approachable about problems, and I think he's very open to looking for solutions.

It would be rather surprising if a social space like Fairmount, with the kind of racial exclusion and racism that had plagued the neighborhood in the past, would have produced a group of adult men where racist feelings or subtle racist behaviors were entirely absent.

The integration of the baseball space certainly did not mean this. But the extent to which the leadership of FSA reached out on a regular basis to a stream of new Black families, and sponsored their entry with a welcoming stance, was remarkable. Their willingness to do this, while holding their "race bulldogs" mostly in check, set the stage for the race integration that followed.

Coupled with the sponsorship of early Black children into FSA by strategic leaders, the relatively low level of interest of their parents in getting very involved in the organization of FSA meant they posed little threat to insiders. The first Black parents who entered the organization lived largely outside the neighborhood, in Center City or surrounding areas, and were primarily interested in a safe space for their children that would not require a large time commitment. As one Black lawyer expressed it:

> I don't feel like they necessarily need me to do anything, and that's fine. I'm just happy that we have the league. If they can handle it, fine. But nobody really asked me to participate in any leadership way anyway. . . . But I don't have the time. There's a lot about FSA that I would like to see changed, but I don't have the time to really make it happen, so there's no point to complain about something you can't do a thing about.

Beyond the organizational leadership, at the city level, the consolidation of Black politicians in strategic positions of power, including as neighborhood representatives to the city council, added an additional incentive to facilitate the smooth reception of new Black families into FSA. One White Fairmount mother contrasted the current openness of the organization to the past she remembered in this way:

> I think it can happen now because of the way the laws are set up. It kind of ties your hand. Where 20 years ago I think them laws were like stuck in a box somewhere. And everybody just closed their eyes to it. Ignorance. Whatever you want to call it.

And 20 years before, a White leadership also dominated the city, and baseball was strictly a neighborhood affair. A Black father, William, who gave several FSA leaders the bulk of the credit for welcoming in families of color, nonetheless noted the importance of this background political climate and two strategic African-American politicians:

> Well I think the leadership set the tone. I think the other thing, from a practical standpoint, the leadership, Fairmount's Sport Association, has received a lot of support from John Street and he was the councilman then and now from, what's his name, Darrell Clark. You know they get state money. They get city money. And I think they understand that part of that, in order to do that, you have to show that there is some, you know some positive, affirmative kind of plan for the . . . for what they do, and it's worked out fine.

Remote race sponsorship by a few strategic leaders, however, could not bring about the kind of race integration seen at FSA if it were not also occurring in multiple ways at a more grassroots level as well. In addition to sponsorship by leaders, and greater accountability to Black leaders, more intimate forms of race sponsorship were also significant to the integration process. Numerous Black professional parents I interviewed mentioned that they originally found out about FSA through their child's White friends at the private school they attended outside the neighborhood. These friendships structured the context of entry, such that an exclusion of one child could easily translate into conflicts with another, whose exclusion could not be justified along racial lines and whose parents might have had more social resources to resist.

Helena, the Black professor, and her family, whom I described above as one of the early Black families in Fairmount who had been tormented by hostile teenagers, provides another example of race sponsorship. This family's very entrance into the neighborhood had been sponsored originally by a Black real estate agent who rented them their first apartment in Fairmount.

> Helena: "Michelle [a Black real estate agent] used to live above us and owned the building. They were an interracial marriage, and they would catch it upstairs, and we would catch it downstairs. They [the neighbors] would really just throw things at them. So when Earl, my husband, went out there and took care of them, it slowed up a lot because they just thought he was crazy."
>
> S.G.: "So when you guys lived up there, were those two apartments the only Black people in the neighborhood? On that block?"
>
> Helena: "Almost in the neighborhood. There were very few African Americans in the neighborhood. Michelle was probably the pioneer. And then, she rented to us. Later she sold us this house."

But it was sponsorship into baseball that provided their eventual social acceptance in the neighborhood. One year, a very competitive coach who lived on their block "discovered them" before the draft and recruited them into FSA. They entered under his direct personal sponsorship, although they had already formed an opinion about the organization from another professional Black mother whose daughter had played the year before with no problems.

> But if it weren't for that [baseball] we would probably never have really gotten involved with the neighborhood. It forced us to become "Fairmounters." That's basically what happened. Real Fairmounters! Accepted by Fairmounters! You know, it's hard to be a Fairmounter. You almost have to be in the sports. One thing that puts you in their league is the sports team. . . . I just think that Fairmount is a unique little area. It really is, when you think about it. There's a 2- to 3-mile radius, and it never ceases to amaze me. Even this little block, my neighbors. They are interesting people. There's the different cultures, the different economic brackets. One person lives over here and makes $500,000 and another person doesn't work.

Interracial couples or mixed-race families constitute obvious instances of "intimate race sponsorship." Those prone to exclude a Black child, for example, may come to see the child in a different light when his behaviors are regularly being interpreted by his White father with little social distance from the racially suspicious. As one Black mother, married to a White man, Fritz, who was active in the league for years, explained her son's positive experience in FSA: "Want to know why Sonny had such a good experience down there [the field]? One and only one reason: Fritz. They could all relate to Fritz. So I tried to keep a distance and just watch from far off."

Similarly when two middle-class children of different races demonstrate a casual comfort, as well as an implied history, despite the fact that they may have different cultural styles, their friendship proves a model for those with no such experience. The modeling might be for other racially exclusive children, or it might be for their own, wary parents. Shawn, a Fairmount parent in the league who had described his own adolescence as one constant battle with Black kids, expressed amazement at how his son, Jimmy, had Black friends from the ball field who ran in and out of his house "like nothing."

As a different kind of example, a Black parent who suspects a White coach is treating his child unfairly might be less likely to read in racial motives if the coach regularly selects a Black parent as his assistant, and this Black parent can testify by example of a non-exclusionary style of the suspected coach. In this case, the Black parent is sponsoring the acceptance. Intimate race sponsorship is vital, because the reception and the interpretation of the behaviors of those defined as "the other" always happen in a context, and the extent to which the context links the potentially excluded to internal bases of support, via distant or intimate race sponsorship, the more likely the entry will be smooth and judgments about behaviors tolerant, or at least not overtly hostile.

Although the integration process at FSA occurred relatively harmoniously, it also happened unevenly. I noticed over the years, and numerous parents I interviewed also brought up, that the children of color were often not randomly distributed among the White coaches; certain White coaches were more likely to have more Black kids on their teams than others. This pattern of "selective recruitment" resulted from a variety of factors. Some coaches worked hard to recruit known neighborhood kids who were largely White. Others either had no such preferences, or once they had a Black child on their team they tried to draft him again because he was known to them. Black parents who had had positive experiences with a coach sometimes volunteered to assist with the coaching so as to secure a place on this coach's team for their child. In any case, these coaches carved out a safe social space for these new children and their parents, which served as an important filter for their overall interpretations of the organization. Sal was one such coach, whom a Puerto Rican father had included in his list of a handful of White coaches he viewed as most likely to have more mixed teams. In my interview with Sal, he described how he perceived his role in the racial encounter of the organization:

> The direction of this interview was interesting to me because it's stuff I think about all the time—when you asked me about race. I watch these interactions all the time. I'm supposed to . . . and I'm not one of these crusaders. I'm not gonna come out and say [pause]. I mean I have to coexist here. But I don't agree all the time with what's going on. . . . Last year I had a lot of Black kids on my team again. Years ago, I used to work as an exterminator, and I worked in some Black homes where the kids would come up to me and touch my arms, like they had never seen a White person in their lives. I always remembered that. My experience here has been such that, having these kids on my team, I don't try to be anything special. I'm jus', I'm just a White guy who's not half bad. That's what I'm trying to be. White kids get a lot of preconceptions from their parents and so do Black children—what to expect. There's a guy, Phil, a Black janitor where I work, who lives way up North Philly and told me he wanted his kids to play baseball and experience other types of children. So he came down and I got him on my team. The kid got the sportsmanship award, for being there all the time. . . . They said he had a great time and is coming back.

When asked how he could explain the overall smooth integration in the league:

> Why is it so smooth? Because of the diversity of the White people. You have people with better educational backgrounds; it's not all the [pause]. I don't know how to explain this. I think about this a lot, but I can't verbalize it. I think there were more non–Fairmount Whites who could lessen the impact of the change. Does that make sense?

Jessie, a White Fairmounter, whose small neighborhood business brings her into frequent contact with newcomers, also mentioned the impact of more liberal professional attitudes on neighborhood change:

> No, I think it [race integration] has been relatively smooth, considering this neighborhood

> and its background. . . . I guess you gotta give credit where credit's due. If the yuppies didn't move in, I don't think there wouldn't be any change. I think they moved in with different attitudes, and you kind of got a little eye opening here and there and you start to think. Well, you know, they're right. . . . And I think time itself.

Recognizing the segmented nature of the racial integration that did occur in FSA is crucial to understanding the uneven process by which the transformation occurred. Its unevenness also meant that not all families of color who played baseball at FSA came away with good feelings. Some were isolated on teams whose coaches were less sympathetic, or were concentrated on teams whose coaches were in disfavor with the leadership or umpires, and came away with judgments that race issues were still alive and well at FSA. But many more families of color stayed and found enough welcoming space at FSA to transform the organization into a multicultural one.

CLASS AND COMPETING COMMUNITY VALUES

The professionals gentrifying Fairmount and Spring Garden fit the description of the "cultural new class" (Ley 1994) or the liberal sector of the middle-class that concentrated in the social and cultural fields of the economy typically unconnected to the corporate sector, i.e. doctors, lawyers, professors. The newcomer coaches and parents I interviewed also came almost exclusively from the sector of the middle-class consisting of social and cultural professionals. Almost all of the 20 newcomer coaches and parent interviewees held professional jobs in governmental, educational, or legal services unconnected to the corporate sector. Almost half of them were educators—teachers, principals, and professors. When describing their motivations for moving to this area of the city, newcomers often spoke of their preference for the cultural lifestyle of the city, and, specifically, the diversity of the city as a plus. Many had working-class parents who had helped them achieve upward mobility through educational advancement, and they remained positive toward, and emotionally comfortable with, the social style of many of the Fairmounters.

Part of the intensity that Fairmounters felt about the outcomes of games and championships stemmed from their definition of baseball as the only sport, perhaps the only social activity, that mattered. A Fairmounter coach complained that newcomers' overinvolvement in multiple leisure activities and other sports translated into "jack of all trades and master of none," namely, their general lack of baseball talent. Part of what was at stake for Fairmounters as newcomers entered their sports association was not just organizational control but the preservation of baseball itself, the game as it was meant to be played and had been played in the neighborhood: adeptly, thoughtfully, strategically and with discipline. Playing baseball well was a source of pride for many in Fairmount. Seeing local boys compete in city-wide competitions, representing the neighborhood at Philadelphia's Veterans stadium, and following the championships of local teams were important neighborhood rituals. But essential to maintaining a respectable neighborhood baseball identity was the dedication of a cadre of coaches who both knew enough about the game and its intricacies and had enough time to train the next generation of players. But as time passed, there weren't enough old-timers to do this job and newcomers and outsiders were brought in.

The gap in the amount of time dedicated to maintaining the FSA by an inner core of mostly old-timer volunteers, whose participation ranges from 10 to 53 hours every week of the season (or an average of 270 hours each season per "activist"), and the outer circle of regular parents, who contribute only four hours once during a season, is a source of significant resentment by insiders in the organization. The different degrees of involvement in the FSA became a central focus of tensions between oldtimers and the newcomers in FSA; tensions, as we have seen, already established in the neighborhood. But time devoted to the organization was just one symbolic issue that divided them. Just as Fairmounters complained that newcomers had weak ties to the neighborhood with little local mixing, instrumental friendships, and minimal community support, they saw newcomers approach the baseball organization in a similar manner—for the instrumental needs of their individual children and not as a neighborhood treasure that needed nurturing. Many newcomers were oblivious to this resentment. Others countered with their own complaints about Fairmounters' coolness to outsiders, about unfair access to insider information about teams and opportunities, about the adult-centered, competitive way that Fairmounters ran an organization for children.

The Fairmount tradition established in the 1960s of neighborhood men volunteering to coach baseball, whether or not they had a son in the league, continued in a modified way for decades. In the 1990s, many teams in the FSA were still associated with a Fairmounter coach who "kept his team" year after year. That is, a particular man coaches the Rangers, or the Angels, in the 7–9 age division year after year. Teams came to be identified as "The Padres—John's team," or "The Grays—Bob's team." Most newcomer coaches, on the other hand, were father-coaches and often coached, unlike Fairmounters, their sons in other sports, like soccer. Their reference group was more their own son, and other players and parents on the team, rather than spectators outside this small group. They were less likely to stay with the same team or the same age division over time and more likely to move up age divisions as their sons did.[11] They almost never coached or maintained contact with the organization beyond the playing careers of their children. This way, they established less identification with a particular team and less of an investment with the organization beyond their team.

If Fairmounters saw newcomers as individualistic and not community minded enough, newcomers would counter that, at least, it was a child-centered individualism. The sharpest newcomer critique related to their view that the FSA prioritized adult socializing over children's interests. While Fairmounters might devote lots of time to the organization, they argued, a good amount of that time was devoted to hanging out in the clubhouse and drinking beer, which set a bad example for the kids. The clubhouse has a keg refrigerator so that cold beer is always on tap. Insiders have only to grab a plastic cup, pull down a lever, and fill up.

The complaint that the FSA was adult-centered went beyond discomfort with beer drinking in the clubhouse. Actually many newcomers thought that drinking beer in the staff office and using the clubhouse year round as a hangout place was perfectly acceptable, even appropriate compensation for the hours they spent holding the organization together. When newcomers said that the organization wasn't enough about children they usually had in mind an emphasis on winning games, winning championships, and winning in the city-wide league. Among the parents I interviewed, it was disproportionately newcomers who felt the FSA leaned excessively in the competitive direction and who longed for more emphasis on individual instruction of players. In contrast, Fairmounter parents tended to see the organization as more balanced, with an appropriate emphasis on teaching skills as well as competitively winning games.[12] Typical among newcomer parents were this father's comments,

> At FSA they are very much playing games to win, very competitive. This is one of the things I don't like. See, certain kids are not going to get a base hit because the coach just teaches them to bunt, so he can win the game. They learn to bunt but should be learning to hit and [then they would] have a slightly better chance to get on base than by [just] bunting. I prefer to teach kids how to play baseball and not how to win.

Another newcomer father described FSA as "less instructional and more about winning" and related it to the need of coaches to have bragging rights in the neighborhood. This argument relates back to the issue of "clubhouse teams" versus the newcomer teams. Baseball as a central element of Fairmount neighborhood's identity meant that losing a game, especially for a "clubhouse team" took on a weighted significance. The association of particular teams with insiders focused energy on the importance of winning to prove something to some other group of *adults*. Many newcomers thought that that somebody was them.

The differences in the way that Fairmounters and newcomers related both to the neighborhood as described above, and to the league, reflected a competing set of cultural values related to individual responsibility, group solidarity, and how best to promote children's interests. The different orientations toward the community could be described as hierarchical communalism versus child-centered individualism. While there was a range of opinion about most of these concerns within the two groups, when differences did appear, they often took this form. Fairmounters, on the one hand, regularly brought up resentments about the way newcomers used the organization for the narrow benefit of their own children without appropriate levels of support, or deference, to the needs of the broader group and its leadership, similar to their approach to the neighborhood. Newcomers complained that their interests were ignored, that Fairmounters too often listened only to other Fairmounters and ran the organization to benefit themselves and their adult friends, with children a distant secondary concern.

A UNITED "INNER-CITY" IDENTITY

Despite the emphasis in this discussion on the divisions and tensions between Fairmounters and more affluent newcomers, there were also many forged understandings and feelings of connection across these groups. Indeed, the cross-class sympathies may even have been stronger than some of the strains between the deep insiders and newcomers. Most importantly, many newcomers cherished being a part of the FSA, despite its warts and their somewhat marginal position. In the words of one newcomer, "We represent some of the outsiders. But I think the mixture of kids here is terrific. I'm not aware of any tensions. I think it's one of the few places where kids of different colors, different ethnicities, and different socioeconomic incomes come together for a common purpose in this city. It's wonderful."

The sympathies that emerged across class and racial lines at the FSA were especially apparent in encounters that the ball club had with the outside world, such as in traveling team championships played in remote neighborhoods of the city and suburbs. Professional parents at the FSA were sometimes surprised to learn that suburban teams viewed Fairmount in an undifferentiated way, as a low-class, inner-city team. The generalized apprehension of suburbanites for anything inside the city translated into nervousness about even neighborhoods as affluent as Spring Garden had become. This external judgment stimulated community loyalty. This was salient one year when the Fairmount's 12-and-under traveling team faced an all-White, extremely affluent, suburban team. FSA's team was about one-third boys of color and their team was all White. Neighborhood men and women had driven over an hour to see this important Fairmount game, many with no child on the team. After the Council Rock parents had left their BMWs and slick SUVs in the immense parking lot behind their practice field, Fairmounter adults began lining behind FSA's dugout. Seeing the crowd of adult Fairmounters outside our neighborhood, all of us looking particularly ragtag compared to the well-dressed suburban parents we faced, I could see the "insider/newcomer" problem slip away. As the game proceeded, many Fairmounters shouted out non-stop, encouraging comments to each of the Fairmount players. Although some were still strangers to me, they called out my son by name. They called out also the names of our Black catcher and third baseman in a raucous, public testimony of solidarity for the community we sometimes achieved.

Although Fairmounters had many complaints about newcomers' individualism, some also recognized the importance of contributions by professionals who were strategically placed in the city. Newcomers were sometimes generous in tapping their networks and resources to provide a different kind of financial support, one that was more lucrative than "booster day," where ball players knocked on neighborhood doors with FSA cups asking for donations. As one FSA staffer acknowledged, "They're [the newcomers] able to get us sponsored money. Where in the past, we used to knock on doors. Now they just email each other, and it's here. That really helps. So it's less work for the twelve people most involved. It's less work because, they can call two friends and a check comes in the mail. It's beautiful." While receiving mailed-in checks might produce more revenue, knocking on doors builds community support for the field and connects the baseball children with locals who might not have children in the league. It was this combination of both orientations, reaching inward to capitalize on community solidarity, and reaching outward for inclusion and external support, which built on the strengths of the two worlds of Fairmounters and newcomer professionals.[13] So while different cultural orientations divided some Fairmounters from some newcomers within the FSA, important cross-class ties of solidarity and understanding coexisted in this local public space of sports, more so than the organizational gatekeepers acknowledged.

SOMETHING ABOUT BASEBALL

This article has explored the factors behind a delicate process of racial and class integration in the neighborhood baseball league of these two Philadelphia neighborhoods. Turning to the role of sports itself, we could extend the question and ask, "Were all the features mentioned above sufficient to bring about the transformation of this exclusive, white, baseball league into a relatively harmoniously integrated recreational space? Were all these factors, the passion of the neighborhood men for preserving the integrity of the game when faced with a scarcity of local children, mixed-race alliances and the race sponsorship of new children, the lure of the visible new clubhouse, and the new accountability to black politicians, enough?" We could further ask, "Did it matter that it was baseball? Would the same thing have happened if it had been football, or soccer, or a neighborhood basketball league? Could the social change that happened in Spring Garden and Fairmount have been embodied in any other sport?" My answer would be no. Something about baseball itself did matter to this transformation.

For one thing, baseball is a highly structured encounter, inherent in which is a great deal of waiting. And it is precisely because of all that waiting, that requirement of patience while tracking the contingencies and possibilities of a play, that baseball offers such social opportunities. Think of the spectators' experience of the game, not just that of the players. Parents sit together on bleachers, often separated from the parents of the other teams who are sitting on different bleachers, each team's parents sitting with their child's teammates' parents. Parents of different backgrounds sit together, but in a very highly structured context. They do not have to figure out how to relate to one another. The differences that might cause problems among them are not right on the surface, or are at least deflected by the bigger concern: the game. You're part of this team, and you're part of that team. You just sit, and wait, and you don't have to do anything. But at the same time, there is a bonding that goes on, because, at least for this season, you share a common fate. And this common fate produces conversation: what the other team did wrong, what the other coach should have done, what our coach should have done, how Rickie didn't fall asleep until midnight worrying about the playoffs, what if the sun goes down before we score? Over a fairly short period of time, a deep sense of "we" develops. Parents don't like it, for example, when parents from another team forgetfully sit on their bleachers (even when they know one another). They want to be able to feel happy with "their group" when the poor little seven-year old on the other team strikes out. They want to feel okay about it, to mumble, "Thank God." So there is that structure to baseball. There is enough time between the moments of intensity to permit human connections. Precisely what looks like a boring moment to baseball's detractors, is often a deeply felt moment of shared wonder to the informed spectator. And those who don't at first "get the religion" are often seduced into believing by the collective reverence around them. Because baseball is a game of waiting for long periods with occasional, intense peaks of emotion, it provides a conducive space for parents and children of diverse backgrounds to sit patiently, controlled by a ritualistic drama, clustered in teams not of their own choosing, while trying to figure each other out.

Baseball is also a game of hope, and a game that spotlights individual failures. Pitchers break down. Batters fail. Fielders drop the ball. There are a lot of collectively shared feelings about the errors and mishaps of individual players, most of whom, almost all of whom, will not be your own son or daughter. A kind of identification evolves, not just with the group, but with particular kids over what happened to them that day, that game. We now care intensely about what happened today to the kid we didn't even know three weeks ago. Mothers will commiserate with each other with a, "You're gonna have a rough night tonight!" when one of the boys has three strikeouts in a game.

So the slow pace of baseball, punctuated as it is by moments of such intensity and drama—that long plateau with its occasional upsurges—matters. It allows parents of different backgrounds to come together on the bleachers and feel comfortable, without the need to do much, and yet to share the passion, the disappointments, and the triumphs. And just before all this "we" feeling gets out of control (at least usually before), the season comes to an end. And then comes the reshuffling. So that, the next season the parents are on the same bleachers, but with a different group of people. And after four seasons, they have come to know a lot of people in the community, and learned a lot, very specifically, about different individuals and their children. While they may at first have thought of a given child as a "jerk," after months on the bleachers with that child's parents they often learn more about why a given child behaves poorly, and may feel less removed from that child's "problem."

On the bleachers, parents share that baseball "suspension of time." In contrast, parents who sit together watching basketball do not get the same opportunities. In basketball, too much happens against the pressure of the clock. The same is true for soccer. So, it mattered that it was baseball. Because it was baseball, we waited, and hoped together, and experienced moments of communion, pain, and redemption in the process.

Last but not least, Fairmount baseball is played on that lush, green, rectangle of grass and red earth, before the backdrop of the open skyline of Center City, Philadelphia, and its most majestic museums. This space offers all its participants a constant grounding in beauty on a scale grander than the baseball diamond. The deep longing begins around the end of February. "When will practices start?" "Has your coach called yet?" Opening Day becomes an aesthetic reentrance into a community of friends, neighbors, and former strangers where, just as you feel the first warmth of the spring, you begin tracking the inevitable growth and changes in this year's crop of children. "Oh, my gosh, look at how much Jonathan grew." "I can't believe George is no longer afraid of the ball." "Look at that green! I say to my wife, you want a yard? A yard? This is all the grass I need."

To say that the racial integration of FSA occurred relatively smoothly and without major conflicts is not to say that there were not tensions, grumblings, or conflicts, including stacking, selective recruitment, and questionable calls against outsiders, in which racism played a real or perceived role. These certainly did happen. But given the history of racial conflict in this neighborhood, the fact that the central cleavages to emerge in this organization were not along racial lines, but, rather along lines of class, or along the divide between the old timers and the new professionals, is striking. One of the sweetest intricacies of baseball is the rule about a dropped third strike. This rule permits a player who strikes out the chance to run to first base if the catcher drops the ball on the third strike. It builds a strong element of hope into baseball. While individual failures are spotlighted in baseball, small possibilities of redemption like this are laced throughout the game. In reviewing the history of baseball in this neighborhood, we have seen that old-timer residents cared enough about baseball to turn their backs on their exclusionary past and make room for outsiders, first their "class competitors" and, second, children of color. Did the newcomers get to be deep insiders? For the most part, no. But their children were allowed in and gathered rich experiences in a beautifully orchestrated game. And all this happened in a city that had distinguished itself as having one of the last professional teams in baseball to integrate in the mid-1950s.[14] A neighborhood that had represented the ugly racial segregation that marked many American cities, which had racially defended itself against outsiders with violence, had a chance to redeem itself in the later decades of the 20th century, and took it. Responding to population loss, and in the context of a new scrutiny by Black politicians in a post-civil rights era, locals watched as children and parents of color were sponsored in. The neighborhood reformed itself, slowly and unevenly, to move beyond its failures, at least on the turf of baseball. It received a second chance and took it—just like a dropped third strike.

NOTES

1. This article draws on research that was conducted with the aid of a study leave from Temple University and a research grant from the Department of Sociology, Temple University. I wish to thank John Landreau, Debbie Rogow, Gideon Sjoberg, Nancy Theberge, and Michael Messner for comments and criticism that helped to improve the quality of distinct parts of this paper. I am grateful to Kevin Delaney for his help and collaboration on an early rendition of this project, and to Joshua Freely and Dylan Galaty for their research assistance in the fieldwork for this project, and to Nadine Sullivan for her assistance in finalizing this piece.
2. For a more detailed description of my research methodology and additional ethnographic reflections see Grasmuck (2005: 206–222).
3. Lidz (1991, p. 84) distinguishes a "participant observer" from an "observing participant," in that the former, "enters the group or situation to be studied as a natural member meeting all the usual qualities or requirements of participation. . . . One is a member who then asks the group for permission to carry out social scientific observation in conjunction with one's other activities of membership." As a "bench Mom" for years, I then requested permission to study the organization.
4. Whalen's data (2001, p. 186) extends the area defined as Spring Garden to include an additional census tract 133, one tract to the east of tract 134.
5. Cybriwski (1978, p. 22) calculates the rates of homeownership in Fairmount as even higher, almost three quarters of Fairmount residents in the 1960s, based on real estate directories.
6. See Taylor (1988, pp. 79–131) for a conceptual discussion of socially defended territories.
7. Ley and Cybriwsky (1974, p. 503) report two cases of large anti-Black actions against Black families settling in the area in the early 1970s.
8. Although I wanted to include the real name of Tom O'Connors in recognition of his important historical role in the creation of the ball club, he preferred that I use a pseudonym in describing his involvement.
9. Although some Puerto Ricans and other Latinos do self-identify as both Latino and White, the use of *White* here refers to non-Latino Whites, unless otherwise specified.
10. This occurred in the early Jackie Robinson days, in 1947, when Pee Wee Reese left his short-stop position to walk to first base and stand with his arm around his lone Black teammate on the Dodgers, Jackie Robinson, as they confronted racist taunts from the Cincinnati fans. Roger Kahn considers this the greatest moment in the history of American sports (MacNeil/Lehrer, 1997). This is not to portray Reese as more heroic than Robinson. It just underscores the need of all heroes and heroines for help from friends.
11. Between 1996 and 1999, 65% of Fairmounter head-coaches agreed to take a team when they had no son playing in the division compared to only 20% of the newcomer head-coaches who had a son on the team they coached over this same period. After 1998, newcomers came to dominate numbers, hovering around 60 percent of head-coaches over the next several years. This ushered in an increase in "father coaches" since newcomers typically coached only when they had a son on the team, 80% of those managing the 7–12 age groups between 1996 and 1999 compared to 35% of their Fairmounter counterparts.
12. Seven of the ten newcomer parents described the FSA as stressing competition (playing games to win) over instruction (teaching individual and team skills), whereas only two of the 10 Fairmounters described the ball club as relatively competitive. Most Fairmounters saw the FSA as appropriately balancing competition with instruction.
13. Putnam (2000) makes a distinction between "bonded social capital" and "bridging social capital" similar to this inward and outward reaching set of networks of Fairmounters and newcomers and the need for communities to have both.
14. In the mid-1950s, the Phillies had the only all-White baseball club in the National League, with their first Black member, John Kennedy, arriving in 1957 (see Kuklick, 1991, p. 148). Two years later, the Red Sox signed Pumpsie Green, making it the last team in Major League Baseball to integrate, with the Phillies coming in next to last (see Bryant, 2002).

REFERENCES

Bryant, H. (2002). *Shut out: A history of race and baseball in Boston.* New York: Routledge.

Coakley, J.J. (2001). Sport in society: An inspiration or an opiate? In D.S. Eitzen (Ed.), *Sport in contemporary society: An anthology* (pp. 20–36). New York: Worth.

Cybriwsky, R. (1978). Social aspects of neighborhood change. *Annals of the Association of American Geographers,* 68, 17–33.

Edwards, H. (1970), *The revolt of the Black athlete.* New York: Free Press.

Edwards, H. (1973). *Sociology of sport.* Homewood, IL: Dorsey Press.

Edwards, H. (2001). An end of the golden age of Black participation. In D.S. Eitzen. (Ed.), *Sport contemporary society: An anthology* (pp. 285–291). New York: Worth.

Eitzen, D.S. (1999). *Fair and foul: Beyond the myths and paradoxes of sport.* Lanham, MD: Rowman & Littlefield.

Ericksen, E.P., Bartelt, D., Feeney, P., Foeman, G., Grasmuck, S., Martella, M., et al. (1985). The state of Puerto Rican Philadelphia. Philadelphia: Institute for Public Policy, Temple University.

Gatz, M., Messner, M.A., & Ball-Rokeach, S.J. (Eds.). (2002). *Paradoxes of youth and sport.* Albany: State University of New York Press.

Goodman, C. (1979). *Choosing sides: Playground and street life on the Lower East Side,* New York: Schocken Books.

Grasmuck, S. (2005). *Protecting Home: Class, Race, and Masculinity in Boy's Baseball.* Piscataway, N.J.: Rutgers University Press.

Hoch, P. (1972). *Rip off the big game: The exploitation of sports by the power elite.* Garden City, NY: Anchor Books.

Kuklick, B. (1991). *To every thing a season: Shibe Park and urban Philadelphia, 1909–1976.* Princeton, NJ: Princeton University Press,

Lapchick, R. & Benedict, J. (1993). Racial report card: improvement badly. *Crisis,* 100, 38–40.

Ley, D. (1994). Gentrification and the politics of the new middle class. *Environment and Planning D: Society and Space.* 12, 53–74.

Ley, D., & Cybriwsky, R. (1974). Urban graffiti as territorial markers. *Annals of the Association of American Geographers,* 64, 491–505.

Lidz, V. (1991). The sense of identity in Jewish-Christian families. *Qualitative Sociology,* 14, 77–102.

MacNeil/Lehrer Productions. (1997). *Memories of summer: The golden days of baseball.* Transcript of interview between Roger Kahn and David Gergen, Online News Hour: www.pbs.org/newshour/gergen/april97/kahn.

Molotch, H., Freudenburg, W., & Paulsen, K. (2000). History repeats itself, but how? City character, urban tradition, and the accomplishment of place. *American Sociological Review,* 65, 791–823.

Putnam, R. D. (2000). *Bowling alone: The collapse and revival of American community.* New York: Simon and Schuster.

Sage, G. (2001). Racial inequality and sport. In D.S. Eitzen (Ed.), *Sport in contemporary society: An anthology* (pp. 275–284). New York: Worth.

Sparkes, A.C. (2002). Fictional representations: On difference, choice and risk. *Sociology of Sport Journal,* 19, 1–24.

Taylor, R. (1988). *Human territorial functioning: An empirical, evolutionary perspective on individual and small group territorial cognitions, behaviors, and consequences.* Cambridge: Cambridge University Press.

Whalen, C.T. (2001). *From Puerto Rico to Philadelphia: Puerto Rican workers and postwar economics.* Philadelphia: Temple University Press.

CHAPTER 14

Rooting the Home Team: Why the Packers Won't Leave—and Why the Browns Did

David Morris and Daniel Kraker

On the last Sunday in January, an elated John Elway stood on the gridiron where his Denver Broncos had just beaten the Green Bay Packers 31–24, and announced to millions of worldwide television viewers that the best part about finally winning the Super Bowl was how much it meant to his longtime fans, the people of Denver. Mere months later, the owners of the newly crowned Super Bowl champions announced they might move the team to another city if Denver fails to come up with $250 million for a new stadium—even though the team itself is valued at only $182 million.

Denver's predicament is not uncommon. More than 50 million Americans in almost 30 urban areas stand to lose a professional sports team in the near future unless their local governments agree to subsidize new, amenity-laden stadiums. But why should a community pay millions more than a team is worth simply to keep it local for another 10 or 20 years—especially since tax revenue generated by a stadium is usually less than the cost of the subsidy? How can a city keep its home team without emptying the municipal coffers into the hands of a private owner?

The best answer to this last question may be provided by 1998's Super Bowl losers, the Green Bay Packers, the only community-owned team in America. Rather than paying a continuous stream of subsidies to fickle owners, communities ought to be able to emulate Green Bay and buy their teams outright. Community ownership, combined with effective revenue sharing within professional sports leagues, would prevent teams from leaving home and would save taxpayers huge amounts of money by protecting fans and taxpayers from owners who bid their team out to the city offering the best stadium and the biggest subsidy.

FAITHFUL FANS

Professional sports is modernity's mass religion. The sight of Green Bay Packers fans baring their chests and wearing foam-rubber cheese on their heads leaves little doubt as to just how fanatic these modern zealots can be.

Yet support for a local professional team is more than frenzied enthusiasm. Stadiums bring together Americans from all walks of life—black and white, old and young, assembly-line worker and CEO—to share civic pride as they root for the home team. Detroit's population doesn't congregate in bars to watch Ford or Chrysler workers build cars; Seattle residents don't cluster around their televisions to watch Microsoft programmers design software. But the cities do root communally for the Tigers and the

Seahawks. This intimate connection between fan and team is what makes it so unbearable for some people to see their favorite team shipped around the country like a packaged good.

But civic pride is not equivalent to job creation or tax revenue. The same year that Cleveland unsuccessfully offered $175 million to refurbish Memorial Stadium to prevent the Browns from leaving for Baltimore, the city closed 11 schools for lack of funding. Although team owners claim that the economic benefits created by building new stadiums justify sweetheart deals, new stadiums have little impact on residents. Andrew Zimbalist, a professor of economics at Smith College who has written extensively about sports, argues that professional sports teams are actually a "slight net drag on the local economy."

In the past six years, eight teams have changed addresses, uprooting themselves from Minneapolis, Quebec, Cleveland, Los Angeles (the Rams and the Raiders), Winnipeg, Houston, and Hartford. They moved either because their host cities wouldn't build them a new stadium or because competing cities made a relocation offer that owners couldn't resist. During the same period an additional 20 cities paid the extortion that team owners demanded, building a new facility or remodeling an existing one. And yet another 44 teams are planning a new stadium, or have expressed dissatisfaction with their current one, and are demanding new subsidies from their city governments. All told, $7 billion is expected to be spent on new sporting facilities by 2006, most of which will come from taxpayer pockets.

FAILED STRATEGIES

Communities have tried to use the law to stop wayward teams from leaving town. Oakland in 1982 and Baltimore in 1984 tried to invoke their legal authority to seize privately owned property to prevent their National Football League teams from moving, but the courts denied them that power. In the wake of the Cleveland Browns' move, Ohio Representative Louis Stokes and Senator John Glenn introduced the Fans Rights Act of 1995, which would have provided for a narrow antitrust exemption, shielding a league from a lawsuit if it blocks a relocation.

Most of the efforts at the national level have been focused on increasing the cost to cities that subsidize teams. New York Senator Daniel Patrick Moynihan introduced legislation two years ago to prohibit tax-exempt bonds from being used to build professional sports stadiums.

Yet no bill to curb the right of teams to move has ever made it out of a congressional committee, much less come up for a vote in either chamber. Cities are reluctant to support a limitation on tax-exempt borrowing for sports teams for fear that Congress would eventually limit their borrowing authority for other purposes. Also, for every two senators trying to keep a team in their home state, there are two more wrangling for a team for their state; for every city struggling to fund a stadium, there are two more cities claiming a willingness to pay whatever it takes.

When Baltimore built Camden Yards in 1992 and Cleveland opened Jacobs Field two years later, local residents were enthusiastic. Located downtown, these new baseball stadiums are smaller and more intimate than their predecessors and have great sight lines, modern amenities, and a traditional feel. Both were financed almost entirely by public money, and city leaders and urban experts alike touted them as sparks that would revive languishing city centers.

But the fiscal bottom line has been disappointing. Despite the Orioles' success on the field and at the ticket office, taxpayers haven't seen a return on their investment. Bruce Hamilton and Peter Kahn, economists at Johns Hopkins University, estimate that Camden Yards generates about $3 million annually in economic benefits but costs Maryland taxpayers $14 million a year. The new stadium for the Baltimore Ravens, built adjacent to Camden Yards, was much more difficult for politicians to approve, partly because its projected fiscal deficit is even higher than that of Camden Yards.

With the cost of sports arenas soaring, other cities are looking more closely at the promised economic benefits, and public opinion has taken a decidedly negative turn. Voters, when asked directly whether they would fund a sports facility, are increasingly refusing—as residents of Minneapolis, Pittsburgh, Columbus, and San Francisco have done. Last November the citizens of Minneapolis voted to amend the city charter to require any city contribution in excess of $10 million for a sports facility to be approved by voters in a special referendum. San Francisco Bay-area voters struck down six public financing initiatives for a new Giants ballpark in the last decade before the team owners finally agreed to finance a stadium themselves—the first 100 percent privately financed stadium in this country in 30 years.

In some cities, residents voted down proposals to finance a stadium with public funds only to watch helplessly as their legislators bypassed their votes with financing plans of their own. In 1995, by a margin of 64 percent to 36 percent, Milwaukee voters defeated a proposal to pay for a stadium with a sports lottery. A few months later, by a single vote, the state legislature passed a plan for $160 million in direct public funds, when Senator George Petak "changed his mind" at the eleventh hour. While the stadium circumvented the public will, Petak could not; he was immediately recalled by angry citizens and lost re-election, causing Republicans to lose their majority in the state senate.

Even the referenda that have succeeded have been extraordinarily close, and all were tainted by gross spending disparities. In Seattle in 1996, Paul Allen, cofounder of Microsoft and the third wealthiest human being on earth (with a fortune of some $17 billion), agreed to buy the NFL's Seahawks (who were close to moving to Los Angeles) on the condition that the state put up 75 percent of the $425 million cost of a new stadium. In an unprecedented step, Allen personally paid the $11 million for a referendum, then saturated the media with a $5 million pro-stadium advertising blitz and spent $1.7 million lobbying the Washington legislature. Stadium foes spent about $100,000 total. The result was a 51 to 49 percent victory for Allen.

Just a year earlier King County taxpayers had narrowly defeated a financing initiative for a Seattle Mariners ballpark despite facing the same spending disparities (the *Seattle Times* even donated free ad space to the pro-subsidy campaign). The next month, apparently stirred by the Mariners' playoff victory over the Yankees, Washington legislators appropriated $270 million in public funds for a new stadium. The stadium, still under construction, is way over budget, putting taxpayers on the hook for yet greater subsidies.

San Francisco voters passed a referendum on June 4, 1997, calling for $100 million in public funds to help finance a new stadium complex for the NFL's 49ers. It passed by the squeakiest of margins—1,500 votes out of more than 173,000 cast—and only after closing a 20 percent gap in the polls in the final two weeks. Stadium proponents outspent their foes by $2.5 million to $100,000 and enlisted the aid and rhetorical agility of Mayor Willie Brown, whose office allegedly went so far as to set up special polling places at selective public housing projects where support for the stadium referendum was especially high but voter turnout was historically low.

COMMUNITY OWNERSHIP

For some years now, most communities with pro sports teams have been paying large subsidies to keep the teams around. But it is only recently that team owners have been demanding more public money than their teams are worth. Minnesota Twins owner Carl Pohlad tried to extract $250 million from the Minnesota state legislature for a state-of-the-art retractable roof stadium, but the team is only worth around $100 million (see "Team Values vs. Stadium Subsidies," below).

The best way to reverse this trend and keep teams at home is to allow communities to own their teams. The Green Bay Packer organization is the poster child for community ownership of professional sports teams. Pre-NFL football champions in 1929, 1930, and 1931, and winners of Super Bowls I, II, and XXX, the Packers were incorporated in 1923 as a private, nonprofit, tax-exempt organization. Their bylaws state that the Packers are "a community project, intended to promote community welfare." The team can move only through dissolution, in which case the shareholders receive only the original value of their shares. A board of directors, elected by the stockholders, manages the team.

This nonprofit status has been threatened only once, in 1949. The Packers needed to raise more than $100,000 to avoid insolvency, but instead of becoming a profit-making venture the board chose to authorize 10,000 shares of common stock at $25 a piece—4,628 of which were issued—and dissolve the stock that had been sold in 1923. To ensure that no one individual or company had too much control, each shareholder was limited to a maximum of 200 shares.

Green Bay's model works. While its surrounding metropolitan area is home to fewer than 200,000 people, the Packers rank in the top 20 percent of all professional teams in terms of franchise value. Extravagant player salaries have driven many cost-conscious franchises into competitive irrelevancy as they fail to bid for the best free agent players. Observing this trend, Packer team shareholders decided in late 1997 that more revenue needed to be raised for the

Table 14.1 Team Values vs. Stadium Subsidies

Team	*Year Funding Was Approved*	*Amount of Public Subsidy (in millions)*	*Franchise Value (in millions in Year Subsidy Was Approved*
Baltimore Orioles	1992	$210	team sold for $70 in 1989
Cleveland Indians, Cleveland Cavaliers	1991	$295	(two stadiums) $162 combined value
Cincinnati Bengals, Cincinnati Reds	1996	$540 (projected cost)	(two stadiums) $270 combined value
Milwaukee Brewers	1995	$160–310 (projected)	$96
St. Louis Rams	1993	$260	$148 (as L.A. Rams)
Seattle Mariners	1995	$340 (projected)	$80
Seattle Seahawks	1997	$300 (projected)	$171
Florida Panthers	1996	$171	$45
Tennessee Oilers	1996	$220–292 (projected)	$159 (as Houston Oilers)

team to remain competitive. The 10,000 shares issued in 1950 were split into 10 million shares—400,000 of which were made available to the public at $200 a piece. A disclaimer on the opening page of the stock offering reads: "It is virtually impossible for anyone to realize a profit on a purchase of common stock or even to recoup the amount initially paid to acquire such common stock." Even so, by March the team had raised $24 million dollars, far short of its $80 million goal but enough to double its available cash, and ample capital to invest for the future construction of a new stadium 20 or 30 years from now.

Wisconsin residents support the team even through dismal seasons. Games at Lambeau Field have been sold out for more than 30 consecutive seasons, even through years of mediocrity in the 1970s and 1980s. Streets are deserted for three hours on autumn Sunday afternoons. The waiting list for season tickets is 36,000 names long for seats in a stadium that holds 60,000. It is common for season tickets to be willed from one generation to the next and to be hotly contested in divorce proceedings. For better or for worse, the Packers are like a community religion (even for the truly religious: nuns in northern Wisconsin proudly sport Packer T-shirts when doing social work in the community). Literal and figurative community investment in the team fuels such loyalty.

LEAGUE RULES

If community ownership can make sports teams less transient, then why isn't it more widespread (though it should be noted that the Canadian Football League, the NFL's struggling junior sibling to the north, boasts four successful community-owned teams)? One simple reason, mainly: professional sports leagues have prohibited community ownership.

The NFL formally banned community ownership in 1961 at the same time that it adopted a radical revenue-sharing plan that distributes all revenue from merchandise, television, and gate receipts equally among all teams. It took NFL Commissioner Pete Rozelle two years to convince Congress to enact this essentially socialist redistributive mechanism. Revenue sharing made small-market teams viable. In fact, had the league not chosen to ban community ownership at the same time, we might now be rooting for NFL teams from Akron, Ohio, and Gary, Indiana. Major-league baseball has also managed to prohibit fan ownership, though without enacting a formal policy against it. In the 1980s when Joan Kroc, widow of McDonald's founder Ray Kroc, offered to donate the Padres to San Diego along with $100 million to cover operating expenses, the owners nixed the idea. Bud Selig, baseball's current acting commissioner—who as owner of the Milwaukee Brewers coerced Wisconsinites into building him a new stadium—has vowed to kill any community ownership proposal because it would be an "awkward" arrangement for the league.

Though clearly successful where implemented, community ownership remains illegal in most professional leagues. A bill introduced in the House of Representatives by Earl Blumenauer, a Democratic congressman from Oregon, would change that. The Give Fans a Chance Act of 1997 would override all league rules against public ownership. Under the bill, if a league refused to allow a community to purchase its team, the league would lose its sports broadcast antitrust exemption. The bill also would require leagues to take into account fan loyalty and whether an investor is willing to keep the franchise in its home community when considering whether to allow teams to relocate. If enacted, Blumenauer's bill would give fans the opportunity to give the home team genuine roots.

Community ownership is attracting increasing interest at the grassroots level. In 1995, Kansas City Royals owner Ewing Kauffman donated his team to charity with two conditions: the charitable foundation had to sell it to someone who would commit to keeping the team in Kansas City, and the proceeds from the sale had to go to local charities. The IRS approved the donation. While this arrangement does not call for community ownership, it does tie the team permanently to the city.

In Minnesota, Twins owner Carl Pohlad has offered to donate the club to a local foundation as part of a deal for a new publicly financed ballpark (as long as his accumulated losses of around $85 million are covered). Considering this an invitation to community ownership, several legislators have introduced a bill that would have the state buy the team and then sell a majority share to the fans within a year. If the fans failed to buy the shares, showing themselves unwilling to put their money where their cheers are, the team would go back on the market.

History indicates that fans are willing to pay top dollar for the home team. The Boston Celtics went public in 1986 as a rare "pure play" limited partnership, meaning someone buying shares got part ownership in a company made up entirely of the basketball team and all its parent corporation's holdings. Shares in the Celtics were grossly overvalued at $18.50, did not grant voting rights, and lacked even the endorsement of star player Larry Bird, who deemed them "not a good investment." Still, 2.6 million shares, a 40 percent interest in the team, were sold in one day, raising $48 million dollars—more than triple the $15 million the team's owners had paid only three years earlier. Celtics shares are trading today for only around $20, but have paid out more than $16 per share in dividends since 1988. This comes to a healthy 10 percent annual return on investment.

REVENUE SHARING

Yet community ownership, while necessary, is by itself an insufficient remedy for the disease currently afflicting professional sports. The Green Bay Packers, though the paragon of community ownership, would have died long ago if not for the NFL's revenue-sharing policy—which ensures that, for example, its recent $17.6 billion television contract will be divvied up among all the teams.

Baseball and—increasingly—basketball and hockey, on the other hand, are tied to the fortunes of their owners and the skybox-revenue generating capacity of their stadiums. The four most victorious baseball teams in 1997 also had the largest payrolls; six of the eight top-spending teams have had stadiums built since 1989. As the same well-positioned teams continue to win while the small-market clubs flounder in division cellars, fan enthusiasm will erode, taking with it the leagues' financial vitality. If baseball, basketball, and hockey are going to retain an interesting level of competitiveness, small-market vitality, and national fan support, these leagues must emulate the NFL's revenue-sharing system.

But revenue sharing alone will not make sports franchises less nomadic. In fact, the NFL's revenue-sharing policy has effectively encouraged team migration—the NFL has experienced more relocations than any other league over the last decade—because sharing revenue permits small cities to compete for teams. But since revenue from corporate suites, club seats, and other stadium sources are excluded from the revenue-sharing arrangement, owners feel compelled to demand new stadiums with more and bigger skyboxes. Despite average game attendance of more than 75,000, the highest TV ratings in the NFL, and Cleveland's 72 percent approval of a $175 million tax increase to redo Memorial Stadium, the Browns left for Baltimore in 1995 to enjoy a fancier, heavily subsidized stadium. Cleveland Mayor Michael White and Ohio federal legislators failed to keep the Browns from leaving, but they did reach a compromise that enabled Cleveland to retain the Browns name. The league also promised that Cleveland would receive an expansion team within three years. This kind of compromise should be the third element, with community ownership and revenue sharing, of a comprehensive solution to the professional sports problem.

Under such compromises, teams would remain free to move, but the league would be penalized when they do. If Los Angeles and Cleveland were granted expansion franchises when their teams left, each team's share of the league's total revenue would decrease because of the two additional teams that would join the league. In other words, by moving their teams to increase short-term revenue, the owners of the Rams and Browns would have decreased the average value of NFL teams in the long run. Owners would therefore have to weigh the short-term advantages of relocation against the long-term financial advantages of league stability.

Professional teams have become an integral part of our community fabric and our emotional and civic lives. This may justify stadium subsidies in certain communities, but common sense dictates that when an owner demands a subsidy two to three times the value of the team itself, fans would be much better off purchasing the team themselves.

Professional sports may be in decline. As taxpayers spend more on new stadiums, team values, player salaries, and ticket prices all increase. Many fans can no longer afford to attend games and will grow increasingly uninterested in sports. For fans and communities to reclaim their teams, they need to rewrite the rules of ownership to give priority to the civic value of teams; for leagues, new rules of ownership may be the smartest option even if it's not yet in their playbook.

Excerpted from David Morris and Daniel Kraker, "Rooting the Home Team: Why the Packers Won't Leave—and Why the Browns Did" in *The American Prospect* 9, no 40 (September 1, 1998). Reprinted with the permission of The American Prospect, 1710 Rhode Island Avenue NW, 12th floor. Washington, DC 20036.

CHAPTER 15

Football, Television, and the Supreme Court: How a Decision 20 Years Ago Brought Commercialization to the World of College Sports

WELCH SUGGS

Twenty years ago last week, the U.S. Supreme Court rewrote the rulebook for college sports.

Siding with the boards of regents for the Universities of Georgia and Oklahoma in 1984, the court declared that college football games, particularly ones played on television, were an ordinary business practice —not an idealistic venue for universities to promote amateur sports and academic ideals. Because of that, the court ruled, the National Collegiate Athletic Association had no right to force its members to abide by a central plan to broadcast games.

The decision freed colleges to pursue their own broadcast contracts, enabling them to make millions of dollars. In doing so, it brought economic competition to college sports, making money at least as important as the games on the field.

The "haves" of college sports signed their own television deals, setting one athletic conference against another in the race for network dollars.

The ultimate result was today's athletic landscape, in which a few universities control the most-lucrative bowl games, conferences are raiding each other for members, and the NCAA has little control over any of it.

"When one looks back, the tipping point for the commercialization of collegiate sports began with the victory by Georgia and Oklahoma against the NCAA," says Sheldon E. Steinbach, then and now the general counsel of the American Council on Education.

CHALLENGING THE NCAA

From the earliest days of the medium, the NCAA exercised complete control over which football teams got to play on television. Its purpose, according to the association's officers, was to protect colleges from losing fans who would stay home and watch television instead of paying to see games in person.

The NCAA was more aggressive about television than it ever was about scandals or rules violations. The only college ever to lose its membership in the association was the University of Pennsylvania, which tried to defy the NCAA and schedule its own broadcasts in 1951. (Penn relented quickly and was restored to full membership.)

The NCAA also used the television agreement to structure its membership. In the late 1970s, the association's executive director, Walter F. Byers, tried to persuade lower-tier colleges to move from Division I-A to Division I-AA by promising them television time if they made the move.

By the 1970s, universities like Oklahoma and Georgia with big-time football teams had become fed up with the system. Their squads were the ones the networks wanted, but the NCAA insisted on limiting each institution to one or maybe two television appearances per year. In addition, the entire membership voted on the terms of the NCAA's contracts with CBS and ABC, so the powerhouse colleges were effectively outnumbered.

"The NCAA kept watering down the scotch," says Charles M. Neinas, then the Big Eight commissioner. "The NCAA started having more requirements for the networks to carry certain games, and at same time did not increase the number of appearances for those that actually drove the TV engine."

In 1977 the Atlantic Coast, Big Eight, Southeastern, Southwest, and Western Athletic conferences formed the College Football Association, along with major unaffiliated institutions like Pennsylvania State University and the University of Notre Dame, to lobby for their interests within the NCAA. They hired Mr. Neinas as director.

Four years later, the group struck its own television deal with NBC. At the time it was the second-largest sports television contract ever signed, according to the association's lawyer, Philip R. Hochberg. Even though its bylaws said nothing about television rights, the association threatened to ban from championship events every team in every sport, not just football, from any college that participated in the CFA deal.

Oklahoma and Georgia then sued in federal court, arguing that the NCAA was acting as a monopoly in violation of the Sherman Antitrust Act. "It evolved into Oklahoma and Georgia suing to protect their property rights," recalls Mr. Hochberg. "They had not ceded to the NCAA all of their property rights, and that was a fundamental aspect of why the lawsuit was brought."

Despite the NCAA's argument that it was protecting its members' gate receipts and preserving competitive parity among football teams, Judge Juan G. Barciaga ruled that the association was behaving like a "classic cartel," inflating prices and restricting output to make more money.

Moreover, he and a majority of judges on the U.S. Court of Appeals for the 10th Circuit and the Supreme Court said that "live college football television" was a unique product that consumers desired, just like professional football on television or even Coca-Cola. The NCAA could pass and enforce some kinds of rules, like scholarship limits and requirements that athletes were amateurs, but it had no right to restrict its members' opportunities to make money from televising football games.

"The NCAA plays a critical role in the maintenance of a revered tradition of amateurism in college sports," wrote Justice John Paul Stevens in the Supreme Court's majority decision. "The preservation of the student-athlete in higher education adds richness and diversity to intercollegiate athletics and is entirely consistent with the goals of the Sherman Act. But consistent with the Sherman Act, the role of the NCAA must be to preserve a tradition that might otherwise die; rules that restrict output are hardly consistent with this role."

The court's decision could not have come at a better time for the television industry. Cable was just gaining a foothold in American households, and ESPN and other channels desperately needed programming.

"The immediate reaction is that since more games were available, the price of each game went down, and the number of games went up," says James E. Delany, then the commissioner of the Ohio Valley Conference and now of the Big Ten Conference. "As you might expect, those unable to fend for themselves in the marketplace were losers, whether they were in Division I-AA or II or III, and the winners were those schools that were strongest in the marketplace—the CFA, the Big Ten, and the Pac-10."

Athletics departments were hungry for new sources of income, Mr. Neinas says. The passage of Title IX of the Education Amendments of 1972 and the NCAA's 1981 decision to begin holding women's championships had forced colleges to add an assortment of teams for women, and those teams needed money to operate.

The College Football Association took over the NCAA's role in orchestrating television appearances for football teams at most of the country's elite sports conferences. However, even that kind of organization was too restrictive for the most-popular members, leading Notre Dame to defect in 1991 and the Southeastern Conference to do the same in 1994. That put the CFA out of business.

HIGH STAKES

The NCAA, for its part, was essentially shut out of the business side of football. The association received a legal opinion two years after the Supreme Court's decision saying that it could not exercise any control over postseason bowl games either, leaving conferences free to make deals with bowls and television networks for their teams.

The financial stakes quickly became enormous. The Southeastern Conference divided $16-million in revenue among its members in 1990; this year, the league will distribute almost $109-million. Nearly all of Division I-A has been rearranged over the past 14 years as colleges have tried to make the best television deals: The SEC grew from 10 to 12 teams; the Big Eight acquired four members of the Southwest Conference to form the Big 12; and most recently, the ACC reached far beyond its Tobacco Road roots to create a league stretching from Boston to Miami.

Salaries for top football coaches have shot past $1-million, and the best-paid, Nick Saban of Louisiana State University, will make roughly $2.5-million this year, following the Bayou Bengals' national championship in January. And costs for all colleges playing Division I-A football have skyrocketed: The average program budget in 2002–3 was $6.6-million, up 63 percent from a decade earlier.

Along the way, the NCAA's arguments about the need to protect attendance at football games and to preserve amateurism have been disproved. Attendance at college football games has soared, and most Division I-A institutions have expanded their stadiums dramatically to keep up with demand. Ohio State University, Penn State, the University of Michigan, and the University of Tennessee will all draw more than 100,000 fans per game this year, even though almost all of their games will be televised.

College football is as amateur as it ever was. Over the past two years, the NCAA has introduced sweeping reforms to relax standards for incoming players and to increase requirements for athletes already in college. Players get scholarships, but none are paid overtly.

AN IMPORTANT DISSENT

The Supreme Court ruled 7 to 2 in favor of Oklahoma and Georgia in 1984, with Justices William H. Rehnquist and Byron R. White dissenting. Justice White, who had been an All-American football player at the University of Colorado at Boulder, argued that his colleagues had misconstrued college sports.

"The Court errs in treating intercollegiate athletics under the NCAA's control as a purely commercial venture in which colleges and universities participate solely, or even primarily, in the pursuit of profits," he wrote.

Rather, the NCAA's purpose is to regulate amateur sports that enhance higher education, he wrote, and such a system could not exist in a purely commercial marketplace.

The NCAA's limitations on television appearances would not be countenanced as an ordinary business practice, but neither would its rules preventing athletes from being paid, limiting the number of coaches a team could have, or limiting the scholarships teams may award, he wrote.

And permitting a small number of colleges, even popular ones, to have unlimited television appearances "would inevitably give them an insuperable advantage over all others and in the end defeat any efforts to maintain a system of athletic competition among amateurs who measure up to college scholastic requirements," Justice White predicted.

The second part is debatable, but the first part has certainly come true. The colleges in the six current elite conferences—the ACC, Big East, Big Ten, Big 12, SEC, and Pacific-10—have much more money, much better facilities, and for the most part, much better teams than the rest of the NCAA. That worries William C. Friday, president emeritus of the University of North Carolina and chairman of the Knight Foundation Commission on Intercollegiate Athletics.

"I am one who thought Judge White was correct in his dissent," Mr. Friday says. "What he predicted is going on now, and . . . academic institutions are not as free to act as they ought to be."

Colleges must ratchet up spending on sports, especially football, continue paying coaches exorbitant amounts, and take on more and more capital debt to maintain their visibility, Mr. Friday says.

For that reason, the Knight Commission voted 9 to 2 (with Mr. Friday abstaining) in May to call on the NCAA to take control of football's bowl games as an initial step toward controlling the commercialism of college sports. The games are now managed by television networks and conference commissioners. They tend to be more overtly commercialized than the NCAA's own championships. The NCAA does not sell naming rights for its events, for example, and stadiums and arenas are precluded from having most sponsors' signs visible to spectators or cameras, unlike at bowl games.

The court's decision defined the NCAA's right to maintain certain kinds of rules. But if colleges continue to ratchet up their pursuit of money through sports, Mr. Friday warns, the Internal Revenue Service could determine that athletics departments are business entities and not part of the nonprofit mission of a university.

"It's a huge business, and we can't go on giving it a tax exemption when it goes on building what it builds," Mr. Friday says. "No other part of an institution has such a situation."

Mr. Hochberg, the NCAA lawyer, says that's possible, but there are other reasons to control the bowls and other commercial aspects of college sports.

"I'm not sure it would necessarily play out the way President Friday would say, but I see an even more imminent impact," says the lawyer. "With so many bowl games, you're going to have half the schools in Division I-A needed to fill out the bowl schedule, and you're going to start having teams with losing records. I think that weakens the entire bowl structure."

In 1951 Congress voted to give the National Football League an exemption from antitrust laws so it could negotiate collective television deals for its teams. The NCAA, Mr. Hochberg says, passed up the opportunity to apply for an exemption of its own, believing that it didn't need one because of its ties to higher education.

The rising cost of college sports, along with continuing questions about scandals and rules violations, are causing more people to question how strong those ties really are, and the Knight Commission and even Congress have begun talking again about the question of an antitrust exemption and other solutions. Something, Mr. Friday says, has to be done.

"The issue without a doubt is the pursuit of money, and what money does in excessive coaches' salaries and greater bonding debt," he says.

"Intercollegiate sports has got to stop this arms race."

CHAPTER 16

Money, Myth and the Big Match: The Political Economy of the Sports Media

David Rowe

The influence of television is felt in the ever increasing number of on-site advertising banners and logos and sponsorship tie-ins. Some athletes have become walking billboards for their multiple sponsors and equipment suppliers . . . The commercialization of sports, even at amateur level, continues apace, justified by the constant need to bring in more money, and limited only by initial resistance from the public, which inevitably overcomes its outrage and learns to accept yet more blatant salesmanship in sport as a necessary evil which subsidizes the undertaking. If in junk sports, it's tough to separate the junk from the sports, then in all sports it's equally tough to separate the business from the sport.

(Klatell and Marcus 1988: 21)

INTRODUCTION: VALUING SPORT

As Toby Miller (1999: 115) has argued, expenditure on sport has heretofore seemed immune to 'conventional business cycles' and 'has grown through most recessions'. In recent memory, therefore, words like downswing and contraction have found little expression in the lexicon of the media sports cultural complex. It has been difficult, therefore, to question the 'article of faith for broadcasters that sports programming was a river of gold' (Maiden 2002: 33). But nothing undermines business faith more than the arrival of the receivers and the administrators, as has occurred in such high-profile media sport cases.

The fortunes of individual sports and also of media companies can, in the ordinary course of things, shift rapidly in response to the involvement of sponsors, crowd attendance and TV ratings, broadcast rights, and so on. It is useful, then, to appraise the major forces in media sport, the ways in which they cooperate and conflict, and the consequences of this economic activity for sport and the wider society and culture. If no single party can be said to dominate the media sports cultural complex or to control its 'image bank', it can hardly be denied that the presence of major economic entities has resulted in far-reaching changes to the sport we see and read about, and to the culture in which it is located. To illustrate this point, we need only point to the cut-throat competition and multi-million dollar and pound investment involved in acquiring such mega media sports properties as the broadcast rights to the:

- Summer and Winter Olympics
- English Premier League soccer
- US National Football League

(Rowe and McKay 2003)

That media sport involves serious money is obvious, but the cultural and economic consequences for media sports texts are less apparent. For this reason, we need to delve further into the place where economic and sporting muscles are flexed.

SPORT, MEDIA AND CAPITAL ACCUMULATION

In the intersecting development of sport and media, arguing that each institution had something that the other wanted – and with increasing urgency. The initial reluctance which both parties displayed in forming a deep alliance was, in part, due to the unprecedented nature of the economic and cultural relations that developed speedily from the late nineteenth century onwards (that is, consumer capitalism and national state-sanctioned media were 'feeling their way'), and partly because their initial economic base relied on direct exchange. So, when most of the revenue for sports enterprises stemmed from paying customers going through the turnstiles to watch sport in person in highly localized settings, not much in the way of mass marketing and promotion was needed. Word-of-mouth, wall posters and some rather staid newspaper advertisements were the major means of informing the paying public about forthcoming sports events, and the technological means did not exist (and when they did, were not initially welcomed) to record and transmit proceedings for those not present (Stoddart 1986; Whannel 1992; Boyle and Haynes 2000). To understand precisely how the media sports text becomes such a valuable economic and cultural object, it is necessary to view it in terms of large-scale social, economic and cultural transformations (as occurred in Chapter 1), and also to appreciate the specific ways in which that object is desired or can be made to be or seem desirable.

Within the history of capitalist development, the sports media are not essential commodities: they are not vital for the maintenance of life like food, shelter and clothing, or 'consumer durables' that preserve food, wash clothes or transport whole families to work and school. Nobody has ever died as a direct result of media sport starvation, although passionate sports fans can do striking impressions of zombies during TV blackouts. Seen in this way, media sports texts are not very useful goods but they are, paradoxically, highly prized. This is so because they exist in an economic environment where, as many goods have become easier to mass produce and standardize, only a relatively small proportion of their total price is attributable to the cost of raw materials, labour and manufacture.

If cultural factors are emerging as central to economic processes – and most contemporary analyses suggest that they are – then sport and the sports media, as cultural goods *par excellence*, are clearly a central element in a larger process (or set of processes) that is reshaping society and culture (Throsby 2001).

There is a well-known argument (e.g. Novak 1976) that sport is a secular religion, having taken over from the church as the primary place of collective and individual ritual, belief, ecstasy, and so on. When sports fans have their ashes spread on the 'hallowed turf' of their favourite sports stadium, the spiritual qualities of sport are very evident. When on occasion a sports team receives a blessing from a religious leader before a major sports event, it may appear that 'sacred sport' is supporting orthodox religion, rather than the other way round. If sport and religion have certain qualities in common, they also share an involvement with business, especially where the religion is, as Max Weber pointed out, the Calvinist form of Protestantism, which he argues supplied many of the values crucial to the formation of capitalism. Indeed, in one (unconsciously) prescient passage in *The Protestant Ethic and the Spirit of Capitalism*, Weber links all three institutions by stating that:

> In the field of its highest development, in the United States, the pursuit of wealth, stripped of its religious and ethical meaning, tends to become associated with purely mundane passions, which often actually give it the character of sport.
>
> (Weber 1930: 182)

If Weber's lifespan had stretched a few decades beyond the year of his death (1920), he would have seen not only 'the pursuit of wealth' in the USA and other capitalist nations given 'the character of sport', but also leisure pursuits like sport take on the character of the pursuit of wealth. He would also have seen sport appropriate many of the functions of established religion in increasingly secular societies dedicated to the worship of the god of conspicuous commodity consumption.

Irrespective of whether sport and its values are religious in the strict sense, in broad economic terms (concerned more with profits than prophets, to use a rather old pun) it is one of the key contemporary sites where the expression of strong emotions is translated into the generation of substantial capital. Or, more expansively, where (following Lash and Urry) aesthetic and informational signs meet popular emotion (which sometimes looks like mass hysteria) in a manner readily convertible into commodified pleasure. Media sport has, as we have seen, a proven capacity to bring potential consumers to the marketplace in numbers ranging from the respectable to the staggering. It is able at particular moments symbolically to reconstruct disparate human groups, to make them feel at one with each other (and perhaps, in the case of the Olympics and the World Cup of association football, the world). When contemporary advertising relies so heavily on making very similar items (such as sugared drinks, cars with shared components and 're-badged' computers) appear different, sport's capacity to stimulate emotional identification with people and things is priceless. Sport can connect the past, present and future, by turns trading on sepia-tinted nostalgia, the 'nowness' of 'live' action and the anticipation of things to come. Furthermore, even when our human sports 'subject' is being reflexively critical, rather than getting carried away by sporting affect, they can take an ironic, playfully post-modern approach to it, mocking the mangled language of sports commentators.

Media sports texts are perhaps, then, at the leading edge of this culturalization of economics: they cannot be eaten or worn yet billions of people desire them in a bewildering variety of types, and media corporations are willing to expend billions of units of currency to supply them, often 'free of charge', to the user. In return, as we have seen, invaluable access is given to audiences, on a global scale, which can be cashed in for large sums of money exchanged between sporting associations, clubs, officials and players, TV and sports management companies, sponsors, advertisers and governments. Media sports texts are particularly valuable assets because of their flexibility and interconnectedness. A single sports 'live' TV broadcast can be shown in 'real time' and endlessly afterwards, and can be cut up and packaged in myriad ways, with its soundtrack separated from its visual images so that both can be continually manipulated and reproduced. The sports print media, both newspapers and magazines, can help stimulate interest before the event and 'keep it alive' for a lengthy period afterwards, aided and abetted by the celebrity status of elite sportspeople. In multi-media environments like the Internet, virtually any media sports text can be put to use in the virtual world. All manner of goods and services, from sports equipment and 'designer' leisurewear to beer, banking and tobacco, can invoke or be directly associated with media sports events, the associated messages adapted as necessary to the cultural sensitivities of different audience blocs around the globe (Rowe *et al.* 1994). It is for this reason that television broadcast rights to the major sports are often contested more fiercely than the sports events they are seeking to cover – even when those same media companies complain about how much money they lose by winning them. To understand this apparently economically irrational behaviour (which perhaps has turned out to be irrational after all) means delving further into the media sports cultural complex.

HOW TO MAKE MONEY WHILE LOSING IT IN SPORTS TELEVISION

Having set out the broad economic framework within which contemporary media sport operates, more precise explanations of why media corporations are prepared to expend huge sums on securing the rights to television sport are required. The Olympic Games constitutes a useful example of the economic appeal of broadcast sport and of the extent to which the rights pertaining to it are both protected and infringed. Detailing the statistics is not unlike recounting the latest world record time in the 100 metres sprint or the greatest number of points scored in the World Series, except that (at least until the early twenty-first century) more records have been broken more frequently in buying sports rights than in performing in sport. Taking the example of the USA's NBC television network, it transpires that in 1995 NBC won the US TV rights to the Sydney 2000 Olympics for US$715 million, as part of a deal in which it paid escalating fees of US$793 million and US$894 million for the 2004 and 2008 Olympics, respectively, to show the Games to American audiences in (then) unknown locations (which turned out to be, respectively, Athens and Beijing). Despite its capacity to sell subsidiary rights, charge vastly inflated advertising rates during key events, and make some other returns from various 'spin offs' (selling videos of Olympic highlights, for example), the cost of rights and of producing TV coverage ensured that NBC would lose large sums of money on the deal. But this does not mean that the NBC Board has suddenly become philanthropic, and is prepared to carry out a selfless task of public service by subsidizing the delivery of Olympics TV to the people of the United States of America and the rest of the world. It has a broader economic motive: the huge audiences for the Olympics raise the network's overall ratings, meaning that it is in a stronger position to negotiate advertising rights across its year-round, all-genre programming. The network also hopes for an Olympics 'spillover effect' – that viewers will be exposed to and stay with its other programmes or, even better, that it will 'get the habit' of switching on NBC first. Being the Olympics station brings with it a great deal of *kudos*, especially prima facie evidence (which might in practice be repudiated) that the network can handle with distinction one of the world's largest media events. In an image-saturated age where 'branded sign-value' is paramount, being known as the Olympic network – with all the brand recognition and prestige that the label entails – gives an important competitive advantage in the media industry. Securing the US broadcast rights to the Olympics also has a 'spoiler effect' – ambitious commercial rivals, such as Rupert Murdoch's Fox Network, can be thwarted (McKay and Rowe 1997) and induced to expend equally large sums of money on other broadcast rights on pain of being locked out of major TV sport altogether. They might also gain psychological ascendancy over other networks like CBS boasting a strong sporting culture who have lost out in the fight for key TV sport properties. All these justifications for paying out vast sums on broadcast rights for sport hold as long as it can be demonstrated that, by one means or another, over time benefits outweigh costs. As briefly noted above, and discussed in greater detail below, the orthodoxy that TV sport is more golden goose than dead duck has come under sharp challenge.

Historically, there is great symbolic and economic value to be gained from controlling the production and distribution of symbols and, in the case of Olympic sport, global images do not come any more desirable (Schaffer and Smith 2000a). It is for this reason that there is so much antagonism between Olympic rights and non-rights holders, a struggle that also inevitably draws in sports organizations and even athletes. A diverting parallel game is thus played out, with non-rights holders trying to sneak as much sports coverage as possible, and unofficial sponsors seeking to associate their corporate logo as closely as legally permissible with major sports events. Their official counterparts, in true sporting style, do their best to stop them. If the sporting action is a little dull, especially in out-of-stadium events like cycling, the triathlon and marathon running, television viewers can search for 'ambush' corporate brand imagery strategically planted for the cameras.

By negotiating, honouring, helping police and strategically modifying broadcast rights, sports organizations and personnel become economic allies, even colleagues, of the media. Hence they need to be well versed in the arcane rules that govern rights, such as whether non-rights holders should be bound by the 'three by three by three' rule ('three minutes of Olympic footage three times a day in news programmes at least three hours apart'). Such deliberations also involve national broadcast policy priorities and the copyright laws with which any rights agreement must be in accord, and even whether the Olympics come under the rubric of 'news' (and, therefore, should be more fully reported on public interest grounds) or 'sport' (that is, more subject to broadcast restriction as just another form of entertainment). These issues continue to preoccupy the broadcast media and sports professionals because the entire economics of the media sports cultural complex turn on the careful rationing, packaging and sale of media sports texts in different markets. Hence, the idea of the global media sports spectacle is at its heart quite illusory: the images that appear to be so freely released have been subject to extraordinarily stringent pre-selection and control, and the sanctions taken against those who breach such arrangements (by, for example, implying official Olympic endorsement when it has not been negotiated and paid for) powerful indeed. High-end, especially 'live' broadcast sport appears to be in plentiful supply, but it is, in fact, subject to careful rationing and, as is discussed later in the chapter, would be controlled and harboured even more by highly concentrated commercial interests were it not for intervention by the state in the public interest.

The Summer and Winter Olympics, however, occur only over four-year cycles, which leaves large gaps between orgies of Olympic viewing, although after 1992 these were staggered at two-year intervals to ensure that the world did not have to wait so long for its Olympic television 'fix'. Other great media sports events – international tournaments like the soccer, rugby and cricket World Cups, world championships in sports such as athletics and swimming, and major annual competitions with international involvement like Wimbledon in tennis or the US Masters in golf – have important places on the sports calendar, but they are by their nature intermittent and out of the ordinary. Filling television schedules is a constant task that cannot wait for the next global media sports spectacular. The 'bread and butter' of sports television, then, is annual competition within nations.

NBC had become accustomed to its position as the main sports network and, not coincidentally, the top rating network overall, having the rights to such major US sports as American football, basketball and baseball to supplement its Olympic fare. Yet in 1998 it found itself 'frozen out of football for the first time in 33 years' (Attwood 1998: 39). Given that American football is the most important television sport in the USA, with broadcast rights valued in 1998 at US$2.25 billion a season, the scramble for broadcast rights to it is vigorous to say the least. This contest takes place over rights to a game that is barely played, understood or watched in other countries (although not for want of trying; see Maguire 1999), thereby revealing the pre-eminence of the USA as a media sport market in its own right. As noted above, their direct economic value is almost overshadowed by the image of being a 'winner' (analogous to that of breaking a world record while winning an Olympic gold medal). As Attwood states:

> Several morals can be drawn from this US price war. One is that, more than ever, sport is *the* most important commodity for TV. Another is that the desperation of grown men, most of whom have never played top-level sport themselves, to feel as if they are part of the game should never be underestimated.
>
> (Attwood 1998:39)

The struggle for television sport can be seen to be more than a fight for profit: it reveals the cultural power of sport, particularly in the higher ranks of large corporate enterprises, where aggressive, competitive masculinity is as evident in the boardrooms as in the locker rooms (McKay and Rowe 1997). For example, the loss by the CBS network of its rights to Sunday football in 1993 to a Fox network prepared to pay over three times the amount for them (US$1.58 billion as opposed to US$500 million), had a demoralizing impact on the entire network that went beyond the concomitant fall in ratings. As Attwood (1998: 39) goes on to say, the four networks which paid unprecedented sums for the right to televise American football into the early part of the twenty-first century 'regard football as so crucial to their credibility and programming that they are prepared to pay almost any price', and that this phenomenon is not confined to the boundaries of the United States, but 'demonstrates how crucial major sporting events are to networks, worldwide, in an increasingly competitive TV market'. Thus, as Singer (1998: 36) notes, 'today's rule of thumb mandates that any viable network must have sports to help raise the profile of its other properties'; here he means literally to 'have sports', listing the direct ownership of sports teams in the late 1990s by US media conglomerates, including Cablevision (the Knicks basketball and Rangers ice hockey franchises), Disney (the Angels in baseball and Mighty Ducks in hockey) and (the now AOL-merged) Time Warner (the Braves in baseball and Hawks in basketball). As Law *et al.* (2002) have demonstrated, media sport involves intricate 'supply chains' that go well beyond the 'usual suspects' (Disney, News Corp and AOL Time Warner) and the more obvious 'circuits of promotion' (Whitson 1998). While the cross-promotional possibilities of jointly owned media and sports enterprises are attractive, it is the cultural appeal of sport that ensures that old fears of club owners of 'oversaturation' and that '"giving away" the product on TV would kill the gate' are as 'misguided as Hollywood's fear of the VCR [video cassette recorder]' (Singer 1998: 36). Such popularity also allays the concerns of media proprietors in countries like the USA that sport is not worth the asking price:

> There's good reason why sports is a TV staple: It's human drama at a base level, it's cheap to produce and it's live. One can't minimize the power of immediacy in this time-shifting era when sports are the last remaining live coast-to-coast events – the Oscars, the Emmys, even 'Saturday Night Live' are tape delayed to the West Coast. Only sports has the nation, and sometimes the world, watching the same thing at the same time, and if you have a message, that's a potent messenger.
>
> (Singer 1998: 36)

Once again, the power of sports television to create and connect nations fragmented by space, time and social difference is shown to be its crowning economic advantage. With this power, though, comes contest and even chaos.

THE 'STRATEGIC CHAOS' OF MEDIA SPORT

Network free-to-air television is, it should be noted, not the only player in the sports market. The fierce 'internal' competition between networks is replicated in the struggle between the network and pay television sectors. In some cases, as with Rupert Murdoch's News Corporation (which owns the Fox network and various pay satellite services like British-based BSkyB and the Hong Kong-based Star) or the Walt Disney Company (which owns both the ABC network and the leading sports cable channel ESPN), the enterprise is 'horizontally integrated' (that is, spread across different media and modes of delivery) and so is involved in both free-to-air and pay sports television. The continuing and accelerating realignment of organizations and convergence of technologies (as discussed in the Afterword) ensures that sports television will continue to be in a dynamic (which is often a euphemism for unstable) condition.

While it is premature to conclude that there is a single, integrated global sport or sports media market – for such a thing to exist much greater cultural homogeneity and economic rationalization would be necessary – there is a marked globalizing trend in media sport that makes it increasingly hard to insulate any aspect of sport and media in any particular country from external, disruptive forces (Maguire 1999; Roche 2000). Just how much power the media wield over sport can be seen through some brief case studies. In Australia, for example, a large country with a medium-sized population (now 19 million – as Turner [1990] has noted, a country with a land mass comparable to that of the USA and a population similar to that of Holland) some distance from the centres of power in media sport, there has been turmoil in sports television as the belated introduction of pay TV (in January 1995) precipitated a convulsion in the industry that is far from approaching a settled state. The intimidating presence in the free-to-air and pay TV market of Rupert Murdoch (who was born in Australia but gave up his citizenship to purchase key media assets in the USA) and his great commercial rival (and sometime strategic ally) Kerry Packer, owner of the top-rating Network Nine and (in)famous TV pioneer of one-day cricket, alongside a host of other 'players' like Telstra (the partially privatized national telecommunications company). Its two most powerful media barons retained and extended their influence. Sheehan's assessment of Murdoch's inevitable triumph in TV sport is not, however, universally shared – the *Los Angeles Times* in 1997, for example, described Murdoch's expensive attempt to control the sport of rugby league in Australia, Britain, France, New Zealand and the small number of other countries in which it is played as 'one of News Corp.'s bigger blunders' (quoted in Miller 1998b: 5). Expensive acquisition has, however, been a major part of News Corporation's global strategy (Andrews 2004). When a big financial player like Murdoch is sufficiently determined to make a major impact on a sport, the outcome is inevitably far-reaching, and the means by which that influence is exerted always involves media, especially television coverage. Thus, while Murdoch's strategy includes taking a stake not just in the sports media but in sport itself (hence his purchase of major stakes in rugby union and rugby league, and the ownership of individual sports outfits like the Los Angeles Dodgers baseball team), it is always the promise of wider TV coverage and cross-media exposure through his newspaper and magazine interests that forms part of the 'pitch'. Furthermore, when new forms of delivery involving subscription are involved, no media identity understands the importance of sport more than Rupert Murdoch. Not only have these contracts, with their strong elements of exclusive 'live' rights, had the effect of raising subscription levels, but also they have in some cases (including boxing and soccer) included a pay-per-view element, with its opportunities for the kind of direct economic exchange between sports provider (now via an intermediary) and sports spectator that once existed only at the turnstiles of sports stadia.

By turning the television set-top decoding box into an electronic turnstile, pay-per-view and subscription sport are, paradoxically, via new media delivery technology, recreating an older cash nexus. But now sports themselves are ceding to the media, for a handsome price, responsibility for the presentation of great sporting occasions to the largest component of the audience. The political implications of this shift are serious (as is argued more fully later), in that the new services – and many of the old ones – are now available only to those citizens with the capacity to pay.

Murdoch's £623 million bid in 1998 for Manchester United, the world's best known and richest football club, highlighted the economic desirability of simultaneously owning both broadcast rights to sport and the sports teams that are being broadcast (Brown and Walsh 1999). Despite enthusiastic support by Murdoch newspapers like *The Times* and *The Sun,* the bid was opposed by the Blair Labour Government (despite its warm relationship with Murdoch) and blocked 'in the public interest' by the (then) UK Monopolies and Mergers Commission. The grounds were that it would reduce competition in the broadcasting industry (Murdoch would be on both sides of the negotiating table in buying and selling TV rights) and that it would damage the already weakened fabric of English football by exacerbating the inequalities between the clubs in the Premier League and the rest.

The changing economics of broadcasting popular sports events – sometimes held in check as we have seen by public political values or by the desire of major sports organizations like the IOC to ensure maximum television exposure – nonetheless continually modify the conditions under which media sports texts are made. For example, the timing of 'live' sports broadcasts is now dictated by the need to stagger them over several days and nights, and/or to give a number of parties the opportunity to show whatever material to which they have gained access. Thus, while as recently as the 1970s most professional British soccer matches or Australian rugby league games started and ended on the same weekend day within 15 minutes of each other, the 'festival' of football now stretches over much of the week in the sports media equivalent of continuous process production. As seasons have extended and competitions proliferated in deference to the media hunger for sport –

and to sport's appetite for media money – the prospect of creating a media sports cultural complex that defies the constraints of time and space – just as the first factory owners began to do in the eighteenth century – approaches closer. The difference, however, is that much of the population is now viewing the production process from the domestic sphere rather than participating within the factory walls. Watching, in this sense, is essential to complete the production cycle of relayed movement, meaning and imagery.

The constant availability of sport on television, though, is not necessarily coterminous with its popularity, even for some major sports events. This is because, despite occasional appearances to the contrary, even sports fans have to work, sleep, go to the supermarket, clean the toilet and offer emotional support to their families and friends. In other words, they have to make choices about when and what to view, in real time ('live') or otherwise. For this reason, the concept of prime time may have been stretched, but it has not been rendered meaningless. Grant Farred (2001: 3) makes this point about the Sydney 2000 Olympics, which he judges 'will be remembered as the Olympics that weren't' by East Coast American viewers at least. Despite then IOC President Juan Antonio Samaranch declaring these to be 'the best Games ever' at its Closing Ceremony, various factors made it for Farred and others 'turn-off television'. These included: 'the fact that 15-hour tape delay (if you're on the East Coast) produces bad Nielsen ratings tells us not only that time-zone is everything, but that the old North-South economic paradigm is pivotal to culture' (Farred 2001: 3). It is suggested here that US TV sport viewers are accustomed to watching at convenient times and discomfited by too much distance from a land that, it should be recalled, describes its national domestic baseball competition as the World Series. Significantly, Farred argues that many viewers preferred the Internet's instantaneous provision of the 'pleasure of information' to the delayed 'pleasure of spectacle' (p. 4) offered by television. In such circumstances, television may attempt to be 'plausibly live', simulating events as if they are happening and shaping them into smoothly assimilated live narratives that are, in fact, recordings (Rivenburgh 2003). The Internet's developing capacity to marry informational and spectacular forms of pleasure threatens to reconfigure the economic structure of media sport, and is a strong motivation for the merging of media and Internet service providers, most spectacularly the (so far disastrous) 2000 merger of Time Warner and AOL (Hesmondhalgh 2002). The exciting prospect of radical vertical and horizontal integration of the Internet, media, sport and entertainment has faded somewhat, with AOL Time Warner reporting a US$98.7 billion loss for 2002, having a group debt in 2003 of US$26 billion (*Sydney Morning Herald* 2003: 33) and attempting to sell off various assets including its sports teams and events, which include:

> The Atlanta Thrashers, the NHL's most recent expansion team . . . NBA [National Basketball Association] and MLB [Major League Baseball] teams in Atlanta, TNT Sports, the Goodwill Games, World Championship Wrestling, the CNN/SI sports network, *Time*, and *Sports Illustrated*, and is the NBA's cable partner.
>
> (Miller *et al.* 2003: 66)

Television sport can, in strictly economic terms, be seen as a battlefield between media corporations seeking to generate revenue from all manner of sources – advertisers, sponsors, subscribing viewers and even from sports themselves (the more unfortunate ones who need TV exposure so much that they are prepared to pay for it).

This state of affairs means that media mogul Rupert Murdoch frequently tops the *Sporting News*'s annual list of the most powerful people in sport rather than global sports celebrities like Michael Jordan, Tiger Woods, Serena Williams and David Beckham; powerful sports administrators like current IOC President Jacques Rogge or FIFA President Sepp Blatter (Rowe and McKay 2003); or sport and leisurewear entrepreneurs like Nike founder Phil Knight. Why such a person is at the centre of power in sport can be explained succinctly by the following opening paragraphs from a newspaper feature article on Rupert Murdoch as the 'champion of world sports':

> Last month [January], American television networks spent [AUS]$26 billion on the broadcast rights for American football games for the next eight years. That is not a misprint. That's $26 *billion*. It works out to almost $1 billion for each of the 30 teams in the National Football League (NFL).
>
> This stratospheric number is a foretaste of the revolution that is about to engulf television, and Rupert Murdoch's global sporting empire is playing a central role in that revolution. The revolution will occur on several fronts, all at the same time.
>
> (Sheehan 1998: 4)

Given that, in 1980, NBC paid only US$72 million for the broadcast for the Summer Olympics, the coming revolution in television has clearly already arrived. Perhaps, in Trotsky's (1969) famous formulation, it is in a state of 'permanent revolution'.

It can be seen that the global sports television market is, despite attempts to portray it as a single entity following predictable trends, a series of smaller national, regional and local markets occasionally linked by spectacular mega media events or by the more routine circulation of content from core markets to secondary ones. In fact, as O'Regan (1992: 76) points out, there is a tendency to exaggerate the extent to which television programmes, especially from the United States, flow freely around the world. Culture has continued to be a major sticking point in attempts to create an open global market for good services with, as Ann Capling (2001: 165) has pointed out, the 'the audiovisual sector, especially films, videos and television programs' being an 'extremely contentious' area in multilateral trade negotiations. There are few more highly charged areas of audiovisual culture than sport, with many nations intervening in the TV marketplace to protect the broadcast of listed events of national significance – almost all of them sporting (Rowe 2002). Cunningham and Jacka (1996: 40), furthermore, observe that most sports programming does not travel well in the global mediascape, so that 'Of the various genres of television . . . most are locally specific, and are not heavily traded', and genres like sport 'except for major international events like Grand Slam tennis, the Olympics, World Cup soccer, or Formula One Grand Prix motor racing . . . are usually entirely local in character'. The aforementioned example of American football is just such a game that has had little success in its attempts to 'export itself' as popular sports television (Maguire 1990, 1999; McKay and Miller 1991). However, as Hollywood film and US network television discovered many years ago, a successful if expensive-to-produce item in a domestic market is doubly successful when it can be distributed and promoted 'fully formed' in other markets.

For this reason, there is an unending search for new ways to exploit the same or partially modified economic goods and, as Cunningham and Jacka (1996: 40–1) recognize, 'under the pressure of burgeoning channel capacity and commercialization, new tradeable international formats are emerging', including those 'prompted by new forms of delivery like pay television', leading to the 'growth of specialist sports channels [which] will lead to the televising of sports not previously considered television fare, in order to fill the demand'. Sports like boxing have been quick to appreciate the international economic potential of 'pay-per-view' bouts involving heavyweight (in more than one sense) stars like Mike Tyson and Lennox Lewis, where all the resources of the broadcast and print media can be used, through staged pre-fight confrontations between the combatants and other devices, to stimulate an urge to pay to see the event on screen as it happens. Avid sports fans have been lured over time in respectable numbers to subscribe to pay TV, especially when the siphoning of their favourite live sports from free-to-air television means that they have no other home viewing option (as has occurred with the rugby union in New Zealand).

SPORT AS SCREEN FILLER

Where sports are hoping to cultivate a new audience (and sometimes paying or subsidizing the broadcasters for the privilege), what is being offered for exchange is not TV sport for interested viewers but TV viewers for interested sports. The 'market' is constructed around the need to patch the holes created by technologically induced abundance; the opportunity to offer sports that cannot command huge broadcast rights revenue the chance to do so in the future by contacting some kind of television audience; and accommodation of those sports with more modest ambitions of receiving some valuable media coverage in the knowledge that some committed fans are willing to pay for it (Moore 1996). This form of sports TV delivery, unlike the networked free-to-air television that is heavily reliant on 'blockbuster', ratings-based viewing figures, is in principle amenable to smaller-scale, targeted, niche-marketed, post-Fordist sport (Giulianotti 1999), as is indicated by the development of a cable channel for golf in the United States and a women's sport TV network in Canada.

The 'bonanza' for minority sports promised by multi-channel pay TV has not yet eventuated, with claims of increased broadcast sports diversity more closely resembling political and marketing rhetoric than the actual practice of expanding the range of sports on television. As Crosswhite (1996: 58) has pointed out in the Australian context, for example, women's sports have often been required to pay broadcasters (both free-to-air and subscription) to get on screen, have come under pressure to be more 'watchable', and so have been forced to confront such questions as 'Should athletes go into Lycra outfits, or the sport alter the size of the playing area, or speed up the flow of the game, or change the venue, increase the crowd, etc?' Appleton (1995: 32), however, is less concerned by television changing sport than the need for sports organizations to cater better for television. This means for her mobilizing to secure greater genuine broadcast sports diversity rather than the 'resort to entertainment of the ilk of demolition derbies and mud wrestling rather than "real" sport'.

Free-to-air mega sports events like the Olympics will continue to exist for the foreseeable future because, as the International Olympic Committee has recognized, their greatest economic (and cultural) asset is the massive popularity that can give billions of people the sense of simultaneously having the same sporting experience (Wilson 1998). On the other hand, smaller sports TV audiences can be catered for, targeted or (even if notionally) created through various forms of direct purchase. What Holger Preuss (2000: 122) calls 'match TV: A combination of free TV and pay-per-view' he believes to be 'the most probable variant for future

Olympic coverage' given the globalization of television infrastructure. It should be remembered, of course, that television is not the only means by which sports culture is framed, disseminated, peddled and circulated. Radio and print are also integral components of the media sports cultural complex, their products just as pervasive in the everyday world. Yet, while radio rights are contested for popular international and national sports, newspapers are committing greater resources to the sports pages, expanding print and photographic coverage and headhunting their competitors' 'name' sports writers; and new general and specialist sports magazines are launched (and closed) every year, in sports television lies the most compelling expression of naked economic power in the media sports cultural complex. Accompanying this economic power to make media sports texts for vast audiences comes, as noted earlier, considerable political and cultural power.

MEDIA SPORTS POLICY, POLITICS AND MYTH

It is probable that many times a day, somewhere in the western world, a talkback radio host or caller pronounces that 'sport and politics don't mix' or proclaims that 'politics should be kept out of sport'. Such comments are a little curious, given the many ways in which sport and politics interrelate. These include: deciding public spending priorities, such as allocations by national, state and regional governments to sporting organizations (Cashman and Hughes 1998) and by local governments for civic sports amenities (Mowbray 1993); anti-discrimination policies (such as Title IX section of the US Education Amendments Act of 1972, which denied 'federal financial assistance' to 'any education program or activity' that discriminated against any person 'on the basis of sex', and so had a substantial, positive impact on women's and girls' sport; see Guttmann 1991; Heywood 2000); and government restrictions on the advertising and sponsorship through sports such as Formula One motor racing and cricket of unhealthy products like tobacco and alcohol (Harris 1988). Sport and identity politics would also have to be forever separated (Baker and Boyd 1997; Bloom 2000), and uncomfortable questions about, for example, the relationship between sport and violence against women suppressed (Benedict 1997). To be really vigilant about keeping sport and politics apart, it would be necessary to ban politicians from using sports metaphors like 'going the distance', 'levelling the playing field' and 'moving the goalpost after the game has started' in political speeches and interviews (Rowe 1995). The task of keeping sport and politics forever separate is, then, not only difficult, but inherently futile.

The media, in various ways, are called upon to:

- provide good, wholesome family entertainment through sport;
- offer sensationally dramatic coverage that will attract healthy audiences (but perhaps for 'unhealthy' reasons);
- describe and show what happened to those who were not present or who want to see it again and differently;
- subject sport to intense scrutiny as part of the media's Fourth Estate function;
- support local, regional and national sporting efforts; and
- further the Olympian ideals of sport by transcending petty, partisan politics in the name of international peace and good will.

No single organ of the media can fulfil all of these expectations (some of which are seen as unfortunate obligations), just as different types of media sports text are better suited to the performance of some tasks than others. To develop this logic to its fullest extent absolves the sports media of any general responsibility for their actions beyond the minimal observance ('actionable', in any case) of the laws of defamation, obscenity, and so on. The sports public, it is claimed, is provided with what it wants from the media on orthodox, market principles – if a demand exists for a type of sports coverage, then the market will provide it. To take the sports media simply at their word and to accept this account of their motives, operations and effects would be as unwise as to confine analysis only to the surface properties of media sports texts. By pointing out the latent and sometimes manifest political significance of their practices, it is made more difficult for the sports media to evade the proposition that with cultural power comes political responsibility.

An intellectually respectable political economy of the sports media, therefore, must seek to be aware of the many influences – strong and weak, constant and intermittent, predictable and unpredictable – on the making of media sports texts.

In illustrating this argument, it is useful to examine briefly some instances where the cultural politics of media sport are played out in contrasting ways. For example, in looking at the gender order in media sport above, it was clear that women have been subject to subordination and/or under-representation in two key organizational complexes – in media corporations as owners, senior executives and 'rank-and-file' professional personnel (Creedon 1994a,b) and in sporting organizations on governing bodies and as professional athletes (Jennifer Hargreaves 1994; McKay 1997). The intimate, longstanding linkage between sport and masculinity has helped secure the dominance of male sport in the media and of males employed to cover sport in the media. Yet, pressure to change this pattern of male predominance in media sport is coming from various sources. Sport is, somewhat belatedly, one of the important fronts on which battles for sexual equality are being waged, with both governments and feminist groups demanding an end to male exclusionism in sport (Jennifer Hargreaves 1994; Hall 1997). Women workers in the sports media have mobilized to improve their positions within media organizations (Cramer 1994), while women's sports organizations have demanded more air time and column inches, sponsorship and broadcast rights revenues (Crosswhite 1996). To a lesser extent, sport is also emerging as a site of contestation over gender and sexuality, with, for example, the Gay Games offering a challenge to the longstanding association of sport and 'hegemonic masculinity', Connell's (1987) conception of physically assertive, white male heterosexism that has historically dominated the institution of sport (Krane and Waldron 2000; Symons 2002).

These have not, however, all been external pressures; within the media sports cultural complex itself there has been a gradual realization that it is economically and otherwise senseless to alienate a large proportion of a market, which, if segregated too strictly on gender lines, would in the case of some sports (like the football codes) be close to saturation (Miller 2001). This is even without mentioning the key decision-making position of women in household consumption. Then there is the potential of new media technologies to provide more diverse sports fare, and the requirement for public and commercial broadcasters who have been outbid for sports broadcast rights by their rivals to make a virtue of necessity in 'signing up' some women's sports like basketball and netball. As a result, sports broadcast programmers and print editors have sought (with signal success in sports like soccer and rugby league) to attract substantial female audiences by adopting strategies such as overtly sexualizing sportsmen (see Chapter 5), explaining arcane rules to the uninitiated, giving greater and more sympathetic coverage of sportswomen, employing female sports commentators and writers, and so on (Miller 2001). The issue of sex and gender equality in sport and media sport, and the ways in which it is confronted by governments and business enterprises, raises the wider question of the role of media sport in the whole domain of 'cultural citizenship'.

FIGHTING FOR THE RIGHT TO WATCH

The concept of cultural citizenship is a broadening of the traditional idea of the rights and responsibilities of states and citizens in recognition of the increased 'culturalization' of society. In making informed choices, contemporary citizens need to have ready access to highly detailed information about the values, histories, performances and intentions of the various parties engaged in formal and informal political processes. Therefore, they must possess the means of ready communication in the public sphere.

This model of cultural heritage encompasses quite recent historical developments, like the twentieth-century practice of broadcasting major public events to the entire nation. Because sports events have become the most important, regular manifestations of this national culture (Rowe *et al.* 1998), and despite the move towards their supply to the citizenry by commercial rather than by public broadcasters (Wilson 1998), media sport has become a major aspect of contemporary cultural heritage. Sport and television are, therefore, deeply implicated in debates about cultural citizenship in a way that would horrify cultural elitists (Tomlinson 1999).

Once, then, free-to-air television provided major national and international sports events at nominal direct expense to viewers, and these cultural items had been counted among the major rituals of national significance, they became incorporated into the citizen's cultural 'treasure house'. As a result, there would need to be compelling grounds indeed for the 'free list' of major television sport to be fully commodified, yet this is precisely what is threatened. The political value of (virtual) universal entitlement in the west has been challenged by market-based values, with the idea of abundant choice of television sports texts as the overriding imperative – a choice that involves a 'user pays' principle and one which positions sport as simply another commercialized entertainment option in an unforgiving and, ideally, unfettered cultural marketplace. The only rights that need to be safeguarded from this point of view, then, are those of sports media consumers from fraud, deception and other crimes of commercial practice, rather than in terms of any higher concept of the protection of significant cultural rights. The completed commodification of television sport would be consistent with its current direction, but would ultimately destroy the values associated with serving all citizens in favour of identifying, targeting and privileging affluent viewers. As Stan Correy puts it:

> Sporting tradition dictates that whatever the game, it was originally played for pure and honest motives. Money was the servant of the players not the master.
>
> In the 1990s, it's clear that sports tradition has lost out badly to commerce. The sports field is the battleground on which global TV corporations are fighting to test new television technology. The reward is not a gold-plated trophy but the traditional sports consumer. Profile: Male, 18–35, with enough disposable income to attract the sponsors with the big dollars.
>
> (Correy 1995: 80)

Debates about the rights and responsibilities in sports television are played out differently according to national context. In most European countries and various former British colonies, for example, broadcast sport was first dominated by public broadcasters, their control gradually loosened first by commercial free-to-air broadcasters and then by pay TV companies. In the USA, with its much weaker commitment to non-commercial broadcasting, the sports media marker developed much earlier (Wenner 1989), although this did not destroy network free-to-air sports television, which has survived and prospered through a combination of anti-trust legislation, broadcast synergies and the economic power of the networks deriving from television audiences captured for mass advertising rather than targeted for subscription and pay-per-view. There is, then, a complex intrication (that is, perplexing entanglement) of the economic, the political and the cultural in the determination of how televised sport is to be delivered and to whom.

REFERENCES

Andrews, D.L. (2004) Speaking the "universal language of entertainment": New Corporation, culture and the global sport media economy, in D. Rowe (ed.) *Critical Readings: Sport, Culture and the Media*. Maidenhead: Open University Press.

Appleton, G. (1995) The politics of sport and pay TV, *Australian Quarterly*, 67(1): 31–7.

Attwood, A. (1998) Football crazy, *Sydney Morning Herald*, 17 January.

Baker, A. and Boyd, T. (eds) (1997) *Out of Bounds: Sports, Media, and the Politics of Identity*. Bloomington, IN: Indiana University Press.

Benedict, J. (1997) *Public Heroes, Private Felons: Athletes and Crimes Against Women*. Boston, MA: Northeastern University Press.

Bloom, J. (2000) *To Show What an Indian Can Do: Sports at Native American Boarding Schools*. Minneapolis, MN: University of Minnesota Press.

Boyle, R. and Haynes, R. (2000) *Power Play: Sport, the Media & Popular Culture*. Harlow: Pearson Education.

Brown, A. and Walsh, A. (1999) *Not for Sale: Manchester United, Murdoch and the Defeat of BSKyB*. London: Mainstream.

Capling, A. (2001) *Australia and the Global Trade System*. Melbourne, VIC: Melbourne University Press.

Cashman, R. and Hughes, A. (1998) Sydney 2000: cargo cult of Australian sport?, in D. Rowe and G. Lawrence (eds) *Tourism, Leisure, Sport: Critical Perspectives*. Melbourne, VIC: Cambridge University Press.

Connell, R.W. (1987) *Gender and Power*, Sydney, NSW: Allen & Unwin.

Correy, S. (1995) Who plays on pay?, *Media Information Australia*, 75: 80–2

Cramer, J.A. (1994) Conversations with women sports journalists, in P.J. Creedon (ed.) *Women, Media and Sport: Challenging Gender Values*. Thousand Oaks, CA: Sage.

Creedon, P.J. (1994a) Women in toyland: a look at women in American newspaper sports journalism, in P.J. Creedom (ed.) *Women, Media and Sport: Challenging Gender Values*, Thousand Oaks, CA: Sage.

Creedon, P.J. (1994b) From whalebone to spandex: women and sports journalism in American magazines, photography and broadcasting, in P.J. Creedon (ed.) *Women, Media and Sport: Challenging Gender Values*. Thousand Oaks, CA: Sage.

Crosswhite, J. (1996) Pay TV and its impact on women's sport, in R. Lynch, I. McDonnell, S. Thompson and K. Toohey (eds) *Sport and Pay TV: Strategies for Success*. Sydney, NSW: School of Leisure and Tourism Studies, University of Technology, Sydney.

Cunningham, S. and Jacka, E. (1996) *Australian Television and International Mediascapes*. Cambridge: Cambridge University Press.

Farred, G. (2001) TV's time's up: the forgotten Games, *Journal of Sport & Social Issues*, 25(1): 3–5.

Giulianotti, R. (1999) *Football: A Sociology of the Global Game*. Cambridge: Polity.

Guttmann, A. (1991) *Women's Sport: A History*. New York: Columbia University Press.

Hall, M.A. (1997) Feminist activism in sport: a comparatives study of women's sport advocacy organizations, in A. Tomlinson (ed.) *Gender, Sport and Leisure: Continuities and Challenges.* Aachen: Meyer & Meyer Verlag.

Hargreaves, Jennifer (1994) *Sporting Females: Critical Issues in the History and Sociology of Women's Sports.* London: Routledge.

Harris, K. (1988) What do we see when we watch the cricket?, *Social Alternatives,* 7(3): 65–70.

Heywood, L. (2000) The girls of summer: social contexts for the "Year of the Women" at the '96 Olympics, in K. Schaffer and S. Smith (eds) *The Olympics at the Millennium: Power, Politics, and the Games.* New Brunswick, NJ: Rutgers University Press.

Klatell, D. and Marcus, N. (1988) Sports for Sale: Television, Money and the Fans. New York: Oxford University Press.

Krane, V., & Waldron, J. J. (2000). The Gay Games: Creating our sport culture. In K. Schaffer & S. Smith (Eds.), *The Olympics at the millennium: Power, politics, and the Olympic Games* (pp. 147–164). New Brunswick, NJ: Rutgers University Press.

Law, A., Harvey, J., & Kemp, S. (2002). The global sport mass media oligopoly: The three usual suspects and more. International Review for the Sociology of Sport, 37 (3–4), 279–302.

Maguire, J. (1990) *More than a sporting touchdown: the making of American football in Britain 1982–1989,* Sociology of Sport Journal, 7(3): 213–37.

Maguire, J. (1999) *Global Sport: Identities, Societies, Civilizations.* Cambridge: Polity.

Maiden, M. (2002) Odds blow out on TV sports gamble, *Sydney Morning Herald,* 25 February.

McKay, J. (1997) *Managing Gender: Affirmative Action and Organization Power in Australian, Canadian, and New Zealand Sport.* Albany, NY: State University of New York Press.

McKay, J. and Miller, T. (1991) From old boys to men and women of the corporation: the Americanization and commodification of Australian sport, *Sociology of Sport Journal,* 8(1): 86–94.

McKay, J. and Rowe, D. (1997) Field of soaps: Rupert v. Kerry as masculine melodrama, *Social Text,* 50(1): 69–86.

Miller, T. (1998b) Hopeful signs? Arthur Ashe/working-class spectatorship (editorial), *Journal of Sport & Social* Issues, 22(1): 3–6.

Miller, T. (1999) Competing allegories, in R. Martin and T. Miller (eds) *SportCult.* Minneapolis, MN: University of Minnesota Press.

Miller, T. (2001) *Sportsex.* Philadelphia, PA: Temple University Press.

Miller, T., Lawrence, G. and McKay, J. (2003) Globalization the over-production of US sports, and the new international division of cultural labour, *International Review for the Sociology of Sport,* 38(4): 427–40.

Moore, D. (1996) Pay TV: the Confederation of Australian Sport perspective, in R. Lynch, I. McDonnell, S. Thompson and K. Toohey (eds) *Sport and Pay TV: Strategies for Success.* Sydney, NSW: School of Leisure and Tourism Studies, University of Technology, Sydney.

Mowbray, M. (1993) Sporting opportunity: equity in urban infrastructure and planning, in A.J. Veal and B. Weiler (eds) *First Steps: Leisure and Tourism Research in Australia and New Zealand.* Leisure Research Series No. 1. Sydney, NSW: ANZALS.

Novak, M. (1976) *The Joy of Sport.* New York: Basic Books.

O'Regan, T. (1992) The international, the regional and the local: Hollywood's new and declining audiences, in E. Jacka (ed.) *Continental Shift: Globalisation and Culture,* Sydney, NSW: Local Consumption Publications.

Preuss, H. (2000) *Economics of the Olympic Games: Hosting the Games 1972–2000.* Petersham, NSW: Walla Walla Press/Centre for Olympic Studies, University of New South Wales.

Rivenburgh, N.K. (2003) The Olympic Games: twenty-first century challenges as a global media event, in A. Bernstein and N. Blain (eds) *Sport, Media Culture: Global and Local Dimensions,* London: Frank Cass.

Roche, M. (2000) *Mega-Events and Modernity: Olympics and Expos in the Growth of Global Culture.* London: Routledge.

Rowe, D. (1995) *Popular Cultures: Rock Music, Sport and the Politics of Pleasure.* London: Sage.

Rowe, D. (2002) 'Producing the Crisis: The State of Leisure Studies', *Annals of Leisure Research,* 5(1): 1–13.

Rowe, D., Lawrence, G., Miller, T. and McKay, J. (1994) 'Global Sport? Core Concern and Peripheral Vision', *Media, Culture & Society,* 16(4): 661–75.

Rowe, D., McKay, J. and Miller, T. (1998) 'Come Together: Sport, Nationalism and the Media Image' in L. Wenner (ed) *MediaSport: Cultural Sensibilities and Sport in the Media Age.* New York: Routledge, 119–33.

Rowe, D and McKay, J. (2003) 'A Man's Game: Sport and Masculinities' in S. Tomsen and M. Donaldson (eds) *Male Trouble: Looking at Australian Masculinities.* Melbourne: Pluto, 200–16.

Schaffer, K. and Smith, S. (eds) (2000a) The Olympics at the Millennium: Power, Politics, and the Games. New Brunswick, NJ: Rutgers University Press.

Sheehan, P. (1998) Game, set and match: Murdoch, the champion of word sports, *Sydney Morning Herald – The Guide,* 23 February – 1 March.

Singer, T. (1998) Not so-remote-control, *Sport,* March, p. 36.

Stoddart, B. (1986) *Saturday Afternoon Fever: Sport in the Australian Culture.* North Ryde, NSW: Angus & Robertson.

Sydney Morning Herald (2003) AOL Time ponders radical editing to reduce $44bn debt load, 3 February.

Symons, C. (2002) The Gay Games and community, in D. Hemphill and C. Symons (eds) *Gender, Sexuality and Sport: A Dangerous Mix.* Petersham, NSW: Walla Walla Press.

Throsby, D. (2001) *Economics and Culture.* Cambridge: Cambridge University Press.

Tomlinson, A. (1999) Olympic spectacle: opening ceremonies and some paradoxes of globalization, *Media, Culture & Society,* 18(4): 583–602.

Trotsky, L. (1969) *The Permanent Revolution, and Results and Prospects.* New York: July/August, pp. 34–7.

Turner, B.S. (1990) Australia: the debate about hegemonic culture, in N. Abercrombie, S. Hill and B.S. Turner (eds) *Dominant Ideologies.* London: Unwin Hyman.

Weber, M. (1930 [1904/5]) *The Protestant Ethic and the Spirit of Capitalism.* London: Unwin University Books.

Wenner, L.A. (ed.) (1989) *Media, Sports, and Society.* Newbury Park, CA: Sage.

Whannel, G. (1992) *Fields in Vision: Television Sport and Cultural Transformation.* London: Routledge.

Whitson, D. (1998) Circuits of promotion: media marketing and the globalization of sport, in L.A. Wenner (ed.) *MediaSport.* London: Routledge.

Wilson, D. (1998) Television's *tour de force*: the nation watches the Olympic Games, in D. Rowe and G. Lawrence (eds) *Tourism, Leisure, Sport: Critical Perspectives.* Melbourne, VIC: Cambridge University Press.

CHAPTER 17

Supporters, Followers, Fans, and *Flâneurs*: A Taxonomy of Spectator Identities in Football

Richard Giulianotti

No one would deny that world football (or soccer, as it is sometimes known) has undergone a fundamental structural transformation. At the elite level, football's finances have grown exponentially, while there have been major changes in the cultural organization of the game as experienced by players, spectators, and media commentators. The United Kingdom (particularly England) has perhaps witnessed the most dramatic change in football's social and economic standing, because in the mid-1980s the English game was synonymous in the global public imagination with spectator violence and an entrenched infrastructural decline.

One area of substantial discussion over the past decade has concerned the impact of football's new political economy on its grassroots custodians, the football spectators. In the United Kingdom, there have been persistent criticisms of this boom on the basis that established (but relatively poorer) football spectators are being squeezed out of any stakeholder position within their clubs, most notably the biggest ones, in exchange for wealthier new spectators.[1] The *Guardian* newspaper described these disenfranchised spectators as "football's new refuseniks."[2] Football's burgeoning popularity, its increasingly serpentine ties with corporations and other business institutions, the reduction of stadium capacities to create high-priced seating, and the advent of pay-per-view television are four key ingredients identified in this process of commodification. A government-appointed football task force, with a mandate to identify and recommend on spectator interests, produced two rival, concluding reports and has had a negligible effect beyond promoting antiracist work within the game. Nevertheless, concern with the impact of this commodification remains strong in the public sphere, notably in the United Kingdom and also in Spain, Germany, Italy, and France.

In this article, I seek to examine the impact of football's commodification on spectator identities relative to their association with professional football clubs. I set out a model of four ideal-type spectator identities that may be found in the contemporary football world. In doing so, I seek to redefine more precisely and sociologically four particular spectator identities, and these are supporters, followers, fans, and *flâneurs*.

The analysis mapped out here applies principally to professional football clubs, particularly those whose corporate structures are owned or controlled on market principles by individuals or institutions. These privately owned clubs are most apparent across Western Europe (with the partial but declining exception of some clubs in France, Germany, Scandinavia, Spain, and Portugal) and increasingly in Eastern Europe. Similar processes of commodification look set to affect other football societies and other sporting codes. In Latin America (as in Iberia), clubs have traditionally existed as private associations, under the ownership and political control of their many members (socios). However, there are signs, notably in Brazil, that future legislation will enable single investors or institutions to buy a controlling interest in football clubs. In North America, elite baseball, basketball, American football, and, to a lesser extent, ice hockey have all undergone extensive commodification and remarketing, resulting in different and new kinds of spectator relationships to clubs.[3] In Australia, there have been intensive attempts in recent years to construct national leagues for elite level clubs in Australian Rules Football (AFL), rugby league, and soccer (A-League). The AFL appears to have been most successful in constructing a popular, lucrative national profile for its sport and in the process generating new kinds of spectator identification, which have experienced resistance from more traditional supporters (Hess & Stewart, 1998). This apparent trend toward a homogenization of the corporate structures of professional sports suggests that the arguments presented here do not just pertain to football but, instead, have a cross-code and cross-cultural purchase.

The article develops critical sociological and normative arguments presented elsewhere on the nature of football's commodification (Giulianotti, 1999; Giulianotti & Gerrard, 2001a; Walsh & Giulianotti, 2001). Following earlier work, I take commodification to mean that process by which an object or social practice acquires an exchange value or market-centered meaning. Commodification is not a single process but an ongoing one, often involving the gradual entry of market logic to the various elements that constitute the object or social practice under consideration. As I argue below, the marked intensification of this process in recent years is of a different order to that which was experienced up until the late 1980s, and so might now be described as a period of hypercommodification.

Football's contemporary commodification—its hypercommodification—has been driven by extraordinary and different volumes of capital that have entered the game from entirely new sources: satellite and pay-per-view television networks, Internet and telecommunications corporations, transnational sports equipment manufacturers, public relations companies, and the major stock markets through the sale of club equity.

Concomitantly, a new set of social and cultural relations have arisen since the late 1980s, notably featuring the greater migration of elite labor, a gradual proliferation of continental and global competitions, astronomical rises in elite player salaries, new media outlets for football (for example, satellite television, club television stations, the Internet, and in future, mobile telephones), and new forms of cultural encoding of football through these media.

These transformations have been symptomatic of the contemporary condition of "disorganized capitalism" identified by Lash and Urry (1987, 1994). It is characterized by the genesis of intensified flows between individuals, social groups, objects, and institutions across an increasingly globalized terrain, rather than through a more organized chain of relations within national boundaries (cf. Lash & Urry, 1994, p. 10). Part of this transformation involves the increased social and sociological relevance of communication flows, not merely in the electronic media, but also in terms of the aestheticization of consumer culture and the semiotic expression of social identity within an information age (cf. Castells, 1996).

The old institutions and organizations that had regulated economic and cultural relations throughout the 20th century entered what may be a terminal decline toward the new millennium (Lash, 1994, pp. 213–214). Within football, that transformation may well be illustrated through the rising power and influence of transnational corporations (TNCs) and the political and economic decline of some national or continental associations. Among the rising TNCs, we might certainly list major media corporations and sports merchandise corporations, but increasingly top football clubs such as Manchester United, Real Madrid, and Juventus possess transnational characteristics in consumer profile, flexible labor recruitment practices, and the global diffusion of corporate symbolism. The most powerful of these "superclubs" have formed an organization called (with some statelike irony) the "Gl4." Following warnings of an impending breakaway from established football structures, Union des Associations Européennes de Football (UEFA—European football's governing body) agreed in 1999 to amend Europe's top club tournament (the Champions League) to suit G14 demands for more lucrative fixtures. Reflecting the disorganized political structure within European football, continuing speculation has surrounded the future format of top club tournaments, as a range of institutional actors (old and new) jockey for positions that are most advantageous economically to their respective owners, shareholders, and officials. Finally here, as I have indicated, these transformations are all constituent of the broader, immensely complex process that is the contemporary globalization of football.

In what follows, I concentrate on one critical social relationship that has undergone transformation throughout football's modern and postmodern eras of hyper-commodification. I refer to the identities of spectators and their relationships to football clubs.

CONTEMPORARY SPECTATOR IDENTITIES: THE PRINCIPLES BEHIND THE TAXONOMIES

I argue that there are four ideal-type categories, into which we may classify spectators. The main criterion for classifying spectators relates to the particular kind of identification that spectators have toward specific clubs.

As Figure 17.1 demonstrates, the four spectator categories are underpinned by two basic binary oppositions: hot-cool and traditional-consumer. Thus, there are four quadrants into which spectators may be classified: traditional/hot, traditional/cool, consumer/hot, consumer/cool. The four quadrants represent ideal-type categories, through which we may map the historical changes and cultural differences experienced by specific spectator communities in their relationships with identified clubs. The traditional/consumer horizontal axis measures the basis of the individual's investment in a specific club: Traditional spectators will have a longer, more local and popular cultural identification with the club, whereas consumer fans will have a more market-centered relationship to the club as reflected in the centrality of consuming club products.

The hot-cool vertical axis reflects the different degrees to which the club is central to the individual's project of self-formation. Hot forms of loyalty emphasize intense kinds of identification and solidarity with the club; cool forms denote the reverse. The hot-cool opposition is indebted to at least two sources. First, theorists of the mass media, such as Marshall McLuhan (1964) and Jean Baudrillard (1990), have employed this opposition to explain the cool social relations that structure the communicative processes involving the electronic media. Second, the hot-cool distinction is also derived from an essay by Bryan Turner (1999) on the changing historical and cultural meanings of body marks.

Turner argued that in more traditional societies, body marks were relatively obligatory and employed to designate hot forms of loyalty to the collective. Conversely, in postmodern societies, identification with the collective is voluntary and transient, reflecting cooler, postemotional forms of personal identity. Thus, tattoos in Western societies have traditionally demarcated the individual's hot and permanent masculine loyalty toward a specific social entity (such as the nation, family, female partner, military unit, football club, etc.). Latterly, postmodern tattoos have emerged that are impermanent, are unisex in bearer, are heavily aesthetic (often borrowed from Eastern cultures in design), and reflect a cool or nonexistent association with a specific social group. Turner also employed the binary distinction between thick and thin forms of solidarity. These latter categories tend to be congruent with his earlier binary, so that hot loyalties reflect "thick" forms of social solidarity, whereas cool identification produces "thin" forms of social solidarity.

By way of redeveloping Turner's model, it is important to return to the cultural form and to the social relations surrounding the game itself to map out the spectator identities. Each of the four spectator categories shows a distinctive synthesis of hot, cool, traditional, and consumer qualities. Each category displays distinctive kinds of identification with a specific club and a particular motivation for such a personal association. Each category evidences a particular form of spatial relationship to the club. As ideal types, these categories do allow for degrees of empirical variation and difference among their constituents, for example in their relative manifestations of thick or thin solidarity.

TRADITIONAL/HOT SPECTATORS: SUPPORTERS

The traditional/hot spectator is defined here as a supporter of the football club. The classic supporter has a long-term personal and emotional investment in the club. This may

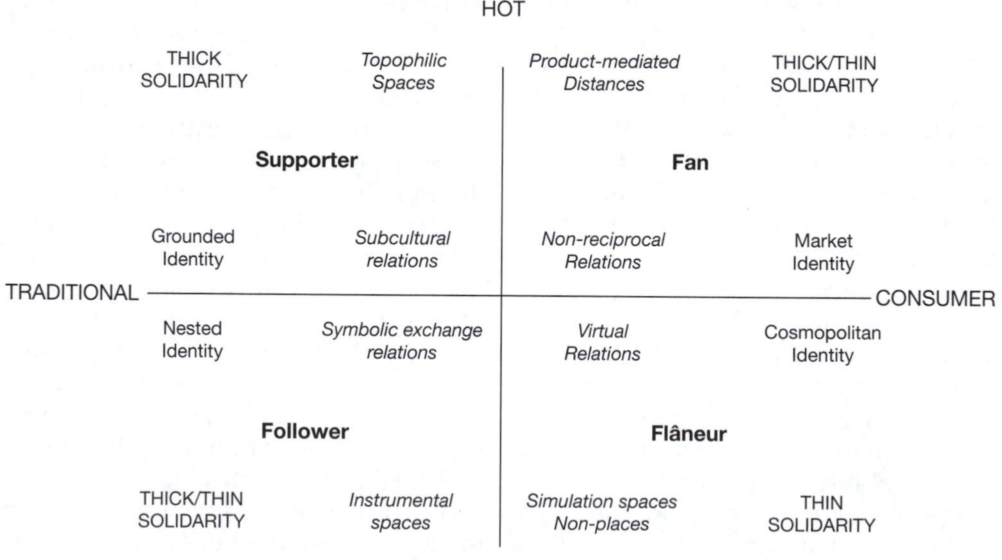

Figure 17.1 Taxonomy of spectator identities

be supplemented (but never supplanted) by a market-centered investment, such as buying shares in the club or expensive club merchandise, but the rationale for that outlay is still underpinned by a conscious commitment to show thick personal solidarity and offer monetary support toward the club. Showing support for the club in its multifarious forms (including market ones) is considered to be obligatory, because the individual has a relationship with the club that resembles those with close family and friends. In South America, supporters talk of their respective clubs as "mothers," whereas they are its "sons" or "children." More routinely, whereas the players at the club may change, the ground is always "home." Renouncing support or switching allegiances to a rival club is impossible; traditional supporters are culturally contracted to their clubs.

Traditionally, the club is an emblem of its surrounding community, from whence it draws its core supporters. To establish themselves, clubs may have "raised the banner of town chauvinism, and prospered under it" (Hopcraft, 1968, p. 186), but the social and cultural impact of a club is always more relevant to local supporters than its unstable economic impact. Localist solidarity is strong, although some clubs with ethnic traditions might retain the deep affections of diasporic supporters. To continue the Durkheimian metaphor, the club might be seen as a totemic representation of the surrounding community. Thus, the various supporter rituals surrounding match day (not least the chanting of the club's name and the oldest supporter songs) coalesce to become a ceremony, through which the supporters worship themselves. The body becomes a key vehicle for communicating these hot and permanent forms of solidarity with club/community: Club crests are tattooed onto arms and torsos; club colors are worn perennially; during matches, the supporter corpus comprises hands, arms, and bodies that move in unison as part of the various supporter chants.

Supporters attend regularly, coming to know the ground's nooks and crannies in a very familiar, personal manner. The ground enhances their thick solidarity with fellow supporters, crowds of whom generate an atmosphere on match days that is considered to be special or unique. Supporting the club is a key preoccupation of the individual's self, so that attending home fixtures is a routine that otherwise structures the supporter's free time.[4] Supporting the club is a lived experience, rooted in a grounded identity that is reflected in an affectionate relationship to the ground that is regularly revisited. Moreover, the supporter's emotional investment in the club is reciprocated in several ways. The club might be seen to repay that faith by winning some matches or even some trophies, but less instrumental elements of reciprocated affection are at least as crucial. The club's players might play in a style that is favored by the supporters and the club's traditions (whether this is flamboyant, fluent, tough, or efficient), perhaps even reflecting some distinctive local values. Outwith match day, supporters may enjoy some community benefits through use of club facilities or social engagements with officials and players.[5]

Supporters themselves husband these strong senses of hot, traditional identification in a subcultural manner. New generations of supporters are socialized into the core subcultural values by their parent groups or by older peers. Key forums for the debating of local club questions and the reproduction of subcultural values emerged through the creation of specific supporter associations, or latterly through the production of "fanzines" that are sold on the streets outside the ground. Yet within the support, there are inevitably various status gradations. To borrow from Thornton's (1995, pp. 8–14) development of Bourdieu

(1984), some supporters seek to display greater volumes of "subcultural capital" to authenticate their support to the extent of claiming greater status over their fellow supporters. In the United Kingdom, subcultural capital is really reserved for those supporters who continued to attend and to live through those periods when their clubs were unsuccessful rather than become part-time supporters; distinction is also acquired by those football spectators who did not emerge during the post-1990 boom in the sport's fashionability.[6] The embodiment of key values is also accorded status, such as dedication to the club or vocal appreciation of the aesthetics behind the team's playing style. Moreover, the supporters' commitment to the team's cause does not preclude a deep interest and understanding of the various qualities and subcultural values of other clubs and their players. Supporters are both custodians of football qua game and hot participants in active rivalries with other clubs, notably those from neighboring communities (Armstrong & Giulianotti, 2001). For traditional/hot supporters, one cannot acquire subcultural capital in a purely market manner simply by purchasing the latest club commodities.

TRADITIONAL/COOL SPECTATORS: FOLLOWERS

The traditional/cool spectators are followers of clubs, but they are also followers of players, managers, and other football people. The follower is so defined not by an itinerant journey alongside the club but, instead, by keeping abreast of developments among clubs and football people in which he or she has a favorable interest. The follower has implicit awareness of, or an explicit preconcern with, the particular senses of identity and community that relate to specific clubs, to specific nations, and to their associated supporter groups. But the follower arrives at such identification through a vicarious form of communion, most obviously via the cool medium of the electronic media.

Traditional/cool followers may evince either thin or thick forms of solidarity toward their favored football institutions. In its thin solidarity form, the follower might be drawn to a particular club because of its historical links to his or her favored club, such as in one club hiring the other's players or manager. The distant club might have ideological attractions for specific individual followers, such as the anarcho-leftist St. Pauli club in Hamburg, the ethno-national culture of Barcelona, or the fascistic subcultures at clubs such as Lazio, Verona, Real Madrid, or some clubs from the former East Germany. In its thick form of solidarity, groups of followers might establish friendship relationships with the traditional/hot supporters at these clubs. In Italy, for example, there are complex, subcultural lineages of friendship and strong rivalry that exist across club supporter groups, which might, for example, encourage Sampdoria supporters to be Parma followers.[7] In the United Kingdom, there are friendships that link club supporter groups through religious-ethnic sentiments.[8] Among some hooligan groups in particular, there are signs of informal transnational friendship networks, such as those between English firms and hooligans in the Benelux countries, or Scottish groups with ties to some English club hooligans and some ultras in southern Europe.

Informal communities are ritually cemented through the symbolic exchanges of football paraphernalia and the generous hosting of visiting friends. In its fullest sense, very thick senses of social solidarity might be reproduced through the club in a nationalist sense, enabling the "imagined community" to be socially realized—such as when Turkish clubs visit Germany and find that the local "guest workers" are in massive attendance, magically recreating their national identity whereas their actual identification with the specific club is typically a cool, instrumental one.

In both thick and thin versions of solidarity, we have a set of noneconomic, symbolic exchange relationships involving the follower and the favored club. The latter is accorded the interest or backing of the follower, but the favored club does offer something in return that accords with the follower's habitus or established football interests, such as in terms of employing a favored player or in the club's cultural politics. The follower may seek to authenticate in normative terms this association with the club by appealing beyond principles of mere football success to more abstract social and cultural values. Typically, these values harmonize with those associated with the follower's other, more established focus for support. Followers may define themselves against consumer values to authenticate their traditionalist motives, such as through a stylized denial of the role of team success or "fashionability" in inspiring their club allegiance (as one finds among Scandinavian followers of such unlikely football teams as Cowdenbeath or Stenhousemuir in Scotland).

To borrow from Cohen (1978), the notion of a set of "nested identities" might help to explain how the self seeks to integrate these different objects of allegiance.[9] There may be no simply ranked pyramid set of affiliations that the follower has for organizing his or her allegiances. Instead, these affiliations may be composed in a rather complex manner, with no obvious way of determining which identification is favored when different favored entities rub up against one another (such as when a favored manager comes up against a favored team). Nested identities instead function to provide the follower with a range of favored clubs and football people in different circumstances, ensuring that the follower's football interest is sustained when his or her supported true team is no longer competing. The proliferation of televised football now means that, to sustain the traditional spectating habit of favoring a particular team, the viewer must become a follower of some clubs. But, the follower is suitably inured with the cultural politics of football to know that certain elements cannot combine to construct a viable nest: Only flâneurs (see p. 257), for example, would declare a penchant for both Liverpool and Manchester United, or Fiorentina and Juventus.

Moreover, the follower lacks the spatial embedding of the supporter within the club and its surrounding communities. For followers, football places may be mere practical resources with few symbolic meanings: a stage upon which favored players and officials might pitch up to perform before moving on. In circumstances of thicker solidarity, the public geography surrounding the favored club may be respected by followers, but from a distance, typically with no deep personal knowledge or engagement within this particular lifeworld.

THE HOT/CONSUMER SPECTATORS: FANS

The hot/consumer spectator is a modern fan of a football club or its specific players, particularly its celebrities. The fan develops a form of intimacy or love for the club or its specific players, but this kind of relationship is inordinately unidirectional in its affections. The fan is hot in terms of identification; the sense of intimacy is strong and is a key element of the individual's self. But, it is a relationship that is rather more distant than that enjoyed by supporters. Football's modern move into the market and its more recent hypercommodification have served to dislocate players and club officials from supporters, particularly in the higher professional divisions. The individual fan experiences the club, its traditions, its star players, and fellow supporters through a market-centered set of relationships. The fans' strength of identification with the club and its players is thus authenticated most readily through the consumption of related products. Such consumption might take the direct form of purchasing merchandise, buying shares, or contributing to fundraising initiatives. More significantly in future, more indirect forms of consumption come into play, particularly purchasing football magazines and pay-per-view or other subscription rights to the club's televised fixtures. The consumer relationship to the club is thus at its strongest among the wealthiest of football clubs.

The hot/consumer spectator can incline toward relatively thicker or thinner versions of social solidarity. In its thicker manifestation, bordering on the supporter identity, the fans' consumption practices are orientated toward enhancing the collective consciousness, intensifying the rituals of support. If large groups of fans attend matches in club shirts or other trademarked colors, then this striking display of visual solidarity may energize the players during matches. Thinner forms of solidarity are evinced from a greater distance. In its more extreme manifestation, buying into club regalia or shares becomes one of the few means by which fans scattered across the world may continue to signify their deep allegiance to a local team.

The fan recognizes that in contemporary professional sport, the amoral free market dominates, consequently the club's survival and successes are dependent upon greater financial contributions from all kinds of backers relative to the wealth of other clubs. Purchasing shares in clubs may be investments in football's boom time, but fans are reluctant to sell in the interests of personal profit. The brand loyalty and inelastic demand of fans for club shares and merchandise are consciously intended to provide the club with financial stability, typically to enable the purchase of better players (Conn, 1997, p. 155). But in promoting the transformation of its spectators into rather consumer-centered fan identities, the club tends to generate a set of utilitarian conditions for its consumers to continue attending. If the club fails to deliver on its market promises (such as "brand improvement" of the team), then the fans may drift into other markets (other leisure activities, other football leagues, though probably not supporting rival teams) in the deculturalized pursuit of "value for money." If solidarity is rather thicker, then fans may collectivize and agitate to unseat the incumbent controllers, such as by sacking the board or forming independent shareholder associations. Most typically, the club's fans are politically passive, strong in their affections for club and players, probably geographically removed from the club's home, and especially separated from the entertainment "star system" in which the players circulate.

Consequently, football fans resemble the fans of leading musicians, actors, and media personalities, through their largely unidirectional relationship toward these household names. Thompson (1997) described this social framework in terms of "non-reciprocal relations of intimacy with distant others" (pp. 220–222). Fans refer to stars by first name, discuss their private lives and traits, collect biographical snippets, surround the family home or workplace with their images, and perhaps even fantasize about a loving, sexual relationship with their objects of affection. Star footballers, like other celebrities, are rarely in a position to reciprocate. Football matches before live audiences only afford a temporary break in the distance between stars and fans, but in any case, the divisions are symbolically retained. Football players at matches, or even when signing autographs or visiting sick children in hospital, continue to play the star role. Their "work with the public" is a form of emotional labor, necessitating a form of professional "deep acting," which Hochschild (1983) has previously documented. Thompson viewed fan identity as a strategy of the self, a deliberate entry into a relationship that is fundamentally different from those founded on face-to-face interaction. Consequently, we may add that such a relationship is dependent on specific media that allow for a continuous and multifarious flow of star-related signs toward the fan. In the West particularly, this must mean capital-governed signifiers, through product endorsement, television interviews, and even forays into other realms of popular culture, such as pop music. Again, for such public relations, football players and club officials are trained to draw upon an ever-expanding reservoir of clichés and dead metaphors to confirm typified public constructions of their personality. These more shallow, mediated forms of acting help to preserve the highly profitable, parallel football universe that has been constructed to supply the fan market.

The commodity-centered mediation of football qua entertainment intensifies, so the fan identity comes under pressure to enter the realm of the flâneur, the unreconstructed cool consumer. This process is most apparent as market representations of football are increasingly telescoped onto playing stars and their celebrity lifestyles (rather than what they do on the field of play). The process first appeared in the United Kingdom with the public identity of George Best, but it has reached a new category of representation with Beckham, whereas in global terms, Ronaldo is the tragic exemplar.[10] As commodity logic comes to prevail, we encounter a redoubled fetishizing of the star's exchange value, beyond merely transfer worth and club wages, but into the highly unstable environment of general marketability, fashion, and exposure in popular media. Thus, football stars are quickly nudged out of the limelight by new performers and are liable to experience a decline in their "rating" among distant fans to a degree that far outstrips their continuing regard among supporters or those within the game. The hot identification that fans once attached to stars embarks upon a categorical decline, as fans generally learn to cool their affections, in expectation that the next player qua commodity sign will arrive sooner than ever.

COOL/CONSUMER SPECTATORS: FLÂNEURS

The cool consumer spectator is a football flâneur. The flâneur acquires a postmodern spectator identity through a depersonalized set of market dominated virtual relationships, particularly interactions with the cool media of television and the Internet.

The flâneur constitutes a distinctive. urban social type first chronicled and characterized by Baudelaire in the mid-19th century, remolded sociologically by Simmel, expounded upon more critically by Walter Benjamin (1973, 1999) during the 1930s, and latterly the flâneur has been the subject of substantial debate among cultural theorists.[11] In its original sense, the flâneur was a modern urban stroller: Male and bourgeois, typically in full adulthood, he would promenade through boulevards and markets. For the true flâneur, "kaleidoscopic images and fragments whose novelty, immediacy and vividness, coupled with their fleeting nature and often strange juxta-position, provided a range of aesthetic sensations and experiences" (Featherstone, 1995, p. 150). Benjamin's (1999) flâneur is understood in part as an idler and traveler, a student of physiognomy and character among the passing throng, essentially semidetached in his engagement with the crowds and commodities of the labyrinthine metropolis.

In its contemporary manifestation, I would suggest the flâneur is less gender specific. Class differences must remain, because the flâneur has the economic, cultural, and educational capital to inspire a cosmopolitan interest in the collection of experiences. Accordingly, the flâneur's social practices are increasingly oriented toward consumption.

The football flâneur may tend to be more male than female, but not by definition. The flâneur is more likely to be bourgeois and thus in pursuit of a multiplicity of football experiences. The flâneur adopts a detached relationship to football clubs, even favored ones. A true football flâneur, the cool consumer belongs only to a virtual community of strollers who window-shop around clubs. In the most extreme manifestation, national allegiances may also be exchanged on the grounds of competitive successes or mediated identification with superstar celebrities. The adornment of a team's attire is in tune with a couture aesthetic, drawn to the signifier (the shirt color, the shirt design, its crest, even its sponsor logo) rather than to what is signified conceptually (the specific, grounded identity of the club or the nation). The flâneur thereby avoids any personal consumption by the appended signs but instead consumes these signifiers in a disposable and cliché-like fashion, as if adopting a temporary tattoo. Moreover, the football flâneur's natural habitat is increasingly the virtual arena, seeking the sensations of football as represented through television, Internet, or perhaps in the future, the audiovisual bodysuit. Thus, television presentation of football is tailored toward a flâneur-type experience. Television compresses time-space differences, distilling entire matches or tournaments into 100-second transmissions of blinding, aestheticized action, to an accompanying backbeat that drifts between techno and opera.

The cool/consumer seeks relatively thin forms of social solidarity with other fellow fans. Within the context of a postemotional panoply of social relations, the flâneur is definitively low in genuine collective affect. Nevertheless, there are occasions when flâneurs congregate and thus come to simulate in a playful manner the football passion that they have witnessed in prior media representations of those who appear to be true supporters.[12] The cool consumer is a cosmopolitan, but not in the classical sense whereby constant perambulations produce a worldly merchant in ideas. Rather, this cosmopolitan has relatively little biographical or strategic interest in discerning an underlying meta-narrative from the medley of football signifiers around which the flâneur dances, save for the instrumental identification with an avant-garde, winning brand. Flâneurs evidence the "transferable loyalties of the postmodern passenger" (Turner, 1999, p. 48); accordingly, they are liable not only to switch a connection with teams or players, but also to forsake football for other forms of entertainment. And the true cosmopolis, the cultural setting, for the community of strollers is the non-place, such as the airport departure lounge or the most contemporary shopping mall (Augé, 1995).

Some of the largest world clubs have provided the flâneur with an increasingly welcoming shop window in which to gaze, thereby creating a quasi-community of cosmopolitans. And thus, relatively more committed, regular forms of engagement with these clubs (so long as they continue to win or to be chic) encourages the germination of a proxy form of narcissistic self-identity for the cool consumers. Invariably, association with winning is particularly favored, but so too are cosmopolitan signifiers of conspicuous wealth, European sophistication (French, Italian), or an avant-garde setting (high-tech stadium). Clubs thus become appendages, selected for what they may say about the flâneur's personality.

Flâneurs may seek to authenticate their cosmopolitan identity through direct and unfavorable representation of spectators that possess traditional or hot characteristics. Traditionalists are constructed as regressive figures from the past—chauvinists, romanticists, xenophobes—in sum, truculent locals who refuse to reconcile themselves to the ineluctable hegemony of neoliberal principles within football. Flâneurs might try to depict hot spectators as emotionally driven and thus intellectually incapable of appreciating the fineries of the game. Yet as we have noted, the real identity of the flâneur is rooted in persistent motion, classically in material terms but increasingly in virtual terms, through switching affiliations like television channels. Thus, the flâneur who endeavors to authenticate a stable football identity relative to other spectators is something of a contradiction in terms.

MOTIVES, LANDSCAPES, AND THE PARADOXES OF CROSS-CATEGORY RELATIONSHIPS

The four spectator categories examined have been distinguished according to their different football identities and the distinctive, underlying relationships that they have toward the game. I shall avoid treating the reader as a flâneur and providing a highlighted recapitulation of arguments, but it is useful to elucidate briefly these categorical differences by reference to two analytical heuristics—the specific motivations and the spatial relationships of these spectator identities.

In terms of motive, supporters give their support to clubs because they are obligated to do so. The club provides the supporter not simply with an element of personal identity but a complex and living representation of the supporter's public identity. Followers forward various allegiances to clubs because it helps to sustain and spread their personal senses of participation in football. This diffusion of allegiances is structurally facilitated by an increasingly complex, mediated networking of football information and images. Fans are motivated to produce non-reciprocal relationships with distant others, which are qualitatively different to face-to-face relationships and which promote a consumption-oriented identity to bridge symbolically the socio-spatial divide. Finally, flâneurs are motivated to seek sensation, excitement, and thus to switch their gaze across clubs, players, and nations. The greater commodification of football, and emphasis on association with success, structures the flâneur's peripatetic pursuit of winning or chic teams.

In terms of their relationship to the material environment, supporters have inextricable biographical and emotional ties to the club's ground, which is a key cultural emblem of the surrounding community. Similarly, followers are cognizant of the symbolic significance of the ground to the club, but their dependency on mediated representations of favored clubs reflects their circumscribed ties to this other community. Fans experience a distant socio-spatial relationship to favored clubs and their stars. Consumption of star-focused products might affirm and demonstrate fan loyalties, but the communicative divisions remain even in face-to-face interludes as stars consciously reaffirm their celebrity identity. Finally, the flâneur's preferred habitat is replete with audiovisual stimulation, such that high-tech electronic media are particularly favored. As a mobile cosmopolitan, the flâneur lives in a cosmopolis of consumption and thus has no capacity to secure personal alignment with a club qua locally defined institution. Instead, club signifiers are adorned in a cool, market-oriented style, such that the most congruous landscapes for these displays must be the character-free non-places of what Augé would prefer to term "supermodernity."

The model forwarded here suggests a structural relationship between the various spectator categories. Fans and followers share some primary, paradoxical qualities in their basic constitution. As hot/consumers and traditional/cool spectators, their dichotomous identities border on oxymoron. Followers have a traditional position in regard to the game's culture, but that is tempered by a cool relationship toward the clubs followed. Fans possess a hot sense of loyalty to players and to clubs, but that is tempered by a market-centered approach toward surmounting symbolic distances. Consequently, this synthesis of apparently conflicting qualities ensures that followers and fans can display relatively thick and thin forms of social solidarity. Historically, we may also view these spectator categories as intermediary retreats, as part of a strategy of negotiation and accommodation, whereby gradually the traditional/hot properties of the supporter are dissolved into the cool/consumer practices of the flâneur, although this does point toward a deeper social paradox.

As presented here, supporters and flâneurs are literally in diametrical opposition to one another, but they do appear to be dependent on each other for different reasons. In an increasingly neoliberal financial environment, local supporters practicing realpolitik come to recognize that the club must attract the custom of cosmopolitan flâneurs to preserve its status and perhaps push on for more successes. But can the same be said of the wealthy cosmopolitan who flits over the locals? After all, the contemporary structures of football are geared toward global consumption. Football is dominated by transnational corporations, particularly the merchandise companies (Nike, Reebok, Adidas), the world's governing bodies (notably the Fédération Internationale de Football Association and UEFA), and the largest football clubs. Unquestionably, the football flâneur is the cultural consumer that these transnational corporations are committed to seduce; their overtures are motivated by the rather hazardous aim of securing the flâneur's attention and thus securing his or her conversion into a warmer (more regular) consumer. Such a fundamental transformation in football, as in other sports or other realms of popular culture, threatens a Pyrrhic victory for the neoliberal agenda. As the political philosopher Michael Walzer has argued in a broader context, "There is a sense in which the cosmopolitan is parasitic on people who are not cosmopolitans . . . you could not exist if there were not people who sat still and created the places that you visit and enjoy" (as cited in Carleheden and Gabriëls, 1997, p. 120).

Otherwise stated here, if supporters become flâneurs, then the spectacle that is created by the spectators themselves will be threatened. There will be no more curious displays of football tribalism past which to stroll or on which to gaze.[13]

Excerpted from Richard Giulianotti, "Supporters, Followers, Fans, and Flaneurs: A Taxonomy of Spectator Identities in Football" in the *Journal of Sport and Social Issues* 26.1 (February 2002): 25–46.

NOTES

1. See, for example, Conn (1997), Horton (1997), Fynn and Guest (1994), Giulianotti (1999), Lee (1998), Perryman (1997), Dempsey and Reilly (1998), and the more accommodative work by Szymanski and Kuypers (1999). At least two separate editions of the British Broadcasting Corporation's Panorama series have also assessed, with strong criticism, the affect of football's financial boom on its established grassroots spectators and players.
2. In highlighting the abandonment of match attendance by an architect and his wife, the relevant article pointed out that the poorest spectators were not alone in feeling financially and culturally marginalized from football (*The Guardian*, August 22, 1999, www.guardian.co.uk/Archive/Article/0,4273,3894685,00.htm).

3. There is a reasonable range of literature in this area. On North American sports generally, see Alt (1983); on Canadian sports and North American ice hockey, see respectively Gruneau (1983) and Gruneau and Whitson (1994); on basketball, see Andrews (1995).
4. As one football journalist explained, "It is difficult for those who care about their game and, more particularly, care about their team, to comprehend life without this obsession" (Allsop, 1997, p. 95).
5. In South America, most clubs remain private member associations, so that their swimming pool, gym, and other recreation facilities are all available to members in return for a modest annual fee.
6. By far the most successful text on UK football during the 1990s was Nick Hornby's *Fever Pitch,* which became a major bestseller, acquiring numerous awards before being turned into a stage play and film. Hornby's book is a kind of autobiography, in which the author claims that his football obsession has determined his life course. However, the "subcultural capital" of Hornby as genuine football man has been revalued; for example, some critics point disparagingly to his abandoning of Arsenal as a supporter during his time at university. More generally, some traditionalist supporters also refer critically to spectators who came into football during its 1990s boom as "post-Hornby fans."
7. For example, in Italy during the early 1990s, Sampdoria's ultras were "friendly" with Verona, Inter, Atalanta, Cremonese, and Parma fan groups; they were strongly opposed to fans from the lineage linking Genoa, Torino, Bologna, and Pisa (cf. Roversi, 1992, p. 58).
8. For example, there are the pro-Irish nationalist sentiments of some fans of Celtic and Manchester United, or the "Blues Brothers" network of Unionist fan groups (Chelsea, Glasgow Rangers, and Linfield of Norrhern Ireland).
9. I am indebted to Bea Vidacs for the first application of this concept to football identity and to her provision of the reference to Cohen.
10. For a discussion of how specific football players appear to fit into traditional (Stanley Matthews), modern (George Best), and postmodern (Paul Gascoigne) identity categories, see Giulianotti and Gerrard (2001b).
11. See, for example, Tester (1994), Featherstone (1995), and Weinstein and Weinstein (1993).
12. This is increasingly apparent at major tournaments such as the World Cup, when the carnival atmosphere before and during matches is often a strikingly sanitized, simulated version of supporter passion. The most extreme illustrations occur when a dead atmosphere among thousands of fans suddenly changes into highly animated collective behavior when the television cameras come into view.
13. Nor should one assume that an attempt to protect the interests of traditional supporters is an act of xenophobia toward those who want to join the football spectator community. There is no credible a priori argument that states that other spectator categories, including flâneurs, are incapable of harboring deeply intolerant attitudes towards some other communities. In addition, as Walzer (in Carleheden & Gabriëls, 1997, p. 129) himself argued, one may quite easily identify those genuinely intolerant communities and seek to remove such traditions, but all the while encourage the community members to adapt to the new conditions, to redefine their values.

REFERENCES

Allsop, D. (1997). *Kicking in the wind: The real life drama of a small-town football club.* London: Headline.

Alt, J. (1983). Sport and cultural reification: From ritual to mass consumption. *Theory, Culture and Society,* 1(3), 93–107.

Andrews, D. L. (1995, September 7–9). *The [trans]-national basketball association: American commodity-sign culture and global-local conjuncturalism.* Paper presented at the First Annual Conference for Popular Culture, Manchester UK.

Armstrong, G., & Giulianotti, R. (Eds.). (2001). *Fear and loathing in world football.* Oxford UK: Berg.

Augé, M. (1995). *Non-places: An introduction to the anthropology of supermodernity.* London: Verso.

Baudrillard, J. (1990). *Seduction.* London: Macmillan.

Benjamin, W. (1973). *Charles Baudelaire: A lyric poet in the era of high capitalism.* London: NLB.

Benjamin, W. (1999). *The Arcades Project.* Cambridge, MA: Belknap.

Bourdieu, M. (1984). *Distinction.* London: Routledge and Kegan Paul.

Carleheden, M., & Gabriëls, R. (1997). An interview with Michael Walzer. *Theory, Culture and Society,* 14(1), 113–130.

Castells, M. (1996). *The network society.* Oxford, UK: Blackwell.

Cohen, R. (1978). Ethnicity: Problem and focus in anthropology. *Annual Review of Anthropology,* 7, 379–403.

Conn, D. (1997). *The football business.* Edinburgh, Scotland; Mainstream.

Dempsey, P., & Reilly, K. (1998). *Big money, beautiful game: Saving soccer from itself.* Edinburgh, Scotland: Mainstream.

Featherstone, M. (1995). *Undoing culture.* London: Sage.

Fynn, A., & Guest, L. (1994). *Out of time: Why football isn't working.* London: Simon & Schuster.

Giulianotti, R. (1999), *Football: A sociology of the global game.* Cambridge, UK: Polity.

Giulianotti, R., & Gerrard, M. (2001a). Cruel Britannia? Glasgow Rangers, Scotland and "hot" football rivalries. In G. Armstrong & R. Giulianotti (Eds.), *Fear and loathing in world football* (pp. 23–42). Oxford, UK: Berg.

Giulianotti, R., & Gerrard, M. (2001b). Evil genie or pure genius? The (im)moral football and public career of Paul "Gazza" Gascoigne. In D. L. Andrews & S. Jackson (Eds.), *Sport stars: The politics of sport celebrity* (pp. 124–137). London: Routledge.

Gruneau, R. (1983). *Class, sport and social development.* Champaign, IL: Human Kinetics.

Gruneau, R., & Whitson, D. (1994). *Hockey night in Canada.* Toronto, Canada: Garamond.

Hargreaves, J. (1986). *Sport, power and culture.* Cambridge, UK: Polity.

Hess, R., & Stewart, B. (Eds). (1998). *More than a game: An unauthorised history of Australian Rules football.* Melbourne, Australia: Melbourne University Press.

Hochschild, A. R. (1983). *The managed heart: Commercialization of human feeling.* Berkeley: University of California Press.

Hopcraft, A. (1968). *The football man.* London: Simon & Schuster.

Horton, E. (I997). *Moving the goalposts.* Edinburgh, Scotland: Mainstream.

Lash, S. (1994). Expert-systems or situated interpretation? In U. Beck, A. Giddens, & S. Lash, *Reflexive modernization* (pp. 198–215). Cambridge, UK: Polity.

Lash, S., & Urry, J. (1987). *The end of organized capitalism.* Cambridge, UK: Polity.

Lash, S., & Urry, J. (1994). *Economies of signs and space.* London: Sage.

Lee, S. (1998). Grey shirts to grey suits: The political economy of English football in the 1990s. In A. Brown (Ed.), *Fanatics!* (pp. 32–49). London: Routledge.

McLuhan, M. (1964). *Understanding media.* London: Routledge.

Perryman, M. (1997). *Football United: New Labour, the task force and the future of the game.* London: Fabian Society.

Robertson, R. (1992). *Globalization: Social theory and global culture.* London: Sage.

Roversi, A, (1992). *Calcio, tifo e violenza* [Football, the fan, and violence]. Bologna, Italy: Il Mulino.

Szymanski, S., & Kuypers, T. (1999). *Winners and losers: The business strategy of football.* London: Viking Press.

Tester, K. (1994), *The flâneur.* London: Routledge.

Thompson, J. B. (1997). *The media and modernity: A social theory of the media.* Cambridge, UK: Polity.

Thornton, S. (1995). *Club cultures: Music, media and subcultural capital.* Cambridge, UK: Polity.

Turner, B. S. (1999). The possibility of primitiveness: Towards a sociology of body marks in cool societies. *Body & Society,* 5(2–3), 39–50.

Walsh, A., & Giulianotti, R. (2001). This sporting mammon: A normative analysis of the commodification of sport. *Journal of the Philosophy of Sport,* 28, 53–77.

Weinstein, D., & Weinstein, M. A. (1993). *Post-modern(ized) Simmel.* London: Routledge.

CHAPTER 18

The Football-Fan Community as a Determinant Stakeholder in Value Co-creation[1]

Patrizia Zagnoli and Elena Radicchi

INTRODUCTION

The new complexity of the sport sector has a strong impact on the implementation of sport products that nowadays are an expression of manifold subjects. Planning, production, distribution and communication of sports content involves numerous actors who participate in the implementation of sport with diversified roles and importance: sport organizations, athletes, institutions and local administrations, sponsors, media, etc. Fans and supporters are of course of central importance to sport-service production. The passion, excitement, involvement expressed by the audience has a crucial role for event implementation and value creation. Due to the importance of fans as 'co-producers' of the sport service, the hypothesis of this research is that a fan community is a salient stakeholder in the value co-creation process.

This research focuses on the fan community of a specific professional football club, *ACF Fiorentina* – the Florence, Italy, football club – a 'rich' example for identifying and analysing the manifold influences and interactions that fans can engage in with their team, the local context and the network of actors as a whole. The knowledge of this case study has profited from several investigations, research and theses carried out within the Master's Degree in Sport Management at the University of Florence. We started to monitor the football club and the relations with the local stakeholders in the year 2003 – after the club's failure and its 'rebirth' when the team went to an owner that, for the first time ever, was 'non Florentine' – up to the last 2009/2010 football season.

To develop this case study a quali-quantitative methodology was used. The analysis of the fan community starts with an examination of Fiorentina's season-ticket-holders database that highlights their socio-economic features.[2] One-to-one interviews and focus groups with fan-club representatives, the local chief of police, sport institutions, members of the football club (coach, managers, etc.) were also organized.[3] Further information was retrieved through the monitoring of sport magazines and national newspapers, and the site searching of the ACF Fiorentina official website, blogs and fan-club websites, in order to better explain data collected from interviews, focus groups and the database.

The complex context where fans move was studied by analysing different subjects with a specific interest in the football club. The mapping of actors who are more or less linked to the existence of Fiorentina was guided by the *stakeholder theory*. Nonetheless, this analytical tool does not seem to thoroughly explain all the relations developed within the sport sector. This approach is somewhat 'corporate-centred' and considers mainly the relationships activated by the 'focal organization' with its stakeholders.[4] It further aims to understand how a firm can create value through transactions and relations established with each stakeholder.

The present research takes a different focus. It analyses the relations within the sport network by focusing on a specific stakeholder, that in economic terms constitutes the demand for which the product or service is destined, in respect to the focal organization. The local fan community, Fiorentina's 'user', interacts with manifold actors such as the players and coach, owners, local citizens, institutions, media, sponsors and suppliers. By drawing on the theoretical tools of the *network analysis* it is possible to map the relations between the football club and its fans, as well as between fans and other stakeholders.[5] More particularly, it is possible to emphasize the special network of Fiorentina both in terms of internal dynamics as well as in regard to its connections with the external competitive football environment.

Even though the theoretical framework offered by stakeholder theory and the network analysis give us the analytical lens for exploring the system of relationships developed around the football club, these approaches have not offered specific analytical categories able to 'read' the peculiarities of a sport community until now. By not exhaustively highlighting the role of the fan community in the value creation process, these theories leave space for a *typological articulation* related both to the fans' behaviour in regard to the match, and to strategic behaviour adopted by the various subgroups of fans in the football sector.

MAPPING STAKEHOLDERS OF A PROFESSIONAL FOOTBALL CLUB

The theoretical framework we decided to use to explore football-fan communities is referred to as the Service-Dominant (S-D) Logic approach.[6] One of the fundamental premises of this research recognizes a central role of networks and interactions in value creation. Many of the actors in sport, with their different roles and capabilities, *co-participate* in the sport service and create a 'constellation' of relations[7] that produce value by implementing the sport product.

Stakeholder theory[8] enables us to map the actors involved within the sport system. From the stakeholder's perspective a firm, or more generally a 'focal organization' (company, corporation, etc.), is at the centre of a network of stakeholders.[9] According to the definition proposed by Freeman that is: 'groups and individuals who can affect, or are affected by the strategic outcomes of a firm'.[10] Actors who are vital to the continued growth and survival of the organization can be grouped as *primary stakeholders* (e.g., customers, employees, manager, owners, suppliers, sponsors, local communities), while other groups that can affect or be affected by the focal organization, are called *secondary stakeholders* (e.g., competitors, media, government, consumer advocate groups, special interest groups).[11]

A case such as ACF Fiorentina football club gives us some interpretative insight into the system of stakeholders in regard to a professional football club. In recent years Fiorentina has undergone relevant changes in terms of ownership that for the first time ever is 'not Florentine'. This event has triggered a relationship process among the actors involved within the local system (fans, institutions, media, coach, top management, etc.) that enriches the empirical framework as shown in Figure 18.1.

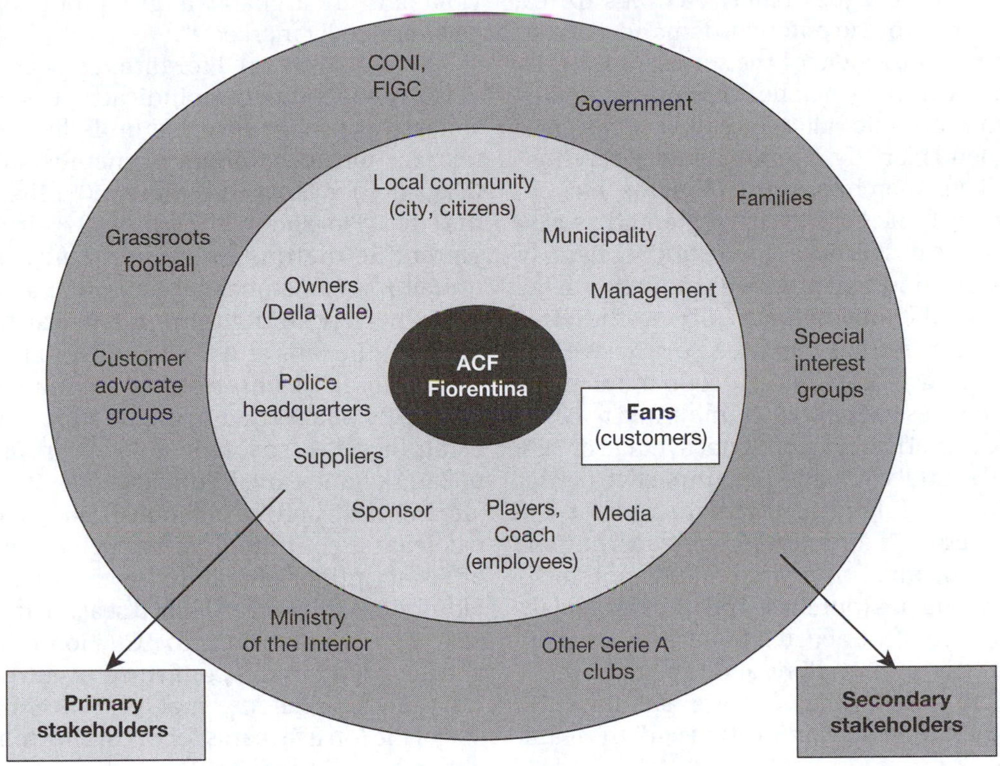

Figure 18.1 A stakeholder map for the Fiorentina football club.

Note: Adapted from Freeman, Harrison and Wicks, *Managing for Stakeholders.*

Fiorentina, the only professional football club of Florence, is at the centre of a network of relationships with fans, spectators, players, coach, top management, media, sponsor, facilities managers, etc., who interact to implement the match end-product (see Figure 18.1). The football club is the actor around which many subjects and interests rotate. The team is the entity that satisfies the emotional need of fans. These fans are citizens and therefore the local and governmental institutions are involved in managing sport facilities, logistics, road conditions and liveable spaces that enable the team to carry out matches, for their direct and mediated enjoyment. In the following paragraphs we propose an interpretative and dynamic mapping of the main primary stakeholders that in different ways interact with the football club in Florence. The fulcrum of our analysis is therefore the fan community, which we will analyse both in socio-demographic and organizational terms.

CUSTOMERS: THE 'VIOLA' FANS

The *viola*[12] are fans, spectators, supporters of Fiorentina. These individuals can be considered as *customers* of the football team's product, whose emotional involvement is derived by attending the match. Subscribers and spectators of Fiorentina are a crucial support in producing the game and make it possible to deliver the sport event. They play a meaningful role in value creation since fans are the 'demand' and are able to drag friends, colleagues, family, etc. Fans are real activators of the potential demand. Fans, as direct consumers of the service offered by the sport club (matches), assume an important economic value since their satisfaction depends largely on football club revenues (tickets, merchandising, TV rights, etc.). In the case of Fiorentina, single and season ticket sales are an important source of income and of continuous growth,[13] being 10% of the total football club revenue. This datum is further reinforced by the average percentage of stadium[14] occupation, which in the season 2008/2009 amounted to 68%[15] in comparison to a national average of 59% of the total capacity. The ample live participation of fans is therefore one of the strengths of Fiorentina. This means the football club must offer services and apply technical policies (purchase and transfer of players, type of game, etc.) to be able to satisfy the fans' expectations and especially those of the season ticket holders who have the highest level of identification with the team.

SOCIO-DEMOGRAPHIC FEATURES OF THE 'VIOLA' FANS

Fiorentina fans can be considered a 'tribe' of people who share the same passion for the Florence football team. The concept of community used in this research is that of 'tribe' in the *anthropological* sense, rather than sociological or marketing sense.[16] The territorial bonds among city, fans and team in this case are particularly important. One anthropological definition of a tribe is a 'group of individuals united by a family bond and by the sharing of a territory'.[17] Following a sociological approach, Maffesoli uses the metaphor of the 'postmodern tribe' to point out 'micro-groups of people that share an affective drive'.[18] In the case of Fiorentina, this is a tribe of people who are passionate about a football team. Thus, while some historical football teams' fans, such as fans of Milan, Inter or Barcelona, are plurilocalized, viola fans are arguably a 'group of people geographically marked'[19].

The research on Fiorentina's season-ticket-holders database indicates a strong viola collective identity that underlines the relevant territorial origin of membership-ticket-holder fans.[20] Of these, 50% live in the city of Florence with a further 37% in the Florentine metropolitan area. Thus, this overall 87% of membership subscribers confirms the very strong territorial tie existing between the fans and the team (see Figure 18.2). This also implies that the stadium can easily be reached by many supporters using bicycles, scooters or even on foot, making it handy and immediate. The strong identification between Florence and its football team is confirmed by the high number of subscriptions purchased every year by Florentines. In the 2007–2008 season, there were 22,856 subscribers to ACF Fiorentina, a value pretty much confirmed as a trend for the last seasons, making Fiorentina one of the top five teams for maximum number of subscriptions sold.[21]

The bond between Florence and its football team has always been very strong. Even when the team downgraded to Division C2 following its bankruptcy in the 2001–2002 season, the number of supporters and membership-season-ticket holders remained the same as when it was in the First Division with about 17,000 subscribers. The collective viola identity emerges even in the current 'turbulent' football environment. Notwithstanding sporadic episodes of violence, increases in average ticket prices, alternative viewing choices for enjoying sports events (digital TV, internet, etc.) and the continuous change in the schedule of games, the 'active' participation of fans remains stable and relevant.

Fans are predominantly male, aged between 25 and 44, have supported the 'Viola' for a long time, and can be divided into three socio-demographic profiles: the core fans, young people and seniors. Most

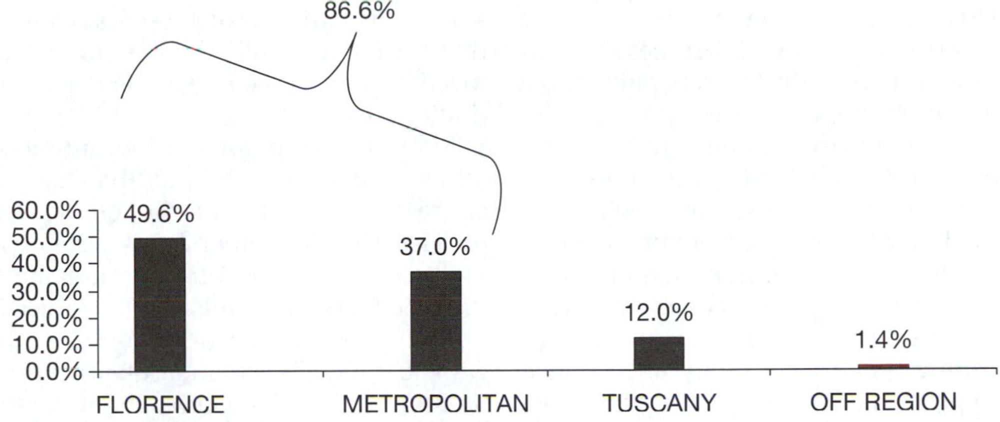

Figure 18.2 The strong collective 'viola' identity.

of the *core group* (25–44 years) are male, live in Florence or in the metropolitan area and belong to the middle class. They have a high-school diploma and are white-collar workers. Many of these supporters choose a particular sector of the stadium (the Curva Fiesole).[22] This means not only 'watching' the match but engaging in the role of supporters who really incite their team. *Young people* (6–24 years) (students, apprentices, etc.) have a presence 'en masse' in the Curva Fiesole, the sector of the stadium with the liveliest fans who have a desire to join in and share the team's fortunes, emulate and admire the 'more expert' and better known supporters, and be part of the historical groups of the 'Curva' sector. *Seniors* (over 44 years), due to their mature age, tend to watch the game itself carefully rather than seek an active participation in supporting activities. They are more interested in comfort and safety, hence they are likely to occupy 'quiet' seats of the stadium like Maratona and Tribuna.

The socio-cultural level of fans is predominantly middle class[23] thus confirming that football is a mass sport. Nevertheless, the viola fans' social status seems to reflect the city's socially productive sector: workers, students, entrepreneurs, merchants, etc., who have an active role towards Fiorentina, considered by everyone as common 'property'. The structure of the fan community on the whole appears varied, encompassing those with very great or lesser degrees of 'fanaticism', those who enjoy going to bars[24] or a recreational facility, and who are affiliated with a fan club.

The dimensions and attributes of the viola fan community make it a remarkable phenomenon in the local context. On the occasion of every match the team can count on about 45,000 spectators between real and mass-media audience. The most relevant segment is the *membership subscribers* (around 23,000 in the season 2008/2009) who express their loyalty to the team through live participation in all home games and many of those out of town. There are about 9000 *live spectators* at home matches.[25] There are about 9000 *media spectators* who watch the matches on Sky television, the pay satellite TV station which broadcasts every Fiorentina game,[26] as well. Since 2007 the games are even broadcasted by the digital terrestrial TV[27] at half the price of Sky, and the estimated audience is around 8000 spectators. There are also many enthusiastic fans who do not go frequently to the stadium or watch the games on television, but who have an interest in the team's fortunes by reading newspapers and 'posters', and these numerically might involve a great part of the local population. Even if they are not interested in football, they feel represented by the team and involved in its successes and failures. The fan's community is further amplified if we consider the grassroots football schools and young sectors connected to the team that constitute a sort of local 'breeding ground', not only for the next champions but also for growing fans. The Fiorentina team in Florence seems to be, therefore, the only 'event' able to mobilize, more or less simultaneously, the interest of tens of thousands of people, since fans share their passion with families, friends, colleagues, etc., making the team a meaningful expression of the city.

FANS' ORGANIZATIONAL STRUCTURE: THE VIOLA CLUBS

Analysing the manifold components that constitute the viola fan community, an ample group of 'organized' fans or members of the so-called 'Viola Club' emerges. As a whole, the structure of the supporters' community appears as a variegated and composite network of micro-groups, a sort of 'tribal constellation'[28] (see Figure 18.3). Although there are some national and international fan clubs (i.e., Scandinavia, Malta, etc.), most of the population of Viola Clubs is rooted in the Florence metropolitan area, confirming the identity between the city and the fans.

Some Viola Clubs act autonomously. There are historical groups that for a long time have done their activities (single-ticket and season-ticket selling, websites, house organ dedicated to the supporters, etc.) without having higher coordination, such as the 'Settebello' founded in 1965. The *autonomous Viola Clubs* segment is quite small. The attitude of Fiorentina fans is therefore that of collaboration, or 'playing together' to achieve success and the continuity of the city team.

Many fan clubs of the Fiorentina are affiliated with associations that have an active supportive role in the football-club policies. The most important associations of Viola Clubs are the Centro Coordinamento Viola Club (ACCVC) which includes around 220 clubs, the Associazione Tifosi Fiorentini with 30 fan clubs and the Collettivo Autonomo Viola, which includes about 10 clubs specifically located on the Curva Fiesole. The size of Viola Clubs can vary from 20–30 people up to more than 500. If we hypothesize that the average number of fans enrolled within a single fan club is around 180–200 supporters, these create a community of fans affiliated to a Viola Club that accounts for about 50,000 people. Of these, a remarkable share are membership subscribers as well (23,000). The others are fans of Fiorentina who may not have a season ticket because they are not living in Tuscany, but they express their own attachment to the team through membership in a fan club, where they can share with others their enthusiasm for the Viola.

Fiorentina is aware of the importance of having good collaborative relationships with fan clubs. The representatives of the three main associations are often guests at official meetings, congresses, press conferences, operational groups for security,[29] to express points of view regarding decisions that concern the football club not only on technical terms, but also strategic and managerial (i.e., facilities management, training fields, out-of-town game management, etc.). Figure 18.3 shows the affiliation of each Viola Club to a higher organization, hence the connections among these actors are illustrated. The Viola Club associations have many activities for single fan clubs that can be grouped as follows:

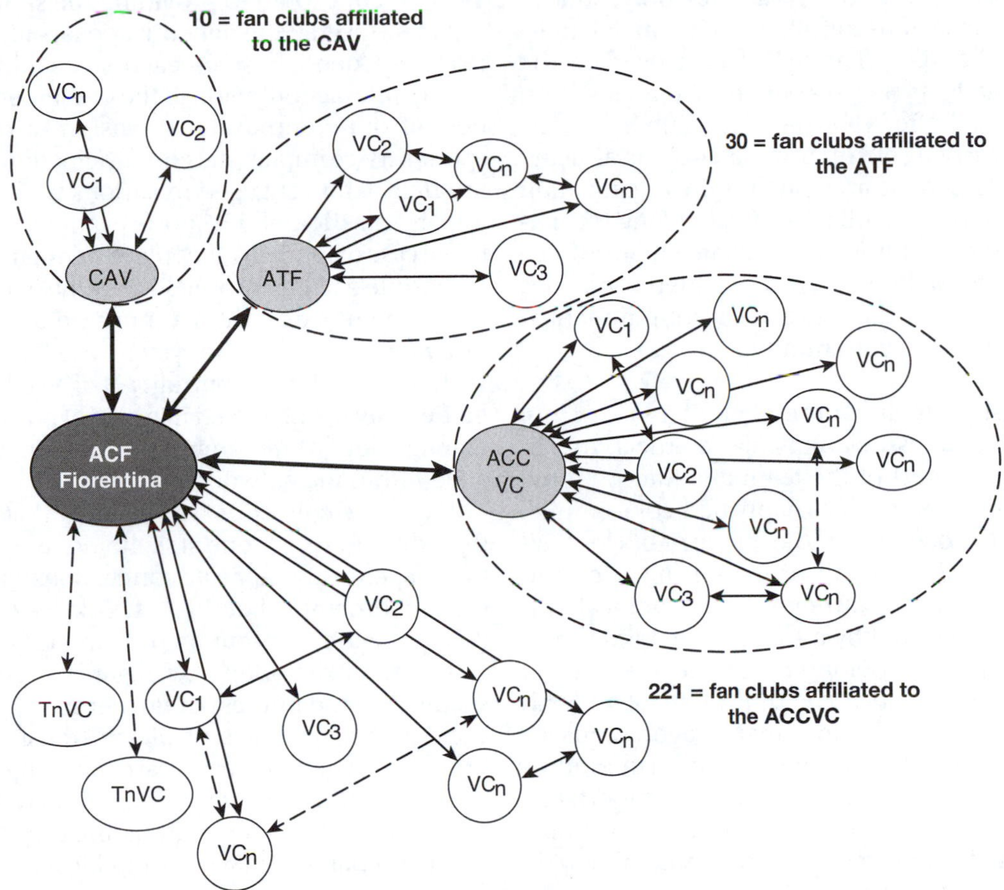

Figure 18.3 ACF Fiorentina fan community organisational structure.

- support of home game tickets and membership subscription selling;
- support of out-of-town game ticket selling and the organization of packages (ticket plus journey) for members who want to go to the match venue or even stay abroad for longer;
- organization and management of the typical supporters' activities in the stadium, like banners, chants, drums, choreography, etc;
- support of new Viola Club start-up and growing implementation;
- management of the information and communication process towards the fans through the use both of new technologies (mobile phones,[30] websites) and traditional tools (i.e., magazines of the association of Viola Clubs);
- production and commercialization of 'non official' merchandising. Even though a good percentage of supporters

buy Fiorentina material, only 30% of those fans purchase the official merchandise. The fans feel 'closer' to the gadgets (i.e., scarves, hats, hanging keys, etc.) offered by the Viola Club;[31]

- carrying out of convivial and 'social' activities in the area, such as the organization of parties, billiards and bowling tournaments, besides the management of five football fields and the athletic activities for children, with evident commitment to the local community.

Besides their coordination of a Viola Club, fan-club associations play a crucial role in the support of the team in addition to the mere sport itself as happened, for example, on the occasion of the failure of the football club. The rebirth of Fiorentina occurred thanks to the strong stimulus of local citizens[32] started by a small group of fans and supporters belonging to the main Viola Clubs, who became directly involved with the local institutions in the negotiations for the football club,[33] and pressured the appropriate institutions.[34] Despite the importance of the organizations of Viola fans, the number of supporters who are *not* members of a Viola Club is high. These participate in the team's activities by going to the stadium, following matches on TV, or staying informed about the sport results through the press.

THE SOCIAL NETWORK OF ACF FIORENTINA

Network analysis can be used to place the fan community within a network of relations where it operates using different strategies and adopting different policies.[35] The structure of ACF Fiorentina's network is characterized by a multi-directional set of relations (*polyadic network*).[36] In fact, one may observe the presence of a multiplicity of stakeholders (*nodes*) interacting with each other, such as, the team, the fans, the institutions, the media, the owners, etc. (see Figure 18.4), to contribute to providing the sports service.[37] Overall the network appears to be relatively 'dense'[38] since each stakeholder sets up interactions with all the other members of the community. Provision of the sports service implies the co-participation of multiple actors engaged in various ways in the organization of the sports event, which in the case of football takes place frequently.

Despite each team, and Fiorentina in the case in point, being the actor positioned *ab origine* at the core of the system (see Figure 18.4), the relational 'centrality'[39] of a stakeholder may be measured in terms of power, management of relations, specific importance within the network, etc.[40]

Using the concept of 'closeness', that is the extent to which one stakeholder is able to 'independently' activate connections with the other members of the network, we can define the fan community of Fiorentina as a central stakeholder.[41] As regards events keeping up the interest of fans in the club, such as the dynamics of player transfers, the introduction of the fan card, building of a new stadium etc., Fiorentina fans play an active role in the network, relating directly to the football-club owners and local institutions, and expressing their opinion both 'officially' (press releases, open letters, etc.) and 'diffusely' (intervening in the many local sports transmissions, blogs, online articles published on the net, etc.).

As regards interaction within the network, the fan community is particularly 'opinionated', putting pressure not only on the other stakeholders, such as local community institutions, but even in some cases considerably influencing the football club's strategic choices. But then the fan community strongly identifies with the team and, in the effort to maintain this identification, is open to dialogue and to collaboration, constantly pressing the owners to improve the team's technical competitive qualities. The ownership[42] and the management are thereby forced to assume a position in which it involves the fans and negotiates with them, asserting their role as protagonists of the city and therefore of its football, which in Florence is based on the strong ties between the football club, team of players, fans and institutions. A *virtuous circle* is thus created wherein, thanks to the collaboration of the various stakeholders, in part induced by relations of power, the entire local context pivots on the value created.

The case study enables us to identify, as well as the variables used in literature to delineate a network (density, centrality, etc.), further dimensions which seem to influence the structure of the specific ACF Fiorentina system and the relations between the stakeholders who compose it. One variable which is decisive in structural terms is the *territory*, with the cultural aspects, values and principles which have, over time, instilled themselves in the people inhabiting a specific local context. The high level of interpenetration between the local environment, specific features of the territory and of civil society affects people's behaviour, delineating a largely atypical network structure compared to other networks of actors in the sports sector. For example, in terms of fans' behaviour, social exclusion and juvenile unease seem to be relatively limited phenomena at a regional level[43] so that the absence of forms of 'social deviation' throughout the territory may explain the almost total absence of violence among Fiorentina fans. The fans' tendency to continuously challenge the football club and institutions so as to 'fight' for something which they feel is theirs derives from the 'Florentine outlook' which 'enjoys a verbal scuffle and manifest dissent, which is diffident, suspicious, ever inclined to believe that someone wants to rip them off'[44] and therefore ready to 'shout' its opinion at anyone attempting to lay their hands on its heritage, whether the city itself, a monument or a football club.

On the sports side, a close connection emerges between Florence's social and economic features and the structure of the local football system. The situation of Fiorentina must be interpreted in the light of the Tuscan social-economic context, a region characterized by a dense network of medium-sized cities and which, compared to other Italian regions, has undergone a process of 'light industrialization' placing it in a 'peripheral' economic position.[45] Top-class clubs like Milan, Inter FC, Juventus, etc., are able to create top-performing teams not just because of the considerable financial resources provided by selling TV-rights but also because they are backed by large industrial groups that can afford to buy champion players and ensure organized and efficient technical management. In the case of Fiorentina, despite the owners being a business group at the higher end of the leather goods market, they are still a family firm, the expression of the economy of the *third Italy* characterized by the predominance of a system of small to medium-sized enterprises far from the process of economic development typical of historically industrialized regions such as Lombardy, Piedmont and Veneto.[46]

On one hand, the strictly 'local' nature of the supporters is a strong point, especially in moments of difficulty when they are able to mobilize the entire city, however on the other, this nature also reduces its 'appeal' to television networks. The game's local popularity make Fiorentina a 'minor' team in terms of audience: preventing it from negotiating consistent fees for broadcasting matches and denying it the significant resources needed to purchase top coached and players.[47] There is therefore a discrepancy between the perceived position of the club at a national and international level and its locally desired 'status'. Indeed the city would like to see its team among the top teams but comes up against a competitive, external environment dominated by the big teams with relative skills and resources. The continual gap between top-level competitive goals on one hand and

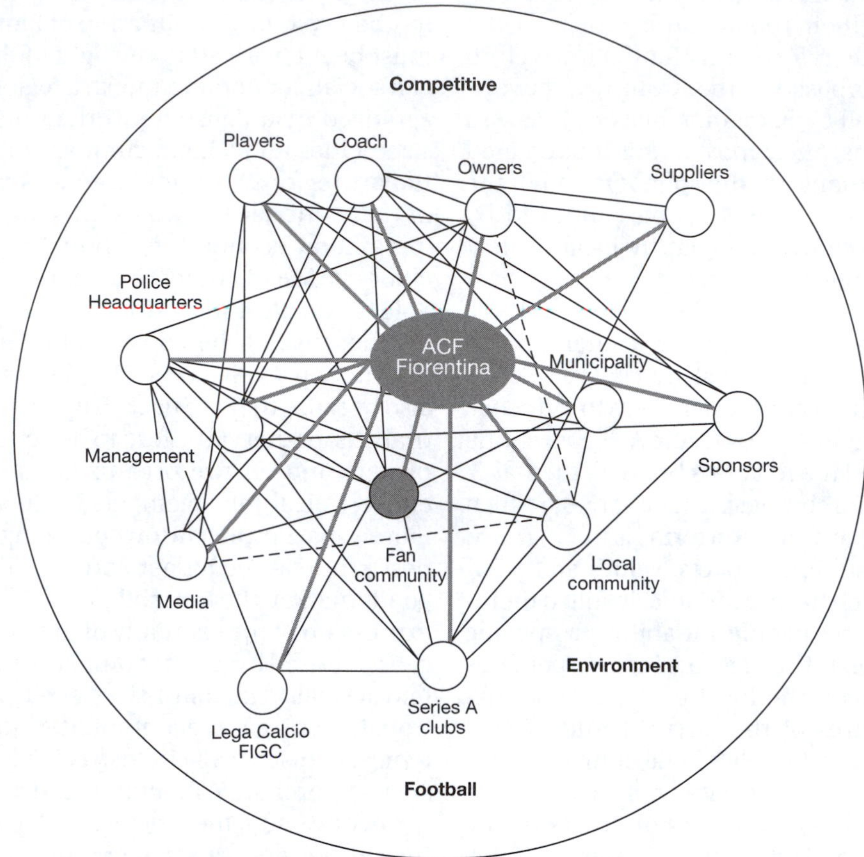

Figure 18.4 The social network of ACF Fiorentina.

strategic and economic restraints on the other affects the structure and relations within the network via the constant dialogue between fans, institutions, media and the football club which keeps the network of relations alive at a local level.

The dominant driving force in the Fiorentina network is the will to win. External competition triggers cooperative interaction of the various actors evident in the competitive commitment of the coach and players, economic investments by the owners, support of the team by fans, commitment of the institutions to ensuring the correct use of local facilities and logistic resources. In the last few years, subsequent to going bankrupt in 2002, an unusual situation has arisen in which the stakeholders have behaved according to a network logic, aimed at ensuring the success and continuity of the team. Despite the absence of star players, the cooperative boost of the coach, owners, sports director and management has led to important results being achieved. Each stakeholder therefore acts as part of a network with a strong local and sports identity in which each plays their role. The competitive strategy of Fiorentina over recent years has been to pursue ambitious goals (such as achieving classification in the Champions League) of an intermediate level in relation to the financial and economic resources available, valorizing to the utmost the resources of each individual stakeholder. This strategy has been adapted to external circumstances, shaping the football club's abilities to the competitive environment. Thus the distinctive capability of Fiorentina has been its ability to create a single project in which the owners, players, coach, fans and institutions collaborate.

The viola fan community sees the team as part of its cultural, historic and artistic heritage. Not only does it respect the team but it plays a role as central stakeholder helping to create value through commitment and social participation which seem, given the results achieved, to compensate for the technical performance discontinuity and scarcity of economic and financial resources.

TOWARDS A TYPOLOGY OF SPORTS FANS' ROLES AND BEHAVIOUR

In the light of the empirical evidence gathered we propose a first typology of fans' roles and strategies to add to current analysis classifying fans' behaviour with reference only to the sports event itself.[48] This paper analyses the fan community not only to show the roles assumed by fans at the stadium, but above all to underline the variety of ways in which fans behave as stakeholders of their own team.

To represent fans' roles and behaviour we built a simple matrix (see Figure 18.5) where on the ordinate axis we put the variable 'fans' level of identification with the team', while on the abscissa the 'type of participation in the event'. According to Sutton et al., fans' identification is defined as 'the personal commitment and emotional involvement people have with a sports organization' and can be highly varied in degree: from low levels of participation (*low*) when the fan does not feel 'part' of the club but is more interested in satisfying a need for entertainment, to an intense (*high*) level in which *soccer identity* subtends a *common social identity* that expresses the fan's affiliation to a sports club and/or to a specific local context.[49]

Fan participation in the event can be direct or indirect. Real or *live spectators* are those who directly watch the match, while *indirect spectators* enjoy the game through free-view television, digital, satellite and terrestrial television, radio, the internet and mobile phones. Sometimes the choice between direct or mediated participation seems correlated to numerous variable factors that are, in nature, *organizational* (change in schedule of games), *social* (friends and family's influence), *economic* (increase in average ticket prices), *distributive* (ever-increasing 'virtual' choices for enjoying sports events), *technical-sportive* (match location, team combination, refereeing), and related to *safety* and *security* (episodes of violence occurring inside and outside stadiums. Such factors can influence fans' choices to attend sports events. Moreover fans themselves, in turn, modify their participation by adopting broadly diversified behaviour depending on the intensity of identification and the 'importance' of the match, apart from the various participation options, compatibility with the timing of games, sport facilities and other commitments (work, family, etc.) (see Figure 18.5).

In terms of direct participation, *live occasional spectators* 'consume' sport as with any other type of entertainment such as

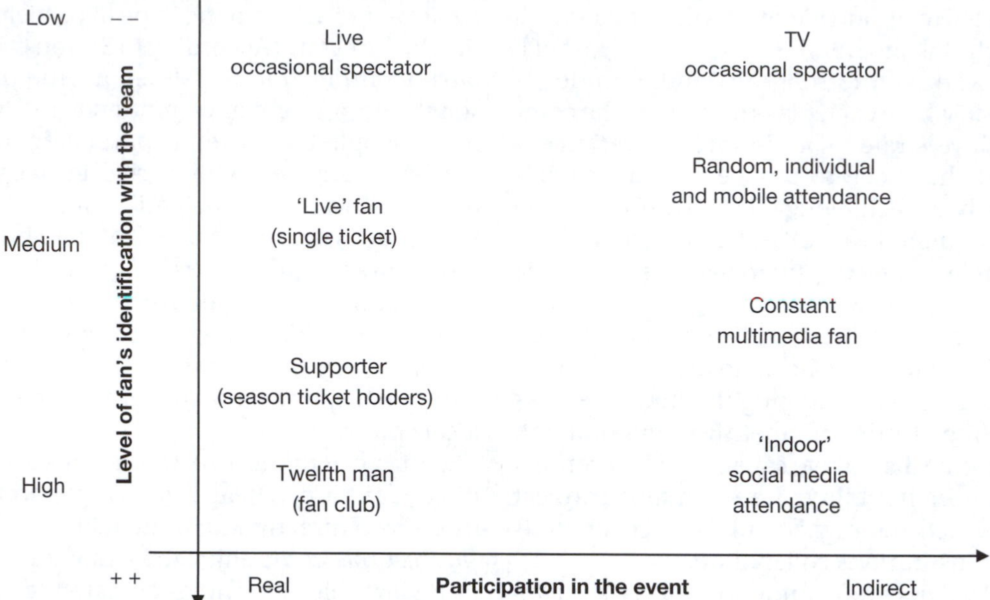

Figure 18.5 Fans' roles.

movies, music concerts, etc. In this group we can also include those people who go to the stadium sporadically to capture the 'aesthetic' dimension of the event, the atmosphere and the 'neat play' on the field.

For the *live fan*, participation in the event is not continuous, but motivated by the importance and the 'drama' of each match. Live fans do not buy a season ticket. Their choice is guided each time in part depending on the 'social' dimension: going to the stadium is a moment of aggregation with other people, friends, family, a way of having a good time together. The *supporter* is not just a spectator, but 'participates' in the event continuously, by purchasing his season ticket to the home games. Despite following each match with excitement the supporter is not an active member of the fan club, even though he/she feels highly motivated and part of the team.

The 'twelfth man', as the term suggests is an essential support to the game and the success of the team as much as the players and coach are. The actions performed by fans during the game (ritual chants, songs, banner waving, etc.) motivate the team and 'intimidate' the other side and thus to an extent, fans' emotions, passions and moods can influence the result of the match. The twelfth man seems to actively and passionately follow every match, both home and away, in national championships and international tournaments. Fans truly believe they must 'participate' in the game to 'help the team win'.[50] What strengthens and distinguishes the role of the twelfth man compared to that of the supporters is the importance he gives to rituals (which he spends a great deal of his time in) and in planning the celebratory routines, the wording to put on the banners, the songs to be chanted, and the coordination of the fan clubs. During pre-match days, fans meet up to discuss their 'scenographic' strategies and keep themselves up-to-date with the line-ups of their own team and the opponents', as well as downloading online statistics on players' performance.

In terms of indirect participation, the growing use of new technologies is largely responsible for the reduction of live spectators. Opportunities offered by the new media have modified fans' behaviour in relation to how they enjoy a game which for years characterized the sports culture rooted in our country.

Occasional TV spectators are those who watch the most important matches both at national and international level (Champions League finals, European and World football championships, etc.) on television. In this case the level of identification with a single team is quite low. What influences the type of participation is the passion for sport. Even when they do not have a 'favourite team', the competitive spirit of football makes them 'take sides'. Spectators' motivation to be a fan of a club can be influenced by multiple intangible factors such as the popularity of a football player, the fame of a club or the passion for a specific jersey or other tangible aspects, such as the country of origin of the teams competing on the pitch, the participation of star players and the refereeing.

Within the segment *random, individual and mobile attendance* we have classified sports fans that 'sporadically' follow football, mainly but not exclusively through websites and mobile phones. Having a general interest for sport, they do not limit themselves to attending matches of a single team but, for example, download onto their laptops and/or phones the most thrilling highlights. Fans included in this category often combine viewing the match with 'live betting' services, where betting on the event is streamed on websites or mobile phones. With the new media, traditional 'passive' participation in a football match is enriched by additional contents which can be enjoyed wherever the spectator is, by maximizing his level of entertainment as being a football (content) and new media (tools) expert.

Constant multimedia fans create virtual communities of people with whom to share their passion for the same team. These fans usually attend matches on pay-TV or through websites that offer live football services. Through multimedia match attendance, fans are not only able to follow their own team, but can even have real-time exchanges of information with other fans, strengthening their own 'ties' with the team. Despite there being no direct participation, the use of new media can increase the fans' voice and the flow of information and comments, increasing the level of attention paid to the team.

The *indoor social media attendance* segment includes fans who *usually* meet up in small groups in public places like cafes, fans' clubs, etc., or in friends' and families' houses for championship and Champions League matches and very often recreate a sort of 'stadium atmosphere'. Although they express a high sense of identification with the team, this group of fans prefers to attend the match by buying a seasonal membership card to a digital or satellite television network, mainly on account of the increasing cost of live matches, the continuous schedule changes, the 'distance' from the venue, etc.

The typology of roles proposed does not set out to be exhaustive, but provides some interpretative indications of the multiple combinations of fans' behaviour in the light of empirical evidence. The representation of roles is not static. The positions (fans' role classification) assumed by fans are closely related to the strategies of the football club both in technical and managerial terms, the role played by the owners, the competitive position of the team, the calendar of events, the media channels on which the sport content is provided (matches, interviews with players and coaches, dedicated channels, etc.), and to social and personal relationships (family, social class, income, etc.). Since *success* is what drives the popularity of a football club, a winning team can generally guarantee greater attendance in terms of fans and spectators. Fan loyalty is in fact a variable 'depending' first and foremost, on the success of a team.

Being included in important championships, achieving victories on the field, together with popularity, history, legend and the international flavour acquired over time by a team, are the prime factors influencing fans' involvement. Nevertheless, the construction of a continuous club-supporters relationship aimed at preserving a certain level of fan loyalty and avoiding lower levels of identification and participation, is developed though the ability of each individual football club to undertake new sports-technical challenges and to set up initiatives able to involve the fans. These initiatives might include tangibles such as the modern management of football venues, an exciting team performance, appealing merchandising, the organization of collateral events, and the offer of additional services (call centre, services online for the fans such as games and chat, info services on mobile phones, etc.).

STRATEGIC POSTURES OF FANS AS A STAKEHOLDER

In concluding this paper the need emerged to explore and offer a possible classification of strategies adopted by fans as stakeholders of a football club. Figure 18.6 was built by counterposing the fans' *inclination to cooperate* with their *inclination to be a threat* to the football club and for the network as a whole. The analytical framework used here is drawn from the theoretical tools proposed by Freeman et al., to outline the strategic behaviour of a firm's stakeholders.[51] The variables in Freeman's model – 'relative cooperative potential' and 'relative competitive threat' – can be applied to the fan community to delineate a first typology of fans' 'strategic postures' and outline the different ways in which the latter are able to influence the decisions of the football club. The graphic representation of Figure 18.6 highlights a continuum of strategic behaviour: from maximum cooperation (*partner*) to dysfunctional behaviour.

Partners have very high cooperative potential, but at the same time may have great control over the football club's decisions and can therefore shape its strategic outcomes. Partner fans can be defined as 'rule setters' and may be particularly opinionated and able to voice their concerns towards the football club. This can be done not only through open letters to the football-club chairman and owners, press releases, speeches on local radio and TV (traditional media), blogs and websites (new media), or sit-ins involving the entire local community, but also through direct contact with the football club's top management, coach and local institutions. Partners are generally an inner circle of fans who do not 'speak' as individuals, but rather it is the fan club which interacts with the other stakeholders (football club, media, local government, etc.). Apart from their official duties of coordinating fans, supporting the team and assisting the football club in managing ticket sales, fan clubs have over the years moved away from being almost 'piloted' by the owners – since it was the club itself which elected the official representatives and chairmen of the fan clubs[52] – to assuming an independent role not only towards the football club, but also towards other stakeholders such as the municipal government and related institutions. Partners' strategic behaviour is therefore distinguished by a high level of freedom of opinion and action toward the football club, but also by their inclination to be 'propositively open'. At the same time, the football club acts towards the partners in a spirit of dialogue and negotiation, involving them in its strategic choices. For example, it usually invites them to official meetings and

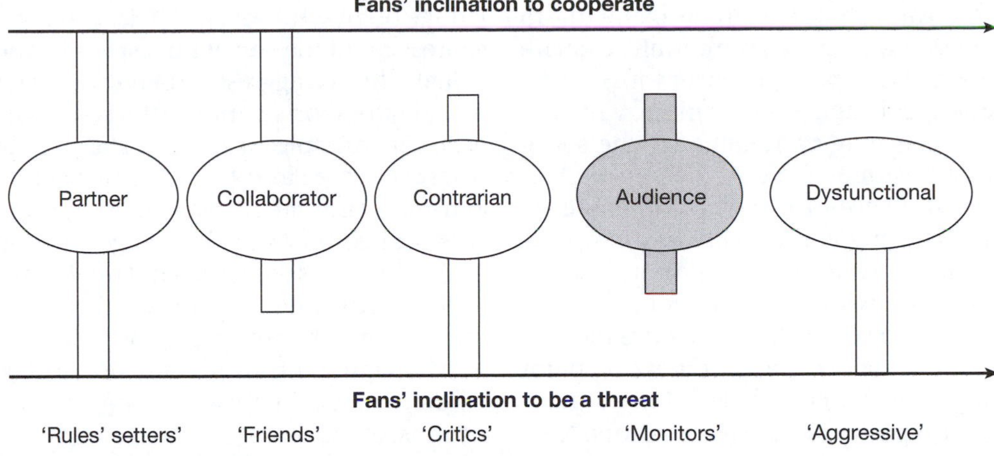

Figure 18.6 Strategic postures of fans as a stakeholder.

Note: Adapted from Freeman, Harrison and Wicks, *Managing for Stakeholders.*

local and national conferences where other stakeholders (e.g., local government, local police, etc.) take part.

The group defined *collaborator* is characterized by a high level of cooperation and a relatively low threat potential. As with partners, the activities performed by this segment of fans assume a 'collective' dimension; it is not the single fan who acts, but rather the association coordinating the fan clubs. The strategic behaviour of the collaborators aims to find 'friendship and dialogue with the football club, thinking of football merely as an exciting sports event'.[53] Their aim is to keep in contact with, and coordinate, each fan club's activities, to maintain direct relationships with football clubs and local institutions, and restore the human side to the match-event; for example, by seeking moments of encounter with the opponents' supporters through the organization of convivial meetings, twin fan clubs, exchanges of team flags and jerseys, etc. Collaborators are an active but moderate part of the fan community. They play an important role in the success of the event in terms of safety and security. The friendly attitude of the fans towards their opponents' supporters[54] can help football clubs, local government and the institutions responsible for public order to manage public safety, welcoming away-fans and controlling the areas around the stadium.

In stark contrast, our model poses *contrarians* as a strong threat to the football club, while having very limited collaboration potential. The contrarians' strategic behaviour enables fans to continually influence the football club's choices responding specifically to an action or a decision of the latter, by spreading counter arguments, refusals, criticisms, etc. This is a rather dangerous strategy for the football club, since this segment of fans does not seem willing to negotiate and collaborate. At the same time, the football club cannot 'ignore them' since they may have a strong influence on achieving competitive goals. If the contrarians do not approve of the football club's decisions, they are openly 'critical' and tend not to activate relationships with other stakeholders, but rather express their own opinions through the new media, such as, blogs, social networks and fans' websites. The threat deriving from this kind of behaviour is amplified by use of the new media: digital technologies contribute to *viral spreading*[55] a general complaint due to the tendency of the fan community to share their emotions and experiences with friends, relatives, colleagues, etc., online, which in some cases may even influence the social and sports atmosphere.

The *audience* are fans who are characterized by having contextually low cooperation and threat levels. This group does not specifically express its position, whether supportive or critical, towards the football club; the audience does not make its point through the media or the fan clubs, as happens with partners and collaborators. Nevertheless, their strategy is not 'neutral' since this stakeholder is an important asset for a football club: by not going to the stadium or not purchasing a pay-TV subscription, they can considerably influence the football club's revenues both in terms of single-ticket and season-ticket sales, and in terms of the audience on television networks. The variation in number of 'indirect' consumers can influence the value of a match's broadcasting rights thus decreasing this segment of revenues. Fans included within the audience react in an indirect way to the choices of the football club, for example, as regards the team line-up and its technical level, the purchase and/or transfer of players, increases in the average prices of tickets and season tickets, etc. Nevertheless, the audience's behaviour is able to negatively influence the number of spectators of the team.

The *dysfunctional*[56] group appear to have a very high threat level and non-existent attitude to collaboration. For these people, the football event is merely an occasion to yell out their anger, frustration and personal dissatisfaction through oral and physical abuse of power, destructive fury and violence towards things and people. Their aggressive behaviour and their violent gestures are scarcely related to the results of the match. Violence is mainly the result of a long process starting in the mind of the individual before the event. It is usually an expression of the social unease of the individual.[57] In fact, aggressive behaviour occurs outside the sports context (the stadium) as well, for example near train stations, bus stops, subways, and takes the form of out-and-out criminal actions (devastation of cars, trains, buses and damage to shops, etc.). The aggressiveness is not only a threat to the football club, but also disrupts the value created by generating negative feedback affecting the entire network of stakeholders (fans, institutions, media, local citizens, etc.).

CONCLUSIONS

A number of articles have been written about the football-fan phenomenon both in the popular press and in academic papers, but not much systematic research has been found related to the role of a football-fan community as regards the way it behaves as stakeholder of its own team. This paper aimed to increase our understanding of the concept of value co-creation in the football sector. Therefore our main research question was: *how can a football-fan community participate in value co-creation?*

To answer this question we referred to the empirical case of ACF Fiorentina, by studying the interaction among all the actors involved within the local social network and trying to highlight the central role of the fan community. Although we are aware of the limits of single case study research, the case of Fiorentina can nevertheless be considered a kind of active and dynamic 'laboratory' from where we tried to draw a first classification of fans' roles and strategic behaviours.

The empirical research illustrated a variety of fans' roles connected to the intensity of the identification with the team and to the type of participation in the event (direct or mediated). The typological articulation of fans' roles goes from a live occasional participation where sport is consumed as with any other type of entertainment (movies, music concerts, etc.) to a continuous participation with the submission of a season membership (*supporter*). The highest level of participation corresponds to the twelfth man, a component as essential to the game as the players and coach. In terms of indirect participation, new media modify fans' behaviour in relation to how they enjoy a football game. Different roles emerged depending on the media channels (TV, mobile phones, internet) through which the game is enjoyed; which, in turn, is closely related to several variables (e.g., the calendar and the location of the matches, the behaviour of friends and relatives with whom to watch the game, etc.).

In terms of strategies adopted by a fan community as a stakeholder of a football team, this paper develops a first classification of *strategic postures* that have been built by matching the 'inclination to cooperate' with the 'threat potential' of the fans. Building on Freeman's work, the empirical case highlights a variety of strategic behaviours that move along a continuum. On one extreme side there are *partners*; this group of fans have a great cooperative potential, but at the same time they are particularly opinionated and often they can considerably influence the football club's strategic choices. Nevertheless partners are propositively open to dialogue and negotiation. On the other extreme we found fans that have a very high level of threat to the club (*dysfunctional*) and their aggressiveness disrupts the value created for the social network. In the middle of the continuum we have identified three other strategic positions of fans. *Collaborators* are an active but moderate part of the fan community. They play an important role, especially on the sport side of the team, by helping the club to maintain a safe and secure environment. *Contrarians* are fans that can pose a strong threat to the football club since they do not want to collaborate. If contrarians do not approve of the club's decisions, they are openly critical and tend not to activate relationships with other stakeholders. The *audience* are fans with contextually low cooperation and threat levels. They do not specifically express their position, whether supportive or critical. Nevertheless, their strategy is not neutral since by not going to the stadium or not purchasing a pay-TV subscription, they can considerably influence the football club's revenues.

The typological articulation of roles and strategic postures proposed here is not exhaustive and therefore does not exclude the exploration of additional fan behaviours through further research. However, the empirical evidence of Fiorentina illustrates the viola fans' specificity as stakeholder of their team. In a global football environment where 'productive resources' like players and coaches come from different countries and not within their team's local context, and where football ownership is often the expression of foreign investors, fans frequently develop 'emotional relations' with top international teams (e.g., Manchester United, Inter, Barcelona, etc.). Indeed, the media broadcasting of football matches and the process of global branding pursued by several clubs have favoured the growth of worldwide supporters' communities.

Against these currents, the Fiorentina football club is an example where the strong local identity between the fans and the club is still persistent, irrespective of the fact that other stakeholders, like players, the coach and the owner are 'non Florentine'. The territorial identity between the team and the fan community is an intangible asset that is crucial to the continued growth and survival of the club. Indeed Fiorentina's fans are repositories of the history and the Viola cultural continuity. They play a role that goes beyond that of the twelfth man: fans do not only support the team by following every match, but through the fan clubs they can speak their voice, they interact with the football club and other stakeholders (owner, coach, local institutions, etc.), and they are involved in its strategic choices. The viola fans play a leading role within the social network of Fiorentina by helping to create value through commitment, collaboration and social participation, which seems to compensate for the continuous evolutions and changes of the technical results, the players, the owners and the coach. The very strong territorial tie existing between the fans and the local context, the attachment to the 'viola jersey' in itself, and the high level of identification with the city and the team make the viola supporters a key determinant stakeholder for the value creation process within the Fiorentina's social network.

NOTES

1 Although the authors have shared their research work, Patrizia Zagnoli has written: Introduction; Mapping stakeholders of a professional club; Towards a typology of sports fans' roles and behaviours. Elena Radicchi has written: Customers: the 'Viola' fans; Socio-demographic features of the 'viola' fans; Fans organizational structure: the Viola Clubs; The social network of ACF Fiorentina; Strategic postures of fans as a stakeholder; Conclusions.
2 See Zagnoli et al., 'L'identità collettiva viola'.
3 Associazione Centro Coordinamento Viola Club, Associazione Tifosi Fiorentina, Collettivo Autonomo Viola.
4 Freeman, Harrison and Wicks, *Managing for Stakeholders;* Harrison, Bosse and Phillips, 'Managing for Stakeholders'; Rowley, 'Moving Beyond Dyadic Ties'.
5 For network analysis compare Burt, 'Range'; Freeman, White and Romney, *Research Methods;* Håkansson and Snehota, 'Analysing Business Relationships'; Gummesson, *Marketing Relazionale;* Mitchell, Agle and Wood, 'Toward a Theory'; Rowley, 'Moving Beyond Dyadic Ties'; Salvini, *Analisi delle reti sociali;* Scott, *Social Network Analysis;* Wasserman and Faust, *Social Network Analysis.*
6 Lusch and Vargo, 'Service-dominant Logic'; Lusch and Vargo, *Service-dominant Logic of Marketing.*
7 Normann and Ramirez, *Le strategie interattive di impresa.*
8 Freeman, *Strategic Management;* Harrison *et al.*, *Managing for stakeholders.*
9 Harrison, Bosse and Phillips, 'Managing for Stakeholders'.
10 Freeman, *Strategic Management,* 25.
11 Freeman, *Strategic Management;* Harrison Bosse and Phillips, 'Managing for Stakeholders'.
12 The term 'viola' means 'violet', i.e., a bluish-purple colour, and this is the colour of 'la Fiorentina's' jerseys, hence the fans team formal name *viola.*
13 The season tickets sales for the ACF Fiorentina rose from more than six million euro in 2007/2008 to eight million euro in 2008/2009. Source: Poesio, 'Poveri, ma belli', 10–11.
14 The stadium where the Fiorentina plays its home games is named 'Artemio Franchi'.
15 See Lega Calcio, *Analisi del trend.*
16 Muniz and O'Guinn, 'Brand Community'.
17 Sitz and Amine, 'Consommation at groups de consommateurs', 3.
18 Maffesoli, Le temps des tribus, *18.*
19 Zagnoli et al., 'L'identità collettiva viola'.
20 Ibid.
21 See Lega Calcio, Analisi del trend.
22 Curva Fiesole is the place to be for chants, songs, drums and non-stop team support; thus it is the area in the stadium where most young people are found.
23 The number of subscribers that hold a university degree is lower than that with a high-school diploma and a middle-school certificate.
24 The place where traditionally young and senior Fiorentina's supporters meet up to discuss matches results, technical aspects of the team, players performance, etc., is the 'Bar Marisa', which is located near the stadium Artemio Franchi.
25 Average number of live spending spectators for each match. Source: Lega Calcio, *Analisi del trend.*
26 Average number of Sky spectators for each match. Source: Lega Calcio, *Analisi del trend.*
27 Mediaset Premium broadcasts Champions League matches, while Dahlia TV offers a full package with all the Fiorentina home and away games.
28 Cova, 'Community and Consumption'.

29 The Operational Group for Security includes representatives of the police headquarters, local municipality, fire department, health service, besides representatives of the guest team and local fan clubs.

30 For example, the ACCVC, one of the most well organized supporters associations, has implemented an SMS service to communicate in real time with all the Viola Club Chairmen. This service enables each club to be up-to-date on changes of instructions, new services and general meetings of the Association.

31 Some fan clubs have registered a trademark – the *Indiano* – expression of the Curva Fiesole clubs, to be placed on their merchandise. In this case the Viola Club seem to provide for the football club deficit, by offering products and gadgets that satisfy the particular needs of fans, first and foremost, with regard to the price.

32 During the months before the football club's failure, through the local press and other media, fans succeeded in informing the whole city about the financial crash Fiorentina was heading for. They also organized initiatives aimed at increasing the level of protest, such as the famous torchlight procession of April 2001 in the streets of the city centre which involved over 30,000 fans, or the boycotting of season tickets subscription, and so on.

33 After bankruptcy hit the former owner Cecchi Gori, on 1 August 2002, AC Fiorentina also failed. The same day, in the light of several initiatives, demonstrations, and sit-ins by the supporters and local citizens during the previous weeks, the Mayor and the Sport Councillor of Florence, following the FIGC resolution allowing 'expression' of a team representing the city, founded a new football club: Fiorentina 1926-Florentia Srl, with the Mayor as president. In the following days the football club was transferred to a new owner, the business man Diego Della Valle.

34 *Lawsuits* contemplated by some representatives of Viola Clubs have been central in expressing their disagreement with the decisions made by the Florentine Court, the FIGC and the Lega Calcio. Those acts were aimed at speaking out against a 'sick' football system widespread among many professional teams which were not penalized as Fiorentina was.

35 Håkansson and Snehota, 'Analysing Business Relationships'; Gummesson, *Marketing Relazionale;* Mitchell, Agle and Wood, 'Toward a Theory'; Scott, *Social Network Analysis;* Wasserman and Faust, *Social Network Analysis.*

36 Freeman, White and Romney, *Research Methods.*

37 The graphic representation of the network is the result of qualitative analysis without the use of specific statistical software. The connections between focal organizations and stakeholders were developed by interpreting the results of interviews and discussion groups.

38 Network density is the *extent to which all actors in the network are connected.* It describes the general level of linkage among members and measures the ratio of the number of ties that exists in the network to the number of possible ties, if each network member were tied to every other member (Scott, *Social Network Analysis*).

39 Network centrality refers to an individual actor's position in the network relative to others. Centrality measures the extent to which communication within a network passes through an actor. Network centrality refers to power obtained through the network's structure (Rowley, 'Moving Beyond Dyadic Ties').

40 Burt, 'Range'.

41 On concept of 'closeness', see Rowley, 'Moving Beyond Dyadic Ties'.

42 Following the failure of the football club and its rebirth in 2002, the team went to the well known Italian entrepreneur Della Valle, for the first time ever a 'non Florentine' owner. Although not Florentine, the new owner won support for his operational, technical and business choices. He started a process of creating collaborative relationships in the city, among supporters, institutions and the football team.

43 Istat, *Indagine Multiscopo sulle famiglie 'Aspetti della vita quotidiana'.*

44 Taken from the blog of a Fiorentina fan. See www.blog.libero.it/archiaraviola/5735501.html.

45 Becattini, *Lo sviluppo economico della Toscana.*

46 Bagnasco, *Tre Italie.*

47 By way of comparison, the signing budget of a team such as Inter FC, considered among the top international and national clubs is about 150 million euro a year and coach Mourinho's salary is about eight million euro net per season. In the case of Fiorentina, the annual signing budget is about 35 million euro and the coach Prandelli earns a net salary of slightly under two million euro. See www.legacalcio.it.

48 Harada, Saito and Hirose, 'Segmentation of Sports Fans'; Hunt, Bristol and Bashaw, 'A Conceptual Approach'; Kozanli and Samiei, 'Segmenting the Football Audience'; Tapp and Clowes, 'From Carefree Casuals'.

49 Sutton, McDonald and Milne, 'Creating and Fostering', 15; Finn and Giulianotti, 'Scottish Fans'.

50 As an example consider some banners written by the Fiorentina fans for the Champions League match Fiorentina–Liverpool, 29 October 2009: *'Our faith is your strength', 'Fedelissimi', 'A unique city, a never ending love'.*

51 Freeman, Harrison and Wicks, *Managing for Stakeholders.*

52 In Italy, the control of the fan club by the football club was justified by the relevant economic support given to the former, which very often in return entailed the possibility for the owners to name the majority of fan clubs' representatives and chairmen. See Papa and Panico, *Storia sociale del calcio in Italia.*

53 See Sancassani, *La voce dei tifosi.*

54 For example, for the Champions League match Fiorentina–Liverpool (29 September 2009), some fans from the Collettivo Autonomo Viola launched a twin fan club initiative with the English supporters, called the 'Reds' after the colour of the team's jerseys, welcoming them before the match outside the stadium, exchanging flags and jerseys and expressing their friendship through chants and banners such as 'Reds, your name is a legend'.

55 Wilson, 'Six Simple Principles'.

56 Hunt, Bristol and Bashaw, 'A Conceptual Approach'.

57 Elias and Dunning, *Quest for Excitement.*

REFERENCES

Bagnasco, A. *Tre Italie. La problematica territoriale dello sviluppo italiano.* Bologna: Il Mulino, 1977.

Becattini, G. *Lo sviluppo economico della Toscana, con particolare riguardo all'industrializzazione leggera.* Firenze: IRPET, 1975.

Burt, R.S. 'Range'. In *Applied Network Analysis. A Methodological Introduction,* edited by R.S. Burt and M.J. Minor, 176–194. Beverly Hills: Sage, 1983.

Cova, B. 'Community and Consumption. Toward a Definition of the Linking Value of Products or Services'. *European Journal of Marketing* 31, no. 3 (1997): 297–316.

Elias, N., and E. Dunning. *Quest for Excitement. Sport and Leisure in the Civilization Process.* Oxford: Basil Blackwell, 1989.

Finn, G.P.T., and R. Giulianotti. 'Scottish Fans, not English Hooligans! Scots, Scottishness, and Scottish Football'. In *Popular Culture. Production and Consumption,* edited by C.L. Harrington and D.D. Bielby, 314–27. Oxford: Blackwell Publishing, 2001.

Freeman, E.R. *Strategic Management: A Stakeholder Approach.* Boston, MA: Pitman, 1984.

Freeman, R.E., J.S. Harrison, and A.C. Wicks. *Managing for Stakeholders: Survival, Reputation, and Success.* New Haven and London: Yale University Press, 2007.

Freeman, L.C., D.R. White, and A.K. Romney, eds. *Research Methods in Social Network Analysis.* Fairfax, VA: George Mason University Press, 1992.

Gummesson, E. *Marketing Relazionale.* Milano: Hoepli, 2006.

Håkansson, H., and I. Snehota. 'Analyzing Business Relationships'. In *Understanding Business Markets,* edited by D. Ford, 151–75. London: The Dryden Press, 1995.

Harada, M., R. Saito, and M. Hirose. 'Segmentation of Sports Fans Using the Experiential Value Scale'. Conference Proceedings, 17th Annual European Sport management Conference EASM, Amsterdam, 16–19 September 2009.

Harrison, J.S., D.A. Bosse, and R.A. Phillips. 'Managing for Stakeholders, Stakeholder Utility Functions and Competitive Advantage'. Working Paper, University of Richmond, VA, February 2009.

Hunt, K.A., T. Bristol, and R.E. Bashaw. 'A Conceptual Approach to Classifying Sport Fans'. *Journal of Services Marketing* 13, no. 6 (1999): 439–52.

Istat. *Indagine Multiscopo sulle famiglie 'Aspetti della vita quotidiana'.* Roma: Istat, 2008.

Kozanli, A., and M. Samiei. 'Segmenting the Football Audience. A Market Study Based on Live Attendance'. Master Thesis, Stockholm University School of Business, 2007.

Lega Calcio. *Analisi del trend degli spettatori allo stadio e degli ascolti televisivi della Serie A TIM e della Serie B TIM,* 30 May 2009.

Lusch, R.F., and S.L. Vargo. 'Service-dominant Logic: Reactions, Reflections and Refinements'. *Marketing Theory* 6, no. 3 (2006): 281–8.

Lusch, R.F., and S.L. Vargo, eds. *The Service-dominant Logic of Marketing: Dialog, Debate, and Directions.* Armonk, NY: ME Sharpe, 2006.

Maffesoli, M. *Le temps des tribus, le decline de l'individualisme dans les sociétérs postmodernes.* Paris: La Table Ronde, 1988.

Mitchell, R.K., B.R. Agle, and D.J. Wood. 'Toward a Theory of Stakeholder Identification and Salience: Defining the Principles of Who and What Really Counts'. *Academy of Management Review* 22, no. 4 (1997): 853–86.

Muniz, A.M., and T.C. O'Guinn. 'Brand Community'. *Journal of Consumer Research* 27 (March 2001): 412–32.

Normann, R., and R. Ramirez. *Le strategie interattive di impresa.* Milano: Etas Libri, 1995.

Papa, P., and G. Panico. *Storia sociale del calcio in Italia.* Bologna: Il Mulino, 1993.

Poesio, E. 'Poveri, ma belli'. *Corriere della Sera,* 3 July 2009.

Rowley, T.J. 'Moving Beyond Dyadic Ties: A Network Theory of Stakeholder Influences Author(s)'. *The Academy of Management Review* 22, no. 4 (October, 1997): 887–910.

Salvini, A., ed. *Analisi delle reti sociali: teorie, metodi, applicazioni.* Milano: Franco Angeli, 2007.

Sancassani, M. *La voce dei tifosi*, Italian Federation of Football Club supporters, June 2009.

Scott, J. *Social Network Analysis: A Handbook*. London: Sage, 2000.

Sitz, L., and A. Amine. 'Consommation at groups de consommateurs, de la tribu postmoderne aux communautés de marque: Pour une clarification des concepts'. Colloque 'Societè et Consommation', Rouen, 11–12 March 2004.

Sutton, W.A., M.A. McDonald, and G.R. Milne. 'Creating and Fostering Fan Identification in Professional Sports'. *Sport Marketing Quarterly* 6, no. 1 (1997): 15–22.

Tapp, A., and J. Clowes. 'From Carefree Casuals to Professional Wanderers: Segmentation Possibilities for Football Supporters'. *European Journal of Marketing* 36, no. 11–12 (2002): 1248–69.

Wasserman, S., and K. Faust. *Social Network Analysis: Methods and Applications*. New York: Cambridge University Press, 1994.

Wilson, R. 'The Six Simple Principles of Viral Marketing'. *The Web Marketing Today*, no. 70, 2000.

Zagnoli, P., D. Fanti, E. Radicchi, and E. Lamanna. 'L'identità collettiva viola: Analisi socio-economica degli abbonati della ACF Fiorentina (2003–2004)'. Università di Firenze, Giugno, 2004.

SECTION 4

The Political Economy and the Politics of Sports: Dynamics and Diffusion

In 1936, Harold Lasswell wrote a book about politics; its title became the popular definition of the term: *Who Gets What, When and How* (Lasswell, 1936). As we discussed in Section 1, **power**—the central dynamic of politics—is at the root of the explanation for how valued resources are distributed.

In this Section, we will be examining how sport, in its many manifestations, intersects with power and politics. We begin with a short "note on power" that re-orients the reader to one of the central concepts we use to understand the sport/society relationship. We then move to examine the many ways that sports and politics ostensibly do not—and, as many believe, should not—mix. And, we explore the many ways that they *do*. We then introduce "**political economy**" as a prism through which we can understand sport as a big business that faces economic challenges but does so in a political context. Next we examine the power of the media in sport, which shifts the context to a more global level and leads us to consider global labor mobility, national differences in support for sports, and how variations in countries' ideological and political commitments affect sports. Drawing on these ideas about power and politics, we explore how groups mobilize (or do not) to contest power differentials within sports and society, and how these vary by sport, country, league, team, and individual athletes.

POWER, THE "PURITY" OF SPORT, AND POLITICAL ECONOMY

In order to explore how sport affects and is affected by the specific distribution of power that exists in a given society, it is important to have a clear idea of what we mean by power, how it manifests itself, and how it seeps into existing societal arrangements. In contrast, sport presents itself as a "world apart"—a space that is imbued simply with fair competition and love of the game. As a frame for this chapter on power and politics, however, we discuss the ways that sport, politics, and power are deeply implicated with one another. This is where the idea of political economy comes in; it is central to understanding the economic and political dynamics discussed in the remainder of the Section.

A NOTE ON POWER

As discussed in Section 1, we focus extensively on power relations as fundamental to our understanding of society and of sport in society.[1] When there is a direct conflict between two parties, we can easily see who wins and who loses; usually, it is simply the one with greater resources on her/his side.[2] These resources may be the kinds of **capitals** that Bourdieu refers to as **economic**, **cultural**, and **social**. We can also notice power being used to prevent people from even competing for a given outcome. So, the powerful elites who wish to build a stadium may prevent the group that wishes to stop it from even getting on the agenda of the city or state agency that will decide the issue.

We can also imagine situations in which people "naturally" act in ways that seem contrary to their own interests and consistent with the interests of those with whom we might expect them to be at odds. When this happens, we might say, with Marxist theorists (see Section 1), that we have a situation in which a particular ideology is **hegemonic**. When people simply act "naturally," that is, according to their **habitus** (as Bourdieu would say), they are in essence following a cultural inheritance that is very difficult to resist. Bourdieu suggests that this "natural" inclination becomes inscribed in the body, such that people simply follow their quasi-instinctual notions: "The most successful ideological effects are those which have no need for words, and ask no more than complicitous silence" (Bourdieu, 1977: 188).[3] There is an "unthinking" aspect to this notion of power. Barrington Moore tries to capture this idea, using a broad array of "motivations" (cited by Lukes, 2005:122):

> The assumption of inertia, that social and cultural continuity does not require explanation, obliterates the fact that both have to be recreated anew in each generation, often with great pain and suffering. To maintain and transmit a value system, human beings are punched, bullied, sent to gaol, thrown into concentration camps, cajoled, bribed, made into heroes, encouraged to read newspapers, stood up against a wall and shot, and sometimes even taught sociology. To speak of cultural inertia is to overlook the concrete interests and privileges that are served by indoctrination, education, and the entire complicated process of transmitting culture from one generation to the next.
>
> (Moore, 1967: 486).

Power, then, is ubiquitous but it is often difficult to notice because it appears to be operating quite "naturally." So, when the corporate elites in a given city are aligned with the masses on spending millions for a new stadium while the schools are starved for basic educational resources, we can think about how power is implicated in this "natural" love for our sports team.

THE PURITY OF SPORT AND ITS IRONIES

When we watch our favorite teams and sports stars, we generally don't think about—or want to think about—their political opinions. Our devotion to the idea of an apolitical "purity of sport" is such that an athlete or other sports figure who makes a political statement is likely to attract considerable controversy and criticism. Indeed, during the run-up to the Iraq war in 2003, a silent protest by Toni Smith, a Manhattanville College student and basketball player—turning her back to the US flag during the national anthem—led to press conferences, sold-out basketball games in the 300-seat arena, and counter-protests that vilified Smith for her anti-war, anti-veteran, anti-flag behavior (Pennington, 2003). Although we are accustomed to movie actors getting involved politically, we don't want our more athletic entertainers doing so.

Why is this? What is behind this idea that our sports should be, somehow, pure and unsullied by the "dirt" of politics? In part, our aversion to mixing sports and politics is due to the fact that many of us play and follow sports precisely because it is something that occurs outside the stresses and vicissitudes of daily life. It is our way of escaping from concerns about money and politics. This is probably why fans often complain about the money that athletes make, but not about the profits of the owners who pay those athletes—as if the ballplayers, since they're playing a game, should *not* be concerned about money but the owners, who are managing the game, are simply doing what business folks do.

Further, many of us are attracted to sport because we truly love to experience the wonders of the human body engaged in intentional, competitive play. This was our orientation the first time we caught, threw, hit, or kicked a ball (or ball-like object) and this encounter captivated us. As we matured, we grew to play more and follow more, engaging more deeply with our own, our favorite players', and our favorite teams' progress (and regress). Since only a miniscule percentage of us play sports professionally, we have an *amateur's* appreciation of this domain of social life. The root of the word "amateur" is "to love." So, when we think about sports, we think—not about money. . .not about power and politics—but about something we love.

Yet today, the concept of the "purity of sport" is laden with ironies. First, despite our love of our teams, we have also come to recognize just how impure the professional game is, affected by the cash nexus and all its ramifications. Indeed, during the course of the last half-century, we have witnessed massive changes in the nature of capitalism and, since sports are a part of this system, in sports. Major sports organizations have transitioned from family capitalism to corporate capitalism,[4] with all the baggage that that implies. The era in which bonds of loyalty connected owners and employees, or teams and cities, has ended. Just as corporate manufacturing firms relocate plants in pursuit of higher profits, corporate sports owners (usually with the assent of the league and their fellow owners) leave cities and their fans in pursuit of better deals in terms of stadiums, parking, concessions, and the like.

Second, it is ironic that the very organization (in the US, at least) that touts athletic purity—where amateurs play for the "love of the game"—runs one of the most lucrative businesses on the sports scene. For its Division I basketball championship tournament (March Madness—a 68-team tournament that occurs in a three-week period), the National Collegiate Athletic Association (NCAA) signed a contract in 2010 with CBS and Turner for almost $11 billion over a 14-year period (at least $740 million per year) (Wolverton, 2010). Contracts for Division I football are more complicated to summarize, since they are signed by individual conferences and involve a financially complicated Bowl Championship Series. *Forbes*, however, has calculated "the most valuable conferences in college sports" (Smith, 2013) using NCAA tournament payouts, bowl game revenues, and television deals. According to their figures, as of 2013 the Big Ten is the most valuable conference with revenues of $310M per year, followed by the Pac-12 with $303M, and the SEC with $293M. With deals being renegotiated and the conferences realigning with different teams, these figures and rankings will change; how lucrative the business of college sports is will not.[5] We will discuss the NCAA later.

Third, it is certainly ironic that we think of sports and politics as somehow disconnected when so many powerful forces have intervened in how the games have been played. Don't we need to invoke politics and power—who gets what, when, and how—to understand blacks' exclusion from baseball from the 1880s until 1947, Jewish sprinter Marty Glickman's exclusion from the 1936 Berlin Olympic Games, and the singing of the national anthem and/or "God Bless America" at baseball games? In the Middle East, the connections among royals, the military, and soccer teams could not be closer.[6] There has even been an actual war between countries—the Honduras-El Salvador Soccer War of 1969—that is directly connected to a sports contest (see Barrett et al., 2013). So, the idea that sports is or should be "pure"—somehow, above or separate from politics—is, at best, idealistic, and at worst, ludicrous.

WHAT IS POLITICAL ECONOMY?

"Political economy" was the term used to describe the kinds of analyses produced by Adam Smith, David Ricardo, and Karl Marx in the eighteenth and nineteenth centuries. This approach recognizes that economic activities occur within a political context and that attention to power is fundamental to an understanding of both economic and political transactions. You might recognize this approach as consistent with the kind of field analysis that we introduced in Section 1. In thinking about how players, owners, teams, and leagues operate as they pursue their interests, we need to be aware of the resources that are available to them as well as to their competitors. These actors have particular political orientations, reflecting their social origins, their current structural location, and the ideological contexts in which they have been immersed. Thus, in this Section, we will explore the ways that those involved in sports pursue their interests in a power-laden context.

SPORT IS BIG MONEY: TWO EXAMPLES

If it is not already obvious from the previous discussion, we need to recognize that sport is big business and its reach is long. We reviewed the industry financial data in Section 1 but it is worth re-emphasizing. When we discuss sport—and this varies in different countries—we are sometimes discussing government ministries, economic elites, public policy, "the media," and international networks of conflict and cooperation. We are also discussing taxation and public expenditures: how much people are taxed and how those monies are used. Are public funds used to support stadium construction or schools? Olympic training facilities or health care? Finally, we are talking about the conditions under which people (for example, sports team owners) invest and the conditions under which they labor (say, professional athletes). All of this adds up to a significant segment of the national and global economy.

BIG BUSINESS IN COLLEGE SPORTS

To delve into the thorny thicket of the sports business, let's examine college sports in the United States.[7] Imagine a fictional college football program from Football State University (FSU).[8]

This representation of FSU's organizational field[9] orients us to the many constraints and opportunities that a football program faces. The opportunities involve its ability to attract

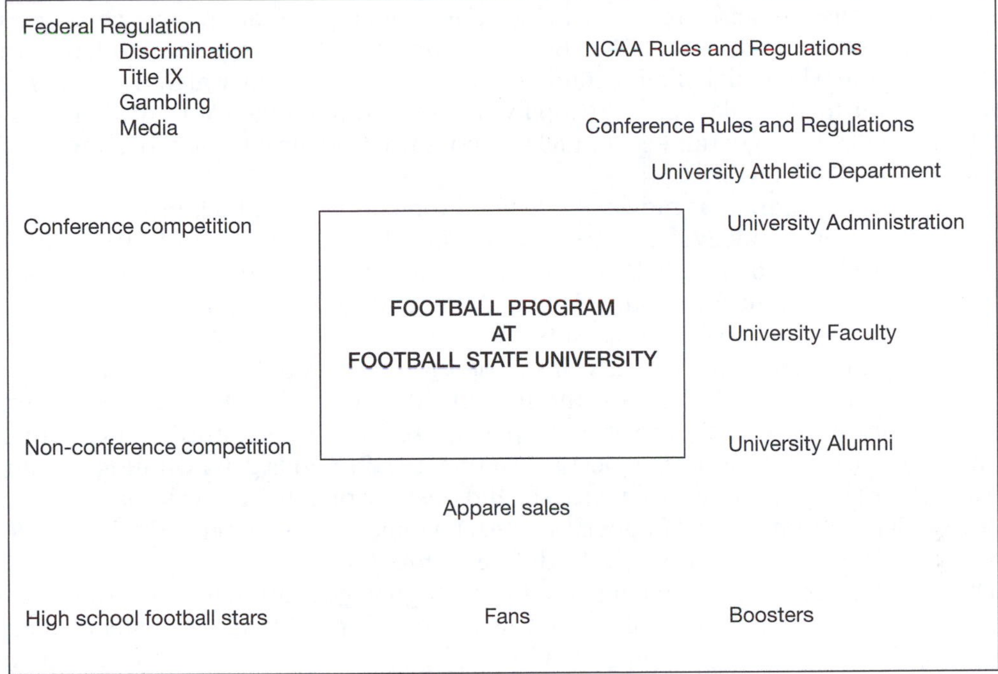

Figure 4.1 Football State University's resources and hopes/dreams for its football program are dependent on many other actors. In a different context, Benford (2007) sees this as a "multiorganizational field." See Washington and Karen (2010: xviii)

funds—ticket and apparel sales are obvious sources—and recruit players for its team. This is not, however, something the team or athletic program can do by itself; beyond its alumni and boosters (though not to minimize these), its ability to raise money and recruit blue-chip athletes is dependent largely on its connection to the NCAA, its conference's money deals, and television exposure.[10] High school athletes, especially those with aspirations for a professional career, are very much attracted to programs that have a high proportion of their games on television. The constraints have to do with getting various university stakeholders (for example, an often reluctant faculty) to support them, other expenses that confront the athletics department (e.g., supporting non-revenue producing sports as well as women's sports—thanks to Title IX), and the rules and regulations that affect recruitment efforts (especially, NCAA rules and regulations—when can contact be made? Under what circumstances? How often?).[11]

In thinking about the organizational field for a Division I football program, then, we must recognize that its aspirations and strategies for success are rooted in a political and economic context that is shaped by powerful forces in the larger society. Large football programs are multi-million dollar businesses that are almost always the largest component of a university's athletics budget. They have enormous expenses, ranging from the often astronomical salary for the head coach[12] down to the costs of equipment, travel, and staffing the ticket office. Since there is usually no additional expense associated with having a media contract,[13] media corporations strongly affect the amount of money that is available to sustain these programs. In fact, one could argue that the large corporations that pay for television rights (ESPN/ABC, CBS, Fox, etc.) encourage the "athletics arms race" across the whole higher education sector.[14] According to the Knight Commission's report, "Restoring the Balance,"[15] the top five athletic conferences (ACC, Big Ten, Big 12, Pac 12, and SEC) have guaranteed annual revenues from media contracts of almost $1.1B (as of October, 2011).

At the same time, there is radical inequality in the degree to which institutions profit from their athletic endeavors. According to *USA Today*'s analysis of 2012 athletics expenditures, only 23 of the 228 Division I public institutions covered their expenses and only seven (!) did not receive a subsidy from their institutions. A number of institutions had to rely heavily on institutional subsidies: in 2012, for example, Rutgers athletics covered its $28M deficit with $17.5M from the university and $9.5M from student fees (Berkowitz et al., 2013). Public institutions subsidize their athletic teams with funds garnered from state subsidies; so, state taxpayers are, in effect, supporting these athletic teams. From the institution's perspective, all they need to do is get a winning season or two and their ticket revenues will skyrocket and postseason revenues will soar. This, they believe, will put them in good financial shape. Obviously, the numbers, which have been relatively stable from year to year, tell a different story.[16]

The political economy perspective situates higher educational institutions in an organizational field and, as we will explain, also helps us understand the higher education tuition crisis. In Table 4.1, we compiled the Knight Commission data (referred to above) on changes in spending for athletics and academics from 2005 to 2010.

Table 4.1 shows clearly that as one moves from the most competitive FBS to the less competitive FCS to the non-football schools, the increases get smaller. More damning of the sports focus is the ratio of athletics spending per athlete to the spending per full-time-equivalent student. In 2010, at the high end, the Southeastern Conference (SEC) median was more than twelve times the median academic spending per student. The conference at the low end of the athletic/academic ratio was the Mid-American (MAC) conference at "only" four times. In general, at FBS schools, athletics spending outpaced academic spending by a factor of 6.7; at FCS schools, by a factor of 3.1; and at non-football schools by 3.3. While spending on head coaches explains part of this imbalance, there are many other costs associated with athletics that have no parallels on the academic side. Insurance for athletes, field/stadium/arena upkeep, equipment, and athletic staff are just some of the costs of doing business in this expensive venture.

Table 4.1 Increases in Median Spending for Different Types of Higher Educational Institutions

	% Increases in median spending from 2005 to 2010		
	**FBS*	*FCS*	*D-I-NF*
Athletics spending per athlete	51	48	39
Institutional funding for athletics per athlete	61	42	38
Academic spending per student	23	22	11

* FBS: Football Bowl Subdivision; FCS: Football Championship Subdivision; D-I-NF: Division I—No Football

Source: Knight Commission (2012).

At the same time, we have to understand all of these cost pressures in the context of fiscal pressures on governments. Other than the impact of the 2008 recession, state government tax revenues have not trended in any reliable way. According to the Tax Policy Center (Urban Institute and Brookings Institution), "State own-source revenue[17] measured as a share of GDP [Gross Domestic Product] increased 27 percent between 1977 and 2008 from 5.9 percent of GDP to 7.5 percent. The Great Recession has caused a slight drop in state own-source revenues to 6.8 percent in 2010." Thus, over the last 33 years state own-source revenues grew by only 15 percent (less than 0.5 percent per year). Another major source of state tax revenues, personal income taxes, held constant (proportionately) at 10 percent of all revenues through this period. In the context of these relatively stagnant state revenues, the changes in state appropriations for higher education since 2008 are stark: 48 of 50 states have decreased their contributions to higher education, with 37 of them decreasing their appropriations by over 20 percent. At the same time, all states increased their tuition and fees, with over half increasing them by over 20 percent.[18] So, from a political economy perspective, when we think very concretely about universities' athletics spending in the context of a state fiscal crisis, we see just how consequential these athletic expenditures can be. State contributions to higher education decline, athletic expenditures soar (compared to academic expenditures) and tuition, therefore, must go up.

To understand better why this very rich industry is only profitable for a few institutions, let's examine the revenues and expenditures of one institution—the University of Michigan—that generally receives no subsidy (or only a small one). Using figures from the Athletic Director's report to the Regents for the 2010–2012 operating budgets (University of Michigan Regents, 2011), we see that in Fiscal Year 2010, Michigan's athletics personnel expenses came to $34M. Sports program expenses (such as equipment, recruiting, training, and medical expenses) were $15.6M. Facilities, including repairs, supplies, and utilities, cost $8M. Finally, other operating and administrative expenses (everything from postage and insurance to Big 10 conference dues) were $5.7M. Thanks largely to having one of the largest football stadiums in the country, net revenues for spectator admissions for Michigan athletic teams' home games was $38.4M. In addition, they received almost $20M from selling premium luxury seats at the Big House and a similar amount from the Big 10 for television, the NCAA for the basketball tournament, and for football bowl games. With help from these revenue sources, Michigan emerged in the black. The point is that the University of Michigan Department of Athletics, all by itself, is a very large business! And this large business would not be successful—that is, avoid deficits—if all the different revenue sources weren't producing at full steam.

STADIUM CONSTRUCTION AND THE PUBLIC PURSE

Professional sports teams develop very strong connections with their localities. In the US, for example, the Boston Red Sox, the Dallas Cowboys, and the Los Angeles Lakers are identified strongly with their cities. Since leagues have been given control over issues of expansion and contraction through exemptions from US antitrust laws (officially, only in baseball, but leagues usually work with their franchises to control team mobility), teams are assured that they will only have local competition (for example, the NY Knicks and Brooklyn Nets in New York City or the White Sox and Cubs in Chicago) if the league as a whole approves. No upstart basketball team can simply locate itself in, say, Indianapolis and challenge the Pacers, unless the NBA approves. At the same time, the Pacers can make demands on the local and state governments to provide incentives for them to stay in town rather than leave for greener pastures. Indeed, the Conseco Fieldhouse (now named the Bankers Life Fieldhouse), built in 1999, was almost entirely (96 percent)[19] financed by Indiana taxpayers while the profits are, of course, pocketed by the team owners. And this is not an isolated case; facilities built or renovated since then for which taxpayers also bore at least 96 percent of the capital costs (Long, 2013: 110ff.) include Buffalo's Ralph Wilson stadium (100 percent public share of capital cost—1999); Oklahoma City's Ford Center (100 percent—2002); Houston's Toyota Center (100 percent—2003); Memphis' FedEx Forum (100 percent—2004); and Pittsburgh's Consol Energy Center (96 percent—2010).

Long (2013:110ff.) goes further in her analysis of public costs by estimating the public share of capital costs PLUS ongoing costs. She explains that the real, full public costs can only be estimated because they should include not only the construction costs (including land and infrastructure) but also operations, demolition, re-purposing—the full life-cycle of the project. The estimates are affected by whether the project is an arena or a stadium (arenas cost less to build, have lower foregone property taxes, and can be used for many more purposes such as being home to both an NBA and NHL team) as well as market size (larger markets have a better chance to recoup the costs). To provide a sense of just how much of a share the public may end up contributing to these projects, consider Memphis, estimated to contribute 144 percent of the capital plus ongoing costs, and Oklahoma City, at 129 percent. Canadian cities, by contrast, tend to cluster at the lower end (Montreal—9 percent and Ottawa—11 percent). In the US, two of three cities with the lowest public shares of capital plus ongoing costs were big markets (Boston and New York).

Long's reminder that the public share of the cost of a facility should be based on its full life-cycle is important insofar as many facilities seem to meet their demise or lose their high-profile tenants well before the debt is repaid. According to data from 2010 (McGinty et al., 2010), Giants Stadium in the Meadowlands was demolished in 2010 with $266M remaining to be paid on the Meadowlands complex; and the Astrodome, known as the eighth wonder of the world when it opened in 1965, still had $32M remaining to be paid, despite not having had either the Astros or the Oilers since 1998.

As Delaney and Eckstein explain in Chapter 21, there are some serious issues about how much of a voice the populace has in some of these stadium deals. Certainly, with great needs for public funding of education and health care, public expenditures on arenas and stadiums that are privately managed or owned and that generate private profits is a luxury many states and municipalities can ill afford. At the same time, Delaney and Eckstein (2003) describe very well how important many civic leaders believe it is to be considered "a major league city." In Cincinnati, they tell us, leaders expressed fear that the Reds leaving would mean that their city would be . . . Dayton!

THE SPORTS–MEDIA COMPLEX AND ITS EFFECTS

The political economy of sport in today's world occurs within the context of what scholars of sport have variously called the **sports–media complex** (Jhally, 1984), "the Golden Triangle" (Nixon, 2008), the Sports/Media/Commercial Complex (Messner et al., 2000), and the global media–sport production complex (Maguire, 1999; 2011). These authors are referring to powerful networks that bring together elites from the sports world, the media, other large corporations, and governments[20] that present a particular view and understanding of the world. This view can be broadly construed as consistent with the interests of the dominant groups in given societies. To the extent that men, whites, and corporate elites are dominant, it will be their values, ideologies, and interests that dominate media discourse and that we will see in media's presentation of sports. This "complex" or "golden triangle" can be thought of as an institutional framework that consists of a playing field so familiar to us that we can't conceive of alternatives. Ideologies of hegemonic masculinity, of "faster, higher, stronger," of private property ownership prerogatives, of race-coded team and league aspirations, and other ways of reinforcing dominant power relations are taken as given.

Slowly but surely, our understanding of sports has become not only consistent with, but defined by, interests that have nothing to do with the contest that we are watching. These days, we are all accustomed to "media time-outs" during college basketball games. We have come to understand that coaches wait for these opportunities rather than using one of their allotted time-outs. Media incursions have thus become part of a game's strategy! We have come to expect that the lineup announcements will be corporate-sponsored: the "Firestone starting lineup," for example. Our favorite announcers do their work in the "Sunoco Broadcast Booth." The authors of this volume remember when sports presentations were different; the readers of this book probably don't. It is important to recognize that the games that we watch are mass-mediated presentations organized in line with the profit goals of the media corporations and the corporations to which they sell air time for commercials. The media corporations are enriched by the massive amounts paid by other corporations to corporate-identify time-outs or scoreboard-updates in order, ultimately, to sell their products. There may be technological constraints in sports presentations that have to do with the mechanics of television, cable, or radio production and distribution, but the particular ways that we receive these programs are unique to our specific political–economic context.

As Maguire's label makes clear, this is a global phenomenon. Of course, the specific institutional framework is different in different locales. The structure of professional sports in the US is different than in Europe: The stability of the teams in the US major leagues is based on the monopoly power of its leagues (rooted in various forms of cartel power and an **antitrust exemption**[21] granted by the government), while the **promotion and relegation system** in European football leagues is based on the idea that any team has a chance to rise to the major leagues (Szymanski, 2009). Nonetheless, when we observe sports in our city or country, we have a particular set of expectations about what they will look like, how they operate, how we interact with it, and what we can expect from it. In the US, we would never go to a game of the Lehigh Valley Iron Pigs (the highest level minor league affiliate of the Philadelphia Phillies) and hope that a win will have any effect on the team's likelihood of playing Major League Baseball. On the other hand, fans of Cardiff City in Wales were able to celebrate the team's promotion to the Premier League in 2013 after 51 years outside the top division (Clutton, 2013). Despite these differences, fans of both teams have become much more comfortable with—indeed, excited about!—rosters comprising many foreign stars, thanks to the more global sports labor market. Both sets of fans would be familiar with the particular prerogatives of ownership in each league and adjust their expectations about everything, from the type of play to the relative luxury of facilities to the products available at arenas/stadiums or online. Indeed, we all become accustomed to how our favorite sports teams operate in their local political economies.

GLOBAL LABOR MARKETS

While it is clear how *teams* move within and between leagues on different continents, there have been some relatively new developments in how *players* move. Over the past half-century, the major restrictions on player mobility have been lifted. Compared to the 1960s, when teams controlled their players' capacity to move from team to team (in the US, this was through some form of the "**reserve clause**" and in England, there was a league-wide maximum wage for footballers until 1961), the situation now is very fluid. Though there are many rules about how players move from country to country, one can reasonably say that there is a truly global labor market. Some of the mobility restrictions have to do with agreements between leagues: in 2013, for example, Japanese baseball players could move to a US MLB team only if the MLB team that bids on the player paid a "posting fee" of $20M to the Japanese team. In 1995, the European Court of Justice issued the "Bosman ruling," which essentially granted free agency to soccer players.[22] Although it was originally a European Union ruling, FIFA applied it worldwide. Ultimately, the ruling made it possible for foreign players to sign with a team without regard to how many domestic players were on the team. The free agents with expiring contracts or, "Bosman players," as they are known, have transformed the salary structure in European soccer, with teams paying more to their stars than teams in any league. According to ESPN and Sportintelligence.com using data from 2012–14 (Jones and Marrinson, 2014), of the top 10 teams paying the highest average annual salaries, six are European soccer teams, two are MLB teams (Dodgers and Yankees), and two are NBA teams (Nets and Bulls).

The era of free agency in European football has significant implications for the promotion and relegation system. If a relatively poor team somehow does get promoted to a top league, it will be very difficult for it to stay there. Not only will the team not be able to bid for the top players in the world, it is likely that its top players will be raided by the richer teams. Eibar, a Spanish team, was promoted to La Liga in 2014 but doesn't really have the money to compete at this level. Not only does the league have minimum capital requirements but they also require stadiums to be of a certain size.[23] While very exciting for Eibar fans, promotion may be extremely fleeting and not be all it's cracked up to be.

FIFA's decision to permit increased labor mobility now means that any player from any country can play for any other country, as long as the player has played for only one country in a FIFA-sanctioned international match. [24] As Andrei Markovits (personal communication, 2014) stated, a country can get 11 players from anywhere in the world, grant them citizenship, and these 11 could be their national team. Of course, that nation's legislature might have to be willing to relax citizenship rules, but thus far this has not seemed to be a problem.

Baird (Chapter 19), in her comparison of US and Cuban baseball leagues, provides another example of how political economy and different institutional frameworks lead to different outcomes. Her analysis illustrates the key point that a political economy approach to sports recognizes that economic markets do not exist in a vacuum. There may be more (as in Cuba) or less (as in the US) direct government regulation of markets but its extent is a function of ideology and politics. As the Cuban case makes clear, both internal politics and international politics have shaped the development of Cuban baseball. Similarly, and ironically, it was government intervention in the US—in the form of court decisions that opened the baseball major leagues to free agency—that *ended* a specific form of market constraint. We will come back to this issue later when we discuss player unions.

SPORT AND POLITICS AT THE NATIONAL LEVEL AND BEYOND

When we discuss politics and sport, it is important to think comparatively. A cross-national perspective reveals some radical variations in how different societies deal with sport. While the US, Canada, and Mexico do not have cabinet-level departments or ministries of sport, a quick internet search revealed that the following countries do have ministries that included "sport" in their titles (a random, non-exhaustive list): India, England, France, Swaziland, Trinidad and Tobago, Poland, Georgia, Russia, Myanmar, Cuba, and Zambia. This doesn't speak to effectiveness or policy breadth and it doesn't mean that countries with departments or ministries without sports in the title don't have comprehensive sports policies. Many countries use sports as a fundamental aspect of their health policy. For example, England, Sweden, and Finland have adopted sports and fitness policies that attempt to close the participation gaps—by age, social class, gender, etc.—in athletic activities (Bottenburg et al., 2005). As we noted in Section 2, this approach speaks to our "pipeline" dimension of fairness. Countries that do not have such policies are necessarily making other public policy choices.

In the United States, as we have discussed, there are many intersections between politics and sport. Although at the level of policy, Title IX is probably the most extensive and effective example, many other sport–politics connections occur in terms of nationalism and patriotism. For example, many sporting events feature "flyovers" from the US Air Force. Military personnel take part in color guards when the national anthem is played at the beginning of ballgames. Indeed, the singing of the national anthem at the start of an athletic contest is a near-universal feature of both amateur and professional sports in the US. These rituals can be seen as some of the ways that the society attempts to reinforce unity and a semblance of collective effervescence.[25]

One of the most interesting studies of the relationship between sport and a country's politics and culture is C. L. R. James' (1983) *Beyond a Boundary*. Though we cannot capture here the nuances of James' analysis, we wish to highlight his argument that a sport may, in various ways, be a symbol both of oppression and of liberation. James analyzed how cricket was played in the West Indies and what it meant: It was both a source and reminder of imperial oppression as well as a means of resistance and liberation. As cricket moved from being a sport played by foreign elites to one played by poor West Indians—in other words, as it became a more level playing field—its symbolic role in the society was transformed into a more humane and inclusive one.

While a global perspective reveals differences across nations, it also highlights similarities, especially in the current context of the increasing globalization of particular sports. Despite the relatively small fan base for soccer in the US, 26.5 million watched ESPN/ABC and Univision's presentation of the final match of the 2014 World Cup between Germany and Argentina. The Associated Press (Bauder, 2014) reported that, according to the social media companies, "(t)he month-long World Cup also was responsible for more than 3 billion interactions on Facebook and 672 million messages on Twitter." The Germany–Argentina final also produced record viewership in Germany (ESPNfc.com, 2014a). Though the US record for the World Cup final pales in comparison to the 111 million who watched the 2014 Super Bowl,[26] the growth in soccer viewership is likely to continue at an accelerated pace. According to Nielsen, "(t)he average viewership for all 64 World Cup matches was up 39 percent over 2010 on ESPN and its sister station ABC and 34 percent on Univision." We see a four-fold increase in average number of viewers per game from the 2002 to the 2014 World Cup (ESPNfc.com, 2014b). Although final figures are not available, it is likely that over one billion people watched the 2014 World Cup final. Even skeptics of globalization would recognize this as a global phenomenon.

In some ways, though, the more interesting manifestations of these global processes occur at the individual level in the form of, for example, what pieces of athletic clothing are worn where. The presence of Lionel Messi jerseys in Denver and Michael Jordan shoes in Beijing reflects commercial and cultural penetration at a very deep level. Large transnational corporations bring images of media stars from around the world emblazoned on shoes, shirts, hats, and other products that cross national boundaries. While it would clearly be a stretch to see this as evidence of a unitary global sports culture—the Messi jersey means something different and makes different claims in Denver than it does in Rosario, Argentina (Messi's hometown) or Barcelona, Spain (where he plays)—we believe that the spread of global sport creates new possibilities for more similarities emerging in many different places (DiMaggio and Powell, 1983).[27]

ATHLETES AND OWNERS ORGANIZING FOR AND AGAINST CHANGE

Over the course of the past century, athletes in a variety of contexts have organized to challenge the prerogatives and power of dominant groups. These challenges range from forming unions to increase compensation in sports leagues to organizing international boycotts to protest apartheid in South Africa. In the US, the most famous and consequential "event" along these lines was Jackie Robinson's breaking the baseball color line, in place since the 1880s' "gentlemen's agreement" to keep blacks out of baseball. Robinson's signing by Branch Rickey in 1945 preceded the integration of the armed forces (via Executive Order from President Truman), the unanimous Supreme Court decision in *Brown v. Board of Education* that integrated schools, and the various federal civil rights laws that were passed in the 1950s and 1960s. Yet like these events, Robinson's breakthrough also had its roots in the years of organizing by the National Association for the Advancement of Colored People (NAACP), which challenged school segregation in the 1930s and voting rights laws in the 1940s, and the work of Wendell Smith, a reporter for the *Pittsburgh Courier*. So, in thinking about the political context of sports, we need to include government challenges by mobilized grassroots organizations and mass media pressure on the sports' powers that be.

The deep commitments of individuals in and around sports to make sports a more inclusive, democratic space are recounted in other places (Lapchick, 2005; Zirin, 2005; 2009). Here, we focus on just a few examples of the ways that actors in the sports world have engaged politically—despite the claim, discussed above, that "never the twain shall meet."

Aside from the general ways that a political economy approach forces us to consider how those politics and the economy affect sports, politics and sports also come together in the context of attempting to make a profit for one's team. Though teams are ostensibly putting the best team on the field with the goal of winning games, they are also trying to make a profit by putting fans in the seats and getting web-surfers to buy their team's merchandise. Thus, teams are always marketing themselves to their perceived fan base. If the team is perceived to have a "bad rep," for whatever reason, this is a problem for the owners (and the league). We know that many teams came late to signing African-American players, even as the success of Dodgers after Robinson joined the roster (six World Series trips in 10 years) demonstrated that signing black players was a "winning idea." We know that, even as the NBA came to be dominated by African-American players, there have been owners who felt that their team just had to have some white players.[28] Calvin Griffiths, owner of the Washington Senators, when asked why he moved his team to Minneapolis-St. Paul in 1961, replied: "It was when we found out you only had 15,000 blacks here. Black people don't go to ballgames, but they'll fill up a rassling ring and put up such a chant it'll scare you to death. We came here because you've got good, hard-working white people here" (*New York Daily News*, 2014). Though it is a much more subtle organizational argument, these are the kinds of issues raised by Carey in Chapter 24 on "Hoosier Whiteness and the Indiana Pacers." When a team or league is perceived to be associated with criminality, deviant behavior or marginalized groups, team officials may attempt to change course and appeal to those who are disaffected. One of the most prominent examples of this was NBA Commissioner David Stern's 2005 imposition of a dress code for players who were on the bench. Among the banned items were headwear of any sort and chains and pendants, items seen as much more likely to be worn by African-American players (Rovell, 2005). In essence, we are reinforcing the point we made in Section 2 that, when particular ways of viewing the world become hegemonic, there are implications for how social life is organized. The examples of Stern and Griffiths (and others) suggest that their[29] "common sense" notions of what their fans like or don't like have important consequences, not only for whether a team is putting its best team on the field (or even where that field is located), but also for the freedom of cultural expression for particular groups.

Recall that in Section 1 we proposed a conception of sports that includes different dimensions of fairness; with this in mind, we will examine two examples of athletes' struggles for fairness in the form of greater equality and inclusion. Since it is so central to the ways that professional sports operate in the contemporary United States, we will discuss the development and role of players' unions. And since disabled athletes are at the nexus of a worldwide movement for greater inclusiveness in sports, [30] we will discuss some of the more recent developments in that arena. We will then briefly turn to a discussion of the politics of individual athletes.

FREE AGENCY, ANTITRUST, AND THE RESERVE CLAUSE

A recurring issue in the operation of professional sports leagues in the United States is the degree to which they are a monopoly, controlling the country's supply of baseball, football, hockey, and basketball.[31] The Sherman Antitrust Act was passed in 1890 to protect the consumer from the immense power of monopolies to set prices (since they have no competition). Sports leagues have tried to sidestep these prohibitions against monopoly so that the league itself can regulate how franchises within their leagues compete with one another and so that it can keep out other leagues. The leagues' business model depends on restricting competition within a given geographical area[32] and maintaining competitive balance within the league. To achieve the latter, they had to devise a means to restrict player movement so that the richest teams didn't simply buy up the best players. This was best exemplified by Major League Baseball's "**reserve clause**." This clause, inserted in each player's contract, reserved to current teams the right of first refusal of a player's services for all future years. Needless to say, since this meant that the player could only play for one team and therefore could not sell his services to the highest bidder, it kept down players' salaries. In baseball, MLB's antitrust exemption had been challenged unsuccessfully many times since the Supreme Court granted it in 1922, interestingly because the Court deemed that baseball was not a business, it was a sport. Yes, teams might travel across state lines to play games but the focus, according to Justice Oliver Wendell Holmes, is "giving exhibitions of base ball, which are purely state affairs" (FEDERAL CLUB v. NATIONAL LEAGUE, 259 U.S. 200, 208 (U.S. 1922)).

The other major professional sports leagues were never granted this exemption and players have used the antitrust law to challenge the power of the owners and the leagues. As we will explain, these conflicts were usually resolved through court actions and/or collective bargaining agreements. Nevertheless, leagues were often able to maintain monopoly power by crowding out attempts by other leagues to encroach on their business prerogatives. When there were challenges (such as those mounted by the World Hockey League, the American Football League, or the American Basketball Association), they often led to player salary increases—but ultimately, to league mergers as well. Team owners have resisted attempts by players to increase their bargaining power. In fact, according to an author who studied the Cleveland Browns' franchise during its 1940–50s heyday, Paul Brown, the owner for whom the team was named, felt that "it was both just and necessary that management could cut, trade, bench, blackball and own in perpetuity anyone and everyone that it wanted" (Piascik, 2010: 268).

Thanks to the courage of Curt Flood, who challenged baseball's reserve clause, all leagues now have some version of free agency. Flood, an excellent outfielder for the St. Louis Cardinals, was traded to the Philadelphia Phillies in 1969. . .but he refused to go.[33] He told the Commissioner of Baseball Bowie Kuhn that "I do not regard myself as a piece of property to be bought or sold." Since baseball had its antitrust exemption, Kuhn figured that Flood's claim had no legal grounding. Indeed, Flood's case went to the Supreme Court, which, once again—*in a narrow and close decision*—argued that it was up to Congress to remove this exemption. Despite Flood's loss, baseball's union was emboldened to bargain for binding arbitration on grievances and, in 1975, two excellent pitchers, Andy Messersmith and Dave McNally, agreed to play a season without a contract and were declared by an arbitrator to be free agents.

To this day, all the professional sports leagues have both some version of free agency as well as various means of restricting player bargaining power and mobility. These restrictions are not challenged as part of antitrust practices because they are usually written into collective bargaining agreements between unions and leagues. Since both parties agree, the restrictions are not considered relevant to antitrust (i.e., power) concerns. Some of the ways that player bargaining power and mobility are restricted are: the draft; rookie contract maximums; restricted free agency (subject to a team being able to match another team's offer); transfer fees paid to teams when a player leaves Team A to go to Team B;[34] salary caps (maximum salary expenditures per team) and luxury taxes (imposed when a team overspends a set maximum); and many others that vary from sport to sport and from league to league.

SALARY CAPS

In light of our discussion in Section 1 about dimensions of fairness, we want to pay special attention to the idea of salary caps in relation to the issue of competitive balance. Our concern about resource fairness had to do with the ability of "rich" teams simply to outspend "poor" teams for the best players. Though salary caps certainly restrict compensation to players (a team cannot pay Madame Superstar her full market value and still have enough money to fill out a roster), they make it impossible for, say, the New York

Yankees to buy up all the good players from a small-market team, which may have good prospects but little money. The idea is that having a salary cap "levels the playing field" in a particular way, thus leading to a more competitive environment (as already noted, the necessity to outspend one's competition in La Liga is the concern for Eibar). This question is ripe for empirical investigation but difficult to study, since no two leagues have exactly the same salary cap arrangement. On the face of it, though, it appears that there is much greater stability (that is, less competitive balance) among the top teams in the various European football leagues, where there is no salary cap, than in any of the US top sports leagues, each of which has a semblance of one.

UNIONS IN US PROFESSIONAL SPORTS

All four major professional sports leagues in the US currently have well-established players' associations. These labor unions have been able to negotiate collective bargaining agreements (CBAs) with their respective leagues, ensuring employee benefits ranging from high(er) salaries—for free agents as well as for rookies making the minimum—to health care benefits to pensions. The mobilizations required to establish and maintain these organizations were long and hard; the bare-knuckled images of labor-organizing struggles in industries ranging from mining to automobiles to steel are well-reflected in sports as well. Players in all four major sports made significant attempts at unionization in the 1950s, when the percentage of workers unionized in the private sector was at its zenith.[35] Conditions for players at that time were quite dire: low pay, poor health coverage, and often no compensation for non-league/exhibition games. It wasn't until the 1960s that each player's association had some degree of success in establishing itself as a bargaining unit to be reckoned with.

In baseball, attempts to unionize came as early as 1885 (Brotherhood of Base Ball Players) and 1900 (Players Protective Association); the current Major League Baseball Player Association was begun in 1952 (Staudohar, 1997) but didn't get much traction until 1966, when it hired an old Steelworkers Union hand, Marvin Miller. Miller transformed the union into an organization that, within a decade, had organized a strike, implemented salary arbitration, and overcame the reserve clause, establishing free agency.

In football,[36] players attempted to extract concessions from the league and owners as early as 1956, relying on some of the most prominent stars of the game to take a stand. Even though a majority of the players in the league had signed on, the owners ignored them. Their demands? "[A] minimum $5,000 a year salary, uniform per diem pay for players, a rule requiring clubs to pay for players' equipment and, more importantly, a provision for the continued payment of salary to an injured player."

NBA players attempted unionization in 1954 at the urging of the highly skilled, popular player Bob Cousy.[37] He got stars from most teams to join him and presented a list of demands to the NBA commissioner at the 1955 All-Star game. It wasn't until 1957, though, that the NBA finally recognized the union. According to Cousy's own account, his "biggest win was getting the meal money bumped from $5 to $7. Getting that concession made me a hero" (McClellan, 2004). His other "successes" included shorter training camp, limiting to three the number of exhibition games *during* the season, and—these two seem so quaint!—"*considerate* treatment for the player in regards to radio and television appearances" and "*reasonable* moving expenses for a player traded during the season" [emphasis added]. The real breakthrough for the union occurred when, before the 1964 televised All-Star game, players indicated that they would not play if a pension agreement weren't reached; the commissioner agreed.

Even the National Hockey League, the smallest and least lucrative of the leagues, had early union activity.[38] Two of the league's stars (Ted Lindsay and Doug Harvey) helped organize the NHLPA in 1957–58 and demanded changes to the pension plan. The NHL fought back by getting Detroit to trade Lindsay, their captain, and getting Toronto to trade Jim Thomson, the Leafs' player representative, to the Chicago Black Hawks. After filing an antitrust suit claiming that the NHL was a monopoly (along with other legal actions), the union eventually won some minor concessions from the league: a minimum salary of $7000 (which, in fact, was already being followed); increasing to $4000 the winning player's share for the Stanley Cup playoffs; limiting exhibition games; and a few others. "In return, the Players agreed to drop all pending union certification applications and the antitrust litigation" (Ross, 2010). Finally, in 1967, the NHL Players Association was officially established.

To provide a sense of how much of an impact unions have made since those early years, let's look at changes in minimum and average salaries in baseball. We noted above that Marvin Miller was a transformative figure for the baseball players' union. In 1968, he negotiated the first collective bargaining agreement in professional sports and the minimum salary was raised from $6000, where it had been stuck for two decades, to $10,000 (MLB Players). As Table 4.2 shows, by 1970, the minimum salary had doubled to $12,000 and, by 2014, it reached half-a-million dollars per year. The average salaries show an even more remarkable pattern of increase, from under $30,000 in 1970 to almost $4M in 2014. Other professional sports leagues have also realized significant average salary increases over the same period. As of 2014 (based on the estimated 2015–16 salary cap), the NBA, which has the fewest number of players on their rosters, has the highest average salary: $6.1M. The NHL average salary (2012 data) was $2.4M. The league with the largest rosters, but also the biggest profits—the NFL—has the lowest average salary: $1.9M.[39] Each of the four major US professional sports leagues has a collective bargaining agreement (CBA) with its respective unions that provide 50–55 percent of the revenue to player salaries. While there are battles over what gets included as revenue (Do jerseys count? Usually, yes!) these are good estimates of how revenues are divided between players and teams/leagues.

Table 4.2 MLB Minimum and Average Salaries, 1970–2014

Year	*Average Salary*	*Minimum Salary*
2014	$3,950.000	$500,000
2010	$3,297,828	$400,000
2005	$2,632,655	$316,000
2000	$1,998.034	$200,000
1995	$1,071,029	$109,000
1990	$578,930	$100,000
1985	$371,571	$60,000
1980	$143,756	$30,000
1975	$44,676	$16,000
1970	$29,303	$12,000

Sources: CBS Sports; Baseball-Reference.com; Staudohar (1997); Blum (2014)

The world of sport has certainly been transformed since the days when professional athletes had to find jobs in the off-season, as so many did in the 1950s and 1960s. When Jim Gentile, the Orioles' first baseman, finished the 1961 season with 46 home runs and 141 runs batted in, he went to a job at a car dealership (Finkel, 2013). Many others sold real estate or insurance.[40] The struggles for union recognition and CBAs have radically changed the lives of many professional athletes. It is worthwhile to remember, however, that many excellent athletes never make it to the highest level leagues and that, among those who do, the average career length is very short.

How have players' unions been able to be so successful at winning concessions from team owners and the leagues—especially during a time when union power has been declining dramatically in other sectors of the economy? The short answer is that the leagues are generating enormous revenues through media contracts (as discussed earlier) and thus franchises are rapidly increasing in value. According to *Forbes* (Badenhausen, 2014), in 2014 the New York Yankees were worth $2.5 billion, the highest of any non-soccer team in the world. Of the top 50 most valuable sports franchises in the world, 39 are in North America. Twenty-nine of the top 50 are NFL franchises (23 of them are valued at $1B or more), five are MLB teams, four are from the NBA, and one (Toronto) is from the NHL. According to an analysis completed in 2008 (Phillips and Krasner, 2008), many of the ownership transfers in the US professional sports leagues showed compound annual growth rates (CAGR) of over 10 percent. One of the examples they cite is the New York Jets, which sold in 2000 for 635 times its 1963 $1M price tag, a CAGR of over 19 percent. Between global expansion (new media deals, new tournaments, new teams) and lucrative stadium deals (expanded seating, luxury suites, other amenities that are not part of revenue-sharing with other teams), owners can expect value increases for many years to come. Union successes may thus be, at least in part, a result of owners' recognition that people are paying to see the players and that a rapidly expanded pie rewards them enormously even if the players benefit as well.

DISABILITY SPORT

As discussed in Section 2, our consideration of disability and sport is based on a notion of disability that is sociologically contextualized. Rather than focusing on any inherent limitation that is relevant to sports participation, a sociological model of disability examines the social context of inclusion. Thanks to their political mobilization *as* disabled (Shapiro, 1993), new opportunities have developed to "become visible in sport as disabled athletes" and even "becoming visible in sport as athletes" (DePauw, 1997). DePauw (1997: 426) identifies "access, accommodation, and transformation" as "stages of inclusion" for people with disabilities. As Nixon (2007) and Fay and Wolff (2009) have shown, many sports can be adapted in ways that would be much more welcoming to those with "different" abilities. Both sports and our conceptions of ability have been changed by these developments (see Le Clair, Chapter 11).

The recent international mobilization around the right to sport for people with disabilities presents a major challenge to normative conceptions of sport (United Nations, 2006). By conceptualizing access to sport for people with disabilities as a *human right*, the United Nations has lent its prestige to a broadened notion of fairness in sports (along the lines we suggested in Section 1). Article 30.5 of the UN's Convention on the Rights of Persons with Disabilities states the following (United Nations, 2006: 22):

> With a view to enabling persons with disabilities to participate on an equal basis with others in recreational, leisure and sporting activities, States Parties shall take appropriate measures:
>
> a. To encourage and promote the participation, to the fullest extent possible, of persons with disabilities in mainstream sporting activities at all levels;
> b. To ensure that persons with disabilities have an opportunity to organize, develop and participate in disability-specific sporting and recreational activities and, to this end, encourage the provision, on an equal basis with others, of appropriate instruction, training and resources;
> c. To ensure that persons with disabilities have access to sporting, recreational and tourism venues;
> d. To ensure that children with disabilities have equal access with other children to participation in play, recreation and leisure and sporting activities, including those activities in the school system;
> e. To ensure that persons with disabilities have access to services from those involved in the organization of recreational, tourism, leisure and sporting activities.

This kind of comprehensive approach, which expands access, increases training opportunities, and empowers excluded groups to develop their own versions of sporting activities, occurs only rarely and it is a response to the challenges and resistance by marginalized groups. Needless to say, these are political struggles that have to be waged in country after country, and will need to be sustained if the goals of Article 30.5 are to be realized.

CONTINUING COLLECTIVE STRUGGLES

Perhaps the most important global struggle surrounding sport is one that has been dubbed by the United Nations "Sport for Development and Peace." This initiative sees sport as a universal language that has the power to accomplish a wide range of goals: advance gender equality; improve physical and mental health; include everyone, regardless of abilities; promote respect and dialogue; and enhance life skills of children and youth (United Nations Office on Sport for Development and Peace [UNOSDP], 2014). The UN sees this initiative as a means of harnessing the potential of sport for the "promotion of human rights, the achievement of inclusive and sustainable development,. . .and peace-building objectives" (United Nations Office on Sport for Development and Peace, 2013: 9). This Office has helped organize country- and even community-level programs that focus on including young adults in activities that foster inclusion and community development. While the work of this Office must be implemented locally in order to maximize its effects, a worldwide network of sports activists has already materialized and begun its work. We mention just two examples from the UNOSDP 2012 Annual Report: (1) in Haiti, almost 2000 persons with disabilities were supported and the Disability Project co-hosted a National Disability Sport Festival; and (2) in Tajikistan, the National Taekwondo and Kickboxing Federation began a project focused on improving girls' capacity to participate in sports and promote human rights (UNOSDP, 2013: 25).

THE POLITICS OF INDIVIDUAL ATHLETES

While there may be a general expectation that athletes, as athletes, should not be political actors, this has not prevented some athletes from venturing onto explicitly political terrain. Former US President Gerald Ford, who was an All-American football player at University of Michigan, didn't follow that "rule." There are quite a few well-known athletes who hold (or have held) very important political positions in their respective countries. In the US, former baseball player and "perfect game" hurler Jim Bunning has served as US Senator from Kentucky. Bill Bradley, a Rhodes Scholar and twice a National Basketball Association champion with the NY Knicks, served as a US Senator from New Jersey and ran for the Democratic Party nomination for president. Two great NBA guards have been mayors of major US cities (Dave Bing—Detroit; Kevin Johnson—Sacramento). Many other athletes have served in the US House of Representatives. Internationally, the most famous congressperson in the world is probably Manny Pacquiao (sometimes referred to as the best "pound for pound" boxer in the world) of the Philippines. Another internationally known boxer, Vitali Klitschko, former heavyweight champion, is mayor of Kiev. In Canada, one of the most famous NHL players and a Hall of Famer, Frank Mahovlich, was a Senator from Ottawa for many years. Far from a hindrance to their political aspirations, these athletes have found their status to be a net positive, if only for the platform that athletic celebrity provides.

Why, then, is there such consternation when an athlete utters a political opinion, as opposed to other types of celebrities? Craig Hodges, two-time NBA champion with the Chicago Bulls and three-time three-point shooting champion at NBA All-Star Weekend, was a committed community leader who believed that the US should do more to help low-income black communities. At a White House celebration of the Bulls' championship,[41] he gave President George H. W. Bush a letter that encouraged exactly that. Shortly thereafter, he was cut by the Bulls and, despite contacting every single general manager in the league, not a single other team ever signed him.[42] If ever there were a good example of the "social significance of statistically insignificant events," as Michael Schudson has dubbed this phenomenon (cited in Illouz, 1997:19), this is it. After what happened to Craig Hodges, what athlete would venture to suggest that current public policies—of whatever sort!—need to be changed? In the essay below (Chapter 25), Candaele and Dreier discuss the conditions that militate against athletes getting involved in political issues. Ironically, one of the huge disincentives to expressing political dissent is the fact that athletes have so much money to lose, which, of course, would not be the case had the athletes that came before them not gotten involved politically in their own labor conflicts.

POWER, POLITICS, AND FAIRNESS

This Section provided an overview of the many ways that politics and power articulate with sports. We have recounted examples of the powerful maintaining or even increasing their power and examples when mobilization from below opened up new opportunities for the marginalized and dispossessed. The underlying point is that, as groups jockey for advantage, struggle is a constant and the terrain is tilted in favor of the powerful. Usually, the battles take place within an institutional framework that "naturalizes" the resources, societal arrangements, and world-views of the powerful. Sometimes, though, we see contestation over the nature of the terrain itself. When there is struggle over the terrain, as we see when groups mobilize for access to new sports, to new venues, and to new training opportunities, we consider that a victory for subordinate groups. That victory, though, is, of course, just the beginning; the battle continues . . .

NOTES

1 Much of the following discussion draws from Lukes (2005).
2 But see the excellent book by Marshall Ganz (2010), *Why David Sometimes Wins: Leadership, Organization, and Strategy in the California Farm Worker Movement.*
3 This is also Wacquant's point in Chapter 2.
4 Some might say that we have transitioned from *feudalism* to family capitalism to corporate capitalism.
5 As of this writing, the Ed O'Bannon case (O'Bannon v. NCAA) figures to affect just *how* lucrative the NCAA and its conferences are.
6 Dorsey (2011) notes: "In football-crazy Egypt, about half of the Egyptian PremierLeague's16 teams are owned by the military, the police, government ministries or provincial authorities. Military-owned construction companies built 22 of Egypt's soccer stadiums. Similarly, Iran's Revolutionary Guards have in recent years taken control of a number of prominent soccer teams. In the Gulf, soccer association and club boards are populated by royals. The Syrian military and police own and operate two of the country's most important teams with Al Jaish (The Army) [and] have long been virtually synonymous with the national team."
7 If we were discussing college sports in any other country, we would not be discussing sports as big business! The US is unique in this regard.
8 We intend no association with or reference to Florida State University.
9 See the definition in Section 1, p. 16.
10 Its television exposure is a function of a Supreme Court decision about property rights, as explained by Suggs (Chapter 15 of this volume). This decision gave much more power to individual universities and conferences to negotiate their own television deals.
11 To give you an idea of how extensive and legalistic these restrictions are, see www.ncaa.org/student-athletes/resources/recruiting-calendars?division=d1
12 According to *USA Today* (http://www.usatoday.com/sports/college/salaries), in 2013, there were 70 head football coaches who received total compensation packages in excess of $1M.
13 Of course, the more successful the program and its conference, the more money will be available. Thus, expenses associated with recruitment of top players and coaches could be seen as relevant to television contracts. Programs *may* decline to pursue top coaching and athletic talent.
14 Not only do university athletic departments strive to put themselves in a position to gain or keep this lucrative revenue source but the facilities that they build become part of a standard for the industry as a whole.
15 See the updated financial data at (Knight Commission, 2012): www.knightcommission.org/resources/press-room/787-december-3-updated-financial-data
16 As we discussed in Section 2, it appears that these institutions have the same kind of lottery mentality that D-I athletes exhibit as they aspire to pro careers.
17 This is state revenue that doesn't come from federal or local sources.
18 See Mitchell et al. (2014). Center for Budget and Policy Priorities, Changes in State Appropriations per Student and Tuition, 2008–14 (Related Excel tables: http://www.cbpp.org/cms/index.cfm?fa=view&id=4135).
19 See Table 4.5 of Long (2013). This table includes historical data on all facilities from US professional baseball, basketball, football, and hockey leagues.
20 Maguire (2011: 966) reminds us that "(o)ther global flows that structure this system include technology, capital, migrant labour, and national symbols and ideologies."
21 Below, we will explain one of the key elements of the antitrust issue as it relates to player movement: the reserve clause.
22 Ask (2014) summarizes this ruling.
23 See the article by Minder (2014).
24 There are differences for youth leagues and, of course, "friendlies" don't count.
25 A Durkheimian analysis would see the ritual in this way while, from a conflict perspective, these rituals would be seen as elites attempting to impose a perhaps false unity.
26 Indeed, during the 2013 NFL season, there were 15 *regular season* telecasts that equaled or exceeded the 26.5 million viewers of the World Cup final (Bibel, 2014).
27 Since different corporations, state policies, and other national differences are involved in the different organizational fields, DiMaggio and Powell's hypothesized isomorphic outcomes will be somewhat attenuated.
28 In 1980, Ted Stepien, owner of the Cleveland Cavaliers, made such a statement (as reported in the *New York Daily News*, 2014).

29 Their powerful positions made *their* common sense quite consequential.

30 See Chapter 22 by Lenskyj for a discussion of mobilization by gay athletes.

31 For an excellent overview of these issues, see Szymanski (2009).

32 This restricts the "supply" of a given sport to a given number of fans and allows the franchise to set prices at an artificially high level.

33 Information about Flood challenging the reserve clause is from Barra (2011).

34 When Ronaldo moved from Manchester United to Real Madrid in 2009, the transfer fee was £80M or €94.4M (*The Guardian*, 2009).

35 According to the *New York Times*' Steven Greenhouse, "The peak unionization rate was 35 percent during the mid-1950s, after a surge in unionization during the Great Depression and after World War II." www.nytimes.com/2011/01/22/business/22union.html?_r=0

36 This information comes from the NFL players association website: www.nflplayers.com/about-us/History

37 Information about the NBPA comes largely from Robert Bradley's Association for Professional Basketball Research: http://www.apbr.org/labor.html

38 Most of this information is garnered from the excellent piece by J. Andrew Ross (2010).

39 Salary data were compiled from Doyle (2013) and from NBA, NFL, and NHL players' association websites.

40 According to J.G. Preston (www.prestonjg.wordpress.com/2014/01/12/off-season-jobs-of-major-league-baseball-players-in-the-winter-of-1958–59/), *The Sporting News* compiled off-season job information for many baseball players in its October 8, 1958 issue.

41 The US President meeting with championship teams from major sports organizations (NBA, NFL, NCAA, etc.) is a routine event. Its celebratory nature attempts to deny the sport–politics connection even as it reinforces it.

42 Granderson (2008) and Berkow (1996) discuss this case in depth. Hodges sued the NBA for "blackballing" him but he lost.

REFERENCES

Ask, Mathias. 2014. "Bosman Still Struggling with Ruling That Rewards Soccer's Free Agents." *Wall Street Journal.* July 2. http://online.wsj.com/articles/the-jean-marc-bosman-ruling-benefited-soccers-free-agents-but-the-man-himself-is-still-struggling-1404327335

Badenhausen, Kurt. 2014. "The World's 50 Most Valuable Sports Teams 2014." July 16. *Forbes.* www.forbes.com/sites/kurtbadenhausen/2014/07/16/the-worlds-50-most-valuable-sports-teams-2014

Barra, Allen. 2011. "How Curt Flood Changed Baseball and Killed His Career in the Process." *The Atlantic.* July 12. www.theatlantic.com/entertainment/archive/2011/07/how-curt-flood-changed-baseball-and-killed-his-career-in-the-process/241783

Barrett, Lindsey, Colby Leachman, Claire Lockerby, Steven McMullen, Matthew Schorr, Yuriy Veytskin. 2013. "The Soccer War," at Soccer Politics Pages, http://sites.duke.edu/wcwp/research-projects/the-soccer-war

Baseball-Reference.com. www.baseball-reference.com/bullpen/minimum_salary

Bauder, David. 2014. "The World Cup Final Was the Most Watched Soccer Game in U.S. History." July 14. Associated Press. www.huffingtonpost.com/2014/07/14/world-cup-final-viewers-record_n_5585861.html

Benford, Robert D. 2007. "The College Sports Reform Movement: Reframing the 'Edutainment' Industry." *Sociological Quarterly* 48(1): 1–28.

Berkow, Ira. 1996. "Basketball: Still Searching for the Truth." February 18. *New York Times.* www.nytimes.com/1996/02/18/sports/basketball-still-searching-for-the-truth.html

Berkowitz, Steve, Jodi Upton and Erik Brady. 2013. "Most NCAA Division I Athletic Departments Take Subsidies." July 1. *USA Today.* http://www.usatoday.com/story/sports/college/2013/05/07/ncaa-finances-subsidies/2142443

Bibel, Sara. 2014. "NFL 2013 TV Recap: 205 Million Fans Tuned In; 34 of 35 Most Watched Shows This Fall." January 8. www.tvbythenumbers.zap2it.com/2014/01/08/nfl-2013-tv-recap-205-million-fans-tuned-in-34-of-35-most-watched-shows-this-fall/227726

Blum, Ronald. 2014. "Dodgers Top Spender, Ending Yanks' 15-Year Streak." March 26. Associated Press. www.bigstory.ap.org/article/dodgers-top-spender-ending-yanks-15-year-streak

Bottenburg, Maarten van, Bas Rijnen, Jacco van Sterkenburg. 2005. *Sports Participation in the European Union: Trends and Differences.* Niewegein, The Netherlands: Michel vanTroost, Arko Sports Media.

Bourdieu, Pierre. 1977. *Outline of a Theory of Practice.* New York, NY: Cambridge University Press.

Bradley, Robert. "Association for Professional Basketball Research." www.apbr.org/labor.html

CBS Sports. www.cbssports.com/mlb/salaries/avgsalaries

Clutton, Graham. 2013. "Premier League Promotion Party Starts at Cardiff City after 0–0 Draw Against Charlton Athletic." *The Telegraph*, April 17. www.telegraph.co.uk/sport/football/teams/cardiff-city/9999495/Premier-League-promotion-party-starts-at-Cardiff-City-after-0–0-draw-against-Charlton-Athletic.html

Delaney, Kevin J. and Rick Eckstein. 2003. *Public Dollars, Private Stadiums: The Battle Over Building Sports Stadiums.* New Brunswick, NJ: Rutgers University Press.

DePauw, Karen P. 1997. "The (In)Visibility of Disability: Cultural Contexts and 'Sporting Bodies.'" *Quest* 49(4): 416–430.

DiMaggio, Paul J. and Walter W. Powell. 1983. "The Iron Cage Revisited: Institutional Isomorphism and Collective Rationality in Organizational Fields." *American Sociological Review*, 48(2) (April): 147–160.

Dorsey, James M. 2011. "Soccer: A Middle East and North African Battlefield." November 6. www.papers.ssrn.com/sol3/papers.cfm?abstract_id=1955513

Doyle, Frank. 2013. "How to Make Money in Pro Sports – Infographic." October 24. www.news.sportsinteraction.com/sports/how-to-make-money-in-pro-sports-infographic-45774/?utm_source=feedburner&utm_medium=feed&utm_campaign=Feed%3A+SportsInteractionBlog+(Sports+Interaction+Blog)

ESPNfc.com. 2014a. "World Cup Final Sets Viewing Record." July 15. http://www.espnfc.com/fifa-world-cup/story/1950379/world-cup-final-sets-germany-tv-record

ESPNfc.com. 2014b. "World Cup Final Sets U.S. TV Record." www.espnfc.com/fifa-world-cup/story/1950567/world-cup-final-most-watched-soccer-game-in-us-historymore-than-26m-viewers July 15

Fay, Ted and Eli Wolff. 2009. "Disability in Sport in the Twenty-first Century: Creating a New Sport Opportunity Spectrum." *Boston University International Law Journal* 27(2): 231–248.

FEDERAL CLUB v. NATIONAL LEAGUE, 259 U.S. 200, 208 (U.S. 1922). www.casetext.com/case/federal-club-v-national-league#.U8wcBfldV8E

Finkel, Jon. 2013. "Mickey Mantle, Roger Maris and Jim Gentile: The Story of Baseball's Forgotten 1961 Sensation." The PostGame.com. May 13. www.m.thepostgame.com/blog/men-action/201305/mixing-it-mantle-and-maris-story-forgotten-star

Ganz, Marshall. 2010. *Why David Sometimes Wins: Leadership, Organization, and Strategy in the California Farm Worker Movement.* New York, NY: Oxford University Press.

Granderson, L.Z. 2008. "Trying to Define Craig Hodges." February 15. ESPN. http://sports.espn.go.com/espn/blackhistory2008/news/story?page=granderson/080211

Greenhouse, Steven. 2011. "Union Membership in U.S. Fell to a 70-Year Low Last Year." January 21. *New York Times.* http://www.nytimes.com/2011/01/22/business/22union.html?_r=0

Illouz, Eva. 1997. *Consuming the Romantic Utopia: Love and the Cultural Contradictions of Capitalism.* Berkeley: University of California Press.

James, C.L.R. 1983. *Beyond a Boundary.* New York, NY: Pantheon.

Jhally, Sut. 1984. "The Spectacle of Accumulation: Material and Cultural Factors in the Evolution of the Sports/Media Complex." *Insurgent Sociologist* 12(3): 41–52.

Jones, Maya A. and Ross Marrinson. 2014. "The Salary Survey Says. . ." ESPN The Magazine. April 14. www.espn.go.com/espn/story/_/id/10709445/sportingintelligence-global-salary-survey-espn-magazine

Knight Commission. 2012. December 3, 2012 – Updated Financial Data. www.knightcommission.org/resources/press-room/787-december-3-updated-financial-data

Lapchick, Richard. 2005. *100 Heroes: People in Sports Who Make This a Better World.* Orlando, FL: NCAS Publishing.

Lasswell, Harold. 1936. *Politics: Who Gets What, When, and How.* Whittlesey House: McGraw-Hill Book Company, Incorporated.

Long, Judith Grant. 2013. *Public/Private Partnerships for Major League Sports Facilities.* New York and London: Routledge.

Lukes, Steven. 2005. *Power: A Radical View.* Second Ed. Hampshire, England and New York, NY: Palgrave Macmillan.

Maguire, Joseph. 1999. *Global Sport: Identities, Societies, Civilizations.* Cambridge, England: Polity Press.

Maguire, Joseph. 2011. "Globalization, Sport, and National Identities." *Sport in Society: Cultures, Commerce, Media, Politics* 14(7–8): 978–993.

Markovits, Andrei S. 2014. Personal communication. July 23.

McClellan, Michael D. 2004. "Captain Fantastic: The Bob Cousy Interview." February 9. Celtic Nation. www.celtic-nation.com/interviews/bob_cousy/bob_cousy_page7.htm

McGinty, Jo Craven and Griff Palmer. 2010. "Still Paying for the Demolished and Underused." *New York Times*. September 7. www.nytimes.com/interactive/2010/09/08/sports/20100908-stadium-sidebar.html?ref=sports

Messner, Michael A., Michele Dunbar, and Darnell Hunt. 2000. "The Televised Sports Manhood Formula." *Journal of Sport and Social Issues* 24(4) (November): 380–394.

Minder, Raphael. 2014. "A Tiny Club's Uneasy Rise." *New York Times*. July 23. www.nytimes.com/2014/07/24/sports/soccer/eibar-a-rare-debt-free-team-in-la-liga-faces-stiff-challenges.html?_r=0

Mitchell, Michael, Vincent Palacios, and Michael Leachman. 2014. "States Are Still Funding Higher Education Below Pre-Recession Levels." May 1. Center for Budget and Policy Priorities. Changes in State Appropriations per Student and Tuition, 2008--14 (Related Excel tables: www.cbpp.org/cms/index.cfm?fa=view&id=4135

MLB Players. www.mlbplayers.mlb.com/pa/info/history.jsp

Moore, Jr., Barrington. 1967. *The Social Origins of Dictatorship and Democracy: Lord and Peasant in the Making of the Modern World*. Boston, MA: Beacon Press.

NFL Players Association. www.nflplayers.com/about-us/History

New York Daily News. 2014. "Marge Schott, Calvin Griffith and Ted Stepien among Sports' Dumbest Owners." April 27. www.nydailynews.com/sports/dumb-owners-article-1.1770468

Nixon, Howard L., II. 2007. "Constructing Diverse Sport Opportunities for People with Disabilities." *Journal of Sport and Social Issues* 31(4): 417–33.

—— 2008. *Sport in a Changing World*. Boulder, CO: Paradigm Publishers.

Pennington, Bill. 2003. "COLLEGE BASKETBALL; Player's Protest Over the Flag Divides Fans." February 26. *New York Times*. www.nytimes.com/2003/02/26/sports/college-basketball-player-s-protest-over-the-flag-divides-fans.html

Phillips, Jeff and Jeremy Krasner. 2008. "Professional Sports: The Next Evolution in Value Creation." www.srr.com/assets/pdf/professional-sportsthe-next-evolution-value-creation.pdf

Piascik, Andy. 2010. *The Best Show in Football: The 1946–1955 Cleveland Browns – Pro Football's Greatest Dynasty*. Boulder, CO: Taylor Trade Publications.

Preston, J.G. www.prestonjg.wordpress.com/2014/01/12/off-season-jobs-of-major-league-baseball-players-in-the-winter-of-1958–59

Ross, J. Andrew. 2010. "Trust and Antitrust: The Failure of the First National Hockey League Players' Association, 1957–1958." *Business and Economic History On-Line*, Volume 8. www.thebhc.org/publications/BEHonline/2010/ross.pdf

Rovell, Darren. 2005. "Stern Sure Players Will Comply with Dress Code." October 20. ESPN. www.sports.espn.go.com/nba/news/story?id=2195141

Shapiro, J. 1993. *No Pity: People with Disabilities Forging a New Civil Rights Movement*. New York, NY: Times Books.

Smith, Chris. 2013. "The Most Valuable Conferences in College Sports." January 16. Forbes. www.forbes.com/sites/chrissmith/2013/01/16/the-most-valuable-conferences-in-college-sports

Staudohar, Paul D. 1997. "Baseball's Changing Salary Structure. Compensation and Working Conditions." Fall. Bureau of Labor Statistics. www.bls.gov/opub/mlr/cwc/baseballs-changing-salary-structure.pdf

Szymanski, Stefan. 2009. *Playbooks and Checkbooks: An Introduction to the Economics of Modern Sports*. Princeton and Oxford: Princeton University Press.

The Guardian. 2009. "Manchester United Confirm Real's One-off £80m Payment for Cristiano Ronaldo." www.theguardian.com/football/2009/jul/01/cristiano-ronaldo-one-off-payment-real

United Nations. 2006. "Convention on the Rights of Persons with Disabilities." Final report of the Ad Hoc Committee on a Comprehensive and Integral International Convention on the Protection and Promotion of the Rights and Dignity of Persons with Disabilities. www.un.org/disabilities/convention/conventionfull.shtml

United Nations Office on Sport for Development and Peace. 2013. Annual Report 2012. www.un.org/sport

United Nations Office on Sport for Development and Peace. 2014. April 6. www.un.org/wcm/content/site/sport/home/unplayers/unoffice/idsdp

University of Michigan Regents. 2011. www.regents.umich.edu/meetings/06-11/2011-06-X-13.pdf

Urban Institute and Brookings Institution. www.taxpolicycenter.org/briefing-book/state-local/revenues/overtime.cfm

USA Today. www.usatoday.com/sports/college/salaries

Washington, Robert and David Karen. 2010. *Sport, Power, and Society: Institutions and Practices*. Boulder, CO: Westview.

Wolverton, Brad. 2010. "NCAA Agrees to $10.8-Billion Deal to Broadcast Its Men's Basketball Tournament." April 22. *Chronicle of Higher Education.*

Zirin, Dave. 2005. *What's My Name, Fool? Sports and Resistance in the United States.* Chicago, IL: Haymarket Books.

Zirin, Dave. 2009. *A People's History of Sports in the United States.* New York, NY: New Press.

CHAPTER 19

Cuban Baseball: Ideology, Politics, and Market Forces

Katherine E. Baird

In the United States, the business of professional baseball is mostly driven by the ideology of a free market economy. Teams are privately held and purchased in a competitive market; teams compete for the best players, with players going to the highest bidder; and player pay tracks each player's marginal revenue of product (how much money he generates for owners). The organization of Cuban baseball offers a sharp contrast to the organization of professional U.S. baseball. In Cuba, insofar as the concept of team "ownership" applies, teams belong to the state; players earn a minimal state salary; players play for their regional team with virtually no player mobility; there is no advertising in the stadiums, on radio, or on television; and games cost just pennies to attend. Despite or because of these differences, the caliber of play in Cuba is remarkable, especially given its size (population 11 million). Until 1997, the Cuban national team went decades without losing an international competition.

Some suggest that Cuban baseball represents a superior way to organize and structure the game. Fans of U.S. baseball increasingly criticize the seemingly perpetual imbalance among teams, the huge player salaries, taxpayer-financed stadiums, and the frequent labor disputes between extremely wealthy players and the even more wealthy team owners. Not surprisingly, some Major League Baseball (MLB) fans point approvingly to the lack of commercialization in Cuban baseball, the absence of gimmicks and distractions at the ballpark, and the greater access the average fan has to players. Whitesmith (2001) writes about the thrill of discovering the past in Cuban baseball: "To the devout baseball fan, it's a trip to the pure well of a kind of baseball the rest of the world has strayed from—the veritable Vatican of baseball: Cuba" (see www.baseballthinkfactory.org/files/main/article/Whitesmith_2001-04-17_0).

This article addresses the question of whether the Cuban model of organizing baseball along less market-driven criteria leads to more desirable outcomes. Many analysts believe the answer is yes.[1] Richards (2003), for example, proposes a quite radical transformation of MLB that would give ownership of teams to the public, would severely limit player mobility, would introduce a salary structure based on seniority, and would assure affordable tickets. With that in mind, a close analysis of the Cuban system—how it works, what outcomes it generates—can be instructive.

Cuba offers one example of league play that purports to uphold egalitarian rather than market values. This case study is not meant to be generalizable to all examples (real or hypothetical) of league play under nonmarket rules. However, the article is meant to demonstrate that alternatives to market-driven sports leagues inevitably have their own downside. In the case of Cuba, the article shows that the attributes of the Cuban baseball system that observers most approve of—regionally based teams, high-caliber play, players motivated by the love of the game, and a seeming lack of profit motive—are achieved through the government's exploitation of players, its extreme control over the choices of players, and a persistent imbalance in team composition.

A BRIEF HISTORY OF BASEBALL IN CUBA

Baseball in Cuba has a long history, as organized league play dates to 1878 (roughly the same time as U.S. baseball). From Cuba's independence from Spain in 1898 through the first half of the 20th century, American interests dominated Cuban politics. One result was that during this period, the two countries developed close political, economic, and cultural ties. Before Cuba's revolution in 1959, professional baseball in Cuba was closely associated with professional baseball in the United States. For example, many MLB teams played exhibition games or their entire spring training schedule in Cuba. The best (White) Cuban players played in the major leagues, Americans often played for Cuban teams, and major league players would often play in Cuba's winter league. In 1946, the Havana Cubans joined the Florida International League as an affiliate of MLB's Washington Senators, and thus, Cuba then became a direct participant in U.S. professional baseball.

Cuba's 1959 revolution dramatically changed baseball in Cuba. The revolution struck at the heart of American interests in Cuba in that most private property became state property; this, coupled with Cuba's emerging ties with the Soviet Union, led to growing hostility between the two countries. First to change in baseball were the formal relationships between Cuba and MLB. In 1960, the International League voted to relocate the Cuban Sugar Kings (previously known as the Havana Cubans) to Jersey City. Eleven Cuban players, faced with the option of remaining in their country or playing professional baseball, chose the latter and left their country (Rucker & Bjarkman, 1999, p. 8). Shortly after the loss of the Sugar Kings, Cuba's winter league circuit was forced out of business (Rucker & Bjarkman, 1999, p. 185).

Second to change in Cuban baseball was its organizational structure. Part of Castro's plan for revolutionizing Cuba entailed revolutionizing sports. This eventually led to the country's adoption of a model of so-called physical culture prevalent in the Soviet Union and other socialist countries (Pettavino & Pye, 1994, pp. 10–12). According to both Marx and Lenin, an individual's physical and mental development are linked and must be shaped by socialist society to assure strong character and values. Mass physical culture is one way to accomplish this, which also serves as an additional means of promoting state ideology among the masses (Pettavino & Pye, 1994). Mass physical culture in Cuba today remains important and involves a highly structured system of physical education within the schools as well as an extensive system of special sports schools where talented young athletes develop skill in dozens of sports (Pettavino, 2004).

Unlike mass participation in sports, the socialist emphasis on developing champions is done largely for strategic and nationalist reasons. Pettavino and Pye (1994, p. 14) state, "through competition in sports, the other peoples of the world could observe the differences between the socialist and capitalist systems, and compare them." Under socialism, it was believed that talented athletes would be motivated by patriotic duty to perform for their country, rather than by money. A new socialist basis for the relationships among players, fans, and the sport would result in a higher caliber play, greater fan appreciation, and a stronger public identity with sports—in short, a superior system.

Across the decades, the particular role of baseball in Cuban ideology and politics has remained obvious in the public pronouncements of officials and in the public statements of players. Cuba's vice president recently was quoted as saying that in Cuba, sports are "not only the fruit, but also the symbol of our Socialist revolution" (Price, 2000, p. 35). In Cuba, athletes are expected to be political as well as athletic examples for others to emulate. Moreover, promotion within the sports system is based not only on talent but on the degree of an individual's perceived support of the government (Pettavino & Pye, 1994). One of Cuba's best baseball players, Antonio Pacheco, is the epitome of the ideal athlete. In 2000, he made the following statement in a program aired in the United States, in response to questions about why he does not defect:

> I think I represent to the fans the athlete formed by my country; the athlete that all Cubans want to see; the athlete who is a role model for all the Cubans who put their trust in me; the athlete who will never leave his people; the athlete who will never betray them; the athlete who will defend his flag with love and dignity. I think that is where the fan's admiration and respect come from. . . . Cuba for me is like my mother, and I will never abandon my mother.
>
> (Clift & Skvirsky, 2000)

POSTREVOLUTIONARY BASEBALL IN CUBA TODAY

In 1962, the Castro government replaced Cuba's professional baseball system with a new amateur baseball league called the Cuban League. Post-revolutionary baseball in Cuba was to be based on a socialist model of amateur sports not driven by money but by national ideals. Cuba's commissioner of baseball, Carlos Rodríquez Acosta, underscores this ideal:

> The people have an incredible sense of ownership over Cuban baseball. It's a symbol. I'd say like the flag, like the coat of arms, like the national anthem. Baseball has been a symbol of nationalism for more than 120 years. And therefore, when we're organizing the championships, we have to be very aware that we're not just dealing with some baseball game; but rather with the most important spectacle that exists in Cuba, the Cuban National Championship Series.
>
> (Clift & Skvirsky, 2000)

Organization of play. The Cuban League remains relatively unchanged since 1962. It consists of 16 teams playing a 90-game schedule, teams are divided into an East and West Sector, and after the regular season, postseason play leads to the Eastern champion playing the Western champion. Each of the 16 teams in the Cuban League represents a different Cuban province, with the exception of the province of Havana City, which hosts two teams. Teams do not move nor, for the most part, do the players. The regional structure to games, with players originating from the province itself, is thought to heighten interest, rivalries, and the level of play. Rucker and Bjarkman (1999) note that "regional pride and socialist ideals of sportsmanship have replaced professional salaries as the driving force of championship play" (p. 9).

At the end of each play-off season, government officials from the sports ministry select the Cuban national team to compete in international tournaments. Cuba's national team has won the vast majority of international baseball tournaments it has entered since the revolution, attesting to the success of Cuba's system of developing talented athletes. In theory, the national team is comprised of the most talented Cuban players. However, team members are sometimes selected for political reasons rather than athletic performance (Fainaru & Sánchez, 2001; Jamail, 2000; Rohter, 1997b). Because international play outside Cuba gives players an opportunity to defect, players with so-called questionable political loyalty may not be selected. Commissioner Rodríquez confirms that political factors figure into the government's selection of the national team:

> An athlete is selected to defend our country. . . . If he doesn't have an attitude where we . . . can have confidence in him, then he will never have the right to represent Cuba in an international event. . . . On top of everything he must be patriotic, dignified, and participate like the athlete he is.
>
> (Price, 2000, p. 109)

PLAYER MARKETS AND DEFECTIONS

As is true of talented athletes in many present and past socialist countries, baseball players in Cuba are developed through an extensive and highly organized player-development system run by the sports ministry. Talented players are identified as early as age 10 and move into one of the regional sports boarding academies that are found throughout the country.[2] Here they have access to specialized trainers, facilities, and coaches. The best players eventually earn a spot on their province's team or, in rare cases, are assigned to another province's team.[3] As is true of all state workers in Cuba, changing jobs or locations (teams) is very difficult and involves state approval. All players receive a salary from the state, which today generally ranges from about 250 to 350 pesos per month (currently $10 to $15 per month; Arturo González, personal communication, March 26, 2003). This pay is equivalent to that earned by the vast majority of the workforce that is likewise employed by the Cuban government. Officially, there is no difference in pay between the best and worst players. Informally, as is true throughout much of the government-controlled labor market, players (workers) identified by the government as deserving may receive additional gifts. This might include a vacation, a car, a washing machine, or smaller items such as movie tickets, a restaurant meal, or a spare part for a broken television set. However, such gifts are unpredictable, and players occasionally complain about their size (Clift & Skvirsky, 2000; Fainaru & Sánchez, 2001).

Because of the lure of higher salaries from playing with teams abroad, such as in Japan, Italy, or other Latin American countries, government rules prohibit players from earning money by playing baseball overseas. Unless they defect, players are expected to play Cuban baseball until they are too old to play well, at which point the government reemploys them elsewhere. Within Cuba, all defectors are officially regarded as traitors, although among the general population, defecting ballplayers remain very popular and their careers are closely watched (Fainaru & Sánchez, 2001; Jamail, 2000; Price, 2000; Rohter, 1997a).

Since 1990, economic hardship has brought many changes to Cuba, including to the rules prohibiting Cubans from playing overseas. Before 1990, the Soviet Union provided Cuba with about $6 billion per year in aid (Mesa-Lago, 1998), as well as favorable commercial arrangements. The fall of the former Soviet Union brought tough times to Cuba. Between 1989 and 1993, Cuban exports fell from $5.4 billion to $1.7 billion, and GDP fell by 40% (Jatar-Hausmann, 1996). Exacerbating this, in 1992, the U.S. Congress passed the Cuban Democracy Act, an act ostensibly intended to hasten Castro's demise (Purcell, 2000). The act prohibited subsidiaries of U.S. companies from conducting business with Cuba, prohibited U.S. citizens from traveling to Cuba, and made it more difficult for Cubans in the United States to send remittances home. In 1996, the U.S.'s grip on Cuba tightened further with the Helms-Burton Act (Purcell, 2000). This act placed additional restrictions on foreign subsidiaries doing business in Cuba, allowed U.S. citizens to sue foreigners who make use of Cuban property supposedly still owned by U.S. citizens, and denied entry into the United States to such foreigners.[4] For baseball, the economic difficulties wrought by these changes worked to undermine rules proscribing players from playing overseas, as discussed below.[5]

In 1991, René Arocha, a pitcher on Cuba's national team, shocked Cuba by defecting to the United States while returning from an exhibition game in Tennessee. One prominent Cuban, baseball journalist Gilberto Dihigo, went so far as to call the first defection by Arocha a "dagger in the heart [of] the regime" (quoted in Jamail, 2000, p. 77). Although clearly an exaggeration, this defection did publicly reveal that not all players shared the official view of Cuban baseball. Two years after defecting, Arocha (playing for the St. Louis Cardinals) compiled an 11–8 record with a 3.78 earned run average, and earned $109,000.[6] Arocha's experience confirmed to Cubans that their players could compete with the best professional baseball players in the world, could do so without retribution, and could also earn unimaginably large salaries. This knowledge, along with Cuba's worsening economy and fervent efforts by baseball scouts to facilitate defections (Fainaru & Sánchez, 2001), led to more than 80 Cuban baseball players defecting between 1991 and 2000 (Clift & Skvirsky, 2000).

In 1995, the government responded to this crisis by making a number of changes. First, it reassigned or demoted many baseball officials; second, and most significantly, it established *Cubadeportes*, a marketing arm of the government's sports ministry. Among other things, *Cubadeportes* began actively seeking contracts abroad for Cuban athletes, as Cuba's best athletes would now be allowed to "retire" early, before the natural end of their careers. These early retired athletes were then allowed to play, perform, or coach overseas—with the caveat that about 80% of their earnings would go to the Cuban government (Clift & Skvirsky, 2000; Jamail, 2000; Price, 2000).

The response in baseball to this new rule was immediate: during 1995, more than 50 baseball players took early retirement from Cuban baseball (Rohter, 1997b), and went to play for teams throughout the world. During a three-year period, about 85 baseball players retired to play abroad (Jamail, 2000, p. 70), and more than 1000 athletes and coaches in total left Cuba (Price, 2000, p. 18). The Cuban government drew significant revenue from these contracts (Baxter, 2002); although official figures are not available, Price (2000, p. 65) estimates the amount to be $40 million.

The ability to make more money playing baseball relieved the pressure on players to defect. But this also created another political problem: dissatisfaction from Cuban baseball fans. After winning every official international tournament in which it had played during the previous 10 years, and after compiling a 152-game winning streak in the process, the Cuban national team lost the Intercontinental Cup to Japan in 1997. Moreover, fans perceived that the quality of play in the Cuban League had declined. According to Jamail (2000, p. 70), fans believed that players were playing poorly so that they could be allowed to retire, and they bemoaned the loss of their best players to foreign teams. Interest in baseball plummeted, and fans became increasingly dissatisfied with the political management of baseball. In 1997, attendance during the usually wildly popular championship series was very low, sometimes no more than a few thousand fans per game (Jamail, 2000).

In 1998, after a three-year experiment, the Cuban government decided to end its so-called early retirement plan. Predictably, many Cuban athletes were unhappy with this decision. With the option of playing overseas gone, the pressure to defect increased, and within months, Cuba's star pitcher, Adrían Hernández, defected and signed a $4.4 million dollar contract with the New York Yankees (Clift & Skvirsky, 2000). During the 2000 season alone, Cuba lost 11 more of its baseball players to defections (Clift & Skvirsky, 2000). According to Pettavino (2004, p. 31), in the late 1990s, defections of athletes had become so common that a Canadian newspaper held a "count the defectors" contest where readers competed by guessing how many Cubans would defect during the 1999 Pan American Games in Winnipeg.[7]

PROFITS: ARE CUBAN PLAYERS EXPLOITED?

With a single employer, Cuban baseball players have no bargaining power in the setting of player salaries. The government is free to pay all players (and citizens because it has a virtual monopoly on the labor market) a reservation wage—which is approximately what it does by paying everyone about $15 a month.[8]

Are players exploited, though? In this case, the exploiter would be the government because it is the residual claimant on any revenue generated by government workers (players). Jamail (2000), a critic of the Cuban government's restrictions on baseball players, thinks players are exploited. Commenting on why the government bans from baseball any player who it thinks is considering defecting, he writes, "bannings were a reminder that making money off baseball was still an activity reserved for the state" (p. 89).

The main way that Cuban baseball generates money is through ticket sales. In MLB, ticket sales are only one of many sources of revenue. In Cuba, there is no commercial advertising in stadiums, nor is there any advertising on television or radio. Very little food is sold at the stadium, and for those who drive (few do), parking is free. Items such as baseball caps, jerseys, and baseball cards are almost nonexistent. In short, very little money is made on baseball other than through ticket sales.

Before 1994, baseball games in Cuba were free. In 1994, economic hardship led the government to start charging admission. The price charged in 1994 is the same price charged throughout the country today: one peso (about 4 cents), or three pesos for box seats behind home plate. However, complimentary seats are frequently distributed in large quantities to select groups. If, in the most generous approximation of ticket revenue, 10,000 people pay 1 peso for each game played, ticket sales in the Cuban League would raise about 7.2 million pesos per year.

An equally rough approximation can be made of the Cuban League's expenses. If each player makes 300 pesos a month, and there are 24 players on each team, then player salaries in the Cuban League would be approximately 1.4 million pesos a year. Assume all other expenses—staff, travel, equipment, stadium upkeep—roughly equals the players' salary (which is true in MLB; Fort, 2003, p. 275). Then, in the best-case scenario of baseball revenue, players receive only about 24% of the net revenue that they generate, with the balance going to the government.[9] If, on the other hand, revenue estimates were reduced by 50% and nonsalary expenses doubled—both of which may be more reasonable approximations—then the government loses money on baseball. Certainly, it lost money before it began selling tickets in 1994.

In sum, it is possible that Cuban baseball players are exploited by their government, but if so, probably not by much, at least in terms of what a free internal market would provide them. The exception to this is in foreign contracts, where the government's share of 80% (or more) of player pay is a clear case of exploitation. Indeed, the profits generated by Cuba's elite group of athletes and coaches are in large part what now keeps Cuba's entire sporting structure afloat (Pettavino, 2004).

Many baseball players in Cuba can also be seen as exploited in a different sense. The government's prohibition against playing in foreign leagues is an instance where the government restricts players from generating their value. These rules exist not so that the government can gain some financial advantage but rather that it can obtain some political gain. In this sense, many players can be thought of as exploited by their government for political rather than economic gain.

The government's response to this characterization of its policy is two-fold. First, any narrow estimate of the revenue and expenses associated with the Cuban League leaves out the entire period of player development. As previously stated, the government begins investing in players when they are as young as 10. Commenting on U.S. scouts' continual efforts to acquire Cuban talent, Cuba's baseball commissioner Rodríguez says,

> It's pillaging. They come to see what they can take. But you didn't train them. You didn't develop them. You didn't spend one single cent on them. Now you want to come take them? I also want them for my team.
>
> (Clift & Skvirsky, 2000)

However, for highly paid athletes, the government's share from a foreign contract gives it many times over its investment in the athlete. Second, the Cuban government would argue that baseball in Cuba is not based, as it is in the United States, on a market ideology. The sport is managed for the good of the people, not for the individual, and players' participation is part of the social contract Cubans have with one another. The question this raises is whether the values of the government are the same as those of the governed. That many players seek to defect suggests that for some at least, the answer is no.

THE DISTRIBUTION OF TALENT AND COMPETITIVE BALANCE: DOES CUBA GET IT RIGHT?

A third issue in the evaluation of an organized sports league is competitive balance: how evenly is talent distributed among teams? Uneven distribution leads to less interesting match-ups and fan dissatisfaction over a perceived unfairness in competition. In MLB, a widespread belief exists that persistent competitive imbalance is undermining the sport. This issue concerned MLB enough that the owners recently commissioned a study that documented the problem of imbalance and proposed ways to improve it (Levin, Mitchell, Volcker, & Will, 2000).

In MLB, talent goes to the team that is most willing to pay for it; imbalance is largely a result of differences among the teams in their willingness to pay for talent, which is usually determined by market size. In Cuba, talent is distributed (with some caveats, discussed below) according to the players' origin. Thus, one might reasonably expect that teams drawing from a larger population would have better players and compile better records. This proposition is examined below.

. . . A simple and common method of measuring competitive balance is to calculate the standard deviation—a measure of spread—in team records. One can then compare this with the expected standard deviation if all teams were equally talented so that the results of any match-up were equivalent to the flip of a coin. This is called the *ideal* standard deviation. The ratio (actual standard deviation/ideal standard deviation) provides a measure of competitive balance. . . . A higher ratio thus implies greater imbalance (wins are more concentrated with certain teams), a lower ratio better balance (wins more evenly spread across all teams). Quirk and Fort (1997) use this measure to compare competitive balance across time and across professional sports in the United States. Based on annual winning percentages, they find that in MLB, this measure of balance has averaged around 2 during the last 50 years, although during the last 25 years, this indicator of balance has declined to approximately 1.7.

Table 19.1 shows this competitive balance indicator for the Cuban League during the period of 1978 to 2002. The first column is the indicator based on teams' annual winning percentage. This indicator has averaged 2.8 during the 25-year period, revealing that play in the Cuban League is historically more imbalanced than in MLB. Figure 19.1 compares competitive balance between the Cuban League, the American League, and the National League during the same 25 years and reveals that in most years, the Cuban League was more imbalanced than either of MLB's leagues.

Column 2 in Table 19.1 presents competitive balance indicators based on the previous five-year accumulated winning record of each team. By this measure, league play in Cuba is much more imbalanced, as the spread in team winning percentages is almost four times larger than expected if the league had been comprised of teams with an equal chance of winning. This shows that in the Cuban League, teams that win (lose) in one year tend to also win (lose) in subsequent years—something characteristic of professional leagues in the United States as well (Quirk & Fort, 1997).

Figure 19.2 graphically shows trends in competitive balance in the Cuban League, based on both annual and five-year records. Balance based on the past five years of play reveals that balance worsened during the 1980s but has steadily improved during the past decade. It may be that defections and early retirements during the past decade have improved balance in the Cuban League. Anecdotally, baseball powerhouses —notably the Havana *Industriales*—have lost their best stars during the past decade. During the first half of the 1990s, the *Industriales* compiled a winning record of .678; during the second half, its winning record was .566. The opposite trend is evident in a number of the weaker teams; for example, *Guantánamo* improved its record from .330 in the first half of the 1990s, to .444 during the second half. Although likely of little consolation to fans, it appears that defections and early retirements at least have improved the prospects of the weaker league teams.

Finally, Table 19.2 shows the cumulative win-loss record during the past 25 years of the 16 teams currently playing in the Cuban League. *Pinar del Río* has been a perpetual winner, winning 67% of its 1,559 games, whereas *Las Tunas* has won just 35% of its 1,561 games. Examining cumulative winning records in the Cuban League reveals a league more imbalanced than MLB's leagues.

As suggested by evidence in Table 19.2, the spread in cumulative winning records during the past 25 years is significantly smaller in MLB than it is in the Cuban League. The last column in Table 19.2 indicates the percentage of the Cuban population in 1990 living in the region that each team represents. This can be used to approximate the relative size of the pool from which each team's players are drawn. The correlation between teams' accumulated winning percentage and their region's population is .65; this means that 65% of the differences among teams' winning records can be explained by the size of the region's

Table 19.1 Competitive Balance Indicators in the Cuban League, 1978 to 2002 (actual/ideal standard deviation)

Year	*Annual Record*	*Previous 5-year Record*
1978	1.86	
1979	2.13	
1980	2.03	
1981	1.73	
1982	1.68	3.11
1983	2.08	3.10
1984	2.03	3.22
1985	2.21	3.48
1986	2.23	3.48
1987	2.02	3.72
1988	2.53	3.41
1989	2.34	3.41
1990	2.34	4.06
1991	2.01	4.08
1992	1.99	4.27
1993	2.24	4.16
1994	2.16	3.86
1995	2.09	4.05
1996	2.12	4.24
1997	2.28	4.24
1998	1.97	3.83
1999	1.61	3.58
2000	2.04	3.56
2001	2.19	3.67
2002	2.18	3.63
Average	2.08	3.72

Source: Author calculations are based on annual records retrieved from Cuba's Radio Coco (www.radiococo.cu/totalbeisbol).

population. Thus, market size in Cuba seems to be an even more important determinant of team quality in Cuba than it is in the United States.[10]

In sum, competitive balance in the Cuban League appears to be no better, and probably worse, than competitive balance in MLB. Imbalance in MLB is largely a result of differences in the market size in which teams operate. Ironically, Cuban baseball confronts the same problem. In the case of MLB, differences in market size mean that some teams are willing to pay to obtain the best talent, whereas teams in small markets are not. In the case of Cuba, market size does not influence the amount of revenue that top talent generates but rather influences the size of the labor pool from which the talent is drawn. Yet in both cases, the resulting distribution of talent is unbalanced—and is more so in the case of Cuba. To the extent that the Cuban government allows some mobility of players, it does not appear to be the case that these decisions are made so as to improve the distribution of talent. The evidence also suggests that defections may be improving competitive balance.

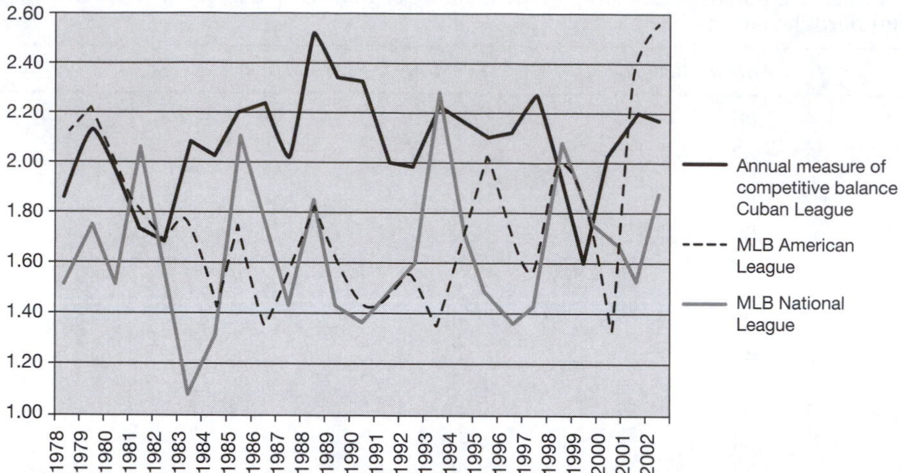

Figure 19.1 Competitive balance: Cuban League versus Major League Baseball, 1978 to 2002.

Source: Author calculations are based on team record data retrieved from Cuba's Radio Coco (www.radiococo.cu/total beisbol) and Rod Fort's Website for Major League Baseball (http//users.pullman.com/rodfort/sportsbusiness/BizFrame.htm).

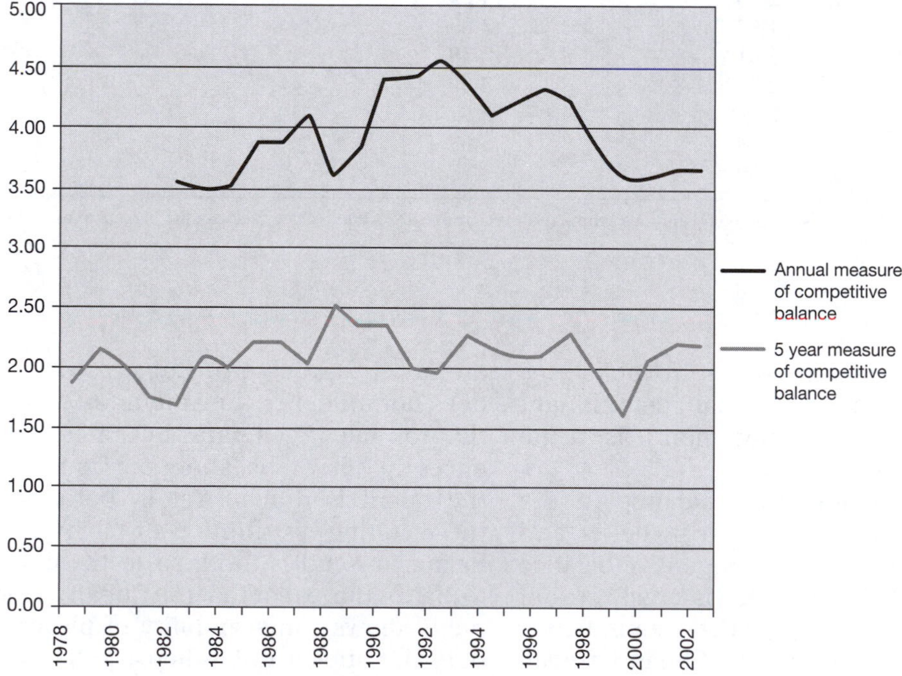

Figure 19.2 Competitive balance in the Cuban League, 1978 to 2002.

Note: Values shown are derived by dividing actual standard deviations by idealized standard deviations.

Table 19.2 Cumulative Records of Cuban League Teams, 1978 to 2002

Region	*Wins*	*Losses*	*Winning Percentage*	*Share of Population (1990)*
Pinar del Río	509	262	.660	6.6
Isla de la Juventud	619	940	.397	0.7
Matanzas	389	384	.503	5.8
Metropolitanos	755	799	.486	10.0
Sancti Spíritus	658	906	.421	4.1
Industriales	959	594	.618	10.0
La Habana	818	734	.527	6.1
Cienfuegos	659	900	.423	3.4
Villa Clara	969	588	.622	7.6
Camagüey	847	715	.542	7.0
Ciego De Ávila	646	913	.414	3.4
Las Tunas	543	1,018	.348	4.7
Holguín	717	845	.459	9.0
Santiago De Cuba	951	613	.608	9.4
Guantánamo	661	903	.423	4.7
Granma	819	744	.524	7.5

Source: Team records are retrieved from Cuba's Radio Coco (www.radiococo.cu/ totalbeisbol); population data is taken from Smith (1997).

DISCUSSION AND CONCLUDING REMARKS

In many respects, Cuban baseball under Castro can be seen as a great success, as its achievements in international competition are remarkable. These successes have come about through extensive government regulation, most notably through public investments in player development, and through strict control over both the labor markets and the gains generated therein. This is in stark contrast with baseball in the United States and elsewhere, where market forces play a central role in determining the development of talent, the allocation of talent, and the distribution of baseball's gains.[11]

Cuba's high level of talent and consistency of team composition is ensured through, on one hand, stifling individual freedom, and on the other, a loss of political legitimacy as too strict of control over the labor market fosters defections. The conflict between Cuba's ideology and the quality of its baseball has led the Cuban government to attempt striking a balance between the official egalitarian rhetoric and the easing of restrictions on player compensation so as to reduce defections. The dilemma is that the regulation of baseball for ideological purposes places a very high cost on those from whom the government most wants support.

For the time being, defections, the fear of continued defections, and the government's continuing need for hard currency have led the government to once again compromise its commitment to egalitarian ideals and a sports ideology that exalts amateur athletes. After bringing the practice to a halt in 1998, the Cuban government has once again begun negotiating contracts with foreign teams. In 2002, it negotiated contracts with Japanese teams for Cuba's five top baseball players ("Linares to play," 2002), the most famous of the five being Omar Linares and Germán Mesa.[12] In his first year in Japan,

Omar Linares's contract provided him with $12,000 (Continental Baseball Association, 2002). The Cuban government's share of the contract was not made public, but top stars in Japanese baseball—and the expectation was that Linares would become one—easily make more than $1 million a year.[13] In all likelihood, the Cuban government received significantly more than 80% of Linares's earnings. Although it is less clear if the average Cuban player is exploited, those who are able to play overseas are clearly exploited by the Cuban government.

Ironically, in terms of competitive balance on the field, the government's control over player mobility does little to help smaller provinces compete with larger provinces. In fact, it may do just the opposite, as smaller regions in Cuba have little ability to field a winning team, no matter how much they might want one. What sounds ideal—player immobility—in fact may be bad for fairness on the field. This is a lesson that many have also drawn from MLB's old reserve system that tied players to teams (Butler, 1995; Fort, 2003; Maxcy, 2002; Rottenberg, 1956).

In Cuban baseball today, government policy continues the pursuit of an organization structure based on egalitarian and amateur values. This pursuit is increasingly in conflict with both the economic incentives facing players and the economic incentives facing the government to capture the value players can generate abroad. How the government manages these three competing forces—ideology, the threat of defection, and economic expediency—will likely be determined by the government's assessment of the importance of each to maintaining its power. The dilemma facing the Cuban government in its management of these forces in baseball is in many ways also emblematic of its larger problem of maintaining political control in the face of adverse economic changes.[14]

With respect to the applicability of the Cuban case to the optimal way to organize a sports league, the Cuban case points out that markets fail to perform for the public interest insofar as an alternative system would do better. A case study of Cuba does not offer a definitive answer—yes or no—to the question of whether government regulation can improve on market outcomes. Rather, it is illustrative of the often unintended results that are associated with government regulation of any market. That government regulation of sports markets is superior to the use of market forces, as suggested by (among others) Richards (2003), is an argument that still needs to be made.

NOTES

1 For a popular account of the woes facing Major League Baseball (MLB), and proposals to remedy them, see Costas (2000). For a similar analysis (financed by MLB), see Levin, Mitchell, Volcker, & Will (2000).

2 The system currently includes 15 schools for sports instruction, 14 schools for superior athletic refinement, 162 sports academies, and two centers for high performance located in Havana (Pettavino, 2004).

3 In 2003, for example, the *Cienfuegos* team included three players from other provinces (González, 2003).

4 These two acts strengthened policy (commonly referred to as *the embargo*) dating to 1962 that prohibited the sale of all goods to Cuba originating in the United States. In 2001, Cuban wages remained about 40% (and GDP about 20%) below their 1989 levels (Mesa-Lago, 2001).

5 In fact, the economic hardship of the 1990s brought many instances of market liberalization, as discussed in Jatar-Hausmann (1996).

6 See http://www.baseballlibrary.com/baseball library/teams/1993cardinals.stm.

7 The exodus during the 1990s has not been limited to ballplayers. According to Pedraza (2002), about 25,000 Cubans a year are leaving the island.

8 A reservation wage is the lowest wage for which a worker will accept work.

9 1.4 million/(7.2million – 1.4 million) = 24%.

10 Here, the term *market size* is used differently for MLB and the Cuban League, although both can be approximated by the size of population within the vicinity of each team. In Cuba, the market that differs for each team and that determines the distribution of player talent is the player market; in the United States, each MLB team faces the same player market because it is a national market. What market matters for the acquisition of talent in MLB is the consumer market, and it is this that differs for each team.

11 The government's role in U.S. baseball (the financing of stadiums and the inapplicability of antitrust laws in particular) is certainly crucial in understanding baseball outcomes in the United States. With this important caveat, market forces do explain most of what happens in MLB.

12 Long considered the best baseball player in Cuba—and perhaps one of the best in the world—Linaras reportedly was once offered $40 million by MLB to defect (CBA, 2002). Mesa is one of numerous star players who have at one time or another been banned from Cuban baseball for allegedly considering defection; he is currently coaching baseball in Japan ("Linaras to play," 2002).

13 See http://japanesebaseball.com/players/index.jsp.

14 See Corrales (2002) for greater discussion on the government's responses since 1990 to conflicting state interests.

REFERENCES

Baxter, K. (2002, June 11). Trio of Cubans's services sold to Japanese Industrial League. *Baseball America News*. Retrieved from www.baseballamerica.com/today/news/cubans061102.html

Butler, M. (1995). Competitive balance in Major League Baseball. *American Econo- mist, 39*(2), 46–52.

Clift, R. A., & Skvirsky, S. A. (Producers and Directors). (2000). *Stealing home: The case of contemporary Cuban baseball* [PBS television special]. New York and Washington, DC: Public Broadcasting Service.

Corrales, J. (2002). The survival of the Cuban regime: A political-economy perspective. *Cuba in Transition: Proceedings of the Fifth Annual Meeting of the Association for the Study of the Cuban Economy, 12*, 493–506. Retrieved from www.lanic.utexas. edu/project/asce/publications/proceedings/

Costas, B. (2000). *Fair ball: A fan's case for baseball*. New York: Broadway Books. Cummings, S. (2003, May 13). Baseball on 12 cents a seat. *Seattle Times*, p. C1.

Fainaru, S., & Sánchez, R. (2001). *The duke of Havana: Baseball, Cuba, and the search for the American dream*. New York: Villard.

Fort, R. (2003). *Sports economics*. Englewood Cliffs, NJ: Prentice Hall.

González, A. (2003). Personal communication. March 26.

Guillermoprieto, A. (2004). *Dancing with Cuba: A memoir of the revolution*. New York: Pantheon.

Jamail, M. (2000). *Full count: Inside Cuban baseball*. Carbondale: Southern Illinois University Press.

Jatar-Hausmann, A. (1996). Through the cracks of socialism: The emerging private sector in Cuba." *Cuba in Transition: Proceedings of the Fifth Annual Meeting of the Association for the Study of the Cuban Economy, 6*, 202–218. Retrieved from www.lanic.utexas.edu/project/asce/publications/proceedings/

Levin, R., Mitchell, G., Volcker, P., & Will, G. (2000). *The report of the independent members of the commissioner's blue ribbon panel on baseball economics*. Retrieved from www.mlb.com/mlb/downloads/blue_ribbon.pdf

Linares to play for Chunichi Dragons. (2002, July 6). Retrieved from www.espn.go. com/mlb/news/2002/0706/1402758.html

Maxcy, J. (2002). Rethinking restrictions on player mobility in Major League Baseball. *Contemporary Economic Policy, 20*(2), 145–159.

Mesa-Lago, C. (1998). Assessing economic and social performance in the Cuban transition of the 1990s. *World Development, 26*, 857–876.

Mesa-Lago, C. (2001). The Cuban economy in 1999–2001: Evaluation of performance and debate on the future. *Cuba in Transition: Proceedings of the Eleventh Annual Meetings of the Association for the Study of the Cuban Economy, 11*, 1–17. Retrieved from www.lanic.utexas.edu/project/asce/pdfs/volume11/

Pedraza, S. (2002). Democratization and migration: Cuba's exodus and the development of civil society. *Cuba in Transition: Proceedings of the Fifth Annual Meeting of the Association for the Study of the Cuban Economy, 12*, 247–261. Retrieved from www.lanic.utexas.edu/project/asce/publications/proceedings/

Pettavino, P. (2004). Cuban sports: Saved by capitalism? *NACLA Report on the Americas, 37*(5), 27–32.

Pettavino, P., & Pye, G. (1994). *Sport in Cuba: The diamond in the rough*. Pittsburgh, PA: University of Pittsburgh Press.

Price, S. (2000). *Pitching around Fidel.* New York: HarperCollins.

Purcell, S. K. (2000). Why the Cuban embargo makes sense in a post–cold war world. In S. K. Purcell & D. J. Rothkopf (Eds.), *Cuba: The contours of change* (pp. 81–103). Boulder, CO: Rienner.

Quirk, J., & Fort, R. (1997). *Pay dirt.* Princeton, NJ: Princeton University Press.

Richards, D. (2003). A (utopian) socialist proposal for the reform of Major League Baseball. *Journal of Sport and Social Issues, 27,* 308–324.

Rohter, L. (1997a, October 19). Marlins star is a hero Cuba ignores. *The New York Times,* p. A4.

Rohter, L. (1997b, November 3). Havana journal: No joy in Cuba, as its baseball team strikes out. *The New York Times,* p. A8.

Rottenberg, S. (1956). The baseball players' labor market. *Journal of Political Economy, 64,* 253–256.

Rucker, M., & Bjarkman, P. (1999). *Smoke: The romance and lore of Cuban baseball.* Kingston, NY: Total/Sports Illustrated.

Smith, R. F. (1997). Cuba. In *World book encyclopedia* (Vol. 4, pp. 1168–1179). Chicago: World Book.

Whitesmith, G. (2001, April 17). *Window on Cuba: A pilgrimage to the Vatican of baseball.* Retrieved from www.baseballprimer.com/articles

CHAPTER 20

Public Dollars, Private Stadiums, and Democracy

Kevin J. Delaney and Rick Eckstein

WHERE'S THE DEMOCRACY?

Overall, the process of building private stadiums with public dollars in the United States is more akin to plutocracy and oligarchy than to democracy. Here, we include both a procedural definition of democracy (in which everyone affected by policy decisions has a meaningful say in making them) and a substantive definition (in which policy decisions reflect the real interests of affected parties without those interests being manipulated). Sometimes the anti-democratic processes are blatant and unmistakable, sometimes they are more subtle, and sometimes they are obfuscated by the workings of normal politics. Residents in and around Pittsburgh and Phoenix were crystal clear about not wanting to spend public dollars on private stadiums. But in both cases, powerful stadium advocates simply trampled on public sentiment and built the stadiums anyway.

Sometimes the threats to democracy are more subtle, although still obvious if you look in the right places. In Philadelphia, for instance, there was no need to blatantly trample on popular sentiment because the public was never given any say on the matter except indirectly through city council and state representatives. When a Pennsylvania state representative explained to us the inner workings of the legislature, it seemed to have little in common with democracy as we conventionally define it. He explained exactly how Pennsylvania decided to put up two-thirds of the money for the four new stadiums in Pittsburgh and Philadelphia:

> Ninety-five percent of the calls we get on this issue are against it. . . . For dynamic issues like these that are wildly unpopular, the legislative leaders decide it will happen; and then they decide how many votes each side [Republican and Democratic] will give up and which representatives are least vulnerable—so they don't get taken out [for voting for something so unpopular].

This representative was clear that, even though Pennsylvania residents were overwhelmingly opposed to using public dollars for the four new stadiums, the legislative leadership did it anyway. The leaders selected which representatives would vote for the "wildly unpopular" issue by determining who was in a safe district and would thus be insulated from voter backlash. So, for example, a Democrat in a district that is 90 percent Democratic is cajoled into voting for the unpopular issue because she or he will be unlikely to lose reelection. Of course, that Democrat will not vote "correctly" without some serious horse trading. When we interviewed the representative just quoted a few months before the final vote, he predicted, "I would bet this [funding for new stadiums] will happen because most members have their price" in terms of pet projects (such as, acquiring park land or resurfacing bridges), which others will vote for in exchange for supporting the stadium issue. It turns out he was correct.

In fact, we were told that one of the big inside fights on this issue concerned the fact that Republicans wanted to provide fewer than half of the total *yes* votes needed to pass the stadium bill. The Democratic leadership, however, argued that because Republican governor Tom Ridge wanted the bill so badly, the Republicans should give up more than half of the votes. The Republican leadership countered that because the stadiums would benefit the two largest cities in Pennsylvania, which are largely Democratic, the Democrats should give up more than half of the votes. All of this finagling may not surprise a cynical observer, but it is not exactly what you read about democracy in a high school civics text.

While such blatant and clandestine power plays pose clear threats to democratic institutions, we think there are even more sinister threats within the everyday political process. Here, the trappings of democratic procedure often mask very undemocratic social policies. The best ongoing examples are the referendums that seem to indicate community support for new publicly subsidized stadiums, apparently demonstrating that policies allocating public dollars for private stadiums reflect popular sentiment. But this belief assumes that the referendum process is balanced and fair—that all interested parties have an equal opportunity to influence public policy.

Referendum campaigns are anything but fair arenas for hashing out the advantages and disadvantages of using public dollars for new stadiums. Subsidy advocates have much more power in the referendum process than do stadium opponents. At the most basic level, advocates directly outspend opponents by at least ten to one and sometimes, as in San Diego, by much more. These powerful individuals and organizations also have far superior "unofficial access" to decision makers than do average citizens—access that often occurs in stadium luxury boxes! We heard a story in Pittsburgh about a city council member who spent Sundays at Three Rivers Stadium, not watching the Steelers but keeping track of who was meeting whom in the corporate boxes. In this way, the council member knew what was going on behind the scenes when certain people or companies tried to influence city policy.

In addition to these obvious advantages in the referendum process, stadium advocates also have a third-dimensional[1] advantage: citizens grant more legitimacy to powerful people (the so-called experts) than to average people such as themselves, especially when it comes to complex issues like stimulating economic growth. This advantage is paralleled by a political system that also grants much more legitimacy to the opinions of powerful individuals and organizations than to more ordinary ones. In a sense, then, stadium supporters rarely have to fight city hall to achieve their goals. With important exceptions, the default position among many political elites is to equate new stadiums with economic growth or heightened community self-esteem. Subsidy opponents have to convince politicians *not* to believe what they have already been conditioned to believe.

WHY GROWTH COALITIONS?

We have argued throughout the book that unraveling these stadium battles is best accomplished by examining the structure of each city's local growth coalition (or its proxy) and the strategies these coalitions use to build private stadiums with public dollars. As we have shown, the strength and unity of the growth coalition shapes the stadium battles in American cities. Both the structure of growth coalitions and the decisions they make are deeply embedded in the unique social characteristics of each city. Some combinations of structure, decisions, and social characteristics carve out relatively uncomplicated paths to publicly subsidized stadiums, while other combinations create many more challenges. Either way, no route is a shining testament to democracy in action.

We have built our analytical framework around growth coalition theory because it allows us to identify some of the covert threats to democratic institutions. We believe these threats are not just sporadic and temporary breakdowns of a fair, self-regulating system but are embedded in the workings of the system itself. Most academic and nonacademic studies of new sports stadiums, good as they usually are, miss an important part of the story because they focus only on the most obvious public-policy players: the politicians and the sports teams. But guided by our search for local growth coalitions, we have discovered a world of less discernible players; and they have tremendous power over the policies allocating public dollars for private stadiums. Like more public players, these individuals and organizations stand to gain from new stadiums, but in less noticeable ways. Because growth coalitions can be so powerful, because they are largely invisible, and because they are mostly unaccountable to other social actors, we think it is imperative to understand how they are involved in the battles over new stadiums and how this involvement poses an especially insidious threat to a democratic society.

This point has not been emphasized enough, even in critical discussions of sports-stadium funding. Instead, conversations on the issue generally take a corporate welfare approach, castigating wealthy team owners who ask for handouts and local governments that universally grant these requests. But team owners are acting in the way that team owners are *supposed* to act; so the brunt of criticism, from the corporate-welfare perspective, ends up being aimed at the spineless politicians who sell out the rest of the community for a private seat in the owner's luxury box or a future campaign contribution. In contrast, our growth coalition approach insists that we must also look at the large nonsports corporations in a community (with multibillion-dollar gross revenues) rather than just the teams themselves (with gross revenues close to $100 million) in assessing who might benefit from the public financing of new stadiums.

These corporations are far more powerful than any local sports team; and their influence over the policymaking process may be ideological (that is, third-dimensional), not just a matter of throwing their money around or threatening to take their huge companies elsewhere. Local politicians "naturally" turn to the leaders of corporations for advice on important matters. Executives are invited to sit on economic development task forces and be part of municipal stadium authorities. If these successful business leaders, who are also involved with local philanthropic organizations, think that publicly financed stadiums are good for the local community, then why should policymakers (or the general community) think otherwise? Thus, corporations' particular parochial vision of suitable growth strategies comes to rule the day. Too often, however, this vision is not portrayed as particular, parochial, or self-interested but as civic-minded and altruistic. In this regard, nonsports corporations can more easily than sports teams conceal their organizational self-interest and maintain that community welfare is driving their interest in new publicly funded stadiums—if anyone even knows they are interested in the matter.

THE CORPORATE ARM OF THE GROWTH COALITION

Why do the corporate members of a growth coalition want new stadiums? We found that business leaders (sometimes including team owners) were more likely than politicians to promise social rewards from new stadiums, such as increased civic pride or a closer-knit community. While politicians talked more of economic activity to justify opening the public coffers, business leaders knew very well that there were better ways to create jobs than by subsidizing a huge stadium that operates either eighty-one days per year (baseball) or ten days per year (football). Thus, when we interviewed growth coalition leaders about their advocacy of public dollars for private stadiums, they talked about "wearing their civic hat" rather than stimulating economic growth. But this attitude only begs the question: Why promote sports stadiums rather than any other type of civic good? What underlies corporate executives' interest in advocating public dollars for private stadiums?

We think a number of factors have led corporate elites to favor building new stadiums. First, corporations want to be able to use stadiums—especially their luxury boxes—and the aura surrounding professional sports to attract new executive talent. Many of the corporate executives we talked with spoke about the challenges they faced recruiting top talent to their city. This is a particularly strong sentiment in small cities with little allure for graduates from top law schools and business schools. Business leaders in Cleveland and Cincinnati told us that, when competing with firms in New York and San Francisco, the new stadiums gave them something to show off. We can't help but wonder whether a gender bias exists here. Of course, women can be interested in professional sports. But in all our conversations with executives about recruiting A-level talent, they always seemed to be talking about men. Although we aren't even sure whether A-level talent cares all that much about stadium luxury boxes, clearly the "real truth" doesn't matter. As long as current executives believe that future executives will care, they continue to treat new stadiums as part of their recruitment effort. And why not have the local government subsidize this particular recruitment tool?

We speculate that the growth coalitions in larger, more exciting cities have less success in emphasizing new sports stadiums as an executive recruitment tool. Places such as New York, San Francisco, Boston, Philadelphia, and Los Angeles have so many other amenities that they don't really need (or think they need) new sports stadiums to attract the A players. This is one reason why there has been little, or only very deliberate, progress toward new publicly financed stadiums in these cities. Simply put, in the minds of the local growth coalitions of mid-sized cities, the consequences are severe if they don't get a new ballpark. Therefore, getting a stadium is high on their agendas.

The recruitment effort put forth by local growth coalitions is also linked with the larger notion of community self-esteem. Many corporate executives desire an image of a city on the move. Cities such as Cleveland and Hartford, for example, seem to radiate negative impressions to the surrounding world. They are looked upon as decaying urban holes with declining and increasingly impoverished populations. Again, these images may be exaggerated far beyond empirical reality. But as long as the local growth coalition *believes* this is the projected image, corporate leaders will do tangible things to address it. Thus, members may see a flurry of new stadium construction as a visible and relatively fast way to counter the image of a city in decline. In hindsight, it seems to have been at least a moderately effective strategy. Outsiders are now more inclined to talk about turnarounds in places such as Cleveland and

Baltimore, having absolutely no evidence except the presence of new stadiums and the growth coalition's constant reiteration that things have turned around.

It is also important to note that some corporate executives are simply big sports fans. They enjoy professional sports and want to be associated with building a new sports palace. Wearing their civic hats, executives will find it a lot harder to improve the test scores of inner-city schools (although a few do gallantly try) than to build a new stadium. Most want a visible monument to their efforts, and the stadium can serve that purpose. If you are a big-time sports fan, what better way to show your civic pride than to help give the team a new place to play and the community a new place to watch games? It would be grander still if you could manage to have the new stadium named after your company.

Today, many postindustrial cities in the United States are filled with hollow corporations: companies that split their administration from their production, the former staying in the home city and the latter moving elsewhere in the United States or even offshore. Thus, when we say that a firm's headquarters are located in a city, often this simply means that the company employs several hundred, or at most a few thousand, top managerial and administrative staff who work in the city. The production workers have left town—or perhaps more accurately, their jobs have left town—leaving only very low-wage workers who provide support services for executives. The result is a polarized social-class dynamic: cities have very well paid and very poorly paid workers on either end, with fewer people in the middle. The two polarized groups have very different stakes in the city itself. For the high-paid members of the local growth coalition, the city is a transient station for work and play before returning home to suburbia or moving on to their next outpost in another city. Their urban priorities include good roads or commuter rails, decent restaurants, and cultural diversions, which might include new sports stadiums with plenty of available parking. For minimum-wage workers, the city is usually a permanent place to work and live. Their urban priorities are more likely to include good schools, reliable buses, safe neighborhoods, clean streets and playgrounds, and decent grocery stores. Given the recent wave of using public dollars for private stadiums, it seems clear that the needs of the growth coalition are winning out over the needs of poorer urban residents.

This disparity was illustrated for us by a Cleveland business leader, who said that among many of the top corporations in the city, *no* employee had ever been directly exposed to the Cleveland public schools. This astounding statement would not have been made fifty years ago, when these companies still had relatively well paid production workers living in Cleveland. Gone are the Fisher Body Division workers from the Euclid plant (which closed for good in 1993) as well as members of the United Steel Workers, whose Cleveland-area membership dropped from 47,000 in 1980 to slightly more than 20,000 in 1990. Urban neighborhoods, which were built around such factories, increasingly face economic and social decay when the facility leaves town. This reduces the overall tax base and puts even more strain on the public sector to maintain services (such as schools) and deal with the fallout (such as crime) from deindustrialization. Unfortunately, in cities like Cleveland, the powerful local growth coalition and its political champions have been subsidizing new stadiums rather than decent housing, further exacerbating the metamorphosis of the city into a playground for suburbanites.

The frontier cities have very different development histories. Here, suburbanization was a major factor from the beginning rather than a threat to an older urban tradition. Thus, the frontier cities have a power structure with less entrenched political expertise and a wider field for stadium battles to play out. The population explosion in these cities sometimes mitigates the issue of fighting over a shrinking pie, which is so common in Rust Belt cities. At the same time, however, citizens in frontier cities opposed to the particular growth strategies of subsidized stadiums often find few political champions with either the will or the political acumen to take up their cause.

THE POLITICAL ARM OF THE GROWTH COALITION

Clearly, the corporate arm of the local growth coalition has reasons to be interested in new publicly funded sports stadiums and has the power to help turn this interest into reality. Ultimately, however, local government is still responsible for the actual policies that will direct public dollars to private stadiums. As a result, local governments become important components of coalitions. In cities with weak or absent corporate communities, the local government often (but not always) takes the lead on new stadium projects. Why do some governors, mayors, and other political leaders want stadiums if they are increasingly unpopular? Why do they risk their political lives on this issue?

As we have suggested throughout the book, the coalition between local government and the corporate community can take different forms. One form, which we refer to as second-dimensional power, occurs when the corporations capture and control policymakers through campaign contributions, relocation threats, membership on key task forces, or other overt types of influence. The other form, which we call third-dimensional power, occurs when policymakers "naturally" see a convergence between corporate interests and the overall community's interests without the application of any overt influence. These two types of relationships are by no means mutually exclusive, and it is not particularly important which type of power prevails. We saw them overlap in Cleveland through the relationship between the mayor's office and Cleveland Tomorrow. The business group had produced an economic blueprint for the city, which the mayor completely supported. This alignment seemed predictable enough because the executive director of Cleveland Tomorrow at the time had previously been the mayor's chief assistant for economic development, illustrating what some have called a "circulation of elites." But the fact that the new mayoral assistant (who replaced the person now directing CT) also completely agreed with this blueprint suggests that the convergence of corporate and government interests is more than just a personal matter. Whatever the case, alternatives to the corporate vision of local economic growth are not seriously considered.

This more systemic bias is reflected by politicians who genuinely believe that, for their city to survive, they need to transform it into a tourist destination—and they are betting on stadiums to do the job. Particularly in cities that have experienced substantial decline, politicians may be understandably desperate to hold on to businesses and residents. Professional sports and, in particular, new stadiums are seen as a highly visible way to indicate that a city is still powerful and important. But when politicians make these choices and place huge monetary bets on them, they neglect other urban needs. Cleveland was once a well-known manufacturer of basic durable goods. In fact, its pattern of industry originally attracted many of the corporations that subsequently located their headquarters there. With this history in mind, Norman Krumholz, a professor of urban studies at Cleveland State University and a former planning official in the city, is critical of the new civic tourism strategy:

> We haven't spent money on tool-and-die, metal bending, or steel, or certainly not comparable to the money we are spending reforming our image. It's at least worth a guess whether if we spent this kind of money on less spectacular but basic things, whether we'd put more of our industries back to work in jobs that people of this city could do.

You could, of course, argue that less visible factors are more important to the vibrancy of a city. For example, we were told by business leaders in several cities that the office sector would benefit most from improvements that were not stadium-related: enhancing Internet infrastructure, nurturing small business development through seed money, improving education beyond the most basic skills, and developing reliable and affordable mass transit. These kinds of improvements, however, are far less sexy, far less visible, and therefore far less attractive to politicians. You often see politicians holding a shovel during a stadium groundbreaking or throwing out the first pitch on opening day. But how many politicians are photographed sitting in the driver's seat and opening the doors on one of the city's brand-new low-pollution buses? Perhaps it is naïve to ask them to choose bread over circuses, but the question is still worth asking.

Some politicians fear threats (direct, implied, or imagined) that a sports team might leave town on their watch. Professional sports truly are different from any other kind of business because much more attention and emotion are attached to the home team. If a nonsports business that employed 150 people left town, hardly anyone would notice. But if that business were a professional sports team, thousands of hours of talk radio, hundreds of pages of print media, and millions of e-mail messages would be devoted to the news. Some politicians must also believe that they can contain the anger of citizens who are opposed to publicly financed stadiums, although many mentioned that they tried to schedule tax referendums as far away as possible from their own reelections. Some, too, believe that they just know better than the opponents of public funding, dismissing them, during several of our interviews, as "naïve," "nay sayers," "CANEs" (Citizens against Nearly Everything), or "crazed Naderite types," among even unkinder names.

In cities with a strong local growth coalition, elected leaders are better able to take a low profile in stadium initiatives, although, they may choose not to. Politicians offer to serve as watchdogs over the political process, while the local growth coalition exercises its power behind the scenes. Conversely, in cities with weak or fractured growth coalitions, the teams or the politicians are forced to take the lead. This is much more problematic: if the teams are taking the lead, they are accused of holding the city hostage for a handout; if local government takes the lead, the entire process assumes the messy trappings of procedural democracy such as public hearings and rancorous city council meetings. These situations can sometimes derail a stadium initiative or at least slow it down, as in San Diego, Philadelphia, and Minneapolis. They usually also result in making the teams pay for a larger share of the new stadium. We aren't claiming that some cities are more democratic than others. But in cities with weaker growth coalitions, politicians often have trouble avoiding grass-roots input.

THE MEDIA ARM OF THE GROWTH COALITION

In every city we studied, the main local newspaper editorially favored using public dollars for private stadiums. Fortunately, this editorial bias rarely interfered with a relatively fair reporting of the stadium initiatives, and journalists and columnists often wrote scathing and embarrassing stories about the stadium-building process.

Publishers and high-level editors often seem to share the same ideologies and visions as the local growth coalition. This may be due in part to their sense that they know better than the masses. It may also be due to the fact that, as newspaper companies come to be part of larger media conglomerates, they are increasingly indistinguishable from the corporate arm of the growth coalition. High-level editors frequently rub elbows with growth coalition members and come to share a vision of what is needed for correct growth. Only in Pittsburgh did we find a maverick newspaper publisher with a strong set of libertarian beliefs who promoted significant media criticism from the top of the company. The opposition of the *Tribune* (and the Allegheny Institute for Public Policy) was a significant irritant to the growth coalition's plans to acquire public dollars for private stadiums. If more cities had competing mainstream media voices, their stadium initiatives might have taken much different paths.

WHAT IS A MAJOR LEAGUE CITY ANYWAY?

During our interviews, we repeatedly encountered the socially constructed notion that professional sports teams are a necessary condition of being a major league city. The more teams you have (taking population into account), the more major league you are. In some ways, we understand that having sports teams gives a city the stamp of authenticity by providing publicity and media exposure. Stadium advocates have taken this idea, however, and manipulated it to extract maximum public financing. They argue that, without a new stadium like those popping up in other places, their city will quickly become second-rate. Its fall from grace will be even faster and more embarrassing if the sports team actually leaves town. Increasingly, however, there is no actual threat that a team will leave without a new stadium (although the threats are still occasionally verbalized). And often the team owners aren't even the ones making this argument; rather, the corporate and political arm of the local growth coalition is making the claim. Policymakers, it seems, have internalized the assumption that "a new stadium" equals "the team stays" (or "a new one comes") equals "our city is first-rate."

Ironically, those cities with other sources of community self-esteem are more immune to this kind of manipulation. Rarely do pro-subsidy advocates in New York, Los Angeles, Philadelphia, or San Francisco claim that the city will cease being major league without a new sports stadium. The reason is obvious: these cities do not need the imprimatur of a sports team to make them major league in their own eyes or the eyes of the world. They have a diverse economy, vibrant downtowns open after bankers' hours, and great restaurants. Can you imagine somebody saying, "Without new stadiums, New York will be just another Hoboken with tall buildings," or "San Francisco will only be Sacramento with a bay view"? Los Angeles lost its NFL team in the 1990s because the city refused to build a new publicly financed stadium. At last look, L.A. had not become second- or third-rate.

San Francisco, in fact, is a great example of how the manipulation of community self-esteem is ineffective in cities that are already first-rate. The new Pacific Bell Ballpark opened in 2000[2] and has been touted as the only privately financed ballpark among the recent wave of new stadiums. While this claim is an exaggeration, as we will explain, it is true that the public share of the stadium is significantly below average. Although some view the Giants as magnanimous in not asking for handouts, this perception misreads the history. The Giants got fewer public dollars to be sure, but not for lack of trying! The new stadium went to public votes four separate times and lost each referendum. The team wandered around the Bay Area looking for some municipality to pay for their new ballpark and failed each time. Finally, the team's most recent ownership group, headed by Peter Magowan, decided to build a stadium largely with private financing. The Giants raised about $65 million from the sale of personal seat licenses and another $121 million from naming rights and other corporate partnerships, with Chase Financing backing much of the remainder. The price of the stadium reached nearly $307 million, although, as in all of the cases in this book, ongoing debate continues about the true cost.

A certain amount of public money has gone into the project, despite proclamations to the contrary. San Francisco used a tax-increment financing plan to provide money for infrastructure and neighborhood improvements around the new ballpark. The Giants received some tax breaks; and the city agreed to fund the construction of all needed amenities outside the park, including a light-rail stop and street lighting, and provided all water, sewerage, and other public service connections. Nevertheless, the Giants are able to say that the park itself was built with 100 percent private financing and no public dollars.

Despite some linguistic maneuvers, the important point still holds; the Giants got fewer public dollars for their new stadium. The key to this difference is the chemistry between San Francisco's growth coalition and the potential efficacy of manipulating community self-esteem. San Francisco certainly has a corporate community far stronger and more cohesive than those in Hartford and Minneapolis and probably just as strong (or stronger) as those in Cincinnati, Cleveland, and Pittsburgh. But San Francisco's local growth coalition doesn't really need a stadium to attract executive talent or create the image of being first-rate. The rest of San Francisco can do that all by itself. Property values in the city are among the highest in the nation, and it would be laughable to argue that those values will decline if the Giants leave town.

Equally important, San Francisco has an affluent population and a large number of corporations willing to buy seat licenses (at least for now). Recognizing the unique features of the city, Jack Bair, the Giants' senior vice president and corporate counsel, said in an interview on Minnesota Public Radio (www.news.mpr.org/features/199911):

> I can't speak for other communities. We faced our unique problem here in San Francisco and tried to fashion a solution that would work here. We also are blessed with having a community that has enjoyed great economic times and also is the home to many of the most successful companies: . . . the gateway to Silicon Valley. We have a very affluent population here. And so we have been successful where other communities might not be able to be successful.

Despite San Francisco's powerful local growth coalition, appeals to community self-esteem would have fallen on deaf ears. Many residents seemed perfectly willing to let the team walk away: after all, they voted down stadium deals over and over again. Eventually the Giants chose to stay and build their own park, but that decision may not work in cities without a strong demand for private seat licenses or enough money to buy them. Clearly, midsized cities and those fighting population decline are more vulnerable to being manipulated by arguments about major league status.

STADIUM BATTLES AND COMPETING VISIONS OF CITIES

Stadium battles are struggles over competing and contested views of cities in the United States. Are cities meant to be tourist attractions? Are they places to improve exchange value (that is, drive up real estate costs for speculators, sometimes at the expense of poor and middle-class residents)? Should they be designed to attract high-priced corporate talent—the A players of the world? Are they places where people live and care about schools, parks, libraries, public safety, traffic congestion, and transportation systems?

The desire to become a tourist destination often informs the ideology of local growth coalitions as they press for new stadiums. In the postindustrial economy, many cities, desperate for new revenues, have been chasing elusive tourist dollars, hoping to attract visitors to their city. There is often a certain faddishness to these attempts. For a while, many cities were trying to build festival markets in imitation of Faneuil Hall in Boston (Ehrlich and Dreier 1999). Then cities began closing streets to create pedestrian shopping malls, mimicking malls in the suburbs. For the past ten years, building new sports stadiums has seemed to be the way to get tourists. What we have learned from these experiences, however, is that the copy cats tend not to do as well as the originals because the novelty quickly wears off.

Being a tourist destination also depends in large part on uncontrollable things like weather and location. Only the most die-hard football fan will visit Cleveland in early January just to see a football game in the new lakefront stadium. Pittsburgh is also likely to have a difficult time attracting tourists, despite two new stadiums and the grand dreams of city politicians. Unlike Baltimore, Pittsburgh cannot count on a large population within easy driving distance that will come to the new stadium. For a time, Pittsburgh planners considered placing a major tourist attraction between the two new stadiums, but some joked that a steel industry museum might be too depressing. Others imagined a high-tech amusement park but had trouble articulating exactly what that might be. Perhaps they envisioned a very fast roller coaster, with cars shaped like ingots, careening through an abandoned steel plant.

There is also a clear downside to becoming a tourist city. Tourist economies are highly dependent on the health of the national economy; and in recessions, tourist spending lessens significantly. In addition, those economies provide a large number of low-wage service jobs, which can increase inequality in cities. For example, in Phoenix, several proposals are in the works for new single-room occupancy (SRO) housing in the downtown area near Bank One Ballpark. The demand for such housing is intimately related to the quality of jobs produced not just at ballparks but in the tourist economy as a whole. Hotel desk clerks, hot dog vendors, and ticket takers do not make high enough salaries to afford a place to live. Three developers have approached Phoenix Downtown Partnership with plans to build new, modern SROs. They are repackaged versions of the old flophouse hotel, only with amenities such as a security system and a fax machine for residents' use. Despite the high-tech wiring, however, the SRO illustrates a way to provide a very cheap, single room for someone who works in and around the ballpark, the hotel industry, or the restaurant industry and is simply not paid well enough to live anywhere else. A business leader who focuses his attention on downtown development described it this way:

> This is a step above homelessness, obviously. . . . [SROs] are meant to house hospitality workers, students, and others on fixed incomes. They are very small units, your typical SRO, but they have security at the front door, cable TV, a little refrigerator. They have "business centers" in them, a whole bunch of amenities that obviously aren't flophouse amenities. . . . Because our economy is built so much on the hospitality industry, I think there is a pretty good market for it here.

To be fair, some political leaders really do not know how to make their cities more vibrant. They are not sure if investment in schools or basic work force training will pay off in the long run. Dependent on being reelected, politicians tend to favor a more visible project over a less visible investment in job training or public schools that might pay off only gradually over several decades. Sadly, though, sports stadiums may not be our urban saviors. As we showed in chapter 2, a growing body of anecdotal experiences and systematic research show they stimulate little economic growth. They probably provide notoriety and good publicity in the short run as well as temporarily shoring up a city's reputation. Nevertheless, this advantage is surely waning as the stadium boom peaks. These days, people seem much less excited about the next new stadium. Baltimore can only happen once. Recent data show that the increase in attendance at new stadiums is declining and that the honeymoon effect is lasting for a shorter period. Nine major league baseball teams have established new lows for single-game attendance in their stadiums, and all nine built new stadiums in the 1990s or 2000s (*Philadelphia Inquirer*, April 28, 2002, D18).

Stadiums don't seem to promote the kind of mixed residential, retail, and business development that actually builds vibrant neighborhoods in the long run. When urban governments finance new stadiums, they are really spending hundreds of millions of dollars to entertain suburbanites. Unfortunately, the political relationship between city and suburb is often so contentious that there is little regional cooperation between poorer and wealthier municipalities in funding stadiums. In Philadelphia, for example, the city decided to put a rental-car tax in place to help fund the stadium. City leaders approached suburban leaders about the possibility of instituting this tax in all of the counties surrounding Philadelphia. Not surprisingly, the suburbs politely declined. (Some local officials, we were told, actually laughed out loud.) As a result, the rental surcharge applies only to renting a car *in the city*. So city residents, who are generally poorer, must pay an extra tax for a rental car. Granted, this particular tax was designed as a visitor tax, but it will still have a detrimental effect on city residents who need a rental car.

OPPOSITION AND THE GROWTH COALITION

It's tough being opposed to new sports stadiums, especially when you are up against a powerful local growth coalition that can obfuscate its vested interests in such social policies. Although we have described the role of opposition groups in the cities we have studied, we now want to place this opposition into the larger context that frames our conclusions. That is, what does the plight of new stadium opponents have to say about the state of democracy in the United States? We have seen several well meaning and occasionally well organized opposition groups rolled over by pro-subsidy forces. Supposedly democratic venues like referendums are almost inherently unfair because opposition groups cannot raise anywhere near the money generated by stadium advocates. Indeed, in cities such as San Diego, new stadium advocates wanted very much to have a public referendum because they thought it would be easier to manipulate the general public than to get prompt action from the local government without a public mandate. And what are opponents to think when apparent referendum victories such as those in Pittsburgh and Phoenix are simply ignored by stadium advocates? Why even bother?

There is no monolithic pattern to these opposition groups. Like the growth coalitions they battle with, their existence, shape, and form are firmly tied to the social characteristics of a particular city. In Minneapolis, they coalesce around an anti-corporate welfare position that has roots in Minnesota's longstanding populist tradition. In Pittsburgh, one of the most effective opposition campaigns came from a wealthy newspaper owner with a libertarian streak, who just happened to live there. If Richard Scaife had lived in a different city, the opposition in Pittsburgh would have been far less effective. Arizona's relatively elderly population generated a fairly formidable opposition in Phoenix that was rooted almost totally in an anti-tax philosophy. They were simply ignored, however; and their single-minded anti-tax focus prevented them from forming more sustainable alliances with smaller bands of opponents with different philosophies. Members of Philadelphia's relatively middle-class opposition were effective in preventing a downtown baseball stadium from being built in their neighborhood but were largely irrelevant to the more general issue of building the ballpark in the first place.

How can citizens build more effective opposition to subsidizing private stadiums with public dollars? One reform might be to create spending limits on referendums that concern stadium funding. This would at least even the playing field. Our research shows that proponents typically outspend opponents by at least a ten-to-one margin and sometimes much more. At the same time, we are aware that such a reform might not make a difference in the long run. Stadium proponents have ways to manipulate the community even without a funding disparity. Newspapers can still run an avalanche of editorials and print home team press releases documenting the economic pain that the franchise is enduring. Corporate elites can still pressure politicians or more subtly influence the political discussion over "correct" forms of economic growth and development. The teams can continue to threaten that they will leave the city, and politicians can wring their hands over the tragedy of becoming a minor league city. We are also wary of campaign finance reform because ultimately the referendums only seem to matter if ballpark proponents win, not if they lose. With that in mind, opposition groups might decide not even to bother trying to influence the outcomes via a popular referendum.

Stadium opponents often try to pressure the local sports teams who seem to benefit most from these policies, arguing that using public money for private stadiums is a form of corporate welfare for wealthy team owners. Opponents might publicize the finances of the team and its owners (in hopes of embarrassing them) or organize a boycott. But based on what we have learned in our research, these tactics might not be very effective. For one thing, it is no surprise that teams are trying to use tax money to build their stadiums. They are forever trying to increase revenues through soaring ticket prices and six-dollar beers, so why not try to get the community as a whole to pay for a new stadium? Owners are lodged in an economic system (professional sports) that leads them to press for more than the other guy gets. So an obvious reform, suggested by other observers, involves pressing for reform of the economic structure of the leagues, which would benefit all teams and cities: for example, national legislation limiting the amount (or percent) that a municipality can spend on a sports stadium or laws mandating that leagues pay a substantial share of new stadium costs. Other possibilities include placing limits on teams' mobility (particularly after receiving a large public subsidy in the stadium), thereby undercutting any future threat to leave town.

More important, however, our identification of the growth coalition's leading role in building publicly financed stadiums suggests a different tactic for any opposition. Opponents need to target these nonsports organizations and try to raise awareness about their manipulation of policymakers and their influence over dominant ideologies. So instead of pressuring sports teams, opponents might pressure local businesses that advocate using public dollars for private stadiums. In Cincinnati, this could mean boycotting Chiquita bananas. In Pittsburgh, this might mean pulling accounts from PNC Bank or refusing to buy Heinz ketchup.

A successful opposition should also adapt to the shifting strategies of local growth coalitions and other stadium advocates. While some attention still must be paid to critiquing the alleged economic benefits of new stadiums, even more should be paid to countering arguments that link new stadiums with community self-esteem and community collective conscience. In other words, opponents must have a good response to "Keep Cincinnati a Major League City" and "Keep Cleveland from Becoming Akron." They must articulate ways in which public dollars can be better spent to keep their city vibrant and remind people that the public coffers are not bottomless. A stronger connection must be made for community development, stronger neighborhoods, lower crime, a vibrant downtown, and better schools instead of new ballparks. It might be easiest for opponents to highlight these community trade-offs in cities where advocates have mostly abandoned strategies that justify new stadiums in economic terms. By admitting that stadiums will not expand the public till, advocates can no longer make arguments that there will soon be enough money for new stadiums *and* new libraries *and* new public schools.

Thus, opponents must force a public realization that there are actual choices to be made about which of these amenities contributes most to enhancing community self-esteem and community collective conscience. At the moment, sports stadiums have been cornering the market on what makes a city first-class. But this perception is not inevitable, even though it will be hard to change. Perhaps political representatives and corporate leaders can be educated about the possible consequences of "wearing their civic hats" or "leaving their marks" through new stadiums rather than in less visible ways. For example, in 2001, racial unrest erupted in Cincinnati just as the city built two new sports stadiums that were supposed to enhance community collective conscience. We think that unfortunate situation in Cincinnati may foreshadow events in other cities where good stadiums have been defined as more socially important than good jobs, good libraries, and good schools.

So long as cities keep spending lots of public dollars on new sports stadiums rather than on public schools, affordable health care, and safe neighborhoods, social conditions will continue to deteriorate for a great number of urban residents. Perhaps we need an entirely new vision for what makes an American city a major league city.

Excerpted from Kevin J. Delaney and Rick Eckstein, *Public Dollars, Private Stadiums: The Battle Over Building Sports Stadiums.*

NOTES

1. The third dimension of power (Lukes 1974) is the deepest level of power. Though not entirely uncontested, it operates as a strong hegemonic ideology. [Eds.]
2. Due to various corporate changes, the name was changed to SBC Park & is now AT&T Park. [Eds.]

REFERENCES

Ehrlich, B. and P. Dreier. 1999. *The New Boston Discovers the Old: Tourism and the Struggle for a Livable City.* In D.R. Judd and S.S. Fainstein (eds), *The Tourist City.* New Haven: York Universaity Press.

Lukas, Steven. 1974. *Power: A Radical View.* London: Macmillan, 1974.

CHAPTER 21

Sport, Masculinity, and Black Cultural Resistance

Ben Carrington

> *On sport's level playing field, it is possible to challenge and overturn the dominant hierarchies of nation, race, and class. The reversal may be limited and transient, but it is nonetheless real. It is, therefore, wrong to see black sporting achievement merely as an index of oppression; it is equally an index of creativity and resistance, collective and individual.*
>
> —*Marqusee (1995, p. 5)*

This article traces the meanings associated with cricket in relation to Black masculinity by examining the role of sport as a form of cultural resistance to the ideologies and practices of White racism. The article then shows the absences within contemporary sociology of sport theorizing around race, which has led to incomplete understandings of the complex ways in which gender operates in and through discourses of race. It is argued that it is necessary to produce more critical theorizations of the intersections of race with gender, nation, and class if we are to fully appreciate how social identities are constructed. A theoretical account follows of the historical and contemporary significance of sport within racialized societies (the racial signification of sport).

The theoretical arguments are then explored in more detail by an extensive empirical analysis. Drawing on participant observation and in-depth semistructured interviews, an account is given of how a Black cricket club in the north of England is used by Black men as both a form of resistance to White racism and as a symbolic marker of the local Black community. Three themes are traced in this regard, namely (a) the construction of Black sports institutions as Black spaces, (b) the use of Black sports clubs as symbolic markers of community identity, and (c) the role of cricket as an arena of both symbolic and real racial and masculine contestation. The theoretical framework developed and the empirical analysis presented begin to provide a more critical understanding of the complexities of racial identity construction and resistance in sport than has so far been developed within the sociology of sport. . . .

BLACK MASCULINITY AND THE LIMITS TO SPORTS SOCIOLOGY THEORIZING

In analyzing the historical development and social significance of sports during the 19th and early 20th centuries, it is now commonplace within the sociology of sport to assert that sport functioned as a key male homosocial institution whereby "manly virtues and competencies" could be both learned and displayed as a way of avoiding wider social, political, and economic processes of "feminization." Sport, in effect, symbolized and reinforced a patriarchal structure of domination over women. However, such accounts have consistently failed to acknowledge that this view can only be sustained if the inherently racialized nature of social relationships and the position of Blacks, and in particular Black males, within Western societies, generally, and within sport, in particular, is ignored. Historically, the entry of Black males into the social institutions of sport was conditional with formal segregation, particularly in the United States, often imposed. When Black males did compete directly and publicly with Whites, such competition was organized on the premise that the "White man" would eventually win, thereby maintaining the racial order, and where this could not be guaranteed the prohibition of Blacks was quickly instated.

Thus, the claim that is repeatedly made concerning sport's early development as the preservation of male authority needs to be critically reexamined as it more accurately relates to the preservation of certain notions of White male identity and authority. To acknowledge this challenges many of the Eurocentric accounts that have themselves been guilty of reproducing racist discourses that have denied both the importance, and the very presence, of Black peoples throughout the modern history of the West.[1]

One notable exception to such accounts can be found in the work of Michael Messner (1992), who has argued that men's historical and contemporary experiences in sport clearly demonstrate that it is overly simplistic to view sport as a patriarchal institution that reinforces men's domination and power over women. Rather, "the rise of sport as a social institution in the late nineteenth and early twentieth centuries had at least as much to do with men's class and *racial relationships* [italics added] with other men as it did with men's relations with women" (Messner, 1992, p. 17). Messner continues,

> We can see that the turn-of-the-century "crisis of masculinity" was, in actuality, a crisis of legitimation for hegemonic masculinity. In other words, upper- and middle-class, white, urban heterosexual men were the most threatened by modernization, by changes in the social organization of work, by the New Woman's movement into public life, by feminism, and by the working-class, ethnic minority, immigrant, and gay men.
>
> (p. 18)

Such a radical reconceptualization of the meaning of sport's historical development would help us to better understand the heightened significance of sport within colonial and contemporary societies and, specifically in relation to this article, the critical role that sport continues to play in narrating relations between Black men and White men. . . . Kobena Mercer (1994) has drawn attention to these questions in criticizing the Eurocentrism of many of the theoretical approaches to masculinity that have stubbornly refused "to recognize that not all men in the world are white or even that white masculinities are informed by the ethnicity of whiteness" (Mercer, 1994, p. 153).[2] The historically constructed social position of Black males, which raises profound questions for contemporary sports sociology theorizing, is accurately described by Mercer when he writes,

> Whereas prevailing definitions of masculinity imply power, control and authority, these attributes have been historically denied to Black men since slavery. The centrally dominant role of the white male slave master in eighteenth- and nineteenth-century plantation societies debarred black males from patriarchal privileges ascribed to the masculine role. . . . In racial terms, black men and women alike were subordinated to the power of the

> white master in hierarchical social relations of slavery, and for black men, as objects of oppression, this also cancelled out their access to positions of power and prestige which in gender terms are regarded as the essence of masculinity in patriarchy. Shaped by this history, black masculinity is a highly contradictory formation of identity, as it is a subordinated masculinity.
>
> (pp. 142–143)

It is clear then that we need to move toward more sophisticated and nonreductionist models of analysis that do not treat the significance of race as being epiphenomenal to the development of modern sports and that take seriously the "intersectionality" (Brah, 1996) of race, gender, nation, class, and the other multiple relational identities individuals have.

THE RACIAL SIGNIFICATION OF SPORT

> When you talk about race in basketball, the whole thing is simple: a black player knows he can go out on the court and kick a white player's ass. He can beat him, and he knows it. It's that simple, and it shouldn't surprise anyone. The black player feels it every time. He knows it from the inside.
>
> (Rodman, 1996, p. 129)

Given that sport is one of the few arenas where public displays of competition, domination, and control are openly played out (Birrell, 1989), it is not surprising, as bell hooks (1994) suggests, that, historically, "competition between black and white males has been highlighted in the sports arena" (p. 31).

Messner (1992) highlights the way in which sport provides opportunities for subordinated groups to challenge the established order. Messner argues that subaltern groups are able to "use sport as a means to resist (at least symbolically) the domination imposed upon them. Sport must thus be viewed as an institution through which domination is not only imposed, but also contested; an institution within which power is constantly at play" (p. 13). Therefore, within racially inscribed societies we can see how the sociocultural, psychological, and political meanings of public displays of sporting contestation come to take on specifically racial significance. . . .

A further, pertinent, question would be to ask what happens when sporting contests between Black men and White men actually take place? What is the significance for those involved, both Black and White, and how do wider racialized discourses affect the game itself?

Michael Messner's (1992) arguments pertaining to the role of sport in allowing for the realization of a masculine identity for subaltern groups is relevant here. Messner suggests that "subordinated groups of men often used sport to resist racist, colonial, and class domination, and their resistance most often took the form of a claim to 'manhood'" (p. 19). It is precisely this attempt to reconstruct Black masculinity, which colonialism had configured "as feminised and emasculated" (Verges, 1996, p. 61), that is central to Frantz Fanon's (1986) analysis of colonial racism, and further shows why it is impossible to separate, in any simple way, questions of masculinity from race. . . .

It is not surprising then that it is the traditionally highly masculinized arena of sports through which Black men often attempt to (re) assert their Black identity, that is, gender acts as the modality through which a racialized identity is realized (Gilroy, 1993, p. 85). As the quote from the enigmatic basketball player Dennis Rodman suggests, sports can therefore be seen at one level as a transgressive liminal space where Black men can attempt, quite legitimately, to (re) impose their subordinated masculine identity through the symbolic, and sometimes literal, "beating" of the other, that is, White men.[3] Therefore, what we might term the "racial signification of sport" means that sports contests are more than just significant events, in and of themselves important, but rather that they act as a key signifier for wider questions about identity within racially demarcated societies in which racial narratives about the self and society are read both into and from sporting contests that are imbued with racial meanings.

CRICKET, COLONIALISM, AND CULTURAL RESISTANCE

> The whole issue [of racism] is quite central for me, coming as I do from the West Indies at the very end of colonialism. I believe very strongly in the black man asserting himself in this world and over the years I have leaned towards many movements that follow this basic cause.
> (Richards, 1991, p. 188)

It is within this context that we can begin to more fully understand the centrality of sports to Black resistance. As Douglas Hartman (1996), correctly in my view, points out, sport has "long constituted an important, if under-appreciated, set of activities and institutions in the black community providing many of its leaders and one of its most established spaces for collective action (second only perhaps to the Church itself)" (p. 560).[4] In the Caribbean, complex class, gendered, and racial antagonisms within the Caribbean itself, and of course between the West Indians and the British, were most often played out in the arena of cricket. C.L.R. James's (1963/1994) seminal work *Beyond a Boundary* is testament to what he saw as the inherent relationship between culture, and in particular cricket, politics, and Black resistance in the anticolonial struggles of the time. James argued that cricket was central in helping to shape a political sense of West Indian identity during the period of colonial rule by the British. In a way, cricket could be seen as being more than a metaphor for Caribbean politics; in many ways, it was Caribbean politics.[5]

Cricket, in particular, due to its position both as perhaps the cultural embodiment of the values and mores of Englishness and its "missionary" role within British imperialism and colonialism, occupied a central site in many of the anticolonial struggles both within the Caribbean and elsewhere within the Empire. Thus, the game itself assumed political importance in narrating unequal power relations between the British and the West Indians: "beating them at their own game" taking on deeper and more profound meanings. In discussing this, Grant Farred (1996) has argued that it "is precisely because the colonised were immersed in and observant of the codes of the native British game that they were able to transform the sport into a vehicle for Caribbean resistance" (pp. 170–171).

Viv Richards (1995), captain of one the most successful West Indian teams in cricket history, extends this connection between sport and Black resistance to the Black diaspora, when he reflects; "In my own way, I would like to think that I carried my bat for the liberation of African and other oppressed people everywhere" (p. vii).[6] Cricket, especially for certain generations of West Indian men, came to occupy a central position in their social identities, whether they were living in the Caribbean or elsewhere within the Black diaspora. As Ossie Stuart (1996) notes, for many Black men cricket itself occupied a symbolic position in articulating an empowered sense of self within White supremacist societies; "cricket represented social status, social mobility, it meant modernisation and it meant West Indian success" (p. 125). It is to ground these theoretical issues, relating to the importance of cricket and notions of cultural resistance in the lived experiences of Black men, that I now turn.

THE SETTING: THE RACIALIZATION OF CHAPELTOWN

This study focuses on the Caribbean Cricket Club (CCC), which is situated near an area of Leeds, a large city in the north of England, where the majority of the city's Asian and Black residents live.[7] The 1991 census data for Leeds showed that those classified as Black-Caribbean numbered just under 7,000, of whom nearly 60% lived within the two wards known as Chapeltown (Policy Research Institute [PRI], 1996). Because of the relatively large concentration of Black people, Chapeltown has come to be known in the city as a Black area, and as such, has been subject to a racialized discourse, fueled by local and national media representations (Farrar, 1997) that have labeled the area (and by default the Black residents of Chapeltown) as a deviant, dangerous, and sexually promiscuous place.

In keeping with many of Britain's multiracial, inner-city areas, Chapeltown is a largely working-class area with few public amenities and considerable economic problems, such as higher-than-average levels of unemployment and poor housing conditions (Farrar, 1997; PRI, 1996). Partly as a result of these socioeconomic conditions, the area has twice seen major disturbances, which attracted both regional and national attention in 1975 (see Farrar, 1981; Gilroy, 1987; Sivanandan, 1982) and during the summer of 1981, when many areas of Britain were gripped with violent Black and working-class political revolts (see Farrar, 1981). Despite, and probably because of, these economic conditions and the difficulties faced by the city's Asian and Black populations, the large number of political and cultural organizations in the area, of which the cricket club is a central part, have maintained, and even increased, their importance to social life.

THE CLUB: CARIBBEAN CRICKET CLUB

The CCC is one of the oldest Black sports clubs in Britain. It was originally formed in the late 1940s as a social and sporting club by a group of West Indian soldiers who had fought in the Second World War and had settled in the city (Wheatley, 1992; Zulfiqar, 1993). Over the years, the club became more successful, culminating in the late 1970s when it won the league three years running and won the treble on a number of occasions. In the late 1980s, the CCC moved on to play in one of the strongest leagues in Yorkshire County, the Leeds League, where it has played for the past 10 years. It currently has three senior men's teams and three junior boy's teams. Nearly all of the senior players are Black except for three Asian players and three White players.

The club's current ground, called The Oval, is a relatively new acquisition. With money from the local council, wasteland just outside of Chapeltown was transformed, over many years, into a cricket pitch and a few years later the club's current pavilion was built—the plaque inside proudly confirming the opening as "The Realisation of a Dream." The surrounding area is largely overgrown grassland, overlooked by a working-class council estate and tower blocks on one side, with a panoramic view of the city's skyline on the other.

The clubhouse has been the constant subject of vandalism and break-ins over the years—another break-in occurred during the research, in which the television, phone, drinks, and money from the till and pool table were stolen. The most serious setback to the club has been an arson attack that unfortunately destroyed nearly all of the club's memorabilia. This has left the clubhouse looking somewhat empty without all the team photos that usually adorn cricket clubhouses. There is often talk within the club that such attacks are racially motivated, with the prime suspects being the youths from the nearby, predominantly White, council estate, although on each occasion the police have been unable to prosecute anyone. Earl, the third team wicket-keeper, suggested,

> I think it's down to, "Oh, it's a Black club, we don't want them to get far." I think it's a racial thing again because I've seen words daubed up, "Niggers Out," and things like that. Because once you've been done over once, and it happens again, you know there is a pattern to it.

The spacious wasteland of the surrounding area tends to attract youngsters riding motorbikes and sometimes cars. Presumably due to this activity, a police car or two, and sometimes even a police helicopter, will circle the ground (as occurred on my very first visit to a game at the club). The well-documented history of police and state regulation, surveillance, and harassment of Black community spaces within Britain (Gilroy, 1987; Hesse, 1997b; Keith, 1993; Sivanandan, 1982), a key factor in the disturbances in Chapeltown in 1975 and 1981, gives this constant police activity (that symbolically infringes on the bounded space of the club) heightened significance. This inevitably leads to the feeling among many that the police are keeping an eye on the club as much as looking out for the joyriders. The location of the club and its somewhat troubled history seems to give the club and its members an embattled feel and adds to the widely held notion of the club's struggle both on and off the pitch.

BLACK SPACE AS CULTURAL RESISTANCE

I wish now to explore briefly how members of the club use the CCC as a discursively constructed Black social space.[8] In relation to the racialization of space, Farrar (1997) remarks,

> In everyday speech, many residents of an urban area of black settlement would readily comprehend a phrase such as "black space" . . . in terms of their effort to forge discourses and practical activities in a particular part of town which are, to some extent, "free" from the discourses and practices which they associate with a coercive white power structure. Establishing nearly autonomous territory is the conscious aim of all sorts of actors in the black inner city—in churches, mosques, temples, community centers, clubs, pubs, and in certain "open" spaces.
>
> (p. 108)

Such movements to create nearly autonomous spaces are an attempt to resist what might be described as the "terrorizing white gaze" (hooks, 1992) within public spaces. Here, Black people, and Black bodies, become subject to a panoptic form of "white governmentality" (Hesse, 1997b) that seeks to oversee, control, and regulate the behavior of Black people and is underpinned by the constant threat of racial harassment and violence. In this sense, we can see how the club's significance goes beyond merely being a cricket club and assumes a heightened social role as a Black institution within a wider White environment, providing many of the Black men with a sense of ontological security. This can operate on a number of related levels, from being a space removed, albeit not entirely, from the overt practices of White racism, as a social and cultural resource for Black people, and as an arena that allows for Black expressive behavior. These elements can be traced in the various ways in which the importance of the CCC was discussed by its members. The club was often labeled by the players and members in the interviews and discussions as a *Black space*, by which was often meant a place where Black people could be themselves (for example, in being able to tell certain jokes and speak in Caribbean patois), free from the strictures imposed by the White gaze. Thus, the club's importance transcended its sporting function.

The current chair and manager of the CCC, Ron, came to Leeds in the late 1950s and joined the CCC in the 1970s, when in his early 20s. For Ron, it was important to acknowledge the historical social role of the club within the area. When asked whether he saw the club as being more than just a sporting club, he replied,

> Oh yeah, because when it started in '47 it wasn't just a sports club, it was a focal point for those people who were black and in a vast minority, because in 1947 I don't think there were the amount of black people in Leeds that there are now. It was a focal point, it was a survival point for the people that were here. So it was more than a club then and it's still more than a club now, so it will always be that.

The use of the language of survival is interesting. It highlights the historical significance of the club in providing a safe space within a wider (hostile) environment for the earlier Caribbean migrants, which is then mapped onto the present, showing the continuities of the club and its role in the light of the persistence of racism: "It was more than a club then and it's still more than a club now, so it will always be that."

Nicholas, a 17-year-old who played for both the senior and junior sides, referred to the CCC as an important social space for Black people. As he played for another junior cricket team in another part of Yorkshire, he was able to contrast his experiences of playing for White and Black teams. Nicholas had experienced racial abuse from an opposing player while playing junior cricket for his other team, Scholes, which had increased his feelings of isolation at his predominantly White club.

> Nicholas: Some teams, if you're batting against them, and you start hitting them all over the place they always have to come out with their racist remarks to try and put you off. . . . It even happened to me this season when we played a team from Garforth, and I was hitting the opening bowler who has played for Yorkshire [Juniors]. I was hitting him for quite a lot of fours, and then he started to go on and call me names on the pitch . . . and then he got me out, and then, he was all "mouthy mouthy."
>
> BC: But how did that make you feel?
>
> Nicholas: Well, it's the first time it's happened, it made me feel kind of funny. I didn't know whether to answer him back or to walk away from him.
>
> BC: If you were playing for Caribbean do you think he would have said it?
>
> Nicholas: If I were playing for Caribbean he wouldn't have dared say it because if he was saying it to one person he's really saying it to the whole team . . . but at Scholes there is only two of us there, and all the rest are White, so it was more easier for him to say it there.

Such incidents compounded his feeling of isolation and otherness in a White setting, and he thus felt more relaxed and secure when at the CCC. In this sense, the CCC can be seen as providing Nicholas with an environment where his Blackness takes on a lesser significance and offers, in both a symbolic and very real sense, protection from the more overt practices of White racism.

The achievement of creating and sustaining a cricketing Black space within a White environment was often reflected on, somewhat nostalgically, by the club's members, particularly the older ones. There was a sense of pride among many of the players and members that despite all the problems the club had faced, including increasing financial pressures, the CCC was still going and now had its own ground and pavilion. Pete, one of the older players, who had come to England from Barbados in the late 1960s, echoed these views, while being interviewed in his car at The Oval. He said,

> I tend to think there are people out there who don't want us to have this. . . . But I hope we can carry on. I mean look at this [he gazes at the panoramic view across the ground overlooking the city], this is great as far as I'm concerned!

COMMUNITY, RESISTANCE, AND CRICKET

It is important to remember the wider context of the CCC's recent development. Its current ground and clubhouse materialized in the 1980s and can be seen as emerging from a wider Black political struggle that was taking place during this period. Following the violent disturbances of the early 1980s, there was a shift in government spending toward social expenses as a means of trying to placate inner-city tensions. The provision of leisure facilities was a key part of this process, even while government expenditures were generally being squeezed as the welfare state was restructured (Henry, 1993). Although state funding of such leisure provisions has been criticized as a form of "soft policing" (Hargreaves, 1986) that increased state control of Black and working-class communities and simultaneously diverted attention away from the underlying economic causes of the social deprivation these areas were facing, the outcomes of these policies were more ambiguous. Although it was clear that the primary motive behind such funding was designed to (re)-impose social integration, many Black organizations were willing to take the money available and to use it to their own advantage. Thus, the negotiations with the local state to achieve the aims of the CCC were contradictory. To a degree, this allowed the state to use sport, as John Hargreaves (1986) suggests, to further its own ends, while the Black community fought for space to negotiate a different set of cultural possibilities (cf., Hall, 1996).

Ron, who worked for the local council and was instrumental in securing local government funding for the development of the ground and the subsequent building of the clubhouse, was well aware of the underlying political motives of such a provision.

> It was after 1981, the uprisings, or the disturbances, whatever you want to call them. The authorities decided that they had to keep the "natives" happy, and they looked at something that the natives liked, and obviously cricket was what the natives liked.

Ron's deliberately ironic self-description of the "natives" is instructive. It highlights how the colonial discourse of British imperialism still resonates as a point of reference within the popular contemporary White imaginary in relation to Black people living in Leeds. Indeed, as late as the 1970s Chapeltown was actually referred to in the local press as "the colony within" (Farrar, 1996), reinforcing popular local misconceptions of Chapeltown and its residents as alien and potentially violent, a place to be overseen and policed as a colonial settlement.

The "natives," then, had, after almost 40 years, secured their own ground and pavilion—a physical marker of the club's (and in some ways, Chapeltown's Black communities') presence and progress in the area. However, it is argued here that although the CCC now has a physical presence, that is, a clubhouse and a pitch, the sense in which the club comes to represent the community for some of its members is largely as a symbol, that is to say, it is imagined. As Cohen (1985, p. 19) notes, "Symbols are mental constructs: they provide people with the means to make meaning. In so doing, they also provide them with the means to express the particular meanings which the community has for them."

The polyvocal nature of signs can be seen in the way in which the CCC is itself used interchangeably with the Black community in discussions at the club, standing as a symbolic marker of the community (which depending on the context can take on both local, that is, Chapeltown, or wider, that is, diasporic, dimensions), and assumes a specifically racial, that is, Black, association. We can see then that the language of community, especially for Blacks living in Britain, connotes both political (as a form of resistance) and moral (as a place of transcendence) associations. What we might term "Black community discourse" (Back, 1996) is used strategically as a way of articulating wider Black struggles within a specific locality by labeling it as a Black area. The Black community discourse can be understood as a narrative that locates a particular area "as the site of Black struggles and institutions, a place where Black people have fought to make something their own. This construct is also invested with a notion of political agency and locates Black resistance to racism and self-affirmation in this particular area" (Back, 1996, p. 113). Such attempts at establishing (partially) autonomous institutions and spaces, such as the CCC, as part of wider community projects are mechanisms in the development of "communities of resistance" (Sivanandan, 1990), which are inherently political maneuvers. As Gilroy (1987) notes, the invocation of community refers to more than just the concentration of Black people within a particular bounded area.

> It has a moral dimension and its use evokes a rich complex of symbols surrounded by a wider cluster of meanings. The historical memory of progress from slave to citizen actively cultivated in the present from resources provided by the past endows it with an aura of tradition. Community, therefore, signifies not just a distinctive political ideology but a particular set of values and norms in everyday life: mutuality, co-operation, identification and symbiosis. For black Britain, all these are centrally defined by the need to escape and transform the forms of subordination which bring "races" into being.
>
> (Gilroy, 1987, p. 234)

Thus, given the symbolic significance attached to the club and its central position within the local Black community discourse, the success of the club on the field came to be seen as reflecting on the standing of the Black community of Chapeltown too. For example, during team meetings, management and other senior players would often stress the need for the players to be aware that they were not just playing for themselves, or even the team, but also for the community as a whole: "for everyone down at Chapeltown" as Ron once put it. Despite the CCC's achievements over the years, the club had not won the Leeds League since its acceptance, after a number of unsuccessful applications, in 1988, and this was a constant source of frustration for many at the club. Both Ron and Earl felt the need for the club to win the league title.

> Ron: Because we need to be champions one day.
> Earl: For the community as well as the club.
> Ron: And it would lift the community like Earl says. . . .

For Pete, the CCC was important to Chapeltown because "it's the only sporting club, cricket club, that black people have got in the area, and when I say black I mean West Indian." Pete was aware that the CCC was perceived by White people as a Black club and symbolically represented Chapeltown and Black people in general to them, therefore, it was vitally important that the club was not only successful but run well: "I've had my hands down the loo! 'Wash this, wash that.' Because I'm buggered if I want anyone to come up here and believe, 'Ah, is this the way Black people live?'" He therefore spoke disparagingly and with a sense of bewilderment and incomprehension about those members who did not realize the wider social significance of the club: "Most members come up here and all they want to do is play cricket!"

CRICKET AND RACIAL CONTESTATION

C.L.R. James (1963/1994, p. 66) noted long ago the wider social significance of cricket contests: "The cricket field was a stage on which selected individuals played representative roles which were charged with social significance." Given that the CCC has a predominantly Black membership (and its name, and location, as suggested earlier, signify the club as Black) and given too that it plays its cricket in a league in the heart of Yorkshire (a regional identity historically constructed through a notion of Whiteness), the racial meanings invested in the actual matches are heightened even further.[9] Many of the players felt sure that the opposing teams were well aware of the wider racial significance of the contests and that the cricket matches were more than "just a game"; the war metaphor was often used to describe the contests.

Overlaid on this of course, as outlined earlier, is the specificity of cricket itself as a cultural practice and its central, almost metaphoric, position as a site of hegemonic struggle between the British and the West Indians. The competition between Black and White men within this context becomes a symbolic and real contestation of masculine and racial pride, and specifically for the Black participants a way of attempting to reassert a unified sense of self, and of rejecting, even if temporarily, the notion that their Black identity is a subordinated, and inferior, identity. As Westwood (1990, p. 68) notes in her brief analysis of a Black men's football team, the victory of Black teams over White teams "is, in effect, an injury to White masculine pride and a source of power and celebration to Black masculine pride when White teams are beaten."

These themes emerged constantly during the discussions at the club and the interviews conducted. For instance, referring to opposing White sides, Nigel said, "I think they see us purely as colour first, end of story, and then the cricket club comes [second]." Nigel was therefore dismissive of the notion that the cricket arena was somehow free of racial contestation and significance and that it could bring people together. When I suggested this to him, he replied,

> Oh come on, come on! We are talking about cricket here aren't we Ben? We're talking about the one county that we're based in being the one that always said, [puts on a strong mock Yorkshire accent] "You can't play for Yorkshire unless you're born in bloody Yorkshire lad!" That's still got to come through and that's been so strong within Yorkshire, the country on its own inside of another country, that's almost how strong they feel, and particularly around cricket.

This passage is important as it pulls together a number of key issues. It shows how a regional identity can become conflated with notions of nation and indeed race. The view that Yorkshire is a "country on its own inside of another country" is a powerful one that gives the county a particularly strong regional identity. That sport, and in particular cricket, is central to this, and that until recently only those born in Yorkshire could play for Yorkshire, excluding Asian and Black immigrants from being "true Yorkshiremen" and thus giving the identity a racial connotation, means that the players come to assume representative roles that are charged with social significance; the games themselves become, in effect, Black (West Indian)/White (Yorkshire) contests.

For example, Pete was clear, as he saw it, on the wider significance of the CCC and the matches within a context of a racist society. The relationship of the players to the actual national West Indian Test team went beyond a rhetorical identification and extended to the view that they actually were in some sense part of the West Indies side:

> Pete: As far as I'm concerned we're just an extension of the West Indies national team.
>
> BC: Is it more than just a cricket game to you?
>
> Pete: Yes it is. You see I've heard the opposing teams talk you see. I've been at a game when we've lost and I've heard the words coming out of the dressing room, "We've beaten the fucking Black bastards dem, again!" [thumps steering wheel] So then it takes the game away from being a game, it's war then.

Such views were reflected in a number of the interviews undertaken in this study. Errol, who was in his 30s and had played for the club for a number of years and who had also played with a predominantly Asian cricket team, similarly noted the racial, and hence national, significance that was attached to the games: "They [White teams] don't want a West Indian team to beat them or they don't want an Asian team to beat them. For them it's like, England versus the West Indies, or England versus India." Errol suggested that White teams would consciously raise their game to ensure they were not beaten by a Black side:

> Errol: At the end of the day we are living in England. Nobody want us to do better. It's like if there were an English [i.e., White] team in the West Indies, there's no way that the West Indies players or teams are gonna want them to win.
>
> BC: How do you think other teams see Caribbean?
>
> Errol: It's like, to me, they don't want a Black team to beat them. We've played against teams who never win a game but yet when they're playing Caribbeans you'd think that they were unbeatable! . . . It's because they don't want a Black man to beat them.

We can begin to see here how the wider discourses of the racial signification of sport become constituted in the actual contests themselves. The view that other teams played differently against the CCC because they were seen as a Black club was widely held among the players and supporters. . . .

Given the racial signification of the contests, the immense emotional and personal investment made in the games for the Black men was significant. At both a symbolic and very real level, winning became a way of challenging the logic and efficacy of the racism they faced in their day-to-day lives, even if the victories were always, ultimately, transitory. As Bob, an older player in his 40s, acknowledged, racial and masculine pride was at stake in contests between the CCC and other White sides, thus it became paramount for the CCC, and the players themselves, not to lose.

> At the end of the day you don't want to be beaten. You think "Let's show these lads who's the boss here." You try your best because you don't want to be beaten because it's like they go away all cocky and that, "We showed them, they can't play cricket, English game's the best!" all that business. You want to go out there and hopefully shut them up.

CONCLUSION

Westwood (1990) has argued that as "a counter to racism black masculinity is called up as part of the cultures of resistance developed by black men in Britain" (p. 61). This article has shown how for a number of Black men, sport, and in particular cricket, can provide a modality through which Black cultural resistance to racism can be achieved. Sports provide an arena whereby Black men can lay claim to a masculine identity as a means of restoring a unified sense of racial identity, freed, if only momentarily, from the emasculating discourses imposed by the ideologies and practices of White racism.

However, we should be cautious not to overstate unproblematically the benefits of such sites of resistance. For one, Black women often occupy marginal positions within sports clubs such as the CCC (especially those that do not have women's teams), which are perhaps more accurately described, as I have tried to make clear throughout, as Black men's cricket clubs. Without acknowledging such limitations, the complex positioning of Black women, in particular, within "white supremacist capitalist patriarchal societies" (hooks, 1994) gets overlooked. Thus, any claims for such cultural practices as being in some way emancipatory must be qualified. Otherwise, as Black feminists have consistently pointed out, the requirements for Black resistance become equated with the need for Black male emancipation. The overcoming of the crisis of Black masculinity is frequently misrecognized as the panacea for the Black community as a whole, thereby silencing the voices and needs of Black women; the politics manifest within certain (conservative) Black nationalisms being the most obvious example of this.

There is also, of course, the further problem with the zero-sum notion of resistance and power, most evidenced in the competitive sports arena, which inevitably leads to a conceptualization of resistance that can only be understood via notions of domination and physical conflict. Richard Burton (1991, 1997), for instance, has provided an interesting analysis in arguing for cricket to be situated within carnivalesque aspects of Caribbean street culture. Burton suggests that the carnival's symbolic subversion is central to how cricket is watched and played, as a more diffuse and stylized site of popular cultural resistance in challenging dominant social hierarchies.[10] This should alert us to the point that such modes of resistance as have been analyzed here should not be thought of as the only positionings possible. They ultimately need to be embedded within wider struggles.

It is perhaps necessary therefore to understand and explore both the benefits that such forms can have for a number of Black men while simultaneously acknowledging the limitations of sport as a modality of resistance to racism. Only when we have more ethnographically informed analyses in a greater variety of different communities across differing locations will we be able to more fully understand the complexities of Black cultural resistance through sport and its emancipatory possibilities.

NOTES

1. Eurocentrism is used conceptually to refer to those discourses and relations of power that privilege culturally hegemonic European notions of Western universality and that therefore elide, within its frame of reference, the voices of others, both within and outside the West. In another sense,

Eurocentrism can be understood as an attempt to recenter the West in conditions when its universality can no longer be guaranteed due to the multifaceted interrogations of the West by various postcolonial movements and critical multiculturalisms (cf., Hesse, 1997a; Sayyid, 1997; Shohat & Stam, 1994).

2. It is worth mentioning here that if the literature within the sociology of sport and leisure studies (and indeed elsewhere), on race, racism, and sport is inadequate, then the acknowledgment within these fields of study of White ethnicity is even worse. There are too few studies that have seriously considered how sport is central to the construction of White racial identities or even demonstrated an awareness of the fact that Whiteness is a racial category. As researchers, "we" are in the habit of equating race with the Black (and/or Asian) experience (just as in an earlier period gender equaled female experience), which as a number of scholars have demonstrated, only serves to reinforce current racist discourses and obscures the normalizing power of Whiteness (see Bonnett, 1996; Dyer, 1988, 1997; Feagin & Vera, 1995; Frankenburg, 1993; hooks, 1992; Ware, 1992).
3. Interestingly, Rodman's comments were echoed by a Black professional rugby league player when interviewed as part of a survey looking at racism within rugby league (Long, Tongue, Spracklen, & Carrington, 1995). He said, "I think a lot of Black players play rugby league, in my opinion . . . as they see it as a way to get their own back, or to take their aggression out on people, white people. . . . You couldn't do it on the street, but you can do it on the pitch" (as cited in Long, Carrington, & Spracklen, 1996, p. 13; see also Long, Carrington, & Spracklen, 1997). It is also within this context that we can understand the comments made by the cricketer Brian Lara, currently captain of the West Indies, after his side's inexplicable loss to Kenya in the cricket World Cup in 1996. In private remarks to the Kenyan side after the game, which were eventually reported by the media and for which he later apologized, he said, "It wasn't that bad losing to you guys. You are Black. Know what I mean. Now a team like South America is a different matter altogether. You know, this White thing comes into the picture. We can't stand losing to them" (as cited in Marqusee, 1996, p. 136). St. Pierre (1995) similarly suggests, in relation to cricket, that West Indian Test players "will tell you, privately, that a victory against England carries with it a special savour" (p. 77). Clearly, as I explore further in the rest of the article, the significance of these last two examples has as much to do with historical colonial and political relationships as it has with race.
4. There is a complex history, which is yet to be fully theorized, or indeed written, concerning the connections, crossovers, and interplay between the roles and lives of Black athletes and Black political radicals within the Black diaspora. I have begun to tentatively map this out elsewhere via the concept of the "sporting Black Arlantic" (see Andrews, Carrington, Jackson, & Mazur, 1996). I am thinking here, for example, of the relationships between figures such as C.L.R. James and Learie Constantine (see Note 6) and Muhammad Ali and Malcolm X, and in a somewhat different context, the quite literal connections made by Jean-Michel Basquiat in his painting *All Colored Cast (Part II)* (1982), between the boxer "Jersey" Joe Walcott and Toussaint L'Ouverture.
5. The continuing relevance of, and insights from, James can still be seen in contemporary writings on cricket and the Caribbean that demonstrate the inherent relationship between Black political struggle and cricket. Consider the titles of recent books on cricket and the Caribbean, all of which are heavily influenced by a Jamesian analysis; for example, see Beckles's (1994) *An Area of Conquest: Popular Democracy and West Indies Cricket Supremacy*, Beckles and Stoddard's (1995) *Liberation Cricket: West Indies Cricket Culture;* and Birbalsingh's (1996) *The Rise of West Indian Cricket: From Colony to Nation.* See also the essays by St. Pierre (1995), "West Indian Cricket as Cultural Resistance," and Yelvington's (1995) "Cricket, Colonialism, and the Culture of Caribbean Politics."
6. Richards can be seen to be operating within a longer lineage of great West Indian cricketers who were aware of the wider significance of cricket. This can be traced back to Learie Constantine. The grandson of a slave, Constantine was a vocal advocate of West Indian independence and spoke out against racial injustice, both within cricket and more generally, eventually serving in Dr. Eric Williams's government in Trinidad and Tobago from 1957 to 1961 (Birbalsingh, 1996). Indeed, C.L.R. James credits Constantine as being a central figure in James's political development in relation to his racial awareness, anticolonial sensibility, and views on West Indian nationalism. As James (1963/1994) remarks, "Constantine had always been political, far more than I had ever been. My sentiments were in the right place, but I was still enclosed within the mould of nineteenth-century intellectualism. Unbeknown to me, however, the shell had been cracked. Constantine's conversations were always pecking at it" (p. 113).
7. The research is based on my doctoral study. In-depth semistructured interviews conducted between 1995 and 1997, and participant observation

during the summer cricket seasons of 1995, 1996, and 1997, have been used to collect the data. Pseudonyms for the players and club members are used throughout. I am using the nomenclatures Black and Asian to refer to those groups who, due to the process of racialization, are visibly marked as belonging to different races. Within this context, those referred to as Black are those people of sub-Saharan African descent and those referred to as Asian are of South Asian descent.

8. The concept of space invoked here is not used simply as reference to a geographically bounded area, although clearly this is a dimension of any use of the term, but rather refers to the social production of space, that is, the ways in which socioeconomic, cultural, and political discourses construct spatial relations and the ways in which individuals themselves negotiate and reconstruct these discourses. As Lefebvre (1976) argues, space should be seen as having been "shaped and moulded from historical and natural elements . . . this has been a political process. Space is political and ideological. It is a product literally filled with ideologies" (as cited in Farrar, 1996, p. 295).

9. Due to a number of high-profile incidents of racist abuse from supporters at Yorkshire cricket grounds and statements, widely seen as racist, by prominent members of the Yorkshire County Cricket Club over the years, the county has a reputation as an "unwelcoming territory for Black cricketers" (Searle, 1990, p. 43; see also Searle, 1996). As Marqusee (1994) accurately notes, "The roots of racism in Yorkshire cricket are set deep in the county's peculiar regional chauvinism, a chauvinism warped by years of cricket failure. . . . The powers that be at Yorkshire have for many decades preferred the spurious roots of racial and cultural identity to the living roots of the game as it is actually played in the locality. It stands proudly not for the mixed culture of contemporary Yorkshire—industrial and urban, black and white, immigrant and native—but for a reified, hollow culture of boastfulness and bigotry. It is, at its core, profoundly exclusive" (pp. 143–144).

   Despite over a century of Asian and Black involvement in cricket throughout England at both the county and national levels, Yorkshire disgracefully remains the only County Cricket Club never to have fielded a British-born Asian or Black cricketer in its first team. Although Yorkshire County Cricket Club now officially promotes an open policy in its selection, evidence suggests that racial discrimination is still prevalent in Yorkshire cricket, despite the work of a number of committed individuals at the club to change this situation (see Long, Nesti, Carrington, & Gilson, 1997). The county's emblem, a white rose, has therefore become a powerful signifier for racist sentiments in the county in wanting to keep the "white rose white."

10. In fact, following Michel de Certeau, Burton (1997) makes the distinction between resistance, that is, those forms of contestation from outside a particular discursive regime, and opposition, that is, those forms of contestation from within a system. Discerning readers will have noticed that I have used the term resistance rather more generally and descriptively in this article when perhaps opposition would have been more analytically precise. Such distinctions have not been central to my arguments in this article.

REFERENCES

Andrews, D., Carrington, B., Jackson, S., & Mazur, Z. (1996). Jordanscapes: A preliminary analysis of the global popular. *Sociology of Sport Journal*, 13, 428–457.

Back, L. (1996). *New ethnicities and urban culture: Racisms and multiculture in young lives*. London: University College London Press.

Beckles, H. (Ed.). (1994). *An area of conquest: Popular democracy and West Indies cricket supremacy*. Kingston, Jamaica: Ian Randle.

Beckles, H., & Stoddard, B. (Eds.). (1995). *Liberation cricket: West Indies cricket culture*. Manchester, UK: Manchester University Press.

Birbalsingh, F. (1996). *The rise of West Indian cricket: From colony to nation*. Antigua, Jamaica: Hansib.

Birrell, S. (1989). Racial relations theories and sport: Suggestions for a more critical analysis. *Sociology of Sport Journal*, 6, 212–227.

Bonnett, A. (1996). Anti-racism and the critique of "White" identities. *New Community*, 22, 97–110.

Brah, A. (1996). *Cartographies of diaspora: Contesting identities*. London: Routledge.

Burton, R. (1991). Cricket, carnival and street culture in the Caribbean. In G. Jarvie (Ed.), *Sport, racism and ethnicity*. London: Falmer Press.

Burton, R. (1997). *Afro-Creole: Power, opposition and play in the Caribbean*. London: Cornell University Press.

Cohen, A. (1985). *The symbolic construction of community*. London: Routledge.

Dyer, R. (1988). White. *Screen*, 29, 44–64.

Dyer, R. (1997). *White*. London: Routledge.

Fanon, F. (1986). *Black skin, White masks*. London: Pluto.

Farrar, M. (1981). Riot and revolution: The politics of an inner city. *Revolutionary Socialism*, 2, 6–10.

Farrar, M. (1996). Black communities and processes of exclusion. In G. Haughton & C. Williams (Eds.),

Corporate city? Partnership, participation and partition in urban development in Leeds. Aldershot, UK: Avebury.

Farrar, M. (1997). Migrant spaces and settlers' time: Forming and de-forming an inner city. In S. Westwood & J. Williams (Eds.), *Imaging cities: Scripts, signs, memory.* London: Routledge.

Farred, G. (Ed.). (1996). *Rethinking C.L.R. James.* London: Basil Blackwell.

Feagin, J., & Vera, H. (1995). *White racism: The basics.* London: Routledge.

Frankenburg, R. (1993). *White women, race matters: The social construction of Whiteness.* London: Routledge.

Gilroy, P. (1987). *There ain't no Black in the Union Jack: The cultural politics of race and nation.* London: Hutchinson.

Gilroy, P. (1993). *The Black Atlantic: Modernity and double consciousness.* London: Verso.

Hall, S. (1996). Politics of identity. In T. Ranger, Y. Samad, & O. Stuart (Eds.), *Culture, identity and politics: Ethnic minorities in Britain.* Aldershot, UK: Avebury.

Hargreaves, J. (1986). *Sport, power and culture.* Cambridge, UK: Polity.

Hartman, D. (1996). The politics of race and sport: Resistance and domination in the 1968 African American Olympic protest movement. *Ethnic and Racial Studies,* 19, 548–566.

Henry, L (1993). *The politics of leisure policy.* London: Macmillan.

Hesse, B. (1997a). It's your world: Discrepant M/Multiculturalisms. *Social Identities,* 3, 375–394.

Hesse, B. (1997b). White governmentality: Urbanism, nationalism, racism. In S. Westwood & J. Williams (Eds.), *Imaging cities: Scripts, signs, memory.* London: Routledge.

hooks, b. (1992). Representing Whiteness in the Black imagination. In L. Grossberg, C. Nelson, & Treichler, P. (Eds.), *Cultural studies.* London: Routledge.

hooks, b. (1994). *Outlaw culture: Resisting representations,* London: Routledge.

James, C.L.R. (1994). *Beyond a boundary.* London: Serpent's Tail. (Original work published 1963).

Keith, M. (1993). *Race, riots and policing: Lore and disorder in a multi-racist society.* London: University College London Press.

Lefebvre, H. (1976). Reflections on the politics of space. *Antipode,* 8, 2. Trans. by Michael Enders from the French journal *Espaces et Sociétiés,* No. l, 1970.

Long, J., Carrington, B., & Spracklen, K. (1996, April). *The cultural production and reproduction of racial stereotypes in sport: A case study of rugby league.* Paper presented to the British Sociological Association annual conference, Reading, UK, April.

Long, J., Carrington, B., & Spracklen, K. (1997). "Asians cannot wear turbans in the scrum": Explorations of racist discourse within professional rugby league. *Leisure Studies,* 16, 249–260.

Long, J., Nesti, M., Carrington, B., & Gilson, N. (1997). *Crossing the boundary: A study of the nature and extent of racism in local league cricket.* Leeds, UK: Leeds Metropolitan University Working Papers.

Long, J., Tongue, N., Spracklen, K., & Carrington, B. (1995). *What's the difference? A study of the nature and extent of racism in rugby league.* Leeds, UK: The Rugby Football League/Leeds City Council/ The Commission for Racial Equality/Leeds Metropolitan University.

Marqusee, M. (1994). *Anyone but England: Cricket and the national malaise.* London: Verso.

Marqusee, M. (1995). Sport and stereotype: From role model to Muhammad Ali. *Race and Class,* 36, 1–29.

Marqusee, M. (1996). *War minus the shooting: A journey through South Asia during cricket's World Cup.* London: Heinemann.

Mercer, K. (1994). *Welcome to the jungle: New positions in Black cultural studies.* London: Routledge.

Messner, M. (1992). *Power at play: Sports and the problem of masculinity.* Boston: Beacon.

Policy Research Institute. (1996). *Community profile of Chapeltown Leeds.* Leeds, UK: Leeds Metropolitan University.

Richards, V. (1991). *Hitting across the line; An autobiography.* London: Headline.

Richards, V. (1995). Foreword. In H. Beckles & B. Stoddard (Eds.), *Liberation cricket: West Indies cricket culture.* Manchester, UK: Manchester University Press.

Rodman, D. (1996). *Bad as I wanna be.* New York: Delacorte.

Sayyid, B. (1997). *A fundamental fear: Eurocentrism and the emergence of Islamism.* London: Zed Books.

Searle, C. (1990). Race before wicket: Cricket, empire and the white rose. *Race and Class,* 31, 31–48.

Searle, C. (1996, August 18). Running a gauntlet of hate at Headingley. *The Observer,* p. 12.

Shohat, E., & Stam, R. (1994). *Unthinking Eurocentrism: Multiculturalism and the media.* London: Routledge.

Sivanandan, A. (1982). *A different hunger: Writings on Black resistance.* London: Pluto.

Sivanandan, A. (1990). *Communities of resistance: Writings on Black struggles for socialism.* London: Verso.

St. Pierre, M. (1995). West Indian cricket as cultural resistance. In M. Malec (Ed.), *The social roles of sport in Caribbean societies.* Luxembourg: Gordon & Breach.

Stuart, O. (1996). Back in the pavilion: Cricket and the image of African Caribbeans in Oxford. In T. Ranger, Y. Samad, & O. Stuart (Eds.), *Culture, identity and politics: Ethnic minorities in Britain*. Aldershot, UK: Avebury.

Verges, F. (1996). Chains of madness, chains of colonialism: Fanon and freedom. In A. Read (Ed.), *The fact of Blackness: Frantz Fanon and visual representation*. London: Institute of Contemporary Arts.

Ware, V. (1992). *Beyond the pale: White women, racism and history*. London: Verso.

Westwood, S. (1990). Racism, Black masculinity and the politics of space. In J. Hearn & D. Morgan (Eds.), *Men, masculinities and social theory*. London: Unwin Hyman.

Wheatley, R. (1992). *100 Years of Leeds League cricket*. Leeds, UK: White Line Publishing.

Yelvington, K. (1995). Cricket, colonialism, and the culture of Caribbean politics. In M. Malec (Ed.), *The social roles of sport in Caribbean societies*. Luxembourg: Gordon & Breach.

Zulfiqar, M. (1993). *Land of hope and glory? The presence of African, Asian and Caribbean communities in Leeds*. Leeds, UK: Roots Project.

CHAPTER 22

Gay Games or Gay Olympics? Implications for Lesbian Inclusion

Hellen Jefferson Lenskyj

The Purpose of the Gay Games is "to foster and augment the self-respect of lesbians and gay men . . . and to engender respect and understanding from the non-gay world."

—*Federation of Gay Games (1997)*

When the first Gay Games, at that time called the "Gay Olympic Games," were held in San Francisco in 1982, they were hailed as an empowering sporting and cultural celebration organized by and for lesbians, gays and their allies on the principles of inclusion and participation. (The Gay Games are open to participants who are gay, lesbian, bisexual, transgendered, queer, and heterosexual, but the terms most often used in reference to the Gay Games–related communities are *lesbian and gay*. Since most of the discussion here concerns events of the 1980s and 1990s, the terms lesbian and gay are historically appropriate.)

From their inception, discrimination based on "sexual orientation, gender, race, religion, nationality, ethnic origin, political belief(s), athletic/artistic ability, physical challenge, or HIV status" was prohibited. Since their modest beginnings in a San Francisco football stadium, the Gay Games have grown into an international sporting spectacle and business enterprise, with more than 20 core sporting events, a high level of competition between bidding cities, budgets exceeding US$7 million, corporate sponsors and more participants than most Olympic Games have attracted.

ORGANIZING FOR SOCIAL CHANGE

For many Canadian and American lesbian and gay activists in the early 1980s, an enterprise such as the Gay Games represented a radical departure from their usual political work, in that it was primarily a proactive initiative—a sport and cultural festival designed to celebrate lesbian and gay existence. Unlike activists lobbying for legislative or policy change, Gay Games founders were less interested in reforming the mainstream than in creating an alternative, inclusive model of sporting competition. Although, for many, the Games represented a reaction to homophobia in mainstream sport, significant numbers of participants with little prior sporting involvement were attracted by the principle of inclusion and the promise of community that the Games offered.

GAY GAMES ORGANIZING AND ACTIVISM

The first two Gay Games were organized by San Francisco Arts and Athletics, a group founded by former Olympic decathlete Tom Waddell in 1981. By 1989, this organization had become the Federation of Gay Games (hereafter the Federation) and included board members from a number of participating countries outside North America. Gender parity in committee structures was a key principle from the outset. The year 1990 marked the first Gay Games held outside the U.S., with the Metropolitan Vancouver Athletic/Arts Association (MVAAA), Canada, hosting the event with 29 sports and more than 7,000 athletes. It is noteworthy that the words *lesbian* and *gay* were not part of the names of these first organizing groups, an omission that at least one critic viewed as an attempt to blend into the mainstream (Syms, 1990).

The 1994 Gay Games in New York, with 11,000 athletes from 45 countries, marked the first time that there had been competition between two bid cities; for the 1998 Games, there were three bids, and for 2002, five. The total cost of all five bids for the 2002 Gay Games exceeded the budgets for the first two Gay Games themselves (Boson, 1998), an indication of the growing trend towards emulating the Olympic model.

In the early 1980s when Waddell and others first began organizing the Gay Games, the principle of inclusion had different connotations—different for Waddell, a closeted gay man for much of his athletic career, and for most lesbian and gay athletes. Billy Jean King's experience of homophobic backlash and her loss of commercial endorsements amply illustrated the safety of the closet for competitive athletes. Similarly, jobs in coaching, sport administration and physical education were in jeopardy if sport leaders' lesbian or gay identities became public knowledge, while athletes at every level risked harassment and ostracism if they came out. Twenty years later, with sport still representing the last bastion of sexism and homophobia, legislative and policy changes are addressing some—but certainly not all—of the problems of discrimination facing lesbian and gay athletes.

Gay Games founders sought to provide an opportunity to participate in an openly lesbian and gay sport festival. As Waddell explained, "[T]he message of these games goes beyond validating our culture. They were conceived as a new idea in the meaning of sport based on inclusion rather than exclusion" (cited in Coe, 1986; 7). He envisioned the Gay Games as a way of raising consciousness and enlightening people both outside and inside lesbian and gay communities (Messner, 1984). Participation in the Games would challenge homophobia in the heterosexual world, and sexism, ageism, racism and nationalism among lesbian and gay people. He hoped that his dream of an "exemplary community" would be achieved through inclusive policies and practices: age-group competition, recruitment and outreach to ethnic minority athletes and those from the developing countries, and social and cultural events to break down the barriers of gender, class, ethnicity and dis/ability among gays and lesbians. Two decades later, there are continuing debates about the realization of these goals.

MEDIA REPRESENTATIONS OF THE GAY GAMES

In most written accounts of the Gay Games, lesbian and gay commentators seemed just as eager as their non-gay allies to *normalize* this sporting spectacle and its participants. There was a consistent emphasis on similarity rather than difference: "We" (lesbian and gay athletes) can break "their" (heterosexual) records; we can organize events that are officially approved by their international federations; and we can produce one of the biggest international sporting spectacles in the world.

In the extensive lesbian and gay media coverage, there is a clear emphasis on using conventional sporting practices to counter homophobic stereotypes and to achieve lesbian and gay visibility and empowerment. In *The Story of Gay Games II*, Roy Coe described them as "an important demonstration of our love for each other and our presence in the world community. Our statement as a minority group was clearly made through the wonderful spirit of camaraderie and friendly competition" (Coe, 1986; 7). And, in the 1990 photo-journal of Gay Games III, the editors stated that the Games

> symbolized for thousands of gay men and women one more step along the road of self-discovery. And for one astounding week in time it was a road they could travel without ever having to apologize for their existence, or even having to suffer the strain of maintaining an appearance alien to their very nature.
>
> (Forzley and Hughes, 1990; 110)

Although the emphasis on empowerment is valid, to reduce the idea to simply "being oneself" and publicly showing "love for each other" is to overlook the sociocultural diversity of lesbian and gay communities. The choice whether to "be oneself" or to "pass" as a member of the dominant group is not available, for example, to lesbians and gays who are Black, or to those who have disabilities. Liberal individualistic notions of self-discovery and self-expression are insufficient for authentic, universal empowerment because they overlook the double or triple oppressions suffered by minority members of lesbian and gay communities. Furthermore, simply bringing together diverse groups of lesbians and gay men in sport does not in itself guarantee "love for each other," and it is naive to hope that sexism, racism, ableism and other entrenched forms of discrimination that divide communities will simply evaporate during Gay Games. On a more grandiose scale, Olympic industry rhetoric calls for peace and harmony, and presents Olympic competition as a transcendent human experience, at the same time ignoring the labour practices and human rights abuses of its multinational sponsors, its impact on low-income and homeless people in host cities, and countless other negative social and environmental impacts (Lenskyj, 2000, 2002a).

Although lesbian and gay community newspapers are an obvious forum for Gay Games debate, they face competing pressures. On one hand, they are expected to generate support for upcoming bids and games, to congratulate organizers and participants, and to celebrate the event as a success story in a homophobic world. On the other hand, since they are the most accessible source of analysis and critique of the Gay Games movement, they will fail in that role if they avoid controversy and self-criticism.

A brief review of selected newspaper coverage of Gay Games III in Vancouver shows few differences between mainstream and lesbian/gay media. *Kinesis*, a Vancouver feminist newspaper, published a supportive information article in July and a five-page, mainly favourable report in September; in Toronto, the coverage in *Xtra*, the major lesbian and gay paper, was mostly positive. In both papers, the only serious criticism was reserved for the homophobic Christian fundamentalists who picketed sporting and cultural events, and threw bottles at Gay Games participants. The American lesbian and gay magazine, *The Advocate*, was similarly uncritical. Mainstream Canadian newspapers, such as the *Toronto Star*, the *Globe and Mail* and the University of Toronto student paper, *The Varsity*, were largely supportive of the Games and critical of right-wing backlash (Brunt, 1990; MP, 1990; UBC, 1990; Vancouver, 1990).

One of the most obvious attempts to support MVAAA at all costs was Esther Shannon's commentary published in *Kinesis*. Discussing some anecdotal accounts of the Games, she wrote the following:

> A friend of mine told me about . . . getting a politically correct earful from two British lesbians . . . according to them, the Games were nothing more than an appalling white, middle-class North American spectacle. My friend . . . knew these earnest criticisms were valid but she kept thinking, "they're missing the point." [Vancouver] Gay Games organizers are at pains to keep "politics" out of the Games . . . [They] kept public debate on the Games' shortcomings to a minimum.
>
> (Shannon, 1990; 13)

> One might argue that, in the face of the right-wing backlash, a public united front was crucial to the success of the Games. However, the naive aim of keeping "politics" out of sport—also a popular notion among Olympic boosters—is especially inappropriate in relation to a sporting event that is by its very nature political.

Rites, a Toronto lesbian and gay newspaper, published some of the few critical commentaries. Anne Vespry, a *Rites* collective member, and Shawn Syms, an athlete, identified a number of organizational problems that threatened the Games' commitment to inclusion and visibility. Syms was critical of the composition of the MVAAA board: seven white, university-educated members, four men and three women (Syms, 1990), Vespry focused on the shortcomings of the cultural events, including access problems for people with disabilities, failure to subsidize tickets for low-income participants, and under-representation of people of colour (Vespry, 1990).

Both Syms and Vespry targeted the MVAAA's assimilationist approach to advertising. Its "straight looking, straight acting" board members, they claimed, opted for a "puritan image," and rendered lesbian and gay people invisible by omitting the words *gay* or *queer* from advertising in mainstream media. Although MVAAA might have argued that their low-key advertising and sanitized public image were justified in light of virulent right-wing opposition, Vespry and Syms are persuasive in their argument that the Games' principle of inclusion requires, at the very least, unequivocal solidarity with openly lesbian and gay members of the community, including the large numbers who reject assimilationist strategies (Syms, 1990; Vespry, 1990).

Given the increased levels of competition among bid cities, pressure on community media to limit negative commentary will be especially strong during the Gay Games bidding process. There was evidence of this trend in Sydney's major lesbian and gay newspaper, the *Sydney Star Observer*, which published mostly positive articles and encountered criticism from Team Sydney (the Sydney Gay Games bid committee) whenever it didn't, or when the timing of a particular article (e.g., Boson, 1997b) did not "suit" Team Sydney's purposes. This did not prevent the *Star*'s sport reporter, Mary Boson, from writing, among other critical articles, an insightful piece titled "Are we cheap dates?" in which she identified the danger that lesbian and gay organizations like Team Sydney would abandon their social justice agendas in the rush to get government and corporate funding, and in their efforts to demonstrate the power of the (gay male) "pink dollar" to the non-gay world (Boson, 1997a, 1997c). Given the double economic disadvantage experienced by lesbians—as women and as members of a stigmatized sexual minority—Boson's analysis was particularly cogent.

GAY GAMES OR GAY OLYMPICS?

Since their inception, Gay Games have involved a number of sport celebrities and former Olympic athletes, including Tom Waddell, Betty Baxter, Bruce Hayes, Martina Navratilova and Greg Louganis, and the biographies of Federation representatives and bid committee members usually include their athletic credentials (except for those organizing the cultural festival). The liberal notion of lesbian and gay celebrities serving as "role models" appears to hold sway in the Gay Games movement, and undoubtedly their positive examples and personal courage are inspirational to many. At the same time, however, this emphasis serves to entrench the mainstream competitive sporting ethos modelled on the Olympics, rather than to promote genuinely alternative and inclusive visions of sporting participation, where winning is less important than participating.

Research studies on lesbian and gay community sport demonstrate that it is difficult for those who have been socialized into the ethos of mainstream sport to abandon their often unexamined acceptance of competition and the "no pain, no gain" mantra for an alternative model that values fun, friendship and the pure pleasure of bodily movement. Socialized gender differences make it somewhat easier for women than men to embrace a new ethos of cooperation rather than competition in sport contexts (Lenskyj, 1994a). Greater involvement of feminist women in leadership roles would no doubt help the Gay Games movement to achieve its original radical goals. One troubling trend remains: Only 25 percent of Gay Games III and about 36 percent of Gay Games IV participants were women (Verry, 1998). This increased to 45 percent for Gay Games V in Amsterdam, largely as a result of the Women's Outreach Committee and direct marketing efforts.

From 1982 to 1986, Gay Games organizers were engaged in a lengthy and unsuccessful court battle against the United States Olympic Committee (USOC) to keep their original name, the Gay Olympic Games. Ambivalence over the key political question, "Gay Games or Gay Olympics?" was evident when Sara Lewinstein (Waddell's partner) told the press, "The perception has been created that somehow gays hate the Olympics . . . we love the Olympics. We just don't like the dumb bureaucrats who run the USOC" (Waddell and Schaap, 1996; 234). She went on to cite the improved sport facilities that would result from a successful Olympic bid.

In light of these early events, it is somewhat ironic that Sydney hosted the Summer Olympic Games in 2000, two years before Gay Games VI. In fact, according to Sydney's Gay Games bid book, most events would be using facilities constructed in the 1990s for Sydney 2000. Equally important, widespread popular support for Sydney 2000, achieved in large part by the Olympic Bid Committee's pressure on the mass media to suppress any negative reports (Booth and Tatz, 1994; Lenskyj, 2000, 2002a) helped pave the way for lesbian and gay community efforts to win Gay Games VI. The Gay Games bid book stressed the excellence of the Olympic facilities, and stated that the New South Wales government would provide these venues either free of charge or with major subsidies (Sydney 2002, 1997: 57). One section, however, presented an unexpected critique of the Olympic Games: "The [Gay] Games' ideals and prominent sporting participants will be used to contrast the elitism of the modern Olympics and to gain [media] coverage in the run-up to Sydney's Olympic Games in 2000" (15).

The Gay Games represent an alternative to the Olympic Games, but they are modelled in large part on an international sporting competition with over 100 years of checkered political history (and, in the late 1990s, a seriously tarnished image; see Lenskyj, 2000). From the outset, Gay Games' winners were named and recognized, medals were awarded, records were kept, and some events were "sanctioned" (conducted according to international federation standards); highly trained and talented athletes whose careers had been impeded by homophobia now had their own "Olympics." Only a minority of commentators problematized these trends.

CONCLUSION

The issues examined here confirm that tension remains between the radical view of the Gay Games as an alternative, inclusive and empowering lesbian and gay community event, and the liberal goal of mounting an income-generating, international sporting spectacle modelled on the Olympic Games. The key principle of inclusion, particularly in relation to lesbians, low-income people, participants from developing countries, and people with disabilities, is unlikely to be realized if organizers allow the Olympic model to dominate. However, if leaders can maintain an uncompromising political stance on the issues of inclusion, participation and accessibility, the Gay Games movement has transformative potential.

Excerpted from Helen Jefferson Lenskyj, "Gay Games or Gay Olympics? Implications for Lesbian Inclusion" in *Out on the Field: Gender, Sport and Sexualities* (Toronto: Women's Press, 2003), pp. 135–144. Earlier version appeared in *Canadian Woman Studies* 21.3 (2002): 24–28.

REFERENCES

Booth, D. and Tatz, C. (1994). Sydney 2000: The games people play. *Current Affairs Bulletin* 70 (7), 4–11.

Boson, M. (1997a). We won! Government Goes for Gold. *Sydney Star Observer* (November 20) [www.sso.rainbow.net.au]

——. (1997b). Gay Games License: Sydney hit with $1.4 million fee. *Sydney Star Observer* (December 11).

——. (1997c). Are we cheap dates? *Sydney Star Observer* (December 18).

——. 1998. Games bids "too costly." *Sydney Star Observer* (May 1).

Brunt, S. (1990). Inside the gay 90s: the name of the Games is pride. *Globe and Mail* (August 4), A24.

Coe, R. (1986). *A Sense of Pride: The Story of Gay Games II.* San Francisco: Pride Publications.

Federation of Gay Games. (1997). The Purpose [www.gaygames.org].

Forzley, R. and Hughes, D. (Eds.). (1990). *The Spirit Captured: The Official Photojournal of Celebration '90 – Gay Games III.* Vancouver: For Eyes Press.

Lenskyj, H. 1994a. Girl-friendly sport and female values. *Women in Sport and Physical Activity Journal* 3 (1), 35–46.

——. 2000. *Inside the Olympic Industry: Power, Politics, and Activism.* Albany, NY: SUNY Press.

——. 2002a. *The Best Olympics Ever? Social Impacts of Sydney 2000.* Albany, NY: SUNY Press.

Messner, M. (1984). Gay Athletes and the Gay Games: An Interview with Tom Waddell. *M: Gentle Men for Gender Justice* 13 (Fall), 22–23.

MP Praises Gay Games as "rainbow" of diversity. (1990). *Toronto Star* (August 6), A2.

Shannon, E. (1990). Can you believe the roar of the crowd? *Kinesis* (September), 12–14.

Sydney. (2002). *Sydney Gay Games VI: Under New Skies.* Sydney: Bid Book, 1997.

Syms, S. (1990). Celebration Æ90: Physique and Critique. *Rites* (September), 13.

UBC. (1990). UBC Condemns Homophobic Ad in Daily Papers. *The Varsity* 7 (November 20: 7).

Vancouver holds the third and largest Gay Games. (1990). *Globe and Mail* (August 6), A7.

Verry, C. (1998). Gay Games 2002 – Sydney. *Womensport Australia Newsletter 14* (March): 14.

Vespry, A. (1990). Reflections on the Gay Games. *Rites* (September), 11–13.

Waddell, T. and D. Schaap. 1996). *Gay Olympian: The Life and Death of Dr. Tom Waddell.* New York: Knopf.

CHAPTER 23

Argentina's Left-Wingers

Leslie Ray

On April 18th, 2004, Diego Maradona was admitted to the Swiss Clinic in Buenos Aires in an extreme condition. A crowd immediately began to form outside and soon developed into a mass vigil of a quasi-religious kind—devotees clutched candles, Virgin Mary statuettes, rosary beads and flowers, and held banners declaring 'Jesus in Heaven and Diego on earth'; 'Diego of the soul, after so many joys, give us one more'; 'God forgive the journalists, they know not what they do.' For British observers, there was an obvious parallel to be made with the collective grief following the death of Princess Diana.

That 'San Diego' (St Diego) is much loved is no surprise in a country so crazy about football, but why such reverency? For huge swathes of Argentina's working class, despite his dalliance with drugs, Maradona encapsulates their own religiosity, nationalism and political identity to an extent that would be inconceivable with a player in Britain. But while millions adore him, Argentina's elite and its beleaguered middle classes loathe him with an equal intensity for declaring himself a Peronist, as the presence of the populist demagogue whose presence still looms large over Argentine politics, decades after he was in power.

In Argentina, football is divided along political lines: if you are a Boca Juniors fan, you are likely to be a working-class Peronist; if you follow River Plate, you tend to be a middle-class radical, Argentina's other main political grouping. The origins of this division are probably rooted in early twentieth-century differences of geography, wealth and nationality. Boca is the port area where the poor immigrant Italians first settled, while River Plate is in more affluent Liniers, in northern Buenos Aires, where the middle-class Spanish and Jewish tended to live. Radical River fans cannot forgive Maradona for his very public association with communism—he has a tattoo of Che Guevara displayed prominently on his forearm—and with Castro's Cuba. Yet this support for Cuba has a nationalist, rather than an internationalist, slant; after a meeting with Fidel, Diego said of him: 'He defends his flag, in Argentina we gave ours away to the United States.'

The twin tracks of nationalism and socialism have been constants in Argentina's footballing history. The nationalism is easily recognized by England or Scotland supporters, as it mirrors their own. As historian Eric Hobsbawm has said, 'the imagined community of millions seems more real as a team of eleven named people'. England and Argentina have a World Cup history of great pitch battles: Michael Owen's winning goal in 2002, David Beckham's leg wave at

Simeone, his subsequent disgrace and rehabilitating penalty, in 1998; England's victory over Rattin's hackers in 1966, when Sir Alf Ramsey called the Argentine team 'animals', and of course Maradona's unforgivable crafty 'hand of God' in Mexico in 1986. Argentine fans are often keener to bring up this particular bone of contention with England than the Falklands/Malvinas War. For them, the stadium is not just a battlefield; it is also the terrain of class struggle, nationalistic fervour and ecstatic religious experience. This is not unique to Argentina, of course, but the intermingling of these elements on the football pitch seems all the more obvious here.

Curiously, the founding of Argentina's football clubs around the turn of the twentieth century would seem to be due in equal measure to the empire-building efforts of the British bourgeois elite and to the organizing forces of socialism. The English names of major clubs are many: Racing Club, Boca Juniors and River Plate are Argentina's three leading clubs. However, it is Newell's Old Boys, from the Primera Division A, which has the strongest connection with England. It was founded in 1903 in honour of Isaac Newell, originally from Kent, who was the headmaster of the Anglo-Argentine College in the city of Rosario from 1883 to 1900, where he taught the boys the skills and values of this character-forming sport. In 1903 his son Claudio and other alumni of the school founded Newell's Old Boys in Isaac's honour. The club's red and black shield have prompted many Argentine anarchists to believe that its founders had anarchist sympathies, though the club's official history stresses that in fact black was supposed to represent eloquence and red wisdom.

In Argentina Rosario is renowned for developing two great traditions: attacking football and radical politics. Gabriel Batistuta, Argentina's star striker of the 1990s, learnt his football on the streets of Rosario, and his first club was Newell's. An even more famous local boy was Maradona's hero, a certain Ernesto 'Che' Guevara. Che was in fact a keen rugby player, but chronic asthma forced him to abandon the oval ball in favour of the round one. His chosen position was in goal, so he could be close to his inhaler. In the 1940s—as today—most Argentine youngsters supported River or Boca, but Che, ever on the side of the underdog, decided to follow his local team, lowly Rosario Central.

Football was looked upon rather ambivalently by the theorists of the left. In 1917 the anarchist newspaper *La Protesta* condemned it as the 'pernicious reducing to idiocy through the repeated kicking of a round ball'. But socialists and anarchists were in the forefront of Argentina's new football enthusiasts. Founded in 1904, the Club 'Mártires de Chicago' (Martyrs of Chicago), later to become Argentinos Juniors and now in Primera B Nacional, was named in homage to the Chicago Haymarket Martyrs, hanged in 1886 for demanding an eight-hour working day. The Club El Porvenir (The Future), from predominantly working-class southern Buenos Aires, also in the Primera B Nacional, was founded by utopians; Chacarita Juniors, in the Primera División A, by the members of a libertarian library, appropriately enough on May 1st, International Workers' Day. Independiente, also in the Primera, was another socialist club, so named because it considered itself independent of the factory in Avellenada where its players worked.

As the twentieth century developed, football gradually divested itself of its British identity (though British referees were still invited to preside over matches to ensure that they were played in a proper, ethical fashion) and became increasingly associated with the urban working class of Italian and Spanish origin. The powerful forces of 'fanaticism' that football unleashed began to be exploited by politicians pursuing a nationalist agenda. Juan Domingo Perón loved football, but he also recognized the part it could play in building the nation. Perón wanted Argentina to occupy a more prominent role on the world stage, and he saw it as essential to modify the elitist profile of many of the country's institutions, including sports, and open them up to the popular sectors. In a 1998 article for *Entrepasados* magazine, Eugenia Scarzanella describes how the Peronist government contributed to the expansion of sport: 'Racing drivers, marathon runners, boxers and footballers received decorations and favours. New football stadiums and sports facilities were built. Children were given free entry to matches and special tournaments were organized under the aegis of Evita.' Such forceful promotions of football, along with other sports, might have led to success at the 1950 World Cup, had the event not been held in Brazil, with whom Argentina's relations were—not for the first or last time—rather strained at the time.

Perón had seen that soccer could play an important role in forging a modern national identity for Argentina, but it was later generals who were the most determined to tap its immense power. So it was that when Argentina hosted the World Cup in 1978 during the military junta of Jorge Rafael Videla, the so-called 'Dirty War'—perhaps the greatest battle between ideologies in Argentine history—was waged inside and outside the stadiums. The Junta had spent an estimated $700 million on the World Cup project, seriously increasing Argentina's already large national debt. Although 60,000 foreign tourists were expected, only 7,000 actually turned up, most of whom were journalists. So the panicking government commissioned the American PR firm Burson & Marsteller to improve the country's image. Theirs was the slogan that was seen all over Argentina during the 'Mundial': *los argentinos somos derechos y humanos* ('we Argentines are upright and humane')—a pun that subverted and downplayed the accusation that grave abuses of human rights (*derechos humanos*) were taking place in the country at the time.

The national side progressed all the way through the competition—not without controversy, as when they beat a suspiciously supine Peru team 6–0—eventually making it to the final against Holland, which was played at the River Plate Stadium. It was somehow fitting that the great showpiece event pitted against the Generals' team a side from a liberal democracy whose 'total football' was more than just a tactical system, it was the egalitarian principle in practice, as every player was capable of playing in every position, with commitment, empathy and without hierarchy. Mixed among the sea of blue and white banners, and the occasional orange one, were others drawing attention to Argentina's thousands of 'disappeared'. The cameras strained to avoid them, but by this stage it was too late, the cat was out of the bag. Every day during the World Cup, despite attempts to silence them, the Mothers and Grandmothers of the Disappeared had walked silently and courageously around Plaza de Mayo in Buenos Aires, their white headscarves embroidered with the names of their missing loved ones. Amid the fuss surrounding the final—with thousands demonstrating their passion for the game, others their outrage at the Junta's repression—the great but irremediably elitist writer Jorge Luis Borges showed his utter disdain for the whole event by intentionally calling a conference on the theme of immortality on the very day, at the very time, that the Argentine team was playing. Few attended.

Argentina won 3–1, and the head of the Junta, Videla, gleefully handed the trophy to captain Daniel Passarella. Glory then, but anger or indifference now. Last year, to mark the twenty-fifth anniversary of the victory, a paltry crowd of just over 6,000 watched a match between a current Argentine side and a team including three members of the 1978 World Cup winning side. Once again many held banners inside and outside the stadium denouncing human rights' abuses. One banner read, 'Inside they played a World Cup. Outside, a country was being lost.'

One irony of Argentina's victory was that the team's manager was Cesar Luis Menotti, who has never made a secret of his left-wing views. Menotti has always been understandably defensive about his work in 1978. He has said 'Revolution is not made by footballers, musicians or actors.' He was on tour in the USSR when the coup that brought Videla to power took place in 1976, and he has since confessed that he hesitated over whether to return to his country or go into exile. Return he did, his high profile and match-winning importance to the regime keeping him safe, despite his views.

Angel Cappa is a former midfielder and coach, and was Menotti's right-hand man when he managed Boca Juniors in 1987 and later Atlético Madrid. What makes Cappa unusual for a footballer is that he is truly a soccer intellectual, a professor of philosophy and sociology, who has written a number of books on the sociological aspects of the beautiful game. He is also the living demonstration of the fact that socialist ideas are still alive and well in football. Cappa believes with former Liverpool manager Bill Shankly that 'football isn't a matter of life and death: it's much more serious'. In an interview earlier this year he criticized the way that European soccer drains Argentina of two hundred players a year:

> Eduardo Galeano once said that the South sells not only arms to the North, but also legs. The centre of world footballing power has a permanent 'factory' of players in South America and other marginalized regions, some of whom are already in Europe without ever having played in our own premier leagues. At best, in their countries of origin they are only ever seen on TV. This is nothing but total dependency on the centres of economic power.

In December 2001, at the peak of the social upheaval in Argentina, when thirty people were killed and hundreds injured as the government struggled to maintain the rule of law, the decision was made to allow the final day's matches on the fixture list to be played—thus ensuring that Racing won the championship for the first time in three decades. Three years later, this still arouses Cappa's bitter condemnation:

> It was disgusting. A cruel way of accepting that money is what counts most for those in power, perhaps it is the only thing that counts. Undoubtedly it was television, and the other sectors profiting from Racing winning the championship after so long, that needed the matches to be played. It's one thing to sell products taking advantage of fresh euphoria and quite another to allow too much time to pass. Money has no patience. The same happened with the bombs in Madrid on March 11th [2004], when some Spanish teams didn't want to play in the European tournaments, and were forced to, with the whole country in shock. If anything were needed to show that all they care about is money, that is the proof.

Today Argentina's stability is precarious, but at the time of the millennium it was a country in ferment. Many factory owners, unable to meet their debts, abandoned their businesses. Faced with no jobs, the workers at a number of factories decided to run them themselves. One of these was Zanon, in Neuquén, Patagonia. In the late 1990s Zanon had a trades union leadership that was corrupt and complicit with the bosses. Surprisingly, it was football that enabled a group of activists to wrest the control of the unions from the bureaucrats and plan the factory occupation. Syndicalist Raul Godoy tells the story:

> We decided to hold a soccer tournament, with every sector of the factory taking part, as there was much rivalry between them. There was a team for each sector, and each team had its own delegate, so there we took advantage to talk to everyone. We talked about organizing the tournament, but we also began to chat about other things, the problems in the factory. So a network formed within the factory with comrades from different places, and we were able to find out their views, when we went to play, because you were not allowed to talk openly inside the factory. That's how it came about. First it was matches, nothing more, every Sunday spent barbecuing sausages, selling beer and playing football. It was tough, but it was worth it, because it meant we were eventually able to organize.

Even though a hundred years have passed since some of Argentina's first football clubs were founded by left-wingers, the country's soccer-socialists are still organizing.

Excerpted from Leslie Ray, "Argentina's Left-Wingers" in *History Today* 54.12 (December 2004): 36–38. Reprinted with the permission of History Today Limited.

CHAPTER 24

Hoosier Whiteness and the Indiana Pacers: Racialized Strategic Change and the Politics of Organizational Sensemaking

R. Scott Carey

NEED TO STRATEGICALLY CHANGE THE PACERS' 'IMAGE PROBLEM'

Between October 2006 and January 2008, seven different players of the Indiana Pacers (National Basketball Association, NBA) were implicated in a number of off-court events that sparked the anxieties of those within and outside the organization. Brought under scrutiny for their possession and/or use of marijuana, David Harrison and Shawne Williams' names were cast on the public realm. Harrison was caught violating the NBA's drug policy, while Williams was pulled over for 'driving infractions' leading police officers to eventually find the substance in his car.[1] Overlooking the deeper set of politics under which these players were constructed as criminals and/or miscreants (e.g. the NBA drug policy and its castigation of recreational drug use as opposed to performance enhancing drugs; 'driving while black'), many commentators decidedly chastised Pacers' athletes for what they considered to be irresponsible, juvenile, or delinquent behaviour. Shawne Williams' name was, once again, brought forth to the public as he housed a childhood friend who was suspected of murder.[2] Similarly, an alleged rape took place in the home of Marquis Daniels during a small party, where he was not found to be involved.[3] Jamaal Tinsley was shot at, and chased down, in his vehicle after leaving a nightclub on one occasion; and was also involved in a separate incident along with Daniels, Stephen Jackson, and Jimmy Hunter (whereby a car purposely struck Jackson in the parking lot of a different establishment).[4] Lastly, an alleged altercation took place at a third nightclub, after a man attempted to steal the coats belonging to Tinsley, Daniels, and Keith McLeod.[5]

Even though many of the athletes were victims of assault, acting in self-defence, and/or unfairly linked by association, they were rarely (if ever) portrayed by the media in this light. The author does not wish to suggest that each player be exempted from suspicion with regards to their involvement in these acts. Instead, it is the author's intention to question the effects that this criminalizing, racializing discourse had on the sensemaking processes of individuals responsible for enacting the Pacers' strategic change initiative. Set against the backdrop of the infamous brawl that took place on 19 November 2004 between Indiana Pacers' players and Detroit Pistons' fans, the Pacers were seen to be an organization in a state of crisis. Suspecting that its fanbase had begun to formulate a negative image of the team, the franchise leaders hired a professional pollster to determine the validity of this assumption. Of the fans who were polled, only 43% noted they had a 'favorable opinion of the team' by the end of 2007.[6] According to the pollster, Frank Luntz, 'the fans had said "I've had enough"; and they were telling us that they weren't going to come back . . . they wanted the players to be people that their kids could look up to – role models'.[7] Driven by the results of this research, the Indiana Pacers' leaders identified community and character as being central to the organization's change, and it is to this issue that the author focuses his critique.

Answering the call for sport management research to address epistemological racism,[8] this paper shall evaluate the Indiana Pacers' change by resituating organizational sensemaking theory underneath the lens of critical race theory (CRT). In doing so, the author also hopes to fill a perceived gap in the sport management fan literature – one that has yet to frame 'race' from a critical lens. With the recognition that sport fans shape and construct their identity by associating or dissociating with teams,[9] it is imperative to acknowledge how such decisions become influenced by racial judgments. As such, the Indiana Pacers' image reconstruction provides the perfect backdrop to further explore racialized identities and their respective role in the shaping of organizational strategic change.

Within academic circles, the NBA has already received critical analysis from scholars seeking to expose the inherent corporatized Whiteness that remains embedded in the league's decision-making, policies, and discourse.[10] However, individual franchises have yet to be analysed from a similar perspective. As this paper hopes to make clear, context matters. Taking matters into their own hands, the Indiana Pacers went beyond the NBA's white, normalizing routines and surveillance techniques (e.g. dress code, age policy) to use a more symbolic set of changes aimed at appeasing Indiana's predominantly white demographic. Whiteness, Blackness, basketball, masculinity, Indiana, the 'Hoosier identity', and the Pacers franchise thus represent a series of socially constructed, historically contingent, and contextually meaningful signifiers. Wanting to avoid essentialist notions of race, it is therefore necessary that we critically interrogate the space(s) where these forces come to intersect and produce meaningful racialized subjectivities for individuals on a personal and organizational level. Henceforward referred to as 'Hoosier Whiteness', it is argued that basketball's cultural significance within the state of Indiana is understood from this deeply institutionalized ideological nexus of race, masculinity, the Hoosier identity, and 'purity'. Thus, perceived to have diverged from its logic, the Indiana Pacers appealed to its external constituents by adopting the familiar sensemaking process into the organization's strategic change initiative. Racial stereotypes were deployed, reinforced, and rearticulated within Indiana's symbolic basketball territory, allowing those beyond the organization to collectively construct a 'dark' past and 'bright' future for the franchise. Activated through purposeful action and suggestive language, this paper examines four sites at which the organization's commitment to 'Hoosier Whiteness' came to be known and understood by the Indiana public. First, the increased power that was afforded to Larry Bird by the Indiana Pacers will be placed under closer scrutiny, as he represents an embodied form of Hoosier Whiteness. Second, the drastic changes to compose a 'Whiter' roster will be critiqued as a significant act based on racial stereotypes. Third, the unjust banishment of one particular player from the team[11] will be understood for its symbolic value and widespread acceptance; and, lastly the organization's 2008–2009 marketing campaign will be analysed for its role in infusing the aforementioned changes with a particular ideology (i.e. Hoosier Whiteness).[12]

CONCEPTUAL FRAMEWORK

Before interrogating these matters from a resituated organizational sensemaking perspective, it is first necessary to explain sensemaking theory and CRT in more detail. Sensemaking theory, as conceived by organizational scholars, argues that an individual's knowledge structure is the most fundamental concept in organizational decision-making.[13] Described as being a 'mental template that individuals impose on an information environment to give it form and meaning',[14] knowledge structures are both cognitive and social in nature. Theoretically then, the study of sensemaking must take into account broader social forces and embedded hierarchies of power that come to influence one's schematic processing. In choosing how to make sense of a particular information environment, cognitive decisions are complexly intertwined with notions of legitimacy. Those self-evident or institutionalized ways of understanding often emerge as such, in part due to the privileged and/or dominant voice(s) that construct and uphold these 'truths' (thereby reinforcing their own power). As a result, entire groups of people can be persuaded into conferring on the same (read: 'common sense') knowledge structure to better comprehend the events or actions taking place before them.

Levine, Resnick, and Higgins referred to these homogenized knowledge structures as sociocognitive beliefs,[15] in that they represent a shared system for meaning creation within a given environment. However, if one is to properly understand the institutionalizing forces responsible for the development of sociocognitive beliefs, Antonio Gramsci's hegemony theory acts as a useful theoretical lens. Gramsci used the term hegemony to denote the dominance of one social group over others. Extending on Marxist thought, he theorized that ideology, language, and symbolism worked in conjunction with existing economic inequalities to formulate and/or uphold hegemonic power relations in society.[16] These become articulated and/or performed through various political, pedagogical, ideological, or cultural outlets so as to normalize relations of power; and in turn, garner consent among ruled populations who actively participate in their own subjugation.[17] Consent – rather than force or coercion – remains at the centre of Gramsci's hegemony theory. And, it is through the ability of the ruling class to convince others of the legitimacy on which the existing social order rests, that hegemonic structures are upheld and reproduced by beneficiaries and the oppressed alike. That is not to suggest that Gramsci purported an absolute, top-down conception of power with no potentiality for resistance. In fact, he argued that consent is characterized by a 'contradictory consciousness' whereby individuals are constantly engaged in an internal struggle between hegemonic common sense and their own critical voice.[18] In other words, they do not passively admit defeat to the resounding logic(s), but rather ambivalently and superficially adhere to these dominant ideologies while experiencing conflicting feelings and/or desires.

Yet, professional organizations (sport or otherwise) are subject to the logics of capitalist hegemony. Consequently, to generate profit, they look to curb uncertainty by producing a coherent 'package' with which external constituents can identify and consume. From a Gramscian perspective, the organization thereby acts as one of many pedagogical or cultural institutions responsible for the articulation and reinforcement of dominant ideologies. Such a belief seems to fall in line with Weick's request for sensemaking theorists to 'pay more attention to sufficient cues for coordination such as a generalized other, prototypes, stereotypes, and roles, especially considering that organizations seem to drift towards an "architecture of simplicity"'.[19] Therefore, as organizations strive to repress Gramsci's notion of 'contradictory consciousness' by appearing congruent with legitimate or common sense norms and values,[20] sensemaking theory seems to offer an inherently critical voice capable of disrupting and illuminating invisible power relations. Proceeding forward with the understanding that organizational sensemaking aims to 'construct, filter, frame, create facticity, and render the subjective into something more tangible',[21] the Pacers' mobilization of race and a racialized ideology (i.e. Hoosier Whiteness) to accomplish this task deserves our attention.

At this point, it is useful to briefly introduce CRT so as to further expound on the notion of Whiteness. CRT has emerged as a viable theoretical tool to reshape our ontological understanding of sport.[22] By placing 'race' at the forefront of analysis, researchers embark on a quest to uncover and explain racism's highly institutionalized and covert nature as it is/becomes embedded in structures and embodied in people. Situated within a particular space and time, 'races' are always dialogic, fluid, and socially constructed signifiers developed by, and for, hegemonic forces in society: 'Not objective, inherent, or fixed, they correspond to no biological or genetic reality; rather, races are categories that society invents, manipulates, or retires when convenient.'[23]

Nonetheless, discourse surrounding the topic of 'race' has tended to perform through a process of Othering, whereby a group of 'Others' are made hypervisible in their difference(s) to an invisible Whiteness – the '"inside", "included", "powerful", the "we", the "us", the "answer"'.[24] In turn, Whiteness is afforded with considerable power and privilege, as its normalizing gaze seeks to define, control, and oppress those labelled outside its sphere. Functioning underneath the protective sheath of colour-blindness, Whiteness has become particularly invisible in today's 'post-racial era' where racism is no longer seen to exist (amplified by factors such as the election of a Black president and the material success of Black athletes in professional sports). Instead, all people are seen to have the same opportunity in life, providing some with the dangerous illusion that they exist as raceless beings. Not surprisingly, CRT advocates that researchers question this invisibility by interrogating Whiteness as a racial category that society has also invented and manipulated. Additionally, liberalist notions of race-neutrality must be problematized as being one of the contributing factors to the invisibility of Whiteness and its intrinsic racism. As Sefa Dei, Karumanchery, and Karumanchery-Luik pointed out, the 'ordinary' nature of racism today has become so intertwined within the very fabric of democracy, that the oppressed are seen as being responsible for their own oppression.[25] In other words, dedication to a humanist philosophy that positions everyone as equal and responsible for their own success largely marginalizes and overlooks the many structural inequalities that exist today.

Thus, Whiteness is a difficult concept for many to accept in that it asks one to challenge the meritocratic assumptions on which Western discourses of individualism owe their legitimacy. In this regard, the reconceptualization of an imaginary egalitarianism for something with far less moral integrity requires white folks to critically reflect on their own achievements as benefitting from an unequal, invisible centre of power and privilege (an introspective task that some are unable or unwilling to explore). But, as many CRT scholars have been right to point out, Whiteness exists as more than a discourse.[26] It is, as Leonardo stated, also 'a world-view which, according to Gibson, projects a "delusional world", "a racial fantasyland", and "a consensual hallucination"', that constructs the world in a partitioned manner.[27] In other words, this White epistemology owes much of its deluded nature to the way it conceives of history as a fixed concept that is fragmented from the present. Leonardo noted the repercussions of this type of thinking: 'This allows the white psyche to speak of slavery as "long ago", rather than as a legacy which lives today . . . It can only be concerned with "how things are and not how they got to be that way"'.[28] That is not to say that White people are the only ones who remain prone to its obfuscated portrayal of reality. In actuality, those who are traditionally positioned as Other can also be allured into adopting the normalized/normalizing world view (consistent with Gramsci's notion of hegemony and consent). And most importantly, there is great incentive for individuals to deny its existence as it would consequently infer that one accept some responsibility for contributing to social injustice and oppression. Nonetheless, since Whiteness is a 'particular pattern of localized and global cognitive dysfunctions (which are psychologically and socially functional)',[29] it seems to coincide with many of the central propositions of sensemaking theory.

To resituate sensemaking theory underneath the lens of CRT, it is therefore necessary to think about Whiteness as this cognitive dysfunction and/or world view that distorts the way people conceive of history, race, racism, and racialized subjects. Pervading all spheres of Western democratic life, the ubiquity of Whiteness represents an ideology of privilege that has managed to elicit widespread academic critique. And, while scholars within the broad disciplinary field of sport studies have begun to elucidate the ideological value of a corporatized/corporatizing NBA Whiteness, a closer look at individual franchises reveals the dialectical complexities, pluralities, and negotiations at work. As the NBA continued to promote a 'safe' (commercialized) articulation of hip hop aimed at attracting youth markets (even after the announcement of a dress-code policy),[30] the Indiana Pacers sought to distance themselves from hip-hop signifiers altogether by the late 2000s. Wanting to rid the organization of this perceived moral threat, the Pacers instead opted to embrace Indiana's own, hegemonic ideology of 'Hoosier basketball' into their sensemaking process. Thus, borrowing from Gramsci (1971) that ideology is a 'spontaneous philosophy' situated in 'language itself, which is a totality of determined notions and concepts . . . "common sense" and "good sense" . . . popular religion and, therefore . . . the entire system of beliefs, superstitions, opinions, ways of seeing things and acting . . . collectively bundled together under the name of "folklore",'[31] this paper uses a discourse analysis methodology to better understand the meanings attributed to 'Hoosier basketball' by the Indiana Pacers.

Discourse analysis is a useful methodological tool for researchers hoping to uncover hidden regimes of power. As Foucault (1978) describes: 'Discourse transmits and produces power; it reinforces it, but also undermines it and exposes it, renders it fragile and makes it possible to thwart it.'[32] In other words, discourse plays an important role in shaping people's experiences; but, as individuals become subjected to a variety of competing discourses, a critical perspective is useful in explicating the inherent contradictions and discontinuities of subject positions (i.e. how individuals come to know, construct, and subject themselves through discourse) to subsequently offer a potential site for resistance.[33] For example, the identities of Indiana Pacers' athletes, fans, and organizational leaders were not unitarily constructed according to their respective affiliation with the NBA, but rather governed by a number of competing and intersecting discourses including 'Hoosierness', race, masculinity, and class. Existing underneath this complex discursive landscape, the language used by the organization (e.g. its leaders, marketing department), community, and media serves as the foundation on which this paper analyses the Indiana Pacers' strategic change. Through these linguistic processes, individuals come to experience, know, and construct the reality in culturally and historically contingent ways. And, in a Gramscian sense, 'language becomes one of the means by which common sense is transformed into philosophical good sense'.[34]

Wanting to understand the ideological 'good sense' attributed to 'Hoosier basketball' – and more specifically, examine its appeal in creating a 'sensible, sensable'[35] knowledge structure under which the Indiana Pacers hoped to legitimize itself and regain support from the broader community – this paper uses a wide variety of sources. To appreciate the sensemaking at the top of the organization, transcripts from media-conducted interviews (available online) with decision-makers and/or leaders were included in the analysis. Furthermore, the team's 2008–2009 marketing campaign and related messaging were also brought under scrutiny. News reports were incorporated to account for the media's role in producing hegemonic beliefs; and lastly, Internet message board postings and personal interviews provided a means to insert the voice(s) of the community and/or fans of the team.[36] To compensate for the criticism that a focus on discourse too often presupposes a 'simple translation between reality and language',[37] the emergent narratives were always situated alongside actualized events and/or decisions being made within the organization: 'Narratives matter because they do ideological work which has material consequences'.[38] Focusing on these discursive *practices* thus shaped the ensuing themes and codes used in analysis, illuminating what 'truths' were responsible for people's understanding and construction of the reality around them (i.e. the Indiana Pacers' strategic change).

However, placing a priority on the material consequences evinced by the Indiana Pacers' ideological shift (i.e. racialized symbols and events resulting from the change) subsequently affected the hermeneutic process of enquiry, in that 'meaningful' data/language was closely linked to racial politics and themes. Of course, a macro-discourse analysis might reveal other meaningful narratives[39] that either intersects with the racialized arguments put forth in this paper, or provides an alternative reading altogether. That is not to suggest that the author proceeded forth with an essentialist perspective towards race (e.g. the impending analysis does indeed make connections to masculinity, nationality, commercial forces); although, it is recognized that the focus of this paper was to explore the conjuncture of race, power, and the NBA on a micro-political level as opposed to the macro perspective used in the existent scholarship. Consequently, data analysis was driven from a radically contextualized, localized orientation grounded in the dialectical historicism of Indiana's (racist) basketball tradition, 'to see how broader formations of discourse and power are manifest in the everyday, quotidian aspects of texts in use'.[40]

RECLAIMING HOOSIER BASKETBALL

The dominant, institutionalized cultural notions of what constitutes as uniquely 'Hoosier' (that is, Indiana) basketball have been widely professed, publicized, and represented throughout the state's history. Far from being static in nature, this perceptual lens has evolved from a much broader White discourse that existed as part of Indiana's political landscape well before Hoosiers began to embrace basketball. In fact, the omniscient power of Hoosier Whiteness has largely stemmed from its inconspicuous fluidity. This ability to adapt, reformulate, and reinscribe values that conform to much larger discursive interdependencies are what provide Hoosier Whiteness with a veiled, taken-for-granted illusion of truth.

To demystify this complex concept, it is therefore necessary to deconstruct the word 'Hoosier' as a starting point to unconceal its racialized essence.

Sefa Dei, Karumanchery, and Karumanchery-Luik stated: 'By deconstructing how words and meanings function relative to power, we interrogate the political nature of language and its role in the maintenance of oppression.'[41] Seen in this vein, the word 'Hoosier' poignantly draws our attention. The state of Indiana – officially nicknamed the 'Hoosier State' – continues to embrace this label as a means for characterizing its citizens. Moreover, the word has become an established part of Indiana's everyday cultural lexicon (particularly as it refers to a distinguished style of basketball). Unquestionably then, the word flaunts a considerable degree of power as it lays claim to both Indiana's political *and* cultural landscape. Yet, the majority of Indiana natives remain unclear as to the true derivation of the word, and instead pay homage to a variety of glorified but competing folkloric tales.[42] While the differences in these etymological origins are varied to some degree, Whiteness acts as the common denominator from which they all make sense. Most historians have been quick to propose theories that position Indiana's original, White settlers as the referents to the word – in turn, creating a rustic, rural, and White image that has been embraced as the popular representation of a true and authentic Hoosier. Contrastingly, those theories which project a Black sense of the word[43] have been pushed into the shadows of history with far less support or popular representation (despite convincing scholarship). This process of burying and/or concealing history is symptomatic of the 'institutionalized white supremacy [that] puts in place structures for the dissemination of knowledge' and attempts to create forgetfulness on the part of populations.[44] As a result, the word Hoosier has maintained its concealed Whiteness in all contexts. Beyond Indiana's borders, the word has been used as a slang term to connote imagery surrounding stereotypic 'rednecks' or 'hillbillies'. Within Indiana, however, the word is embodied proudly, and represents something closer to an ideology that maintains its Whiteness in a specifically tailored, contextualized form.

With the partial understanding that basketball is a fundamental component to the Hoosier identity, it is important to trace this socio-cultural development. Historically, Indiana basketball began to appropriate its social meaning in the first half of the twentieth century, as it coincided with the migration of a largely rural image:

> While searching for economic opportunity amidst the industrialized North, the preponderance of transplanted southerners might explain why so many Hoosiers looked suspiciously upon the dawn of modernity . . . those from a Southern tradition had an instinctive mistrust of outsiders and change, especially when they apparently came in one big package. With the forces of change all around, Hoosiers searched for ways to define their communities around very traditional, pre-industrial values.[45]

Thus, the argument stood that Indiana's displaced White, rural, conservative, Southern demographic used high-school basketball as a 'social and cultural response' to the effects of industrial capitalism. Not surprisingly, the team was meant to embody and rearticulate the values of 'discipline, teamwork, obedience, and self-sacrifice'[46] that were seen as '*exclusively* associated with the state's white, Protestant, and native-born culture'.[47]

However, Indiana's 'social and political response' to industrial capitalism was the emergent rise of the Ku Klux Klan; producing its highest state membership (leading to political victories) between 1922 and 1925.[48] This hate for the 'Other' (e.g. a newly migrated Southern, Black population) permeated into the realm of high-school basketball when all-Black schools were deemed ineligible to play in officially sanctioned games and tournaments by the Indiana High School Athletic Association in 1927. As such, a racialized dichotomy had been established whereby the perceived threat of a 'different' 'urban, Black basketball' stood in direct opposition to what had been claimed as the aforementioned values and meaning of a 'rural, White basketball'. On integrating all-Black schools into statewide competition, Pierce suggested that the 1951 high-school team, Crispus Attucks Tigers, came to challenge this simplistic binary opposition. By recognizing their political significance as an all-Black team, the coaches and players from Crispus Attucks 'emphasized sportsmanship, rather than winning' in the state finals.[49] Despite losing the game (attributed largely to biased officiating), White Indianapolis residents supported the team 'but it appeared that whites were more wary in their acceptance, as if supporting the team was part of a civic responsibility'.[50] This would suggest that, at the time, White audiences were still largely adhering to the notion that 'urban, Black basketball' presented a possible threat to the established (and exclusively) 'rural, White basketball' norms – but were reluctantly willing to support the team so long as they conformed to remaining within the established system of domination.

Therefore, concern arose when 'the image of the farm-boy ballplayer began to lose its social and cultural significance' with the onslaught of urban, Black basketball players who 'revolutionized' the game in the 1960s.[51] On the heels of losing basketball's symbolic and ideological constitutions to a Black, stylistic, free-flowing and artistic game that was nothing like the 1951 Crispus Attucks Tigers team (thereby reinforcing the dichotomized imaginary landscape of 'Black' and 'White' styles), Indiana's White citizenry were longing for a symbol of their past; or, more aptly, a symbol of who they were as 'Hoosiers'. Indiana University head coach, Bob Knight, became that symbol in 1971 and similarly worked to reinscribe Hoosier Whiteness 'as the last mainstay of half-court, rural white basketball in a game completely redefined by black players, artistry, and style'.[52] More importantly, Knight came to represent 'a racially entangled part of both basketball and state history in Indiana, an era of containment for which many people still long'.[53] In placing restrictions and impositions on each player's individuality (on and off the court), and coaching wildly disproportionate White teams, Knight became a symbol of White supremacy and patriarchy who was read through a rearticulation of Hoosier Whiteness. While he continued to preach the values of 'Indiana basketball', he also symbolized a colonialist force on what was perceived as a threatening 'Black style' that emphasized competing values of individualism, flash, and innovation in need of control.

This imagined 'Black style' came under further attack in the 1986 film *Hoosiers* through the retelling of the often romanticized and glorified 1954 state championship game which featured a small, rural, all-White school (Milan High) upsetting a larger, urban, all-Black (Muncie Central) school.[54] More importantly, the film functioned as an important location for the reconstruction of Hoosier Whiteness in that cultural forms (i.e. film) work as an ideological apparatus to maintain racial identities.[55] Predictably, the claimed rural, White values of 'decency, innocence, hard work, ingenuity, discipline, and sense of team or community' were embodied in the all-White school and, juxtaposed against the all-Black team 'which threaten[ed] not only the homogeneity of the small town but also white control of a sport such as basketball'.[56]

Most problematic of all, however, was film director David Anspaugh's attempt to 'render invisible the racial context of black basketball in Indiana'.[57] As Pierce so poignantly described, Indiana high-school basketball in the 1950s came to have political meaning for all-Black schools operating within the Civil Rights movement. Anspaugh's film, however, neglected to portray the racial politics involved; instead opting for an 'American-dream' narrative that emphasized the values of hard work and obedience (embodied in the rural, all-White team from 'Hickory High') in the determination of success. Furthermore, the all-Black team represented in the state finals of the movie was not rooted in any historical truth, as Oscar Robertson pondered:

> I ask you this: when the fictional version of Milan – a team named the Hickory Huskers – reaches the championship game in *Hoosiers*, what does it mean that the filmmakers twisted the truth? Instead of having Milan defeat Muncie Central and an integrated team with two black guys on it, which is what happened in real life, Hickory defeated a fictional team of black players, coached exclusively by black men, whose rooting section consists of black men, women, boys, and girls.[58]

Robertson's critique has been pushed to the margins by the hegemonic force of 'Hoosier basketball', but his critical voice is an important one. As a Black, Indiana native who played high-school basketball throughout the 1950s,[59] he is well aware of the racial politics that were, and still are, a part of Indiana's cultural obsession with basketball. However, in the colour-blind era under which he now finds himself (and thanks to the romanticized narratives in movies such as *Hoosiers*), Robertson's commentary is seen as leftover resentment from the 'racist era' in which he grew up. Asked to make sense of Robertson's contemporary critique during a personal interview, one White interviewee in his sixties suggested: 'There's some leftover . . . there is bound to be some bitterness for how people were treated.' Whether this history continues to exist and influence the experiences of racialized Others does not seem to be in question. But clearly, according to the logic, White bodies have managed to disjoint themselves from this same history, creating what is now a post-racial, colour-blind cultural phenomenon that is no longer open to Robertson's 'antiquated' or 'biased' critique. In other words, the 'race-neutral', post-Civil-Rights era where we find ourselves today has contributed to the fact that 'Hoosier basketball' of the late twentieth and early twenty-first centuries no longer derives its symbolic cultural value from the sport's racialized past. In turn, the (depoliticized) ideology rooted in Whiteness has become a common sense way to perceive the uniqueness of Indiana basketball.

EMBEDDING THE SENSEMAKING

Therefore, it should come as no surprise that the Indiana community became largely disillusioned with the Pacers' franchise in the light of the off-court behaviour of (Black) athletes who were perceived as undermining or threatening the hegemonic sensemaking of 'Hoosier basketball'. Pfeffer suggested that 'one of the important ways of generating external support for a given organization is to make that organization's operations and outcomes appear to be consonant with prevailing social values and useful to the larger social system'.[60] Falling in line with this idea, the Indiana Pacers were confronted with the opportunity to implement Hoosier Whiteness into their own sensemaking. The ideology, having already identified community values as an essential characteristic, was perfectly suited to explain the organization's past while paving a viable future – albeit in racialized terms. The players responsible for the organization's woes were conspicuously un-Hoosier in their upbringing (many of them raised in poor, inner-city environments from other US states) and appearance/demeanour (representing a dangerous and threatening hip-hop culture). As such, they could not be depended on to behave in line with 'normal' Hoosier life, nor represent 'Hoosier basketball' in its purest form. Instead, these were – and always had been – the values one learned growing up in small, quiet, rural towns of Indiana (which, to this day, continue to be overwhelmingly populated by White bodies).

One of the first steps involved in the strategic change was to acutely outline a commitment – an important type of organizational 'action' that is expounded on in the sensemaking literature by Karl Weick. According to his work, actions and beliefs play an integral and synergistic role in the development of meaning construction: 'Sensemaking starts either with the action or the outcome, but in both cases, beliefs are altered to create a sensible explanation for the action or the outcome'.[61] That is to say, it is important for organizations to clearly delineate what types of actions warrant their attention before a belief structure can be imposed on the action to generate meaning. In so doing, organizations (and the people inside/outside its realm) are provided with the opportunity to construct their identity around these choices.

As part of their strategic change initiative, the Indiana Pacers unveiled a commitment to off-court community behaviour of athletes; an area that had, up to that point, been interpreted by the organization with ambiguity and weariness. According to Weick, this is something to avoid as 'an inability or unwillingness to choose, act, and justify leaves people with too many possibilities and too few certainties'[62] and can provoke the onslaught of negative emotions. In fact, the organization's unwillingness and/or inability to trade, cut, or harshly punish their 'misbehaving' athletes was interpreted by fans as a type of complacency or reinforcement of anti-Hoosier ideals and values. However, by committing to off-court actions, the Indiana Pacers and its constituents became outfitted to retrospectively identify and make sense of these events together, as a way to build support towards the future. It is precisely at this point where beliefs were invoked. Weick argued that such beliefs can manifest themselves in the form of expectations, which have 'an effect on what was noticed, what was inferred, what was remembered, and most important . . . an effect on what was done'.[63] Similarly, the Pacers' expectation that athletes embody the ideals of Hoosier Whiteness seems to have influenced the organizational sensemaking process. Those players that did not embody the expected values of the community (i.e. threatening Black athletes, as Hoosier Whiteness professes) were judged on the basis of their character. Management and fans inferred that these types of players were not the 'right' basketball players for the Indiana Pacers, and these individuals were promptly banished from the team (a symbolic process that is explored in later sections of the paper in more detail).

With a belief and action-driven process for sensemaking in place – laced in a commitment to Hoosier Whiteness – the Indiana Pacers began to enact their strategic plan for change. Gioia et al. defined strategic change as 'either a redefinition of organizational mission and purpose or a substantial shift in overall priorities and goals to reflect new emphases or direction'.[64] This description seems to accurately capture the Indiana Pacers' change in philosophy, as team-owner Herb Simon expressed the desire to incorporate positive community image into what was once a myopic strategy based on winning: 'We're talking about restructuring, re-thinking, all the things you do when your team is in crisis . . . winning is important, but also how we present ourselves to the community. In that case, we've all done a horrible job.'[65] While this quotation provides the reader with a very limited comprehension for the organization's strategic plan, Gioia et al. recommended an examination of the 'symbolism, sensemaking, and influence processes that serve to create and legitimate the meaning of the change'.[66] Or, in this case, what did the Indiana Pacers specifically do and/or say (and how did they do/say what they did) to convince the external environment of their more 'friendly' community vision? The remainder of this paper subsequently aims to elucidate the meaning behind four symbolic acts, casting each under the critical lens that has heretofore been argued as Hoosier Whiteness.

THE LARRY BIRD FACTOR

Executive succession is an important location for the symbolic construction of meaning: 'The voluntary or involuntary departure of a chief administrator provides the occasion to select a replacement. This act of choosing a successor itself can take on important symbolic meaning'.[67] This scenario became a reality for the Indiana Pacers when it was announced that general manager, Donnie Walsh, would be leaving the organization at the end of the 2007–2008 season. While his decision to leave was completely voluntary in nature, the fact remained that team-owner, Herb Simon, was left with the task of choosing a successor. The eventual replacement would unquestionably need to represent a commitment to the organization's strategic plans moving forward.

Coincidentally, Indiana native and NBA hall-of-famer, Larry Bird was chosen for the position. Bird had worked alongside Donnie Walsh for five years in a coactive role; yet, placing him in firm control of the organization's basketball affairs portrayed a commitment to Hoosier Whiteness that would coincide wonderfully with the organization's strategic change. Herb Simon further elaborated on this notion in the following quotation: 'We couldn't be more enthused about Larry's passion for the game, *his understanding of what our fans want* and his experience as a player, coach and president.'[68] Automatically, Larry Bird was perceived as a legitimate replacement because of his understanding of what the fans wanted. After all, his experiences as a player, coach, and president were all, at one point in time, contextualized within Indiana's basketball environment (a sharp contrast from his predecessor, Donnie Walsh, who was born and raised in New York). Essentially, Larry Bird knew what Indiana fans wanted because his own experiences and upbringing in Indiana's basketball environment suggested to audiences that he could be relied on to make decisions according to the legitimate knowledge structure of Hoosier Whiteness.

Theoretically, the decision to promote Bird reaffirmed the argument that individual actions are conceptualized as something more institutional in nature:

> When we look at individual behavior in organizations, we are actually seeing two entities: the individual as himself and the individual as representative of his collectivity . . . thus, the individual not only acts on behalf of the organization in the usual agency sense, but he also acts, more subtly, 'as the organization' when he embodies the values, beliefs, and goals of the collectivity.[69]

In this sense, Bird's own schematic knowledge structure (one of Hoosier Whiteness) was prepared to coincide wonderfully with the values of the Pacers' strategic change initiative. Furthermore, as the representative embodiment of these values, it can be theorized that Larry Bird would confer on their 'positive' merit to project a favourable self and organizational image. Dutton and Dukerich confirmed this position as an integral part of the sensemaking process:

'The close link between an individual's character and an organization's image implies that individuals are personally motivated to preserve a positive organizational image and repair a negative one through association and disassociation with actions on issues.'[70] From Herb Simon's perspective (and similarly, the fanbase to which he was interested in appeasing), Larry Bird's personal motivations were well equipped to make sense on a much larger scale that extended beyond the direct organization.

Not only did they make sense, but Bird's symbolic value as one of – if not the best – White, American-born basketball players to ever play the game cannot be overlooked. Nor can his upbringing in the small, rural town of French Lick, IN. As a player for the Boston Celtics, Bird fuelled the 'Hoosier basketball' ideology with hope, suggesting to audiences that learning to play the 'right' or 'pure' way could still lead to success in a sport that was increasingly dominated by 'physically superior' Black athletes. In the 1980s, when the Celtics visited Indiana to play against the Pacers, the number of people cheering for Larry Bird would routinely outnumber those cheering for the hometown Pacers, as Bird acknowledged: 'I know I'm a draw here. Fans realize I have a talent that they like. I play the way they like.'[71] The actual game between the Pacers and Celtics seemingly became less important than the ideological war between 'Hoosier basketball' and the threatening 'Other' style(s) embodied in much of the NBA's Black athletes.[72] Similarly, the Indiana Pacers called on Bird's corporeal significance to articulate the same type of ideological battleground – only this time, from his office chair. Insomuch that Bird appealed to the hegemonic, institutionalized White norms and values that required protection from the Black athlete, the Indiana community was provided with the opportunity to engage in a form of psychic wealth.

Bird became the symbolic heir to Bob Knight's throne as the protector of a Hoosier ethos, using its legitimated and embedded structure as the basis for his decision-making: 'This thing is going to be put together the way the fans of Indiana perceive basketball [should be played].'[73] Of course, how it *should* be played was no longer how it *was* played in a league featuring the same threatening Black bodies responsible for the Pacers' 'moral decay'. But at the very least, Larry Bird represented a trustworthy, household name to the Indiana community. A 'Great White Hope' that Hoosiers vociferously supported throughout his basketball career. And though his playing days had long-since passed, fans were given the opportunity to once again cheer for Bird's old racialized symbolism (i.e. the embodiment of 'Hoosier Whiteness') in a new competitive landscape (i.e. the managerial 'game' of which he now found himself a part of).

Certainly, Larry Bird was promoted, in part, due to his 'Hoosier' brand of basketball acumen, and similarly encouraged to confer on this knowledge structure to make organizational decisions. Weick argued that such a strategy can lead managers to act on 'impoverished views of the world',[74] while Gioia noted the added potential for stereotypic thinking.[75] To understand Larry Bird's stereotypes as they relate to a player's 'race' and basketball/athletic ability, one must consider the following quotation:

> As far as playing, I didn't care who guarded me – red, yellow, black. I just didn't want a white guy guarding me. Because it's disrespect to my game . . . But it is a black man's game, and it will be forever. I mean, the greatest athletes in the world are African-American.[76]

Clearly, Bird seemed to fall in line with antiquated biological notions of 'race' that project Black athletes as naturally, athletically superior to their White counterpart.[77] Yet, the Indiana Pacers' strategic change efforts were directed less towards 'basketball/

athletic ability', and more concerned with an individual's character and values as he related to the off-court community. In the light of these facts, the racial changes to the Indiana Pacers' player personnel between the years 2006 and 2009 are of particular interest. Despite their supposed 'athletic inferiority', the number of White, American-born athletes went up from one to six. Contrastingly, Black, American-born players were reduced from thirteen to nine (eight of whom had not been a part of the team in 2006).[78] Apparently, an entirely different set of stereotypes existed within Bird's conception of 'race' as it pertained to an individual's character. As well, he believed fans would begin to embrace the team as a result of these racialized decisions:

> I think it's good for a fan base because as we all know the majority of the fans are white America. And if you just had a couple of white guys in there, you might get them a little excited.[79]

Thus, a deeper examination of the symbolic nature behind these player personnel changes is necessary to gain a more comprehensive understanding of Hoosier Whiteness and its role in the Indiana Pacers' strategic sensemaking.

'BLEACHING' THE PACERS

To demonstrate their commitment to community image, the Indiana Pacers also made a conscious effort to reflect this change in the 'types' of athletes they showcased. After implementing Hoosier Whiteness into their own sensemaking, the Indiana Pacers' leadership began to retrospectively impose meaning on those players who fell outside its acceptable boundaries. Those who did, according to owner Herb Simon 'didn't belong in *our* community'[80] and were promptly traded or released from the team. More importantly, these Black (American-born) bodies were often replaced by White (American-born) bodies.[81]

Weick proffered that extracted cues play a fundamental role in organizational sensemaking, offering one potential way to read these changes. He described these as 'simple, familiar structures that are seeds from which people develop a larger sense of what may be occurring'.[82] Moreover, context seems to play a crucial role in deciding *what* cue becomes extracted, and *how* that cue is interpreted. Not surprisingly, an athlete's Blackness became the cue that was summoned by Hoosier Whiteness as an identifiable and recognizable site for the negotiation of difference, and construction of meaning. As Abdel-Shehid described: 'Blackness becomes synonymous with physicality and acts as the opposite side, or 'other' that illuminates, constructs, and highlights whiteness, which itself becomes synonymous with rationality'.[83] Thus, Larry Bird's beliefs regarding Black athletic superiority begin to make sense (for the purposes of arguments presented in this paper), as it dualistically deployed stereotypes regarding one's capability to reason, an important facet to acceptable off-court behaviour.

Another stereotype from which the Indiana Pacers' leadership appeared to work (and from which external constituents read) was the generalized representation of Black male bodies as deviants. In turn, many of these athletes were framed as criminals after the organization's leaders and fans enacted their sensemaking processes – subsequently invoking the dominant culture's fear of Black masculinity.[84] A considerable portion of this fear arises from a perceived lack of control or power over the 'immorally predispositioned' Black body. It has been suggested that the NBA as a collectivity has dealt with such anxieties by popularizing management strategies that are masked in corporate objectives, but actually seek to capitalize on the White imaginary (that is, a White need to exert control over Black subjects).[85] Similarly, Larry Bird and other members of the Indiana Pacers' management team appear to have adjured the same philosophy by reinforcing 'Whiteness and management while conveniently, even strategically, avoiding altogether specific questions about race'.[86]

Trained to 'think away' these unconscious racial judgements, the Indiana Pacers' fans and leaders instead focused their attention on the legitimacy of these assumptions. Extending far beyond Indiana's basketball context, these powerfully embedded fixtures exerted their force on the organization in the form of status beliefs. Such status beliefs represent what most people think, and give one the 'appearance of consensuality . . . that allow status beliefs to function as legitimizing ideologies'.[87] Therefore, the notion that Black athletes raised in poverty (who often embodied a dangerous and threatening hip-hop culture) were somehow more likely to be 'bad people' compared to their White counterparts seems to have been an accepted discourse by fans, as one interviewee retrospectively suggested:

> They had some thugs on the team – call it what it is – they're thugs. And unfortunately you're seeing a lot of NBA players with that mentality. Maybe they're going back to the way they were raised; they were raised in that environment and they just . . . that's the way it's supposed to be.

This type of attack on a demonized 'Black culture' has become the focus of many contemporary scholars' attention, suggesting that racism now operates with a focus on 'culture' rather than its biological focus of the past:

> a sort of cultural discourse that promote[s] an essentialist masternarrative of Black violence, thereby excusing collective White cultural practices of racism. According to this narrative, White racism is not in fact what it appears, but rather a rational and even necessary response to the practices of a deeply troubled Other culture.[88]

These ideas shine forth in the light of the Indiana Pacers' personnel changes, as Hoosier Whiteness also began to present a solution to Black, hip-hop culture.[89] In addition to the influx of White players, many of the new Black players were not seen to (overtly, at least) identify themselves with signifiers of hip-hop culture – a stark contrast from the many individuals they replaced. Moreover, many of the new Black players had completed at least three years of post-secondary education – demonstrating perhaps an increased likelihood to 'rational thinking' based on White hegemonic values. Lastly, playing basketball under the college system connoted a player's willingness to abide by the values espoused by Hoosier Whiteness (e.g. learning the importance of fundamentals, teamwork, and discipline from an authoritative coach). These players, then, were positioned to contrast with the criminalized Black athletes who preceded their tenure. Coincidentally, one of the remaining players from the demonized group of Black athletes was strategically used to convey this message to fans, as a constant reminder that he and his exiled teammates were 'different' from the new players on the team.

THE MEANING BEHIND JAMAAL TINSLEY

At the beginning of the 2008–2009 NBA season, only two players remained from what was framed as the Pacers' 'troubled past': Jeff Foster (the lone, White American-born player from San Antonio, TX) and Jamaal Tinsley (a Black American-born player from Brooklyn, NY). Foster was awarded a new contract before the season began, while Tinsley (and his contract) were desperately unwanted by the organization. Despite Larry Bird's best efforts to trade him, other teams were largely discomforted by the negative labels that were being attached to Tinsley (atop the millions of dollars he was contractually owed). As such, Tinsley was perfectly healthy and under contract by the start of the NBA season; yet, the Indiana Pacers' leadership team had, what they felt to be a new roster of athletes who better reflected Hoosier Whiteness. In response, the decision was made to banish Tinsley from the team altogether, thereby exerting control over the 'deviant' Black body.[90] One could argue that this decision became a part of the Indiana Pacers' strategic efforts to send a strong intimation to its new, Black players and the entire fanbase. Read amidst the other connotative and symbolic gestures put forth by the organization, Jamaal Tinsley's exile came to represent a clear attempt to institutionalize a set of organizational norms that were shaped by the Pacers' new sensemaking process (i.e. Hoosier Whiteness).

To completely sequester all reminiscence of Jamaal Tinsley from the team (both on and off the court) – despite contractual obligations and issues of procedural fairness – is to engage in a highly symbolic act that extends far beyond basketball: 'The Pacers told him he wasn't invited to training camp, not welcome at Conseco Fieldhouse. He's not in the media guide or a part of anything they're doing.'[91] Consequently, one must begin to analyse how such prejudiced means were interpreted as fair and/or legitimate. Surely, many of the propositions put forth thus far all lend a certain degree of insight into this matter. Nevertheless, this particular symbolic site for sensemaking had the added dimension of contractual obligations, which should have served to confuse those inside/outside the organization in determining its legitimacy. Why then, did the Indiana Pacers take the risk of unjustly suspending Tinsley (permanently) from the team, and how did the fanbase come to support such a decision?

With Tinsley and Foster being the last remaining players from the Pacers' 2004–2005 roster, they came to symbolize an important year in the history of the Indiana Pacers. For it was during that season when the famous 'Malice in the Palace' took place between players from Indiana and fans of Detroit.[92] Unquestionably, the actions of those athletes who partook in the brawl do not coincide with the principles of Hoosier Whiteness, but it is important to remember that the organization had not yet adopted this knowledge structure into its own sensemaking process. Consequently, general manager Donnie Walsh spoke passionately about supporting his players – whom he believed to be wrongfully and exclusively punished for the transgression of events in Detroit.[93] Moreover, those athletes who decided to appeal their suspension in federal court were also provided with support from Donnie Walsh and the rest of the organization.[94] By standing up for these athletes who had partaken in 'anti-Hoosier' activity, many fans were left to decide between the legitimacy of their own sensemaking process (i.e. Hoosier Whiteness) and the alternative sensemaking advocated by the Pacers organization. With the team remaining relatively successful, some fans were willing to reluctantly adopt the organization's 'lenient' sensemaking process – but as the community relations 'disasters' began to accumulate between 2006 and 2008, the fanbase overwhelmingly reverted back to the sociocognitive belief structure of Hoosier Whiteness. Those who remained steadfastly committed to Hoosier Whiteness throughout it all could proclaim 'I told you so', and were reaffirmed in their sensemaking. In contrast, those who had wavered from Hoosier Whiteness were presented with its predetermined legitimacy and 'racialized explanation' to construct meaning on the more recent (and recurring) image problems.

It is no wonder, then, that part of the organization's strategic plan was to rid themselves of these Black, hip-hop identifying players and replace many of them with White, American-born players who fell more closely in line with the organization's new sensemaking process of Hoosier Whiteness. In fact, by committing so strongly to this knowledge structure, the organizational leaders had little alternative than to do away with Black players from the brawl, as fans had retrospectively made sense of them (and their culture) as the main contributors to the Indiana Pacers' image problems. Therefore, when Larry Bird was unable to trade Jamaal Tinsley by the start of the 2008–2009 season, the organization was faced with a dilemma. Under the sensemaking of Hoosier Whiteness, Tinsley had come to symbolize antithetical qualities to the franchise's strategic change initiative. Rather than allow for such contradictory messages, the organizational leaders felt it best to use Tinsley in a way that could demonstrate their full commitment to Hoosier Whiteness. Subsequently, the decision was made to banish him from the team as if he was no longer a member of the roster (nor was he permitted to use any of the practice facilities for personal use). This eventually led Tinsley and his agent to speak out against this injustice and file an official grievance with the team.

According to message board postings, his voice was heard; but, its legitimacy was met with varying degrees of support. Indeed, some fans questioned the fairness involved with Tinsley's banishment from a strictly legal perspective, prompting one to question whether his punishment was therefore perceived as ethically justifiable by the community. Many fans were far less willing to analyse the situation altogether, leaving some to begrudgingly offer Tinsley a spot at the end of the bench (in dress clothes); while others became even more upset over Tinsley's willingness to even make it an issue, writing: 'Let him rot and fight this' and 'It must be nice to complain about getting paid millions of dollars to do absolutely nothing'. Acting in terms that might have satiated the resounding public opinion, the Pacers continued to 'let him rot' – waiting less than one week before the arbitration hearing (months later) to finally waive him from the team and part ways. Not only did this exertion of power serve to appease fans (who could feel more comfortable in supporting a remapped 'safer' team), but it also served as what Cialdini, Bator, and Guadagno termed a critical event: '[one] that occurs early in a newcomer's tenure on the job, where the purpose of the incident and the consequences of the action can be easily understood by the newcomer . . . to shape their normative beliefs and their behavior'.[95] Recognizing the parallels between normative beliefs, behaviour, and sensemaking, this critical event became one more way for the Indiana Pacers to invoke its strategy on six newly signed Black players. These athletes were connotatively encouraged to adopt a sensemaking strategy that more closely mirrored that of Jeff Foster (i.e. Hoosier Whiteness) who was rewarded with a new contract, rather than Jamaal Tinsley. Similarly, the public could begin to feel more comfortable in aligning their identity with the team, knowing that the organization was taking a firm stance against those who did not fall in line with the professed values of Hoosier Whiteness.

MARKETING THE 'NEW' PACERS

For those who required a reminder as to what these values were, the 2008–2009 marketing campaign was a key strategy to reclaim/reestablish the ideology of Hoosier basketball and link it to the Pacers' new (racially symbolic) team. This articulation of an ideology is hugely important according to Pfeffer, who argued:

> One way in which identity and inclusion become known and developed is through the articulation of an ideology or world view and the acceptance of that view, at least to some degree, by those included in the organization . . . These understandings, these shared meanings, provide organizational participants with a sense of belonging and identity.[96]

Before the 2008–2009 season, fans had begun to express distaste for the team's marketing, as it did not coincide with their 'Hoosier basketball' beliefs. As an Internet forum poster wrote:

> The team/marketing department seem totally disconnected from what the fans tell them. Are they using an out of town marketing group because they sure don't seem to understand the locals and what it takes to get them excited . . . We are asked to support a team that not only seems out of touch with the constituency but are apparently ambivalent toward the local fan.

Therefore, it should come as no surprise that the organization's 2008–2009 marketing campaign primarily focused on 'emphasizing the *character* and *determination* of team members [and] the *core values* of basketball in Indiana: *hustle and hard work by team players*'.[97] Most fans, working from the sense-making process of Hoosier Whiteness, were led to believe these values ceased to exist as a part of the organizational identity of the Indiana Pacers, thereby causing many to dissociate their own identity/belonging with the organization. But, through expressing these familiar shared beliefs the team became outfitted to regain fan support on a level that made sense to citizens (*particularly* as the message coincided with a Whiter team).

Beyond the words themselves, the Indiana Pacers' home stadium (Conseco Fieldhouse) also came to represent changes as a part of the marketing campaign. Such physical spaces (e.g. the venue) can also provide leaders with an additional opportunity to construct meaning.[98] In this respect, the changes 'harkening back to Indiana's high school basketball glory days [allowing fans to] hear the squeak of the sneaker'[99] became further evidence that the organization had firmly committed itself to Hoosier Whiteness. Hip-hop signifiers, such as the team's long-time official disc jockey, were replaced by more 'authentic' symbols of Indiana's basketball history (e.g. a pep band). Staged within the White, ruralized symbol of a 'Fieldhouse', these changes were clearly meant to engender the authenticity of Indiana's pure basketball origins. More specifically, they were juxtaposed with a perceived dangerous 'Other' – that is, the NBA's more traditional marketing practice of a commodified and 'safe' hip-hop culture.[100] For the Indiana Pacers, hip hop served little to no commercial value underneath the hegemonic force of 'Hoosier basketball', and instead acted as the demonized 'Other' to which Hoosierness owed its own successful commodification and financial worth.

Therefore, if Pfeffer was correct in his premise that articulating a world view can assist in reinforcing or establishing one's identity – it makes sense to believe that the Pacers' marketing campaign was specifically targeted towards a White audience. After all, Hoosier Whiteness (like any model of Whiteness) maintains a racialized undertone that strives to present White hegemonic values as 'right' and 'good' (at the expense of the 'Other'), benefitting Indiana's overwhelmingly White population. Those fans who were apprehensive to support a team with which they could not identify (i.e. Black, hip-hop affiliated, outspoken athletes) were subsequently provided with an alternative model that fell more closely in line with their Hoosier identity. Suddenly, the franchise began to remodel itself in a way that made sense from a historical point of view that was laced in racialized discourse from both the past and present.

Yet, problematically the 2008–2009 marketing campaign's synchronicity with a 'Whiter' team (in both material and symbolic forms) reinforced the notion that White athletes are intelligent, hard working, and persevering.[101] This was of course bifurcated through a subsequent attack on Black athletes, and more specifically, those who suggestively related to hip-hop culture. Therefore, the suspect timing of the Indiana Pacers' marketing campaign to coincide with the team's roster changes was meant to unconsciously reflect this racialized dichotomy that has forever persisted at the foundation of Hoosier Whiteness. And, in the new-found absence of Black athletes and hip-hop culture, the campaign insinuated that these individuals were primarily to blame for the team's 'troubled past' (working from contemporary White stereotypes and conservative fears of Black masculinity, and more specifically hip-hop culture). Therefore, inclusion and identity within the Pacers were being framed (and embraced by a White majority) as 'good', 'pure', and 'right' – and to reject those values and their hegemonic force was to reflect poorly on one's own character and identity as a real Hoosier.

CONCLUSION

To conclude, we might ask ourselves whether the strategy has worked for the Indiana Pacers. Attendance rates, television ratings, and opinion polls – although limited in their explanatory power – can begin to provide some insight into this question. For the 2007–2008 season, the Pacers witnessed one of the lowest attendance rates in recent franchise history, featuring only 12,221 fans per game. This number increased to 14,182 and 14,202 fans per game in each of the following two consecutive seasons.[102] And although home attendance once again declined to 13,538 fans per game for the 2010–2011 season, the organization's television ratings were their highest in five years.[103] Lastly, the 2007–2008 opinion poll suggesting that only 43% of fans had a 'favorable opinion of the team' was re-administered before the 2008–2009 season illustrating a considerable shift in public opinion as the number increased to 67%.[104] Certainly, it would be remiss to suggest a simple, causal relationship between these numbers and the arguments advanced thus far. While the racialized significance of the organization's change may have had some influence in the way people identified with (and supported) the franchise, it merely represents one piece of a complex, multitudinous puzzle. Rather than to try to precisely identify how important these racial politics were in effecting change, it might be more useful to ask what kind of impact it has had on the 'Hoosier' sensemaking process.

Asked whether Larry Bird's 2008 promotion was perceived as a strategic choice for the Pacers, one interviewee responded by saying:

> Yeah, I thought it was pretty obvious. I mean, he's from Indiana, he wanted to rebuild, and they needed a figurehead. I think since Larry Bird's been here [in charge of player personnel], he's made a conscious effort to try and get the Pacers back to hoosier fundamentals basketball.

However, if the Pacers are now seen to represent 'Hoosierness' (in line with the organization's strategic plan), they have managed to do so through a complex dialogic process rather than simply impose this meaning to audiences. In other words, audiences are simultaneously called on to remember the 'Other' (in this case, a criminalized, demonized group of hip-hop identifying Black male athletes) to create the necessary *difference* that signifies the 'new' Pacers as 'Hoosier'.[105] Without this difference, 'meaning could not exist'.[106] Thus, as the public have been asked to remember the organization's 'troubled past', many of their original stereotypes and anxieties regarding Black male athletes and hip-hop culture have been reaffirmed, leading another interviewee to comment:

> I think they've rebuilt their image . . . When they brought in some of the players – they brought in Artest and some of these kinds – everybody was saying 'What are they doing there? Why?' Because we knew their history. We knew what kind of player they were and it didn't fit the mould of what that purist, Indiana basketball was all about.

In conclusion, it would seem as though the Pacers' strategy seems to have capitalized on, and reinforced the underlying racial logics embedded within Indiana basketball. With the hope of regaining fan support, the organization has constructed itself as protecting the symbolic ideological value of Hoosier basketball; the 'pure' origins of the sport (which are not so innocent) that have since been compromised in the twenty-first century; and the Indiana community at large from a threatening, inner-city, Black, male presence and hip-hop culture. Whereas the NBA has continued to associate its image with hip-hop culture for commercial reasons, the Indiana Pacers have taken the opposite approach – distancing themselves from hip hop's dangerous signifiers (and bodies), and replacing them with 'safe' and culturally meaningful symbols (and bodies) of 'Hoosier basketball'. In this respect, the Indiana Pacers have sought to distinguish themselves apart from the NBA altogether, as a sort of moral sanctuary that stands up to the NBA's 'poverty of morals and wretched excess', [107] reminding people that 'In 49 states, it's just basketball . . . but this is Indiana'.

NOTES

1 'Indiana Pacers Center David Harrison Suspended 5 Games for Violating Drug Policy'. *ESPN Associated Press*, January 11, 2008. www.sports.espn.go.com/espn/wire?section=nba&id=3192141; 'Bird Statement on Williams arrest'. *Indiana Pacers Press Release*, September 11, 2007. http://www.nba.com/pacers/news/bird_williams_070911.html. To appreciate the local contempt for these (and other) 'athlete misbehaviours', as they were constructed in the media, see clippings from *The Indianapolis Star*.

2 'Pacer to Miss Game Amid Murder Mystery'. *NBC Sports Associated Press*, February 28, 2008. www.nbcsports.msnbc.com/id/23381055.

3 'Police Say Daniels Not Suspect in Rape Reported at his Home'. *WSBT Associated Press*, February 25, 2008. www.wsbt.com/sports/local/15958912.html.

4 'Emotions Mixed After Latest Tinsley Incident'. *Conrad Brunner*, December 9, 2007. www.nba.com/pacers/news/tinsley_incident_071209.html; 'Pacers' Jackson Hit by Car, Fires Handgun, Police Say'. *ESPN Associated Press*, October 10, 2006. www.sports.espn.go.com/nba/news/story?id=2615124.

5 See Emily Udell, 'Pacers Players Free After Being Booked'. *The Washington Post*, February 22, 2007.

6 See Daniel Lee, 'Pacers Use Marketing to Win Back Fans'. *The Indianapolis Star*, November 2, 2008.

7 'Frank Luntz, the Word Doctors, CEO'. *Inside Indiana Business*, October 22, 2009. www.insideindianabusiness.com/video-player.asp?id=10622.

8 Singer, 'Addressing Epistemological Racism in Sport Management Research'.

9 See, for example, Cialdini et al., 'Basking in Reflected Glory'; Funk and James, 'The Psychological Continuum Model'; Mahony, Madrigal, and Howard, 'The Effect of Individual Levels of Self-Monitoring on Loyalty to Professional Football Teams'; Wann and Branscombe, 'Sports Fans'.

10 de B'béri and Hogarth, 'White America's Construction of Black Bodies'; Hughes, 'Managing Black Guys'; McDonald and Toglia, 'Dressed for Success?'.

11 Jamaal Tinsley was banished from the Indiana Pacers at the beginning of the 2008–2009 NBA season despite being healthy and under contract.
12 The 2008–2009 marketing campaign was an attempt by the Indiana Pacers to firmly embed Hoosier Whiteness as part of its own organizational identity.
13 Walsh, 'Managerial and Organizational Cognition'.
14 Ibid., 281.
15 Levine, Resnick and Higgins, 'Social Foundations of Cognition'.
16 Gramsci, *Selections From the Prison Notebooks.*
17 Rowe, 'Antonio Gramsci'.
18 Gramsci, *Selections From the Prison Notebooks.*
19 Weick, *Sensemaking in Organizations,* 42.
20 Humphreys and Brown, 'Narratives of Organizational Identity and Identification'.
21 Weick, *Sensemaking in Organizations,* 14.
22 Hylton, *'Race' and Sport.*
23 Delgado and Stefancic, *Critical Race Theory,* 7.
24 Hylton, *'Race' and Sport.*
25 Sefa Dei, Karumanchery, and Karumanchery-Luik, *Playing the Race Card.*
26 Ibid.; Leonardo, 'The Souls of White Folk'.
27 Ibid.
28 Ibid.
29 Mills, *The Racial Contract,* 18.
30 McDonald and Toglia, 'Dressed for Success?'.
31 Gramsci, *Selections From the Prison Notebooks,* 323.
32 Foucault, *The History of Sexuality, Volume 1,* 101.
33 Markula and Pringle, *Foucault, Sport and Exercise.*
34 Mumby, 'The Problem of Hegemony', 366.
35 Weick, *Sensemaking in Organizations,* 4.
36 Personal interviews were conducted by the author between January and March 2011. Therefore, it is important to note the context under which interviewee responses were provided. Much of this paper focuses on the implementation of the organization's strategic change that began towards the end of the 2007–2008 and beginning of the 2008–2009 seasons. As such, conversations with interviewees were much more reflexive than they were reactionary to this organizational change. This provided the author with an interesting perspective from which conclusions could be made regarding the effects of the organizational initiative; however, the responses given were situated in a different space and time than what other sources (taken directly from the years 2006–2009) revealed.
37 Markula and Pringle, *Foucault, Sport and Exercise,* 31.
38 McDonald and Birrell, 'Reading Sport Critically', 295.
39 For example, a gendered critique might point to the white male power structure in the NBA (and its franchise owners/managers) who remain vested in preserving or reclaiming a hegemonic masculinity on which sport is seen to have its roots (see Walton and Butryn, 'Policing the Race: US Men's Distance Running and the Crisis of Whiteness). Or, perhaps a class-focus might offer the reading that the values ascribed to 'Hoosier basketball' have less to do with race, than to do with class (see Holt, *Sport and the British: A Modern History*).
40 Luke, 'Text and Discourse in Education', 11.
41 Sefa Dei, Karumanchery, and Karumanchery-Luik, *Playing the Race Card, 17.*
42 See, for example, Graf, 'The Word Hoosier'.
43 See, for example, Webb, 'Introducing Black Harry Hoosier'.
44 hooks, *Black Looks,* 184.
45 Paino, 'Hoosiers in a Different Light', 66.
46 Ibid., 75.
47 Ibid., 68, emphasis in original.
48 Ibid.
49 Pierce, 'More Than a Game', 14.
50 Ibid., 16.
51 Paino, 'Hoosiers in a Different Light', 75. Paino also goes into further detail/analysis of this decline through an examination of attendance figures.
52 Lane, *Under the Boards,* 149.
53 Ibid.
54 *Hoosiers.* In the movie, Milan High and Muncie Central are given different names. The 1954 state championship, often referred to as 'The Milan Miracle', is arguably one of the most culturally important events to Indiana basketball. One cannot underestimate the power of its (mis)representation through a popularized medium such as film, and its subsequent impact on transmitting the 'constructed' story throughout future generations.
55 Sefa Dei, Karumanchery, and Karumanchery-Luik, *Playing the Race Card.*
56 Briley, 'Basketball's Great White Hope and Ronald Reagan's America', 15.
57 Ibid.
58 Robertson, *The Big O,* 40–1.
59 Robertson led Crispus Attucks to back-to-back high-school state championships in 1955 and 1956 (the years directly following the glorified tale of the 1954 Milan Indians). The first all-Black high school to win a state championship(s) – let alone back-to-back – in the United States, one begins to question why the 1954 tale of small-town Milan was more fit for a movie titled *Hoosiers* than the story of Crispus Attucks?
60 Pfeffer, 'Management as Symbolic Action', 21–2.
61 Weick, *Sensemaking in Organizations,* 168.
62 Ibid., 160.
63 Ibid., 151.

64 Gioia et al., 'Symbolism and Strategic Change in Academia', 364.
65 'Simon Optimistic of Quick Turnaround'.Pacers.com, March 7, 2008. www.nba.com/pacers/news/herb_simon_qna_080307.html, 4.
66 Gioia et al., 'Symbolism and Strategic Change in Academia', 364.
67 Pfeffer, 'Management as Symbolic Action', 39.
68 'Walsh Will Not Return to Pacers'. *Pacers.com*, March 24, 2008. www.nba.com/pacers/news/walsh_release_080324.html, 5, emphasis added. Larry Bird was given final decision-making authority on all basketball-related decisions; while fellow Hoosier and team-owner, Herb Simon, assumed Walsh's business-related duties.
69 Chatman, Bell, and Staw, 'The Managed Thought', 211.
70 Dutton and Dukerich, 'Keeping an Eye on the Mirror', 548.
71 See David Benner, 'Larry Bird Comes Home, So Do Fans as Former ISU Star Draws Faithful'. *The Indianapolis Star*, December 2, 1981.
72 The relationship between Larry Bird and Magic Johnson certainly reflected this dichotomization of styles.
73 See Mark Montieth, 'Bird Sticks to Plan in Indiana Amid Often-Skeptical Pacers Fan Base'. *Sports Illustrated.com*, September 2009. www.sportsillustrated.cnn.com/2009/basketball/nba/09/16/bird/.
74 Weick, 'Cognitive Processes in Organizations', 68.
75 Gioia, 'Conclusion'.
76 See Rudy Martzke, 'Bird: NBA Needs More White Stars'. *USA Today*, June 8, 2004, 3.
77 Hoberman, *Darwin's Athletes.*
78 See www.basketball-reference.com/teams/IND/.
79 See Rudy Martzke, 'Bird: NBA Needs More White Stars'. *USA Today*, June 8, 2004, 3.
80 'Simon Optimistic of Quick Turnaround'. *Pacers.com*, March 7, 2008. www.nba.com/pacers/news/herb_simon_qna_080307.html, 2, emphasis added.
81 This evolutionary process occurred through trades, waiving, free-agent signings, and the draft. By the start of the 2009 NBA season, the Indiana Pacers no longer had any of the Black players remaining from their 'troubled past', and instead featured the continued likes of Jeff Foster, as well as Travis Diener, Mike Dunleavy, Tyler Hansbrough, Josh McRoberts, and Troy Murphy (all of whom are White, American-born players). It is important to note these White players as American-born in a global NBA era. White bodies are not subject to the same universal discourse (e.g. White, European athletes are often positioned as 'soft' compared to their American counterpart) – and thus, nationality must be recognized for its role in forging a distinctly 'Hoosier' brand of Whiteness.
82 Weick, *Sensemaking in Organizations*, 50.
83 Abdel-Shehid, *Who Da Man?*, 48.
84 See, for example, Brown, 'Allan Iverson as America's Most Wanted'; de B'béri and Hogarth, 'White America's Construction of Black Bodies'; hooks, 'We Real Cool'.
85 For example, the NBA dress-code policy that articulates the need to present a more 'professional' (i.e. White) image to its largely corporate (i.e. White) audience, instead of the 'unprofessional' (i.e. Black, hip hop) styles that are embraced by many of its athletes.
86 Hughes, 'Managing Black Guys', 181.
87 Ridgeway, 'The Emergence of Status Beliefs', 258.
88 Vaught, 'Writing Against Racism', 579.
89 Hip hop, as a cultural art form, has grown from a space of critical consciousness and social and political commentary to resist everyday mainstream society. However, in its appropriated, mainstream format bell hooks (2004) has argued that '. . . it is just a black minstrel show – an imitation of dominator desire, not a rearticulation, not a radical alternative' (p. 143). Either way, hip hop is positioned as a threat to the existing power structures of society.
90 See Chris Broussard, 'Sources: Tinsley May File Grievance'. *ESPN The Magazine*, February 3, 2009. www.sports.espn.go.com/nba/news/story?id=3880962.
91 Ibid., 6.
92 The incident began once Pistons player, Ben Wallace, looked to persuade Pacer Ron Artest into fighting. Artest, wanting to avoid the situation, stayed clear of the fray but was hit with a cup of beer thrown from the stands. Running into the stands to confront the supposed suspect, Artest and many of his Pacers teammates became involved in physical altercations (both in the stands, and on the playing surface) with Detroit Pistons fans. Many of the spectators continued to throw various items onto the court, and some even stormed onto the hardwood to confront players. The NBA (i.e. Commissioner David Stern) placed the majority of the blame at the shoulders of Pacers' athletes, culminating in suspensions and fines that indicated as much, further activating White anxieties concerning the Black male body.
93 See, for example, Liz Robbins, 'NBA Bars 4 After a Brawl Involving Fans'. *The New York Times*, November 21, 2004; Oscar Dixon, 'Five Pacers, Seven Fans Charged in Palace Brawl'. *USA Today*, December 8, 2004.
94 See Sekou Smith, 'O'Neal to Return on Christmas Day'. *The Indianapolis Star*, December 24, 2004.

95 Ibid.
96 Pfeffer, 'Management as Symbolic Action', 13.
97 See Daniel Lee, 'Pacers Use Marketing to Win Back Fans'. *The Indianapolis Star,* November 2, 2008, 2, 41, emphasis added.
98 Ibid.
99 See Daniel Lee, 'Pacers Use Marketing to Win Back Fans'. *The Indianapolis Star,* November 2, 2008, 3.
100 Leonard, 'The Real Color of Money'; McDonald and Toglia, 'Dressed for Success'.
101 See, for example, Boyd, *Am I Black Enough For You.*
102 See www.espn.go.com/nba/attendance.
103 See www.ibj.com/the-score/2011/05/12/pacers-games-earn-higherst-tv-ratings-in-five-years/PARAMS/post/27121.
104 See Daniel Lee, 'Pacers Use Marketing to Win Back Fans'. *The Indianapolis Star,* November 2, 2008.
105 A queer-theory reading might examine how this 'Other' becomes managed by the hegemonic force of 'Hoosier basketball' through a politics of difference to maintain its power.
106 Hall, 'The Spectacle of the "Other"', 234.
107 Wertheim, *Transition Game,* 152.

REFERENCES

Abdel-Shehid, G. *Who Da Man? Black Masculinities and Sporting Cultures.* Toronto: Canadian Scholars' Press, 2005.

Boyd, T. *Am I Black Enough For You: Popular Culture From the 'Hood and Beyond.* Indiana: Indiana University Press, 1997.

Briley, R. 'Basketball's Great White Hope and Ronald Reagan's America: Hoosiers (1986)'. *Film and History* 35, no. 1 (2005): 12–19.

Brown, T.J. 'Allan Iverson as America's Most Wanted: Black Masculinity as a Cultural Site of Struggle'. *Journal of Intercultural Communication Research* 34, no. 1 (2005): 65–87.

Chatman, J.A., N.E. Bell, and B.M. Staw. 'The Managed Thought: The Role of Self-Justification and Impression Management in Organizational Settings'. In *The Thinking Organization,* edited by H. Sims and D. Gioia, 191–214. San Francisco, CA: Jossey-Bass, 1986.

Cialdini, R.B., R.J. Borden, A. Thorne, M.R. Walker, S. Freeman, and L.R. Sloan. 'Basking in Reflected Glory: Three (Football) Field Studies'. *Journal of Personality and Social Psychology* 34, no. 3 (1976): 366–75.

de B'béri, B.E., and P. Hogarth. 'White America's Construction of Black Bodies: The Case of Ron Artest as the Model of Covert Racial Ideology in the NBA's Discourse'. *Journal of International and Intercultural Communication* 2, no. 2 (2009): 89–106.

Delgado, R., and J. Stefancic. *Critical Race Theory: An Introduction.* New York: NYU Press, 2001.

Dutton, J.E., and J.M. Dukerich. 'Keeping an Eye on the Mirror: Image and Identity in Organizational Adaptation'. *Academy of Management Journal* 34, no. 3 (1991): 517–54.

Foucault, M. *The History of Sexuality, Volume 1: An Introduction.* London: Penguin Books, 1978.

Funk, D.C., and J. James. 'The Psychological Continuum Model: A Conceptual Framework for Understanding an Individual's Psychological Connection to Sport'. *Sport Management Review* 4, no. 2 (2001): 119–50.

Gioia, D.A. 'Conclusion: The State of the Art in Organizational Social Cognition: A Personal View'. In *The Thinking Organization: Dynamics of Organizational Social Cognition,* edited by H. Sims and D. Gioia, 336–56. San Francisco, CA: Jossey-Bass, 1986.

Gioia, D.A., J.B. Thomas, S.M. Clark, and K. Chittipeddi. 'Symbolism and Strategic Change in Academia: The Dynamics of Sensemaking and Influence'. *Organization Science* 5, no. 3 (1994): 363–83.

Graf, J. *The Word Hoosier.* Available from www.indiana.edu/~librcsd/internet/extra/hoosier.html (accessed 14 October 2008).

Gramsci, A. *Selections From the Prison Notebooks.* New York: International Publishers, 1971.

Hall, S. 'The Spectacle of the "Other"'. In *Representation: Cultural Representations and Signifying Practices,* edited by S. Hall, 223–91. London: The Open University, 1997.

Hoberman, J. *Darwin's Athletes: How Sport has Damaged Black America and Preserved the Myth of Race.* New York: Houghton-Mifflin, 1997.

Holt, R. *Sport and the British: A Modern History.* New York: Oxford University Press, 1989.

hooks, b. *Black Looks: Race and Representation.* Cambridge: South End Press, 1992.

hooks, b. We *Real Cool: Black Men and Masculinity.* New York: Routledge, 2004.

Hoosiers [DVD]. *Directed by David Anspaugh.* Brownsburg, IN: De Haven Productions, 1986.

Hughes, G. 'Managing Black Guys: Representation, Corporate Culture, and the NBA'. *Sociology of Sport Journal* 21, no. 2 (2004): 163–84.

Humphreys, M., and A.D. Brown. 'Narratives of Organizational Identity and Identification: A Case Study of Hegemony and Resistance'. *Organization Studies* 23, no. 3 (2002): 421–47.

Hylton, K. *'Race' and Sport: Critical Race Theory.* New York: Routledge, 2009.

Lane, J. *Under the Boards: The Cultural Revolution in Basketball.* Lincoln, NE: University of Nebraska Press, 2007.

Leonard, D.J. 'The Real Color of Money: Controlling Black Bodies in the NBA'. *Journal of Sport and Social Issues* 30, no. 2 (2006): 158–79.

Leonardo, Z. 'The Souls of White Folk: Critical Pedagogy, Whiteness Studies, and Globalization Discourse'. *Race Ethnicity and Education* 5, no. 1 (2002): 29–50.

Levine, J.M., L.B. Resnick, and E.T. Higgins. 'Social Foundations of Cognition'. *Annual Review of Psychology* 44, no. 1 (1993): 585–612.

Luke, A. 'Text and Discourse in Education: An Introduction to Critical Discourse Analysis'. *Review of Research in Education* 21 (1995–1996): 3–48.

Mahony, D.F., R. Madrigal, and D. Howard. 'The Effect of Individual Levels of Self-Monitoring on Loyalty to Professional Football Teams'. *International Journal of Sports Marketing and Sponsorship* 1, no. 2 (1999): 146–67.

Markula, P., and R. Pringle. *Foucault, Sport and Exercise: Power, Knowledge and Transforming the Self.* New York: Routledge, 2006.

McDonald, M.G., and S. Birrell. 'Reading Sport Critically: A Methodology for Interrogating Power'. *Sociology of Sport Journal* 16 (1999): 283–300.

McDonald, M.G., and J. Toglia. 'Dressed for Success? The NBA's Dress Code, the Workings of Whiteness and Corporate Culture'. *Sport in Society* 13, no. 6 (2010): 970–83.

Mills, C. *The Racial Contract.* Ithaca, NY: Cornell University Press, 1997.

Mumby, D.K. 'The Problem of Hegemony: Rereading Gramsci for Organizational Communication Studies'. *Western Journal of Communication* 61, no. 4 (1997): 343–75.

Paino, T. 'Hoosiers in a Different Light: Forces of Change v. The Power of Nostalgia'. *Journal of Sport History* 28, no. 1 (2001): 63–80.

Pfeffer, J. 'Management as Symbolic Action: The Creation and Maintenance of Organizational Paradigms'. In *Research in Organizational Behavior,* edited by L. Cummings and B. Staw, 1–52. Greenwich, CT: JAI Press, 1981.

Pierce, R.B. 'More Than a Game: The Political Meaning of High School Basketball in Indianapolis'. *Journal of Urban History* 27, no. 1 (2000): 3–23.

Ridgeway, C.L. 'The Emergence of Status Beliefs: From Structural Inequality to Legitimizing Ideology'. In *The Psychology of Legitimacy,* edited by J. Jost and B. Major, 257–78. London: Blackwell, 2001.

Robertson, O. *The Big O: My Life, My Times, My Game.* Pennsylvania: Rodale Inc., 2003.

Rowe, D. 'Antonio Gramsci: Sport, Hegemony and the National-Popular'. In *Sport and Modern Social Theorists,* edited by R. Giulianotti, 97–110. Basingstoke: Macmillan, 2004.

Sefa Dei, G.J., L.L. Karumanchery, and N. Karumanchery-Luik. *Playing the Race Card: Exposing White Power and Privilege.* New York: Peter Lang Publishing, 2004.

Singer, J.N. 'Addressing Epistemological Racism in Sport Management Research'. *Journal of Sport Management* 19, no. 4 (2005): 464–79.

Vaught, S.E. 'Writing Against Racism: Telling White Lies and Reclaiming Culture'. *Qualitative Inquiry* 14, no. 4 (2008): 566–89.

Walsh, J.P. 'Managerial and Organizational Cognition: Notes from a Trip Down Memory Lane'. *Organization Science* 6, no. 3 (1995): 280–321.

Walton, T., and T. Butryn 'Policing the Race: U.S. Men's Distance Running and the Crisis of Whiteness'. *Sociology of Sport Journal* 23, no. 1 (2006): 1–28.

Wann, D.L., and N.R. Branscombe. 'Sports Fans: Measuring Degree of Identification With Their Team'. *International Journal of Sport Psychology* 24, no. 1 (1993): 1–17.

Webb, S.H. 'Introducing Black Harry Hoosier: The History Behind Indiana's Namesake'. *Indiana Magazine of History* 98, (2002): 30–41.

Weick, K.E. 'Cognitive Processes in Organizations'. In *Research in Organizational Behavior,* edited by L. Cummings and B. Staw, 41–74. Greenwich, CT: JAI Press, 1979.

Weick, K.E. *Sensemaking in Organizations.* Thousand Oaks, CA: Sage, 1995.

Wertheim, L.J. *Transition Game: How Hoosiers Went Hip-Hop.* New York: G.P. Putnam's Sons, 2005.

CHAPTER 25

Where Are the Jocks for Justice?

Kelly Candaele and Peter Dreier

Adonal Foyle, 29, is a 6-foot, 10-inch center for the NBA's Golden State Warriors.[1] Like most pro athletes, he spent his youth perfecting his game, hoping for a shot at big-time sports. But off the court he's an outspoken critic of America's political system. "This mother of all democracies," Foyle insists, "is one of the most corrupt systems, where a small minority make the decisions for everybody else."

Three years ago Foyle started a grassroots group called Democracy Matters (www.democracymatters.org). Its goal is to educate young people about politics, mobilize them to vote and bring pressure on elected officials to reform the nation's campaign finance laws. When he's not playing basketball, Foyle is frequently speaking at high schools, colleges and conferences about the corrupting role of big money in politics. "I have lots of support [from fellow players] and I explain to them a lot what I'm doing," says Foyle, "The players understand that I want people to be excited about the political system."

Foyle's activism is rare in the world of professional sports. Many athletes visit kids in hospitals, start foundations that fix inner-city playgrounds, create scholarship funds to help poor students attend college and make commercials urging kids to stay in school and say no to drugs. But when it comes to political dissent, few speak out on big issues like war, sweatshop labor, environmental concerns or the increasing gap between rich and poor. While Hollywood celebrities frequently lend their fame and fortune to candidates and causes, athletes are expected to perform, not pontificate. On the few occasions when they do express themselves, they are often met with derision and contempt.

Last year, for example, just before the United States invaded Iraq, Dallas Mavericks guard Steve Nash wore a T-shirt to media day during the NBA's All-Star weekend that said No War. Shoot for Peace. Numerous sports columnists criticized Nash for speaking his mind. (One wrote that he should "just shut up and play.") David Robinson, an Annapolis graduate and former naval officer, and then center for the San Antonio Spurs, said that Nash's attire was inappropriate. Flip Saunders, coach of the NBA's Minnesota Timberwolves, told the Minneapolis *Star-Tribune*: "What opinions you have, it's important to keep them to yourselves." Since then, no other major pro athlete has publicly expressed antiwar sentiments.

Although political activism has never been widespread among pro athletes, Foyle is following in the footsteps of some courageous jocks. After breaking baseball's color line in 1947, Jackie Robinson was outspoken against racial segregation during and after his playing career, despite being considered too angry and vocal by many sports writers, owners and fellow players. During the 1960s and '70s some prominent athletes used their celebrity status to speak out on key issues, particularly civil rights and Vietnam. The most well-known example, boxing champion Muhammad Ali, publicly opposed the war and refused induction into the Army in 1967, for which he was stripped of his heavyweight title and sentenced to five years in prison (he eventually won an appeal in the Supreme Court and didn't serve any time). Today he is among the world's most admired people, but at the time sportswriters and politicians relentlessly attacked him.

Many others were also unafraid to wear their values on their uniforms—and sometimes paid the price. Coaches and team executives told Dave Meggyesy, an All-Pro linebacker for the St. Louis Cardinals in the late 1960s, that his antiwar views were detrimental to his team and his career. As he recounts in his memoir *Out of Their League,* Meggyesy refused to back down, was consequently benched, and retired at age 28 while still in his athletic prime. Tennis great Arthur Ashe campaigned against apartheid well before the movement gained widespread support. Bill Russell led his teammates on boycotts of segregated facilities while starting for the Boston Celtics. Olympic track medalists John Carlos and Tommie Smith created an international furor with their Black Power salute at the 1968 Olympics in Mexico City, which hurt their subsequent professional careers. When St. Louis Cardinals catcher Ted Simmons came to the majors from the University of Michigan in 1967, some teammates were taken aback by his shaggy hair and the peace symbols on his bat, but they couldn't argue with his All-Star play. In 1972, almost a year before the Supreme Court's landmark *Roe v. Wade* ruling, tennis star Billie Jean King was one of fifty-three women to sign an ad in the first issue of *Ms.* magazine boldly proclaiming, "We Have Had Abortions." Washington Redskins lineman Ray Schoenke organized 400 athletes to support George McGovern's 1972 antiwar presidential campaign despite the fact that his coach, George Allen, was a close friend of McGovern's opponent, Richard Nixon.

Contemporary activism hasn't infiltrated the locker rooms as it did in the past, in large measure because of dramatic improvements in athletes' economic situation. A half-century ago, big-time sports—boxing and baseball in particular—was a melting pot of urban working-class ethnics and rural farm boys. Back then, many professional athletes earned little more than ordinary workers. Many lived in the same neighborhoods as their fans and had to work in the off-season to supplement their salaries.

Today's athletes are a more diverse group. A growing number come from suburban upbringings and attended college. At the same time, the number of pro athletes from impoverished inner-city backgrounds in the United States and Latin America has increased. Regardless of their backgrounds, however, all pro athletes have much greater earning power than their predecessors. Since the 1970s, television contracts have brought new revenues that have dramatically increased salaries. The growing influence of players' unions—particularly in baseball, since the end of the reserve clause in 1976—has also raised the salaries of stars and journeyman jocks alike. For example, the minimum salary among major league baseball players increased from $16,000 in 1975 to $100,000 in 1990 to $300,000 last year, while the average salary during those years grew from $44,676 to $578,930 to $2.3 million. Even ordinary players are now able to supplement their incomes with commercial endorsements. At the upper echelons of every sport, revenue from product endorsements far exceeds the salaries paid by the teams superstars play for or the prize money for the tournaments they win.

Thanks to their unions, pro athletes now have more protection than ever before to speak out without jeopardizing their careers. But, at the same time, they have much more at stake economically. "Athletes now have too much to lose in endorsement potential," explains Marc Pollick, founder and president of the Giving Back Fund, which works with pro athletes to set up charitable foundations. "That has neutralized their views on controversial issues. Companies don't want to be associated with controversy."

A few years ago labor activists tried and failed to enlist basketball superstar Michael Jordan in their crusade to improve conditions in Nike's factories. But with a multimillion-dollar Nike contract, he was unwilling to speak out against sweatshop conditions in overseas plants. In 1990 Jordan had refused to endorse his fellow black North Carolinian Harvey Gantt, then running for the US Senate against right-winger Jesse Helms, on the grounds, Jordan explained at the time, that "Republicans buy sneakers, too." (The criticism must have stung. Six years later he contributed $2,000 to Gantt's second unsuccessful effort to unseat Helms. And in 2000, like many NBA players, he publicly supported former New York Knicks star Bill Bradley's campaign for President. In March he contributed $10,000 to Illinois State Senator Barack Obama, who recently won the Democratic Party's nomination for an open US Senate seat.)

Early in his professional career, golfer Tiger Woods stirred some political controversy with one of his first commercials for Nike after signing a $40 million endorsement contract. It displayed images of Woods golfing as these words scrolled down the screen: "There are still courses in the United States I am not allowed to play because of the color of my skin. I've heard I'm not ready for you. Are you ready for me?" At the time Woods told *Sports Illustrated* that it was "important . . . for this country to talk about this subject [racism]. . . . You can't say something like that in a polite way. Golf has shied away from this for too long. Some clubs have brought in tokens, but nothing has really changed. I hope what I'm doing can change that."

According to Richard Lapchick, executive director of the National Consortium for Academics and Sports at the University of Central Florida, and a longtime activist against racism in sports, Woods was "crucified" by some sportswriters for the commercial and his comments. Nike quickly realized that confrontational politics wasn't the best way to sell shoes. "Tiger seemed to learn a lesson," Lapchick says. "It is one that I wish he and other athletes had not learned: no more political issues. He has been silent since then because of what happened early in his career." Woods remained on the sidelines during the 2002 controversy over the intransigence of the Augusta National Golf Club, host of the annual Masters tournament, on permitting women to join.

Like Lapchick, former New York Yankees pitching ace Jim Bouton, whose 1970 tell-all book *Ball Four* scandalized the baseball establishment, bemoans the cautiousness of today's highly paid athletes. "I'm always disappointed when I see a guy like Michael Jordan, who is set up for life, not speaking out on controversial issues," said Bouton. Today's athletes, he observed, "seem to have an entourage around them that they have to consult before making a statement or getting involved in something. Ali was willing to go to jail and relinquish his boxing title for what he believed in. He was a hero. It's a scared generation today." And it may be no coincidence that some of today's more outspoken athletes grew up outside the United States. Foyle, now a US citizen, is from the Grenadines, and the Mavericks' Nash is a Canadian.

American sports—from the Olympics to pro boxing to baseball—have long been linked, by politicians, business leaders and sports entrepreneurs, to conservative versions of nationalism and patriotism. At all professional sports events, fans and players are expected to stand while the national anthem is played before the game can begin. No similar expressions of patriotism are required, for example, at symphony concerts or Broadway shows.

Over the past century presidents have routinely invited championship teams to the White House for photo ops. A few weeks after 9/11 President Bush attended a World Series game at Yankee Stadium. His press secretary explained that Bush (who once owned the Texas Rangers) was there "because of baseball's important role in our culture." In January, just before the Super Bowl, Bush invited New England Patriots quarterback Tom Brady to sit in the gallery during his State of the Union address. Of the more than 900 Americans who have died in Afghanistan and Iraq, none were singled out for as much attention—by the media or politicians—as Arizona Cardinals safety Pat Tillman, who was killed in Afghanistan in April. Sometimes politicians' efforts to align themselves with sports figures can backfire. In 1991, for example, when President George H.W. Bush invited the Chicago Bulls to the White House to celebrate their NBA championship, Bulls guard Craig Hodges handed Bush a letter expressing outrage about the condition of urban America.

While most pro athletes are silent on political issues, many team owners regard political involvement as essential to doing business. Owners like Jerry Colangelo of the Phoenix Suns and Arizona Diamondbacks, Art Modell of the Baltimore Ravens, Charles Monfort of the Colorado Rockies and George Steinbrenner of the New York Yankees make large campaign contributions to both Republicans and Democrats; invite elected officials to sit next to them at games; and lobby city, state and federal officeholders on legislation and tax breaks for new stadiums.

The emergence of professional players' unions should have been a voice for athletes on political and social issues. According to Ed Garvey, who ran the NFL Players Association from 1971 until 1983, racial turmoil was critical to the union's early development. The union "was driven by the African-American players, who knew there was an unwritten quota on most teams where there would not be more than a third blacks on any one team," says Garvey, who now practices law in Wisconsin. "And they knew they wouldn't have a job with the team when their playing days were over." The players also understood that team owners were "the most powerful monopoly in the country," he says.

Garvey brought the association into the AFL-CIO—the only professional sports union to do so—to give the players a sense that they were part of the broader labor movement. In the early 1970s several NFL players walked the picket lines with striking Farah clothing workers, joined bank employees in Seattle to boost their organizing drive and took other public stands. But "now they're making enough money, so they want to keep their heads down," he says. When Marvin Miller, a former Steelworkers Union staffer, became the first executive director of the Major League Baseball Players Association (MLBPA) in 1966, he sought to raise players' political awareness. "We didn't just explain the labor laws," he recalls. "We had to get players to understand that they were a union. We did a lot of internal education to talk to players about broader issues."

But those days are long gone. Bouton believes that athletes' unions now consider themselves partners in the sports business. They are "part of the same club," Bouton says, negotiating mainly to give players a greater share of proceeds from ticket sales, television contracts and the marketing of player names and team logos. Donald Fehr, the MLBPA's executive director, argues that players' unions should stick to the issues that directly affect them. "It is not our role to go around taking positions on things for the sake of taking positions," he insists. "Only if it's a matter involving baseball or the players do we look at an issue and determine what to do."

Like its counterparts in other sports, the MLBPA occasionally goes beyond the narrow confines of business unionism. For example, Fehr sent letters asking ballplayers to honor the recent United Food and Commercial Workers picket lines in Southern California and gave verbal support to the striking workers of the New Era Cap Company, who make major league baseball's caps in a Derby, New York, facility.

The players associations could usefully go beyond such symbolic gestures. After the 234-day 1994–95 strike ended, catcher Mike Piazza, then with the Los Angeles Dodgers, donated $100 for every home run he hit to the union that represented the concessionaires, who lost considerable pay while 921 games were canceled. It was an individual gesture of empathy with Dodger Stadium's working class—ushers, ticket takers, parking-lot attendants and food vendors—that generated tremendous good will among the Dodgers' fan base. As an organization, the MLBPA could have followed Piazzas example and set aside a small part of its large strike fund to help stadium employees who were temporarily out of work.

A glaring example of the MLBPA's shortsightedness is its reaction to a recent exposé by the National Labor Committee (NLC, www.nlcnet.org/campaigns), reported in the *New York Times*, revealing that Costa Rican workers who stitch Rawlings baseballs for the major leagues are paid 30 cents for each ball, which is then sold for $15 in US sporting-goods stores. According to a local doctor who worked at the Rawlings plant in the 1990s, a third of the workers developed carpal-tunnel syndrome, an often-debilitating pain and numbness of the hands and wrists. When the *Times* asked Fehr about the situation, he said he didn't know about it, despite the fact that the Rawlings plant had been the subject of news stories for several years. (Another recent NLC report documented that NBA sweat shirts are made in Burmese sweatshops.)

Echoing growing concern about corporate responsibility and runaway jobs, professional players associations could demand that teams purchase their uniforms, bats, helmets and balls solely from companies —in the United States and abroad—that provide workers with decent wages, working conditions and benefits. The associations could send fact-finding delegations of athletes to inspect the working conditions factories where their uniforms and equipment are made. The associations could demand that teams provide a living wage for all stadium employees, encourage politically conscious athletes to express their views and endorse candidates for office, support organizations like Adonal Foyle's Democracy Matters and even walk picket lines and do commercials for labor causes. As Foyle understands, taking stands on such issues could help the players forge better relations with the community whose support is critical to their continued economic success.

Foyle has refused to be intimidated by those sportswriters and fans who object to his beliefs. "How can we say we are creating a society in Iraq based on democracy and freedom and tell people here who have the audacity to speak out to keep quiet?" he says. "If people shut down because they are afraid the media is going to spank them or fans are going to boo them, then the terrorists have won." A history major at Colgate University, Foyle says, "The 1960s generation was against the war, people coming home in body bags, dogs gnawing at black people's feet. Today issues are more complicated, and you have to read between the lines. When you talk about campaign finance reform, you are talking about all of the issues—war, civil rights, environment, gender, globalization—because they are all connected." He adds: "If people want us to be role models, it's not just saying what people want you to say. It's pushing the boundaries a bit, saying things that you may not want to think about. That's good for a society. Morality is much bigger than athletics."

Excerpted from Kelly Candaele and Peter Dreier, "Where are the Jocks for Justice?" in *The Nation* (June 28, 2004). For subscription information, call 1-800-333-8536. Portions of each week's *Nation* magazine can be accessed at www.thenation.com.

NOTE

1 Foyle is now retired. [Eds.]

SECTION 5

Breaking the Normative Rules: The Problems of Deviance in Sports

A SOCIOLOGICAL CONCEPTION OF DEVIANCE

- A male teenager wants a smart phone to stay in touch with his friends and to play video games but he can't afford to buy one; so he snatches a smart phone from the hand of a woman he passes on a busy street;
- A man regarded as one of the most successful investment brokers on Wall Street is discovered by government investigators to be running an illegal Ponzi scheme through which he defrauded his unwitting clients of millions of dollars;
- A powerful United States Congressman is expelled from Congress for illegally diverting government funds to his private bank account and is sentenced to three years in prison.

Each of these examples depicts actual situations of social deviance, which constitutes one of the most ubiquitous, intriguing, and disturbing realities of life in modern societies. According to one generally accepted sociological definition: "Deviance is behavior, beliefs, or characteristics that are likely to generate a negative reaction in others" and result in a process by which the deviant individual's "character is tainted, stigmatized, and inferiorized"(Goode, 2011: p.3).

Deviance matters because it violates normative rules which are the bases of social organization. Ranging from whole societies to schools, corporations, and families, all social organizations need general compliance with their normative rules to sustain stability and achieve objectives. But normative compliance is hardly automatic. Some people are motivated to commit deviant acts. As can be observed in everyday life experiences: some businesses evade income taxes; some public officials accept bribes; some lawyers defraud their clients; some students cheat on exams; and some motorists drive while intoxicated. Hence all social organizations must deal with deviance as a fact of life.

Typically social organizations counteract both potential and actual deviance by relying on two basic means of defense. The first defense is socialization, teaching newcomers the normative rules, getting individuals to internalize and accept the legitimacy of rules as guidelines for individual behavior. Families, police departments, banks, factories, armies, hospitals . . . as well as sports programs . . . are all examples of social organizations using socialization to induce compliance with their organization's normative rules.

Though essential, socialization is seldom sufficient to induce everyone to conform to the rules—the normal social expectations. Take the example of the teenager cited above who stole the cell phone. He was no doubt taught as are almost all children that stealing is wrong. But some individuals, despite having been socialized to conform to the rules, choose to follow their personal impulses and violate the rules in anticipation of some personal benefit. This is why social organizations also rely on a second means of defense, **external social controls—punishment** by means of **negative sanctions**—that may range from public shaming, financial penalties, job loss, imprisonment and, in extreme situations, even death.

It is not just the punishment but also the threat of punishment, the risk associated with being caught, that makes external social control so effective. Take the simple example of a big city mayor who is offered a $10,000 bribe to award a city construction contract to a builder incapable of winning the contract in a open process of competitive bidding. The mayor feels tempted to accept the bribe though he knows it is illegal. But he rejects the offer because of the risk he would be caught, facing public dishonor, forfeiting his future political career, and, worst of all, the risk of going to prison. This applies to many situations where individuals comply with normative rules. The risk posed by external social controls operate as a powerful deterrent.

CHANGES IN NORMATIVE RULES

Though social organizations need compliance with their normative rules to sustain their stability and to achieve their objectives, it is important to note that normative rules may change. In light of this fact, it is useful to think of social organizations as entities with normative boundaries, which over time may expand (become less restrictive) or contract (become more restrictive) and, thereby alter the categories of deviant behavior. When the normative behaviors expand, a behavior that had been previously regarded as deviant is normalized—loses its stigma—and becomes acceptable. This can be illustrated by several examples resulting from changed social attitudes. Consider the case of norms regulating the days of the week retail business could operate. Many states prohibited retail stores doing business on Sundays because of conservative religious beliefs—which fostered so called "Sunday Blue Laws." But as religious attitudes in the nation became less conservative, shopping and conducting business on Sundays ceased to be deviant. One needs only to visit shopping malls throughout the United States to realize that Sunday is one of busiest shopping days of the week in many communities. Divorce was considered deviant in the United States up until the later part of the twentieth century; divorce carried a stigma. Many political analysts believe that both Adali Stevenson and Nelson Rockefeller failed in their efforts to be elected president of the United States because they had been divorced. In fact, it was not until the election of Ronald Reagan in 1980 that a divorced individual was elected to the presidency of the United States. Divorced individuals faced disadvantages in applying for employment, bank loans, and private club memberships, as well as in other situations that entailed character evaluations.

Similarly gambling was another activity that was traditionally prohibited in most of the United States. Individuals caught gambling could be arrested, fined, and sentenced to prison. Gambling now in the United States, in the early twenty-first century, is viewed as being not only acceptable behavior but also an essential source of government revenue, supplementing conventional taxes. We see this today in many cities and states which conduct lotteries and license casinos to attract gambling dollars. Perhaps the most significant shift in normative boundaries in the recent history of the United States pertained to pre-marital sex. Considered deviant for much of American history, pre-marital sexual activity is now generally accepted throughout most of the United States, a fact attested to by the relative absence of public debate about it. These are all examples of normative boundaries governing previously prohibited behaviors that have loosened.

But change can move in the opposite direction. Normative boundaries can narrow, with the effect that previously acceptable behaviors are prohibited—as can be in the changed normative status of such behaviors as spousal abuse, uninvited male sexual overtures to women, and harsh parental corporeal punishment of children. Prior to the mid-twentieth century, parents using harsh corporeal punishment to discipline their children were viewed as exercising their legitimate authority; some even defended the practice by quoting the biblical maxim: "spare the rod and spoil the child." Husbands hitting or slapping their wives was at one time generally tolerated behavior in the United States. So too was the behavior of men who persistently made unwanted sexual overtures to female employees, subordinates, or acquaintances and refused to acknowledge the women's negative responses. This was regarded during most of American history as harmless "flirting," as normal masculine behavior, that sometimes even became a source of humor among men.

The normative boundaries pertaining to each of these behaviors changed, over the past half-century, by becoming more restrictive, with the result that they are now regarded as deviant. This is reflected in their recently acquired stigmatized labels of "wife battering," "child abuse," and "sexual harassment," respectively. Individuals engaging in those behaviors risk stigmatization as well as other negative sanctions. These shifts in normative boundaries, which were strongly influenced by the women's movement, along with several others social movements during the decades of the 1960s and 1970s, reconstructed the meanings of these behaviors.

We noted above that in general unpunished normative transgressions weaken social organization; however, it is important to note that sometimes violations of norms mark the beginning of social change, the beginning of new normative rules. This occurs when deliberate violations cause changes in public attitudes and become the basis of a new pattern of social organization. We can see a dramatic example of this in the history of the black American civil rights movement which openly violated the normative rules of racial segregation in the American South which led to a period of protracted conflict, with the result that the old southern social organization based on racial segregation was transformed.

To reiterate the theme of this Section: a social organization's or community's categories of deviant behavior are subject to change. This is why sociologists regard deviance not as an inherent or permanent quality of the act—but rather as a socially constructed meaning.

We will now turn to a consideration of the strength or weakness of a behavior's deviant status. To say that a behavior is deviant does not necessarily mean that everyone agrees with that judgment. For example, smoking marijuana is a behavior about which public attitudes are divided. Some people regard it as deviant whereas others regard it as non-deviant—as an acceptable and pleasant means of recreation—like drinking a beer or a martini.

By contrast, most people would agree that committing a bank robbery is deviant. This highlights a distinction between what is termed "low consensus deviance"—e.g., smoking marijuana—and "high consensus deviance" (Goode, 2011: 8). It is the behavior linked to high consensus deviance that is least tolerated and most threatening to social organization because it violates widely shared normative rules. Low consensus deviance, by contrast, tends to be tolerated, if not ignored. (Sometimes this is a matter of social context.)

The different levels of tolerance versus repression of deviant behaviors can be perhaps best illustrated with the metaphor of traffic light signals, with the green zone denoting acceptable behavior; the yellow zone denoting problematic (contested) behavior; the red zone denoting deviant (prohibited) behavior. Throughout this essay we will use the shorthand terms green zone behavior, yellow zone behavior, and red zone behavior to refer to the different normative statuses of social behaviors. Yellow zone behaviors are especially interesting because, while not deviant, they are contested behaviors which are the focus of conflict and tensions as well as pressures to shift them to the red zone. Many behaviors occupy this yellow zone status before being relegated to a deviant status. To take one of the above examples, spousal abuse existed as yellow zone behavior in a large sector of the American population before it was relegated to a deviant status, labeled "wife battering," and made illegal. Social movements often play a vital role in transforming the normative status of behaviors.

It is important to recall that we will use the terms "hard deviance" and "soft deviance" to distinguish those designated red zone behaviors that arouse strong general negative reactions (high consensus deviance) from those that arouse mild or placid reactions. This distinction will be especially helpful in explaining the different types of punishments imposed on deviant behaviors in sports.

In summary, deviance, which consists of violations of normative rules of behavior, occurs in all social organization—ranging from societies and large corporations to schools, families, and sports teams. The two most important mechanisms used by social organizations to minimize deviance are: socialization and negative sanctions. The first seeks to teach individuals the guidelines for proper conduct needed to perform their social roles; whereas the second, coming into play when socialization is insufficient, imposes external controls by using various means of punishment. This punishment does more than penalize the deviant individual; it also operates as a deterrent to others who may feel tempted to engage in similar behavior, by signaling the harsh consequences it would entail. However, not all deviant behavior has bad outcomes. Sometimes deviant behavior—like the above noted American civil rights movement—leads to changes in normative rules that reform the pattern of social organization. How do we distinguish between beneficial and harmful deviant behavior?

It is impossible to make any generalizations about the normalcy or deviance of a behavior apart from the specific social context within which it occurs. Thus we repeat the sociological conception of deviance: it is not an inherent quality of the act but the meanings others attach to that act.

Now that we have introduced the general sociological conception of deviance, we will explore the meaning and significance of deviant behavior in the social world of sport. This discussion is divided into three distinct sections. The first introduces major types of sports deviance based on two factors: their competitive orientation and their visibility; we then use this typology to examine different empirical patterns of deviance in the sports world; our third section presents multiple social theories of deviance and evaluates their utility for explaining the causes and effects of deviant behavior in sport. Finally, our essay concludes by explaining how the various readings in this Section on Deviance relate to our sociological overview of the subject.

THE NATURE OF DEVIANCE IN SPORT

We are reminded almost daily by news media reports about deviance in the sports world ranging from athletes taking performance enhancing drugs and teams using illegal means to recruit players, to Olympic officials accepting bribes from governments seeking to influence the selection of sites for future Olympic games. Media pundits and fans typically react to these transgressions with expressions of moral indignation.

While violations of normative rules in sports usually entail unethical conduct, it would be a mistake to regard unethical behavior and social deviance as the same thing. Ethics is concerned with general principles of right and wrong from a philosophical perspective. The principles of ethics consist of abstract universal rules which are thought to be valid everywhere—regardless of the historical and social context. Simply put, conceptions of ethical/unethical behavior are philosophically constructed. Thus what is thought to be ethical in United States would apply equally to assessments of behavior in Ethiopia and Japan. By contrast, conceptions of normal/deviant behavior are different because they do not derive from abstract universal principles but rather from ideas, attitudes, and beliefs of social groups—typically expressed through social organizations—for which these conceptions operate as actual rather than ideal behavior. This is what sociologists mean by saying that "deviance is socially constructed." Viewing these acts from a moral/ethical perspective would fail to comprehend their meaning and significance for social organization.

The core of all sports is the sports contest—a social organization of competition between opponents—governed by uniform and fair rules. The contest objective is to determine a winner. Deviance occurs when those rules governing the organization of the contest are violated.

Imagine watching two boxers in a heavyweight boxing match in which one boxer, feeling that he is losing, suddenly bear hugs his opponent and bites off the top part of his left ear. This bizarre event actually occurred in a boxing match, in June 1998, between Mike Tyson and Evander Holyfield. In response to Tyson's act, the referee immediately stopped the fight and declared Holyfield the winner. That heavyweight championship fight revealed a clear example of sports deviance in that Mike Tyson, by biting Holyfield's ear, gained an unfair advantage by violating the rules governing the organization of the contest. It was the job of the referee to impose negative sanctions, to protect the integrity of the contest, which is precisely what he did.

Most sports fans regard sports deviance as behavior that is relatively easy to understand like the actions of Mike Tyson noted above—or that of a professional baseball player (Sammy Sosa) using an illegal corked bat or an Olympic sprinter like Marion Jones ingesting prohibited drugs. Sports deviance apparently consist of cheating to win. Though this seems perfectly logical given the objective of the sports contest, it fails to grasp the actual complexity of sports deviance, because not all sports deviance is motivated by the desire to win. Some sports deviance is counter-intuitive—because it is motivated by the desire to lose. In short, there exist different types of sports deviance, which we must understand to gain a perspective on the varied social factors behind the motivations to commit acts of sports deviance.

Table 5.1 distinguishes major analytical types of sports deviance. Based on the relationship between two factors—the competitive orientation of the deviant behavior and the visibility of the deviant behavior—we can distinguish four major types of sports deviance: (1) hidden non-competitive; (2) hidden competitive; (3) open competitive; (4) open non-competitive.

TYPOLOGY I: PATTERNS OF DEVIANCE: VISIBILITY AND COMPETITIVE ORIENTATION

		VISIBILITY	
		HIDDEN	*OPEN*
COMPETITIVE ORIENTATION	NO	1	3
	YES	2	4

1. Hidden Anti-Competitive Deviance (e.g. gambling corruption)
2. Hidden Competitive Deviance (e.g. doping, recruiting violations)
3. Visible Anti-Competitive Deviance (e.g. slackers)
4. Visible Competitive Deviance (e.g. impulsive violence)

HIDDEN ANTI-COMPETITIVE SPORTS DEVIANCE: PLAYING TO LOSE

This pattern of sports deviance arguably evokes the most angry and shocked reactions from media pundits and fans because it violates the objective of sport contests: the quest to win. The practitioners of hidden anti-competitive deviance are "fixers"—who play to lose to gain some non-sports objective. If sports contests, according to their generic meaning, are competitive events with uncertain outcomes, then fixers transform sports contests into pseudo events, manipulated performances, with scripted outcomes.

Hidden anti-competitive deviance is linked inextricably to gamblers. Infiltrating sports environments from external criminal subcultures, they typically supplant the desire to win sports contests with the desire to win money. If unchecked, this pattern of sports deviance poisons and destroys the integrity of sports, causing disillusionment and cynicism among fans. The decline in the popularity of professional boxing can be attributed, in part, to increased doubts about the sport's integrity due to its association with organized crime.

Viewed from the standpoint of athletes, their involvement in gambling corruption, in contrast to competitive deviance, is typically motivated by the prospect of immediate financial or other material rewards. Reaping the benefits of quick cash payments takes priority over the joys of competing to win. Or, as has happened sometimes in boxing, the boxer may agree to lose a fight (to lay down in a match) in order to get an opportunity for a genuine contest with a ranked opponent in the future. These deals were usually transacted by corrupt promoters, who controlled the boxers access to big name opponents. In any case, hidden anti-competitive deviance consists of fraudulent athletic performances usually in the form of players receiving bribes or some other favors from gamblers to scale back their efforts in order to achieve a pre-determined outcome.

Sports gambling is an established and lucrative reality of life in the contemporary world. Looking at an affluent industrial society such as the United States, we can discern the scale of sports gambling. Sports betting in Nevada, the center of legal American sports gambling, represents only a small fraction of the American total. Notes one report: "Overall, Nevada's legal sports wagering represents less than 1 percent of all sports betting nationwide. In 2011, $3.45 billion was legally wagered in Nevada's sports books" (American Gambling Association, 2012). This is in sharp contrast to estimates of illegal betting, which is the primary source of sports corruption. "The National Gambling Impact Study

Commission (NGISC) estimates that illegal wagers are as much as $380 billion annually." The scale of betting on highly popular single sport events is also quite revealing: According to the FBI, "more than $2.5 billion is illegally wagered on March Madness . . . the premier NCCA college basketball championship tournament." But by far the sports event that attracts the most illegal wagers is the Superbowl, which is the object of more bets "than on any other single day sporting event of the year" (American Gambling Association, 2012).

Viewed in a wider global context, sports gambling has grown enormously. According to one study which tracks internet gambling, online sports betting generated $4.29 billion in revenue in 2005. This was more than double the 1.7 billion generated by online sports betting in 2001 (American Gambling Association, 2012). Though only rough estimates, these huge sums of money suggest that illegal gambling represents a great potential danger of sports corruption. Ever mindful of this potential danger, the major professional sports employ special investigators to monitor any suspicious activity of players and game officials.

While the prototypical form of gambling corruption involves a player being bribed by a gambler to lose a game, there are several variations of this prototypical form. In the first variation, a referee rather than a player is paid to alter a game's outcome, which usually means manipulating the game to favor the underdog or alter the point spread. In the second variation, a player is paid to decrease his scoring without losing the game. That is what's termed "point shaving", which is a more subtle form of anti-competitive deviance. Because it does not aim to alter the game's expected outcome, point shaving is likely to be more appealing to players than throwing the game. Nevertheless, players involved in point shaving open themselves to potential "entrapment."

In this way, point shaving may escalate easily into efforts to manipulate the game's expected outcome.

VULNERABILITY TO GAMBLING CORRUPTION

Players who receive little or no pay in high revenue sports may find it easy to rationalize accepting bribes as a "way of getting paid," getting compensation for their talents in a situation where they feel powerless and exploited. In major league baseball, for example, many players felt they were being exploited by cheap owners during the the early history of the sport, before players achieved the right to free agency. Certain sports have been more vulnerable to gambling corruption than others—particularly in reference to the point spread—because the scoring can be easily manipulated by one or several players. This no doubt explains why athletes on big time American college basketball teams were targeted by gamblers far more often than were athletes on big time college football teams. Other factors linked to vulnerability are the player's age and phase of career because they are likely to influence the player's calculation of the relative risks, particularly in professional sports that have low player salaries and no pensions. However, older and more marginal players typically have less opportunity to play a major role in the sports contest.

Finally, financial debt is likely to operate as a major incentive to game fixing, especially if the player gambles and has incurred large losses. For this reason, players who gamble are perceived by teams as special risks. Some sports journalists have speculated that Michael Jordan's decision to leave the NBA and pursue a career in major league baseball for several years was prompted by the NBA commissioner who suspended Jordan for gambling. Many sports programs are wary about signing such athletes. A closely related factor of vulnerability exists for players who socialize with gamblers and organized crime figures. It is for this reason professional sports organizations such as Major League Baseball and the National Basketball Association employ private investigators who monitor the conduct and associations of players, managers, and referees.

Before examining varied examples of gambling corruption in sports, we will consider the Chicago Black Sox Scandal, the infamous case of gambling corruption, which transformed the normative boundaries of major league baseball.

CONSTRUCTING A RED LIGHT ZONE OF HARD DEVIANCE: THE 1919 CHICAGO BLACK SOX SCANDAL

The Chicago Black Sox baseball scandal shocked the sports world and became the most notorious American case of sports gambling corruption in the twentieth century (Asinoff, 1963). In 1919, during the early phase of MLB's development as a professional sport, eight Chicago White Sox players accepted bribes from a Boston gambler to deliberately lose a game in the World Series. When the conspiracy was discovered almost a year later, after the World Series, the players were arrested and charged with fraud by the Chicago District Attorney. But they failed to be convicted; the files containing their confessions mysteriously disappeared from the courthouse. The scandal significance derived not from the criminal trial which ended in acquittals but from the swift and harsh reactions of the baseball commissioner, Judge Kenishaw Landis. Installed in 1920 as the first person to occupy the newly created office of commissioner, Landis was determined to protect the integrity of the game, which entailed establishing new normative boundaries for players' behavior. So shortly after the trial, despite the players having been acquitted, he imposed the ultimate sports negative sanction—he banned all eight players for life.

Seen from the standpoint of deviance and social control, Landis' decision established a new red line category of hard deviance for major league baseball players, which was revealed in his announcement of the new rule:

> Regardless of the verdict of juries, no player who throws a ball game, no player who undertakes or promises to throw a ball game, no player who sits in confidence with a bunch of crooked ballplayers and gamblers, where the ways and means of throwing a game are discussed and does not promptly tell his club about it, will ever play professional baseball.
>
> (Ginsburg, 1995: 144)

In establishing this new rule, Landis sent a message to all current and future players: accepting bribes to fix games would result in a career-ending death penalty. By creating this new and harsher level of social control on gambling, Landis did not just restore the league's integrity; he solidified its development as a social institution. Gambling corruption in major league baseball virtually disappeared. Baseball's response to the Black Sox Scandal illustrates a situation where the toxic effects of anti-competitive deviance were successfully repelled.

The continuing impact of that normative rule in the modern era was illustrated by the fate of Pete Rose, one of baseball's greatest all-time hitters. Rose was discovered to be betting on major league baseball games when he was managing the Cincinnati Reds major league baseball team. He at first denied the charge but the evidence from baseball investigators was irrefutable. Despite subsequent protests from Rose and many fans, he was banned for life in August, 1989 (Rodenberg, 2014). This indicates the continuing force of Landis's anti-gambling rule almost a century later. All of Rose's efforts to have the decision reversed have failed.

NOTABLE CASES OF COLLEGE SPORTS GAMBLING CORRUPTION IN THE UNITED STATES

Revelations of gambling corruptions in American college sports were especially prevalent in the mid-twentieth century. The first revelation of a major case of gambling corruption in college sports hit the American sports world like a huge bomb explosion in 1951. The scandal involved several powerhouses of college basketball—the City University of New York, the University of Kentucky, and New York University. It was revealed through the investigations of a New York City grand jury that at least 86 games between 1947 and 1950 had been fixed by players, who had been bribed by gamblers to keep the scores within the point spread (Paciella, 2007: 1).

Despite the shocked responses to these revelations in 1951, gambling corruption in college basketball hardly ended with the New York City scandals. From 1959 to 1971, it was revealed that 37 players from 22 schools had been involved in point shaving scandals (Paciella, 2007: 1–2). The man behind many of these fixed games, Jack Molinas, a former NBA basketball player associated with organized crime (Rosen, 2001) who became perhaps the most notorious fixer of the era, was later killed allegedly by organized crime figures.

It should be noted that most college basketball players, in contrast to professional basketball players, typically had short careers and fewer incentives to resist bribes. Most were not risking the possibility of financially lucrative professional careers.

Some of the most publicized cases of college basketball corruption within the past years (from the 1970s through the 1990s) occurred at Boston College. In the 1978–79 basketball season, gamblers linked to organized crime arranged to fix nine Boston College games with the assistance of three Boston College players (Paciella, 2007). One of the players, Rick Kuhn, was convicted and served a two-and-a-half-year prison term. In 1989, Boston College suspended four football players for betting on football games. In 1996, 13 football players were suspended for gambling; two had bet against their team. Thirteen other players were suspended for gambling.

In the 1984–85 season, four Tulane starters, including John "Hot Rod" Williams, and one reserve were accused of manipulating the scoring in two games (Goldstein, 2003). Testimony revealed that they shaved points in exchange for money and cocaine. None of the players were convicted. But the university suspended its basketball program for four seasons. In 1997, two Northwestern University players were found guilty of point shaving. Investigation revealed that 15 of 22 fraternities were involved in illegal campus gambling networks. In 1998, four players were charged with fixing the outcome of three games during the 1994–95 season. In a separate indictment, a former Northwestern football player was charged with running a bookmaking operation on Northwestern's campus (Dedam, 1998, p. 1).

Given that the highly publicized cases represented only the major cases of gambling corruption in American college sports that were revealed, it seems reasonable to assume other cases of gambling corruption in college sports went undetected.

Significantly, by contrast, the only case of betting corruption revealed in the National Basketball Association involved a referee—Tim Donaghy—who bet on games and sold tips on games to bookmakers (Beck and Schmidt, 2007: 7). He was publically denounced by the league commissioner, convicted, and served 11 months in prison. Though Donaghy claimed that other NBA referees were also involved in betting corruption, no other violators were discovered by the league's investigators. Again, it is important to bear in mind that other instances of gambling corruption may have occurred in the NBA which remained hidden. The high salaries and lucrative careers of NBA players provide strong incentives to avoid corruption.

SPORTS GAMBLING CORRUPTION OUTSIDE THE UNITED STATES

While major cases of sports gambling scandals have occurred in the United States, particularly in college basketball, they have been hardly as extensive as the cases of sports gambling scandals in other parts of the world.

Among some of the most noteworthy international cases of sports gambling revealed in the global sports world, the Australian Cricket Federation, in 1995, secretly suspended two players for passing information to Sri Lankan gamblers (Forest et al., 2009). In another highly publicized case, in 2000, Indian police learned that the captain of the South African cricket team, had accepted bribes from India and elsewhere to fix the result of a test match against England (pp. 15–16). The South African captain offered no apology for his involvement in match fixing because it entailed point shaving that did not affect the outcome of the game. But the league thought otherwise. Following an official inquiry, the team captain and two fellow players received lifetime bans. In the German soccer league, in August 2005, it was alleged that a referee fixed the outcome of a match because of the suspicions aroused by dubious penalties he imposed (p. 17). In reaction to the apparently biased decisions, officials conducted an inquiry, which resulted in the referee confessing to prosecutors and receiving a 29-month prison sentence.

Sports gambling corruption is not restricted to any region of the world. We also see revelations of serious cases of sports gambling corruption involving South Asian nations. In 2010, for example, three Pakistani cricket players were found guilty in a London court of conspiring to cheat in a match between Pakistan and England. The players were sentenced to jail for two years, one year, and six months, respectively. The players were suspended from the sport for periods ranging from five to ten years.

One of the biggest recent sports scandals occurred in the Indian Premier League, in 2013 (Agarwal, 2013: 1). Delhi police arrested three Rajasthan players for allegedly spot-fixing. Eleven bookies were arrested at the same time, including one who was a former Rajasthan player. The team's owner was also suspended for participating in betting corruption. Significantly these punishments for gambling corruption in cricket did not receive a lifetime ban which indicates that it is tolerated deviance. In many of these societies, gambling corruption exists as soft deviance: behavior that is disapproved of but not stigmatized.

Because gambling corruption often involves enormous sums of money, its effects often extend beyond players and referees to police and political leaders who perceive sports as a lucrative businesses that can be exploited for extra income. The sports values of fair competition under uniform and impartial rules have not been strongly institutionalized in many societies where there are also long traditions of political corruption. Is there a link between sports gambling corruption and general political corruption in a society? Cultures that impose strong sanctions on political corruption may also have little tolerance for gambling corruption in sports. There exists no definitive answer to this linkage between political and sports gambling corruption but it deserves to be studied.

THE CHALLENGE: DEVISING EFFECTIVE SOCIAL CONTROLS OF SPORTS GAMBLING CORRUPTION

Sports face formidable challenges in attempting to detect and control gambling corruption. First, there is the problem of lax and ineffectual sports associations. As noted by a recent Transparency International report on gambling corruption, "few national sports associations seem to see it as their task to address match-fixing as part of promoting integrity in sport" (Transparency International, 2009: 1). Controlling the problem of match-fixing will require not only that sports associations broaden the conception of their mission to include combating sports gambling corruption; but also that they implement new investigative tools, administrative resources, and harsher punishments. Second, there is the ironic problem of autonomy of sports organizations from the state. Noted one perceptive observer: "The claim of autonomy from the state may protect national sports bodies from being politically misused but it also may prevent accountability in their decision making processes" (p. 6). Because sports associations often regulate themselves, they are vulnerable to possible corruption among the sports officials. Hence there is a need in many nations for oversight of sports associations by the state agencies rather than direct state administration of sports, which risks subjecting sports to political manipulation. This negative effect of direct state administration of sports occurred in Eastern Europe during the cold war period when authoritarian governments misused and corrupted sports for political ends. What is needed is a system of checks and balances rather than the autonomy of sports organizations from the state. For instance, in the corruption case of the above noted Indian Premier Cricket League, in a sports association plagued by match fixing scandals, the Indian Supreme Court refused to hear the case, stating that sports were outside its purview. In effect, this leaves the Cricket League without effective social control of gambling (Agarwal, 2013: 1).

Effective social controls over sports gambling corruption where the sports league is complicit requires more than state oversight of sports; it also requires vigilant journalistic reporting as well as efficient investigative agencies which can routinely monitor major sports activity and gambler networks to gather information about suspicious contacts between gamblers and athletic personnel (e.g. players, coaches, referees). The process that resulted in the revelation of the 1919 Chicago Black Sox Scandal began with the initiative of a Chicago journalist who became suspicious after examining game scorecards (Asinoff, 1963).

Monitoring referees is especially important. Referees generally earn low incomes relative to the players and coaches and are therefore likely to feel a stronger temptation to accept bribes. As noted by one astute observer, "referee corruption has been produced not only in the NBA but also in Czechoslovakian, Chinese, German, and Italian football leagues." The fact that these cases were discovered only "by chance, suggests that sports governing bodies should have a very proactive program to guard against corruption involving officials—especially in sports like football (soccer) or cricket where judgements on individual incidents routinely determine the outcome of the contest and where the decisions are difficult and so subjective that apparent errors do not stand out as suspicious."

On an optimistic note, directly related to improved monitoring, sports are increasingly being subjected to forensic statistical analyses of team scoring patterns; though in the early phase of development, these statistical analyses promise to provide more effective means for detecting sports gambling corruption in the future.

Despite potential advances in the social control of sports gambling corruption, there is one problem that is likely to constitute a more formidable obstacle to social control of sports gambling corruption. That is the problem posed by transnational gambling. As one observer has noted, "strict regulation of one country's betting sectors does not guarantee to protect its domestic competitions from corruption since betting is international." Future expansion of internet communications along with increasingly sophisticated means for encrypting messages will no doubt exacerbate this problem of international control.

But no matter how sophisticated the technology for detecting gambling corruption, effective social control of this activity cannot occur in a social vacuum. It must be situated within an organizational culture which relegates gambling corruption to the red light zone of hard deviance. Anything short of this is unlikely to succeed.

HIDDEN COMPETITIVE DEVIANCE: EVADING RULES TO WIN

We turn now to a type of sports deviance that is most familiar to fans. In fact, competitive deviance in sports is seldom viewed as irrational or shocking behavior. That is because it reflects the ultimate objective of sports contests—the quest to win. But it pursues that objective by ignoring the principles of "fairness." Embracing an attitude that seeks to win by any means—an attitude tempered only by the fear of being caught—makes deception inevitable. This "win by any means" attitude often extends beyond the individual deviant athlete to a deviant organizational culture, which may include not only team mates but also coaches and even administrators, for whom winning takes priority over all other concerns.

The appearance of new normative rules seldom marks the end of a particular competitive deviant practice if it relegates the behavior to the red zone of soft deviance. That is because both fans and athletic teams may favor illicit practices that help their team win if the penalties are not too costly. This tolerance of rule breaking is likely to prevail in anomic societies which are characterized by an obsessive emphasis on winning. We see this particularly in situations where winning yields huge rewards—in the form of multi-million dollar prizes, salaries, lucrative endorsement contracts, and acclaim, as well as huge symbolic honors for the institutions or communities they represent. The Olympic games have been the sites of much competitive deviance, driven by quests for the recognition and prestige bestowed on winners of gold medals. Where rule breaking exists in the yellow light zone of soft deviance, competitive sports often degenerates into cynical practices of deception and cheating as routine practices.

In contrast to anti-competitive deviance like gambling corruption, hidden competitive deviance poses the most difficult problems of social control where it is not subject to zero tolerance, it tends to arouse ambivalent attitudes toward rule breaking.

In a famous declaration, Willard Waller, a leading American sociologist in the 1920s and 1930s, argued that social problems exist because people do not want to solve them. Solving them, Waller maintained, would entail changing cherished values (Waller, 1936). In other words, social problems like hidden competitive sports deviance derive from contradictory values: the values that emphasize both winning and meritocratic practices. While both are fundamental values in sports. it is winning that garners the reward and the acclaim.

Thus, even though it violates the principle of fairness, hidden competitive deviance "makes sense" to sports fans who value winning—whereas anti-competitive deviance does not—because it reflects the objective of all sports competition. Hence the ambivalence, especially among some fans and coaches who are on the winning side due to cheating.

Also, some sports leagues officials may respond with ambivalence by "looking the other way" when they hear allegations of cheating, especially if they think the rule breaking enhances fan interest and revenues. Some argue that this happened in major league baseball in the 1990s, when steroid use by some players boosted the number of home runs and increased fan attendance. Actually Alex Rodriquez, the New York Yankees superstar third baseman who tested positive for peds, recently revealed that he was given permission to use steroids several years ago by League officials (Schmidt, 2014).

Why not impose severe punishments in order to end the deviance? Severe punishment such as a lifetime ban on the deviant athletes would weaken the quality competition by removing some of the best athletes; whereas ignoring competitive deviance would undermine the sport's integrity. Hence social controls typically entail compromise, balancing competing interests, which merely reduce rather than eliminate hidden competitive deviance.

It is worthwhile to contrast this situation to major league baseball's response to gambling corruption in the Chicago Black Sox scandal, an act of anti-competitive deviance which betrayed the ethos of sports competition and imperiled the sport's survival. In the opinion of the baseball commissioner Landis, that situation hardly warranted compromise: It was a malignant tumor that had to be exorcised before it spread and destroyed the sport. Baseball could ill afford public doubts about the players' commitment to winning—which would have amounted to ignoring the cancer. No equivalent to this threat is associated with competitive sports deviance.

JUICING THE BODY: THE MENACE OF DOPING

Doping may be the most widespread and elusive problem of deviance confronting sports in the modern era. This view seems to be supported by the findings of a 2009 survey conducted in European Union countries which indicated that doping was seen as the number one threat to sports (72 percent), followed by commercialization (55 percent) and corruption (41 percent). This view was no doubt influenced by the increased number of news reports about doping in sports (Transparency International, 2009, p4).

We should begin by placing public awareness of doping in historical perspective. Arising from scientific advances in molecular biology and pharmacology, doping practices gained public attention, following the death of a Danish cyclist, Knut Jensen, during the Rome Olympics in 1960 (Mukhopadhyay 2012: 2). A few years later, researchers introduced anabolic steroids for increasing muscle development. This was followed by the development of EPO, a drug for treating anemia, that attracted the interest of athletes because it allowed them to increase their capacity to utilize oxygen during competition. According to some informed observers, EPO remains popular because it is difficult to detect. Nevertheless, by the late 1960s, both sports authorities and the public were very much aware of doping in sports.

While media publicity focusing on performance enhancing drugs (peds) began in the 1960s the timing of the diffusion of these drugs into different sports, as reflected by media coverage, varied. In the view of one sports sociologist, drug use in the Olympics, which constitutes a good barometer, reached its high point between 1972 and 1998 (Luschen, 2000: 473). While it is impossible to know whether there will be a future surge in Olympic drug use, we know that the first widely publicized instance of a doping scandal in the Olympics occurred in 1988.

At the Olympic games in Seoul, South Korea, Ben Johnson broke from the starting blocks and flashed past the finish line ahead of his opponents to become the only Canadian to win the gold medal for the 100 meters sprint. Jubilant Canadian fans had barely begun to celebrate when Olympics officials announced that Johnson had been disqualified because tests revealed prohibited steroids in his urine. The gold medal was awarded instead to Carl Lewis, the American runner and Johnson's arch rival, who had come in second (Slot, 2003). The humiliated Ben Johnson, permanently tarnished by the doping disclosure, quickly faded from the spotlight of international fame into the obscure dustbin of sports history.

But Johnson was not the only celebrated Seoul Olympian track star who had been using peds. Fifteen years after the Seoul Olympics, a newspaper article revealed that Carl Lewis, the sprinter who had received the 1988 100 meter gold medal by default, had failed three drug tests in the 1988 Olympics trials but the ban imposed on Lewis was overturned by the United States Olympic Committee (USOC) when Lewis gave the excuse that he had mistakenly taken herbal supplements. On hearing this news, an irate Johnson demanded that Lewis be stripped of his medals from Seoul. However, the International Olympic Committee (IOC) decided not to review the case, because the three-year statute of limitations had passed. Asked to comment on the newspaper article, Lewis replied—"Who cares I failed drug tests" (MacKay, 2003). The USOC's handling of Lewis' failed drug test caused many to conclude that its decision had been motivated by a patriotic bias toward an American athlete.

Perhaps the highest profile American Olympic athlete punished for doping was Marion Jones, the women's 100 and 200 meter champion in the 2000 Sydney Olympics, who was stripped of her medals and sentenced to six months in a federal prison for lying to a federal agent about her use of peds (Pilon, 2013: Kelly and Rao, 2008). The conviction ended Jones' athletic career. Oddly it was Jones' estranged husband, also an athlete, who had informed officials about her drug use. After Jones' conviction, the USA Track and Field president expressed no sympathy for what he termed the "Jones saga," which he described as a "vivid morality play that gradually illustrates the wages of cheating in any phase of life, on or off track" (Kelly and Rao, 2008). This was no doubt an attempt to convince sports fans that doping in Olympic sports could no longer remain hidden, a questionable opinion when we realize that Jones' deviance was discovered by her estranged husband who informed Olympic officials about her drug use. Other cases of doping were revealed. For example, among elite American Olympic sprinters, Charles Gaitlin was penalized in 2009. His Olympics gold medal was annulled after peds were discovered from blood tests he took. Who could say how many elite athletes were doping, especially when some peds could not be detected by the available tests?

The Olympics led the way in highly publicized cases of doping in competitive sports; whereas major league baseball, in contrast, lagged more than a decade behind. Media-reported rumors of doping in major league baseball escalated sharply in response to the extraordinary home run production of Barry Bonds. The rumors became especially intense when Bonds surpassed Babe Ruth's all-time home run record, one of the most cherished achievements in American sports. Some refused to believe that Bonds was capable of surpassing Ruth's record without assistance from peds. The rumors of doping focused on Bonds soon spread to other outstanding major league players—including such stars as Mark McGwire, Sammy Sosa, Roger Clemons, Jose Caneseco, and Alex Rodriquez—casting shadows of suspicion over their performances.

REACTIONS TO SUSPICIONS OF PEDS

In 2006, a book was published by two San Francisco Chronicle investigative reporters, that attempted to present detailed evidence of Barry Bonds' steroid use, beginning several years before he broke Babe Ruth's record (Katutani, 2006). In response to the atmosphere of mounting media allegations and widespread rumors about steroid use in major league baseball, the league's commissioner Bud Selig appointed George Mitchell, a former U.S. Senator, to investigate the problem of doping in baseball, in March 2006.

After a 21 month investigation into the use of steroids and growth hormones in MLB, Mitchell released a report in December 2007, which named 89 athletes who had used steroids and other peds (Mitchell Report). Significantly, the report focused on only high profile players, but avoided commenting on the alleged or actual roles of MLB teams in encouraging or facilitating players' use of peds. An earlier more limited report based on random testing of players from 2003 to 2005, Mitchell noted, found 5 to 7 percent of the players tested positive. But it was impossible to determine the actual prevalence of doping among players in those earlier years from an admittedly incomplete report.

The Mitchell Report itself presented several important conclusions:

> that MLB's 2002 response to steroids use resulted in players switching to (then) undetectable growth hormones; that the entire baseball community is responsible for failing to recognize the problem sooner; that an extensive investigation to determine which players had used peds would not be helpful; that MLB should employ an independent testing organization to conduct future tests.
>
> (Mitchell Report Summary and Recomendations, p. 6)

The Mitchell report marked a historical watershed in baseball's response to the growing problem of doping, which had begun to raise serious questions in public discourse about the game's integrity. Before the report appeared, MLB's response to allegations of doping had been tepid: one announced random test each year for every player and selective tests of random players in the off-season. But most revealing were the mild punishments for violations: first offense 10 days' suspension; second offense 30 days; third offense 60 days; and fourth offense one year.

In effect, doping in major league was regarded as soft deviance, which was evidenced by mild punishment and relatively weak stigma. Not surprisingly many players continued to use prohibited drugs. But the league soon realized its public credibility as a sport governed by rules of fairness was being endangered. Not since the Black Sox scandal had the league faced such a challenge. The Mitchell Report helped the league to recognize the gravity of the situation, by making clear the urgent need for serious reform. The Report set forth tough recommendations that called for increases in both testing and punishment: Unannounced random tests twice a year for all players as well as unannounced random tests for selected players throughout the year and tests for seven different peds, along with tests for human growth hormones (which now had a reliable test). Without question, its most far reaching reforms focused on social control—punishment of offenders—which became more severe. The suspension for first offense increased from 10 days to 50 days; second offense from 30 days to 100 days; and the third offense, from 60 days to a lifetime ban, the death penalty ending an athletic career. Though not quite zero tolerance, the new punishments shifted closer to that standard.

In short, drug use shifted from yellow zone soft deviance to red zone hard deviance. In response to the widespread revelations of doping in baseball during the 1990s and the obvious unfair advantage gained by drug users, some sports commentators argue that the entire period of widespread doping should be marked in the record books with an asterisk (*)—a permanent stigma attached to performances.

DOPING IN CYCLING

Suspicions about doping in sports continued to spread. In recent years several American cyclists came under scrutiny, John Landis, the American winner of the 2006 Tour de France, was later stripped of his title after tests disclosed peds in his urine sample (Zeigler, 2010). Landis protested and appealed the decision for several years; but in 2010, he finally confessed to having used peds. Tarnished by the scandal, he was unable to find a new team willing to sign him to a contract and retired from cycling in 2011. Though newsworthy, Landis's doping scandal paled in comparison to the scandal involving Lance Armstrong, who many had considered to be the greatest cyclist in the history of the sport.

In addition to his reputation as a great cyclist, Armstrong had attained the status of an American cultural icon due to his successful experience in overcoming cancer and his subsequent founding of a foundation to assist cancer patients. It would hardly be an exaggeration to say that Armstrong was admired by tens of millions of people who knew nothing about the largely European sport of cycling. But Armstrong's iconic image later changed. In June 2012, the United States Anti-Doping Agency (USDA) accused Lance Armstrong of doping and trafficking in drugs. Armstrong immediately denied the charges and filed a law suit against the agency, in July 2012, to defend his reputation. But the USDA refused to back down.

Armstrong lost the law suit and a few days later, in August 2012, the USDA voided all of his titles between 1998 and 2012 and, apparently convinced that he was bad for the sport of cycling, imposed a lifetime ban (Macur and Austen, 2013). Throughout the whole process, Armstrong continued to claim that he was innocent. But after it became clear that he had no possibility of reversing the decision, he dropped his defense. The moment of truth had apparently arrived. Shortly after the USDA decision, he arranged to appear on the Oprah Winfrey show, a popular television program with a very large, mostly female audience, to make a confession. Though he finally admitted on the show—publicly—that he had used peds, he expressed little contrition or regret about using drugs to gain a competitive advantage. This attitude can be seen in an interview he gave to a reporter from the French newspaper, *Le Monde*, which was reported in *USA Today* (*USA Today*, 2013).

> (Interviewer): "When you raced was it possible to perform without doping?"
>
> (Armstrong): "That depends on which races you wanted to win. The Tour de France? No, impossible to win without doping. Because the Tour is a test of endurance where oxygen is decisive."

Armstrong, the shattered cultural icon, not only lost his championship titles and fame; but also, and no doubt equally devastating, he lost millions of dollars of income he earned annually from advertisers and organizations for endorsing products, making promotional appearances, and giving speeches.

Due to Armstrong's downfall and dozens of other revelations of doping in cycling, the sport's officials realized it was in crisis. Much like major league baseball responding to the doping crisis, professional cycling entered a period of self-reflection and reforms.

DOPING: SOCIAL CONTROLS AND SANCTIONS

Social control of doping in sports requires effective means of testing and detection. But these are difficult to sustain as new drugs and new means for masking peds are continually being developed in response to new tests. The situation resembles the proverbial game of cat and mouse with a seemingly endless chain of actions—reactions—actions—reactions. . . .

Testing for peds in sport has a relatively long history. Following the appearance of anabolic steroids, testing began in 1967. A few years later, in the 1970s, the International Olympics Committee (IOC) introduced a standard test for anabolic steroids. This was followed by new tests for testosterone in 1982 and blood doping in 1984.

It has been argued that the turning point in the control and conviction of sports drug use occurred at the Pan Am games in Caracus, in 1983, marking the end of uncontrolled usage without risks of detection (Luschen, 2000: 464). Probably the most significant development in the international effort to control doping occurred in 1999 with the establishment of the World Anti-Doping Agency (WADA). As a creation of the IOC, "it works with intergovernment organizations, governments, public authorities, and other public and private entities to stay at the forefront of the fights against sports doping." In addition to maintaining an extensive list of banned drugs and methods for performance enhancement, WADA supports research investigations in molecular biology, biochemistry, chemistry and pharmacology to fight doping practices (Mukhopadhyay, 2012: 2).

Nevertheless, there remains the problem of international disunity. In the words of one observer, "internationally the variety and inconsistency of doping control is high. So far there is no clear set of rules that is consistent throughout national and international sport federations. Moreover, only recently has a common movement emerged among sport organizations that doping must be controlled by sport itself lest it lose its moral authority and autonomy" (Luschen, 2000: 469).

UNESCO attempted to overcome this disunity in 2005 when it published its official international convention against doping in sport. This was significant because it went beyond sports federations and involved governments.

> For the first time governments around the world . . . gathered to apply the force of international law to anti-doping. . . . The convention provides the legal framework governments can (use) to address specific areas of the doping outside the domain of the sports movement. Hence the convention helps to formalize global anti-doping rules, policies, and guidelines in order to provide an honest and equitable playing environment for all athletes.
>
> (Marriott-Lloyd, 2008)

Though this Unesco convention marks a significant point of progress by helping "to ensure the effectiveness of the WADA code," it hardly succeeded in its objective, because the convention lacks a consensus" about the means the governments use. In short, it did not oblige the governments to embrace specific means to attain the objectives. It was thus largely a symbolic gesture—which is not to say it is unimportant but rather that it marks only the beginning phase rather than the actual achievement of effective international controls.

Some have argued that it is better to begin with each league or federation as distinct organizations with responsibility for implementing and enforcing anti-doping rules; and that international sports organizations should oversee national federations and impose punishments on those who fail to implement anti-doping rules.

Viewed from a broader analytical perspective, doping in sports poses formidable problems not simply because it appeals strongly to athletes but also because it confronts two inherent characteristics of sport: (1) its conflicting ideologies; and (2) its conflicting organizational interests.

The conflicting ideologies of sport are seen by some as the major obstacles to effective controls of doping. In the words of one commentator:

> While sport is seen to be a natural promulgation of positive values and moral education, it also has to be constrained . . . by a raft of positive sanctions to secure the best outcome. This essentially protective and authoritarian view can be summarized as a "social engineering and brand protection ideology." But . . . elite sport produces a highly competitive culture, or opposite ideology that encourages its participants to do all that is necessary to secure an advantage over their rivals.
>
> (Stewart et al., 2012: 95)

Second, and manifested at a different level, are conflicting interests of sport organizations, which explains the lax attitude some sport organizations display toward doping. It is deviance in pursuit of a goal all share: winning.

CUTTING CORNERS IN AMATEUR SPORTS: VIOLATIONS OF RECRUITING AND ELIGIBILITY RULES

Now we turn to another sphere of conflicting organizational interests. Most people understand that sports involve on-field competition but few understand its off-field competition—the game outside the game—the intense rivalries to recruit the best athletes. This is hugely important because the quality of the athletes a team recruits largely spells the difference between a successful and a mediocre sports program. This concerns the domains of sports program management and competitive organizational deviance in sports. While organizational deviance exists in both professional and amateur sports, it is at the amateur level that we find most frequent rule violations. That is because amateur sports impose tighter constraints on player recruitment and financial compensation, which is why most stories in the news media about recruiting and eligibility violation focus on colleges. In contrast to professional sports like the NFL, MLB, and the NBA, which have league-controlled player drafts, college and other amateur sports are obliged to compete with restricted resources in an open market, with the result that some feel compelled to cheat. Like doping and other forms of hidden competitive deviance driven by the desire to win, these actions violate the principle of competitive fairness. But unlike doping these violations are regarded as less serious threats to the integrity of sports because they occur off-field, apart from actual sports contests. Hence the tendency to treat them as soft deviance.

NOTABLE EXAMPLES OF RECRUITING AND ELIGIBILITY VIOLATIONS

1. Illegal Payments to High School Prospects: Sweetening the Deal

Financial payments to exceptional high school prospects is one means used by big time college basketball and football programs to improve their success. This practice is likely to be especially appealing to marginal big time athletic programs which find it difficult to compete against more prestigious programs for highly talented prospects. This explains why illegal recruiting is often practiced by teams aspiring to upward mobility in national rankings of big time basketball and football programs. That these programs are willing to risk penalties and a tarnished reputation to gain a higher level of national recognition reflects the powerful inducement of the lucrative rewards bestowed on highly rated programs. Among these rewards are multimillion dollar media contracts, which we will discuss in the chapter on sports communities and media.

In 1981, Clemson University's football program paid several outstanding high school prospects to attend Clemson (Watt, 2012). The illegal payments were discovered and Clemson's football team received a penalty of two years probation. Though only a few athletic programs have been discovered using illegal financial payments to recruit players, it seems reasonable to assume many more violate the rules and manage to avoid getting caught. Financial inducements are likely to be especially appealing to teenage athletes from economically disadvantaged backgrounds, where they may have had very little money to spend on clothing and entertainment. They are likely to have few ethical qualms about accepting payments. They may also see the money as an affirmation of their self-worth in a society which has relegated them and their families to poverty.

Sometimes the illegal inducements are simply parties and other pleasurable recreation financed by an athletic program. For example, at the University of Colorado, in 2001, it was revealed that the football program was using sex and drugs to recruit players, practices that turned out to have a bad outcome when some of the recruits were charged with sexual assault and rape (Watt, 2012: 1; OnlineCollege.Net, 2013). Several years after this scandal broke the head coach was dismissed. There have been numerous examples of using attractive females and entertainment to induce young prospects to attend a particular university and play for its basketball or football team.

Illegal payments and gifts to recruits are often difficult to detect because they may involve "third parties"—boosters or agents—who are not officially employed by the athletic program. Nevertheless, these individuals may be operating with the knowledge or even co-operation of the athletic staff, who deliberately remain in the background to avoid possible allegations of rule breaking. We see an example of this at Central Florida University, in 2012, where outside third parties were involved with recruits and student athletes, with the knowledge of the football team staff, who facilitated this activity during its recruiting period (Fish, 2011). These activities, while prohibited by NCAA rules, actually constitute soft deviance. They are likely to persist insofar as the relative mild punishments are perceived as worth the risk relative to the potential rewards of gaining superior recruits and producing winning programs.

2. Providing Under the Table Benefits: The Problem of Illegal Compensation

This is often more serious than illegal recruiting because it involves players who are already participating in big time college sports; it risks jeopardizing the legitimacy of the game outcomes. In fact, this compensation places the student athlete in a quasi-professional status of "being paid" for their performance. Athletic programs involved in "paying players under the table" may gain a competitive advantage over their opponents by attracting star players who might have attended another school. We can illustrate the nature of this practice with a few examples.

In 1986, SMU football players were paid through a slush fund from boosters—which was administered by university officials. The NCAA penalized the team by canceling its 1987 season (Watt, 2012: 1–2). Though it continued its football program after the suspension ended, the team failed to regain its national prominence. Was this because it lost the unfair advantage and was unable to compete for recruits with more prestigious programs?

In 1993, Florida State University was placed on probation for one year because some of its players had received illegal compensation—in the form of shoes and other items—from a sports agent who was trying to get them to sign contracts (Online College.net, 2013: 3–4).

In a highly publicized case in the 1990s, the University of Michigan basketball team was penalized because several of its star players had received payments from a team booster, who was a gambler (Paciella, 2007: 1–2). This situation shook the NCCA officials because Michigan, at the time, ranked among the nation's top five teams. In an effort to remove the taint of scandal, which affected all high profile college basketball programs, the NCAA voided the team's records as well as its two tournament finals. Though the players involved in the scandal had graduated, the school basketball program was placed on probation for two years and the team's coach was fired.

In a more recent highly publicized case of illegal compensation, involving a star athlete—Reggie Bush—who had graduated, the USC football team was hit with a two-year post-season ban and the loss of 30 scholarships after the NCAA learned that Bush had received several hundred thousand dollars from an agent while he was playing at USC (Coventry, 2012).

All of these are examples of the "creeping professionalization" of some big time college basketball and football programs, where the financial rewards to the school and coaches for winning are so large that cheating to stay on top is difficult to resist.

3. Academic Cheating: Subverting the Educational Mission

The third major form of hidden competitive deviance extends beyond sports and involves violations of the normative rules governing academic institutions. These consist of manipulating test scores, grades, and other academic records in order to maintain a player's eligibility for sports. Big time college sports programs usually have some players who lack academic preparation for college and the challenge faced by many college sports programs consists of finding ways to make these players eligible. Unfortunately, most college sports programs do not perceive this as an educational challenge, which demands taking measures to enhance the players' intellectual development. Instead, most perceive it as an eligibility challenge, which demands finding ways to subvert the college's academic standards. Because most big time college sports programs have little interest in the college's educational mission or the athlete's occupational future, they resort to cheating or devious techniques of rule evasion to keep their academically deficient players eligible. The pressure to "bend the rules" is especially strong if the players are outstanding athletes whose presence in games could affect the outcome.

Sports-driven academic cheating highlights the tensions between the goals of big time sports programs and the educational mission of colleges. When academic cheating is encouraged and condoned for the sake of attaining success in sports, the educational mission is betrayed. Because academic cheating—like its counterparts, illegal recruiting and illegal compensation—is hidden, we have no way to determine its actual prevalence. It seems reasonable to assume that the cases that are exposed are only the tip of the iceberg. The following few examples illustrate the seriousness of the problem.

A huge academic cheating scandal surfaced at the University of Minnesota in the 1990s when it was revealed that the athletic department had hired an employee to write term papers for basketball team members (Paciella, 2007: 1). The scandal involved not only players and coaches but also professors. The team was placed on probation for four seasons and obliged to forfeit all of the records and titles it had attained over a period of five years, extending from 1993 to 1998; also, they lost five scholarships for three years.

In contrast to this University of Minnesota case, more recent sports cheating scandals have operated on a smaller scale. In 2002, at the University of Georgia three basketball players received bogus grades in a course that had been taught by the coach's son—who was also an assistant coach (Online College.net, 2013: 5). After the cheating was discovered, both the coach and his son were fired. The coach, it turned out, had a tarnished background from a previous coaching job where he been dismissed—for submitting false expense reports.

In one of the most egregious cases of academic cheating, St. Bonaventure University in New York admitted a basketball player whose only academic credentials consisted of a welding certificate which was credited as a sociology course (Online College.net, 2013: 4–5). The president of the college, after admitting he had violated NCAA and university rules, was forced by the college's board of trustees to resign. The student was barred from playing basketball and the university's basketball team was prohibited from playing in the conference post-season tournament. Finally, in one of the more recent highly publicized cases of academic cheating at the University of Memphis, in 2009—a player paid another student to take a SAT exam for him, apparently with the knowledge of the basketball team staff. The NCAA responded by forcing the team to forfeit all games in the 2007–8 season.

Academic cheating is unlikely to disappear so long as it remains in the zone of soft deviance.

OPEN COMPETIVE DEVIANCE: ILLEGITIMATE VIOLENCE

- In a NBA game between the L.A. Lakers and the Houston Rockets, in December 1977, a fight broke out involving several players. In the ensuing confusion, one of the Lakers' players (Kermit Washington) swung around and visciously punched a Lakers' player (Rudy Tomjanovich), who collapsed on the court. Tomjanovich suffered a fractured cheek bone and brain damage from the force of the blow. That fight marked a watershed in the NBA's rules about fighting (Feinstein, 2003).
- The French superstar, Zinedine Zidane, reacting to an alleged verbal insult in a 2006 soccer World Cup match, brutally headbutted an Italian player, which resulted in Zindane's ejection from the game and, ultimately, France's loss of the championship (*The Guardian*, 2014).

In contrast to hidden competitive deviance, open competitive deviance is manifested through illegitimate violence which tends to arouse immediate hostile reactions. Where hidden competitive deviance results from strategic actions prior to the sports contest that make it difficult to detect (and in some cases it is never detected), open competitive deviance results from lapses of discipline (usually impulsive actions) that are easily detected because they occur during the sports contest, in plain sight, disrupting the flow of routine in contest interactions. In short, it is violence that transgresses the normative boundaries of the sport. Think of the difference between the Lance Armstrong doping scandal (clever hidden competitive deviance) and the Mike Tyson ear biting spectacle (impulsive open competitive deviance).

Violence is an integral part of many sports; however, each sport sets different normative limits to the violence it permits. The levels of violence permitted by different sports is illustrated by this simple continuum.

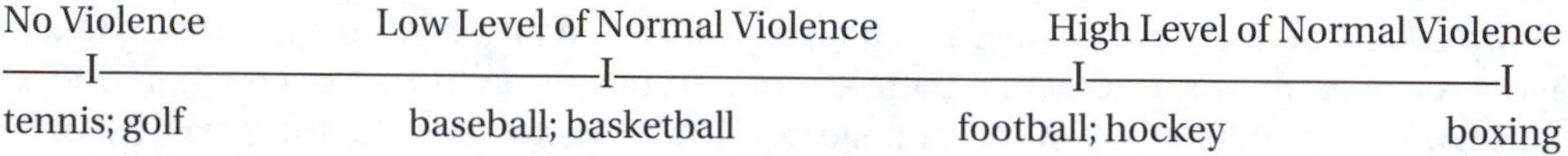

Thus the range of permitted violence varies widely among sports. Or to state this in terms of our metaphorical traffic lights, we can say that sports like football and hockey have a broader green light zone of violent acts than do baseball and basketball, which have more narrow zones. We can classify the normative status of violent acts in each sport into one of three categories:

1. Green Light ((Normal) Zone
2. Yellow Light (Problematic) Zone
3. Red Light (Illegitimate) Zone

The meaning of these normative statuses can be illustrated with an example. Consider the physical act of a player deliberately smashing into his opponent and knocking him to the ground. This would be in the green light zone in football, the yellow light zone in baseball, and a red light act zone in tennis. Note that in baseball the normative zone of this type of physical act is very narrow. It is normative (acceptable) in only one situation: when a base runner smashes into an opposing player who is attempting to block his path and prevent him from touching a base or home plate. Any other deliberate physical collision with an opposing player in baseball would enter the red light zone of illegitimate violence. In contrast, in football or hockey this physical act fits into a broad green light zone of normal violence. Though football and hockey are clearly violent sports, all sports must place limits on their "normal violence." What are the limits in football and hockey? Deliberately kicking a player in his face after he has been tackled in football and "high sticking" (swinging the hockey stick at an opponent's head) in hockey are examples of red light violence in these two sports. Even boxing, which is probably the most violent popular sport, sets limits to normal violence. As was revealed in the earlier cited example of Mike Tyson biting his opponent's ear in a heavyweight boxing match, this crossed into the red zone of illegitimate violence in the boxing—which is why the contest was immediately ended. Tyson was disqualified because his actions violated the normative boundaries of permissible violence in prize fighting.

It should be noted that the punishments imposed on prohibited red zone violence, like punishments of deviance in ordinary social life, vary in severity because they are calibrated to fit the gravity of the act. Here we see the distinction between soft and hard red zone deviance as the punishment may range from ejection from the contest or suspension from multiple contests to expulsion from the sport, the so-called the death penalty, which is reserved for what the sport regards as the most egregious acts of illegitimate violence: red zone hard deviance.

SERIOUS INJURIES: THE SPUR TO NARROWING THE NORMATIVE BOUNDARIES OF SPORTS VIOLENCE

This brings us to the problem of sports injuries and their potential for creating pressures for change. Acts that frequently result in serious sports injuries tend to be placed in a problematic (yellow light) zone of behavior, which generate negative public reactions, which sometimes result in reforms. We can see an example of this in the movement to curtail injuries in college football, which became controversial in the early history of the game. In response to the death of 18 players in the season of 1905, President Theodore Roosevelt joined the crusade. Waging a war to eradicate brutality from the game, Roosevelt declared:

> I believe in outdoor games, and I do not mind in the least that they are rough games, or that those who take part are occasionally injured . . .(but) "brutality playing a game should awaken the hardiest and most plainly show of contempt for the players guilty of it.
>
> (Teddy Roosevelt quoted in Associated Press, 2011: 2)

Pressured by public criticisms, college football subsequently was reformed by narrowing the boundaries of permissible football violence and requiring safer equipment. Similar criticisms directed at the brutality and injuries in boxing were followed by reforms which narrowed the green zone of permissible violence. In the contemporary era, we are witnessing increasing controversy focused on football violence and the problem of concussions, particularly in professional football. This controversy was spurred by news media reports of mounting evidence that concussions from football collisions, for many players, resulted in long-term brain disease and dementia. Noted one recent report:

> Research on NFL retirees has shown that those players who sustained three or more concussions during their careers were significantly more likely to fall into clinical levels of depression later in life for no apparent reason other than the concussions.
>
> (Mayeda, 2008: 1)

The increased awareness of the dangers posed by football-related concussions was created, in part, by vivid personalized descriptions of individuals, like the former NFL star defensive back, Andre Waters.

> After suffering a long period of depression, Andre Waters, a former Philadelphia Eagles football player, committed suicide (at the age of 44). A leading forensic pathologist said that 'the condition of Waters brain tissue was that of an 85 year old man. . . The doctor said he believes the brain damage had come from or had been quickened by successive concussions.'
>
> (Farray, 2007)

Since the Waters' story surfaced, there have been not only many other articles describing the plight of former NFL players suffering from dementia but also lawsuits filed by some these former players against the NFL.

Perhaps the most significant indication that concussions have become matters of serious public concern was the recent White House summit on concussions convened by President Barack Obama. Speaking to over 200 sports leaders, athletes and parents, Obama said:

> Concussions are not just a football issue. . . . They don't just affect grown men who choose to accept some risk to play a game that they love and that they excel at. Every season, you've got boys and girls who are getting concussions in lacrosse and soccer and wrestling and ice hockey, as as well as football.
>
> (Brennan, 2014:p1)

Although the problem remains unresolved, the NFL has made several rule changes to narrow the green zone of normative violence. It also has agreed to pay the medical expenses of former players suffering from dementia and cognitive impairment under certain stipulated rules. Because the problem of serious injuries from sports violence goes beyond football and professional sports to college, high school and other amateur sports, it is unlikely to disappear. Noted a recent study: "About 135,000 children between the ages of 5 and 18 are treated in emergency rooms each year for sports related concussions and other head injuries" (Lavigne, 2012) This is already causing parents to steer their children away from playing certain sports. As noted by an ESPN survey:

> The concussions, violent hits seen on TV, lawsuits over health, and suicides among players have taken their toll on parents, who see a connection between what's happening in the pros and the risks their children face on the field down the street, an "Outside the Lines survey" finds. About 57% of parents in an online survey of more than 1000 people conducted by ESPN Research and the Global Study Group in early August said that recent stories about the increase in concussions in football have made them less likely to allow their sons to play in youth leagues.
>
> (Lavigne, 2012: 1–2)

Also, sports violence raises ethical issues which are another source of pressure for change in professional and big time college sports. One of the most hotly debated issues concerns the pressure on injured athletes to play and ignore the risks of long-term negative effects on their health. Two notable examples are from the experiences of professional basketball players—Andrew Toney (a former Philadelphia 76er) and Bill Walton (a former Portland Trailblazer). Both complained that they suffered permanent impairment of their mobility because they were pressured to play on an injured foot. Often such pressures to play are accompanied by pressures to use pain killing drugs to deaden the sensation of the injury. Managing injuries so that the athlete can return to the contest exists within the problematic (yellow light) zone of behavior, in many sports, prompting serious questions. Are athletes who are pressured to play injured being exploited? Are they aware of the possible long-term effects on their bodies? What are the athletes' rights? These remain hotly debated issues. On one side of the debate are those who argue that the pressures on the injured athletes to play exploits them because their bodies are being sacrificed for someone else's benefit. However, on the other side of the debate are those who view the athlete's situation in terms of what is called "risk transfer."

> This suggests that . . . administrators and coaches minimize their own financial, commercial, sports related risk (of failure or losing) by getting athletes to be willing to sacrifice their bodies 'for the good of the team.' Unable to define the boundaries of acceptable risks themselves, athletes assume substantial physical risks as 'part of the game' and absolve management of its responsibility to assure the safety of athletes.
>
> (Murphy and Waddington, 2007)

In short, this presents a risks/benefits contractual argument that views the athlete as someone who accepts the risks of injury much like coal miners or lumber jacks who sign on to do dangerous work. But this raises the question of "false consciousness." To what extent is the athlete aware of the actual risks?

A closely related issue concerns the ambiguous situation of the sports team doctor. As a medical professional and a team employee, team doctors are often in situations of role conflict. To whom should the doctor be accountable—the athlete who is his patient or the team who pays his salary?

OTHER TYPES OF SPORTS-RELATED DEVIANCE

We now turn to a brief consideration of deviant behaviors of athletes and fans that violate societal laws. The primary focus here is on off-field violence of athletes and fan violence, which often involve crimes and law enforcement.

1. Off-field Violence: A Different Type of Game

> Even the coverage of the murder trial of O.J. Simpson . . . seems so far to have avoided dealing with the possibility that football players, as surely as combat soldiers, have been programmed and rewarded for a kind of violence that can't always be turned off.
>
> (Lipyste, 1994)

The most serious social problem of deviance involving male athletes, apart from sports, is that of off-field violence. We can easily discern this problem of criminality among athletes from the following research findings:

- A three year study shows that while student athletes comprise 3.3% of the population, they represent 19% of sexual assault perpetrators and 36% of domestic violence perpetrators.
- One in three college sexual assaults are committed by athletes.
- In 1996, while only 8.5 percent of the general population was charged with assault, 36.8% of athletes were charged with assault.
- 20% of college football recruits in the top 25 Division I teams have criminal records.

(Benedict and Crosset, 2012)

Despite numerous incidents of male athletes engaging in bar room fights, domestic abuse, rape, and other types of physical assaults, this problem has received little public discussion. Many of these incidents are not reported in the news media, especially if they involve high profile stars. Their misconduct is often covered up by coaches and schools, with the result that these athletes become accustomed to breaking laws with impunity.

Some sports journalists and social scientists argue that it is a result of learned aggression which male athletes simply extend to all aspects of their social lives. But does this mean males athletes in all sports are prone to violence—or just athletes in certain sports? According to the findings of a recent empirical study by Derick A. Kraeger, football players and wrestlers, in contrast to other athletes, are significantly more likely than non-athlete males to be involved in a serious fight (Kraeger, 2007). This study is especially impressive because it is based on a rigorous statistical analysis. A broad cross-national study, including athletes from a variety of sports, is needed to test further these findings.

Given that athletes in certain sports seem to be more prone to violence, the question is why? Before considering the competing arguments that attempt to answer this question, it is important first to make a distinction between the individual athlete acting alone and athletes acting in a group. As to the individual athlete involved in such violent deviant acts as rape and domestic violence, some analysts see this as the outcome of a learned disposition, arguing that the off-field violent behavior of athletes like Aaron Hernandez (the New England's Patriot's football player accused of multiple homicides) and Lawrence Taylor was conditioned by their socialization into a sport which celebrated and rewarded their violence. As has been noted in the case of Lawrence Taylor, the former New York Giant all pro player:

> The greatest defensive football player of the century, the troubled Lawrence Taylor, caused havoc in the hallways of his high school and college and then went onto the streets as a pro or, more recently as a jock out of water. Felony arrests among pro and college athletes may or may not be rising, but better reporting makes it clear that many of them can not turn off their aggressive behavior at the Buzzer.
>
> (Lipsyte, 1994)

A somewhat broader but related argument is presented by analysts who suggest that violence of individual athletes, such as rape and domestic violence, derive from hegemonic masculinity, which causes male athletes to internalize a belief in their gender superiority, particularly as males playing a hyper-masculine sport; it encourages them to inferiorize and abuse women, who they see as weak and subservient, as sex objects to be used. The hegemonic masculinity argument can apply to both individual violence and group violence, where it is often viewed as operating along with other social influences (see Chapter 10).

Much of this off-field violence occurs in groups. Highlighting this fact, Robert Messner argues that the interpersonal bonds of athletes, like those of juvenile gangs and college fraternities, provide social support for deviance of athletes, which results in them doing things they would never do if they were acting alone.

The actual prevalence of off-field violence by athletes is no doubt much greater than cases revealed by media reports because some the incidents are kept secret, particularly in the case of star athletes. Coaches, administrators, and even law enforcement officers sometimes "cover up" the violent crimes to protect the athlete's reputation and future career, as well as the school's image.

2. Fan Violence

Fan violence is a widespread problem of sports-related social deviance, which often results from the intense emotional passions and frustrations aroused by sports contests. Some fans involved in violence experience it as a way of participating in the sports contest—by extending it to physical confrontations with fans of the opposing team. We see this phenomenon especially in the violence of soccer hooliganism in Europe. Other fans may see violence as a way to vent their anger. The targets of such fan violence may be opposition players, game officials, and, in some unusual situations, players of their own team who they attack for losing.

Typically fan violence is social deviance that is dealt with by the local criminal justice system. We will discuss fan violence more extensively in the section on fan community, where we examine it as a dark side of sports social capital.

THEORETICAL PERSPECTIVES ON SPORT DEVIANCE

We will now turn to major sociological theories of deviance and their implications for understanding the recurrent patterns of deviant behavior in the sports world. The typical media and public response to sport deviance attributes it to individual character flaws. In contrast, these sociological theories explain the social factors that lie behind patterns of deviance linked to sports. Focusing on these social factors is important because they not only draw attention to the *social contexts* of those behaviors, they also indicate the type of social changes that are needed to bring about reform.

ANOMIE THEORETICAL PERSPECTIVE

This theoretical perspective, which derives from the writings of Emile Durkheim, influenced several different theories of deviance. We will begin here by presenting some of the key ideas of this theoretical perspective; and then we will focus on one specific **anomie theory** that is especially relevant to deviant behavior in sports.

In general, the anomic theoretical perspective focuses on societies that are characterized by weak normative rules. It suggests that many individuals living in such societies tend to ignore its normative rules due to the absence of effective social controls. Durkheim argued that modern societies are especially vulnerable to anomie because they lacked strong and stable forms of community life. In contrast to traditional societies where social community was characterized by agriculturally based rural and small town communities, where people shared similar values and lifestyles, modern urbanized societies have diverse populations working in varied occupations, practicing different religions, and pursuing an array of lifestyles. One major consequences of this diversity, along with the declining influence of religion, Durkheim argued, was a weakening of normative rules or anomie, which would be evidenced in higher rates of crime, juvenile delinquency, suicide, and other types of deviant behavior. While Durkheim believed that modern society was especially vulnerable to anomie, he did not believe anomie was an inevitable outcome of modernization.

Durkheim, however, was wary about the capacity of modern urban societies to develop new forms community. In retrospect, a fair assessment of Durkheim's theoretical projections about the future development of modern urban societies would have to conclude that the picture is mixed.

On the one hand, as we pointed out in our discussion of sports fandom, Durkheim failed to anticipate the emergence of sports generated social capital—in the form of vibrant urban sports fan communities—which have become a major feature of modern urban societies. But on the other hand, his anticipation of the problems of anomie in modern societies—at least in part—have proven to be accurate.

The specific Durkheim-influenced contemporary anomie theory that seems especially relevant to sports deviance is the institutional anomie theory developed by Messner and Rosenfeld. Focusing on modern capitalist societies such as the United States, the authors argue these societies are characterized by institutional anomie because of their exaggerated emphasis on materialistic values (i.e., making money, acquiring material objects, commercializing all aspects of human life) and an under-emphasis on moral values that can restrain the extreme materialism. The authors suggest that institutional anomie is being driven by the ideology of "free market capitalism," promoting a world view that opposes all regulations of the economic market by weakening non-economic institutions such as religion, family, education, and government to economy—and, thereby, creating institutional imbalance.

In reference to sports, institutional anomie theory is especially relevant to three prevalent types of deviant behavior: gambling corruption, doping, and college sports' routine violations of recruitment and eligibility rules. Take the example of doping, which is perhaps the most serious manifestation of institutional anomie in modern sports.

The enormous material rewards linked to winning sports contests have spawned an anomic modern sports culture in which the desire to win, for many athletes, takes precedence over all considerations of fairness. The deviance of such athletes as Lance Armstrong, Ben Johnson, Carl Lewis, Marion Jones, Alex Rodriques, to name only a few of the outstanding examples, illustrates this exaggerated emphasis on the material rewards and acclaim.

What are the implications of the institutional anomie theory for solutions to the problems such as gambling corruption and doping in sports? As suggested by the theory, these problems stem not from sports but from the larger society, whose values are diffused into the sports world. At the societal level, the theory highlights the need to strengthen the institutions of family, religion, education, and the media as counter-balancing constraints on economic materialism. This is obviously not easy to do. Nevertheless, the first step consists of public recognition of the problems. The media has enormous potential influence in mobilizing public opinion by calling attention to problems of cheating and corruption in sports.

Next, the theory suggests the need for tighter social controls, including more investigative scrutiny and harsher penalties, on athletes and sports organizations who violate the rules of contest fairness. Such acts should be defined as fraud, transgressions similar to manipulating stocks on Wall Street or selling counterfeit paintings.

Finally, the theory suggests that societies need to celebrate and honor outstanding athletes who exemplify the morality of fairness in sports competition. There should be annual awards in recognition of those who achieved athletic pre-eminence while playing within the rules of the game. Sports Halls of Fame selections should highlight the values of integrity and competitive fairness in their induction ceremonies.

DEPRIVATION THEORETICAL PERSPECTIVE

This theoretical perspective, which was developed by Robert Merton in reference to American society, highlights the effects of social inequality on rates of deviant behavior. Focusing on the contradiction between the society's materialistic culture, which all Americans are encouraged to embrace, and its unequal opportunity structure, the theory predicts that the poor in an affluent society like the United States, will have higher rates of materialistically motivated deviance. This theory suggests that it is not simply poverty but poverty in society where most people are affluent that will result in feelings of deprivation among the poor. Thus, in these societies, we see higher rates of robbery, auto-theft, drug dealing, and other types of materialistically motivated crimes, committed disproportionately by the poor.

When extrapolated to sports, **deprivation theory** focuses our attention on working class athletes in affluent societies like United States. It suggests that these athletes are more likely to be involved in financially profitable deviance than are athletes from the middle class and upper class backgrounds. This can be illustrated with several examples.

First, we have examples of gambling corruption involving working class athletes in schemes to fix games for money. Not surprisingly, this typically occurs in big time college athletics where players receive no salary. The offer of bribes are likely to be more tempting to working class athletes who may see this offer as a chance to make money—for the first time in their lives. The New York City basketball scandals in the early 1950s and the derailed basketball career of Connie Hawkins are examples of this.

Second, the predominant examples of deprivation-driven deviance in sports are the players involved in violations of the rules regulating college sports. This is by far the area characterized by the most entrenched and widespread deviance involving working class athletes. This usually entails either recruiting violations or illegal compensation—which are often linked. The athlete is paid secretly to sign an agreement committing him/her to play for a particular college. These recruiting violations often include an arrangement for continuing payments to the athlete while he is attending college. These payments, in effect, provide the working athlete illegal compensation for playing. Few working class athletes express remorse about violating these athletic rules because they know that the college, the coaches, and others affiliated with the athletic program are being paid generously for successful teams. The experiences of Reggie Bush at USC, Chris Webber at the University of Michigan, Marcus Camby at the University of Massachusetts—to cite only a few cases—illustrate this inclination of many working class college athletes to accept prohibited "payments."

TYPOLOGY II: MERTON'S SOCIAL STRAINS THEORY

	(Cultural Goals) *Societally Prescribed Cultural Goals*	*(Opportunity Structure)* *Societally Prescribed Means*
I. Conformity	+	+
II. Ritualism	–	–
III. Innovative (Deviance)	+	–
IV. Rebellion	+/–	+/–

Source: Robert Merton K. Social Theory and Social Structure. New York: Free Press, p. 132.

In addition to its implications for explaining sports-related deviance of working class athletes, deprivation theory also has relevance to non-sports-related deviance of working class athletes, who are sometimes involved in conventional crimes to acquire money. There are examples of working class black athletes getting involved in robberies or thefts while enrolled in college. One of the most publicized cases was that of Maurice Claret of Ohio State who was convicted for having committed two armed robberies in Columbus, Ohio. Two Drexel University basketball players were charged with armed robbery; two University of Kansas football players were charged with aggravated robbery; and a Marshall University football player was charged with felonious robbery—a few examples of working class athletes becoming involved in robberies and thefts.

What are the implications of deprivation theory for a solution to the problem of materialistically motivated deviance among working class athletes? There are two possible solutions—implied by deprivation theory. The first, and more preferable solution, would entail government social policies that expanded the opportunity structure and improved public schools in poor communities, measures that would raise the standard of living in the society. Significantly reducing working class economic deprivation would benefit not just working class athletes but all groups in the society. Because this is unlikely in the foreseeable future, a perhaps more feasible solution, in the short term, would be to establish legal means to compensate working class athletes for their athletic labor. This would end the legal fiction of "amateur college athletics"—a profitable enterprise in which everyone gets paid except the athletes. But most important, it would reduce financial strain among working class college athletes in revenue producing sports.

While deprivation theory provides useful insights into some types of deviance in sports, what it cannot explain is perhaps the most egregious practice of deviance in collge sports: the recruiting violations committed by college coaches, athletic directors, and boosters. To explain the behavior of these individuals, who are hardly poor, we have to look at the subcultural and white collar theoretical perspectives.

THE CHICAGO SCHOOL INTERACTIONIST/DIFFERENTIAL ASSOCIATION THEORETICAL PERSPECTIVES

Both the institutional anomie and deprivation theoretical perspectives explain deviant behavior by means of macro-social analysis, focusing on social conditions in the larger society. In contrast, the current theoretical perspectives are based on a micro-social or social psychological level of analysis, which focuses on interpersonal and peer group influences on individual behavior. It argues that deviance is the result not of individual psychopathology but rather of interpersonal relationships, influences from friends or significant others, who model and encourage deviant behavior. This theoretical perspective argues that those who socialize with individuals or groups involved in deviant behavior (e.g. using drugs, stealing, gangbanging) are highly likely to both learn and become involved in that same behavior. This perspective is captured perhaps best by the old maxim "birds of a feather flock together." Which is to say, individuals tend to reflect the attitudes and behavior of the people with whom they associate.

In reference to sports, this perspective suggests that deviant behavior is unlikely to derive from isolated individual athletes. Whether it is gambling corruption, doping, or violating recruitment/eligibility rules, the deviance will tend to involve multiple individuals—a supportive social network which may range from several friends to a larger group or organization. We see a clear example of this in the 1919 Chicago Black Sox baseball scandal. That scandal involved eight players on the team who, through their friendships, had developed bonds of mutual trust, which made it possible for them to manipulate the outcome of games.

SUBCULTURAL THEORETICAL PERSPECTIVE

Related to the social psychological approach, the subcultural theoretical perspective also views deviant behavior as being derived from interpersonal influences. However, unlike the interactionist/**differential association** perspective, it focuses explicitly on the position of the group relative to the mainstream social structure. Typically the subculture is not a group of individuals whose deviant behavior is the result of momentary impulses like a crowd of drunken college students engaged in smashing shop windows and overturning cars to celebrate a basketball championship. Rather a subculture is a socially marginalized group which is committed to alternative, non-mainstream norms.

Behaviors such as participating in group rapes or group indulgence in illegal drugs like cocaine, or bar room fighting are subcultural insofar as the participants perceive their behavior as being acceptable, from the standpoint of alternative social norms. Existing as marginal groups in the society, subcultures matter because they provide rationales and supports for deviant behavior that make it resilient and resistant to reform. We see this, for example, in the deviant criminal subcultures such as the Mafia or terrorist groups like the Klu Klux Klan. Arresting and imprisoning individual members of a deviant subculture is seldom sufficient to eliminate the behavior.

In reference specifically to sports, subcultures can be powerful influences on behavior. The practice in some Hispanic and Black American neighborhoods of staging dog fights is an example of subcultural sports deviance. Though dog fighting is illegal, those organizing the fights view it as a legitimate sport like hunting or horse racing. Michael Vick, the NFL pro-football quarterback was convicted and sentenced to several years in federal prison for organizing dog fights.

Turning to legitimate organized sports, we find that the subcultural theoretical perspective is relevant to a varied range of deviant behaviors in both on-field performances and off-field administrative practices. Two major types of deviances that are especially illuminated by **subcultural theory** are: gambling corruption and doping. In the case of the first, gambling corruption, the source of the deviance typically exists outside the sports world, in criminal subcultures, who prey on sports because of the enormous amounts of money bet on sports contests. This is one reason gambling corruption is one of the most widespread and persistent problems confronting sports throughout the world. The role of organized crime in the Chicago Black Sox Scandal, in Jack Molinas' fixing of basketball in what became the New York City basketball scandals, and in many cases of gambling corruption in Europe and South Asia—all reflect the capacity of subcultures to produce gambling corruption in sports.

Doping, in contrast, derives from a very different type of deviant subculture, a subculture comprised of athletes and medical technicians or trainers, who are the primary suppliers of the peds. While the participants in the doping subcultures know their use of peds violates normative rules, as reflected by their efforts to keep their doping practices hidden, they derive support from a social network who not only provide information about specific drugs and techniques of evading detection, but also help to legitimize doping by providing support and encouragement. Because athletes are willing to pay large amounts of money to access peds, the doping subculture yields huge financial profits, which explains why it is difficult to eliminate. We see examples of this subculture in the labs that developed the peds, and that supplied peds to athletes such as Barry Bonds and Alex Rodriquez.

Subcultural theory also has relevance for understanding the deviance we see in some big time college sports programs which exhibit a persistent pattern of rule violations in recruiting and compensating players. This is also related to white collar deviance and deviant organizational culture, which are the last theoretical perspectives we will explore.

WHITE COLLAR DEVIANCE AND DEVIANT ORGANIZATIONAL CULTURE

White collar deviance is probably the most neglected topic in discussions of sports deviance. Focused specifically on the elites or privileged managerial class in sports, it attempts to explain the role and behaviors of the most powerful and wealthy operatives in the sports world. This includes owners, coaches, athletic directors, general managers, physicians, boosters, and league officials, as well as the organizational cultures they create and manage. We find examples of elite deviance in the corruption of Olympic officials who accept illegal bribes that influence their decisions, college coaches and athletic directors who are involved in illegal recruitment and payment of athletes and assisting academic cheating, covering up for athletes' crimes.

In contrast to the deviant behavior of athletes, deviant college sport programs tend to receive little media attention and weak negative sanctions. How many big time college presidents or athletic directors have been fired for rule violations of their football and basketball teams? How many boosters have been punished for making illegal payments to athletes? How many coaches have been arrested and prosecuted for covering up for their players who committed crimes? The recent scandal at Penn State University, which brought down both the football coach and president of the university is a rare exception. Unlike most sport deviance, this went beyond sports to cover up criminal pedophilia behavior by a former assistant coach. The routine Penn State athletic department practice of covering up deviance failed in this situation because it involved a serious crime. We see a similar failed effort to cover up a crime of murder by a basketball player at Baylor University.

But ordinarily, sports elites escape accountability for sports deviance. This appears to be largely due to the deference and respect they receive. Occasionally there will be media reports of a coach or sports official being fired for rule violations but these reports are typically brief and superficial. Like elites in other institutions of society, sports elites are typically subject to milder negative sanctions for rule violations—whereas athletes are more likely to be featured in banner headlines and in-depth articles that may persist for weeks.

There remains a need for more research on the roles of sports elites and the organizational cultures they create.

Also related to this theory is the practice of illegal grade fixing to get working class athletes admitted to college or, afterwards, to keep them eligible. Coming from sub-standard high schools in poor communities, these athletes often lack the academic backgrounds needed to succeed in college.

REFERENCES

American Gambling Association. 2012. "Sports Wagering." www.americangaming.org/industry-resources/research/fact-sheets/sports-wagering

Asinoff, Eliot. 1963. *Eight Men Out.* New York, NY: Henry Holt & Company.

Associated Press. 2011. "NFL Urging States to Pass Youth Football Concussion Laws" February 23.

Agarwal, Pankai. "India Premier League Corruption Must Be Dealt With." Transparency International. www.blog.transparency.org/2013/05/28/indian-premier-league-corruption-must-be-dealt-with-now

Beck, Howard and Michael Schmidt. 2007. "N.B.A. Referee Pleads Guilty to Gambling Charges." www.topics.nytimes.com/top/reference/timestopics/people/d/tim_donaghy/index.html

Benedict, Jeff and Todd Crosset. 2012. "National Coalition Against Violent Athletes." www.national coalition against violent athletes.org

Brennan, Christine. 2014. "Brennan: Like Many Parents, Obama Worried about Concussion." *USA Sports.* May 29, p. 1. www.usatoday.com/story/sports/christinebrennan

Coventry, Andrea. 2012. "Biggest College Football Recruiting Scandals of All Time." 23 Kam. www.yahoo.com

Dedam, Bill. 1998. "College Football: 4 Are Indicted in Northwestern Football Scandal." *New York Times.* December 4. www.nytimes.com/1998/12/04/sports/college-football-4-indicted-in-northwestern-football-scandal.html

Forest, David, Ian Hale, and Kevin McAuley. "Risks to the Integrity of Sport from Betting Corruption." www.epma-conference.net/salford report/22012009/—feb 8

Farray, Tom. "Pathologist Says Waters Brain Tissue Had Deteriorated." sport.espn.go.com/espn

Fish, Mike. 2011. "NCAA Alleges Violations at UCF." ESPN College Sports. Espn.go.com/college/sport/story/u-c-f-knights-accused-recruiting violations

Feinstein, John. 2013. *The Punch, the Lives, and the Fight That Changed Basketball Forever.* New York, NY: Little Brown.

Ginsburg, David E. 1995. *The Fix Is In: A History of Baseball Gambling and Game Fixing Scandals.* Jefferson, NC: McFarland.

Goldstein, Joe. 2003. "Recent Scandals: BC, Tulane, and Northwestern." www.espn.go.com/classic/s/basketball_scandals_recent.html

Goode, Erich. 2011. *Deviant Behavior.* Saddle River, NJ: Prentice Hall.

The Guardian. 2014. "World Cup: 25 Stunning Moments . . . no.5 Zindane Zidame's Head Butt." March 11. www.theguardian.com/football/world-cup-moments

Kakuta, Michiko. "Barry Bonds and Baseball's Steroids Scandal." *New York Times.* www.nytimes.com/2006/03/23/books

Kelly, Jessica and Mythill Rao. "Track Star Marion Jones Sentenced to Six Months." www.cnn/2008/crime/o1/11/jonesdoping

Kraegar, Derek. 2007. "Unecessary Roughness? School Sports, Peer Networks, and Male Adolescent Violence." *Amer. Soc. Review* 72(5): 705–724.

Lavigne, Paula. 2012. "Concussion News Worries Parents." Espn.com

Lipsyte, Robert. 1994. "Why Male Athletes Assault Women." *New York Times* November 11. B14.

—— 1999. "The Jock Culture." *New York Times.* May 9.

Luschen, Gunther. 2000. "Doping in Sport as Deviant Behavior and Its Social Control." *Handbook of Sports Studies,* edited by Jay Coakley and Eric Dunning. Thousand Oaks, CA: Sage Publishers.

Mackay, Duncan. 2003. "Lewis: Who Cares I Failed Drug Test?" *The Guardian.* www.guardian.co.uk/sport/2003/apr/23/athlectics

Macur, Julietr and Ivan Austen. 2013. "Amid Tears, Armstrong Leaves Unanswered Questions." *New York Times.* January 13. nytimes.2013/01/19/sports/cycling/amid-tears-armstrong

Mayeda, David. 2008. "Sporting Violence: The Injuries." July 13. Bleacher report.com/articles/37370 –sporting-violence-the-injuries

Mitchell, George. 2007. "The Mitchell Report." www.files.mlb.com/mithrpt.pdf

Mukhopadhyay, Rajendrani. 2012. "Sports Doping: An Extreme Game of Biology." *Annual Review of Biochemistry.* June. www,asbmb.org/asbmbtodayu/article.asps/od-17038

Murphy, Patrick and Ivan Waddington. 2007. "Are Elite Athletes Exploited?" *Sport in Society*10(2): 239–255.

Marriott-Lloyd, Paul. 2008. www.unesco.org/new/en/social and human sciences?/antidoping

OnlineCollege.Net. 2013. "Top 10 Scandals in College Sports." www. Online.College.Net

Paciella, Joe. 2007. "Worst Basketball Scandals." Doc's Sports Service, November 15, pp. 1–2. www.doc sports/current worse-college-basketball-scandals

Pilon, Mary. 2013. "Top Sprinters Test Positive, Jolting Track World." nytimes.com/2013/07/15/sports/tyson-gay-tests-positive-for-banned-substance

Rodenberg, Ryan. 2014. "Pete Rose's Reckless Gamble." *The Atlantic.* www.the atlantic.com/entertainment/archive/2014/08/why-pete-rose-still

Rosen, Charles. 2001. *The Wizard of Oz: How Jack Molinas Almost Destroyed the Game of Basketball.* Seven Stories Press. New York, N.Y.

Schmidt, Michael S. 2014. "Baseball Let Rodiquez Use Testosterone in Big Year, Book Says" *New York Times.* www.newyorktimes.com/2014/07/03/sports/baseball-let/roddriquex-use-testosterone

Slot, Owen. 2003. "Ambition, Naivety and the Tantalizing Prospect of Inheriting the World." *The Times.* January 18. www.times.co/uksports/athletics/article

Stewart, Bob, C. Aaron, and T. Smith. 2012. *International Review of Sport Sociology* 45(2): 187. p. 95

Transparency Intertnational. 2009. "Corruption and Sport: Building Integrity and Preventing Abuses." Working Paper March 2009. www.transparency.org

USA Today. www.usa.today.com/story/sports/cyclying/2013/06/28/lancearmstrong-impossible-to-win-tour-de-france-doping/2471413

Watt, Kristin. 2012. Yahoo Sports. "Top 5 College Football Scandals."www.yahoo.com/ncaa/footballnews

Waller, Willard. 1936 "Social Problems and Mores." *American Sociology Review.* 1(6): 922–933.

Zeigler, Mark. "Landis Admits Doping, Says Armstrong Did Too." *San Diego Union-Tribune.* www.signon sandiego.com/news/2010/may/19/cyclist-landis -admits-doping-reprts-says

CHAPTER 26

Creating the Frankenstein Athlete: The Drug Culture in Sports

Fran Zimniuch

"The use of performance-enhancing drugs like steroids in baseball, football and other sports is dangerous, and it sends the wrong message—that there are shortcuts to accomplishment, and that performance is more important than character."

—President George W. Bush, State of the Union address, January 20, 2004

As sure as the sports section in every morning newspaper across the country reviews sporting events from the previous day, an increasingly troublesome trend in the world of sports is that the morning paper also often includes news of yet another athlete's involvement in the use of illegal drugs. For many outside the sports spotlight, their only experience with illegal drugs is the occasional use of the recreational kind. But in the high-powered world of sports, where fortune and fame can be decided by a millisecond, any means by which one athlete can gain even the slimmest edge has become acceptable. The drug culture in sports has reached such a crescendo that we've gone well beyond jocks doping to win events. Now, many are doping just trying to keep up with their competitors. It is a vicious circle that has fans doubting the validity of just about every outstanding athletic achievement.

If a big, powerful home run hitter like Ryan Howard hits a gargantuan tater, fans will whisper—even though most players are just like Ryan Howard: honest, hardworking, nondoping athletes who strive to be the best they can be the old-fashioned way. It's just not fair.

Most fans, who live their lives out of the spotlight and who have been so disappointed by so many athletes, are certainly against the use of performance-enhancing drugs—particularly when that use filters down to local college and high school athletes trying to ensure their piece of the pie. That's when it gets dangerous—and hits home.

The amateur and professional sports world has reacted—albeit a day late and a dollar short—in an attempt to put an end to the widespread use of illegal drugs on every level. But when confronted by talented, aggressive, extremely competitive athletes surrounded by throngs of enablers who also want *their* piece of the pie, the recipe for dishonest disaster is always percolating.

Unless our culture decides that it wants überleagues of doped-up, raided jocks with watermelon-sized heads and pea-sized testicles performing their sport as if there was no such thing as gravity, then stringent measures need to be taken.

We're only human, and many of us have opinions about issues we really don't understand. Just look at the wide variety of—sometimes underinformed—opinions about any political campaign or particularly controversial topic. So it seems prudent to take a step back and try to get a better understanding of just what we're dealing with.

Before talking about the use of steroids, particularly in baseball, history dictates that we should discuss greenies, otherwise known as peptos. Greenies are an amphetamine—speed—which helps a player boost his effort. But a clear distinction should be made between greenies and present-day steroids. Decades ago, players might pop a few greenies prior to a game or sip from a special pot of "hot" coffee in the clubhouse, which was for players only. Greenies helped players to get loose more quickly and play through stretches of the long season when they just weren't able to get up for the game. But greenies, unlike steroids and human growth hormone, did not enable a ballplayer to do things he was normally unable to do. Instead, they gave him what amounted to an extreme caffeine rush to get his ass in gear, loosen up, and play through pain or fatigue. But they never allowed anyone to play beyond his natural ability.

"You have to distinguish greenies, or peptos, as they were called, from steroids," says former pitcher Jim Bouton, who authored what might be the greatest book ever on baseball, *Ball Four*. "Greenies only allowed you to play up to your ability. If you didn't get a good night's sleep, or you had a hangover, it would allow you to play up to your ability, or at least some players thought that. It did not create a different human being. It did not change your physical makeup. It did not allow you to play beyond your ability, your normal ability, as steroids do and human growth hormone does."

"Greenies were performance *enablers*, not enhancers."

Greenies, named for the color of the pills, were introduced to the game in the 1940s. Amphetamines speed up the heart rate and have been proven to fight fatigue, increase alertness, and sharpen reaction time. They were actually considered harmless pep pills until 1970, when they were made illegal without a prescription. They have since been found to be addictive and can cause heart attacks and strokes.

Baseball's love affair with greenies officially ended before the start of the 2006 season, when Major League Baseball began testing players for them. Now, a player who fails the test once is sent to counseling. The second strike results in a twenty-five-game suspension.

The pharmaceutical industry—and baseball—have come a long way since the days of greenies, with the introduction of steroids. While everyone has an opinion about steroids, not as many people understand just what they are. What do steroids do to make the long-term health risks so acceptable to so many of today's athletes?

According to the National Institute on Drug Abuse, anabolic-androgenic steroids are man-made substances related to male sex hormones. "Anabolic" refers to muscle building and "androgenic" refers to increased masculine characteristics. "Steroids" is the name of the class of drug. These types of drugs are available legally only by prescription, to treat conditions that occur when the body produces abnormally low amounts of testosterone, such as in delayed puberty and some types of impotence. They can also be prescribed to treat body wasting in patients with AIDS and other diseases that result in loss of lean muscle mass. Abuse of anabolic steroids can lead to serious health issues, some of which are irreversible.

Today, athletes and others abuse anabolic steroids to enhance performance and improve physical appearance. Anabolic steroids can be taken orally or injected, and are used in cycles of weeks or months, rather than continuously, in a practice known as cycling. Users often combine several different types of steroids to maximize their effectiveness while minimizing negative effects. This is known as stacking.

The major side effects of anabolic steroid abuse include a litany of serious health issues, including liver tumors and cancer, jaundice (the yellowish color of skin, tissues, and body fluids), fluid retention, high blood pressure, and an increase in bad cholesterol and decrease in good cholesterol. Abusers may also suffer from kidney tumors, severe acne, and trembling.

Men who abuse steroids often suffer from gender-specific side effects such as shrinking of the testicles, reduced sperm count, infertility, baldness, development of breasts, and increased risk for prostate cancer. For women, side effects can include the growth of facial hair, male-pattern baldness, changes in or cessation of the menstrual cycle, enlargement of the clitoris, and a deepened voice.

And for adolescents who make the misguided decision to abuse steroids, side effects include permanently halted growth as a result of premature skeletal maturation and accelerated puberty changes. So adolescents risk being shorter than they would normally have been for the remainder of their lives.

"We have a guy in our book, Tim Montgomery, who said that if he could break the 100-meter record, he didn't care if he dropped dead after he crossed the finish line," says Lance Williams, coauthor of *Game of Shadows*. "In *Ball Four* by Jim Bouton, they have guys sitting in the bullpen talking about if you would take a pill that could make you become a twenty-game winner, even if it took five years off your life. Athletes are young men and women and they don't have the perspective that an older person—even in their thirties and forties—has. They think they'll never die. They think the future will never come. The rewards are so incredible. Financially, it's a tremendous temptation."

A 2005 report by the President's Council on Physical Fitness and Sports titled *Anabolic-Androgenic Steroids: Incidence of Use and Health Implications* treated the subject of steroid use and abuse in great detail. The report concludes: "Although anabolic steroids are illegal, and their use is banned by virtually every sport's governing body, survey and drug-testing data indicate continued use by competitive athletes at all levels. That fact that the level of steroid use appears to have increased significantly over the past three decades among adolescents, women, and recreational athletes is also of growing concern. The use of anabolic steroids presents an interesting public health challenge. While these drugs are associated with deleterious physical and psychological outcomes, they are being used to achieve what many consider socially desirable ends: being physically attractive and being a winner."

But, as so many sports fans have learned over the past decade, steroids are not the only synthetic drugs of choice by today's injectors. Human growth hormone ís another well-known performance-enhancing drug that many don't understand. The difference between steroids and HGH can be described as follows: steroids are like heroin while HGH is like marijuana. Unlike steroids, HGH has not been proven to increase weightlifting ability and it has a greater effect on muscle definition than it does on muscle strength.

So why would an athlete risk suspension and suspicion by using HGH? On the surface, it makes no sense. A baseball player can beef up on steroids and improve his performance as a result. HGH, on the other hand, is often used to attempt to reverse the effects of aging. What's the connection?

"One possibility is that the drug really does enhance performance but that the effect is too subtle to measure in a controlled setting," according to Daniel Engber in "The Growth Hormone Myth: What Athletes, Fans and the Sports Media Don't Understand about HGH," at *Slate*. "An elite athlete might be able to detect very slight improvements in strength and agility that would be invisible to lab scientists or statistical tests. At the highest levels of sport, a tiny edge can make a big difference. Athletes might also derive some added benefit by mixing HGH with other drugs—anti-aging doctors often prescribe growth hormone in combination with testosterone."

"It's also possible that baseball players aren't using HGH to beef up at all. Almost everyone who gets caught red-handed claims they were using the drug to recover from an injury. This might be more than a ploy to win sympathy: Some doctors believe that growth hormone can speed up tissue repair. There isn't much clinical work to support this idea, however."

"The most likely reason that athletes use HGH, though, is superstition. A ballplayer might shoot up with HGH for the same reason we take vitamin C when we have a cold: There's no good reason to think it does anything, but we're willing to give it a try. The fact that the major sports leagues have banned growth hormone only encourages the idea that the drug has tangible benefits. Why would they ban something unless it worked?"

"This mentality has put doping officials and athletes into a feedback loop of added hysteria. The World Anti-Doping Agency (WADA) will ban any drug that athletes use, whether or not it has an effect. The WADA code points out that the use of substances, 'based on the mistaken belief they enhance performance is clearly contradictory to the spirit of sport.' In other words, it doesn't matter if HGH gives athletes an unfair advantage. If Jerry Hairston believes he's cheating, then he really is cheating."

According to the Mitchell Report, which investigated and reported on the use of illegal steroids and human growth hormone in professional baseball, it seems that many of the players implicated for the use of HGH were actually trying to recover from an injury. Whether the drug actually does speed up tissue repair, thus enabling players to recover and return sooner from injury, is not known for certain. What is known is that growth hormone stimulates the synthesis of collagen, which is necessary for strengthening cartilage, bones, tendons, and ligaments.

Jason Grimsley reportedly used the drug in combination with the anabolic steroid Deca-Durabolin to recover from ligament replacement in just nine months—half the usual estimated recovery time for pitchers.

When you combine anabolic steroids and HGH, the result is apparently very conducive and potent—sort of like combining a triple espresso martini with a double shot of Jägermeister. The stronger connective tissues developed through the use of HGH not only work better and heal faster, but they are better equipped to handle the oversized muscles often associated with steroid use.

HGH also increases red blood cell count, boosts heart function, and makes more energy available by stimulating the breakdown of fat. Users also have noticed improved eyesight, better sleep, and better sex.

HGH users can sometimes be identified by the characteristic side effects of the hormone. Use of HGH can cause acromegaly, a condition characterized by excessive growth of the head, feet, and hands. In people with acromegaly, the lips, nose, tongue, jaw, and forehead increase in size, and fingers and toes can widen. Excessive use of HGH can also lead to diabetes.

Another drug that has made the rounds among athletes is andro, short for androstenedione, which was manufactured as a dietary supplement. Andro—a hormone produced in the adrenal glands that increases testosterone production and protein synthesis, resulting in increased lean body mass and strength during training—was commonly used by MLB players, including Mark McGwire, throughout the 1990s.

On March 12, 2004, the Anabolic Steroid Control Act of 2004 was introduced into the United States Senate. It amended the Controlled Substances Act of 1970, placing both anabolic steroids and prohormones on a list of controlled substances and making possession of the banned substances a federal crime. The law took effect on January 20, 2005.

When McGwire was attacking record home run seasons, he openly admitted to taking andro, which was, at the time, a legal over-the-counter muscle enhancement product. So when he took andro, McGwire was not breaking any rules—either those of baseball or those of society.

But the abuse of such dangerous substances by athletes did not just begin with steroids and other performance-enhancing drugs. They are simply the latest of an ever-growing list of dangerous man-made substances used to help create the Frankenstein Athlete. The history goes well beyond even the historical period where Mary Shelley wrote *Frankenstein* in 1831.

We've seen the impact of pharmaceuticals on performance on the field, but it will be interesting and perhaps tragic to see what health-related ramifications drug use will have on these athletes later in life. They may have raised the bar significantly on the playing field. What happens in their future is a crapshoot, because this past generation of performance-enhanced athletes are also guinea pigs who may very well pay a huge price for their athletic achievements.

Has our society become aware of the problem soon enough? Will the risks of such behavior preclude future jocks from crossing over the line? The United States has yet to experience the long-term effect of the use of steroids and performance-enhancing substances, but the same cannot be said of other countries.

Excerpted from Fran Zimniuch, "Creating the Frankenstein Athlete: The Drug Culture in Sports" in *Crooked: The History of Cheating in Sports.*

CHAPTER 27

Discourses of Deception: Cheating in Professional Running[1]

Peter G. Mewett

I stood in the crowd clustered near to the circle races [2] finish line. I could not help but hear the conversation between two men beside me. One man clearly had a deep knowledge of the sport and he was telling the other one about it, including, it seems, about how athletes run dead to secure a lighter handicap. On learning about this, the second man questioned the honesty of the sport, to which the first replied, 'If everybody's a cheat, it's not dishonest'.

(fieldnotes)

Cheating, it seems, occurs in all sports. This is not to claim that all sports players cheat, but rather that each sport contains some who cheat. Revelations about athletics, cricket, cycling, baseball, the football codes, swimming and more have come to light in recent years. There is nothing new about cheating in sport, though there are numerous historical references to it from the commencement of modern sports over two hundred years ago.[3]

Although cheating may be more widespread than many people suspect, in this paper I examine a sport, professional running, in which it is commonplace. Yet, as with other sports, the public image projected by professional running is that of a sport in which the cheat is weeded-out and dealt with by impartial, vigilant officials. These officials, invariably former professional runners, include people who, it may be assumed, routinely cheated in their running careers, know all the ruses of cheating, are aware that cheating is taking place in the meetings they supervise, but intervene and impose penalties only when it becomes obvious. Competitors then, have to carefully conceal their cheating; successful professional runners seldom lack the art of deception. This form of cheating—'clean' cheating—features in the everyday construction of the sport. The ways of clean cheating form a significant discourse in the sport and serve to underpin its reproduction. The art of the official, to detect and penalise this cheating, forms a second discourse that, although publicly denying clean cheating as constitutive of the sport, implicitly recognises this to be the case. A further discourse centres on the continuing tussle between runners and officials, all knowing what is 'really' occurring but publicly denying the centrality of cheating in their dealings. Another form of cheating, 'dirty' cheating, does not form a part of the officials' discourse. Although the terms clean and dirty cheating are my terminology, they reflect an emic typology used in the sport to distinguish between unconscionable actions and the esoterically expected, accepted ways in which the sport is played out. Dirty cheating usually involves a personal financial gain made from a betrayal of trust or from some form of subterfuge; it is widely condemned and spoken of either in anger or in the guarded terms of the unmentionable.

My concern in this paper is to present the forms of cheating that occur in professional running and to demonstrate how clean cheating promotes discourses central to the reproduction of the sport. This is mostly an exercise in ethnographic description blended with grounded theory; as such, it is based on emic constructions, but I also draw on Bourdieu (1978, 1986) to point to how cheating in this sport may be placed in a wider social context. Methodologically, it is based on two years' observation of the professional running circuit in the Australian State of Victoria, a close association with a 'stable'[4] of runners, approximately 100 semi-structured interviews with runners, trainers and officials, and considerable historical research. Clearly, there are beguiling comparisons to be drawn between professional running and cheating in other sports. Such comparisons go beyond the bounds of this paper, however. Indeed, cheating in sport in all its forms, varieties and significances requires a much larger treatment than can be afforded in one article.

Given the rich rewards afforded top-line runners in 'mainstream athletics',[5] professional running is now perhaps something of a misnomer. As a sport it is the present day version of 'pedestrianism', which originated in eighteenth century Britain and came to Australia in the mid-nineteenth century (Mewett 1999). Today, the sport retains its strongest presence in Australia, particularly in Victoria where Stawell is located—this country town being the site of the sport's most prestigious meeting. Spurned by 'athletics', its amateur offspring, professional running has remained a mostly plebeian sport closely linked with gambling. In Australia it is a sport associated with 'battlers', those for whom each dollar is hard earned and life is a struggle against adversity.

Professional running differs from many other sports—such as soccer, rugby league, cricket, baseball—that are 'professional' in the sense that while the players are waged, they are expected to refrain from betting on the outcome of a game. Professional runners are not paid wages to run, however. Rather, they compete for cash prizes and they routinely bet on the outcome of races in which they are participating:[6] this gambling is a part of the sport for professional runners and, for a few, it has provided the money to 'set them up' for life. Many of the ruses and much of the cheating in professional running derive from the strategies and tactics used to rake in gambling winnings and, as Vamplew (1988: 51) has pointed out for horse racing, 'with gambling comes the danger of corruption'. Indeed, the 'unsavoury' nature of gambling to the British higher social orders in the latter half of the nineteenth century was an argument they used to differentiate between their supposedly 'pure' amateur sports, and, to them, the unrespectable, sullied professional sports of the working classes. Although much of the upper class hyperbole served as social markers, an important difference was centred on those who had the financial means to uphold the amateur ethic[7] and those who used sport as a source of income.

Often using sporting metaphors, an ideology of 'fair play' pervades Western-type capitalist societies and perhaps provides a reason for the widely expressed aversion to cheating. In sport, this ideology came from and has been associated most strongly with the ethos of amateurism that emerged from the English 'Greater Public Schools' and Oxford and Cambridge Universities in the second half of the nineteenth century.[8] It is an ideology that remains in many sporting arenas and with it comes the illusion that people compete simply on the basis of their innate, albeit highly trained, abilities: the 'best' competitor or team wins. Although in practice numerous cheating tactics may be used and sometimes detected—weeding-out a cheat every now and then gives the appearance that they are an aberrant few and the sport as a whole is honest—the public face of many major sports present an image of fairness and honesty. But this imagery is a throw-back to the amateur fair-play ethos. As an avowedly professional sport closely associated with the working classes, pedestrianism for a long time was shrouded in disrepute, being viewed through the amateur lens as corrupt, 'ungentlemanly' and demeaning. But sport means different things for the working classes than it has for the upper classes, a point made abundantly clear by Bourdieu (1978, 1986). For the lower classes, the opportunity costs of participating in sport are significant, at the time of participation and for their futures. Unlike wealthy amateurs, they cannot afford to support themselves while preparing for competition. They need to make money from the time spent in sport. Pure competition is not an option for them, because the opportunity costs can be too high. Only when the chance involved in sport has been manipulated into an assessable, calculable risk and the promise of financial gain beckons, does the sacrifice of time from alternative income sources in favour of sport become a viable option. Cheating blunts pure competition and permits players to manipulate chance in their favour to increase the probability of a positive outcome. Bourdieu (1978: 835) notes that 'class habitus defines the meaning conferred on sporting activity, the profits expected from it'. For the wealthy amateur, the acquisition of social capital, for example, may have constituted the 'profits'. But lower class athletes needed to convert their physical capital into cash. Running and competing supposedly for the thrill of it was not enough: the habitus framing their lives promoted dispositions that supported the manipulation of chance and the minimisation of risk.[9]

While increasing personal incomes over the last half century have lessened the economic imperative associated with participation in professional running, the prospect of the winnings from a big race remains a significant pull for many competitors. Although the really 'big' money now is in mainstream athletics, professional running continues to provide the battler with the chance of a 'kick-on' in life. Over the years, winners of major races have used their winnings to purchase businesses, further careers, buy houses or expensive items that would otherwise bind them in years of debt, and so on. Even though the economic imperative may have lessened—it is now a lifetime away from the Depression years when some men survived from this sport—the ways of succeeding in the sport, including cheating, have remained remarkably similar.

RUNNING DEAD

[. . .]

What makes professional running so interesting is that its practitioners, from neophyte runner to peak organisation officials, present a public face of an untainted sport, one in which the cheat is a deviant to be dealt with swiftly by fine and suspension. Yet new runners are taught the tactics of the sport, which involve running in a way to gain a favourable handicap. This is a sport that uses handicaps (also called 'marks') in the form of staggered starts, with the more poorly performed runners starting the race in front of and running a shorter distance than the better performed ones. In theory, handicapping means that differences in ability are levelled by giving the less able an advantage, increasing the uncertainty of a race's outcome thereby making for a more open betting market. But to reduce uncertainty athletes 'run dead', or deliberately lose races while pretending to win, so that by the time that they 'go-off' (that is, attempt to win) they have secured a more favourable handicap than their true ability would warrant. Accordingly, it is common practice for runners to disguise their ability and form and run dead to gain an advantage that they unleash in their targeted races. Such tactics improve the chance of winning a big race, its associated prize money and, hopefully, a princely swag from the betting ring, but this success requires careful concealment of the runners' potential until they go-off. Running dead, a major part of clean cheating, has to be concealed from the watchful eyes of the sport's officials and its followers, the latter factoring into their betting equations any evidence of a runner holding back. Many of the plays in this sport centre on trying to work out what others are doing and planning. Accordingly, to optimise gambling winnings it is important for all players to deceive, to conceal their objectives from others (Mewett 2000; Mewett with Perry 1997).

Runners are in the public gaze when they compete at meetings, which they need to do in order to get the 'lifts'[10] from the handicapper that will give them an advantageous mark. Handicappers and other officials will penalise athletes that they detect running dead. Successful concealment is recognised as that needed to deceive officials into thinking that runners are trying as hard as they can but need a lighter handicap to give them a chance of winning. Perhaps it is more a case, though a generally unspoken one, that the game being played with the officials is not so much one of pretending not to cheat—because runners and officials alike know that cheating is taking place—but rather one of concealing cheating in such a way that it is not obvious to the official and to the public gaze. Cheating has a self-regulatory quality: a runner will cheat in a way that maintains the officials' face. The consequences of ignoring these self-regulatory practices is to suffer the officials' ire and retribution.

Officials are charged with the responsibility of detecting cheating, punishing it and with keeping the sport free of rogues. But, with very few exceptions, the officials are ex-runners, many of whom had followed the ways of the sport in their own athletic careers. Their job, apart from ensuring the smooth organisation of meets, is to detect instances of running dead, 'inconsistent performances' and so forth, in order that, to the public eye at least, the sport presents as well-regulated, with cheats being detected and the perpetrators punished. Perhaps it is only the poor runner incapable of securing a win who need not cheat. In reality, only those runners with inadequate, readily detectable techniques of cheating are penalised. They, and the officials pulling them up, are well aware that there are others, cheating more effectively, that are not being spotted. Within the sport it is accepted that runners will routinely cheat in order to win; the winners are often those who can cheat most effectively. Handicappers and stewards seek the 'blanket finish', the ideal race of professional running, when all of the competitors cross the winning line very close together.[11] Although this is rarely realised in practice, the officials' nightmare is to be 'embarrassed' by having a winner succeed by a large margin over the next finisher. This makes obvious their failure to detect deception, to weed out the cheat.

[. . .]

Deception, then, occurs in multiple ways. Gambling, taken from the wagering closely associated with horse-racing, often lurks behind the deceptive practices. The manipulation of outcomes for pecuniary advantage is hidden from public view, however. The means of cheating change little in a sport, but, when cheating comes to light and creates a scandal, administrators act to impose measures that, in the public eye at least, serve to suppress it. It is important, especially in gambling sports, to deal severely with overt cheating and perpetuate the myth that the probabilities of winning can be calculated from the known performances of the competitors. Cheating only results in large gambling winnings if the bookmakers take in a significant amount of money on a race: winnings are proportional to the total money that is bet.[12] Certainly, those in the sport lay bets on their own hopefuls and on their evaluations of what others could be doing. But to succeed in gambling, bets need to be laid by other, losing punters. Some of this money will come from a public that may not be fully aware of the deceptions being played out before their eyes. The betting public has to be kept interested in the sport, but it has turned away from professional running on several occasions when cheating became too obvious, to come back to the sport only when the controlling authorities had taken measures designed to demonstrate to spectators that cheating had been stopped. Obvious cases of cheating are dealt with by the sport's officials to avert a drop-off in attendance by spectators, including the loss of gate money (Bull 1959: 64–6).

Professional runners do not try to win every event that they enter. Their objective is to win a particular, specified race: in the argot of the sport, the one for which they are 'set'. The set race often is several years away and the athlete's training and running tactics are organised with it in mind. The 'handling' of the runner, typically in the form of the ruses dictated by the trainer, in this long preparatory period is vital to securing a successful outcome. Much of the routine and expected cheating associated with the sport takes place in this lead-up to the runner's set race.

Harry Boyle once said to me that 'handicap is everything' in professional running. Rob Monaghan, a man who ran through the years of the Depression and trained runners for several decades more, had an explicit strategy of letting his runners go-off only when they had achieved a very favourable handicap, even if this meant years of running dead. Rob also went to considerable lengths to ensure that his runners were concealed from the gaze of those who might realise their potential, pick the race in which they were going-off and take the 'cream' of the 'market'.[13]

Running dead is a skill learned from the start of a professional athlete's participation in the sport. The actual techniques can differ between sprinters and distance runners, although runners of all distances commonly put in a very hard training session or run the evening or the morning before a meeting so that carry-over fatigue prevents them from performing to their true ability. Roger Best explained how he managed his running dead:

> I was standing to run well and we were going to a meeting . . . I went to Monash University on the way and I ran two flat out four hundreds, one after the other, until I was physically sick and then I went to the meeting. As well as that I was fortunate in that I could run reasonably dead, I mean in ten years I was never picked up.
> (taped interview)

Cheating also occurs on the track. Heavier running spikes can be worn, sometimes through the addition of lead; while this is heavily proscribed, lead has been used by runners who were unable to run dead by using the more common tactics. John Whitson was one such runner. An excellent athlete and a good prospect for a major race, his chances of winning were tempered by his inability to run dead without being detected. Whitson told me:

> I didn't have the ability, as the term was in those days, 'to run a dead un'. I couldn't run dead and not get caught. And so, what we did . . . Wilf [Whitson's trainer] came to training one night with a pair of inner soles and he said, 'Here, put these in your [running] shoes'. He gave them to me and my hand went down like that. He had actually lined the underside of the

inner soles with lead and each one weighed about half a pound. So, for all of that season . . . I ran . . . with these lead weights in . . . [T]he only way that you would get caught was if somebody was around when you took your shoes off, and then they had to pick them up because they looked like any other pair of shoes with inner soles . . . Didn't let anybody else pick your bag up because it had to [be] the heaviest bag in town. I got right through the whole season without even being spoken to [by the stewards] . . .

(taped interview)

More commonly, on-track cheating involves such things as not breathing during a sprint, 'short-striding',[14] the deliberate use of a poor arm action, adjusting blocks to hinder sprint starts, starting a distance race too hard and then fading, and more. The important point is that this has to be done skilfully. As the runner progresses in the sport, skill at cheating becomes increasingly important to avoid being 'picked-up' by a steward. Asinoff (1963: 71ff) makes a similar point for baseball when he argues that a very fine line separates effective play from deliberately missed play. A deliberate loss requires great care and considerable expertise.

Race stewards, in Australia appointed by the sport's state-based regulating bodies, know all of the means of cheating that are used to deceive and conceal. Moreover, they know that among the runners who they are carefully watching, many will be running dead. [. . .]

'The tactics used to run dead and to keep secret runners' abilities involves what I refer to as 'clean' cheating. It is clean because it is anticipated by those in the sport that others will be playing it this way. Harry's acclaim as a 'shifty bastard' refers to his success in effecting successful concealment of his runners. Shifty can refer to the ways of effecting deceptions, but it refers especially to trainers because of their cunning and subterfuge: renowned trainers are often called 'old foxes' or it has been said of some that 'their left hand doesn't know what their right hand is doing'. Used in this context, shifty is a term of praise. To be called a shifty bastard is to be lauded. Over that weekend Harry was a top trickster, the shiftiest of the shifties. There is an aesthetic appreciation of those who succeed in manipulating the ways of the sport to their advantage and it was clear that Harry's achievements won for him considerable kudos. The wins had come from a classic type of professional running strategy and this was recognised as such by others in the sport. In this way these actions were not dishonest because many others had also tried to achieve the same result through cheating, except that they did not cheat as effectively on that occasion. Apart from beating the handicapper, effective clean cheating involves outwitting others who are trying to do the same thing. This is exactly what many consider must be done for a runner to score a significant win. Officials aside, people in the sport frequently openly admire the performer who has outwitted them.

COLLUSION

Trials are sometimes held between hopefuls from different stables for a major race. For example, a secret trial between contenders for the Stawell Easter Gift, the sport's pre-eminent race in Australia, saw the losing trialist run last in the final of this race. The deal on this occasion was that the losing trialist would be permitted to lay a predetermined bet at long odds on the winning one, who knew that part of the competition had been eliminated before arriving at the meeting. To be sure, this is collusion and cheating, but it is also a way of minimising risk. Both runners, from different stables, had put considerable work into getting prepared for the Stawell Gift. Much was at stake. They both increased the probability of making a return from their efforts by colluding to control the outcome of the event. As it turned out, the winning trialist went on to take out the major race and, with it, a sackful of money. The losing trialist also scored a hefty reward, from betting on himself to win his heat and semi-final as well as from the money he was allowed to bet on the race winner at long odds.

Collusive practices have been used to fix the outcome of races and have given a means for the better performed, known runners—often handicapped out of any significant chance of winning[15]—to fix races to make certain of a return for their efforts. Morrie Gilson had a good career on the professional track. His uncle, a Stawell Gift winner, had been a noted runner in the tough Depression years. In the following interview Morrie told me some of his deceased uncle's stories about race fixing in that period:

> *Gilson:* . . . he told about the races they fixed and the way they ruined betting, . . . he said they would pick a pea as they called it. And they'd, in the Depression days no-one had much money, SO they picked one to be the winner, and they'd go and back him . . . and in match-races too. I think match-races killed off the betting for a while because they'd set up a match race and pick one to win . . . He told me many tales of the great Phil Burke and those people.
>
> *Mewett:* And they were all involved in the fixing of races?
>
> *Gilson:* Yes.
>
> *Mewett:* And this was to make money from the bookies during the Depression?
>
> *Gilson:* Yes, to make sure they didn't gamble with their money and lose their money. . . . There's only one winner.
>
> *Mewett:* How did you make sure that the others didn't win?
>
> *Gilson:* Well, you'd go and take money off each of those and say right we'll back so and so as the pea. They'd [each] put in a quid.
>
> *Mewett:* Oh OK. To make sure the bookies kept up a reasonable price . . . it had to be staged in such a way that the punters were still putting money on the other runners?
>
> *Gilson:* Yes, well he had to only win by an inch, and it was a good finish.
>
> (taped interview)

Morrie's stories of his uncle's exploits demonstrate the necessity of the 'good finish'. Without this, and the illusion to punters that they lost their bets by the slightest of margins, the money that must be put on the other runners for the 'pea' to realise a good return from gambling winnings, would not be forthcoming: thus Morrie's claim that match-racing, in which cheating can be more difficult to conceal, discouraged punters from laying bets. Achieving a close finish suits all players. The officials, particularly the handicappers, are satisfied because it gives the appearance of them having done a good job in matching the abilities of the runners. The runners need to have the money coming in on other competitors for them to get their bets on at longish odds. And, for this to occur, the punters must think that they have a reasonable chance of placing a winning bet.

Collusion is not restricted to pacts between runners. One ex-runner told me of how he had survived through the Depression by being part of a bookmaker's 'team'. He would do the circuit of meetings with the bookmaker, running to their mutual advantage. Another ex-runner explained how a bookmaker had paid him a considerable sum (£100 in 1935) to 'run out' a competitor on whom he had set inappropriate odds and stood to make massive losses had this man won. Harry Boyle said that bookmakers approached him to let them know when his runners were not going to win. The idea is that the bookmaker then stretches out the odds that he offers on them in order to draw in more bets on known losing runners; the money taken on them is split between the bookmaker and the trainer. But Harry said that he knocked back these approaches, because, had he accepted, it may have become more difficult for him to have concealed from these bookmakers the races when one of his runners was to go-off.

Fixing races is not confined to the collusion between runners or with bookmakers. Allan Goddard is a runner from more recent years and a Stawell Gift winner. He told me of an instance when race organisers in another state were involved in the fixing and manipulation of events:

> *Goddard:* I went to [another state] one year for a 300 metre race and I was paid to come third.
>
> *Mewett:* So they [the organisers] actually set it up? Who they wanted to win?
>
> *Goddard:* It was their own race. They wanted somebody in the final, for instance, like a Stawell Gift winner. I didn't know who was going to win first place, but they didn't want me to win. So they said come third.
>
> (taped interview)

Manipulation of races by organisers can be an unpredictable part of the sport. My guess is that organisers are seldom responsible for the type of occurrence reported by Allan Goddard. It is the predictability of the cheating practice that marks the division between where clean cheating ends and dirty cheating begins. Clean cheating is anticipated and, done well, it can be appreciated. Moreover, getting a return from clean cheating still involves considerable effort, or 'work' as the expenditure of considerable time and effort is called. Work is put into the long hours of training as well as into the strategies devised to effect a win. Dirty cheating is when a relatively unpredictable advantage is gained by someone who has not put in the work.

THE UNMENTIONABLE

The more straightforward instances of dirty cheating include snooping, such as surreptitiously timing a trial, often from a hidden position.[16] Knowledge gained in this way can allow the snooper to take the longest betting odds on a runner and reap a considerable financial benefit without having put in the work. Many stories record how runners, ready to go off in a major race, turn up on the day only to find that they have 'lost the market', which is the term used to refer to someone else getting the best of the betting on them. Faced with a lost market, runners must decide whether to go-off as planned and accept the reduced pay-out if successful, or 'pull-up' and set themselves for another race.

At the heart of dirty cheating is the use of what is seen to be privileged knowledge to one's own advantage. Leo Rumsey did not make the winnings from the Stawell Gift that he had anticipated. Although he trained full-time in secret, his keep was met by a man who recognised his potential and wanted to make a gambling coup from Rumsey blasting onto the scene and winning this big race as a complete unknown. When this strategy of training hard but seldom competing is in play, it is common for the runner to trial against another who is competing on the circuit, to gauge what the hidden runner's performance might be. Les Michaels, his 'trial-horse', as the other runner is referred to, was a 'known' athlete, having scored some significant wins. According to Leo, this was when the problems for him started:

> Michaels was very, very greedy. . . he trained with me and he [Rumsey's sponsor] took him into his confidence and that was the worse thing that could ever have happened to us. He just got greedy. As a result of my ability—he had to find out whether I could produce it under pressure—so I used to train with Michaels. Anyway, there wasn't much he [Michaels] could do about me, he couldn't give me starts, and that was when the problem really started. We had blokes . . . would be

> standing there with a bit of paper, watching me run . . . Every time we had a trial, a tree moved . . . We didn't know how the word was getting out until something happened just before Stawell . . . We had to get away from Michaels. What had happened was he went to a place called . . . and run about 12 inside[17] with a gale behind him. But then he tried to give me a start and couldn't give me much . . . so he knew what we was doing. And then we had to drop him off because he was talking too much. This was when the trouble started. Really started. A [State] athletic official . . . he used to bet on the Stawell Gift a month before and all of a sudden a bet was laid. And the fellow was Eric Connelly . . . he laid the bet. . . . That in itself started a snowball type of effect so what we had to do then, we had to get away from Michaels. So, we then had to go and train and trial with [another runner] . . . in the meantime, the damage had been done. But, I've got to tell you this, Peter: I didn't know until 10 years later who had laid that bet. But we found out in the meantime that Les Michaels was sleeping with his [Connelly's] daughter, he was stopping with Eric Connelly, you know, and he just mentioned to Eric Connelly, 'If there's a world series next year, this bloke'll be in it'. And in the final trial we had, he [Michaels] tried to give me a three yard start and couldn't give it to me. I was equal to him. . . . Then it just snowballed and snowballed and snowballed. By the time that we got there [to Stawell], the price had gone off . . .
>
> (taped interview)

Many successful runners have seen the prospect of sought-after riches—and they are riches for people from the working class backgrounds of most professional runners disappear because others, some 'low down buggers' as one ex-runner referred to them, have made use of privileged information to take the cream of the betting market.

If someone from within the runner's own stable makes use of privileged information for their own advantage the hurt is deeply felt. A stable is supposed to act collectively, its members not revealing to others what takes place within it. The stables constitute professional runners' 'teams'. When a stable's runner goes-off, all members of the stable can benefit through collective betting on their representative. Runners in successful stables can expect a steady trickle of money in this way, with a major prize coming their way should they win a big race. A strong sense of camaraderie characterises the successful stables and with it occurs a reinforcement of the secrecy essential for its triumphs. The reality, however, is that leaks occur from stables, sometimes inadvertently and sometimes by design. Many trainers keep as much as they can to themselves, or share information only with their senior runners, to reduce the risk of a secret slipping out. But when members of a stable use privileged information to their own advantage, the resentment is real and the hurt is deeply felt. Harry Boyle was highly aggrieved that one of his runners had cheated by placing a bet on a fellow runner before the stable had laid its collective stake-money. When a runner is about to go-off, stable members usually pool their stake-money which is bet in the form of a 'plunge'—a well coordinated procedure in which several bookmakers are 'hit' simultaneously. If a member of the stable bets before the plunge, they can get the longest odds and privilege themselves at their stablemates' expense; they can also alert the bookmakers to the runner who is going-off.

Perhaps the most despised form of dirty cheating occurs when trainers cheat their runners. Many runners build close and very fond relationships with their trainers, some claiming that these mentors even changed their lives. The more prominent and well regarded trainers are known not just for their legendary prowess in preparing athletes and managing brilliant deceptions, but also for their honest dealings with their runners. But some trainers have cheated their wards. Greg Parker did not make as much money from his win of the Stawell Easter Gift as he had anticipated. Parker soon discovered, to his lasting anger, that he had been cheated by his trainer, Dan Gore. Other than the early bets taken by some Melbourne bookmakers, betting on the Stawell Gift opens on Good Friday evening, but some stables will not bet until the following morning, when the running starts, executing their plunge just before or during the running of the Gift heats. This is especially the case for those going into Stawell with a 'dark horse', a runner that others do not think to be a chance for the big race. By delaying the betting plunge, it is hoped that sufficient money will have been laid on other runners for the bookmakers not to shorten their odds too quickly when the stakes go on one's own competitor. Parker, a dark horse for the race, claimed that they had agreed to delay their plunge until the Saturday morning.

> *Parker:* . . . We had an agreement not to bet on the Friday night and they organised it so they would hit the betting ring on the Saturday morning before the heats. Unfortunately, the price was only . . . it opened at about 15 to 1 or something like that. Subsequently, we found out that Dan and—there was another fellow called Bernie Dawson, he was our punter, he was a professional punter. He had a lot more money than we had and he was going to take the odds and sling back. And Bernie, never saw him back. Unfortunately, Gore and Dawson got into the ring on the Friday night.
>
> *Mewett:* They took the odds?
>
> *Parker:* Bloody true. We . . . were still at Stawell when we actually found out. We had so many relatives in Stawell. . . . and it didn't take long . . . it came back to us that they [Gore and Dawson] were peeling off wads of notes and putting the money on on the Friday night. And Bernie Dawson was at the Dandenong trial—that was the final run before Stawell. He wanted to have a look and hold the clock on me.
>
> *Mewett:* Did he have a good knowledge of professional running?
>
> *Parker:* Oh yes.
>
> *Mewett:* Did you feel used?
>
> *Parker:* I certainly did. . . .
>
> *Mewett:* What [odds] did you open at [on Friday evening]?
>
> *Parker:* 60s I think.
>
> *Mewetti:* So there was quite a bit of money laid to take it down to [15s]
>
> *Parker:* Thousands of pounds. Thousands of pounds. And, of course, when the 'hit the ring' time came about [on Saturday morning], they put money on and the effect of the previous night's betting was well, and truly registered with the bookies at that stage, so it didn't take much money for them to drop it down really low.
>
> (taped interview)

Many years after the rort, Parker remained aggrieved at Gore's treatment of him. Other runners do not know how they lost the market, some surmise dirty cheating but are unwilling to voice their suspicions.

DISCOURSES

As Bourdieu (1978) has pointed out, the sports available for people to take-up result from the history of the activities' emergence and development; an individual cannot change this, he or she must choose between contemporaneous sports. A correlation exists between socioeconomic factors and the distribution of sports in a population, moreover. In part this linkage of class and sport arises from differences between people in their availability of spare time, economic capital and cultural capital, but it is essential also to take into account the different meanings given to the practice of their sports by specified sections of the population. These meanings derive from the dispositions born of particular class habituses; upper class sport is a very different thing from that of the lower classes (Bourdieu 1978: 834).

But the hegemonic power of the upper classes ensures that working class sports at least pay lip service to the ideology of fair play, even if, as in professional running, it is turned into a useful masking device for the concealment and deception that necessarily occurs. Publicly, the discourses of clean cheating present an image of a sport that is relatively free from corruption and shady dealings. Beneath the public image, these discourses, from the runners' and their trainers' points of view, are all about how to cheat; about how it is necessary to cheat to win; and about how others are cheating. Their concern is with deception, concealment, beating the handicapper, sowing false leads, and with detecting the subterfuges of others. The officials, from the same habitus as the runners, control the sport and impose penalties when they detect infringements of the rules. But the interesting aspect of the officials' discourse is that they know clean cheating is constitutive of the sport, so they attack the tip of the iceberg while disregarding the submerged mass. The third discourse centres on the tussle between runners and their trainers on one side, and the officials on the other. Tacit understandings about how the sport is constituted underpin an often unspoken complicity between these parties. The sport continues in a well-organised, seemingly amicable manner provided that these games-within-games are played by the unstated, informal rules. This complicity involves keeping the clean cheating to reasonable levels and maintaining the appearance of fair play essential to ensure the participation of a gambling public. Runners are aware that embarrassing the officials by flouting how well they have deceived the handicapper, for instance, will lead to retribution. The revenge may not be limited to the runner but can extend to all of the runners under the same trainer, because these mentors are major players in deception and concealment. Apart from finding a reason to fine or 'rub-out' (suspend) a runner who has embarrassed them, officials may penalise all the athletes in the runner's stable by not giving them expected handicap lifts. A fine line exists between working the sport to one's advantage and offending the officials. The largely unspoken discourse between runners and officials succeeds partly because the latter have come from within the sport, which ensures that all these participants share the same esoteric knowledge. But it is predicated on the shared meanings that all bring to the sport, meanings that derive from a working class habitus.

The participants in professional running bring with them the dispositions of their class habitus. Although this may account for a readiness to embrace this sport—to select it and participate in it from among those available—and for a predisposition towards the ways in which it is played out, it cannot fully explain what goes on within professional running, which has its own subculture, folklore and layers of esoteric knowledge. Although 'sport' as a category may form what Bourdieu (1978: 821) refers to as a 'field of competition', professional running produces a field in its own right. Despite their habitus disposing them towards this sport, there is much for neophytes to learn after entering it. That which is learned—and here it is necessary to consider the 'ways' constitutive of the sport, more so, perhaps, than the techniques of acquiring fitness and athletic skills—accords with aspects of the runners' social origins.

CONCLUSION

An ideology of fair play—a hegemonic imposition of the wealthy upper classes—has little to offer working class people. Fair play insofar as it exists occurs between those in specified alliances for specific ends. Fair play is expected in the dealings between members of the same professional running stable. Trainers sometimes form links to trial their runners against one another. To betray the trust cementing these often labile consociations of individuals and groups is underhand, it is dirty cheating.

Possibly sports people such as professional runners have a more realistic perspective on success than those struggling with ideas of fair play. They see people who have succeeded in business through sharp or shady practice, and they see those possibly using privileged information to strike it rich off the stock market. What is 'fair' about that? How does one succeed in an acquisitive capitalist society, if not by stacking the odds in one's favour? Clean cheating is all in the game—the sporting game that is simply a part of the game of life. This necessitates alliances with others, all of whom can benefit to some greater or lesser extent. When the deceptive ploys are being worked on people outside these alliances, the cheating is an accepted and anticipated part of play. Perhaps an irony of professional running is that the financial returns that may accrue from clean cheating hinge on the exercise of trust between those on the 'inside'. The unacceptable form of cheating occurs when someone within the alliance uses their privileged knowledge for their personal advantage.

Within professional running, working class athletes have manipulated chance through tactics involving secrecy, deception and the tactical concealment of ability. Done effectively, with the skill that eludes detection by others, it can result in a handsome payout, rewarding the opportunity costs of participation and providing a 'kick-on' for the person's post-sport career. The promise of a reward from the investment of time and effort in the sport justifies the opportunity costs necessarily incurred. The working classes have not been able to afford the dilettantism of amateurism. The model of pure competition is an ideology of the society at large as well of amateurism: embracing it involves more risk than the working classes can allow, it is a luxury that they cannot afford. For the less well off, risk-averse behaviour equates with the avoidance of penury. Cheating is the risk reduction strategy pertinent to the field of professional running. It occurs because the runners bring to the sport the risk-averse dispositions of their social origins.

Excerpted from Peter G. Mewett, "Discourses on Deception: Cheating in Professional Running" in *The Australian Journal of Anthropology* 13.3 (2002): 292–308.

NOTES

1. This research, conducted jointly with John Perry, was supported by grants from the Australian Research Council and from Deakin University.
2. 'Circle races' are those, from 400 metres upwards, that involve one or more full circuits around the running track.
3. See Radford's (2001) biography of Captain Barclay for accounts of cheating in prize-fights in Regency Britain.
4. Professional runners are mostly organised in close-knit groups called 'stables'. A stable usually is under the control of one 'trainer', although the occasional stable is run by two trainers.
5. I use the term 'mainstream athletics' to refer to the relatively recent development from the so-called 'amateur athletics' that dominated global track and field competition for a century. Mainstream athletics has the World Championships and the Olympic Games as its most prestigious meets.
6. I thank an anonymous reviewer for pointing out this difference between professional running and other forms of professional sport. Clearly, as the recent revelations about cricket testify, involvement with gambling may occur as a covert part of any sport. Also see Asinoff (1963) for an account of the infamous 'Black Sox' case in baseball.
7. Horse racing certainly continued as a gambling sport significantly supported by the upper classes, but whether these were the same people that

condemned plebeian gaming is a matter of conjecture—and an important area for historical research.

8. Amateurism emerged in the second half of the nineteenth century with the 'cult' of upper class athleticism associated with the more prestigious British private schools. Mangan (1981) has described the development of athleticism in these schools.
9. The poolroom 'hustlers' described by Polsky (1971) were also of lower-class origins. It is arguable whether the cheating that occurs in horse-racing (Scott 1968) can be understood in the same way, though.
10. A 'lift' is the term used to describe the acquisition of a lighter handicap. Handicaps are measured from 'scratch', so in a 100 metre race, for example, a person on a handicap of zero starts from scratch and runs the full 100 metres. Another runner, on a handicap of two metres, starts the race in front of the person on scratch and runs 98 metres to complete the race. However, if the runner is re-handicapped to 2.5 metres, which is referred to as getting a 'lift' of 0.5 metre, then 97.5 metres needs to be covered in the race. Conversely, a 'pull' refers to being moved to a harder handicap, so if the handicap was reduced (pulled) by 0.5 metre, to 1.5 metres, the runner would need to run 98.5 metres in the race.
11. The term 'blanket finish' comes from the image of being able to cover all of the close-finishing runners with a blanket.
12. Briefly, the betting on a race is assessed in terms of two variables: the price, or odds that can be obtained or runners and, second, the amount of money, or stake, that can be put on them. Long odds refers to winning more for a specified bet than short odds (for example: a bet laid at 20 to 1 stands to win five times more than one laid at 4 to 1). Bookmakers shorten odds as the bets laid against a runner increase, but the rate at which they shorten depends on the amount of money being laid against the other runners in the same race. If plenty of money is being taken against other runners, then the odds will shorten more slowly against a particular runner. Also, the more money being bet on a race, the more ready that bookmakers are to take larger stakes against runners before, perhaps, refusing to take any further bets against them. The objective in betting is to lay the total stake money at the longest average odds that can be achieved.
13. The 'cream' of the 'market' refers to the longest odds given by the bookmakers against a specified runner in a race. If the betting on a runner opens at 50 to 1, then the betters getting those odds have taken the cream of the market, because the odds will shorten quickly when money is laid against that competitor. The objective of a runner and stable is to get the cream for themselves.
14. Short-striding involves putting in shorter than normal steps while moving the legs at the same speed. Done effectively, it gives the appearance of running at full speed.
15. A win involves the re-handicapping of the runner to a tighter mark. Also a different handicapping logic comes into play following a win, because the bigger the monetary value of the race won, the bigger the pull received by the winning runner. Many winners of major races have been handicapped out of further wins.
16. See Mewett (2000) and Mewett with Perry (1997) for some examples of snooping and of the precautions taken by trainers when training their runners.
17. A measure of runners' abilities is how far they can run 'inside' or 'outside' 'evens'. Evens refers to 'even time', which is 10 seconds for the 100 yards, for example. An even-time runner is a good athlete. But the more exceptional athletes–those sprinters capable of running sub-10 seconds over 100 yards, for instance—are referred to as running inside evens, their actual performance being measured as the number of 'yards inside [even-time]'. A similar logic applies to slower runners, those who are 'outside evens'.

REFERENCES

Anonymous, 1868. Pedestrianism in Britain. *Every Saturday* 6:46–50.

Asinoff, E. 1963. *Eight Men Out: the Black Sox and the 1919 World Series.* New York: Holt Rinehart and Winston.

Bourdieu, P. 1978. Sport and social class. *Social Science Information* 17:819–40.

Bourdieu, P. 1986. *Distinction: A Social Critique of the Judgement of Taste* (transl. R. Nice). London: Routledge.

Bull, J. 1959. *The Spiked Shoe,* Melbourne: National Press Pty. Ltd.

Mangan, J.A. 1981. *Athleticism in the Victorian and Edwardian Public School: The Emergence and Consolidation of an Educational Ideology.* Cambridge: Cambridge University Press.

Mewett, P.G. 1999. The emergence of athletics in colonial Victoria. In R. Hay *et al. Sport in History Reader.* Geelong: Faculty of Arts, Deakin University.

Mewett, P.G. 2000. History in the making and the making of history: stories and the social construction of a sport. *Sporting Traditions* 17:1–17.

Mewett, P.G. with J. Perry, 1997. A sporting chance? The 'dark horse strategy' and winning in professional running. *Sociology of Sport Journal* 14:121–42.

Polsky, N. 1971. *Hustlers. Beats and Others.* Harmondsworth: Penguin.

Radford, P. 2001. *The Celebrated Captain Barclay: Sport, Money and Fame in Regency Britain.* London: Headline.

Scott, M.B. 1968. *The Racing Game.* Chicago: Aldine.

Vamplew, W. 1988. Odds against: the punter's lot is not a happy one. *Sporting Traditions* 5:51–60.

Wilson, G. 1815. *Memoirs of the Life and the Exploits of G. Wilson, the Celebrated Pedestrian, who Walked 750 Miles in 15 Days. etc.* London: Dean and Munday.

CHAPTER 28

Male Athletes, Injuries, and Violence

Michael A. Messner

MEN'S VIOLENCE AGAINST OTHER MEN

In February 2000, a professional basketball player with the San Antonio Spurs, Sean Elliott, announced his impending return to play following a life-threatening illness that resulted in a kidney transplant. Elliott's return was met with considerable media discussion and debate about whether it was appropriate for him to return to play at all, given the grave risks he might face should he receive a blow to his kidney. Lakers star Kobe Bryant, when asked how he would respond to playing against Elliott, said, "As soon as he steps on the court, that means he's healthy. I'll have no problem putting an elbow in his gut."[1] This statement spoke to the routine nature of bodily contact and aggression in basketball. Players and coaches know that in order to be competitive enough to win, they will need to "put their bodies on" opposing players in ways that could cause bodily harm. In football and ice hockey, the overt aggression against other players is even more intense. One former National Football League player told me that before a playoff game, his coach implored his defensive players to hurt the opposing star running back if they had an opportunity to do it. This is apparently not that unusual. A 1998 *Sports Illustrated* cover story on "the NFL's dirtiest players" admiringly described San Francisco 49ers guard Kevin Gogan's tendencies, sometimes even after a play has been whistled dead, to "punch, kick, trip, cut-block, sit on or attempt to neuter the man lined up across from him." Gogan's coach, Steve Mariuchi, expressed his approval: "Coaches want tough guys, players who love to hit and fly around and do things that are mean and nasty. Not everyone can be like that, but if you can have one or two players who are a little overaggressive, that's great."[2]

Bodily aggression toward opponents on the field or court, whether of the "routine" kind that takes place within the rules or of the "dirty" illegal kind that aims to injure an opponent, is often assumed to end when the players cross the boundaries back into the "real world." The story of the "gentle giant" football player who growls, curses, and tears opponents limb-from-limb on the field but is a kind and caring teddy bear off the field is part of our national lore. But is aggression on the field against other men related to aggression off the field? Former Dallas Cowboy football star John Niland now says that he and many of his former teammates were involved in drugs, alcohol, and spouse abuse:

> I'm not going to name names, but my wife at the time knew of other wives who were

> abused. . . . We're paid to be violent. We're paid to beat up on the guy across from you. When you're in the game and your emotions are so high and the aura of the whole environment is so unbelievable. When the game's over, technically, it's to be turned off. But you can't. . . . Quite frankly, if you got every player who did drugs or alcohol or played stoned or who was a spousal abuser, you couldn't field an NFL team. It's still going on.[3]

And consider a comment by NBA coach Pat Riley, of the Miami Heat. Bemoaning an unusually long break between his team's playoff games, Riley said, "Several days between games allows a player to become a person. During the playoffs, you don't want players to be people."[4] If it is acknowledged that the supposedly civilizing influences of a player's life outside sports can (negatively!) humanize him, then doesn't it follow that it might also work the other way—that dehumanizing attitudes and experiences within sports might spill over into life outside sports? Indeed, sport studies scholars have found evidence that points to this conclusion. Jeffrey Segrave and his colleagues found that Canadian minor league (fifteen- and sixteen-year-old) ice hockey players were more likely than nonathletes to engage in physically violent acts of delinquency.[5] And sociologist Howard Nixon found that male athletes in team contact sports, especially if they reported having intentionally hurt other athletes on the field, were more likely to hurt others outside sports.[6] To understand this connection, it is necessary to look more closely at the ways that boys and men develop their identities and relationships within the culture of sport.

BOYS' EMBODIMENTS OF TOUGHNESS

In an earlier book, *Power at Play*, I explored the meanings of athletic participation through life-history interviews with male former athletes. One man, a former NFL defensive back who had been known and rewarded for his fierce and violent "hits," had injured many opposing players in his career, some seriously. I asked him to describe how he felt the first time he had hurt someone on a football field, and he said that hitting and hurting people had bothered him at first:

> When I first started playing, if I would hit a guy hard and he wouldn't get up, it would bother me. [But] when I was a sophomore in high school, first game, I knocked out two quarterbacks, and people loved it. The coach loved it. Everybody loved it. You never stop feeling sorry for [your injured opponent]. If somebody doesn't get up, you want him to get up. You hope the wind's just knocked out of him or something. The more you play, though, the more you realize that it is just a part of the game—somebody's gonna get hurt. It could be you, it could be him—most of the time it's better if it's him. So, you know, you just go out and play your game.[7]

This statement describes a contextual normalization of violence: "you realize it is just a part of the game." It also illustrates an emotional process, a group-based suppression of empathy for the pain and injury that one might cause one's opponent. Most children are taught that it is unacceptable to hurt other people. In order to get athletes (or soldiers) to be willing and able to inflict harm on others, the opponent must be objectified as the enemy, and the situation must be defined as "either him or me": "somebody's gonna get hurt. It could be you, it could be him—most of the time it's better if it's him." The most obvious force behind this suppression of empathy is the rewards one gets for the successful utilization of violence: "The coach loved it. Everybody loved it." And it's not just this sort of immediate positive reinforcement. The man quoted above, for instance, received a college scholarship, all-America honors, and eventually all-pro status in the NFL.

But rewards do not tell the whole story behind athletes' suppression of empathy for their opponents. In fact, when I probed athletes' early experiences and motivations in sports, I found stories not of victories, trophies, and public adulation. Instead, these men were more likely to drop into stories of early connection with others, especially fathers, older brothers, uncles, and eventually same-aged male peers. Some found sports to be the primary, sometimes the *only*, site in which they experienced connection with their otherwise emotionally or physically absent fathers. Many also said that they felt alone, unsure of themselves, cut off from others and that it was through sports participation, especially for those who had some early successes and received attention for these successes, that they found acceptance.

Why sports? An important part of the answer is that most boys' early experiences teach them to appear to be invulnerable. This means, don't show any fear or weakness. And little boys begin to learn this at a very young age. Learning to embody and display toughness, even if it is a veneer that covers up a quivering insecurity inside, can be a survival skill that helps boys stay safe in a hostile environment. In his eloquent description of street life for African American boys in poor communities, Geoffrey Canada describes how learning to fight, or at least displaying an attitude that you are ready and willing to fight, was necessary. Losing a fight, and "taking it like a man," was far better (and ultimately *safer*) than being labeled a coward.[8] Learning early to mask one's vulnerability behind displays of toughness may help boys survive on the street, but it can also contribute to boys (and, later, men) having difficulties in developing and maintaining emotional connection with others. Though in an emotional straitjacket, boys and men retain a human need to connect with others. And for those who have some early athletic successes, sports can become an especially salient context in which to receive a certain kind of closeness with others.[9]

A key, then, to understanding male athletes' commitment to athletic careers lies in understanding their underlying need for connection with other people and the ways that society thwarts emotional connection for boys. And there is often an additional layer of emotional salience to sports participation for boys and men from poor and ethnic minority backgrounds. African American men, in particular, when asked about their early motivations in sports, were far more likely to drop into a discussion of "respect" than other men were. Early sports successes, for them, offered the discovery of a group context in which they could earn the respect of family members, friends, schoolmates, and communities. White middle-class men in my study did not talk about the importance of respect in the same way. This is because African American boys and young men are far more likely to face a daily experience of being *suspected* (of a potential crime of violence, of shoplifting in a store, of cheating on an exam, etc.) than of being *respected*. Schools are a major source of African American boys' experience of disrespect. Sociologist Ann Arnett Ferguson observes that elementary school teachers and administrators often treat African American boys as "troublemakers" who are already "beyond redemption."[10] By contrast, most white middle-class boys and men begin each day and enter each situation with a certain baseline, taken-for-granted level of respect that includes an assumption of our competence and trustworthiness, which is then ours to lose. To receive the benefits of this baseline of respect, we simply have to show up. This respect is not earned; rather, it is an unacknowledged but very real benefit that Peggy MacIntosh has called "the invisible Knapsack of White Privilege."[11]

In short, boys' relational capacities and opportunities for expressions of emotional vulnerability tend to be thwarted and suppressed. Some boys find in their early athletic experiences that sports offer them a context in which they can connect emotionally and gain the respect of others. Ironically though, as one moves further away from the playful experiences of childhood into the competitive, routinized institutional context of athletic careers, one learns that in order to continue to receive approval and respect, one must be a winner. And to be a winner, you must be ready and willing to suppress your empathy for other athletes. In the context of sports careers, you do not experience your body as a means of connecting intimately with others; rather, your body becomes a weapon, which you train to defeat an objectified, dehumanized opponent.[12] It's a dog-eat-dog world out there; you gotta have that killer instinct.

BOOZE, BONDING, AND FIGHTING

The lessons learned on the field are important, but athletes also spend large amounts of time not playing sports—in classrooms, at parties, and at other social events with friends. And the kinds of relational patterns that boys and men learn on athletic teams sometimes spill over into these nonsport contexts. Timothy Curry found that college male athletes described life at the campus bar as one of "drinking, picking up women, and getting into fights":

> . . . the athletes would try to "own" every bar they frequented. Often, this meant staging bar fights to demonstrate their power. Several of the athletes were good fighters, and they were typically the ones to start the fight. Often, these fighters would pick out a particular victim based on the fact that he looked "queer." The victim need not do anything provocative—sometimes victims were chosen because "they didn't want to fight." After the first punch was thrown, others in the group would enter in, either throwing punches of their own or attempting to break up the fight. The team always backed up its most aggressive members, so that the victim seldom had much of a chance.[13]

Since the athletes were of such high status, Curry explains, they rarely got into any trouble from this fighting. Instead, most often the victim was thrown out of the bar by the bouncer, and the players would be given free drinks from the bartender and would celebrate their "victory" as "a way of building team cohesion and expressing masculine courage."[14] Alcohol consumption is obviously a key part of this process.[15] The athletes would compete among themselves to see who could consume the most free (or nearly free) drinks at the bar. The heavy drinking, an athlete told Curry, is "to prove you're not a pussy."[16]

Curry's description of the sports bar scene mirrors the interactional dynamics of male peer groups that I described earlier concerning violence against women. In the sports bar, we see a premeditated incident of violence, staged to build in-group cohesion (albeit this time in a public place, with a male victim). The victim is a vulnerable-looking man, who is degraded by the group as looking "queer." As a result, the line between "the men," who are inside the group, and others outside the group, be they "queers" or women who are marked for later sexual conquest, is created and reinforced both by the collective act of violence and by the public approval it receives.

This sort of homophobic bullying of nonathlete boys is also a common occurrence on high school and college campuses. A window was opened on this dynamic in 1999, when Eric Harris and Dylan Klebold, armed to the teeth, entered Columbine High School, in Littleton, Colorado, and proceeded to kill thirteen and wound twenty-one of their schoolmates and teachers. "All jocks stand up," the killers yelled when they began their slaughter. "Anybody with a white hat or a shirt with a sports emblem on it is dead."[17] Much of the aftermath of this tragedy consisted of media and experts discussing the origins of the anger and violence expressed by the two boys, dubbed "the trenchcoat mafia," and how in the future to predict and prevent such individuals from violently "going off." Very little discussion centered on the ways that such outsider boys are so commonly targeted as the "nerds" and symbolic "pussies" that serve as the foil for high-status athletes' construction of their own in-group status. Indeed, Columbine High School was like many other high schools in this regard. There was a "tough little group" of about seven guys, mostly football players and wrestlers, who were known for leading painfully degrading hazing rites among younger male athletes, for harassing and physically abusing girls, for destroying property, and basically getting away with it all. They also abused the outsider boys in the "trenchcoat mafia," one of whom was shoved into a locker by three football players who taunted him, "Fag, what are you looking at?"

Homophobic taunting and bullying does not always result in such serious physical violence.[18] But it is a common part of the central dynamic of male peer groups. The role homophobia plays within male peer groups is akin to Elmer's glue being used to bond two pieces of wood. Once the white glue is dried, it becomes clear, nearly invisible, and it acts simultaneously (and paradoxically) as a bond that holds the two pieces of wood together and as an invisible barrier, or shield, that keeps the two pieces of wood from actually touching each other. Homophobia works the same way. While it bonds boys together as part of the in-group (we are men, they are faggots), it also places clear limits on the extent to which boys and men can make themselves vulnerable to one another (don't get too close, emotionally or physically, or you will make yourself vulnerable). And this, again, is where alcohol often comes in. While it is part of the system of competitive status-enhancement to drink a lot of alcohol, young men also find that one of the short-term benefits of drinking with the guys is that it loosens the constraints on verbal and emotional expression.[19] The key desires underlying boys' and men's affiliations with each other—acceptance, emotional connection, respect—seem more accessible after a few drinks. The constraints normally placed around expressions of physical closeness among men are often relaxed after a few drinks; the arms draped around a teammate's shoulders and the "I love you, man" expression can be conveniently forgotten in the fog of tomorrow's hangover.

In sum, boys in central, aggressive team sports learn early to use their bodies as weapons against an objectified opponent. The empathy that one might be expected to feel for the victim of one's punches, hits, or tackles is suppressed by the experience of being rewarded (with status and prestige, and also with connection and respect) for the successful utilization of one's body against other men. Empathy for one's opponent is also suppressed through the shared contextual ethic that injury is an expected part of the game. These on-the-field values and practices are mutually constitutive of the off-the-field peer group dynamics, whereby the boundaries of the in-group are constructed through homophobia and violence directed (verbally and sometimes physically) against boys and men who are outside the group.

MALE ATHLETES' VIOLENCE AGAINST THEMSELVES

In June 2000, future Hall of Fame quarterback Steve Young ended several months of speculation by announcing his retirement after fifteen years of professional football. Actually, he had played his last down of football ten months earlier, when a "knock out" hit by an opposing player caused Young's fourth concussion in three years. "I'll miss many things," said Young. "What I won't miss are the hits that made my body tingle."[20] Young's announcement was not surprising. In fact, many had wondered why it took him so long to retire, given the mounting evidence concerning the dangerous cumulative effects of head injuries.[21] But Young's desire to continue playing must be seen in the context of an entire career in which he was rewarded for taking tremendous risks on the football field, playing hurt and with reckless abandon. Steve Young is not unusual in this respect. In November 2000, Denver Broncos quarterback Brian Griese suffered a shoulder separation in the first half of the game. Told by team doctors that he had a third-degree separation, the most severe type, he took a painkilling injection and returned to the game to lead his team to victory.

Football players live with the knowledge that small and moderate injuries are an expected outcome of the game and that a serious, career-ending or even life-threatening injury is always a possibility. Indeed, during the 1999 NFL season, 364 injuries were serious enough for a player to miss at least one game. Knee injuries (122) and ankle injuries (52) were the most common. Eleven were concussions.[22] In U.S. high schools, by far the greatest number of fatal, disabling, and serious sports injuries are suffered by football players (though the injury rates per hundred thousand participants are actually higher in ice hockey and gymnastics).[23] Among children, falls and sports-related injuries are now the leading causes of hospital stays and emergency room visits.[24] A survey of hospital emergency rooms and medical clinics in 1997 found a staggering number of sports injuries among U.S. children fourteen years old and under, led by bicycling (901,716 injuries), basketball (574,434), football (448,244), baseball (252,665), and soccer (227,157).[25] In Canada, injuries—a substantial proportion of which are head, neck, and cervical spinal injuries—among children ice hockey players are also escalating.[26]

THE BODY AS MACHINE

Several years ago, I was watching a football game on television with a friend at his house. A big fan, he knew that his team had to win this game to secure home field advantage for the playoffs. Suddenly, the announcer observed that a key player on my friend's team was hurt. The camera focused on the player, slowly walking off the field and looking at his hand with a puzzled look on his face. His index finger, it turned out, was dislocated and sticking out sideways at a ninety-degree angle. "Oh, good," my friend sighed in relief. "It's only his finger—he can still play." Indeed, a few plays later, the player was back on the field, his hand taped up (and presumably popped back into place by the trainer, and perhaps injected with painkiller). What struck me about this moment was how normal it seemed within the context of football. Announcers, coaches, other players, and fans like my friend all fully expected this man to "suck it up" and get back out there and play. We all have incredibly high expectations of football players' (and indeed, of other professional, college, and even high school athletes') willingness and ability to cope with pain, to play hurt, often risking their long-term health. Injuries and pain levels that in other contexts would result in emergency-room visits, home bed rest, and time off work or school are considered a normal part of the workday for many athletes.

I was struck by the depth to which athletes internalize these cultural standards to endure pain when I interviewed former athletes for *Power at Play*. One man, a former major league baseball player, described an incredible litany of injuries and rehabilitations that spanned not only the everyday aches and bruises that one would expect a catcher to endure but also year after year of ankle, knee, shoulder, neck, and spinal injuries that required several surgeries. In particular, he played out the second half of one season with daily injections of painkillers and cortisone in a shoulder that he knew would require surgery. Players routinely decide to "play hurt," to "give their bodies up for the team" in this way, even with the full knowledge that they are doing so at the risk of long-term disability. But when this man's eleven-year pro baseball career finally came to an end, he described it as a "shock. . . . I had felt that the way I had conditioned myself and taken care of myself that I would play until I was thirty-seven, thirty-eight."[27] Nobody could listen to this man's story and not agree that he had worked very hard and been very dedicated to his craft. But to describe the way he had lived his life as taking care of himself seemed to me to express a particularly alienated relationship to his own body. He, like many other athletes, had a wide range of knowledge about his body. However, this self-knowledge was in some ways shallow; it was not an expansive sense of his body as a living organism, as a self that connects in healthy ways with others and with one's environment.[28] Rather, it was a self-knowledge firmly bounded within an instrumental view of one's body as a machine, or a tool, to be built, disciplined, used (and, if necessary, used up) to get a job done.

This kind of self-knowledge—what psychologist William Pollack calls the "hardening of boys"—starts early in life, especially for athletes.[29] Boys learn that to show pain and vulnerability risks their being seen as "soft," and they know from the media, from coaches, and from their peers that this is a very bad thing. Instead, they learn that they can hope to gain access to high status, privilege, respect, and connection with others if they conform to what sociologist Don Sabo calls "the pain principle," a cultural ideal that demands a suppression of self-empathy and a willingness to take pain and take risks.[30]

Why are so many boys and men willing to take such risks? Again, we must look to the young male's embeddedness in social groups, and again, homophobia and misogyny are key enforcement mechanisms for conformity. The boy who whines about his pain and appears not to be willing to play hurt risks being positioned by the group as the symbolic "sissy" or "faggot" who won't "suck it up and take it like a man for the good of the team." One man I interviewed, for instance, told me that in high school, when he decided not to play in a big game because of an injury, his coach accused him of faking it. And as he sat in the whirlpool nursing his injury, a teammate came in and yelled at him, "You fucking pussy!"[31] Canadian sport studies scholar Philip White and his colleagues cite a similar example of an ice hockey player who, returning to play after a serious knee injury, was told by teammates "not to ice the swelling and not to 'be a pussy.'"[32]

The fear of being seen by the team as less than a man is not the only reason an athlete will play hurt, though. As pro football player Tim Green wrote in his illuminating book:

> Doctors don't coerce players into going out on the field. They don't have to. Players have been conveniently conditioned their entire lives to take the pain and put bodies at risk. Players beg doctors for needles that numb and drugs that reduce swelling and pain. . . . Taking the needle is something NFL players are proud to have done. It is a badge of honor, not unlike the military's Purple Heart. It means you were in the middle of the action and you took a hit. Taking the needle in the NFL also lets everyone know that you'd do anything to play the game. It demonstrates a complete

> disregard for one's well-being that is admired in the NFL between players.[33]

Green's statement—that demonstrating a complete disregard for one's well-being is so admired in the NFL among players—speaks volumes not just about the normalization of pain and injury in pro football but also about ways that bodily risk and endurance of pain serve as masculine performances that bring acceptance and respect among one's peers. Indeed, writing more generally about men's (often dangerous) health behaviors, Will Courtenay has argued that "health behaviors are used in daily interactions in the social structuring of gender and power. . . . The social practices that undermine men's health are often the signifiers of masculinity and the instruments that men use in the negotiation of social power and status."[34] In short, in the context of the athletic team, risking one's health by playing hurt is more than a way to avoid misogynist or homophobic ridicule; it is also a way of "performing" a highly honored form of masculinity.

There are concrete rewards—status, prestige, public adulation, scholarships, and even money—for men who are willing to pay the price. But we must also remember that underlying men's performances for each other is a powerful need to belong, to connect, to be respected. In refusing to play hurt, especially in the context of a team sport, a player risks losing the tenuous but powerful connection he has with the male group. Given both the negative enforcement mechanisms and the positive rewards a player might expect from choosing to play hurt, it should surprise us more when a player decides *not* to risk his long-term health, by refusing the needle, sitting down, and saying "no más."[35]

Excerpted from Michael A. Messner, "Playing the Center: The Triad of Violence in Men's Sports" in *Taking the Field: Women, Men, and Sports*.

NOTES

1. "*They* Said It: Kobe Bryant."
2. Silver, "Dirty Dogs."
3. Glauber, "We're Paid to Be Violent."
4. "Quotebook," *Los Angeles Times*.
5. Segrave, Moreau, and Hastad, "An Investigation into the Relationship between Ice Hockey Participation and Delinquency."
6. Nixon, "Gender, Sport, and Aggressive Behavior outside Sport."
7. Messner, *Power at Play*, 65–66.
8. Canada, *Fist Stick Knife Gun*.
9. I develop this line of argument in much more depth in *Power at Play*, where I argue that the specific kind of connection that boys and men experience in sports is a distant and thus "emotionally safe" form of connection. This has (mostly negative) ramifications for the development of friendships, for intimate relations with women, and for athletes' retirement and disengagement from sports. Psychologist William Pollack reaches a similar conclusion, arguing that boys often find sports to be one place where they find emotional connection. Pollack concedes that "the positive benefits to boys dim when sports cease to be played"; still, he tends to overstate the benefits of sports and ignores the range of social-scientific studies of sport that point to negative outcomes. Pollack, *Real Boys*, 273.
10. Ferguson illustrates how dynamics of gender and race in public schools serve as self-fulfilling prophecies, tracking African American boys into failure in the classroom, into the school's "punishment room," and ultimately (and inevitably, according to some of the teachers) into the criminal justice system. Ferguson, *Bad Boys*.
11. MacIntosh, "White Privilege."
12. Philosopher Brian Pronger has argued that an oppressive territorialization of the male body, which closes off intimate and erotic connection with other bodies and channels desire into violent directions, is the key outcome of modern sport, which he sees as a major expression of fascism. Pronger, "Outta My Endzone"; Pronger, "Homosexuality and Sport."
13. Curry, "Booze and Bar Fights," 168, 169–70.
14. Ibid., 170.
15. Several studies have shown that college male athletes and fraternity members tend to have higher rates of alcohol consumption than other

college students, including more drinks per week and higher rates of binge drinking. Boswell and Spade, "Fraternities and Collegiate Gang Rape"; Leichliter et al., "Alcohol Use and Related Consequences among Students with Varying Levels of Involvement in College Athletics." A study of teen athletes found that male and female teen athletes are no more likely to drink than nonathletes, but "highly involved athletes" are more likely to binge drink than nonathletes. Miller et al., *The Women's Sports Foundation Report.*

16. Curry, "Booze and Bar Fights," 169.
17. Adams and Russakoff, "At Columbine High, a Darker Picture Emerges."
18. Indeed, Messerschmidt points out that although many boys are challenged by bullying, not all respond with violence. Boys' responses to bullying vary, and this variance can be explained by boys' being differently situated in family, school, and peer contexts. Messerschmidt, *Nine Lives.*
19. As Rocco L. Capraro puts it, ". . . college men's drinking appears to be profoundly paradoxical. . . . [They drink] not only to enact male privilege but also to help them negotiate the emotional hazards of being a man in contemporary American college." Capraro, "Why College Men Drink," 307.
20. Young, "Young at Heart," 61.
21. The extent of brain damage to boxers has been well documented for many years. Stories of champions and top contenders suffering from dementia pugilistica (a medical term that describes a malady that used to be called punch-drunk) and other forms of boxing-induced brain damage, such as Floyd Patterson, Muhammad Ali, Jerry Quarry, Sugar Ray Robinson, and Wilfredo Benitez are only the most recent high-profile examples of the logical outcome of boxing. These and other cases led to the American Medical Association in 1986 calling for a ban on boxing. More recent research has increased awareness of the danger and extent of head injuries in other sports, especially football and soccer. Crosset sites recent studies that note a connection between men's head injuries and their violence against women: ". . . batterers are more likely to have sustained moderate or severe head injuries than nonbatterers. . . . A history of significant head injury increased the chances of marital violence sixfold. . . . Like alcohol consumption, head injury is not the direct cause of violence against women but clearly one that may play a role in some athlete violence against women." Crosset, "Athletic Affiliation and "Violence against Women," 160.
22. These statistics, of course, do not include the much larger number of routine, smaller injuries that do not result in a player sitting out a game. Gutierrez and Mitchell, "Pain Game."
23. Young and White, "Researching Sports Injury."
24. Dwyer Brust, Roberts, and Leonard, "Gladiators on Ice."
25. As reported in Gold and Weber, "Youth Sports Grind Is Tough on Body, Spirit."
26. Dwyer Brust, Roberts, and Leonard, "Gladiators on Ice," 27.
27. Messner, *Power at Play*, 122–23.
28. Brian Pronger has written about sport as a disciplinary practice particular to modernity, through which men learn to close off their bodies to connection with others. Instead, the body is experienced as a means of overcoming others, Pronger, "Outta My Endzone."
29. Pollack, *Real Boys.*
30. Sabo, "Pigskin, Patriarchy and Pain." The pain principle in sport can also be seen as paradigmatic of (and indeed, a pedagogy for) a more general cultural view of men's instrumental orientations to their own bodies. A few scholars have recently pointed to gender-related health patterns among men that help to explain the fact that, on average, men die seven years earlier than women do and have higher death rates from suicide, heart disease, accidents, and other major killers. Research points to the conclusion that these health risks among men are closely correlated with boys' and men's conformity to narrow conceptions of masculinity that include risk taking, violence, and instrumental orientations to the body. For excellent general overviews, see Sabo and Gordon, eds., *Men's Health and Illness*; and Courtenay, "Constructions of Masculinity and Their Influence on Men's Well-Being." Taking this observation to a different level, scholars have pointed out how different groups of men—broken down by social class, race-ethnicity, sexual orientation, age, and so forth—have very different levels of vulnerability to certain diseases and dangers. See, for instance, Staples, "Health among African American Males."
31. Messner, *Power at Play*, 72.
32. White, Young, and McTeer, "Sport, Masculinity, and the Injured Body," 171.
33. Green, *The Dark Side of the Game*, 215, 125.
34. Courtenay, "Constructions of Masculinity and Their Influence on Men's Well-Being," 1385.
35. The "no más" reference is to the famous 1980 welterweight championship fight between Roberto Duran and Sugar Ray Leonard. Feeling that he was losing the fight, Duran refused to return to the ring for a new round, saying, "No más." He was roundly criticized for quitting instead of continuing the fight until he was knocked out. I critically examined this idea that boxers must fight until the very end in Messner, "Why Rocky III?"

REFERENCES

Adams, Lorraine, and Dale Russakoff. "At Columbine High, a Darker Picture Emerges: Were Athletes Given Preferential Treatment and Allowed to Misbehave with Impunity?" *Washington Post National Weekly Edition*, June 21, 1999, 29.

Boswell, A. Ayres, and Joan Z. Spade. "Fraternities and Collegiate Gang Rape: Why Some Fraternities Are More Dangerous Places for Women." *Gender & Society* 10 (1966): 133–47.

Canada, Geoffrey. *Fist Stick Knife Gun*. Boston: Beacon Press, 1995.

Capraro, Rocco L. "Why College Men Drink: Alcohol, Adventure, and the Paradox of Masculinity." *Journal of American Collage Health* 48 (2000): 307–15.

——. "Constructions of Masculinity and Their Influence on Men's Well-Being: A Theory of Gender and Health." *Social Science and Medicine* 50 (2000): 1385–401.

——. "Athletic Affiliation and Violence against Women: Toward a Structural Prevention Project." In *Masculinities, Gender Relations, and Sport*, ed. Jim McKay, Michael A. Messner, and Donald F. Sabo, 147–61. Thousand Oaks, Calif.: Sage Publications, 2000.

——. "Booze and Bar Fights: A Journey to the Dark Side of College Athletics." In *Masculinities, Gender Relations, and Sport*, ed. Jim McKay, Michael A. Messner, and Donald F. Sabo, 162–75. Thousand Oaks, Calif.: Sage Publications, 2000.

Dwyer Brust, Janny, MPH, William O. Roberts, MD, and Barbara J. Leonard, Ph.D. "Gladiators on Ice: An Overview of Ice Hockey Injuries in Youth." *Medical Journal of Allina* 5 (1996): 26–30.

Ferguson, Ann Arnett. *Bad Boys: Public Schools in the Making of Black Masculinity*. Ann Arbor: University of Michigan Press, 2000.

Glauber, Bob. "We're Paid to Be Violent: Cost Was High for Ex-Dallas Star John Niland." *Newsday*, Sunday, January 12, 1997, B8, B25.

Gold, Scott, and Tracy Weber. "Youth Sports Grind Is Tough on Body, Spirit." *Los Angeles Times*, February 28, 2000, A1.

Green, Tim. *The Dark Side of the Game: My Life in the NFL*. New York: Warner Books, 1996.

Gutierrez, Paul, and Houston Mitchell. "Pain Game." *Los Angeles Times*, January 25, 2000, D1.

MacIntosh, Peggy. "White Privilege: Unpacking the Invisible Knapsack." In *Gender through the Prism of Difference*, ed. Maxine Baca Zinn, Pierrette Hondagneu-Sotelo, and Michael A. Messner, 247–50. 2d ed. Boston: Allyn and Bacon, 2000.

——. *Nine Lives: Adolescent Masculinities, the Body, and Violence*. Boulder, Colo.: Westview Press. 2000.

——. *Power at Play: Sports and the Problem of Masculinity*. Boston: Beacon Press 1992.

——. "Why Rocky III?" In Michael A. Messner and Donald F. Sabo, *Sex, Violence and Power in Sports: Rethinking Masculinity*, 74–81. Freedom, Calif.: Crossing Press, 1994.

Miller, Kathleen, E., Donald F. Sabo, Merrill J. Melnick, Michael P. Ferrell, and Grace M. Barnes. *The Women's Foundation Report: Health Risks and the Teen Athlete*. East Meadow, N.Y.: "Women's Sports Foundation, 2000.

Nixon, Howard L. II. "Gender, Sport, and Aggressive Behavior outside Sports." *Journal of Sport and Social Issues* 21 (1997): 379–91

Pollack, William. *Real Boys: Rescuing Our Sons from the Myths of Boyhood*. New York: Henry Holt, 1998.

Pronger, Brian. "Outta My Endzone: Sport and the Territorial Anus." *Journal of Sport and Social Issues* 23 (1999): 373–89.

——. "Homosexuality and Sport Who's Winning?" In *Masculinities, Gender Relations, and Sport*, ed. Jim McKay, Michael A. Messner, and Donald F. Sabo, 222–44. Thousand Oaks, Calif.: Sage Publications, 2000.

"Quotebook." *Los Angeles Times*, May 11, 2000, D-2.

——. "Pigskin, Patriarchy and Pain." In Michael A. Messner and Donald F. Sabo, *Sex, Violence and Power in Sport: Rethinking Masculinity*, 82–88. Freedom, Calif.: Crossing Press, 1994.

Sabo, Donald, and David F. Gordon, eds. *Men's Health and Illness: Gender, Power, and the Body*. Thousand Oaks, Calif.: Sage Publications, 1995.

Segrave, Jeffrey, Claude Moreau, and Douglas N. Hastad. "An Investigation into the Relationship between Ice Hockey Participation and Delinquency." *Sociology of Sport Journal* 2 (1985): 281–98.

Silver, Michael. "Dirty Dogs." *Sports Illustrated*, October 26, 1998.

"Six Football Players Arrested for Hazing." *High Desert Star*, November 13, 2000. www.hidesertstar.com/display/inn_news/news1.txt.

——. "Health among African American Males." In *Men's Health and Illness: Gender, Power, and the Body*, ed. Donald Sabo and David F. Gordon, 121–39. Thousand Oaks, Calif.: Sage Publication, 1995.

"They Said It: Kobe Bryant." *Sports Illustrated*, February 21, 2000, 26.

White, Philip G., Kevin Young, and William G. McTeer, "Sport, Masculinity, and the Injured Body." In *Men's Health and Illness: Gender, Power, and the Body*, ed. Donald F. Sabo and David F. Gordon, 158–82. Thousand Oaks, Calif.: Sage Publications, 1995.

CHAPTER 29

The Sprewell/Carlesimo Episode: Unacceptable Violence or Unacceptable Victim?

Theresa Walton

Given the extensive amount of violence associated with sport both on and off the playing courts and fields, it is surprising that any one isolated incident of violence between two men would attract much media attention. Yet the amount of mainstream media coverage surrounding men's National Basketball Association (NBA) player Latrell Sprewell's attack on his coach, P.J. Carlesimo, has been quite remarkable. In the 3 months from the altercation (December 1, 1997) to the arbitration decision (March 4, 1998) not a day went by without several media stories about Sprewell in newspapers, magazines, and on television sports channels and news shows. The ways these stories were constructed revealed various meanings of violence within our society. In this paper I examine the way that violence is understood in sport in relation to the Sprewell/Carlesimo altercation and to the normalization of violence against women in American culture. This media analysis reveals how portrayals of the Sprewell/Carlesimo incident differ from descriptions of anti-woman violence committed by male athletes and coaches and what these differences in representation tell us about the cultural valuing of men over women.

A strong belief in capitalist ideology is prevalent within the media coverage of the Spewell/Carlesimo incident. The threat to capitalism represented by workplace violence is one of the main underlying themes in the media coverage of Sprewell's actions. The discourse of workplace violence that gets taken up creates a space to highlight the economic importance of violence between these two men. The separation between workplace violence and domestic violence works to elevate the violence between Sprewell and Carlesimo above anti-woman violence committed by the same population of men (athletes and coaches). Sprewell's attack on Carlesimo inverts the power relationship between boss and employee. Moreover, this particular incident also inverts the cultural power relationship of black and white. Violence within the workplace, as highlighted with this example, threatens social order, while violence within the home is not considered as culturally significant. Moreover, with this incident preceding the National Basketball Association players' strike, we witness a foreshadowing of the discomfort surrounding the issue of black basketball players (who are written within a "thug" narrative) making millions of dollars. An examination of Sprewell's vilification in the media reveals inversions of power relations that are presented by media coverage as threats to social order. Violence committed by athletes and coaches against women, on the other hand, is not positioned as the same threat to social order and is therefore more normalized within media. Notably, violence against women does not result in the same harsh economic and judicial consequences called for by the media in the case of Sprewell.

THE BASICS OF THE INCIDENT

On December 1, 1997, Latrell Sprewell reportedly attacked his coach, P.J. Carlesimo, while practicing for the Golden State Warriors. Sprewell allegedly "choked" Carlesimo after the coach ordered him to leave practice. According to Warriors owner Chris Cohan, the incident occurred when Carlesimo criticized Sprewell during a passing drill. Sprewell returned 20 minutes later and said to Carlesimo, "I'll kill you. If you don't get me off of this team, that's what I'll do." Reports conflict as to whether Sprewell again tried to attack Carlesimo. Hours after the attack, the Warriors suspended Sprewell for a minimum of 10 games. Two days later, the Warriors organization fired Sprewell, terminating his $32 million contract. Altogether, this would have cost Sprewell $7.7 million for the remainder of the 1997–1998 season, plus $17.3 million that he was due to receive for the next two seasons (Curiel, 1998; Kelly, 1997; "NBA beyond misbehavin," 1997; Stein, 1997).

According to Sprewell, the tension had been building in his relationship with Carlesimo, and he finally "just had enough" of the way the coach treated him (Curiel, 1998, p. 3D). "All the frustrations had built up to the point where I couldn't take it anymore," Sprewell said in an interview (Curiel, 1998, p. 3D). Carlesimo has an abrasive—some say abusive—coaching style and is well known as a "yeller" (Curiel, 1998; Keown, 1997; Steele, 1997a). From the beginning and all through the incident, Sprewell is described in media accounts as having the support of most NBA players who voiced an opinion. Players who previously had trouble with Carlesimo, such as Rod Strickland, were not surprised by the incident. Strickland, who was with the Washington Wizards at the time, said in an interview, "[Carlesimo is] annoying, that's the bottom line. We've been face-to-face many occasions, that's for sure, so I can kind of understand Spree" (Steele, 1997a, p. 5B).

On December 4, 3 days after the episode, the NBA banned Sprewell from the league for one year. Sprewell and the NBA Players Association filed an appeal. Dean of Fordham University Law School John Feerick arbitrated a trial that lasted 2 months. He reduced Sprewell's sentence from 1 year to 7 months and from $22.7 million to $6.4 million, meaning the Warriors had to accept responsibility for the final 2 years of Sprewell's contract. Feerick's decision was met by a media outcry that the penalty was too lenient, despite the fact that it was the "most severe punishment ever meted out for any kind of infraction in NBA history" (CNN/SI, 1998). The next longest sentence was a 26-game suspension of Kermit Washington in the 1977–78 season for punching then Rocket player Rudy Tomjanovich in a fight during the game. In comparison, when Dennis Rodman kicked a court side cameraman during the 1996–97 season he received an 11-game suspension ("The NBA has itself," 1998).

UNACCEPTABLE VIOLENCE?

According to NBA commissioner, David Stern, along with the front office of the Warriors, the severity of the original ban and the termination of Sprewell's contract were merited based on moral grounds. "It was not an economical [sic] decision," according to Garry St. Jean, the Warrior's general manager. "It was about morals and ethics and the right thing to do" ("Ruling elicits," 1998, p. 2D). Carlesimo described the decision as "dramatic and courageous" (Curiel, 1998, p. 3D). Yet, the handling of the incident by the NBA and its construction in the media reveal that it is not simply about violence and what levels of violence are acceptable but rather about social power structures. Many lines of power were crossed. Carlesimo was a white man, Sprewell black. Carlesimo occupies a position of power as coach. Sprewell represents the threat of the insubordinate black man to the control of the white male establishment. While 80% of NBA players are black, less than 15% of the coaches, general managers, and owners are (Stein, 1997).

In the arena of professional male sport where incidents of violence occur on a regular basis, it is instructive to note what types of violence are vilified and which are normalized. Some level of violence, even aggression,[1] is considered integral to popular professional male sports: strategic fouls in basketball, outright fights in hockey, football tackling, and the sport of boxing. Yet violence during play is not the only violence that is normalized. Violence toward women, especially girlfriends and wives, by professional athletes and even coaches is unfortunately prevalent. In understanding this issue, I believe it is important in improving the conditions of women's lives to shed light on instances where (hetero)-sexism contributes to dangers women face in our culture. As sociologist Edwin Schur (1984) notes, 'To understand or to curb the victimization of women, we must not only determine what 'causes' these behaviors to occur. We must also consider the social responses their occurrence elicits" (p. 133).

Examples of violence by athletes and coaches toward women abound. In November of 2000, former National Football Association player, Rae Carruth, was convicted of conspiring to murder Cherica Adams, who was 8 months pregnant with his son. Carruth was also convicted of being part of the group that committed the murder and shot into an occupied car, attempting to kill the baby. Adams was shot four times by associates hired by Carruth. She died 28 days later. Her baby Chancellor Lee, who survived the shooting, was delivered by Caesarian section that night. Media reports refer to Adams' murder as a "double tragedy," implying that the loss of Carruth's promising football career was nearly as tragic as Adams' death. As one fan of Carruth's said, "I feel he was foolish to let a woman take him out of all the hard work he put into getting into the NFL" (Wright, Frazier, & Whitmire, 2001). The title of a Website dedicated to Rae Carruth and the murder reveals the same sentiment: "Shattered Dreams: Two families suffer a terrible loss." Adams, then, is implicated in Carruth's downfall. Representing Carruth's situation as tragic does little to either vilify Carruth or highlight the social importance of such violence.

One of the most infamous cases involved the late Nicole Brown Simpson and her then husband, O.J. The public did not learn until after Brown Simpson's death that Simpson had pleaded no contest to a charge of assault in 1989, and police were called to their home numerous times to intervene in family disputes involving violence (Connelly, 1994, p. 48). Nor did we hear her statement in the police report with her eye blackened and lip split, "You never do anything about him. You talk to him and then leave" (Paterno, 1994, p. 11). As one editor said of the decision not to investigate the incidences, "He was a hero. He came up from poverty. He had a sweet and fine manner and an unbelievable level of athletic prowess and achievement. And I'm going to tear down a guy's life work because he had a fight with his wife?" (Paterno, 1994, p. 11).

Other high profile cases of domestic violence include charges of Warren Moon hitting, scratching, and choking his wife Felicia Moon at their home in Missouri City, Texas in July of 1995. The charges were brought by the state of Texas against the National Football League quarterback. Yet in February of 1996, Felicia Moon portrayed herself in testimony as a temperamental woman who had provoked her husband ("Moon's wife on stand," 1996). Clearly she defended him at the expense of her own reputation despite having sought a divorce and order of protection in 1986 ("Moon's wife on stand," 1996; "Moon's wife denies abuse," 1996). Later that month after an hour of deliberation the jury found Warren Moon not guilty ("Jury rapidly acquits Moon," 1996). In June of 1996, Moon became the highest paid player in Minnesota Vikings history when he agreed to a 3-year $15 million contract extension ("Moon signs big deal," 1996).

Iowa State University's head football coach Dan McCarney faced no repercussions when the media disclosed that he had been charged with assaulting his estranged wife, Brenda McCarney. Fans given voice in newspapers said the assault did not affect McCarney's job as a coach. Fans were unequivocal: "They didn't hire him to be a marriage counselor, they hired him to be a football coach" (Weeks, 1995a, p. 4A). "The offense was serious but irrelevant," said one fan. According to another, "We all make mistakes in life" (Weeks, 1995a, p. 4A). Apparently domestic violence is not an issue that should weigh heavily on the public conscious. As one fan asserts, "I just think there are enough other things we should be concerned about in our society, even right here in Iowa City" (Weeks, 1995a, p. 4A). Perhaps a different (male) victim in a different (public) setting would be one of the "things" that should be of more concern to the public.

Many college athletes, perhaps learning from their role models, have assaulted the women in their lives. A University of Nebraska scholarship basketball player, Kate McEwen, was assaulted by her former boyfriend and classmate, football player Lawrence Phillips in September of 1995. Yet he was suspended from playing for only 6 days and was later drafted by the St. Louis Rams in the first round ("Husker rebuff," 1996). Early in March of 1998, University of Iowa football player Eric Thigpen was arrested for assaulting his girlfriend. He spent the night in jail but was neither suspended nor expelled from either the football team or the university.

Violence against women by male athletes does not receive the same media outcry as the Sprewell case. Professional boxer Mike Tyson was convicted of rape in February of 1992, yet an article in the *New York Times* suggests that he was a victim of a corrupt system that took advantage of him. Tyson was said to be "out of control" since Don King took over his management. His victim was implicated as part of the cause of his downfall in boxing (Berkow, 1992; Shipp, 1992). A week after the trial, a group of ministers gathered where the trial was held with 10,000 signatures on a petition seeking a suspended sentence (Vecsey, 1992). A change in coverage occurred after Tyson twice bit Evandar Holyfield's ears in a heavy weight title fight in 1997. This behavior was deemed, unacceptable violence, arguably because it was against a man and in the "work" environment of the boxing ring. One boxing analyst said after the biting incident. "Tyson is a menace to himself and to boxing" ("A bite out of boxing," 1997, p. 20A).

One of the more heinous cases occurred in 1989 and involved four male high school athletes from Glen Ridge, New Jersey, who used a broom and a full sized baseball bat to sexually assault a female classmate with mental disabilities. According to Bernard Lefkowitz, journalism professor at Columbia

University, the male athletes at Glen Ridge High School were often destructive and "treated female teachers and students with contempt. Repeatedly, the boys of the class of '89 found, there was little or no reprimand—not from teachers or from parents. . . . For them, sports was a means of gaining supremacy" (Lefkowitz, 1997, pp. 84 and 94). Moreover, "these Ridgers were taught that women's main purpose was to be decorative and to please and to praise men. A girl who resisted this role was treated as one more opponent to be bullied into submission" (Lefkowitz, 1997, p. 98). The boys' defense was that their victim had encouraged them with her sexual provocation. Their victim remembered it much differently: "Everyone was laughing. I was crying to myself, but I had tears coming out of my eyes" (Lefkowitz, 1997, p. 83). Unfortunately, these boys were typical gang rapists. They were part of the "popular," "jock" crowd—leaders on sports fields and courts, as well as in school and town. Partly these boys were "regarded as above suspicion on campus, but their elevated status also discouraged them from moral reflection; it made them feel entitled" (Lefkowitz, 1997, p. 97). Four years after the attack, three of the boys were finally convicted of aggravated sexual assault in March of 1993. In a controversial decision, they were released on bail until their appeals were heard and did not go to prison until 1997. While Lefkowitz wrote a very sensitive and critical article, the Glen Ridge boys and others like them were not vilified relentlessly by the media in the way that Sprewell was for his attack on Carlesimo.

Unfortunately, violence against women is so prevalent that these examples barely begin to outline the list of violent acts committed by male athletes and coaches. In part we hear about these particular incidents because they are committed by public figures. According to Marian Meyers in her book, *News Coverage of Violence Against Women* (1997), one of the main guiding principles of reporters and editors choosing one story over another is the "unusualness" of the case. To be reported, a crime must be "quirky, out of the ordinary, rare, and uncommon. Because cases of domestic violence and rape are all too common, they can be dismissed by reporters unless they have an unusual twist" (Meyers, 1997, p. 98), such as being committed by a well-known athlete or against someone who is perceived as a defenseless victim, as with the Glen Ridge case. Yet as Ann Marie Lapinski, editor of the *Chicago Tribune,* said, "We should pay attention to women not as famous as Nicole Simpson who are just as dead" (Paterno, 1994, p. 33). The message being portrayed makes it clear that violence against women, while unfortunate, is not villainized and comes closer to being normalized. Columnist Larry Stewart of the *Los Angeles Times* defended not covering the domestic violence of O.J. Simpson by stating. "What man in this country hasn't yelled at his wife?" (Paterno, 1994, p. 11). Value judgments are made in reporting and editing, which determine the importance and meaning of violence—often according to whether the victim is female or male as well as the prestige of the attacker. According to Meyers (1997), when reporters' decisions of "newsworthiness" are based on ideas of "unusualness," "the complexity and interlocking nature of oppression" (p. 98) is revealed. Thus, she argues a sentiment that critical cultural studies scholars[2] share:

> Patriarchy does not operate independent of racial or class interests; these forms of oppression work together to support, maintain and reproduce dominant ideology, which is reflected within journalists' collective understandings and beliefs concerning newsworthiness and the nature of news.
>
> (1997, p. 98)

Male athletes are neither banned from their sports for attacking women, nor are they daily villainized in the news, as Sprewell was.

In attempting to answer the basic who, what, when, where, how, and why, many journalists miss the mark. According to Meyers (1997), when journalists attempt to determine the "why" of a story of violence against a woman they often look to the abuser's psyche or the actions of the victim. She argues that in our patriarchal culture, the "real why behind the violence is that men believe that they have the right to control women" (p. 123). Thus, the pathology of anti-woman violence is "reflective of a society that devalues and hates women, that views women as an appropriate repository for male rage and blame" (p. 123). A lack of control is sometimes excused as the result of some foreign substance in the abuser's system such as alcohol, steroids, or illegal recreational drugs. Sugar Ray Leonard's assault on his wife, Juanita, was attributed to his admitted use and addiction to cocaine. Moon also talked of the pressure of professional athletics sending him over the edge. Reporters also explore the question of "why" by examining the role of the victim to determine her guilt or innocence in provoking the attack. Felicia Moon blamed herself when she testified that she was a "temperamental woman." These examinations often lead to a blaming of the victim and an absolution of the attacker. Had reporters been more sympathetic to the "why" of Sprewell's case, they would have produced much different stories about the incident.

Unlike the great outcry by the media calling for strict punishment of Sprewell, media source continually downplay violence against women and excuse this violence by male athletes. In fact, these acts of violence, according to Schur (1984), are "closely tied to our society's scenarios of approved male behavior" (p. 135). As Schur points out. "The persistence and the relative tolerance of such victimization represents, therefore, a price we pay for maintaining a dehumanizing and exploitative gender system" (p. 135).

The acceptance of violence toward women comes from the low value placed on "womanhood" and the associated domestic sphere as constructed by our culture. Moreover, there is a failure to effectively stigmatize male offenders for their violent actions toward women. While Sprewell was daily stigmatized after his attack on Carlesimo by the Warrior's organization, the NBA, and the sports media, perpetrators of anti-woman violence get much less attention. The successful vilification of Sprewell may work to reduce actions similar to his in the future. This clearly sends the message that an attack on Carlesimo, a white male in a position of power, is more consequential than an attack of a female "domestic" partner. He is important enough that the man who attacked him was publicly criticized every day for 3 months.

The constant portrayal of women as victims in the media works to control women and heightens feelings of disempowerment of female viewers (Reid & Finchilescu, 1995; Walkowitz, 1997). Violence against women functions to control women with the constant fear of the threat of violence. Yet in a paternalistic capitalistic society like the United States, the very idea of "domestic" violence being a "private" matter contributes to the subordination of women. In 1994, two-thirds of victims of completed rapes did not report being assaulted to the police. Among victims who chose not to report a violent crime to the police, many indicated that they felt the matter was private or personal in nature (Perkins & Klaus, 1994). Violence, such as that committed by Sprewell against an authority figure in the "public sphere" of work, is considered more deplorable than violence committed against a "subordinate" woman in the "private sphere" of home because it threatens social order. Thus, the hierarchizing of the "public" sphere as male and the "private" sphere as female is strengthened and perpetuated, with the public/male sphere being more important than the "other," private/female sphere.

ALTERNATIVE UNDERSTANDINGS OF THE INCIDENT

The work environment of professional sports is not like other work environments, although it is clearly in the public sphere. Sprewell used the pressure of his situation to defend his attack of Carlesimo, thus taking on the role of victim. Professional male athletes are in a work environment over which they have little control. Sprewell had wanted to leave the Warriors, but as a professional player he has little control over his work environment. He has little control over where he works or who works with him. In return, professional athletes are highly paid. One of the underlying tensions hidden within the narratives surrounding Sprewell is a sentiment that he is paid enough to play a game to be expected to deal without complaint with whatever style his coach uses. This may also show uneasiness over the amount of money black players such as Sprewell make to play basketball. According to sportswriters, problems between coaches and players in part occur because players often make more than their coaches. Again this threatens to invert the hierarchy of the social order.

Within sport the role of the coach has been cast as a patriarchal figure. Sprewell is apparently rejecting his resulting casting in the "child-like" role. Rather, Sprewell sees Carlesimo as a professional equal and wants to be treated accordingly—"like a man." This works to again support the public/work sphere as male but inverts the traditional coach/athlete power relationship. Sprewell stepped over the line within the public sphere and attacked a representative of authority, the organization, and by extension the white male power structure.

I contend that it is precisely this threat to (white male) authority that fueled the unprecedentedly harsh ban and fine as both the (large) amount of media coverage of the Sprewell "incident" and the vilification of Sprewell by the media. Sprewell's punishment exceeded the total of all suspensions imposed on all players for physical altercations during the 1995–96 and 1996–97 seasons combined as well as all suspensions imposed for altercations during the 1992–93, 1993–94, and 1994–95 seasons combined. In spite of this, most sports writers were not sympathetic to Sprewell. Michael Kelly (1997) described Sprewell as a "millionaire ballplayer and recent attempted strangler" (p, 27A). Tim Keown (1998) of the *San Francisco Chronicle* called him "spoiled and disturbed" (p. 1B). And *Time* magazine's Joel Stein (1997) reports, "As a talk-radio villain Spree has virtually replaced Saddam" (p. 91).

Not only were many journalists not sympathetic to Sprewell, the consensus was that the sentence was too lenient. David Steele (1997b) of the *San Francisco Chronicle* called Feerick's ruling "a surprising arbitration decision" (p. 1A), revealing his belief that the original sentence was fair. Deputy NBA commissioner Russ Granik said, "I have some concern that fans, and perhaps even players, might unfortunately get the message that no matter what you do, your contract can't be terminated" (Curiel, 1998. p. 3D). NBA commissioner Stern said. "The arbitrator is a very charitable man, and he made a charitable decision in respects to Mr. Sprewell in this decision" (Steele, 1998, p. 1A).

Despite the fact that Carlesimo did not press charges, many sports writers expressed the opinion that Sprewell should have been imprisoned for his actions. In these instances writers lean heavily on ideas of appropriate behaviors in the work place but do not consider how professional sports differ from other job situations. Michael Kelly (1997) of the *Washington Post* wrote:

> Sprewell was not arrested, despite the fact that the acts he had committed certainly seemed to constitute assault and battery. . . . If I had tried to strangle my boss in front of a dozen witnesses, I would expect to lose not merely my job but my freedom.
>
> (p. 27A)

Anastasia Hendrix (1998) of the *San Francisco Examiner* quotes a labor lawyer who says, "Even when an employee so much as shoves a superior, the verdict results in 'industrial capital punishment' . . . a term synonymous with firing" (p. 1A). According to Tim Keown (1998) of the *San Francisco Chronicle*, "The man choked his boss, took a shower, returned to the court, fought his way through assistant coaches and players, took another shot at his boss and still didn't lose his job" (p. 1B). Stern said, "I think the fundamental point is whether you can strike your boss and still hold your job. The answer is that you cannot strike your boss and still hold your job—unless you play in the NBA and are subject to arbitrator Feerick's decision" (Keown, 1998, p. 1B).

Stern and many of the sports writers also questioned Feerick's ability to arbitrate. Ray Ratto (1998) of the *San Francisco Examiner* wrote of the arbitrator's decision:

> Most people see this decision as the latest example of permissiveness gone mad. They look at the facts, they look at Feerick, and they decide a ferret with a GED could have done better, and more sensibly. It's hard to tell them that they're wrong, largely because they are right.
>
> (p. ID)

Keown (1998) calls Feerick's decision an "irrational act" saying his "lengthy and addle-brained decision . . . has the reek of random guesswork to it . . . He decided to uphold an employee's right to drag the boss across the key by his vertebrae. He decided to preserve the sanctity of sociopathic behavior in the workplace" (p. 1D).

The emphasis on the workplace also brings to light the economic ramifications of Sprewell's sentence. The issue is racially charged and underscores basic class issues. According to Michael Kelly, the NBA is afraid to punish Sprewell harshly because they need him for the income he provides for them. Thus, they are exploiting Sprewell for their commercial benefit. He contends that the incident is mostly about "thuggism" but does not acknowledge how racially charged the idea of "thuggism" is. He writes that the Sprewell attack stemmed from the fact that

> The white men who run pro and college sports value athletes like Sprewell too much, in the commercial sense, to care that, by tolerating the rise of a culture of thuggism in their business they are encouraging boys and young men to believe in a world where to be a success means not having to obey the rules.
>
> (1997, p. 27A)

Bruce Jenkins (1997) agrees: "There's a deep-seated anger among athletes from hard backgrounds, an anger stemming from racism, injustice and the constant specter of violence. Players will continue to bring that anger into the professional ranks" (p. 2E).

Yet Kelly goes on with some rather racist remarks claiming that it is acceptable to let white athletes get away with preferential treatment because "white society" will save them if they step over the vague boundaries and become drug addicts or get in trouble for violence. "But for black kids, [stepping over the line is] the passport to a life where the best job they will ever get involves a bicycle or a burger or a Xerox machine" (1997, p. 27A). Kelly manages in one paragraph to perpetuate racial stereotypes, blame "black" society for not stepping in to save "their" kids, and offer the usual paternalistic solution of organizations controlled by white men as the saviors. Within the narrative of "thuggism," acts of violence, such as Sprewell's attack on Carlesimo, as well as domestic violence are seen as a "natural" consequence of black anger and oppression.

CONCLUSION

The power the media has to influence public sentiment can be powerfully witnessed with the coverage of the Sprewell/Carlesimo incident. Media coverage does not offer the same intense and prolonged vilification of perpetrators of anti-woman violence. Apparently, violence committed by the same population (athletes and coaches) upon the bodies of women does not disrupt culturally established lines of power or threaten social order. By establishing "domestic" violence as a "private" matter, media coverage contributes to women's social subordination. Perhaps violence against women would not continue to be so prevalent if it were treated as more serious and significant within media coverage. Couching Sprewell's "choking" of Carlesimo within the language of work place violence, clearly placing it within the public sphere, works to mark it as culturally significant. Representing Carlesimo as the "boss" and Sprewell as the worker positions Sprewell's violence as a threat not just to Carlesimo, but to the social order of capitalism. Carlesimo has the doubly privileged position in our culture of being white and male. Furthermore, he is in a position of power over others—a role often reserved for white men. Sprewell not only attacked the man, Carlisimo, but also then threatened the very privilege that Carlisimo represents. It is not a simple case of violence being unacceptable. Violence is a very accepted aspect of sport, especially male sport. What is unacceptable in this case is the threat to white male privilege as represented by Carlesimo in a position of power. Sprewell's attack of Carlesimo crosses the line and threatens to invert long-standing traditional lines of power.

NOTES

1 A significant amount of sport psychology research deals with the issue of aggression in sport (e.g., Silva & Conroy, 1995; Silva & Husman, 1995; and Thirer, 1993). For the purposes of this paper, I consider aggression to be use of physical force with the intention of causing harm. Violence then is a more general term that can include acts of aggression, such as anti-woman violence, as well as accepted aspects of sport, such as football tackling, which do not necessarily carry with them the intention of causing physical harm. Social psychologists refer to aggressive and violent acts that are expected role-playing behavior, such as football tackling, as institutional aggression.

2 Analysis of unequal power relations unifies critical cultural studies work, especially out of the British tradition. For a useful sport studies discussion dealing with relationships of power along intersecting axes, see Birrell and McDonald (2000).

REFERENCES

A bite out of boxing. (1997, July 1). *New York Times*, p. 20A.

Berkow, I. (1992, February 11). The 'animal' in Mike Tyson. *New York Tunes*, p. 11B.

Birrell, S. & McDonald, M. (2000). *Reading sport: Critical essays on power and representation.* Boston: Northeastern University Press.

CNN/SI. (1998, March 9). *Press Conference.* Time Warner Broadcasting.

Connelly, R. (1994, September 3). Domestic violence and the press. *Editor and Publisher,* 127, 48.

Curiel, J. (1998, March 5). Sprewell's 3-month odyssey. San *Francisco Chronicle,* p 3D.

Hendrix, A. (1998, March 5). Did Sprewell get off easy? *San Francisco Examiner,* p. 1A.

Husker rebuff for Phillip's assault victim. (1996, April 19). New *York Times,* pp. 11B & 16B.

Jenkins, B. (1997, December 6). Warriors' wasteland gets deeper. *San Francisco Chronicle,* p. 2E.

Jury rapidly acquits Moon of spousal abuse charges. (1996, February 23). *New York Times,* p. 12B.

Kelly, M. (1997, December 11). The Sprewell saga. *Washington Post,* p. 27A.

Keown, T. (1997, December 3). Incident puts Carlesimo out of criticism's way. *San Francisco Chronicle,* p. 1B.

Keown, T. (1998, March 5). Irrational act follows another. *San Francisco Chronicle,* p. 1D.

Lefkowitz, B. (1997, June 23). Our guys. Sports *Illustrated,* 83–98.

McCallum, J. (1997, December 15). Foul trouble. *Sports Illustrated,* 68–69.

McCarney apologizes; ISU weighs his future. (1995, March 21). *Iowa City Press Citizen,* p. 4A.

Meyers, M. (1997). *News coverage of violence against women, engendering blame.* Thousand Oaks, CA: Sage.

Moon signs big deal. (1996, June 4). *New York Times,* p. 12B.

Moon's wife denies abuse. (1996, February 20). *New York Times,* p. 8B.

Moon's wife on stand, blames her temper. (1996, February 17). *New York Times,* p. 34.

The NBA: Beyond misbehavin'. (1997, December 8). *Washington Post* [On-line]: Levey Live. Available: www.discuss.washingtonpost.com/wp-srv/zforum/97/levey.htm

The NBA has itself to blame for condoning violence and other misbehavior. (1998, March 5). *San Francisco Examiner,* p. 18A.

Ortiz, J. (1998, March 5). Spree's pals cheer victory for player 'family.' *San Francisco Examiner,* p. 4D.

Paterno, S. (1994, July 23). Covering sports heroes: Sports editors discuss why the 1989 wife abuse arrest of O.J. Simpson was not taken seriously by the media. *Editor and Publisher,* 127, 11, 33.

Perkins, C., & Klaus, B. (1994). *Violent crime. National crime victimization survey.* Government Documents: United States Department of Justice.

Ratio, R. (1998, March 5). Deeper into darkness, my old friend. *San Francisco Examiner,* p. 1D.

Records contradict Moons' statements. (1996, February 16). *New York Times,* p. 10B.

Reid, P., & Finchilescu, G. (1995). The disempowering effects of media violence against women on college women. *Psychology of Women Quarterly,* 19, 397–411.

Schur, E. (1984). *Labeling women deviant: Gender, stigma, and social control.* New York: McGraw-Hill.

Score one for bad sportsmanship. (1998, March 5). *San Francisco Chronicle,* p. 22A.

Shipp, E. (1992, February 11). Tyson found guilty on 3 counts as Indianapolis rape trial ends. *New York Times,* p. 1A, 15B.

Silva, J., & Conroy, D. (1995). Understanding aggressive behavior and its effects upon athletic performance. In: K. Henschen and W. Straub (Eds.), *Sport psychology: An analysis of athlete behavior* (pp. 149–159). Ithaca, NY: Mouvement.

Silva, J., & Husman, B. (1995). Aggression: An historical perspective. In: K. Henschen and W. Straub (Eds.), *Sport psychology: An analysis of athlete behavior* (pp. 149–159). Ithaca, NY: Mouvement.

Sprewell wins his case; Warriors contract reinstated. (1998, March 5). *San Francisco Chronicle,* p. 1D.

Steele. D. (1997a, December 3). Strickland says he can relate to Spree. *San Francisco Chronicle,* p. 5B.

Steele, D. (1997b, December 9). Sprewell, Coach tell each other they're sorry: Player apologizes for attack, Carlesimo for his role in it *San Francisco Chronicle,* p. 1A.

Steele, D. (1998, March 5). Sprewell back with the Warriors: Arbitrator reduces suspension. *San Francisco Chronicle,* p. 1A.

Stein, J. (1997, December 15). Tall men behaving badly. *Time,* 91–92.

Thirer, J. (1993). Aggression. In: R. Singer, M. Murphey, & L. Tennant (Eds.), *Handbook of research in sport psychology* (pp. 365–387). New York: Macmillan.

Thomas's troubled history. (1996, July 14). *New York Times,* Sec, 8, p. 4.

Transcript of Sprewell's public statement. (1997, December 2). *ESPN Sportszone.com* [On-line]. Available: www.espnsportszone.com/nba/news/971209/00488874.html.

Vecsey, G. (1992, February 18). A petition for Tyson. *New York Times,* p. 17B.

Walkowitz, J. (1997). *City of dreadful delight: Narratives of sexual danger in late-Victorian London.* Chicago: University of Chicago Press.

Warriors' Sprewell suspended for attacking, choking coach. (1998, December 3). *San Francisco Chronicle,* p. 5B.

Weeks, S. (1995a, March 21). Coach's home life not key to job success, fans say. *Iowa City Press Citizen,* p. 4A.

What they're saying. (1998, March 5). *San Francisco Chronicle*, p. 2D.

Why women-only self defense? (1998). *Women defending ourselves* [On-line]. Available: www.wdo.org/women.html.

Wright, G., Frazier, E., & Whitmire, T. (2001, January 19). Carruth convicted, but not of murder. *Charlotte Observer* [On-line]. Available; www.charlotte.com/observer/special/carruth/docs/0120carruth.htm

CHAPTER 30

Unnecessary Roughness? School Sports, Peer Networks, and Male Adolescent Violence

Derek A. Kreager

In many U.S. secondary schools, interscholastic sports play crucial roles in structuring student status hierarchies and peer friendship networks. "Star" male athletes are often venerated by their peers and local communities, becoming core members of a school's "in-crowd" (Bissinger 1991; Coleman 1961; Holland and Andre 1994). Similarly, nonathletic friends of popular athletes tend to share elevated social status and gain membership in more exclusive peer groups (Eckert 1989). The predominance and visibility of sports in schools encourages all students, regardless of their gender or athleticism, to orient their behaviors toward these activities and define their own identities in relation to the most popular athletes and athletic cliques.

The salience of athletics in adolescent culture fuels ongoing debates about the social role of youth sports. On the one hand, proponents have long argued that interscholastic athletics positively impact adolescent development. Here, youth sports are viewed as (1) increasing adolescents' bonds to schools, conventional peers, and conventional adults (Crosnoe 2001; Larson 1994; McNeal 1995); (2) socializing adolescents into the basic values of American life, such as competition, fair play, self-restraint, and achievement (Jeziorski 1994); and (3) helping students develop social and physical competence, leading to increased self-esteem, social capital, and upward mobility (Ewing et al. 2002; Otto and Alwin 1977; Spady 1970). Studies, in fact, concur on many of these points in consistently finding positive relationships between sports participation and a host of individual benefits, including increased self-esteem, locus of control, academic achievement, commitment to graduation, educational aspirations, and economic attainment (Eccles and Barber 1999; Fejgin 1994; Mahoney and Cairns 1997; Marsh 1993; McNeal 1995; Otto and Alwin 1977). In addition, some research finds a negative relationship between sports participation and delinquent behavior (Landers and Landers 1978; Langbein and Bess 2002; Mahoney 2000; Stark, Kent, and Finke 1987).

Critical scholars, however, assail traditional views of youth sports as incomplete and problematic. These scholars reveal the contradictions and inequities underlying much of modern sport (see Gatz, Messner, and Ball-Rokeach 2002, for a review). Rather than building socially competent young men and women, it is suggested, the conditions of contemporary athletics embed youth in value systems marred by homophobia, sexism, racism, and ruthless competition. Within these contexts, middle-class white males have the most to gain, while disadvantaged minority and female athletes are either marginalized or forego long-term attainment in favor of short-term status benefits and illusory professional careers.

Critical feminist scholars have taken particular interest in the relationship between sports and gendered violence. Rejecting the view that sports help to curb antisocial behavior, some researchers assert that the hypermasculine cultures characteristic of many contact sports teach violence as an acceptable means of maintaining valued male identities (Burstyn 1999; Coakley 2001; Connell and Messner 1995; Crosset 1999; Messner 1992; Sabo 1994; Young, White, and McTeer 1994). By rewarding physical aggression with on-the-field success and increased prestige, contact sports are portrayed as both elevating athletes above their peers and increasing off-the-field violence toward perceived outsiders and "weaker" students. Masculinized sports then become socially sanctioned stepping-stones toward privilege and power-sites where coaches, peers, parents, and the media encourage masculine identities founded on physical aggression and domination.

Seemingly endless accounts of brawling, sexual assault, and bullying by prominent athletes regularly stream across our televisions and newspapers bolster critical views and prompt the question: "Are these activities promoting the fair play and sportsmanship outlined in their charters, or are they encouraging violence by already privileged elites?" Answering this question has important implications for school-based sporting programs, yet surprisingly little research or methodological rigorous studies have addressed the youth sports–violence relationship.[1]

In this article, I move beyond prior research with theoretically grounded hypotheses and advanced quantitative methods. I rely on three distinct theoretical traditions—social control, social learning, and masculinity theories—to derive competing hypotheses for the sports–violence relationship. I then test these for five very different sports—football, basketball, baseball, wrestling, and tennis—using data from the National Longitudinal Study of Adolescent Health (Add Health). The measures of friendship networks in Add Health also allow one to move beyond prior research and gain leverage on a potential mechanism connecting sports to violence (i.e., embeddedness in sports networks increases the likelihood of individual violence).

THEORETICAL BACKGROUND

SOCIAL CONTROL PERSPECTIVES

Sports scholars commonly invoke social control concepts, particularly Hirschi's (1969) social bonding theory, to examine the linkages between sports participation and adolescent antisocial behavior (Crosnoe 2001; Larson 1994; McNeal 1995). Rather than focusing on delinquent motivations, control theories posit that it is the constraining influence of conventional bonds that explain variations in individual-level delinquency. Schools are seen as important sites for adolescent integration into conventional society. Accordingly, youth who are tightly bonded to school and to their student peers are more likely to refrain from violent behavior than are other, less bonded, youth.

Because interscholastic sports are institutionally sanctioned activities governed by school- connected adults, social control perspectives predict that sports participation should increase adolescents' bonds to conventional society and reduce antisocial behavior (Crosnoe 2001; Larson 1994; McNeal 1995). Hirschi's (1969) elements of the social bond—attachment, involvement, commitment, and belief—are readily applied to individual sports participation. First, sports participation should increase attachments between athletes and their teammates and coaches(Coleman 1961; Messner 1992).These ties should reduce antisocial behaviors by constraining individual tendencies toward aggression and delinquency. Second, athletic participation should build athletes' commitment to conventional lines of action, because the penalty for deviance would include the loss of athletic status and a related decrease in social standing. Third, the time required to practice and succeed in sports should increase adolescents' involvement in conventional activities and decrease, by default, the time available for antisocial behavior (McNeal 1995). Finally, because the rules and values of sports are assumed to lie within the value system shared by conventional society, participation in sports should increase adolescents' belief in the moral order and, thus, prosocial behavior (Larson 1994).

Much of the empirical evidence supports the dimensions of social control theory outlined above. Adolescent athletes are less likely to drop out of high school (Mahoney and Cairns 1997; McNeal 1995), more likely to attend college (Eccles and Barber 1999; Marsh 1993; Sabo, Melnick, and Vanfossen 1993), and less likely to behave delinquently (Landers and Landers 1978; Langbein and Bess 2002; Mahoney 2000; Stark et al. 1987). None of this work, however, addresses violence specifically, nor does it address the possibility of variation in antisocial outcomes by forms of athletic engagement.

Control perspectives assume that the motivation to commit delinquent acts is constant across persons and that group norms supportive of crime are weak or nonexistent (Hirschi 1969). Because organization in favor of crime is thought inconsequential, control theorists dismiss the possibility that individuals may be tightly bonded to groups or subcultures that promote antisocial behaviors. Following this logic, violence by male athletes would be interpreted as evidence that either sports are not conventional activities or that violent athletes are not fully bonded to sports. As there is much evidence suggesting that sports involvement is generally associated with conventional behavior, we are left to conclude that violent male athletes are mavericks within their programs, alienated from other players and the conventional institutions of school and family. It would be this lack of social integration that frees an athlete to behave violently.

SOCIAL LEARNING PERSPECTIVES

In contrast to social control theories, social learning perspectives allow for subgroup variation in attitudes toward violence and law violation. Accordingly, individuals learn antisocial values and techniques within intimate social relations, particularly among friends and family members (Akers 1998; Sutherland 1947). Because some individuals and social groups are thought to have positive attitudes toward criminal behavior (or at least justify such behavior under certain circumstances), social learning theorists assume that individuals may be tightly bonded to others while simultaneously holding attitudes favorable to law violation.

At the heart of social learning approaches is the idea that delinquency, like any other behavior, is learned in social interaction. Sutherland (1947), in his classic work, postulates that delinquency results from individuals learning pro delinquency situational definitions within intimate social contacts. Accordingly, delinquency occurs when a person holds more positive than negative delinquent definitions of a situation. Akers and colleagues (Akers 1998; Akers et al. 1979; Burgess and Akers 1966) have expanded on this by including concepts of operant conditioning from behavioral psychology. This more general model adds specific mechanisms to the learning process. Individual violence and delinquency are thus assumed to emanate from continual and reciprocal processes of social observation, attitude internalization, and real and perceived reinforcements from the behavior of self and others. Research has confirmed the explanatory power of the social learning approach, particularly with regard to the relationship between peer behavior and individual delinquency (Matsueda and Anderson 1998; Warr 2002; Warr and Stafford 1991).

Hughes and Coakley (1991) apply social learning ideas to the seeming paradox of athlete deviance. Rather than suggesting that athletes' antisocial behaviors result from social alienation or the rejection of cultural values, they contend that such behaviors stem directly from the normative definitions learned in sports, a concept they call "positive deviance." They state that the values associated with sports—striving for distinction, sacrificing for The Team, playing through pain, and refusing to accept limits—are generally associated with individual success and conventional behavior. Yet, these norms may also create situations where athletes "do harmful things to themselves and perhaps others while motivated by a sense of duty and honor" (p. 311). They point to the widespread use of performance enhancing drugs as a clear example of such behavior. A similar argument may be applied to aggressive behavior, in that aggression is often an essential element for on-the-field success. By applying lessons learned in sports, athletes may perceive violence and intimidation as acceptable means of achieving off-the-field goals and solving problems unrelated to sports.

Peer relationships play central roles in the learning process, particularly during the status-conscious adolescent years (Coleman 1961). As noted previously, sports provide males with clear avenues toward increased peer status (Eder and Kinney 1995; Holland and Andre 1994). Team sports in particular may also direct individual behavior toward group norms. Ridicule, appeals to group loyalty, and status competition are primary mechanisms for ensuring individual conformity to group expectations (Warr 2002). For male athletes, derisive comments such as "pussy" and "chicken" pose deep threats to status within the peer group, prompting behaviors meant to regain face. Perceived threats to masculine reputations or social status may escalate into "character contests" where violence becomes an acceptable means of resolving the encounter (Goffinan 1967; Luckenbill 1977). Situational research of such "honor contests" consistently finds that peers play important roles in the violent transaction (Polk 1999). As Curry (1998) notes in his study of athlete barroom violence, peers may simultaneously encourage violence against perceived outsiders and bear witness to a group member's fighting prowess: "These fights with other males (never members of one's own team) had a way of building team cohesion and expressing masculine courage" (p. 211). Moreover, such activities also serve to further insulate the athlete from nonathletic peers and increase disdain for those who have not made the sacrifices of sports (Hughes and Coakley 1991; Messner 2002). Violence by male athletes may thus bind teammates into exclusive peer groups where individuals are forced to jockey for status with displays of aggression, risk taking, and ridicule.

MASCULINITY PERSPECTIVES AND CONTACT SPORTS

Qualitative research by masculinity scholars suggests that sports are not equal in their relationships to individual violence. The contention here is that "hypermasculine" contact sports create conditions where violence becomes an acceptable means of "doing" masculinity and maintaining valued masculine identities (Coakley 2001; Connell 1995; Crosset 1999; Messner 1992; Young et al. 1994). By differentiating sporting contexts and emphasizing the gendered nature of sport-related violence, masculinity theorists extend social learning ideas and provide additional hypotheses for the relationship between sports and violence.

Stemming from critical feminist perspectives, masculinity theories focus on male groups to illuminate the processes underlying gendered hierarchies (Connell and Messerschmidt 2005). A central concept for these arguments is hegemonic masculinity, commonly defined as the cultural patterns of action that allow some men to maintain dominance over females and subordinated males. Displays of aggression, independence, competition, and a rejection of femininity are thought to be culturally honored ways of being a man, so that enacting these qualities allows men to "do" gender while also reproducing a system of gender inequality. For masculinity theorists, understanding the reproductive processes associated with hegemonic masculinity allows for the recognition of alternative gender forms and opens possibilities for less oppressive gender regimes.

Within the masculinity literature, heavy-contact sports are typically portrayed as important avenues for males to construct hegemonic masculine identities. Accordingly, these sports become "endlessly renewed symbol[s] of masculinity" that promote the "violence and homophobia frequently found in sporting milieus" (Connell and Messerschmidt 2005: 833). In contact sports, on-the-field violence is intertwined with success, prestige, and essentialist images of "maleness." Contact sport athletes are admired for their strength and determination and rewarded with increased prestige and access to exclusive peer groups. The connection between on-the-field violence and identity should then increase contact athletes' risks of violence beyond the playing field (Crosset 1999; Pappas, McKenry, and Catlett 2004). Such behavior confirms the contact athlete's sense of self, connects him to his teammates, and protects his powerful position relative to subordinated masculinities and femininities.

In their qualitative study of a middle school, Eder, Evans, and Parker (1997) document how young boys are able to construct masculine identities within heavy-contact sports. On football fields and wrestling mats, the authors observe boys setting up "a pattern in which higher status is associated with intimidation of others and lower status is associated with submissive behavior'' (p. 69). Memories of "good hits" and "takedowns" establish the informal social order and identify the leaders as the best fighters. Simultaneously, the aggression modeled on the playing field carries over to disdain for nonathletes, who are derided as being weak and effeminate (e.g., "pussies" and "fags") and, thus, become subject to violent victimization (Eder et al. 1997: 76–78).

PHYSICAL CONTACT AND AMERICAN SPORTS

To understand the relationship between adolescent sports and violence in the United States, we must first understand this country's current sports landscape. Unquestionably, the most prominent team sports in contemporary U.S. society are football, basketball, and baseball. Huge industries help promote and broadcast collegiate and professional games, advertise their merchandise, and capitalize on the celebrity status of successful players. More important for this study, these sports are also found in most secondary schools and are at different points on the "contact" continuum.

Football is a heavy-contact sport because physical bodily contact is an acceptable and necessary component for on-the-field success. It is impossible for a team to win a football game without physically dominating opposing players through tackles, blocks, hits, and other forms of "brutal body contact" (Coakley 2001: 176). In contrast, the rules of basketball prohibit play that is physically violent, allowing contact only when it is incidental to the normal course of a game. Although physical and verbal intimidation of opponents are key strategies (Eveslage and Delaney 1998), bodily contact to the point of violence is expressly forbidden and severely sanctioned (Shields 1999). Baseball lies at the opposite end of the contact continuum. During a game, opposing players occupy separate physical spaces and the goals of the game do not require physically defending those spaces. Only on rare occasions (e.g., preventing a double-play or pitchers "brushing back" batters) are baseball players able to threaten opponents physically, and these instances are closely monitored by officials.

According to masculinity arguments, variations in physical contact across these sports arguably relate directly to the masculine definitions fostered by players. For football athletes, on-the-field violence is likely entwined with male status and identity (Coakley 2001; Messner 1992). Social learning approaches would also expect football players' networks to reinforce violent behavior as a means of maintaining peer status and avoiding ridicule (Akers 1998; Warr 2002). Although basketball and baseball players would associate aggressiveness with definitions of self, these definitions should fall short of violence because physical violence is an unnecessary and unreinforced dimension for athletic success.

But what of individual sports? Social learning theories would expect peers to have greater impact on individual behavior in an interdependent team sport than in the more autonomous environments of individual sports. If so, then comparing team and individual sports with similar levels of physical contact would provide insights into the group nature of male violence. Football and wrestling appear to be ideal candidates for such a comparison. Similar to football, wrestling is an exclusively male contact sport, but the small size of wrestling teams and the individual nature of competition may temper wrestling's peer effects. In addition, a noncontact and gender neutral individual sport, such as tennis, provides a useful comparison at the opposite end of the contact and masculine continuum.

SELF-SELECTION AND SPURIOUSNESS

The above perspectives suggest a direct causal relationship between sports and violent behavior. It is likely, however, that factors prior to athletic participation are influential in explaining subsequent outcomes. For example, athletes may be more likely to possess aggressive traits that increase the likelihood of sports participation, success, and individual violence. Aside from population heterogeneity in aggressive propensities, a spurious sports–violence relationship may also result from early socialization experiences. Messner (1992) finds that childhood relationships with fathers, brothers, uncles, and peers contribute to individuals' definitions of masculinity and subsequent desires to participate in sports. These definitions, as well as the environments encountered in early athletic teams, may select individuals into secondary school athletic programs and explain subsequent violence. Parents and coaches may play similar selection roles as well.

Below, I test several competing hypotheses about the relationship between sports participation and male adolescent violence. From social control theory, one would expect sports participation to inhibit violent behavior by bonding youth to conventional institutions. This contrasts sharply with the hypothesis derived from masculinity perspectives that the contexts of heavy-contact sports produce conditions supportive of male violence. Importantly, the masculinity hypothesis adds a sports-specific dimension and an explicit focus on male behavior. From social learning perspectives, I also examine the possibility that peer athletic participation is an important mediating link. Notably, my final modeling explores whether pre-existing conditions, such as prior levels of fighting, delinquency, or background characteristics, make spurious the sports–violence relationship.

DATA AND MEASURES

SAMPLE

I draw from the National Longitudinal Study of Adolescent Health (Add Health). Add Health is a school-based, nationally representative study of American adolescents in grades 7 to 12. Add Health selected a stratified sample of 80 schools with probabilities proportional to size. Schools were stratified by region, urbanicity, school type, ethnic mix, and size.

From 1994 to 2001, the study collected four waves of data from students, parents, and school administrators. For this analysis, I use data from the first (in-school) and second (Wave I in-home) questionnaires. The in-school survey was administered to all available students in each of the sampled schools. In total, 90,118 students (approximately 80 percent of those listed on school rosters) were surveyed. The questionnaire included basic demographic characteristics, school-related activities (including sports participation), and risk behaviors (including a measure of violence). Also, students nominated their five best male and five best female friends. This allows for the construction of friendship data taken directly from friends, thereby avoiding possible measurement error associated with self-reported friends' behavior. Sixteen schools had less than 50 percent of the students complete the nomination portion of the survey and were dropped from the analysis.

The Wave I in-home survey took place in the year following the in-school survey and consisted of a random sample of approximately 200 students from each of the originally sampled schools (N= 20,745). Nested within 120 schools, 14,396 students completed both the in-school and in-home questionnaires. As my hypotheses are primarily concerned with discerning the prevalence of *male* violence, I restricted my analyses to the 6,397 males who completed both surveys and attended schools with adequate network measures.

DEPENDENT VARIABLE

The dependent variable for this analysis is self-reported violence taken from the first in-home interview. This measure captures students' self-reports of getting into a serious physical fight within 12 months of the in-home interview. Descriptive statistics for this outcome are listed in Table 30.l. The variable is coded 0 if a respondent reported not fighting in the last 12 months and 1 if he reported fighting one or more times. Approximately 40 percent of male respondents reported getting into a serious physical fight.

The serious fighting item was originally measured on an interval scale, with values ranging from 0 (never) to 4 (seven or more times). As the distribution for this variable is highly skewed, I chose to present findings using a binary measure capturing the prevalence of serious fighting. In preliminary analyses, however, I also explored alternative modeling specifications of the ordinal scale and found similar results to those presented here.

INDIVIDUAL-LEVEL INDEPENDENT MEASURES

The primary independent variables are individuals' sports participation, friends' sports participation, and prior levels of violence and risk behaviors. Descriptive statistics for these measures are listed in Table 30.l. Add Health asked respondents about their

Table 30.1 Variable Descriptives (Survey Adjusted) (N = 6,397)

Variable	*Mean*			
	(Percent)	*(SE)*	*Minimum*	*Maximum*
Dependent Measure (Wave I In-Home Survey)				
Serious Fighting	*.40*	*(.01)*	*0*	
Independent Variables (In-School Survey)				
Age	14.83	(.13)	10	19
Black	.15	(.02)	0	
Intact Family	.73	(.01)	0	1
Parent Attachment	4.71	(.01)		5
School Commitment	3.18	(.02)		4
Self-Esteem	4.14	(.02)	1	5
Family SES	6.12	(.10)	0	10
Club Member	.41	(.01)	0	1
Body Mass Index	22.59	(.13)	11.22	54.28
Athlete	.63	(.01)	0	1
Football	.26	(.01)	0	
Basketball	.27	(.01)	0	
Baseball	.22	(.01)	0	
Wrestling	.07	(.00)	0	
Tennis	.04	(.00)	0	
Other Sport	.36	(.01)	0	
Prior Physical Fighting	.57	(.01)	0	1
Minor Delinquency	7.03	(.17)	0	36
No Reciprocated Male Friends	.44	(.02)	0	1
Friends Outside School	1.02	(.08)	0	10
Percent Male Friends Football	.16	(.01)	0	1
Percent Male Friends Basketball	.17	(.01)	0	
Percent Male Friends Baseball	.15	(.01)	0	
Percent Male Friends Wrestling	.02	(.00)	0	
Percent Male Friends Tennis	.03	(.00)	0	
Percent Male Friends Other Sport	.20	(.01)	0	1
Male Friends Average Delinquency	3.84	(.19)	0	36
Percent Male Friends Physical Fight	.31	(.01)	0	

participation in 12 athletic activities. Figure 30.1displays the male participation rates for these activities, as well as the percentage of male nonathletes. Approximately 25 percent of the sampled males participated in each of these activities. The individual sports of interest, wrestling and tennis, have lower participation rates (8 percent and 4 percent, respectively), but they remain adequately represented and have relatively low correlations with the team sports (highest *r*: wrestling-football = .21).

Along with being the most common male athletic activities, football, basketball, and football are also positively related to peer status. Figure 30.2 shows the mean number of friendship nominations received by athletes participating in the various sports, as well as the mean number of nominations going to nonathletes. The greater popularity

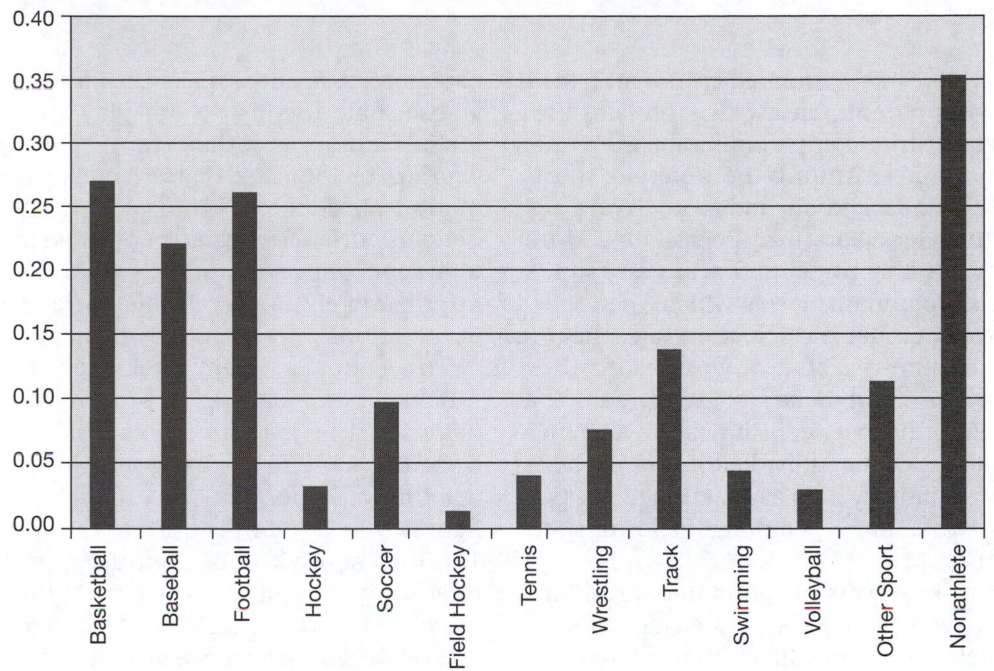

Figure 30.1 Male adolescent sports participation

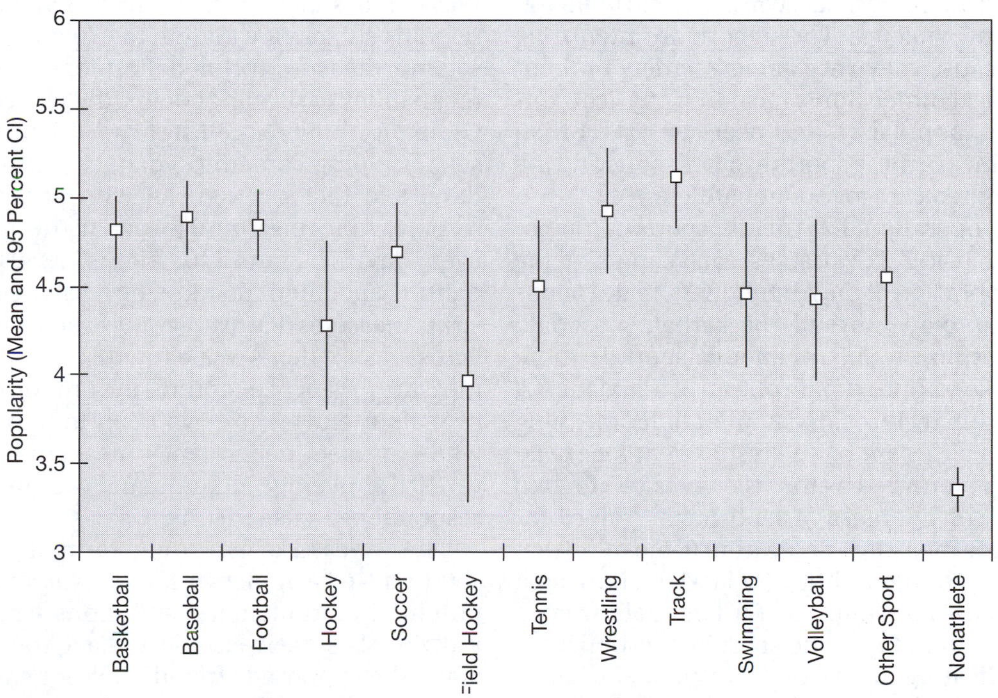

Figure 30.2 Popularity by male adolescent sports participation

of athletes as compared to nonathletes is most apparent. On average, athletes have over one friendship nomination more than nonathletes. Among the different sports, baseball, basketball, and football rate high in their association to peer status. Moreover, the "big three" sports are very similar in their popularity levels, which when added to their similar participation rates, help to reduce the risk that differences on these qualities could make spurious any associations found between the sports and male violence. Of the individual sports, wrestling has a relatively high association to peer status, while tennis is among the lower status sports.

I use two sets of sports measures. First, I create a global sports measure to see if athletes are more likely than nonathletes to be involved in serious fights. I coded 1 if the respondent yes to participating in any athletic activity and 0 otherwise. Second, I look at the independent effects of football, basketball, baseball, wrestling, and tennis on future violence. These sports are interesting because they vary along a variety of theoretical dimensions, including physical contact, popularity, and peer contexts. I then compare these sports to other sports and the omitted category of nonathletes.[2]

I operationalize friends' sports participation using six variables, each capturing the proportion of the respondents' male friends who play football, basketball, baseball, wrestling, tennis, or another sport. To more closely approximate objective friendships, I rely on reciprocated nominations, meaning that a tie sent by the respondent (ego) had to be returned by the receiver (alter) for it to be considered a "friendship."[3] Values for these measures range from 0, meaning that a respondent either (1) lacks reciprocated male friendships or (2) has male friends that do not play the sport in question, to 1, indicating that all of the respondent's male friends play the designated sport. To distinguish between individuals with no reciprocated male friendships and adolescents whose male friends do not play sports, I include a dummy variable for respondents who lack reciprocated male friendship nominations. In addition, I control for the number of reported friendships not listed in the high school or sister middle school rosters. Approximately 15 percent of all friendship nominations were to unknown peers.

To account for potential selection effects, I include two measures of prior antisocial behavior. The first, prior violence, is taken from the in-school survey and indicates whether a respondent was involved in a fight within 12 months prior to the survey. The in-school violence measure does not refer to the "seriousness" of the fight. It is therefore not a true lagged dependent measure. However, its reference to fighting should continue to capture much of the effects of unobserved population heterogeneity. The distribution for this variable has a moderate correlation (.35) between the in-school and Wave I measures, which suggests that there remains sufficient variation to explain. The second measure, prior delinquency, is a mean index of six minor delinquency items (smoking, drinking, getting drunk, skipping school, doing something dangerous on a dare, and racing a vehicle) with possible responses ranging from 0 (never) to 6 (nearly every day). To control for friends' levels of fighting and minor delinquency, I also construct measures that average these behaviors across respondents' male friends. The peer measure of violence captures the proportion of male friends who have been in a fight, while the peer delinquency measure captures the average delinquency among a respondent's male friends.

This measure is often termed the send-and-receive network and overcomes potentially problematic situations where individuals perceive that they have friends while the supposed "friends" do not share the same perceptions. I examined alternative network measures (send-or-receive, just send, andjust receive) with similar results.

Self-esteem and socioeconomic status may also be related both to violence and sports participation (Hughes and Coakley 1991). I construct two indices. The self-esteem measure is an index created from three items ("I have a lot of good qualities,""I have a lot to be proud of,'' and "I like myself just the way I am"). The SES measure captures the highest parents' educational and occupational attainment, as reported by students in the in-school survey. Values in this scale range from 0 (neither parent achieved a high school education or is currently employed) to 10 (at least one parent pursued postgraduate education and has a professional job).

I include individual background and demographic variables to control for concepts that prior research has found to be related to delinquency or sports participation. These variables include measures for age, black race, family structure, attachment to parents, and commitment to school. Of the latter, parent attachment and school commitment are commonly viewed as indicators of social bonding and are therefore important controls for examining the independent effects of sports on violence. Membership in nonathletic extracurricular clubs may also indicate school bonding and confound the relationship between sports and violence. I create a dichotomous measure of club membership with values of 1 for respondents who participated in one of 20 nonathletic activities and 0 otherwise. Finally, I include a measure of respondents' body mass index (BMI). Physical size may be positively related to both male violence (Felson 1996) and sports participation.[4]

MALE VIOLENCE AND SPORTS

I use survey-corrected logistic regressions to predict the binary measure of serious fighting.

Table 30.2 reports five survey-adjusted models of male serious fighting. The first model includes individual background and control variables, as well as a dichotomous measure of athletic participation. The second model disaggregates the athletic variable into the six sports categories with nonathletes as the reference category. The third model addresses issues of selection by including measures of prior individual fighting and minor delinquency. The fourth model adds measures of peer athletic behavior and network structure. Finally, the fifth model examines the effects of peer-reported violence and minor delinquency.

Looking at Model 1, we find few surprises regarding the relationships between individual background characteristics and violence. Consistent with prior research, age, intact family, socioeconomic status, parent attachment, and school commitment are significant negative risk factors for subsequent male violence. Interestingly, involvement in a nonathletic extracurricular activity also decreases the likelihood of getting into a fight by over 25 percent. This finding, along with the negative effects of parental attachment and school commitment, provides support for social control arguments that conventional bonds inhibit youth violence. Model 1 also suggests, though, that athletic participation may not hold similar inhibitory effects. Contrary to the hypothesis derived from social control theory, I find that athletic participation shows a *positive* relationship to serious fighting. Albeit nonsignificant, this runs counter to arguments suggesting that sports participation encourages conventional lines of action and reduces antisocial behavior.

Model 2 examines the independent effects of football, basketball, baseball, wrestling, and tennis participation on male adolescent violence. The results demonstrate that sports differ significantly in their relationships to serious fighting. Only football shows a significant and positive

Table 30.2 Survey-Adjusted Logistic Regressions of Male Adolescent Violence (N = 6,397)

	Model 1		Model 2		Model 3		Model 4		Model 5	
Variable	Beta (SE)	Odds Ratio	Beta (SE)	Odds Ratio	Beta (SE)	Odds Ratio	Beta (SE)	Odds Ratio	Beta (SE)	Odds Ratio
Intercept	4.37*** (.51)		4.29*** (.52)		1.73** (.61)		1.82*** (.63)		1.59* (.65)	
Age	–.17*** (0.3)	.84	–.16*** (0.3)	.85	–.14*** (0.3)	.87	–.14*** (.03)	.87	–.13*** (.03)	.87
Black	.37** (.11)	1.44	.34*** (.11)	1.41	.42*** (.12)	.52	.42** (.12)	.84	.42** (.12)	.85
Intact Family	–.27** (.09)	.77	–.27** (.09)	.77	–.18 (.09)	.84	–.17 (.10)	.97	–.17 (.10)	.97
Parent Attachment	–.12 (0.6)	.89	–.11 (0.6)	.90	.00 (.06)	1.00	.01 (0.6)	.96	.01 (.06)	.96
School Commitment	–.23*** (.05)	.80	–.21*** (0.5)	.81	–.21*** (.05)	.97	–.03 (.07)	.99	–.03 (.07)	.99
Self- Esteem	–.12* (.05)	.89	–.14** (.05)	87	–.14** (.05)	.89	–.11 (.06)	1.02	–.12 (.06)	1.01
Family SES	–.04* (0.2)	.96	–.04* (.02)	.96	–.04* (.02)	.96	–.04* (.02)	1.25	–.04* (.02)	1.23
Club Member	–.31*** (.08)	.74	–.28** (.08)	.76	–.28** (.08)	.79	–.24** (.08)	.90	–.24*** (.09)	.90
Body Mass Index	.002 (.01)	1.00	–.007 (0.1)	.99	–.013 (.01)	.99	–.014 (.01)	1.04	–.014 (.01)	1.04
Athlete	.10 (.08)	1.10								
Football			.34*** (.09)	1.41	.23* (.10)	1.26	.18 (.11)	1.19	.18 (.11)	.81
Basketball			–.01 (.09)	.99	–.02 (.10)	.98	.02 (.10)	1.02	.01 (.10)	.94
Baseball			–.01 (.10)	.99	.22 (.10)	.96	–.02 (.10)	.98	–.02 (.10)	.89
Wrestling			.37*	1.45	.24	1.27	.22	1.25	.21	1.37

			(.14)		(.16)		(.15)		(.15)	
Tennis			–.43*	.65	–.48*	.62	–.45*	.64	–.45*	.64
			(.20)		(.20)		(.20)		(.20)	
Other Sport			–.13	.88	–.14	.87	–.11	.90	–.10	.90
			(.09)		(0.9)		(.09)		(.09)	
Prior Physical fighting					1.40***	4.07	1.41***	4.09	4.10***	4.07
					(.08)		(.08)		(.08)	
Minor Delinquency					.04***	1.04	.04***	1.04	.04***	1.04
					(.01)		(.01)		(.01)	
Peer Network Measures										
No Reciprocated Male Friends							–.08	.93	.04	1.04
							(.09)		(.12)	
Friends Outside School							.04	1.04	.04	1.04
							(.02)		(.02)	
Percent Male Friends Football							35*	1.42	.33*	1.38
							(.16)		(.16)	
Percent Male Friends Basketball							–.20	.82	–.22	.81
							(.15)		(.15)	
Percent Male Friends Baseball							–.20	.82	–.22	.80
							(.15)		(.14)	
Percent Male Friends Wrestling							–.02	.98	–.07	.94
							(.24)		(.24)	
Percent Male Friends Tennis							–.55	.58	–.52	.59
							(.34)		(.34)	
Percent Male Friends Other Sport							–.14	.87	–.12	.89
							(.14)		(.14)	
Male Friends Average Delinquency									–.01	.99
									(.01)	
Percent Male Friends Physical Fight									.31*	1.37
									(.14)	
F-Statistic (df1, df2)	12.88	(10,128)	10.97	(15,107)	37.64	(17,105)	25.64	(25,97)	27.05	(27,95)

*** $p<.001$; ** $p<.01$.; $p<.05$.

relationship with fighting. Playing football increases the risk of getting into a serious fight by over 40 percent, compared to nonathletes, while basketball and baseball participation show no relationship to fighting. Of the two individual sports, wrestling shows a positive effect on fighting that is similar to football, with wrestlers being 45 percent more likely than nonathletes to get into a fight. Playing tennis shows the opposite effect, significantly decreasing the risks of fighting by 35 percent. These results provide strong support for masculinity arguments, in that the two heavy-contact and exclusively male sports show the strongest positive relationships to male violence, while tennis has the strongest negative association with male violence. On the other hand, there appears to be little support for the expectation that involvement in high visibility sports alone increases levels of violence. Neither baseball nor basketball is associated with an increased risk of fighting. Moreover, wrestling, an individual sport with low participation rates, has a strong positive association to male violence. Together, these results suggest a continuum of physical contact and masculinity whereby highly masculinized contact sports increase the risks of violence. Sports low in physical contact and less associated with masculinity, in contrast, seem to curb such behavior. It is possible that the effects of football and wrestling are spurious and explained by latent characteristics or prior socialization. Model 3 gains leverage on this question by including measures of prior fighting and minor delinquency. These variables control for much of the effects of state dependence or selectivity into sports. There is, notably, considerable stability in antisocial behavior over time. Self-reported fighting during the in-school survey increases the risk of being in a serious future fight by over 300 percent. Indeed, these variables attenuate over one-third of the football coefficient and almost one-half the wrestling coefficient, making the latter nonsignificant. Football, however, remains a strong and significant predictor of violence, suggesting that self-selection does not account for the entire relationship.

Model 4 explores the potential mediating role, derived from social learning theories, of friendship network composition on the sports–violence relationship. This model includes peer network measures for each of the six sports categories. The results provide support for combined social learning and masculinity predictions. Males with a high proportion of reciprocated friends playing football are significantly more likely to behave violently than those without football friends. Net of the number of friends playing other sports, individuals whose friends all play football are 38 percent more likely to get into a serious fight than those without football friends.

It is particularly interesting that embeddedness in wrestling networks shows a small negative relationship to violence. This suggests that it is the combination of heavy physical contact and a team setting, and not just the physical contact associated with wrestling, that encourages male violence. Indeed, football friendships fully attenuate the direct effect of individual football participation, decreasing the size of the football coefficient by 35 percent from Model 3. Much of the violence associated with football is thus explained by athletes in this sport having greater contact with other football players. Moreover, embeddedness in a football network significantly increases the risk of serious violence, regardless of an individual's level of football participation. But is the effect of football-playing friends greater for football players than for non-football players? It could be that the relationship between football and violence increases as players are more immersed in football peer networks. To test this possibility, I included an interaction between football and football networks in Model 4 (not reported), yet this interaction was nonsignificant. This suggests that, if anything, football players in football networks are less likely to behave violently than similarly situated non-football males.

To illustrate the effects of athletic friendships, Figure 30.3 presents predicted probabilities of serious fighting across different proportions of football, basketball, baseball, wrestling, and tennis friends. The risk of fighting increases with higher proportions of football friends. Males with all-football friends are expected to have a 45 percent probability of getting into a serious fight, more than 8 percentage points higher than similar individuals with no football friends and almost 20 percentage points higher than males with all-tennis friends. Like Haynie's (2002) examination of the relationship between delinquency and delinquent friendship networks, this analysis suggests that embeddedness in homogeneous peer networks most effectively constrains individual behaviors toward group norms and increases opportunities for group-related behavior. In this case, the norms of football are positively associated with male violence.

As with the potentially spurious relationship between individual sports participation and fighting, it is possible that the effects of peer networks would reflect the possibility that individuals seek friends who are violent and that shared violent tendencies predict both involvement in sports and future individual violence. Model 5 examines this by including measures of the proportion of friends who self-report being in a fight and the average minor delinquency of those same friends. As one would expect, the proportion of friends who have been in a fight is positively associated with individual fighting. Individuals whose friends all report getting into a fight are themselves 38 percent more likely to get into a fight. The delinquency of male friends shows no relationship to serious fighting, net of other covariates. More importantly for my stated hypotheses, the introduction of the two measures does not significantly attenuate the peer football measure. Having a high proportion of friends playing football maintains a significant association with serious violence.

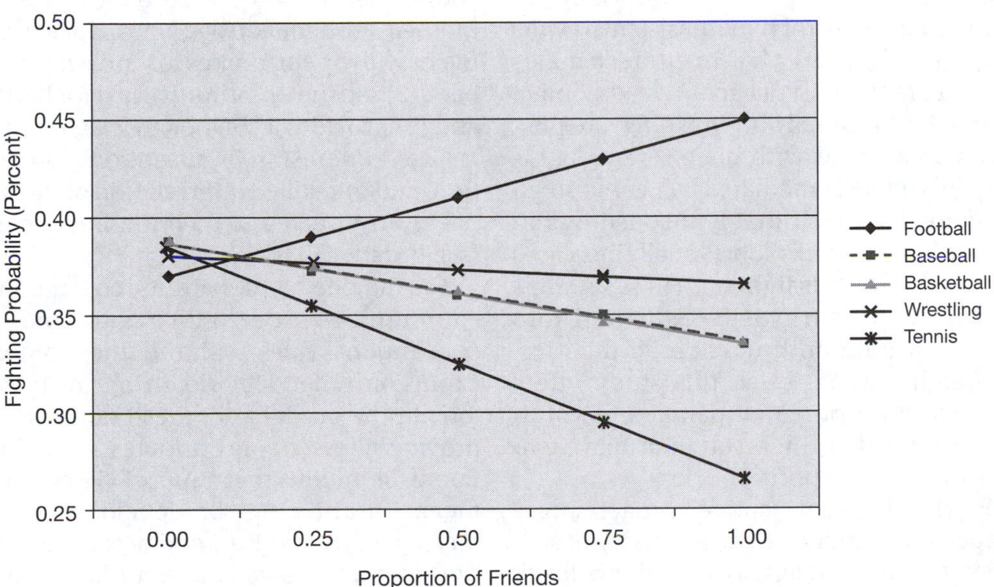

Figure 30.3 Predicted probability of serious fighting by friend's sports participation

To test whether the effects of playing sports or having friends who play sports differ by race, social class, or self-esteem, I include interactions between the sport-specific variables and individual background variables in the final model (not shown). None of these interactions are significant at $p < .05$. Thus, there appears to be little evidence that normative pressures resulting from sports participation should be higher for more disadvantaged or insecure youth.

DISCUSSION AND CONCLUSIONS

This analysis represents a quantitative foray into the relationship between adolescent sports and male interpersonal violence. While prior research has demonstrated that sports participation is associated with many positive outcomes, few studies have focused on the connections between high school interscholastic sports and violence. The sports–violence relationship is a theoretically rich area with competing hypotheses from prominent perspectives. Contrary to the social control hypothesis, my results suggest that sports fail to protect males from interpersonal violence. Indeed, contact sports (e.g., football and wrestling) are positively associated with male serious fighting. This effect is mediated by peer football participation, such that embeddedness in all-football networks substantially increases the risk for serious fighting. These findings are consistent with hypotheses derived from social learning and masculinity theories. Although caveats exist, this study offers leverage on a potential paradox of youth sports, and this understanding may help inform schools' sports policies.

Playing hypermasculine contact sports shapes subsequent violence. This is not surprising, given that aggressive kids are likely to enter contact sports and the coaches of these activities are likely to choose aggressive kids to fill more competitive teams. However, selection does not appear to tell the entire story. Net of prior fighting and delinquency, football remains a significant predictor of serious fighting and is only fully mediated with the introduction of friends' football participation.

The theoretical implications of a positive football–violence relationship are apparent. If we believe that football players generally lie at the center of a school's peer culture it is difficult to explain the football–violence connection as resulting from weak social bonds. The social and individual benefits accrued by male contact-sport athletes do not suggest that they reject conventional norms and lie on the fringes of conventional society, and yet increased rates of violence from these athletes also suggest that they are not altogether conforming. This seemingly paradoxical pattern was recognized at football's inception. Raymond Gettell, a physical educator at Amherst College at the beginning of the twentieth century, echoed the views of many Americans when he described football as an essential tool for preparing young men for war. According to Gettell, football simultaneously (1) provides young males with opportunities for "physical combat," (2) satisfies a "primitive lust for battle," and (3) provides a "higher and distinctively civilized interest in organization, cooperation, and the skilled interrelation of individual effort directed to a common purpose" (see Burstyn 1999: 73).

On the one hand, parents, coaches, and communities expect athletes to abide by conventional rules, with the threat of team expulsion potentially deterring misbehavior. On the other hand, these same groups provide contact-sport athletes with situational definitions that support violence as a means of attaining "battlefield" victories, increasing peer status, and asserting "warrior" identities. Given these conflicting definitions, whether or not male contact-sport athletes behave violently likely depends on the situational contexts in which they find themselves. In the classroom, constraint and conformity validate the conventional identities expected of contact-sport athletes, as well as help to solidify their high status positions within schools. In informal peer situations, however, gendered displays of power and aggression allow the same males to meet group expectations and maintain their superiority within gendered peer hierarchies.[5]

This argument parallels Sutherland's (1940) explanation for white-collar crime. For Sutherland, white-collar crime results from over-conformity to the competitive norms within business and is therefore unlikely to stem from deviant identities or social isolation from conventional society. Like athletes in heavy-contact team sports, businesspeople are often reinforced for behaviors that are at odds with legal rules. Because their behaviors occur within respected and high-status institutional settings, however, both businesspeople and athletes are able to behave in socially unacceptable ways while avoiding deviant labels and identities.

While my findings contribute to our understanding of the relationship between sports and violence, there are obvious limitations. First, it remains possible that *unobserved* heterogeneity explains the association between peer athletic participation and violence. One possibility for addressing unobserved heterogeneity is to look at within—individual change over time using a fixed effects approach. Unfortunately, such an approach is impossible in the current analysis due to a lack of longitudinal sports measures. Without longitudinal data on sports participation, population heterogeneity and selection effects can only be addressed by identifying plausible instrumental variables (notoriously difficult in social science research) or by including theoretically relevant controls.

Second, this study is unable to identify the causal mechanisms that explain the observed relationships. An inability to identify specific mechanisms (e.g., subjects' identification with hegemonic masculinity, objective reinforcement for violence, or victims as "weaker" peers) leaves open the possibility for alternative explanations. This is a problem often associated with cultural, identity, and values research. Qualitative research provides the best hope for understanding the elusive and interparative mechanisms underlying this article's findings. Similar to the work of Eder and colleagues (1997) and Curry (1998), researchers must return to the field to identify the personal and situational characteristics associated with athlete misbehavior. Only ethnographic studies can gain leverage on the intersections of context, opportunity, and motivations that surround sports-related violence. Based on situational research of male-on-male violence (Luckenbill 1977; Polk 1999), I am inclined to believe that athlete violence typically involves threats to masculinity, the presence of an audience, and an informal setting such as a party or schoolyard. It may also be, though, that male athletes actively seek violent encounters to demonstrate their masculine prowess and group worth. Likewise, individual characteristics (e.g., athletic ability or position played) and team characteristics (e.g., win-loss record) may facilitate athlete violence. Future qualitative research could better disentangle the proximal causes of sports-related violence.

Despite such limitations, results suggest that sports, particularly male-dominated contact sports, have important consequences for male adolescent violence. Such findings may also have certain policy implications. As Connell (1996) states in his insightful look at gender and education, the most important step in addressing violence and bullying in schools is to become aware of the masculinizing practices that contribute to gender privilege and hegemonic domination. Sports, he argues, are major contributors to a school's gender regime.

The results of this project clearly demonstrate a link between contact sports and violence, meaning that these activities may be appropriate sites for disrupting male violence. Though, the findings also suggest that much of the connection between contact sports and violence occurs prior to individuals' high school athletic experiences. This possibility makes it all the more important that coaches, parents, and school administrators be conscious of their gatekeeping roles and use their positions to prevent continued athlete violence at all developmental stages. Precluding problematic youth from playing contact sports, not tolerating athletic violence, and fostering a more tolerant atmosphere are three means of breaking the contact sport–violence relationship. These changes necessitate deemphasizing the "winning is everything" mentality, an unlikely proposition given the demands placed on coaches and players to make their schools and communities proud. As Trulson (1986) found when researching martial arts programs, contact sports that emphasize respect for others, self-control, patience, and humility can serve to reduce the violence of aggressive male adolescents. Programs developed according to these ideals may not necessarily win as many matches as those built on aggression and competitiveness, but their attractiveness lies in positively affecting the lives of problematic youth while fostering an environment of inclusiveness and respect.

NOTES

1. Two problems endemic to sport–violence research are (l) a reliance on cross-sectional designs that are unable to distinguish selection from socialization effects and (2) a failure to distinguish effects across different types of sports (see Baumert, Henderson, and Thompson 1998; Begg et al. 1996; Jackson et al. 2002; Nixon 1997; Wright and Fitzpatrick 2006).
2. Correlations between the sports measures range between .04 (tennis-football) to .24 (baseball-football), suggesting that each measure has ample unique variance to minimize problems of collinearity.
3. This measure is often termed the send-and-receive network and overcomes potentially problematic situations where individuals perceive that they have friends while the supposed "friends" do not share the same perceptions. I examined alternative network measures (send-or-receive, just send, and-just receive) with similar results.
4. Add Health's BMI measure does not distinguish physical size from strength or muscularity. Males with relatively high BMI values may therefore be either more muscular or more obese as compared to other males.
5. Recent research also suggests that athletes are at greater risk of alcohol use (Eitle, Turner, and Eitle 2003) and drunk driving (Hartmann and Massoglia forthcoming). These findings, along with positive connections between minor delinquency and popularity (Allen et al. 2005; Kreager forthcoming), support views that "in-crowd" athletes are under pressure to maintain peer status with demonstrations of masculinity and risky behaviors (see also Curry 1998).

REFERENCES

Allen, Joseph P., Maryfrances R. Porter, F. Christy McFarland, Penny Marsh, and Kathleen Boykin McElhaney.2005. "The Two Faces of Adolescents' Success with Peers: Adolescent Popularity, Social Adaptation, and Deviant Behavior." *Child Development* 76:747–60.

Akers, Ronald L. 1998. *Social Learning and Social Structure: A General Theory of Crime and Deviance.* Boston, MA: Northeastern University Press.

Akers, Ronald L., Marvin D. Krohn, Lonn Lanza-Kaduce, and Marcia Radosevich. 1979. "Social Learning and Deviant Behavior: A Specific Test of a General Theory."*American Sociological Review* 44:636–55.

Baumert, Paul W., John M. Henderson, and Nancy Thompson. 1998. "Health Risk Behaviors of Adolescent Participants in Organized Sports." *Journal of Adolescent Health* 22:460–65.

Begg, Dorothy J., John D. Langley, Terrie Moffit, and Stephen W. Marshall. 1996. "Sport and Delinquency: An Examination of the Deterrence Hypothesis in a Longitudinal Study." *British Journal of Sports Medicine* 30:335–41.

Bissinger, H. G. 1991. *Friday Night Lights: A Town, A Team, A Dream.* New York: Harper Perennial.

Burgess, Robert L. and Ronald L. Akers. 1966. "A Differential Association-Reinforcement Theory of Criminal Behavior." *Social Problems* 14:128–47.

Burstyn, Varda. 1999. *The Rites of Men: Manhood, Politics, and the Culture of Sports.* Toronto, Canada: University of Toronto Press.

Chantala, Kim and Joyce Tabor. 1999. "Strategies to Perform a Design-Based Analysis Using the Add Health Data."Chapel Hill, NC: University of North Carolina Population Center. Retrieved January 12, 2007 (www.cpc.unc.edu/projects/addhealth/files/weightl.pdf).

Coakley, Jay. 200 l. *Sport in Society: Issues and Controversies.* 7th ed. Boston, MA: McGraw Hill.

Coleman, James. 1961. *TheAdolescent Society: The Social Life of the Teenager and its Impact on Education.* New York: The Free Press of Glencoe.

Connell, Robert W. 1995. *Masculinities.* Berkeley, CA: University of California Press.

——. 1996. "Teaching the Boys: New Research on Masculinity, and Gender Strategies for Schools." *Teachers College Record* 98:206–35.

Connell, Robert W. and James W. Messerschmidt. 2005. "Hegemonic Masculinity: Rethinking the Concept." *Gender and Society* 19:829–59.

Crosnoe, Robert. 2001. "The Social World of Male and Female Athletes in High School."*Sociological Studies of Children and Youth* 8:87–108.

Crosset, Todd. 1999. "Male Athletes' Violence Against Women: A Critical Assessment of the Athletic Affiliation, Violence Against Women Debate." *Quest* 51:244–57.

Curry, Timothy Jon. 1998. "Beyond the Locker Room: Campus Bars and College Athletes." *Sociology of Sport Journal* 15:205–15.

Eccles, Jacquelynne S. and Bonnie L. Barber. 1999. "Student Council, Volunteering, Basketball, or Marching Band: What Kind of Extracurricular Involvement Matters?" *Journal of Adolescent Research* 14:10–43.

Eckert, Penelope. 1989. *Jocks and Burnouts: Social Categories and Identity in High School.* New York: Teachers College Press.

Eder, Donna, Catherine C. Evans, and Stephen Parker. 1997. *School Talk: Gender and Adolescent Culture.* New Brunswick, NJ: Rutgers University Press.

Eder, Donna and David A. Kinney. 1995. "The Effect of Middle School Extracurricular Activities on Adolescents' Popularity and Peer Status." *Youth and Society* 26:298–324.

Eitle, David, R. Jay Turner, and Tamela McNulty Eitle. 2003. "The Deterrence Hypothesis Reexamined: Sports Participation and Substance Use Among Young Adults."*Journal of Drug Issues* 33:193–222.

Eveslage, Scott and Kevin Delaney. 1998. "Talkin Trash at Hardwick High: A Case Study of Insult Talk on a Boys' Basketball Team." *International Review of Sport Sociology* 33:239–53.

Ewing, Martha, Lori Gano-Overway, Crystal Branta, and Vern Seefeldt. 2002. "The Role of Sports in Youth Development." Pp. 31–47 in *Paradoxes of Youth and Sport,* edited by M. Gatz, M. Messner and S. J. Ball-Rokeach. Albany, NY: State University of New York Press.

Fejgin, Naomi. 1994. "Participation in High School Competitive Sports: A Subversion of School Mission or Contribution to Academic Goals." *Sociology of Sport Journal* 11:211–30.

Felson, Richard B. 1996. "Big People Hit Little People: Sex Differences in Physical Power and Interpersonal Violence." *Criminology* 34:433–52.

Fine, Gary Alan 1987. *With the Boys: Little League Baseball and Preadolescent Culture.* Chicago, IL: University of Chicago Press.

Gatz, Margaret, Michael A. Messner, and Sandra J. Ball-Rokeach. 2002. "Introduction." Pp. 1–12 in *Paradoxes of Youth and Sport,* edited by M. Gatz, M. Messner, and S. J. Ball-Rokeach. Albany, NY: State University of New York Press.

Goffinan, Erving. 1967.*Interaction Ritual: Essays on Face-to-Face Behavior.* Garden City, NJ: Doubleday.

Hartmann, Douglas and Michael Massoglia. Forthcoming. "Re-Assessing the Relationship Between High School Sports Participation and Deviance: Evidence of Enduring, Bifurcated Effects." *Sociological Quarterly.*

Haynie, Dana. 2002. "Friendship Networks and Delinquency: The Relative Nature of Peer Delinquency." *Journal of Quantitative Criminology* 18:99–134.

Hirschi, Travis. 1969. *Causes of Delinquency.* Berkeley, CA: University of California Press.

Holland, Alyce and Thomas Andre. 1994. "Athletic Participation and the Social Status of Adolescent Males and Females." *Youth and Society* 25:388–407.

Hughes, Robert and Jay Coakley. 1991. "Positive Deviance Among Athletes: The Implications of Overconformity to the Sport Ethic."*Sociology of Sport Journal* 8:307–25.

Jackson, James S., Shelley Keiper, Kendrick Brown, Tony Brown, and Warde Manuel. 2002. "Athletic Identity, Racial Attitudes, and Aggression in First-

Year Black and White Intercollegiate Athletes." Pp. 159–72 in *Paradoxes of Youth Sport,* edited by M. Gatz, M. Messner, and S. J. Ball-Rokeach. New York: State University of New York Press.

Jeziorski, Ronald M. 1994. *The Importance of School Sports in American Education and Socialization.* New York: University Press of America.

Kreager, Derek A. Forthcoming. "When It's Good to be 'Bad': Violence and Adolescent Peer Status." *Criminology.*

Landers, Daniel M. and Donna M. Landers. 1978. "Socialization via Interscholastic Athletics: Its Effects on Delinquency." *Sociology of Education* 51:299–303.

Langbein, Laura and Roseana Bess. 2002. "Sports in School: Source of Amity or Antipathy?" *Social Science Quarterly* 83:436–54.

Larson, Reed. 1994. "Youth Organizations, Hobbies, and Sports as Developmental Contexts."Pp. 46–65 in *Adolescence in Context,* edited by R. K. Silberiesen and E. Todt. New York: Springer-Verlag.

Luckenbill, David F. 1977. "Criminal Homicide as a Situated Transaction." *Social Problems* 25:176–86.

Mahoney, Joseph L. 2000. "School Extracurricular Activity Participation as a Moderator in the Development of Antisocial Patterns." *Child Development* 71:502–16.

Mahoney, Joseph L. and Robert B. Cairns. 1997. "Do Extracurricular Activities Protect Against Early School Dropout?" *Developmental Psychology* 33: 241–53.

Marsh, Herbert W. 1993. "The Effects of Participation in Sport During the Last Two Years of High School." *Sociology of Sport Journal* 10:18–43.

Matsueda, Ross L. and Kathleen Anderson. 1998. "The Dynamics of Delinquent Peers and Delinquent Behavior." *Criminology* 36:269–308.

McNeal, Ralph B. 1995. "Extracurricular Activities and High School Dropouts." *Sociology of Education* 68:62–81.

Messner, Michael. 1992. *Power at Play: Sports and the Problem of Masculinity.* Boston, MA: Beacon Press.

——. 2002. *Taking the Field: Women, Men, and Sports.* Minneapolis, MN: University of Minnesota Press.

Nixon, Howard L. 1997. "Gender, Sport, and Aggressive Behavior Outside Sport." *Journal of Sport and Social Issues* 21:379–91.

Otto, Luther and Duane Alwin. 1977. "Athletics, Aspirations and Attainments." *Sociology of Education* 50:102–13.

Pappas, Nick, Patrick McKenry, and Beth Catlett. 2004. "Athlete Aggression on the Rink and off the Ice." *Men and Masculinities* 6:291–312.

Polk, Kenneth. 1999. "Males and Honor Contest Violence." *Homicide Studies* 3:6–29.

Sabo, Donald. 1994. "Pigskin, Patriarchy and Pain." Pp. 82–88 in *Sex, Violence, and Power in Sports: Rethinking Masculinity,* edited by M. Messner and D. Sabo. Freedom, CA: Crossing Press.

Sabo, Donald, Merrill J. Melnick, and Beth E. Vanfossen. 1993. "High School Athletic Participation and Postsecondary Educational and Occupational Mobility: A Focus on Race and Gender." *Sociology of Sport Journal* 10:44–56.

Shields, Edgar W. 1999. "Intimidation and Violence by Males in High School Athletics." *Adolescence* 34:503–21.

Spady, William. 1970. "Lament for the Letterman: Effect of Peer Status and Extracurricular Activities on Goal and Achievement." *Ame can Journal of Sociology* 75:680–702.

Stark, Rodney, Lori Kent, and Roger Finke. 1987. "Sports and Delinquency."Pp. 115–24 in *Positive Criminology,* edited by M. R. Gottfredson and T. Hirschi. Newbury Park, CA: Sage.

Sutherland, Edwin H. 1940. "White Collar Criminality." *American Sociological Review* 5:1–12.

——. 1947. *Principles of Criminology.* 4th ed. Philadelphia, PA: J. B. Lippincott.

Trulson, Michael E. 1986. "Martial Arts Training: A Novel 'Cure' for Juvenile Delinquency." *Human Relations* 39:1131–40.

Young, Kevin, Philip White, and William McTeer. 1994. "Body Talk: Male Athletes Reflect on Sport, Injury, and Pain." *Sociology of Sport Journal* 11:175–94.

Warr, Mark. 2002. *Companions in Crime: The Social Aspects of Criminal Conduct.* Cambridge, UK: Cambridge University Press.

Warr, Mark and Mark C. Stafford. 1991. "The Influence of Delinquent Peers: What They Think or What They Do?" *Criminology* 29:851—66.

Wright, Darlene and Kevin Fitzpatrick. 2006. "Social Capital and Adolescent Violent Behavior: Correlates of Fighting and Weapon Use Among Secondary School Students." *Social Forces* 84:1435–53.

CHAPTER 31

The Dark Side of Social Capital: An Ethnography of Sport Governance

Dino Numerato and Simone Baglioni

The concept of social capital has acquired an influential position in the academic debate on the nature of contemporary sport. This is true not only within the field of sports studies, but also within the more general theoretical framework of social and political sciences. Cooperation, trust, loyalty and respect for rules and adversaries are all considered natural outcomes of social interaction during sport practice or participation in sport governance activities. For this reason, sport practice is considered a 'school for democracy'.

More in-depth theoretical and empirical explorations of the topic, however, have demonstrated that social capital in sport, as in other social spheres, generates both positive and negative consequences for those who practise it as well as for their society. Yet, the negative consequences have not been adequately reflected.

In line with recent literature on the topic, we suggest that academic examination of the relationship between social capital and sport needs to be revisited and informed by a more substantial analysis of its dark dimension. The existence of a dark side was briefly acknowledged by the editors of the recently published book *Sport and Social Capital*, who stated that the phenomenon 'within different geographic and demographic contexts remains relatively untested and given the characteristics of sport organizations and their membership, it is reasonable to suggest that they have the capacity to engender the "dark side of social capital"' (Nicholson and Hoye, 2008: 12). However, more in-depth, systematic and empirically informed research is still missing.

To address this gap, this article focuses mainly on the dark side of social capital created *in* and *through* sports, with a particular interest on the seldom-explored area of sport governance. In particular, the article addresses the following questions: what types of dark side of social capital can we identify by analysing Czech and Italian sport governance? What theoretical implications do the explorations of the dark side of social capital have for further development of research into sport and social capital? What implications does this research have for policy and practice of contemporary sport governance?

In order to answer these questions in the following sections we briefly discuss the dark sides of social capital in general and then move to discuss a conceptualization of the dark side of social capital created *in* and *through* sport. We identify the topics and facets of theory that have remained unexplored. Next, we present the methods for and findings from our own research on the dark side of social capital in sport governance based on two multi-sited ethnographic studies in the Czech Republic and Italy.

THE DARK SIDE OF SOCIAL CAPITAL

Following the vast literature comprehending works based on different epistemological traditions and summarized in different works (e.g. Castiglione et al., 2008; Field, 2008; Keller, 2009; Lin, 2001), some basic and common treats of social capital can be identified. We conceive of social capital as a relational individual or collective resource that is more or less intentionally built and created and is used to achieve defined goals. Such relational resources may be mobilized for very different purposes, for the economic and emotional well-being of an individual or of a group, but also in the interest of a community, an organization or an entire society.

As we argue more extensively throughout this article, contrary to some mainstream conceptualizations of it, we understand social capital as a more ambivalent concept: actions and resources mobilized for the good of an individual or of a group may be detrimental or harmful for another. Although the simultaneous existence of the dark side alongside the positive effects has widely been recognized by existing scholarship and its roots can be traced back to the work of social capital classics (Bourdieu, 1980; Coleman, 1988, 1990; Putnam, 1993, 2000), its further empirical and systematic examination has been rather rare (Field, 2008; Portes, 1998; Warren, 2008). Studies have pointed out that social networks can serve negative purposes, such as terrorism, crime or nepotism, as the cases of Ku Klux Klan, the Michigan Militia or even the Mafia show (Fukuyama, 1999; Gambetta, 1988). Social networks can also work as a tool of social exclusion (Bourdieu, 1980; Crossley, 2008) and increase social inequality (Field, 2008). From the methodological point of view, a contextual and situational analysis of different manifestations of social capital case by case is suggested in order explore a detrimental nature of social action where it is not evident or it becomes an object of competing interpretations (Warren, 2001, 2008).

We define the dark side of social capital as situations in which trust, social ties and shared beliefs and norms that may be beneficial to some persons are detrimental to other individuals, but also to sport movements as well as to the society at large. In the context of sport sociology research we understand the dark side of social capital as attempts to manipulate and misuse trust to achieve a particular interest that is in conflict with more general sports developments objectives. In other words, we conceive of the dark side of social capital not only in terms of a (negative) function that social capital can have, but also in terms of the nature of a social entity, a sport governing body, associated to social capital. To analyse the dark side of social capital therefore means to explore the nature and function of organizational social capital (Schneider, 2009).

While acknowledging the epistemological ambiguity of the social capital concept, we argue that the interconnectedness between different types of social capital must be considered in order to understand the complex nature of civic engagement within sport associations. In this sense, both Bourdieu's and Coleman's understandings of social action can be of particular interest when revisiting Putnam's meso- and macro-socially driven explorations of social capital. To advance knowledge beyond the state of the art we examine the dynamic nature of civic engagement within sport clubs and sport associations throughout the individually possessed volume of social capital or by considering small networks of actors and their interaction. This perspective is not new; it has been employed previously by Blackshaw and Long (2005) and by Burnett

(2006), who revisited Putnam's ideas about social capital through Bourdieu's and Coleman's perspectives, respectively.

This approach also facilitates the re-introduction of the category of power, which has seldom been applied within idealized pro-democracy conceptualizations of the relationship between social capital and sport, although a wide range of literature within the neo-Marxist and hegemony theoretical perspectives (e.g. Hoye and Cuskelly, 2003, 2007; Sugden and Tomlinson, 1998) on sport governance emphasized its significance for the analysis of sport associations.

THE DARK SIDE OF SOCIAL CAPITAL IN SPORT

Scholars dealing with the dark side of social capital in sport have conceptualized the phenomenon in three different ways. First, they conceived of the dark side of social capital in sport as mirroring and reproducing macro-societal negative externalities. Second, they observed the dark side of social capital established in the relations between sport and social spheres external to sport. Third, some scholars emphasized the role of the dark side of social networks jeopardizing the potentially positive values inherent to sport activities.

The majority of writing on the dark side of social capital in sport belongs to the first category. These studies referred to social exclusion and to the negative effects of what Putnam called *bonding social capital*, which reinforces the networks of insiders and excludes outsiders. In this vein, social capital that is built through sport represents a sphere that mirrors and reproduces the same diversities that exist in the overall structure of society. Notions of sport as a facilitator of economically based social exclusion occurred in the overview of the studies on social exclusion and sport presented by Collins (2003), in Jarvie's (2003) remarks on the patterns of privilege and elitism reproduced by sport illustrated using the case of access to private golf clubs, in the example of traditional rugby clubs excluding players or supporters from different socio-economic backgrounds (Skinner et al., 2008) and in Tonts's (2005) study on the role of sport clubs and sport events in rural Australia. Similar attention as to socio-economic factors has been devoted to other socio-cultural factors such as race, ethnicity and gender (Dyreson, 2001; Long, 2008; Palmer and Thompson, 2007).

A second perspective claims that the dark side originates in the interconnectedness between sport practice and the spheres external to sports, namely business. In this manner, Dyreson (2001) suggests that social bonds created in sport are sometimes misused for commercial interests. He notes that social networks created in sport clubs form large communities where market products may be sold.

The third perspective suggests that social capital, which is built in sport, helps to maintain and reproduce a normative framework that is contradictory to idealized myths about sport being exclusively beneficial. Long (2008) emphasized that sports clubs and national sport governing bodies members tend 'to maintain the essence of the sport they know and love', which does not necessarily mean that the sport is safe based on fair play rules and codes of ethics (Long, 2008: 224), but it can rather be normatively framed by values such as winning at any price and top-down domination. Jarvie (2007) similarly noted that sport might contribute to the diffusion of downward levelling or conformity. The dark side of social capital was investigated in the case of sports fans, particularly a group of South Australian football supporters (the so-called 'Groggies'). The dense networks and connections built in relation to sport were analysed in terms of facilitating the diffusion of other detrimental values as malignant behaviour (Palmer and Thompson, 2007). Similarly,

Groeneveld and Ohl (2010) argued that networks built around football can be based on hate, aggression or violence.

While the scope of research on the dark side of social capital in sports has been wide, most studies' primary concern did not expand beyond sport practice or sport supporting. Sport governance, an important topic, was either overlooked or only marginally addressed. In our study, we therefore aim to fill this gap.

Moreover, we suggest that the analysis needs to be strictly anchored within social capital terminology. Namely, studies of the first type (about the exclusive nature of sport practice) run the risk of conceptual slippage, since they employ the term 'social capital' as a linguistic rather than heuristic device. In particular, only a fragile distinction is made between manifestation of the dark side of social capital in sport and the aspects of sport that are simply negative and detrimental. Consistent adherence to the social capital concept requires not only addressing the misuse of social networks but also manipulating trust in sport governance.

Furthermore, following Putnam's ideas, a wide range of evidence has been gathered on *bonding* social capital as a particular form of social capital in sports. Less explicit attention was given to the role of *linking* social capital. We attempted to find evidence of vertically (Côté, 2001) or horizontally *linking* social capital (Woolcock, 2001), connecting actors in dissimilar situations that contribute to the creation of the dark side of social capital.

Finally, when reading the existing literature critically, it is clear that the layers of social capital analysed within studies on the dark side are limited. Attention has been focused on social capital at the micro-level (as an individual) or at the macro-level (as a quality akin to society overall). However, the meso-level of sport association has been overlooked. Our analytical approach addresses the aforementioned issue of the need to analyse various levels of social capital in terms of their dynamics and interconnectedness, especially in relation to micro-level social capital.

METHODOLOGY

The analysis presented in this article draws on a multi-sited ethnographic inquiry among sport movement representatives. The study was carried out in two different countries, the Czech Republic (data collected by the first author) and Italy (data collected by the second author), mainly during the period from January 2007 to early 2008. In this timeframe we carried out fieldwork in Cagliari, Florence, Genoa, Milan, Naples, Rome, Trieste for Italy and geographically covered all the regions of the Czech Republic. During our ethnography we met dozens of persons (100 persons-interviews per country) involved in sport at very different levels: athletes, sport clubs' volunteers, sport governing bodies' managers or officials, representatives of public institutions, sponsors and experts.[1]

The dark side of social capital was not initially an explicit focus of the overarching project, and the respondents of the research were not aware that the dark side of social capital was one of the topics of ethnographic scrutiny. The significance of the dark side emerged contemporaneously with the ethnographic fieldwork and was therefore explored as an inherent part of sport governance.

The dark nature of associational life can be demonstrated by the simple fact that our ethnographic efforts were not always welcomed, and we were occasionally referred to as *spies, inspectors, controllers,* or *allies* (exemplified in first author's field notes from, e.g. observations of a Czech regional handball association's general assembly on 24 March 2007; an interview with a secretary general of a regional football association on

28 May 2007; and observations at a national sailing regatta on 28 September 2007). Some respondents even consulted their colleagues and peers who had met us previously to prove our identity (second author's field notes from an introductory meeting with a secretary general of a national federation on 3 February 2007 and first author's field notes from an interview with a secretary general of a regional football association on 28 May 2007).

The existing distrust within some associations also forced us to be prudent when interviewing our respondents, such as when raising certain sensitive issues or when referring to the respondents to whom we had spoken previously and who provided us with specific information (first author field notes: personal communications with a volunteer for a football association, 26 September 2007; interview with an employee of the Czech football association, 7 November 2007). Repeated formal and informal requests to attend a general assembly of the Czech football association were rejected as well as the request to attend a meeting of the executive board of the Italian national sailing federation (first author field notes from, e.g. phone conversations with employees of the association, 15 and 16 January 2007; second author field notes, 10 March 2007).

Apart from reasons external to this article (an EU project), our choice of countries reflects strong evidence that dark side of social capital exists in real life and are mirrored in a wealth of academic reflections. As shown in studies not related to sport, both Italy and the Czech Republic are countries with relatively frequent episodes of corruption, political clientelism, high institutional distrust, and little respect for the laws (see, inter alia, della Porta and Vannucci, 1999; Frič, 2008; Passmore, 2007).

Needless to say, the aim of this research was not comparative given the novelty and the necessarily exploratory nature of the study. Empirical evidence gathered in different socio-cultural contexts provides the study with a variety of examples on which a solid, coherent and analytically elaborated conceptual model can be built in a future phase of our study.

We used three different techniques; semi-structured interviews were accompanied by observations and secondary analysis of documents. The collected data were thematically analysed both manually and with the Atlas.ti software package. The semi-structured interviews were carried out at the national, regional and local levels of sport federations and clubs for three sport disciplines: amateur football, handball and sailing. We selected three different sports to cover a variety of different sporting cultures and different styles of governance. Our research also touched upon the role of umbrella multi-sport associations as well as the role of public support of sport.

The fact that we did not intend to generalize from and compare partial examples specific to each of the sporting cultures and that we rather aimed to identify ideal types of the dark side of social capital, explains why sometimes no reference is made to a particular sports discipline to avoid challenging the principles of confidentiality and anonymity guaranteed to the respondents; engaging in research on the dark side of social capital creates a need to handle sensitive issues.

Such an exploration requires taking into account several ethical considerations. Interviews were conducted in an overt manner, yet confidentially, using either digital recorders or field notebooks. Throughout the data presentation, the identity of respondents is hidden and anonymized. Some respondents spoke openly about the risk of losing their jobs or positions on boards (first author field notes, e.g. an interview with a secretary general of a regional football association on 26 October 2007 and second author field notes, e.g. an interview with an official of the national sailing federation on 10 March 2007) but felt committed to disclosing the reality 'for the good of the game'.

To better understand certain sensitive issues, observations and informal conversations proved to be useful (especially the off-record parts of interviews and meetings). Additionally, newspaper articles, internet discussion forums and sport association documents such as meeting minutes, charters, norms and resolutions were reviewed. Both participant and non-participant observations were carried out during different sporting events and sport governing bodies' activities, such as general assemblies, executive committee meetings and annual conferences.

THE EVIDENCE

The presentation of empirical evidence is divided into three main sections that present three different types of the dark sides of social capital in sport governance. The first section, entitled 'Winners and losers of the sport governance game', refers to the construction and use of sport-related networks (based on mutual trust and loyalty) as a tool to dispute the control of the material or symbolic resources of a sport governing body. We show that the instrumental use of these ties and the manipulation of the ties of others, existing in the form of *bonding* or *linking* social capital, results in harm to other members, the whole federation, and/or the embedding society.

The second section, entitled 'Sport governance misused for the games played by others', provides an account on those situations in which the social networks created primarily to foster sports development are misused in practice for political or economic interests. In these cases, the social networks that are established for sports development serve different purposes and are connected to the spheres external to sport in the form of *linking social capital.*

The third section, entitled 'Playing at sport governance' provides detailed insights in various instances when trust is deliberately manipulated by manipulating credibility, transparency or interpretations of sport governance processes. The social capital base of sport governance is therefore fragile, secured by a strategically constructed base of false trust.

WINNERS AND LOSERS OF THE SPORT GOVERNANCE GAME

As emphasized by scholars who have focused on the dark side of network-based social capital (Burt, 1992; Lin, 2001; Portes, 1998), networks and the trust developed within them may serve 'exclusive' interests, and their actions may result in damage to individuals or groups. Therefore, due to negative social capital mechanisms, the sport governance games have their winners and losers.

The constellation of winning and losing networks and actors can be first explained at a macro-social level. Sport associations represent potential spheres where macro-societal patterns of exclusion are mirrored and reproduced. In these cases, the bridging potential of social capital fails under the pressure of bonding dark side. This is illustrated by the example of Fórum Ukrajinců (Ukrainian Forum), a football team composed of Ukrainian immigrants[2] and playing in a regional division in the Czech Republic. The Ukrainian team faces discrimination and is kept away from its Czech rivals. Patterns of exclusion are reproduced during football games as well as in the corridors of the local football governing body. This is well documented in the following statement made by a football secretary about the efforts made by Czech clubs' representatives to avoid playing against the Ukrainian team and to use their social networks in order to influence the selection of teams into division groups:[3]

> They [*The team Fórum Ukrajinců*] are now playing in the B division. We have two regional B divisions with 14 teams playing in each [. . .] There are some rather friendly phone calls [*from competitors*] before each season asking us: 'Do not put them in our group.' Nobody wants to play against them. But the system of draw is always the same. This means that half of the teams always get them in their group.

The coalitions built at the micro- or meso-level of sport governance do not only mirror and reproduce macro-societal developments. Additionally, the creation of social capital with a darker side of a slightly different nature tends to be produced within the context of the sport federations' internal power games. Federations are organizations embedded in a precise context: they manage both material and symbolic resources, and as such they are power arenas (Bernardeau Moreau, 2004; Hoye and Cuskelly, 2003; Porro, 2006). In this context, the networks of winners and losers do not reflect wider macro-societal patterns of exclusion, but rather the capacity of individuals to build strategically exclusive coalitions.

In various sports federations, networks are often used by individuals to achieve leadership positions such as presidency or board membership. A person interested in being elected or in maintaining his or her position at the head of the federation needs to be able to count on a network that will assure a majority of votes. Such a majority can be obtained by promising and managing the distribution of available resources, such as event hosting, funding, nominations for international competitions, prestige and victories.

For this reason, material and symbolic resources management may become instrumental to achieve and keep power and have little to do with the merits acquired by a sport club or by regional or local federations. In these constellations, it is rather the strength of relational resources, that is, the social capital, that matters. That is, sports volunteers' and officials' ties (often clientelistic ones) may affect sport governing bodies' decisions more than clubs' or individual performances and this is detrimental to sport development.

There are both relational (social capital) and material resources that are exchanged between sport governing bodies' executives and local branches or clubs. For example, in some cases, sport federations managers can decide autonomously (at least de facto) about the allocation of the organizational budget, particularly the part of the budget devoted to supporting special events such as national or international championships. Some respondents in Italy criticized federations' presidents or presidential candidates who, looking for the support of a certain number of clubs and regional branches, decided to confer a certain amount of federation resources and international and national sporting events to particular clubs and areas that had guaranteed their support at the next presidential elections (second author field notes, 10 March 2007). As we were confidentially told by one of our interviewees:

> These clubs and areas are sometimes not those that are more worthy of hosting important events or receiving extra money based on their performances, but only those that qualify as loyal allies of the current or potential president. Hence, one of the most relevant principles of sport, the supreme role of meritocracy, is discarded for the success of power games.

The social network forms described previously can be understood as the dark side of *vertically linking social capital*, which connects persons with different positions (Côté, 2001) within the structure of sport governance. However, the dark side of social capital as part of the internal sport governance game not only includes active creation of bonding or linking networks, but they are also represented by a manipulation or even a destruction of the networks of competitors. During an interview in Italy, we were told that members of the federal council who openly challenge the president's action are 'for sure not confirmed in the next term' (second author field notes: informal discussion with two officers of a national federation on 12 March 2007).

Potential competitors can be either reconfirmed or directly revoked. In the Czech Republic, the secretary-general of a regional sports association complained about losing his job because his activities and his knowledge could have weakened the position of the president (first author field notes: personal communication, 28 January 2008). As he explained more in detail:

> I was dismissed by the regional executive committee, although everything was working perfectly and there were no complaints from the movement. Obviously, the president and some of his allies felt that their position was jeopardized by my strong connections built during years of regular personal encounters with the majority of the clubs' representatives.

The secretary general possessed valuable symbolic resources, including information that could have eventually led to the revocation of the presidency. Not only was access to decisions at stake, but also the revocation of the presidency could have re-configured the power relations at the national level of the federation. This situation provides evidence of strong links between the micro- and meso-levels of social capital and its dark side.

Finally, publicly available examples of corruption scandals provide further evidence that existing social ties facilitate bribes in both Italy and the Czech Republic. Many examples show that these bribes are not used exclusively to affect the performance of sports practitioners, but that they also tend to be linked with sport governance. Therefore, the bribes might affect the decisions of officials who control the appointment of referees or evaluation of their performance.

SPORT GOVERNANCE MISUSED FOR THE GAMES PLAYED BY OTHERS

Whereas the previous notion of the dark side remained limited to the field of sport, the second notion extends beyond its borders. The dark side is thus produced by the social capital created through sport (at the sport governance or sporting events levels) but serves interests external to sport. In other words, the interconnectedness between the sport and non-sport sectors is sometimes misused for economic or political interests. Metaphorically speaking, sport governance is misused for the games played by non-sport practitioners: politicians, corporations with an economic interest in sport, the media and sponsors.

The role of the social ties is analysed at a micro- and meso-level within the framework of *horizontally linking social capital* that is understood, following Woolcock (2001), as a resource based on ties and networks between individuals, communities and formal institutions: sport volunteers and spheres external to sport. According to experiences from both countries, close ties with politicians are quite common within football movements. This was clearly demonstrated during an interview with one of the leading officials of the Czech football association, whose office was decorated by a photograph of him with the president of the Czech Republic (first author field notes, 28 January 2008):

> Today, it is not only about kicking the ball, but unfortunately also about the fact that the higher [*in the associations' organizational*

> *hierarchy – first author note*] you are, the better for you it is [. . .]. On the one hand, you have politicians who need football in order to be elected. On the other hand, the people from football need the politicians to support their interests in the movement.

In particular, the notion of politicians who need football in order to be elected is striking. To be more specific, the link between sport and politics itself is not a symptom of the dark side of social capital. These ties become problematic when they are detrimental for sports development or some selected sport disciplines or are contradictory to the ethics and morals of sport. Moreover, the networks between sport and politics point out the dark side of social capital as public resources are not allocated to sport according to the criteria of necessity or merit, but rather according to political and personal interests.[4] This may be supported by a legislative framework that allows these distribution patterns and a lack of evaluation mechanisms. This is exemplified by the complaint of a regional official in the Czech Republic:

> We have a terrible thing here, the so-called 'portioning the bear' [*a literal translation from Czech – first author note*]: the deputies of Parliament decide where to allocate a budget surplus at the end of the year. Unfortunately, this money is very often spent in an absurd manner. Sports facilities are constructed in a small village in the middle of nowhere just because the deputy was born there and wants to build his headstone, or because the president of the sporting club is his good friend.

Furthermore, social ties between board members and sponsors are sometimes perceived as constraining sports development. These ties based on relations of trust and reciprocity include agreements for associations to buy and distribute certain products within their membership. Therefore, common members of sport associations are forced to buy products that they do not need (first author field notes, e.g. an observation at the General Assembly of a regional sport association on 27 March 2007). In other cases, the relations between federation top executives and monopolistic sponsors appeared rather opaque and, according to interviewees, prevented other sponsors to get involved in one sport discipline. The very confidential tone of a telephone conversation between a sponsor and a general director of an Italian federation (who after the phone call described the sponsor as 'my dear friend') provided further empirical evidence to the interviewees' opinions on this aspect (second author field notes, 12 March 2007).

The networks with sponsors in several cases represented the dark side of social capital by placing excessive pressure on an athlete's performance, results and manipulation through bribing and match-fixing. Although we did not collect any direct evidence on the issues during our ethnography, the existence of these mechanisms is reflected in dozens of stories, sometimes transformed into myths shared within football movement representatives in both the Czech Republic and Italy (first author field notes: participant observation in a local football club, 20 March 2007; personal communication with a volunteer of the football association, 8 November 2007; second author field notes: participant observation in a local football club, 8 May 2007; interview with a former player of a local football club, 10 May 2007).

PLAYING AT SPORT GOVERNANCE

The actors involved in social ties of a dark nature often acknowledge the importance of what can be called 'social capital at a meso-level', that is relational resources derived from their role in a sport organization and they are willing to manipulate the nature of such ties and their implications, like trust, to pursue their own material and symbolic interests. Therefore, they tend to conceal any paths leading to the disclosure of their detrimental actions and act as if their behaviour followed the maxims of civic engagement and democratic principles. They actually do not behave according to established and shared normative principles of sport governance; rather, they are only playing at sport governance, creating an image of a fair and legitimate authority for the purpose of defending particular interests. In our analysis, we identified three 'dark' strategies employed to manipulate trust: manipulation of transparency, manipulation of credibility and manipulation of interpretations of the sport governance decision-making process.

First, with regard to the *manipulation of transparency*, in some of the analysed federations the official documents used by the executive board to make decisions were not publicly available, they were deliberately shortened, or their electronic versions were changed over time (first author field notes: personal communication with a volunteer at the national level of the football association, 8 November 2007). Decisions may also be altered illegally, as confidentially reported during an informal discussion with a federation official in Italy:

> Sometimes the President changes the decision adopted by the Federal Council afterwards, without even informing the Council. He simply amends the official document as he likes, nobody checks it, and nobody makes a formal protest vis-à-vis such an illegal behaviour.

When transparency is manipulated, a *form* is used to create the idea of transparency and guarantee trust; however, its *content* is deliberately biased. As a Czech football club's local official pointed out:

> The board misuses the fact that the people in clubs have so much to do that they rarely have time to read everything in detail. If they see meeting minutes, they often do not feel the need to question them. It seems that it is an official document and everything stops there.

The correctness of the decisions made and the steps executed is sometimes inadequately justified by referring to a legal expert or to authorities. These strategies are understood as the *manipulation of credibility*. In this vein, some of the leading officials of the Czech football association several times attacked their opponents, employing legal actions to silence critical voices. Since this criticism challenged the distribution of power positions in the association, a specific topic-related discussion could suddenly turn into an examination or even contestation of formal procedures and rules.

An example from a regional football association shows how a decision made by the general assembly at a regional level was revoked by the national executive committee because of non-adherence to legal procedures and, more importantly, because of the vested interest of some of the members of the board. There were rumours about efforts to orchestrate an extraordinary national general assembly that would depose the executive committee, and the voice of the *in pectore* new regional president would have been the last missing voice necessary to convoke the extraordinary meeting. In other words, the decision would have jeopardized the position of the national executive committee (first author field notes: personal communication with a volunteer of a football association on 26 September 2007 and with the coach of a football club on 20 June 2007).

The manipulation of credibility by authorities, whose position is uncontested, represents another way of manipulating trust. In particular, this happened within the Czech football association where UEFA was often referenced to support the official (and often questioned) standpoint of the executive board. To increase the legitimacy of the official standpoint among the membership base, it was presented as approved. However, some of the association members questioned this discursive strategy, as can be seen in the following off-record comment on the General Assembly:

> Yes, it is true that there was an independent delegate from UEFA, so theoretically, everything was all right. But who knows that this 'independent delegate' is a close friend of some of the board members? Those who participated in the assembly could have seen that he left the assembly after two hours to go shopping.

This example touches upon another strategy of trust manipulation: *the manipulation of interpretation* of the sport governance decision-making process. Some cases of bribery and match-fixing demonstrated that the interpreters of the sport governance game are sometimes corrupted in order to provide a biased evaluation and interpretation of the game. Both Czech and Italian corruption scandals in football demonstrated that some journalists and broadcasters were corrupted to prevent them from disclosing illegalities made in sport governance corridors (Numerato, 2009a). Similarly, stories about corruption within Czech football at the lower divisions speak of bribing delegates to force them to evaluate positively corrupted referees (first author field notes: participant observation in a local football club, 17 May 2007).

In sum, sports volunteers and officials active in sport governance can construct the appearance of prosperous civic engagement by *playing at sport governance* and acting *as if* the decision-making process were democratic and transparent. At a more abstract level of interpretation, they strategically build the appearance of trustworthy social capital at the meso-level of a sport association.

CONCLUSIONS AND DISCUSSION

Contrary to mainstream conceptualizations of social capital, we have argued that the nature of social capital cannot be established once and for all as a positive or negative character for the society unless we contextualize it and unless we clarify the point of view from which we make the judgement of value embodied in the concept of social capital.

Drawing on the empirical evidence gathered during one year of multi-sited ethnographic studies in two different countries across three sports, we captured the neglected area of the dark side of social capital by looking at sport governance. Analytically, we distinguished between three different types of the dark side of social capital created *in* and *through* sport. By unpacking the nature of civic engagement which is commonly uttered to represent a good social capital (Driscoll and Wood, 1999; Putnam, 2000; Uslaner, 1999), we have demonstrated how social ties established and reproduced within sports association can be detrimental to other members, the whole federation, and/or the embedding society. We then provided evidence on how social ties created primarily to enhance sports development can be misused for political or economic interests. Finally, we have described different mechanisms through which one of the constitutive elements of social capital, trust, is manipulated.

These three dimensions of the dark side must be understood as interconnected; perhaps the last type, the manipulation of trust, can serve as a way to conceal the first or second type of dark side of social capital. Moreover, stronger social capital established within a sport association at the micro-level of narrow social ties can easily be misused for purposes that originated in spheres external to sport, such as commercial interests or politics.[5]

Although the three different forms of the dark side of social capital were identified in both countries including some very strong similarities (e.g. very often strong ties built between football and politics, distrust in the football movements developed as a consequence of corruption affairs or at a more general level, occurrence of different strategies to manipulate trust), we have explored some nationally specific differences. Some differences were observed in the case of sailing that has two different positions in the Czech Republic and Italy, being a marginal sport discipline in the former and one of the most popular sports in the latter. The popularity of sailing in Italy is connected to higher stocks of material resources (e.g. sponsorship, mega-events, equipment) and the sailing association is therefore exposed to major struggles and conflicts that are though neutralized by a strong and exclusive management of power by the president and by his allies in the executive board. However, the community-based nature of Czech sailing culture (Numerato, 2009b, 2010) and generalized trust created within the association contributes to preventing conflicts. Moreover, typical of the Italian reality is also the existence of strong connections between politics and sport, as leadership positions within Italian federations are connected to high social and political status (Baglioni, 2010), contrary to the Czech situation (with the exception of football) where a leadership position is sometimes considered to be a necessity as there is a lack of volunteers. This aspect of the Italian context enhances a tendency to produce negative effects of social capital, in particular in its horizontally linking form.

Another difference is rather structural than connected to particular positions of analysed sport disciplines and has to do with different historical contexts. The passivity of volunteers, which is characteristic for the Czech sport governance culture and has its roots in the communist regime before 1989, in a way facilitates any efforts to misuse sport governance. On the contrary, Italian volunteers are more likely to be involved in struggles over resources and strategic building of coalitions that can result in detrimental effects for sport development. In other words, whether the Czech examples of the dark side of social capital are frequently based on a deliberate manipulation with resigned, albeit suspicious masses of volunteers, the dark side of social capital in Italy is often characterized by its focus on struggles with opponents.

This study has several implications for both social capital theory and policy and practice. The article has contributed to theory development in two fields: in social capital literature per se and in sport sociology by enhancing a potentially critical role of sport sociology. On the one hand, it has taken the theoretical discussion on social capital further, and it has done it by virtue of a long ethnographic endeavour in multiple sport settings. On the other hand, it has brought back power and power relations in sport sociology with a new, strong body of evidence.

Our analysis confirms some of the findings of previous research on the dark side of social capital in sport. In synergy with previous studies, our ethnographies have demonstrated that bonding social capital can serve as a tool of social exclusion (Collins, 2003; Jarvie, 2003; Tonts, 2005) as well as particularized trust within small social networks that can facilitate anti-social behaviour (Long, 2008; Palmer and Thompson, 2007) or foster particular objectives contrasting with sport development.

Reducing the gap in the contemporary literature in sport sociology and sociology more broadly (Field, 2008; Warren, 2008), we explored the dark side of *horizontally and vertically linking social capital* and emphasized the need to study the manipulation of trust within sport governance. Furthermore, the collected evidence demonstrated that the links of sport field with external societal spheres are not only of economic or commercial nature, as suggested by Dyreson (2001), but also of political nature. Moreover, the analyses of power, hegemony and political-clientelism employed within the studies of sport governance, but omitted from explorations of social capital in sport, provided us with theoretical input that was further informed by empirical evidence. The question of power was not addressed only with an identification of different forms of power games, but also with a deconstruction of the mechanisms through which the power is uttered, in particular deliberate manipulation of social (and not only one's own) networks and trust.

We have deconstructed the main tenets of trust that should theoretically cement members of sport associations and bind organizations through a shared responsibility for sport development. However, several examples demonstrated that these internal bonds are becoming more fragile hand in hand with the increasing importance of power, prestige or economic and political objectives external to sport. Everyday experience of sport volunteers and publicly exposed affairs can nourish distrust and decrease the organizational social capital.

The examination of the ways in which trust is manipulated inspires further theoretical developments of the social capital concept. The fact that sport officials *play at sport governance* and act *as if* their behaviour followed the maxims of civic engagement and democratic principles confirms the notions about the proliferation of the concept of social capital understood as a collective good. The public diffusion of the concept has largely been acknowledged (e.g. Field, 2008; Portes, 1998; Roberts, 2004), yet consequences of the conceptual impact have not been analysed.

Our dialectic approach to understand the impact of the concept's diffusion shows that sport actors may be reflexive about an emphasis which is put on social capital in policy documents related to contemporary sport governance. On the example of the dark side of social capital it is evident that the proliferation of the concept leads not only to the promotion of democratic values, but also to their circumvention. Strategic adaptation of sports actors to these circumstances and a sort of impression management (see Goffman, 1990 [1959]) supports an illusory trust beyond which invisible and detrimental forces of civic engagement can be developed. This idea is in some regard complementary to another critical observation of the perverted role of sport-based intervention programmes, backed up by social capital concept, that can be transformed into tools of social control and regulation (Spaaij, 2009). We argue that further scholarship dealing with sport and social capital shall further examine this dialectic relationship, it shall analyse the dynamics fostered by a practical implementation of the social capital concept, its re-interpretation through the lens of socio-political ideologies and its unintended consequences.

This study also has other implications for further research and stimulates new research agendas as it calls for more informed and critical emphasis on sport governance and its exploration within different geographical and political contexts. Furthermore, it shall also enhance an analysis of different aspects detrimental to sport culture, such as doping, violence or corruption. The role of *horizontally linking social capital* could be explored not only by focusing on the links of sport with the spheres of politics or economics, but also in connection with medicine, as some recent research pointed out (Brissonneau et al., 2008; Malcolm and Scott, 2011).

As regards the implications for practice and policy, a greater understanding of the dark side of social capital could contribute to preventing disputes in sport governance and enhance their efficient resolution. Furthermore, an informed and critical use of the social capital concept by policy-makers could lead to the development of more efficient accountability mechanisms, which can be employed to counteract a strategic misuse of civic engagement associated with sport governance. As our evidence suggests, sport officials are able to reinterpret and adopt existing norms to support their own interests. In this context, a stronger regulation shall not necessarily work as a remedy to struggle negative externalities of sport governance. A promotion of change at an everyday basis of organizational culture rather than a formal intervention in terms of increased regulation could be beneficial. Initiatives promoting youth volunteering and inter-generational cooperation could enhance a collectively shared responsibility for ethically based sport development. Last but not least, a reduction of the dark sides of social capital could be enhanced through a cultivation of critical awareness among sport officials. In particular, a critical capacity to problematize often naturalized, idealized and taken-for-granted allegiances between sport, business and politics and their consequences for sport, can reinforce the democratically based nature of sport governance and thus produce positive stocks of social capital at organizational and societal levels.

NOTES

1. The ethnographic studies in the Czech Republic and Italy were carried out as parts of a larger project 'Sport and Social Capital in the European Union'. This project was focused on sport governance and its social impact in four specific countries of the European Union (Denmark, France, Italy and the Czech Republic).
2. According to a survey representative of the Czech population the Ukrainians are among the less favoured nations, together with Albanians, Romanians, Vietnamese and Russians. On a scale measuring attitude towards other nationals ranging from 1 to 7, where 1 means very sympathetic and 7 very unsympathetic, the average value expressing the Czech attitude towards Ukrainians was 4.48 in 2009, compared to 4.31 in 2008 and 4.31 in 2007 (Červenka, 2011).
3. All the quotations are translated from the Czech or Italian language by the authors, with an aim to keep their colloquial style and authenticity.
4. These interests can also, in a wider perspective, contribute to inadequately prioritize sport over other leisure activities.
5. Simultaneous to the evidence of the dark sides of social capital we also found numerous counter-examples during our fieldwork, positive examples of social capital in action. However, coverage of such issues did not represent the main scope of this article.

REFERENCES

Baglioni S (2010) The social capital of sport organizations in Italy. In: Groeneveld M, Houlihan B and Ohl F (eds) *Social Capital and Sport Governance in Europe*. New York: Routledge, 146–162.

Bernardeau Moreau D (2004) *Sociologie des Fédérations Sportives*. Paris: L'Harmattan.

Blackshaw T and Long J (2005) What's the big idea? A critical exploration of the concept of social capital and its incorporation into leisure policy discourse. *Leisure Studies* 24(3): 239–258.

Bourdieu P (1980) Le capital social: notes provisoires. *Actes de la recherche en sciences sociales* 31: 2–3.

Brissonneau C, Aubel O and Ohl F (2008) *L'épreuve du dopage. Sociologie du cyclisme professionnel*. Paris: PUF.

Burnett C (2006) Building social capital through an 'active community club'. *International Review for the Sociology of Sport* 41(3–4): 283–294.

Burt RS (1992) *Structural Holes: The Social Structure of Competition*. Cambridge, MA: Harvard University Press.

Castiglione D, van Deth JW and Wolleb G (2008) *The Handbook of Social Capital.* Oxford: Oxford University Press.

Červenka J (2011) Názory České veřejnosti na cizince v České republice – prosinec 2010, press release, May. Available at: http://www.cvvm.cas.cz/upl/zpravy/101094s_ov110131.pdf.

Coleman JS (1988) Social capital in the creation of human capital. *The American Journal of Sociology* 94: 95–120.

Coleman JS (1990) *Foundations of Social Theory.* Cambridge: Cambridge University Press.

Collins M (2003) Social exclusion from sport and leisure. In: Houlihan B (ed.) *Sport and Society: A Student Introduction.* London: SAGE, 67–89.

Côté S (2001) The contribution of human and social capital. *Canadian Journal of Policy Research* 2(1): 29–36.

Crossley N (2008) (Net)working out: Social capital in a private health club. *The British Journal of Sociology* 59(3): 475–500.

della Porta D and Vannucci A (1999) *Corrupt Exchanges: Actors, Resources, and Mechanisms of Political Corruption.* New York: Walter de Gruyter.

Driscoll K and Wood L (1999) *Sporting Capital: Changes and Challenges for Rural Communities in Victoria,* March. Available at: www.fulltext.ausport.gov.au/fulltext/1999/vic/sportcapital. pdf.

Dyreson M (2001) 'Maybe it's better to bowl alone: Sport, community and democracy in American thought. *Sport in Society* 4(1): 19–30.

Field J (2008) *Social Capital.* London: Routledge.

Frič P (2008) Světlé a stinné stránky neformálních sítí v postkomunistické společnosti. *Sociologický časopis/Czech Sociological Review* 44(2): 295–319.

Fukuyama F (1999) *La Grande Distruzione.* Milan: Baldini & Castoldi.

Gambetta D (1988) *Trust. Making and Breaking Cooperative Relations.* Oxford: Basil Blackwell.

Goffman E (1990 [1959]) *The Presentation of Self in Everyday Life.* Garden City, NY: Doubleday.

Groeneveld M and Ohl F (2010) Conclusion: Understanding social capital as both metaphor and traditional form of social exchange. In: Groeneveld M, Houlihan B and Ohl F (eds) *Social Capital and Sport Governance in Europe.* New York: Routledge, 181–199.

Hoye R and Cuskelly G (2003) Board-executive relationships within voluntary sport organisations. *Sport Management Review* 6(1): 53–73.

Hoye R and Cuskelly G (2007) *Sport Governance.* London: Butterworth Heinemann.

Jarvie G (2003) Communitarianism, sport and social capital. *International Review for the Sociology of Sport* 38(2): 139–153.

Jarvie G (2007) Sport, social change and the public intellectual. *International Review for the Sociology of Sport* 42(4): 411–424.

Keller J (2009) *Nejistota a důvěra.* Prague: SLON.

Lin N (2001) *Social Capital: A Theory of Social Structure and Action.* Cambridge: Cambridge University Press.

Long J (2008) Sport's ambiguous relationship with social capital: The contribution of national governing bodies of sport. In: Nicholson M and Hoye R (eds) *Sport and Social Capital.* London: Butterworth Heinemann, 207–232.

Malcolm D and Scott A (2011) Professional relations in sport healthcare: Workplace responses to organisational change. *Social Science & Medicine* 72(4): 513–520.

Nicholson M and Hoye R (2008) Sport and social capital: An introduction. In: Nicholson M and Hoye R (eds) *Sport and Social Capital.* London: Butterworth Heinemann, 1–18.

Numerato D (2009a) The media and sports corruption: An outline of sociological understanding. *International Journal of Sport Communication* 2(3): 261–273.

Numerato D (2009b) Revisiting Weber's concept of disenchantment: An examination of the re-enchantment with sailing in the post-communist Czech Republic. *Sociology* 43(3): 439–456.

Numerato D (2010) Czech sport governance cultures and a plurality of social capitals: Politicking zone, movement and community. In: Groeneveld M, Houlihan B and Ohl F (eds) *Social Capital and Sport Governance in Europe.* New York: Routledge, 41–62.

Palmer C and Thompson K (2007) The paradoxes of football spectatorship: On-field and online expressions of social capital among the 'grog squad'. *Sociology of Sport Journal* 24(2): 187–205.

Passmore B (2007) Legitimita, angažovanost a vytváření sociálního kapitálu na českém pracovišti v období pozdní transformace. *Sociologický časopis/Czech Sociological Review* 43(1): 49–68.

Porro N (2006) *L'attore sportivo. Azione collettiva, sport e cittadinanza.* Molfetta: La Meridiana.

Portes A (1998) Social capital: Its origins and applications in modern sociology. *Annual Review of Sociology* 24(1): 1–24.

Putnam R (1993) *Making Democracy Work.* Princeton, NJ: Princeton University Press.

Putnam R (2000) *Bowling Alone: The Collapse and Revival of American Community.* New York: Simon & Schuster.

Roberts JM (2004) What's 'social' about 'social capital'? *The British Journal of Politics and International Relations* 6(4): 471–493.

Schneider JA (2009) Organizational social capital and nonprofit. *Nonprofit and Voluntary Sector Quarterly* 38(4): 643–662.

Skinner J, Zakus DH and Cowell J (2008) Development through sport: Building social capital in disadvantaged communities. *Sport Management Review* 11: 253–275.

Spaaij R (2009) Sport as a vehicle for social mobility and regulation of disadvantaged urban youth: Lessons from Rotterdam. *International Review for the Sociology of Sport* 44(2–3): 247–264.

Sugden J and Tomlinson A (1998) Power and resistance in the governance of world football: Theorizing FIFA's transnational impact. *Journal of Sport and Social Issues* 22(3): 299–316.

Tonts M (2005) Competitive sport and social capital in rural Australia. *Journal of Rural Studies* 21(2): 137–149.

Uslaner EM (1999) Democracy and social capital. In: Warren MR (ed.) *Democracy and Trust*. Cambridge: Cambridge University Press, 121–150.

Warren ME (2001) Social capital and corruption. Unpublished draft paper, June. Available at: http://www.huss.ex.ac.uk/politics/research/socialcapital/papers/warren.pdf.

Warren ME (2008) The nature and logic of bad social capital. In: Castiglione D, van Deth JW and Wolleb G (eds) *The Handbook of Social Capital*. Oxford: Oxford University Press, 122–149.

Woolcock M (2001) The place of social capital in understanding social and economic outcomes. *Canadian Journal of Policy Research* 2(1): 11–17.

CHAPTER 32

Women Athletes as Falsely Accused Deviants: Managing the Lesbian Stigma

Elaine M. Blinde and Diane E. Taub

Gender represents a powerful normative system that both evaluates and controls the behavior of men and women (Schur 1984). This system entails socially constructed conceptualizations of behavior intricately tied to societal perceptions of "masculinity" and "femininity" (Keller 1978).

[. . .] Stigmatization represents a means of social control as it preserves the traditional gender system. Fear of being labeled deviant keeps women "in their place" and reduces challenges to prevailing gender norms (Schur 1984). Not surprisingly, individuals who occupy positions of power or privilege, the "deviance-definers," benefit from continued subordination or suppression of the less powerful (Becker 1963).

Although all women experience devaluation and stigmatization by virtue of being female (Schur 1984), some women occupy roles or engage in behaviors that make them even more susceptible to deviant labeling. This labeling is particularly indicative of women who violate multiple categories of gender norms, including (1) presentation of self (e.g., emotions, nonverbal communication, appearance, speech), (2) marriage and maternity, (3) sexuality (e.g., sexual behavior/orientation), and (4) occupational choice (Schur 1984).

One group of women judged to violate multiple categories of gender norms and thus subjected to various forms of deviance labeling and stigmatization is athletes. Women athletes are frequently perceived to cross or extend the boundaries of socially constructed definitions of "femininity" (Theberge 1985; Willis 1982). In a culture that traditionally equates athleticism with masculinity, women who participate in sport are often viewed as masculine, unladylike, or manly (Willis 1982). Such descriptors imply that women athletes violate presentation of self and occupational gender norms (Schur 1984). Moreover, both the popular press and research literature have examined the assumed conflict between athleticism and femininity (Colker and Widom 1980; Griffin 1987; Hall 1988). This presumed incompatibility, along with equating sport and masculinity, results in a belief system linking women athletes with lesbianism (Lenskyj 1991). The lesbian label, representing a violation of sexuality norms (Schur 1984), is based on the idea that women who challenge traditional gender-role behavior cannot be "real" women (Lenskyj 1991),

The lesbian label as applied to women athletes is particularly significant given the assumed threat of lesbianism (as well as male homosexuality) to the prevailing gender system (Goodman 1977; Lenskyj 1991; Schur 1984). Stigmatization of lesbians is common as the phenomena of "heterosexual assumption" and "heterosexual privilege" ensure that lesbians realize they are indeed norm violators, deviants, and subjects of oppression (Schur 1984; Wolfe 1988). Such stigmatization reflects contempt for those who stretch the boundaries of culturally defined gender roles.

Since the behavior of women athletes is often interpreted to challenge gender norms they may be subject to various forms of devaluation and stigmatization. Although athleticism represents the initial discrediting attribute, its linkage with lesbianism magnifies the devaluation and stigmatization associated with female athletes. The present study examines the manner in which such forms of devaluation and stigmatization impact on women athletes and how they manage the lesbian label (and accompanying masculine image) attached to their sport participation. Not only has there been a paucity of research investigating the specific topic of the stigmatization of women athletes as lesbians, but the entire issue of the perceived presence of lesbianism in women's sport has been neglected (Griffin 1987).

METHODOLOGY

SAMPLE

[. . .]

Three universities (two Midwestern and one Southern) provided names and addresses of all women athletes with at least one year of completed athletic eligibility who were participating in the school's sport programs during the 1990–1991 school year. All sport programs offered by the universities were represented. Varsity women athletes, rather than intramural or informal sport participants, were the focus of this study because of the salience of their athletic identities and their greater sport commitment. [. . .]

These 24 athletes were currently participating in a variety of intercollegiate sports—basketball (5), track and field (4), volleyball (3), swimming (3), softball (3), tennis (2), diving (2), and gymnastics (2). With an average age of 20.2 years and predominantly white (92%), the sample consisted of 2 freshmen, 9 sophomores, 5 juniors, and 8 seniors. The majority (22) were receiving athletic scholarships.

PROCEDURES

Two trained interviewers conducted in-depth and semi-structured tape-recorded telephone interviews that lasted 50–90 minutes. The interview schedule focused on several aspects of the intercollegiate sport experience, one of which related to societal perceptions of women's sport and female athletes. The lesbian topic usually surfaced in responses to questions regarding (1) positive and negative connotations associated with women's sport and female athletes, and (2) stereotypes associated with women athletes. In response to these two questions, 17 of the 24 athletes initiated discussion of the lesbian topic. When asked whether they were aware of the lesbian label being associated with women athletes, 6 of the 7 remaining athletes indicated strong familiarity with this association.

Further, several questions explored how athletes dealt with the lesbian label, for example (1) why they felt women athletes are labeled lesbian, (2) which athletes or teams are most likely to be labeled, (3) who applies this label, (4) how this label affects athletes, and (5) the degree to which athletes discuss this topic among themselves. Questions were open-ended to allow athletes to discuss the most relevant aspects of their own experiences.

[. . .]

Overall, the design of the study allowed for the emergence of concepts from the data rather than imposing preconceived conceptual or theoretical frameworks on the interview protocol and data. Such an approach utilizes the voices of athletes to identify and develop emerging concepts and themes.

In analyzing and reporting the comments of athletes, the intent was not to construct a single profile characterizing the majority of respondents. Rather, realizing that athletes differ and that all comments are important, both similarities and variations in responses are explored.

RESULTS AND DISCUSSION

[. . .]

This article focuses on Becker's (1963) construction of the "falsely accused deviant" and Goffman's (1963) conceptualization of "stigma management." Not only do these two concepts enhance our knowledge of the experiences of women athletes, but the athletes' experiences add further understanding and validation to the conceptualizations of the "falsely accused deviant" and "stigma management."

FALSELY ACCUSED DEVIANT

The vast majority of respondents thought that labeling women athletes lesbian (or at least questioning sexual preference) was quite common. One athlete referred to it as a "societal blanket covering all of collegiate female athletes."

Despite athletes' perception that the lesbian label is prevalent in women's sport and often indiscriminately applied to women athletes, it would be unreasonable to assume all women athletes are lesbian. Although our intent was not to ascertain the sexual orientation of respondents, it was clear that a large majority responded to questions as to suggest that they were not lesbians. For example, phrases like "lesbians don't bother me as long as they don't hit on me," "I have a boyfriend," "the label does not pertain to me," "I'm not really the person to ask about lesbianism because I don't really see enough of it," "people know how I am" (suggesting heterosexuality), or "it's not a problem I'm faced with" were common.

Another way athletes implied distance from lesbianism was through out-group (e.g., "they" or "them") and in-group (e.g., "those of us who aren't" or "we joke about them") terminology. Even though women athletes as a whole frequently are viewed as the out-group in terms of social deviance, a secondary level of deviance exists within the athletic group. That is, within this deviant group, athletes use in-group and out-group terminology to distinguish between the non-lesbian and lesbian athlete.

Given this widespread disassociation from lesbianism, it was assumed that the majority of athletes interviewed were not lesbians. However, since the label is indiscriminately applied to women athletes, many are incorrectly labeled lesbian, typifying what Becker (1963) terms the "falsely accused deviant." One difficulty noted by Klemke and Tiedeman (1990) in the study of false accusations is documenting that accusations are indeed false. Relative to our research, the need of respondents to mislead interviewers should have been substantially reduced as the interviews were anonymous and conducted by strangers over the telephone.

The concept of the "falsely accused deviant" derives from Becker's (1963) original classification scheme of deviant behavior. Basic to Becker's typology are two factors: whether an individual (1) is a rule violator and (2) has been labeled deviant. In contrast to the "pure deviant," correctly labeled a rule violator; the "conformist," correctly labeled a rule abider; and the "secret deviant," a rule violator not labeled as such, the "falsely accused deviant" is an incorrectly labeled deviant.

Unfortunately, Becker (1963) does not systematically examine or discuss the "falsely accused deviant." In fact, this category of deviant is under-researched compared to the other three types. Neglect of the category exists despite its potential to enhance understanding of labeling, especially in terms of conditions and social processes involved in creating false conceptions of social reality (Klemke and Tiedeman 1990). Conceptualizations surrounding the "falsely accused deviant" are particularly useful in understanding why the lesbian label permeates women's sport.

[. . .]

Societal preconditions for false accusation. There are general societal preconditions or organizational factors that increase the probability false accusations will occur (Klemke and Tiedeman 1990). Three factors in particular may account for why female athletes and women's sport, compared to other individuals and domains, are more often targets of lesbian accusations: (1) the growth of women's sport and its perceived threat to the male sport structure, (2) women athletes' lack of power and outsider status, and (3) stereotype adoption.

As the growth of women's sport challenges the male-controlled sport structure, attempts to devalue women's sport by dominant groups can be anticipated. Lenskyj (1986) argues that efforts to preserve sport as a stronghold of male supremacy positively relate to the movement of women into sport. The expansion of women's sport in the past 20 years (due in part to Title IX legislation promoting equal gender opportunity in educational institutions) has been perceived as a threat to men's sport, thus triggering an increased interest in preserving male sport (Blinde 1987). The generalization of the lesbian label to female athletes seeks to discredit and devalue women's sport and ultimately works to keep women "in their place" (Lenskyj 1986).

Second, since women as a group possess relatively little power in the larger society, they are not only more likely to suffer false accusations but also unable to challenge or disprove the label. [. . .] Support for this latter contention was found when athletes indicated that men, especially male athletes, were the most common group labeling women athletes lesbian.

Third, confounding this situation are longstanding stereotypes directed toward women who violate traditional gender norms. In the current example, the societal linkage of athleticism and masculinity increases the likelihood that women in sport will be the target of false charges of lesbianism.

Given the factors that lead to the indiscriminate stigmatization of women athletes, both lesbian and nonlesbian athletes adopt strategies to manage the lesbian stigma. As discussed in the following section, a variety of stigma management mechanisms are utilized by athletes to manage these labels.

STIGMA MANAGEMENT

According to Goffman (1963), stigmas represent discrediting attributes that reflect a discrepancy between individuals' virtual (assumed) and actual (real) social identities. These attributes fall outside the range of what is considered ordinary or natural and generally "spoil" the social identity of the stigma possessor. Since the stigma taints and discredits the individual, attempts are generally undertaken to control and manage the discrediting attribute. The need for such management mechanisms is not necessarily limited to individuals who possess the discrediting attribute; stigma management is arguably the domain of the "falsely accused" as well.

As noted previously, sport participation (especially elite competition) is often considered outside the range of what is ordinary or normal for women. Moreover, given the widespread labeling of women athletes as lesbian and the corresponding stigmatization, women athletes must manage these discrediting attributes.

The particular strategy utilized to manage a stigma largely depends on the degree to which the attribute is visible or perceivable to others. Goffman (1963) distinguishes between individuals possessing attributes easily identifiable (i.e., discredited individuals) and not immediately perceivable (i.e., discreditable individuals). Techniques designed to manage the impact of these two types of attributes differ; the discredited individual manages tension while the discreditable manages information. Although the degree to which others can identify women as athletes varies, athletic status (and the accompanying lesbian label) is generally not immediately perceivable, thus resulting in a discreditable stigma. As Goffman (1963) suggests, such a stigma is associated with the control and management of information.

Concealment. One basic stigma management mechanism noted by athletes was concealment. As an information management technique to prevent association with the lesbian label, women athletes sometimes simply conceal information about their athleticism. Elliott, Ziegler, Altman, and Scott (1990) and Goffman (1963) identify several forms of concealment, including self-segregation, passing, and use of disidentifiers.

Common in the responses of athletes was *self-segregation*, a condition where the stigmatized interact primarily with those sharing a similar affliction or those considered "wise." Wise individuals are familiar and comfortable with the stigmatized but do not have the stigma (Goffman 1963). Athletes frequently indicated that most of their friends are athletes and interaction with the general student body is limited. This compressed social network reduces athletes' interactions with those most likely to react negatively toward their athletic participation. Such avoidance limits disruption in the pursuit of athletic goals (Elliott *et al.* 1990). Although the reason for self-segregation is not exclusively stigma management (e.g., some indicated they relate better to other athletes or that time prohibits developing friendships outside of sport), the comfortable, nonthreatening environment other athletes provide may enhance the prevalence of self-segregation. As one athlete indicated, those outside the women's sport community most commonly initiate the lesbian labeling.

Self-segregation, however, is not without its complications. As Adler and Adler (1987) suggest, self-segregation often isolates athletes both socially and culturally from the university student body. The protective environment of self-segregation is offset by the sometimes narrow and limited athletic subculture.

Since self-segregation is not always practical, women athletes also conceal their athletic identity by *passing.* As information management, passing involves controlling the disclosure of discrediting information about oneself to conceal the stigma entirely (Elliott *et al.* 1990). Several women described techniques they (or other athletes) use so others will not know they are athletes. For example, some simply withhold information about their athletic status in conversations with outsiders. Alternatively, one individual stated athletes sometimes "overtalk" the lesbian topic to disassociate the label from themselves.

Other athletes relied on what Goffman (1963) terms *disidentifiers* to separate themselves from things most stereotypically associated with lesbianism. For example, to contradict the masculine image identified with lesbianism, athletes sometimes consciously accentuated their femininity by wearing dresses, skirts, makeup, and earrings or by letting their hair grow. Others indicated that being seen with men or having a boyfriend is a common technique to reaffirm their heterosexuality. In a few instances this need to identify with men fosters more extreme behaviors including "hanging on men" in public or establishing a reputation as promiscuous with men. Some women athletes take care not to constantly be seen in public with groups of women; others were cautious about the nature of physical contact publicly displayed with women. In all cases, the athlete's presentation of self is consciously monitored or altered to conform to appropriate gender roles.

Although effective in controlling information, passing behaviors and disidentifiers can negatively affect individuals' psychological wellbeing, as well as alienate them from their personal identities (Goffman 1963). Goffman's work suggests that athletes who engage in passing may experience feelings of disloyalty and self-contempt as they disassociate themselves not only from their athletic identities but from qualities representing their personal essence.

In another form of disidentification, some athletes distanced themselves from athletes more seriously "contaminated" or stigmatized. This mechanism is accomplished through techniques such as making "rude comments" about a suspected lesbian teammate, establishing team cliques on the basis of sexual orientation, and being "very critical and mean" to lesbian teammates behind their backs.

Since the lesbian label is not equally applied to all athletes or teams, association with "certain" athletes increases the chance of stigmatization. In response to the question why women athletes are labeled lesbian, athletes identified three categories—appearance, personality characteristics, and nature of the sport activity.

Relative to appearance or externally identifiable characteristics, factors such as dress, hair style, body build, body posture/carriage, muscularity, and mannerisms were mentioned as underlying usage of the labels "dyke," "butch," or "lesbian." Athletes with personality characteristics such as being assertive, outgoing, strong, independent, aggressive, and hard-nosed are most likely to be labeled lesbian.

Regarding the nature of the sport activity, participants in team sports such as softball, basketball, and field hockey are more often recipients of the lesbian label. When asked why team sports are a more likely target, athletes indicated that such activities require more athleticism and strength, involve more physical contact, and are more commonly viewed as sports played by men. These qualities associated with team sports reflect traits socially defined as masculine (Bern 1974). Stigmatization of these team sports may discourage women from both engaging in "masculine sports" and participating in activities with potential to develop cooperation, teamwork, and solidarity among women (Lenskyj 1986). Self-distancing from those more seriously "contaminated," although effective for controlling information, may at the same time prevent women athletes from bonding together as a collective.

In a few instances athletes disassociate themselves from the lesbian label by publicly making fun of lesbian athletes or criticizing homosexuality. This disparaging behavior frequently occurs in the course of conversations with "outsiders" when the topic of women athletes is discussed. As Goffman (1963) suggests, a discreditable individual often finds it dangerous to refrain from joining in the vilification of one's own group. Such a strategy may protect the social identity of the individual athlete but impede the development and maintenance of the collective identity of women athletes.

When concealment is not possible, a stigmatized individual may adopt other stigma management strategies. Included are salience reduction through deflection and direct confrontation through normalization (Elliott *et al.* 1990).

Deflection. Individuals may use deflection to reduce the importance or salience of a discrediting attribute. Representing the original source of stigmatization, the athlete's role is publicly downplayed by athletes. Not only do women athletes use disidentifiers to distance themselves from this role, but they attempt to accentuate the significance of nonsport roles and attributes. It is thus important to many to be viewed as more than an athlete; efforts to demonstrate mastery in other areas (e.g., student role, social role) are common. For example, several athletes mentioned they want to do well in the classroom so that others will not identify them exclusively as athletes. Moreover, some athletes highlighted their social role by mentioning dating and party activities.

Normalization. In some situations it is difficult to reduce the visibility of the discrediting attribute (i.e., athletic status) when it is salient and relevant. This difficulty is particularly true of athletes who are visible on campus or the focus of media and where athletic status frequently impacts on the dynamics of social interaction. Rather than conceal or deflect, the individual has no choice but to directly confront the stigma. The ideal outcome for the athlete is a state of normalization where the discrediting attribute loses its stigmatizing capability. To accomplish normalization, strategies attempt to redefine the stigma and re-educate "normals" (Elliott *et al.* 1990). Although not widespread, redefinition efforts generally emphasize the positive characteristics or contributions of female athletes while re-education consists of athletes informing outsiders that lesbianism is not prevalent in women's sport or that sexual preference should be a non-issue.

Even though most respondents thought the lesbian label is unfairly applied to women athletes, attempts at normalization are difficult given their assumed violation of multiple gender norms. Although some athletes indicated the label did not bother them and that people could "think what they wanted," little evidence existed to suggest that the discrediting attribute of lesbian has lost its stigmatizing capability. Efforts to redefine or reeducate are generally futile since the vast majority of women athletes do not directly confront these labels, preferring to engage in other stigma coping strategies.

This refusal to confront the lesbian label resembles what Elliott and colleagues (1990) term capitulation. Even if false or inaccurate, the lesbian label assumes a master status for the individual (Becker 1963; Schur 1979) and becomes central to her identity and interactions. The stigmatized accept both the stereotypes placed upon them and the accompanying stigmatization. Athletes were generally not proactive in fighting the stereotypes; resistance to these stereotypes and labels usually emerges after a direct confrontation or challenge from an outsider. For example, one respondent stated "I am not an activist," while another indicated she "would not bring up the topic unless something negative was said."

Acceptance of the normative definition of deviance is often true of socially marginalized groups as they (1) rely on others for self-definition, (2) engage in self-hate, and (3) identify with the aggressor (Kitzinger 1987; Nobles 1973; Sarnoff 1951; Thomas 1971). Interestingly, several remarks from respondents demonstrate that women athletes accept and internalize societal stereotypes about themselves and incorporate these images into their identity accounts and personal interactions. For example, internalization of societal beliefs about appearance norms was evident in such comments as "I don't look like an athlete so I rarely am labeled a lesbian" and "I've never seen somebody that looks like a girl called a dyke or lesbian." One athlete dismissed lesbianism as a problem on her team since her "teammates were pretty." This same athlete implied, however, that lesbianism might be more prevalent on other teams since "most of the athletes on these teams looked like guys."

Self-hate was occasionally noted in responses as well. Although generally indicating the lesbian label angers them, athletes also mentioned that it makes them feel "unattractive" and "less desirable to men" and leads some to "always worry about how I look." Identification with aggressors was also evident in that some nonlesbian athletes engage in negative conversations that criticize or mock lesbian athletes.

Nevertheless, the presence of the deviant label does not necessarily garner negative outcomes (Elliott *et al.* 1990; Goffman 1963). As a few athletes' responses indicated, being labeled lesbian makes them stronger individuals and less dependent on what outsiders think of them. For example, learning to cope with the lesbian label helped one athlete "find confidence" in herself and encouraged another to learn more about homosexuality through reading and coursework. Moreover, some athletes claimed exposure to the issue of homosexuality makes them less judgmental and more accepting/respectful of dissimilar others.

Women athletes thus utilize a variety of stigma management techniques to control and manage information about their athleticism. This effort is somewhat paradoxical since most respondents were generally proud to be athletes and viewed their athletic experience as positive. The prevailing negative societal linkage of female athleticism with masculinity and lesbianism often overrides positive self-definitions of their athleticism.

CONCLUSION

[. . .]

The role of labeling is undeniably central to understanding the experiences of women athletes forced to resort to stigma management strategies in the absence of deviant behavior. Female athletes acquire the deviant label because more powerful groups impose their definition of morality on the athletic act (Erikson 1962; Kitsuse 1962). Critical in this labeling are the stigma-laden meanings female athleticism evokes and the processes by which these ideas are perceived and applied. Such meanings are relayed to women, reminding them of "their place" in the gender system (Henley and Freeman 1979).

Overall lack of power confounds the ability of women athletes to actively challenge deviant labels. Not only do women in general lack power, but the discrediting attributes of athlete and lesbian diminish the power position of women athletes even further. Generally lacking organizational backing and viewed as outsiders, women athletes, rather than actively challenge the stigma, rely on stigma management. This passivity not only has negative social and psychological outcomes for the athlete, but enhances the overall power of the label itself. Since athletes resort to actions where silence and denial are central and internalization of deviant labels is frequent, the likelihood of resistance to these labels is significantly reduced.

REFERENCES

Adler, Peter, and Patricia A. Adler. 1987. "Role Conflict and Identity Salience: College Athletics and the Academic Role." *Social Science Journal* 24: 443–455.

Becker, Howard S. 1963. *Outsiders: Studies in the Sociology of Deviance.* New York; Free Press.

Bern, Sandra L. 1974. "The Measurement of Psychological Androgyny." *Journal of Consulting and Clinical Psychology* 42: 155–162.

Blinde, Elaine M. 1987. "Contrasting Models of Sport and the Intercollegiate Sport Experience of Female Athletes." Ph.D. dissertation, Department of Physical Education, University of Illinois, Urbana-Champaign.

Colker, Ruth, and Cathy S. Widom. 1980. "Correlates of Female Athletic Participation: Masculinity, Femininity, Self-Esteem, and Attitudes Toward Women." *Sex Roles* 6: 47–58.

Elliott, Gregory C., Herbert L. Ziegler, Barbara M. Altrman, and Deborah R. Scott. 1990. "Understanding Stigma: Dimensions of Deviance and Coping." pp. 423–443 in *Deviant Behavior*, edited by Clifton D. Bryant. New York: Hemisphere.

Erikson, Kai T. 1962. "Notes on the Sociology of Deviance." *Social Problems* 9: 307–314.

Goffman, Erving. 1963. *Stigma: Notes on the Management of Spoiled Identity*. Englewood Cliffs, NJ: Prentice Hall.

Goodman, Bernice. 1977. *The Lesbian: A Celebration of Difference*. New York: Out and Out Books.

Griffin, Patricia S. 1987. "Homophobia, Lesbians, and Women's Sports: An Exploratory Analysis." Paper presented at the annual meetings of the American Psychological Association, New York.

Hall, M. Ann. 1988. "The Discourse of Gender and Sport: From Femininity to Feminism." *Sociology of Sport Journal* 5: 330–340.

Henley, Nancy, and Jo Freeman. 1979. "The Sexual Politics of Interpersonal Behavior." Pp. 391–401 in *Women: A Feminist Perspective*, edited by Jo Freeman. Palo Alto: Mayfield.

Keller, Evelyn F. 1978. "Gender and Science." *Psychoanalysis and Contemporary Thought* 1: 409–433.

Kitsuse, John I. 1962. "Societal Reaction to Deviant Behavior: Problems of Theory and Method." *Social Problems* 9: 247–256.

Kitzinger, Celia. 1987. *The Social Construction of Lesbianism*. London: Sage.

Klemke, Lloyd W., and Gary H. Tiedeman. 1990. "Toward an Understanding of False Accusation: The Pure Case of Deviant Labeling." Pp. 266–286 in *Deviant Behavior*, edited by Clifton D. Bryant. New York; Hemisphere.

Lenskyj, Helen. 1986. *Out of Bounds: Women, Sport and Sexuality*. Toronto: Women's Press.

——. 1991. "Combating Homophobia in Sport and Physical Education." *Sociology of Sport Journal* 8: 61–69.

Nobles, Wade W. 1973. "Psychological Research and the Black Seif-Concept: A Critical Review." *Journal of Social Issues* 29: 11–31.

Sarnoff, Irving. 1951. "Identification with the Aggressor: Some Personality Correlates of Anti-Semitism Among Jews." *Journal of Personality* 20: 199–218.

Schur, Edwin M. 1979. *Interpreting Deviance: A Sociological Introduction*. New York: Harper and Row.

——. 1984. *Labeling Women Deviant: Gender, Stigma, and Social Control*. New York: Random House.

Theberge, Nancy. 1985. "Toward a Feminist Alternative to Sport as a Male Preserve." *Quest* 37: 193–202.

Thomas. Charles W. 1971. *Boys No More*. Beverly Hills: Glencoe.

Willis, Paul. 1982. "Women in Sport in Ideology." Pp. 117–135 in *Sport, Culture and Ideology*, edited by Jennifer Hargreaves. London: Routledge & Kegan Paul.

Wolfe, Susan J. 1988. "The Rhetoric of Heterosexism." Pp. 199–224 in *Gender and Discourse: The Power of Talk*, vol. 30, edited by Alexandra Dundas Todd and Sue Fisher, Norwood, NJ: Ablex.

SECTION 6

Globalization and Sports

Globalization has emerged as arguably the most dynamic, far reaching, and unpredictable development in the modern world. Despite the eruptions of international tensions, conflicts, and wars, globalization proceeds as a complex and unfolding process of social evolution. Its impact can be observed in the broad array of settings—from the taxicabs of New York City, the factories in China, and the television programs in Lagos to the nightclubs in Tokyo and Berlin. Though scholars differ in their analytic approaches to studying globalization, most regard it as a process manifested in increasing levels of economic, technological, political, and cultural interdependence among nations and peoples throughout the world. Sport has not only been drawn into this process; it stands among the world's leading globalizing institutions, evidenced by its increasing expansion into activities that range from televising sport events and recruiting players to attracting fans across national borders.

CONCEPTUALIZING GLOBALIZATION

According to one formal definition, "globalization is characterized by increasing global interconnections or interconnectivity (for example, greater migration and digital communication; and increasing forms of globality" manifested through the growth of global consciousness) (Giulanotti and Robertson, 2009, xi).

We will begin this section by presenting examples of two conceptual frameworks that present analytical categories for understanding globalization. The first consists of a general conceptual framework which applies to all types of globalization, whereas the second applies specifically to sport.

A GENERAL CONCEPTUAL FRAMEWORK FOR STUDYING GLOBALIZATION

This conceptual framework was developed by an anthropologist, Arjun Appadurai; it delineates five spheres of globalization which he terms "scapes." It provides an analytical vocabulary for categorizing the different distinct spheres of globalization activity (Appadurai, 1990).

- **Ethnoscapes** include mobile groups and individuals (e.g., migrants, tourists, refugees, guest workers) in an ever-changing modern world. For example, the migration of political refugees, farm workers, cooks, teachers, doctors, engineers, and computer scientists to the United States would fit this category. These movements of people from one geographical region of the world to another have consequences for both the country they are entering and the one they left behind. In the sport world, ethnoscapes are manifested in the migration of athletes from one country to another.
- **Techno-scapes** consist of the fluid global configurations of high and low technology—both mechanical and informational—that facilitate the free movement of materials across borders and around the world. Examples include the development of jet travel, which transports people across vast distances in very short time intervals; as well as electronic and digital technologies such as radio, television, and the Internet, which allow people to interact and exchange information across vast distances without even being physically near one another. The distances that previously caused some people to live in isolation and ignorance about the world beyond their immediate local community or region have collapsed as a consequence of modern technological developments. Few geographical areas remain inaccessible and uninfluenced by contacts with the outside world. Virtually every area of the world can be reached quickly by means of travel and technology. The application of techno-scapes to sport can be seen in the technological innovations that facilitate the development of global media and global financial institutions.
- **Media-scapes** are a direct product of advanced techno-scapes; they involve the development and activities of corporate television networks (e.g., Fox, CNN, and Al Jazeera), Internet service providers and websites, the globally oriented movie industry, and corporate-run digitized magazines and newspapers that continuously produce and transmit information and images that circulate throughout the world. The media-scapes' sphere expands the reach of sport events around the world and de-territorializes sport fandoms (e.g., San Antonio basketball fans in China; New York Yankee baseball fans in London).
- **Ideo-scapes** produce ideas and images based on political state ideology—as well as counter ideologies of movements seeking to effect changes in power structures. These ideas and images are facilitated by the modern media-scapes with the result that few ideas can be insulated from criticism and opposing ideas—whether they exist in the form of state laws, religious doctrines, or simply traditional cultural beliefs and practices. For example, the gay rights liberation movement which began in the United States has reverberated through most of the world, influencing the emergence of similar movements in such places such India, Uganda, and Russia. Similar effects have diffused from the women's movement and the human rights movement. All have become part of global ideo-scapes. These spheres affect sport practices of fairness, integrity and inclusion. For example, the pressures on Middle Eastern countries to include women in sports and the anti-apartheid movement against South Africa's participation in the Olympics reflect the circulation of sport-related ideas across national borders.
- **Finance-scapes** involve processes by which huge sums of money are moved through nations and the world at great speeds. These facilitate the growth of global business and other commercial enterprises led by multinational corporations. Modern finance-

scapes also facilitate the globalization of corporate ownership, with stockholders, managers, and facilities increasingly dispersed throughout the world. This sphere facilitates the commercialization of sport, which drives the development of foreign ownership of sport enterprises as well as expansion of media-scapes. Examples of the impact of this sphere upon sport include the ability of an American to become the owner of an elite English soccer team by leveraging financial debt, the purchase of an NBA team by a Russian oligarch, the emergence and growth of multinational sports-media corporations.

A SPORT-FOCUSED CONCEPTUAL FRAMEWORK FOR STUDYING GLOBALIZATION

This second conceptual framework was developed by two leading sport scholars, Richard Giulianotti and Roland Robertson (2009); it highlights four spheres which operate as major social forces within the global field of soccer. The authors maintain that each of the social forces correspond to distinct structural interests or what we can term "institutional logics." Simply put, each operates to promote its distinct interest in professional soccer.

- **Neo-liberalism** is driven by the institutional logic of individual market-centered interests. These interests typically are advanced by transnational corporations which are committed to gaining financial profits from soccer.
- **Neo-mercantilism** is driven by the institutional logic of national interests. These interests tend to be pursued by national governments who seek to use sport to advance the state's political prestige and support.
- **International governance** is driven by the institutional logic of protecting and advancing the interests of a transnational sport; an example is FIFA's relationship to soccer and the World Cup.
- **Global civil society groups** are driven by the institutional logic of human rights. These organizations are committed to using sport and sport venues to advance humanitarian values.

Though this conceptual framework was developed to study soccer globalization, it could be adapted to study the globalization of other sports like basketball and baseball. We will return to discuss some of the broader implications of this framework when we examine the examples of major analytical perspectives and arguments assessing sport globalization as a social process.

ANALYTICAL PERSPECTIVES ON SPORT GLOBALIZATION: NEO-IMPERIALISM OR THE GROWTH OF GLOBAL COMMUNITY?

Proponents of the critical leftist perspectives tend to regard globalization as a manifestation of neo-imperialism, which exploits and undermines the development of poorer nations. In effect, they believe globalization reflects a process of conflict between the interests of the "haves" (affluent nations) and the "have-nots" (poor nations). Though their arguments and emphases differ somewhat, the following three analytical perspectives represent examples of the critical leftist perspectives on globalization.

Sport Globalization as Neo-Colonial Dependency

One of the most provocative leftist analytical arguments on sport globalization is posed by Alan M. Klein in his book *Sugarball*, which focused on the relationship between Major League Baseball (MLB) and baseball leagues in the Dominican Republic (Klein, 1991, 2007). Applying neo-Marxist dependency theory, Klein argues that Dominican baseball is being undermined by its relationship to MLB, which has set up academies in the Dominican Republic and recruited local players to play in the United States. Klein argues that local Dominican baseball leagues were exploited because wealthy American MLB teams, by siphoning off their best players, weakened the local leagues by making them an appendage of MLB.

Klein further asserts that Dominicans do not oppose this exploitation because the nation has been conditioned by U.S. cultural hegemony:

> Cultural resistance in the Dominican Republic is weak relative to its hegemonic opposite. Given the glitter and polish of upwardly mobile baseball heroes, baseball represents an ideal medium for replicating the American cultural domination that exists in other spheres. At the very least it works to soften opposition to American owned corporations.
>
> (Klein, 2007, p. 912).

This situation of baseball globalization, Klein maintains, constitutes neo-colonial exploitation which reflects the earlier history of classical colonialism, when labor and natural resources were extracted from Asia, Africa, and Latin America to enrich Europe and the United States.

Though dependency theory still has some supporters, it has lost favor among most social science scholars. Ironically, this has resulted, in part, from the effects of globalization. The relationships between developed and undeveloped nations have become more complex over the past several decades. The scale of geographical mobility has greatly expanded and the experiences of migrants as well and their ties to their home countries have become more complex. Many migrants transfer resources they earn in affluent nations back home to their families and to investments in local business enterprises they own. Klein makes a distinction between the experiences of individuals and the larger society. He acknowledges that Dominican baseball players who attend MLB academies are ultimately better off than their families. And the ones who sign MLB contracts hit the jackpot as they are propelled to a level of affluence out of reach of ordinary Dominicans. So at this level individual baseball players, Klein realizes, feel satisfied with opportunities for a better life provided by MLB.

His, critique, however, is directed at the societal level, which is where he argues that the impact of MLB has been most damaging because it causes tens of thousands of young Dominican boys to grow up aspiring unrealistically to become MLB players. Similar arguments have been made about the impact of professional basketball in black American communities.

The problem with Klein's argument is that it ignores the agency of Dominicans. Most Dominican youth do not perceive better opportunities for the future and it is doubtful that their futures would be brighter if MLB academies did not exist in the country. Most Dominicans do not share Klein's views for that reason.

In not only the Dominican Republic but also other countries throughout Latin America—Mexico, Venezuela, and Colombia, to name a few—the achievements of star players in MLB are celebrated and encouraged by their local communities and government officials who see them as national heroes. Among Latin American countries, only Cuba remains an exception—though more than a few Cuban players manage to evade government restrictions on players migrating to the United States. Perhaps the best evidence for the demise of the dependency perspective on baseball derives from the fact that Klein himself has moved to a different perspective, which is revealed in his later writing about baseball in the Dominican Republic. We will discuss one of his more recent articles later.

Globalization as Euro-American Hegemony

A related leftist perspective on globalization was developed by Raewyn Connell (Connell, 2007). Unlike Klein's argument, Connell's views do not derive from an actual field study of a sport, but rather from a theoretical analysis of globalization. She argues that globalization operates as a process of cultural hegemony which promotes the interests of the global North (North America and Europe) in exploiting the less developed regions of the global South (e.g., Africa, Asia, and Latin America). Connell maintains that the interests and voices of the global South are ignored in the scholarly writings about globalization.

Connell's argument has encountered various criticisms. One criticism objects to her North–South binary as an outdated conception of the world. Over the past half century, many countries, which were characterized as undeveloped (e.g., South Korea, Taiwan, Singapore, Turkey, and Brazil) have achieved significant economic growth and higher standards of living. Some critics regard the old categories of developed/undeveloped and North/South as too simplistic to make sense of the complexity of the modern world. Other critics dispute Connell's contention that globalization theory excludes voices from the poorer countries of the world: As an example, Arjun Appadurai, who comes from India, is recognized as one of the leading globalization theorists.

"Grobalization" as a Modern Form of Neo-Imperialism

George Ritzer's theoretical writings on what he terms "grobalization" (a blend of *growth* and *globalization*) represent a third example of a critical leftist perspective on globalization. Though he views globalization as a dual process which consists of both grobalization and "glocalization" (a blend of *globalization* and *localization* coined by Robertson), it is Ritzer's argument on grobalization that constitutes an original formulation (Ritzer 2003).

Grobalization, according to Ritzer, focuses on the imperialistic ambitions of nations, corporations, and organizations, which seek to impose themselves on various areas of the world. By emphasizing the role of commodification, capitalism, cultural hegemony, expansion, and exploitation, it highlights the activities of profit making and commercial rationalization. He uses the term "McDonaldization" as the metaphor for grobalization—that is, harmful globalization. Here Ritzer has in mind the activities of corporations like McDonald's fast food restaurants, General Motors automobile plants, Levi's clothing factories, Apple Computer manufacturing operations, and other large corporations, as well as sports organizations like Major League Baseball's academies in places such as the Dominican Republic. Grobalization, in short, corresponds to such pejorative terms for globalization as Americanization, Westernization, or imperialism.

Ritzer's concept of glocalization, in contrast, presents nothing new. It reflects the original meaning of the term developed by Robertson in his theoretical writing on globalization. Ritzer uses it to highlight what he sees as a sharp contrast between the two dimension of globalization: a negative neo-imperial dimension and a positive integrative dimension. The former fosters tensions and conflicts, whereas the latter fosters heterogenization and adaptations to local culture.

GLOBALIZATION AS GLOCALIZED INTERDEPENDENCE

Ritzer's work has encountered strong criticism from Giulianotti and Robertson, two leading theorists of sports globalization. Building on Robertson's earlier theoretical writings on globalization, they have written a recent article which responds to Ritzer's argument (Giulianotti and Robertson, 2012).

Contrary to Ritzer, they argue that globalization does not entail an opposition between the global and the local but rather interdependence. They see glocalization (a term Robertson originated) as being much more widespread than does Ritzer (Giulianotti and Robertson, 2012). Moreover, they criticize Ritzer for focusing so heavily on the commercial aspects of culture—such as fast food restaurants and tourist products—while underemphasizing the non-commerical aspects of globalization. They cite the example of Japanese baseball, noting that Ritzer's analysis would ignore such cultural realities as bodily techniques, self-identities, and meanings of players and supporters. Moreover, Japanese baseball hardly operates as an appendage of MLB. In short, they argue that Ritzer's notion of "grobalization" fails to take into account the complex local heterogenization involved in globalization. They view globalization as largely a process of increasing interdependence, as strongly emphasized in Robertson's earlier writings: "Globalization explains the interpenetration of the local and global. This approach endeavors to move beyond the basic dichotomization of local and global to explain their mutual-interplay and co-presence" (Giulianotti and Robertson 2012, p. 438). Simply put, they reject the neo-imperialist perspective on globalization.

SEEKING AN ACCURATE VIEW OF SPORT GLOBALIZATION

These conflicting arguments lead us to ask: Which of these two perspectives—neo-imperialism or expanding global community—seems to provide the most accurate account of sport globalization? We will attempt to answer this question by examining several studies to see examples of the transactions between external global flows and local reactions in sport.

Israel's National Basketball Team

The first of these examples comes from a study of Israel's national basketball team by Shor and Gality, "Between Adoption and Resistance: Grobalization and Glocalization in the Development of Israeli Basketball" (see Chapter 36). The authors use Ritzer's concept—grobalization—to explain why the team's fans and the media mobilized resistance to the "Americanization" of Israel's national team. They resented having a so-called national team that was actually composed of a majority of American rather than Israeli players. Many of the team's players were African Americans who, in the view of the disgruntled

Israel fans and media—despite the team's successful record—failed to reflect Israel's ethnic-religious identity as a Jewish nation.

The fans and media were eventually obliged to compromise their demands for an all-Jewish national team because of the competitive situation. The team was competing against European teams whose player recruitment was based on free market meritocratic criteria. Here we see the ways in which sport competition facilitates acceptance of meritocratic norms despite fan preferences for local players.

Though the authors use Ritzer's concept of grobalization, it does not actually explain why Israel's team finally accepted having so many American players. Contrary to implications of Ritzer's grobalization argument, "Americanization" was not imposed by imperialistic designs of the United States or American sports organizations; rather, it resulted from choices made by the Israeli basketball coaches and executives. To assemble a competitive team, they needed to play the best players they could find, because ultimately sport involves the quest to win.

Buscom in Dominican Baseball Recruitment

In the second example, we see the transactions between a global cultural flow and a local society in Alan Klein's article "Chain Reaction: Neo-Liberal Exceptions to Global Commodity Chains in Dominican Baseball" (2012b). In this analysis of the role of buscom (loyal brokers) in the development and recruitment of players for MLB in the Dominican Republic (written some 20 years after he published *Sugarball*), Klein shifts from the dependency perspective to a critical but more nuanced argument. Dominican baseball players have become a permanent presence in MLB as they constitute the majority of foreign-born players. In this study, Klein chooses to highlight the way in which Dominicans have adapted that relationship to the local society by creating a local system of middleman local brokers who operate as intermediaries between Dominican players and MLB. Klein notes that MLB disliked the informal system, but could not eliminate it because it was deeply embedded in the local informal economy, and because the brokers had strong ties to the boys' families and local communities.

Klein uses this case study to illustrate a situation in which local intermediaries were able to compromise the power and wealth of MLB by obliging it to adapt to the local society. The brokers filled a vacuum in the MLB recruitment system by serving the function of identifying and developing the talent of very young baseball players—before anyone knew whether they would have enough talent to get a MLB contract. So the brokers took charge of boys' baseball development—a function performed by high schools and colleges in the U.S.—until they were old enough to try out for a MLB team. If a boy turned out to be good enough to sign a contract with a major league team, the broker received a percentage of the signing bonus. The local broker system, in effect, inserted itself into the MLB recruitment process and, thereby, imposed constraints on an external global flow.

Klein characterizes this as a manifestation of counter-hegemonic resistance, which he sees as a form of glocalism, in the Dominican Republic's relations with MLB. This argument departs from the neo-imperial perspective by emphasizing the agency of locals in adapting globalization to the local culture. This hardly corresponds to the grobalization process described by Ritzer which suggests that the local society is dominated by the external global flow.

Nike Sport Gear

In contrast to the above two examples, the third example focuses on a sport consumer item rather than a sport in the globalization process. It explores links between corporate nationalism and glocalization by examining Nike's strategy for representing the "nation" within its Asian advertising campaigns for athletic shoes and other sport gear (Kobryashi, 2012). The author discovered that Nike did not impose imperious control over the production of the ads. Rather he found that "the process worked through a range of global–local negotiations, struggles, and collaborations" (p. 58) that had substantial influence on the content of the ads. In effect, the process of expanding Nike's appeal to Asian consumers obliged Nike to adapt to local cultures. Similar to Klein's conclusion, the author found that the global flow had to adapt to the local society through "local cultural intermediaries."

Japanese Professional Baseball

The fourth example points to the relationship between MLB and Japanese baseball. As noted above, Japanese professional baseball almost 100 years ago developed its own distinctive baseball culture and organization which has remained quite distinct from its American counterpart. Moreover, Japanese baseball has imposed constraints on the ability of MLB teams to sign Japanese professional baseball players (Klein, 2008). This demonstrates a situation in which a local society retains complete control of a global flow.

Assessing the Accuracy of the Neo-Imperial Perspective

As we can see from earlier examples the transactions between global flows and local societies may result in strains, but there is little support for the neo-imperial perspective. Even in the cases of Israeli basketball and Dominican baseball, which were characterized by frictions between the global flows and local culture, these resulted in neither hegemonic domination nor protracted conflicts that disrupted the globalization. Rather, they resulted in adaptive glocalization processes which involved the agency of local actors as intermediaries or brokers in that process. This corresponds to the analytical perspective developed by Giulianotti and Robertson (2009, 2012). But does this mean that globalization—in this case, sport globalization—is resulting in the growth of global community? The answer to this question is complex and hardly warrants a utopian vision of an integrated and harmonious global sport world. As Andrei Markovits and Lars Rensmann demonstrate in their book *Gaming The World* (2010), sport globalization sometimes provokes what they term "anti-cosmopolitanism," antagonistic reactions to globalization, which may be manifested as ethnocentrism, racism, anti-semitism, nativism, or even anti-Americanism. As they observe:

> the anti-cosmopolitan wrath against soccer does not only hail from countries and cultures where the game has come to be seen as an intruder to the established sports culture and a direct competitor to existing hegemonic sports.
>
> They point to the presence of anti-cosmopolitanism in Europe where it frequently erupts in nationalist rages against commercialization and its associated vices. But they go on to note that:
>
> Oddly enough the telling scepter of "Americanization" is frequently invoked in these counter-cosmopolitan attacks on soccer, which is totally odd since the game is anything but American,

> were it not a tell tale word used by all European opponents (left and right) whenever they depict globalization's evils.
>
> (Markovits and Hellermann, 2011, p. 211)

Because major American corporations such as McDonalds and Walmart have high visibility among the major commercial forces of globalization, "Americanization" has become a familiar epithet among people who are troubled by changes, which they believe are de-nationalizing their societies.

The authors make clear that it would be a mistake to view these anti-cosmopolitan reactions as rational responses to "imperious domination" of outsiders, which is the view advanced by nativists. Instead, they argue that these reactions are fed by delusional fears and anxieties aroused by increasing diversity and heterogeneity brought about by expanding globalization. Though anti-cosmopolitanism seems to be particularly strong in some parts of the Middle East, most scholars believe it is a diminishing force in the modern world.

GLOBAL SPORT AS A FORCE CREATING COSMOPOLITAN IDENTITIES

On the opposite end of the spectrum, some sport scholars propose that sport globalization is having a positive effect in the form of creating cosmopolitan identities and values.

Andrei Markovits argues that sport is part of the trend toward progressive and democratic cosmopolitanism derived from the legacy of the 1960s, which promotes a tendency toward universalistic empowerment and inclusion of previously marginalized groups (Markovits 2010). This new culture of cosmopolitanism, he argues, is reflected in the emergence of global sport stars such as David Beckham and Kobe Bryant, who showcase meritocratic norms as the basis of success. He points to the changing patterns of fan loyalties—such as Manchester United soccer fans in Los Angeles and New York Yankee baseball fans in Tokyo—as examples of expanding cosmopolitan identities. While acknowledging, as already noted, that sport sometimes arouses anti-cosmopolitan chauvinistic reactions, evidenced in neo-fascist and racist attitudes among some soccer fans in Europe, he views these as backwaters rather than serious threats to the globalization process.

Franklin Foer makes a somewhat similar argument in his book *Soccer Will Explain The World* (2004), arguing that soccer is advancing the growth of cosmopolitanism. He cites examples of sport being linked to relaxation of conservative restrictions on women in Iran and the leftist cosmopolitan Barca soccer club in Spain to illustrate his argument. However, he also acknowledges that sport sometimes generates hostile chauvinistic reactions toward out-groups as in Serbia and in Glasgow, Scotland, where sport contests operate as platforms for venting ethnic hostility. But overall, Foer thinks soccer globalization will continue to expand cosmopolitan values and identities.

Raffaele Poli presents what is by far the most provocative and radical argument highlighting global sport's impact in increasing cosmopolitanism in the modern world (Poli, 2007). He argues that modern sport operates as a force that is de-nationalizing the world through increasing international migration of players, expanding global sport media, and changing patterns of fan loyalties. These developments, he maintains, are also "de-ethnicizing nations" and "de-territorializing identities"—which perhaps represents the ultimate development of cosmopolitanism. Thus, while agreeing with Markovits and

Foer, Poli goes beyond them by suggesting that sport globalization is fostering a more radical and far-reaching transformation of modern human society.

Interestingly, Giulianotti's *flâneur* type fan, which he sees as increasing in the modern era of global sport and global sport media, parallels Poli's notions of de-nationalization, de-ethnicization, and de-territorialization (Giulianotti, 2012). Both envision sport globalization playing a part in fostering looser and more fluid forms of social community.

There is no question that global sport is contributing significantly to increasing cosmopolitanism throughout the modern world. But what does this mean for human societies? What, if any, are the limits to this cosmopolitanism? How is it related to national citizenship and national identity? What is the relationship between global sport and cosmopolitan identity? Which sports are most likely to be linked to cosmopolitanism? Which segments of modern society are most likely to embrace cosmopolitan sport as well as a cosmopolitan identity? Which are most likely to reject global sport and embrace an anti-cosmopolitan identity? How do the factors of social class and education influence reception to cosmopolitanism and global sport? More research is needed before we can answer these many questions.

THE OLYMPICS: THE GLOBAL VENUE FOR SPORT COMPETITION

The International Olympic Committee (IOC) operates as the quintessential global organization for staging and regulating sport contests involving most nations of the world. Founded by Pierre de Coubertin in 1894, the IOC embraced noble ideals, as articulated in its Fundamental Principles:

> The aims of the Olympic Movement are to promote the development of those fine physical and moral qualities which are the basis of amateur sport and to bring together the athletes of the world in a great quadrennial festival of sports thereby creating international respect and goodwill and thus helping to construct a better and more peaceful world.
>
> (Lapchick, 1986, p. 329)

The IOC, in effect, set out to promote sport contests between individuals in accordance with the normative standards of fair competition. In this regard, it emerged as the first international organization to showcase and affirm those normative standards. Though the Olympic sport contests have often fallen short of the high bar of fair competition, this has hardly diminished their importance. Deviant practices violating that norm were obliged to honor it in the breach by resorting to secrecy and subterfuge to avoid sanctions. This reflected the force of the Olympics in promoting the global diffusion of the norms of fair competition.

Perhaps the most consequential departure from the Olympics' initial objectives occurred in 1908 when the emphasis of the games shifted from individual competitions to competitions between nations. The Olympic games quickly became a venue for displaying national prowess and expressing nationalistic passions. This was—and is—evidenced in such symbolic gestures as wearing national sport uniforms, waving national flags, and counting medals per nation, as well as playing national anthems during victory ceremonies. Though the goals of the Olympic games focused on competition between nations, they played a major role in increasing global consciousness among ordinary people long before international electronic and digital media. This increasing global consciousness was related to the Olympics' initial objectives emphasizing international peace and harmony.

OLYMPICS AND POLITICS

The IOC professed political neutrality. But despite their professed ideals, the Olympics have hardly transcended strains of international politics as they have often been used as a platform for enacting or dramatizing political conflicts. This is illustrated by some characteristic examples.

The IOC's decision to stage the 1936 Olympics in Hitler's Nazi Germany triggered one of the most bitter political controversies in Olympics history. Many non-Germans opposed holding the games in a country that openly promoted racist and anti-Jewish policies as well as international aggression. The IOC's failure to distance the Olympics from Nazi Germany tarnished the organization's image.

Another major political controversy arose at the 1968 Olympics in Mexico City when two black American athletes, Tommie Smith and John Carlos, displayed a "Black power" salute during the playing of the U.S. national anthem. While their gesture was intended to call attention to the problems of racial injustice in the United States, it provoked a major backlash. "The U.S. Olympic Committee suspended them from the U.S. Olympic team, they were thrown out of the Olympic Village, and they were banned for life from competing in the Olympic Games" (Sage, 2010, p. 213). Was this outcome consistent with the Olympics' professed goals of promoting international peace and harmony? Those goals were ambiguous and hollow when political injustices within member nations were protested during the Olympics. The IOC chose simply to remain silent.

The murder of 11 Israeli athletes at the Olympic games in Munich, Germany, in 1972 remains the most shocking and violent expression of political antagonism at an Olympics venue. In 2012, the IOC was criticized for refusing to allow a brief commemoration of the 40th anniversary of that tragic event. This illustrates that the IOC's professed commitment to international peace and harmony typically turns out to be impotent when the Olympics is confronted with actual political conflicts.

The decision of many African nations to boycott the 1976 Olympics as a protest against the participation of apartheid South Africa aroused considerable controversy. The Africans took the action in response to the IOC's refusal to bar South Africa from Olympic competition while the apartheid policy of racial discrimination remained law in that country. Many groups, including the United States Olympic Committee and most American sports media, supported the IOC on the grounds that politics should have no place in the Olympics. Nevertheless, in the 1980 games the IOC reversed its decision and barred apartheid South Africa from participating, a development that many observers believe contributed significantly to the eventual downfall of South Africa's apartheid government.

At the same time, 1980 brought about a an even larger political controversy centered on the Olympics: the United States government's decision to boycott the 1980 Olympics in Moscow, made in reaction to the Soviet Union's military involvement in Afghanistan (Sage, 2010, pp. 205–207) In an interesting shift of opinion, many American sport pundits who opposed the South African ban, because it would bring politics into sport, supported the U.S. boycott of the Moscow Olympics. Most American Olympic athletes, who had trained several years for the games, opposed the decision. Meanwhile, the IOC refused to intervene. The Moscow Olympics took place without U.S. participation.

The most recent example of the Olympics being used to highlight political conflict occurred during the Beijing Olympics in 2008, when several international human rights groups staged protests against China's repression of political dissent and occupation of Tibet, among other things (Sage, 2010, p. 201).

While the IOC has remained neutral in these political conflicts, the Olympic games, by providing a venue for showcasing political protests, have no doubt contributed to advancing international norms of social justice. Some sport scholars argue that these types of political protests are likely to increase along with the expanding reach of global sport media. The Olympic games deliver a global audience (Giulianotti & Robertson, 2009, pp. 160–170).

OLYMPIC CORRUPTION

A different and deeply rooted problem confronting the IOC focuses on corruption. In 1998, for example, IOC members were alleged to have accepted bribes from local officials in Salt Lake City, Utah, in exchange for deciding to stage the Winter Olympics in their city (Shepard, 1999). Although it was determined that the officials had accepted ethically questionable gifts, the investigation uncovered nothing strictly illegal in the negotiations. Nevertheless, the IOC expelled 10 members and sanctioned another. It also implemented several organizational reforms such as placing limits on the value of gifts members could receive from government officials and establishing new term and age limits on members. Feeling that the committee would benefit from more input from individuals who had actually competed in the Olympics, the IOC added 15 former athletes to its ranks.

These changes have scarcely succeeded in eliminating allegations and suspicions of IOC corruption. Because IOC officials have considerable power in making decisions about future sites for the Olympics, prizes that are valued highly by governments, they remain vulnerable to the temptations of corruption. Maintaining high standards of integrity in its operations remains one of the largest challenges facing the IOC as the Olympics operates under the omnipresent gaze of increasingly vigilant and globalized media.

Another major problem that confronted the IOC centered around athletes' amateur status as a requirement for Olympics participation (Sage, 2010, pp. 87–88). For decades, many athletes violated the rule. The problem became especially contentious during the Cold War era when Eastern Bloc governments such as East Germany and the Soviet Union paid salaries to their athletes. Many American athletes accepted money under the table which allowed them to devote full time to training without having to work to support themselves. Such violations became so frequent and pervasive that IOC decided to eliminate the amateur requirement in the early 1990s. In a highly commercialized sport world, which was generating billions in revenue and signing professional athletes and coaches in major sports to multi-dollar contracts, it no longer seemed reasonable to expect world class Olympic athletes to perform without financial compensation. This decision opened Olympics' doors to professional athletes such as National Basketball Association players. As we will discuss, this rule change not only elevated the Olympic competition in basketball, it exposed professional basketball superstars to global audiences, which accelerated the globalization of the NBA.

GLOBALIZATION OF OLYMPIC ATHLETES

In contrast to the problem of amateurism, the problem of athletes' eligibility to represent a country other than the one of their birth has become more contentious due to the increased geographic mobility of athletes. Olympic rules, like those of FIFA, require athletes to represent their native countries in sport competition. But many modern athletes may choose not to represent their home countries. Some have migrated to an adopted country and become citizens, a situation that IOC regards as a legitimate basis for not representing their native country in the Olympics.

But other situations may fail to gain IOC approval. In some cases, the athlete is enticed financially to take up citizenship in a country specifically to represent that country in the Olympics. These situations in a world characterized by international migration of athletes are widespread as revealed by the following examples.

- The first Olympic medal awarded to the small oil-rich Kingdom of Qatar was won in 1992 by Somali-born runner Mohammed Suleiman.
- In 2008 Bahrain's top Olympic woman track hopeful was Maryam Yusuf Jamal, an Ethiopian athlete who lives in Switzerland.
- All of Russia's Olympic boxers at the 2008 Beijing Olympics were foreign.
- Over fifty foreign-born athletes were on Canada's Olympic boxing team.

(Sage, 2010, p. 89)

This practice is hardly restricted to developing nations, a recently reconfigured Russian state or an underpopulated Canada. The United States also participates in this practice of importing Olympic athletes. The United States had eight foreign-born Olympians at the 2006 Winter Games in Turin, Italy. Included among U.S. athletes at the 2008 Olympics in Beijing were "four Chinese-born tennis players, a kayaker from Britain, Russian-born world champion gymnast Nastia Liukin . . . (on the) men's 1500-meter (track) squad—Kenya native Bernard Lagat; Lopez Lomong, one of the lost boys of Sudan's civil war who spent a decade in a refugee camp" (Sage, 2010, p. 89).

In light of the increasing geographical mobility of athletes, has the notion of the Olympics as competition between nations weakened? Is globalization likely to change the meaning of the Olympics? The popularity and the global reach of the Olympic games is indicated by the growth of its broadcasting and total revenues.

The Olympics exists as the leading sport institution showcasing and diffusing norms of competitive fairness throughout the globe. That influence will no doubt continue as was

Total Revenue Generated By Olympics in Five 4-Year Periods

	1993–96	*1997–2000*	*2001–04*	*2005–08*	*2009–12*
Broadcasting	1,215	1,845	2,232	2,570	3,914
Total	2,630	3,776	4,189	5,480	n/a

" Olympic Marketing File," 2012 edition.

* All numbers in the chart have been rounded to the nearest US $1million

Source: www.olympic.org/document/ioc marketing/olympic-marketing-fact-file-2012.

evidenced by the impact of its policy initiatives in punishing performance-enhancing drug users and showcasing women athletes competing in sports formerly forbidden in some traditional societies. The Olympics institution is the elephant in the living room of global sport culture. Its actions matter.

SOCCER: THE PRE-EMINENT GLOBAL SPORT

Soccer—or football, as it is known outside the U.S.—prevails as the world's most global sport. Founded in England in the late 1880s, the game subsequently spread to other European countries, which led to the establishment of the International Soccer Federation (Fédération Internationale de Football Association, or FIFA) in 1904 (Giulianotti and Robertson, 2009, pp. 5–27). This was followed a generation later by the founding of the World Cup in 1930. FIFA operates today as the world's largest international sport association with some 309 national associations—which exceeds the member states of the United Nations.

As noted by Sage, "FIFA's scope at the beginning of the 21st century includes more than 250 million people from more than 200 hundred countries regularly played soccer" (Sage, 2010, p. 72). Taking into account the vast range of soccer's reach throughout the world, Sage went on to make the striking observation that "there may be no world practice more global than soccer" (p.71]). None of the world's great religions such as Islam and Christianity approximate soccer's global reach.

SOCCER AND THE FREE LABOR MARKET

Not only does soccer prevail as the most globalized sport, it possesses the world's freest labor market. Scholars generally agree that soccer achieved that status in 1995 when the European Union initiated what it termed the Bosman Rule. This rule removed all restrictions on the mobility of soccer players within the English and European Leagues. As a result of this rule, notes one economist, soccer represents not just the world's freest profession but also "the most advanced development of globalization."

The following table listing the presence of foreign players in European and English clubs in 2007 reveals the extent of globalization of soccer players.

The national teams in these countries have been experiencing declining representation of native-born players due to increased free market labor migration, a development that has caused nativist resentment and backlashes among some soccer fans. This increasing globalization of the soccer market has had two contradictory effects on European leagues:

	Percentage of Foreign-Born Soccer Players on European Soccer Clubs
England	55.4
Germany	44.8
Spain	34.3
France	32.2
Italy	28.9

Source: Sage, 2010, p. 73.

It has elevated the overall quality of the play but decreased the quality of intra-league competition (Milonvic, 2000, pp. 1–2). This demonstrates that meritocratic normative practices of player recruitment do not necessarily produce fair outcomes. If the resources for acquiring the best players are distributed unequally, as in the case of European soccer leagues, free labor markets result in unequal competition—oligopolistic domination by wealthier teams.

But equally important, soccer's free labor market is de-nationalizing the sport clubs by abolishing national barriers to players' mobility. This development was aptly described by one soccer observer: "Last season, when the British soccer team Liverpool FC played Real Madrid, the number of Spanish players on Liverpool's team outnumbered those playing for Madrid" (Kaplan, 2009). What does it mean to refer to a team as an English team when the majority of its players and a large portion of its fans are not English? What does the team represent or symbolize—a locality? A corporate brand? An outdated history? These questions are related to the argument of Poli noted earlier.

Significantly, FIFA counteracts this de-nationalizing trend by placing restrictions on player mobility. In general, to be eligible to participate in the World Cup competitions, players are required by FIFA to play for their national home teams. Thus, by suspending the free labor market and maintaining greater competitiveness between teams, the World Cup re-asserts the linkage between soccer and nation states. The intense emotional passions generated by World Cup matches, typically manifested in nationalistic expressions of loyalty, arouse unparalleled feelings of national unity every four years, even in societies deeply divided by class, ethnic, and religious fault lines. Soccer madness prevails as World Cup matches cause people to transcend everyday strains of social stratification.

FIFA, like the IOC, is an international sports organization with enormous power, as well as a reputation for corruption and inefficient governance. Recent allegations have surfaced that bribery lay behind the FIFA's choice of Russia and tiny oil rich Qatar for the 2018 and 2022 World Cup. As one of FIFA's greatest challenges in the future, this problem demands organizational reforms that make FIFA officials accountable to external oversight and regulation.

SOCCER IN THE UNITED STATES

As part of its continuing global expansion, soccer has experienced increasing popularity in the United States over the past two decades. The U.S. has a professional league which began playing in 1996; it now has 15 teams divided into two conferences, with one team based in Canada. The U.S. long had the distinction of "American Exceptionalism" for being a nation which rejected soccer as a major sport, but that situation is apparently changing as the American soccer league continues to gain fans (Sage, 2010, p. 73).

Recognizing that the most talented soccer players are located in Europe, Africa, and Latin America, the U.S. league implemented an unusual rule designed to expand its global reach by attracting more foreign players. This rule (the Designated Player Rule) allows each club to exceed the league's salary cap to sign two foreign players. Foreign players who currently comprise approximately one-third of the U.S. professional league have not only elevated the quality of competition; they have also improved the skills of American-born players (Sage, 2010, p. 75). That improvement was illustrated clearly by the impressive performance of the U.S. national team in the 2014 World Cup competition in Brazil, where it advanced to the semi-finals before being defeated by an exceptional German team, which went on to win the World Cup.

The improved quality of play in the U.S. professional league has undoubtedly helped to increase the popularity of soccer among young American boys and girls. "Now some 10,000 teams and 4.8 million young boys and girls are playing [soccer]" (Sage, 2010, p. 73). In his book *How Soccer Will Explain the World*, Franklin Foer offers an explanation for the increased popularity of soccer among young white Americans. He argues that, despite soccer's existence as a minor professional sport in the United States, it appeals to white middle class and professional parents as the preferred sport for their children for several reasons linked to their rejection of the big three major American sports: (1) baseball is rejected because it too stressful and ego deflating; (2) football is rejected because it is too violent; and (3) basketball is rejected because it is too tainted by its ghetto associations. This argument derives from speculations unsupported by empirical data. Nevertheless, American soccer definitely is attracting an increasing fan base. Another significant source of that increase derived from the increasing population of immigrants in the U.S. from soccer-first nations in Europe, Latin America, and Africa. They form part of soccer's globalizing fan base.

GLOBALIZATION OF AMERICAN SPORT

While soccer definitely leads the sport world's globalization, the three major American professional sports have each embarked on global expansion over the past 25 years with mixed results.

PROFESSIONAL BASEBALL

Founded as the National Association of Professional Baseball in 1871, baseball became the first professional sports league. From the 1890s to 1947, it operated as a racially exclusive white professional sport. During its early history, though many white major leaguers played in the winter leagues in the Caribbean and Central America, no recruitment of locals from those regions occurred until after the Brooklyn Dodgers broke the color barrier by signing Jackie Robinson as the first black American to play in the major leagues. The Dominican Republic had a long history of playing baseball, which extended back to 1890 when its first local baseball league was founded. But it took nine years after Robinson's breakthrough for major league baseball to sign its first Dominican player. Oscar Virgil became the first player from the Dominican Republic to play major league baseball.

Once major league baseball ceased to exist as a racially exclusive white sport, teams began to scout and recruit players from the Caribbean and Central America. Modern day major league baseball has not only become a racially and geographically inclusive sport; some of its most celebrated superstars come from countries south of the U.S. border. The percentage of foreign-born players has increased significantly over the past half-century as is indicated by the table on p. 529.

Oscar Virgil's signing marked the beginning of a strong relationship between MLB and the Dominican Republic. Since then, approximately 450 Dominican players have played in the major leagues. The Dominican Republic now has the largest percentage of major league players, second only to native-born Americans (Sage, 2010, p. 82).

Year	*Percentage of Foreign-Born Players in Major League Baseball*
1958	4
1960	7
1978	9
1988	12
2010	28

Source: mlb.com/2010.

On opening day of the 2014 season, MLB had 223 foreign-born players (26.1%) of its 853 players. They came from 16 countries and territories. The Dominican Republic led the group with 82 MLB players, followed by Venezuela (59) and Cuba (19). Among the most diverse teams, the Texas Rangers leads with 15 players from nine countries. Perhaps the most striking indication of the future direction of this trend toward diversification is revealed by the percentage of foreign-born players in the baseball's minor leagues in 2009: 48 percent (Sage, 2010, p. 82; MLB.COM). These numbers indicate that MLB is increasingly globalized—at least in its player recruitment. But is this enough?

Alan Klein in his recent book, *Growing the Game* (2007), says no. He argues that global expansion no longer exists as an option for major league baseball. Due to its dwindling domestic base of fans and players, Klein maintains, baseball must expand globally to remain financially viable. As indicated by recent data on the popularity of American sports, baseball no longer occupies the position of America's number one sport. It was supplanted by professional football over a decade ago. Moreover, Klein observes, it is losing fans.

The baseball commissioner's office apparently understands this. MLB has created an international division in its headquarters which aims to grow baseball's global audience. MLB's international division has classified the world into three tiers (Klein, 2012a, pp. 332–333).

- **Tier 1:** denotes those countries with strong baseball cultures. Examples: Japan, Dominican Republic, Venezuela, Mexico.
- **Tier 2:** denotes countries with moderate baseball cultures; game exists at semi-pro and amateur levels. Exanples: Italy, Australia, the Netherlands. Klein notes that baseball culture is expanding in Australia, which looks like a good prospect for Tier 1 development.
- **Tier 3:** denotes long shots because they have weak baseball cultures. Examples: Germany, England, and South Africa. These countries require much work to create strong baseball cultures.

Interestingly, Klein notes that MLB's international office has targeted South Africa and has begun to create programs in the public schools to attract students to baseball (p. 337). The international division sees this as a long-term project with a large potential payoff. South Africa is attractive because its national government expressed enthusiasm about the project. Unlike the established sports in South Africa, which began under the racial system of apartheid, baseball, the government believes, gives it an opportunity to develop a national sport that is untarnished by the history of racial division. This constitutes an unusual venture in sport globalization.

Looking at the global initiatives of specific major league franchises, Klein singled out two as especially noteworthy: the Los Angeles Dodgers organization, which represents the globalization frontrunner among the big-market teams; and the Kansas City Royals, which occupies a similar front-runner position among small-market teams. Klein believes the L.A. Dodgers is continuing the pioneering legacy of Walter O'Malley, who owned the racially progressive late 1940s Brooklyn Dodgers. Now run by Walter O'Malley's son Peter, the Dodgers have built especially strong ties in Japan and the Caribbean. The Kansas City Royals, in contrast, having more limited resources, has focused its initiative on undeveloped baseball regions such as Europe and South Africa, where they are helping to develop the game and seeking new prospects. This effort looks likely to yield some benefits: Seven South Africans have signed MLB contracts; three are still playing in the minors; two with Royals.

Baseball's global footprints are wide and varied, as indicated in the following table:

South Korea	manufacturing baseball caps
Costa Rica	manufacturing major league baseballs
South Africa	public schools program
Japan	broadcast corporation recently signed $275 million contract to televise MLB games
Japan	a Japanese team is currently playing in a California minor league
Dominican Republic	proliferation of baseball academies

Source: Klein, pp. 333–336. Note: this table does not appear in the article. It was constructed from the text for this essay.

OTHER BASEBALL GLOBALIZATION ACTIVITIES

Baseball globalization goes beyond major league baseball. The three most important examples of baseball's extensive and expanding global reach are Japanese baseball, the World Baseball Classic, and Little League Baseball.

Japanese Baseball

Baseball has a long history in Japan dating back to the late nineteenth century, and thrives today as Japan's most popular sport. Having established its first professional league in 1936, it now has two professional leagues, which play the game at a high level. Though not as diverse as MLB, the Japanese leagues do recruit foreign-born players. For example, in 2008, 62 foreign players—including some from the United States—played in the Japanese leagues. As noted earlier, Japanese baseball not only remained autonomous relative to MLB, it restricts the freedom of Japanese players to play in the United States (Klein, 2007). Japanese players must play 10 years in Japan before they are eligible to sign a MLB contract. MLB teams must engage in an expensive process of bidding in order to qualify to negotiate a contract with the player, yet another expensive process. Due to these complex restrictions, relatively few Japanese players have played in MLB. However, that appears to be changing. The number of Japanese players in MLB has gone from 1 in 1964 and 6 in 1990 to 18 in 2009 (Sage, 2010, p. 84; source Japanese BallPlayers.com).

The World Baseball Classic

Is baseball likely to develop into a global sport with a single world championship series like soccer? This is unlikely in the near future, but the organizational platform for that potential development already exists. As one sports journalist noted:

> The growth of the international game has been stunning. Anyone who hadn't caught on to this notion got more than an eyeful at the inaugural World Baseball Classic, in 2006. By the time this event reached the equivalent of the Final Four, what we like to think of as baseball's home team, the one representing the United States of America, was nowhere to be found. But Cuba, the Dominican Republic, Korea, and Japan were still in the competition.

He went on to make a projection about the implications of this series.

> Japan emerged the eventual champion, but the overall winner was probably the cause of baseball globalization. The quality of the baseball was undeniably good, and it was undeniably good before a truly international audience.
>
> (Bauman, 2008, p. 1)

This event is the World Baseball Classic (WBC). It is sponsored by the International Baseball Federation (IBAF). Both deliberately reflect soccer's global sport model, which they aim to replicate in baseball. These baseball developments followed the International Olympic Committee's decision to drop baseball as an Olympic sport. WBC series take place every four years and it has had a noticeable impact. One American commentator observed:

> Baseball can no longer be contained within the borders of America's 50 states. In March, 16 nations will compete in cities around the globe to prove their nation's skills in an ever-growing sport. In the first round of competition, teams played in Mexico; San Juan, P.R.; Tokyo; and Toronto.
>
> (McMaster, 2009, p. 1) bleacherreport.com/article/the-globalizationofbaseball, 18 May, 2009

The WBC world series has continued to flourish. The last one, which occurred in 2013, was won by the Dominican Republic. The next one will take place in 2017.

The national teams of the IBAF members feature professional players from the major leagues and around the world—representing their home countries. Though the WBC has attracted little attention in the United States, it achieves very high media ratings in other countries such as Taiwan and Japan. No doubt a major reason it attracts little attention in the U.S. is because few MLB stars participate. Given MLB's commissioner's interest in growing the global baseball audience, encouraging its star players to compete in the WBC would no doubt increase the series popularity in the United States and attract more international fan interest in MLB.

Little League Baseball: The Ignored Global Sport

Little League typically is overlooked in discussions of globalization because it operates as an amateur sport which is perceived as a local community institution with little potential for attracting a mass audience. Other factors that make Little League baseball different include the age of the athletes, the absence of labor migration, and the absence of athletes with celebrity status. Nevertheless, Little League baseball matters because it has operated as an important international force helping to grow baseball's global culture by exposing peoples around the world to baseball.

Founded in1939, in Williamsport, Pennsylvania, with three teams, Little League baseball has demonstrated a remarkable capacity for growth (SportingNews.Com, pp. 1–6). After expanding to 12 leagues in Pennsylvania during the early 1940s, it established its first team outside Pennsylvania in New Jersey in 1947. By 1950, 300 Little Leagues were operating in the United States. The year 1951 marked a major milestone when it established its first league outside the United States, in British Columbia, Canada, making Little League a North American sport.

Just 18 years after its founding, a non-U.S team—Monterrey, Mexico—won the Little League World Series. This achievement by a Latin American team affirmed the Little League Baseball as a truly international sport. In 1960, the first European Little League was founded in Berlin, Germany; by then the sport had grown to over 5000 Little Leagues. Only a few years later, in 1967, the first Far Eastern Asian team won the world series.

Further expanding baseball culture internationally, during the year of its 50th anniversary, in 1989, Little League baseball established a league in Poland, the first league in a former Eastern Bloc country.

Equally noteworthy, Little Leagues forged new areas of inclusion with the establishment of Little League softball programs for girls in 1974. Sixteen years later, in 1990, the Little League challenger division was established for mentally and physically disabled children.

By the end of the twentieth century, approximately 60 years after it was founded, Little League baseball spread to a record number of 100 countries—when the African nation of Burkino Faso established a Little League. While it is difficult to determine the actual impact of Little League baseball, it no doubt has contributed significantly to the global growth of baseball culture, a development that will yield benefits for MLB's future globalization.

PROFESSIONAL BASKETBALL

The NBA has advanced farther than Major League Baseball in globalization, in part because basketball has a stronger presence throughout the world. Basketball has the distinction of being second to soccer as a global sport. In Latin America, in Europe, in Africa, and in Asia, basketball leagues have become part of the sport landscape. In Europe, in particular, where there are professional national teams in countries such as Germany, Spain, Greece, and Turkey, the quality of both the players and the competition have reached high levels.

The NBA's history, like that of other major American sports, evidenced a gradual shift from racial insularity to increasing diversity and inclusion. Its first significant change occurred in the early 1950s when the first African-American players were admitted into the league. During its early history up to the early 1990s, the NBA, like American professional baseball and football, showed little interest in recruiting players from foreign countries. This era featured such great NBA superstars as Bob Cousy, Bill Russell, Wilt Chamberlain, Oscar Robertson, Jerry West, Elgin Baylor, and Bob Petit—when hardly any coaches or executives in the NBA thought foreign players could compete at the NBA level.

But that changed in 1992, when the U.S. team in the Olympics, in Barcelona, Spain, was represented by a group of NBA superstars that became known as the Dream Team. Many sports media commentators believed the team comprised perhaps the greatest assembly of American basketball players in history (Hancock, 2013; Forbes.com). Featuring such iconic basketball talents as Michael Jordan, Larry Bird, Magic Johnson, Chris Mullin, and Karl Malone, the Dream Team dominated the Olympics tournament as they defeated their opponents by an average of 44 points. Not surprisingly, they won the Olympic gold medal. But what turned out be actually surprising was that they encountered some foreign players who displayed exceptional talents.

NBA Commissioner David Stern changed his attitude about the NBA's future direction after the Dream Team Olympics. He recognized the enormous global potential of NBA basketball. In fact, his aim was to transform the National Basketball Association into The International Basketball Association, beginning with the location of several NBA franchises in Europe. Though Stern did not achieve his dream before he retired in 2014, the NBA has definitely established a large global footprint. In the words of one sports news reporter:

> Basketball sits alongside soccer and, to an extent, cricket as a truly global sport. Football reigns but children in Italy recognize Kobe Bryant almost as readily as they recognize Lionel Messi. Turkey has become a regular holding space for players outside the foyer of the NBA. Chinese fans built a statue to honor Stephon Marbury.
>
> (Watanabe, nesn.com)

But beyond the increased international visibility of star NBA players, during the 20-year period following the Dream Team's Olympic appearance, the league has embarked on serious recruitment of foreign players. This included such exceptional talents as Tony Kukuch (Croatia), Dirk Nowitzki (Germany), Akeem Olajawon (Nigeria), Tim Duncan (Virgin Islands), Manny Genoble (Argentina), Tony Parker (France), and Yao Ming (China).

The NBA had a record number of 92 foreign players from 39 countries during the 2013–14 season, an increase from 85 foreign players from 36 countries during the 2012–13 season. Significantly, the winner of the 2013–14 NBA champion title is also the team with the most foreign players. The next NBA teams with the highest number of foreign players are the following: Cleveland Cavaliers (6); Minnesota Timberwolves (6); Milwaukee Bucks (5). These were followed by seven teams with four and three teams with three foreign players (NBA.com).

The foreign countries most represented among NBA players are: France (9), Russia (4), Argentina (4), Canada (8), Brazil (4), Israel (2), Australia (5), Italy (4), Spain (5), and Turkey (4) (nba.com 2013).

This increased presence of foreign players, note some observers, will certainly increase, a development that will yield major dividends because the presence of these players will expand the NBA's global fan base, particularly in the players' home countries. This was illustrated by the impact of Yao Ming—the Houston Rocket's center—in China, where his presence in the NBA "attracted tens of millions of viewers and sponsors" (Longman, 2013, p. 2). By expanding the league's global fan base, the foreign players create opportunities for the NBA to increase revenues from broadcasting, advertising, and selling consumer products in new markets.

While David Stern had dreamed of locating NBA teams in Europe, the key global strategy the NBA developed under his leadership prioritized expanding the media audience for NBA games.

> Despite the old adage, it's not location, location. Geography is not the most important factor any more. Interest in European soccer is soaring and the lack of a premier league in the US hasn't hindered the popularity of the English Premier League in the states. LeBron James and Kevin Durant are the most popular players in the NBA despite the fact that the vast majority of fans have never seen and will never see either play live. Believing fans need to be in the same building as a team in order to watch it play is a quaint anachronism from a by-gone age. . . .
>
> After the Dream team revealed the international potential decades ago, Stern realized the key to expanding the NBA—or any league—globally was not to put teams in foreign cities, but to put them in foreign living rooms.
>
> (Watanabe, p. 1)

Put simply, contemporary global sport is a creature of global media, not stadiums.

AMERICAN FOOTBALL

The National Football League faces the most formidable obstacles in its attempts to expand American football culture globally. Commissioner Roger Godell aims to accelerate the NFL's globalization. In pursuit of this goal, the NFL has embarked on several international ventures. It attempted to establish an American football league in Europe, which was used primarily as minor leagues for the NFL. It began in 1991 with the name World League of American Football and was reorganized in 1998 and re-named the European Football League. (www.world league of American football.com). This new incarnation, which had five teams in Germany and one in Amsterdam, was terminated in 2007 because it failed to attract sufficient fan support. The decision to locate the restructured league largely in Germany may have been influenced by the presence of U.S. military bases there. Over the past few years the NFL has shifted its focus to London, where it has played several pre-season games a year. Roger Godell now aims to establish an NFL franchise in London and to try to grow a fan base there with the hope that interest in the game will expand to continental Europe. He feels London holds the key to the league's expansion beyond its U.S. fan base (Jordan, bleacher report.com, p. 1). An NFL fan club already exist in London.

According to one sports journalist, Mexico has considerable untapped potential NFL support. In Mexico City, in 1994, the Dallas Cowboys played the Houston Oilers in a preseason game that attracted over 112,000 fans. Apparently this was no fluke, because over 103,000 fans attended a later regular season game in Mexico City (Jordan, bleacher report.com, p. 1). It remains unclear what portion of those fans had traveled from the U.S. But Mexico may be more lucrative because many Mexicans watch NFL games on television.

Nevertheless, most commentators agree the NFL confronts a difficult future in its efforts to expand its global audience. In the words of one informed NFL observer:

> Every other league in the United States has taken way bigger steps to not only become a better league in the world but also to have stars from other countries now able to play in their respective sports.
>
> (Jordan, bleacher report.com)

> Meanwhile the NFl has an overwhelming majority of American born players, and it cannot get players from overseas due to a lack of exposure that gets outside North America.
>
> (Jordan, bleacher report.com, p. 1, bleacherreport.com/articles/355662/globalization, "Globalization: The NFL's Future Depends On It: 3 March, 2010)

In short, the NFL faces not one but a set of obstacles in its attempts to globalize. American football does not travel well because it is harder to understand outside the United States and Canada; it lacks a global culture (Emmons, p. 3). This explains its dearth of foreign players. Where would boys in Japan, Hungary, and Turkey learn to play American football? Football globalization is unlikely to succeed until it grows a global culture. It needs to follow the model of MLB activity in South Africa. But this is unlikely to succeed in a country like South Africa which already has an established football-related sport in rugby. The road the NFL will have to travel will be difficult because it will have to travel it alone. Both basketball and baseball sport cultures grew without direct support from the NBA and MLB. The NFL does not have that luxury.

GLOBAL PLAYER MIGRATION

We conclude this essay with an assessment of the phenomenon of athletes migrating from one country to another, a quintessential manifestation of globalization in sport. Indeed, player migration operates as a major driving force behind sport globalization. Informed sports observers generally agree that sport labor migration has four positive effects on sport:

> 1. it improves the skills of athletes playing the sport;
> 2. it increases the global popularity of the sport;
> 3. it expands media coverage; and
> 4. it broadens the fan base.
>
> (Sage, 2010, p. 94)

We typically think of sport migration as a simple process—an athlete signs a contract, travels to a city in a foreign country, settles in, and commences playing for a new team. Most of the studies on player migration have focused on soccer, the most prevalent area of sport migration. They suggest that the migration process tends to be more complex and problematic than is generally assumed.

MIGRATION TRANSFER NETWORKS

As Raffaele Poli demonstrates in his article on soccer player migration to and within Europe, these player migrations typically involve "transfer networks" which consists of human intermediaries—agents—who navigate the migrant players through a series of "soccer geographical spaces with the objective of reaching the highest level of soccer, their desired destination" (Poli, 2010). The first space, which Poli terms "platform space," denotes the first country the migrant reaches. After negotiations of the intermediary agents, the player moves to a stepping stone space which, as the name implies, is regarded only as a temporary stop where the players land to get access to another country with a higher level of soccer and a more financially rewarding championship. If the player successfully traverses several other intervening geographical spaces by demonstrating his superior soccer skills, he reaches the destination space with the wealthiest leagues and championships in the world—which is England (p. 502).

Poli undertook this analysis to show the difficult and unpredictable migration channels through which players travel guided by human transfer networks, with the objective of reaching the high-level soccer leagues in Europe. He argues that these migration chains constitute "the social relations of circulation" which differ from the more familiar Marxist "social relations of production" (p. 503). In the case of soccer, where the relations of production are fragmented, these transfer networks compensate for that fragmentation by providing an alternative mechanism for organizing and channeling soccer labor through human intermediaries. These intermediaries exercise power by controlling the movements of soccer players through migration channels, increasing the value of their human capital as the players move up to more lucrative soccer spaces.

MOTIVATIONS FOR MIGRATION

Poli's study implies that soccer migration is economically motivated. Looking at soccer and other sport migration, analysts have identified multiple factors influencing the motivations of athletes who migrate. Economic rewards are certainly among the major factors. Also important, some analysts point to the opportunity structure within the athlete's home country (Sage, 2010, pp. 90–91). How do opportunities for a professional career in the home country compare to those in foreign countries? Is there an oversupply of talented athletes playing the sport in the home country? Examples of this factor are widespread: Many talented American college football players who fail to get contract offers from NFL teams migrate to Canada to play Canadian professional football; a large number of American college basketball players migrate to Europe, Turkey, and Israel to pursue professional basketball careers; American baseball players, including some former major leaguers, migrate to Japan to play in a professional Japanese baseball league. The importance of differential opportunity structures for professional sport careers will grow stronger as the number and variety of professional sport leagues increase throughout the world.

Closely linked to opportunities, the economic and political conditions in the athletes' home country also operate as important factors influencing migration, particularly among athletes in undeveloped societies. Many athletes in poor countries migrate to developed or politically stable societies to attend college, to access better training facilities, to live in safer and more democratic societies. The United States, for example, has attracted many athletes because of the excellent sport programs and training facilities in U.S. colleges and universities. Some of these athletes after graduating from college decide to become American citizens and represent the United States in the Olympics and other international sport competitions. We will return to this issue of athletes migrating from undeveloped societies later when we discuss some of the controversies and debates surrounding sport labor migration.

Migration decisions are often influenced by other issues of contextual characteristics of the foreign country (Maguire and Stead, 1998, pp. 71–72). Is there a colonial link to target country? Colonial links can exert significant influence because the athlete may speak the language and understand the culture of the target country, making the transition easier.

Geographic proximity to the target country may make it easier for similar reasons. The ease of labor mobility in the target country is cited by some analysts because it gives the athlete the freedom to shift to different team if a better opportunity arises. One of the most important contextual factors, the target country's reputation for tolerance of outsiders and openness to diversity is likely to have a major influence on athletes' migration decisions—particularly in light of the racist and nativist reactions to foreign players in some European countries.

The role of the media can also figure importantly in sport labor migration. The opportunity to showcase one's talents via the global media can be a strong incentive for wanting to play in a high-profile sport league.

CONTROVERSIES IN SPORT LABOR MIGRATION

Despite the many ostensible benefits of sport labor migration, it also has generated criticisms and controversies. One criticism highlights the problems experienced by young sport migrants such as the promising youth soccer players recruited by English soccer clubs. These recruits are often too young to cope with the difficulties of adapting to foreign cultures without family support. Reports also indicate their problems of loneliness, inadequate language skills, and educational deficiencies (Weedon, 2012).

A more contentious debate focuses on the issue of exploitation. Seen from the standpoint of the undeveloped countries who lose their star athletes through migration, some argue that this pattern of sport migration produces a "brawn drain"; by taking these valuable athletic resources from poor countries, it undermines and weakens their home sport culture. In effect, echoing the argument of dependency theory, these critics view sport migration as serving the interests of the "haves" at the expense of "have nots" (Sage, 2010, pp. 93–94).

The Cuban government's policy restricting migration of its athletes can be seen as a response to the "brawn drain." However, that policy has failed to stop the migration of Cuban athletes, mostly baseball players, to more lucrative sport opportunities in the United States. Given that international sport labor flows are an irreversible reality of expanding globalization, Cuba's restrictive policies seem doomed to failure (see Chapter 37).

Nevertheless, there remain genuine problems of inequality and fairness in sport relations between wealthy and poor nations. These problems deserve further study and critical debate about how best to expand the normative ideal of fairness beyond the game on the field to the game outside the game—that is, the struggle to create a more equitable distribution of competitive resources not only within sport but also nations.

REFERENCES

Appadurai, Arjun. 1990. *Globalization, Knowledge, and Societies.* London: Sage.

Bauman, Mike. 2008. "Baseball Knows No Global Borders." March 19. m.mlb.com/news/article/2442391

Connell, R.W. 2007. "The Northern Theory of Globalization." *Social Theory* 25(4): 368–385.

Emmons, Gary. www.hbs.edu/stories:supersizing the nfl

Foer, Franklin. 2004. *How Soccer Will Explain the World.* New York, NY: Harper Collins.

Forbes.com. www.Forbes.com.sites/sap/2013/06/17/the-globalization-of-the-nba.

Giulianotti, Richard and Roland Robertson. 2009. *Globalization and Football.* Thousand Oaks, CA: Sage Publications

——2012. "Mapping the Global Football Field: A Sociological Model of Transnational Forces in the World Game." *British Journal of Sociology*, 63(2), pp. 33–58.

Hancock, Benjamin. "The Globalization of the NBA." http://www.forbes.com/sites/sap/2013/06/17/the–globalization–of–the–nba

Lapchick, Richard. 1986. "A Political History of the Modern Olympic Games." Pp. 329–345 in *Fractured Focus*, edited by Richard Lapchick. Lexington, MA: D.C. Heath & Co.

Kaplan, Daniel. "The Soccer Theory of Globablization." aidwatchers.com/2007/the-soccer-theory-of-globalization.

Klein, Alan. 1989. "Baseball Underdevelopment: The Political Economy of Sport in the Dominican Republic." *Sport in Society* 10(6): 896–915.

—— 1991. *Sugarball: The American Dream, The Dominican Dream.* New Haven, CT: Yale University Press.

——2007. "Growing the Game: The Globalization of Major League Baseball." *American Studies*, 48(3), pp. 175–176.

—— 2008. *Growing the Game: The Globalization of Major League Baseball.* Binghamton, NY: Vail–Ballou Press.

—— 2012a "Growing The Game – The Globalization of Major League Baseball." Pp. 1–9 in *Sport in Contemporary Society* edited by D. Stanlely Eitzen, 9th ed. Boulder, CO: Pardigm Publishers.

—— 2012b. "Chain Reaction: Neo-Liberal

Kobryashi, Koji. 2012. "Country Nationalism and Glocalization of Nike Advertising in Asia: Production and Represetation Practices of Global Intermediaries." *International Review for Sociology of Sport* 47(1): 27–42.

Longman, Jere. 2013. "Globalization Sweeps Away Misgivings About Foreign Team Mates." *NYTimes.* 14 October. nytimes.com

Markovits, Andrei. 2010. "The Global and Local in Our Contemporary Sports Cultures." *Society* 47(6): 503–509

Markovits, Andrei and Steven Hellerman. 2001. *Offside: Soccer and American Exceptionalism.* Princeton, NJ: Princeton University Press.

Markovits, Andrei and Lars Rensmann. 2010. *Gaming the World.* 2010. Princeton, NJ: Princeton University Press.

McMaster. 2009. May, bleacher report.com/article/the globalization of baseball

Maguire, Joseph and David Stead. 1998. "Border Crossings: Soccer Labor Migration and the European Union." *International Review for the Sociology of Sport* 33(1): 54–73.

Milonvic, Banko. 2000. *Yale Global Online.* 15 June, "The World at Play: Soccer Takes On Globalization." yaleglobal. Yale.edu/content/world-at-play-soccer-takes-on-globalization

NBA.Com. 2013. nba.com/global/nba-off-201314_season-with-record-international-presence-2013–10–24-hmtl.

Olympics. Org. 2012. "International Olympic Marketing File." www.olympic.org/document/ioc marketing/olympic-marketing-fact-file-2012

Poli, Raffaele. 2007. "The DeNationalization of Sport: De-Ethnicization of the Nation and Identity Deterrorialization" *Sport in Society* 10(4): 646–661.

——2010. "Understanding Globalization Through Football: The New International Division of Labour, Migratory Channels, and Transnational Trade Circuits" *International Review for the Sociology of Sport* 45(4): 491–506.

Ritzer, George. 2003. "Rethinking Globalization: Glocalization/Grobalization and Something/Nothing." *Sociological Theory*, 21(3), pp. 1932–209.

——2011. "Appadurai's Landscapes." Social Theory. New York: McGraw Hill pp. 589–590. Based on Appadurai, Arjun, *Modernity at Large: Cultural Dimensions of Globalization.* Minneapolis: U. of Minnesota Press.

Sage, George. 2010. *Globalizing Sport,* Boulder,CO: Paradigm Publishers.

Shepard, Alicia. 1999. *American Journalism Review,* "An Olympic Scandal." ajrarchive.org/article.asp

SportingNews.com. "History of Little League" www.sportingnews.com/archives/littleleague/year.html

Watanabe. nesn.com/2014/01/david-stern

Weedon, Gavin. 2012. "'Glocal boys' Exploring experiences of acculturation amongst migrant youth footballers in Premier League academies" April 2012. *International Review for the Sociology of Sport* 47(2), pp. 200–216 www.irs.sagepub.com/content/47/2/200

World League of American Football www.world league of american football.com

CHAPTER 33

Theorizing Sport in the Global Process

Joseph Maguire

Let us export our oarsmen, our fencers, our runners into other lands. That is the true free trade of the future; and the day it is introduced into Europe the cause of Peace will have received a new and strong ally.

Pierre de Coubertin, paper presented at the Union des Sports Athlétiques, Sorbonne, 25 November 1892

That the representatives of cultures communicate, compete, emulate and/or distinguish themselves from others across a range of global networks has seemingly become so much part of the lives of late twentieth-century Westerners that it is viewed as 'second nature' and treated in an unproblematic way. Clearly, the export of the Olympics, that de Coubertin called for, has proved to be so successful that people do not question its history, though George Orwell's comments about international sport being, 'war minus the shooting', should make people more circumspect about whether the Olympics add to global peace and harmony.

Several issues arise when examining cross-cultural processes. Though there was a range of contacts between peoples in the so-called 'ancient worlds', the games at Olympia being one example, the frequency, form and depth of interaction has, over time, intensified. Though people have become more aware of making comparisons between 'others', they show little sensitivity to how this process has emerged out of the past and is structured in the present. A high degree of hodiecentric or 'today-centred' thinking is evident (Goudsblom, 1977: p. 7), In addition, when people make comparisons, they do so on the basis of a taken-for-granted international rank order of worth and a valorization of identities, values, customs and cultural forms. The meaning, experience and consumption of global sport are no exception to this general process. How then are we to make sense of this global cultural interchange? Here, I will examine the broad debate concerning globalization processes and then consider how the study of global sport reflects the general issues and questions that characterize this debate. In doing so, a broad review of the existing pool of social scientific knowledge regarding the global sport process will be provided.

MAKING SENSE OF THE GLOBALIZATION DEBATE

Use of the term *globalization* has become widespread in academic and media discourse over the past two decades. The meaning and usage of the term has been, however, marked by confusion, misinterpretation and contentious debate. Perhaps because the term diffused so rapidly into 'everyday' use, commentators, politicians and academics have taken fairly rigid positions over its precise meaning. In addition, the term appears to provoke a degree of moral judgement, as if its use, in itself, implies support for or criticism of the existing world order. The following remarks offered by Tony Mason, a historian, are symptomatic of this kind of thinking when applied to the study of sport. Comparing Brazilian and European soccer, Mason observes:

> In 1994 it could be argued that this footballing dichotomy of styles no longer exists. All teams now play in a similar fashion with teamwork and organization paramount . . . Caution is the watchword; the game is not to lose. Perhaps this is an aspect of that globalization or homogenization of the sporting world about which sociologists excitedly chatter . . . But if the homogenization theory is true something which made football vital and attractive will have been lost.
>
> (Mason, 1995: pp. 156–7)

In these observations, globalization is unequivocally equated with homogenization and is seen as a 'threat' to some idealized notion of what football was or is. Yet, the local meanings and patterning of sport in general and of football in particular, were influenced by global diffusion processes in quite complex ways. The contrasts between playing styles may have diminished but new varieties of playing formations have emerged. Equally, the perspective offered by sociologists on globalization is, ironically, not as homogeneous as Mason's observations suggest.

Indeed, several traditions have sought to compare and contrast the development of different societies. These traditions include: the modernization perspective, theories of imperialism, dependency theory, world-system theory, hegemony theory and 'globalization' research. Each finds expression in the current debate surrounding globalization. I do not intend simply to review the degree to which these traditions – or specific pieces of work within them – have variously advanced our collective fund of relatively adequate social scientific knowledge. Rather, I want to identify several key issues and themes that characterize the debates, within and between these traditions, regarding globalization. In turn, when consideration is given to the emergence and diffusion of sport cultures, a number of these issues and themes are also evident.

Several key features associated with the term globalization can be detected in the literature. Reference is repeatedly made to the idea that globalization involves some form of greater interdependence between the local and the global.[1] A series of local–global nexuses can be identified. These include: local responses to economic practices; local resistance to ideological processes; local revivals of traditional customs; local celebrations of diversity and local initiatives to combat global pollution. It is clear that every aspect of social reality, our activities, conditions of living, belief systems, knowledge base and responses, is affected by interconnections with other groups, both 'near' and 'far' away. For Anthony Giddens, globalization entails 'the intensification of world-wide social relations which link distinct localities in such a way that local happenings are shaped by events occurring miles and miles away and vice versa' (Giddens, 1990: p. 64).

These interconnections are seen to have deepened and also to have stretched across the globe. The world becomes 'compressed' as the scope and intensity of global interconnectedness has increased. Central in this regard have been the emergence of a world economy, an international nation-state system, a global diffusion of technology and division of labour, and a system of military alliances and treaties (Giddens, 1990: pp. 63–77). Hand in hand with these interconnections, the scale, velocity and volume of globalization processes gathered momentum.

This much is clear. Understood in this light, we can see that a series of interconnections also characterize global sport. Consider the example of basketball. Citizens of countries spread across the globe regularly tune in by satellite broadcasts to National Basketball Association (NBA) games. In these games perform the best male players drawn from North America and Europe. The players use equipment – balls, shoes, uniform, etc. – that is designed in a range of European and North American locations, financed in the USA and assembled in the Pacific Rim. This equipment is then sold on to a mass market across the globe. This equipment, basketball boots for example, is made out of raw materials from 'developing countries', the molecular structure of which was researched and patented, in the case of Nike, in Washington State (USA) and fabricated in Taiwan. Several other transnational corporations are also involved in the production and consumption phases of this global cultural product. The product is itself provided by a global media sport production complex and is viewed on a television that was itself manufactured as part of a global telecommunications network. The beguiling appeal of the slogan 'Just Do It', and of the transnational cultural icon Michael Jordan, hides the stark reality of the global sports industry complex.

Several writers have sought to discern a pattern, or structure, to these interconnections. Appadurai (1990), for example, refers to a series of diverse, fluid and unpredictable global flows. These 'scapes' include the movement of capital, technologies, people and mediated images. As a consequence of the diverse and unpredictable nature of these movements, a series of 'disjunctures' marks these 'scapes'. Hannerz (1990) also views globalization in terms of 'cultural flows'. These flows include: cultural commodities, the actions of the state in organizing and managing meanings, the dissemination of habitual perspectives and dispositions and the activities of social movements. Though he emphasizes diversity as opposed to uniformity, Hannerz observes that, 'the world has become one network of social relationships, and between its different regions there is a flow of meanings as well as of people and goods' (Hannerz, 1990: p. 237).

The idea that the world 'has become one network' has been taken up by several writers (Giddens, 1990; Robertson, 1992; Wallerstein, 1974). In this connection it is useful to highlight Robertson's notion of a global field. In mapping what he terms the 'global human condition', Robertson stresses four aspects of the global field. These are: nations/societies; individuals or selves; relations between nations/societies; and humankind as a whole. The pattern of this global field stems from the interweaving of these aspects (Robertson, 1992). People have become aware of the global condition, and of the 'finitude and boundedness of the planet and humanity' (Featherstone, 1991a). For Featherstone and Lash, an understanding of this 'global human condition' requires new types of thinking, and for them, 'the global *problematique* represents the *spatialization* of social theory' (1995: p. 1). In this endeavour, sociologists have been joined by geographers who examine the geography of global change, focusing on place, space, 'power geometry' and identity politics; the local/global scales of economic processes and the interconnections between human activities and ecological sustainability (Dickens, 1992; Harvey, 1989; Johnson et al., 1995; Massey, 1994; Yearley, 1996). Some of these concerns have also surfaced in the geography of sport (Bale, 1994).

If these are some of the broad themes and issues where a degree of consensus is evident, when it comes to understanding the periodization of globalization, the main dynamics involved, and the impact that such processes have, then what emerges is a sharp division of opinion and position. Let me try to illustrate some of the tensions and major fault lines that characterize these debates. A series of binary oppositions can be detected. Are globalization processes unidimensional or multidimensional? Are monocausal or multicausal factors the main dynamic of global processes? Do globalization processes lead to a form of 'unity', or perception of 'unity' or of fragmentation? Are globalization processes the intended or the unintended result of intended social actions? Do globalization processes lead to homogenization or heterogenization? At this stage, it is appropriate to examine the claims of the various contributors to these debates.

MAKING SENSE OF CROSS-CULTURAL PROCESSES: COMPETING TRADITIONS

Several traditions of sociological thought have, as noted, sought to examine trans-societal development. The modernization approach, closely linked to functionalism, was the dominant paradigm in this research area until the early 1970s. Essentially concerned with how traditional societies reach modernity, this approach has focused on the political, cultural, economic and social aspects of this process. Consideration is given to the development of political institutions that support participatory decision-making. The growth and development of secular and nationalist ideologies is also examined. The emergence of a division of labour, the use of management techniques, technological innovations and commercial activities have been the subject of attention. These changes are seen to be accompanied by urbanization and the decline of traditional authorities. The modernization approach also tends to assert that the 'effects' of these trends leads to homogenization. Societies in different parts of the globe 'eventually' follow the Western model of development.[2]

Some or all of these themes have surfaced in 'comparative' studies of sport where a 'critical' approach has failed to take hold (Baker, 1982; Jokl & Simon, 1964; Pooley, 1981; Seppanen, 1970). This, of course, relates to a major criticism that other traditions have of the modernization approach: issues of conflict, exploitation and under-development are ignored (Hettne, 1990). Cultural imperialist analyses have proved more popular in accounts provided by sport historians and sociologists of sport (Klein, 1989; Mangan, 1986). Ironically, though cultural imperialist accounts stress issues of conflict and exploitation, they share an important feature in common with the modernization approach, that is, an emphasis on the alleged homogenizing impact of these processes. Equally, these approaches tend to stress the unidirectional character of these global developments – from the West to the 'rest' – and deploy a monocausal explanation, technological or economic, to explain these changes.

In cultural imperialism accounts, terms such as 'Westernization' or 'Americanization' are used to capture the homogenizing tendencies said to be involved in cross-cultural processes. Cultural flows are identified with the activities of representatives of nation-states and/or multinational corporations. These activities entail a form of domination of one culture over another. Issues of power, control and the ability of 'indigenous' people to interpret, understand and/or resist cultural manipulation and domination arise in evaluating these types of studies. The idea of the 'invasion' of an indigenous culture by a foreign one is the usual way of understanding the processes involved (Tomlinson, 1991).

Two main emphases in cultural imperialism accounts of global cultural flows can be identified. In one, the focus is placed on a 'world' made up of a collection of nation-states in competition with each other. One manifestation of this is 'Yankee imperialism'. The 'hearts and minds' of foreign people are said to be at stake. Another approach views the 'world' as an integrated political-economic system of global capitalism. Here the focus is on the activities of multi- or transnational corporations. Whether attention focuses on the imperatives of multinational capitalism, or on the spread of a specific nation's 'value-system', an alleged homogenizing trend is identified. While the scale and pace of the process are disputed, the general drift towards the convergence of cultures is accepted.

Studies within this Marxist tradition explain the colonialism of specific nation-states, especially Western nation-states, in terms of the necessity for capitalist expansion. At least three dimensions of these colonial ventures have been noted. These include the search for new markets in which to sell products, the search for new sources of raw materials and the search for new sources of 'cheap' or 'skilled' labour power. This process is seen to help Western economic development while impoverishing the rest of the world. Large business corporations, as well as state organizations, have played and continue to play a leading role in these developments. While the formal possession of empires has largely disappeared, with the concomitant rise in self-governing countries a form of economic neo-imperialism has developed. Western countries are thus able to maintain their position of ascendancy by ensuring control over the terms upon which world trade is conducted. Ideas of this kind have surfaced, as will be developed shortly, in the literature on sport.

In several respects dependency theory links with neo-imperialist accounts. Dependency theorists argue that the global economy cannot be conceived as a system of equal trading partners and relations (Frank, 1967; Larrain, 1989). The superior military, economic and political power of the 'centre' imposes conditions of unequal exchange on the 'periphery'. Former colonial countries remain dependent on the West. Concerned with the uneven manner and form of global development, advocates of dependency theory also stress the integrated and systematic nature of modern global capitalism. Though the origins and nature of the dependency of specific nations vary according to how far a country was colonized, and by whom, those countries located at the 'periphery' experience unequal access to markets and unequal exchange for their raw materials. These materials include cash crops, such as sugar, or 'human crops', such as athletes.

There are, however, several strands, including dependent underdevelopment, dependent development and dependency reversal, that are evident in this tradition. In the first strand, it is argued that the global capitalist system operates actively to underdevelop the 'third world'. This is done largely, but not exclusively, through multinational corporate activity. The impoverishment of third world countries is the direct result of their subordinate position compared with the industrialized countries. The wealth of the industrialized countries is at the expense of third world countries, the latter being economically dependent on the former. Exponents of this strand argue that no genuine development is possible if this system is in place. Western ownership and control of the major governing bodies, the media–sport complex and the sports equipment manufacturing and services nexus ensure that this is also the case in world sport.

Yet, this dependent underdevelopment strand appears unable to account for the growth of some 'third world' countries. Hence, advocates of this approach coined the idea of dependent development. That is, the growth of some third world countries is acknowledged, but this is viewed as limited in nature. Examples include South Korea and Taiwan – both nations which have become bases for the manufacture of sports goods such as tennis racquets and shoes. While dependent development is conceived of as possible, such an approach still does not appear to grasp that certain countries can break out of the 'double bind' of dependent development. In this context, a further revision of the basic approach is evident in which reference is made to dependency reversal. In this approach, it is viewed as possible that certain third world countries, and/or institutional sectors of third world countries, can escape and reverse the previous disadvantageous relations with developed countries. Successful individual or team performances by representatives of third world countries could be considered as evidence of such an 'escape', but these countries remain locked into a structure of world sport controlled by the West. Despite the fruitfulness of the dependency perspective, attention has increasingly been given, if not in the study of sport, then certainly in other fields of social science, to 'world-system theory'.

Associated with the work of Wallerstein (1974), the main theme of world-system theory centres on the historical dynamics of capitalism. The logic of capitalism permeates global processes. Several key elements of this approach can be identified. Dating from the sixteenth century onwards, a 'world system' of commerce and communication has developed. Based on the expansion of a capitalist world economy, this world system has produced a series of economic and political connections. For Wallerstein, the world capitalist economy is orientated around four sectors. The core states dominate and control the exploitation of resources and production. Their wealth derives from their control over manufacturing and agriculture, and is characterized by centralized forms of government. Those states that are linked in various kinds of dependent trading are referred to by Wallerstein as being semi-peripheral to the core. Peripheral states are those that depend on selling cash crops directly to the core states, and are seen as at the outer edge of the world economy. For Wallerstein, however, there were states that were, until colonial expansion, relatively untouched by commercial development. Their dependency, and indeed that of those states at the periphery of the world economy, has been established and maintained by the legacy of colonialism. These nations are enmeshed in a set of economic relations that enrich the industrial areas and impoverish the periphery. The driving force of globalization is seen to be located in the logic of the capitalist world economy. As yet, this latter approach has not been taken up extensively by scholars studying global sports and leisure development. It is not difficult, however, to view the trade of sports talent from 'peripheral' countries to 'core' countries from this perspective. Think of the recruitment of African athletes to American college sport programmes (Bale & Sang, 1996).

This approach alerts us to the extent to which hegemonic powers exploit other nations in their search for new markets to sell sport forms, leisure products, equipment and cultural merchandise. Further, in the context of sports and arts labour migration, the activities of hegemonic states centre on the search for new sources of 'skilled' labour whose early development was resourced by these former colonial countries. From this perspective, the global sports and leisure system can be seen to operate largely but not exclusively through multinationals or organizations dominated by first world nations. This system operates actively to underdevelop the third world by excluding third world countries from the centre of the global political decision-making process and from the economic rewards derived from the world sports/leisure economy.

Indeed, it could be argued that the core states dominate and control the exploitation of resources and production. A deskilling of semi-peripheral and peripheral states occurs on the terms and conditions set by core states. The most talented workers, in which peripheral or semi-peripheral states have invested time and resources, are lured away to the core states whose wealth derives from their control over athletic and artistic labour and the media–sport/leisure production complex. Non-core states are thus in a position of dependent trading, their athletic or artistic labour being the equivalent of the cash crops that they sell in other sectors of the world economy.

While the existence of these relatively autonomous transnational practices must be recognized, it is also important not to overlook another key feature of the global media–sport complex. In seeking to avoid slipping into a homogenization thesis, the analysis must not overlook how transnational practices are subject to control and manipulation. This can involve the actions of transnational agencies or individuals from the 'transnational capitalist class' (Sklair, 1991). Transnational agencies such as the International Olympic Committee (IOC), the International Amateur Athletic Federation (IAAF), the International Marketing Group (IMG) or International Sport and Leisure (ISL) seek to regulate access to cultural flows. Individuals who belong to the 'transnational capitalist class' (such as, Juan Antonio Samaranch, Primo Nebiolo, Mark McCormack and the late Horst Dassler) are also centrally involved as these are some of the key players whose plans and actions interweave in attempting to develop a global media–sport complex. Such interventions cause cultural struggles of various kinds and at different levels.[3]

Several of these themes, as will be emphasized later in this chapter, have been fruitfully employed by scholars in sport history and the sociology of sport. Any account of global sport that does not consider the issues of power, exploitation and cultural control that such work highlights would be deficient. Yet, it has also to be noted that there are several problems associated with cultural imperialist and world-system theory accounts. These can best be summarized as several 'sensitizing' questions that need to be asked about these accounts. What constitutes Westernization and/or Americanization? Is it simply a question of the presence of a cultural product from a 'foreign' culture or does it involve a shift in the conscious and subconscious make-up of people? How 'intended' is the process described? How complete does the process have to be for domination to be said to have occurred? What ability do people have to understand, embrace and/or resist these processes? What constitutes the 'indigenous/authentic' culture that the foreign culture threatens? The problems associated with a modernization account of convergence have already been noted. Ironically, by emphasizing a unidirectional and monocausal explanation, evident in some cultural imperialism accounts, the contested and contradictory nature of global change is overlooked.

Writers such as Featherstone (1991a), Nederveen Pieterse (1995), Robertson (1990b) and Tomlinson (1991) have concluded that this is a non-productive line of thinking, and have sought to reconceptualize the debate, suggesting that the globalization concept helps reorientate the analysis. Several objections to variants of dependency theory are thus raised by exponents of globalization research. Whereas dependency theories use monocausal explanations, for example Americanization, to explain the global condition, some globalization research emphasizes the need for a multicausal analysis. Globalization research also disputes whether there is a trend towards homogenization. In contrast, Robertson and Featherstone maintain that the unity of nation-states is being dissolved, identity pluralized and a partial mixing of global cultures is occurring. Indeed, in some globalization accounts, emphasis is placed on the emergence of global diversity (Nederveen Pieterse, 1995). Citizens of different nations are becoming aware of 'otherness' and recognizing difference. Polyculturalism, not homogenization, is said to be one of the main features of global processes.

A feature that reinforces these processes is the reassertiveness of 'local' identities. Global cultural products are also seen to be actively interpreted and used by those who consume them. From this, some observers have concluded that the dynamics of globalization are powered by an 'infinitely varied mutual contest of sameness and difference' (Appadurai, 1990: p. 308). Globalization is viewed as a far less coherent or culturally directed process and occurs as a result of the complex dynamics of political, economic and cultural practices. These do not, of themselves, aim at global integration, but nonetheless produce it. The effects, then, of globalization are to weaken the cultural coherence of nation-states. This includes those nations who are more powerful within the interdependent world order (Tomlinson, 1991).

In stressing the formation of a global culture, the danger is thus to overstate the case for homogeneity and integration (Featherstone, 1990). This tendency is due to associating the idea of a global culture with the culture of any one nation-state. The tendency towards dichotomous thinking regarding global culture reinforces this weakness. Instead of endlessly arguing about whether homogeneity or heterogeneity, integration or disintegration, unity or diversity are evident, it is more adequate to see these processes as interwoven (Nederveen Pieterse, 1995; Robertson, 1992). Moving the analysis to an examination of what Sklair (1991) describes as transnational practices, the observer is better placed to note that there is something more at work than solely flows between nation-states. Transnational practices, which take a variety of cultural forms, gain a degree of *relative autonomy* on a global level.

Referring to what he terms trans-societal processes, Robertson (1990) maintains that it is these that sustain the exchange and flow of goods, people, information, knowledge and images. By utilizing terms such as *transnational* and *trans-societal*, both Sklair and Robertson are seeking to move beyond the nation-state as the sole reference point for understanding the 'integration' of the world. It is not difficult to conceive how the media–sport production complex is an integral part of this general process. Think of the technological advances involved in the media coverage of the modern Olympics and how satellites now relay powerful images across the globe in an instant. For Real (1989b), these images, however briefly and superficially, reflect and help sustain the emergence of a global culture.

How then to navigate a route round or through these competing explanations? Robertson tries to steer a middle course. Others, as will be noted, seek to move away from a homogeneity thesis altogether. Though Robertson sees globalization as referring, 'in its most general sense, to the process whereby the world becomes a single place' (Robertson, 1992: p. 135), he is also keen to avoid the suggestion that this notion of a 'single place' entails a crystallization of a cohesive system. Yet, he maintains, globalization does involve the development of a global culture. This culture, he argues, is not a homogeneous, binding whole, but refers to a 'general mode of discourse about the world as a whole and its variety' (Robertson, 1992: p. 133). Concerned to trace the way in which the world is ordered, Robertson maps out, as noted earlier, what he refers to as the 'global field'. In tracing the pattern of this global field, Robertson maintains that reference to a single causal process must be avoided. Globalization is not the direct outcome of inter-state processes. Rather, these processes need to be understood as operating relatively independently of conventionally designated societal and sociocultural processes. He stresses the relative autonomy and 'logic', and the long-term nature of the processes involved. While he refers to the development of a global culture, Robertson also stresses, as noted, that globalization processes do not lead to homogeneity. For Robertson, global processes involve both the particularization of universalism and the universalization of particularism (Robertson, 1992: p. 130). That is, these processes are marked by heterogeneous tendencies and characteristics. In sum, 'globalization is . . . best understood as indicating the problem of the form in terms of which the world becomes "united" but by no means integrated' (Robertson, 1992: p. 51).

The process by which people have come to understand the world-system as a whole has a long history. In mapping out the global condition, Robertson identifies five main phases (germinal, incipient, take-off, struggle for hegemony and uncertainty phase) in this long process (Robertson, 1992). Lasting from around the 1870s until the mid-1920s, the third phase involves the process through which the 'increasingly manifest globalizing tendencies of previous periods and places gave way to a single, inexorable form' (Robertson, 1992: p. 59). These globalization processes are evident in several areas: the growth of agencies that straddle the globe; the establishment of global awards and prizes; the emergence of a global communications system; and the emergence of a standardized notion of human rights. As part of this general framework, Robertson is also keen to explore how standardized notions of 'civilization' emerged during this period. Robertson does not view ethnic reassertiveness as running counter to globalization processes. These processes are not mutually exclusive. Indeed, he suggests that 'the contemporary concern with civilizational and societal (as well as ethnic) uniqueness – as expressed via such motifs as identity, tradition and indigenization – largely rests on globally diffused ideas' (Robertson, 1992: p. 130). Roudometof and Robertson have recently further developed these ideas. Rejecting the idea that the process of globalization is a phase of capitalist development, and that economic integration necessarily leads to cultural convergence, they conclude:

> Cultural homogeneity and heterogeneity are consequences of the globalization process. Although cultural diffusion can transform a locale, the recurrent 'invention of tradition' makes it possible to preserve, create or recreate cultural heterogeneity at the local level.
>
> (Roudometof & Robertson, 1995: p. 284)

Significantly, it was in the third phase identified by Robertson that contemporary notions of national/ethnic identity and culture were formed. During the period of intense globalization (roughly 1880 to 1920), Featherstone (1991b) suggests that more nations were drawn together in a tighter global interdependency and set of power balances. Representatives of national cultures sought both to reinvent traditions of the nation and to marginalize local ethnic and regional differences. For Featherstone, this entailed the invoking of a collective memory. This was done through the performance of ritual, bodily practices and commemorative ceremonies. Royal Jubilees, the Olympic Games, international competitions and national days all performed this function. These practices became 'echoes of the sacred' where the fundamental elements of national culture and identity were revealed. Leisure events came to express myths, invoke memories, emphasize heroes and embody traditions. These tied popular consciousness together (Featherstone, 1991b). Significant issues arise from these observations.

In this earlier phase of globalization, leisure practices functioned to bind nations together around *specific* invented traditions. In contrast, the more recent phase of globalization, dating from the 1960s, is forcing nation-states to reconstitute their collective identities along more pluralistic and multicultural lines. Significantly, leisure practices also take on new meanings. Featherstone notes in this connection:

> . . . festive moments [such as Woodstock] in which the everyday routine world becomes transformed into an extraordinary sacred world enabled people to temporarily live in unison, near to the ideal. Subsequent gatherings often incorporate rituals which reinvoke the aura of the sacred. . . . Televised rock festivals such as the Band Aid, Food Aid, the Nelson Mandela concert and other transnational link-ups may also invoke a more direct sense of emotional solidarity which may reawaken and reinforce moral concerns such as the sense of common humanity, the sacredness of the person, human rights, and more recently the sacredness of nature and non-human species.
>
> (Featherstone, 1991b: p. 122)

Although global consumer culture can be perceived to be destroying local culture, Featherstone argues that it can also be used for reconstituting a sense of locality. Given the moral concerns about humanity, human rights and environmentalism, identified by Featherstone as permeating some leisure events, it is not surprising that he believes that global consumer culture is leading to polyculturalism and a sense of otherness. Global leisure practices do not automatically involve a homogenization process. In contrast, for Featherstone, 'the tendency . . . within consumer culture to reproduce an overload of information and signs would also work against any coherent integrated universal global belief on the level of content' (Featherstone, 1991b: p. 127). More recently, Featherstone and Lash developed this argument further, and noted that analyses must 'become attuned to the nuances of the process of globalization and seek to develop theories which are sensitive to the different power potentials of the different players participating in the various global struggles' (Featherstone & Lash, 1995: p. 3). The very prevalence of images of the 'other' contained in global sport and leisure practices may both decentre the West and put other cultures more centre stage. Sport practices, such as the Olympic movement, will also be part of this global cultural contest. An even more robust case for viewing globalization as involving hybridization of the kind noted comes from the work of Nederveen Pieterse (1995).

For Nederveen Pieterse, there are many modes and forms of globalization. Seeking to avoid the potential Eurocentric and modernization connotations that can be associated with the concept, he stresses the plural, multidimensional and open-ended nature of the process. His approach is primarily a critique of essentialism. Advocating a geographically 'wide' and historically 'deep' analysis, Nederveen Pieterse emphasizes the flows between the West and the non-West and how globalization processes precede the recent 'rise of the west' to relative predominance. For Nederveen Pieterse, the problem of globalization involves a diverse range of currents and counter-currents, entails an active and critical reception by 'locals', and is leading to creolization of cultural forms and a hybridization of people's identities. For Nederveen Pieterse, cultural experiences have not been moving in the direction of cultural uniformity and standardization, but rather towards a global *mélange*. As he concludes:

> How do we come to terms with phenomena such as Thai boxing by Moroccan girls in Amsterdam, Asian rap in London, Irish bagels, Chinese tacos and Mardi Gras Indians in the

> United States? . . . Cultural experiences, past or present, have not been simply moving in the direction of cultural uniformity and standardization. This is not to say that the notion of global cultural synchronization is irrelevant – on the contrary – but it is fundamentally incomplete.
>
> (Nederveen Pieterse, 1995: p. 53)

In reaching this conclusion, Nederveen Pieterse argues that the global cultural synchronization thesis fails to note the influence that non-Western cultures exercise on each other, leaves no room to explore crossover cultures, overstates the homogeneity of the West and overlooks the fact that many of the standards and cultural forms exported by the West and its cultural industries turn out to be of a culturally mixed character. Adopting a long-term perspective allows him to stress that 'Europe', until the late fourteenth century, was the recipient of cultural influences from the Orient. While such observations provide a powerful corrective to the excesses of the homogenization thesis, in either its modernization or cultural imperialist guise, there is a danger that the analysis veers too far in the opposite direction.

It is important to push the globalization process timeframe back beyond the so-called 'modern' period and also to account for the influence of non-Western cultures on the West. Likewise, it is important to probe the hybridization of cultural identities. Equally, the creolization of sport cultures does, to some degree, parallel similar processes at work in the areas of music, art and food. Nevertheless, the analysis must not lose sight of the need to account for interrelated processes; that the contrasts between cultures have also diminished over time and that powerful groups do operate to construct, produce and provide global sport processes. This much is clear from the dependency and world-systems theorists. An uncritical deployment of concepts like hybridization and creolization can lead to a position where the individual is assumed to be sovereign and where people freely choose from the global sport *mélange*. The insights of scholars of cultural imperialism, dependency or world-system theory would thus be overlooked. That is too high a price to pay. At this juncture, it is appropriate therefore to see how the themes, questions and issues raised above have found expression in the cross-cultural study of sport.

STUDYING SPORT IN THE GLOBAL ORDER: THE STATE OF PLAY

Judging by the number of perspectives that currently provide a range of competing explanations for the structure, meaning and significance of contemporary global sport processes, perhaps it is surprising that there is greater consensus regarding the origins of sport. Though the use of globalization concepts is a relatively new feature of research studying sport processes, cross-cultural analyses have been attempted for some time.[4] Johan Huizinga's 1949 work, for example, developed a cross-cultural account of the origins of modern sport and remains compelling reading. This is what Huizinga concluded:

> The great ball-games in particular require the existence of permanent teams, and herein lies the starting-point of modern sport. The process arises quite spontaneously in the meeting of village against village, school against school, one part of a town against the rest, etc. That the process started in nineteenth-century England is understandable up to a point, though how far the specifically Anglo-Saxon bent of mind can be deemed an efficient cause is less certain. But it cannot be doubted that the structure of English life had much to do with it. Local self-government encouraged the spirit of association and solidarity. The absence of obligatory military

> training favoured the occasion for, and the need of, physical exercise. The peculiar form of education tended to work in the same direction, and finally the geography of the country and the nature of the terrain, on the whole flat and, in the ubiquitous commons, offering the most perfect playing-fields that could be desired, were of the greatest importance. Thus England became the cradle and focus of modern sporting life.
>
> (Huizinga, 1949/1970: p. 223)

There are several features of this argument that require qualification. At this stage, it is sufficient to note that scholars accept the basic premise that 'England became the cradle and focus of modern sporting life' (Dunning & Sheard, 1979; Gruneau, 1988; Guttmann, 1991). Here the consensus breaks down. Different interpretations exist with regard to the dynamics underpinning the emergence and subsequent diffusion of modern sport (Dunning & Sheard, 1979; Gorn & Goldstein, 1993; Hargreaves, 1986; Hargreaves, 1994; Mandell, 1984). Similar themes, issues and questions that characterize the broader debate regarding global cultural flows also surface in discussing modern sport. Not surprisingly, similar fault-lines regarding homogeneity/heterogeneity, monocausal/multicausal, unidimensional/multidimensional, unity/fragmentation, universalism/particularism are also evident. In the following section, I identify key research, and outline where such work is positioned along these fault-lines.

The clearest exposition of the modernization thesis as it applies to sport can be found in the work of Eric Wagner. Reviewing a diverse set of trends that are said to characterize global sport, Wagner correctly observes that 'Americanization is part of these trends but it is only one part of much broader processes; it is not by itself the key process' (Wagner, 1990: p. 400). Yet, Wagner mistakenly assigns central status to what he terms 'international modernization' (Wagner, 1990: p. 402). While he acknowledges important caveats, such as 'sport culture flowing in all directions', and a 'blending of many sport traditions', Wagner does appear to downplay the conflictual nature of these processes, to overemphasize the ability of people to pick and choose as they wish from global sport cultures, and to see such development as a sign of progress. His concluding comments echo many of the features, and weaknesses, of the modernization perspective. This is what he had to say:

> I think we make too much of cultural dependency in sports when in fact it is people themselves who generally determine what they do and do not want, and it is the people who modify and adapt the cultural imports, the sports, to fit their own needs and values. Bringing sports into a new cultural context probably serves more as examples available for people to pick up or trade if they wish, rather than any imposed or forced cultural change. . . . The long-term trend has to be, I think, towards greater homogenization, and I don't think there is anything bad or imperialistic about this; rather, these sports trends ultimately must reflect the will of the people.
>
> (Wagner, 1990: p. 402)

Though modernization was one of the first approaches within the field, ideas of this kind still surface in the literature on sport. Consider Baker and Mangan's collection of papers on sport in Africa (1987), Cashman's exploration of the phenomenon of Indian cricket (1988), Arbena's evaluation of literature relating to Latin America (1988) and papers published in comparative sport studies edited by Wilcox (1995). In his early writing on this subject, Allen Guttmann supported this position, arguing that Wagner was 'correct to insist that we are witnessing a homogenization of world sports rather than an Americanization', and that 'the concept of modernization is preferable because it also implies something about the nature of the global transformation' (Guttmann, 1991: pp. 187–8). Though he acknowledges that terms like '*Gemeinschaft* and *Gesellschaft*, the traditional and the modern, the particularistic and the universalistic' employ an 'admittedly simplified dichotomy', Guttmann still works within a modernization time frame, and overlooks what Robertson describes as the universalization of particularism' and not just the 'particularization of universalism' (Robertson, 1992). This is odd. In other work by Guttmann, important lines of enquiry are opened up when he refers to the diffusion of game forms in the ancient world and to the influence of the Orient on the West (Guttmann, 1993). Guttmann's solution, as we shall see later, has been to adopt a cultural hegemony position and to concentrate on more recent events. While advocates of a cultural imperialist and dependency theory approach would reject several, if not all of the premises outlined by Wagner and Guttmann, these perspectives do share a common assumption that we are witnessing the homogenization of world sports. Within sport history research, informed by a cultural imperialist perspective, several insightful case studies of the connection between the diffusion of sport and imperialism have been provided (Mangan, 1986; Stoddart, 1989). The diffusion of sport, out of its European heartland, moved along the formal and the informal lines of Empire – particularly, though not exclusively, the British. But it was not just the diffusion of specific sports, such as cricket, that reflected this broader process (James, 1963). From a cultural imperialist perspective, what was also at stake was the diffusion of a cultural/sporting ideology and a form of Western cosmology. This argument can be highlighted with reference to the work of Henning Eichberg, John Bale and Johan Galtung.

Eichberg's study probes several of the issues identified. He suggests that Olympism is a 'social pattern' that reflects the 'everyday culture of the western (and east European) industrial society' (Eichberg, 1984: p. 97). He emphasizes several negative consequences of Olympism, including drugs, violence and the scientification of sport. Eichberg maintains that these excesses are not accidental or marginal, but logically related to the configuration of Western Olympic sport, with its emphasis on 'faster, higher, stronger'. Olympism is seen to reflect the colonial dominance of the West, and its spread across the globe has been remarkably successful. While it is possible to agree with Eichberg on this, Wilson overstates this case when he suggests that 'the major impetus for the globalization of sport was the Olympic movement' (Wilson, 1994: p. 356). The dynamics underpinning the globalization of sport are more multifaceted than this. Indeed, as Eichberg argues, Western domination is increasingly subject to resistance. Alternatives to Olympism are emerging. These alternatives include a resurgence of national cultural games, open-air movements, expressive activities and meditative exercises. He concludes that 'the age of Western colonial dominance is coming to an end – and with it the predominance of Olympic sports', and that, 'new physical cultures will arise . . . from the different cultural traditions of the world' (Eichberg, 1984: p. 102). Not all, as we shall see, share Eichberg's optimism.

Tackling these issues within the subdiscipline of sports geography, John Bale paints a more conflict-ridden and destructive picture of the impact of the diffusion of sport along the lines of Empire. As Bale records, 'western sports did not simply take root in virgin soil; they were firmly implanted – sometimes ruthlessly – by imperialists' (Bale, 1994: p. 8). For Bale, such 'sports colonisation' marginalized, or destroyed, indigenous movement cultures and, 'as cultural imperialism swept the globe, sports played their part in westernising the landscapes of the colonies' (Bale, 1994: p. 8). There is much in this latter argument and Bale's pioneering study raises our understanding of sport landscapes to a new level. There are, however, grounds for suggesting that the homogenization process is not as complete as these observations appear to indicate. This reservation is not, however, shared by Galtung. In similar vein to Bale and Eichberg, Galtung sets up his analysis with the following question: 'What happens when there is massive export of sports, radiating from Western centers, following old colonial trade and control lines, into the last little corner of the world, leaving cricket bats, soccer fields, racing tracks, courts of all sorts and what not behind?' (Galtung, 1991: p. 150). For Galtung, the answer is clear. Sports carry the sociocultural code of the senders, and those from the West 'serve as fully fledged carriers of the combination typical for expansionist occidental cosmology' (Galtung, 1991: p. 150). Unlike Eichberg, however, Galtung detects no hopeful alternatives. Whatever the merits of his overall argument, Galtung rightly points to the role of the body in these processes, and insightfully observes that, as people learn these body cultures at an early stage in their lives, they leave 'imprints that may well be indelible' (Galtung, 1991: p. 150).

Although the research highlighted above emphasizes a cultural imperialist perspective, variants of dependency theory have been used in the study of sport. Several studies have also examined Latin and South America (Arbena, 1993; Mandle & Mandle, 1988). Alan Klein's study of Dominican and Mexican baseball are examples of dependency research at its very best (Klein, 1991, 1997). Grounded in a careful and sophisticated anthropological approach, he probes the contradictory status and role of baseball in relations between the Dominican Republic and the USA. Klein skillfully observes:

> Because baseball is the only area in which Dominicans come up against Americans and demonstrate superiority, it fosters national pride and keeps foreign influence at bay. But the resistance is incomplete. At an organizational level American baseball interests have gained power and are now unwittingly dismantling Dominican baseball. Therefore, just when the Dominicans are in a position to resist the influence of foreigners, the core of their resistance is slipping away into the hands of the foreigners themselves.
>
> (Klein, 1991: p. 3)

Despite noting, in similar fashion to Eichberg's interpretation of the Olympic movement, that 'Caribbean baseball is rooted in colonialism', Klein does not convey the sense of uniformity, or of total domination, that Galtung does. On the contrary, while pointing to the unequal nature of power relations, Klein remarks, 'having struggled in obscurity to refine the game Dominicans have made it their own, a game marked by their cadence and color' (Klein, 1991: p. 156). Local responses to broader processes are acknowledged. Klein goes further, and argues that 'the Dominicans are a beleaguered people who may someday rebel; to predict when the flash point will occur, look first to the firefights being waged in a game that has inspired their confidence. Look first at Sugarball' (Klein, 1991: p. 156). In studying the US–Mexican border, baseball and forms of nationalism Klein makes the same incisive case. As he remarks, 'an examination of the sport and the subculture of baseball in this region illustrates these nationalisms as well or better than other kinds of studies' (Klein, 1997: p. 13).

Other scholars working within this broad cultural imperialist/dependency theory and cultural hegemony tradition either straddle these perspectives or downplay the role of Americanization and, instead, stress the role of global capitalism. Sugden and Tomlinson, for example, appear to draw on aspects of these traditions. Take, for example, their following remarks, 'although on the one hand

FIFA has served as a forum for Third World resistance, on the other hand it has undoubtedly aided and abetted neocolonialist forms of economic and cultural exploitation' (Sugden & Tomlinson, 1998b: p. 314). In studies that Donnelly (1996) refers to as being located within a cultural hegemony position, the contested nature of global capitalism is highlighted. Guttmann, for example, argues that 'cultural imperialism is not . . . the most accurate term to characterize what happens during the process of ludic diffusion. Cultural hegemony comes closer' (Guttmann, 1994: p. 178). For Donnelly, the advantage of this cultural hegemony perspective lies in avoiding an overdeterministic view of Americanization: the transfer of cultural products is not one way, the ideological messages are not fixed and those who are exposed to such products have a degree of freedom to interpret and reinterpret these messages and products. As Donnelly concludes, 'cultural hegemony may be seen as a two-way but imbalanced process of cultural exchange, interpenetration, and interpretation' (Donnelly, 1996: p. 243). Yet, interestingly, while Guttmann (1994: p. 179) also sees merit in this perspective, he argues that cultural hegemonists overstate the intentionality involved in ludic diffusion processes. Perhaps this is so, but equally important is the fact that the unintentional dynamics involved in global processes are overlooked. In addition, non-occidental influences on the West and the linkages between non-occidental societies and their impact on each other are still not accounted for. Civilizational struggles of a quite complex kind are the key to unlocking aspects of global processes.

Bruce Kidd's study of sport in Canada, located within a broader analysis of the development of Canadian national culture, insightfully explores the role of global capitalism (Kidd, 1981). Noting the potential importance of sport in the strengthening and enunciation of national identity, Kidd observes that the commodification of Canadian sport has served to undermine this potential. Focusing on the National Hockey League (NHL) as a 'critical case' in this regard, he highlights how both the ideological marketing strategy of the NHL and the general process of commodification between the two world wars served to 'accelerate the disintegration of beliefs and practices that had once supported and nurtured autonomous Canadian institutions' (Kidd, 1981: p. 713). For him, an explanation of these processes lies not in Americanization *per se* but in a critique of capitalism. Kidd observes:

> Explanation lies neither in U.S. expansion nor national betrayal, but in the dynamics of capital. Once sport became a sphere of commodity production . . . then it was almost inevitable that the best Canadian hockey would be controlled by the richest and most powerful aggregates of capital and sold in the richer and more populous markets of the U.S. The disappearance of community control over Canadian hockey strengthened a much larger process – the centralization of all popular forms of culture.
>
> (Kidd, 1981: p. 714)

Whereas Kidd deals with issues between 'core' economies, George Sage (1995) draws on the work of Wallerstein and adopts a more 'world-system model' to explain the global sporting goods industry. Surveying the social and environmental costs associated with the relocation strategies of multinational corporations such as Nike, Sage concludes that such companies have been 'following a model which places exports over domestic needs, profits over worker rights, growth over the environment', and that a 'neo-colonial system of unequal economic and political relationships among the First and Third World countries envisioned by Wallerstein's world-system model of global development becomes abundantly evident to even a casual observer' (Sage, 1995: p. 48).

While noting the obvious American influences on Australian popular culture, McKay and Miller (1991) adopt a similar stance to Sage. They view the concept of Americanization to be of limited help in explaining the form and content of Australian sport. For them, the political economy of Australian sport can best be analysed by concepts such as post-Fordism, the globalization of consumerism and the cultural logic of late capitalism. Though McKay and Miller (1991) and McKay, Lawrence, Miller and Rowe (1993) prefer the term 'corporate sport', Donnelly has argued that the 'notion of corporate sport may easily be extended to indicate the Americanization of sport, given that most of the conditions for corporate sport are either American in origin, or have been more fully developed in the United States' (Donnelly, 1996: p. 246). It would seem, however, that neither Sage, nor McKay and his fellow researchers, would accept this interpretation. As McKay and Miller remark, 'in the discourse of the daily report from the stock exchange, the Americans are not the only players in the cultural game' (McKay & Miller, 1991: p. 93).

Yet, Donnelly (1996) would have much in common with these writers. In certain respects his position, as noted, represents a modified and more sophisticated form of the Americanization thesis. Eschewing the excesses of the Americanization as imperialism argument, Donnelly views Americanization as a form of cultural hegemony with resistance and accommodation evident and also with other imperialist influences at work.

Although McKay and Miller de-emphasize the pervasiveness of American control, and concentrate on the dynamics of global capitalism *per se*, the work by David Andrews would, at first sight, appear to be more in keeping with the position adopted by Donnelly. Andrews, for example, examines the 'global structure and local influence of the National Basketball Association (NBA) as a transnational corporation, whose global ubiquity inevitably contributes to the hyperreal remaking of local identities' (Andrews, 1997: p. 72). Andrews goes on to argue that the NBA has been turned 'into one of the popular commodity-signs which had usurped the material economic commodity as the dynamic force and structuring principle of everyday American existence' (Andrews, 1997: p. 74). In language sometimes akin to that used by Adorno and his fellow contributors to the Frankfurt School, Andrews argues that during the 1980s, 'the NBA became a hyperreal circus whose simulated, and hence self-perpetuating, popularity seduced the American masses' (Andrews, 1997: p. 74). This 'success' is not confined to the USA. Though it may be unwise to overestimate the knowledge of the powerful and underestimate the ability of 'locals' to reshape, resist, or simply ignore, the marketing strategies of multinationals, Andrews is correct to observe that the NBA does 'have a vivid global presence' (Andrews, 1997: p. 77). The source of debate, however, as he himself acknowledges, is 'the extent to which the circulation of universal American commodity-signs has resulted in the convergence of global markets, lifestyles and identities' (Andrews, 1997: p. 77). Despite the manner in which he formulates the early part of his argument, Andrews stresses the 'built-in particularity (or heterogeneity) in terms of the ways that products and images are consumed', and that, products, images and services from other societies 'to some extent . . . inalienably become indigenized' (Andrews, 1997: p. 77). As with the broader globalization literature, sociology of sport research is divided over the precise form and blend of homogeneity and heterogeneity characteristic of the global sport process.

What kind of assessment can be made regarding the state of play of the sociological study of global sport? Several writers have attempted some overall review (Donnelly, 1996; Harvey & Houle, 1994; Houlihan,

1994). While there are clear fault-lines along which the literature lies, reflecting the more general globalization debate, there is also some overlap. Research from both a modernization and a cultural imperialism perspective concludes that a homogenization process is occurring. This common ground can be seen in Guttmann's work. While his early work endorsed a modernization perspective, his more recent contribution has swung in favour of a form of cultural imperialism (Guttmann, 1991, 1994). While issues of cultural struggle and contestation are much more to the fore in this latter work, and in the work stemming from a cultural hegemony perspective, the common denominator is still a continued emphasis on homogenization.

Within the broad 'Marxist' tradition (cultural imperialism, dependency theory, world-system theory and hegemony theory), common emphasis is placed on power, exploitation and the role that multinationals play in local markets. While the relative role of Americanization and/or global capitalism is disputed, what is agreed upon is that modern sport is structured by a political economy in which multinationals play a decisive part. In some instances, as we have seen, a particularly unidirectional and mono-causal focus is used to explain these processes. More recently, work by Andrews and Klein illustrates, to a greater extent, issues of local resistance, reinterpretation and indigenization. In this, they are in keeping with a trend in the more general globalization literature that emphasizes heterogeneity (Nederveen Pieterse, 1995). Harvey and Houle summarize aspects of this debate that have surfaced in the sociology of sport when they conclude:

> Thus, linking sport to globalization leads to an analysis of sport as part of an emergent global culture, as contributing to the definition of new identities, and to the development of a world economy. Therefore, the debate between globalization and Americanization is more than a question of vocabulary. Indeed, it is a question of paradigmatic choice, which leads to completely different interpretations of a series of phenomena.
>
> (Harvey & Houle, 1994: p. 346)

While the observations made in this chapter would endorse these writers when they argue that different interpretations of globalization more broadly, and global sport processes in particular, are 'a question of paradigmatic choice', there is room to doubt whether such interpretations are as polarized as they suggest. This chapter reveals a degree of common ground and a basis on which to build future work. It is not necessary to discard research from other traditions simply because we do not have all assumptions and concepts in common. What is clear from the literature reviewed in this chapter is that the study of global sport processes is a vibrant area, and that narrow, natiocentric analyses do not capture the complexity of modern sport in the late twentieth century.

NOTES

1 Globalization research has taken various forms and has been subjected to extensive debate. For further discussion, see Beyer, 1994; Chase Dunn, 1989; Featherstone, 1990, 1991a, 1991b; Featherstone, Lash & Robertson, 1995; Friedman, 1994; Giddens, 1990; Gilpin, 1987; Hall, 1991; Hall et al., 1992; King, 1991; McGrew, 1992; Robertson, 1990a; Rosenau, 1980; Sanderson, 1995; Sklair, 1991; Waters, 1995; Wolfe, 1991.

2 For further discussion of this, see Blomstrom & Hettne, 1984; Frank, 1967; Hettne, 1990; Larrain,

1989. For consideration of how this approach has been applied to the development of sport, see Gruneau, 1988.

3 For examples of how this cultural imperialism approach has been applied to the media more generally, see Emanuel, 1992; Mattelart, 1977; Rollin, 1989; Schiller, 1969; Tunstall, 1977.

4 Examples of these cross-cultural studies include Bale, 1985; Clignet & Stark, 1974; Jokl & Simon, 1964; Krotee, 1979; Mandell, 1984; Wagner, 1989.

REFERENCES

Andrews, D. (1997): "The (trans)national basketball association: American commodity-sign culture and global-local conjuncturalism", in Cvetkovich, A. & Kellner, D. (eds), Articulating the Global and the Local: globalization and cultural studies. Westview Press: Boulder, Colo., pp. 72–101.

Appadurai, A. (1990): "Disjuncture and difference in the global cultural economy", Theory, Culture & Society 7, pp. 295–310.

Arbena, J. (ed.) (1988): Sport and Society in Latin America: diffusion, dependency and the rise of mass culture. Greenwood Press: Westport, CT.

Arbena, J. (1995): "Sport and Nationalism in Latin America, 1880–1970: The Parade of Promoting and Performing 'European Sports'", *History of European Ideas* 16, pp. 837–844.

Baker, W. (1982): Sports in the Western World. Rowman & Littlefield: Totowa, NJ.

Baker, W. & Mangan, J.A. (eds) (1987): Sport in Africa: essays in social history. Africana: New York.

Bale, J. (1985): "Toward a geography of international sport." Occasional Paper 8, Department of Geography, University of Loughborough.

Bale, J. (1994): Landscapes of Modern Sport. Leicester University Press: Leicester.

Bale, J. & Sang, J. (1996): Kenyan Running: movement culture, geography and global change. Frank Cass: London

Beyer, P. (1994): Religion and Globalization. Sage: London.

Blomstrom, M. & Hettne, B. (1984): Development Theory in Transition. Zed Books: London.

Cashman, R. (1988): "Cricket and colonialism: colonial hegemony and indigenous subversion" in Mangan, J.A. (ed.) Pleasure, Profit and Proselystism: British culture and sport at home and abroad 1700–1914. Frank Cass: London, pp. 258–72.

Chase Dunn, C. (1989): Global Formation: structures of the world economy. Blackwell: Oxford.

Clignet, R. & Stark, M. (1974): "Modernization and the game of soccer" in Cameroun, International Review of Sport Sociology 9, pp. 81–98.

Dickens, P. (1992): Global Shift: the internationalization of economic activity. Paul Chapman: London (2nd edn).

Donnelly, P. (1996): "The local and the global: globalization in the sociology of sport", Journal of Sport and Social Issues 20, pp. 239–57.

Dunning, E., & Sheard, K. (1979). Barbarians, gentlemen, and players: A sociological study of the development of rugby football. New York University Press: New York.

Eichberg, H. (1984): "Olympic sport – neo-colonialism and alternatives" International Review for the Sociology of Sport, 19 (1), Pp. 97–104.

Emanuel, S. (1992): "Culture in space: the European cultural channel", Media, Culture & Society 14, pp. 281–99.

Featherstone, M. (1990): "Global culture: an introduction", Theory, Culture & Society 7, pp. 1–14.

Featherstone, M. (1991a): "Local and global cultures", Vrijetijd en Samenleving 3/4, pp. 43–58.

Featherstone, M. (1991b): Consumer Culture and Postmodernism. Sage: London.

Featherstone, M. & Lash, S. (1995): "Globalization, modernity and the spatialization of social theory: an introduction", in Featherstone, M., Lash, S. & Robertson, R. (eds) Global Modernities. Sage: London, pp. 1–24.

Featherstone, M., Lash, S. & Roberston, R. (eds) (1995): Global Modernities. Sage: London.

Frank, G. (1967): Capitalism and Under-development in Latin America. Monthly Review Press: New York.

Friedman, J. (1994): Cultural Identity and Global Process. Sage: London.

Galtung, J. (1991): "The sport system as a metaphor for the world system," in Landry, F., Landry, M. & Yerles, M. (eds) Sport. . .the third millennium. University of Laval Press: Quebec, pp. 147–56.

Giddens, A. (1990): The Consequences of Modernity. Polity Press: Cambridge.

Gilpin, R. (1987): The Political Economy of International Relations. Princeton University Press: Princeton.

Goudsblom, J. (1977): Sociology in the Balance. Blackwell: Oxford.

Gorn, E.J. & Goldstein, W. (1993): A Brief History of American Sports. Hill & Wang: New York.

Gruneau, R. (1988): "Modernization or hegemony: two views on sport and social development", in Harvey, J. & Cantelon, H. (eds) Not Just a Game. University of Ottawa Press: Ottawa, pp. 9–32.

Guttmann, A. (1991): "Sports diffusion: a response to Maguire and the Americanization commentaries", Sociology of Sport Journal 8, pp. 185–90.

Guttman, A. (1993): "The diffusion of sports and the problem of cultural imperialism", in Dunning, E.G., Maguire, J.A. & Pearton, R. (eds) The Sports Process:

a comparative and developmental approach. Human Kinetics: Champaign, Ill., pp. 125–38.

Guttman, A. (1994): Games and Empires: modern sports and cultural imperialism. Columbia University Press: New York.

Hall, S. (1991): "The local and the global: globalization and ethnicity", in King, A.D. (ed.) Culture, Globalization and the World-system. Macmillan: London, pp. 19–39.

Hall, S., Held, D. & McGrew, T. (eds) (1992): Modernity and its Futures. Polity Press: Cambridge.

Hannerz, U. (1990): "Cosmopolitans and locals in word culture", Theory, Culture & Society 7, pp. 237–51.

Hargreaves, Jennifer (1994): Sporting Females: critical issues in the history and sociology of women's sports. Routledge: London.

Hargreaves, John (1986): Sport, Power and Culture. Polity Press: Cambridge.

Harvey, D. (1989): The Condition of Postmodernity. Blackwell: Oxford.

Harvey, J. & Houle, F. (1994): "Sport, world economy, global culture and new social movements", Sociology of Sport Journal 11, pp. 337–55.

Hettne, B. (1990): Development Theory and the Three Worlds. Longman: London.

Huizinga, J. (1949/1970): Homo Ludens: a study of the play element in culture. Temple Smith: London.

Houlihan, B. (1994): "Homogenization, Americanization, and creolization of sport: varieties of globalization" Sociology of Sport Journal 11, pp. 356–75.

James, C.L.R. (1963): Beyond a Boundary. Stanley Paul: London.

Johnson, R.J., Taylor, P. J. & Watts, M.J. (1995): Geographies of Global Change: remapping the world in the late twentieth century. Blackwell: Oxford.

Jokl, E. & Simon, E. (eds) (1964): International Research in Sport and Physical Education. Charles Thomas: Springfield, Ill.

Kidd, B. (1981): "Sport, dependency and the Canadian state", in Hart, M. & Birrell, S. (eds) Sport in the Sociocultural Process. Wm. C. Brown: Dubuque, Ia, pp. 707–21.

King, A.D. (ed.) (1991): Culture, Globalization and the World-system: contemporary conditions for the representation of identity. Macmillan: London.

Klein, A.M. (1989): "Baseball in the Dominican Republic," Sociology of Sport Journal 6, pp. 95–112.

Klein, A.M. (1991): Sugarball. The American game, the Dominican dream. Yale University Press: New Haven, Conn.

Klein, A.M. (1997): Baseball on the Border: a tale of two Laredos. Princeton University Press: Princeton, NJ.

Krotee, M. (1979): "The rise and demise of sport: a reflection of Uruguayan society" Annals of the American Academy of Political and Social Science 445, pp. 141–54.

Larrain, J. (1989): Theories of Development. Polity Press: London.

Mandell, R. (1984): Sport: a cultural history. Columbia University Press: New York.

Mandle, J. & Mandle, J. (1988): Grass Roots Commitment: basketball and society in Trinidad and Tobago. Caribbean Books: Parkesburg, Ia.

Mangan, J.A. (1986): The Games Ethic and Imperialism. Viking Press: London.

Mason, T. (1995): Passion of the People? Football in South America. Verso: London.

Massey, D. (1994): Space, Place and Gender. Polity Press: Cambridge.

Mattelart, A. (1977): Multi-national Corporations and the Control of Culture: the ideological apparatuses of imperialism. Harvester: Hassocks.

McGrew, A. (1992): "Conceptualizing Global Politics." From A. McGrew, P.G. Lewis, et al. (eds.) Global Politics: Globalization and the Nation-State. Polity Press: Cambridge.

McKay, J. and Miller, T. (1991) "From old boys to men and women of the corporation: the Americanisation and commodification of Australian Sport", Sociology of Sport Journal 8: 86–94.

McKay, J., Lawrence, G., Miller, T. and Rowe, D. (1993) "Globalisation and Australian sport", Sport Science Review, 2 (1): 10–28.

Nederveen Pieterse, J. (1995): "Globalization as hybridization", in Featherstone, M., Lash, S. & Robertson, R. (eds) Global Modernities. Sage: London, pp. 45–68.

Pooley, J.C. (1981): "Ethnic soccer clubs in Milwaukee: a study in assimiliation", in Hart, M. & Birrell, S. (eds) Sport in the Sociocultural Process. Wm. C. Brown: Dubuque, Ia, pp. 430–47.

Real, M. (1989b): "Super bowl football versus world cup soccer: a cultural-structural comparison", in Wenner, L. (ed.) Media, Sports and Society. Sage: Newbury Park, Calif., pp. 180–203.

Robertson, R. (1990a): "After nostalgia: wilful nostalgia and the phases of globalization", in Turner, B.S. (ed) Theories of Modernity and Postmodernity. Sage: London, pp. 45–61.

Robertson, R. (1990b): "Mapping the global condition: globalization as the central concept", Theory, Culture & Society 7, pp. 15–30.

Robertson, R. (1992): Globalization: social theory and global culture. Sage: London.

Rollin, R, (ed.) (1989): The Americanization of the Global Village. Bowling Green University Press: Bowling Green, Ohio.

Rosenau, J. (1980): The Study of Global Interdependence. Francis Pinter: London.

Roudometof, V. & Robertson, R. (1995): "Globalization, world-system theory, and the comparative study of civilizations: issues of theoretical logic in world-historical sociology", in Sanderson, S.K. (ed.) Civilizations and World Systems. Alta Mira: Walnut Creek, Calif., pp. 273–300.

Sage, G. (1995): "Deindustrialization and the American sporting goods industry", in Wilcox, R. C. (ed.) Sport in the Global Village. Fitness Information Technology, Inc." Morgantown, W.Va, pp. 39–51.

Sanderson, S. (ed.) (1995): Civilizations and World Systems: studying world-historical change. Alta Mira: Walnut Creek, Calif.

Schiller, H. (1969): Mass Communication and American Empire. Beacon Press: Boston, Mass.

Seppanen, P. (1970): "The role of competitive sports in different societies," Paper presented at 7th World Congress of Sociology, Varna, Bulgaria, September.

Sklair, L. (1991): Sociology of the Global System. Harvester: London.

Stoddart, B. (1989): "Sport in the social construct of the lesser developed world: a commentary", sociology of sport journal 6 pp. 125–35.

Sugden, J. & Tomlinson, A. (1998b): "Power and resistance in the governance of world football: theorizing FIFA's transnational impact", Journal of Sport & Social Issues 22, pp. 299–316.

Tomlinson, J. (1991): Cultural Imperialism: Pinter Publishers: London.

Tunstall, J. (1977): The Media are America. Constable: London.

Wagner, E. (ed.) (1989): Sport in Asia and Africa: a comparative handbook. Greenwood Press: Westport, Conn.

Wagner, E. (1990): "Sport in Africa and Asia: Americanization or mundialization?" Sociology of Sport Journal 7, pp. 399–402.

Wallerstein, I. (1974): The Modern World System. Academic Press: New York.

Waters, M. (1995): Globalization. Routledge. London.

Wilcox, R.C. (ed.) (1995): Sport in the Global Village. Fitness Information Technology: Morgantown, WV.

Wilson, J (1994): Playing by the Rules: Sport, Society, and the State. Wayne State University Press: Detroit.

Wolfe, Alan (1991), "The Single European Market: National of Euro-Brands," International Journal of Advertising, 10 (1), 49–58.

Yearly, S. (1996): Sociology, Environmentalism, Globalization: Reinventing the Globe. Sage: London.

CHAPTER 34

The Denationalization of Sport: De-ethnicization of the Nation and Identity De-territorialization

Raffaele Poli

INTRODUCTION

The concept of denationalization was first used in the 1970s in economic studies as a synonym for privatization. For two decades, most of the articles in which the notion has been employed referred to the sale of State-owned companies. More recently, the concept has come to be used among others, such as deterritorialization, transnationalism, post-national, etc., as a means to circumvent 'methodological nationalism' or 'state-centrism' which has been dominant in the social sciences for many years.[1] Neil Brenner has defined the latter approach as the tendency to conceptualize 'space as a static platform of social action that is not itself constituted or modified socially' and state territoriality 'as a preconstituted, naturalized, or unchanged scale of analysis'.[2] The increasing importance of phenomena such as the development of transnational corporations, the intensified deployment of information technologies, the advent of 'a consciousness of the world as a whole',[3] the formation of transnational communities of migrants, etc., has encouraged researchers to develop concepts allowing them to transcend the limits of state-centric based theories. As in the case of deterritorialization, latent in the notion of denationalization, there is the idea that the territoriality of state is an historical construction that is not the 'natural' container of economic, political or social life.

From a spatial point of view, Brenner defines the 'denationalization of the State' as the process by which 'the role of the national scale both as a self-enclosed container of socioeconomic relations and an organizational interface between sub- and supra-national scales' declines.[4] According to Saskia Sassen, denationalization can be defined as the filtering and embeddedness of the global in what has historically been thought, represented, constructed and institutionalized as national. Thus, one central task of contemporary social sciences is 'to decode particular aspects of what is still represented or experienced as "national", which may in fact have shifted away from what had historically been considered or constituted as national'.[5]

From this standpoint, the aim of the essay is to test under what conditions and under which forms it is possible to speak of a denationalization process taking place in sport. Without careful analysis, it may seem to the casual observer that sport is not affected by any form of denationalization. Sportsmen continue to compete for nation states and every international competition is preceded or followed by a national anthem. Media and spectators also play an active role in the (re)production of this national semantic. This is noticeable in collective sports, where TV audiences are generally greater when a national team or club is competing. In 2004, for example, in France, the four biggest recorded sport audiences were during matches of the national football team.

The particular way in which sporting competitions are organized also tends to perpetuate the geopolitical division of the world in nation states, reproducing a spatial fetishism where blocks of territory, thought as homogeneous, are juxtaposed and never superimposed. In the contemporary globalized world, as Pascal Boniface suggests, the elite sports worldwide spectacle seems primarily to be an activity by which nations find new meaning and homelands are glorified.[6] While in the context of European unification, nationalist feelings and sentiments are rekindled through international sporting competitions.[7] As a consequence, the idea according to which state territories are the natural physical container for identity is reactualized. Nationalist feelings reinforced through sport tend also to justify the existence of borders and hide the imagined nature of national communities.[8] In this respect, Duke and Crolley underline that 'football captures the notion of an imagined community perfectly. It is much easier to imagine the nation and conform national identity, when eleven players are representing the nation in a match against another nation'.[9]

Without neglecting these aspects of sport, the goal of this essay is to show that sport also plays a role in the deterritorialization and reterritorialization of identities. The first form of denationalization on which this essay is centred is linked to increasing migratory movements, partially provoked by professional sport itself, and the increasing tendency towards naturalizations of sportsmen and nationality changes. The second form is linked to the global broadcasting of images and information and to the increasing possibilities to identify with teams and sportsmen representing geographical entities on different scales (from the town to nation states), located thousands of miles away from the supporter's place of residence. While these two forms of denationalization may appear as marginal when compared to the importance of the state-national basis on which international sports events are still grounded, the author considers it of major importance to take them into account.

If these two distinct forms of contemporary sport denationalization cannot be considered as dominant trends from a historical perspective, it is possible to understand them as incipient changes, intervening in the broader context of globalization, of which researchers—sociologists above all—have to be aware. The results of further investigation of these two phenomena could thus be interpreted as premises to bigger changes that may progressively lead to a redefinition of both sports' organizational structure and the popular understanding of sporting events on a greater scale than is actually the case. The essay's intention is neither to judge negatively the interpretation of sport according to a state national grid, nor to propose radical changes to eligibility conditions for international competitions. The goal is rather to stimulate a debate in the academic field on a topic—identities—that has predominantly been treated from a state-centric perspective. This has, up till now, prevented many researchers from taking into account processes such as the changing character of nations and the new expressions of identity occurring both in and through sport. Thus, the purpose of the essay is to draw attention to the impact on the playing field of processes that have been discussed abundantly in other domains.[10]

The essay is divided into three parts. First of all, the author has considered it useful to take a step back and examine how elite sport became nationalized and some of the reasons for this. Indeed, some aspects that can appear as being naturally nation-based in today's organization of sport are in reality historical constructs. The first section furnishes the elements that allow us to understand why we can speak of a new trend towards denationalization. The second and third sections focus on the analytical description of two sets of processes causing denationalization, which either stimulate a de-ethnicization of the nation or lead to a deterritorialization of identity. If these two forms of denationalization are different both in terms of their origin and in their consequences, the author considers that they are intrinsically linked and have thus to be analyzed in conjunction with each other. Even if international migratory flows and changes of nationality do not directly bring about a deterritorialization of identity, and the global broadcasting of sports events does not necessarily provoke a de-ethnicization of the nation, both sets of processes in different ways result in a denationalization in sport in which the 'natural' correspondence between a State, an identity and a territory is called into question.

THE NATIONALIZATION OF SPORT

At their very beginning, modern sports in England stimulated more the competition between members of upper classes (university students, aristocrats) than competition between territorial groups.[11] The advent of national and global diffusion of modern sports was then accompanied by the appearance of a strong territorial significance, according to which clubs and players did not symbolically represent social classes but geographical areas. This was followed in the early years of the twentieth century by the emergence of national football teams outside of Great Britain.[12] The Fédération Internationale de Football Association (FIFA) was founded in 1904 and the international fixtures organized between teams representing nation states helped to 'dramatize senses of national difference and cultural opposition'.[13] Nevertheless, the idea of having only players with a national passport in national teams was not yet completely integrated. For example, in April 1900, nine foreigners played for Italy against Switzerland in Turin. According to Papa and Panico, 'the concept of "national" was understood by football pioneers in a purely residential way'.[14] This was a reflection of the overrepresentation of expatriates in football clubs and, more generally, proof of the early internationalism of modern sports.[15]

With the growth of nationalism that preceded the First World War, elite sport was imbued with strong political meaning. Between the two World Wars, two European countries in particular used sport for political ends: Italy and Germany. According to Holt and Mason, sport in these countries was considered as 'a device of the strength of the State' and 'has been used as a weapon of foreign policy'.[16] Arnaud underlines that in France too, since the beginning of the 1920s, sport has become a State matter. Indeed, a national Office of Physical Education and Sport was created. The goal of this office, placed under the aegis of the Ministry of Public Instruction, was to 'promote (the) sport at a high level in order to restore France's image in the world'.[17]

Inside national borders, sport has become instrumental in the construction of a national consciousness. According to the ideological project that dominated for many years the building of nation states, this construction had to be realized through an uniformization of the citizens living inside national borders. In fact, instead of taking into account the variety of its populations, the internal logic of the nation state was to encompass the cultural unity of all, as this was considered as the only means of creating a national identity.[18] According to Lefebvre's view, 'the modern state is grounded intrinsically on the drive to rationalize, unify, and homogenize social relations within its territorial space'.[19]

The direct consequence in sport of this ideological project has been the exclusion of non-national sportsmen in national teams, followed by the introduction of quotas limiting the presence of foreign sportsmen in national clubs. From the 1920s onwards, all major national federations of collective sports had introduced these kinds of restrictions. Having become accustomed to thinking not only in national but also in nationalist terms, sport federations up until this day continue to act to maintain these limitations, even at the risk of infringing rights such as the EU one regarding free movement of workers. Thus, it is not by chance that the free movement of communitarian sportsmen in European Union countries resulted from a juridical decision, the 'Bosman' decree of December 1995, rather than from an internal choice taken by sport bodies.

Sports federations have been intrinsically linked to the project that creates a correspondence between national territories and national societies, and have helped states to attain the objective of building a nationalism grounded in ethnic and cultural homogenization. On an international level, federations worked also to both create and preserve a nation-based reading grid. In 1932, in reaction to the employment of former Argentinean football players in the Italian team, such as Raimundo Orsi and Julio Libonatti, FIFA introduced a new rule according to which each player had to wait at least three years before playing for another national team. In the 1950s, after having been confronted by Laszlo Kubala's case,[20] FIFA introduced a rule, still in force, according to which a player, even if he has dual nationality, cannot play for more than one national team at a senior level. On 17 March 2004, FIFA's Urgency committee decided to forbid the employment in national teams of players that, even if they have received the passport of their host country, have not lived at least two years consecutively in the territory of the football association concerned. This decision followed rumours about a possible recruitment of the Brazilian forward Ailton by the Qatari selection. After different cases of nationality changes through naturalization, the International Olympic Committee in turn decided in 2000 to introduce a period of three years before which a sportsman can compete for his new country.

These examples show that in sport, nationalization is inscribed in an historical trend, which tends towards the preservation of the concept of a nation based on cultural homogeneity rather than pluralism. More recently, apart from ideological convictions according to which a national consciousness is only possible where there exists an ethnic and cultural uniformity, governing bodies of sport also act to preserve national identities for commercial reasons. UEFA's former president Lennart Johansson, for example, declared, 'our game is founded on traditional values, such as the pride in the jersey, national or regional identity and other mixes of social-cultural phenomena that are not financially related. And if television is so interested in football as a product today, it is thanks to these factors. Thus they have to be preserved with care if we want to guarantee a sustainable future for it.'[21]

MIGRATIONS, NATURALIZATIONS AND THE DE-ETHNICIZATION OF THE NATION

The 'label of origin'[22] is omnipresent in modern sports. This label, which is usually represented in the media via the inscription of the code of the nation state for which sportsmen compete, is largely employed not only for collective sports, but also for individual ones, such as, among others, cycling.

Table 7.4.1 is one example of the media's tendency to 'label' sportsmen's results by referring to the national code of the country that they symbolically represent.

Medias [sic] and state officials also encourage the reading of sporting performances on a nation-based grid. Every four years, during the Olympic Games, the total number of the medals won by national teams and athletes serve to elaborate a ranking in which some of the most powerful states in the world usually occupy the top positions. In 2004, this special ranking classified consecutively the United States, China, Russia, Australia, Germany, Japan, France, Italy, South Korea and Great Britain. If the sportsman has dual nationality, the medals he wins cannot be attributed to more than one state. This illustrates sports organizations' incapacity to take into account dual nationalities. The negative perceptions associated with dual nationality are linked to elite sports' ethno-nationalization process described above and, more generally, to the crucial role played by sport in competition between nation states. According to Saskia Sassen: 'the aggressive nationalism and territorial competition among European states in the eighteenth, nineteenth and twentieth centuries made the concept of dual nationality generally undesirable, incompatible with individual loyalties and destabilizing of the international order'.[23] This is also the case in sport. As a consequence, a considerable number of sportsmen have to choose whether they want to compete for their native country or whether they prefer to compete for their adoptive one. As in a state of war, simultaneous loyalty to two countries is simply unthinkable in sport.

Due to the acceleration of migratory flows occurring in the context of globalization, the inability of sports organizations to take into account dual nationalities is rendered problematic.[24] On the one hand, sport is often a means by which young immigrants participate in local societies, which favour their integration. On the other hand, sports organizations do not accept plural identities and oblige dual nationals to choose one nationality over another. States' citizenship models play a crucial role in the management of migratory flows. The waiting period that applicants must adhere to before obtaining the right to be naturalized varies considerably from one country to another. This is true also at a European level. The shortest delay is in Belgium (three years of uninterrupted stay) and the longest is in Liechtenstein (30 years).[25] Similar to the

Table 34.1 Overall Standing of the Tour de France 2005, after the 15th Stage (www.letour.fr)

Pos	*No.*	*Name Surname*	*Team*	*Nat.*	*Gaps*
1	001	ARMSTRONG Lance	DSC	USA	
2	021	BASSO Ivan	CSC	ITA	02 46″
3	057	RASMUSSEN Mickael	RAB	DEN	03 09″
4	011	ULLRICH Jan	TMO	GER	05 58″
5	031	MANCEBO Francisco	IBA	ESP	06 31″
6	164	LEIPHEIMER Levi	GST	USA	07 35″
7	066	LANDIS Floyd	PHO	USA	09 33″
8	019	VINOKOUROV Alexandre	TMO	KAZ	09 38″
9	101	MOREAU Christophe	C.A	FRA	11 47″
10	014	KLÖDEN Andréas	TMO	GER	12 01″

latter country, the right to nationality in Switzerland is based on *ius sanguinis.*[26] Foreign people, even if they are born on national soil, have to wait 12 years before being eligible to apply for nationality. Despite this, in the under 20-year-old Swiss national football team that participated in the 2005 World Cup in the Netherlands, nine players out of 11 had foreign origins. National coach Bernard Challandes declared that 'instead of discriminating against players with foreign origins, we must promote them and do everything that we can do to convince them to choose to play for the Swiss team'.[27] Germany, another country where the right to nationality is grounded in *ius sanguinis*, tends also to employ a growing number of foreign-born sportsmen. In 2001, Gerald Asamaoah, a Ghanaian-born forward, became the first black player to play for a German football team. In June 2005, during the Confederation Cup, the German national trainer Jürgen Klinsmann asserted that 'to open national teams to immigrants' sons is important. It gives a better image of our country.'[28] These changes in the conception of who can be part of the 'national' indicate the existence of a trend towards a de-ethnicization of the nation. This process is accelerated by the fact that professional sport itself stimulates migrations, sometimes on a global scale.[29] A considerable number of sportsmen migrating for sport-related reasons are confronted with the dilemma of changing nationality, such as in the well-documented Wilson Kipketer case.[30]

During major sporting competitions, States' and national federations' authorities try to reinforce their selection by naturalizing athletes. In France's case, every four years, before the Olympic Games, a special department of the national Olympic and sport committee select and submit to the international Olympic executive committee a list of sportsmen that France wishes to naturalize. For the 2004 Olympic Games, 270 naturalized athletes were present (2.7 per cent of the total). Detailed statistics show that most of them have grown up in less well off countries and actually compete for more powerful States. Indeed, the balance in naturalizations on a continental or subcontinental scale is positive for Western Europe (+ 67), America (+ 22) and Oceania (+ 12) and negative for Eastern Europe (–47), Africa (–36) and Asia (–18).[31]

In football, the final example of an instrumentalized naturalization attempt occurred shortly before the 2006 World Cup, in the case of Salomon Kalou. The Dutch national trainer Marco Van Basten, wishing to convoke the Ivorian forward of Feyenoord Rotterdam, encouraged him to ask for a new passport. Finally, after a long juridical battle, the immigration minister Rita Verdonk refused his request. This is not always the case. Indeed, some countries have allowed exceptions for sportsmen regarding the right to nationality. In Slovenia, for example, a special law has been passed in order to make possible naturalizations of celebrities such as artists or sportsmen. Since then, 93 persons have obtained a Slovenian passport. Most of them did not have any Slovenian origins, as in the case of the former Jamaican sprinter Marlene Ottey or the former Austrian skier Josef Strobl. Speaking about the latter example, the head of Slovenian international cooperation, Zoran Verovnik, maintained that 'ski professionals supported his candidacy for Slovenian citizenship. We trust the opinion of the individual sport branch. If the sportsman wins several times, this is a good promotion for the State.'[32]

A much better known case in comparison with the examples cited above has been that of the nationality change of the former Kenyan runner, Stephen Cherono. In 2003, just before the World championships, the pre-eminent specialist of the 3,000 meters steeple agreed to become Qatari and to change his name to Saif Saïd Shaheen. He admitted having made this choice for financial reasons. Qatari officials promised him a life pension of 1,000 dollars per month. Shortly after the naturalization, his agent, the Briton Ricky Simms, confirmed that Cherono 'will continue to live between London and Kenya, even if the Qatari federation puts a house at his disposal'.[33] Another East African runner, the former Ethiopian Zanebech Tola, who first unsuccessfully sought asylum in Switzerland, finally decided to accept the proposal of adopting Bahrain nationality. On 26 January 2005, a messenger from the Bahrain National Youth and Sport's Ministry came to Geneva to reach an agreement with her. She finally flew to Bahrain after being promised 1,100 euros per month and a special award of 80,000 euros. She actually lives in Switzerland and runs for Bahrain under the name of Mariam Jamal.

These brief examples show that there is an increasing tendency in modern sport competitions to include in the 'national body' sportsmen who, because of their origins, do not correspond to the historical ethnic composition of the citizens of the state for which they compete. These instrumental and commercial naturalizations occurring without sportsmen putting down roots in their new homeland challenge the traditional vision of the nation as a group of people belonging to the same culture and having the same ethnic origin. If in the past sport has contributed to the historical construction of a correspondence between the State and a specific 'national culture', nowadays, the study of sport helps to highlight the historical character of this construction. While it is undeniable that football still 'offers the possibility for nationhood to be represented through (. . .) fixed archetypes', it can also be considered as a platform from 'which the circumscriptions of the national body politic—particularly in terms of race—can be breached'.[34] The 'Black-Blanc-Beur' French football national team is perhaps the best example to illustrate this.

The case of rugby is an excellent instance that reveals an incipient process consisting of a progressive dissociation between nationality and citizenship in sport. Many authors have underlined that the historical project of the nation state in most European countries has been to link the rights granted to citizens with the holding of the requisite nationality. Thus, nationality has become a key component of citizenship and the two concepts tend to converge.[35] In the cases of the above-mentioned naturalization of sportsmen, the acquisition of nationality remains a prerequisite condition to have the right to represent a State, but this is no longer the case in rugby. The international rugby board now permits the employment of up to three foreign players at any one time. Even if their employment is conditional on them having played for at least three years in their 'country of adoption' and not having already played for the national team of their country of origin, these new rugby rules on nationality could prefigure a revolution in the world of sport. In fact, the incorporation into the national team is here partially disconnected from the nationality of the sportsman, giving rise to a sport citizenship, which is not based on nationality.

[. . .]

WORLDWIDE SPORTING STARS, TRANSNATIONAL ADOPTION AND IDENTITY DETERRITORIALIZATION

This essay evokes the relationship between the global mediatization of sporting events arising from developments in telecommunications and the resulting changes in identification processes. Competitions can be viewed worldwide much more easily than in the past. For example, the most important football matches of European clubs are regularly broadcast live on all continents.

As a consequence, sportsmen have become worldwide stars. Because sport is an activity in which the identification process has a very important emotional aspect,[36] the possibility to follow a competition or a match live throughout the world is a major factor in increasing the geographical areas of people affected by the event. Thus, identification appears to become less subject to state borders and territorial criteria. In an article based on the example of Norwegian fans of English clubs, Hognestad suggests that, 'as a hugely popular phenomenon in Norway, football becomes interesting as a possible generator of identities that are liberated from the role of carrying its key national symbols', and that 'the attraction of English football provides a possible creative space of hybridization, in which the geographical distance itself generates options for a more liberated and imaginative playing with identities'.[37] Bourgeois and Whitson explain the identification with geographically distant clubs by the growing overlap between sport events and promotional activity: 'the owners of teams look for bigger markets and woo rich consumers and corporate bodies'. There is a resulting deterritorialization of identities that is closely linked to the capitalist system. Within this type of society, 'the identity is expressed by the choices available to consumers' and no longer by 'a feeling of belonging to a place' or by 'any implication in a collective destiny'.[38] Following a similar train of thought, Giulianotti and Robertson draw an analogy between big European football teams and trans-national corporations (TNCs), and evoke the existence of 'deterritorialized communities of global consumers' underlining that 'transnational clubs like Manchester United, Juventus and Bayern Munich have global communities of supporters and merchandise consumers that are similar in size, if not patterns of identification, with the citizenry of nations'. In their view, these football communities, that they call 'self-invented virtual diasporas', 'are forged from the global dispersal of club-focused images and products, and from the voluntaristic identification of individuals with club-related symbols and practices'.[39]

From the points of view of the authors cited above, the identification of Japanese supporters with European clubs, for example, is primarily linked to the marketing politics pursued by these clubs. Players are transformed into commercial products and are called upon to play the role of mediators between the supporter and the team for which they play, in order to encourage the allegiance of the former to the latter. As a consequence, the resulting identification with the club is not inscribed in a territorial reading grid. The identity that emerges does not operate through clubs representing cities, regions or countries, but by the personal identification with stars that are part of a global star system. For example, supporters do not follow Real Madrid because it is a Spanish club, but because the team had strongly publicized players such as David Beckham in the squad. Because of this, before his move from Manchester United to Real Madrid, Reuter's correspondent in Asia, Jason Szep, asserted, 'the allegiance of millions of Asian fans is likely to move with him'.[40]

The increasing spatial reach of sports broadcasting gives rise to a pluralization of the ways in which people identify with modern sporting heroes. Besides the label of origin, other criteria of identification appear, such as, among others, aesthetic, lifestyle, biographical or behavioural ones. By stating this, the objective is not to deny the importance of territorial aspects in the identification processes to sportsmen and teams, but to show that these aspects are less and less important when taken into account. Concepts such as deterritorialization and denationalization allow us to shed light upon phenomena that have been ignored in the past. For example, if the transnational adoption of foreigners is inscribed in football's history, these players having very often represented the best expression of talent and fantasy, only a few studies exist on the cultural meaning of this acceptance.

In 2005, the Argentinean Diego Armando Maradona returned to Naples almost 15 years after his departure. More than 70,000 hysterical people attended the match in which he participated in the San Paolo stadium. More than any Neapolitan player, Maradona has been adopted and adored by Neapolitan fans who have elevated him to cult status. This devotion dates back to the 1980s, when Maradona enabled SSC Naples to win two Italian championships and, above all, to take an historical revenge against the well-off clubs of the wealthy northern cities of the Peninsula, Milan and Turin. During the semi-final of the 1990 World Cup played between Italy and Argentina in Naples, many Neapolitans preferred to support Argentina instead of Italy, which resulted in an increase in the historical tensions existing between the Southern and Northern parts of the country. Maradona's case merits particular attention because it shows that, in the context of a growing migratory circulation of sportsmen, the geographical origin of the latter is not a hindrance to identification. On the contrary, the individual identification with a foreign sporting star can sometimes surpass the criterion of national belonging when it comes to choosing which team to support.

[. . .] In terms of identities, denationalization can be defined as the loss of importance of the label of origin in the identification process with sportsmen and teams. The decreasing impact of the label of origin reflects the growing disconnection between identities and territories. This disjuncture[41] is linked to the migratory movements of people, both inside and outside professional sport, and to the development of global media. Occurring at every geographical level, from the national to the local, this disconnection induces deterritorialization.

CONCLUSION

Even if they continue to support ethnic nationalisms and the division of the world into nation states, sporting competitions can also play an opposite role by promoting a double movement of denationalization. Firstly, the integration of sportsmen of foreign origin in the national selections of their host countries, coupled with the global circulation of sports workers and the naturalizations linked to these migrations, favour the acknowledgement of a cultural pluralism within countries and encourage a de-ethnicization of the nation through sport. The appearance of a sporting citizenship in rugby not directly related to nationality shows that sport could even play an avant-garde role regarding denationalization. While leading sport authorities are still accustomed to thinking in state-national reading grid terms, they are also concerned with issues linked to nationality that occur outside of this framework. [. . .] The idea of creating a 'special independent commission' that could allow athletes to compete for a country without having the national passport would go some way towards dealing with the intensification of mobility of professional sportsmen.

Secondly, the worldwide diffusion of the sports spectacle heralded by the development of global media has stimulated a new playing with identities, resulting in spectators becoming interested in countries or areas that are sometimes very distant from their home. This also makes possible the transnational allegiance of supporters to global stars whose label of national origin doesn't play a key role in the process of identification. As an activity that is part of a worldwide popular culture, sport assumes here the role of precursor in the identity deterritorialization process challenging the postulate according to which there exists a perfect correspondence between a state, a territory and an individual identity. [. . .] By resituating the state-national reading grid of sport, which is often regarded as a given, into its historical context of genesis and development, its socially constructed nature becomes apparent. This should enable us to consider contemporary changes in the representation of the nation through sport as part of an evolution occurring within a broader, nonlinear historical process, which previously had the tendency to ethnicize the nation and to territorialize identities and which actually tends to de-ethnicize the first and deterritorialize the second.

NOTES

1. Wimmer and Glick Schiller, 'Methodological Nationalism and Beyond. Nation-State Building. Migration, and the Social Sciences'.
2. Brenner, 'Beyond State-Centrism? Space, Territoriality, and Geographical Scale in Globalization Studies', 45.
3. Robertson, *Globalization: Social Theory and Global Culture.*
4. Brenner, 'Beyond State-Centrism?', 52.
5. Sassen, 'Globalization or Denationalization?', 15.
6. Boniface, *La terre est ronde comme un ballon. Geopolitique du football.*
7. Maguire *et al.*, 'The War of the Words? Identity Politics in Anglo-German Press Coverage of EURO 96'.
8. Anderson, *Imagined Communities: Reflections on the Origin and Spread of Nationalism.*
9. Duke and Crolley, *Football, Nationality and the State*, 4.
10. Habermas, *Apres I'Etat-nation: une nouvelle constellation politique;* Appadurai, 'Global Ethnoscopes. Notes and Queries for a Transnational Anthroplogy'; Soysal, *Limits of Citizenship; Migrants and Postnational Membership in Europe; Beck, What is Globalization?;* Sassen, 'The Repositioning of Citizenship: Toward New Types of Subjects and Spaces for Polities',
11. Armstrong and Giulianotti, 'Introducing Global Football Oppositions'.
12. The first international match recorded was played between England and Scotland in 1872.
13. Armstrong and Giulianotti, 'Introducing Global Football Oppositions', 2.
14. Papa and Panico, *Storia sociale del ealcio in Italia*, 73.
15. Lanfranchi, 'Football, cosmopolitisme et nationalisme'.
16. Holt and Mason, 'Le football, le fascisme et la politique étrangère britannique: l'Angleterre, 1'Italic et I'Allemagne (1934–1935)', 79 and 89.
17. Arnaud, 'Des jeux de la victoire aux jeux de la paix? (1919–1924)', 135.
18. Schnapper, 'De l'Etat-nation au monde transnational. Du sens et de l'utilité du concept de diaspora'.
19. In Brenner, 'Beyond State-Centrism?, 49.
20. Laszlo Kubala was born in 1927 in Hungary to a Hungarian father and a Czech mother. He first played for the Hungarian national team. During the Second World War he moved to Czechoslovakia and played for the Czech national team. In 1949, he moved to Spain, where he received political asylum. He obtained Spanish nationality in 1952 and he also played for the national team. However, FIFA did not allow him to play for Spain in the qualifiers for the 1954 World Cup.
21. *I Quaderni del calcio*, 3, Second trimester 1999.
22. Calmat, 'Sport et nationalisme'.
23. Sassen,' The Repositioning of Citizenship', 3.
24. Papastergiadis, *The Turbulence of Migration, Globalization, Deterritorialization and Hybridity.*
25. Clarke *et al.*, 'New Europeans: Naturalisation and Citizenship in Europe', 49; Weil, 'L'accès à la citoyenneté. Unc comparaison de vingt-cinq lois sur la nationalité'.
26. Piguet, *L'immigration ans Suisse. 50 ans d'entrouverture.*
27. Personal interview, February 2003.
28. *Guerin Sportivo*, 27 (1554), 5–11 July 2005.
29. Lanfranchi and Taylor, *Moving with the Ball. The Migration of Professional Footballers;* Poli, *Les migrations internationales des footballeurs;* Bale and Maguire (eds), *The Global Sports Arena: Athletic Talent Migration in an Interdependent World.*
30. Poli, 'Conflit de couleurs. Enjeux géopolitiques autour de la naturalisation de sportifs africains'.

31. Gillon and Poli, 'Naturalisation de sportifs et fruite des muscles. Le cas des Jeux Olympiques de 2004'.
32. *Courrier des Balkans,* 9 January 2005 (www.balkans.eu.org).
33. *Le Monde,* 17–18 August 2003.
34. Back *et al. The Changing Face of Football.* 270.
35. Sassen, 'The Participation of States and Citizens in Global Governance'; Sassen, 'The Repositioning of Citizenship'; Courtois, 'Habermas et la question du nationalisme: le cas du Québec'; Déloye, 'Le débat contemporain sur la citoyennété au prisme de la construction européenne'.
36. Bromberger, 'Se poser en s'opposant. Variations sur les antagonismes footballistiques de Marseille a Téhéran'.
37. Hognestad, 'Long-distance Football Support and Liminal Identities among Norwegian Fans', 97 and 108.
38. Bourgeois and Whitson, 'Le sport, les médias et la marchandisation des identities', 157 and 160.
39. Giulianotti and Robertson, 'The Globalization of Football: A Study in the Glocalization of the "Serious Life'", 551.
40. Reuters, 13 June 2003.
41. Appadurai, 'Disjuncture and Difference in the Global Culture Economy'.

REFERENCES

Anderson, B. *Imagined Communities: Reflections on the Origin and Spread of Nationalism.* London: Verso, 1983.

Appadurai, A. 'Disjuncture and Difference in the Global Culture Economy'. *Theory. Culture, and Society 7* (1990): 295–310.

Appadurai, A. "Global Ethnoscapes. Notes and Queries for a Transnational Anthroplogy." In *Recapturing Anthropology. Working in the Present,* edited by R. G. Fox. Santa Fe: School of American Research Pr., 1991: 191–210.

Armstrong, G. and R. Giulianotti. "Introducing Global Football Oppositions." In *Fear and Loathing in World Football,* edited by G. Armstrong and R. Giulianotti. Oxford: Berg, 2001: 1–5.

Arnaud, P. "Des jeux de la victoire aux jeux de la paix? (1919–1924)." In *Sport et relations Internationales,* edited by P. Arnaud and A. Wahl. Metz: Universite de Metz, 1994: 133–55.

Back, I., T. Crabbe and J. Solomos. *The Changing Face of Football. Racism, Identity and Multicultture in the English Game.* Oxford: Berg, 2001.

Bale, I. and J. Maguire (eds). *The Global Sports Arena: Athletic Talent Migration in an Interdependent World.* London: Frank Cass, 1994.

Boniface, P. *La terre est ronde comme un ballon. Géopolitique du football.* Paris: Seuil, 2002.

Bourgeois, N. and D. Whitson. 'Le sport, les médias et la marchandisation des identitiés', *Sociologie et sociétés* 27, no, 1 (1999): 151–63.

Brenner, N. 'Beyond State-Centrism? Space, Territoriality, and Geographical Scale in Globalization Studies'. *Theory and Society* 28, no. 1 (1999): 39–78.

Bromberger, C. 'Se poser en s'opposant. Variations sur les antagonismes footballistiques de Marseille à Téhéran'. In *Football et identités. Les sentiments' appartenance en question,* edited by R. Poli. Neuchâtel: CIES, 2005: 35–55.

Calmat, A. 'Sport et nationalisme'. *Pouvoirs,* 61 (1992): 51–6.

Clarke, J., E. van Dam and L. Gooster. 'New Europeans: Naturalisation and Citizenship in Europe'. *Citizenship Studies 2,* no. 1 (1998): 43–54.

Courtois, S. "Habermas et la question du nationalisme: le cas du Québec." *Philosophiques* 27, no. *2* (2000): 377–401.

Déloye, Y. 'Le débat contemporain sur la citoyenneté au prisme de la construction européenne'. *Etudes européennes* (www.etudes-europennes.fr), (2004): 1–9.

Duke, V. and L. Crolley. *Football, Nationality and the State.* London: Addison Wesley Longman, 1996.

Gillon, P. and R. Poli. 'Naturalisation de sportifs et fuite des muscles. Le cas des Jeux Olympiques de 2004'. In *Sport et nationalité. Enjeux et problèmes,* edited by D. Oswald. Neuchátel: CIES Editions (2007): 47–72.

Giulianotti, R. and R. Robertson. "The Globalization of Football: A Study in the Glocalization of the "Serious Life"." *British Journal of Sociology* 55, no. 4 (2004): 545–568.

Habermas, J. *Aprés I'Etat-nation: une nouvelle constellation politique.* Paris: Fayard, 2000.

Hognestad, H. "Long-distance Football Support and Liminal Identities among Norwegian Fans." In *Sport, Dance and Embodied Identities,* edited by N. Dyck and E. Archetti. Oxford: Berg, 2003, pp. 97–113.

Holt, R. and T. Mason. 'Le football, le fascisme et la politique étrangère britannique: 1'Angleterre, l'Italie et l'Allemagne (1934–1935)'. In *Sport et relations internationales,* edited by P. Arnaud and A. Wahl. Metz: Université de Metz, 1994: 73–95.

Lanfranchi, P. "Football, cosmopolitisme et nationalisme." *Pouvoir* 10 (2002): 15–25.

Lanfranchi, P. and M. Taylor. *Moving with the Ball. The Migration of Professional Footballers,* Oxford: Berg, 2001.

Maguire, J., E. Poulton and C. Possamai. 'The War of the Words? Identity Politics in Anglo-German Press Coverage of EURO 96'. *European Journal of Communication* 14, no. 1 (1999): 61–89 Berg, 2001.

Papa, A. and G. Panico. *Storia sociale del calcio in Italia.* Bologna: II Mulino, 2002.

Papastergiadis, N. *The Turbulence of Migration. Globalization, Deterritorialization and Hybridity.* Cambridge: Polity Press, 2000.

Piguet, E. *L'immigration en Suisse. 50 ans d'entrouverture.* Lausanne: Presses polytechnique; et universitaires romandes, 2004.

Poli, R. *Les migrations internationales des footballeurs. Trajectoires de joueurs camerounais en Suisse.* Neuchátel: CIES, 2004.

Poli, R. 'Conflit de couleurs. Enjeux géopolitiques autour de la naturalisation de sportifs africains'. *Auirepart,* 37 (2006): 149–61.

Robertson, R. *Globalization: Social Theory and Global Culture.* London: Sage, 2002.

Sassen, S. "Globalization or Denationalization?" *Review of International Political Economy* 10, no. 1 (2003): 1–22.

Sassen, S. 'The Participation of States and Citizens in Global Governance'. *Indiana Journal of Global Legal Studies* 10, no. 5 (2003): 5–28.

Sassen, S. 'The Repositioning of Citizenship: Toward New Types of Subjects and Spaces for Politics'. *Campbell Public. Affairs Institute* (www.campbellinstitute.org), (2004): 1–15.

Schnapper, D. 'De I'Etat-nation au monde transnational. Du sens et de lutilité du concept de diaspora'. *Revue Européenne des Migrations Internationales* 17, no. 2 (2001): 9–36.

Soysal, Y. *Limits of Citizenship: Migrants and Postnational Membership in Europe,* Chicago: The University of Chicago, 1994.

Weil, P. "L'accés à la citoyenneté, Unc comparaison de vingt-cinq lois sur la nationalité." *Travaux du centre d'études et de prévision du Ministre de I'Intérieur* (2002): 9–28.

Wimmer, A. and N. Glick Schiller. "Methodological Nationalism and Beyond. Nation-State Building, Migration, and the Social Sciences." *Global Networks* 2, no. 4 (2002): 301–34.

CHAPTER 35

The Global and the Local in our Contemporary Sports Cultures

Andrei S. Markovits

In his singularly impressive and important work, *Guns, Germs and Steel: The Fates of Human Societies,* Jared Diamond demonstrates more convincingly than anybody in my opinion why Europe "won," or put differently, why it was this relatively small archipelago, appended to a huge Asian landmass thumbing into the Atlantic Ocean, that created the preconditions and the fundamentals for a system of society, governance, warfare, economy, and culture that was to conquer the rest of the world. Best known under the term "capitalism," the search for and analysis of its origins and nature gave rise to virtually every discipline of what we have come to know as the social sciences. And capitalism's trials and tribulations continue to nurture them. In his own magnum opus, *The Modern World System,* Immanuel Wallerstein analyzes capitalism's rise to a "world system" by assigning it a core, a semi-periphery, and also a periphery. To no one's surprise, capitalism's core rests in the northwestern part of the Atlantic Ocean anchored in the Low Countries and, most important, Great Britain.

Few, if any, items have confirmed Wallerstein's conceptual framework more powerfully and lastingly than the world of sports, with the possible exception of the English language's becoming the global lingua franca. By transforming previously local and disorganized games into rule-driven and institution-bound novel entities, and by exporting this to its empire's (and the world's) semi-peripheries and peripheries, sports developed into one of Britain's most lasting contributions to our global civilization. Of the many sports that Britain bequeathed to the world, none became more globally successful than the game of Association football, best known to Americans, Australians and others by the term "soccer" which constitutes an Oxbridge colloquial abbreviation of the more cumbersome "Association" and denotes this kicking code of the family of football games as opposed to its running codes of Rugby Union, Rugby League, American and Canadian football. The term "football" came to signify each culture's dominant code. Thus, in America, football means its American version just like in New Zealand it implies Rugby Union whereas in New South Wales it stands for Rugby League and in neighboring Victoria Australian Rules. Thus, the term soccer is ubiquitously used in every culture in which a rival football code emerged hegemonic in the course of the past 150 years. For the purposes of this analysis, I will conform to the American vernacular by referring to the game of Association football as "soccer" rather than by the globally more common "football" which in the United States denotes a related but different game.

Soccer's global success can best be gauged by the following three developments: first, the game penetrated the world's most distant peripheries and is played literally everywhere on earth; second, one of its semi-peripheries, meaning continental Europe, soon joined the motherland in becoming the core of this game, where it continues to reside to this day; and third, the other semi-periphery, namely Latin America, developed decidedly into the core's equal as far as the quality of its game and players have been concerned, yet simply never attained a level of capitalism to compete with Europe's becoming the unquestioned core of global soccer. Thus, not by chance, hundreds of Latin American players, led by the continent's superstars, ply their trade in Europe with virtually no European of any significance playing in Latin America.

One of Britain's former semi-peripheries was to emerge as a burgeoning core in its own right in the course of the nineteenth century, precisely the era when Britain introduced sports to the world. But as a semi-periphery that had successfully surpassed the British core and that busily and self-consciously was forging itself into a bigger and more powerful one, the United States remained largely impervious to Britain's sports exports. Still, America accepted them briefly only to convert them into its self-contained systems where they developed into languages all their own. Of course, these American sports continued to share essential commonalities with their British relatives in that both featured all the essential attributes of being profoundly modern constructs. Moreover, in the first (1860–1914) and the second (1990–present) globalization, the sports worlds across the Atlantic helped create forms of "cosmopolitan citizenship." They developed new transnational bonds and languages reaching far beyond their respective shores. The "best of the best" evolved into popular icons that enjoy global recognition. Still, while the deeper structures of the two sports worlds on either side of the Atlantic share great similarities in form and content, and both have spawned global players, their actual expressions and their hegemonic manifestations—their languages—remain divergent for good.

My concern in this essay pertains solely to the world of these two cores: on the one hand Europe-centered soccer; on the other hand the America-centered Big Four of baseball, football, basketball, and hockey. What matters most to me, however, is capturing the interaction of these cores in their personae as semi-peripheries (even peripheries), which is exactly what their relationship has been in the realm of sports cultures for more than one hundred years. America has been peripheral to Europe's core in soccer and continues to exhibit every aspect of such a relationship, as amply depicted by Wallerstein and other "dependency" theorists. The best American players have to go to Europe to play at the highest level of the game and to make the most money because the best teams and the best leagues are in Europe, as is the highest remuneration for players. Simply put, the greatest weight of the game, its core, its best-of-the best, remains firmly in Europe.

The exact obverse pertains to the Big Four. The very best basketball players come to America, as do the very best hockey players. The best leagues are in America, and the most money is there as well. Again, there is no doubt that the greatest weight of these games, their core, their best of the best, continues to reside in America. America, of course, furnishes the uncontested core in baseball, with Japan, the Caribbean, South Korea, Taiwan, Australia, and a few other countries assuming the role of semi-periphery. Much of Europe is relegated to the game's periphery although Holland, Italy, and Russia have made recent strides possibly qualifying them as members of the "more advanced" semi-periphery. American football constitutes the lone outlier among these sports in that it enjoys no meaningful concentric circles outside the United States in terms of the game's production side, though it most certainly has both ample semi-peripheries and peripheries in the successful consumption of its American-based products—ranging from its jerseys to its televised games, with the Super Bowl having actually developed into a globally followed television event very much denoting the powers accorded to a true core.

There is thus no question that the semi-peripheral roles of Europe in American sports and America in Europe's have substantially gained in stature in the course of what I have come to call the second globalization. And there can also be no question that each side will do its best to succeed in the other's core. Moreover, in China and other "new" areas currently "in play," there is little doubt that the two cores have entered the contest to attain major footholds in these open spaces and have assigned substantial resources to render these places—with China being the real prize—into a semi-periphery beholden to their particular core. But pursuant to the immense changes wrought by the second globalization, it would not be surprising to witness the mutation of formerly peripheral and semi-peripheral regions into core ones. For example, in the world of soccer, countries that until the new global age were on the fringes of the game's periphery, such as Australia, Japan, the two Koreas and China, have with little doubt made major progress that puts them well on the road to enter the game's core in the next two to three decades.

One need not be a committed Marxist to realize that the two most powerful capitalist entities of this world, North America and Europe, battle each other in their own backyards just as they do in these newly available spaces. Moreover, it is quite evident that money has played a very important role in the increasing commercialization of these sports cultures on the global level. Thus, *SportsBusiness Journal* estimates that the annual organized global sports industry is as large as $213 billion. This figure includes all economic activities that are ancillary to sports themselves, such as advertising, media contracts, gambling facilities, construction projects, operating expenses, transportation, and lodging. Taking slightly less encompassing categories into consideration, the accounting firm Deloitte & Touche estimates that the entire English Premier League, far and away the richest soccer league in the world, received revenue in excess of $2.3 billion in 2006–7 (with its debt being much higher). Reports by MLB Commissioner Bud Selig had Major League Baseball enjoying over $6 billion in revenue in 2007. The NFL's annual revenue for 2005 was nearly $6 billion as well. And the noted sports economist Andrew Zimbalist estimates that the annual revenue of all the Big Four North American sports amounts to around $15 billion. Furthermore, the nearly $2 billion price tag for teams like the New York Yankees, the Dallas Cowboys, the Washington Redskins, Manchester United, and Real Madrid, is anything but trivial and has grown precipitously during the era of the second globalization. Thus, Takeo Spikes, the eloquent linebacker for the San Francisco 49ers, was spot on when he said in November 2008, "I always tell today's young quarterbacks who enter our League that with their arm and brain and legs, they are actually in charge of a one billion dollar plus corporation. Because it is clear that any professional football team's ultimate worth is decided by its quarterback's overall performance, quarterbacks in essence have the fate of their team's value on their shoulders."

I do not need to belabor the fact that global players plying their trade in the top leagues on both sides of the Atlantic have reached heights in their remuneration that were unimaginable only two decades ago, let alone five, when, for example, most players contesting that legendary Baltimore Colts vs. New York Giants NFL championship game on December 28, 1958 had to tend to their "regular" day jobs during the off-season to supplement their income from football, which only paid very few stars the kind of money that accorded them a comfortable lifestyle. Identical patterns pertained to basketball, baseball, and hockey in America as in European soccer. There were a few rich individual sports stars prior to the second globalization—for example, Babe Ruth, who made more money than the president of the United States, at least for one season. But collectively, players in top leagues have only attained anything resembling wealth in recent decades.

Let us not forget that these much-maligned mega-salaries of our era also bespeak the victory of a merit-based cosmopolitanism that rewards the very best performances completely irrespective of their producers' social backgrounds. These new player migrants are not only expressions of the second globalization. They also help create transnational publics and cosmopolitan communications beyond the confines of the nation-state. And they are instrumental in promoting diversity and cultural cosmopolitanism "from below," that is cultural change and diversity accepted by "the masses." We witness this on the local level. Over time, players who make their team better, no matter their origins, are loved even by a team's most ardent "localist" fan community and, at least if they succeed, are seen to be "worth every penny." If a player's performance pleases a team's fans, then the alleged exorbitance of his salary bears no adverse sentiments whatsoever. Ditto with doping, best demonstrated by the fact that fans readily forgave self-admitted or suspected culprits provided their performance helped the team win on the field, ultimately the only measure that truly matters to sports fans the world over. Just think how Alex Rodriguez (one of the highest-paid athletes in the world and an admitted user of performance-enhancing drugs) mutated from pariah to hero for Yankee fans in a matter of months solely by virtue of his accomplishments on the baseball diamond that contributed to the Yankees' winning their 27th World Championship. (Truth be told, fans ultimately do not much worry about the money that the players make or the type of substances that they inject or ingest as long as these players perform to the best of their abilities and—most important—thus help their teams win; ditto with all the strikes, lock outs, and corruption scandals that have occurred with constancy on both sides of the Atlantic. The scenario is always identical: Fans are up in arms whenever these disruptions commence and their cause becomes public. But in due course, fans forgive and forget, their passion takes over and fully restores the status quo in which they once again are glued to the issue at hand—following their beloved game and hoping [even against hope] that their team wins in every contest in which it performs.) Rodriguez and culturally diverse players exhibiting rare and much-appreciated skill levels comparable to his in other sports have rendered different communities around the world ever more inclusive. Thus, the handsome reward of top achievement entails a socially inclusive dimension that sports share with few other venues, since the clear-cut criteria of good and bad, successful and unsuccessful, and winning and losing that lie at the very heart of modern sports are much less clear-cut in other endeavors.

The clear-cut nature of sports, the dichotomy between winning and losing, seems to be a major reason for sports' attractiveness to men. In a brilliant scene in the film *White Men Can't Jump*, the character played by Woody Harrelson describes to his girlfriend (played by Rosie Perez) why he loves to play street basketball for money: at the end of every game, there is a clear winner and a clear loser—no ambiguities, no complexities, nothing left unclear. Needless to say, the girlfriend disagrees and tells him that sometimes the winners are losers and vice versa, in other words that reality—even in sports—is much murkier than apparent at first. Of course, the couple splits up.

With all this said, mega-sports still remain puny in their economic dimensions compared to many other industries and commercial activities. I looked at the Fortune 500 largest U.S. corporations and the Global 500 as well. Neither of them lists any sports team. Indeed, on the latter ranking, the last company listed, Fluor, had roughly $17 billion revenue in 2007, which exceeds by $2 billion the entire annual revenue generated by the Big Four sports in America according to the Zimbalist data. On the domestic U.S. list, all of the revenue generated by the Big Four would have weighed in at 170, between the Paccar Company in Bellevue, Washington and Computer Sciences in Falls Church, Virginia. "Even the biggest teams, such as the Yankees, generate revenues of $300 million per year or less. While this is a lot of money, it is only comparable to a large department store. In a typical big league city, a business like this hardly is a blip in the economy. . . . In 2005, the combined revenues that year of the Seahawks . . . the Mariners, and Sonics"—the three top-league professional teams of the Seattle-Tacoma community, the fifteenth largest U.S. metropolitan area comprising a $182 billion economy—"accounted for $449 million—less than one quarter of one percent of total economic activity in the metro area." Even the Green Bay Packers—representing a virtually unique situation in big-league American sports in that this top-notch, arguably most pedigreed, team in professional football calls a community of less than 250,000 its home—have a marginal economic effect. "The team's $194 million revenues represent only 1.5 percent of the surrounding area's $13 billion economy." (See Kevin G. Quinn, *Sports and Their Fans: The History, Economics and Culture of the Relationship Between Spectator and Sport* [Jefferson, NC: McFarland & Company, Inc., Publishers, 2009], p. 26.) Moreover, owners of sports teams do not gauge their investment in terms of monetary rewards but almost solely in the social status and prestige that such ownership and association bestows on them, their entourage, and their community large and small.

I realize that number games of this kind are fraught with inaccuracies and need to be gauged with extreme caution. Still, my point is simple. Sports' most important capital is cultural, political and social, not economic. The power and global attractiveness of their teams and actors have little to do with the wealth and the money involved. Rather, these entities speak to emotions that create a bevy of "bridging" and "bonding" capital that are often competing, yet both are important in the creation and maintenance of key collective identities. As such, sports are much more akin to museums or operas and similar kinds of cultural institutions than to major international corporations, to which they have come to be compared in recent times, wrongly, I believe, both from an empirical as well as a normative viewpoint.

I believe that the disapproval of, even anger toward, the money involved in these global sports—of which the players (rarely, if ever, the team owners, agents or others earning millions off the players' excellence) get the brunt though notably not so much by the fans themselves for whom winning is the only thing that matters but by the public at large—has much to do with their immense popularity and imagined simplicity since, after all, sport is a form of play, and child's play to boot. Whereas millions upon millions of hitherto mainly men have engaged in these sports primarily as children and youngsters, they thus deem themselves experts at something that, after all, cannot be that difficult since not too long ago, they, too, practiced it. Thus, the public on both sides of the Atlantic is much more likely to begrudge sports its commercialization, and global players their huge incomes, as compared to, say, musicians, actors, or any other professionals rewarded for excelling at a métier that appears less facile and common than sports. After all, how difficult can it really be to kick or throw a ball for a living? Indeed, the alleged simplicity of sports serves to discredit them as needing special physical and mental skills. Rarely are sports' exceptional practitioners accorded the honor and esteem bestowed on highly skilled workers, artisans, and artists who deserve to have their labor and product rewarded by whatever the market bears. My experience in the academy convinces me that it is this perceived lack of sophistication that renders so many of my colleagues studiedly ignorant of popular sports.

The put-down of sports as "simple" is also common in the ever-extant inter-sport competition that has heated up between America and Europe, and across the globe, in the course of the second globalization. The discrediting of a foreign rival is often coupled with the newcomer's being boring and not manly enough. How often have I heard all three of these negatives—simple, boring, not tough enough—from fans of the Big Four in their resistance to soccer? Conversely, European soccer fans disparage the Big Four American sports for their lack of toughness—yes, including collision-based American football which, to "real" men, would be played with no padding, like rugby—and, of course, disdain "feminized" American soccer. The powerful attraction of manliness, coupled with a defiant localism that spurns all forms of outside intrusion as "female," "weak," "commodified," and "foreign" provide constant challenges to the "sportization" of sports. Thus, for example, as Maarten Van Bottenburg and Johan Heilbron perceptively demonstrate in their research on "ultimate fighting" and other so-called "No Holds Barred Events," these sports arose precisely as local oppositions to the overruled, overregulated (i.e., overly "sportized" and cosmopolitan) pugilist venues such as boxing, wrestling, and the martial arts. Men wanted to find out who was the last guy standing after a fight with virtually no rules, who was the best of the best so to speak in a rule-less (i.e., "desportized") context not dictated by any outside (i.e., global) authority or any distant bureaucratic federation. They wanted to ascertain who is the best fighter, period, not the best wrestler or boxer or judoka. But once these local contests proved to be popular, they soon became "resportized" in that they spread all over the world which, of course, meant that they acquired rules, regulations, venues, television contracts—once again demonstrating that in our contemporary world, with its speedy and ubiquitous channels of communication, even the most local of discourses quickly attain global dimensions, thus emerging as quintessentially "glocal."

There exists absolutely no compelling reason for the global topography of sports to remain essentially unchanged, since its establishment in the mid to late nineteenth century. After all, why should a world created by English students in elite public schools and at Oxbridge, and the industrial working class of the Midlands, as well as that of their social counterparts in the United States established pretty much at the same time, last forever? Indeed, there exists every reason for the best basketball players to hail from China in, say 2040. And, the Italians and the Dutch might lead the world of baseball by then, and Americans might become the globe's best soccer players after having won the World Cup repeatedly. One could go even further and argue that these very sports languages, which were, after all, creations of a specific time and space, and are thus random, need not persevere forever. Who knows, maybe the real global game will be Quidditch in centuries to come. After all, the world witnessed in 2009 the first Quidditch World Cup video game in which the United States, England, France, Germany, and Scandinavia united as the Nordic Team and played against a joint squad comprising Japan, Spain, Australia, and Bulgaria.

But note, even in this Quidditch World Cup, long-established entities called nation-states formed the key organizational core of the players. Thus, there is ample evidence that the immense cultural resilience and social stamina of this bizarre world established 150 years ago called modern sports will continue to prevail and flourish in the foreseeable future. I agree with Simon Kuper and Stefan Szymanski that by virtue of the second globalization American soccer fans have come to follow and identify with the European core's mega clubs just like British football fans have become totally conversant with the NFL. In a globalized world, real fans follow the best of the best regardless of time and space. But this development has not eliminated affection for and identification with local variants of these top performers such as MLS or even United Soccer League (USL) teams for American soccer fans, and "some bunch of no-hopers playing on a converted rugby field a few miles from your house" in the case of British fans of American football (see Kuper and Szymanski, *Soccernomics*, pp. 177, 178). Far from "crowding out" the second or third-rate local, the best of the best global in fact fosters such developments by giving fans a real live experience to practice and hone their newly acquired language as participants and spectators that they would otherwise only enjoy as television viewers. Thus, for a soccer-loving resident of Utah, being a Real Madrid fan does not obviate one's passion for Real Salt Lake. Instead, the two reinforce each other. Ditto for American football fans in Vienna whose love for the Minnesota Vikings does not displace their affection for the Vienna Vikings but, if anything, strengthens it. The Metropolitan Opera's widely available performances enhance, instead of diminish, the local opera fan's interest in the productions staged by her or his local opera company. The second globalization has widened horizons and has facilitated the reception and appreciation of the best of the best on local levels, but it has not displaced local experiences and identities. Instead, it created new ones that have become congruent with the global as in Real Salt Lake's case with Real Madrid and that of the Vienna Vikings with their namesake in Minnesota. In the course of the second globalization, layers of culture, consciousness, and identities emerged in the topography of sports in Europe and America that were unimaginable before the late 1980s.

Permit me to invoke James Flege's speech-learning model as an apt analogy to what I am trying to convey here. In this model, Flege demonstrates that a person's "phonetic space" becomes committed very early in her or his life and that any acquisition of a new language becomes increasingly difficult because these newcomers will have to fight for room in a construct that has already been occupied. In a sense, not only is the space limited, but even in the areas in which the newcomers might be accommodated, the terrain will have been predisposed by the original language. The later one learns another language, the less possible it becomes to sound native in it. In a study of Italian-English bilinguals who differed in their age of arrival in Canada, Flege found that the earlier in life one arrived in Canada, the less of an Italian accent one had in English. Indeed, it is very rare for anybody to speak a new language, acquired after the age of twelve or thirteen, like a native. One's hearing as well as sound reproduction has been hopelessly compromised by one's native language that continues to shape one's phonetic space for life. This finding is corroborated by onomatopoeia, which curiously is immensely language-specific in its reception and reproduction. Every language renders identical sounds in its own way that is different from other languages, meaning that both our hearing of sounds and their reproduction are particular and local. Thus, even though presumably pigs make identical sounds in German-speaking and English-speaking regions of the world, German-speakers reproduce the pigs' sound as "gruntz, gruntz" whereas English speakers say "oink, oink." Thousands of other examples abound.

This in no way means that one cannot learn to speak, read, and write a new language perfectly and master it even better than its native speakers. It merely means that one's ability to emulate its sounds like a native is severely compromised, actually well-nigh impossible. A comparably rigid path dependence pertains to our world of sports. Every day, baseball speakers become fluent soccer speakers as well as vice versa; and both can, and do, master the languages of basketball or cricket or hockey or rugby. But they will pronounce these newly acquired sports languages with accents that will be unlike a native speaker's—neither better nor worse, just different. In our cacophonous and interconnected world, purity of accents might become as obsolete in the world of sports as it has in many other forms of communication, language included. This is the essence of what Lars Rensmann and I have come to characterize as "cosmopolitanism" in our book *Gaming the World: How Sports are Reshaping Global Politics and Culture* published by Princeton University Press in June of 2010.

Essential to this cosmopolitanism have been the fundamentally democratic and progressive legacies of the 1960s with the unmistakable tendency in all advanced industrial democracies to include the hitherto excluded, to empower the formerly disempowered. Barack Obama is as much testimony to this remarkable societal and cultural transformation as is the fact that nearly 50 percent of law and medical students in the United States are female and that the presidents of such fine universities as Harvard, Princeton, Penn, Brown and Michigan are women. And the struggle is far from over since there are still massive areas in all these democratic societies where the formerly disempowered still constitute little more than tokens. Be it among the tenured professoriate, particularly in subjects belonging to the STEM fields of science, technology, engineering, and mathematics; or among CEOs and CFOs of large and powerful companies; women continue to be underrepresented. But the thrust of the struggle remains crystal clear: full inclusion on equal terms.

And yet, there is one domain in which the modus operandi and ultimate aim have been "separate but equal" from the very beginning: sports, particularly the dominant team sports that are not only performed on a popular basis but also avidly followed. Short of certain religions (an arena in which, too, the struggle for equality has had some remarkable successes), one would be hard put to point to *any* institution of such importance in our society in which such "sexual apartheid" (to use Paul Hoch's apt terminology though I prefer "gender apartheid") is not only tolerated but actively enforced, perhaps even feted as progress.

To be sure, Title IX's empowering legacy and major contribution to the inclusive and thus democratizing process hailing from the late 1960s, is nothing short of transformative, indeed revolutionary. Just think of the national prominence of the University of Connecticut's women's basketball team or that of the United States women's national team in soccer to mention just two of many other relevant examples. And yet, Title IX and its empowering legacy merely aspired to a situation of "separate but equal" in the culturally crucial world of sports.

Why have few, if any, feminists—at least to my knowledge—never demanded that the quarterback position of the Green Bay Packers, the point guard of the Los Angeles Lakers, and one of the closers for the New York Yankees be occupied by a woman the way they have successfully asked that university presidents, doctors, lawyers, mathematicians, chess players, even presidents of the United States, be women? Or why have there not been any movements afoot to change the rules to have every football team consist of six men and five women (or vice versa) in effect making them into mixed-gender teams like the Dutch game of "korfball," a kind of basketball played by four men and four women on the same team in which, however, only men can guard men and women can play against women thus in essence perpetuating the gender apartheid within this game itself?

I am, of course, talking only about sports at the top level, not in amateur leagues in which we have indeed observed a large degree of integration since the late 1960s and early 1970s. Just think of the thorough gender integration of intramural sports teams on many college campuses. But why do we make such a discriminatory exception for the highest echelons of sports, i.e. the world of the physical that we would never tolerate in the world of the mental or intellectual or political? The equivalent in education would be for us to foster gender-integrated elementary and secondary schools, but then only allow men to enter and compete in the top universities with women relegated to lesser institutions even though the value of their effort in terms of degrees or championships attained would be nominally equal; or, to offer an analogy from the world of politics, women only permitted to run for state and local though not for national offices.

Does the logic of citius, altius, fortius—swifter, higher, stronger—by definition exact our currently practiced and legitimately perceived sexual apartheid at the very top level of sports since the most accomplished men will always run faster, jump higher, and be stronger than the most accomplished women? If we continue to define "the best," which is such an integral part of any sport, by our current criteria, then this separate but equal world will never change. But if we construct alternate logics to what constitutes "the best"—include metrics of cooperation and style, for example, in computing winners and losers, or create truly gender-integrated teams in which the women's output would be weighted more heavily (e.g. assign five points to baskets scored by female players as opposed to the two by males) thereby creating real incentives to have the women be welcomed as positive additions to these teams, as has been the case in the aforementioned intramural contests—then we might actually arrive at a truly integrated sports world which would thus be congruent with virtually all important public institutions of our contemporary democratic world. It is only with such a major reform that the cosmopolitan powers of sports cultures would truly attain their well-deserved potential.

FURTHER READING

Kuper, S., & Szymanski, S. 2009. *Soccernomics: Why England loses, why Germany and Brazil win, and why the United States, Japan, Australia, Turkey—and even Iraq—are destined to become the Kings of the World's most popular sport.* New York: Nation Books.

Kurasawa, F. 2004. A cosmopolitanism from below: Alternative globalization and the creation of solidarity without bounds. *European Journal of Sociology*, 45(2), 233–255.

Teed, K. C., Delpy-Neirotti, L., Johnson, S. R., & Seguin, B. 2009. The marketing of a NHL hockey team.

International Journal of Sport Management and Marketing, 5(1–2), 226–246.

Van Bottenburg, M., & Heilbron, J. 2006. De-sportization of fighting contests: The origins of no holds barred events and the theory of sportization. *International Review for the Sociology of Sport*, 41(3–4), 259–282.

Walley, A. C. 2007. Speech learning, lexical reorganization and the development of word recognition by native and non-native English-speakers. In O.-S. Bohn & M. J. Munro (Eds.), *Language experience in second language speech learning: In honor of James Emil Flege* (pp. 315–330). Amsterdam: John Benjamins Publishing Company.

CHAPTER 36

Between Adoption and Resistance: Grobalization and Glocalization in the Development of Israeli Basketball

Eran Shor and Yair Galily

Sport constitutes one of the most dynamic and sociologically illuminating domains of globalization (Giulianotti & Robertson, 2004). Over the last two decades, a growing number of scholars have looked at the intricate relationship between global processes and sports (Giulianotti & Robertson, 2007; Maguire, 1999; Miller et al., 2001). Most notably, studies have focused on the various dimensions of globalization—economic, political, and cultural—and on the effects that each of these dimensions has had on the development of modern sports. While some of the studies emphasize the homogenizing effects that globalization has had on the practices, regulations, and discourses surrounding sport, others have focused on local resistance and the challenging of hegemonic practices by various nation states and local audiences.

In this article we examine the tension between what George Ritzer (2004) called "the grobal and the local" (see next section for more details) through the case of Israeli basketball. Israeli basketball is a unique case: it is located geographically in Asia, competes in Europe, but is dominated by American players, culture, language, and values. Despite this uniqueness, it also shares many commonalities with other cases in both Europe and in Asia, mainly in terms of the way in which the game has developed and in the intricate interaction between grobal processes of Americanization and glocal processes of resistance and uniqueness. We examine this tension between grobal and glocal processes and highlight both the differences and the similarities between the Israeli case and other cases. Most notably, we examine the unique national, religious, and racial discourses surrounding Israeli basketball and the way these discourses draw from similar global discourses to challenge and defy the American domination of the game.

GLOBALIZATION, GLOCALIZATION, AND GROBALIZATION IN THE STUDY OF SPORTS

Over the last two decades a growing number of theoretical and empirical studies have made use of Roland Robertson's (1992, 1995; Robertson & White, 2003) conceptualization and theoretical development of the term *glocalization.* Robertson coined the term drawing from the Japanese word *dochakuka,* meaning "global localization," or "indigenization." The term represents the recognition that globalization, at least in part, features the critical construction and reinvention of local cultures vis-à-vis other cultural entities. Rather than passively accepting global forms, local cultures construct or even invent local traditions or forms of particularity. They adapt to and redefine any global cultural product to suit their particular needs, beliefs, and customs.

Some of the most prolific work on globalization and glocalization practices has been conducted in the sociology of sports (e.g., Bairner, 2001; Donnelly, 1996; Maguire, 1999). According to Robertson, the sports field provides one of the most salient representations of the glocalization process (Giulianotti & Robertson, 2004). Indeed, a growing number of studies seem to provide empirical support for the manifestation of glocalization processes in various sports. Many of these studies have focused on the glocalization of football (soccer) (e.g., Giulianotti & Robertson, 2004; 2006; Lee, Jackson & Lee, 2007), but other sports, such as basketball, baseball, cricket, and sailing have also been studied (Cho, 2009; Falcous & Maguire, 2005; Kaufman & Patterson, 2005).

Reviewing this growing body of literature, Ritzer in his book *Globalization of Nothing* (2004) warned against putting too much emphasis on the local when analyzing through the framework of glocalization. Ritzer criticized what he called the hegemony of the concept of glocalization in recent research endeavors. This hegemony, he claimed, produces work that overtly and covertly gives an advantage to the idea of glocalization and underestimates processes such as homogenization, Americanization, and McDonaldization. He argued that this body of work often accords far too much attention to glocalization, while underplaying the significance of what he terms *grobalization*: "the imperialistic ambitions of nations, corporations, organizations, and the like and their desire, indeed need, to impose themselves on various geographic areas" (p. 73). Ritzer criticized analyses of sports that emphasize unique and distinct local sports practices and resistance to global conformity, while underplaying the roles of commodification, capitalism, cultural hegemony, expansion, and exploitation.

According to Ritzer (2004), "glocalization" suggests an interaction between global and local, where there are parallel shifts toward global and local. He, therefore, advocated analyses that emphasize the tension between localization and grobalization, and the continuum between the two. Anything that at one time could have been thought of as local is today strongly influenced by the grobal, or in Ritzer's words—we are witnessing "the death of the local" (p. 159). Following Robertson (1992, 1995; & White, 2003) and Ritzer (2004), in this paper we employ a theoretical framework that highlights the continuum between grobal and glocal processes to examine the case of basketball in Israel.

GROBALIZATION IN ACTION: THE AMERICANIZATION OF ISRAELI BASKETBALL

As indicated earlier, Israeli basketball is largely influenced by European and American basketball cultures. However, it is also an important research site in which to examine the glocalization of Asian sports. This is both because of Israel's geographic location in the Middle East, an area in which sociological studies of sport have been quite scarce (Calabrese, 2010; Shor & Yonay, 2011), and due to the commonalities it shares with the basketball cultures of other Asian countries in terms of the interaction between grobal American influence and local resistance. In many ways the story of Israeli basketball and its fight to maintain a unique identity and character has also been the story of basketball in many other Asian countries. Although each case maintains some unique political and cultural characteristics, similar processes to the ones described below have been taking place in other Middle Eastern countries such as Lebanon, Jordan, Turkey, and even Iran (Harrison, 2005; Millman, 2010). These processes can also be found in many East Asian nations, in countries such as South Korea, Japan, Taiwan, and China (Houlihan, Tan & Green, 2010; Yep, 2009).

While Israeli basketball teams (including the national team) have been competing in Europe from Israel's early days, this is largely the result of political rather than geographical reasons. Before the state of Israel was established, local basketball teams traveled to compete in neighboring Arab countries such as Egypt and Lebanon. But following the 1948 war with its Arab neighbors Israel became politically ostracized in the Middle East and Israeli teams had to find a different venue in which to compete internationally. During the 1960s and 1970s the Israeli national team participated in both European and Asian tournaments. In consequent years, however, the Israeli team was no longer allowed to participate in these games and moved to compete only in the European arena.

Israeli basketball has had a strong American influence from its early days.[1] This is not surprising, given that basketball was invented in North America and largely developed in the United States as a popular game. Yet, American influence over Israeli basketball is to some extent even more pronounced than it is in other countries. This is due to the unique relationship between Israel and the US, a relationship that has been significantly fortified over the years. Indeed, it would be hard to understand the developments on the basketball court without first examining the general process of Americanization in Israeli society. The United States has been Israel's biggest (and at times only) ally from Israel's early days. American–Israeli relations are in many ways unique. Both countries are nations of immigrants, places of refuge seen by many as "promised lands." Since the establishment of the state of Israel, the United States has expressed its commitment to Israel's security and well-being and has devoted a considerable share of its worldwide economic and security assistance to Israel. However, this support is not unconditional. Large parts of the grants provided to Israel are in the form of American credit to purchase American goods and military supplies. In addition, the free trade agreement signed in 1984 between the two nations not only makes American products relatively cheap and therefore worthwhile imports, but also ties in the Israeli currency with the fate of the American dollar (Podhoretz, 1998). The American influence on Israel goes far beyond mere economics. American culture and cultural products have widely penetrated the Israeli way of life. In fact, American cultural influence is so widespread that many places in Israel sometimes seem like a transliterated America (Garfinkle, 1996). For example, Avraham and First (2003) showed that American symbols have been widely used to market an array of consumer goods in Israel. Various products are marketed with some sort of an American angle by invoking US values, symbols, landscapes, and lifestyle. In many cases product names and store names may be in English, but these names are written in Hebrew letters (e.g., Best Buy, Super Farm, Club Market, and Super Center).

The Americanization of Israeli society is further evident in various other social spheres, including language, movies, television, and the political culture. Many Israeli politicians visit and stay extensively in the United States. Many of Israel's leading politicians, judges, academics, and business people have studied in the United States, and both former Prime Minister Yitzhak Rabin and the current Prime Minister Binyamin Netanyahu served as Israeli Ambassadors to the United States (Caspi, 1996). American values have also permeated Israeli society, including the ethos of individualism, competitiveness, and the belief in the free market economy. The rise of these values has coincided with the gradual dismantling of various Israeli social support systems, its welfare system and its social cohesion.

This process of Americanization is clearly manifested in the field of sports, particularly in basketball. Basketball in Israel follows only soccer as the country's most popular sport. It is played by amateurs of all ages and at all levels, as well as by highly skilled and very well-paid professionals. Thousands of people throughout the country crowd arenas to watch basketball games, while many others watch these games on television. Israel's competitive basketball achievements have been substantial. In 1977, 1981, 2001, 2004, and 2005 Maccabi Tel Aviv (the nation's premier basketball team) won the European Club Championship, while in 1979 the Israeli national team finished as runners-up to the Soviet Union in the European National Championship.

These successes can largely be attributed to the growing influx of American players, who increasingly have come to dominate Israeli basketball. At present, more than 100 American-born basketball players—both men and women—play in the top two Israeli professional basketball leagues. They occupy most starting positions on the court, and almost without exception lead the most important statistical categories in the game, such as scoring, rebounding, assisting, and blocking. However, this has not always been the case. It was not until 1965 when American players began to take part in Israeli basketball.

THE EARLY YEARS: 1935–1965

Before the establishment of the state of Israel in 1948, basketball was not a very popular sport in the territory then called Palestine; the games of soccer and handball were far more popular. However, in the mid-1930s this began to change, as a group of Jewish immigrants from the United States introduced the game of basketball to the local inhabitants, and the game slowly gained popularity.[2] The first formal basketball game played in Israel took place in 1935, as part of the second "Maccabiah" games (the "Jewish Olympic games"). Basketball competitions included teams from Syria, Egypt, Turkey, and Palestine. The first Jewish basketball club in Palestine, Maccabi Tel Aviv, was also founded in 1935 and an outdoor basketball court was built in the center of the new city of Tel Aviv. During the following years, the popularity of the game grew steadily (Galily, 2003).

This growth in popularity continued in the early 1950s, after the establishment of the state of Israel, largely thanks to another American immigrant, Nat Holman (Galily, 2003). Holman, a member of the first Boston Celtics basketball team, a senior basketball coach in the United States, and an avid Zionist, was responsible for laying the foundations for Israeli basketball and the Israeli basketball league. Holman brought with him modern coaching techniques from the United States and taught them to many of Israel's future coaches. At the time Israel was prevented from participating in international sports competitions, due to its geopolitical stance within the Middle East. Therefore, in the early 1950s the International Basketball Federation (FIBA) invited Israel to compete in Europe.

INTENSIFIED AMERICANIZATION: 1965–1979

Following the seventh Macabbiah Games in 1965, the Maccabi Tel Aviv basketball team was quick to sign Tal Brody, a young Jewish American basketball player who had excelled in the games. Due to the Israeli *Law of Return*, which grants immediate citizenship to any Jew immigrating to Israel, Brody was allowed to participate in the local league, as well as represent Maccabi Tel Aviv in its European competitions. During the same year, Maccabi's biggest rival, *Hapoel Tel Aviv*, was able to convince an American physical educator, Bill Wald, to join the team. Wald later on became the first American-born Israeli to play for the Israeli national team. During the subsequent seasons, the presence of Jewish American immigrates in Israeli teams continued to grow. Within a few years the number of Jewish Americans playing in Israeli basketball increased from two players in the 1966–1967 season, to eight in the 1968–1969 season, and to ten in 1972–1973. By 1974–1975, twenty four American-born players (40% of the "starting fives") were playing basketball in the Israeli major league (Galily & Bar-Eli, 2005).

The new American players brought with them significant changes in playing style. The game quickly became faster, more dynamic, and more physical, with greater emphasis placed on defensive efforts. The leading values of the game were transformed as well. Instead of the traditional English-influenced values, emphasizing the importance of participation, fair play, and amateurism, teams and players began to adopt the American ideology which stressed victory above all (Galily & Sheard, 2002). The decline in amateurism also brought with it a change in the work ethic. Teams that formerly practiced only twice or three times a week began to practice every day, and some players began working with weights. Part of this change may also be attributed to Israeli players who went to play in American colleges and brought back with them the American working habits and discipline (Galily & Bar-Eli, 2005).

The 1970s saw what some refer to as the "golden age" of Israeli basketball. The success of Israeli teams (especially Maccabi Tel Aviv) in both the European and Asian arenas increased (largely due to the boost from Jewish American players), and with it the popularity of Israeli basketball. This success culminated in the 1976–1977 season. On February 1977 Maccabi Tel Aviv, playing in the European Championship Cup, within two days beat the champions of two Eastern European basketball powerhouses: Zabriobzka Berno (Czechoslovakia) and CSKA Moscow (the Soviet Union). The game against the Soviet army team was much more than just another basketball game, as sport carried a particular social and political significance in the development and maintenance of Communist society at that time (Riordan, 1986).

In the Israeli media the game was presented as a battle between the East and the West. The fact that a few American-born Jews were playing for the Israeli team added to the charged atmosphere, as it symbolized for many the personification of the struggle between American capitalism and Soviet communism. When Maccabi, whose starting five consisted of four players born in the United States, defeated the Soviet team, the game became an instant classic, and the win remains ingrained in the Israeli collective memory to this day. The win also guaranteed the team for the first time a place in the European Cup finals against the Italian champions Mobilgirgi Varese. In April 1977, when Maccabi beat the Italian team to win its first European Cup, it became Israel's highest and most memorable basketball achievement to date (Galily & Bar-Eli, 2005).

The Israeli national team also profited from the influx of Jewish American players. In June 1979 the Israeli national team traveled to Italy for the European National Championship. The expectations before the tournament were not very high, but the Israeli team's performance far surpassed any expectations. The team, once again led by a number of American-born Jews, was able to beat Yugoslavia, the reigning world champions, and to reach the finals of the tournament where it lost to the Russian team. The silver medal in the European national championship is today considered by many to be the greatest achievement of Israeli basketball in all times.

AN AMERICAN FLUX: AFTER 1979

During the 1979–1980 season the executive committee of the Israeli Basketball Association decided that for the first time players who were not Israeli citizens would be allowed to take part in the Israeli league. In addition to one foreign player, each team was now allowed to include in its roster one player in the process of becoming a naturalized Israeli. The immediate result of the decision was that twelve more American players joined the Israeli league. In addition, an increasing number of non-Jewish American players sought to receive Israeli citizenship, many of them through marriages of connivance (and convenience). The entrance of American players into the Israeli league continued to grow during the 1980s. In 1985 it was decided that to halt the abuse of naturalized-player status, three years would have to elapse before naturalized players could become eligible to play in the Israeli teams. However, at the same time it was also decided that the number of foreign players allowed in each team would be raised to two (Galily & Sheard, 2002).The number of foreign athletes playing for Israeli basketball teams gradually continued to increase during the next two decades. By the mid-2000s four foreign players were allowed to play in each team (taking up 80% of the starting positions).

Then, before the 2006/2007 season the last limitations on the number of foreign players were removed, as the league adopted "The Russian Ruling" (named after a similar regulation in the Russian basketball league), stating that a team may have as many foreign players as it wishes, as long as at least two of the five players on the court at any given moment are Israeli (in effect, some of these Israelis were American-born naturalized players).[3,4]

Galily and Sheard (2002) emphasized the role of internal politics and domestic power struggles within the Israeli Basketball Association in influencing decisions and policies concerning foreign players. While these were certainly important in determining policies and regulations, one should not underestimate the role of the European basketball institutions and the isomorphic effects of policies and regulations passed in other European nations.

First, we should examine concurrent developments in the policies of individual European countries regarding foreign basketball players. Italian teams, for example, were for many years (especially during the 1970s and 1980s) among the fiercest competitors of Israeli teams in the European arena. In 1965 the Italian Basketball Association for the first time allowed the employment of one non-Italian player per team. This number was increased to two players starting in 1977 (Addesa, 2011). Similar changes were occurring in other European countries during the same years. By 1986 the average number of foreign players per team in all of the European basketball leagues was more than two. By 2007 this number had increased to almost six (Alvarez et al., 2009), with some leagues (e.g., the Italian league) employing almost ten foreign players per team (Addesa, 2011). The increasing pressures for competitive isomorphism (DiMaggio & Powell, 1983) meant that Israeli basketball had to adapt and allow the growing penetration of foreign (mostly American) players to maintain a competitive stance in the European arena.

Another significant development occurred in 1995 on the transnational front, when the European Court of Justice passed the Bosman Ruling, which transformed the landscape of sport and the movement of players in Europe. The ruling came about following the case of Belgian football player Jean-Marc Bosman, who applied to the Court asking that restrictions be removed on foreign EU members within the national leagues. The Court's decision effectively allowed athletes to ply their trade anywhere in the European Union, in line with the rules applying to other workers. Although Israel is not part of the European Union, the decision had an effect on Israeli basketball, due to the many Israeli teams competing in Europe. To adjust to the new ruling, the Israeli league decided that each team would be allowed to bring one foreign player holding citizenship in one of the EU countries (a "Bosman" player). In effect though, many of these new players were also Americans who held an additional citizenship in one of the European countries.[5] While today other European basketball leagues are also inundated by foreign players, in Israel, Americans completely dominate the scene. The Bosman Ruling, thus, paved the way for the further Americanization of the league.[6]

The Bosman ruling also opened the door for Israeli players to move and play in various European leagues. Since the beginning of the new millennium multiple Israeli players (especially those holding an EU citizenship) have been playing in various European leagues, including in France, Germany, Italy, Spain, Russia, Poland, and the United States. This export of players represents another stage in the globalization of Israeli basketball.

Perhaps more interesting is the success of Israeli basketball coaches in the European arena. During the 2000s, largely due to the successes of Maccabi Tel Aviv and other Israeli teams in the European arena, a number of prominent Israeli coaches began coaching in leading European teams, including national teams. Most notable among these coaches is David Blatt, an American Jew who immigrated to Israel in the 1980s. During the 2000s, Blatt has coached a number of leading European teams, including the Russian national team. One of the interesting things about Blatt's success is that it is often ascribed to the mix of Israeli creativeness and inventiveness and American systematic and methodic coaching style. For many, Blatt thus encapsulates the successful glocalization of the game in Israel (see for example Lev Ari, 2010; Eshed, 2012).

The growing Americanization of Israeli basketball was manifested in more than just the number of Americans in each team. It has also influenced the values guiding the game, the dominant training and work ethic philosophies, the game's growing commercialization, the increasing use of statistics, the ways in which it is covered by the media, and perhaps most notably its language. Over the years, both spoken and written Hebrew have adopted a host of foreign terminology. Many of these terms are taken from the English language, mainly under the influence of American culture. English terms have penetrated almost every domain of daily life in Israel, including the business sphere, various popular culture products (movies, books, TV shows, commercials, and more), organizations (private as well as governmental and third sector), popular idioms, and product names.

In no field has the penetration of (American) English terminology into local everyday language been felt as strongly as it has in basketball. The sweeping move toward English terminology in basketball was not only influenced by the growing number of Americans on the teams, but also by the Israeli media revolution of the early 1990s that brought NBA games (and broadcasting norms) to Israeli TV. Consequently, over the last three decades the language of the game has become a mixture of Hebrew and a growing number of terms and expressions taken from the American basketball culture. In a typical newspaper report or a broadcasted game, one is likely to encounter terms such as offense, assist, baseline, block, backdoor, jump-shot, double-team, hook-shot, weak-side, time-out, transition, penetration, lay-up, match-up, fast-break, mismatch, small forward, pick-and-roll, low-post, triple-double, money-time, garbage-time, coast-to-coast, cross-over, point guard, winner-shot, and in-your-face (written in Hebrew lettering or pronounced with a Hebrew accent). These terms have gradually replaced the equivalent Hebrew terms (in cases where such terms existed) and have come to dominate the language of media reporting and everyday discourse on basketball in Israel.

This Americanization of the language reflects a common sentiment among Israeli basketball people: To uphold the American standards of playing and broadcasting one has to adopt the language in which the game was created and has been developed. Furthermore, while the language in newspapers and television broadcasts is a mixture of Hebrew and English, the language on the court has become solely English. Unlike other prominent European basketball countries, such as Spain, France, and Russia, in which the local language still dominates trainings and games, in Israel the trainings and games are entirely conducted in English (Tzadik, 2010).

With the language also often came practices. When the Hebrew word "*hagana*" becomes "defense," this entails not only a change in terminology, but also in mindset—a stronger emphasis on defense as a way to win games and a growing defensive orientation among many Israeli basketball coaches and players. Similarly, importing the wealth of terminologies from the more professional NBA league allowed Israeli coaches to develop new and more sophisticated strategies on both the defensive and the offensive ends of the floor. Israeli basketball fans, on their part, gradually came to value many of the aspects which are most valued in American basketball: Show-time, assists, dunks, and more sophisticated types of defensive and offensive plays (which have received an appropriate terminology, allowing commentators to point them out and fans to notice and appreciate them).

Tensions Between Grobalization and Glocalization: Discourses of Religion, Nationality, and Race

Over the last decade, we have followed closely and analyzed systematically the Hebrew media discourse surrounding foreign and naturalized athletes in the major men's soccer and basketball Israeli leagues. We examined all of the major relevant reports in the daily newspapers (*Yediot Ahronot, Maariv*, and *Haaretz*), television channels (*Channel 1, Channel 2, Channel 5*, and *Channel 5+*) and internet Websites (*Sal-news.com, Sport5.co.il, Safsal.co.il, One.co.il*, and *Ynet.co.il*). We also analyzed a large sample of internet surfers' talkbacks (see Kohn & Neiger, 2007; Shor & Yonay, 2011; Sikron, Baron-Epel & Linn, 2007)—short interactive responses appearing at the end of articles. Overall we conducted qualitative content analysis of more than 300 long reports, articles and interviews from the written press, television, and internet websites and over 600 talkbacks on selected articles.

Our extensive media content analysis reveals a few important themes which are relevant to the issues examined here. Alongside the clear Americanization of Israeli basketball, one can also detect continuous expressions of resistance and glocalization in both the practice and discourse surrounding the game. Already in the early 1980s the first signs of resistance began to appear, many of them involving a religious component. The new regulations allowing each team to include in its roster one player in the process of becoming a naturalized Israeli began to come under attack. Up until the 1970s foreigners coming to play basketball in Israel were white Jewish Americans, many of whom coming to Israel as declared Zionists, expressing their wish to make the country their new home and to play for the national team. Given that Israel is largely comprised of Jewish immigrants, this was reason enough for most Israelis to accept these players with a warm embrace and view them as part of the Israeli collective. Tal Brody, who joined Maccabi Tel Aviv in the mid-1960s, exemplified this tendency. An avid Zionist, Brody became not only Maccabi's best and most valuable player, but also the team's new symbol. In 1977, right after the team won its first European Championship, an excited Brody famously declared on national TV "We are on the map, not only in sport, but in everything!" (Galily & Bar-Eli, 2005: 320). This statement demonstrates that many of the American Jewish players who came to Israel during the 1960s and 1970s were clearly accepted as part of the "us" of the Jewish-Israeli collective.

The new regulations of the 1980s increased the number of non-Jewish American players seeking Israeli citizenship, many through bogus conversions to Judaism. It became clear that at least for some of these players the sole purpose of pursuing citizenship was to be able to play for Israeli teams and earn higher wages, rather than a sincere connection to Israel (Galily & Sheard, 2002). These attempts were viewed by religious elements within Israeli society as shameful cheapening of both Judaism and Israeli citizenship, and were harshly criticized.

The local players were also unhappy with the new regulations. Many of them felt that their way to a successful career in basketball was blocked by the new influx of American players. Finally, the general Israeli public, basketball fans, and journalists covering Israeli basketball also began to lament the loss of local identity in the teams. According to Galily and Bar-Eli (2005), the fact that the victories of Maccabi Tel Aviv and the national team during the 1970s and early 1980s were mostly achieved with the help of players not born in Israel (but who were nevertheless White Jews) did not seem to bother most Israeli sport fans. However, over the years this approach gradually changed and the increasing dominance of American players in the teams has received growing criticism.

One case which clearly marks this change in attitude is that of Elitzur Netanya in the late 1980s. In 1986 a successful businessman, Neil Gilman, decided to invest in the team. Wanting to make the team a commercial product that would sell more tickets and generate higher public attention, Gilman sought to make Elitzur as attractive as possible by bringing as many American players as possible to the team. Gilman signed five American players (four of them Black), and for a short time the team managed to draw substantial public attention and achieve professional success (Galily & Sheard, 2002). However, much of this public attention was not very positive. Elitzur is a national-religious sports organization and the signing of five American players (although three of them also had an Israeli citizenship) seemed to symbolize the exact opposite of its ideals.

Further evidence for the public and media discontent with the growing Americanization of basketball comes from our analysis of the Israeli media coverage of foreign basketball and soccer players during the 2000s. While the media and fans enjoy the achievements of Israeli teams in the European arena, they often lament what they see as a "sell out"—the reliance on foreigners to achieve international success. The fact that the heroes of victories are mostly foreign clearly makes many in Israeli society uncomfortable. In 2005, following one of Maccabi Tel Aviv's greatest achievements—winning the European Championship for the second time in a row—one internet blogger responding to an online newspaper report of the final game expressed these sentiments:

> I find the recent national erection odd. . . . Not everyone takes part in this sad festival. . . . Let us not forget that the ones who brought us this achievement are three Americans, a Lithuanian and a Croatian [the team's predominant players]. . . . Only when the game was already decided an anemic Israeli came off the bench. . . . This is a Foreign Legion. . . . How can we say that *Maccabi Tel-Aviv* represents Israel, the Jewish state, when so few Israelis play there?
>
> (posted to *Ynet*, May 18, 2005)

This rejection of Americanization in favor of local (Jewish) heroes comes from a mix of national, religious, and even racial elements. First, various studies have emphasized the centrality of ethno-religious identities in the definition of the Jewish nation (Kimmerling, 2004; Peled & Shafir, 2002; Smooha, 1998). The contradiction between local-patriotic feelings and rhetoric on the one hand, and the cosmopolitan nature of present-day international sports on the other hand, is not unique to Israel. Many studies have shown the close relationship between sport, the nation state, and ethnic and religious identities (e.g., Maguire, 1999; Sugden & Tomlinson, 1994; Wong & Trumper, 2002). Bairner (1996) emphasized, however, that the nature of this relationship differs greatly according to the political context.

In a study focusing on naturalized athletes and on athletes who wish to become Israeli citizens, Shor and Yonay (2010) demonstrated that Israeli media and public discourses largely revolve around issues of collective identity related to ethnicity and religion. The Israeli media is preoccupied with the relationship between foreign players, the Israeli nation, and Judaism. Therefore, even when they help the collective to compete with other nations (either by playing for Israeli clubs or, if they are naturalized, by playing for the national team), they largely remain foreigners for many Israelis. Publicist Amir Bogen demonstrated this view in an article on the Maccabi Tel-Aviv basketball club, entitled "The Fake Passport of Israeli Basketball":

> They say that Maccabi represents Israel in Europe against a cruel and anti-Semitic world. Huffman, Parker, MacDonald, *Sharp, Brisker*, Louis, Goree, Vujcic, and *Bluthenthal* are all citizens of the world, and even a bit Israelis (in heart or in passport). Maccabi prefers these foreign workers to the locals.
>
> (Bogen 2002b; emphases by the authors)

Although Bogen knows that some of the players on his list (in italics) are naturalized Israeli citizens as well as American, he clearly believes that this is not enough. They have an Israeli passport, but are not complete Israeli at heart. This estrangement of foreign athletes is largely maintained through an ethno-religious discourse, which emphasizes the fact that most of them are not Jewish. Our analysis shows that the players' religious background is often mentioned in discussions about their desire to become citizens. The fact that they are not Jewish is frequently cited as an objection to their naturalization, and they are often expected to exhibit familiarity with Jewish holidays and customs.

Interestingly, not all the naturalized players in the list above are gentiles. David Bluthenthal (Blu), who has been playing for Maccabi Tel Aviv and the Israeli national team for much of the last decade, is Jewish. In his case, however, this fact is not enough to make him an indisputable Israeli. Another similar case can be found almost a decade later in an opinion article on the basketball team Maccabi Haifa. In the article titled "Foreign to the Club," Journalist Eyal Gil described the team's failure with its foreign players: "We haven't seen such a group of head-cases in Israel in a long time." The article's secondary title reads: "One foreign player has been cut off from the team, a second ran away, the third is unconnected to the team, and the fourth only thinks about Maccabi Tel Aviv [the reporter eludes here to rumors suggesting that this fourth player is sought after by the richer Maccabi Tel Aviv basketball club]" (Gil, 2011). What Gil failed to mention (although he is well aware of it, as the body of the article later demonstrates) is that "the fourth" player on his list, Sylvan Landsberg, is actually a naturalized Israeli player of American origin. In fact, Landsberg is not only an Israeli citizen, he is also Jewish.

Why is it then that both David Blu (Bluthenthal) and Sylvan Landsberg (as well as two other non-Jewish players in Bogen's list above, Mark Brisker and Derrick Sharp) continue to be excluded by many from the Israeli collective despite their Israeli citizenship? One likely explanation is that they are all African-American, revealing the racial component in the discourse over the Americanization of Israeli basketball. Even when the player is Jewish, as is the case with David Blu, reporters have a hard time settling the contradiction between "Jewishness" and "Blackness," as the following quote demonstrates: "An antithesis to the image of the Jewish athlete (smart, scheming and full of faith) . . . David Bluthenthal, 202 centimeters of springy iron muscles, . . . proved his true and definitely non-Jewish potential, grabbing 28 rebounds in one game" (Bogen, 2002a). This racial component of the discourse demonstrates the interplay between the grobalization and the glocalization not only of the practices but also of the *discourses* surrounding the game. The separation between Americans and locals (and thus the resistance to the Americanization of the game) is ironically often maintained through the adoption and glocalization of American (Western) racial stereotypes. These stereotypes are then contrasted with the constructed ethnic stereotypes about Jews (see Shor, 2008b for further discussion of these ethnic constructions).

Already in the late 1980s one could detect racial elements in the discourse over the Americanization of Israeli basketball. The fact that four out of the five American players in Elitzur Netanya were Black was clearly one of the main reasons for the attention devoted to the team. Israeli newspapers echoed the public discourse, exclaiming that for the first time an Israeli team would have four *Kushim* (a word in Hebrew with similar negative connotations to the epithet *niggers* in English) on its roster. Two years later, the Elitzur sports center, unhappy with the team's image, decided to intervene and asked the team to decrease the number of its Black players. This act pushed Gilman out of the team ownership, and eventually led to the team's demise (Elitzur Netanya—Nostalgia, 2011).

The media coverage, as well as the popular public image of Black Americans playing basketball in Israel draws substantially from common racial stereotypes in the American media and public discourse. Studies that examined media coverage of sports in the United States (Burstein, 1999; Sabo & Jansen, 1994), Canada (Wilson, 1997) and in Britain (Whannel, 2002) found that journalists often emphasized the Black athletes' physicality and toughness. The players are portrayed as athletic phenomena, but also as big bad brutes who are frequently embroiled in scandals (usually of a criminal or sexual nature). They were also often depicted as tough- guys, with violent animal-like and savage tendencies. On the other hand they were rarely mentioned in connection to hard work, discipline and intelligence, although these are necessary elements in producing successful athletic performances.

Shor (2008b) found similar tendencies in the Israeli media. Israeli media often depicts Black players as submissive, childlike, impulsive, and unintelligent, but also as physically and sexually superior (making them an object of fantasy and envy) and as tough individuals who are able to handle pressure. Alongside the admiration for their "natural" physical abilities, mental toughness, and sexual prowess, one can find overt racial stereotypes about their violent and criminal tendencies and their inferior cognitive capacities. This duality serves as a binary to the constructed image of Jewish-Israeli players. The latter are often portrayed as physically inferior (both athletically and in terms of size and strength), but as being able to (partially) compensate for these disadvantages with "typical" Jewish characteristics—playing intelligently, scheming, and having faith. This Jewish-Black binary serves as a clear example of the tension between the grobal and the glocal discourses. American discourses on race have been adopted by the Israeli media, but have subsequently been modified and reframed so they can suit the Israeli context.

THE ISRAELI CASE IN A COMPARATIVE FRAMEWORK: THE CASE OF ENGLISH BASKETBALL

The manifestations of resistance discussed above are hardly unusual in the context of the global (and in particular American) cultural influences over national settings in general, and more specifically sports and basketball. Israel is not the only country where local basketball has gone through a process of increased Americanization. In fact, most of the European nations (including European basketball powerhouses such Italy, Spain, France, and Greece), as well as Middle Eastern and East Asian ones (e.g., Lebanon, Turkey, Iran, Japan, South Korea, and China), have gone through similar processes, with a growing influx of migrant basketball players, mostly coming from the United States. In most countries, these growing tendencies have provoked debates and sometimes resistance, but the level of resistance varies according to local characteristics such as the indigenous sport culture and the importance of basketball in it, unique national, linguistic, and religious characteristics, and the country's relationship with the US.

One well researched case that is similar to the Israeli one is that of English basketball. Unlike in Israel, basketball has never been a very popular sport in England. English basketball teams (including the national team) have also not been very successful in the international arena. Despite these differences, there are some similarities between the two countries in the gradual Americanization of the game, as well as in the expressions of local unrest and resistance following this process. Maguire (1988) showed that beginning in the mid-1970s one can find a growing debate surrounding the recruitment of foreign players into English basketball. Much like in Israel, this debate tended to focused on the marginalization of local players and the effect this is likely to have on the national team. The criticism grew stronger in the 1980s, as the number of American players in English basketball continued to grow. As in Israel, much of the criticism focused on players who held dual nationality (in the case of England either through naturalization or through parents of British origin). Some of the discourse also emphasized racial components, talking about a shift away from a game played by "respectable" white Britons to one in which Black Americans and Black Britons dominated. Indeed, between 1977 and 1994 the percentage of Black Britons within the total number of British players soared from 8.8% to 58.9% (Chappell et al., 1996).

During the 1990s the number of foreign players in English basketball continued to grow and by the late 1990s more than half of the players (as well as most of the coaches) were foreigners. Falcous and Maguire (2005) and Maguire (2008) showed that while this increase prompted some further criticism, it did not stir up substantial contention. English basketball supporters by and large now accept the necessity of foreign players in order for "the game to get better." They lament the marginalization of the "local lads" and question the commitment of the foreign players to the clubs and the local community, but at the same time they show no anti-Americanism and acknowledge the importance, even the necessity, of the American players.

At this point one may ask why it is that the case of English basketball seems somewhat less contentious than the Israeli one. After all, alongside the historical alliance and cooperation between the US and the UK, there is also a clear rivalry between the two countries over cultural hegemony. English culture in particular often tries to fend off and maintain its distinction in the face of the growing global dominance of American culture (Biltereyst, 1991; de Grazia, 1989; Fox, 2004). When comparing this to the apparent fascination in Israeli culture with everything American, discussed above, it may seem surprising to find greater resistance to the Americanization of basketball in the Israeli case.

One reason for what seems like a less contentious terrain in the English case may be the fact that the English national team has not gained many international achievements. This may have convinced some within English basketball that the stakes in bringing in Americans are not very high. Religious and cultural dimensions may also play a role in what appears to be a less contentious process of Americanization in English basketball compared the Israeli one. Americans who come to play basketball in England differ in their culture and nationality, but often share a language, a religious background, and, since most English basketball players today are Black, also a racial background. These aspects may help to reduce perceived differences and assuage resentment.

CONCLUSION

This article looked at the ongoing tension between grobalization and glocalization processes, as demonstrated in the case of Israeli basketball. We showed the growing penetration of American ideas, practices, culture, and athletes into Israeli basketball, a process that began in the 1960s and has grown stronger with each passing decade. With time, Israeli basketball has come to be completely dominated not only by American players, but also by American basketball values and work ethic. The game has been commercialized and quantified, largely following the American model (including the media coverage), and English has become the main language of the game in professional as well as semiprofessional settings.

However, we also showed that these processes, although powerful and very influential, did not take place without contention. Over the years, national, religious and racial elements were invoked by the Israeli public and media and have had an effect on both the practice (in the form of changing regulations) and the discourse surrounding Israeli basketball. The growing numbers of foreign players (almost all Black non-Jewish

Americans) have brought a change of attitude, compared with the warm acceptance of the (mostly Jewish American) players who came in the 1960s and 1970s. Israeli public and media have come to pronounce growing discontent with the "flood" of foreign players and the "sell out" of the game. The fact that most of these players are non-Jewish and Black creates a feeling of discomfort and estrangement among many in the Israeli media and public.

The rapidly growing process of Americanization in Israeli basketball, alongside the evident local resistance, once again exemplify the contentious process of glocalization, as it was discussed by Robertson (1992; 1995) and followers. However, the Israeli case also calls for further attention to Ritzer's (2004) reconceptualization of globalization and glocalization. We believe that the Israeli case serves as a good example for the overwhelming influence of American culture, practices, discourse, and players on the ways in which basketball is conceived of and played. We, thus, join Ritzer's call for analyses of the sport field that do not over-emphasize unique and distinct local sports practices and resistance to global conformity ("glocalization"), while underplaying the roles of commodification, capitalism, and (American) cultural hegemony ("grobalization").

We would also like to suggest that further comparisons across cases (like the one we have conducted here between the Israeli and the English cases) are especially important for the future development of the sports-globalization analysis. Such comparisons are highly useful in accounting for global processes and the divergent ways in which they affect local practices (Shor 2008a; 2008c). Many scholars have already demonstrated that grobalization rarely (if ever) penetrates localities without tension and resistance. We believe, therefore, that it is important for empirical studies to move beyond simply trying to show that glocalization exists. Instead, future research should focus on examining the various manifestations of the grobal–glocal interaction in different settings and should make an attempt to understand the similarities as well as the differences that characterize these intricate dynamics as they occur in various locations.

NOTES

1 The difference between the two sports is also manifested in their regulations regarding foreign players. While Israeli basketball is heavily dominated by American players, Israeli soccer is still largely dominated by Israeli nationals. Still, about half of the players in each team playing in the Israeli premier league are foreigners. These foreign players come from a variety of countries, mainly Eastern-European, South American, and African ones (Shor & Yonay, 2010)

2 It should be noted though, that in the first half of the 20th century Jews were a very dominant group in American basketball (Eisen, 1999; Horvitz, 2007).

3 Before the 2011–2012 season the league managers decided to go back to four players of foreign nationality in each team, removing the stipulation regarding the number of Israeli players that must be on the court at any given time. Consequently, in the 2011–2012 season there were over fifty foreign players playing in the eleven teams that make up the major Israeli basketball league (*Ligat Ha'al*). The number of naturalized players (almost all American) in this league was eight. In addition, each team in the secondary league (*Haliga Haleumit*) was allowed to have up to two foreign players, meaning that the number of foreign players in this league was about twenty-five (six naturalized players).

4 The Israeli Women's Basketball League has been adopting similar regulations to those of the men's league (including the "Russian Ruling") regarding foreign players. Therefore, this league is also highly dominated by foreign—mostly American—players (more than forty-five foreign and six naturalized players in the 2011–2012 season).

5 One of the more well known cases demonstrating this phenomenon is that of American basketball player Kenny Williams. In 2001 Hapoel Jerusalem signed Williams as a Bosman player holding a Czech passport. However, it was later revealed that Williams' Czech passport was fake.

6 The Bosman Ruling also opened up the gates for those Israeli players who held a citizenship in one of the EU countries (and later on also to some who were not). Starting in the late 1990s Israeli players began for the first time to play for European teams, in countries such as France, Italy, Germany, and Spain.

REFERENCES

Addesa, F. (2011). Competitive balance in the Italian basketball championship. *Rivista di Diritto ed Economica dello Sport, 7*, 107–125.

Alvarez, J., Forrest, D., Sanz, I., & de Dios Tena, J. (2009). Impact of importing foreign talent on performance levels of local co-workers. Contributi Di Ricerca Crenos working paper 2009/14. Retrieved August 29, 2011 at www.eprints.uniss.it/5405/1/ alvarez_J_Impact_of_importing_foreign.pdf.

Avraham, E., & First, A. (2003). 'I buy American': The American image as reflected in Israeli advertising. *The Journal of Communication, 53*, 182–299. doi:10.1093/joc/53.1.182

Bairner, A. (1996). Sportive nationalism and nationalist politics: A comparative analysis of Scotland, the Republic of Ireland, and Sweden. *Journal of Sport and Social Issues, 20*, 314–334. doi:10.1177/019372396020003006

Bairner, A. (2001). *Sport, nationalism, and globalization: European and North American perspectives.* Albany, NY: SUNY Press.

Biltereyst, D. (1991). Resisting American hegemony: A comparative analysis of the reception of domestic and US fiction. *European Journal of Communication, 6*, 469–497. doi:10.1177/0267323191006004005

Bogen, A. (2002a). David Bluthenthal: A true profit, a false messiah. *Ynet*, March 26, 2002. Retrieved March 26, 2002 at www.ynet.co.il/articles/0,7340, L-623688,00.html.

Bogen, A. (2002b). Maccabi Tel Aviv: The fake passport of Israeli basketball." *Ynet*, September 29, 2002. Retrieved September 29, 2002 at www.ynet.co.il/articles/0,7340,L-2001754,00.html.

Burstein, V. (1999). *The rites of men: Manhood, politics, and the culture of sport.* Toronto: University of Toronto Press.

Calabrese, J. (2010). Introduction. P. 7 in J. Calabrese (ed.), *Sports and the Middle East: A special edition of viewpoints.* Washington, DC: The Middle East Institute.

Caspi, D. (1996). American style electioneering in Israel: Americanization versus modernization. In D. Swanson & P. Mancini (Eds.), *Politics, media and modern society* (pp. 173–193). Westport, CT: Praeger.

Chappell, R., Jones, R., & Burden, A. (1996). Racial participation and integration in English professional basketball 1977–1994. *Sociology of Sport Journal, 13*, 300–310.

Cho, Y. (2009). The Glocalization of U.S. Sports in South Korea. *Sociology of Sport Journal, 26*, 320–334.

de Grazia, V. (1989). Mass culture and sovereignty: The American challenge to European cinemas, 1920–1960. *The Journal of Modern History, 61*, 53–87. doi:10.1086/468191

DiMaggio, P., & Powell, W. (1983). The iron cage revisited: Institutional isomorphism and collective rationality in organizational fields. *American Sociological Review, 48*, 147–160. doi:10.2307/2095101

Donnelly, P. (1996). The local and the global: Globalization in the sociology of sport. *Journal of Sport and Social Issues, 20*, 239–257. doi:10.1177/019372396020003002

Eisen, G. (1999). Jews and sport: A century of retrospect. *Journal of Sport History, 26*, 225–239.

Elitzur Netanya – Nostalgia. (2011). Retrieved September 16, 2011 at www.sites.google. com/site/natanya basketball/

Eshed, I. (2012). "David Blatt – an MVP coach". *Ynet*, January 19, 2012. Retrieved March 23, 2012 at www.ynet.co.il/articles/0,7340,L-4178244,00.html

Falcous, M., & Maguire, J. (2005). Globetrotters and local heroes? Labor migration, basketball, and local identities. *Sociology of Sport Journal, 22*, 137–157.

Fox, K. (2004). *Watching the English: The hidden rules of English behavior.* London: Hodder.

Galily, Y. (2003). Playing hoops in Palestine: The early development of basketball in the Land of Israel (1935–1956). *The International Journal of the History of Sport, 20*, 143–151. doi:10.1080/714001851

Galily, Y., & Bar-Eli, M. (2005). From Tal Brody to European champions: Early Americanization and the "golden age" of Israeli basketball, 1965–1979. *Journal of Sport History, 32*, 401–422.

Galily, Y., & Sheard, K. (2002). Cultural imperialism: The Americanization of Israeli basketball, 1978–1996. *Culture, Sport, Society, 5*, 55–78. doi:10.1080/713999862

Garfinkle, A. (1996). U.S.-Israeli relations after the Cold War. *Orbis, 40,* 557–576. doi:10.1016/S0030-4387(96)90019-8

Gil, E. (2011). Foreign to the Club. *Haaretz,* December 19, 2011 (Hebrew). Retrieved December 19, 2011 at www.haaretz.co.il/sport/opinions/1.1594877

Giulianotti, R., & Robertson, R. (2004). The globalization of football: A study in the glocalization of the 'serious life'. *The British Journal of Sociology, 55,* 545–568. doi:10.1111/j.1468–4446.2004.00037.x

Giulianotti, R., & Robertson, R. (2006). Glocalization, globalization and migration: The case of Scottish football supporters in North America. *International Sociology, 21,* 171–198. doi:10.1177/0268580906061374

Giulianotti, R., & Robertson, R. (Eds.). (2007). *Globalization and sport.* Oxford: Blackwell. Harrison, F. (2005). Basketball in the 'Axis of Evil'. *BBC News,* November 17, 2005. Retrieved December 19, 2011 at www.news.bbc.co.uk/2/hi/4445030.stm

Horvitz, P. (2007). *The big book of Jewish sports heroes.* New York: S.P.I. Books.

Houlihan, B., Tan, T., & Green, M. (2010). Policy transfer and learning from the West: Elite basketball development in the People's Republic of China. *Journal of Sport and Social Issues, 34,* 4–28. doi:10.1177/0193723509358971

Kaufman, J., & Patterson, O. (2005). Cross-National cultural diffusion: The global spread of cricket. *American Sociological Review, 70,* 82–110. doi:10.1177/000312240507000105

Kimmerling, B. (2004). *Immigrants, settlers, natives: The Israeli state and society between cultural pluralism and cultural wars.* Tel Aviv: Am Oved Publishers (Hebrew).

Kohn, A., & Neiger, M. (2007). To talk and talkback: Analyzing the rhetoric of talkbacks in online journalism. In T.S. Altshuler (Ed.), *Online newspapers in Israel. Be'er-Sheva.* The Democracy Library.

Lee, N., Jackson, S., & Lee, K. (2007). South Korea's "glocal" hero: The Hiddink syndrome and the rearticulation of national citizenship and identity. *Sociology of Sport Journal, 24,* 283–301.

Lev Ari, Y. (2010). "Blatt's achievements are similar to those of Phil Jackson". Ynet, September 6, 2010. Retrieved March 23, 2012 at www.ynet.co.il/articles/0,7340,L-3950479,00.html

Maguire, J. (1988). The commercialization of English basketball 1972–1988: A figurational perspective. *International Review for the Sociology of Sport, 23,* 305–323. doi:10.1177/101269028802300403

Maguire, J. (1999). *Global sport: Identities, societies, civilizations.* Cambridge, UK: Polity Press.

Maguire, J. (2008). 'Real politic', or 'ethically based': Sport, globalization, migration and nation-state policies. *Sport in Society, 11,* 443–458. doi:10.1080/17430430802019375

Miller, T., Lawrence, G., McKay, J., & Rowe, D. (2001). *Globalization and sport: Playing the world.* London: Sage.

Millman, J. (2010). Global hot spot: Hoops stars make a fast break for the Middle East." *The Wall Street Journal,* December 10, 2010.

Peled, Y., & Shafir, G. (2002). *Being Israeli: The dynamics of multiple citizenship.* Cambridge, MA: Cambridge University Press.

Podhoretz, N. (1998). Israel and the United State: A complex history. *Commentary (New York, N.Y.), 105,* 28.

Riordan, J. (1986). Communist sport policy: The end of an era. In L. Chalip (Ed.), *National sports policies: An international handbook* (pp. 89–115). Westport, Conn.: Greenwood.

Ritzer, G. (2004). *The globalization of nothing.* Thousand Oaks, CA: Pine Forge.

Robertson, R. (1992). *Globalization: Social theory and global culture.* London: Sage.

Robertson, R. (1995). Glocalization: Time-space and homogeneity-heterogeneity. In M. Featherstone, S. Lash, & R. Robertson (Eds.), *Global modernities* (pp. 25–44). London: Sage.

Robertson, R., & White, K. (2003). *Globalization: Critical concepts in sociology.* London: Routledge.

Sabo, D., & Jansen, S.C. (1994). Seen but not heard: Images of black men in sports media. In M.A. Messner & D.F. Sabo (Eds.), *Sex, Violence and Power in Sports* (pp. 150–160). CA: The Crossing Press.

Shor, E. (2008a). Conflict, terrorism, and the socialization of human rights norms: The spiral model revisited. *Social Problems, 55,* 117–138. doi:10.1525/sp.2008.55.1.117

Shor, E. (2008b). Contested masculinities: The new Jew and the construction of Black and Palestinian athletes in Israeli media. *Journal of Sport and Social Issues, 32,* 255–277. doi:10.1177/0193723508316376

Shor, E. (2008c). Utilizing rights and wrongs: Right-wing, the "right" language, and human rights in the Gaza disengagement. *Sociological Perspectives, 51,* 803–826. doi:10.1525/ sop.2008.51.4.803

Shor, E., & Yonay, Y. (2010). Sport, national identity, and media discourse over foreign athletes in Israel. *Nationalism & Ethnic Politics, 16,* 483–503. doi:10.1080/1353711 3.2010.527239

Shor, E., &Yonay, Y. (2011). 'Play and shut up': The silencing of Palestinian athletes in Israeli media. *Ethnic and Racial Studies, 34,* 229–247. doi:10.1080/01419870.2010.503811

Sikron, F., Baron-Epel, O., & Linn, S. (2007). The voice of lay experts: Content analysis of traffic accident 'talk-backs'. *Transportation Research Part F: Traffic Psychology and Behaviour, 11,* 24–36. doi:10.1016/j.trf.2007.06.001

Smooha, S. (1998). Ethnic democracy: Israel as an archetype. *Israel Studies, 2,* 198–241. doi:10.2979/ISR.1997.2.2.198

Sugden, J.P., & Tomlinson, A. (Eds.). (1994). *Hosts and champions: Soccer cultures, national identities and the United States world cup.* Aldershot, UK: Arena.

Tzadik, G. (2010). Put the ball in the *sal.*" *Haaretz,* October 13, 2010. Retrieved September 23, 2011 at www.haaretz.co.il/sport/1.1225026

Whannel, G. (2002). *Media sport stars: Masculinities and mortalities.* London, New York: Routledge.

Wilson, B. (1997). Good blacks and bad blacks: Media constructions of African-American athletes in Canadian basketball. *International Review for the Sociology of Sport, 32,* 177–189. doi:10.1177/101269097032002005

Wong, L.L., & Trumper, R. (2002). Global celebrity athletes and nationalism: *Fútbol,* hockey, and the representation of nation. *Journal of Sport and Social Issues, 26,* 168–194. doi:10.1177/0193723502262004

Yep, K. (2009). *Outside the paint: When basketball ruled at the Chinese playground.* Philadelphia, PA: Temple University Press.

CHAPTER 37

What Happens While the Official Looks the Other Way? Citizenship, Transnational Sports Migrants and the Circumvention of the State

Thomas F. Carter

INTRODUCTION

In the spring of 2008, Alejandro Rojas[1] will travel from the Dominican Republic to the training facilities of the Chicago White Sox in Tucson Arizona.[2] He will, in all likelihood, travel on a passenger jet in relative comfort, pass through US Immigration with relative ease on his Dominican passport and US work visa, and continue his career as a professional baseball player. Rojas is not Dominican, however; he is Cuban. His ethnicity is not that remarkable. That Rojas will travel across the North American continent for his employment is not especially remarkable either. What is rather remarkable and is often absent from public discourse is the negotiated terms of his travel, terms set by a transnational corporation, Major League Baseball, in conjunction with a national government, the US Government, that regulates, legalizes, and constrains transnational sport labour migration. Even more remarkable and hidden is the means by which Rojas travelled to the Dominican Republic from Cuba. His and others' travels are what is of particular concern in this article.

A decade earlier, Alejandro Rojas was just a boy and I was in Havana. While I have never met Señor Rojas, I have known several other Cuban baseball players. On a brisk January day that Cubans consider cold, I was conversing with Román, a sports journalist and friend, in the street outside his office when he informed me that Juan Pablo was missing. Confused, I queried, 'Missing? What do you mean missing? He's got a game tonight. I just talked to him last week.'

Román shrugged his shoulders, 'He's gone. He's not at home, no one has seen him for three days.' His voice drops *sotto voce*, 'They [baseball officials] do not know where he is.'

'*Pinche*, he promised to give me an interview next week. Where do you think he is?'

Cocking his head to one side and looking at me out of the side of his glasses, Román smiles slightly and says, 'Who knows? All they know is that he is not where he is supposed to be.'

Two weeks later, Román and I meet again to catch up on news, gossip, and to discuss various local issues. Even as he sits down, he raises the subject of Juan Pablo again. 'Juan Pablo is in Costa Rica. So is Gutierrez.' Gutierrez is Juan Pablo's teammate on their *Serie Nacional* team.[3]

I splutter in disbelief, 'Both of them? How'd they get there? What are they doing there?'

Román orders the waiter to bring us two beers. 'No one here knows,' implying that no Cuban official knows. 'They are investigating how they got there. *La Peña* says that

Juan Pablo will sign with the [New York] Yankees for ten million.'[4]

I retort, 'The Yankees? Not without a tryout he won't. And I'm sure he'd have a tryout to show other clubs what he can do as well.' The waiter arrives with our drinks, takes our order, and wanders back to the kitchen leaving us in relative peace. I continue, 'You say no one knows. That's crap. Surely someone knows where he went and how.'

Román laughs briefly and smiles. 'Of course, Tomás. People know he went in a boat. What no one knows is who took him. Except those who organized it and some of them must still be here in Cuba.'

'Why do you say that?' I ask.

'It is simple, really. To do something like that, I imagine, requires coordination with people here and out there (*p'alla*). So some of them, logically, must still be here.'

I finish his thought, 'And that is what the authorities are investigating . . .'

Román finishes this conversational thread, 'Exactly.'

These two episodes, 10 years apart, serve to introduce the main themes of this paper. Both Rojas's sudden appearance in the Dominican Republic in 2007 and Juan Pablo's disappearance in 1997 illustrate the complexities of transnational sport migration and challenge our current understandings of these phenomena. Transnational sport migration (TSM), in all its forms, is dynamic and multifaceted, and capturing the intricacies of TSM requires more analytical sophistication than currently offered by the mainly ahistorical typologies that so far have been proposed.[5] At present, understandings about the transnational migration of sports professionals have been presented in atemporal dichotomies of sundered ties and new relations without any critical examination of the ties that are supposedly cut and the new ones used to replace those that allegedly disappear. These approaches oversimplify the migratory experience in both localities, origin and destination, consequently resulting in an overly simplified portrayal of the processes involved in TSM. The typologies currently on offer simply cannot account for the various factors that inform migratory processes, whether they are economic, political, familial, or one of several other potential factors informing decisions and strategies to move from one locale to another. They also tend to treat transnational sport migrants as individuals who operate in isolation when their decision-making processes clearly involve multiple individuals in the planning, implementation and effect of any such move.[6] Further, the choices of where, when and how to move from one place to another also are absent from these sorts of categorization. Another shortcoming, and the one that is the focus of this particular article, is the absence of the state in such migratory practices. The role of the state in TSM is essential despite pre-eminent texts' much greater emphasis on the global economic and political forces affecting sport in academic literature.[7] While certainly accurate in their accounts of the expanding roles that international non-governmental organizations (INGOs) like the International Olympic Committee (IOC) and FIFA play in shaping TSM, these leading works fail to account for the well established and ongoing effects that state governance of borders has on TSM. To begin to address these limitations, the complexities of Cuban TSM are used to illustrate these processes. Cuban TSM has a number of unique features specific to its recent history that further illuminate the importance of historical specificities that exist in all forms of TSM.

This paper brings the state back into analyses of TSM by looking at strategies migrant athletes have used to skirt bureaucratic attempts to control their movements. Excavating the strategies employed by transnational migrants draws attention to the means by which states channel the flow of TSM and to the particular contests over the control of the movement of individuals. By attending to these key aspects of how 'globalization' itself is ideologically articulated and received, it reveals the tenuously negotiated strategic positions held in the control of professionals' movements. Globalization is not merely the benign force its advocates claim it is; rather it entails conflicts over local ideologies and values that define personhood. Understanding the classificatory schema of citizenship that states construct is therefore essential – both for this paper and for migrants themselves in order to manipulate these controlling mechanisms in their favour. Adopting this perspective permits an investigative consideration of the various positions involved in this contested social process.

This essay is part of a larger project on TSM that attempts to humanize our understandings of these migrants by engaging in 'translocal research'.[8] Translocal research entails making a conscious methodological decision to exchange ethnographic depth for breadth of materials. This larger project makes use of a combination of ethnographic material gathered over the past decade, along with interviews and investigative reports. This was a conscious decision since it was unlikely that I would be able to obtain detailed observational data on the everyday lives of the particular migrants discussed in this paper.[9] Nor could I, realistically, make the same journeys under similar conditions since the migratory moves under scrutiny in this paper entail illegal activities. Consequently, every person identified in this article has been given a pseudonym, even if that person has appeared elsewhere in other publications (including my own) under other names, because the material presented here documents some of the reasoning for and strategies of engaging in illegal activities. Nevertheless, the examples presented here are results of primary fieldwork in which I followed migrants' routes (albeit not necessarily at the same moment in time or using identical methods of travel) and spoke with at least one person in each of the ethnographic anecdotes provided in this article at some point in their travels.

The strategic decision to engage in translocal research echoes Ian Henry's recent categorical rejection of the supposed diminished role of the nation-state in sports policy and supposed irreconcilable difference between the West and its Others.[10] Pursuing anthropologist George Marcus' suggestion to follow the subject and see where it leads shifts the analytic focus of transnational migration and global process from 'place of origin' and 'place of destination' to the strategic moves involved in sustaining a livelihood.[11] Such an approach is likely to take the researcher in unanticipated directions instead of the researcher imposing sui generis expectations of how 'global' practices form and adhere. My reliance on multivocal, translocal fieldwork sacrifices some of the usual ethnographic 'thick description' in favour of a broader expanse of transnational networks.[12] Tracing the movements of transnational sport migrants has led me to variously unanticipated places based on the routes taken by the individuals and not by any design I had on how this study should proceed. Instead, shorter visits to some, but certainly not all, of the other localities where the migrants were present (ideally while those individuals were in those locales) were made in an effort to obtain a better grasp of the routes and challenges migrants face in each state.

ON SPORT AND GLOBALIZATION

> At least 95 percent of all scholars and all scholarship from the period of 1850 to 1914, and probably even to 1945, originates in five countries: France, Great Britain, the Germanies, the Italies, and the United States. There is a smattering elsewhere, but basically not only does

> the scholarship come out of these five countries, but most of the scholarship by most scholars is about their own country. . . . This is partly pragmatic, partly social pressure, and partly ideological: these are the important countries, this is what matters, this is what we should study in order to learn how the world operates.[13]

Immanuel Wallerstein's comments on the historical patterns of scholarly production are undeniably important for those scholars concerned with the study of transnational sport. The vast majority of sport-related scholarship follows a similar pattern in which the predominant production of knowledge on sport is situated and produced within predominantly Anglophile, protestant, capitalist societies.

> [As] a product of modern European civilization, studying any problem of universal history, [a scholar] is bound to ask himself [*sic*] to what combination of circumstances the fact should be attributed that in Western civilization, and in Western civilization only, cultural phenomena have appeared which (as we like to think) lie in a line of development having universal significance and value.[14]

This tendency leads to a rather myopic position that the organization, values and practices found in sport in one culture compared with another are unequivocal evidence of some cosmopolitan universalism identified as 'global sport'. The prevalence of 'global sport' has been widely remarked upon and had a number of its facets addressed yet the methods, manner and meanings of the production and consumption of global sport are embedded in local power struggles and do not reign above them.[15] Globalization advocates speak about ways in which people are transcending localized, spatialized identities in order to become cosmopolitan citizens of a singularly imagined world.[16] Worryingly, the commentators and scholars examining all of these various aspects of what has come to be both popularly and academically called 'global sport' tend to adopt the particular rhetoric and logic of globalization. From this position, sport becomes a global social practice that transcends boundaries via 'diminishing contrasts and increasing varieties' yet simultaneously glosses over the specific disjunctures of hierarchy, power and agency in and across local contexts.[17] The muting of historically forged differences is particularly evident among scholars who have stressed the 'deterritorialized' nature of the contemporary world with respect to the organization of political economies and the reproduction of 'global sport'. Although 'global sport' arguments are frequently peppered with qualifications recognizing important differences among nations, cultures and transnational processes, these differences rarely rise to the level of analysis.

These suppressions of difference exaggerate the autonomy and determinacy of capital vis-à-vis states and leads to perspectives that locate anti-capitalist agency in cosmopolitan subjects who have the wherewithal, sophistication and power to negotiate national borders while calcifying those individuals who do not possess these capacities. It is precisely this lack of attention to the space-forming and space-contingent character of relations of production that has led some to regard late capitalist accumulation as being external to the political field of the state – as waves of 'global' capital that wash over states and, in the process, over important political questions.

> One thing is clear: globalization is not some great carnival of capital, technology, and goods where we are all free to walk away with what we want. What one gets and how much, where one finds a place in the global network of exchanges, indeed whether one finds a place in it at all, depends on several economic and political conditions.[18]

By stressing the deterritorialized character of contemporary capitalism, some have neglected not only the critical role played by states in constituting and disciplining labour power – Foucault's question of 'governmentality' – but also the multi-tiered spatial politics that enable and disable the transnational movement of capital.[19] 'The nation-state – along with its juridical-legislative systems, bureaucratic apparatuses, economic entities, modes of governmentality and war-making capacities – continues to define, discipline, control and regulate' all kinds of capital, including labour, whether in movement or in situ.[20] The tendency to exaggerate the deterritorialized nature of the contemporary world has important theoretical and political consequences. First, it has led to the assertion that globalization is a *fait accompli.* Irresistible and new, the projection of globalization is articulated as having superseded not only the politics of nation-states but their enduring asymmetrical relationships – asymmetries that are firmly rooted in the ongoing histories of imperialism. Second, the deterritorialization argument risks underestimating and obscuring political agency. The oppositional practices of those very agents who are experiencing, theorizing and struggling against 'globalizing' neoliberal economic policies, in particular, become hidden in supposedly hegemonic macro-scale phenomena.[21] Since states still monopolize the legitimate means of force within their borders, for the most part, it is problematic to conceptualize the 'deterritorialization of the state' as any kind of socio-political process entailing the deconstruction of state systems of rulership and power.[22] Far from dismantling state apparatuses and opening borders to free-flowing capital, it is apparent that many states, once presumed to be peripheral, are promoting the reproduction of transnational subjects and in the process reinventing their own role in the so-called 'new world order'.[23] What should be apparent is that the logic of globalization is not a foregone conclusion but is one politically informed ideological discourse engaged in a hotly contested ideological struggle. This contest over the constitution of global interests and identities in relation to the national is better viewed as an argument between multiple social agents instead of as a set of intractable, structural relationships between superstructural 'global' capital whose tentacles dangle and dip into base 'national' economies.[24] Finally, this same contest is one in which state authorities are prominent agents in the struggle and that condition cannot be ignored.

ON CITIZENSHIP AND GLOBALIZATION

Globalization advocates speak about the ways people are transcending localized, spatialized identities and lives in order to become cosmopolitan 'citizens of the world'. This whole concept of a citizen of the world rests on the ideological construct of a singular global culture that supersedes the various spatial restrictions of movement entailed in crossing international boundaries. Quite simply, global citizenship is, as an aspect of globalization itself, an ideological project that is nowhere near fruition. Miller et al. survey the way in which global governance of sport appears to be creating such 'citizens of the world' while sport-related INGOs, such as FIFA, and other supranational bodies of governance define who shall be incorporated into this new form of citizenship through the establishment of transnational industrial labour regulations.[25] In effect, these processes in TSM are part of the creation of a transnational capitalist class – a group of social actors comprising executives, professionals, bureaucrats and consumers who strive to sustain the dominance of capitalism as a social system.[26] These citizens of the world are primarily understood as individual rights holders and not members of a common or cohesive community.[27] Although incomplete, such projects nonetheless do impact states' attempts to regulate movement across borders and creates spaces in which individuals can manipulate those rules in their favour, thereby contravening the gate-keeping desires of the state.

These gate-keeping apparatuses are evident in various countries via the strategic interrogation of individuals requiring the proper kind of social capital. State bureaucracies, emblematic in the ubiquitous forms (filled out in triplicate) necessary to accomplish what should be basic interactions, facilitate the enforcement of a division of labour through the control of social spaces.[28] This gate-keeping work is not only an attempt to keep control of a state's populace, it serves to aid in the application of governmentality. The predominant form of this aspect of governmentality is the state's attempt to prevent unapproved individuals from entering the state's territory. States also attempt to prevent certain kinds of persons from leaving its domain as well.[29] In either direction, this work is partially accomplished through the definition of citizenship criteria and the identification of citizens.

Citizenship consists of disciplinary techniques comprising discourses and practices governing national belonging exercised by state authorities to channel access to social rights and regulate, among other things, the social division of labour. Those without the correct information on their identification often find themselves removed from certain spaces with utmost haste. Attending to the everyday struggles over labour, identity and national belonging highlights critical antagonisms within, and resistances to, the organization and specific practices of governmentality exercised in nation-states' attempts to produce and reproduce specific socio-spatial orders of capital accumulation.

Since the state itself is imagined as occupying a defined space over which it has nominal control of social experience, one of its goals and roles is to protect the sanctity of its borders from uncontrolled and unwanted presences. It does so through the invention and implementation of a variety of practices, one of the most prevalent being the forging of specific immigration policies and practices. The attempt to control entry and exit of this space is paramount to the performance of sovereignty, in which a state has to be seen by both its own peoples and outsiders, to be in control of its boundaries. In conjunction with a sport's national governing body (yet another bureaucratic arm of the state), quotas and definitions of citizenship, of who can and cannot represent the nation-state, are defined and enforced. Citizenship regulations determine who is and who is not a member of any given state. Acting as a 'continuing series of transactions between persons and agents of a given state in which each has enforceable rights and obligations, citizenship constitutes a critical and contested field of power relations and practices'.[30] Indeed, citizenship tests do not establish qualifications for such status but are instead a tool used to control the level and composition of immigration. These sorts of examinations have historically been introduced or modified in line with changing attitudes towards immigration in those states that utilize them.[31] Even with the introduction of 'European citizenship', access at 'this regional or supranational level is still defined at the member-state level'.[32] By controlling membership, a government can delineate who does belong, 'citizens', and who does not, 'foreigners'; and the contested processes of defining persons as one or the other determines access to various rights and goods, like political representation and employment. Yet citizenship is not portrayed as a categorical construct but as a 'natural' or 'biological' quality that effectively masks the actual relation between individual and state, and 'roots' people in territorial soil. Thus, people become 'naturally' linked to a specific space – a state's territory – and by creating 'lineages' of 'genetic material' passed down from generation to generation, the social fluid of 'blood' becomes a determining aspect of citizenship equated with a biological trait.[33] More recently, the concept of citizenship has shifted from inherent embodied right to negotiated commodity even as full membership remains crucial since it defines the scope of opportunity, security and sense of belonging within a state.

States actively recruit and deny citizenship of sports professionals through the use of quotas set by a sport's governing body in a given country. National governing bodies, on their own, with other bureaucratic aspects of the state and in consultation with an international governing body, are one bureaucratic limb of the state and often determine the quantity and quality of professionals allowed to enter and work in that country. These instruments of bureaucratic governmentality are a major restraint on a sport professional's ability to move around the world in search of employment.[34] Because the specificities of citizenship in each state are informed by historical particularities, any particular study of TSM must take the original state, the destination state and the historical political relationship between them into account. Thus, citizenship is a valuable piece of personal, social and political capital that can be deployed strategically within the global sport industry.

This is especially evident in the increasing attempts by athletes to switch nationalities in order to qualify for international competitions, what is euphemistically called 'code switching'. Indeed, this strategic switching of citizenship is becoming so prevalent the International Association of Athletics Federations (IAAF) and the IOC have both set up working groups to investigate the growing question of national representation and nationswitching.[35] One athlete who pursued this strategy of citizenship exchange is Graciela Yasmine Álvarez.[36] As is increasingly common among Cuba's star athletics athletes, Álvarez lived and trained in Europe in recent years. Since 2001 she had lived in the United Kingdom, training and competing in Europe on the IAAF sanctioned circuit. Álvarez applied for British citizenship in 2003 while living with her British husband so she could compete under the auspices of the Union Jack. While British athletics officials were privately thrilled with the potential addition of a world-class athlete, British immigration authorities denied her request for UK citizenship, in part because Cuban authorities refused to allow her to skip the required three-year waiting period for switching nationalities under IOC and IAAF regulations, which meant she would be ineligible to compete in the 2004 Athens Olympics. Having already missed the World Championships because she was effectively stateless, Álvarez decided that she could not accept her situation and pursued other possible nations to represent. Unwilling to return to Cuba, which would, in all likelihood, mean the end of her career and marriage, Álvarez reportedly entered into discussions with the Italian and the Czech governing bodies. When Sudanese officials suddenly approached her willing to grant her immediate citizenship, Álvarez readily accepted their offer.

Graciela Álvarez is one of the more recent world-class athletes in a variety of sports to decide to compete for a country with which she has no historical connection. While athletes can and do switch citizenship to facilitate their economic earning power, this is often done within state-defined rules of who is and who is not a member of the nation, particularly through the 'grandfather rule' as it is sometimes called, based on 'natural' or biological qualities of citizenship rather than based on the individual deployment of strategic capital. When pursuing this strategy, many athletes do not abandon their original 'natural' citizenship but become dual nationals, maintaining citizenship in two states, the country of their birth and the one which they represent in international athletic competition. Cuban athletes, however, do not have that particular option. The restrictions laid upon them by the Cuban state require that they choose rather than multiply their citizenship capital. This situation is by no means unique to Cubans; during the Cold War individuals often found it necessary to illegally migrate within an international political context that framed such moves. The peculiar historical circumstances that currently exist necessitating such strategies inform the particular patterns involved in Cuban TSM. Thus, they are required to renounce their citizenship and obtain new state membership. In short, they have to defect.

The whole concept of defection, a citizen's sundering of a relationship between state and citizen without that state authorities' consent, via a public renunciation of citizenship, is one that is firmly entrenched within Cold War ideological discourses. Ironically, it is not the framework in which the movement of Cuban athletes should be understood despite the vociferous trumpeting by right-wing Cuban exiles each time a baseball player leaves Cuba to try his luck as a professional abroad. Defection is itself an unusual context although political motivations are more prevalent than commonly assumed in TSM literature.[37] Álvarez's cross-border movements should be understood in the discourse of 'code-switching', found throughout the global governance of international sport, in which citizenship, effectively, is being used as a commodity that can be deployed for its use-value or even sold on to a government willing to sponsor the athlete. This is becoming more and more prevalent as citizenship parameters are being defined by non-state actors.[38] Citizenship is transforming from a condition of personhood to a resource, a form of capital, to be flexibly deployed.[39] While many of those who abandoned the Cuban state in the 1990s are baseball players, athletes in other sports have begun to flee the island within the past few of years thereby affecting the strategies used in the Cuban citizenship game.

THE CUBAN GAME OF CITIZENSHIP

The Cuban state's strategies for maintaining and utilizing its sporting excellence reveal the tensions found in the continual negotiation of citizenship. For most of the history of the Revolution, the control of Cuban athletes' movements was limited by Cold War contexts. Cuban athletes willingly accepted these controls as no active Cuban athlete defected in the first 30 years of Revolutionary rule. That situation changed with the onset of the *Periodo Especial en el Tiempo de Paz* (the Special Period in Times of Peace) in which the international relations the Cuban state had nurtured and cultivated over the previous three decades disintegrated along with the Berlin Wall and the Soviet Union. The collapse of European state socialism suddenly threw the ability of Cuban state bureaucrats to meet their obligations towards Cuban citizens into question, thereby causing a traumatic rupture in state-legitimating discourses. Through artful negotiation with its own population, authorities implemented the equivalent of war-time rationing without the experience of state-level violence. Officials positioned themselves, through various state institutions, to act as the primary distributor of imports within the domestic economy while maintaining a monopoly of exports in the global economy. In short, Cuban officials set themselves up as the gatekeepers of Cuban sport, as the structural control of sport moved from a centralized model run wholly under the Cuban Ministry of Sport to a more diffuse control through the creation of CubaDeportes, SA.[40]

During the 1990s, the restructuring of the economy included the following state-led strategic moves: the legalization of hard currency possession by individuals, changing entrepreneurship regulations, renegotiated international trade agreements, and the emergence of novel forms of foreign investment.[41] Many of these strategies emanated from within the government's hallowed halls but these strategies were also reactions to the situations on the ground in which citizens adopted alternative strategies and rejected the sacrifices for which authorities called. This led to the burgeoning of the already existing *bolsa negra*, the black market that thrived on petty theft from state warehouses and other forms of economic exchange that did not involve state institutions. Yet the dire straits in which both state leaders and everyday citizens found themselves led many to pursue alternative strategies to increase the likelihood of personal and familial survival. Numerous strategies were implemented at the behest of or, at the very least, with the tacit approval of state authorities. A few strategies, however, actively challenged the state's controlling mechanisms.

Cuban authorities created CubaDeportes, SA in 1993 to exploit the status and expertise of Cuban sports personnel. Its role over the past 15 years has been to cultivate and develop transnational economic relations with other sporting bodies for the economic benefit of the Cuban sports programmes. One of its primary strategies has been the export of Cuban technical knowledge through the contractual employment of Cuban coaches by foreign national governing bodies.[42] Yet while CubaDeportes officials work to create opportunities for sports professionals, not just anyone is provided the opportunity to become a Cuban transnational sport migrant. State officials keep a close eye on who they permit to leave the country for a number of reasons. The process was explained by several CubaDeportes employees in the following manner:

> Okay, let us say that you want to hire me to coach your team in whatever sport. You as an official of that club would either contact me who would tell you to contact CubaDeportes, or you would contact your sport's officials (of that national governing body) telling them that you want me or a coach with specific qualifications that I have, suggesting that I would be the best to get. Your officials would then contact CubaDeportes who would then check their list of available personnel. If I was the name at the top of that list, CubaDeportes would check on me, talk to my neighbors, to my coworkers, find out what kind of person I am. Is he an angry person? Does he show up for work on time? What's his family situation? Does he get along with others? Does he have *calidad*? And if all of that is positive then they would contact me and say, Señor Fulano, we have an opportunity for you, we want you to go over there.[43]

On the surface it would appear that Cubans would leap at the chance to work overseas. In a short span they could potentially earn five or six times what they normally make in a year, sometimes even more, depending on the country to which they would be sent. What one interviewee made clear though is that the offer of overseas employment is not really optional. 'If they ask you, you have an obligation to go. . . . If you do not, they can make your life *difficult*.' There are repercussions for not taking any opportunity presented since demonstrated reluctance to go can inhibit future opportunities to work overseas.[44] Not only is there an implicit obligation on the part of the individual to accept the offer the state has provided, it is nigh on impossible for a Cuban to find work independently from CubaDeportes. Indeed, it is all but impossible to organize one's own contract or offer. A couple of different individuals described situations in which they had been overseas and had maintained contact with foreign nationals while back in Cuba. They had obtained written invitations to return for further employment but because these offers did not follow proper channels, that is, through CubaDeportes representatives, state officials deemed the offers unacceptable and each individual in question was unable to leave Cuba to take up the offer of a post. This was true despite the glowing reviews their employers had written about their earlier work and the good relationship the migrant in question had developed with the foreign organization. An individual who attempts to play by other rules, so to speak, finds one's own willingness to be properly revolutionary, of one's willingness to engage in *lucha*, to struggle for the good of the Revolution, and be a staunch supporter of revolutionary ideals all called into question by those who do make the rules of the citizenship game. Demonstrating a public unwillingness to act in the manner expressed by state officials makes one's own social position in Cuban society open to reinterpretation vis-à-vis the Cuban state. In short, the relationship between citizen and state is called into question.

Consequently, many Cuban transnational sport migrants draw upon the *doble moral* of contemporary Cuban life in which it is necessary to demonstrate affections for a cause, in which one does not actually believe, all the while being forced to act in a contradictory manner in order to survive.[45] Those athletes who earn the honour of being able to represent Cuba in international competition have demonstrated not only outstanding athletic skill but also embody Cuban socialist ideals. The state's investiture in their bodies makes them essential to its legitimacy. By becoming part of this revolutionary vanguard, athletes demonstrate how the power of the socialist body can be made manifest. Their multiplying victories embody the idealized notion of the New Man and, by shaping their powerful bodies via rigorous discipline, their love for the Cuban people and their *patria*.[46] Patriotic fervour is supposed to provide greater motivation for the individual athlete, theoretically replacing monetary compensation. Ideally, the love of one's country replaces the fear of losing one's job. The problem is that most athletes' motivation for living overseas is the opportunity to earn some prize money (i.e., hard currency). Whether they are ever afforded this opportunity depends on their ability to 'produce' not just with their athletic bodies but also with their socialist bodies. These particular athletes must somehow find a way to incorporate and demonstrate that they embody socialist ideals to state authorities if they are going to earn an opportunity to compete at an international level. The irony is that those who eventually do leave or refuse to return must demonstrate socialist 'techniques of the body' in order to be allowed to compete overseas in international competition.[47] It is only by constructing, at the minimum, a 'revolutionary skin' – a façade that covers one's 'true' body – to demonstrate that one is a proper Cuban citizen that these same individuals can deny the primacy of the Revolutionary body through the act of nation-switching and citizenship exchange.

This *doble moral* leads some individuals to attempt to circumvent the state by engaging in unsanctioned TSM. Unsanctioned TSM refers to professionals who have crossed state borders or remained in a state's territory without the explicit consent of that government. Unsanctioned TSMs unquestionably affect Cuban sport. Two of the more common strategies Cubans employ are the refusal to return while working or competing overseas, or to be smuggled out of the country. While each is a distinct strategy, they share some similarities. They inherently contain a set of risks in that the refusal of state authority can have repercussions for those family members left behind. It can also inadvertently result in the termination of the very career one attempts to maintain. Plus, the uncertainty of finding further work and earning enough to survive makes taking such a decision a huge risk, with the rare exception of high-profile 'star' athletes. Most unsanctioned TSMs never make the international press, or even the national for that matter. Unfortunately, if such unsanctioned Cuban transnational sport migrants do obtain media coverage, they readily slide into a political context informed by Cold War politics.[48] The motivating factors for these unsanctioned movements are individual decisions based on family economics not political ideologies.[49]

The other form of unsanctioned Cuban transnational migration that needs to be addressed is migrant smuggling – the clandestine movement of groups of people from one state to another. Smuggling has a long history throughout the Caribbean and Cuba and continues to play a prominent role in the region.[50] People smuggling, in all its myriad forms, also continues to play a prominent role in transnational migration. Whereas slaves were smuggled past British naval ships into Cuba in the nineteenth century, twenty-first century smugglers attempt to evade US Coast Guard authorities to smuggle people out of Cuba. The popular perception of people smuggling is that globalization created the conditions for greater transnational trafficking of humans, conducted predominantly by violent and greedy professional criminals exploiting weak and (mostly) innocent migrants. That the specific actions by politicians and other state actors in both origin and destination states are largely responsible for creating these conditions remains largely unacknowledged. These smuggling operations are incredibly diverse in scope, scale and integration in local and regional social networks and structures.[51]

Migrant smuggling only began to be a viable and prominent migratory strategy in the 1990s when Cuba's economy changed rapidly and dramatically. The demise of the Soviet-led economic bloc resulted in the loss of 80–85% of Cuba's external trade and 50% of its purchasing power; and it has taken several years for the economy to climb out of that abyss.[52] Tourism replaced sugar as the island's primary source of hard currency.[53] Family remittances and foreign investment partially replaced the subsidies supplied by the Soviet Union. Family remittances increased from the comparatively paltry US$18 million in 1991 to estimates between US$500 and US$725 million in 1999.[54] Foreign investment strategies concentrate primarily on activities related to the use of natural resources, such as tourism, mining, petroleum and agriculture. A consequence of these changes has been a reordering of the class hierarchy in Cuban society with transnational ties suddenly becoming an eminently vital factor in determining one's position in Cuba. This new class is made up of those who played minimal roles in the state bureaucracy but now work with foreign investors in world markets as commercial intermediaries and service providers. Many of these managers are minor government officials who did not have much standing in the hierarchy of government but use their new found relations to augment and raise their own standard of living. This is evident in the changes in savings and new forms of employment. The number of small savings accounts dropped by 50%, yet the monetary value of the most affluent has nearly doubled.[55] In 1996, 12.8% of bank accounts represented 85% of private savings in the economy.[56] Professionals working in sport, however, did not have access to these new transnational links except through CubaDeportes. Sport professionals were losing socioeconomic position in this radical reshuffling of relationships and many individuals felt a need to either change careers or find another way to maintain their status.

As the following vignette illustrates, sport professionals have plans in place, strategies formulated, and a transnational network to implement those strategic moves. Those Cuban transnational sport migrants who take to the seas and risk life, limb, career and family in order to avoid the control of the Cuban state are not fleeing blindly, contrary to the popularly perpetuated myth of the *balsero*.[57] Rather, their moves are informed by the local political conditions in both Cuba and their destinations.

On a hot summer day in 1998, seven Cubans, five of whom claimed to be baseball players, suddenly arrived in a small town on the eastern shore of Nicaragua, aboard a 72-foot pleasure cruiser. The cruiser's tarpaulins were deliberately rigged to cover the vessel's name and the crew initially refused to give interviews when the luxury yacht arrived. Eventually, a convoluted story emerged, which, in each retelling of the circumstances of the Cubans' arrival in Nicaragua, gradually revealed that this arrival was more of a planned smuggling operation rather than a chance encounter at sea.

Allegedly, the group had launched a small boat from the western tip of Cuba with three gallons of water and two cans of tomato juice with the express hope of reaching the Yucatan peninsula, some 130 miles away. After only six hours at sea, they ran into a large pleasure cruiser supposedly on its way from Cozumel, Mexico to Costa Rica. The yacht took them to Nicaragua, where it so happened that four of these seven *balseros* had previously been offered visas by the Nicaraguan government months earlier.[58]

The Cubans claimed that they set out from Pinar del Rio province and encountered the pleasure cruiser by chance. Initially, the boat's owner corroborated the Cubans' story, claiming that they had accidentally happened upon the Cubans, even though he had told the boat's captain to make a several hundred mile detour from the usual route between Yucatan and Costa Rica so he could see the Cuban coast because 'a lot of people are investing in Cuba'. Months later, the owner claimed that he had received a call from an unidentified person asking him to help the players prior to his encountering them. He also claimed earlier that the athletes' escape was similar to a paramilitary operation involving around 20 people. Both statements clearly contradict his initial claims of accidental discovery.

Three months after arriving in Nicaragua, the Cubans suddenly vanished while waiting for their Nicaraguan visas. The current political climate in Nicaragua was in flux and their applications, previously guaranteed by President Alemán, were now being questioned.[59] The Cubans' disappearance was not really noted until they suddenly appeared in San José, Costa Rica. San José is in the middle of the country between two mountain ranges. How they got from the eastern coast of Nicaragua to the Costa Rican capital became another mystery. They fled to Costa Rica because they believed it was doubtful they would be able to obtain the necessary citizenship documents, whereas the differing local contexts in Costa Rica made it much more likely that they would be successful in obtaining a Costa Rican passport than a Nicaraguan one.[60]

In the end, two of those men eventually landed in the USA as legal migrants from Costa Rica and played professionally in the United States. Another secured a professional contract for one season in a Taiwanese professional league before returning to Costa Rica. The others, apparently, have never left Costa Rica and disappeared from sight.[61] The movements of this group from Cuba to Nicaragua, and then to Costa Rica, before pursuing their own separate routes hint at the importance local political contexts have in determining migratory strategies. It is clear from this example, along with others, that transnational migrants carefully consider shifting local conditions while planning their next move(s).[62]

SOME CONCLUDING REMARKS

The importance of local conditions in both the origin state and the destination state of transnational sport migrants cannot be underestimated or ignored. Furthermore, the rules of citizenship are frequently manipulated and exploited to individual actors' own advantages. These manipulations are not done solely by marginalized individuals but by prominent individuals and by state authorities themselves to further their own specific interests. The repercussions of such actions affect sport and society as a whole in both localities thereby heightening the emphasis on historically specific connections rather than broad, sweeping generalized flows. This specificity is evident in the recurring concern over the territorial sanctity of state borders even as those borders become flexible, elastic and increasingly porous. This ever-present concern over the sanctity of state borders challenges the emphasis currently placed on the supposed deterritorialization of transnational sport processes.

The tendency to exaggerate the deterritorialized state risks obscuring political agency and those who are truly shaping the patterns of TSM. In particular, the focus on TSM lends itself to a picture of 'global sport' in which athletes readily move from location to location with relative ease because of 'globalizing' neoliberal economic policies of specific governments and international governing bodies. This projection of globalization is articulated as a *fait accompli* that supersedes not only the politics of nation-states but their enduring asymmetrical relationships – asymmetries that are firmly rooted in the ongoing histories of imperialism. Cuban state authorities act in direct contravention to these supposedly globalizing neoliberal strategies. At the same time, Cuban sports authorities attempt to control the movements of Cuban professionals thereby facilitating their own repositioning in transnational political economic relations within sport.

The constituency of the state is no longer simply a population of citizens defined by territorial borders who demand protection from forces outside of those borders. Increasingly, the global economy and its dominant actors and institutions themselves inform definitions of citizenship and citizenry. Various international actors, such as the IOC, FIFA and MLB, have all assumed some of the defining powers of citizenship within their respective domains. These reformulations are not accomplished despite states but in conjunction with state authorities. The emerging shape of TSM must, as a consequence, include considerations of the historical relationships between states since state-based actors continue to work at maintaining control of the entrance of individuals into their sovereign space and the movement through that geopolitical space. Through a variety of discursive bureaucratic processes, many states not only work at keeping certain individuals from entering the confines of the state's territory but actively attempt to prevent individuals leaving the country without the state's awareness. This is an especially prevalent strategy among those nation-states attempting to prevent the drain of educated and highly skilled citizens, as the loss of these individuals creates further restrictions on the ability of the state's leaders to sustain any economic stability. Thus citizenship is useful for not only keeping certain alien threats out but for state authorities to maintain control of the socioeconomic capital of its own citizens, whether resident or not.[63] Understanding how citizenship is conceived and deployed within the contemporary world system has important theoretical and political consequences that must be attenuated to any consideration of TSM.

The enduring role the nation-state plays in configuring global flows of capital, technology and labour, as well as in structuring the discourses about the nature and future of the 'global', cannot be discounted. However diminished the capacity of nation-states to govern their economies appears to be, the state nonetheless remains a central agent in structuring the specific manner in which transnational movements of capital, people and media are materialized in space, whether as multinational corporate initiatives or in alternative forms. 'Global sport', as an aspect of 'globalization' then, is less a description of the existing world system than a set of contested claims about how the world should be structured in relation to nation-states and their peoples. An assumption about TSM is that migration is predominantly based on individuals' economic decisions influenced by transnational corporate capital's penetration and shaping of domestic markets. Virtually ignored are other variables including the influence of families, state attempts to restrict the influx or flight of capital, including (especially) labour.[64]

The Cuban cases in this article make it apparent that the reach of global sport is not 'the world as it actually exists' but is more a reflection of how certain organizations and its members would like the world to be. Contrary to contemporary ideological discourses within the arena of international politics, whether the stultified remains of Cold War political ideologies or contemporary neoliberal globalization ideologies, Cuban TSM is based on a number of factors that includes individuals' economic decisions, corporate capital's penetration of domestic markets, and local political contexts.

As an initial step towards a greater understanding of the various forces that shape TSM, the ideological constructs and power struggles hidden within 'global sport' need to be extruded. The transnational structures of 'global sport' are historically specific power relations that are informed by and directly impact individuals' lives. How individuals support or challenge these structural relations loosely identified as 'global sport' is of utmost importance. Through their own actions, transnational sport migrants contour the very movements and flows of these processes. The evidence of these struggles may take numerous forms; one of which is the movements of transnational sport migrants. Approaching 'transnationalism from below' so that the apparent *fait accompli* of 'global sport' is taken as a problematic rather than as a sociological given would be an excellent start.[65]

Transnational migrants do not passively accept state-based definitions of citizenship: the surest indicator yet that there is much more work to be done on TSM. The current debates on sport-related labour migration are especially useful as long as it is emphasized that migration is not the rupture of social relations in one location and the forging of replacement ones in another but migrants' ability to transcend various borders and maintain social relations in two or more localities simultaneously – in some cases despite authorities' attempts to control these interactions.[66] What must be more thoroughly and critically documented are the means by which people continue to act while the 'official' looks the other way.

NOTES

1 All individuals identified in this article have been given pseudonyms to help protect their anonymity. Those Cubans who have given of their time, energy and knowledge freely have had their identities changed for two reasons: (1) it is standard ethnographic practice to do so unless the individual in question is someone well known and whose work and life are heavily reported in local if not international media; and (2) the potential repercussions for giving their assistance, which cannot be foreseen, when addressing social issues that involve questions of illegality and state power.

2 Field research for this paper, funded by a British Academy Small Research Grant, SG-43107, examined the experiences of Cuban transnational sport migrants. Earlier fieldwork, informing that study and this paper, on various issues revolving around Cuban identity and sport was funded by the Latin American and Iberian Institute at the University of New Mexico. The Sports Council for Northern Ireland funded a long-range ethnographic study on the impact transnational sport migrants were having on local sports infrastructures after the 1998 Good Friday agreement. The support of all of these institutions is gratefully acknowledged.

3 The *Serie Nacional* is the national baseball league.

4 La Peña is a reference to the peña deportiva or sports group that meets every day in Parque Central in Havana. Members of this group meet daily to argue about sport, especially baseball gossip, commiserate and socialize. See Carter, 'Baseball Arguments', for further discussion.

5 Maguire, *Global Sport*, 97, 127, esp. 105–6; Magee and Sugden, 'The World at their Feet'. Unfortunately, space constraints preclude more detailed discussion of the strengths and weaknesses of these typologies.

6 Carter, 'Family Networks'.

7 Maguire, *Global Sport;* Maguire, *Power and Global Sport;* Miller et al., *Globalization and Sport;* Giulianotti and Robertson, *Globalization and Sport.*

8 Hannerz, 'Being There'.

9 This differs from other publications and research on TSM in which extended ethnographic fieldwork was carried out in numerous locales (see Carter, Donnan and Wardle, *Global Migrants;* Carter, 'Family Networks').

10 Henry, *Transnational and Comparative Research.*

11 Marcus, *Ethnography*, 79–104.

12 Geertz, *Interpretation of Cultures.*

13 Wallerstein, 'Open the Social Sciences', 3.

14 Weber, *Protestant Ethic*, 13.

15 A variety of topics from sport and the media to global governance, international migration, consumerism and commoditization all basically reproduce this theoretical encompassment of the local by the global. I argue that if the two can be separated into different social spaces, and I am highly sceptical that they can, the two are congruent with each other and national and regional spaces – all of which intersect, overlap, and inform each other.

16 Beck, 'Cosmopolitan Society'; Held, *Democracy and the Global Order;* Robertson, 'Mapping the Global Condition'; Venn, 'Altered States'.

17 Maguire, *Global Sport*, 213.

18 Chatterjee, *Politics of the Governed*, 85–6.

19 Foucault, 'Governmentality'.

20 Ong, *Flexible Citizenship*, 15.

21 This includes those states not willingly accepting the neoliberal dream of a global world made in their image. Cuba is one such state. See Carmona Báez, *State Resistance.*

22 There are those exceptions, typically characterized as 'failed states', in which transnational organizations have sent military forces to act as 'peacekeepers'. Examples include NATO intervention in the Balkans, and African Union intervention in Darfur, Sudan.

23 Guarnizo and Smith, 'Locations of Transnationalism', 8.

24 Tsing, 'Inside the Economy of Appearances'.

25 Miller et al., *Globalization and Sport;* see also Dabscheck, 'The Globe at Their Feet: FIFA's New Employment Rules – I'; Dabscheck, 'The Globe at the Their Feet: FIFA's New Employment Rules – II'; Parrish and McArdle, 'Beyond *Bosman*'.

26 Sklair, *Transnational Capitalist Class.*

27 Held, *Democracy and the Global Order.*

28 Herzfeld, *Social Production of Indifference.*

29 This particular aspect of state control is often overlooked and taken for granted by many people from Western liberal capitalist democracies, but is a fact of life in many places around the world, including Cuba. It is manifest in the passport checks undertaken at the airport BEFORE one is allowed to enter the gate area for boarding.

30 Gregory, *Devil Behind the Mirror*, 39.

31 Etzioni, 'Citizenship Tests'.

32 Shachar and Hirschl, 'Citizenship as Inherited Property', 261. Italics in original.

33 Malkki, 'National Geographic'.

34 Clearly, states are not the only agents restraining professionals' movements. INGOs, the European Union and other international organizations also play significant roles in the shaping of migratory patterns through their own regulatory schema regarding national representation. The Bosman ruling also has had an impact on TSM, particularly

in relation to European Union labour law. States, however, are the focus of this article and so the others will have to remain for later consideration.

35 Poli has produced a similar discussion from a slightly different theoretical approach. Poli is addressing the question of nationality and ethnic nationalism whereas the concern here is the strategies and manipulations of citizenship. The two concepts are different yet interrelated and these distinctions need further explication sometime in the future. Where Poli and I diverge is the question of deterritorialization, which I argue is a distraction from actual processes of power and does not constitute an actual removal of spatial concerns, whereas Poli appears to support such claims. See Poli, 'Denationalization of Sport'.

36 This is a pseudonym.

37 Magee and Sugden, '"The World at their Feet": Professional Football and International Labour Migration.'

38 This is apparent as FIFA sets the rules for transnational sports labour migration and was even more apparent when Bud Selig, the Commissioner of Major League Baseball, decreed that he would determine star player Alex Rodriguez's status over which team he would represent in the inaugural World Baseball Classic, the United States or the Dominican Republic, and that Rodriguez had no say in the matter.

39 Ong, *Flexible Citizenship.*

40 Instituto Nacional de Deportes, Educatión Física y Recreatión (National Institute of Sport, Physical Education and Recreation).

41 Carmona Báez, *State Resistance*; Espinosa Martínez, 'Ethics'; Phillips, '"Cuentapropismo" in a Socialist State'; Ritter, 'Cuba's Economic Reorientation'.

42 Carter, 'New Rules to the Old Game'.

43 *Calidad* (quality) is a particular aspect of Cuban personhood evident in how one demonstrates expected morals, mores and values in everyday life. For a discussion on *calidad*, see Carter, *Quality of Home Runs*, 160–5.

44 Carter, 'Family Networks'.

45 Wirtz, 'Santeria in Cuban National Consciousness'.

46 Guevara, *Socialismo y el Hombre en Cuba.*

47 Mauss, 'Techniques of the Body.'

48 See Bjarkman, *A History of Cuban Baseball*, 386–420; Fainaru and Sanchez, *Duke of Havana;* Jamail, *Full Count*, 73–101; Price, *Pitching Around Fidel.*

49 This has been emphasized repeatedly in interviews I have conducted and in press conferences in which Cuban athletes publicly declare their motivations for 'fleeing' as 'to be able to provide for my family' and not in any overt repudiation of the Castro regime. It could be argued that these statements mask migrants' true feelings because of fear for family members still in Cuba. However, considering the anonymity of my consultants I find this particular argument unlikely.

50 Rogozinski, *A Brief History of the Caribbean;* Williams, *From Columbus to Castro.*

51 Kyle and Dale, 'Smuggling the State Back In'.

52 Carmona Báez, *State Resistance*, 86.

53 Monreal, 'Development as an Unfinished Affair'.

54 Ritter and Rowe, 'Cuba', 104.

55 Burchardt, 'Contours of the Future', 61.

56 Hamilton 'Whither Cuban Socialism?', 27.

57 A *balsero* (rafter) is a Cuban who clandestinely builds a homemade raft and then either alone, or (usually) with a few others, launches it into the Florida Straits, a particularly dangerous and swift moving stretch of water.

58 There is insufficient space to provide full detailed accounts for the reasons why these four had already obtained visa offers from another state. Suffice it to say, for the purposes of this article, that those four had made a previously unsuccessful attempt to leave Cuba that had received some publicity thereby attracting the attention of then Nicaraguan president Arnoldo Alemán.

59 Ex-President Alemán is currently serving a 20-year prison sentence in Nicaragua for money laundering in which he used roughly 60 Panamanian bank accounts to launder about US$58 million allegedly stolen from Nicaraguan government coffers.

60 Unfortunately, there is insufficient space to detail the methods used to travel from Nicaragua to Costa Rica in this article. The reasons for their belief are complicated and the space of this article prevents an accurate chronicle of all of the machinations that were involved in their illegal move from Nicaragua to Costa Rica and why they engaged in a second risk-laden journey. Those details will be forthcoming in a larger publication.

61 Anyone's sight, it appears, since I have been unable to trace them since they arrived in San José.

62 Brettell, 'Adjustment of Status'; Chavez, *Shadowed Lives;* Ong, *Flexible Citizenship.*

63 Margheritis, 'State-led Transnationalism'.

64 Corrales, 'Gatekeeper State'; Carter, 'New Rules to the Old Game'.

65 Smith and Guarnizo, *Transnationalism from Below.*

66 I am thinking here of the work of Nina Glick Schiller and Michael Peter Smith, among others, who make this point abundantly clear. See Glick Schiller, 'Transnational Social Fields'; Glick Schiller and Fouron, *Georges Woke Up Laughing;* Smith, 'Power in Place/Places of Power'; Smith and Guarnizo, *Transnationalism from Below.*

REFERENCES

Beck, U. 'The Cosmopolitan Society and Its Enemies'. *Theory, Culture and Society* 19, nos. 1–2 (2002): 17–44.

Bjarkman, P.C. *A History of Cuban Baseball, 1864–2006*. Jefferson: McFarland & Co, 2007.

Brettell, C.B. 'Adjustment of Status, Remittances and Returns: Some Observations on 21st Century Migration Processes'. *City & Society* 19, no. 1 (2007): 47–59.

Burchardt, H-J. 'Contours of the Future: the New Social Dynamics in Cuba'. *Latin American Perspectives* 29, no. 3 (2002): 57–74.

Carmona Báez, A. *State Resistance to Globalization in Cuba*. London: Pluto Press, 2004.

Carter, T.F. 'Baseball Arguments: Aficionismo and Masculinity at the Core of Cubanidad'. *The International Journal of the History of Sport* 18, no. 3 (2001): 117–38.

Carter, T.F. 'Family Networks, State Interventions and the Experiences of Cuban Transnational Sport Migration'. *International Review of the Sociology of Sport* 42, no. 2 (2007): 371–89.

Carter, T.F. 'New Rules to the Old Game: Cuban Sport and State Legitimacy in the Post-Soviet Era'. *Identities: Global Studies in Culture and Power* 15, no. 2 (2008): 1–22.

Carter, T.F. *The Quality of Home Runs: The Passion, Politics, and Language of Cuban Baseball*. Durham, NC: Duke University Press, 2008.

Carter, T.F., H. Donnan, and H. Wardle. *Global Migrants: The Impact of Migrants Working in Sport in Northern Ireland*. Belfast: Sports Council for Northern Ireland, 2003.

Chatterjee, P. *The Politics of the Governed: Reflections on Popular Politics in Most of the World*. New York: Columbia University Press, 2004.

Chavez, L.R. *Shadowed Lives: Undocumented Immigrants in American Society*. New York: Wadsworth, 1997.

Corrales, J. 'The Gatekeeper State: Limited Economic Reforms and Regime Survival in Cuba, 1989–2002'. *Latin American Research Review* 39, no. 2 (2004): 35–65.

Dabscheck, B. 'The Globe at Their Feet: FIFA's New Employment Rules – I'. *Sport in Society* 7, no. 1 (2004): 69–94.

Dabscheck, B. 'The Globe at the Their Feet: FIFA's New Employment Rules – II'. *Sport in Society* 9, no. 1 (2006): 1–18.

Espinosa Martínez, E. 'Ethics, Economics, and Social Policies: Values and Development Strategy, 1989–2004'. In *Cuba in the 21st Century: Realities and Perspectives*, edited by J. Bell Lara and R.A. Dello Buono, 57–100. La Habana: Editorial José Martí, 2005.

Etzioni, A. 'Citizenship Tests: A Comparative, Communitarian Perspective'. *The Political Quarterly* 78, no. 3 (2007): 353–63.

Fainaru, S., and R. Sanchez. *The Duke of Havana: Baseball, Cuba, and the Search for the American Dream*. New York: Villard, 2001.

Foucault, M. 'Governmentality'. In *The Foucault Effect: Studies in Governmentality*, edited by G. Burchell, C. Gordon, and P. Miller, 87–104. Chicago, IL: University of Chicago Press, 1991.

Geertz, C. *The Interpretation of Cultures*. New York: Basic Books, 1973.

Giulianotti, R. and Robertson, R., eds. *Globalization and Sport*. Oxford: Wiley-Blackwell, 2007.

Glick Schiller, N. 'Transnational Social Fields and Imperialism: Bringing a Theory of Power to Transnational Studies'. *Anthropological Theory* 5, no. 4 (2005): 439–61.

Glick Schiller, N., and G.E. Fouron. *Georges Woke Up Laughing: Long-Distance Nationalism and the Search for Home*. Durham: Duke University Press, 2001.

Gregory, S. *The Devil Behind the Mirror: Globalization and Politics in the Dominican Republic*. Berkeley, CA: University of California Press, 2007.

Guarnizo, L.E., and M.P. Smith. 'The Locations of Transnationalism'. In *Transnationalism from Below*, edited by M.P. Smith and L.E. Guarnizo. 3–34. New Brunswick, NJ: Transaction Books, 1998.

Guevara, E. *Socialismo y el Hombre en Cuba*. Atlanta: Pathfinder Press, 1992 [1965].

Hamilton, D. 'Whither Cuban Socialism? The Changing Political Economy of the Cuban Revolution'. *Latin American Perspectives* 29, no. 3 (2002): 18–39.

Hannerz, U. 'Being There . . . and There . . . and There! Reflections on Multi-Site Ethnography'. *Ethnography* 4, no. 2 (2003): 201–16.

Held, D. *Democracy and the Global Order*. Cambridge: Polity Press, 1995.

Henry, I. *Transnational and Comparative Research in Sport: Globalisation, Governance and Sport Policy*. London: Routledge, 2007.

Herzfeld, M. *The Social Production of Indifference: Exploring the Symbolic Roots of Western Democracy*. Chicago, IL: University of Chicago Press, 1993.

Jamail, M.H. *Full Count*. Carbondale, IL: Southern Illinois University Press, 2000.

Kyle, D., and J. Dale. 'Smuggling the State Back In: Agents of Human Smuggling Reconsidered'. In *Global Human Smuggling: Comparative Perspectives*, edited by D. Kyle and R. Koslowski, 29–57. Baltimore, MD: Johns Hopkins University Press, 2001.

Magee, J., and J. Sugden. '"The World at their Feet": Professional Football and International Labor

Migration'. *Journal of Sport and Social Issues* 26, no. 4 (2002): 421–37.

Maguire, J. *Global Sport: Identities, Societies, Civilizations.* Oxford: Polity, 1999.

Maguire, J. *Power and Global Sport: Zones of Prestige, Emulation and Resistance.* London: Routledge, 2005.

Malkki, L. 'National Geographic: The Rooting of Peoples and the Territorialization of National Identity among Scholars and Refugees'. In *Culture, Power, Place: Explorations in Critical Anthropology*, edited by A. Gupta and J. Ferguson, 52–74. Durham, NC: Duke University Press, 1997.

Marcus, G.E. *Ethnography Through Thick and Thin.* Princeton, NJ: Princeton University Press, 1998.

Margheritis, A. 'State-led Transnationalism and Migration: Reaching Out to the Argentine Community in Spain'. *Global Networks* 7, no. 1 (2007): 87–106.

Mauss, M. 'Techniques of the Body'. *Economic Sociology* 2 (1973): 70–8.

Miller, T., G. Lawrence, J. McKay, and D. Rowe. *Globalization and Sport.* London: Sage, 2001.

Monreal, P. 'Development as an Unfinished Affair: Cuba After the Great Adjustment of the 1990s'. *Latin American Perspectives* 29, no. 3 (2002): 75–90.

Ong, A. *Flexible Citizenship: The Cultural Logics of Transnationality.* Durham, NC: Duke University Press, 1999.

Parrish, R., and D. McArdle. 'Beyond Bosman: The European Union's Influence upon Professional Athletes' Freedom of Movement'. *Sport in Society* 7, no. 3 (2004): 403–19.

Phillips, E. '"Cuentapropismo" in a Socialist State'. In *Cuba in Transition? Pathways to Renewal, Long-Term Development and Global Reintegration*, edited by M. Font and S. Larson, 107–24. New York: Bildner Center for Western Hemisphere Studies, CUNY, 2006.

Poli, R. 'The Denationalization of Sport: De-ethnicization of the Nation and Identity Deterritorialization'. *Sport in Society* 10, no. 4 (2007): 646–61.

Price, S.L. *Pitching Around Fidel: A Journey into the Heart of Cuban Sports.* New York: Ecco, 2000.

Ritter, A.R.M. 'Cuba's Economic Reorientation'. In *Cuba in Transition? Pathways to Renewal, Long-Term Development and Global Reintegration*, edited by M. Font and S. Larson. New York: Bildner Center for Western Hemisphere Studies, CUNY, 2006.

Ritter, A.R.M., and N. Rowe. 'Cuba: From "Dollarization" to "Euroization" or "Peso Reconsolidation"?'. *Latin American Politics and Society* 44, no. 2 (2002): 99–123.

Robertson, R. 'Mapping the Global Condition: Globalization as the Central Concept'. In *Global Culture: Nationalism, Globalization and Modernity*, edited by M. Featherstone, 15–30. London: Sage, 1990.

Rogozinski, J. *A Brief History of the Caribbean: From the Arawak and the Carib to the Present.* New York: Meridian, 1992.

Shachar, A., and R. Hirschl. 'Citizenship as Inherited Property'. *Political Theory* 35, no. 3 (2007): 253–87.

Sklair, L. *The Transnational Capitalist Class.* Oxford: Wiley-Blackwell, 2000.

Smith, M.P. 'Power in Place/Places of Power: Contextualizing Transnational Research'. *City & Society* 17, no. 1 (2005): 5–34.

Smith, M.P. and Guarnizo, L.E., eds. *Transnationalism from Below.* New Brunswick, NJ: Transaction Publishers, 1998.

Tsing, A. 'Inside the Economy of Appearances'. *Public Culture* 12, no. 1 (2000): 115–44.

Venn, C. 'Altered States: Post-Enlightenment Cosmopolitanism and Transmodern Socialities'. *Theory, Culture and Society* 19, nos. 1–2 (2002): 65–80.

Wallerstein, I. 'Open the Social Sciences'. *ITEMS, Social Science Research Council* 50, no. 1 (1996): 1–7.

Weber, M. *The Protestant Ethic and the Spirit of Capitalism.* New York: Routledge, 1992 [1904].

Williams, E. *From Columbus to Castro: The History of the Caribbean.* New York: Vintage Books, 1970.

Wirtz, K. 'Santeria in Cuban National Consciousness: A Religious Case of the *Doble Moral*'. *Journal of Latin American Anthropology* 9, no. 2 (2004): 409–38.

GLOSSARY INDEX

Note: Subject headings in bold indicate the presence of a glossary description. Page numbers in bold refer to tables; page numbers in italics refer to figures.